VOLUME 9

# Southwest

ALFONSO ORTIZ

*Volume Editor*

SMITHSONIAN INSTITUTION

WASHINGTON

1979

For sale by the Superintendent of Documents,
U.S. Government Printing Office, Washington, D.C. 20402.
Stock Number: 047-000-00361-0

**Library of Congress Cataloging in Publication Data**

Handbook of North American Indians.

    Bibliography: pp. 625–678
    Includes index.
    CONTENTS:

                  v. 9 Southwest.

    1.  Indians of North America.   2.   Eskimos.
I.   Sturtevant, William C.

E77.H25          970′.004′97          77-17162

*Southwest Volumes Planning Committee*

Alfonso Ortiz, Volume Editor

William C. Sturtevant, General Editor

Richard B. Woodbury, Coordinator for Prehistory and Archeology chapters

Edward P. Dozier

Fred Eggan

Kenneth Hale

Albert H. Schroeder

Douglas W. Schwartz

Gary Witherspoon

# Contents

This map is a diagrammatic guide to the coverage of this volume and volume 10. The prehistory of the whole region is treated in this volume, but for the historic and recent periods only the groups indicated in tone are described in this volume while the others are described in volume 10. This is not an authoritative depiction of tribal ranges, for several reasons. Sharp boundaries have been drawn and no territory is unassigned. Tribal units are sometimes arbitrarily defined, subdivisions are not mapped, no joint or disputed occupations are shown, and different kinds of land use are not distinguished. Since the map depicts the situation at the earliest periods for which evidence is available, the ranges mapped for different tribes often refer to quite different periods, and there may have been many intervening movements, extinctions, and changes in range. Not shown are groups that came into separate political existence later than the map period for their areas. In general, the Pueblo areas are simplifications of the locations known for the 16th century, while the adjoining areas of Athapaskan groups are approximately as in the 18th century as are the boundaries along the Colorado River. The extreme southwestern region shows the 17th-century distribution. Boundaries in the large area south and southeast of the Chiricahua and Mescalero are especially arbitrary, due to the lack of evidence for the 17th and 18th centuries. For more specific information see the maps and text in the accompanying chapters in this volume and volume 10.

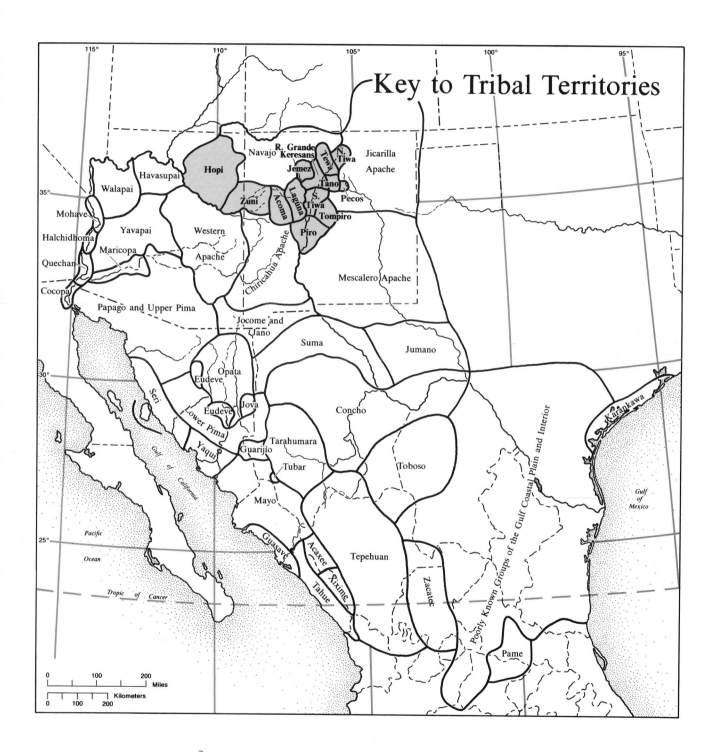

# Key to Tribal Territories

Walapai
Havasupai
Hopi
Navajo
**R. Grande Keresans**
**Jemez**
**Tewa**
N. Tiwa
Jicarilla Apache
Mohave
Halchidhoma
Yavapai
Western Apache
Zuni
**Acoma**
**Laguna**
**Tano**
**S. Tiwa**
**Tompiro**
**Pecos**
**Piro**
Maricopa
Quechan
Cocopa
Chiricahua Apache
Mescalero Apache
Papago and Upper Pima
Jocome and Jano
Suma
Jumano
Opata
Eudeve
Eudeve
Jova
Concho
Seri
Lower Pima
Yaqui
Guarijío
Tarahumara
Toboso
Tubar
Mayo
Guasavé
Acaxee
Xixime
Tahue
Tepehuan
Zacatec
Pame
Poorly Known Groups of the Gulf Coastal Plain and Interior
Karankawa

Gulf of California
Pacific Ocean
Tropic of Cancer
Gulf of Mexico

115°   110°   105°   100°   95°
35°
30°
25°

0   100   200   Miles
0   100   200   Kilometers

# Technical Alphabet

## Consonants

| | | bilabial | labiodental | dental | alveolar | alveopalatal | velar | back velar | glottal |
|---|---|---|---|---|---|---|---|---|---|
| stop | vl | *p* | | *t* | *t* | | *k* | *q* | *ʔ* |
| | vd | *b* | | *d* | *d* | | *g* | *ġ* | |
| affricate | vl | | | *θ̂* | *c* | *č* | | | |
| | vd | | | *δ̂* | *ʒ* | *ǯ* | | | |
| fricative | vl | *φ* | *f* | *θ* | *s* | *š* | *x* | *x̣* | *h* |
| | vd | *β* | *v* | *δ* | *z* | *ž* | *γ* | *γ̇* | |
| nasal | vl | *M* | | *N* | | | *Ŋ* | | |
| | vd | *m* | | *n* | | | *ŋ* | *ŋ̇* | |
| lateral | vl | | | | *ł* | | | | |
| | vd | | | | *l* | | | | |
| semivowel | vl | *W* | | | | | *Y* | | |
| | vd | *w* | | | | | *y* | | |

vl = voiceless; vd = voiced

Other symbols include: λ (voiced lateral affricate), X̣ (voiceless lateral affricate), ˤ (voiced pharyngeal fricative), ḥ (voiceless pharyngeal fricative), *r* (medial flap, trill, or retroflex approximant). Where in contrast, *r* is a flap and *R* is a continuant.

Modifications indicated for consonants are: glottalization (*ł̓, k̓*, etc.), retroflexion (*ṭ, ç, ʒ̣*), palatalization (*tʸ, kʸ, nʸ, lʸ*), labialization (*kʷ*), aspiration (*tʰ*), length (*t·*). For vowels: length (*a·*), three-mora length (*a:*), nasalization (*ą*), voicelessness (*A*). The commonest prosodic markings are, for stress: *á* (primary) and *à* (secondary), and for pitch: *á* (high), *à* (low), *â* (falling), and *ǎ* (rising); however, the details of prosodic systems and the uses of accents differ widely from language to language.

## Vowels

| | front | central | back |
|---|---|---|---|
| high | *i (ü)* | *ɨ* | *u (ɨ)* |
| | ɪ | | ʊ |
| mid | *e (ö)* | *ə* | *o* |
| | ε | | ɔ |
| | | ʌ | |
| low | *æ* | *a* | *a* |

Unparenthesized vowels are unrounded if front or central, and rounded if back; *ü* and *ö* are rounded; *ɨ* is unrounded. The special symbols for lax vowels (*ɪ, ʊ, ε, ɔ*) are generally used only where it is necessary to differentiate between tense and lax high or mid vowels. *ɨ* and *a* are used for both central and back vowels, as the two values seldom contrast in a given language.

---

Words in Indian languages cited in italics in this volume are of two types. Those in Nahuatl (the language of the Aztecs) are in the regularized orthography of Siméon (1963). Italicized words in other Indian languages are written in phonemic transcription. That is, the letters and symbols are used in specific values defined for them by the structure of the sound system of the particular language. However, as far as possible, these phonemic transcriptions use letters and symbols in generally consistent values, as specified by the standard technical alphabet of the *Handbook*. Deviations from these standard values as well as specific details of the phonology of each language (or references to where they may be found) are given in an orthographic footnote in each tribal chapter or an early chapter in each tribal section. Italicized Navajo words are in the standard Navajo practical orthography (described in volume 10), which is phonemic but uses digraphs and trigraphs for some single phonemes.

No italicized Indian word is broken at a line end except when a hyphen would be present anyway as part of the word. Words in italicized phonemic transcription are never capitalized, except that the Navajo orthography follows the English rules of capitalization. Pronunciations or phonetic values given in the standard technical alphabet without regard to phonemic analysis are put in square brackets rather than in italics. The glosses, or conventionalized translations, of Indian words are enclosed in single quotation marks.

Indian words recorded by nonspecialists or before the phonemic systems of their languages had been analyzed are often not written accurately enough to allow respelling in phonemic transcription. Where phonemic retranscription has been possible the citation of source has been modified by the label "phonemicized" or "from." A few words that could not be phonemicized have been "normalized"—rewritten by mechanical substitution of the symbols of the standard technical alphabet. Others have been rationalized by eliminating redundant or potentially misleading diacritics and substituting nontechnical symbols. Words that do not use the standard technical alphabet occasionally contain some letters used according to the values of other technical alphabets or traditional orthographies. The most common of these are c for the *Handbook*'s *š*; ts and tz for *c*; tsh, tj, and tc for *č*; dj for *ǯ*; chr for *ç*; p̓ and ph for *pʰ* (and similarly with some other consonants); hl for *ł*; j for *ž*, *ǯ*, or *y*; ' for *ʔ*; ˤ for *h* (or nondistinctive aspiration); oñ or oⁿ for *ǫ* (and with other vowels, for nasalization); u for *ɨ* (particularly in Hopi and Keresan words); and x or j for *š*, *x*, or *h*, and z for *c* (in early Spanish sources). Other common variants in Spanish are discussed in the section on "Synonymies," p. xiv. All nonphonemic transcriptions give only incomplete, and sometimes imprecise, approximations of the correct pronunciation.

# Nontechnical Equivalents

Correct pronunciation, as with any foreign language, requires extensive training and practice, but simplified (incorrect) pronunciations may be obtained by ignoring the diacritics and reading the vowels as in Italian or Spanish and the consonants as in English. For a closer approximation to the pronunciation or to rewrite into a nontechnical transcription the substitutions indicated in the following table may be made.

| technical | nontechnical | | technical | nontechnical | | technical | nontechnical |
|-----------|--------------|---|-----------|--------------|---|-----------|--------------|
| æ | ae | | $M$ | mh | | $Y$ | yh |
| $\beta$ | bh | | $N$ | nh | | $\check{z}$ | zh |
| $c$ | ts | | $\eta$ | ng | | $\mathcal{3}$ | dz |
| $\check{c}$ | ch | | $\mathcal{N}$ | ngh | | $\check{\mathcal{3}}$ | j |
| $\delta$ | dh | | $\mathfrak{o}$ | o | | $\mathcal{P}$ | ' |
| $\hat{\delta}$ | ddh | | $\theta$ | th | | $\acute{k}, \acute{p}, \acute{t}$, etc. | k', p', t', etc. |
| $\varepsilon$ | e | | $\hat{\theta}$ | tth | | $a\cdot, e\cdot, k\cdot, s\cdot$, etc. | aa, ee, kk, ss, etc. |
| $\gamma$ | gh | | $\phi$ | ph | | $\mathfrak{q}, \mathfrak{e}$, etc. | an, en, etc. |
| $\ell$ | lh | | $\check{s}$ | sh | | $k^y, t^y$, etc. | ky, ty, etc. |
| $\lambda$ | dl | | $W$ | wh | | $k^w$ | kw |
| $\acute{\lambda}$ | tlh | | $x$ | kh | | | |

# English Pronunciations

The English pronunciations of the names of tribes and a few other words are indicated parenthetically in a dictionary-style orthography in which most letters have their usual English pronunciation. Special symbols are listed below, with sample words to be pronounced as in nonregional United States English. Approximate phonetic values are given in parentheses in the standard technical alphabet.

ŋ: thi**ng** (ŋ)
θ: **th**in (θ)
ð: **th**is (ð)
zh: vi**s**ion (ž)
ă: b**a**t (æ)

ä: f**a**ther (a)
ā: b**ai**t (ey)
e: b**e**t (ɛ)
ē: b**ea**t (iy)

ə: **a**bout, gall**o**p (ə)
ĭ: b**i**t (I)
ī: b**i**te (ay)
ô: b**ou**ght (ɔ)

ō: b**oa**t (ow)
o͝o: b**oo**k (ʊ)
o͞o: b**oo**t (uw)
u: b**u**t (ʌ)

ˈ(primary stress), ˌ (secondary stress): elevator (ˈeləˌvātər) *(éləvèytər)* ·

# Conventions for Illustrations

## Map Symbols

•    Indian settlement

■    Non-Indian town

Mountain range, peak

- - — - —   National boundary

- - — - —   State boundary

- - - - - - -   County boundary

River or stream

Intermittent or dry stream

*Santa Fe*    Settlement, site, reservation

*Rio Grande*    Geographical feature

Toned areas on tribal maps represent estimated territory.

Detailed Pueblo maps are oriented in the same direction as the accompanying aerial photographs.

## Credits and Captions

Credit lines give the source of the illustrations (often the copyright holder), or the collections where the artifacts shown are located. The numbers that follow are the catalog or inventory numbers of that repository. When the photographer mentioned in the caption is the source of the print reproduced, no credit line appears. "After" means that the *Handbook* illustrators have redrawn, rearranged, or abstracted the illustration from the one in the cited source. All maps and drawings not otherwise credited are by the *Handbook* illustrators. Measurements in captions are to the nearest millimeter if available; "about" indicates an estimate or a measurement converted from inches to centimeters. The following abbreviations are used in credit lines:

| | | | |
|---|---|---|---|
| Amer. | American | Hist. | History |
| Anthr. | Anthropology, Anthropological | Histl. | Historical |
| | | Ind. | Indian |
| Arch. | Archives | Inst. | Institute |
| Arch(a)eol. | Arch(a)eology, Arch(a)eological | Instn. | Institution |
| | | Lib. | Library |
| Assoc. | Association | Mus. | Museum |
| Co. | County | NAA | National Anthropological Archives |
| Coll. | Collection(s) | | |
| Dept. | Department | Nat. | Natural |
| Div. | Division | Natl. | National |
| Ethnol. | Ethnology, Ethnological | opp. | opposite |
| fol. | folio | pl(s). | plate(s) |
| Ft. | Fort | Soc. | Society |
| | | U. | University |

## Metric Equivalents

| | | |
|---|---|---|
| 10 mm = 1 cm | 10 cm = 3.937 in. | 1 in. = 2.54 cm |
| 100 cm = 1 m | 1 m = 39.37 in. | 1 ft. = 30.48 cm |
| 1,000 m = 1 km | 10 m = 32.81 ft. | 1 yd. = 91.44 cm |

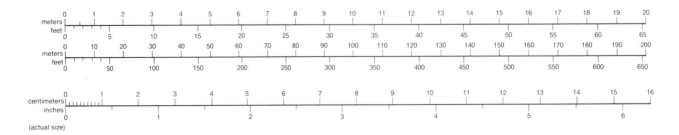

# Preface

This is the third volume to be published of a 20-volume set planned to give an encyclopedic summary of what is known about the prehistory, history, and cultures of the aboriginal peoples of North America who lived north of the urban civilizations of central Mexico. Volumes 5-8 and 11-15 treat the other major culture areas of this region.

The Southwest is the only culture area requiring two volumes. This is because of the great amount of anthropological knowledge of the many peoples of this region, due in part to the fact that distinctive traditional cultures have survived here to a greater extent than elsewhere on the continent. The present volume covers the prehistory, general history, and languages of the entire Southwest, and the cultures and histories of the Pueblo peoples. Volume 10 covers the non-Pueblo peoples of the Southwest and also includes a few surveys of special topics over the entire Southwest. Each volume is separately indexed.

Some topics relevant to the Southwest area are excluded from volumes 9 and 10 because they are more appropriately discussed on a continent-wide basis. Readers should refer to volume 1, Introduction, for general descriptions of anthropological and historical methods and sources and for summaries for the whole continent of certain topics regarding social and political organization, religion, and the performing arts. Volume 2 contains detailed accounts of the different kinds of Indian and Eskimo communities in the twentieth century, especially during its third quarter, and describes their relations with one another and with the surrounding non-Indian societies and nations. Volume 3 gives the environmental and biological backgrounds within which Native American societies developed, summarizes the early and late human biology or physical anthropology of Indians and Eskimos, and surveys the earliest prehistoric cultures. (Therefore the Paleo-Indian or Early Man period in the Southwest receives major treatment in volume 3 rather than in this volume.) Volume 4 contains details on the history of Indian-White relations. Volume 16 is a continent-wide survey of technology and the visual arts—of material cultures broadly defined. Volume 17 surveys the native languages of North America, their characteristics and historical relationships. Volumes 18 and 19 are a biographical dictionary; included in the listing are many Southwest Indians. Volume 20 contains an index to the whole, which will serve to locate materials on Southwest Indians in other volumes as well as in this one; it also includes a list of errata found in all preceding volumes.

Preliminary discussions on the feasibility of the *Handbook* and alternatives for producing it began in 1965 in what was then the Smithsonian's Office of Anthropology. A history of the early development of the *Handbook* and a listing of the entire editorial staff will be found in volume 1. Detailed planning for the Southwest volumes was undertaken at a meeting of the General Editor and the Volume Editor with a specially selected Planning Committee (listed on page v) held in Santa Fe, New Mexico, January 7-9, 1971. At that time a tentative table of contents was drawn up, and qualified specialists on each topic were listed as potential authors. The chapter headings in the final volumes reproduce almost exactly the list decided upon at that meeting, and about two-thirds of the authors were those first invited. Inevitably, some replacements had to be made as people were unable to accept invitations or later found that they could not meet their commitment to write. We especially regret the death on May 2, 1971, of Edward P. Dozier, before he could begin work on several chapters he enthusiastically agreed to prepare. We are fortunate that the organization of the two volumes and the selection of many authors do reflect his important aid during the Planning Committee's discussions.

At the time they were invited, contributors were sent brief indications of the topics to be covered, prepared by the Volume Editor (with the assistance, for the prehistory chapters, of Richard B. Woodbury and Douglas W. Schwartz; for the Yuman chapters of Kenneth M. Stewart; for the Navajo chapters of Gary Witherspoon; and for the Piman chapters of Donald M. Bahr). They were also sent a "Guide for Contributors" prepared by the General Editor describing the general aims and methods of the *Handbook* and the editorial conventions. One convention has been to avoid the present tense, where possible, in historical and cultural descriptions. Thus a statement in the past tense, with a recent date or approximate date, may also hold true for the time of writing. As they were received, the manuscripts were reviewed by the General Editor, the Volume Editor, and usually one or more referees (frequently including a member of the Planning Committee). Suggestions for changes and additions often resulted. The published versions frequently reflect more editorial intervention than is customary for academic writings, since the encyclopedic aims and format of this publication made it necessary to attempt to eliminate duplication, avoid gaps in coverage, prevent contradictions, impose some standardization of organization and terminology, and keep within strict constraints on length.

The editors have adopted a conservative position on the names of Pueblos, sometimes over the objections of authors. We have not replaced official and recognized English names for Pueblos with new borrowings from native names, even when the ordinary names are considered by some to be inappropriate; however, we have attempted to follow the preferences of members of the groups themselves for the standard English spellings of accepted names of tribes.

Many archeological sites have been designated by names borrowed from Indian languages. In a few cases, where it was possible without introducing confusion, the etymologically most appropriate English spellings for such site names have been adopted here, but for the most part the names traditionally used by archeologists have been retained. Many of these names are not the traditional Indian designations, few if any are accurate transcriptions, and a number have not been confirmed by linguistic study.

The first manuscript submitted was received on March 22, 1972, and the last on November 20, 1978; the first final acceptance of an author's manuscript was on May 5, 1972, and the last on November 20, 1978. Edited manuscripts were sent from the Washington office to authors for their approval between October 17, 1977, and January 17, 1979. These dates for all chapters are given in the list of Contributors. Late dates may reflect late invitations as well as late submissions.

## Linguistic Editing

All cited words in Indian languages were referred to consultants with expert knowledge of the respective languages and, as far as possible, rewritten by them in the appropriate technical orthography. The consultants and the spelling systems are identified in an orthographic footnote to each tribal chapter or set of chapters; these footnotes were drafted by the Linguistic Editor, Ives Goddard.

Statements about the genetic relationships of Indian languages have also been checked with linguist consultants, to ensure conformity with recent findings and terminology in comparative linguistics and to avoid conflicting statements within the *Handbook*. In general, only the less remote genetic relationships are mentioned in the individual tribal chapters; the chapter "Historical Linguistics and Archeology" treats more remote rela-

tionships, and further information will be found in volume 17.

The Linguistic Editor served as coordinator and editor of these efforts by linguist consultants. A special debt is owed to these consultants, many of whom took time from their own research to check words with native speakers, for all provided advice and assistance without compensation. The Linguistic Editor is especially grateful to Joe S. Sando and Velma Garcia-Mason for the time they spent providing words in their native languages (Jemez and Acoma, respectively).

In the case of words that could not be respelled in a technical orthography, an attempt has been made to rationalize the transcriptions used in earlier anthropological writings in order to eliminate phonetic symbols that are obsolete and diacritics that might convey a false impression of phonetic accuracy. Lack of accurate transcriptions was particularly a problem in the case of the phonetically complex dialects of Keresan. For many of these no scientific linguistic information was available, and even for those that have been studied religious and ceremonial terms, which are the words most frequently cited in the tribal chapters, were often not obtainable.

In a number of cases words from Indian languages have been used as the standard English designations of certain cultural features in all societies in which these features occur, even though the words were originally borrowed from specific languages and variants or different words may be used in societies speaking other languages. This has seemed especially appropriate for cultural features that have similar designations (clearly historically related) among all or a number of groups, such as Koshare and Quirana (the clown societies), kachina, Sipapu (the Earth Navel or Hole of Emergence from the Underworld), and sipapu (the symbolic representation of Sipapu in the kiva), and for certain other well-established words, such as kiva. In some cases English spellings based on more than one language have been used in order to ensure consistency with the spellings of associated terms, so we write, for example, (Hopi) Koyimse beside (Zuni) Koyemshi, because these forms also appear in the names of ceremonial figures within the respective descriptions of the Hopi and Zuni cultures.

## Synonymies

Toward the end of each tribal chapter (or, sometimes, in an early chapter of a set covering a single tribe or several closely related tribal groupings) is a section called Synonymy. This describes the various names that have been applied to the groups and subgroups treated in that chapter (or set of chapters), giving the principal variant spellings used in English and in Spanish, and often the names applied to the groups in neighboring Indian languages.

Not all spelling variants of names in the earlier Spanish sources have been included: alternations among u, v, and b; between j and x (and occasionally h and g); and between hu and gu (representing [w]), occur more often than indicated. Also ç (for [s]) in manuscript sources has sometimes been miscopied as c (normally used for [k]). Older Spanish spellings also often omit or write the accent in violation of modern rules for accentuation, and they often omit the dierisis over u, writing ambiguously gu for [g] and [gw] (word-medial [(γ)w]) and qu for [k] and [kw].

A number of the synonymies have been expanded or reworked by the Linguistic Editor, who has added names and analyses from the literature, from other manuscripts submitted for the *Handbook* (from which they have then been deleted), and as provided by linguist consultants. When a synonymy is wholly or substantially the work of the Linguistic Editor, a footnote specifying authorship is given.

These sections should assist in the identification of groups mentioned in the earlier historical and anthropological literature. They should also be examined for evidence on changes in the identifications and affiliations of groups, as seen by their own members as well as by neighbors and by outside observers.

## Radiocarbon Dates

Authors were instructed to convert radiocarbon dates into dates in the Christian calendar. Such conversions normally have been made from the dates as originally published, without taking account of changes that may be required by developing research on revisions of the half-life of carbon 14, long-term changes in the amount of carbon 14 in the atmosphere, and other factors that may require modifications of absolute dates based on radiocarbon determinations.

## Binomials

The scientific names of plant and animal genera and species, printed in italics, have been checked by the General Editor to ensure that they reflect modern usage by biological taxonomists. Scientific plant names have been brought into agreement with those accepted by Kearney et al. (1960), while zoological nomenclature has been revised in consultation with Smithsonian staff in the appropriate departments.

## Bibliography

All references cited by contributors have been unified in a single list at the end of the volume. Citations within the text, by author, date, and often page, identify the works in this unified list. Wherever possible the *Handbook* Bibliographer has resolved conflicts between citations of different editions, corrected inaccuracies and omissions, and checked direct quotations against the originals. The bibliographic information has been verified by examination of the original work or from standard reliable library catalogs (especially the National Union Catalog and the published catalog of the Harvard Peabody Museum Library). The unified bibliography lists all and only the sources cited in the text of the volume, except personal communications. The sections headed Sources at the ends of most chapters provide general guidance to the most important sources of information on the topics covered.

## Illustrations

Authors were requested to submit suggestions for illustrations: photographs, maps, drawings, and lists and locations of objects that might be illustrated. To varying degrees most complied with this request. Yet considerations of space, balance, reproducibility, and availability required modifications in what was submitted. In addition much original material was provided by editorial staff members, from research they conducted in museums and other repositories, in the published literature, and from correspondence. Locating suitable photographs and earlier drawings and paintings was the responsibility of the Illustrations Researchers, at first Joanna Cohan Scherer (for this along with all other *Handbook* volumes), and beginning in 1976 Laura J. Greenberg (especially for this volume). Artifacts in museum collections suitable for photographing or drawing were selected by the Artifact Researcher, Cathe Brock (in 1977-1978), by the Illustrations Researcher, Laura J. Greenberg, and by the Scientific Illustrator, Jo Ann Moore. All uncredited drawings are by Moore, except for 19 illustrations redrawn by Brigid Sullivan after published sources.

All maps were drawn by the *Handbook* Cartographer, Judith Crawley Wojcik, who redrew some submitted by authors and compiled many new ones using information from the chapter manuscripts and from other sources. The base maps for all are authoritative standard ones, especially U.S. Geological Survey sheets and Universal Jet Navigation Charts (from the National Oceanic and Atmospheric Administration). When possible, the hydrography has been reconstructed for the date of each map. The detailed maps of Pueblos are revised from the base maps cited in the credit lines, using more recent maps, identifications and occasional sketches from authors and other consultants, and information from 1977 oblique aerial photographs. However, no new surface surveys of the Pueblos have been used.

Layout and design of the illustrations have been the responsibility of the Scientific Illustrator, Jo Ann Moore, who has worked in consultation with Laura J. Greenberg, Judith Crawley Wojcik, and Cathe Brock. Captions for illustrations were usually composed by Greenberg, Moore, or Brock, and for maps by Wojcik. However, all illustrations, including maps and drawings, and all captions have been approved by the General Editor, the Volume Editor, and the authors of the chapters in which they appear, and authors frequently have participated actively in the selection process and in the improvement of captions.

We are indebted to individuals on the staffs of many museums for much time and effort spent in their collections locating photographs and artifacts and providing documentation on them. Many individuals, including professional photographers, have generously provided photographs free or at cost. Donnelley Cartographic Services (especially Sidney P. Marland, III, resident manager) have devoted meticulous care to converting the map artwork into final film.

## Acknowledgments

Especially valuable suggestions for improving and editing chapters were provided by several scholars. Richard B. Woodbury's efforts in this and other respects are recognized on page v. Albert H. Schroeder's knowledge of the historical sources and the archeology was repeatedly placed at our disposal. Fred Eggan provided prompt and sage advice, especially regarding the Hopi and Zuni chapters. Dennis Tedlock was very helpful regarding Zuni ethnography and linguistics. Joe Ben Wheat helped select and document illustrations of artifacts. Antonio F. Garcia assisted in labeling some of the Pueblo maps. Ives Goddard was of particular assistance on matters of historical accuracy as well as on decisions made by the General Editor regarding organization and other editorial procedures.

During the first few years of this project, the *Handbook* editorial staff in Washington worked on materials for all volumes of the series. In early 1976, intensive preparation of this volume began. Especially important contributions were provided over the final three years by: the Editorial Assistant, Betty Tatham Arens; the Production Manager and Manuscript Editor, Diane Della-Loggia; the Bibliographer, Lorraine H. Jacoby; the Scientific Illustrator, Jo Ann Moore; the Cartographer, Judith Crawley Wojcik; the Illustrations Researcher, Laura J. Greenberg; the Artifact Researcher, Cathe Brock; and the Assistant Illustrations Researcher, Nikki L. Lanza.

The Department of Anthropology, National Museum of Natural History, Smithsonian Institution, released the General Editor and the Linguistic Editor from part of their curatorial and research time.

Preparation and publication of this volume have been supported by federal appropriations made to the Smithsonian Institution, in part through its Bicentennial Programs.

The volume editor, Alfonso Ortiz, acknowledges the research and secretarial assistance of Nancy Soulé Arnon during the critical first year of 1971–1972, when the initial great flood of correspondence with authors for both volume 9 and 10 had to be attended to. Rebecca Ann Foulk provided a similar level of assistance during 1972–1973, when the largest number of manuscripts were edited and accepted. His greatest debt, however, is to Margaret Davisson Ortiz, for she provided back-up secretarial services on *Handbook* matters every other year in which the volumes have been in preparation.

Four months of direct support from a Travel and Study Grant from the Ford Foundation in 1971–1972 enabled the Volume Editor to devote much of his time to the *Handbook* during that period. Reduced teaching loads at Princeton University during 1972–1973 and at the University of New Mexico during 1974–1975 further expedited editorial work. The chapters on San Juan and the Introduction were written while the volume editor was a Fellow at the Center for Advanced Study in the Behavioral Sciences at Stanford during 1977–1978. Final editorial responsibilities for Volume 9 were also discharged during this same year. Grateful acknowledgment is made to the National Endowment for the Humanities and to the Rockefeller Foundation for the financial assistance that made possible the Volume Editor's year at the Center.

March 19, 1979                    William C. Sturtevant
                                  Alfonso Ortiz

# Introduction

ALFONSO ORTIZ

"We have lived upon this land from days beyond history's records, far past any living memory, deep into the time of legend. The story of my people and the story of this place are one single story. No man can think of us without thinking of this place. We are always joined together" (Henry et al. 1970:35). This is the statement of a Taos Pueblo man.

So it is in much of Southwestern North America. Here Indian people remain in their traditional homelands, and much that is vital in life remains as it was, timeless. Here is the oldest continuous record of human habitation on the continent outside of Mesoamerica, a habitation that has fashioned this region into a humanized landscape suffused with ancient meanings, myths, and mysteries. Here, as well, is a land of diversity, both of landscape and of ways of life upon that landscape. Volumes 9 and 10 attempt to convey something of the diversity of those ways of life and to give a sense of the timelessness, the meanings, and the mysteries.

When the Southwest was first seen with European eyes, those of Francisco Vásquez de Coronado and the men of his expedition of 1540, both the land and the people of the Southwest were already very diverse and very old. One has only to think of the great multi-hued gaps in the earth, such as Bryce and the Grand Canyon, Zion and Canyon de Chelly, or of the gigantic and majestic spires of red sandstone comprising nature's own sculpture in Monument Valley, to slip into a geological time perspective. One's spatial sense as well as one's temporal sense grows immense in the Southwest before the vast distances and topographical diversity that open out before one's eyes when looking down from any high vantage point. Here, truly, the imagination soars and the very spirit is set free. The spirit is further moved, and the temporal sense further broadened, by contemplation of the various native groups upon this land, many of whom were encountered in 1540 near where they are, and living very much as they do in the last quarter of the twentieth century.

These various peoples have their own rhythms to complement the diverse rhythms of the variegated Southwestern landscape. Within this region one can move, for example, from the Seri fishermen on Mexico's far northwest coast to Yuman, Piman, and Pueblo farmers who live along each of the great watercourses, from a few hundred feet above sea level to more than 7,000 feet

above. Over all of this and beyond, up close to timberline, roamed the hunters, gatherers, and raiders, most of whom mixed the three pursuits with bravado. There are the Yavapai and Walapai, known as the Upland Yumans to distinguish them from the agricultural Riverine Yumans, and the Athapaskan-speaking Apache and Navajo. These groups have been able to retain a somewhat nomadic existence even in contemporary life, through sheep and cattle raising and social events such as dances and rodeos.

Interspersed among these contemporary groups, the evidence of the most ancient inhabitants is everywhere. Some artifacts, like petroglyphs and chipped stone, may date back untold millennia; others, like potsherds and pit houses, may go back only to the time of Christ. Although the knowledge of human events in this area beyond a few millennia removed is as yet far from complete, it is known that cultigens and the knowledge of pottery making had come up from Mexico centuries before the dawn of Christianity. These and other Mesoamerican imports were embraced by the hunting and gathering peoples of the Southwest in diverse ways, which coalesced into four distinctive prehistoric civilizations. These four—Anasazi, Mogollon, Hohokam, and Hakataya—were in the process of formation by the beginning of the European Christian era. It is, indeed, the presence of Mesoamerican influence, in belief systems as well as more tangible realms, that most clearly gives the Southwest an underlying continuity beneath its diversities and distinguishes the Southwest from the areas surrounding it.

This is not to imply that the Southwest can be understood as a frontier or periphery of Mesoamerica. While it is important to trace continuities between Mesoamerica and the Southwest, it is essential to stress that the various peoples of the Southwest fashioned unique cultural syntheses from elements of diverse provenance. This synthesizing activity continues today, in contemporary efforts to combine the eternal verities of native life with the benefits and unavoidable impositions of the encompassing American and Hispanic societies.

The boundaries and characteristics of the Southwest and its status as a culture area have long been debated (Kirchhoff 1954; "Prehistory: Introduction," this vol.). It is important to recognize that, because of the very diversity of the Southwest, various subareas within it, as well as the inhabitants of these subareas, may have more in common with the land and people of regions adjoining them than they do with other tribes within the Southwest. Boundaries should be treated with caution, as they tend to limit and rigidify thought, as is shown by the earlier acceptance of the United States-Mexico boundary as the southern border of the Southwest, despite broad continuities in geography and culture that extend across the border and well into Mexico. The west, which is defined principally by the Colorado River, forms the closest geological and cultural break that there is in the Southwest, but it is only a relative one because there is such a vast expanse of desert west of the river itself. To the northwest, well away from the western slope of the Rockies, the land is very much like the Great Basin, and the people who adjoin it, such as the Hopi, have linguistic and other cultural affinities with tribes of the Great Basin. To the northeast and east, where the Southwest gradually merges with the Plains, the peoples who adjoin also have much in common. Hence the people of the northern Rio Grande Pueblos and the Jicarilla Apache manifest many Plains-derived customs, from arts and adornment to songs and ceremonies. There is, and has always been, free and frequent movement among the peoples of these adjoining areas, whether it be for trading, courting, religious and healing ceremonies, or some other purpose.

An appropriate gateway to the Southwest, and to a closer look at the various peoples and landscapes of the area, is from the northeast through Raton Pass. This pass lies high on the east side of the great continental divide, which runs like a backbone down the middle of the Southwest. Here one may break free of the Colorado Rockies and look down upon the vast expanse of small mountain ranges, mesas, and valleys that make up the northern region of the Southwest. The immense and diverse landscape that opens out before the eye here is truly one of the most breathtaking views in North America. Upon descending Raton Pass one enters the northern region of the Southwest, a landscape of multi-hued bluffs, spires, and canyons. At dawn and dusk, especially, these present a dazzling array of colors and shadows. This northern country is one face of the Southwest, which the Pueblo peoples and, later, the Navajo and Apache have made their own.

Another face of the Southwest is that of the watercourses of the arboreal desert on the west side of the continental divide, principally the Gila and the Salt rivers, where the prehistoric Hohokam culture flourished. The Hohokam adapted very well to the challenges of life on this searing landscape that, apart from the few watercourses that thread their way through, can be most inhospitable. The land is so hot in the summer that the air just above it quivers before the naked eye, as if there were ghostly presences about in broad daylight. At the hottest time of day the vibrations of the earth can cause objects in the distance, or even the horizon itself, to waver so much that one cannot trust one's own eyes. Sometimes the pressures of air, heat, and sand unite in an explosive combination that may send as many as six whirlwinds at a time dancing off across the landscape.

The Hohokam peoples contemplated these whirlwinds and recorded their impressions on petroglyphs and pottery. Before their civilization began to fade early in this millennium they constructed an extensive and efficient system of irrigation canals along both the Gila and Salt rivers. This waterworks system remains their most impressive monument and legacy. The agricultural Pimas and river Yumans, who succeeded the Hohokam on their land and are probably direct descendants of them, also contemplate the whirlwind in song and myth, and they record their own impressions on basketry as well as on pottery. They further respond and give meaning to this otherwise forbidding landscape in dreams and dream journeys, their distinctive form of spiritual expression.

A third face of the Southwest is provided by the rugged Gila Mountains of southwestern New Mexico, where arose the Mimbres culture, a branch of the more far-flung Mogollon prehistoric culture. From here, high up on the Gila River's watershed, one can look over what is the most concentrated topographical diversity in the Southwest. Early in the morning at first light, and at night, one may be treated to sights on these mountain slopes that stir the imagination. In the morning the evergreens appear as if they have wrapped themselves in splendid white garments, for the silver-hued frost shimmers like satin before the gathering light of day. And, during clear nights, one can watch ethereal white fingers of mist creep down the mountain slopes or between canyon walls silently, ever so silently.

If one follows out the many narrow, sparkling, serpentine streams that gather themselves together as the Gila River on the eastern flank of the continental divide, one can, in a relatively short time, traverse through several life-zones, from the snow pack of the Canadian life-zone to the desert of the Lower Sonoran. The floral and faunal life also change, of course, and abruptly. The ancient Mimbres people were quite aware of these topographical, floral, and faunal differences, for they moved regularly through all of them, and their imaginations dwelled upon them. And in this imaginative dwelling lies one key to understanding their greatest cultural legacy, their pottery. They had not much that was impressive in the way of habitations or other cultural artifacts, but they more than made up for it with their pottery, which in design was the finest produced by Indians north of Mexico. The many delicate, graceful, conventionalized designs of beetles, rabbits, turtles, bears, and other animals and insects attest to much imaginative musing on the varied fauna of their ever-changing land. They were equally skilled in executing abstract designs, but, centuries and centuries removed, no one can really be sure what brought these forms into being.

By the beginning of the second millennium A.D., even

2

before the passing of the Hohokam, the Mimbres people were absorbed by the expanding and closely related Pueblo peoples to the north. Some may have also migrated to the south, into modern-day Mexico. The Mimbres people, of unquestionable artistic genius, would remain much more of an enigma to scholars if their continuing influence were not so readily apparent in the pottery made by Pueblo people in every generation since their own passing.

The Pueblo peoples are the only one of the cultural groups identifiable as long ago as two millennia that have survived with clearly unbroken cultural continuity into the last quarter of the twentieth century. In their greatest time, from the tenth through the thirteenth centuries, they built and occupied the great architectural wonders at Chaco Canyon, Mesa Verde, Casa Grande, and numerous other places spread out over what are now five large states. During this time they ranged from mountain to canyon and even to the higher desert elevations. During the persistent drought that haunted the Southwest in the last quarter of the thirteenth century, the Pueblo people began contracting into the great valley of the Rio Grande and its tributaries. Only the Hopi, then as now, enigmatically hung on and persisted in farming successfully in a region with no permanent or semipermanent watercourses.

The other Pueblo groups maintained their way of life—characterized in essence by intensive horticulture, an elaborate ceremonial cycle, and a cohesive social organization—in the villages of adobe and stone that, for the most part, are strung along the Rio Grande and its tributaries like beads upon a crooked string. These villages all blend in with their surroundings so that one never knows one is approaching a Pueblo until one is right upon it. The architecture of the Pueblos is gentle and unobtrusive, as, indeed, are the Pueblo peoples' very character, customs, institutions, and art forms. The Pueblo peoples have shown a genius for maintaining that which is most essential to their lives while also receiving, absorbing, and reinvigorating the decaying "vines"—to use the appropriate and evocative Tewa metaphor—of other ways of life. Hence, the Pueblo legacy has been to endure.

In addition to these four identifiable prehistoric cultural traditions of the northern Southwest, there were others in northern Mexico, but these, with the exception of the Casas Grandes region, are not at all well known. These prehistoric hunter-gatherers and small-scale farmers remain opaque to scholars for the most part because they have been little studied. A major additional group in the Southwest are the late-coming Southern Athapaskans, who arrived in the Southwest as hunters and gatherers not more than a century before the first Europeans.

These Athapaskans came into the Southwest from the north, "threading the labyrinthine canyons with their eyes on the stars" (Waters 1950). Once in the Southwest they divided, with most of the Navajos staying in the northwest country of sandy washes and red bluffs and box canyons. In this dry country, after even a mild rainfall, such fragrances emanate from the land that the earth itself seems to smell grateful for the moisture. The small mountain ranges are widely scattered, and red or pale green limestone bluffs may run for miles. These cliffs gleam at eveningtide, as the shadows skirt their folds. Appropriately enough, one of these long high bluffs is named by the Navajo, Woman's Skirt Mountain.

Yet, the land of the Navajo does not differ from that of the Pueblos along any absolute dimension; the two peoples differ, rather, in how they live upon the land. Unlike the Pueblos, the Navajo remain thinly spread out within the box canyons, or at the base of the cliffs, of their far-flung land. While they have proved themselves to be extremely adaptable, with many becoming quite successful cultivators, sheep herding and raiding were more amenable to them, and they moved about a great deal. In addition to agriculture, the Navajo absorbed many other Pueblo ideas and institutions, along with quite a few Pueblo people themselves, mainly refugees from the Spaniards. What the Navajo have learned from the Pueblos and, later, from the Spaniards and Americans, has been blended with their still seminomadic life-style to form a unique, flexible, and vital synthesis.

What is most distinctive and striking about the Navajo people and their culture is their aesthetic tradition. The woven rugs and silver jewelry, impressive as they are by themselves, ultimately have their roots in the traditional dry paintings of Navajo religion. And the dry paintings, in their turn, are but concrete pictorial representations of the great sings or chants that comprise the living vitality of Navajo religion. Hence, the entire Navajo aesthetic tradition is inspired by what are at once prayers, myths, poetry, and sacred scripture rendered into song.

Their Athapaskan siblings, those who were to be called Apaches, moved onto the higher mountain vastnesses after centuries of raiding with impunity all over the Southwest. There they, in their turn, have stayed, as guardians of the watersheds of some of the major feeder streams of the great rivers.

The diversity of the Southwest was both increased and threatened by the arrival of the Spaniards in 1540 and, further, by the American onslaught beginning in the early nineteenth century. The Coronado expedition into the Southwest was inspired by Fray Marcos de Niza's exaggerated 1539 report of the riches of the region. De Niza had spotted the Zuni Pueblos from afar, presumably at dawn or in the late afternoon sun, when the Pueblos may glow with a golden hue, and assumed he was near the famed cities of gold.

Coronado explored the Pueblo country for two years without finding the hoped-for riches, and his report dispelled Spanish enthusiasm for the region for a half-century. It was not until 1598 that Juan de Oñate set up a colony in Pueblo country, after several exploring expeditions headed by others. The Spanish government demanded labor and tribute from the Pueblos and vigorously attempted to suppress native religion. These practices eventually led the Pueblos to unite in revolt in 1680, and they managed to expel the Spaniards until 1692. In that year Diego de Vargas re-entered Pueblo country, though it was not until 1696 that he gained control over the entire Rio Grande Pueblo area. The Spaniards had learned from the Pueblo Revolt and were gentler in their demands in the next century and a half. However, the Pueblos had learned as well and maintained their ceremonial life out of the view of the Spaniards, while adopting the veneer of Roman Catholicism.

The nomadic tribes and the Hopi were considerably more independent during this postrevolutionary Spanish period and the Mexican period that ensued, from 1821 until 1846. In 1846 the United States took control over that portion of the Southwest north of the Rio Grande and began campaigns to settle the nomadic tribes upon reservations. By 1863 most of the Mescalero Apache had fled into Mexico or submitted to imprisonment at Fort Sumner. Most of the Navajo were forced to join them there in 1864 after Kit Carson's siege upon Canyon de Chelly. Their journey to Fort Sumner is the tragic Long Walk to which they still refer in their stories of those times. In 1868, after four years of heartbreak and starvation, the Navajo were allowed to return to a reservation on their homeland, and four reservations were set aside for the various bands of Apaches. However, few Apaches would submit to settlement, and it was not until 1875 that those Apaches who had not fled to Mexico were confined on reservations.

The other native groups in the Southwest have also retained at least portions of their homelands, though the struggle to gain and keep these lands has been a continuous and often a bitter one. Missionaries and government programs have had an impact upon the native peoples of the Southwest to varying degrees, but this and other historical considerations are explored in depth in volume 4. Contemporary issues are discussed in volume 2. The focus in the two volumes of *Southwest* is on the impressive tenacity with which Southwestern Indians have held on to their homelands, religions, languages, social institutions, and aesthetic traditions. It is this tenacity that attracted the interest of anthropologists, writers, artists, and tourists to the Southwest initially, and it is this very tenacity that makes the detailed accounts in the pages to follow possible.

# History of Archeological Research

ALBERT H. SCHROEDER

## Early Investigations and Accomplishments

In tracing the development of archeology and related fields in the Southwest, one notes that investigators in the East prior to 1846 had not progressed much beyond describing and speculating about the prehistoric structural remains and the living tribes encountered by exploratory parties. The reports of early American travelers and explorers in the Southwest (Pattie 1833; Gregg 1844; Emory 1848; Simpson 1850; Whipple 1854–1855; Ives 1969), like those in the East not only incorporated information based on Indian oral tradition, but also drew on the few Spanish references that treated with and linked the ruins of Casa Grande in southern Arizona to the Aztec migration tradition and derived various Rio Grande Pueblo customs from the same source in Mexico.

In many instances, these explorers were led to ruins by local guides, such as John Moss who led W.H. Jackson to Mesa Verde ruins in Colorado (fig. 1) in 1874, the Wetherills who led others in the following decade (Watson 1959), and other cowboys, such as George McJunkin, who reported the Folsom site in the 1920s.

Coincident with the founding of a number of anthropological societies and the Bureau of Ethnology in the East in the 1870s, trained observers assigned to United States army and other Southwestern projects produced reconnaissance reports, collected specimens, made sketches (fig. 2), and accumulated other data (Jackson 1876; Pinart 1962; Holmes 1878; Putnam 1879a; Powell 1891; Morgan 1880). These and other investigations began to build a base for comparative studies, at that period an unlikely possibility due to the lack of a time-scale by

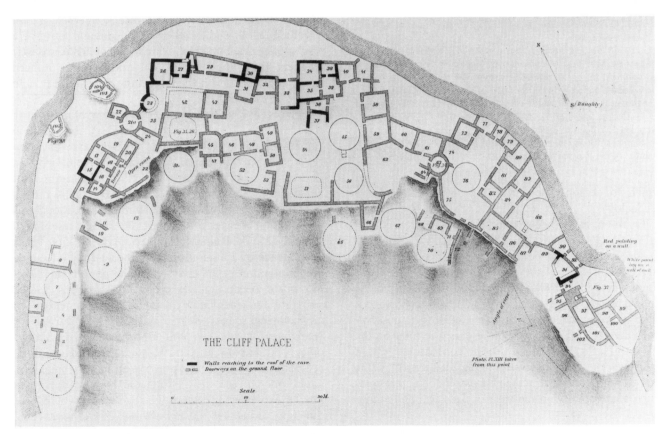

THE CLIFF PALACE

Walls reaching to the roof of the cave.
Doorways on the ground floor

Scale

Smithsonian, Dept. of Anthr.: Nordenskiöld 1893:pl. XI.

Fig. 1. Cliff Palace, Mesa Verde, Colo. Plan published by Gustav Nordenskiöld, a Swedish archeologist who surveyed the ruins in 1891. Fewkes (fig. 3) also excavated and partially restored Cliff Palace (see "Prehistory: Western Anasazi," fig. 13, this vol.) and other Mesa Verde ruins.

Fig. 2. *Cliff House in 1875*. Watercolor sketch of a cliff house at Mancos Canyon (near Mesa Verde), by William H. Holmes, artist and geologist for one of several Hayden Survey parties that explored the Colorado region 1873-1876 as part of the U.S. Geological and Geographical Surveys (see R.A. Bartlett 1962:74-120; F.W. Hayden 1877). Holmes later became chief of the Bureau of American Ethnology. William H. Jackson (1875, 1877), renowned for his photographs of this region (Newhall and Edkins 1974:76), was also a member of the Hayden Survey.

which to demonstrate change or contemporaneity in archeology.

To obtain more precise information, the Archaeological Institute of America in 1880 sent Adolf F. Bandelier to the Southwest to gather information on the living Indians and their history and to investigate the ruins (Bandelier 1883, 1890a, 1890-1892). Working from the known present to the unknown past, he combined knowledge gained at the living Pueblo of Cochiti with observations derived from his survey of prehistoric ruins on the Pajarito Plateau immediately to the north and produced the novel *The Delight Makers* (1890). This represents the first attempt to reconstruct the life pattern of a prehistoric Pueblo community on the basis of historical and ethnological data.

One of the first major efforts at intensive excavation, Frank Hamilton Cushing's expedition to the middle Gila River valley of southern Arizona in 1886-1889, failed to produce final reports (Cushing 1890) on the material objects recovered, which task Emil W. Haury (1945) attempted a half-century later. Through field observations Cushing postulated a class system among the former valley occupants, based on the association of different forms of burial and architectural characteristics. This observation, however questionable, drawn from archeological circumstances rather than existing ethnological situations in the Southwest, is the forerunner of later intensive studies to derive specific sociological and ceremonial conclusions from associated prehistoric material culture (Longacre 1970).

Cushing's associates on the project did produce reports on skeletal studies (Matthews, Wortman, and Billings 1893), documentary research (Bandelier 1890a), observations among the nearby Pimas (Ten Kate 1892), and prehistoric irrigation (Hodge 1893). Not only did this project represent a major scientific field expedition in Southwestern ruins, but also it had the basic aspects of a multi-disciplinary approach. Unfortunately, other investigators did not pursue this fruitful method for many decades to come. Instead, each followed his own field of interest, occasionally drawing on other disciplines.

Jesse Walter Fewkes (fig. 3), after working among the Zunis and Hopis in the late 1880s, turned his attention to prehistoric sites in Arizona and southwestern Colorado. Much of his interpretation concerning the ruins drew heavily on Western Pueblo traditions so familiar to him, a technique followed by others of his contemporaries. He also applied the name Hohokam to the prehistoric desert dwellers along the middle Gila drainage of southern Arizona to distinguish them from the prehistoric Pueblo people of the north.

Fewkes (1896) also recognized the extent of prehistoric trade through the presence of Pacific Coast shells among ruins in northeastern Arizona. Though his excavation reports on sites in Mesa Verde leave something to be desired by later standards, his efforts in cleaning out several ruins and preserving them (1909) qualify him as the father of Southwestern ruins stabilization, though his preservation measures were not the earliest attempted.

Casa Grande Ruins of southern Arizona, first given prominence by Father Eusebio Kino in 1694, attracted much attention in the early American period. In 1877 a movement began for the preservation of this unique structure and, incidentally, for the establishment of an archeological society in Arizona (Fewkes 1912:69). Five years later, Marshall P. Wilder and Edmund F. Slafter, officers of the New England Historic Genealogical Society, petitioned Congress to preserve antiquities on federal lands, only to see their efforts die because a Kansas senator expressed a fear that the government would have difficulty protecting the many ruins in the west (U.S. Congress. Senate. Congressional Record 1882:3777).

Though set back, the preservation movement continued. In 1888 Capt. John G. Bourke led a group of

Smithsonian, NAA.
Fig. 3. Jesse Walter Fewkes (standing at center) supervising the excavation of Far View House at Mesa Verde, Colo., in 1916. (See Swanton and Roberts 1931 for a short biography of Fewkes, including a chronological list of his archeological and ethnographic accomplishments.) Photographer unknown.

Bostonians, including Mary Hemenway who had sponsored Cushing and Fewkes, in obtaining congressional approval for the preservation of Casa Grande (U.S. Congress. Senate 1889) and approving funds for a stabilization project in 1891. The year following, 480 acres were set aside, marking the first federal reservation for a prehistoric site in the United States.

Success did not slow the conservation drive. Fewkes (1896a) pleaded for legislation to protect ruins from vandals, commercial traffic, and untrained excavators. Frank Pinkley, custodian at Casa Grande, recommended in 1902 that fines for defacing the ruins be extended to include unauthorized excavations and the removal of specimens (Van Valkenburgh 1962). Four years later, Edgar Lee Hewett, an educator in New Mexico, assisted Congressman J.F. Lacey of Iowa in drafting the approved federal Act for the Preservation of Antiquities on federal lands (Hewett 1938), which also provided for the establishment of national monuments. So was born the foundation upon which later acts broadened the scope of protection and preservation. The Southwestern states, between the 1930s and 1970, modeled their state antiquities acts after this federal legislation.

Field workers of the late 1800s and early 1900s concentrated on Pueblo and "cliff dweller" sites (figs. 1, 4), including those in northern Mexico, and produced reports of varied quality and scope, being mostly descriptive in content (Nordenskiöld 1893; C. Mindeleff 1897a;

Bandelier 1890–1892; Schwatka 1893) with some efforts devoted to comparative and environmental interpretation (Fewkes 1895; Hough 1897, 1906). Data from these reports and related fields of study began to appear in compendiums on prehistoric and living Indians (Curtis 1907–1930; Hodge 1907–1910). Translations of journals from early Spanish expeditions into the Southwest (Winship 1896; Bolton 1916; Kino 1919) also provided information on Indian customs during the exploration of the 1500s prior to Spanish influence on Southwestern Indians.

With the passage of the Antiquities Act, the Bureau of American Ethnology augmented the data-collecting surge of this period by stepping up its program of compiling an archeological catalogue of sites on federal lands in the Southwest (Holmes 1911:10). Through cooperative efforts, these surveys produced information on areas previously unstudied (Hewett 1906; Hough 1907; Jeançon 1911). They also provided inventories on new monuments established under the Antiquities Act (Fewkes 1911a).

Other contemporaries directed their efforts toward producing new specialized data—architectural typology (Prudden 1903), physical anthropology (Hrdlička 1908), ethnozoology (Lyon 1906; Henderson and Harrington 1914), ethnobotany (Stevenson 1915; Robbins, Harrington, and Freire-Marreco 1916), and ethnogeography (Harrington 1916).

Amer. Mus. of Nat. Hist., New York.
Fig. 4. Navajo workmen excavating room 62 of Pueblo Bonito, Chaco Canyon, N.M., as part of the Hyde Expedition of 1897 (one of several expeditions funded by Fred and Talbot Hyde in association with Richard Wetherill). George Hubbard Pepper, a student of Frederic Ward Putnam who was appointed director of the expedition on Putnam's recommendation, dug several test trenches and made extensive measurements of all the rooms and their contents (taking as many as a dozen photographs of each room to record the various stages of excavation) but stopped short of any stratigraphic analysis of the excavated materials (McNitt 1957:59, 140-151; Pepper 1920). Photograph by Wetherill or Pepper.

## The Pursuit of Time, Space, and Cultures

Early investigators recognized the existence of regional variations in the prehistoric architectural and material remains of the Southwest, all of which they identified with one culture, Pueblo. The differences noted were attributed to migrations or environmental factors. Pepper (1902) provided the first breakthrough on relative chronology in Southwestern sites when he suggested that Basketmaker material represented an earlier development than that of the Pueblo. This led to distinctions between culture areas (Hough 1907:25-26) as well as between early and late ceramic forms and designs. In the following decade, the study of potsherds collected from a number of sites not only provided similar information but also led to a sequence of pottery types in the Rio Grande area (Nelson 1914; Kidder 1915; Kroeber 1916a). This survey technique, checked by the first stratigraphic tests undertaken in the Southwest and double-checked by excavation in various Pueblos (Nelson 1916), was further refined through the use of a quantitative approach (Spier 1917).

The concentration on and interest in Southwestern prehistoric sites attracted the attention of local universities shortly after the turn of the century, and they began to offer courses in archeology. Hewett and Byron C. Cummings set up departments, established archeological societies, directed museums and field expeditions, and ultimately developed the first generation of Southwestern-trained archeologists (Turner 1962; Euler 1963a).

In 1914 and 1915, Alfred V. Kidder and Samuel J. Guernsey (1919) applied the technique of stratigraphy to sites in northeastern Arizona and set up three culture periods for the ruins of that region—Basketmaker, Slab House, and Cliff House. Kidder (1932), between 1915 and 1929, concentrated on Pecos Pueblo (fig. 5) to demonstrate cultural continuity from prehistoric into historic times as Nelson (1914) did in ruins of the Galisteo Basin and Hodge at the Zuni site of Hawikuh between 1917 and 1923 (Smith, Woodbury, and Woodbury 1966). From 1921 to 1927, Neil M. Judd (fig. 6) directed his efforts to a similar large project in the prehistoric sites of Chaco Canyon (1954, 1959, 1964). During the course of this work, he established ceramic and masonry chronologies and worked out the sequence of construction at Pueblo Bonito. Kirk Bryan (1925, 1926, 1954) correlated the geological stratigraphy of the canyon with archeological material recovered from arroyo banks. He suggested that information on deposition and erosion during

Alfred Kidder Guthe, Knoxville, Tenn.
Fig. 5. Alfred V. Kidder (center) in the archeology "shack" at Pecos Pueblo, with Carl E. Guthe (right), his assistant, and Alfred E. Tozzer (left), with whom Kidder had studied at Harvard. (See Woodbury 1973; Wauchope 1965; G.R. Willey 1967.) Photographer unknown, June 18, 1916.

Fig. 6. Frederick W. Hodge (seated at left) at the archeological field camp at the ancient Zuni Pueblo of Hawikuh. Staff members and visitors to the site include Alfred V. Kidder (seated at right), Earl Morris (standing far right), Neil M. Judd (standing second from right), Jesse L. Nusbaum (standing third from left) and the Mayanist Sylvanus G. Morley (standing far left). Photograph by staff photographer Charles Martin, 1920.

the range of human occupation also might be correlated with culture change.

Throughout the 1920s, other surveys and excavations established new local chronologies and more clearly identified regional variations in material culture (Morris 1921; Judd 1926; Martin 1929; F.H.H. Roberts 1930). By the middle 1920s, Kidder (1924) had proposed several prehistoric culture areas to replace what formerly had been considered regional variations. Three years later he invited Southwestern archeologists to his field camp at Pecos Pueblo to discuss the status of Southwestern archeology. At this first "Pecos Conference," the conferees defined eight prehistoric periods based on the stratigraphic record, Basketmaker I-III and Pueblo I-V (Kidder 1927).

Basketmaker I represented a hypothetical period for progenitors of Basketmaker II, probably included because of Cummings's (1928) discovery of man-made artifacts in association with extinct mammals at the Double Adobe site in southeastern Arizona and J.D. Figgins's (1927) recovery of similar information at the Folsom site, New Mexico. These finds, authenticated by geologists, removed previous doubts cast by Aleš Hrdlička (1918) on the possibility of so-called Early Man finds in America. In the 1930s and later years, work in the Clovis-Portales, New Mexico, area also provided important stratigraphic information relating to early man (Wormington 1957).

The late 1920s produced several other significant developments. A.E. Douglass (1929), working on the calendrical possibilities of tree rings—dendrochronology—since 1919, announced the first date derived from a prehistoric timber in 1929. Within a relatively few years, this technique provided archeologists with a means of dating and correlating their finds as well as with leads on fluctuations in precipitation patterns during prehistoric times.

In 1928 Harold S. and Winifred Gladwin founded Gila Pueblo Archeological Foundation, a private research institution, and initiated the largest archeological survey attempted in the Southwest (fig. 7). Three years later they hosted a conference that led to a new taxonomic concept (Gladwin and Gladwin 1934) for classifying then-recognized Southwestern prehistoric cultures into four major categories or roots, broken down into stem and then subdivided into branches. Excavations that followed defined the preceramic Cochise culture (fig. 8) (Sayles and Antevs 1941) and the Mogollon (Haury 1936a).

Also in 1928, Harold S. and Mary Russell Colton (fig. 9) established the Museum of Northern Arizona, Flagstaff, which encompassed a smaller geographical area of interest but included a broader field of natural and social sciences than did Gila Pueblo. Surveys and excavations under Lyndon L. Hargrave and John C. McGregor led to the identification of the Sinagua and Cohonina patterns, distinct from the Anasazi (Colton 1939); and ceramic research resulted in the publication of the first keyed handbooks of pottery types based on taxonomic relationships (Hargrave 1932; Colton and Hargrave 1937). The museum also encouraged Hopi crafts as a part of its activities.

Fig. 7. Members of the staff of Gila Pueblo at the Snaketown excavations, the results of which were published and later revised by Gladwin et al. (1937; Gladwin 1942, 1948). left to right, Emil Haury, Julian Hayden, Evelyn Dennis, Irwin Hayden, E.B. Sayles, Nancy Pinkley, Erik K. Reed, and J.C. Fisher Motz. Photographer unidentified, March 1935.

Fig. 8. Ernst Antevs (left), John Rinaldo (center), and E.B. Sayles on site at Dry Leggett, a stream a few miles north of Wet Leggett, Catron Co., N.M., which was surveyed by Sayles and Rinaldo. Photographer unknown, about 1947.

The Laboratory of Anthropology Incorporated, set up with personal funds from John D. Rockefeller, Jr., provided similar impetus in New Mexico, beginning in 1930 with Jesse L. Nusbaum serving as director, Kenneth Chapman encouraging Rio Grande Pueblos in crafts, Harry P. Mera and Stanley A. Stubbs conducting surveys and excavations, and W.S. Stallings, Jr., working on tree-ring dating.

The last of the privately endowed Southwestern institutions established with a prime interest in archeology

Fig. 9. Harold S. Colton, cofounder and first director of the Mus. of Northern Ariz., in an excavated kiva at Wide Ruin (Kin Tiel), Apache Co., Ariz. Wide Ruin, occupied in the 13th century, covered approximately 30 acres. The high standing walls were vandalized to build the Wide Ruin Trading Post (Colton and Baxter 1932:50). Photographer unknown, 1929.

Fig. 10. Plaza 3–12, which contained 2 rows of macaw breeding bins and hundreds of macaw carcasses, at the site of Casas Grandes in Chihuahua, Mexico, during the second season of excavation. Charles Di Peso (kneeling at center), holds the stone plug to one of the breeding bins (Di Peso 1974, 8:figs. 304–8, 305–8). Camera (at left), photographic reflector (in front of Di Peso), and plane table used for mapping (at right) are being used to record features of the excavated plaza as excavation proceeds in the small room at upper right. See Di Peso (1974, 1:20–41) for description of on-site recording methods. Photograph by Tom Carroll, staff photographer, 1959.

was the Amerind Foundation Incorporated, founded by William S. Fulton in 1937. Fieldwork, mostly limited to southeastern Arizona, later expanded into north Mexico at Casas Grandes (fig. 10) under the guidance of Charles C. Di Peso. These private institutions became prime leaders in probing into the past in the Southwest, investigating different sites and areas rather than concentrating on one site over a period of years as did university field schools of necessity in training students during the 1930s and later, such as the University of New Mexico Chaco Canyon Field School and the University of Arizona Field School at Kinishba and at Point of Pines (fig. 11).

### Ancillary Developments

In physical anthropology, Earnest A. Hooton's (1930) study of a large mass of skeletal material recovered from stratigraphically controlled deposits at Pecos provided detailed documented evidence of skeletal change within a site. This was followed by Hrdlička's (1931) work on material from the collections of the Smithsonian Institution in which he noted close resemblances between Basketmaker and early historic period Zuni crania. Seltzer (1936) expanded this concept and later (1944) provided data supporting his contention that all prehistoric Southwestern crania studied (into Pueblo IV times) were but variations of one Southwest Plateau type except in the Rio Grande where changes appeared earlier at Pecos.

Fig. 11. Emil Haury (right) with Alfred V. Kidder at the University of Arizona's summer field school at Point of Pines, Ariz. Haury was for many years director of the field school, which concluded its first season in Aug. 1946. Photograph by E.B. Sayles, 1947.

This nullified the old idea that the Basketmakers had been replaced by an invasion of Pueblo people.

With a few exceptions (Judd 1926; Martin 1929), areas peripheral to the Anasazi (Pueblo) had received little attention prior to the 1930s when interest surged in an effort to determine relationships and influences on the north (Steward 1931, 1933; Morss 1931; F.H.H. Roberts 1930), east (Jennings and Neumann 1940; Mera 1934), and south in Mexico (Sauer and Brand 1930, 1931; Brand 1935; Carey 1931; Sayles and Antevs 1935; Sayles 1936; Taylor 1956). In southwestern New Mexico, Cosgrove and Cosgrove (1932) excavated a Mimbres site, and in eastern Arizona Mera (1934a) recognized a brownware complex that extended southward from the upper Little Colorado River, much of which area came to be identified with the Mogollon culture (Haury 1936a; Wheat 1955). Work by Gila Pueblo in the mid-1930s identified the full range of Hohokam development at Snaketown along with demonstrations of Mexican influences (Gladwin et al. 1937). A few years later, McGregor (1941) recorded the presence of a Hohokam colony in the Flagstaff area.

Frank H.H. Roberts, Jr., who concentrated on the Chaco-Zuni area, and who first defined the criteria for the different periods of the Pecos Classification, also first (1935) recognized differences between the early Western and Eastern Pueblo cultural remains. While Earl Morris (1939) found the Pecos Classification applicable in the San Juan region, F.H.H. Roberts (1937) revised it for use in the upper Little Colorado drainage area. Colton (1939), on the other hand, adapted Gladwin's classification system to the Flagstaff region. It had become apparent that no one classificatory system could be applied in the same manner to several different cultures and subcultures.

Ethnozoological studies during this period (Castetter and Underhill 1935; Whiting 1939), as well as the application of these specialties (V.H. Jones 1935; Hargrave 1939) to materials recovered from archeological sites, provided new cultural-environmental information. The establishment of the Laboratory of Tree-Ring Research at the University of Arizona in 1937 led to expanded chronologies, to refinement of paleoclimatological data, and later to coordination with other geochronological techniques (Smiley 1955).

The archeological pursuits of the 1930s, in addition to those noted above, left a legacy of specialized studies on sites as well as on various subjects such as pottery, architecture, and lithics (Vaillant 1932; Fulton 1934; Mera 1935; Colton 1936, 1939a; Brand et al. 1937; Martin, Lloyd, and Spoehr 1938; Kluckhohn and Reiter 1939; Chard 1940; Woodbury 1954).

### Organizations and Legislation

Southwestern archeological societies, first organized in the early 1900s, provided considerable impetus to Southwestern archeology. The society in New Mexico was the prime factor in establishing what is now the Museum of New Mexico, Santa Fe, and in bringing the School of American Research to New Mexico. These groups also provided publication outlets for articles on archeology. Only a few of these societies undertook field activities of their own prior to the 1960s.

The idea of the original Pecos Conference was maintained periodically in the 1930s up to 1941 at meetings known as the Southwest Archeological Conference, sometimes referred to as the Chaco Conference. In 1949 it became an annual affair known as the Pecos Conference. These gatherings provided a forum for the continued exchange of ideas, reports on current work, and discussions of problems of the moment.

Increased archeological activities in the Southwest and throughout the country by the 1930s led the professionals in 1934 to establish The Society for American Archaeology, and Southwesterners Roberts, Kidder, and Alfred L. Kroeber drew up the constitution and bylaws. The passage the following year of the Historic Sites Act, which provided for nationwide survey and research, acquisition of such sites, cooperative agreements, markers, and other measures, also included a mandate on structural preservation. The National Park Service inaugurated a formal program of ruins stabilization that, under Charlie R. Steen and R. Gordon Vivian and later under Roland S. Richert, preserved many significant sites in the parks. Coincident with the passage of the act, fieldwork at two historic-period sites, Abó (J.H. Toulouse 1949) and Awatovi (Montgomery, Smith, and Brew 1949), got underway.

The Committee for the Recovery of Archaeological Remains, also created in 1945, with J.O. Brew as chairman for many years, developed a congressionally supported interagency program to salvage sites threatened with destruction by reservoir construction projects. Roberts played a major role in developing the Missouri River Basin aspect of this program (Brew 1961). The passage of the Indian Claims Act of 1946 created the need to establish pre-American period tribal identities, ranges, and interrelationships for the hearings. Historical archeology combined with documentary research produced much of this information and gave needed stimulus to the field of ethnohistory.

## New Directions in Research and Preservation

During the wartime lull in field research, a healthy curiosity developed. Researchers reviewed old ideas, examined alternatives to set new directions of investigation, and provided new syntheses, most of which appeared in print shortly after the war. Haury (1945a) explored the problems of Mexico-Southwest contacts. Brew (1946) questioned several aspects of archeological systematics. Colton (1946) produced a compendium on the Sinagua, and Albert H. Schroeder (1947) suggested that this prehistoric group, not the Salado, introduced northern traits to the Hohokam. Kidder and Cosgrove (1949) in turn rejected the idea that the Salado migrated to Mexico. Erik K. Reed (1946) defined the characteristics of the San Juan Anasazi and the Western Pueblos (1948) and related the different types of skull deformation to specific culture areas (1949). The greatest impact came from Walter W. Taylor's (1948) analysis to resolve conflicts of a theoretical order, in which he suggested a comprehensive approach to the development of a conceptual scheme for archeological research and made a plea to archeologists to investigate interrelationships within a cultural entity.

Within the next few years, new dating techniques became available. The application of carbon-14 dating to material from prehistoric sites, developed by J.R. Arnold and W.F. Libby (1949), proved a boon to chronologically sorting Southwestern early man finds beyond the reach of dendrochronology such as those at Sandia Cave and Bat Cave, New Mexico (Hibben 1941; Dick 1951), and at Ventana Cave and Naco, Arizona (Haury 1950, 1953). New techniques—fluorine, archeomagnetism—provided methods of dating material other than wood or charcoal. The use of palynology—the study of pollen—opened up a new field for reconstructing prehistoric environments and plotting changes that occurred at different periods in time at a given site, the changes providing another relative chronological scale.

The postwar population increase in the Southwest and the resultant development of reservoirs, power lines, highways, and the like created a threat to archeological sites. Jesse L. Nusbaum, as Department of Interior consulting archeologist, concentrated on the enforcement of the Antiquities Act and set the precedent in 1950 of instituting salvage on pipeline rights of way (Wendorf, Fox, and Lewis 1956). This in turn, through negotiations between Fred Wendorf of the Museum of New Mexico, W.J. Keller of the federal Bureau of Public Roads, and the New Mexico State Highway Department, led to highway salvage in 1954 in New Mexico (Wendorf 1954–1956; Peckham 1957–1963) and two years later to the passage of the Federal Aid Highway Act for similar salvage on federally financed projects in all states. The Reservoir Salvage Act of 1960 also included stipulations for the salvage of archeological remains, providing another step in the conservation of the national historical heritage.

Though considerable effort was diverted to salvage projects in the Southwest after 1950, institutions and individuals continued with their own research programs or completed earlier studies (Lehmer 1948; Kelley 1952; W. Smith 1952a; Schroeder 1952a, 1955, 1961a; Holden 1952; Di Peso 1953, 1956; Stubbs and Stallings 1953; Wendorf 1953; Lambert 1954; Lancaster et al. 1954; Morris and Burgh 1954; Ezell 1954; Danson 1957; Jennings 1957, 1966; Kidder 1958; Lister 1958; Breternitz 1959, 1960; Dittert, Hester, and Eddy 1961; Eddy 1961, 1966; Adams, Lindsay, and Turner 1961; Bullard 1962; Carlson 1963; Ellis 1964a; Ellis and Brody 1964; Wasley and Johnson 1965; Aikens 1966; Jelinek 1967; Gumerman and Skinner 1968; Lange 1968; Irwin-Williams 1968). Perhaps the longest investigation of its kind was Paul S. Martin's work on Mogollon sites in western New Mexico, from the late 1930s into the 1950s, and his subsequent shift to the nearby region of eastern Arizona (see, for example, Martin 1940; Martin and Rinaldo 1950, 1950a; Martin, Rinaldo, and Antevs 1949).

Also during the 1950s and 1960s, investigators probed the gap between the better-known Mesoamerican cultures and those of Arizona and New Mexico, in Tamaulipas (Aveleyra Arroyo de Anda 1951; MacNeish 1958), Nuevo Leon (Epstein 1969), Chihuahua (Di Peso 1968), and Sonora (Fay 1958; Johnson 1963). The work accomplished in northeastern Mexico including west Texas has been summarized by Taylor (1966).

The National Park Service multi-disciplinary project on Wetherill Mesa at Mesa Verde (Hayes 1964; Osborn 1965; Swannack 1969; Rohn 1971) and the Navajo Reservoir salvage project in northern New Mexico, under the direction of A.E. Dittert, demonstrated the advantages of this type of approach. Particularly the Navajo Reservoir project developed a renewed interest in Indian rock art (Schaafsma 1963), included a study of vertebrate remains as an aspect of reconstructing past environments in other than early man situations (Harris 1963), and used alluvial and palynological data to produce culturally relevant prehistoric environmental information (Schoenwetter and Eddy 1964).

With the accumulation of so much and so varied data, a few specialized compilations began to appear after the war, such as on flint quarries (Bryan 1950), ceremonial wall paintings (W. Smith 1952), pottery types (Colton 1956), clay figurines (Morss 1954), stone implements (Woodbury 1954), cotton weaving (Kent 1957), and tree-ring dated pottery types (Breternitz 1966). In addition, a series of ceramic seminars, initiated in 1958, coped with the classification of the increasing numbers of new Southwestern types.

Several Southwestern postwar studies produced syntheses and postulations concerned with cross-cultural ties (Martin and Rinaldo 1951; Daifuku 1952), chronology and culture area correlations (Rogers 1945; Colton 1945; Stubbs and Stallings 1953; Wendorf and Reed 1955; J.B. Wheat 1955; Di Peso 1956; Schroeder 1960; Jennings 1966; Ford, Schroeder, and Peckham 1972), and prehistoric groups and language (Davis 1959; Taylor 1961; Trager 1967), all of which revised earlier broad syntheses on the archeology of the Southwest (F.H.H. Roberts 1931, 1935; McGregor 1941a; Wormington 1947; Gladwin 1957). Articles on trends in Southwestern archeology (Judd 1940; Reed 1955) and occasional seminars on the Southwest provided additional review and updating of ideas (Haury 1954; Wauchope 1956; Longacre 1970; Ortiz 1972). Anthropological literature, hypotheses, and methods also received critical review and comment (Taylor 1954; Bayard 1969; Schiffer 1972); and preservation measures continued with the passage of the Historic Preservation Act of 1966, which expanded the federal program into the states.

Research of this period also included the formulation of new ideas on Mexico-Southwest relationships (Ferdon 1955; Kelley 1960; Schroeder 1965, 1966), the concept of a Desert culture (Jennings 1957), the Hakataya culture (Schroeder 1957, 1960), possible new cultural alignments for the Fremont culture (Ambler 1966; Aikens 1967), and configurations of preceramic Southwestern cultural developments (Irwin-Williams 1968).

Detailed work on the part of specialists, working with material recovered from excavations, contributed considerably to reconstructing past developments. Concepts on the use and dispersion of domestic plants in the Southwest and neighboring regions were updated (Cutler and Whitaker 1961; Galinat and Gunnerson 1963; Mangelsdorf and Lister 1956). Paleopathologists probed into the identification of possible prehistoric diseases and abnormalities in skeletal remains (Armelagos 1967; Kunitz 1970). In reconstructing ecological changes of the past (Schoenwetter 1962; Martin 1963), palynologists suggested trends in climate changes counter to former beliefs (Martin 1963a). New techniques and studies (Osborn 1965) have provided Southwestern archeologists with detailed information relative to prehistoric environments.

In addition, a review of modern Pueblo Indian social units and possible implications concerning architectural and geographic relationships (Dozier 1965) has opened up new leads for investigation in prehistoric sites. Archeologists, obtaining data from excavations in known, but abandoned, Indian sites or from related historical documents and ethnological studies, have been filling gaps between present and late prehistoric times in an attempt to more accurately identify groups, culture change, and interaction with other groups (Hester 1962; Ezell 1963; Gunnerson 1969; Schroeder 1972).

Techniques employing random sampling, statistics, and computer analysis have produced inferences derived from research designed to test hypotheses relating to various aspects of cultural processes (J.N. Hill 1966; Longacre 1970). The work of Herbert W. Dick on Picuris Pueblo; Florence Ellis on San Gabriel, the first Spanish settlement in New Mexico; Di Peso (1974) on Casas Grandes; R. Gwinn Vivian on water control devices and roads in Chaco Canyon; and Douglas W. Schwartz on Grand Canyon, along with the new techniques, will certainly open up new vistas.

A variety of physical, natural, and social sciences is being more closely drawn together, and specialized approaches are being developed to provide leads as well as answers in Southwestern archeology. Archeology undoubtedly will continue to grow, as its history demonstrates, by generating schools of thought, developing new techniques, and utilizing the best in other disciplines.

# History of Ethnological Research

KEITH H. BASSO

In 1879 the newly founded Bureau of American Ethnology arranged for one of its employees, a 22-year-old named Frank Hamilton Cushing, to travel to the Territory of New Mexico to inquire firsthand into the customs and beliefs of the Zuni Indians. Cushing, who was a talented naturalist but completely without training in anthropology, stayed with the Zuni for the next four and one-half years. Living as they did and sharing closely in their activities, he mastered their language, received instruction in their myths and rituals (fig. 1), and grew to understand the complex organization of their society as had no non-Indian before him. Much of what Cushing learned was never published, but his major ethnographic work—a detailed and carefully wrought study of Zuni mythology (1896)—set an enduring precedent by demonstrating conclusively what had previously only been suspected: the cultures of Southwestern Indians afforded extraordinary opportunities for anthropological research.

These opportunities have not gone unexploited. Social and cultural anthropologists have applied their discipline in the Southwest for about a century, and they have produced a body of literature on the region's indigenous peoples that in terms of sheer magnitude and variety probably surpasses that of any ethnographic area in the New World. Equally impressive, if not more so, is the extent to which this material reflects the prominent role played by successive generations of Southwestern ethnologists in stimulating and shaping the growth of anthropological thought. Clyde Kluckhohn, an eminent student of culture, once wrote that anthropology was a "mirror for man." One could observe just as correctly that the history of research in the Southwest has been—and still is—a mirror of American anthropology.

Unlike many regions of North America, where Indian populations had been decimated by disease, destroyed by arms, or forcibly removed from their original homelands, the Southwest in the late 1800s contained a number of native societies that persisted in situ and essentially

Smithsonian, NAA.

Fig. 1. Frank Hamilton Cushing at Zuni. left, Dressed in Zuni clothing—woven woolen shirt, wrapped hide leggings over his breeches, moccasins, numerous silver ornaments and jewelry (including looped earrings worn through pierced ears) and a scarf tied round his forehead, Zuni-style—an outfit that Cushing (1941:88-91) said he acquired at the urging of the Zunis. right, Cushing (foreground, in dark clothing) at a ceremony of the War Gods performed by the Bow Priesthood, a society into which Cushing was initiated in 1881 (see Brandes 1965; Pandey 1972:321-325). Photographs by John K. Hillers, possibly 1880-1881 (left) and unknown photographer, probably winter 1881-1883.

Fig. 2. John Wesley Powell (b. 1834, d. 1902) (at extreme left) on one of the Geographical and Geological Surveys, probably that of 1873 (see Stegner 1954); the man to his immediate left may be a Navajo guide. Powell later served as the first director of the Bureau of (American) Ethnology. Photograph possibly by John K. Hillers.

intact. The viability of these societies, coupled with the fact that none of them had been adequately studied or described, presented early anthropologists with a compelling challenge. It was plausibly argued by explorer-ethnologists such as John Wesley Powell (1891) (fig. 2) that nowhere in the United States was ethnographic fieldwork so badly needed and at the same time so eminently feasible as in the Southwest. And nowhere, for the same reasons, was it likely to yield more valuable results.

Just as intriguing was the fact that Southwestern Indian societies exhibited a striking degree of linguistic and cultural diversity. This diversity, together with an abundance of well-preserved archeological sites, suggested that the prehistory of the Southwest had been long and complicated and that archeological investigations, by clarifying what took place in the region's past, could contribute significantly to a clearer understanding of its present. Concomitantly, and in keeping with nineteenth-century theories of cultural evolution, it was assumed that knowledge acquired about extant Southwestern societies could be "reversed," so to speak, and used to interpret archeological materials. In this way—working from the known to the unknown, from the living to the dead by means of analogy—prehistoric cultures could be identified and connected with their surviving descend-

ants. Ethnology and archeology were opposite sides of the same coin.

Concentrating mainly on the Puebloan groups, early ethnologists seized upon information contained in myths and so-called migration legends to construct elaborate hypotheses about the origins and evolution of basic forms of social organization (Bandelier 1883, 1890-1892, 2; Fewkes 1896b, 1900; Mindeleff 1891; C. Mindeleff 1900). Although most of these hypotheses were subsequently rejected as untestable and unduly speculative, they succeeded in drawing attention to important substantive problems and, by reason of their own inadequacy, emphasized a need for more sophisticated method and theory (cf. Taylor 1954; Longacre 1970). A few workers, following Cushing's lead, combined excursions into conjectural history with lengthy descriptions of ongoing cultures. The best of these studies—on the Navajo (Matthews 1887, 1890, 1902), Tewa (Harrington 1916), Seri (fig. 4) (McGee 1898), and Huichol (Lumholtz 1902)—went well beyond the "mere collection of facts" (a facile criticism that is sometimes leveled at all Southwestern studies conducted before 1925) to show that Indian customs and beliefs were rich in symbolic content, extensively detailed, and fully deserving of careful analysis in their own right. Simultaneously, these studies

Fig. 3. Juan José Montoya, Adolph F. Bandelier's principal Cochiti informant (see Bandelier 1966-1976,1), posing with his daughter Ignacio. The photograph was apparently arranged by Bandelier (1966-1976,1:222) to show as many items as possible of Cochiti material culture including: household items such as water jars and bowls, a bread paddle and a mano and metate for grinding corn; items of warfare such as bow and arrows, rifle, and shield; a 3-pronged pitchfork used in farming; and what appear to be a bandolier and rattle (for similar, see "Santa Ana Pueblo," fig. 7, this vol.) for ceremonial use. See "Cochiti Pueblo," fig. 7, and "Santa Domingo Pueblo," fig. 5, this vol. for sketches by Bandelier showing Pueblo architecture and land use. Photograph by George C. Bennett, a Santa Fe photographer who accompanied Bandelier, Nov. 30, 1880.

preserved large amounts of data that are invaluable and irreplaceable.

Shortly before the turn of the century the influential Franz Boas voiced strong dissatisfaction with prevailing theories of cultural evolution, observing that they were grounded in questionable assumptions and that the search for universal developmental laws should be suspended until more accurate information had been collected concerning historical sequences in particular geographical regions. Boas held staunchly to the view that generalizations about the origins and causes of cultural phenomena should be derived inductively and therefore could be formulated only on the basis of systematic empirical research. It was just this kind of research, he emphasized, that had not yet been carried out. In most cases, for example, one simply could not tell whether an item or institution that occurred in several cultures had been invented separately in each, or whether, having been invented in only one, it subsequently spread to others. Boas stressed that questions such as these could not be answered a priori; they depended upon full descriptions of all the cultures within a region as well as detailed investigations of their historical contacts and relations.

In the Southwest as elsewhere the initial effect of Boas's program was to stimulate more ethnography and

a more cautious and responsible approach to the collection and interpretation of ethnographic facts (Spier 1928, 1933; Parsons 1932; Forde 1931a; Gifford 1933; Kroeber 1935). Later, it provided the framework and rationale for studies of cultural borrowing and diffusion (Kroeber 1925, 1939; Strong 1927, 1929; Reed 1946; Spier 1953) as well as a series of attempts to define the perimeters of the Southwest and establish it as a bounded "culture area" (Spier 1929; Beals 1932, 1943; Kroeber 1939; Reed 1946; Kirchhoff 1954). Although this body of research pro-

Smithsonian, NAA.

Fig. 5. Matilda Coxe Stevenson. top, Detail from engraving in the *Illustrated Police News* titled "an assassin red-devil cowed by a white heroine . . ." that accompanied an article allegedly describing one of Stevenson's encounters with the Hopi (Anonymous 1886:9, 15); to her left is Col. James Stevenson, whom she accompanied. bottom, Zia women prepare clay floor for Stevenson's camp at that Pueblo (see Stevenson 1894); photograph by Stevenson 1888–1889.

Smithsonian, NAA.

Fig. 4. WJ McGee (seated at left) securing a Seri vocabulary at the Rancho San Francisco de Costa Rica in Sonora, Mexico (see McGee 1898:pl. 1 for exact location), where approximately 60 Seri were occupying a temporary rancheria. Mashem, a Seri subchief who spoke Spanish, leans on the table across from McGee; Pascual Encinas, the owner of the ranch, is seated between them. Onlookers include Encinas's son and grandson and a Spanish interpreter. McGee's (1898) monograph on the Seri was based on research conducted during an 1894 and an 1895 Bureau of American Ethnology expedition among the Seri (and the Papago). Photograph by William Dinwiddie, expedition photographer, 1894.

16

duced relatively little in the way of general theory, it was valuable for a number of other reasons. To begin with, the true complexity of Southwestern culture history was revealed for the first time, and the relationships of Southwestern cultures to those in adjoining regions were significantly clarified (Kroeber 1925, 1939; Strong 1927; Haury 1945a; Lange 1953b). Culture area studies drew attention to the existence of covariation among subsistence practices and features of the natural environment, thereby raising the important question of how ecological factors operated to influence the development of different forms of social organization (Steward 1937; Kroeber 1939; Goldfrank 1945a). And studies of diffusion, emphasizing as they did the processual nature of culture change, laid the groundwork for pioneering studies of acculturation (Parsons 1930; Parsons and Beals 1934; Reed 1944; Ellis 1951).

It is important to understand that between 1900 and 1925 most Southwestern ethnologists took the position that a culture was commensurate with, and essentially equal to, the number of discrete elements or "traits" that comprised it. Consequently, the exercise of analyzing a culture was seen to consist in making an exhaustive inventory of its component elements, framing minute descriptions of them, and attempting to identify their historical sources. (Explaining similarities among cultures was tantamount to showing that they possessed elements derived from the same source; cultural differences were accounted for by showing just the reverse.)

Fig. 6. Elsie Clews Parsons (b. 1875, d.1941), while doing fieldwork among the Taos (see Parsons 1936). Taos was one of several Pueblos that she visited and studied from 1915 to 1932, leading to numerous articles and books (see Anonymous 1943:48–56) that culminated in Parsons's (1939) classic study of Pueblo religion (see Spier 1943; Kroeber 1943). Photographer unidentified, 1916–1925.

Consequently, overwhelming significance was attached to the *content* of cultures as opposed to their organization, and the *forms* of social institutions were studied to the virtual exclusion of their functions. The effects such institutions had upon individuals, that is, the role of culture in shaping and guiding human behavior, was neglected almost entirely.

By 1930 this conception of culture and ethnography began to change in response to two major developments. One was the increasing sophistication of British functionalist theory as formulated by A.R. Radcliffe-Brown and applied by him and his students to the analysis of kinship and social organization. The other, stimulated by the writings of Edward Sapir (fig. 7) and Ruth Benedict, was a growing interest in cultural patterning and the study of culture as a psychological phenomenon. Although these intellectual currents were in many ways very different, they were alike in one fundamental respect. Both were rooted in the assumption that cultures were much more than aggregates of disparate practices and customs. Every culture formed a system whose parts were related to each other by a set of underlying principles. These principles, which it was the ethnographer's task to discover and make explicit, imparted a structure to the system; and the system's parts, precisely because they were interrelated, could only be fully understood in terms of their place in this structure. Thus emphasis was shifted from the history and external attributes of a culture's elements to its functions—the "contributions" each element made to the system as a whole.

Working with materials from Zuni and Hopi respectively, Kroeber (1919) and Lowie (1929) made early studies of Southwestern kinship systems; however, it was not until the mid-1930s, by which time Radcliffe-Brown had come to the United States to teach, that social organization became a focal point for intensive research. In accepting the basic tenets of functionalism Southwestern ethnologists were reluctant to jettison their established interests in culture history. This proved to be highly significant because it was a successful attempt to combine the two perspectives that enabled them to make genuine theoretical advances. Morris Opler's (1936) elegant reconstruction of Apachean kinship systems clearly foreshadowed the development of a new synthesis, and to a lesser extent so did the work of Elsie Clews Parsons (1939), Leslie White (1930), and others (Spicer 1940; Titiev 1944). However, conclusive evidence that the synthesis had been achieved awaited the publication of Fred Eggan's (1950) masterful comparative study of Western Pueblo social organization. Eggan showed that while a strictly functional approach to the analysis of kinship was extremely useful, it also left important facts unexplained. Cultures were never static, change was fundamental, and principles of historical explanation could not be discounted. To the contrary, Eggan argued, they were essential.

Fig. 7. Linguist-anthropologist Edward Sapir (far right) on the U. of Chicago campus with anthropologists Fay-Cooper Cole (center) and Paul S. Martin (left), as Martin was about to depart on a field trip to Galena, Ill. Sapir conducted linguistic research with several groups (see Boas 1939). From 1927 until his death in 1939, he worked with Navajo, collecting many of his texts during a summer field training program in linguistics, supported by the Laboratory of Anthropology in Santa Fe, which he led in 1929. The bulk of these materials was published posthumously (Sapir 1942; Sapir and Hoijer 1967) under the editorship of Harry Hoijer, who continued Sapir's Navajo work (Hoijer 1974). Martin later did archeological research in the Southwest (Longacre 1976). Photograph by unknown photographer, 1925-1931.

The recognition that functionalist methods could be used in conjunction with those of historical analysis had important consequences for Southwestern research (cf. Hoebel 1954). Problems in cultural reconstruction were attacked with fresh insight and greater conceptual precision, and the scope of ethnography was broadened also. No longer satisfied to describe the manifest form and content of a society's institutions, ethnographers investigated the ways in which these institutions articulated with one another to form unified, coherent structures (Underhill 1939; Spicer 1940; Opler 1941; Kluckhohn and Leighton 1946). The result was a heightened awareness of covert principles of social integration and a more acute understanding of how such principles operated to preserve stability and cohesion in the face of change. A view of Southwestern Indian societies as organized, dynamic wholes began to emerge, and this in turn fostered interest in the full range of cultural mechanisms that had enabled them to adapt to three centuries of contact with Spanish, Mexican, and Anglo-American intruders (Reed 1944; Aberle 1948; Dozier 1951, 1954; Spicer 1954).

It would be wrong to suppose that functionalism alone was responsible for altering the course of twentieth-century Southwestern ethnology. As previously stated, the theory of cultural patterning was equally influential.

Initially formulated by Benedict (1930a, 1932, 1934) on the basis of fieldwork at Zuni (but prefigured by Haeberlin 1916), this theory held that every culture embodied a distinctive ethos, a set of implicit ideological premises that served among other things to define appropriate forms of social behavior. Backed by the unassailable forces of tradition and moral authority, these premises were communicated to children early in life (as much by deed as by word) and in the process of becoming internalized fostered the development of certain basic personality characteristics. These characteristics, which together made up what Benedict called a "psychological type," functioned to place strong constraints upon adult behavior, patterning it in ways that were congruent with the culture's ethos and therefore minimally disruptive of the established social order. A culture, in other words, provided its members with more than language, technology, a kinship system, and the like. It also provided them with an orderly conception of the universe and the proper place of man within it. More fundamental still, it moulded the character of its members in ways that were compatible with this conception. Personality, in short, was a culturally determined product.

In contrast to functionalism, which drew attention to relationships among the components of social systems, Benedict's work emphasized the relationship of culture and the individual. As a result, it was directly instrumental in stimulating research on a variety of psychological topics that previously had been regarded as lying outside the domain of ethnology. Much of this research was conducted in the Southwest between 1935 and 1950, a period when studies of "culture and personality" were numerous, fashionable, and influential. The concept of patterning in culture was clarified and refined (Opler 1946; Kluckhohn 1941), and its utility in describing behavioral regularities was confirmed (D. Eggan 1943; Goldfrank 1945; Thompson 1945; J.W. Bennett 1946; Astrov 1950). Psychoanalytic and psychobiological theories were employed to interpret life-history materials (L.W. Simmons 1942; Leighton and Leighton 1949; D.F. Aberle 1951), the overt content of dreams and myths (Benedict 1935; Goldfrank 1948; D. Eggan 1949), and conditions that influenced the expression of aggression, ambivalence, and anxiety (Opler 1936; Kluckhohn 1944). Observational studies focused upon child-rearing practices and the effects of these practices on personality formation (Dennis 1940; Goldfrank 1945; Kluckhohn and Rosenzweig 1949). Still other works dealt with forms of deviant behavior (Devereux 1937; Devereux and Loeb 1943), the administration and analysis of psychological tests in cross-cultural contexts (Havighurst and Hilkevitch 1944; Kaplan 1954), and the central place of values and "value-orientations" in both cultural and personality systems (J.W. Bennett 1946; Kluckhohn and Leighton 1946; Kluckhohn 1951).

Taken as a whole, this body of research was valuable

on several counts. To begin with, it established that the members of Southwestern Indian societies were neither immune to, nor exempt from, psychological conflict and stress; more significantly, it revealed the existence of a variety of cultural practices and institutions that functioned to relieve these tensions and render them relatively harmless (Opler 1936a; Kluckhohn 1944; Devereux 1948). In addition, the fact of variation in personality was conclusively affirmed. Within any society some persons would be found who exhibited a large number of "typical" personality characteristics; however, other persons would be found who did not. The amount and range of this type of variation was just as great in Indian populations as in Anglo-American populations of comparable size. Finally, and most important, it became clear that processes of personality development were far more complex than had formerly been thought, and that psychological theories (especially those of Sigmund Freud) were inadequate to explain many of the data collected by anthropologists (D.F. Aberle 1951, 1954). By the same token it was recognized that Benedict's theory, though arresting and undeniably important, had been drawn too simply and was therefore of limited utility (Li 1937; Kluckhohn 1954). What was needed was a more general and sophisticated theory that effectively related the development of personality to cultural and social variables as well as to the unique biological heredities and idiosyncratic histories of individuals (Kluckhohn 1954; D.F. Aberle 1954).

Studies of Indian religion had long figured prominently in Southwestern research. Prior to 1900 such studies concentrated mainly upon descriptions of myths and religious beliefs. Later, when problems in diffusion gained importance, they were chiefly concerned with the spatial distribution of elements of "religious culture"—traits such as shamanism, masked dancers, the use of prayer-sticks, and so forth. The advent of functionalism brought with it an explicit interest in how religious institutions operated to maintain community integration and solidarity (Titiev 1944) as well as how the purposes served by these institutions had changed over time (Rapoport 1954). Ruth Underhill (1948) demonstrated the functional interdependence of certain types of ceremonial patterns with distinct forms of economic organization, and pioneering studies of religious symbolism were made by Gladys Reichard (1950) and Parsons (1939). Parsons's contribution, a massive comparative treatment of Pueblo religion, also contained a valuable analysis of the historical development of ceremonial complexes and their relationships to features of social and political systems.

Psychological theories were put to use by a number of workers interested in religion (Benedict 1935), but no one applied them more creatively than Kluckhohn (1942, 1944; Kluckhohn and Leighton 1946). In a series of penetrating studies dealing with the Navajo, Kluckhohn

top, Field Mus., Chicago; bottom, Smithsonian, NAA.
Fig. 8. Museum displays of Southwestern ethnological materials in the 1880s and 1890s. top, Field Columbian Museum life group exhibit showing a Hopi home, which was installed in 1897–1898 and was still on exhibit (in modified form) in 1978; photograph by staff photographer, 1897–1898. bottom, Whewa, a Zuni transvestite who was one of Matilda Coxe Stevenson's informants, constructing a loom (probably for use in a life group similar to the one above) in the Arts and Industries building of the Smithsonian Institution, photographer unidentified, probably 1884–1887.

showed how myth, ritual, and belief in witchcraft contributed to the psychological welfare of individuals by allaying anxiety and imbuing them with a sense of control over the exigencies of life in a harsh and unpredictable environment. In addition, Kluckhohn demonstrated that these institutions gave expression to a set of sophisticated philosophical principles that provided the Navajo with an integrated model of the workings of their universe.

The theoretical growth and diversification that marked Southwestern ethnology during the 1930s and 1940s was accompanied by a substantial increase in ethnographic activity. While interest remained strong in the frequently studied Puebloan peoples, a number of other Indian cultures were investigated extensively and in depth for the first time. Excellent materials were published on the

Chiricahua (Opler 1941, 1942), Jicarilla (Opler 1936b; 1946), Kiowa-Apache (McAllister 1955), and Western Apache (Goodwin 1939, 1942), as well as the Navajo (Hill 1936, 1938; Kluckhohn and Wyman 1940; J. Ladd 1957). Informative works also appeared on the Papago (Underhill 1939, 1946a), Yaqui (Spicer 1940, 1954a), and Tarahumara (Bennett and Zingg 1935). Together with earlier studies of the various Pai and Yuman groups (Kroeber 1925; Spier 1928, 1933; Forde 1931a; Gifford 1932, 1936), these contributions revealed much about the simpler societies of the Southwest and their adjustments to differing ecological settings and historical circumstances.

Shortly before 1950 increasing numbers of ethnologists turned their attention to problems in the area of cultural and social change, especially the processes of acculturation, assimilation, and revitalization. The dominant approach, articulated and exemplified most clearly in the work of Edward H. Spicer (1961, 1962), located analysis at the level of cultural systems and attempted to determine how their content and organization, together with the conditions under which they came into contact, gave rise to particular forms of adjustment. Although these adjustments displayed considerable variation from culture to culture, comparative study suggested that the processes that produced them—fusion, substitution, compartmentalization—were relatively few in number. Another approach, ably illustrated in studies by Vogt (1951) and Adair and Vogt (1949), located analysis at the level of the individual. Here the primary concern was with the ways in which Southwestern Indian people adapted psychologically and behaviorally to the experience of living and participating in cultures other than their own. Consideration was also given to the difficulties encountered by such individuals when they returned home and were called upon to reenter their own society. A third and highly successful approach was to treat a single class of phenomena, nativistic movements, as examples par excellence of adjustments to conditions generated by culture contact. The best of these studies, a meticulous treatment of the rise and spread of Navajo peyotism by David Aberle (1966), combined analysis at all levels to illuminate not only the economic and social causes that prompted the Navajo to adopt and refashion the Peyote religion but also the reasons they found it satisfying and beneficial.

In the early 1960s younger scholars who were dissatisfied with established viewpoints and modes of analysis began to formulate new problems and attack them from fresh perspectives. This willingness to challenge and experiment has been responsible for some significant contributions to Southwestern ethnology, but the introduction of new approaches, together with the persistence of older ones, has also resulted in unprecedented specialization and compartmentalization within the field as a whole (Basso 1973).

Estelle Titiev, Ann Arbor, Mich.

Fig. 9. Ethnological field party (Lab. of Anthr., Santa Fe) consisting of graduate students assembled under the leadership of Leslie White to study the clan and kinship organization of Third Mesa, with particular reference to the 1906 split (see "Hopi History, 1850-1940," this vol.). Shown here at Kyakotsmovi (New Oraibi), they are (left to right): Ed Kennard (Columbia U.), Jess Spirer (Yale U.), Leslie White (U. of Mich.), Fred Eggan (U. of Chicago), and Mischa Titiev (Harvard U.). Photographer unknown, 1932.

In contrast to earlier periods, there is simply no one underlying theme, or two, or three, that can be adduced to integrate the full array of methods and theories with which Southwestern ethnologists in the late twentieth century conduct research. At one end of the spectrum are staunch "behaviorists" who locate structure in patterns of overt social action and seek explanation through the use of statistical models; at the other end are equally enthusiastic "mentalists" who find structure in the symbolic codes that underlie behavior and seek explanation through the analysis of conceptual oppositions and the construction of decision-making models. Intersecting the behaviorist-mentalist continuum is another whose poles are defined by the presence and absence of an explicit emphasis on change. The presence of a concern with change tends to be accompanied by behaviorist methods and is clearly visible in studies of urban migration (W.H. Hodge 1969; Graves 1970), social pathologies (Graves 1971; Levy and Kunitz 1974), systems of resource exchange and distribution (Ford 1972, 1972a), and processes of Indian "modernization" (Hackenberg 1972). The absence of this concern, frequently coupled with mentalist strategies, is most conspicuous in studies of folk classification (Basso 1969; Werner and Begishe 1970; Witherspoon 1971), ritual (C.J. Frisbie 1967; Wyman 1970), and world view (Ortiz 1969; Meyerhoff 1970).

The difficulty with this sort of pigeonholing is that there are many more pigeons than holes. Consequently, it would be deceptive to claim that distinctions of the kind mentioned above do more than provide general points of orientation. On the other hand, it would be just as misleading to pretend that current work in Southwestern ethnology fails to provide evidence of new trends as well as the continuation and demise of old ones.

Interest remains strong in the historical reconstruction of Southwestern Indian societies (Kurtz 1969; Hoijer 1971; Gunnerson and Gunnerson 1971), the dynamics of their relationships with the physical environment and other human populations (Griffin 1969; Dobyns and Euler 1970; Bradfield 1971), and their responses to successive waves of conquest and subjugation by the governments of Spain, Mexico, and the United States (Brugge 1968; L.C. Kelly 1968; Basso 1971). Models of cultural evolution, differing substantially from those employed in the nineteenth century, have also been successfully applied (Dozier 1970). Students of kinship and social organization have done some excellent work (Fox 1967; Lamphere 1970, 1971) but in many cases have tended to ignore the relationships that link Indian institutions to the non-Indian world around them. This is unfortunate because it gives the impression that modern Indian societies are closed systems and/or cultural isolates. In fact, of course, they are neither. Studies of religion exhibit increased sophistication in the analysis of sacred symbols and the expressive functions of ritual in dramatizing covert cultural principles (Ortiz 1969, 1972; Lamphere 1969; Wyman 1970a). In other works, the techniques of ethnographic semantics have been employed to disclose aspects of Indian world view (Leap 1970a; F.H. Trager 1971). However, as Eggan (1972) has observed, the potential of linguistic models has not yet been fully exploited. In almost all spheres there has been a rise in efforts to account for variation within single societies and a concomitant decline in cross-cultural comparisons. Culture and personality studies have come to a virtual halt.

When Cushing first visited Zuni in 1879, anthropologists were firmly convinced that all the Indian cultures of North America were doomed to extinction. So rapidly would native peoples become acculturated, it was feared, that before long all traces of their "Indianness" would be completely and irrevocably gone. Fortunately, this dire prediction did not come true, and nowhere has it been refuted more dramatically than in the Southwest. As the Indians of this region continue to flourish so, undoubtedly, will anthropology.

There are signs, however, that in one essential way the character of Southwestern ethnology may change. For the first time in history respectable numbers of Indian people have become interested in anthropology and either alone or in collaboration with colleagues are studying their own languages and cultures. The fact that these Indians have already made useful contributions to scholarship—and, equally significant, that they have found aspects of anthropology helpful in planning the affairs of their own communities—suggests that research in years to come may be guided by a new spirit of intellectual partnership and cooperation. If this spirit is encouraged and allowed to develop to its full potential the future of Southwestern ethnology will be exciting indeed.

# Prehistory: Introduction

RICHARD B. WOODBURY

The Southwest is both a geographical and a cultural unit of North America, the boundaries and the subdivisions of which have been the subject of long discussion, with no complete agreement achieved, although a consensus has gradually developed as to the meaning and the limits of the Southwest. In the early days of archeological research in the region, it was often called the Southwestern United States, partly reflecting national myopia and partly resulting from ignorance of what lay south of Arizona and New Mexico. Southwestern North America is a more appropriate term, since the international border has no relation to prehistoric or recent aboriginal cultural boundaries.

The concept of the Southwest as a culture area, that is, a portion of the continent having definable cultural unity, rather than mere geographical distinctiveness, has a long history. However, the assumption has usually been made that the definition of the area in terms of its recent and modern Indian cultures would be suitable for prehistoric times, and various names have been used for this Southwest as a cultural unit. For example, O.T. Mason (1907:427–430) listed the "Pueblo Country" as one of 12 "environments" into which he divided North America. Wissler (1922) used the term Intensive Agriculture for this area but later changed this to Southwest; he also specified that the Southwest included "an indefinite portion of Mexico" (Wissler 1938:241). A much clearer definition of the Southwest was provided by Kroeber (1939:32–48), who discussed in detail the Mexican portion of the area. Nevertheless, these boundaries were still drawn on the basis of cultural characteristics of modern Indian groups, and their applicability to prehistoric cultures was uncertain. It was Kidder (1924) who published the first comprehensive archeological summary of the Southwest. His map (Kidder 1924:fig. 3) shows the Southwest as including most of New Mexico (all but the extreme northeast and southeast), Arizona (except the western one-third), most of Utah, the extreme southwest corner of Colorado, and a small and indeterminate amount of northern Chihuahua. These boundaries have been improved upon, mostly by extending them southward, by including all of Arizona, and by eliminating much of Utah, which is considered part of the Great Basin rather than the Southwest. The southern boundary has been greatly enlarged since 1924, to encompass a portion of northwestern Mexico, larger than the part of the Southwest that lies within the United States. Yet this southern region is still poorly known archeologically, in contrast to the northern Southwest. This is because investigators from the United States have rarely carried their work south of the international border and because Mexican archeologists have concentrated their work much farther south, in the region of incipient and developed civilizations, leaving a vast poorly studied zone in northern Mexico.

Understanding of the cultural and geographical meaning of the Southwest was greatly advanced by Beals (1943a:246), who suggested the term Greater Southwest to indicate clearly that it was more than Arizona, New Mexico, and portions of a few adjacent states. As an alternative he also used the term Arid America, already proposed by Kirchhoff. Later, Kirchhoff (1954:550) suggested replacing the concept of the Greater Southwest with a division into two major components, Arid America for the areas occupied by gathering and hunting peoples, and Oasis America for the areas occupied by farming peoples. Unfortunately, the arid zone of North America extends north to the Canadian border and east onto the High Plains, so that the term is misleading when used to identify a much smaller region. Oasis America at best applies only to the last few centuries rather than to the many millennia during which farming played no role or a very minor role in the Southwest, and the term has never been generally adopted.

Therefore, it seems most suitable to retain the long-familiar term Southwest to mean the southwestern part of North America and to recognize that its boundaries as a cultural unit have changed through the many millennia of its occupation. In general terms, the Southwest consists of most of the states of New Mexico, Arizona, Sonora, Chihuahua, Coahuila, Durango, Nueva Leon, and Tamaulipas and includes parts of several others—extreme southern and western Texas, southwestern Colorado, western and southern Utah, and the southern tip of Nevada. It has been said (Reed 1964:175) only half in jest that the Southwest extends from Durango (Mexico) to Durango (Colorado) and from Las Vegas (Nevada) to Las Vegas (New Mexico), and this is close enough to the facts to be a convenient reminder of the Southwest's extent.

Since the Southwest has both a great diversity of prehistoric and historic cultural patterns, and also great geographic diversity, as well as boundaries that shifted through time, it can properly be asked whether it is more than a residual category, a region that lies north of Mesoamerican civilization, south of the Rocky Mountains and the Great Basin area, east of the Pacific coastal cultures and west of the Plains. In fact, it is a meaningful unit, with an identifiable cultural continuity provided by the acquisition of farming from Mesoamerica (both the crops and the techniques) by peoples with old and specialized hunting-gathering economies, and by the gradual increase in importance of farming to a central role in the economy of most Southwestern cultures. The Southwest thus parallels in its growth the Southeastern United States, which also received farming from Mesoamerica as an economic and technological system that gradually transformed the lives of most of its peoples. With possible minor exceptions, these two streams of diffusion were separate, and they brought about quite different kinds of cultural changes in the two regions. Therefore, for studies of culture history and of culture processes the Southwest deserves attention as one of the several distinctive units of North American aboriginal culture.

The specific cultural features that distinguish the Southwest at the height of its prehistoric development can be summarized in terms of numerous details, of varying importance (Jennings 1956:88–89). Among these features are: permanent villages with relatively dense population; regionally differentiated architectural forms, including pit houses, jacals, abobe and masonry structures; specialized religious and ritual structures (kivas, ball courts); patterned settlements; agriculture, with a variety of irrigation and dry-farming methods; domesticated turkeys and dogs; major crops—corn, beans, squash, cotton, tobacco; pottery, with decoration in color rather than texturing, except for corrugated surface treatments; extensive use of marine shells for ornament; weaving; pipes and cane cigarettes for tobacco; weak stratification of society, but with successful communal efforts for building religious structures and for large-scale irrigation; emphasis on ceremonial elaboration and on religious rather than political controls; localized raiding but little or no organized warfare; moderate elaboration of mortuary practices (cremation, mortuary offerings) but little status differentiation; slight development of human sacrifice and taking of trophy heads; and strong continuity with the preagricultural past in many hunting, gathering, and food preparation techniques. No single area or time period within the Southwest displays all these features, but many of them are widespread and persistent, and it is in modifications of them rather than marked departures from them that the minor regional and temporal variations are defined.

## Internal Subdivisions

From the time of the earliest archeological explorations of the Southwest, marked local differences were noted in pottery and in architecture, the least perishable and most conspicuous remains. But there was little or no success in using such criteria for the definition of subareas within the Southwest prior to 1915, when Kidder (1917:112) identified "the northern and eastern" and "the southern and western" divisions and briefly described their distinctive features. Kroeber (1928) emphasized the same twofold division and suggested the names Pueblo and Gila-Sonora. In his synthesis of Southwestern archeology Kidder (1924) proposed a more detailed division into nine geographical subareas and described the distinctive cultural features of each. These areas were the San Juan, Northern Peripheral, Rio Grande, Eastern Peripheral, Little Colorado, Upper Gila, Mimbres, Lower Gila, and Chihuahua Basin, units that to a large extent have continued to be accepted as useful cultural-geographic subdivisions. Kidder emphasized the distinctiveness of the Lower Gila area (approximately the same as his southern and western division outlined in Kidder 1917), seeing it as set apart from all but the Chihuahua Basin in most cultural details. However, the grouping of these nine subareas into fewer, larger units was accomplished only gradually during the next two decades.

When the Pecos Conference, an informal but significant meeting in 1927 of most of the archeologists then active in the Southwest, defined a chronological scheme for the Southwest (Basketmaker I, II, and III, and Pueblo I, II, III, IV, and V), it was tacitly assumed that it was applicable to most of or all the Southwest, although based mainly on information from the San Juan drainage. But in 1931 an archeological conference was held at Gila Pueblo, a private research center in Globe, Arizona, and it was agreed that the Basketmaker-Pueblo region should be recognized as culturally separate from the southern Arizona desert area drained by the Gila and Salt rivers. For the Gila-Salt region's prehistoric culture the name Hohokam was proposed (Gladwin and Gladwin 1933). Gladwin and Gladwin (1934) suggested two additional cultural subdivisions of the Southwest, the Caddoan and the Yuman, but since these are linguistic terms for groups of contemporary Indian languages they had serious drawbacks as applied to archeological cultures for which evidence was lacking as to the languages their bearers spoke. Soon after this the name Anasazi was proposed to replace the cumbersome phrase Basketmaker-Pueblo (Kidder 1936:152), and Mogollon and Patayan were proposed to replace Caddoan and Yuman (Colton 1938). A four-fold cultural division of the prehistoric Southwest was thus established and has continued in general usage: Hohokam, Anasazi, Mogollon, and Patayan. The Southern Athapaskan culture has been recognized as deserving separate identification, Hakataya has been suggested to include the Patayan, and O'otam has been proposed for a portion of the culture sequence previously included within Hohokam.

## Environmental Diversity

The greater part of Southwestern North America is arid or semiarid, has extreme variations in elevation from deserts lying close to sea-level to mountain peaks rising as high as 12,000–13,000 feet, and has relatively few large permanent rivers (fig. 1). It is remarkable for the diversity of its topography, plant and animal life, climate, and soils, all of which were important elements in the resources that could be made use of by prehistoric peoples.

Physiographers (see, for example, Lobeck 1948) identify several provinces, each with its own environmental

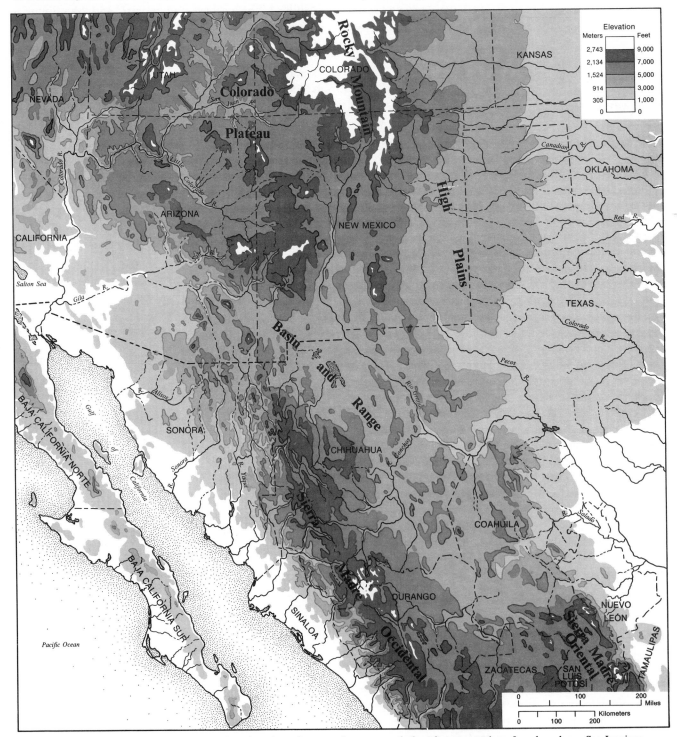

Fig. 1. Geomorphic provinces. Parts of some rivers have been drawn to show courses before the construction of modern dams. See Jennings (1956:fig. 1) for prehistoric culture area boundaries after A.D. 900.

characteristics, which in turn suggest the natural resources available in the past (although recent over-use of some resources has caused conspicuous changes, which must be taken into account in evaluating past landscapes). From north to south these physiographic provinces include, first, the southern Rocky Mountains, extending south through central Colorado into north-central New Mexico, with numerous high, forested mountain ranges, from which the spring run-off of the heavy winter snows provides an important part of the waters of the Colorado, the Rio Grande, and the Pecos. Although valuable for large game animals and heavy stands of coniferous trees, this province has little arable land and a short growing season; therefore, it was sparsely inhabited except in the lower valleys and basins. Second, a major part of the Southwest is occupied by the Colorado Plateaus—western Colorado, eastern and southern Utah, the northern half of Arizona, and northwestern New Mexico. This area is characterized by steep-walled sandstone mesas, deep canyons with intermittent streams, and a few perennial flows (the Colorado being the largest of these). The mountains have pine forests, the mesas support dense stands and scattered clumps of piñon pine and juniper, and both the mesas and the lower elevations have sparse grass and shrubby growth. Third, the Basin and Range province includes the southern half of Arizona, southern New Mexico, Sonora, eastern Chihuahua, Coahuila, and the Mexican states to the southeast. It is marked by broad, nearly level expanses of hot, dry desert separated by steep, rocky mountains of limited extent, their higher portions well-watered, cool, and forested. Fourth, the southwestern edge of the High Plains province extends into eastern New Mexico, occupied by the Pecos Valley and adjacent lands. Just south of the international border two major mountain systems begin and extend southeastward far into central Mexico, comprising the fifth and sixth provinces: the Sierra Madre Occidental to the west along the Sonora-Chihuahua boundary, and the Sierra Madre Oriental to the east, with the southern extension of the Basin and Range province between them. These mountains are high and rugged, cut by deep canyons opening into the desert lands adjacent to them.

The major cultural subdivisions of the Southwest are associated with distinctive patterns of geographical features (see G.R. Willey 1966:179–181).

The Hohokam area consists of low deserts except for interspersed isolated mountain areas. Extremely hot summers with a long rainless period give way to mild to cool winters with light rains. The dominant vegetation is an abundant growth of thorny shrub, cactus, and hardy trees such as mesquite, adapted to extreme dryness. Most streams are intermittent, although not long ago the Gila and Salt and some of their major tributaries flowed permanently.

The Anasazi region has quite variable topography, climate, and flora, including deeply dissected sandstone plateaus with narrow, vertical-walled canyons, and broad, sparsely vegetated valleys with only occasional flowing water. Higher, mountainous areas are cool and well watered but most of the region has a long dry spring and early summer, broken by heavy thundershowers; winters are chilly with considerable snow.

Lying at the southern edge of the Colorado Plateaus, the Mogollon area is one of forested mountains lower than the Rockies, extending from north-central Arizona to southwestern New Mexico, grasslands of intermediate elevation, and numerous small year-round streams. Climate is like the cooler parts of the Anasazi area, in marked contrast to the desert lying immediately to the south. The native rocks are metamorphic and igneous, rather than the sandstones of the plateaus to the north.

The Hakataya subarea lies on both sides of the Lower Colorado River, extending from the Grand Canyon southward; it is a lower, hotter continuation of the deserts and mountains of the Hohokam area.

In the sixteenth century Athapaskan speakers arrived in northeastern New Mexico and gradually spread to the west and south, occupying areas formerly Anasazi and Mogollon. Their descendants are the present-day Apache and Navajo groups.

This varied Southwestern habitat offered its prehistoric occupants an enormous assortment of resources, many of them to be found only in very restricted zones, although often recurring elsewhere. This encouraged and even necessitated the development of greatly differing lifeways in different locations, each adjusted to the resources available and taking advantage of several distinctive micro-environments. An intimate knowledge of these environments was essential to the prehistoric peoples, to permit them to exploit each with the most advantageous techniques at the most appropriate times. Not only was this true of the food-collecting earlier inhabitants, but also after the introduction of farming it was still essential to make use of a large assortment of wild plant and animal resources, both to supplement annual crop yields and to replace them in times of serious crop failure. In addition, farming required the use of many slightly differing environmental niches, to partly compensate for unpredictable and extreme fluctuations in frosts and rainfall, so that failure of crops in one type of location would be balanced by success in another. Therefore, sedentary village life almost certainly went with a continued mobility, with travel over considerable distances, familiarity with large regions, and selection of certain resources from far and wide. Trade and travel are suggested for prehistoric times by the wide distribution of marine shells, for example, and in historic times by the extensive trade in salt from a few prized sources. Therefore, in spite of its regional diversity, the Southwest was knit together to an important degree by its interlocking networks of economic and social relationships, and no portion of it remained long isolated from the others.

## The Southwest and Mesoamerica

A great deal of the culture of the Southwest derived from the civilizations to the south—its ceramics, its agriculture, many details of its architecture, much of its ceremonial, religious belief, and ritual. A comprehensive summary of this relationship states that "the Southwestern cultures have the general appearance of attenuated Mesoamerican cultures, and the distributional evidence suggests strongly that they are peripheral and reduced copies of the Mesoamerican prototypes" (Kelley 1966:95). If Southwestern archeological research had been initiated in Mexico and moved northward, this would have been apparent much sooner. Archeologists coming to the Southwest from the eastern United States, largely uninformed about Mesoamerican civilizations, and later studying it from local Southwestern museums and universities with relatively parochial attitudes, tended to see the evolution of Southwestern culture as taking place in far greater isolation than is now known to be the case. Although it has a distinctive configuration of cultural patterns, the Southwest clearly is peripheral to the centers far to the south from which came its first domestic crops and farming techniques, its pottery making, and later a large number of exotic trade goods, such as copper bells, cloisonné mirror backs, conch-shell trumpets, and parrot feathers. It is important to distinguish ideas that diffused northward from actual objects manufactured in the south and carried to the Southwest, in the later centuries possibly by long-distance traders. Several basic changes occurred in the widespread collecting-hunting culture that existed for several millennia, the Desert culture or Desert Archaic, when the idea of farming and the necessary crops reached it from the south. Gradually, a vast area of northern Mexico and then of the United States saw the start of settled village life. The change had occurred in central and southern Mexico long before, where archeological evidence reveals the slow in-place evolution of the change to village farming life, with local wild plants eventually being domesticated. In the Southwest no new plants were domesticated and no new techniques developed for growing them. The idea of pottery making almost certainly spread from central Mexico northward, from group to group, eventually undergoing changes in some details but keeping others that are strongly suggestive of Mexican prototypes.

Since this cultural continuity persisted for many centuries, grading from more complex in the south to simpler in the north, and new ideas diffused northward by different routes and at different times, the definition of a Southwestern-Mesoamerican boundary is made very difficult. If the boundary is judged to be far south of the

international border, as it is here, it might be appropriate to add to the major regional Southwestern cultures the Chalchihuites culture of Durango and Zacatecas, which was a major transmitter of Mesoamerican culture traits to the north via the central Mexican plateau (see Kelley 1966). Another major route, important after A.D. 1300, when the Chalchihuites culture was disappearing, was by way of the west coast states of Sinaloa and Sonora, a route probably used from far earlier times. The religious florescence that took place in the Anasazi culture about this time was probably based on a complex assortment of Mesoamerican ritual beliefs and practices diffused northward. Eventually, however, as with earlier ideas acquired by Southwestern groups, they were modified and reshaped into distinctive local forms, which has made the recognition of their Mesoamerican origin a slow and controversial task. When the Spaniards conquered and settled the Southwest in the seventeenth century, it had had two or more centuries of relative isolation from Mesoamerica, an ebbing of the long, intermittent contacts that had provided so much of the basic culture that it reworked in its own ways. Therefore, the boundary between the Southwest and Mesoamerica can best be considered as a shifting zone, north of which Mesoamerican culture traits existed only in attenuated and greatly modified form.

## The Southwest and the Great Basin

The vast region lying north and northwest of the Southwest shares a common cultural background, the Desert culture. Until the specializations of the cultures of the Southwest and the Great Basin were recognized as divergent from this shared cultural base, a "boundary" between the areas was not archeologically definable. For several decades many archeologists regarded the Basin as best described in terms of its relationship to the Southwest, using terms such as Northern Periphery and Puebloid culture to suggest a derivative cultural status. This reflects the fact that masonry architecture, village life, pottery making, and—most important of all—agriculture did spread northward to this region. But it fails to take account of the other influences on the Basin, such as those from the Plains and from the Plateau region farther north. And it fails to recognize that Southwestern influence on the Basin was relatively short-lived and did not equally affect all of it. The decision as to where a meaningful boundary between Southwest and Basin is to be drawn and how the historical relationships of the two regions are to be evaluated must take account of the changes through time in their degree of similarity or difference. The most pronounced similarities with the Southwest are in the area of the Fremont culture in east-central Utah, the Sevier-Fremont culture in west-central Utah, and along the Virgin River in extreme southwestern Utah and adjacent Arizona and Nevada. All or most of these areas have been included within the Southwest by some archeologists, but with the recognition that they again diverged from it after a relatively short few centuries of effective contact. Therefore, the boundaries used vary slightly from one scholar to another, depending on time period emphasized and on viewpoint. As Kroeber (1939:5-6) has described it: "The weakest feature of any mapping of culture wholes is also the most conspicuous: the boundaries. Where the influences from two culture climaxes or foci meet in equal strength is where a line must be drawn. . . . Yet it is just there that differences often are slight. . . . It would be desirable, therefore, to construct cultural maps without boundary lines, on some system of shading or tint variation of color."

## The Southwest and the Plains

Until it was recognized that the historic culture of the Plains, with its emphasis on the horse, the buffalo, and mobility, was underlain by a long period of sedentary farming life, it had seemed as though there were few significant similarities and relationships between the two areas. However, as village-farming life spread westward along the major rivers of the Plains, the nonfarming zone between the areas narrowed, and, at least in the Texas Panhandle, was bridged by an intermediate cultural pattern, the Antelope Creek focus, which drew on both Plains farming and Pueblo architecture for its background. It is now recognized that a considerable number of distinctive Southwestern cultural traits may have an eastern origin—the grooved ax, certain effigy forms of pottery vessels, and the stockaded settlements of the Rosa phase, for example (see Phillips, Ford, and Griffin 1951:453; Jennings 1956:98-102). It is also important that the most easterly large Pueblo villages, notably Pecos, carried on a lively trade in historic times with Plains nomads, which may have derived from earlier significant contacts. Therefore, although there is less difficulty in defining a boundary between the Plains and the Southwest than for some other adjacent culture areas, it is, like the others, a fluctuating boundary and a zone of gradually dwindling Southwestern influence that extends a considerable distance eastward onto the southern Plains.

## The Continuity of Past and Present

The archeological study of the Southwest has been deeply influenced from its beginning by the impression, which soon became seen as a certainty, that the present-day Indians of the Southwest were not only directly descended from the Indians responsible for the archeological remains but also continued some past lifeways with few changes. This view has been modified but not abandoned. It is clear that the continuity is not so direct and close for some groups as once thought, but for the Pueblo Indians particularly the knowledge of their culture gained by ethnographic studies is of profound significance in understanding the past. Interpretation of this continuity has advanced beyond an earlier naive belief that migration myths of modern peoples could be used to identify the "tribes" or "clans" that once occupied specific ruins (see, for example, Fewkes 1912a:218). By the late 1930s careful thought was being given to the ways in which the past of the Southwest could be interpreted through the present (Steward and Setzler 1938; Parsons 1940), and in the 1970s the efforts of ethnologists and social anthropologists have been joined with those of archeologists (Longacre 1970) in using data on recent and modern Pueblo society in all its complexities to understand the social and other processes at work in the past. To a limited degree this approach is used in all of American archeology, but in regions where Indian culture was shattered and only small remnants of the population survived, either forced into new locations or submerged by European settlers, there is far less to work with in the resources of historical and ethnographic data. In the Southwest it is possible not only to observe in use material objects such as the mano and metate for corn grinding and thus determine their function, efficiency, and roles (K. Bartlett 1933) but also to consider the "meaning" of prehistoric paintings of ceremonial activities in the light of current ritual practices by the descendants of the original artists (W. Smith 1952). To a great extent a comparable continuity exists in the Arctic between prehistoric cultures and those of the twentieth-century Eskimo, but in much of North America connections are more tenuous and subject to numerous conflicting interpretations.

While archeological remains have been most successfully interpreted by means of ethnographic data in the Pueblo area, there have gradually emerged studies of Mogollon and Hohokam materials that benefit from data on the historic-period Indians. If the controversial but probable continuity of Hohokam and modern Pima is accepted, then prehistoric irrigation practices can be better understood through knowledge of Pima irrigation. On a broader and less specific level, prehistoric materials in many areas have been re-examined in terms of growing insights as to the nature of family and village relationships and land-use systems (see Longacre 1970, 1973). Thus, analyses of possible past cultural processes are being added to reconstruction of events and historical sequences.

## Chronological Frameworks for Southwestern Archeology

No single set of terms and no one framework or chronological classification is "best" for every type of investigation, and therefore Southwestern archeologists have not only tried, through the years, to create "better" chronological systems but also have added new ones to supplement those already proved useful (see, for example, Brew 1946:44-66). This presents a problem to the nonspecialist, who would prefer one framework to many. Southwestern archeologists still use several frameworks in organizing their data. Therefore, in addition to the summary of temporal and spatial units presented below, several of the other systems used in the past few decades or still in use will be summarized.

There are two kinds of frameworks for Southwestern archeology, those that are intended to apply to the entire area and those that are meant for a single subarea or for one of the several major cultural units, such as the Anasazi or the Mogollon.

The first important framework of the general kind was the Pecos Classification, which was devised at the Pecos Conference of 1927 (Kidder 1927). It was expected to be useful for the entire Southwest as then understood archeologically, but eventually it was agreed that it was applicable only to the San Juan drainage or at most to the Anasazi culture. The Pecos Classification was a simple division of the total span of Anasazi culture into eight units, at that time of uncertain length and unknown antiquity, since dating by means of tree rings had not yet been developed to a usable point. The criteria for distinguishing these successive time periods were chiefly architecture and pottery, which not only were the best known and most abundant kinds of evidence but also showed the clearest changes with time. The time periods were defined as follows (Kidder 1927:490). Basketmaker I was preagricultural; Basketmaker II, "the agricultural, atlatl-using, non-pottery-making stage"; Basketmaker III, "the pit- or slab-house-building, pottery-making stage." Pueblo I was "the first stage during which cranial deformation was practiced, vessel neck corrugation was introduced, and villages composed of rectangular living-rooms of true masonry were developed"; Pueblo II, "the stage marked by widespread geographical extension of life in small villages; corrugation, often of elaborate technique, extended over the whole surface of cooking vessels"; Pueblo III, "the stage of large communities, great development of the arts, and growth of intensive local specialization"; Pueblo IV, "the stage characterized by contraction of area occupied; by the gradual disappearance of corrugated wares; and, in general, by decline from the preceding cultural peak"; Pueblo V, the period after 1600.

Changes in these definitions have been made, by adding additional criteria, but the general ideas expressed have stood the test of further research remarkably well, and in 1978 the classification is still often used as a broad-gauge and convenient way of identifying archeological materials, even though finer divisions have been created that are more useful for many purposes.

F.H.H. Roberts (1935) published the first substantial refinements of the Pecos Classification, using information on sandals, basketry, and textiles, as well as architecture and pottery, and suggesting names instead of numbers, a change used for a few years but eventually given up. He recommended abandoning the period called Basketmaker I, since no satisfactory evidence for it existed, and using the following names: Basketmaker (for Basketmaker II), Modified Basketmaker (for Basketmaker III), Developmental Pueblo (for Pueblo I-II), Great Pueblo (for Pueblo III), Regressive Pueblo (for Pueblo IV), and Historic Pueblo (for Pueblo V).

Meanwhile, with recognition in 1931 that the Pecos Classification could not be applied to archeological materials from southern Arizona, and with the creation of the name Hohokam for the culture of this area, a scheme of time periods was proposed by Gladwin and Gladwin (1934) that has continued in use, although with numerous changes in the detailed criteria by which each period is defined, and in the estimated dates that they assigned to each. Their periods were Colonial Period, Sedentary, Classic, Recent, and Modern.

The next major regional culture that was defined and named in the Southwest was the Mogollon (Gladwin and Gladwin 1935; Haury 1936a), occupying an area previously thought of as Puebloan or Pueblo-like in its culture both because its earlier occupation was largely uninvestigated and because it was heavily influenced by Anasazi (that is, "Pueblo") culture after the eleventh century. Argument continued vigorously for a decade or more as to whether the Mogollon culture "existed"—that is, was demonstrably distinct from the Hohokam to the south and west and the Anasazi to the north. Eventually it was generally accepted as a major component of the prehistoric Southwest, although sharing its origins with the Hohokam.

Another proposed terminological refinement met with much less general acceptance. Gladwin and Gladwin (1934) suggested that the Southwest be divided into four "roots" and each root into "stems" and these further subdivided into "branches." This elaborate scheme was clearly influenced by the Midwestern Taxonomic method that McKern (1939) had introduced in the Middle West as an effective way of stating cultural relationships among a large number of units of uncertain age and derivation. A major difficulty of the Gladwin and Gladwin proposal was that Caddoan and Yuman were linguistic terms and there was doubt that they could properly be applied to the prehistoric materials. The stem and branch system remained in use for some time but has not continued as a widely accepted scheme. Colton (1939) devised a similar but substitute system of culture units for northern Arizona, which included as "roots" the four major subcultures that then had been recognized in the Southwest: Anasazi, Mogollon, Hohokam, and Patayan. He substituted "focus" as the smallest unit, equivalent to site, or to "component" in the McKern system, and his terminology has had considerable use in the area of his major attention. However, classifications based on biological analogies or consisting of family-tree diagrams have been increasingly rejected by archeologists, with the growing realization that they rest on unacceptable assumptions as to the nature of culture and culture change.

Dissatisfaction with these overly elaborate, biologically oriented schema and a desire to see the Southwest in its broadest outlines led to two attempts in the early 1950s to devise terminology that would encompass all the regional subdivisions. The first of these was called the Southwestern co-tradition and was modeled on the co-tradition concept of Bennett (1948). As applied to the Southwest by Martin and Rinaldo (1951), it comprised five successive broad stages or time periods, each of which they characterized for the area as a whole, and for which they identified regional variations: Preagricultural and preceramic stage, about 2000 to 1000 B.C.; Early agricultural stage, 1000 B.C. to A.D. 1; Formative stage, about A.D. 1 to 900 or 1000; Classic stage, 1000 to 1350; Renaissance period, 1350 to 1700.

The next year Daifuku (1952) proposed "a new conceptual scheme" that was comparable in aim but differed in all details: Elementary, about 3000 B.C. to A.D. 1; Formative, about A.D. 1 to 700; Florescent, about 700 to 1300; Fusion, about 1300 to 1600; Historic, 1600 onward. These innovative ideas stimulated a great deal of debate, led to the better recognition of broad areal uniformities as well as localized differences, and yet failed to become the permanently accepted and utilized frameworks for archeological discussion and research. But the usefulness of this kind of all-embracing scheme is reflected in the continuing creation of new versions, such as that used in 1955 by the summer seminar that analyzed Southwestern culture from the standpoint of its isolation and external relationships (Jennings 1956). The framework in which the group's findings were reported consisted of five area-wide chronological units, each with identifiable historical-cultural characteristics: the base, 6000 to 1000 B.C.; emergence, 1000 B.C. to about A.D. 700; specialization and divergence, A.D. 700 to 1300; crystallization and resistance, 1300 to 1600; and acculturation, 1600 to the present. Irwin-Williams (1967) has used some of the same terms from earlier schemes, quite differently arranged and defined: Emergent, 6000 B.C. or earlier to about 3000 B.C.; Elementary, 3000 B.C. to about A.D. 1; Formative and Marginal Formative, about A.D. 1 to the present.

Finally, the most detailed chronological system designed to apply to the entire Southwest is that proposed by McGregor (1965): Ancient stage, prior to 10,000 B.C.; Hunter stage, 10,000 to 5000 B.C.; Collector stage, 5000 to 200 B.C.; Exploitation period, 200 B.C. to A.D. 1; Founder period, A.D. 1 to 500; Settlement period, 500 to 700; Adjustment period, 700 to 900; Dissemination period, 900 to 1100; Classic period, 1100 to 1300; Culminant period, 1300 to 1600; Historic period, 1600 to the present.

In spite of this array of schemes for placing cultural data of the entire Southwest into convenient temporal

schemes, it is significant that the preference has increasingly been for the defining of successive time periods within limited geographical areas. Each unit (often called a phase) is then defined culturally and its chronological position determined as far as possible in absolute terms from tree-ring or radiocarbon dates and in relative terms by cross-dating through specific cultural traits, usually pottery types. There has thus arisen in the technical literature of Southwestern archeology an enormous number of local culture units, grouped into geographical "areas" or "regions" somewhat like those proposed by Gladwin and Gladwin (1934) and Colton (1939) and sometimes using their terms, such as Kayenta, Cibola, or Mimbres. However, for more general purposes the approach taken in 1927 by the Pecos Conference has proved to be the most acceptable. For example, in the most comprehensive synthesis of New World prehistory yet attempted (G.R. Willey 1966), the Anasazi area is divided into seven time periods (San José, Basketmaker II and III, Pueblo I, II, III, and IV), comparable numbered subdivisions of Patayan and Mogollon are used, and the Hohokam periods of Gladwin and Gladwin (1934) are still employed.

There is, of course, a need for all these types of chronological-cultural classifications, each for its own purpose. In the chapters that follow some use will be

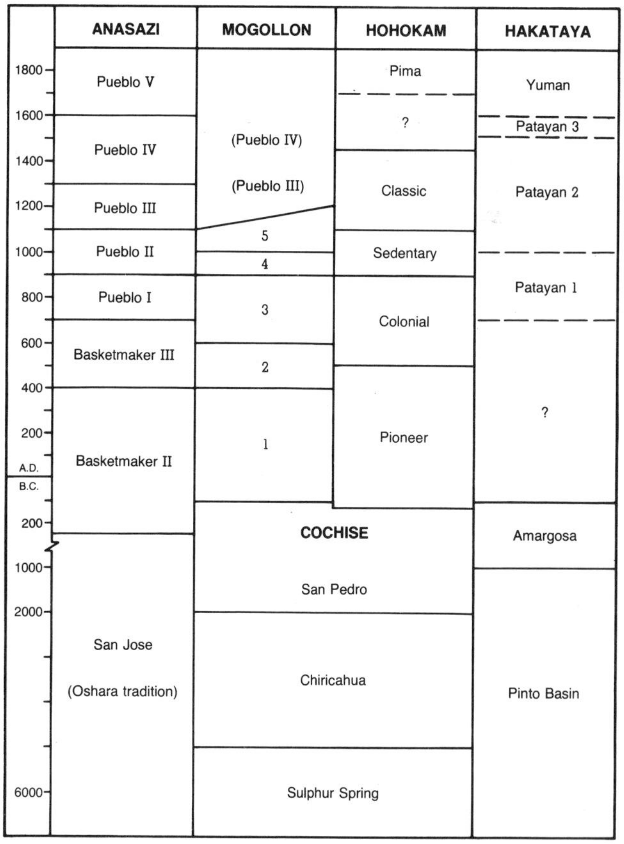

| | ANASAZI | MOGOLLON | HOHOKAM | HAKATAYA |
|---|---|---|---|---|
| 1800 | Pueblo V | (Pueblo IV) | Pima | Yuman |
| 1600 | Pueblo IV | | ? | Patayan 3 |
| 1400 | | (Pueblo III) | Classic | Patayan 2 |
| 1200 | Pueblo III | | | |
| 1000 | Pueblo II | 5 | Sedentary | |
| 800 | Pueblo I | 4 | Colonial | Patayan 1 |
| 600 | Basketmaker III | 3 | | |
| 400 | | 2 | | |
| 200 | Basketmaker II | 1 | Pioneer | ? |
| A.D. / B.C. | | | | |
| 200 | | COCHISE | | Amargosa |
| 1000 | San Jose | San Pedro | | |
| 2000 | (Oshara tradition) | Chiricahua | | Pinto Basin |
| 6000 | | Sulphur Spring | | |

Fig. 2. Chronological subdivision of the 4 major Southwestern archeological cultures.

made of the more detailed schemes for discussing localized cultural developments, but for many purposes it will be sufficient to divide the Southwest into four geographical-cultural areas and each of these into a few successive time periods, as is diagrammed in figure 2.

## Problems of Southwestern Archeology

In spite of the importance that regional chronological schemes continue to have for the ordering of the vast accumulation of data that Southwestern archeologists have achieved, they serve mainly the rather limited purpose of culture history and to a lesser degree set the background for discussions of culture change and the processes of change. The shift in Southwestern archeology from primary attention to historical chronicle and artifacts to a concern with nonmaterial culture, social organization and processes, and problems of interest to other anthropologists was sparked by Taylor (1948) who criticized in strong terms the deficiencies of American archeology for the preceding several decades. Gradually, the goals of Southwestern archeology have shifted, as have those of archeology elsewhere, to "processual" problems and attention to the testing of hypotheses about the functioning and relationships of cultural and biological systems and their environment. In the Southwest a major emphasis has developed on investigating the social organization of prehistoric societies by means of inferences and hypotheses that benefit from the rich ethnographic and historical data available on the descendants of the prehistoric population of the region. This emphasis is typified in the volume edited by Longacre (1970), in which Martin (1970:195) comments:

> One salient point in the papers impressed me, and that was the shift in goals. The papers do not dwell on traits, artifacts, the history of traits, or taxonomy. They are not written in terms of "brown ware people" or "gray ware people"; they do not equate difference in social organization with differences in traits. Archeology is explicitly viewed as anthropology and social organization is viewed as social organization. The goals are the discovery of cultural regularities, the formulation of laws of cultural dynamics, the search for trends in and causes of human behavior, and, finally, the attainment of sufficient sophistication to make predictions with a high degree of probability.

Other kinds of problems not specifically cited by Martin but that are of interest to Southwestern archeologists are the understanding of the economic and ecological systems of prehistoric societies (see, for example, Zubrow 1971; Bohrer 1970) and the distribution of prehistoric populations in terms of relative density, choice of locations for various purposes, and total numbers (see, for example, Gumerman 1971).

If relatively little of these recent viewpoints and conclusions appears in the chapters that follow, it is because few "final" or even extensively tested answers have yet been found to the questions. The time-space frameworks that permit arranging the raw data and the culture chronicles and examinations of processes of change are still fundamental in Southwestern, as in other, archeology. With this foundation now largely complete in all but minor details, more complex and perhaps more significant problems can be studied, hypotheses formed and tested, man-environment relationships investigated, and the data of Southwestern archeology used in continually broadening interdisciplinary research. Therefore, the summaries of the archeology of certain eras and regions that appear in this volume can only suggest and not fully reveal the wealth of detailed and precise information about the prehistoric Southwest that can be brought to bear on a wide range of cultural, historical, and social questions.

## Archeological Sites

The following list includes the names and general locations of important Southwestern archeological sites that are open year-round for visits by the general public. Most are maintained by the U.S. National Park Service.

• ARIZONA  Besh-Ba-Gowa, near Globe; Canyon de Chelly National Monument; Casa Grande Ruins National Monument, near Coolidge; Kinishba Pueblo (National Historic Landmark), near Whiteriver; Kinlichee Tribal Park, near Ganado on Navajo Indian Reservation; Montezuma Castle National Monument, near Flagstaff; Navajo National Monument (Betatakin, Kiet Siel), near Tsegi; Petrified Forest National Park, near Holbrook; Pueblo Grande Museum, in Phoenix; Tonto National Monument, near Roosevelt; Tuzigoot National Monument, 2 miles east of Clarkdale; Walnut Canyon National Monument, near Flagstaff; Wupatki National Monument, about 25 miles north of Flagstaff.

• NEW MEXICO  Albuquerque Petroglyphs (city park), in Albuquerque; Aztec Ruins National Monument, near Aztec; Bandelier National Monument, near White Rock; Chaco Canyon National Monument, about 40 miles northeast of Crownpoint; Coronado State Monument, near Bernalillo; El Morro National Monument, near El Morro; Gila Cliff Dwellings National Monument, 47 miles north of Silver City; Gran Quivira National Monument, 26 miles south of Mountainair; Pecos National Monument, near Rowe.

• COLORADO  Great Sand Dunes National Monument, near Alamoso; Mesa Verde National Park, between Cortez and Mancos.

• UTAH  Arch Canyon Indian Ruin, near Blanding; Calf Creek Recreation Site (administered by Bureau of Land Management), between Boulder and Escalante; Canyonlands National Park, near Moab; Hovenweep National Monument, near Aneth (partly in Colorado); Natural Bridges National Monument, 45 miles west of Blanding.

# Post-Pleistocene Archeology, 7000–2000 B.C.

CYNTHIA IRWIN-WILLIAMS

Despite its intrinsic significance, the long period that preceded the development of sedentary life in the Southwest at about the beginning of the Christian era remains very incompletely investigated and poorly understood. This is due partly to the lower density of population and the concomitant sparsity of archeological remains, and partly to their relatively unspectacular nature, which has resulted in a degree of scientific neglect. However, from the still scanty data certain major patterns are beginning to emerge. These still shadowy outlines reflect the complex interplay of a large number of factors, including the changing climatic and environmental context, technological innovation and adaptations, shifting population size and demographic structure, and the socioreligious network that integrates these elements into human culture.

## The Environmental Context for Human Development

Information on the essential environmental context for long-term early cultural development in the Southwest has been provided principally by research in geology and paleobotany. Geological research since 1900 includes the classic studies of Antevs (1948, 1952, 1955), Bryan (1941, 1950a), and Hack (1942) and the numerous subsequent revisions and refinements by J.P. Miller (1958), Haynes (1968), Malde (1964), Malde and Schick (1964), and others. There are also complementary paleobotanical studies (Martin 1963, 1963a; Mehringer 1965, 1967; Mehringer and Haynes 1965; Mehringer, Martin, and Haynes 1967; Schoenwetter and Dittert 1968; Wendorf 1961). Although there is not yet complete agreement on all phases of the long-term sequence of climatic change, the outlines of that sequence are beginning to emerge (fig. 1).

For some time before 10,000 B.C., climatic conditions of considerably greater effective moisture than the present prevailed in the Southwest. Under these conditions, a juniper savanna occupied the now desolate Las Vegas (Nevada) Valley (Mehringer 1965); shallow lakes dotted an open savanna that included elements of pine and spruce, in the now treeless short-grass plains of the Llano Estacado of eastern New Mexico. This corresponds to geologic deposition Unit A in Haynes's (1968) Southwestern alluvial chronology and to the Tahoka pluvial outlined by Wendorf (1961) on the Llano Estacado. Thick alluvial deposits were laid down by vigorous

effluent Late Pleistocene streams. The faunal assemblage was characterized by a thriving and varied population, including mammoth, horse, camel, *Capromeryx* (antelope), extinct bison, tapir, sloth, peccary, deer, rabbit, turtle, and others.

Between about 10,000 B.C. and 9500 B.C., a period of decreased effective moisture resulted in the desiccation of many of the desert lakes and erosion and soil formation on the earlier deposits (Mehringer 1967; Haynes 1968; Wendorf 1961). This corresponds to the Monahans interval on the Llano Estacado and is correlated with the Two Creek interstadial in the continental glacial sequence (Wendorf 1961).

A return to conditions of somewhat more effective moisture between 9500 B.C. and 9000 B.C. (the Blackwater subpluvial on the Llano Estacado, Wendorf 1961) provided the context for the evolution of the early Clovis culture. Vegetational differences from the present may reflect the equivalent of a three to four inch decrease in annual rainfall and/or a three to four degree decrease in mean annual temperature (Mehringer and Haynes 1965). A Plains-type desert grassland occupied southern Arizona (Mehringer 1967), and stands of pine and spruce survived in favorable niches on the full Plains grasslands of eastern New Mexico. Desert grasslands and high lake levels characterized the desert basins of the western Southwest. The geologic sequence reflects gradually lowering water tables and is characterized by the deposition of alluvial and colluvial sediments of Haynes's (1968) Unit $B_1$. Many elements of the earlier faunal assemblages survived, though probably in different proportions (possibly with the decline of groups such as horse, camel, and *Capromeryx*).

A short period of decreased effective moisture and local erosion separates geologic Units $B_1$ and $B_2$. The latter occurred between about 8600 B.C. and 5000 B.C. and is usually represented by massive alluvial, colluvial, and eolian silts and local pond deposits. Evidence from both soil formation and palynology indicates a general long-term though fluctuating trend toward decreased effective moisture. By the end of the period, at about 5500–5000 B.C., conditions approximated those of the present (Mehringer 1967). As a whole, the period correlates to Antevs's (1955) Anathermal and to the Lubbock subpluvial Yellow House interval and Portales subpluvial on the Llano Estacado (Wendorf 1961). The most significant of the recognizable internal fluctuations toward increased effective moisture occurred between about 6500 B.C. and 6000 B.C. (Portales subpluvial) and may have had an important influence on the distribution of game species and human populations (Irwin-Williams and Haynes 1970). As a whole, the period witnessed crucial changes in the Southwestern faunal resource base. Remains of mammoth, horse, camel, *Capromeryx,* and several other Pleistocene forms are absent, and the dominant game species were evidently *Bison antiquus* (early) and *Bison occidentalis* (late). The distribution of these animals was probably closely linked to the extent of the fully developed grasslands, which shrank slowly from the western Southwest and strongly influenced human demographic patterns. This long period of gradual desiccation witnessed the later Paleo-Indian cultures (Folsom and Cody) in the east. It probably also encompassed the earliest development of economically eclectic Archaic cultures such as San Dieguito in the west and Sulphur Springs Cochise in the south.

The period represented by geologic Unit $B_2$ was terminated by erosion and soil formation and probably by the onset of conditions of markedly decreased moisture (Antevs 1955; Haynes 1968; Mehringer 1967). Because of this, the environmental record of the subsequent period of about 5000–3000 B.C., termed the Altithermal by Antevs (1955), is very poor indeed. Deposits dated within this time span are not common and are frequently eolian (Haynes geologic Unit $C_1$) or locally alluvial or colluvial (Haynes geologic Unit $C_2$) (Haynes 1968; Williams and Orlins 1963). More commonly, the period is represented by an erosional break preceded by a pollen profile of decreasing effective moisture and succeeded by one of increased effective moisture. Martin (1963), on the basis of work in the San Pedro Valley of southeastern Arizona, presented an alternative hypothesis in which the Altithermal is seen as a period of increased rather than decreased effective moisture. However, there is a break in the local deposition sequence at about 5000 B.C. that probably, in fact, represents the Altithermal. A reinvestigation of the problem at the Murray Springs locality supports this interpretation and indicates a major break between 5000 and 3000 B.C. Pollen sequences from upland dune sites in northwestern New Mexico dating from this period (4800–3600 B.C.) lend further support to the interpretation of decreased effective moisture (James Schoenwetter, personal communication 1967; Peter Mehringer, personal communication 1967). Certainly, near the beginning of the period the last of the Pleistocene megafauna became extinct, and all species represented are entirely modern. The effect of these relative environmental extremes on the human population was also marked, and generally the archeological record is rather poor (Irwin-Williams and Haynes 1970). Dated Archaic remains include the initial Jay and Bajada phases of the Oshara tradition in the northern Southwest. The related

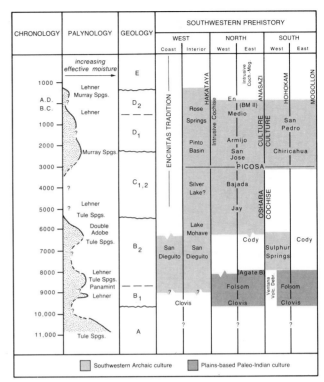

after Irwin-Williams and Haynes 1970:fig. 1.

Fig. 1. Schematic correlation between principal geologic units (after Haynes 1968), climatic change in terms of effective moisture (after Mehringer 1967), and archeological cultures in the Southwest.

Lake Mohave and Silver Lake complexes in the west, the distinctive Red Sand complex at Ventana Cave, and the Buff Sand complex at Bat Cave are probably also referable to some part of it.

A period of greater effective moisture than present (Antevs's Medithermal) beginning by 3000–2500 B.C. is indicated in several pollen records and is frequently represented by the formation of a prominent soil on the top of geologic Unit $C_2$ (Antevs 1955; Mehringer 1967; Malde 1964; Malde and Schick 1964; Haynes 1968). Deposits that were laid down unconformably upon Unit C during this time (3000 B.C. to about A.D. 500–600) comprise Units $D_1$ and $D_2$. Within the period, the two recognizable subdivisions are usually separated by a minor unconformity and a period of less effective moisture about 500 B.C., which may coincide with Antevs's Fairbank Drought (Antevs 1955; Agogino and Hibben 1958). In many respects the Southwestern environment during this period, particularly in its early stages, was much more favorable than before. This is apparently reflected in a notable expansion in the size of the human population (as indicated by site size, site number, and territorial coverage). It is also a period of rapidly improving communications within the Southwest, as shown by the unity underlined in the Picosa concept (Irwin-Williams 1967). Concomitant expansion of communication between the Southwest and other areas is indicated by the penetration of elements of the basic agricultural complex from Mexico and the growth of interareal sharing of stylistic and technological components (Dick 1965a; Haury 1957; Lister 1953). Unit D₂ was usually terminated by a brief erosional cycle that probably occurred about A.D. 500–700 and was occasionally topped by a minor soil. This hiatus (probably equivalent to Antevs's Whitewater Drought), while brief, had a very marked effect on the character of many of the semisedentary cultures that were evolving at the time (Antevs 1955; Schoenwetter and Dittert 1968; Irwin-Williams 1973).

## The Paleo-Indian Period

The Paleo-Indian complexes labeled Clovis, Folsom, Agate Basin, and Cody, and the associated climatic, faunal, and geological data (fig. 1) are treated in volume 3 (see especially "Paleo-Indian Period: Plains and Southwest"). Much of the Southwest at this time may be considered an extension of the Great Plains, in terms of its rich faunal resources and overall configuration. The Paleo-Indian cultural adaptations to that environment also represent a Plains-based big-game-hunting way of life. Clovis finds, relatively sparse everywhere, have been reported over essentially the entire Southwest and much of the adjacent Great Basin. By the beginning of Haynes's geologic Unit B₁, conditions suitable to the survival of large herds of grazing animals such as bison probably no longer existed in the western Southwest: Folsom materials are concentrated east of the Arizona–New Mexico border. In the central and northern Southwest, there is an apparent occupational hiatus after Folsom times, although occasional remains of the Agate Basin complex, centered to the north, occur in central and eastern New Mexico (Irwin 1967). A brief return to conditions of relatively greater effective moisture (Haynes's Unit B₂) was accompanied by the spread of the Cody complex widely and, locally, densely over much of the eastern and northern Southwest (Irwin-Williams and Haynes 1970). The tool kit recovered from Cody sites in the Southwest apparently differs only slightly from that known elsewhere on the High Plains.

## The Archaic Period

Following the disappearance of the Cody complex, there is no further evidence of the occupation of the Southwest by Plains-based hunting-oriented groups.

Early Archaic cultures, characterized by an eclectic or at least less centralized economy, may be as early in some parts of the Southwest as Clovis, Folsom, and Cody materials. There is, at present, no evidence for any direct relation between these Early Archaic cultures and the Plains Paleo-Indian nor for their origin in the latter. They and their derivatives are sometimes characterized as belonging to the widespread Desert culture, originally defined by Jennings (1956), largely in terms of its eclectic

adaptation to an arid or semiarid environment. It is now apparent that this identification is valid at the broad adaptational level, but that on a historico-genetic level the term Desert culture should be confined to the area of original definition in the Great Basin (C.N. Warren 1967; Irwin-Williams 1967). At this level of reference, the West is considered to have been occupied by a number of distinctive cultural traditions, whose external boundaries and internal dynamics and continuities reflect the existing patterns of interaction, communication, and identity. In the Southwest four such cultural traditions may be recognized. They are referred to here in brief as the Western or San Dieguito-Pinto tradition (southern California, western Arizona, and southern Nevada); the Southern, Cochise tradition (southeastern and east-central Arizona, southwestern and west-central New Mexico); the Northern, Oshara tradition (northern Arizona, southeastern Utah, southwestern Colorado, and northwestern New Mexico); and the poorly known Southeastern tradition, represented by the Fresnal and Hueco and related complexes (fig. 2). These traditions have been treated here in terms of their early and late developments, not only for convenience but also because the two are set apart by a series of pan-Southwestern events that occurred about 3000 B.C.

## The Early Archaic

Within the early range, cultural development took place in the context of frequent and significant climatic change—first, the fluctuations of the early post-Pleistocene (before 5000 B.C.), with its effects on the distribution of the Plains Paleo-Indian cultures; and second, the conditions of fluctuating but general desiccation between about 5000 and 3000 B.C. These climatic alterations were critical to the development and distribution of Southwestern Archaic cultures (fig. 1).

### The West: San Dieguito-Pinto Tradition

In the western area the earliest well-defined cultural remains very closely resemble those of the Clovis culture to the east. Similarities of tool kit, parallel distribution patterns of the remains of extinct fauna (Davis and Fortsch 1970), and the occurrence of these materials on the high beaches of Pleistocene lakes—all suggest an adaptation roughly similar to that represented at the excavated localities farther east.

An understanding of the early Archaic in this area is hampered by the paucity of excavated data, despite more than 50 years of archeological attention. Except for the C.W. Harris site in southern California and Ventana Cave in southwestern Arizona (C.N. Warren 1967; Haury 1950), chronologic relations have been erected largely on the basis of surface distributions, relation to geologic features, and weathering of artifacts (Campbell and Campbell 1937; Amsden 1937; Rogers 1938, 1939; Hau-

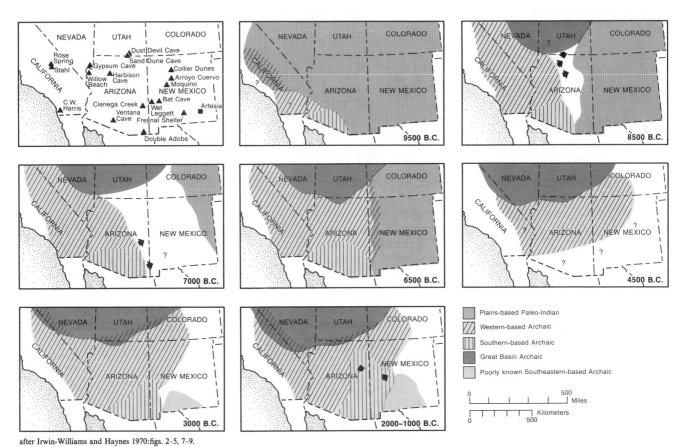

after Irwin-Williams and Haynes 1970:figs. 2-5, 7-9.

Fig. 2. Archeological sites and suggested distribution of early Southwestern cultures.

ry 1950; Rogers et al. 1966; C.N. Warren 1967; Davis, Brott, and Weide 1969).

The cultural materials from the Basal Volcanic debris stratum at Ventana Cave (the Ventana complex) indicate that the earliest occupation of the western Southwest may date back as far as 9300 B.C. (Rogers et al. 1966). However, these materials are exceedingly difficult to assess. The crude concave-based point recovered is unlikely to represent either the Folsom (as originally thought) or Clovis phenomenon. The associated tool kit of percussion-flaked scraper planes, choppers, and side-struck flaked scraping and cutting tools is comparable to other Southwestern Early Archaic assemblages, particularly those of the Cochise culture. Rogers (in Haury 1950) assigned the material to the putatively very early San Dieguito I or Malpais Industry, which he felt to be ancestral to the later better-known San Dieguito III complex (represented at the Harris Ranch site) and also the Lake Mohave complexes. However, the absence of additional data makes placement of these materials uncertain. The Malpais Industry itself was otherwise known only from heavily patinated surface collections from mesas and rocky terraces in a limited area of California and adjacent southwesternmost Arizona. It was frequently associated with the stone-outlined remains of circular structures ("sleeping circles"), "ceremonial rock alignments," and trails marked by stone cairns.

Given the absence of excavated sites and the specific environmental patterning of the assemblages, its relation to the better-defined San Dieguito complex (Rogers's San Dieguito III) represented at the Harris site is still unclear.

• SAN DIEGUITO COMPLEX   The earliest dated assemblage belongs to the San Dieguito complex recovered at the Harris site (Rogers 1938; C.N. Warren 1967; Warren and True 1960-1961). Carbon-14 dates from the Harris locality indicate an occupation between 7000 B.C. and 6500 B.C. (C.N. Warren 1967). Related materials occur widely over southern California (fig. 2), usually on the raised beaches of ancient lakes such as Lake Mohave, China Lake, Owens Lake, and in Death Valley. They have also been found in southwestern Nevada, near Tonapah and Carson Sink, and in southwestern Arizona, in the Colorado River basin (Campbell and Campbell 1937; Campbell 1949; Amsden 1937; Rogers 1939, 1958; Hunt and Tanner 1960; Rogers et al. 1966; Davis and Fortsch 1970). They have been referred to as the Playa complex, the San Dieguito II and III complexes (Rogers et al. 1966; C.N. Warren 1967), the Lake Mohave complex (Amsden 1937), and incorporated as part of the Western Lithic co-tradition (E.L. Davis 1968). C.N. Warren (1967) considers all these materials to represent a single unified complex termed San Dieguito. He defines this in terms of a tool kit comprising a wide range of scrapers, including ovoid side scrapers, oblong side and

34

end scrapers, triangular end scrapers, large domed scrapers, simple flake scrapers, rare crescents, and bifacial leaf-shaped knives (fig. 3). The characteristic projectile points include elongated leaf-shaped forms (San Dieguito points), very slightly shouldered specimens with contracting stems (Lake Mohave points), and shorter specimens with well-defined shoulders and short, straight, or contracting stems (Silver Lake points). Warren concludes that this material reflects an ancient indigenous stratum of unspecialized hunters and gatherers, with ties to the northwest, to phenomena represented at contemporary localities such as Lind Coulee in Washington and the Five Mile Rapid site in Oregon.

Given the variability of the artifact assemblages and the rarity of excavated and dated material, as well as the general lack of associated fauna, an evaluation of San Dieguito chronology and internal systemic organization is hazardous. The materials do, in fact, show a degree of consistency. However, wide variations within the tool kit and the uneven occurrence of the several projectile point styles and other artifacts, such as choppers, suggest the possibility of internal temporal and spatial development. Working in Owens Valley, California, E.L. Davis (1963) recovered the typical Lake Mohave points on the valley floor, but many of the smaller Silver Lake-like ("Mohave-Silver") points at higher, more montane localities. She suggests that this pattern may reflect a shift with time from the pursuit of lowland herbivores toward a pattern of mixed seasonal upland-lowland hunting and gathering. In addition, materials from the Red Sand deposit at Ventana Cave in southeastern Arizona (Haury 1950), which date after 5000 B.C. (on the basis of the geologic context), show many similarities to the Silver Lake

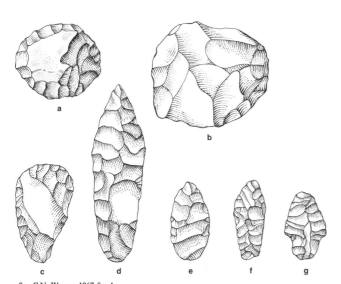

after C.N. Warren 1967:fig. 4.
Fig. 3. Lake Mohave artifacts from San Bernardino Co., Calif. a, Ovoid scraper; b, domed scraper; c, triangular end scraper; d, leaf-shaped knife; e, leaf-shaped point; f, Lake Mohave point; g, Silver Lake point. Length of d 9.3cm (see also "Post-Pleistocene Archeology, 9000-2000 B.C.," fig. 4, vol. 8).

portion of the San Dieguito complex. In brief, it seems probable that materials included in the San Dieguito complex reflect a relatively long-term development falling between perhaps 7000 B.C. and sometime after 5000 B.C. Within this development, the San Dieguito materials proper probably occupy an early position, with the Lake Mohave and Silver Lake materials occurring respectively later.

### The North: Oshara Tradition

The northeastern and southeastern portions of the Southwest were the last to be abandoned by Plains-based big-game-hunting groups represented by the Cody complex, which probably lasted until about 6000 B.C. By this time, the San Dieguito-Lake Mohave development was well under way in the western sector, and Cochise foragers already inhabited the south.

Between these terminal Paleo-Indian cultures and the succeeding Early Archaic, there is a brief hiatus that reflects the demographic withdrawal of the big-game-hunting groups in reaction to environmental stress. Subsequently, the northern Southwest was the focus of a long-term continuous development within the Archaic spectrum, which culminated ultimately in the formation of the central core of the relatively well-known sedentary Anasazi (Pueblo) culture.

Since 1940, surface collections in the northern Southwest have recorded scattered fragments relating to this continuum. These include the Rio Grande complex of northern New Mexico (Renaud 1942); the San Jose complex of northwestern New Mexico (Bryan and Toulouse 1943; Agogino and Hester 1956); the Concho complex of eastern Arizona (Wendorf and Thomas 1951); the Aneth and Moab complexes of southeastern Utah (Mohr and Sample 1959; Hunt 1960).

Between 1964 and 1971 Irwin-Williams and her associates carried out a long-term research program aimed specifically at defining the character of the Archaic continuum that underlay the evolution of sedentary Pueblo society. This research centered in the Arroyo Cuervo Valley in the Rio Puerco (East) drainage of northwestern New Mexico. On the basis of the work done there and distribution studies elsewhere in the northern Southwest, it was concluded that the Archaic continuum defined in this region and termed the Oshara tradition is representative of the northern Southwest generally between about 5500 B.C. and A.D. 400 (fig. 4).

The type region itself comprises a zone of sandstone canyons and gravel uplands between the Puerco and Jemez rivers in northwestern New Mexico. The characteristic vegetation is one of cholla- and yucca-dotted grasslands alternating with juniper-piñon savannas in uplands and along water courses. A large portion of the native vegetation could be utilized as a food resource, and the complexion and shifting distribution of these floral resources were closely tied with human occupation of the

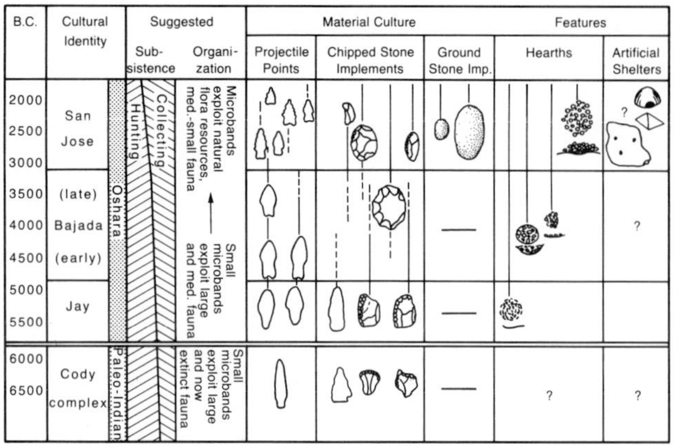

| B.C. | Cultural Identity | Suggested | | Material Culture | | | Features | |
|---|---|---|---|---|---|---|---|---|
| | | Subsistence | Organization | Projectile Points | Chipped Stone Implements | Ground Stone Imp. | Hearths | Artificial Shelters |
| 2000 2500 3000 | San Jose | Hunting / Collecting | Microbands exploit natural flora resources, med.-small fauna | | | | | ? |
| 3500 4000 4500 | (late) Bajada (early) | Oshara | Small microbands exploit large and med. fauna | | | — | | ? |
| 5000 5500 | Jay | | | | | — | | |
| 6000 6500 | Cody complex | Paleo-Indian | Small microbands exploit large and now extinct fauna | | | — | ? | ? |

after Irwin-Williams 1973:fig. 7.

Fig. 4. Synopsis of the Oshara tradition as represented in the Arroyo Cuervo region.

Irwin-Williams 1973:fig. 2.

Fig. 5. Jay complex artifacts. a, Bifacial knife; b, projectile point; c, concave-edged side scraper; d, straight-edged side scraper; e, convex-edged side scraper. Length of a 7.7 cm.

area. Of the 12 principal microhabitats defined, 6 were of critical importance to Archaic populations: canyon head clifftop dunes, canyon head cliff-base springs, canyon rims, ephemeral ponds, low mesaland, and upland arroyo-edge dune ridges. The 500 archeological sites excavated, tested, or collected represent all periods from Clovis to historic Pueblo.

• JAY PHASE   Within the Arroyo Cuervo region, Paleo-Indian occupation is represented by remains belonging to the Clovis, Folsom, and Cody complexes. The earliest Archaic materials recovered in place, belonging to the Oshara tradition, have been termed the Jay phase and date between about 5500 and 4800 B.C. The Jay phase differs so greatly in tool kit (technology, typology, and functional classes), settlement patterns, and other aspects from the preceding Cody complex and other Paleo-Indian phases that there is evidently no essential connection between them. However, detailed similarities between this material and early Archaic assemblages in the western Southwest suggest ultimate derivation from this area.

Within the Arroyo Cuervo region, Jay phase sites may be divided into base camps and small specialized activity sites. The former are uniformly located in the very favorable environment represented by the canyon-head complex, while the position of the latter depends upon their focus on hunting (sites located near ephemeral ponds or in the higher mountains), generalized foraging (sites located on the low mesa), or quarrying (mountain obsidian quarries). Base camp debris evidently represents repeated returns to the same locality but does not show seasonal or other differentiation. Where isolated, as at the excavated Dunas Altas locality, the camps were relatively small (covering less than 50 square meters) and thin. The tool kit (fig. 5) recovered includes large slightly shouldered projectile points (reminiscent of those termed Lake Mohave in California and Arizona), well-made bifacial knives, and a range of well-made side-struck side scrapers. In general, the tool kit, limited faunal evidence, and

repeated reoccupation of favorable localities suggests a mixed spectrum of subsistence activities adapted to a year-round exploitation of a fixed group of local resources.

Distribution studies indicate that materials similar to those of the Jay phase occur widely in northwestern New Mexico and southwestern Colorado (Rio Grande complex, Renaud 1942); in northeastern Arizona (Concho complex, Wendorf and Thomas 1951); and southeastern Utah (Aneth complex, Mohr and Sample 1959; Moab complex, Hunt 1960).

On the basis of this distribution and the detailed similarities of the material to the contemporary or immediately antecedent San Dieguito-Lake Mohave remains in California and western Arizona, it may be postulated that the Oshara phenomenon derives its origins from slow, low-level demographic movements from the west, which spread progressively into the niche left by the withdrawal of the Paleo-Indian groups (fig. 2 center right).

• BAJADA PHASE   The next phase of Oshara development in the Arroyo Cuervo region was termed Bajada and was radiocarbon-dated between 4800 and about 3300 B.C. It occurred during the major part of the period of less effective moisture termed the Altithermal. The Bajada settlement system was essentially the same as the Jay, and despite this apparent climatic deterioration, the population (as represented by number of base-camp sites) may have increased somewhat. Within the tool kit (fig. 6) the projectile point form shifted from an early variety distinguished from the Jay principally by the presence of basal indentation and basal thinning to a later variety with increasingly well-defined shoulders and decreased overall length. The accompanying nonprojectile point elements include survivals of the well-made side scrapers and, more rarely, bifacial knives, together with an in-

36

Fig. 6. Bajada complex artifacts. a, Projectile points; b, crude irregular flake scrapers; c, well-made scraper. Length of c 7.7 cm.

creasing number of large chopping tools and poorly made flake side scrapers. The choppers and side scrapers are believed to be better adapted to the processing of coarse plant foods.

In general, the Bajada phase reflects considerable continuity from the preceding Jay phase. The possible increased population and the shifts in tool kit apparently reflect increasingly effective adaptation to a broad-spectrum localized resource space.

Similar materials have been reported widely on the surface in northern New Mexico, southwestern Colorado, southeastern Utah, and northeastern Arizona in the same generalized long-term complexes in which the Jay phase materials occurred.

• DESHA COMPLEX  Of considerable interest in an understanding of the early distribution of the Oshara tradition and its relation to contemporary developments elsewhere is the Desha complex of south-central Utah and a small section of adjacent north-central Arizona. Excavations near Navajo Mountain at Sand Dune and Dust Devil Caves produced very early Archaic remains dating between 6000 and 5000 B.C. (Lindsay et al. 1969; Richard Ambler, personal communication 1968). Diagnostic materials included elongated shallow side-notched points, open twined sandals, and one-rod foundation-interlocking stitch basketry. The general character of these materials is completely distinct from those of contemporary complexes to the west or east (Lake Mohave, Jay, Bajada) but suggests instead strong relations to the Great Basin to the north (Jennings 1957).

*The South: Cochise Tradition*

• SULPHUR SPRING PHASE  The crude chipped-stone assemblage from the base of Ventana Cave (the Ventana complex) indicates that by 9000 B.C. parts of the southern Southwest were already occupied by economically eclectic groups, although the specific relationships of these materials are not clear. However, this is not the only evidence for early Archaic occupation of the southern

Southwest. Sayles and Antevs (1941) defined the Sulphur Spring phase of the long-lived Cochise culture (Whalen 1971). The ultimate origins of this widespread tradition are obscure, but limited surface evidence suggests that it may represent the northern extremity of a general northwest Mexican hunting-gathering culture (Dick 1965a). All the sites belonging to this earliest Sulphur Spring phase (a total of six) are located in southeastern Arizona in the Sulphur Spring Valley and Whitewater Draw. The type site of Double Adobe has produced radiocarbon dates indicating an age between 7000 and 6000 B.C. for the materials excavated there (Haynes 1968; Whalen 1971).

The lithic industry recovered is dominated by thin flat milling stones and cobble manos, as well as a chipped stone complex characterized by percussion flake choppers, flake scrapers, and flake knives. To date, no projectile points have been recovered (Sayles and Antevs 1941). Surprisingly, at the type site, this kind of assemblage was accompanied by the bones of extinct megafauna such as horse, mammoth, bison, and dire wolf, as well as modern species such as rabbit, coyote, goose, and duck. The directness of these associations has been questioned (Haury 1960).

The absence of projectile points, the presence of extinct megafauna (some of which are generally considered to have become extinct before 7000 B.C.), and the rarity of Sulphur Spring age materials combine to leave a number of questions concerning this earliest Cochise phase unanswered. However, the available evidence does seem to indicate that by 7000–6000 B.C., well before the onset of Altithermal climatic conditions, the south-central Southwest was already occupied to some degree by groups with a mixed gathering-hunting economy, who already employed well-developed ground stone implements for processing plant foods.

Cochise development between this Sulphur Spring phase at about 7000–6000 B.C. and the relatively well-known Chiricahua phase at about 3500–1000 B.C. is still obscure. After their initial investigation, Sayles and Antevs (1955) discovered several additional localities in the Double Adobe area that yielded material generally similar to the Sulphur Spring except for the presence of projectile points. Carbon-14 dates from apparently associated sediments indicated an age between 4000 and 3000 B.C., and the investigators conclude that this represented a post–Sulphur Spring phase, termed Cazador. Whalen (1971) considers these deposits to be approximately contemporary with the Sulphur Spring phase and to represent its hunting facies. However, examinations of the stratigraphy of the type area by Irwin-Williams (1968c) and others reveal problems in the stratigraphic relationship of the Cazador materials to the carbon-14 dates and to the Sulphur Spring remains. In addition, the Cazador materials themselves do not parallel Sulphur Spring very closely, and, in fact, the projectile points exhibit detailed similarities to the local late Chiricahua phase. Accordingly, the postulated Cazador phase cannot be verified either as a separate phase or as a part of the Sulphur Spring. This leaves a hiatus between Sulphur Spring and Chiricahua, which encompasses all or most of the Altithermal, and which may reflect either a sparsity of population or a paucity of research.

### The Late Archaic

Evidence from geology and palynology indicates that during the period between about 3500 B.C. and 2500 B.C. there occurred a marked trend toward increased effective moisture in the Southwest (Antevs 1955; Mehringer 1967; Mehringer, Martin, and Haynes 1967; Haynes 1968). For the same time period, the significant increase in the number of archeological sites may well reflect an increase in population and/or expansion of population distribution. It seems possible that the existing economically eclectic Southwestern Archaic cultures, conditioned to maximum exploitation, underwent expansion with the amelioration of local resource bases and the removal of some existing constraints on population increase. For the remainder of the Archaic, hypotheses concerning large-scale development rest on somewhat firmer substantive ground.

#### Picosa Culture

It has been suggested that by about 3000 B.C. the Southwest was occupied by a broad continuum of interacting culture systems that have been termed the Picosa or Elementary Southwestern culture (Irwin-Williams 1967). This is the first time in prehistory that the Southwest may be considered a distinct culture area. The principal feature of the Picosa phenomenon is the existence of a large-scale low-level communication network, which is reflected in the rapid spread of subsistence elements and the interareal sharing of stylistic patterns. The three principal subdivisions that can be recognized within the Picosa continuum correspond to developments from earlier Archaic bases already outlined (in the west, north, and south). In addition, the existence of an as yet poorly known southeastern sector has become apparent.

#### The West: San Dieguito-Pinto Tradition

• PINTO BASIN COMPLEX Information on the late Archaic in the western Southwest is somewhat more abundant than for the earlier periods but is still sparse and largely derived from surface collections. The earliest materials related to this development are those recovered from the Red Sand deposit at Ventana Cave and termed Amargosa I by Rogers (in Haury 1950). These materials bear close resemblance to those of the Silver Lake portion of the San Dieguito-Lake Mohave-Silver Lake continuum and probably represent a very late development within it. Neither Silver Lake nor Red Sand materials are

apparently common or widespread and may reflect the somewhat more difficult climatic conditions of the late Altithermal. The derivative Pinto Basin (Amargosa II) assemblages of southern California and western Arizona evidently represent groups with a mixed foraging economy adapted to lake-edge, river-valley, and succulent-desert environments, in a period of notably more effective moisture than the present. These materials have been found in excavations at Ventana Cave (Haury 1950), at the specialized, probably late, Stahl site in southern California (M.R. Harrington 1957), at the very late Harbison Cave site in western Arizona (C.H. Jennings 1971), and probably at Gypsum Cave in southern Nevada (M.R. Harrington 1933). Surface materials have been recovered in many of the old lake basins in southern California, such as the Pinto Basin (Campbell and Campbell 1935), the Panamint Valley (E.L. Davis 1968), the Owens Valley region (E.L. Davis 1963), and Death Valley (Hunt and Tanner 1960). They also occur widely in the Colorado River Valley (Rogers 1939), western Arizona (C.H. Jennings 1971), and in southern Nevada (M.R. Harrington 1933). Inadequate carbon-14 dating and geologic position suggest an age of about 3000 B.C. to about 1000-500 B.C. for these materials (M.R. Harrington 1957; Haury 1950). However, it is probable that improved chronologic control will permit temporal divisions within this range.

As presently known, the tool kit (fig. 7) is dominated by chipped-stone implements, including cobble and thick flake choppers, scraper planes, flake scrapers and cutting edges, and a variety of projectile points. Most of the points are variants of a straight-stemmed shouldered or unshouldered concave base serrated form. Excavations at Ventana Cave and the Stahl site indicate late shifts toward increasingly expanded stems, more abrupt shoulders, and, in some instances, absence of basal concavity. Ground-stone implements, principally shallow-basined grinding slabs and cobble manos, are present; but, possibly because of the specific economic activities represented, they are relatively rare on the open desert sites.

The Stahl site near Little Lake in southern California presents a rare opportunity to examine the Pinto Basin

Southwest Mus., Los Angeles.
Fig. 7. Pinto Basin projectile points. Materials are: a-b, obsidian; c, rhyolite; d, jasper. Length of a, about 3.7 cm (see also "Post-Pleistocene Archeology, 9000-2000 B.C.," fig. 11, vol. 8).

cultural system in a stable and abundant environmental situation (M.R. Harrington 1957). Located at the junction of a tributary stream and a permanent lake, the site measures more than 500 feet in diameter and produced a concentrated and prolific cultural deposit. The seven or more structures uncovered were circular in outline, with a southern entrance, and were marked by post holes and shallow depressions. Several of these overlap and reflect repeated reoccupation of this desirable locality. Extensive storage pits and the concentration of cultural debris combine to suggest relatively long-term occupations. Food preparation involved the use of large cobble-filled hearths (ovens). Unfortunately, little research was done on the details of the subsistence pattern represented. The extensive tool kit suggests the potential range and complexity of the Pinto Basin pattern in a favorable environment. The excavations recovered a variety of well-made scrapers, flake knives, scraper planes, keel scrapers, perforators, bifacial disks, and a few bifacial knives. The ground-stone inventory included several variants of the shallow-basined and also the semitroughed milling stone, as well as cobble manos. Exotic items included polished stone pendants and ornaments of bone and shell. The range of projectile points included shouldered and unshouldered Pinto points, leaf-shaped points, contracting-stem points, and a few barbed specimens. The complexion of the whole assemblage suggests a relatively late (perhaps 2000–1500 B.C.) age for the site, but no radiocarbon data are available. On the whole, the site appears to reflect a situation of repeated, possibly seasonal, population aggregation and relatively long-term occupations. Elsewhere in southern California, material of comparable or slightly later age than the Stahl site has been recovered at the Rose Spring site at the base of a sequence leading in to the better-known Amargosa III period (Lanning 1963).

The northeastern extension of cultural systems similar to those represented at the Stahl and Rose Spring localities is known from materials recovered on the surface and in excavation on the Coconino Plateau of northwestern and north-central Arizona (C.H. Jennings 1971). Red Butte phase materials from Harbison Cave are very similar to the late Pinto Basin complex represented at the Stahl site and early Rose Spring deposits to the west, on the one hand, and also to remains identified with the Armijo phase of the Oshara cultural tradition to the east. They evidently represent the middle range of the cultural continuum existing between the two areas (fig. 2, bottom left and center).

At Ventana Cave in southern Arizona the extensive material cultural inventory recovered represents a wide range of activities and provides an indication of the character of culture change through time (Haury 1950). Gypsum Cave in southern Nevada yielded a limited and probably specialized assemblage dominated by the contracting-stem point form. The possibility of the associ-

ation of these materials with extinct fauna (giant ground sloth) and the very early date originally attributed to them (Wormington 1957) initially obscured their relations, but they are now believed to be coeval with other Pinto and Pinto-Gypsum assemblages.

• AMARGOSA III PHASE  The cultural developments that followed the Pinto Basin phase in California and western Arizona may be briefly outlined. In California, the very late preceramic Amargosa III and Amargosa IV assemblages were derived from the preceding Pinto Basin (Amargosa II) phase. They are represented in excavation at the Rose Spring locality (Lanning 1963) and in extensive surface collections from California and western Arizona. They also parallel many of the stylistic-technologic developments recorded in the northern Southwest. In northwestern Arizona, related materials were recovered in the Red Horse phase at Harbison Cave on the Coconino Plateau (C.H. Jennings 1971). Developments of this kind in Arizona and California ultimately culminate in assemblages such as the Basketmaker II materials recovered at Willow Beach (Schroeder 1961a). In general, these very late Archaic assemblages are characterized by the addition of an extensive bifacial chipped-stone complex (stemmed and barbed points, bifacial knives, drills) to the basic chopper and flake scraper industry. Although there are suggestions of population increase, evidence for the development of agriculture and semisedentarism is absent except locally in the west.

*The North: Oshara Tradition*

• SAN JOSE PHASE  Slightly before 3000 B.C. a series of systemic changes gradually initiated a new phase of the Oshara tradition in the northern Southwest that has been termed San Jose and that lasted until about 1800 B.C. Climatic evidence indicates that toward the beginning of this period the Southwest witnessed a general shift toward increased effective moisture, dune stabilization, and soil formation.

At this time in the Arroyo Cuervo region of northwestern New Mexico, Irwin-Williams (1968c, 1973) noted an increase in the number of canyon-head-based camp sites, in the size of these sites (averaging about 100–150 square meters), and in the concentration of camping debris. Irregular post-hole patterns at the Collier Dunes site suggest simple structures. Extensive fire-cracked cobble-filled earth ovens are well represented. The limited faunal assemblage is dominated by the remains of medium- and small-sized game animals. Special activity sites in the Arroyo Cuervo region continue to be present (gathering sites, quarries), although relatively few ephemeral pond-edge hunting sites have been noted. The possibility of relatively large special activity groups is suggested by one hunting site, which produced 15 hearths.

The tool kit from the San Jose phase (fig. 8) is dominated by increased numbers of large, heavy chopping tools and poorly made flake side scrapers and

Irwin-Williams 1973:fig. 4.
Fig. 8. San Jose complex artifacts. a, Projectile points; b, ovoid bifacial knife; c, elongated bifacial knife; d, irregular flake scraper; e, chopper, edge view of use area. Length of c 10.1 cm.

cutting edges. Projectile point forms differ from those of the preceding phase principally in the use of serration of the projectile point blade and decreased stem length; there is a trend in time toward decreasing overall length and toward expanding stems. Important additions were shallow-basined grinding slabs and simple cobble manos, which permit the more effective use of wild grass and other seeds. On the whole, the assemblage parallels those identified as Pinto Basin to the west.

In general, the evidence suggests an increasingly successful and localized adaptation focused principally on the favorable canyon head environments. More effective resource utilization and improved technology, together with somewhat more moist climatic conditions, may have permitted a slight population increase.

Materials similar to those recovered in the Arroyo Cuervo region have been found in excavation in Colorado, in the Apex complex (Irwin-Williams and Irwin 1966), and near Acoma, New Mexico (A.E. Dittert, personal communication 1967). Related surface materials were recovered from northern New Mexico (San Jose complex, Bryan and Toulouse 1943; Gallegos complex, Hadlock 1962), southwestern Colorado (Rio Grande complex, Renaud 1942), northeastern Arizona (Concho complex, Wendorf and Thomas 1951), and southeastern Utah (Moab complex, Hunt 1960; Aneth complex, Mohr and Sample 1959). This distribution, which complements and overlaps that of Pinto Basin in northern Arizona, together with the detailed similarity of the two assemblages, suggests that they form the extremities of a continuum (fig. 2, bottom left). This may well reflect in part their common earlier derivation.

40

## The South: Cochise Tradition

• CHIRICAHUA PHASE  Developments in the southern sector remain relatively distinct from those in other areas of the Southwest. The earliest materials belonging to a Chiricahua (or pre-Chiricahua) Cochise pattern were recovered in the Buff Sand layers of Bat Cave in western New Mexico and probably date from 3000 B.C. or earlier (Dick 1965a). As originally defined, typical Chiricahua materials are known from excavations and surface collections in southeastern Arizona, in the San Pedro Valley (Sayles and Antevs 1941; Whalen 1971), and at the Cienega Creek site (Haury and Sayles 1947). Limited Chiricahua materials occur in the moist midden levels of Ventana Cave, mixed with a predominantly Pinto Basin assemblage (Haury 1950). In western New Mexico excavated materials are available from Bat Cave (Dick 1965a), the Wet Leggett site (Martin, Rinaldo, and Antevs 1949), and at the Moquino site in northwestern New Mexico (Irwin-Williams and Beckett 1973). Surface collections in north-central and northeastern Arizona (for example, included within the Concho complex) indicate a strong penetration of that area during Chiricahua phase times (Wendorf and Thomas 1951). In New Mexico, Beckett (Beckett 1973) indicates a distribution of Cochise materials largely west of the Rio Grande River as far north as the Moquino locality. At the opposite extreme, "Chiricahua" materials have been reported as far south as southern Chihuahua (Dick 1965a). Radiocarbon dates from the Wet Leggett, Bat Cave, and Moquino localities indicate a time range of about 3500-3000 to about 1500-1000 B.C.

The tool kits recovered from Chiricahua sites evidently reflect a mixed foraging economy with emphasis on a well-developed ground-stone assemblage dominated by shallow-basined milling slabs and cobble manos. The chipped-stone assemblage is characterized by crude choppers, scraper planes, simple scrapers, flake scrapers and cutting edges, and a range of projectile points. The points are distinctive and include the large side-notched concave-based Chiricahua form (fig. 9), the diamond-shaped Pelona style, and the widespread contracting-stemmed Augustin type (Dick 1965a).

Whalen's (1971) study of Cochise sites in the San Pedro Valley indicates that the subsistence system there focused on the exploitation of two environmental habitats, river valley and hill slope. The economic cycle represented

Eastern N.M.U., Paleo-Indian Institute, Portales, N.M.
Fig. 9. Projectile points from Chiricahua Cochise level at Moquino site, Sandoval Co., N.M. Length of left 2.4 cm.

evidently utilized the floral and faunal sources of both of these without developing a markedly seasonal (transhumant) pattern. Both base camps and specialized activity sites were identified on the basis of the range of proportion of tools represented and the presence or absence of hearth materials. Using modern foragers as analogues, Whalen postulated a small band of about 25 persons as the basic population unit.

A primitive variety of maize was probably introduced into the southern Southwest by about 2500–2000 B.C. and spread rapidly through all but possibly the western sector. In the Cochise area, this maize (a primitive Chapalote variety) was accompanied by domestic squash. In terms of the relative proportions of domestic versus wild flora represented in the diet, the significance of these plants was probably limited, at least until the introduction of a more productive form of maize about 750 B.C. (Mangelsdorf and Lister 1956). However, research in the northern sector of the Southwest indicates that a small seasonal surplus made possible by small-scale cultivation may have been of great importance in the development of seasonal population aggregation and ultimately a sedentarism. Further research in the Cochise situation may produce comparable indications. In addition to the data on early agriculture, Bat Cave also produced evidence of basketry, textiles, and sandals, which must have played an important part in the original Chiricahua material culture.

*The Southeast*

Although intermittent investigations have been carried out since the 1930s, southeastern and south-central New Mexico and the adjacent southwesternmost portions of Texas are very poorly known for the Archaic period. Clovis, Cody, and Folsom remains in this area fall within the distribution patterns already discussed. Sporadic excavations at well-preserved rockshelters (for example, Cosgrove 1947; Sayles 1935) produced materials that have been lumped under the general term Hueco Basketmaker and that were initially believed to be coeval with the Anasazi Basketmaker at about A.D. 1. However, it is now apparent that these and related materials reflect a relatively complex long-term development going back to at least 2000 B.C. and suggesting intriguing possibilities of early Mexican contacts.

Excavations at Fresnal Shelter near Alamogordo, New Mexico, near Carlsbad, New Mexico, and near Artesia, New Mexico, all have produced materials generally identifiable with the Hueco complex (Irwin-Williams 1970, 1971, 1971a; Roney and Irwin-Williams 1971; Wimberly 1972; Mark Strong, personal communication 1970). At the Fresnal Shelter, the sequence of development dates from about A.D. 1 back to at least 1600 B.C. and will ultimately permit internal chronologic segmentation. The earliest materials here are characterized by

Photograph by Peter B. George, San Francisco, Calif., 1971.
Fig. 10. Projectile points from Fresnal Shelter, Otero Co., N.M. Left two are earlier, right two later; length of left 3.7 cm.

Photograph by Peter B. George, San Francisco, Calif., 1971.
Fig. 11. Well-made small end scrapers from Fresnal Shelter, Otero Co., N.M. Length of left 3.0 cm.

shouldered straight-stemmed concave- or straight-based projectile points, contracting-stemmed projectile points (fig. 10), well-made small end scrapers (fig. 11), choppers, flake scrapers, and manos and metates.* In addition, preserved remains include coiled and twilled basketry bags and sandals. Of critical importance are food remains, including not only wild plants (such as cactus, sotol, grass seed, and wild squash) but also, even in the earliest deposits, Chapalote maize, a smaller eight-rowed maize, and domestic beans. This early agricultural complex differs considerably from that represented at the contemporary Cochise site of Bat Cave, which produced maize and domestic squash but no beans. Later deposits at the same site include a variety of expanding-stemmed and side- or corner-notched projectile points and shifts in other artifact classes. Coarse brown pottery was added to this kind of assemblage just after the beginning of the Christian era, and the material has been termed the Jornada Mogollon (Lehmer 1948).

Although knowledge of this material is in an embryonic state, limited comparisons are possible. The Fresnal and/or Hueco remains show few similarities to the contemporary Cochise culture to the west or the Oshara to the north, and most of these are of a generalized adaptive nature. Distributional studies in southwestern New Mexico indicate that Cochise sites occur principally

---

* The term metate is widely used in the Southwest and by anthropologists to refer to a milling stone with shallowly troughed top that is used to grind corn (and sometimes other substances) by rubbing with a smaller stone muller called a mano. Both words are borrowed from the Mexican Spanish names for the objects, where *metate* is derived from Nahuatl *metlatl* (the name for the artifact) and *mano* is literally 'hand'.

41

Photograph by Peter B. George, San Francisco, Calif., 1971.
Fig. 12. Perishable materials from Fresnal Shelter, Otero Co., N.M. a, Slotted foreshaft of atlatl dart; b, bone awl; c, bone gaming pieces; d, string and feather ornament. Length of a 8.7 cm.

west of the Rio Grande River and Fresnal-related materials to the east (particularly in the Tularosa Basin and eastward). The adjacent area of northern Mexico, immediately to the south, is poorly known. However, Taylor (1966) has identified a generalized widespread Archaic entity termed the Frontera complex in the north Mexican states of Coahuila, eastern Chihuahua, and in a small portion of westernmost Texas. This large-scale long-term but as yet little-defined cultural phenomenon goes back to at least 7500 B.C. at Frightful Cave in Coahuila (Taylor 1966). Remains from the later phases of this development (identified as the Coahuila complex) show remarkable similarities to those from Fresnal Shelter, in both the lithic and the textile inventories.

In brief, although the data are very sparse, they suggest that, for at least 2000 years before A.D. 1, the eastern periphery of the Southwest was occupied by groups whose origins lie to the south, east of the Sierra Madre Occidental Range in north-central Mexico.

On the whole, the long record of the preceramic period in the Southwest indicates the kind and degree of cultural complexity that was basic to the later, better-known developments in the area.

# Agricultural Beginnings, 2000 B.C.-A.D. 500

RICHARD B. WOODBURY AND EZRA B.W. ZUBROW

A hunting and gathering economy with a band social organization has been judged the most stable and hence the most successful form of economic and social adaptation that mankind has achieved. Its stability is documented by the fact that for almost all the time that man has been on earth he has been a hunter and gatherer. In the North American Southwest there is evidence that only by about 2000 B.C. this adaptation was beginning to change, and then only very gradually.

The reconstructed picture of life in the Southwest at about 2000 B.C. suggests a sparse population living a life of seasonal movement in order to exploit systematically all possible environmental resources (not just wild plants and animals, but fibers, stone materials, pigments, for example, and, of course, seasonal water supplies). The usual historic analogy for this Desert culture or Southwestern Archaic, is the Great Basin Shoshoni—small bands of family size or perhaps larger but closely kin-related groups, living on a diet of grass seed, piñon nuts, berries, roots, mice, rats, insects, rabbits, birds, and so on, without substantial or permanent dwellings but seasonally occupying rockshelters, windbreaks, and perhaps huts as substantial as an Apache wickiup.

According to Lee and DeVore (1968) and Martin and Plog (1973) any hunting and gathering economic system was based upon three propositions concerning production, consumption, and redistribution. First, production of food was based on the sexual division of labor; males did the hunting and females the gathering with the addition of child care. Second, consumption was almost immediate and the producers and consumers were members of the same small kin-related group. Third, redistribution was based upon kin ties within the group and therefore was closely related to immediate demand.

The social organization was based upon two propositions. First, the mobility necessary for production made the accumulation of wealth impossible. Thus, without differences in wealth, long-term hierarchies were impossible to maintain and the social organization was egalitarian. Second, kin ties provided the social organization. Such a life, for all its immediacy and occasional hardships, did not preclude a rich verbal, conceptual, musical, artistic, and ceremonial life, yet for these sectors of Southwestern life in the last two millennia B.C. there is no direct evidence. The discussion that follows is necessarily limited to the economic, demographic, and social aspects of life as interpreted from relatively imperishable remains that have been studied by archeologists.

Numerous local minor variations on the general hunting and gathering pattern would reflect the many ecological niches to which man in the Southwest had adapted during the preceding millennia. For example, Binford (1968) has argued that in environments with a large amount of ecological diversity, the entire household moves as part of the hunting-gathering group from one locus of production to another. Where ecological diversity is low, specialized hunting groups of men move from one area to another, following the movements of herds and other game, while more generalized gathering groups (mostly women and children) remain in the immediate area of a base camp for longer periods of time. Entire households therefore move less frequently.

Regional variation increased through time, as tool kits and skills were elaborated and passed from person to person. The results increased the chances for survival through more efficient exploitation of natural resources but at the same time increased the dependence for a particular group of people on the specific environment and resources that they manipulated. Important technological innovations would permit improved hunting methods—for example, very large, strong rabbit nets, in contrast to small individual snares. The excavation of wells was another important new technique, making possible a dependable water supply in an area where water scarcity might have precluded full use of its food resources. The wells at the Cienega Creek site, dug shortly after 2000 B.C., may not be unique but only a lucky archeological find skillfully interpreted, and an example of one of the ways people increased their chances for survival by permitting fuller use of the food resources of a water-scarce area.

Archeological evidence from the Southwest indicates that perhaps as early as 2000 B.C. and at least by 1500 to 1000 B.C. a significant modification began in this hunting-gathering pattern, with the introduction of agriculture from Mexico. But the domesticated maize and squash that came first played such a minor role in the economy initially that the way of life of those groups that adopted the new foods was changed hardly at all. A few groups of people planted some small patches of corn in favorable spots, tended them cursorily while keeping up their essential round of hunting and gathering activities, or left

*43*

the area until late summer, and then returned to gather a small harvest from these plots. However, in the last few centuries before A.D. 500, farming was developing into a significant subsistence base for some Southwestern groups, first in the settled villages along the Gila and Salt rivers, where irrigation on a substantial scale had appeared by about 300 B.C. Here, at least one village of 50 or so families (Snaketown) was a year-round rather than a seasonal settlement, with reliance on wild foods greatly reduced by the regular production of domestic crops. Elsewhere in the Southwest details are known for only 12–15 villages prior to A.D. 500 that seem to have been permanently occupied with at least 15 houses (and in a few 30 to 40) in simultaneous use. If not lived in through the entire year, they were returned to each fall as a permanent base and were supported by an efficient subsistence system, of which agriculture was one major component.

Yet what is significant when one examines archeological data for a period of 2,500 years is the small role that agriculture played in the Southwest before A.D. 500. The critical questions for Southwestern archeologists are not only where and when agriculture began or even how it came to the Southwest, but also why agriculture was adopted and how it continued for two millennia or more to play only a minor part in the economy. It is clear that the prerequisites for agricultural adoption existed in the Southwest by 2000 B.C. First, the Southwest was a marginal agricultural area with increasing population density. Binford (1968) and Flannery (1968) have argued that populations under conditions of economic stress react more favorably toward the adoption of innovation. Second, there existed in the Southwest a variety of ecozones, so that artificial adaptive radiations could have begun as man introduced new crop plants to particular ecozones. Third, the eventual existence of multiple varieties of corn in the Southwest suggests a single introduction of several varieties (which is not supported by the archeological record), or successive introductions of multiple varieties. Fourth, small artificial environments were being created by human activities that disturbed the soil, causing greater productivity of certain species. These prerequisites having been met, the increased use of plants would result in increased modification in the direction of increased productivity, which would have a cyclic feedback toward greater utilization of these agricultural products. Nevertheless, in the Southwest the archeological record fails to show any such substantial change and instead there is some 2,000 years of stability in agriculture, at a very low level of production and economic dependence. This stability extends to social and technological sectors of Southwestern culture as reflected in the material record of the period.

Without doubt, the domestic crops came from Mexico, where they are known at much earlier times. But the methods of preparation and cooking were strongly influ-

enced by the continuing tradition of the Desert culture, with sun-drying, parching in baskets with coals, and grinding dried seeds (now corn, earlier wild grasses) all continuing in use.

An important addition to the food technology was the use of large, secure storage pits, which permitted large quantities of food, such as corn, to be protected for months and even years. Present evidence indicates that storage pits only came into common use many centuries after farming began in the Southwest. Pottery also offered an important new means of storage, dry and safe from rodents and insects. Baskets, snares, bags, tumplines, and other specialized devices probably date back much earlier than open sites permit the proof of; in the Great Basin they were in use several thousand years earlier. The assortment of perishable objects found in Tularosa Cave, dating to the last few centuries B.C., strongly suggests a long tradition, not a sudden, late start for a variety of highly specialized crafts and tools. One possible late development—coming only about A.D. 500—is the bow and arrow, which replaced the spear-thrower; but even there, lack of earlier evidence may be misleading, and the bow and arrow may be older by far than known examples can show.

Excavated and recorded archeological sites for the time span of 2000 B.C. to A.D. 500 are spread from northern Chihuahua to southern Colorado and Utah but heavily concentrated in a few regions: the upper Gila (Pinelawn-Reserve area); southern Arizona, south and east of Tucson; the San Juan; and the Rio Grande near Albuquerque. This concentration may be mostly the result of where archeologists have looked the hardest, and the lucky circumstances of preservation and then rapid erosional exposure and discovery, without complete destruction. The variety of elevations, topography, and vegetation zones represented by known sites suggests that large parts of the Southwest where information is lacking could have been similarly occupied by small, scattered, sedentary or semisedentary bands during this time period.

The changes that can be seen by A.D. 500 may be the result of a fortunate combination of circumstances. First, population was slowly increasing, with more efficient subsistence techniques. The increase would justify, or require, a minority of the population becoming part-time specialists, to produce more and better traps, weapons, clothes, carrying bags, and so on. The results would be cumulative, the specialists being the source of further complexity of culture and greater efficiency in meeting basic group needs. Gradually the continuing face-to-face group would grow from the nuclear family to the extended family and perhaps further. Another set of reasons for change may involve the arrival of new strains of corn from farther south, so that yields were larger and farming was becoming too promising to be a minor or casual pursuit. If harvests were large enough, and if means of storage were secure and ample, the need for annual movements of the group would decrease. Sedentary life requires and makes worthwhile the effort of building a more permanent dwelling, and this in turn permits the accumulation and preservation of more material objects. As groups became larger, more specialization was possible, in ceremonial and symbolic activities as well as in economic pursuits and craft work. For all the foregoing there is little archeological evidence, except the fact that during the first five or six centuries A.D. there were settled villages in many parts of the Southwest, whereas before that they were neither numerous nor widespread.

The elaborate material objects of Tularosa Cave and the Basketmaker II rockshelters suggest plenty of leisure for intricate craft work—elegant designs made in difficult techniques, rather than mere utilitarian products. The "cost" in human productivity was doubtless large but supportable and the returns in esthetic or symbolic values satisfactory. Evidence from open sites farther south, such as those of the Cochise culture, lack information on similar perishable objects, but no doubt the same skilled crafts existed and produced corresponding objects.

In summary, a comparison of the situation at 2000 B.C. to the most advanced areas of the Southwest at A.D. 500 shows a significant but very slow change in cultural adaptation. There were changes in man's interrelationship with his environment, his demographic characteristics, his economy, and his social organization. However, these changes were slow and partial, and there was considerable stability and continuity.

## An Ecological Perspective On Agricultural Development

### Agriculture as an Invasion

It is possible to look at the beginning of agriculture in the Southwest as the artificial introduction of a series of plants into an already developed natural ecological community. Invasion is the process by which an organism spreads from its parent community to a new community and successfully adapts to its new habitat. Agriculture is the artificial introduction of plants for human use into a new habitat—that is, an artificially produced invasion.

Energy is transferred by a food chain, as a result of the consumption of one type of organism by another. For example, herbivores consume plants, and carnivores then consume herbivores. Food chains may vary in complexity and in the number of different types of organisms that are dependent upon each other. To measure the complex series of food chains that forms an ecological community, the concepts of stability and diversity are useful. By stability is meant the persistence of an ecological system, which may be measured in local or global, or in structural terms. Diversity is a nontemporal measure of the distribution of the biomass, usually relating the number of species

to the size of the population of each species. The development of agriculture can then be viewed as an invasion that takes place in communities with expanding diversity indices and with short food chains.

The invaders, whether they are supposedly beneficial plants such as new agricultural strains or are harmful pests, have certain common biological characteristics: the ability to adapt to a variety of new environments, since they are versatile (carrying much genetic variability); a relatively high reproduction rate; competitive advantages that allow them to obtain dominant or even exclusive occupation of their niches; and relatively more transience than most species. Early agricultural species that entered the Southwest conform to these general characteristics.

Man's association with agricultural invaders has emphasized the first characteristics. The cultivation of plants tends to create a monoculture, an artificially simplified plant community, by weeding out competitors and thus increasing production of the chosen species. This reduction of the variability of the community is reinforced in two ways. First, man's conscious attempt at herbivore control, even at such a simple level as keeping animals out of the fields, reduces the range available to the herbivores and decreases the number of species actually subsisting off the fields. Second, this change in herbivores is reflected in unintentional changes in the carnivore distribution (Elton 1958).

Invaders are most likely to succeed and result in a population explosion of one or more plant species in natural communities with low diversity indices (that is, species-poor communities). There are fewer competitors and predators even at the start. There are three kinds of species-poor situations: new communities, where the number of species is increasing; severe environments, where small changes cause large abiotic results; and unpredictable environments, where there is large spatial and temporal variation.

If one places in chronological order the Southwestern archeological sites and strata with evidence of agriculture, the number and variety of invaders increases through time. This can be seen as an artificial increase in the diversity of the crop plant communities from their initial low diversity. It was probably not until late in this process, with the major irrigation system of Snaketown, that the local ecological communities were being artificially simplified on a broad scale. The conscious artificial reduction of the complexity of a large plant and animal community would seem to require labor forces similar in scale to those used in the construction of major irrigation projects.

### The Desert Culture and the Archaic Pattern

In many ways Southwestern North America 4,000 years ago closely resembled its appearance, in terms of wildlife and landscape, at the time that Europeans began displacing its Indian inhabitants only four centuries ago. The greatest difference was in the pattern of life of the human occupants, who were small in number, mobile in their seasonal movements, and dependent on collecting a large variety of wild plant foods and hunting the wild animals. The earlier extinction of the Pleistocene megafauna had left the smaller grazing animals (deer and antelope), numerous edible rodents and birds, and the smaller carnivora. When the concept of Desert culture was proposed and defined (Jennings and Norbeck 1955) it was considered to be a widespread cultural pattern with relatively minor local variations, extending from the Plateau region, throughout the Great Basin, and into the Southwest. As a foraging economy with emphasis on plant foods and smaller game, it contrasted with the big-game hunting tradition of the Southwest and High Plains. The definition of Desert culture was regarded as ending the need to search for the hypothetical Basketmaker I, since it was the base from which Southwestern cultures developed—the Anasazi in the north, the Hohokam in the southern deserts, and the Mogollon. This view has now changed somewhat, and the Desert culture is better considered both as a regional manifestation in the Great Basin of the continent-wide Archaic cultural pattern and as including smaller areal distinctions. Nevertheless, it is instructive to retain the idea expressed as the core of the Desert culture concept (Jennings 1964), a pattern of exploiting arid environments for a successful but mobile life by small bands of families, which resembled in many ways the life of the Numic peoples who occupied the Great Basin in the nineteenth century and were observed briefly before their traditional culture changed (Steward 1938; Fowler and Fowler 1971).

By about 3000 B.C. there were several localized variants of the Archaic in the Southwest, a western (San Dieguito-Pinto tradition), a northern (Oshara tradition), a southern (Cochise tradition), and a southeastern ("Post-Pleistocene Archeology, 7000–2000 B.C.," this vol.). The distinguishing features of these traditions represent gradually developing technological variations that do not obscure the essential broader cultural similarities. Tool types, food preferences, and perhaps other aspects of culture, such as size of social grouping and degree of seasonal mobility, were beginning to show the local differentiation that was eventually to become so conspicuous in the final centuries of Indian cultural dominance in the Southwest.

## The Southwest as Marginal to Mexico

When the western hemisphere's cultural development is viewed as a whole, through the span of the many millennia from its first human occupation, it is clear that the two major regions of innovation and rapid change that culminated in the pre-Columbian civilizations were the Andean and Mesoamerican, in each of which a sequence of changes led from simple farming villages to complex states achieving control of large areas. Beyond each central region were vast areas that felt the influence of their cultural developments without significant direct contact. More specifically, the Southwest from about 2000 B.C. onward can be best understood in terms of its marginal relationship to Mesoamerica, from which it received important cultural stimulation. Before about 5000 B.C. the Southwest and Mesoamerica were more similar, culturally, than they were different. However, from this time on, with the development of agriculture and village life, Mesoamerica advanced socially, economically, and ideologically far more rapidly than did the Southwest, which was viewed as the remote and "barbaric" north, beyond the limits of civilization as it existed in Mesoamerica. Even the Hohokam, closest culturally to Mesoamerica and most directly derivative from it, lacked the urbanism and accompanying traits of civilization that had developed to the south. On the other hand, Casas Grandes, in northern Chihuahua, was once considered a "peripheral Southwestern" center but is now better understood as an outpost of Mesoamerica (Kidder 1962:321; Di Peso 1966:21–23).

Mexico was the source, directly or indirectly, for many of the changes that began in the Southwest about 2000 B.C., especially agriculture and various technological innovations. Nevertheless, these often took forms quite different from their southern prototypes. Much of the attention of Southwestern archeologists for nearly a century has been directed to identifying Mexican antecedents for Southwestern culture traits or distinguishing the minor but distinct local variations in the Southwest that grew up after their initial introductions (Vaillant 1932; Kelley 1966).

Domestic plants, as the primary Mexican contribution to the Southwest, did the most to transform the life of its inhabitants. The introduction of pottery making from Mexico was less basic but of archeological importance because of the abundance of imperishable evidence it supplies.

## The Introduction of Domestic Plants

### Domestication of Maize in Mexico

Maize is now generally believed to be descended from teosinte, a wild grass widespread in Mexico (Beadle 1972; Harlan 1967; Galinat 1970, 1971; Flannery 1973; "The Origin of Maize," vol. 3). This theory has replaced the hypothesis that cultivated maize is derived from a wild ancestor of the same species that no longer exists (Mangelsdorf 1974). Cobs of an early variety of maize have been identified by Mangelsdorf in material found in dry cave deposits in the Tehuacán Valley of central Mexico, dated at about 5000 B.C. (Mangelsdorf, MacNeish, and Galinat 1964, 1967; MacNeish 1967). The ears were tiny, and the food value of the plant would have been quite modest. By about 3500 B.C. the Tehuacán maize was certainly being cultivated, along with a number of other plants native to the region (squash, beans, gourds, chili peppers, avocados, and amaranth).

Cultivation is a term generally used to mean the improvement of the immediate environment of a cultigen, by weeding (a mechanism to decrease competition), watering (a mechanism for increasing productivity), and the retention each year of seed for planting a future crop (a mechanism for increasing production stability). From these mechanisms came adaptive change in the maize plant. By about 1500 B.C. corn of considerably greater size was being grown, partly as a result of hybridization of the earlier corn with wild teosinte. Greater variability as a result of this hybridization offered farmers corn with differing characteristics for selection in terms of yield, resistance to drought, suitability to growing season and temperature, and other desirable features. Eventually many "races" of corn were developed in Mexico, including the predecessors of the Chapalote and Nal-Tel, which spread to the Southwest. Evidence from other parts of Mexico is much less complete than for the Tehuacán Valley, but many similar ecological zones elsewhere in highland Mexico also took part in the domestication and development of corn. Gradually it diffused northward, first into northern Mexico and then into the Southwest. This probably occurred slowly, kernels of maize passing from group to group, along with the knowledge of how to grow it, but there is no record of the transmission except the evidence that at an early date it reached the Southwest. It took between 1,500 and 3,500 years to travel about 2,000 miles (depending on what dates for earliest domestication and for arrival in the Southwest are used).

It is significant for understanding the manner of transmission of corn northward from Mexico that the complete complex of associated techniques for growing corn and preparing it for eating was not carried to the Southwest. The widespread Mexican technique of soaking kernels in a lime solution to soften the pericarp (hull) prior to crushing them on a stone slab was not necessary in the Southwest, where the type of corn, with floury kernel, could be crushed easily in the dry state (Walton C. Galinat, personal communication 1974). The dried kernels were ground on a metate and only subsequently moistened for cooking. This is a strenuous and time-consuming technique and perpetuates the very old (Archaic) tradition that had been used for wild grass seeds. Another ancient technique consisted of roasting fresh ears over the coals of a shallow hearth, then removing the kernels and grinding them coarsely (Ford 1968a). Ford observes that this method preserved the nutrients as fully as cooking the ground meal in water yet required no utensils except the basin metate and one-hand mano grinder.

*Evidence from Sites*

• BAT CAVE, THE EARLIEST SOUTHWESTERN MAIZE Almost 2,000 miles north of the Tehuacán Valley lie the San Augustín Plains of western New Mexico, a dry, flat basin that once held a Pleistocene lake. In the low rocky mountains of its southern border is Bat Cave, a disturbed rockshelter in which Dick found remains of corn in 1948 and 1950, along with artifacts left by the contemporary occupants of the shelter (Dick 1965a; Mangelsdorf, MacNeish, and Galinat 1964; Mangelsdorf and Smith 1949). Their exact age is still uncertain, because of differing interpretations of the stratigraphy of the cave and the associated carbon-14 dates. One viewpoint, based on geochronological evidence, puts the date at 3500 B.C.; the other places it at 1500 B.C. on the basis of various stratigraphic and dating problems (the carbon sample, for example, is pooled from a number of smaller samples, was dated by the solid carbon method, and has not been rechecked by more modern techniques). Mangelsdorf, who studied the Bat Cave corn as well as the Tehuacán corn, favors the date of about 3600 B.C. on the basis of the primitive nature of the corn itself. The corn consist of tiny, strawberry-shaped ears, which carried kernels that were both pod (each covered by its own husklike glume) and pop (had kernels capable of exploding when heated, and thus becoming edible without grinding or other cooking). These "primitive" features cause most archeologists to favor the earlier dating, even though the evidence for it is not fully satisfactory. The importance of the Bat Cave corn is its early date, its central location in the Southwest, and its similarity to the early corn of Mexico, the pre-Chapalote corn of Tehuacán. In the entire intervening area there has not yet been found evidence of equally early corn.

The cultural material associated with the earliest Bat Cave corn belongs to the Chiricahua stage of the Cochise culture, which has been thought of as having an essentially plant-gathering and small-game-hunting economy, on the basis of numerous sites in southwestern New Mexico and southeastern Arizona. The presence of a small amount of corn does not change this view significantly, for it could have contributed only a small percentage to the varied subsistence resources. In addition, squash (*Cucurbita pepo*) was also grown by these Chiricahua stage occupants of Bat Cave, an important nutritional accompaniment of maize, since squash provides the amino acid tryptophan, which maize lacks (Ford 1968a).

In the succeeding San Pedro stage of the Cochise culture the occupants of Bat Cave added beans (*Phaseolus vulgaris*) to their farming, making the trio of basic Southwestern domestic food complete by about 1000 to 400 B.C.

Bat Cave, at an elevation of 7,900 feet, has a growing season averaging 130 days, only just long enough in terms of present-day Southwestern Indian farming. The present average annual precipitation of the Plains of Augustín is 13.32 inches. Climatic evidence for a minor fluctuation to warmer and/or drier at the time of the occupation of Bat Cave suggests that this would have been a more desirable farming location then than today. There is no archeological evidence for deriving the Bat Cave maize directly from Tehuacán, but a route through the central cordillera of Mexico, the Sierra Madre, would have offered almost continuous elevations of 5,000–6,000 feet and avoided the unsuitable hot and dry lowlands and coasts (Haury 1962). This interpretation has two implications—either the adaptation of maize to more arid (and lower) environments occurred subsequently within the Southwest (the "Mogollon dispersal" concept) or lowland races of maize spread separately into the Southwest from Mexico.

• LA PERRA CAVE   Although not within the most probable cordilleran route of diffusion of corn from central Mexico to the Southwest, the occurrence of corn at about 2500 B.C. in extreme northeastern Mexico at La Perra Cave is additional evidence that corn growing had spread widely at this time and had entered new climatic and topographic zones. The earliest corn was of the Nal-Tel race, which still exists in Mexico, having cobs a little larger than those of the earliest Bat Cave corn (MacNeish 1958; Mangelsdorf, MacNeish, and Galinat 1956, 1964). This supports the idea of multiple diffusion of different races of maize. The occupants of the cave also grew squash but most of their diet was wild plants, with lesser amounts of wild animal food, and farming only playing a small role. The kinds of tools and the range and quantities of plant remains that were found suggest that they camped there in the course of their annual foraging movements (MacNeish 1964), which, of course, may also have been true of Bat Cave.

• SWALLOW CAVE   At an elevation of about 6,000 feet in a deep valley in the eastern edge of the Sierra Madre Occidental of northwestern Chihuahua, Swallow Cave is a deep rockshelter (Mangelsdorf, MacNeish, and Galinat 1964; Mangelsdorf and Lister 1956). In the lowest levels of its refuse some tiny corn cobs were found, identified as prototypes of the Chapalote race. They have not been dated but are associated with preceramic remains. If an early date could be assigned to them, they would fit well with the idea of the spread of maize through the central mountain zone by people who nevertheless continued their foraging economy.

• CIENEGA CREEK   The Cienega Creek site lies in a mountain valley in east-central Arizona, at an elevation of about 6,000 feet, 100 miles southwest of Bat Cave. It has a long record of occupation from about 2000 B.C. (Haury 1957). Pollen from the lower levels indicates that corn was being grown there at that time (Martin and Schoenwetter 1960). The cultural material contemporary with the pollen is assigned to the Chiricahua phase of the Cochise culture and thus is related to contemporary Bat

Cave. The early farmers at Cienega Creek also left evidence at the site that they had dug wells, probably to secure water for domestic purposes (not farming), digging down many feet to reach the water table, which was being lowered by the down-cutting of the adjacent arroyo.

• TULAROSA CAVE   Tularosa Cave is a small, deep cave in the Mogollon Mountains near Reserve, in west-central New Mexico, at an elevation of about 6,000 feet. Its excavation in 1949 and 1950 yielded a very large assortment of perishable materials, including domestic plant remains (Martin et al. 1952; Cutler 1952). It was occupied from a "Pre-Pottery" level dated at about 350 B.C. through the San Francisco phase of the Mogollon, that is, until about A.D. 1000. The Pre-Pottery level artifacts are generally similar to the latest phase of the Cochise culture, and no marked break is apparent in the subsequent cultural development of the cave's occupants.

The maize in Tularosa Cave shows a major change in Southwestern corn, as a result of the introduction from Mexico of a new race, which Cutler (1952) concluded had been substantially modified by mixture with the wild grass teosinte. An alternative explanation would be that this simply reflected local adaptation, since maize is an immensely variable plant capable of relatively rapid modification by selection to meet new conditions. The changes in Chapalote corn that resulted include a greater drought resistance, which permitted its spread to many new regions (fig. 1). Similar teosinte-influenced corn was found in the middle levels of Bat Cave, dated only a century or two earlier than the Pre-Pottery level of Tularosa Cave, indicating that the spread of this modified Chapalote corn was already under way. This corn is the basis for Basketmaker and Pueblo farming in the subsequent centuries, and by A.D. 300–400 it had spread to southern Utah and southwestern Colorado wherever local conditions were favorable for farming.

The information on corn summarized thus far here suggests that the Mogollon area served as a secondary center of dispersal of corn to the rest of the Southwest, with the probable exception of the Hohokam area. Although wild plants continued to be important to the Southwest Indians (and have been in the twentieth century, Whiting 1939), the relative importance of corn, supplemented by beans and squash, was significantly greater from about 500 B.C. onward, at least during periods of assured agricultural yield.

• SNAKETOWN   At about 300 B.C. a village was founded on the north bank of the Gila River in southern Arizona by a small group of farmers who were already skilled in irrigation, as demonstrated by the large and skillfully constructed canals (see "Prehistory: Hohokam," fig. 11, this vol.) that were uncovered by archeological research there in 1934–1935 and 1964–1965 (Haury 1937b, 1976). Conditions of plant preservation were poor, but there is evidence of maize from the time of the initial occupation, and of beans, cotton, and squash in the subsequent

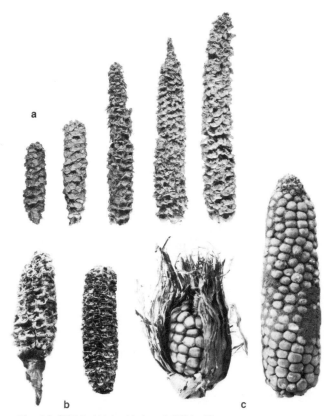

a, Mangelsdorf 1974:fig. 14.1; b-c, Martin et al. 1952:fig. 172.

Fig. 1. Maize from archeological sites. a, Chapalote-type cobs from the middle and upper levels of Bat Cave, Catron Co., N.M. The size, especially the length, of the cobs increases from the lower to the upper levels though smaller cobs persist in all levels. b-c, Maize from Tularosa Cave, Catron Co., N.M.; b, cobs typical of the lower levels; c, ear with husk and large ear from Pre-Pottery phase with lower kernel-row numbers probably the result of selection of strains more resistant to drought. Length of c right about 12.3 cm, rest same scale.

centuries (Bohrer 1970). By the analogy of recent Pima Indian farmers in the same area, the Snaketown corn farmers probably grew two crops a year, planting in March and August, when fields could be irrigated from the Gila River flow. Nevertheless, these farmers of the early Hohokam culture made substantial use of wild plant foods as well, from the nearby growth of grasses, mesquite, cactus, and other plants.

Although the corn grown by these irrigators on the Gila River has not been identified as a distinct or new importation from Mexico, the technique of canal building almost certainly must be. There is no evidence of canal irrigation elsewhere in the Southwest at this time, and no antecedents in the form of simpler irrigation from small ditches, springs, or the control of surface runoff. The first Southwestern evidence for these small-scale water controls actually comes from at least a millennium later (Woodbury 1961, 1961a, 1962). It must be concluded, therefore, that the idea of large-scale riverine irrigation was brought fully developed from central Mexico where substantial water-control systems had

already been developed by 600 B.C. (Woodbury and Neely 1972). This, then, is a major departure from the long, slow development of small-scale farming as represented by sites such as Tularosa Cave. From this time onward, two kinds of farming were present in the Southwest, and in time, the technologically more advanced type practiced by the Hohokam significantly influenced farming methods throughout the region. But it took 1,000 years for irrigation to develop on the Colorado plateaus, adapted perhaps from the southern Arizona desert model.

• HAY HOLLOW  A small village in central Arizona, about 10 miles east of Snowflake and at an elevation of about 5,700 feet, Hay Hollow is probably typical of many such small settlements that have been overlooked or left unexamined by archeologists in their zeal for larger sites yielding more impressive artifacts. It was occupied from about 200 B.C. to A.D. 300 and probably never had more than 10 houses at any time (Martin 1967; Fritz 1974). Such sites demonstrate the transition from foraging to farming, and the beginning of sedentarism. Maize kernels were found in some of the small pits at the site, the chief use of which was not storage but roasting. This maize has been tentatively assigned to the Reventador race, a teosinte-influenced Chapalote with small, hard flint kernels. But the addition of maize at Hay Hollow village is estimated to have increased the caloric intake of the occupants by only about 4 percent, with wild plants and animals providing the major part of the subsistence base (Zubrow 1971a). Thus it appears that the transition to a farming economy was far from complete.

• BOCA NEGRA CAVE AND SITE BR-45  Site BR-45 is about 12 miles west of Albuquerque at an elevation of 6,100 feet and consists of two small pit houses of the Alemeda phase of early Basketmaker III (about 25 B.C.). Boca Negra Cave lies a few miles to the east, close to the Rio Grande, and is a repeatedly used campsite (about A.D. 370). Maize from these two sites includes Chapalote, which had been long established in the Southwest prior to this time. In addition, there was also a race of maize that has been termed Maíz de Ocho, in reference to its eight-rowed characteristics. It was a new introduction from Mexico and provided both productivity and vigor in the maize plant as a whole, as well as larger, softer kernels that were easier to shell and to grind (Galinat, Reinhart, and Frisbie 1970). A closely related hybrid, called Pima-Papago, was also found at these sites. Both of these new kinds of corn would have stimulated increased dependence on corn, and they may have contributed substantially to corn's spread eastward to the Plains and eastern United States.

• OTHER SITES  In the northern Southwest, several additional sites indicate that in the first three centuries A.D. a new hybrid maize was being grown increasingly widely (Galinat and Gunnerson 1963). These include Cave du Pont in south-central Utah, White Dog Cave and other

Basketmaker II sites in the Marsh Pass area of northeastern Arizona, and Talus Village near Durango in southwestern Colorado. In addition, sites in the central part of the Southwest have provided sure evidence of corn prior to A.D. 500, including the Flattop site in Petrified Forest National Monument (estimated occupation A.D. 300–600); site LA-4257 of the Los Pinos phase, on the Pine River in northern New Mexico (estimated date A.D. 1–400); Tumbleweed Canyon, near Saint Johns in eastern Arizona (dated about A.D. 275); the SU site of western New Mexico (estimated at 250 B.C. to A.D. 600); and the Armijo Rockshelter in north-central New Mexico, believed to have been occupied as early as 1800 B.C.

By 200 B.C. to A.D. 1, then, it appears that maize growing had spread to localities scattered over much of the Southwest and before A.D. 500 was associated with an increasingly sedentary way of life that included the building of larger villages than heretofore. Some conservative groups doubtless still farmed little or not at all, and hunting and collecting were continued as important subsistence activities by even the best-established farmers. This mixed economy continued to be basic to Southwestern societies throughout the ensuing centuries.

*The Introduction of Beans*

In Mesoamerica the common or kidney bean *(Phaseolus vulgaris)* may have been domesticated by about 6,000 years ago. Pods or seeds have been found in both Tamaulipas and Tehuacán caves (L. Kaplan 1967:205) and are interpreted as cultivated rather than wild. However, they were not grown in significant amounts until much later, eventually becoming an important part of the diet in combination with corn and squash. In the Southwest there is no evidence that beans were introduced until some 2,000 years after maize (or nearly contemporaneously with it if the later dating for Bat Cave is accepted).

Beans are a valuable supplement for a diet to which maize contributes a significant amount, because they supply the amino acids lysine and tryptophan to complement the amino acid zein, of corn. L. Kaplan (1967:203) has said in this connection:

> because the nutritional insufficiency of plant-seed proteins is the result of limiting amino acids rather than low total protein content, raising the total protein content would not make it [the plant used, in this case corn] much more effective in the diet. The answer to the problem of lysine as a limiting amino acid in corn in indigenous America has been the supplementation of corn with beans, rather than changes in the total proteins or in the array of amino acids of corn.

Beans were generally dried, stored, and later soaked and boiled. This process greatly lessens the chance of preservation for the archeological record. Beans are absent in the Southwest before Level IV of Bat Cave, which is estimated to date at about 600 B.C. (possibly as early as 1000 B.C.). If they were, indeed, not yet being grown in the Southwest prior to this, the fact would help explain the limited extent to which corn was used, as corn remained an inadequate mainstay in the diet except insofar as its combination with squash could make up its deficiencies in the amino acids.

It should be noted that in contrast to maize, which shows considerable natural variability from generation to generation, beans (and also squash) show little variation from which prehistoric farmers could have selected for desirable characteristics. This means that beans spread and were adapted to new environments more slowly than maize.

The Bat Cave beans are *Phaseolus vulgaris* and show no botanical change through the subsequent centuries of the site's occupation. Only two other sites in the Southwest have sure evidence for beans before A.D. 500. At Snaketown, charred remains of beans have been found in the Estrella phase (Bohrer 1970), but probably they were brought in with maize, when the first settlers of the village introduced agriculture there about 300 B.C. In Tularosa Cave there were beans and bean pods in the Pre-Pottery levels (about 350 B.C.) and also in the succeeding Pinelawn levels.

*The Introduction of Squash*

The record for squash is nearly as scant as for beans but begins much earlier. In association with the earliest maize in Bat Cave there was squash *(Cucurbita pepo),* and it also occurs in all the later levels, with no significant change in form. Therefore, its absence from many other sites is best explained as a gap in the archeological record, due to squash being so seldom preserved in charred form or in dry deposits. From about 3600 B.C. onward it was probably associated with maize in the incipient stage of Southwestern farming. Much later, at Jemez Cave, New Mexico (from about 1000 B.C. to A.D. 300) there are remains of squash (Ford 1968a).

In Tularosa Cave, beginning about 250 B.C. in the Pre-Pottery phase, squash occurs, and at the Basketmaker II sites near Durango, Colorado, there is squash about A.D. 250. At Snaketown a pollen grain of some species of curcurbit comes from about A.D. 500, possibly but not certainly *Cucurbita pepo.*

The seeds of squash provide 20 times the calories of the flesh, twice the calcium, and substantially more vitamins. Its dietary contribution may have been as much through the seeds, dried for winter use, as from the flesh, eaten fresh after boiling, or dried in strips. Squash also is a valuable supplement to corn in the diet, because of its amino acid tryptophan.

The bottle gourd *(Lagenaria siceraria)* has left traces of its use in only a few early sites; its dried shell was a convenient container, fragile but inexpensive. It may have been more commonly used than the archeological record demonstrates, but it was never a garden crop.

## Cotton

Domestic cotton *(Gossypium* sp.) was grown widely in the Southwest after A.D. 700 (Kent 1957:467) and undoubtedly spread north from Mexico before this, although the record is poor for earlier sites. In Tularosa Cave a single specimen of cotton yarn was found in the Pre-Pottery phase (about 350 B.C.) and one more in the next phase, Pine Lawn. At Snaketown, cotton seeds are reported for the Sweetwater phase (about A.D. 200) and also in later phases; all were charred, suggesting that they had been parched for eating, as the Pima and Papago did in historic times (Bohrer 1970). The seeds are, of course, rich in oil. Fibers of cotton were also found at Snaketown and their use in weaving is probable. None of these specimens can be identified as to species.

## Other Possibly Domestic Plants

Sunflower seeds occurred in Tularosa Cave, the first reported in an archeological context in the Southwest, but they are a wild species. Although in historic times the sunflower was cultivated by Indians of the Southwest, there is no evidence for its prehistoric cultivation (Heiser 1951:436).

Stone tubes, which might have been used for tobacco smoking, have been found as early as the Chiricahua stage of the Cochise culture, and a few have had traces of tobacco remaining in them, as at Ventana Cave (Haury 1950:329–332). There is no evidence that the tobacco was cultivated, and wild tobacco, occurring widely in the Southwest, was extensively used in late prehistoric and historic times. It was smoked in small reed cigarettes and in stone and pottery pipes. In addition to being smoked, it was chewed in quids of yucca wrapped around the tobacco, which was mixed in lime; such quids (identified as *Nicotiana attenuata*) have been found in Basketmaker III sites in the San Juan River drainage (Jones and Morris 1960).

## The Slow Establishment of Agriculture

Important as the evidence is of the domestic plants grown in the Southwest from about 3600 B.C. onward, it is insufficient to determine either why they were of such minor importance for so long or why settled farming communities eventually became typical of the larger part of the Southwest. For two millennia after the introduction of maize to the Southwest the pattern of subsistence continued little changed from the past, with each small, mobile band pursuing an annual cycle of hunting and collecting activities at a series of locations selected for their particular seasonal advantages. Thus, the innumerable small environmental niches of the Southwest, which is an area of unusually varied topography and natural resources, came to be thoroughly understood and exploited with appropriate techniques—as simple as gathering cholla cactus buds as a succulent tidbit or as

complex as cooperative deer drives for a major protein supply. The intimate knowledge of the Southwestern landscape that the early inhabitants acquired would have made it possible, when maize was introduced, to select those widely scattered localities where its special needs could be met—loose, well-drained soil with sufficient soil warmth to promote germination, rains and warm days and nights during the phase of growth and filling, and late enough killing frosts to permit its relatively long maturation period (Schoenwetter and Dittert 1968:43). The alluvial soils of small canyons provided one of the better locations, unless drainage of cold air at night offset the advantage of stored warmth from rocky canyon walls. Maize, and eventually both beans and squash, were doubtless planted in small, irregular plots, using only the simple digging stick as planting, cultivating, and weeding tool. Harvests were small, unless special efforts were made to protect the plants from rodents, deer, and birds; this required members of the band or family to remain at the fields throughout the summer, which was impossible as long as the group depended on important hunting and collecting activities elsewhere during the summer. Therefore, the autumn harvest would have differed little from other plant collecting, except for the new species involved, invaders from Mesoamerica. Yields would have been modest and highly variable from year to year, providing little or no surplus for storage and later usage.

In short, between 2000 B.C. and A.D. 500 cultivation of several new species of food plants was introduced into the Southwest. But the potential of this fundamentally different set of technological and subsistence techniques was not realized, and it had little economic significance until later.

## Other Innovations

### Wells

One of the factors in the natural environment of the Southwest that required constant and careful consideration was the supply of water for domestic purposes. A human adult requires at least three quarts of water a day (and much more when active in hot, dry regions), and it is impossible to "learn to do with less" despite popular beliefs to the contrary (D.H.K. Lee 1963). The Southwest has relatively little surface water, since many stream channels run only very briefly after a rainstorm, and subsequently their flow is through subsurface alluvial deposits. Ground water exists, also, of course, in many of the apparently waterless parts of the Southwest, and here and there emerges in the form of springs.

On their annual rounds, hunting-gathering bands required detailed and reliable knowledge of where such springs were to be found and at what seasons they were dependable, to supplement the few and widely dispersed lakes and ponds at which they could camp. But a water supply is relatively useless if food is not available nearby. At least 4,000 years ago the prehistoric Southwesterners learned to produce water by excavating wells where surface water was lacking. Thus far, evidence comes from only two locations, both chance finds resulting from keen observation of profiles in excavated soil layers. These revealed, in cross-section, pits that would have reached down to former ground-water levels and appear to have been dug for this purpose. Near Clovis, New Mexico, wells have been observed that can be only approximately dated to the period 3000 to 2000 B.C. (Evans 1951; F.E. Green 1962). At the Cienega Creek site, a series of wells was found that is dated to about 2000 B.C. (Haury 1957) and was associated with an occupation assigned to the Cochise culture. These wells were 0.8 to 1.5 meters in diameter, with depths from 1.0 to 3.7 meters. It is safe to assume that if this important technique was known by two foraging groups, it was known by many others and the evidence of the use of wells in other locations is merely lacking. A group that could provide water by well digging at dry locations could camp where food supplies could not otherwise be used, since a dry camp must necessarily be a brief one.

### Storage Pits

A major problem for any foraging group is to preserve for future use any food not needed immediately. Mobility sharply limits the quantity of food, no matter what the preservation technique, that can be taken with the group, but food preserved and left behind for future use is subject to the hazards of weather and of discovery by insects, rodents, and other animals. Meat can be sun-dried or smoked, reducing its weight and aiding its preservation, and thus furnish a high-nourishment, light-weight food; nevertheless, only a few days' or weeks' supply can be carried from place to place. Some plant foods must be consumed almost immediately—greens, for example—but seeds will last for many months, if kept dry. In short, as long as convenient long-term storage of any current food surplus is lacking, the value of such a surplus is greatly limited.

During the last two millennia B.C. in the Southwest there was developed (or learned from elsewhere) a very successful technology for food storage by means of pit storage. This was suitable especially for wild seeds and for the seeds of corn, beans, and squash that were being grown in small quantities.

In the San Pedro stage of the Cochise culture, in several sites of Mogollon I, in the En Medio phase in northwestern New Mexico and in the Basketmaker II sites of the San Juan drainage, there occur well-constructed storage pits, both indoors and outdoors. For example, at Pierce:8:4 in southeastern Arizona, a San Pedro house has about one-third of its floor occupied by a deep circular pit, the sides undercut slightly so that the opening in the floor was smaller than the bottom; with a diameter

of 1.5 meters and a depth of 0.5 meter, its capacity would have been relatively enormous in relation to the storage needs of the family occupying the house. Although when found it had no covering, it can be assumed that this, like other pits, was covered with clay or mud, which dried to form a hard, relatively impervious seal for the contents. Some pits were slab-lined, to reduce the crumbling of the walls when dug into poorly consolidated soil, and some were clay lined (but not fired). The fact that similar pits were used for cooking, almost invariably outdoors, raises the question of whether one innovation led to the other. However, pits used for trash disposal probably reflect abandonment of the storage pit for its original use; likewise, occasional use for burials is probably incidental to the initial purpose.

Individual storage pits vary greatly in size and shape but are usually nearly as deep as wide, and round in plan; some are jug-shaped, the mouth slightly constricted. They occur at numerous sites 400 B.C.-A.D. 1 and subsequently. Among the most varied and carefully made are those of Basketmaker II rockshelter sites in the San Juan drainage, particularly those at Talus Village, near Durango (Morris and Burgh 1954). Here there were five shapes: jug-shaped, flat-bottomed with sloping sides, the same with domed clay cover rising above floor level, basin shaped, and finally a domed clay enclosure on the flat floor. Some were lined with mud plaster, but more often they were lined with neatly fitted stone slabs, plastered into place. One of the largest cists was 1.8 meters in diameter and 1.2 meters deep, with a capacity of about 3,000 liters—over two tons of corn (if such a quantity had been available) and more likely a highly varied collection of corn, beans, wild foods, and perhaps tools and clothing also. Of these storage cists at Talus Village, Morris and Burgh (1954:51) report that "not a floor was without a storage cist and in at least one instance there had been six in a single dwelling, at least five of which had been usable up to the time of abandonment." This is a village of fully established farmers of A.D. 1-400, and a pattern of systematic and substantial storage for the future had clearly emerged.

### Pottery

The explanation for the initial appearance of pottery in the Southwest that requires fewest unproved assumptions is that it spread northward from Mesoamerica, where it has far greater antiquity. A local Southwestern invention is extremely improbable and lacks solid evidence, and diffusion from the eastern United States cannot be demonstrated except for certain special traits after the initial spread from the south (Jennings 1956:84-86). Nevertheless, the route and means of diffusion from Mexico into the Southwest are still uncertain, largely for lack of sufficient evidence from northern Mexico.

Contrary to a belief once held by archeologists, pottery making did not spread with farming, but much later and quite separately. Nor did it have the profound influence on the socioeconomic organization of the Indians of the Southwest that farming eventually did. However, it did represent a significant technological change, offering a means of making receptacles of many shapes and sizes, at a considerable saving in time over the labor involved in making basketry containers. Pottery had another advantage over basketry, the material previously most used for containers of all sorts: it held water or other liquids excellently and could be used in direct contact with a fire for cooking. Basketry can be, and was, made waterproof by coating with pitch, but this requires the difficult process of warming the pitch for application, and the finished vessel is a fire hazard. Cooking in baskets is possible, stirring constantly a few fire-heated rocks placed in the liquid contents (stew, mush, or soup), but this is slow and inconvenient. Large pottery containers for storage offer a great improvement, whether for water or dry food materials, as they are safe from insects and rodents, can be sealed with a clay or stone and clay cover, and do not become fragile with age due to drying, as do baskets. The extensive use of pottery does presume a relatively sedentary existence, as clay pots are not easily transported in large numbers, and their advantages are best exploited by settled villagers. Basketry continued to be made, of course, throughout the Southwest, even after some of its functions were taken over by pottery. Similarly, gourds and skin containers continued in use, although playing a less important role, perhaps, than previously.

The introduction of pottery making to the Southwest has probably been overemphasized by archeologists because of its importance to them, as a basis for their study of prehistory. It can be made in so many varying ways, each detail culturally determined, that it is an ideal clue to determining the spatial and temporal relationships among its makers, as a means of constructing basic culture-historic frameworks by which other data from the past may be placed in context. It has played a major role in the relative dating of archeological sites and in defining regional and local subcultural units. Therefore, it has received attention as an archeological tool of investigation far beyond its importance as an aspect of prehistoric technology, economics, or even art.

In spite of the general evidence that pottery is one of the many Southwestern traits deriving from Mexico, certainty as to its source is still lacking. The earliest Southwestern pottery consists of plain (that is, undecorated by either painting or texturing) brown or red-slipped vessels of simple shapes (shallow bowls, globular jars) (see "Prehistory: Mogollon," fig. 9, this vol.) found in southern Arizona and southern New Mexico by 300 B.C. These are not crude experiments; they are expertly made, even though simple, utilitarian objects. The brown and red surfaces are suggestive of plain pottery made in central Mexico at this and earlier times, but no specific

Mexican prototypes have been identified. In the intervening northern Mexican regions through which pottery making can be presumed to have spread, archeological information is still scanty in spite of efforts to bridge the gap. There are pottery types from Zacatecas and Durango, of the first few centuries A.D., that resemble these earlier Southwestern types, and it is reasonable to assume (even in the lack of proof) that they are a continuation of a plain red and brown ceramic tradition that spread northward through the central highlands during 1000 B.C.–A.D. 1. This does not imply any major movement of people, nor any organized trade effort from central Mexico, but rather the diffusion of pottery making as a cluster of technological skills from one farming community to another by means of constant intervillage contacts for small-scale trade and for social and ceremonial interaction. The Chalchihuites culture of Durango offers the fullest details for such a presumed diffusion (Kelley 1966), although its earliest pottery is no older than about A.D. 300.

The gradual northward spread of pottery making continued from the early Hohokam and Mogollon villages but did not reach the northern Southwest until about A.D. 400–500. Basketmaker II sites, such as Talus Village, Ignacio, White Dog Cave, and others lacked ceramics (hence their original identification with basketmaking), although clay-lined baskets, found in several sites in the San Juan region, were once thought to represent a transition to pottery making. It is more probable that these were simply devices for parching seeds in the time-honored technique of placing them with hot coals and shaking them constantly so that the basketry tray would not be charred and damaged. A thin clay lining offered excellent protection for the basket.

Decorated pottery begins in both the Hohokam and Mogollon areas with simple, broad-line decoration in red on the kind of brownware already being made. The Estrella Red-on-gray pottery ("Prehistory: Hohokam," fig. 3, this vol.) of Snaketown, possibly made as early as 100 B.C., uses a design layout in which the bowl interior is divided into quarters, each with identical decoration of nested chevrons or broad, parallel lines (Gladwin et al. 1937:figs. 92, 93, 111, 112). The painted pottery that first appears early in Mogollon 2 (A.D. 400–500) is similar, Dos Cabezos Red-on-brown having broad-line nested chevrons, parallel lines, and quartered layouts (Sayles 1945:pl. and fig. 29; J.B. Wheat 1955:84–85).

Farther to the north, where pottery making began somewhat later, the earliest painted pottery appears to copy basketry decoration rather than follow the simple designs just described. This suggests that as the techniques spread they were revised locally to fit esthetic standards and traditions, thus beginning the bewildering variation that occurs in Southwestern pottery in the succeeding centuries.

Along with the making of bowls and jars, the earliest

Southwestern pottery making included small, simple figurines ("Prehistory: Hohokam," fig. 4, this vol.), for which a Mexican inspiration is suspected. Figurine making was a major craft early in the development of the Hohokam culture, although elsewhere in the Southwest figurines occur only in small numbers. The figurines of the initial Hohokam phase, the Vahki, are crudely modeled with the fingers, the features pinched into shape or indented. General similarities with central Mexican figurines have been proposed (Gladwin et al. 1937:241). If they are assumed to have ritual or symbolic significance and if the idea came to southern Arizona with the new irrigation technology that appears at about the same time, there would seem to be a faint, peripheral reflection of the religious ideas that arose in central Mexico in the Late Formative period, related to fertility, agricultural productivity, and weather control.

## The Atlatl and the Bow

From very remote antiquity, at least 10,000–12,000 years ago, the atlatl or spear-thrower may have been in widespread use in North America for hunting large game.

It probably propelled the heavy darts or spears that were tipped with Clovis and later with Folsom points and continued with subsequent types of relatively heavy projectile points. In some parts of the New World such as the Arctic, Mexico, and the Southeastern United States, the atlatl continued in use into historic times, but in most regions it was eventually replaced with the bow.

The atlatl (fig. 2) is a fairly short, rigid board or stick, from about 20 to 25 inches long, with a spur or pin at one end, against which the butt of a spear or dart can rest. The projectile is propelled with an overhand motion and great force is imparted by what is, in function, an extension of the hunter's forearm. Well-preserved atlatls have been found in several dry caves in the San Juan area (Broken Roof, White Dog, and Kinboko Cave I), in Utah (Hogup Cave), and in Nevada (Lovelock Cave), dating from perhaps 6000 B.C. to about A.D. 400 (see Grange 1952:338; Aikens 1970:154; Grosscup 1960:30). Most of these have a groove near the distal end of the upper surface, at the end of which a small spur is carved, to engage the concave butt of the spear; they also have a pair of leather loops near the proximal end, through which the first two fingers could pass to grip the shaft of

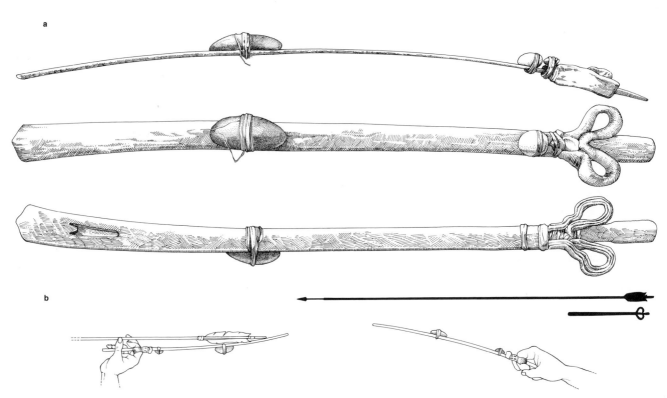

a, after Guernsey 1931:pl. 50; b, after Grant 1968:50.

Fig. 2. a, Basketmaker II atlatl viewed from side, top, and bottom from Cist 1, Broken Roof Cave, Apache Co., Ariz. Made of smoothly finished oak with a spur and groove (front view) to position dart. Finger-loops are made of 3-ply dressed skin and secured with sinew. A small black nut, a light colored moonstone, and dark red stone, possibly charms rather than for balance, have been fastened to the back of the shaft with sinew. The shaft is shorter and thinner than average and the present curved shape is due to warping. Length about 53.4 cm. b, Method of use of atlatl for throwing dart and relative proportions of atlatl and dart.

the spear while the thumb and other fingers gripped the atlatl (see Kidder and Guernsey 1919:178–179, for their detailed description of the technique, based on both experiment and a study of sculptures at Chichén Itzá, Yucatán). Experiments (Browne 1940; Howard 1974) have indicated that the atlatl can increase the force with which the spear is thrown by about 60 percent over simply throwing with the hand. Longer spears, up to about six feet, are more stable and accurate than shorter, and a stone head within the size range of Folsom points is preferable to larger or smaller.

However, projectile point size is not a sure indication of whether it was used on a spear or an arrow, since a wide range of sizes (and weights) can be effective on each, and many large "projectile points" turn out on examination of the wear of the edges to have been knives. Therefore, the trend toward smaller projectile points and the shift from stemmed to corner- or side-notching, which occurred about 1000 B.C. (see, for example, Irwin-Williams 1967:fig. 1), is not a certain indicator of the replacement of the atlatl by the bow, although the change may have taken place at about this time. Evidence of bows and arrows from dry caves is rare prior to about A.D. 500 in the Southwest, but in the Great Basin there are substantial indications that the bow and arrow came into use at least 500 years earlier (Lovelock Cave, Nevada; Grosscup 1960) and probably 1,500 years earlier than in the Southwest (Hogup Cave, Utah; Aikens 1970). This makes the previously held view of a southern entry of the bow and arrow into the Southwest (Grange 1952:341; J.A. Brown 1954) far less likely to be correct. In any case, in the Great Basin the atlatl and the bow were in use simultaneously for several hundred years, with the atlatl finally abandoned at about the same time that the bow first reached the Southwest in the first few centuries A.D.

The acceptance of the bow and arrow was probably chiefly on the basis of their greater accuracy (Browne 1940), although the shorter and lighter arrow would have permitted the carrying of more weaponry on a long hunt. Although arrows can be used with stone tips as heavy as are used for darts or spears, they can also be effective with much smaller and lighter tips, a change that occurred progressively in the Southwest following the adoption of the bow and arrow.

## Early Houses and Villages

The gradual but profound change from the small, temporary campsites of the Paleo-Indian and Archaic eras to the permanent villages of well-built houses of later times cannot yet be traced in all its details, for lack of sufficient evidence.

Many structures in the Southwest have been termed pit houses, but the term is rarely defined and the distinction between pit and surface structures is arbitrary (see

Bullard 1962:99). Floors a few inches below the ground surface were probably the result of simply clearing away loose material to secure a firm floor, whereas in pit houses several feet deep, the side of the pit forms an essential part of the house wall. Here the term pit house will be used only for the second and deeper type. Pit houses gained protection from both cold and heat by being sunken into the ground but, of course, increased drainage problems.

### San Pedro Stage, about 2000–100 B.C.

Sites in southern Arizona and southern New Mexico, representing the final phase of the Cochise culture, have only occasionally provided information on living arrangements. Many of them were probably campsites at which only the flimsiest of structures were built or none at all. At others, no traces happen to remain or have been found.

At Ventana Cave (Haury 1950), important for the length of its occupation and the abundance of artifactual evidence, there were no architectural clues found in spite of extremely careful excavation. It is a rockshelter about 35 meters long, varying from 5 to 10 meters in depth, with numerous irregularities in its floor. It could have housed several families, perhaps with a maximum of 25 to 30 people, and was probably used only intermittently, as one campsite among many used in the course of a year.

At an open site of the San Pedro stage, Benson:8:3 in southeastern Arizona, part of a shallow, oval house floor was found, about 4.0 meters long and 2.5 meters wide (area about 9 square meters) dug only 0.5 meters into the former land surface. Ash in the central floor area suggested use as a fireplace or a depository for coals brought in for warmth, and at one end of the floor was a large storage pit, 1.5 meters deep. There was no indication of how the house was roofed (Sayles 1945).

A similar, better-preserved house at Pearce:8:4 a few miles away to the southeast had a floor about 0.4 meters below the former land surface, oval, and 3.0 by 2.4 meters (area about 6 square meters). It was entered from the west with one step cut into the earth bank. About one-third of the floor, at the north end, was taken up by a large jug-shaped storage pit 0.6 meters deep. Traces of depressions that held roof supports indicate a light framework of poles; they could have been covered with brush, grass, or even hides. Although other floors were not found at Pearce:8:4, the total area that was once occupied, as shown by ash and refuse, was about one-quarter by three-quarters miles, an area of over five million square feet (about 480,000 square meters). The locality must have been a preferred campsite for many centuries, families building simple but snug structures like the one described for occupation during a suitable season of the year, returning each year, but it is unlikely that more than a small fraction of the area was ever occupied at any given time.

*Armijo Phase, about 1800–800 B.C.*

Armijo, a precursor of Basketmaker II in northwestern New Mexico between the Puerco and Jemez rivers (Cynthia Irwin-Williams, personal communication 1972), was characterized by several kinds of settlement: base camps on cliff tops from which both mesa and canyon resources could be collected, small mountain camps for quarrying obsidian and for hunting, and fall or fall and winter canyon-bottom settlements where a relatively large group came together seasonally for several months. This last type is best represented by Armijo Shelter, for which the phase is named. It is located under a large cliff overhang at the head of a canyon with nearby water from a seepage spring. The living floor, littered with tools and debris, and the remains of large cobble-filled cooking pits, gradually increased from about 300 to 450 square meters. Irwin-Williams (1967) has suggested that this area would have accommodated a group of 30 to 50 people. This size was made possible by the farming, on a modest scale, which was carried on in the adjacent canyon bottom each summer. There is no evidence of additional occupation areas outside the shelter.

*Pine Lawn Phase, about 300 B.C. to A.D. 250*

Three villages of Pine Lawn, the initial phase of the Mogollon culture, provide substantial information on settlement, two of them with five to seven houses each and one, the SU site, with about 25 houses. The first, the Promontory site (Martin, Rinaldo, and Antevs 1949), in the Pine Lawn Valley of west-central New Mexico, consisted of five pit houses dug less than one meter into the top of a small mesa. They were roundish in shape, with diameters of 3.6 to 5.8 meters (area 9 to 26 square meters). The roofing arrangement is not clear from the occasional post hole that could be identified, but since there were no large central posts or regular spaced peripheral poles, roofs may have been insubstantial domes of small poles and brush. The individual houses straggle along the mesa without orderly arrangement. The single large structure has been interpreted by Martin to mean that certain group activities, probably social and ritual, took place apart from the individual family dwellings in a structure built specially for this purpose. Other Pine Lawn phase villages also have large "communal" gathering places, suggesting a kind of coordinated social or ritual activity that was absent previously in the Southwest. However, this interpretation from ethnographic analogy has not yet had formal testing based on archeological evidence.

At the Hay Hollow site (Martin 1967; Bohrer 1972; Fritz 1974) near Snowflake in east-central Arizona, there were at least five houses, possibly six or seven, with diameters of three to five meters (area about 7 to 20 square meters); none was of significantly larger size than the rest. A population for the village, estimated from the area of house floors, would have been 25 to 40 people. Careful examination of surrounding areas makes the absence of other houses quite certain. In plan, the village was irregular, covering an area 60 by 100 meters (about 5,000 square meters). Numerous outdoor work areas and pits were found, the pits probably both for cooking and for storing surplus food at harvest time. Since Hay Hollow, like other contemporary villages, was in a transition to farming and much of the stored food was probably from wild sources, such as piñon nuts, grass seed, and amaranth seed, the villagers probably spent a significant part of each year away from the village or undertook frequent, brief collecting forays to nearby resources. Although it is not assigned to the Pine Lawn phase in a taxonomic sense, it is discussed here because it is both contemporary with and shows general similarities to Pine Lawn villages. Martin (1967) has inferred localized unilateral exogamous groups with a single house representing the home of a nuclear family.

The SU site (pronounced ˈes ˈyōō) (fig. 3) in western New Mexico (Martin 1940, 1943; Martin and Rinaldo 1947) lies on a low ridge with 25 to 30 houses in two clusters, arranged irregularly, some close together and some as much as 50 meters from their neighbors. House shapes vary greatly but tend to be roundish with narrow sloping entrances or a simple step entrance at the east side. There was usually a heavy central post with one or more additional roof supports near the walls, and roofs probably had several heavy horizontal beams covered with brush and earth, making a well-insulated, snug year-round shelter. Although there were no interior fireplaces, there were pits containing firecracked rocks, apparently brought in from outside fireplaces to provide warmth—a sensible precaution against the constant danger of destructive fires. Dotting house floors were also numerous pits for storage, most of them probably sealed except when being filled or emptied. Each of the two clusters of houses included one that was somewhat larger and deeper than the rest, kidney-shaped, and about 9.5 and 10.5 meters (areas about 70 to 85 square meters) in diameter. Although they had artifacts of domestic use on their floors, they probably also served for community ceremonial functions (by analogy with modern Pueblo kivas where many ordinary domestic activities take place when ritual activities are not in progress). At SU the individual houses cannot be dated precisely enough to determine how many were simultaneously occupied, but if half were lived in at the same time, the village would have consisted of perhaps 75 to 100 people. The location of SU, as with many other early Southwestern villages, on a low ridge, is probably not related to "defense against enemies" but the preference for good drainage to assure dry houses and perhaps the wish for a sweeping view across nearby fields and paths.

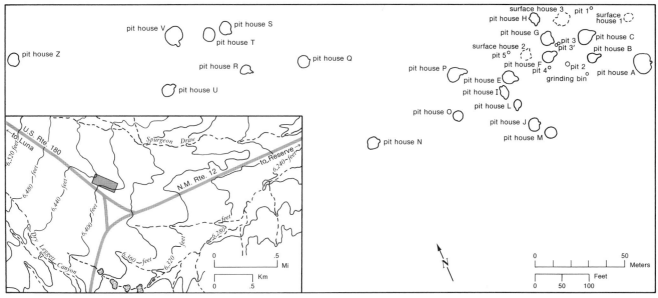

after Martin 1943:maps 13,14; Martin and Rinaldo 1947:map 25.
Fig. 3. Village plan of SU site, Catron Co., N.M., with random arrangement of pit houses (see "Prehistory: Mogollon," fig. 6, this vol.).

*Peñasco Phase, Mogollon Culture, about 300 B.C.–A.D. 100*

A regional variant of the early Mogollon culture, roughly contemporary with the Pine Lawn phase, the Peñasco phase lies at the edge of the region of the Mogollon culture. One of its important sites, Cave Creek Village (Sayles 1945) near Portal at the foot of the Chiricahua Mountains of southeastern Arizona, consists of seven houses located on the outwash fan of Cave Creek, which was then a grassy valley crossed by several small streams. The houses are dug very shallowly into the ground, probably only enough to provide a firm floor of native soil, and are round to rounded-rectangular in shape. A central post hole and sometimes traces of a few other irregularly placed poles leave the form of the roof uncertain. A short passage or single step in the east wall indicates the position of the entrance. The houses are from 3.5 to 4.0 meters across (area 10 to 14 square meters), and each had a shallow fireplace in its floor, usually near the entry. Deeper pits in the floors were for storage.

The contemporary village of San Simon (Sayles 1945), about 40 miles to the northwest, had 15 houses occupied in this time period (and in later centuries about 50 more, but not all occupied simultaneously). They are similar to the Cave Creek houses, shallowly dug into the ground, roundish or with one flattened side (bean shaped), or with four flattish sides. Some have fireplaces and storage pits, and entrances are usually at the east. The houses lie in three widely separated groups, from two to seven houses in each, which may reflect kin or other social relationships of the families living in them, but specific kinds of

social groupings (clans, moieties, and so on) cannot be demonstrated.

*Vahki Phase, Pioneer Period of Hohokam, about 300 B.C.–A.D. 1*

The only village about which abundant information has been secured is Snaketown (Gladwin et al. 1937; Haury 1976). A population of at least 100 persons is estimated for the initial settlement (Haury 1976:75, 150). Four houses can be assigned to the Vahki phase, three to the Estrella phase, which followed, and slightly larger numbers to subsequent phases. The earliest houses are squarish, about 12 meters on a side (area about 145 square meters) with no interior details except a fireplace. However, one Vahki house has two entryways and two fireplaces, suggesting occupancy by more than a single family, or perhaps an extended family.

About 20 miles east of Phoenix a contemporary (Pioneer period) village, Red Mountain, has been found; architectural details are not available (D.H. Morris 1969), but it seems to have been a smaller settlement. Other Pioneer period sites, scattered from south of Tucson to within 40 miles of Flagstaff and from Safford to Gila Bend, have supplied no architectural information and are identified only from the presence of diagnostic pottery.

*Basketmaker II, about 100 B.C. to A.D. 400*

More sites of Basketmaker II have been investigated, mainly in the San Juan drainage, than for any other small part of the Southwest, but many of them are rockshelters used mainly for burial purposes, or used only intermittently and casually as campsites.

57

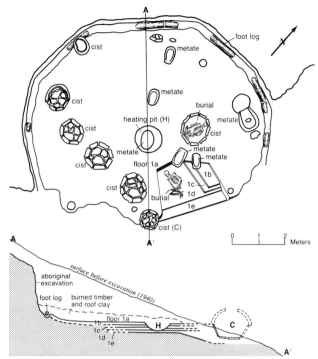

foot log

cist
metate
metate
burial
metate
heating pit (H)
cist
metate
cist
metate
cist
floor 1a
metate
cist
metate
1b
1c
cist
1d
burial
1e
cist (C)

0    1    2
Meters

A                                                    A'

surface before excavation (1940)
aboriginal
excavation
foot log
burned timber
and roof clay
floor 1a
1b                    H                    C
1c
1d
1e
A                                                    A'

after Morris and Burgh 1954:fig. 5.

Fig. 4. Floor plan and cross-section of house from Talus Village, La Plata Co., Colo., with slab-lined storage pits (cists).

At Talus Village (fig. 4) near Durango, Colorado (Morris and Burgh 1954), a steep slope overlooking the bottomlands of the Animas River had been occupied long enough for some of the house floors to have been repeatedly rebuilt and repaired. As many as 10 houses may have been occupied at the same time. These were shallow, saucerlike depressions, oval, with maximum diameters of four to nine meters (area 12 to 50 square meters), walled with horizontally laid timbers set in mud, and probably crudely domed or cribbed. The floors had no hearths, but there were shallow basins in which rocks heated outside were placed to give warmth—a clean, safe, and efficient heating system. Storage pits were dug into the floors, some slab-lined and covered with clay domes to seal the contents. Similar houses were built in two rockshelters nearby, North Shelter having perhaps five houses occupied at the same time, and South Shelter about the same or fewer. Therefore, it can be estimated that as many as 10 families were farming the alluvial soil of the Animas River and wintering in these substantial homes nearby. Long summer hunting and collecting trips were probably carried out by at least some of the group.

At the Ignacio site (Fenenga and Wendorf 1956; Eddy 1966:472–478), 20 miles southeast of Durango, an area of about 150 by 175 feet on a small mesa spur has about 20 circular areas that contain charcoal and fractured rocks and burned clay with stick impressions, probably marking the location of circular houses of 20 to 30 feet in diameter (area 315 to 700 square feet). They were built on the surface or very slightly scooped and may have had

light walls and roofs supported by small poles. About 25 baking pits were scattered between (not inside) the houses.

Other sites contemporary with Ignacio and similar to it, along the Pine River in northwestern New Mexico (assigned to the Los Pinos phase of Basketmaker II), include houses with a small antechamber connected to the main room by a short passage and houses with "log masonry" similar to that of Talus Village. A distinctive feature of many was a cobble-paved area ringing the outer wall of the house, perhaps a walkway that would not be muddy in wet weather. These settlements, ranging in size from 1 to 11 houses, were usually on a low ridge close to arable land along small permanent streams.

The White Dog focus or phase of northeastern Arizona and adjacent Utah and Colorado is named from White Dog Cave in Marsh Pass, near Kayenta (Guernsey and Kidder 1921; Colton 1939). The cave contained no houses but was used extensively for burials and storage by people who probably lived nearby in small villages now destroyed by erosion. In Utah's Red Rock Plateau region, 75 miles to the north, contemporary settlements have been found (Lipe 1970) in shallow rockshelters. One example is the Lone Tree Dune site, where there was one circular house floor about 20 feet in diameter, with a large jug-shaped storage pit five feet in diameter nearby and an outdoor slab-lined firehearth about 70 feet away. Other sites housed no more than two or three families at most. In addition, there were campsites apparently occupied by several families while on seed-gathering trips, and also outlying storage sites where small dry rock alcoves were used for numerous storage pits. As with other early farming communities, settlements appear to have been located where not only farmland but also upland sources of wild foods, both plant and animal, were accessible.

Intermediate in location between these Basketmaker II sites and the Pioneer phase sites of the Hohokam is the Verde Valley. In its middle reaches is the Calkins Ranch site (Breternitz 1960), a village of this same time period or only slightly later, with six shallow "pit houses" of rectangular shape, the only one at all well preserved being 2.5 by 4.5 meters (area about 11 square meters). Below their floors jug-shaped storage pits suggest permanent or protracted winter occupation, with a surplus from harvests of both farmed and wild plants to require storage for the future.

Another site, intermediate in location and also probably contemporary with Calkins Ranch, is the Flattop site about 18 miles southeast of Holbrook, Arizona (Wendorf 1953). It lies on a small mesa and consists of at least 25 houses, circular in shape, dug about 50 centimeters into the ground surface and sometimes into the bedrock of the mesa. They average about three meters in diameter (area 7 square meters) and have narrow entrances on the east or north side. Shallow basins in the floor may have held rocks heated outside, rather than indoor fires—a method widely used in early farming settlements. Roofs were probably of light poles and brush held in place with mud and flat slabs of stone.

## Georgetown Phase, about A.D. 100-400

Sites of Georgetown, the later half of Mogollon I, do not differ greatly from those that preceded them, although there are more often houses of quadrangular shape, with well-defined lateral entrances, sometimes long sloping passages, and some houses have interior fireplaces, usually just inside the entry. Some of the sites are still small, for example, five houses at the Harris Village (Haury 1936a) and four at Starkweather (Nesbitt 1938). Others are larger: 13 at Bluff Ruin (Haury and Sayles 1947), and at Crooked Ridge Village (J.B. Wheat 1954, 1955), 17 excavated with as many as 50 approximately contemporary still undug. At all these sites, as elsewhere, it cannot be certain how many houses were lived in simultaneously, so that house counts cannot be easily turned into population estimates. But in the Mogollon region and probably also in the Hohokam region to the south, at least a few villages were reaching populations of 100 to 300 people.

## Early Village Patterns

There are at least 30 additional sites reported in print for the centuries prior to A.D. 500, many from emergency salvage in advance of construction. However, information on them is incomplete.

In an exhaustive analysis of early Southwestern architecture, Bullard (1962) concludes that Anasazi and Mogollon houses developed along similar lines, from quite shallow to deeper structures (true pit houses with much of the wall consisting of the side of the pit), with a passage entrance, and heavy, post-supported roofs. Hohokam houses continued to be shallower and larger, a rounded rectangle rather than round to oval, but also with an entry passage. It is interesting to note that the floor plans of both these pit houses and the Hohokam surface houses were bilaterally symmetrical, although houses were combined in unpatterned, asymmetric villages. Much later, in the Anasazi area, the interior layout of individual rooms was usually asymmetrical, but rooms were clustered in complex patterns that often tended toward bilateral symmetry.

More important than the increasingly complex details of house architecture, as it developed A.D. 1–500, is the evidence that these villages supply of settled life by groups composed of tens or scores of families. Although not every village had one or two structures much larger than the rest, communal ritual activity, for which such places were probably built, doubtless became a regular feature of village life, an essential technique for repeatedly emphasizing the common beliefs and coordinated efforts that held the group together in spite of the frictions of continued close contact. The enormous complexity of

ritual activity that characterizes the Indians of the Southwest in historic times suggests a great time-depth, so that even two millennia ago there was probably an elaborate annual series of ceremonies related to the basic social and economic needs of the group—individual progress through the stages of life, security and health, and economic well-being.

The dependence on farming that made these villages possible had probably made it important, before A.D. 500, that they be located where extensive farmland was close at hand. Small canyon-bottom plots would not be enough, although even in later times a great variety of farming locations was used, some permitting larger fields but some greatly limited in size. The trend would have been toward the use of the larger alluvial stream valleys, while farming outlying well-watered plots in addition. Planting crops in many different locations, varying in their susceptibility to minor fluctuations in temperature and moisture, was a simple insurance against total loss; in a wet year when floods washed away stream-side fields, drier hillsides would still yield a harvest, although in dry years they would have been the places that produced nothing.

In addition, the wild plant and animal resources of the environment were exploited by techniques little-changed from the past. Therefore, even the most "settled" village was probably partly deserted periodically when groups went to more distant locations to secure important seasonal resources. Boundaries of the areas used by individual villages cannot be reconstructed with any precision but were doubtless well known by both a village's own occupants and those of neighboring settlements. The high mountain slopes may have been generally shared for game hunting, whereas a choice locality closer to home was the preserve of a single village. In late prehistoric and historic times, "hunting shrines" not only represented tangible aspects of hunting magic (effigies, offerings) but also served as clear reminders of territorial rights.

## Conclusion

Viewing the Southwest from 2000 B.C. to A.D. 500 as a whole, many innovations can be observed, but with only slow and moderate changes and with conspicuous stability particularly in the first 1,500 years. If growth is regarded as an increase in size without significant structural changes, in contrast to development, in which structural alterations occur, then this era in the Southwest can be divided into two contrasting periods. The first, up to about 500 B.C., is marked by slow growth, probably in population and certainly in the addition of specific traits diffused northward from Mexico. The second period, 500 B.C. to A.D. 500, is a time of development, with basic changes such as the shift from seasonal to permanent occupation of settlements.

In the first period (or earlier, according to one view of the dating at Bat Cave), maize (pre-Chapalote) and squash were introduced, followed by new varieties of maize (Chapalote and then Nal-Tel), and then by teosinte-influenced maize. Considerably later than the first maize and squash, there was the addition of beans to this small list of domestic crops. Farming of a technologically simple kind gradually spread widely geographically but remained of minor significance economically. Settlements through this period were small, probably with 25 to 30 people at the most, and people used caves and rockshelters as well as open sites with simple, impermanent structures, some of them little more than windbreaks. Specialized economic activities consisted of hunting every available kind of game, collecting wild plant foods, quarrying, tool making, and the making of various kinds of nets, bags, and baskets. Food procurement, a major daily activity, was carried on at a relatively low level of efficiency, that is, most of the population was continually involved in it with little surplus to permit long periods of time for other activities. Property was probably viewed as of little value per se, since the mobility of each band required that its possessions be few and easily portable. In general, this was a time of stability in spite of innovations that would ultimately prove important, and no basic changes in the patterns of social and economic life occurred. At the end of this period, as at the beginning, a group supported itself relatively briefly in a specific locality and then moved to another to repeat the same pattern of activities. Throughout the yearly cycle emphasis changed from one food resource to another, but from year to year and century to century, the annual pattern was little changed, even when small amounts of maize, beans, and squash were added to the diet.

The second period, approximately 500 B.C. to A.D. 500, saw structural changes in the cultural pattern of the ancient Southwesterners such as the shift to permanent villages with houses built to last years instead of weeks or months, dependence on storage pits for long-term food accumulation, the manufacture of pottery with all its advantages over basketry for cooking and storing, and new types of tools for many purposes. Part of this was, in economic terms, an investment of scarce goods or labor in future needs rather than in meeting immediate material needs; for example, the labor of building a house or excavating a large storage pit was at the expense of time for hunting or gathering or for farming, but the trade-off produced a house or storage system usable for long enough to be of ultimate advantage. With the establishment of permanent villages it is possible that patrilineal kin groups making up mobile bands were succeeded by new kinds of social groups. It is also probable that development, rather than merely slow or unchanging patterns, was partly because innovations in clusters provide the reinforcement essential for the effective adoption of any particular innovation. If irrigation had been introduced without the associated and supporting innovations of social mechanisms for canal maintenance and water distribution, for example, it would probably not have continued and developed as it did. The building of houses required several new associated skills in construction of their components—sturdy walls, weatherproof roofs, firm floors, changes in the systems of cooking and heating, and probably also changes in the spatial relationships (proxemics) of the family groups that occupied them.

The successful innovations that began even before 2000 B.C. with the introduction of farming and began to work significant changes in the last few centuries B.C. and the first centuries A.D. laid the basis for far more extensive and complex changes later in the Southwest. The pace of culture change was remarkably slow for nearly two millennia but gradually increased, with mere expansion of population and resources giving way to structural changes in social and economic aspects of life that can be inferred from the archeological record of material remains. By A.D. 500 the culture patterns that set off the Southwest from the rest of North America had emerged in elementary form and succeeding centuries saw their elaboration.

# Prehistory: Mogollon

PAUL S. MARTIN*

Before 1920, many sites in southwestern New Mexico and southeastern Arizona had been excavated along or near the drainages of the Rio Grande, the Animas, the Little Colorado, the Dolores, the Puerco, the San Juan, the San Francisco, the Upper Gila, and the Mimbres rivers. These sites were usually thought of by the archeologists of the time as regional variations of what is now called the Anasazi or Pueblo culture.

As more work was done, especially after the first Pecos Conference in 1927 (Kidder 1927), archeologists came to recognize that there were several subcultures, rather than one grand culture that covered the entire Southwest. Some of the divisions were in part based on geographical provinces—the Colorado Plateau province, the Basin and Range province, and the mountainous zone that is on the southern edge of the Basin and Range province (see "Prehistory: Introduction," fig. 1, this vol.). It is this mountainous terrain that was the homeland of the Mogollon culture. The name Mogollon (ˌmugēˈyōn) is taken from the rugged Mogollon Mountains, which lie at the center of the Mogollon cultural heartland.

H.S. Gladwin, founder of Gila Pueblo Archaeological Foundation, a research center in Arizona (discontinued in 1951), and his assistant, Emil W. Haury, were the first to recognize that the cultures of this area differed from the Hohokam of the southern Arizona desert and from the Anasazi of the Colorado Plateau. This recognition occurred as early as 1930 or 1931 (Gladwin and Gladwin 1935). In 1936 Haury (1936, 1936a) excavated two villages that were the first to be characterized as Mogollon, thereby setting forth the taxonomic differences between the Mogollon and other Southwest cultures. Although the two villages that Haury excavated were the first to be called Mogollon, Hough (1920) of the United States National Museum had earlier published the results of his excavations of a large pit-house village at Luna, New Mexico, that would now be classified as Mogollon.

An expert can readily distinguish among the material facets of the three great subcultures of the Southwest, but actually there is a majestic parallelism of likeness among them. For the most part, the recognizable differences between the Hohokam, Anasazi, and Mogollon seem to reflect the existence of functionally different ecological niches. Such differences are found in the form of cultural activities and artifacts but do not necessarily indicate differences in the ways cultural activities are linked to local ecological communities (Binford and Binford 1968:324). For example, if two cultural systems base their subsistence principally on hunting and gathering, and yet one group occupies a well-watered mountainous environment and the other a desert, one would expect food-procurement and food-processing activities to be carried out in special and different ways. The daily activities would have special, adaptive forms and styles that would be related to gross differences in the environments and the foods being exploited. Since both cultural systems are hunting and gathering societies, they occupy comparable ecological niches in their different environments—that is, the general character or means of subsistence would be the same, but the different foods being collected would lead to different patterns of behavior among the different groups. These differences could have been the reasons for differences in form and style of various aspects of material culture—houses, tools, pottery.

Structural differences in ecological niches refer to different ways of integrating (or articulating) cultural activities with ecological communities (Binford and Binford 1968:324). These differences are related to the exploitation of quite different types of environmental resources. In order to utilize the different resources, human groups require significantly different kinds of social organization and implements. For example, the Hopi and Navajo Indians of Arizona live side by side in the same gross environment. The Hopi emphasize farming; the Navajo, herding. Each cultural system occupies its own distinct ecological niche and is linked with different environmental elements. There are different material and organizational elements in the two groups; these elements are integrated in different ways and they are differentially related to the ecological communities.

In the case at hand, there are functional and perhaps structural differences between the adaptations represented by the Hohokam, the Anasazi, and the Mogollon; and similarly, both kinds of differences occur through time in each of the areas taken individually. When comparisons are made it is important to keep in mind the level of cultural development of the groups whose artifacts are being compared. It is my feeling that the most important structural differences in the Southwest are to be found in

* Final editorial revisions on this chapter were made by Richard B. Woodbury and Alfonso Ortiz after the author's death.

61

the change from food collecting and hunting to increasing dependence upon agriculture, which occurred throughout the region. The differences among the three main Southwestern subcultures, at any given level of development, seem to be primarily functional rather than structural. The environmental and cultural variables that directed the changing adaptations in the various regions are more important than the specific differences in material culture, and it is the similarity of these changes that relate the three subcultures, making one wonder if the differences in forms of artifacts are significant enough to warrant their designation as distinct and independent cultural entities.

To deal with the adaptive aspects of the Mogollon culture specifically, it will be necessary to discuss both the resources exploited and the modes of exploitation used by the Mogollones through time and to relate selected aspects of the Mogollon culture to these factors. This method will aid conceptualization of the ways in which these people adapted to their particular niche. The dispersal of the material remains of a fossilized cultural system is not capricious but patterned. An analysis of these remains in the context of the natural and social environment in which they functioned is essential for grasping some of the processual changes that occurred in the cultural system of the Mogollon. The Mogollon will be considered both from a time-space orientation, in which artifacts, architecture, chronology, and spatial distribution will be discussed, and from a processual point of view, in which the Mogollon will be treated as a continuing adaptation within a particular area.

## Territory and Environment

The geographic location of the Mogollon culture may be roughly placed as sitting astride the Arizona-New Mexico border. This may be considered the "core" area, but actually the area covered by this culture is very large (fig. 1).

The topography of this area is the most maturely dissected in the Southwest, with deep valleys and high mountains. Average rainfall varies according to elevation from about 13 inches a year at Mimbres and about 11 inches in the Reserve, New Mexico, area, to 19 inches for Cibecue, Arizona. The valleys, though well watered, were often not optimally suited for agriculture due to their narrowness, altitude, and short growing seasons. The best agricultural locations in the area were in the Little Colorado, Blue, San Francisco, Gila, San Pedro, and Salt river valleys, especially where the valleys opened out into broad flats. It is in these valleys that the largest concentration of villages occurred. Surprisingly, villages also occurred in some narrow, not very well-watered valleys— for example, Pine Lawn Valley, Wet Legget Wash, and the SU Wash—all west of Reserve, New Mexico, and close to the Arizona border. Although many Mogollon

sites are in New Mexico, important work has been carried out at sites in and around Vernon, Arizona (Martin and Rinaldo 1960), and at Show Low, Forestdale, Snowflake, Pinedale, Concho, Saint Johns, and Springerville, to name only a few contemporary areas in Arizona.

## Chronologies

The initial attempts at establishing a chronology for the Mogollon area were based on the division of the known archeological remains into phases. A phase is an abstraction that defines arbitrary cultural units that are limited in time and space. Ideally each phase represents a cluster of specific attributes of architecture, ceramics, tool types, and other material remains that distinguish it from other similarly defined phases. For example, if one found at a particular site the pit houses, plain ceramics, and stone tool types of the Pine Lawn phase, plus painted pottery, then the site would be of a later phase, perhaps the San Francisco.

It became apparent as work proceeded in the Mogollon area that there were minor regional differences in the phases. The point to be noted here is that attributes that define phases appeared at different times and changed at different rates in the various regions of the larger Mogollon area. No satisfactory scheme that applies to the whole area has yet been devised. However, J.B. Wheat (1955) does provide a classification of phases for different subareas of the Mogollon region. His regional variations or "branches" include Mimbres, Cibola, Forestdale, San Simon, Black River, and Jornada. Some of the famous sites are given in table 1.

The Mogollon culture as a whole developed more or less uniformly out of the Desert culture but with regional differences in the temporal occurrence of certain attributes of material culture; however, the general development of Mogollon material culture will be discussed here without reference to specific stages in specific areas, except where it is relevant.

## Culture

The Mogollon culture was probably an evolutionary development from the Cochise culture, which in turn was a local adaptation in New Mexico and Arizona of the widespread Desert culture of the Great Basin and Southwest during the last five or six millennia before the Christian era. In fact, all the major cultural variations in the Southwest (Anasazi, Hohokam, Mogollon, Patayan, etc.) seem to have evolved from regional variants of the Desert culture.

The people of the Desert culture hunted, fished if they were near lakes or streams, and gathered wild foods. Concentrations of mortars and pestles and grinding mills (metates and manos) in this cultural stage lead one to suspect that grinding and crushing operations were im-

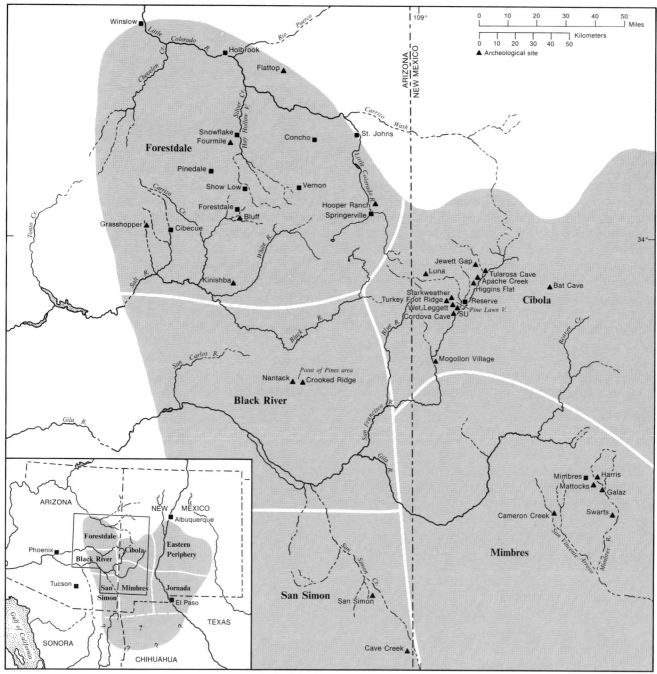

Fig. 1. Archeological sites. Inset shows approximate Mogollon area and its branches.

portant. Whether this activity was confined to wild seeds and nuts or whether corn was also used as a supplementary food is not known for the San Simon and San Pedro drainages. In the central Mogollon area, work in Tularosa and Bat caves (Martin et al. 1952; Dick 1965a) demonstrates stratigraphically not only the presence of maize and squash as early as approximately 2000 B.C. but also the presence of the types of tools (mortars, pestles, manos, metates, choppers) that are characteristic of the Chiricahua and San Pedro stages of the Cochise culture in southern Arizona. It seems likely, then, that corn was present throughout the Mogollon at an early date.

In the San Simon drainage, Sayles (1945) discovered prepottery pit houses of the San Pedro period (about 500 B.C.). The same or similar house type carried over into the next phase (Peñasco, about 300 B.C. to A.D. 100), along with older types of stone tools; but at this juncture brown and red pottery also appeared. This seems to be more evidence for hypothesizing that Mogollon is an outgrowth of the Cochise culture, or rather is a manifestation of late Cochise development, the great difference being that ceramics were introduced and used. It is not known precisely where corn and ceramics came from, but it is most probable that they appeared as the result of the

**Table 1. Mogollon Branches**

| Sites | Dates | Sources |
|---|---|---|
| Mimbres branch | | |
|     Swarts Ruin | A.D. 900–1200 | Cosgrove and Cosgrove 1932 |
|     Harris Village | 600–850 | |
|     Mogollon Village | 700–850+ | Haury 1936, 1936a |
|     Starkweather Ruin | 750–1150 | Nesbitt 1938 |
|     SU site | 300–500 | Martin 1940, 1943; Martin and Rinaldo 1947 |
|     Promontory site | 500 | |
|     Turkey Foot Ridge site | 650–900 | Martin and Rinaldo 1950 |
|     Twin Bridges site | 850–925 | |
|     Tularosa Cave | 2500 B.C.–A.D. 1100 | Martin et al. 1952 |
|     Cordova Cave | 300 B.C.–A.D. 1 | Martin and Rinaldo 1950a; Martin, Rinaldo, and Antevs 1949; Martin et al. 1952 |
|     Cameron Creek site | A.D. 850–1200 | W. Bradfield 1931 |
|     Galaz Ruin | 750–1400 | B. Bryan 1931 |
| Cibola branch | | |
|     unnamed sites | | Danson 1957 |
| Forestdale branch | | |
|     Bluff site | 200–600 | Haury and Sayles 1947 |
|     Flattop site | 400 | Wendorf 1950 |
| Black River branch | | |
|     Nantack Village | 900–1000 | Breternitz 1959 |
|     W:10:51 | | Wendorf 1950a |
|     Crooked Ridge Village | 200–900 | J. B. Wheat 1954 |
| San Simon branch | 300 B.C.–A.D. 1000 | Sayles 1945 |
|     Cave Creek | | |
|     San Simon Village | | |
| Jornada branch | A.D. 800–1400 | Lehmer 1948; Mera 1943a |

SOURCE: J. B. Wheat 1955.

interchange of information and trade from Mexico, where pottery and maize were already several millennia old.

*Subsistence and Settlement*

The key to the development of Mogollon culture lies in the patterns of subsistence. Because of the wealth of preserved food remains in Tularosa Cave deposits covering at least 3,000 years (Martin et al. 1952), scholars have a very good idea of what the people were eating and can guess that the diet of the entire Mogollon area may have been similar. A few of the plants found were as follows (a complete listing is contained in the Tularosa Cave report, Martin et al. 1952): piñon nuts, Indian rice, corn, mariposa lily bulbs, walnuts, acorns, kidney beans, prickly pear, wild tomato (wolfberry), squash, and sunflower seeds. There were over 40 different genera used for food, medicines, sandal and clothing making (figs. 2–3), and perhaps ritual performances. In addition to these plant foods, deer bones were found in great abundance, as well as bones of bison, turkeys, and muskrats.

From about 2000 B.C. to A.D. 500, maize became more and more frequent relative to wild foods. The earliest corn found at Bat and Tularosa caves is classified as pod corn. The cobs were small, primitive, and yielded proportionately less food than the later types. At A.D. 500 to about A.D. 700, cave analysis reveals that the amounts of cultivated foods decreased about 80 percent with a proportional increase in the amounts of wild foods that were collected. Why? Were the Mogollon farmers temporarily forced out of the area by the hunter-gatherers? Was there a decline in rainfall or a microclimatic shift? Was there factionalism? No one knows. And since no other caves in the Mogollon area have yet been found with such a long record of plant deposits, it is not known if this decline in agriculture is a unique event for the Pine Lawn, New Mexico, area, or whether it was a widespread phenomenon. If it is assumed that the Mogollon people persisted and were not replaced by a simpler society, it is a remarkable case of adaptation to changing circumstances; their existence went on and the culture survived even though it was impoverished in a variety of ways. It is possible that this period in which the use of cultivated foods declined was the result of inefficient techniques during the period when the system made a more or less complete commitment to an agricultural subsistence

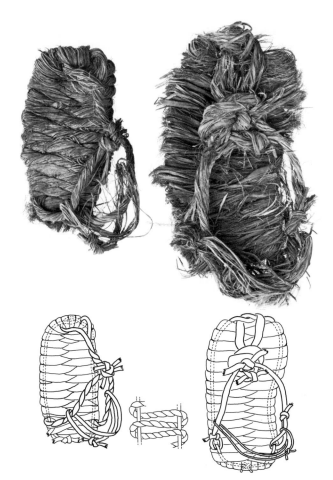

top, Field Mus., Chicago: 260674, 260687; bottom, after Martin et al. 1952:fig. 88b,c.
Fig. 2. Sandals. top, 2-warp wickerwork sandals of yucca leaves excavated from Tularosa Cave, Catron Co., N.M. (Martin et al. 1952:259–266); length of left sandal 16.7 cm. bottom, Construction of sandals.

Field Mus., Chicago: 260830.
Fig. 3. Fragment of cotton cloth with geometric design woven in green, black, and natural, excavated from Tularosa Cave, Catron Co., N.M. The design of different colored and interlocking weft elements is similar to those found on Reserve Black-on-white pottery (Martin et al. 1952:299). Length 8.7 cm.

base. There is no reason to assume that there was any gap in the continuity of Mogollon culture. All the signs strongly suggest this conclusion.

After A.D. 700, agriculture (maize, beans, and squash) again became important and wild foods declined in popularity. The races and strains of corn were improved by hybridization, the number of kernel-rows dropping from 16 to 14 to 12 and finally to 8 rows. This meant more efficient maize since each kernel was larger and more nourishing. Along with this improvement in agriculture came other important cultural developments.

It is not possible to describe the earliest (2000 B.C.) settlement patterns of the Mogollon, since so few sites of this era have been reported on. The Cochise homeland (Sayles and Antevs 1941) is an important exception. The period 2000 B.C.–A.D. 1000 was one of little change, characterized by long, slow, nearly static developments. Between A.D. 900 and 1050 significant changes took place in many parts of the core area. The major changes concern the location of villages, surface masonry, multiroomed Pueblos, and pottery. These developments all followed soon after the surge in agriculture.

Some parts of the Mogollon area were abandoned after A.D. 1100: the Pine Lawn Valley, the San Simon Valley, and the Forestdale Valley. Some continued for a short time longer, such as the Mimbres Valley, which was inhabited until about A.D. 1200, and the Reserve–Apache Creek areas. Other areas lasted longer and flourished after 1000. The Grasshopper Pueblo grew to over 500 rooms and was not abandoned until about 1400 (Longacre and Reid 1974), and the Jornada area around El Paso was also not vacated until about this time. The period 1000–1400 was marked by rapid change. It was a relatively short span in which the metabolism of the culture speeded up. The reasons for this are not surely known, but it may have been due in part to innovations that seeped in from surrounding cultures and to the increasing efficiency in agricultural techniques. Mogollon culture in late times took on a different character, one that reflected both the old and the new (Anasazi) influences. It is possible that at this late time the Mogollon-Anasazi culture was functionally and structurally the same as or more similar to the Anasazi than to the Mogollon. Thus, the development of Mogollon culture will be considered in terms of two large time periods: early, 500 B.C.–A.D. 1000, and late, A.D. 1000–1400.

• VILLAGES  Almost all the villages of the early period were built on high mesas, bluffs, or ridges, well back from the mainstream of travel. Some of the villages on high ridges were provided with crude walls placed on the approachable side of the village, while steep escarpments protected the other three sides. The steep sides of the mesas and fortifying walls sealed off avenues of easy accessibility. In other words, the early villages tended to be easily defensible. One reason for this may have been that these sites were the outgrowth of tension between early farmers and those populations still carrying out hunting-gathering activities as their principal subsistence pattern.

By recourse to a different kind of subsistence pattern (semisedentary agriculture) than had previously existed, the early farmers were effectively restricting the geographic range of contemporaneous hunters while effectively increasing their own range of potentially exploitable resources by means of raids. This could easily have led to hostilities between the hunter-gatherers and the agriculturalists. The results of such strife may have been the construction of fortified, easily defensible sites where the agriculturalists would be less likely to lose the stored staples upon which the existence of the community depended.

As knowledge of techniques for exploiting cultigens increased, the early farmer would have been able to exert greater control over the physical environment than the hunter-gatherer. This meant that the hunter-gatherer either had to adopt a sedentary agricultural life cycle or face extinction (Naroll 1970:1243).

These results can be noted in the distribution of the later Mogollon sites (after A.D. 900–1000). These both increased in number over earlier periods and tended to be located in more accessible topographical positions—such as in valleys near streams or rivers, where agriculture and irrigation could be carried out. Defense was no longer essential, and the people took advantage of river valleys where arable land was plentiful. Irrigation is known to have been practiced near Jewett Gap, New Mexico (Joan Kayser, personal communication 1972), in the Hay Hollow Valley (Plog 1969), and at the Grasshopper site near Cibecue, Arizona after A.D. 1000.

*Structures*

The villages of the early period consisted of roundish pit houses ranging from four or five houses a village to upward of 50. A pit house is a neatly excavated hole, 10 to 16 feet in diameter and two to five feet deep, over which a roof of poles, brush, and mud was constructed. Pit houses came into vogue in northeastern Europe about 25,000 years ago (Klíma 1954); they were popular because of their advantages of warmth and protection from the elements in winter. The use of pit houses spread across Europe and northern Asia (Siberia), and the idea for building this type of house may have been brought into the New World by the ancestors of the American Indians. Pit houses are the earliest structure in many parts of the west and Alaska, and certainly in the Southwest.

There were many variations in Mogollon pit houses, but some generalizations can be made. Most of the early houses were roundish or irregular in shape, some with a short entry way and others with a longer one, something like that of an igloo. A few were bean-shaped, D-shaped, or ovoid. Most were one meter to one and one-half meters

Fig. 4. Flexible cradle with sotol *(Dasylirion wheeleri)* warps, twined yucca wefts, and grass bedding excavated from Tularosa Cave, Catron Co., N.M. Length 80 cm.

Fig. 5. Desiccated female burial being excavated by John Rinaldo from Tularosa Cave, Catron Co., N.M. The flexed corpse with well-preserved hair was wrapped in a fur blanket and placed upon a rush mat (Martin et al. 1952:459–460).

(about 40 to 58 inches) deep. The areas varied from about 12 to more than 35 square yards. The reasons for this variation in size and shape of houses even within the same village of the same period are not known. One can guess that the larger houses may have been homes for extended families. Or, house differences may have denoted lineages or some other social affiliation or ownership. They may have varied because of social differences, although there is no evidence of rank.

Some entryways were inclined, others were merely a step; most of them faced east or southeast, but a few faced west or northeast. The roof was supported in one of four major ways, the two most popular being the "umbrella" type with one central upright post and a type that used four upright posts set in a square (fig. 6).

Since food storage would have provided greater control over the environment, it is not surprising that a high frequency of storage pits was found. The storage pits were usually outside the house proper; but in the Pine Lawn area many floor pits existed, some only a few centimeters in depth (3 to 10 inches), others from a meter to almost twice that depth. It is assumed that food or other materials were stored in these pits and that they were floored with planks. Burials were frequently made in them, and the pits then plugged with earth, while the family continued to live in the house over the remains of the deceased.

Hearths or fire pits were sometimes a mere depression, sometimes stone or clay lined. In many cases, no fire pit existed. Evidence indicates that frequently the fire was built on the floor. In a few cases, there is no evidence of reddening or burning of the earthen floor, and perhaps this indicates that fires were not used often in some of the houses. This might suggest seasonal occupation (spring and summer times), although there is no evidence to support the idea. Fire pits were also found outside the houses.

In the earliest villages, houses were grouped in an apparently haphazard way, without any particular plan. Of course, the village layout depended somewhat on topography. On a long ridge, they were scattered out along the high point of the ridge. The larger pit houses were sometimes placed at the ends of rows of houses; others were more or less centrally located. These larger and somewhat more specialized structures are associated with every branch of the Mogollon pit-house villages except San Simon (J.B. Wheat 1955:57). Actually, the specialized features are not very pronounced. The ceremonial structures—kivas—are usually twice as large as the largest houses, and some are more than that. They range from about 315 square feet to about 1,089 square feet. Depths average from 40 to 50 inches. All of them until A.D. 900 are roundish, bean-shaped, ovoid, or D-shaped. In later times, they were quadrangular and generally smaller, about 135 to 504 square feet. Three of them (SU site, Bluff, and Crooked Ridge Village) are

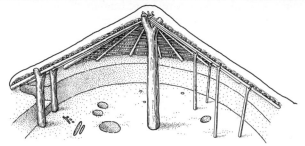

top, Field Mus., Chicago; center, after Martin 1943:fig. 43; bottom, after Martin 1940:fig. 39.

Fig. 6. Pit houses, SU site, Catron Co., N.M. top, View to the south of excavated Pit house J. Entrance on east side is flanked by two postholes, with central large posthole for roof support. Boulder mortars in entrance and south of 50 cm magnetic north arrow. Small holes are the result of root and rodent activity. center, Reconstruction of Pit house J roof and step entrance. bottom, Generalized reconstruction of a pit house with 4 roof posts and tunnel entrance.

supplied with floor grooves. Those in the SU site kiva had five elongated grooves shaped like a half-log and bearing bark impressions in the troughs. The one at the Bluff site had a groove cut in the sandstone floor completely about the periphery. The grooves at Crooked Ridge Village resembled those at SU site.

The entryways to the kivas were short and stubby or long and sloping downward. Most of them faced east or southeast, but a few faced other cardinal directions. Hearths were found in most of them, and sometimes there were pits in the floors. Masonry was used frequently to line the facing of the dirt walls of the kivas after A.D. 900, especially in those of quadrangular shapes. Usually everyday utensils were lacking in these structures, as were subfloor burials.

Aside from these unimpressive special features, there is really no solid evidence for calling these structures ceremonial. However, at one site, Tularosa Cave, materials were excavated that from a western point of view have no practical use or value. Life could have gone on without these items. If this assumption is true, then it might be inferred that these "useless" articles were symbolic or ritual in nature. Among the articles found that fit into this category were bone flutes, dice of wood, minerals that may have been used for body paint (reds, blacks, and whites), small mortars in which paint materials had been ground to a fine powder, quartz crystals, odd-shaped stones, animal claws, animal and human effigies of clay, reed cigarettes, prayer sticks, toy or miniature bows and arrows (before A.D. 300), and pipes of stone in which wild tobacco was smoked.

After A.D. 700, pit houses tended to be basically rectangular. They were carefully excavated and finished on the interior. Most of them were equipped with a side entryway, many of which were provided with ramps that sloped upward from the floor of the house to the outside ground level. The later period saw a startling innovation in house types. Later villages consisted of surface rooms of masonry numbering from four to six rooms per village to the very large ones, like Grasshopper Ruin, that contained 500 rooms or more. The houses were built on the surface of the ground in cellular fashion, so that many rooms had common walls. Masonry was very crude, consisting of randomly selected cobbles held in place by copious amounts of mud mortar. In some cases, the masons tried to achieve an overall flat vertical surface, but the stones used were not tooled and coursing was virtually absent. In general, the masonry may be called dry masonry with voids filled with mud. These were the first surface masonry structures in Mogollon history. Those villages of a few rooms were either built in a straight line on a north-south axis or in a square. The later large villages were composed of rooms erected around a plaza and were often two stories high. The rooms were very large (as at Grasshopper), and usually faced inward toward the plaza. The aggregation of people represented by these changes in site form may relate to the increasing proficiency in agricultural techniques and perhaps to the necessity for increased numbers of people to construct and maintain water control systems.

Most of these Pueblos, especially in the northern part of the Mogollon area, were only one story high. Farther south, in the Gila Cliff–Mimbres areas at Kinishba and at the Grasshopper Ruin, two stories were more frequent.

Associated with many of the later sites in the north were also subterranean pit-house kivas (fig. 8). These were constructed of masonry and rectangular. They were usually provided with a ventilator apparatus, a fire pit, mealing bins containing one to five metates, and sometimes floor drums. Near the ventilator opening one often finds a redware jar, and polychrome bowls on the floor. In some villages, there was just one such structure, while in others there were four to six. The exact function of these subterranean rooms is not known, but because of the presence of mealing bins and other tools, probably they served in part as activity centers.

In the later Pueblos food storage was more easily achieved. Rooms of solid masonry with floors covered with stone slabs were used, a situation in which stored foods would have been subject to less damage from rodents or dampness. If specialization was evolving in

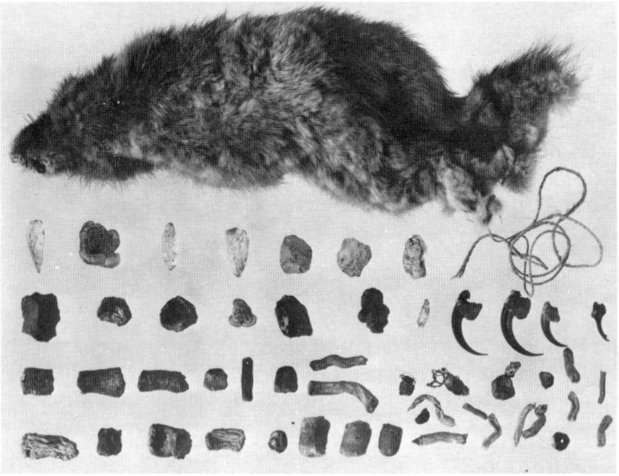

Field Mus., Chicago: 261080.
Fig. 7. Medicine man's muskrat skin bag with contents excavated from Tularosa Cave, Catron Co., N.M. top row, left to right, Quartz crystals, concretions; second row, obsidian flakes, claws of great horned owls, rhinoceros beetle head with horn; third and fourth rows, fragments of vegetal materials. Length of bag 25 cm.

Field Mus., Chicago.
Fig. 8. View from the northeast of kiva 2, Higgins Flat Pueblo, Catron Co., N.M. with slab-lined fire pit near 50 cm magnetic north arrow. Ventilator opening near meter stick against southwest wall.

certain work arrangements, for example, exploitation and preparation in building, in ceremonies, specific work areas and the like, it might be expected that the Mogollon social organization was becoming less generalized and perhaps stronger (Naroll 1970:1243–1245). Furthermore, there were present perhaps the seeds of urbanization, because societies tend to become more complex through time. In later Pueblos (Grasshopper, for instance) where social stratification may have been present, there was perhaps a shift from the simple sharing and reciprocal exchanges of the hunter-gatherer society to a tendency toward hoarding of wealth (Naroll 1970:1245).

## Pottery

The earliest Mogollon pottery, like most early pottery found everywhere in the world, was plain and unpainted. The origins of this pottery are unknown, although it is assumed to be the result of interchange of ideas with Mexico. It was probably not a local development. Pottery making was known just a few hundred miles to the south in the Hohokam area as early as 300 B.C. and in the San Simon drainage as early as 500 B.C.

The earliest wares were polished brown and polished red. Interestingly, polished brown (Alma Plain) (fig. 9) and polished red (San Francisco Red) continue throughout the entire Mogollon history. There are brown textured wares, plain browns, and bowls with brown exteriors and smudged interiors (Reserve Smudged, a derivative ware from plain brown pottery that appeared about A.D. 300). Along with the plain brown polished ware, a thicker brown type also appeared, very rough and unpolished, but its popularity waned about A.D. 400. Texturing (neck-banded, corrugated, incised, scored) appeared as early as A.D. 300–400 (fig. 9). The vessel forms of this plain ware were bowls and jars.

It seems probable that Mogollon pottery was made by the coil method, although there is evidence that some vessels were molded by hand. About A.D. 300–400, the first decorated painted pottery occurred, but it did not become popular until about 600. This is a beautiful ware, bearing broad line designs in red on a brown background (Mogollon Red-on-brown). A little later (about 800–900) a new type appeared called Three Circle Red-on-white (fig. 9). The use of a white background is somewhat startling. J.B. Wheat (1955:90) believes the white is due to Anasazi influences, but Haury (1936:20) and Martin believe that its origin was south in the Mimbres area. This type seemed to evolve into a more sophisticated black-on-white pottery called Mimbres Bold Face Black-on-white. When Martin and Rinaldo (1950) traced the development of design elements from the earliest decorated pottery (Mogollon Red-on-brown) through Three Circle Red-on-white to Mimbres Bold Face, they showed that parallel, medium-width lines constituted the principal design element in all these types, and that there was an evolution in design styles from the earliest to the latest. Stylistically, there seem to be some grounds for continuity in the evolution of these types.

Bowls, jars of many shapes, and cups were the forms that were most popular. There is a remarkable uniformity in shapes over the entire Mogollon area, although a few exotic forms appeared in the Forestdale area in Arizona. There may have been functional differences for utility wares versus painted types.

left to right, Martin 1940:fig. 35; after Martin 1940:fig. 38; Field Mus., Chicago: 207687.

Fig. 9. Mogollon pottery. left to right, Alma Plain jar excavated from SU site, Three Circle Red-on-white bowl excavated from SU site, and Neck Incised Corrugated pottery jar excavated from Wet Leggett Pueblo. All sites in Catron Co., N.M. Diameter of left 9.2 cm, rest same scale.

There was a noteworthy change in the types of pottery that became fashionable after A.D. 900–1000. Allover indented brown corrugated pottery was slowly taking the place of the earlier types. However, the most surprising change took place in the painted ware. The red-on-whites and red-on-browns were completely replaced by a black-on-white type that, while locally made, was inspired by Anasazi types that prevailed to the north of the Mogollon area. No one knows for certain the origin of this black-on-white pottery, but it was probably from the Zuni-Klagetoh-Manuelito-Gallup area of the Little Colorado River basin of western New Mexico and eastern Arizona. The mechanism by which this Anasazi influence became dominant is not known, but it is likely that the people of the above-mentioned area were budding off, forming daughter communities, and expanding in every direction, especially southward into the Mogollon area.

There was a proliferation of ceramic types that may have been the result of increasing functional specificity in the Mogollon culture. More shapes are encountered, such as pitchers, jars, ladles, effigy vessels, and eccentric shapes. Without doubt, the most singular, extraordinary black-and-white pottery to have developed in the entire Mogollon area was Mimbres Bold Face and Mimbres Classic Black-on-white (from about 900 to 1200) (fig. 10). The designs are not only geometric but also naturalistic, depicting animals, fish, humans, insects, and composite creatures. Mimbres Classic pottery demonstrates such originality and such care in draftsmanship that it is in a class all by itself; no prehistoric Southwestern pottery can compare with it as an expression of the sheer ecstasy of living.

Very soon after 1100 or perhaps before, more experimentation in embellishing pottery occurred: polychrome pottery with designs executed in black and white paints on a red slipped background. A few of the more famous

Smithsonian, Dept. of Anthr., Archeol.: a, 326256; b, 326291; c-e, after Cosgrove and Cosgrove 1932:pls. 218a, 148c, 190a.

Fig. 10. Mimbres Black-on-white pottery bowls with animal and bird figures and geometric patterns, painted in black on white-slipped interior surface (see also "Pueblo Fine Arts," fig. 2, this vol.). Bowls found in graves were often ritually "killed" by striking a hole through the bottom (Cosgrove and Cosgrove 1932:28). Diameter of a 25.2 cm, b same scale, diameter of c about 24.0 cm, d-e same scale.

70

polychrome types found in the later Mogollon sites are called St. Johns, Houck, Querino, Gila, Tonto, Pinto, Showlow, Four Mile, Pinedale, Cibecue, El Paso—all stunningly beautiful. Some of these (Houck, Querino, Gila, Tonto, and Pinto) may have been trade wares, made outside the Mogollon area.

The unpainted, textured brown pottery types continued and increased in quantity. The kinds of texturing multiplied almost beyond credibility. If there is any one feature that characterizes the textured pottery of the period, it is the prevalence of smudging and of patterning created by tooling the surfaces, the corrugations, or the coils. The number of types is large: plain corrugations, indented corrugations, filet rims; plus incising, punching, scoring, and bulging, all occurring on the corrugation to produce symmetrical and asymmetrical designs. Almost all variations were carried out so as to produce geometrical straight line patterns such as triangles, alternating hatched triangles, cross hatching, diagonals, stepped elements, and zigzags. These variations are found throughout the Mogollon area, after 900 up to and through Classic Mimbres phase, about 1200.

The brownish color of the pots may be due to firing and/or the volcanic clays that were available to the potter. These fired red or brown naturally. Sometimes where Anasazi influences were present and sedimentary as well as volcanic clays were available, one finds some gray textured wares, although brown predominates.

*Tools*

Although slow to develop in architecture and ceramics, one gets the impression that the Mogollon were stone workers par excellence in the variety and quantity of stone artifacts. In this they seem more closely allied to the Hohokam than to the Anasazi. However, broadly speaking, Mogollon tools are not very well made; they tend to be less well-shaped than those from other areas. Since most of the tools in the pre-900 period represent a heritage from the Cochise tradition, it is not too surprising that they are not well worked and are relatively crude.

• GROUND AND PECKED STONE   One of the most important parts of the tool kit was the metate, or milling stone. The earliest and most frequent were basin metates. As the name implies, this implement was a shallow depression in a stone slab. The unifacial handstone or mano that was used in this type of metate was held in one hand and was ovoid in shape. This type became less popular as time went on and disappeared by 800-900. Mortars of stone with crude, little-shaped pestles were in use from earliest times to about 900 (fig. 12). The troughed metates with one end closed were popular from earliest times to 900, also. In some areas, the closed end of the metates served as a resting place for the handstone—this is called the "Utah" type. A larger handstone was employed with the troughed metate. Both the upper and lower faces (bifacial) served as the grinding surface, and some were large enough to be used with two hands. About 800, a metate-type appeared that is called "through trough" because the grinding area or trough was open at both ends. A large, bifacial handstone, with flat or convex grinding surfaces (rocker bottom manos or beveled grinding surface) was used with the through-trough type.

Then there were stone dishes, polishing stones, grooved mauls and hammerstones, and axes with a groove that encircled only three-quarters of the surface (top and sides). Full-grooved axes began to be used about 900. Even the three-quarters grooved is rare and crudely made. Stone "hoes" (perhaps used for cultivating) occurred now and then.

Tubular stone pipes, made to be used with a bone or wooden mouthpiece, are fairly common. In early times, they were crudely made and very large. A little later (perhaps by A.D. 600) a shorter cylindrical pipe came into fashion and displaced the large, clumsy early ones. The

Field Mus., Chicago.
Fig. 11. Mealing bins with 3 stone metates arranged for grinding meal from coarse to fine, excavated from Apache Creek site, Catron Co., N.M. Manos lie in foreground. Pottery bowls placed below the lower ends of the metates serve as receptacles to catch flour. 50 cm arrow points magnetic north.

Martin 1943:figs. 66, 67.
Fig. 12. Pebble mortars with pecked cup-shaped depressions and stone pestles, from SU site, Catron Co., N.M. Diameter of largest mortar 27.5 cm, rest same scale.

inference that can be made as to the use of these pipes for tobacco, based on the analogy with historic Southwest Indian cultures, is that they were used only in ceremonies.

Atlatl or spear-thrower weights, stone balls, stone rings, and stone discs complete this brief listing of ground and pecked stone tools.

• CHIPPED STONE   The chipped artifacts were for the most part fairly crude. Fine chipping was occasionally done, but most of the tools were made with a minimum of effort. Many were merely simple flakes, the working edge of which was produced by the removal of a few flakes by means of percussion flaking. Those with pressure chipping on all surfaces were in the minority. Many of the scrapers and knives have only a little secondary chipping along one edge; and some are simply raw unretouched flakes. Projectile points with diagonal notches were the most frequent of the chipped tools, followed by knives, scrapers, choppers (very crude and heavy), drills, and even chipped axes. The large choppers were widely distributed, used up to A.D. 1000 and even later, and were merely big cores or cobbles with a bifacially, percussion flaked cutting edge. J.B. Wheat (1955:129) lists 16 different projectile types. This indicates that there was no single preferred Mogollon point. Some were stemless; others were provided with stems.

Generally, the artifacts that were popular early in the Mogollon culture continued to be made and used even after 1000. They fortify the theory that the Mogollon culture was slow to change or to adapt innovations.

• BONE AND SHELL   The most common bone tool was the awl made from deer leg bones that were split or splintered, the ends then ground to a sharp point. There were several types. Some had the head of the bone intact, others had the head removed. Sometimes, awls were fashioned from turkey bones or rabbit bones. Skewers, needles, fleshers, tubes, flakers, and whistles occur sporadically. The tubes and whistles were usually made from bird bones. Awls, skewers, and needles would have been useful in basketmaking, piercing hides, and sewing.

Bracelets were cut from a bivalve *(Glycymeris gigantea)* (fig. 13). Beads, rings, and pendants were manufactured from shell. Most of these objects are rare before A.D. 500 and became more popular in later periods. The shell for the bracelets came from the Pacific Ocean, probably by means of trade.

• DEVELOPMENT   By and large, the stone tools of the later period demonstrate the continuity of the Mogollon culture. The Cochise ancestry of the tools and the styles of the older periods such as those of the Pine Lawn and San Francisco phases were still very marked and in the majority. The principal types of tools, such as manos, metates, choppers, scrapers, flake knives, projectile points, and stone bowls are much the same as in earlier periods although the frequencies may be somewhat different. Rinaldo (Martin, Rinaldo, and Barter 1957:39) stated that if the artifacts of this period were to be mixed

72

Field Mus., Chicago: 207650, 206543.
Fig. 13. Shell trade bracelets imported from the Gulf of California, excavated from Wet Leggett Pueblo and SU site, dating A.D. 1200 and A.D. 200. Both sites are in Catron Co., N.M. Left diameter 5.8 cm.

with those of the earlier phases, it would be impossible to separate many of the late ones from the early ones.

Along with the continuation of the older styles of tools came some innovations. Beveled manos were used on flat, slab metates, and metates were placed in mealing bins; side-notched projectile points were made; grooved axes were gradually displacing the choppers of the older periods. One also finds arrow-shaft straighteners and rectangular stone bowls. In the Mimbres area, notched stone slabs, jar covers, door slabs, and tablets for grinding minerals for paint were innovations. More ornaments occur, such as shell bracelets, pendants of shell and stone (fig. 14), and Mexican copper bells.

Bone tools likewise showed a mixture of many older types and a few newer ones. Bone rings became more common. Some changes were related to other changes. For example, tabular manos increased along with an increase in through-trough metates; the number of metates with trough openings at one end only and the frequency of mortars and pestles decreased. Perhaps the

Field Mus., Chicago: 263548, 206476.
Fig. 14. left, Turquoise pendant excavated from Higgins Flat Pueblo, Catron Co., N.M.; length 1.7 cm. right, Soapstone bird effigy from SU site, Catron Co., N.M., dating from A.D. 200; length 5 cm.

increase of small, triangular, lateral-notched projectile points was related to the increased use of the bow and arrow (Rinaldo, in Martin, Rinaldo, and Barter 1957:40).

## Salado Horizon, A.D. 1300–1500

In the portion of New Mexico south of Glenwood, in the Gila Valley, in the Mimbres area near El Paso, Texas, and in southeastern Arizona, the final occupation is tentatively named the Salado horizon. Very little is known about this occupation, as only 8 or 10 sites of this period have been investigated. Many of them are near or on top of earlier Mogollon pit houses or Pueblos of the Mimbres phase and in valley bottoms. It seems that after the lower Mogollon area in New Mexico and perhaps southeastern Arizona (Johnson and Thompson 1963) was abandoned (about 1200) by the Mogollon, a hiatus of about 100 years occurred after which the Salado people from the Tucson-Phoenix areas may have moved south and east into southeastern Arizona and central southern New Mexico. These sites are fairly large, perhaps 100–200 rooms (Fitting 1972:17). The villages consisted of surface Pueblos with walls composed of river cobbles or vertical slabs set in the ground that served as a base for the coursed or puddled adobe walls. They were frequently multistoried. They may have roughly resembled the Big House at Casa Grande, Arizona. In the Ormand Village (Hammack, Bussey, and Ice 1966:29) a ceremonial structure (about 20 by 34 feet) was found in the middle of the interior plaza. It is the first one to have been reported for any Salado site in this area. Cremation in bowls and jars was the major method for disposal of the dead.

The most common pottery types were Gila and Tonto polychromes, although Hopi wares, Zuni Glazes, El Paso Polychrome, and various wares from northern Mexico also occurred.

Stone tools occurred but are not fully analyzed (Fitting 1971, 1971a, 1971b; Fitting, Ross, and Gray 1971; Baker 1971; Burns 1972; and Lekson, Ross, and Fitting 1971).

Thus, the Mogollon area was occupied for a long time, perhaps 2,000 years, and the final occupation was non-Mogollon.

## The Later Mogollon

After A.D. 900–1000, the following trends are apparent in the Mogollon area. Surface Pueblos of from 4 or 5 to 500 rooms predominated. The number of dwelling units increased until about A.D. 1250 at which time the number of occupied villages in many areas (Pine Lawn, Reserve, Mimbres, Hay Hollow, Jornada-El Paso) dropped to near zero. Concurrently, other Mogollon areas continued to grow, for example, Show Low, Pinedale, Four Mile, Point of Pines, the Grasshopper regions. Black-on-white pottery, especially Reserve, Tularosa, and Mimbres types

were dominant. Along with these black-on-white wares, one finds an ever-increasing vogue in red-on-black, polychromes, and bowls with shiny, polished black (smudged) interiors. Dwellings changed, from those housing perhaps an extended family, to those accommodating only nuclear families, and finally to Pueblos, in which several extended families and perhaps lineages lived in comfort and style. Metate types shifted from a basin type, to trough types, and lastly, to flat tabular types set in grinding bins, which were perhaps the most efficient for grinding corn quickly and easily. Pit-house kivas accompanied the surface Pueblos at a rate of one to six per village (they should not be confused with kivas proper). Their functions are unknown, but the evidence suggests a workroom area, especially for milling corn and for food preparation; a sleeping place for young uninitiated males; or single-family "chapels" and space for religious cults. Great Kivas were developed, mostly rectangular, but sometimes, inexplicably, round. An increase in ritualistic paraphernalia such as painted-stone animal effigies, painted-stone tobacco pipes, "sun" disks, and masks (evidence from pottery bowls depicting masked dancers) is evident (fig. 15). A large increase in jewelry may also be noted: stone and bone rings; copper bells; turquoise, jet, and stone pendants; stone and shell beads, and shell bracelets.

The spread of Anasazi elements from the north to the Mogollon area causing a blending of both Mogollon and Anasazi characteristics, including perhaps rituals as well as social organization, is not easily explained. Merely saying that daughter communities were expanding due to population growth is too simplistic, although this was probably a factor. Why did not the Mogollones resist innovations? Several hypotheses may be advanced, none of which has been tested: generalized societies are replaced by more specialized ones (Frederick T. Plog, personal communication 1970); simple organizations tend to become more complex (Naroll 1970:1244); the law of cultural dominance that states that "if two or more different kinds of sociocultural systems occupy adjacent environmental zones, the one that can be altered or adapted to fit the adjacent environmental zones will expand at the expense of the resident system" (the Mogollon, in this instance) (Binford and Binford 1968:331; Sahlins and Service 1960:69–92).

## Conclusion

In conclusion, this brief analysis of the settlement-subsistence system has hinted at the configuration of the exploitative and maintenance activities, suggested changing adaptations of the system to the total environment, noted the levels of technology achieved by the people, and has intimated some aspects of the social institutions and the reasons for the changes in the Mogollon culture.

The Mogollon evolved out of an essentially hunting

Fig. 15. Ceremonial cache from Great Kiva, Hooper Ranch Pueblo, Apache Co., Ariz. left, View through ring slab cover of crypt in kiva floor containing stone kachina and decorated miniature vessel filled with beads. Crypt is about 30 cm square and 30 cm deep. Sides and floor are lined with fitted sandstone slabs. 50 cm arrow points to magnetic north. right, Anthropomorphic stone effigy with body painted in alternating bands of black, yellow, green, and red, which is thought to be color-directional symbolism (Martin et al. 1962:69–74); length 20 cm.

and gathering and probably seminomadic population. As agriculture became increasingly important as a mode of subsistence, the Mogollones effected a specific sedentary adaptation to what may be characterized as a primarily mountainous zone. In adjacent areas of the greater Southwest, similar structural changes were going on, but, like the Mogollon, they too had their special functional reactions to general environments. The developments in other areas are important (especially Anasazi) to an understanding of the development of the Mogollon, since they probably influenced the character of the Mogollon adaptation.

# Prehistory: Hohokam

GEORGE J. GUMERMAN AND EMIL W. HAURY

The Hohokam (ˌhōhōˈkäm), the desert farmers of the American Southwest, were centered in the middle Gila and Salt river drainage basins in the semiarid Sonoran Desert of Arizona (fig. 1). The Hohokam were strikingly adept at articulating with the desert environment, as the Anasazi to the north adapted to the piñon-juniper country of the Colorado Plateau environment, and the Mogollon to the north and east adapted to the pine-clad mountainous terrain (see "Prehistory: Introduction," fig. 1, this vol.).

Hohokam culture is usually characterized by a number of distinctive traits that emphasize its difference from the better-known Anasazi and Mogollon cultures. The Hohokam lived in villages of scattered perishable brush structures constructed in shallow elongated pits with no apparent formalized village plan. Many of these villages were sustained by extremely large and complex canal systems, and the larger settlements usually had a ball court. Unlike the customary earth burials of the other two major Southwestern cultures, the Hohokam practiced human cremation. Ceramics were characterized by a plain ware ranging in color through grays to browns, and by red-on-buff decorated pottery, both kinds constructed by the paddle and anvil technique rather than by coiling and scraping. Distinctive luxury or religious artifacts include a variety of shell products, objects of bone, clay human figurines, and sculptured receptacles and palettes of stone.

Many of these elements peculiar to the Hohokam vary considerably in form or frequency of occurrence throughout southern Arizona. These variations have been ascribed to subtle adaptations to subenvironments or to contacts with other cultures, especially Mesoamerican peoples. Both factors—environmental adaptation and culture contact—are important considerations in Hohokam archeology, and they must be understood in order to comprehend the nature of Hohokam culture.

## Environment

The Sonoran Desert of southern Arizona and northwestern Mexico is within the physiographic zone of alternating mountains and plains known as the Basin and Range Province. The landscape is characterized by north-northwest and south-southeast trending isolated mountain ranges separated by nearly level basins or plains. The mountains, which rise from 1,000 to 3,500 feet above the intervening basins, were important as a source of natural water in springs and rock tanks and as a collector of rain as runoff for floodwater farming. The mountains also added substantially to the subsistence base by providing subenvironmental zones for natural food resources different from those in the riverine valleys and plains.

The major streams, now all intermittent because of modern dam constructions, have their origins outside or near the edge of the desert. These streams, especially the Gila and Salt rivers, were the lifelines of Hohokam culture because they provided the water for hundreds of miles of irrigation canals. Secondary and more ephemeral drainages tributary to the Gila and Salt, such as the Santa Cruz and San Pedro rivers, supported variations on the main Hohokam cultural theme.

High temperatures, low humidity, and little rain characterize the desert climate. Rainfall is usually less than 10 inches annually with the western area seldom receiving more than six inches. Most of this scanty precipitation comes during torrential summer storms. Consequently, little of it could be utilized by the Hohokam, a factor that further tied them to the river systems.

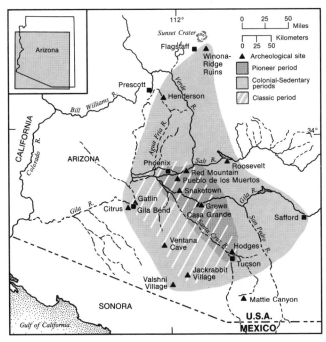

Fig. 1. Hohokam distribution and major archeological sites.

75

The semiarid desert, botanically characterized by mesquite, creosote bush, saltbush, and many species of cactus, was not so desolate prehistorically as it appears today. Although most evidence suggests that the climate was essentially the same when the Hohokam lived in southern Arizona as it is in the late twentieth century (Martin 1963), the present more arid appearance and less lush conditions result from the damming of rivers upstream, from overgrazing, and from the deforestation of the timbered flanks of the mountains. The more vegetated conditions of the past would have provided a better collecting environment than the present condition.

The environment of the Sonoran Desert should not be thought of as a uniform and constant factor. Available water determined in large part both the possibility and the variety of cultural activities. What has been identified as characteristic Hohokam is concentrated in the Gila and Salt river valleys, and these are the regions of the greatest available water. Tributaries to the Gila and Salt rivers have produced varieties of subcultures of the Hohokam that, together with the Gila and Salt manifestations, have been called River Hohokam. In contrast, the much drier southwestern section of Hohokam territory west of the modern city of Tucson, the present-day Papago Reservation, or Papagueria, was the location of the Desert Hohokam (Haury 1950). This is a region of lesser rainfall and no permanent but a few intermittent streams. As a result, the prehistoric population was smaller and the cultural manifestations less spectacular. Canal irrigation from streams was not feasible, but ditches for gathering runoff and other water-control devices are known. These variations in the cultural pattern have had a profound effect on how different archeologists have viewed the Hohokam.

### History of Research

The first archeological investigations in the Hohokam region were accomplished in the 1880s (Bandelier 1890-1892; Cushing 1890; C. Mindeleff 1896) and in the early 1900s (Moorehead 1906; Turney 1924; Fewkes 1907a, 1912). All the early investigators considered the archeological remains as a variation of the northern Pueblo ruins until Kidder (1962:298) perceived that the desert remains were "so aberrant that . . . we had overstepped the limits of the Southwestern culture area."

The most ambitious, and one of the first truly interdisciplinary projects, was the Hemenway Southwestern Archaeological Expedition of 1887-1888 under the direction of Frank Hamilton Cushing (Haury 1945). However, it was the work of the Gila Pueblo Archaeological Foundation under the direction of Harold S. Gladwin in the 1930s that first truly defined the Hohokam culture and established its range and a phase sequence. Gila Pueblo's work at Snaketown on the Gila River Indian

Reservation (Gladwin et al. 1937) was the most rewarding of their explorations.

After 1940 the archeology of the Hohokam was neglected with the exception of excavations in the Papagueria at the Jackrabbit Ruin (Scantling 1940), Valshni Village (Withers 1944), and the important work on the pre- and early Hohokam remains in Ventana Cave (Haury 1950). Since the late 1940s the Amerind Foundation, under the direction of Charles DiPeso, has devoted its efforts to unraveling the prehistory and ethnohistory of the eastern periphery of the Hohokam and, more specifically, the San Pedro Valley (Tuthill 1947; Di Peso 1951, 1953, 1956, 1958). Haury (1976) conducted extensive excavations at Snaketown in 1964-1965. The findings of that effort constitute the basis for much of this chapter. Both the Arizona State Museum of the University of Arizona and Arizona State University have been active in Hohokam salvage archeology (Wasley 1960; Wasley and Johnson 1965; Wasley and Benham 1968; Johnson 1964; Doyel 1974; Goodyear 1975), but the extensive information that has been gathered has not as yet been synthesized.

Although systematic studies of desert archeology began nearly a century ago, about as early as the first efforts to understand the Anasazi, two factors have contributed to a spotty and inconstant record of investigating the Hohokam: Hohokam villages lack the romance and dramatic visual appeal of cliff dwellings and large pueblos, and the heat of the desert discourages summer work when most scholars, usually university affiliated, are free to engage in field activities. Fortunately, interest developed in the Hohokam in the 1970s and syntheses and theoretical articles have appeared largely as a result of contract archeology.

### Cultural Sequence: Chronology

Since its proposal in 1937 (Gladwin et al. 1937), the Hohokam chronology has been subjected to revision of dates in every conceivable manner. Phases have been deleted or merged, and the Pioneer period has been removed from the Hohokam sequence and assigned to peoples called the Hakataya, Mogollon, or O'otam (Gladwin 1942, 1948; Di Peso 1956; Bullard 1962; Schroeder 1975). Major reasons for the lack of agreement are the absence of good chronological controls as provided by tree-ring dating in other parts of the Southwest and varying ways of viewing the evidence by different scholars. The original dating was basically derived from the association with Hohokam remains of closely dated black-on-white sherds from the Western Anasazi region.

The 1964-1965 Snaketown excavations (Haury 1976) generally confirmed the 1937 chronological formulation. The importance of the chronology rests on the fact that Snaketown is the only known Hohokam site that demonstrates a continuous occupation from the beginning of the

Pioneer period until the end of the Sedentary period. The succession of developmental stages in the culture is based on replicated stratigraphic evidence. Calendrical year assignments were derived by other means. Although there are some internal inconsistencies in the data, the year values shown in table 1 are derived from: tree-ring dated intrusive sherds from the Anasazi culture to the north, archeomagnetic dates, and radiocarbon dates. Preliminary studies of obsidian hydration and alpha recoil track densities on mica platelets are yielding promising results.

The dates in table 1 are applicable to the central Gila-Salt drainage system. There is probably some variation in this temporal framework in Hohokam manifestations some distance from the core area.

The origin of the Hohokam has long been disputed. The debate centers on whether they represent an indigenous development with strong Mesoamerican relationships or whether the Hohokam were the result of a direct migration of Mesoamerican people from the south. There is no doubt that the stimulus for settled village life in the Southwest is indirectly attributable to the intensive cultivation of primitive varieties of maize that appeared in the Mogollon region from Mexico about 2500 B.C. (Dick 1965a; Martin et al. 1952). Haury (1962) has postulated a diffusion of agriculture along the Sierra Madre Corridor of Mexico into the highland Mogollon area with its eventual adaptation to the desert environment by the Hohokam. However, the introduction of domesticated plants and the occurrence of settled villages as early as the San Pedro stage of the Cochise culture suggests that the beginning of agriculture may have preceded the farming practices of both the Hohokam and Mogollon.

Similarities in some artifact assemblages between Hohokam and Mogollon suggest that they shared a common parentage, San Pedro Cochise (Haury 1943, 1950: 535-536). Evidence for this continuity was believed to exist in Ventana Cave (Haury 1950) and in the Tularosa and Cordova caves (Martin et al. 1952). Increased reliance on agriculture and the addition of ceramics to the artifact inventory signaled the transition from San Pedro Cochise to Hohokam and Mogollon. These changes were attributed to Mesoamerican stimuli. The apparent common heritage out of Cochise for both culture types, in part, led Gladwin (1948) to group them under one rubric during the early phases, and Di Peso (1956) has considered them, at least in the San Pedro valley, as one group.

Snaketown excavations (Haury 1976), suggest that the origins of Hohokam may have been due to a direct migration from Mexico and that their culture did not develop from an indigenous base. The earliest Hohokam manifestation, the Vahki phase, dating from about 300 B.C. to A.D. 1, appears with a well-developed ceramic complex, clay figurines, cremations, a sophisticated and lengthy canal system, excavated wells, shaped trough metates, stone bowls with sculptured surfaces, turquoise mosaics, and a well-developed shell industry. These traits appear as a cluster in southern Arizona with no local indigenous antecedents. As a result, some archeologists believe that the Hohokam came into the Gila and Salt river drainages from Mexico as migrants, attracted by the living desert streams and the abundance of adjacent irrigable farmlands. Territorial conflict between them and the indigenous Cochise people was avoided because intensive farming and gathering result in the exploitation of different zones of the arid environment.

Two other hypotheses of Hohokam origins also recognize a migration from Mexico, but they propose that the earliest period, the Pioneer, was really an indigenous development of existing peoples and that the Hohokam did not arrive until A.D. 600 or even as late as 900. Schroeder (1953, 1975) feels the earliest Hohokam people were the Hakataya who originated in the Lower Colorado River region. Di Peso (1956) calls the people of the Pioneer period the O'otam. The O'otam, he believes, were displaced by the northward-advancing Hohokam and retreated to the uplands. However, excavations at Snaketown and at Red Mountain, near Phoenix (D.H. Morris 1969), reveal on the basis of cultural continuity that the earliest occupations of the Pioneer period were indeed Hohokam and that they can be traced back to about 300 B.C. There appeared at that time a constellation of elements ushering in a new way of life that had no prototypes in the Southwest.

Although the details of a migration from the south, the place of origin and the time of occurrence, the nature of continuing contacts through the centuries, and the nature of the donor culture may be disputed, there is reasonable agreement that the Hohokam were a northern frontier Mesoamerican society (Kelley 1966; Haury 1976). Wasley (1967), in his survey of northern Sonora for the Arizona State Museum, was unsuccessful in his search for Hohokam sites, suggesting a rapid migration rather than a slow northward expansion of Hohokam progenitors. Whether the Hohokam relationship with Mexico after their arrival was one of continual independent trade or the domination of them by Mesoamericans is debatable.

**Table 1. Cultural and Temporal Sequence**

| Period | Phase | Dates |
|---|---|---|
| Classic | Civano | A.D. 1300-1450 |
| | Soho | 1100-1300 |
| Sedentary | Sacaton | 900-1100 |
| Colonial | Santa Cruz | 700-900 |
| | Gila Butte | 550-700 |
| Pioneer | Snaketown | 350-550 |
| | Sweetwater | 200-350 |
| | Estrella | 1-200 |
| | Vahki | 300 B.C.-A.D. 1 |

SOURCE: Haury 1976:338.

Whichever way the data eventually lead, it seems certain now that the Hohokam society strongly reflects Mesoamerican societies with modifications due to their distance from the original homeland and their adaptation to the southern Arizona environment.

*Pioneer Period*

The data from the earliest phase of the Pioneer period come mainly from Snaketown and the Red Mountain site (D.H. Morris 1969). As might be expected, Vahki phase sites are few in number and are mostly concentrated in the central Gila-Salt area, although Vahki phase ceramics are found at the Hodges site at Tucson (Gladwin et al. 1937) and possibly in Mattie Canyon in southeast Arizona (Eddy 1958).

Early Pioneer period settlements were small, but they had a large enough population to construct long, wide canals and to produce quantities of luxury goods. The oldest houses were unusually large, 10-15 meters in diameter, and nearly square in plan. The large size, and two entries and two hearths in one instance, suggest the dwellings were for extended families. Later in the period the houses were smaller. Most Hohokam structures were shallow and in many cases were constructed after removing the loose desert soil to the depth of a hard caliche, (calcium carbonate) layer, sometimes a matter of a few centimeters.

During most of the Pioneer period two traditions of house construction appear to have been in vogue. A floor plan that was rectangular with right angle corners and shallow in depth existed side by side with slightly deeper structures that were more square with rounded corners. The superstructures of these two types of houses were similar and consisted of a flat central roof with sloping sides of poles covered with brush or grass laid up against the interior supporting framework.

The square structures have a four-post quadrilateral roof support system, the large posts having been sunk into the floor near each corner. The smaller posts of the walls were placed in shallow holes around the periphery of the structure. The more rectangular buildings had a series of roof support posts placed in the floor near the walls. Occasionally, major roof support posts were also placed along the central axis of the house.

Unlike the villages of other prehistoric Southwestern societies, Hohokam settlements demonstrate a loose dispersal of the houses. Houses were scattered haphazardly with no established directional orientation. The perishable nature of the dwelling meant a short life-span for individual houses. As a result, a village that was occupied for a long period of time usually evidences many overlapping house floors that provide the basis for determining the architectural evolution (fig. 2).

Well-constructed canals appear in the earliest Vahki phase. These canals were used to irrigate fields of economically useful plants, notably maize. The evidence shows that the Hohokam were growing the common bean in the Estrella phase and that cotton was cultivated in the Sweetwater phase. The Hohokam could, apparently, produce two crops a year in their temperate habitat by utilizing the spring runoff from the rivers with the late summer storms permitting a second crop (Bohrer 1970). Undoubtedly, the irrigation canals also helped provide the domestic water needed in the villages; but it is known that from earliest times ground water was also tapped by digging wells.

Although the Hohokam were experts at producing farm crops, evidence at Snaketown suggests that there were times of considerable subsistence stress. Collecting saguaro fruit in summer and mesquite beans in fall provided important supplementary calories (Bohrer 1970), and dependence on all kinds of animals gave them much needed protein. It has been estimated that at the time of Spanish contact, the Pima, who lived as irrigating farmers in the Gila-Salt basin, depended on gathered rather than domesticated foods for up to 50 percent of their diet (Castetter and Bell 1942).

The earliest ceramic products were simple, although technically well constructed. Most of the pottery was thin and plain, ranging in color from brown to gray and fired in an oxidizing atmosphere. Along with this type, known as Vahki Plain, the Hohokam potters also made a red slipped type known as Vahki Red. Both Vahki Plain and Vahki Red, as a pottery tradition, are comparable to the earliest ceramics of Mexico and western North America. The earliest Mogollon and Hohokam ceramics have much in common, although the former finished pottery by coiling and then scraping the surface, and the latter

U. of Ariz., Ariz. State Mus., Tucson.
Fig. 2. Aerial view of a portion of Snaketown, Pinal Co., Ariz. with about 50 exposed house floors representing about 1,000 years of architectural history. Photograph by Helga Teiwes, 1965.

usually finished their vessels by the paddle-and-anvil technique.

Early in the Pioneer period some vessels were decorated with a red paint (fig. 3). The designs are simple geometric forms, usually made with wide lines. By the Sweetwater phase, hatched decoration and occasionally scroll elements appear. Throughout the Pioneer period there was a gradual shift from dark gray to a light buff background, and painted designs underwent a corresponding change in complexity of layout and composition of motifs.

Though most Hohokam pottery was finished by paddle-and-anvil technique, the coiling method was also known, usually limited to small bowls. Sometimes the coils were not smoothed externally and the ribbed effect was further accentuated by mechanically deepening the joints between coils. This lead to exterior grooving, either simulating the effect of coils, or, when texturing the surfaces of paddle-and-anvil-made pottery, a patterned effect. Through time there was a progressive deterioration in grooving, going from a high degree of precision to slap-dash execution. The treatment started early in the Pioneer period and it passed out of existence early in the Colonial period.

Ceramic figurines (fig. 4) were manufactured by hand modeling from the Vahki phase to the Classic period. Most of the figurines represent the human form. Pioneer period figurines are crude with minimal modeling of anatomical features. They generally occur in trash while the later and more realistic examples are associated with cremations. Most archeologists (Morss 1954) suggest that the Southwestern figurine complex is related to that of Mexico, a derivation that is particularly evident for the Hohokam figurine. Explanations of function are usually related, as they are around the world, to fertility.

The famous stone and shell industries of the Hohokam also had their genesis early in the Pioneer period. Carved stone bowls are found in the Vahki phase. Later in the

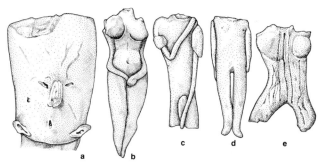

after Haury 1976: fig.13.14.

Fig. 4. Pioneer period ceramic figurines excavated from Snaketown, Pinal Co., Ariz. a-b, Vahki phase figurines of wedge-shaped head form and pregnant female; c-d, figurines of Estrella phase and Pioneer period illustrating arm positions; e, Snaketown phase torso with body incising. Length of a 4.1 cm, rest same scale.

Pioneer period and culminating with the most elaborate forms in the Colonial period, the stone bowls are executed with entwined snakes, horned lizards, birds, and other animals, including humans, sometimes paired and representing both sexes (fig. 5). The recovery of mutilated stone sculptures in caches or as cremation accompaniments suggests religious or votive functions.

Another stone object distinctive of the Hohokam was the palette (see "Prehistory: O'otam," fig. 5, this vol.) on which paints were prepared (Gladwin et al. 1937:122). Pioneer period palettes were well-shaped tablets of hard stone with depressed paint-holding areas but with no further elaboration. By the end of the period they were evolving into rectangular plates of schist with decorated borders and some were even made in effigy form during the Colonial period.

The Hohokam were famous for their stone axes fitted with J-shaped handles in a groove that passed three-quarters around the head (see "Prehistory: O'otam," fig. 8, this vol.). Of particular interest is the fact that the oldest axes, those of the Pioneer period, were the most complicated in concept and the most difficult to make. The groove was framed with ridges to provide a better seat for the handle and the ungrooved edge was provided with a channel paralleling the ax blade designed to receive a wedge with which the haft could be tightened. These attributes were discarded during the Colonial period.

The Hohokam are justly famous for their profuse work in shell (fig. 6), an industry that they practiced from the beginning of the Pioneer period. Shell was used for beads, pendants, rings, bracelets, and as material, along with turquoise, for the production of mosaics. The mosaic art was employed as early as the Vahki phase.

Univalves were often strung whole and used for beads, and sometimes larger shells were cut and ground into disks for stringing. Large bivalves were the primary source for the cut or ground pendants of life and geometric forms as well as the source for bracelets.

after Haury 1937:figs. 93r, r', 89e, g.

Fig. 3. Earliest decorated pottery sherds excavated from Snaketown, Pinal Co., Ariz. a-b, Estrella Red-on-gray with characteristic geometric line designs; c-d, Sweetwater Red-on-gray with scroll motifs. Width of c 20 cm, rest same scale.

U. of Ariz., Ariz. State Mus., Tucson: a, A-26896; b, A-26755; c, A-26763; d, A-26900; e, A-26782; f, A-26757; g, GP-44468; h, GP-43864.

Fig. 5. Pioneer and Colonial period stone sculpture excavated from Snaketown, Pinal Co., Ariz. a-f, Censers with relief carving of snakes, humans, and toads; g-h, effigies, possibly representing horned toads (see also Haury 1976:fig. 11.19-11.24). Length of b 15.8 cm, rest same scale.

Bracelets were fashioned from one-half of *Glycymeris* shells by breaking out the interior of the shell and grinding down the edges. After the Pioneer period the bracelets were often carved with geometric or life forms, especially in the area of the umbo, or hinge, of the shell. The snake, frog, and bird were common motifs. Sometimes near the umbo where the shell was thicker, the carving became so deep as to portray the animal in almost full-round form. The sophisticated acid etching of shell (fig. 7) was invented in the Sedentary period.

Almost all the shell used by the Hohokam originated from the Gulf of California and lesser amounts from the Pacific coast. A single shell found at Los Muertos, a Classic period site, was from the Gulf of Mexico (Haury 1945). The occurrence of red abalone *(Haliotis rufescens)* indicates at least some shell came from the coast of California, not the Gulf of California. Freshwater and land shells were used infrequently because of their fragile nature.

Shell was probably obtained by collecting trips to the ocean and gulf shores as well as by trade with peoples closer to the raw material. The Gila and Salt rivers provided an easily accessible route to the west. Brand (1938) and Hayden (1970) both suggest a trade route from the Gulf of California through northern Mexico to the Gila-Salt drainage. Scattered Hohokam sherds, suggesting campsites and trail use, have been reported from the northeast coast of the Gulf of California (Gifford 1946:217-219).

Technological studies of shell wastage demonstrate clearly that the Hohokam developed a shell industry unique to them and that the trade network indicated not only the importation of raw shell but also the export of finished products to the Mogollon and Anasazi.

The basic utilitarian tools were grinding stones consisting of the nether stone known as the metate, and the companion handstone, or mano. Although similar tools had been used for several thousand years by the people of the Cochise culture, the Hohokam metate was usually of the trough variety (fig. 8) fitted with a two-handed mano, as opposed to the more usual older basin form, in which a one-handed mano was used. The Hohokam were the first people in the long history of the implement to shape the exteriors by pecking to bring them to a symmetrical form, a treatment that persisted into later periods. Chipped tools, such as projectile points (fig. 9), were stemmed.

Treatment of the dead, beginning in the Vahki phase, was traditionally by cremation. Inhumation was acceptable (D.H. Morris 1969) during all periods but it was not

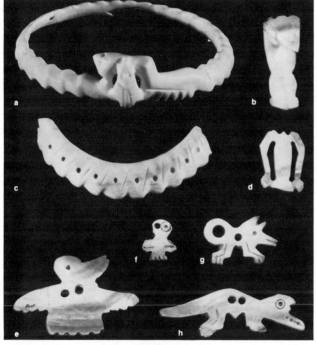

U. of Ariz., Ariz. State Mus., Tucson: a, GP-45456; b, A-25859; c, A-22954; d, A-26339; e, GP-44930; f, GP-43536; g, GP-44930; h, GP-05117.

Fig. 6. Carved and cut shell bracelets and pendants excavated from Snaketown, Pinal Co., Ariz. (see Gladwin et al. 1937:142-144; Haury 1976:fig. 15.17, 15.28). Diameter of a 8 cm, rest same scale.

a popular alternative. The San Pedro Cochise practiced both cremation (Haury 1957) and inhumation (Sayles and Antevs 1941; Haury 1950).

The earliest cremations were not left at the site of the crematory fire. Rather, the few remaining bones were placed with shattered vessels in an elongated trench or in pits. Later in the Pioneer period stone artifacts were also found with the cremations. None of the Pioneer period cremations appears to have been of the primary type, that is, left where they were cremated. Cremation not only destroyed or damaged most of the funerary offerings placed on the fire but also destroyed the physical remains of the people, thereby denying the archeologist much of the information usually gleaned from skeletal studies.

## Colonial Period

As suggested by the name, the Colonial period was one of expansion for the Hohokam. Their range was extended into drainages tributary to the Salt and Gila rivers. There is evidence also of increased social interaction with Mesoamerica in the form of newly introduced traits,

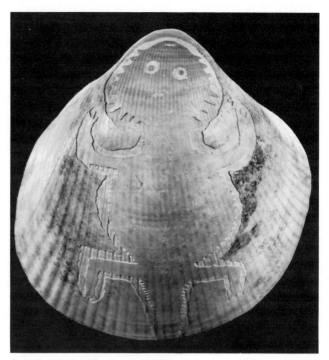

U. of Ariz., Ariz. State Mus., Tucson: GP-44691.

Fig. 7. Acid and wax etching of horned toad on *Cardium* shell excavated from Snaketown, Pinal Co., Ariz. Diameter 10.2 cm.

including the ball court. Existing artifact types, especially luxury items, were elaborated in ways that suggest inspirations from the south. Flamboyance in arts and crafts and the peak of excellence in their production distinguish the period. In most respects the Colonial period was, in fact, the apogee of the Hohokam.

Colonial period sites have been the object of more excavation than those of any other period. Excavations in villages, such as the Grewe site (Woodward 1931) and Roosevelt:9:6 (Haury 1932), as well as Snaketown and sites worked on in salvage operations have provided more information than for any other period in the Hohokam sequence.

For as yet poorly understood reasons, the Hohokam extended their territory out from the Gila and Salt valleys to the north up the Verde River toward the Flagstaff region, north and west along the Agua Fria River toward Prescott, into the San Pedro and Santa Cruz valleys of southeastern Arizona, and east along the Gila River to the Safford region (fig. 1). The incursions into new areas were not solely isolated outpost villages far removed from other Hohokam settlements. Rather, these major streams, whose courses apparently served as the routes of migration, were lined with numerous Hohokam sites.

U. of Ariz., Ariz. State Mus., Tucson: A-26128, A-26571.

Fig. 8. Trough metates of basalt excavated from Snaketown, Pinal Co., Ariz. Length of right 53.5 cm, other same scale.

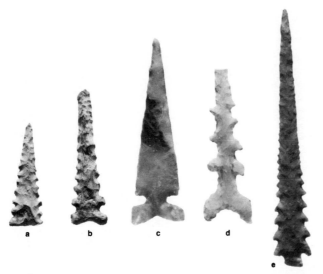

Fig. 9. Hohokam projectile points excavated from Snaketown, Pinal Co., Ariz. a-d, Sedentary period points; e, Colonial period barbed point. Long barbed projectile points may represent the work of specialized craftsmen or be imported items (Haury 1976:296). Length of e 7.6 cm, rest same scale.

The reasons for the expansion were probably manifold. The Hohokam had introduced a successful technique of irrigation farming that produced food surpluses stimulating population increases. These techniques were then adapted to other areas of low native population in regions peripheral to the major Gila-Salt area, in turn allowing a much more productive use of the lowland environments than during the pre-Hohokam occupation. Concomitantly, there was increasing interaction with the higher cultures to the south in Mesoamerica, with perhaps some population incursions into Arizona from the region and, therefore, increased stimulus for trade and territorial expansion.

Although there was a cultural continuum from Pioneer to Colonial the changes in Hohokam culture appeared relatively suddenly, so that the Gila Butte phase, the first in the Colonial period, has been described as "transitional in every meaning of the word" (Gladwin et al. 1937:256). It is this phase when many new traits made their appearance.

There was little change in domestic architecture; rather there were slight modifications of existing patterns. Villages were larger and sites more numerous, reflecting the expanding population. Houses are randomly scattered throughout the settlements.

The architectural additions to Hohokam culture, the platform mound and the ball court, are organized around ceremonial and communal functions, obviously having their origin in Mesoamerica. The concept of the platform mound was introduced earlier than that of the ball court, and perhaps in an informal way as early as the Snaketown phase of the Pioneer period (Haury 1976:93). Early

in the Pioneer period trash was randomly scattered in thin sheets or pits around the village. Only later was rubbish piled into mounds, which were sometimes shaped and made level and plastered with caliche. This provided a hard-surfaced mound that could support a structure or be used for dancing or serve as an area for sacred functions. Like the Mesoamerican platform mound, Hohokam structures of this type were frequently remodeled. The real florescence of platform mound construction was not until the Sedentary and Classic periods.

The Hohokam ball court (fig. 10) is an elongated, slightly oval, and unroofed structure excavated into the soil. There are two types of court. The Snaketown type, which is relatively large, from 52 to 65 meters long (Wasley and Johnson 1965:82), is usually oriented east and west with expanding bulbous end fields. The sides are relatively parallel near the center of the court. The Casa Grande type is smaller, ranging from about 18 to 35 meters, and tends to be oriented to the north and south. The Casa Grande type is more oval than the Snaketown type and, although it has ramp entries on both ends, there are no end features. Both types of court usually have stone end and center markers. The end markers are placed at equal distances from the center marker, resembling the deployment of floor features in Mesoamerican courts. The Snaketown type of court is a hallmark of the Colonial period, and the Casa Grande type, of the Sedentary and Classic periods (Wasley and Johnson 1965:84).

Although early investigators referred to these oval depressions with encompassing ridges as reservoirs, wells, corrals, and sun temples, and they have even been suggested as dance plazas (Ferdon 1967), their primary function as ball courts seems the most likely explanation. Although lacking some of the features of the Mesoamerican types, notably stone rings in side walls and usually

Fig. 10. Colonial period ball court I at Snaketown, Pinal Co., Ariz. with west half completely excavated showing concave curve of south and north walls. Court length about 60 m. Photograph by E.B. Sayles, 1935.

masonry lining of the walls, the Hohokam ball court shares enough characteristics to make the relationship obvious. Mesoamerican ball courts are found as far north as Casas Grandes in the state of Chihuahua (Wasley 1959:148, 1960:245; Di Peso 1974:410ff.) although the major concentration is in central Mexico and the Maya region. Rubber balls have never been found associated with a Hohokam ball court, although two have been excavated in Hohokam sites (Amsden 1936; Haury 1937a).

There were obviously many functions to the ball court and platform mound, but by analogy from Mesoamerica it can be inferred that the platform mound was used for religious activities and the ball court for a semisacred game. Both types of structures have the function of integrating a community or communities allowing for rites of intensifications and the exchange of goods. In all likelihood, they also reaffirmed the social ties to Mesoamerica. Therefore, it can be inferred that the Colonial period was one in which there was less community autonomy and more intercommunity contact.

The irrigation canals (fig. 11) of the Colonial period undergo a great expansion in length providing a large increase in the acreage under irrigation. Not only are the

U. of Ariz., Ariz. State Mus., Tucson.

Fig. 11. Four overlapping irrigation canals of the Colonial to Classic periods (ca. A.D. 800 to 1400), excavated at Snaketown, Pinal Co., Ariz. Photograph by Helga Teiwes, 1965.

canals longer, but also they are narrower and deeper, carrying more water with less evaporation. Canals were also sometimes used primarily for domestic water supply during the Colonial period. The Henderson site near Prescott (Weed and Ward 1970) had a small canal diverting water from a spring through the village and into a cistern.

Cremation, either of the primary or secondary type, was still the preferred method of disposal of the dead during the Colonial period. In primary cremations, pits were dug and the body and offerings cremated in place and then buried; in the case of secondary cremations, the ashes were removed from the crematorium along with the remnants of offerings and they were placed in a specially prepared pit or trench. The pit cremation appears most commonly in the Colonial period (Wasley and Johnson 1965:87). By the Colonial period definite crematory areas are often distinguishable at large sites rather than simple random scattering of cremations throughout the villages.

There is modification of form and painted design in Hohokam ceramics at the beginning of the Colonial period, that is, during the Gila Butte phase. Use of life forms (fig. 12) increased as did a variety of geometric forms, some resembling letters in the English alphabet. These elements are repeated over and over in bands circling the vessel, which gives a flowing and lively appearance to the design layout. During the Gila Butte phase the percentage of painted ceramics to plain ware increases dramatically and there is the first appearance of legged vessels. The careful incising of bowl exterior, which begins to degenerate by the end of the Pioneer period, is shallow and poorly controlled during the Gila Butte phase. The trait is no longer present in the Santa Cruz phase types.

Colonial period ceramic figurines are somewhat more realistic than earlier forms. The majority of the human figurines are female and often depict sexual characteristics but do not exaggerate them. In the Colonial period bits of clay are added to the figurine to represent articles of clothing, headresses, and head, arm, and ankle bands. Black and red paint were occasionally added to represent body painting or tattooing.

During the Colonial period work in stone becomes much more elaborate, although there is little change in the fashioning of utilitarian stone tools. The long, narrow, barbed projectile point is a popular form during the Santa Cruz phase. Often hundreds are found in cremations, warped and brittle from the crematory fire. These points were obviously produced solely to be used as funerary offerings. The three-quarter grooved ax loses its distinctive raised ridge in the late Colonial period. It is during this stage that there is a burst of enthusiasm for the carving of nonutilitarian stone artifacts. Small stone bowls, sculptured in the form of all manner of animals, especially snakes, toads, and birds, are common. Undecorated stone bowls are also manufactured, and there are

83

Fig. 12. Santa Cruz Red-on-buff ware from Snaketown, Pinal Co., Ariz. painted with repeated bird and human motifs. left to right, Plate decorated with quails with top-knot feathers, miniature jar with figures of hand-holding dancers, and sherd with burden carriers. Plate diameter 20 cm, rest same scale.

some stone effigies that do not have a bowllike cavity. A great many of these stone effigies and bowls are found deliberately destroyed in caches that are unassociated with cremations or other features.

The elaborate stone palettes with decorated borders were fashioned during the Gila Butte phase for the first time. For these highly stylized items Mesoamerican prototypes are known from western Mexico in the states of Guererro and Michoacán (Haury 1976:289). By the Santa Cruz phase the palettes become more elaborate with finely carved borders and are sometimes constructed as human or animal effigies. The artistic format of palette decoration became so complicated, and yet to a degree stereotyped, that the Hohokam palette is a good relative dating device.

Not only was stone more important as a medium of artistic expression during the Colonial period, but also the carving of shell became more common and the artifacts and designs much more varied, especially in the late Colonial period. Many small pieces of shell were carved or ground as pendants into geometric or animal forms similar to the stone carving. Shell beads increase in number and variety, and bracelets often have animal or bird figures carved in the umbo. In addition, shell is used as a mosaic material, an art form that becomes greatly elaborated.

The mosaic plaque, or mirror, is first found in the Colonial period and is yet another instance of contact with Mesoamerica where they were made. Most existing specimens have been badly damaged by the crematory fire. On a circular stone, 10 to 25 centimeters in diameter, thin iron pyrite plates, laboriously cut from crystals, were carefully pieced together and set into an adhesive. The cutting of the hard reflective mineral, the occasional pseudo-cloisonné decoration, in fact the entire artifact, is evidence of Mexican craftsmanship.

### Sedentary Period

Hohokam boundaries are relatively stable during the Sedentary period, except for expansion to the north, near Flagstaff. In addition, there was a conservatism manifest in arts and crafts. With a few notable exceptions, the great flamboyance and experimentation in new art and craft forms that was the hallmark of the Colonial period was toned down by the Sedentary period. This is not to deny that there were important elaborations on earlier art and architectural forms; however, in general, most artifacts seem to be mass produced with a consequent loss of quality. There were apparently more craftsmen and fewer artists.

The intrusion of the Hohokam into the region east of Flagstaff in the Sedentary period has been explained as a result of an improved farming situation due to the eruption of Sunset Crater in A.D. 1066 and 1067 (Colton 1960). With the eruption of the volcano, a thin layer of cinder and ash covered a vast area, which permitted precipitation to seep into the soil but retarded evaporation, thereby vastly improving farming conditions. After this eruption there was a significant influx of population, including Hohokam, into the cinder-covered area to exploit this agricultural potential, so some of the large sites have a considerable Hohokam component, especially Winona and Ridge Ruins (McGregor 1937, 1941) east of Flagstaff.

Domestic house forms continued the trend toward greater length to width, although a minor tradition of a square house with rounded corners also persisted.

There is some evidence that plazas were constructed at least at one site during the Sedentary period. At the Citrus site (Wasley and Johnson 1965) a 20 by 35 meter caliche floor was apparently purposely laid down over some 30 centimeters of trash. Houses were scattered randomly around the plaza. This floor probably served as a dance plaza and communal activity area.

Again, the most impressive changes in architecture lie in the realm of ceremonial structures. The platform mounds become not just a plaster-capped rubbish heap but are most often a structure constructed solely for religious functions.

The most impressive Hohokam platform mound is at the Gatlin site near Gila Bend (Wasley 1960). The major mound went through five construction stages, a typical Mesoamerican characteristic. The main part of the mound was composed of earth and trash fill with clay and caliche veneers. The general outline of the mound is oval with sloping walls. No evidence of a ramp or stairs, so characteristic of Mesoamerican mounds, was found. During some construction stages, secondary platform mounds were connected to the major mound by clay walls. Two levels of construction had hearths on top of the mound, and on the fourth stage the post hole outline of a rectangular structure was delineated. It is interesting to note that there were few domestic structures at the Gatlin site and that the cremations were unusually rich, leading Wasley (1960) to the conclusion that the Gatlin site may have been a ceremonial center. Mound 16 (fig. 13) at Snaketown is a one-meter-high mound about 14 meters in diameter that had been remodeled eight times. Each time the mound was remodeled it became flatter so that after the last remodeling a stockade was placed around the perimeter to more sharply define its limits (Haury 1976:84ff.).

All types of cremation activity from earlier periods continued to be employed in the Sedentary period, and, in addition, an occasional cremation is found that had been placed in a jar, sometimes covered by an inverted bowl (Wasley and Johnson 1965:87), a practice more common in the Classic period. Extended inhumation appears to be more common in Sedentary period sites than in earlier periods (Johnson 1964), a pattern that becomes the mode during the Classic.

There is considerable change in ceramic design and in vessel form during the Sedentary. The large storage vessels with the Gila shoulder (a sharp angle formed by the upper and lower parts of the jar) are common. There are also many types of small, thick-walled vessels, animal effigies, and footed vessels. Life forms are rarely present as painted design elements, and geometric designs are extremely complicated with offset panels of solids, fringed lines, interlocking scrolls, and other motifs that are evenly and accurately proportioned over the entire vessel surface. The percentage of decorated to plain vessels increased, so that by this period almost 40 percent of all ceramics was decorated. Plain redware, which was no longer produced during the Colonial period, is again manufactured in small amounts.

Ceramic human figurines in the Sedentary consist solely of realistically executed heads. Impressions in the

U. of Ariz., Ariz. State Mus., Tucson.
Fig. 13. Platform Mound 16 at Snaketown, Pinal Co., Ariz. top, Flat-topped mound of the Sedentary period (Haury 1976:84–91); bottom, incremental additions and final encirclement of the structure with a palisade as suggested by the postholes. Photographs by Helga Teiwes, 1965.

hollow clay head at the neck suggest that the bodies of the figurines were manufactured of perishable textiles or plant fibers. Ceramic animal figurines are sometimes found in caches, purposely destroyed.

The utilitarian stone artifacts of the Sedentary period show little change over the earlier stages, although there is a greater variety of projectile point types, especially those with lateral notches. However, the nonutilitarian stone artifacts show less skill in execution and less variety of form than in the Colonial period. Stone effigy bowls and palettes, for example, are not so ornate; they appear to be more hurriedly manufactured and are less numerous than in earlier periods. Stone effigies without the bowllike depressions were no longer manufactured.

Much of the creative energy seemed to be diverted from the carving of stone to the working in shell with new artistic modes and new techniques. All earlier artifact types and manufacturing techniques were carried over from previous periods and the number of utilized species of marine shell increased. In addition, shell was painted and etched, and whole shell trumpets are found for the first time.

The painting and etching of shell went hand in hand. Large *Laevicardium* shells were coated with a pitch in geometric or animal designs and then immersed in a weak acid solution, probably produced from the fermented fruit of the saguaro cactus. Exposed surfaces of the shell were eaten away by the acid leaving the pitch-protected areas to stand out in relief. Often the shell was then painted, usually in red and green or blue. Large trumpets were fashioned by grinding off the spines of *Strombus galeatus* or *Melongena patula* shells, although they, like etched shell artifacts, were never abundant. Shell mosaics continued to be manufactured and even increased in complexity.

The mosaic plaques become more elaborate during the Sedentary period. The pyrite incrustation does not extend to the edge during this period, but the beveled edge and sometimes the opposing side is highly decorated. The surface to be decorated was usually heavily coated with a sizing substance into which a design was cut. The excised parts were then filled with white, red, yellow, or blue pigments. The mosaic plaques are exactly like those manufactured in Mesoamerica (Lothrop 1936:54; Mason 1927:206; Kidder, Jennings, and Shook 1946) and also have the same typological sequence. In all likelihood, the majority of the plaques found at Hohokam sites are of Mesoamerican origin.

Copper bells, of Mexican origin, are first found in the Sedentary period. Spectrographic analysis suggests that the source of the copper is western coastal Mexico in the states of Jalisco and Nayarit (Meighan 1960; Pendergast 1962:376–377). The bells are small, usually not more than 2.0 centimeters long and 1.5 centimeters wide. Manufactured by the lost wax technique, they have eyelets for suspension and slits in the resonators, which have pebbles or copper nodules for rattlers.

The end of the Sedentary period is signaled by many changes in Hohokam society. There is a movement of people from sites that were occupied for hundreds of years. Seldom does Classic period trash overlie Sedentary rubbish (Haury 1945:204), and Schroeder (1952:331) demonstrates that in the Gila Basin only 8 percent of the sites show a continuous Sedentary to Classic period occupation. Apparently the Sedentary-Classic period transition is a result of a different type of articulation with the desert environment; but what occasioned this change, be it climate variation, different types of social interaction, or modification of edaphic conditions, is at present unknown.

## Classic Period

Classic Hohokam was a period of great change with evidence of social interaction from several sources. Con-

sequently, the events of this last stage of Hohokam are subject to more varied interpretations than any other period since the Pioneer. Most of these innovations in Hohokam society have been ascribed to increased contact, or even invasion, by the Salado culture from the northeast (Haury 1945). Other archeologists have ascribed the change to increased contact with Mexico or to a Sinagua penetration from the Flagstaff area (Schroeder 1960). However, some archeologists (Wasley 1966) see much of what was once thought to be intrusive into the Hohokam as the result of internal development.

There is so much change due to apparent contact with other groups that the Classic Hohokam period is often thought of as a misnomer, as it may no longer be truly Hohokam. Additions attributed to the Salado peoples who moved into the Salt and Gila basin from the Tonto basin-Globe-Roosevelt Lake area include multistoried buildings; Gila, Tonto, and Pinto polychrome pottery; inhumations; compound enclosing walls; and hoes and adzes (Haury 1945; Doyel 1974). Schroeder (1960) has said that this complex of traits was introduced earlier, about A.D. 1150 and not A.D. 1300, by the Sinagua, and that the Hohokam were driven out or totally acculturated; however, in the light of later studies, Schroeder's ideas are difficult to support. Some archeologists (Ferdon 1955) see some of the traits in the Classic period as evidence of continued interaction with Mexico.

The Classic period is divided into an earlier Soho phase, which represents a period of some change and increased experimentation, and a later Civano phase, which evidenced even greater innovation and departure from earlier Hohokam traditions due to increased interaction with other peoples.

There was great territorial contraction of the Hohokam at the end of the Classic. Although there was only a slight reduction of the Hohokam core area in the Gila-Salt valleys, many of the frontierlike Hohokam extensions into areas such as the Upper Verde and Agua Fria valleys show no evidence of Hohokam occupation during the Classic. The contraction of Hohokam territory was not an isolated phenomenon, but part of a pan-Southwestern episode. Whatever the reason for the movements of people affecting the areal distribution of cultures in the Southwest, it was not confined to the Hohokam. Not only is there change in the areal distribution of the last period of the Hohokam, but also there is a definite shift in the settlement pattern with a tendency in some areas to construct villages at some distance from the rivers where domestic water was supplied by canals.

There is also architectural innovation during the Classic. By the end of the Sedentary the Hohokam were building wattle and daub or jacal houses in pits, but they also began to experiment with new types of wall structures including solid clay walls and clay walls reinforced with posts (Haury 1945; Hayden 1957). These types of construction were elaborated on during the beginning of the Classic and became more common, although the typical Hohokam house in a pit continued to be constructed. Sometimes the surface, clay-walled structures consisted of contiguous rooms, but there were no multi-story houses in the Soho phase as were so characteristic of the later Civano phase. Clay- and post-reinforced structures were sometimes constructed on top of massive walled mounds two meters or more in height. The mounds were constructed of thick clay walls and supporting interior walls, forming a honeycomblike structure. Rubbish and earth were used to form the fill between the walls (Hayden 1957; Hammack 1969). The enclosing compound wall becomes a common architectural format in the Classic. The long axis of these rectangular enclosures is usually oriented in a north-south direction and within are houses on mounds or at ground level. Some of the compound walls of clay or stone were no more than one meter high, but others were constructed to a height of more than seven meters. Often there are no entries to the compound, which meant access by a ladder; in other cases there is a single portal for entry.

Even with the advent of new and more complex architectural forms there is no discernible village orientation. Clay-walled houses, clay-walled houses on artificial mounds, and houses in pits were scattered randomly around the village. The Classic communities were larger than Sedentary villages, and this, along with the concept of contiguous houses rather than scattered houses in pits, must have given the village a more compact, crowded appearance.

By the Civano phase multistory houses, or "great houses," with massive clay walls enclosed in rectangular compounds were constructed, the most prominent example of which is figure 14. The clay walls of the "great houses" were sometimes over two meters thick in order to support the upper stories. At Los Muertos there were 25 compounds (Haury 1945) giving an indication of the large population of this community. The settlement was approximately one mile long and one-half mile wide. Even with a community this large, no village layout is apparent. Although the Classic villages were larger, there were fewer of them so the population was becoming more concentrated, a pan-Southwestern phenomenon at this time.

The function of the compound wall is not known, although it has often been suggested as a defensive measure or a means of separating different social classes of people. Although there are analogies of the compound villages of southern Arizona with the walled settlements of the Anasazi to the north, many investigators feel the Hohokam compound is a Mexican trait (Ferdon 1955; Wasley 1966).

The function of the "great houses" like the one at Casa Grande is also unknown. They have been suggested as priests' houses, ceremonial structures, observatories, and communal storage houses. Ball courts continue to be

Smithsonian, NAA.
Fig. 14. Northeast view of multistoried "Great House" at Casa Grande, Pinal Co., Ariz. representing the 14th-century intrusion of Puebloid architecture to the Hohokam (see C. Mindeleff 1897; Fewkes 1912). Photograph possibly by C. Mindeleff, 1890.

constructed but are not so numerous and are usually the Casa Grande type.

Canals reach their largest extent during the Classic period, yet some of the villages remained close to the rivers. Pueblo de Los Muertos and Casa Grande, for example, are large sites supplied with water by canals from river sources approximately six miles away. With the great extension of canals large villages were no longer restricted to the immediate areas along the river systems. In some areas, such as the Gila Bend region, canals were not constructed, suggesting alternate methods of farming (Wasley and Johnson 1965:80). The use of alternate farming techniques can be demonstrated in the lower Agua Fria drainage, where canals are used in the Classic period as well as dry farming techniques, terrace systems, and floodwater farming (Gumerman and Johnson 1971).

Hohokam burial practices during the Classic period shifted to a preference for secondary cremations. Ashes were placed in jars, often with a bowl inverted over the neck of the jar. Primary cremations are also occasionally found. Inhumation increased in popularity during the Classic period and has often been suggested as a Salado-introduced practice. Haury (1945:43–44) has pointed out that at Los Muertos the extended inhumations usually have associated Salado ceramics, Gila and Tonto polychromes. The cremations are usually in red or red-on-buff vessels. Some excavations (Wasley 1966) have indicated that the dichotomy between burial types and ceramic types is not so clear-cut and also that inhumation, although not common, was practiced by pre-Classic Hohokam. However, the weight of evidence does suggest that the popularity of inhumation in the Classic may be attributed to the Salado.

Ceramics also change considerably in form and decoration during the Classic period. There is an appreciable decline in the amount of red-on-buff pottery being manufactured, decreasing from the high of about 40 percent in the Sedentary to 3 or 4 percent in the Classic. The Gila shouldered vessel appears with less frequency, and thick-walled ceramic vessels disappear. Life forms are absent as a decorative element, and designs tend to be geometric with interlocking elements. There is more use of free space incorporated in the designs, although the use of repetitive banding is common. Undecorated ceramics, especially red ware, increase in frequency. Gila and Tonto polychrome, indicative of Salado contact with the Hohokam, represent a relatively small percentage of the total ceramics in the central Gila and Salt drainages (Wasley 1966). Yet, it is widely distributed in southern Arizona and probably locally made (Danson and Wallace 1956; Pailes 1964).

There is no major change in utilitarian stone tools from Sedentary to Classic, indicating more continuity than in most other realms of material culture between the two periods (Weed 1972; Weaver 1972). Exceptions are the presence of adz, double bitted ax, and hoe, suggesting perhaps a change in agricultural techniques also evidenced by the different types of agricultural plots mentioned above. Luxury stone items decrease in number and in sophistication of craftsmanship. Stone palettes are rare. Mosaic pyrite mirrors are no longer in use.

More shell artifacts, especially as mosaic pieces, are produced in the Classic than ever before, but there is a reduction in the number of species worked and type of products manufactured. The etching of shell is no longer an artistic medium.

The Classic period is perplexing with many varied interpretations for the rapid innovation (Doyel 1974). Most archeologists see the Classic period Hohokam as a people who were adjusting to the environment in somewhat different ways by attempting more varied agricultural techniques and by shifting their settlement pattern. Probably a more important influence is the adjustments that had to be made due to the Salado contact and perhaps changes in the type of Mesoamerican influence. The prevailing opinion is that the Salado, although influential in accelerating change among the Hohokam, probably did not "invade" Hohokam territory or even migrate into it in large numbers. Rather, Classic Hohokam is seen by some as a logical evolutionary step from pre-Classic and that for some as yet unexplained reason, the interaction with Salado was greatly increased at this time.

The end of the Classic, between about 1400 and 1450, is also the end of the Hohokam as an archeologically describable culture in southern Arizona. The reasons for the void in the archeological record, created by the abandonment of the towns and villages, the dispersal of the population, and the decline of a lifeway that had grown progressively more complex over 1,400 years, has

been the subject of much speculation. Among the factors that have been proposed are disease, factional contentions between or among the Hohokam and Salado, nomadic invaders such as the Apache, shifts in the climatic regime, and even earthquakes. Among some of the more favored ideas are those that view the Hohokam as dependent on Mesoamerican traders; with the collapse of the high cultures to the south, the Hohokam could no longer sustain themselves (Di Peso 1968, 1968a). Another hypothesis attributes the end of the Hohokam to the failure of the irrigation systems as a result of the lack of maintenance, climate change, or erosion or salinization of the soil (El Zur 1965). It is also possible, if the Salado were really present in large numbers and filled high sociopolitical positions, that when they left, they may have created a leadership vacuum that the Hohokam could not fill. There is some evidence that the Hohokam remained in Salado communities after the dispersal of the Salado, since Hohokam houses in pits have been constructed over and through Salado structures (Haury 1945:212; Hammack 1969). Most likely there was not a single reason for the decline of the Hohokam, since most so-called cultural declines cannot be attributed to a single overriding factor. Many of the causes listed above, or others not suggested, may have been responsible.

There is then a gap in the archeological record from the mid-fifteenth century to the arrival of the Spanish. No sites have been excavated or even surely recognized for this period. Most archeologists believe that with a dispersed population and a simple life the post-Classic sites are difficult to detect. Concerted efforts to find these sites have not been made. There is also the suggestion by Di Peso (1956) that the Classic lasted almost until the arrival of the Spanish and that there really is no void.

What was the fate of the Hohokam? Most archeologists (Ezell 1963) feel that the Hohokam became the present-day Pima, who were living in houses in pits, had a dispersed settlement pattern, and were practicing irrigation agriculture upon the arrival of the Spanish. Di Peso (1956), on the other hand, believes the Pima were the original native population who returned to the area after the retreat of the Hohokam to Mexico. For whatever reason, the inhabitants of the Gila and Salt valleys were living a much simpler life at the time of the Spanish entrada than they were during the Hohokam era.

## Regional Variation and Social Organization

The Hohokam culture, like any other, was not uniform over its entire areal distribution. There were many local variations on the idealized patterns presented here, especially beginning in the Colonial period in the northern river valleys (Breternitz 1960), the Santa Cruz and San Pedro river valleys (Zahniser 1966), and in the Papagueria (Haury 1950; Goodyear 1975). Some of these variations are a result of local environmental differences, such as the distinction between the River and Desert Hohokam (Haury 1950). It was simply not possible to sustain a more elaborate culture without irrigation in the extremely arid Papagueria. Other examples of environmental adaptation are found at the Henderson site near Prescott, where house plans are typical Hohokam, but the brush superstructures were coated with clay because of the severe winters (Weed and Ward 1970). The local clays and tempering materials also affected the appearance of the regional Hohokam ceramics.

Environmental differences cannot, of course, explain all regional differences, such as the preference for inhumation rather than cremation in the Papagueria (Haury 1950:547) and the preference for extended burials at the Henderson site (Weed and Ward 1970). Much of the regional variation can be explained by different types of, and more intense, interaction with other cultures at the periphery of the Hohokam region.

Still other explanations of regional variation may involve the Hohokam social organization. In the Central Gila and Salt drainage, the heartland of the Hohokam, irrigation was extensive, sites large, and the production and use of luxury items common. It would be surprising if the Hohokam did not have a weakly stratified society to engineer, construct, and maintain the canals and supervise the production and distribution of the luxury items. A number of canals link several villages, suggesting intervillage cooperation and perhaps even dominance of one village over others. It is not difficult to imagine Snaketown being a special type of community with satellite villages. The two ball courts and numerous platform mounds at Snaketown suggest the village may have provided the social, religious, and economic integrating force for a number of villages. The farther one goes from the major streams, the simpler and smaller become the sites and the artifacts. It would be logical to assume that these dispersed and simpler Hohokam settlements depended on the larger sites for certain functions and services. Certainly, the obvious difference between the riverine villages and the desert communities demands a different type of social organization. What is unknown is the degree of autonomy or dependence of the riverine communities with one another and with the smaller more desert-oriented sites.

## Ties with Mesoamerica

Throughout this chapter mention has been made of the relationships between the Hohokam and Mesoamerica, largely on the basis of artifactual and architectural similarities. In fact, the evidence from the Snaketown investigations suggests that the Hohokam themselves were a group that migrated from Mexico several centuries before Christ. Later, especially between A.D. 500 and 1200, there was massive contact, evidenced by the platform mound, ball court, macaws, stone palettes, copper bells, mosaic plaques, and some Mesoamerican sherds (Haury 1976:343ff.). What has not been discussed is the infinitely more complex subject regarding the nature of these relationships.

The Mesoamerican traits, with the exception of the platform mound and ball court, indicate solely contact and not the type of relationship between Mesoamerica and the Hohokam. The two specialized architectural forms suggest the Hohokam had a somewhat Mesoamerican-like, if obviously less elaborate, socioreligious system. Whether these architectural forms served the same functions in both areas or indicate religious control of the Hohokam by the Mesoamericans is not understood. Although Di Peso (1968, 1968a) has stated that the entire Southwest as far north as Wichita, Kansas, was dominated by Mesoamerican groups in order to control trade in turquoise, copper, salt, peyote, and slaves, it is doubtful if actual physical dominance, in the guise of religion, could be maintained over such a large area. Other archeologists, such as Haury (1976), see a less formalized interaction system based on barter with little or no control of the Hohokam by the Mesoamerican people—rather a mutually beneficial, or symbiotic, trading relationship. With this view the similarity in religious structures would be due to common historical roots and attempts at imitating the civilizations to the south.

Although the exact source of Mesoamerican contact with the Hohokam is difficult to locate with precision, many of the individual, earlier traits, such as copper bells and stone palettes, seem to derive from far to the south in western Mexico—the states of Guanajuato, Michoacán, Jalisco, and Nayarit. Therefore, it would seem likely that the contact between the two areas was by long-distance traders, so often depicted as burden-carrying individuals in Hohokam ceramic design elements. By A.D. 1200 the Mesoamerican contacts become less apparent, perhaps due to the crumbling of the Toltec empire to the south and the weakening of the connections of Casas Grandes in Chihuahua as a link between the Southwest, especially the Anasazi, and Mesoamerica.

The relationships south to north are now obvious and if the present international border between Mexico and the United States were 150 miles farther north, the northern peripheral Mesoamerican character of the Hohokam would probably have been more readily recognized some time ago. The task now is not to document more evidence of contact but rather to understand the nature of these relationships.

## Summary

The Hohokam entered southern Arizona from Mexico in approximately 300 B.C. to start settled village life based on large-scale irrigation. Villages were small and located along the riverine environment at first.

By the Colonial period the amount of land under

cultivation had increased greatly as had the territorial expansion of the Hohokam. In addition, the Colonial period saw increased contact with Mexico as evidenced by artifact types and, more important, ceremonial and communal structures such as the ball courts and platform mounds. These architectural features and the extensive canal systems serving several villages suggest intervillage cooperation, if not control, based on social, religious, and economic ties. The Colonial period emphasizes the success of Hohokam culture based primarily on the exploitive technique of large-scale irrigation along with social and economic ties to higher cultures to the south. It is probably no accident that this is the period that also had great flamboyance and experimentation in the arts and crafts.

During the Sedentary period there was a slight contraction of Hohokam territory, but there is no evidence of decreased contact with Mexico or a less stable subsistence base. Some of the arts and crafts declined in quality, but there was also new experimentation in some areas. The end of the Sedentary period was a time of change. In many areas there was a shift in the settlement pattern from areas at some distance from the major streams to the floodplains or first terrace; in other regions the settlements are located farther from the rivers. Few Classic sites overlay Sedentary villages. It appears that there may have been a slight climatic change or a change in the quality of the agricultural plots, since different types of agriculture were attempted in environmental situations not utilized before.

The Classic period is one of true innovation. Architecture changed to more surface structures, compounds, multistory houses, and houses on platforms. Extended inhumation and cremation were the customary burial methods, and some additions and deletions were made to the artifact inventory. It has been suggested that this innovation was due to: invading or migrating intrusions of the Salado people from the north; subtle, but unexplained, Salado influence; infusion of ideas or people from Mexico; or primarily an indigenous development out of Sedentary Hohokam.

The end of the Classic marks the end of the Hohokam. When the Spanish arrived they found the Pima, the probable descendants of the Hohokam, practicing canal irrigation but living a much simpler life in essence than the Hohokam. The cause for the decline of the Classic is not known, but most archeologists feel it was due to a failure of the canal systems for a variety of reasons or to the collapse of a supportive Mesoamerican culture. Whatever the reason, it brought to a close an amazingly successful effort to produce a good livelihood for a large population in the deserts of southern Arizona.

# Prehistory: O'otam

CHARLES C. DI PESO

Some 180 years after the echo of the first conquistadors' steel reverberated throughout New Spain, the Jesuits entered upper Pimeria and constructed their missions of penetration (Kubler 1940:17) among the so-called heathen O'otam. These Jesuits were the first to put to paper Christian reactions to the indigenous Chichimecs who occupied this arid northern rim of Christendom (Bolton 1936). They described the territory as that portion of the Gran Chichimeca (Di Peso 1968, 1968a) that lay west of the continental divide and, more specifically, south of the Gila Valley, east of the Colorado River, west of the San Pedro drainage, and north of the middle Yaqui River system (fig. 1). Within these 168,000 square kilometers lived various groups of linguistically related Piman speakers who, in turn, were closely associated in language to the Tepehuan folk who occupied a long curving inland crescent, which stretched southward beyond the Tropic

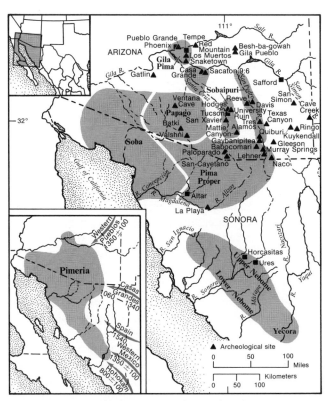

Fig. 1. 18th-century O'otam concentrations and modern archeological sites. Group names are derived from those in the 17th-century Spanish records. Inset shows outside cultural influences A.D. 800–1540.

of Cancer from the Yaqui to the Rio Santiago in Jalisco (Sauer 1934:55–57; Kroeber 1939:125). According to the available eighteenth-century Spanish writings, these indigenes wrested their livelihood by diverse means from this harsh portion of the Mesoamerican frontier (Sauer 1934:82; Hayden 1970). The ancestors of the Soba (Hayden 1970) accepted the environmental challenge in the Papaguería (the Papago region) and were able to glean a living from this desperate land without noticeably changing their biome. However, their Papago neighbors initiated seasonal farming (Underhill 1939, 1946a). Still others of this group, such as the Gila Pima, went even further, actually harnessing their rivers in order to irrigate, thus changing the face of the earth to suit their subsistence needs. Through time, each of these subgroups developed its own particular complement of material culture that, though different in specific detail, remained generically similar. These differences were sufficient to permit the Spanish observers to classify the O'otam into a general Upper (northern) group consisting of five or six subdivisions and a Lower (southern) contingent with three subclusters.

The term O'otam ($'\bar{o}^{\gamma}\bar{o}_1$täm) has been introduced (Di Peso 1956) as a designation for the prehistoric ancestors of the Piman-speaking groups; it is derived from the Upper Piman self-designation 'o'odham 'tribesman, person, human being' (the cognate in the lowland dialect of Lower Pima being 'o'odam) (see the Pima and Papago synonymies in vol. 10; for other evidence on Piman ancestry, see "Historical Linguistics and Archeology," this vol.).

It is the explicit seventeenth-century body of descriptions that must be referred to when constructing the historical continuum for Upper Pimeria, as the earlier, sporadic, mid-sixteenth-century references are too vague in their descriptions of questionable cultural groups such as the protohistoric kingdoms of Marata and Totonteac (Hammond and Rey 1940). However, even these, when studied in the light of archeological data, imply that the old O'otam populations were even then drifting to the west, resulting in a geographic retraction of their eastern border from the San Simon Valley to that of the San Pedro River (Arizona).

Unfortunately, the historical information supplied by the padres for the southern O'otam (Nebome) has not had the support of archeological data. As a consequence, this chapter is necessarily biased in favor of the northern Pimans who occupied southern Arizona, and these data are further distorted by an overemphasis on the very important pre-Spanish Hohokam archeological sequence. The long history of the peoples of Upper Pimeria is couched in terms of the significant excavations of Snaketown, from which there has developed a description of unilinear developments with 200-year intervals of change (Gladwin et al. 1937; Haury 1945, 1967; Wasley 1960; Ezell 1963; Wasley and Johnson 1965; Johnson 1964). Only a few, such as Schroeder (1960), Di Peso (1956:19, 363, 553-568, 1958:12-13), and Hayden (1970), have attempted to approach the history of the Pimeria in terms of culture conquest (Foster 1960) and have come to recognize the Colonial and Sedentary period Hohokam as donors and the Pioneer period as a reflection of either indigenous Hakataya or O'otam. All these interpretations are meaningful although they differ, primarily in terms of the individual scholar's personal bent but also in the specific dates assigned. The dating discrepancy is due to the lack until recently of dating tools satisfactory for this desert tract so that it was necessary to rely upon ceramic cross-dating, which, of course, is an unreliable device (Johnson 1963:182-183). In addition, the O'otam have had a most complicated history involving outside influences from merchant donors such as the Hohokam and the Casas Grandes people (Di Peso 1968, 1968a) as well as from intrusive whole settlements (Willey et al. 1956:9-11; Di Peso 1958:13-16), each of which has had different effects upon the various O'otam subareas. For example, the donor Hohokam intrusion all but submerged the O'otam recipients living in the Gila-Salt area but had much less impact on those who lived away from this target zone.

Each new archeological venture in the Pimeria has added to knowledge of these people, and it becomes more obvious that there is a meaningful correlation between the historical O'otam subgroup territories and recognized pre-Spanish archeological zones, which have been referred to in the literature as the San Simon branch (Sayles 1945:65-66), the Dragoon complex (Fulton 1934; Fulton and Tuthill 1940; Tuthill 1947, 1950), the Red-on-brown people (Gladwin 1957), the Desert Hohokam (Haury 1950:546-548; Johnson 1960, 1963), and the O'otam (Di Peso 1956, 1958). The archeological data have been variously synthesized (Fontana et al. 1962:84-94; Bullard 1962:87-93; McGregor 1965:253, 353-355, 428-430; G.R. Willey 1966:235-236).

It seems evident that these indigenes, who were offshoots of the much older Cochise culture (Sayles and Antevs 1941; Sayles 1945), played the recipient role throughout their long history whenever they came into direct contact with the various Mesoamerican merchant groups (called *pochteca* in Nahuatl) or with the Western Anasazi (Di Peso 1958). Further, they seem to have

reacted to these prehistoric contacts much as they did to the Spanish Christians.

This indigenous desert culture was characterized by loosely arranged, unprotected villages, which consisted of oval to rectangular, shallow pit houses with wall step or inclined covered passageways; a dense brownware, unsmudged redware, and red-on-brown pottery, stone polished over simple rectilinear patterns and including some interior-decorated hemispherical bowls. These part-time farmers made block- or basin-shaped metates; triangular, side-notched projectile points; simple three-quarter grooved axes; and proto-palettes; as well as a cluster of other forms of lithic tools that originated with the Cochise culture (Sayles 1945; Haury 1950:547). They generally buried their dead in a flexed position in pits located randomly about the village premises.

The various pre-Hispanic intrusions that occurred in this district can be defined in social terms and can be compared to the seventeenth-century Spanish penetration and its introduction of an alien Christian iconography, new architectural forms, foreign tool complements, strange modes of subsistence involving domesticated animals and plants, life-taking diseases, and a host of other material and nonmaterial culture traits, all of which were created and developed outside the indigenous area. The pre-Hispanic intrusions of the Western Pueblo people and of the Hohokam and Casas Grandes merchants were each marked by a specific set of cultural traits, which can be recognized archeologically and applied to the reconstruction of early O'otam history.

### Formative Plainware Period, about A.D. 1-650 ± 50

O'otam roots lie deep in the old Cochise desert dweller matrix (Sayles and Antevs 1941; Haury 1943)—and perhaps even in the Paleo-Indian Llano culture because of the presence of a number of Pleistocene megafauna kill sites, such as the Naco (Haury 1953), Lehner (Haury, Sayles, and Wasley 1959), and Murray Springs (Hemmings and Haynes 1969) finds in the upper reaches of the San Pedro drainage, which formed the eastern sector of Pimeria. In any case, the reality of the Cochise continuum has been clarified by the discoveries made at Cave Creek, San Simon (Sayles 1945), Mattie Canyon (Eddy 1958), Ventana Cave (Haury 1950:530-545), Snaketown (Gladwin et al. 1937:251), and Red Mountain (D.H. Morris 1969:47-48). Sometime before A.D. 1, preceramic desert dwellers settled at these locations, built crude, shallow pit houses over their storage pits (Sayles 1945:3-4), and later developed into their Peñasco and Vahki phases. It was in small, insignificant communities such as these that pottery was first made, in the form of small (eight-liter), crude brownware and redware vessels. These O'otam, who made their stone tools and buried their dead after the fashion of their Cochise ancestors (Sayles 1945:62-64), settled into their specific territories and, as small extended families, there farmed and gleaned their lands. There was no apparent centralized authority to spark further cultural achievements, as these groups continued to live in balance with nature and remained static through a number of generations. In time, a few of these widely scattered groups began seasonal dry farming and pottery making after the fashion of their Mountain Mogollon (Sayles 1945:45, 66; Haury 1936a:92-93) and Formative Casas Grandes relatives (Di Peso 1974).

There is conflicting evidence regarding forms of disposal of the dead, originally defined as cremation (Gladwin et al. 1937:95), and house form, which included two large rectangular structures that were 15 times the size of the normal contemporary O'otam dwelling (Gladwin et al. 1937:74-77; Bullard 1962:188); consequently, it has been suggested that the Hohokam were different from the indigenous O'otam. However, evidence from both Mattie Canyon (Eddy 1958) and Red Mountain (D.H. Morris 1969) indicates that some Vahki phase houses were smaller and more in keeping with the conformation of the Cave Creek houses and that inhumation rather than cremation was practiced. Further substantiation of these clues would support the hypothesis of O'otam cultural unity. Moreover, data from the later Snaketown excavations (Haury 1976) cast additional light on this intriguing subject. Evidently the Vahki phase folk were influenced by Mesoamerican traders several hundred years before Christ (Haury 1965, 1967; K.F. Weaver 1967), and these donors, among other things, inspired an intensive irrigation program on the banks of the Gila and Salt rivers. If so, this Hohokam population became mass production farmers almost a millennium before their immediate neighbors, such as those in the San Simon area (Sayles 1945:65-66).

However, most of these indigenes lived in small, shallow, roundish or D-shaped pit houses that were sometimes entered by means of a wall step or a short inclined entry. Inside, they were quite barren, save for a crude fire hearth and a central post (J.B. Wheat 1955:34-65; Bullard 1962:109-174). They were sometimes constructed near one another and formed small, informal villages that lacked an outer wall enclosure, community or ceremonial house, fixed house orientation, formalized burial areas, or irrigation (J.B. Wheat 1955:35; Bullard 1962:109). These frontiersmen clung to the tool designs of their ancestors and likewise buried their dead in pits, sometimes covering these with stone cairns (Sayles 1945:62-64, 66).

### Formative Painted Ware Period, A.D. 650 ± 50-800 ± 100

During the Painted Ware portion of the Formative, which Sayles (1945:67-68) has identified as the San Simon Intermediate period, the Dos Cabezas and Pinaleño phase ceramists added to their brownware and red-slipped stock-in-trade by embellishing their potteries with broad- and thin-line pendant triangles (fig. 2). These they suspended from the rims of their hemispherical bowl interiors and on the sides of their globular jars and, in this, their patterns were indistinguishable from those of their Mogollon and Casas Grandes neighbors (Sayles 1945:45-46; I.T. Kelly 1961). These frontiersmen continued to live in loosely formed village clusters made up of separate rectangular houses (fig. 3) that were several square meters larger than those of their ancestors (Bullard 1962: 120-125). These were entered by short, inclined, covered passageways, and the roofs were supported by a central post pattern (Sayles 1945:23-27; Bullard 1962:116). A variation of this general Pimeria style was noted at Snaketown during its Pioneer period (Gladwin et al. 1937:73), where the single Estrella phase structure was found to have a bulbous, covered passage entry and a more complicated roof-support pattern. The O'otam dead continued to be interred flexed in pits randomly scattered about the village, and for the first time the people (Sayles 1945:62-64) began to place funeral furniture with the deceased. In contrast, the Hohokam Estrella phase folk are assumed to have cremated (Gladwin et al. 1937:95-96, pl. 33). In addition, the O'otam excavated special pit ovens (fig. 4) that were peculiar to them (Trischka 1933; Fulton and Tuthill 1940:20-25).

The native workers continued to use the age-old tool designs and added to their inventory a three-quarter grooved ax form (Sayles 1945:pl. 43f), a proto-palette design (pl. 45), a tubular stone pipe (pl. 46), and triangular and corner-notched projectile points with rounded bases (pl. 42). They were even then trading for marine shell from the Gulf of California, which they made into thin bracelets (Sayles 1945:57, pl. 51a).

### The Hohokam Intrusion, A.D. 800 ± 100

Most students recognize the Hohokam intrusion into the Gran Chichimeca as the Snaketown Colonial period, during which they spread their influence not only through the Pimeria but also far beyond its borders to the Sinagua (McGregor 1941; Weed and Ward 1970) and the Anasazi (D.H. Morris 1970) who lived north of the Gila River, and to the Mimbreños (Cosgrove and Cosgrove 1932) who resided to the east of the San Pedro. This intrusion has been variously dated to about A.D. 500 (Gladwin et al. 1937:216), A.D. 550 (J.B. Wheat 1955), A.D. 800 (Gladwin 1942, 1948; Bullard 1962:93), or possibly A.D. 900 ± 100 (Di Peso 1956). But the truth cannot be ascertained until these Pimeria ruins can be accurately dated. The only meaningful observation that can now be made is to recognize the sequential position of this specific historical event and to perceive its results in terms of the geographical distribution of known Gila-Salt drainage Hohokam traits in neighboring O'otam subareas. This archeological horizon marker involves identifiable Hohokam trade

Fig. 2. O'otam bowls with star designs consisting of rim-suspended pendant triangles. top row, Dragoon Red-on-brown bowls excavated from Gleeson and Tres Alamos sites, both of Cochise Co., Ariz.; bottom row, Anchondo Red-on-brown bowl excavated from Convento site, Chihuahua, Mexico; Trincheras Purple-on-red bowl excavated from Paloparado site, Santa Cruz Co., Ariz.; Dragoon Red-on-brown bowl excavated from Texas Canyon site, Cochise Co., Ariz.; and Tanque Verde Red-on-brown bowl exterior excavated from Paloparado site. Diameter of lower left bowl 22.2 cm, rest same scale.

ceramics; the production of large ceramic receptacles (more than 55 liters); solid clay human figurines (see "Prehistory: Hohokam," fig. 4, this vol.) (Morss 1954); a warrior cremation complex with its attendant central Mexican Tezcatlipoca iconography, including the pyrite mirror (fig. 7) and the bird-snake motif; cotton textiles (Wasley and Johnson 1965:114); sherd spindle whorls (Sayles 1945:59, pl. 58d-e); the long, narrow, gable-roofed house with a covered, bulbous entry; ball courts (Wasley and Johnson 1965:81-86), sometimes referred to as dance areas (Ferdon 1967) or as intercommunity structures (Schroeder 1966:690-698); platform mounds (Wasley 1960); the increased production of shell artifacts (see "Prehistory: Hohokam," figs. 6-7, this vol.); and a host of new lithic forms including the open trough metate, two-hand manos, three-quarter grooved axes (fig. 8), palettes, and the embellishment of stone dishes. The degree of this Hohokam cultural influence can be determined in the excavation of any recipient O'otam village, save perhaps in the Gila-Salt district. This clearly demonstrates the modes of dissemination of the Hohokam in the Pimeria, as well as individual village patterns of accept-

ance and rejection. The pre-Spanish mercantile pattern has been observed at contemporary O'otam villages such as San Simon (Sayles 1945), Tres Alamos (Tuthill 1947), Gleeson (Fulton and Tuthill 1940), Hodges (I.T. Kelly

Fig. 3. Pit house at San Cayetano site, Santa Cruz Co., Ariz., dating A.D. 650-800; view looking east; note east side entrance and postholes in east and west walls (see Di Peso 1956:178-179). House length 7.6 m.

94

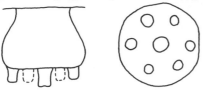

top, Amerind Foundation, Dragoon, Ariz.; bottom, after Trischka 1933:fig. 13.

Fig. 4. Bell-shaped pit oven in house floor with fired adobe inner walls. Used for cooking with heated stones (see Fulton and Tuthill 1940:20–25). top, Pit oven no. 12 of Gleeson site, Cochise Co., Ariz., partially excavated showing vertical cross-section with marked outline of oven. bottom, Section and plan drawing.

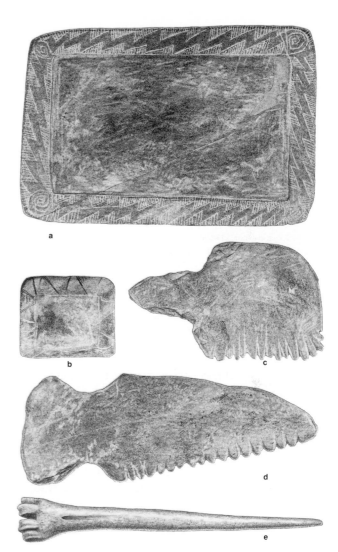

a–e, after Fulton and Tuthill 1940:pls. 18a,e; 19a; 19c; 26l.

Fig. 5. Formative O'otam stone and bone tools excavated from site near Gleeson, Cochise Co., Ariz. a, Stone paint palette, made of mica schist, with raised border covered with zigzag incised design; b, stone paint palette made from portion of larger palette, with the broken edge smoothed and a new border line scratched along it, while the original incised design can be seen along the other three sides; c–d, stone combs possibly used in hair dressing, in weaving, as musical rasps (see Fulton and Tuthill 1940:31), or as hafted saws for cutting down saguaro fruit; e, bone awl. Length of e about 22 cm, rest same scale.

1961), and San Cayetano (Di Peso 1956) and at the La Playa site in Sonora (Johnson 1963). In each of these villages the acceptance and rejection processes can be measured in terms of burial mode, that is, O'otam inhumation versus Hohokam cremation (Haury 1945:44; Tuthill 1947:43–46, 1950); in architecture, as for example in Hohokam and O'otam house types and the presence or absence of ball courts; and in the amounts of indigenous and imported Hohokam ceramics and the impact of the ceramics upon the local ceramists in imitations of forms and motifs (fig. 9).

### The Casas Grandes Intrusion, A.D. 1060–1340

In the mid-eleventh century, while the Hohokam donors were still busily engaged in plying their trade in the O'otam area, a new exploiting group entered the Gran Chichimeca. These Paquimé people settled immediately east of Upper Pimeria in the archeological zone of Casas Grandes, in what is now northwestern Chihuahua (Sayles 1936, 1936a; Lister 1958; Di Peso 1974). These traders (Di Peso 1968, 1968a) organized and directed a sophisti-

cated culture that held sway in this portion of the northern frontier for almost 300 years. In the beginning, their presence had little effect upon the O'otam, who were living through their Sosa phase in the San Pedro Valley (Di Peso 1958), Fairbank phase in the Huachuca area, Tanque Verde phase in the Santa Cruz (Zahniser 1966), Topawa phase in Papagueria (Haury 1950:9–11), and Sacaton-Soho phases in the Gila-Salt homeland of the Gila Pima (Gladwin et al. 1937:260–264). The indigenous ceramic style of the moment (post-A.D. 1100) has diversely come to be known as Tanque Verde Red-on-brown, San Carlos Red-on-brown, or Casa Grande Red-

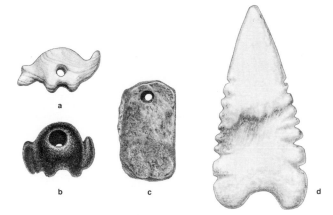

Fig. 6. Formative O'otam stone ornaments excavated from site near Gleeson, Cochise Co., Ariz. a, Sandstone gopher effigy pendant; b, polished steatite animal effigy pendant, possibly representing a skunk; c, rectangular tungsten ore pendant with burnished copper appearance; d, chipped and ground calcite arrow point for nonutilitarian purposes (see Fulton and Tuthill 1940:32-34). Length of d about 6 cm, rest same scale.

on-buff. These three related pottery types have been recognized as a "tripartite manifestation of essentially the same decorative complex" (I.T. Kelly 1961:110), and they are found in association with simple pit house villages that were occupied by the indigenous folk who had absorbed varying amounts of the Hohokam culture.

The first Casas Grandes-O'otam contacts came not on their mutual frontier, but rather in the northern sector of Pimeria. For some unexplained reason, a few of the Gila-Salt Hohokam at the site of Sacaton:9:6 (Gladwin 1928;

Gladwin and Gladwin 1929:31-38) constructed a Casas Grandes-like, thin-walled, puddled adobe compound in the vicinity of the site of the famed Casa Grande, during their Sacaton phase. This was done about the same time that their neighbors living in the Safford portion of the Gila Valley constructed their Bylas phase compounds (Johnson and Wasley 1966). Yet neither of these groups is thought to have traded ceramics with the Paquimé. This particular economic liaison was first noted farther

Fig. 8. Hohokam miniature stone three-quarter grooved ax of the ridged type, Pioneer period (see also Haury 1976:292), a type imported to the O'otam. Excavated from Snaketown, Pinal Co., Ariz. Length 7.2 cm.

Fig. 7. Hohokam pyrite mirror from cave near Tempe, Maricopa Co., Ariz. left, Mirror in original cotton and deerskin wrapping, secured by yucca cord and gum; right, mirror face of fitted pyrite fragments on stone disk. Diameter 10.8 cm.

Amerind Foundation, Dragoon, Ariz.: I/3475, G39/61.
Fig. 9. Hohokam influence on O'otam pottery. left, Hohokam jar with Gila shoulder (see Tanner 1976:128), Texas Canyon site, Cochise Co., Ariz. right, O'otam imitation of Hohokam ware, Gleeson site, Cochise Co., Ariz. Height of left 15 cm, other same scale.

south and nearer to their common border, when, sometime around A.D. 1250, the indigenes of the Ringo site (Johnson and Thompson 1963:479) began a direct ceramic trade in both Casas Grandes and Gila polychromes. This new influx of mercantile contact was felt across the Sulphur Springs Valley (known to Spaniards as Playa de los Pimas) at prehistoric towns such as the Kuykendall village, which has produced archeomagnetic construction dates of A.D. 1385 ± 23 and A.D. 1375 ± 18 (Mills and Mills 1969:168), and westward into the San Pedro–Huachuca area, where a series of surface puddled adobe compound villages was built by the Babocomari folk (Di Peso 1951) who abandoned their pit house villages, as did the inhabitants of Tres Alamos (Tuthill 1947). This influence also spread to the Santa Cruz River, particularly to University Ruin (Hayden 1957), as well as

Di Peso 1974, 2:figs. 224-2, 245-2, 246-2.
Fig. 11. Tinklers and bells excavated from Casas Grandes, Chihuahua, Mexico. top, Shell tinklers worn as necklaces and earrings, and attached to dance kilts. bottom, Copper globular and turtle-shaped bells (crotals) made with the lost wax method and used as necklace, belt, shield, and headdress ornaments. Diameter of turtle about 8 cm, rest same scale.

Smithsonian, Dept. of Anthr., Archeol.: 323872, 323757.
Fig. 10. Casas Grandes pottery. left to right, Ramos polychrome painted jar and effigy jar from Casas Grandes, Chihuahua, Mexico. Left diameter 11.5 cm, other same scale.

to Los Muertos in the Gila-Salt region (Haury 1945). Apparently, these particular recipients variously accepted donor cultural items such as contiguous puddled adobe surface compounds, granaries, road and communication systems, upslope protective irrigation devices, new Casas Grandes trade potteries (fig. 10), copper ornaments, Conus shell tinklers (fig. 11), scarlet macaws, and a host of other items including iconographic elements such as the plumed serpent representing the central Mexican deity Quetzalcoatl (Di Peso 1974). As in the case of the Hohokam, the Casas Grandes complex was not equally accepted by all segments of the Pimeria folk, as many villagers, such as those at San Cayetano (Di Peso 1956), did not choose to participate in the new cultural influence and conservatively held to their old pit-house village ways. In so doing, they set up another donor/recipient pattern.

### West Mexican Trade Contacts, about A.D. 1350

Even while the impact of the Casas Grandes culture was making itself felt throughout different sections of Pimeria, another culture contact was beginning. This time, the Guasave folk of west Mexico exerted influence of sorts, as certain items from this area appeared in various contemporary O'otam villages. These traits included hand-modeled spindle whorls (fig. 12) (Haury 1950:17-18; Di Peso 1956:393-397), striated redware pottery, overlap manos, and possibly shoe-pot cooking vessels (Dixon 1963:612), which apparently were not part of either the Casas Grandes or Hohokam cultural inventories.

This protohistoric period is very complicated and, as yet, little known. In the Casas Grandes area, the culture core was violently destroyed about A.D. 1340 by social disorders that may have been part of a widespread Gran Chichimeca social turmoil. Contemporary communities such as Besh-ba-gowah, Gila Pueblo, and Los Muertos in Arizona were similarly annihilated by fire, and some of

the inhabitants were left unburied where they fell. In the Casas Grandes area, recognizable elements of the culture are found much less frequently and then only in the periphery, where the people existed into the Spanish contact period. This also seems to have been the case with the Babocomari, San Cayetano, and University Ruin folk. But there was no break in the O'otam continuum. Life went on, perhaps in a recession, but still able to react to a new cultural intrusion, such as was implemented by the Anasazi.

### Anasazi Site-Unit Intrusions, about A.D. 1450

Some Anasazi groups moved into the lower San Pedro River valley and set up housekeeping at intrusive site-units such as the Reeve Ruin (Di Peso 1958) and the Davis site (Gerald 1958). These have been identified by the presence of Puebloan stone architecture (fig. 13), slab-lined hearths and entry boxes, stone-lined metate bins, courtyards, and both subterranean and surface rectangular kivas, which appear to have an affinity with the Tsegi phase (late Pueblo III) Kayenta Anasazi (Lindsay et al. 1969:6-8, 365; Lindsay 1969:388-390). However, these intruders into Pimeria did not use similar pottery, but rather Gila and the Kayenta-like (Danson 1957a: 226-229) Tucson polychromes, smudged redwares, perforated rims with a Sobaipuri coil, and very little indigenous Tanque Verde Red-on-brown. The Reeve people cremated, while the Davis folk inhumed, and there is historic evidence to the effect that the eastern Sobaipuri

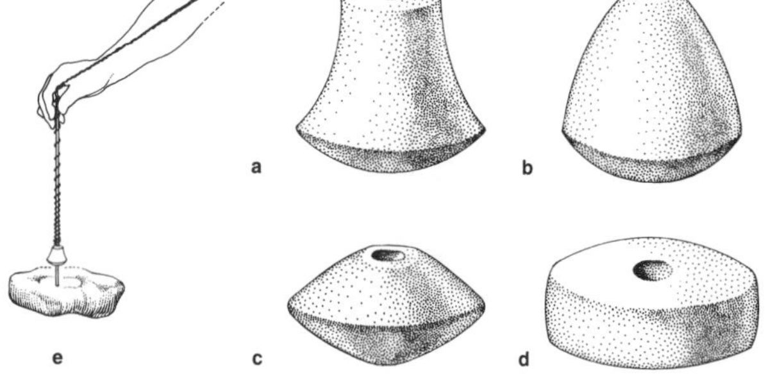

Amerind Foundation, Dragoon, Ariz.
Fig. 13. Anasazi stone architecture, Room 21-3, Reeve Ruin site, Pima Co., Ariz. 50 cm arrow points to north. East and south walls constructed of shaped sandstone blocks set in mud mortar; north and west wall masonry of unshaped stones set in puddled adobe mortar (see Di Peso 1958:35, 52). Stone step entry box in north wall is combined with square slab-lined hearth in floor.

after Di Peso 1956:fig. 57.
Fig. 12. Modeled ceramic spindle whorls of types used by the O'otam and excavated from San Cayetano, Santa Cruz Co., Ariz. a, Truncated cone whorl; b, conical whorl; c, biconvex whorl; d, ellipsoidal whorl; e, truncated cone whorl in use. Height of a about 2 cm, rest same scale.

of this district took on a number of Western Pueblo traits during this period (Di Peso 1958:150-163) that, in the eyes of the seventeenth-century Spaniards, set them apart from their O'otam brothers.

In summary, it would seem that for 800 years, commencing in the ninth century, the people of Upper Pimeria were very much involved with various cultural intrusions that effected a complicated series of events and resulted in the cultural innovations that the Spanish recognized as O'otam. Unfortunately, these have not as yet been formally arranged into a meaningful history. For example, far too little is known of the pre-Spanish career of the Soba, who were found living in an area that contained the remains of the older Trincheras culture. Similarly, it is known that the hostile Papagueria environment was used by the conservative Papago and their ancestors for generations, but still their history consists of hazy inferences. Only a bit more is known of the Santa Cruz Valley folk, such as those who occupied University Ruin (Hayden 1957) and San Cayetano (Di Peso 1956), where it appears that a number of conservative O'otam lived until the Spanish arrived. It is also known that the Pima Proper of the Huachuca area held to their territory until contacted by Father Eusebio Kino, as did their San Pedro Sobaipuri neighbors who, though absorbing a tremendous amount of foreign influence, survived until forced to move westward into the Papagueria at the turn of the eighteenth century, when they were absorbed by the Papago, who, in turn, are now being heavily influenced by the Anglo culture that envelops them.

# Prehistory: Hakataya

ALBERT H. SCHROEDER

The Hakataya (ˌhäkəˈtäyu), a pottery-making people, had a culture distinct from their contemporary prehistoric neighbors, the Anasazi, Mogollon, Hohokam, Sonoran, Coastal California, and Great Basin cultures (Schroeder 1957). They occupied an extensive area (fig. 1) between the coastal ranges on the west and the Mogollon Rim of Arizona on the east, the northern portion of Baja California and the Gila River marking the approximate southern margin, and a line through the Mojave Desert of California passing north of the Providence Mountains

and across the southern tip of Nevada to the Grand Canyon forming the general northern limits.

Basically, all Hakataya were "rock-oriented" people—note their rock-outlined jacales, gravel or boulder alignments, rock-filled roasting pits, rock-pile trail shrines, thick dry-laid, low-walled rock or boulder structures, rockshelters, and bedrock milling stones—who made paddle- and anvil-thinned, sometimes crudely decorated pottery; had a chopper complex; manufactured a few simple ornaments of stone or slightly altered shell;

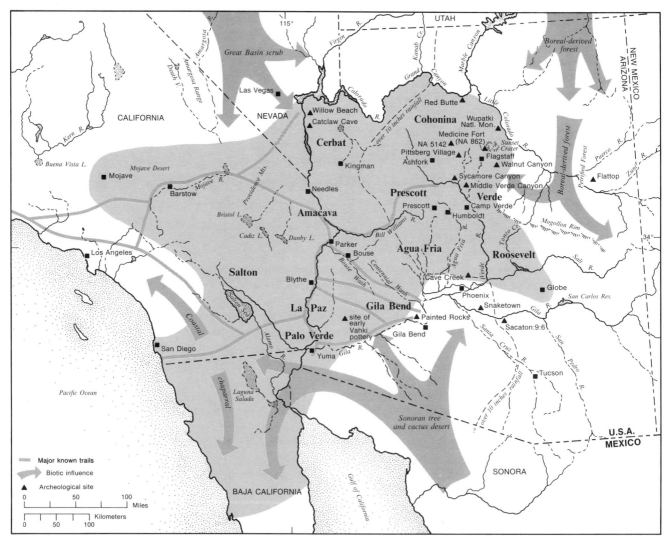

Fig. 1. Hakataya area about A.D. 600 and biotic influences. Branches of Hakataya are named.

Fig. 2. Split-twig animal figurine from a cave overlooking Marble Canyon, Coconino Co., Ariz. made by twisting and wrapping partly split willow twigs; found hidden in caves and rockshelters, probably to improve hunting. Length 11 cm.

preferred medium to long unnotched, triangular points with a concave to convex base; and lived in small camps or villages of scattered units or in small Pueblos with small farm plots.

In contrast, the Hohokam were "dirt-oriented" people—as evidenced by caliche pits, trashmounds, mud and wood jacales, ball courts with earthen embankments, canals, caliche walls, platform mounds—who made intricately decorated paddle and anvil pottery; manufactured ornately fashioned stone and shell work; favored long serrated, unstemmed or stemmed points or nonserrated side-notched points; and lived in sizable rancherias alongside extensive farmlands.

The Hakataya also differed from the "formalized agriculturally oriented" Anasazi, with their pit houses with storage units, kivas in front of Pueblos, multistoried Pueblos with kin or architectural groupings, and towers, dams, reservoirs, and shelters in their fields. These people made coil-scrape black-on-white pottery, manufactured a variety of usually unembellished stone tools and ornaments from quarry sources, favored medium long corner-notched and side-notched points, and fashioned a variety of ritual items.

In contrast to the "sameness" of the Hohokam, there was as much, if not more, material culture variation among Hakataya groups as among the Anasazi. This variation among the Hakataya appears to reflect differences brought about by a wide variety of environments in combination with different cultural influences from neighboring non-Hakatayan people.

## Environment

The Hakataya country, basin and range for the most part, is one of dry lakes in the west half, hot springs in the east, a few streams throughout, extreme variation in seasonal and daily temperatures, and relatively light precipitation and high evaporation. Vegetation varies but the major portion of the region is desert in character, most of which receives less than 10 inches of precipitation annually.

Cultural differences between sites and sectors within the large area under consideration, during both preceramic and ceramic times, undoubtedly resulted to some extent from the effects of the variety of environments involved (Gumerman and Johnson 1971). Three major geographic regions are represented—mountains and low flat desert valleys with playas in the Californias, the broad lower Colorado River valley, and the mountains and valleys of the upland area of western Arizona (see "Prehistory: Introduction," fig. 1, this vol.). Only in the southwestern part of Arizona does the country resemble that west of the Colorado River. Biotic influences (fig. 1)—desert tree and cactus from the south, chaparral on the west coast, Great Basin scrub from the north, and boreal off the plateau on the north and east—flowed into Hakataya country, distorting the makeup of each geographic region.

Covered for the most part with desert soils supporting sparse vegetation and subjected to seasonal temperature extremes and low precipitation, the Hakataya land is biologically fragile. The soils paralleling the region below and a short distance west of the Mogollon Rim tend to produce poorer crop yields over periods of prolonged use as the upper soils become more coarse and the lower more dense. Good stands of different plant types do occur in favorable locales along river valleys, on mountain slopes, or in areas receiving more than 10 inches of precipitation (Prescott-Agua Fria drainage and east). Most of the habitat is of a type in which people without agriculture normally develop a mobile society, following the ripening of the wild foods on a seasonal cycle in pursuit of subsistence and creating specialized sites for hunting, gathering, and quarrying resources.

Humidity zones and precipitation averages shift little compared to temperature belts in the area occupied by the Hakataya. For this reason, dry farming could be pursued only in those areas with sufficient moisture for the crops and a long enough growing season, such as the upper Agua Fria and Prescott areas, middle Verde valley, the plateau country to the north, and the Tonto basin. Moisture for crops in less favorable places came from other sources—spring floods along the lower Colorado River terraces to germinate seeds, springs with good outflow to support a small farm patch, or volcanic ash and cinders that held moisture in the soil as in the Flagstaff, Arizona, area. Those Hakatayas living near the Hohokam adopted at various times their man-made devices to increase agricultural potential, specifically irrigation canals, ditches, check dams on shallow arroyos, or rock-enclosed plots in level areas to slow run-off or to retain rainfall (C. Mindeleff 1896a; Fewkes 1912a:214; Weed and Ward 1970:fig. 6).

## Preceramic Origin

The ancestry of the Hakataya (formerly labeled Yuman, a term that was discarded because of its ethnological connotations—see Schroeder 1957; "Historical Linguistics and Archeology," this vol.) is uncertain. Pinto sites, later than San Dieguito and earlier than Amargosa, originally recorded at Lake Mohave (Amsden 1935; Rogers 1939), have been found over a large area, including Baja California (Massey 1959), Papagueria (Haury 1950; Ezell 1954:pl. 5), southern Nevada (M.R. Harrington 1957; Hunt 1960), Red Butte south of Grand Canyon village (McNutt and Euler 1966), middle Verde valley (Shutler 1950), and the east Verde-Tonto basin area (Olson 1963:94). About 3,000 to 4,000 years ago, in at least a part of the same area, a new preceramic pattern, Amargosa, developed out of the Pinto base (Hunt 1960:62–63; Lanning 1963:267–270). Perhaps not coincidentally, split-twig figurines (fig. 2) of 3,000 to 4,000 years ago have been recovered from sites in southern Nevada; the Barstow, California, area; and Grand Canyon, Walnut Canyon, and Sycamore Canyon in the middle Verde valley (Euler and Olson 1965; Euler 1966).

Rogers (1958) postulates an eastern expansion of the Amargosa out of the Mojave Desert into Arizona about 1000 B.C. Irwin-Williams (1968a:50) suggests that a west-to-east expansion out of California occurred as early as 7500 B.C. By about 3000 B.C., the western sector of the Picosa culture is comprised basically of a Pinto-Amargosa complex (Irwin-Williams 1967). Though the preceramic origins of the Hakataya appear to be related to the area occupied by the Amargosa, more work is needed to demonstrate or reject this relationship.

## Culture

Hakataya sites, especially those west of the lower Colorado River (Wallace 1962:177–178), generally exhibit characteristics of a low dependence on a sedentary way of life: thin trash deposits, preference for jacales or low rock-walled structures, lack of a ceremonial lodge, dependence on simply manufactured ornaments made in small numbers probably for individual use, occurrence of relatively little chipped stone, rare decoration of pottery, and lack of developed craft specialties. Mobile-oriented aspects of Hakataya society, in addition to its rather sparse material culture, include high development of trails; multiplicity of camp, trail, rockshelter, and roasting-pit sites in specific gathering (and hunting?) areas; bedrock milling stones; and percussion food reduction with a hand muller. Scattered jacal structures in sites throughout the Hakataya country as well as in areas far removed from arable lands suggest seasonal occupation. Only in some of the eastern Hakataya areas are there Pueblo-like sites that might have been occupied on a year-round basis.

### Pottery

In addition to environmental factors, the Hakataya at different times came under the cultural influences of groups bordering on their country—West Coast, Hohokam, Anasazi, and Mogollon.

Ceramics best illustrate the sources and directions from which various material culture traits were derived by the Hakataya. Paddle- and anvil-thinned pottery, usually undecorated or poorly so, became the hallmark of the Hakataya, obviously spreading out of the middle Gila River valley. In almost all instances, the brown plainware contained mica in the tempering material. Only in the north did any pottery take on a gray color, probably

left to right, U. of Ariz., Ariz. State Mus., Tucson: GP-45646, A-27806.

Fig. 3. Hohokam plainware pottery from Snaketown, Pinal Co., Ariz. left, Vahki Plain jar. right, Gila Plain jar. Diameter of left 25 cm.

Mus. of Northern Ariz., Flagstaff: 1376/NA4725 P1, P38.

Fig. 4. Adamana Brown ceramic jar, and duck effigy excavated from Flattop site, Apache Co., Ariz. Jar diameter 36.6 cm, other same scale.

resulting from the Kayenta Anasazi influences on the Cohonina to the west (Wilder 1944), who passed the idea on to the south (Verde Gray), or from the Virgin branch Anasazi of southern Nevada, which may have affected pottery manufacture to the south and west (Pyramid Gray).

The first pottery, and the earliest in the Southwest, Vahki Plain (fig. 3), appeared along the middle Gila River, supposedly about 300 B.C. (Gladwin et al. 1937: fig. 106; Haury 1967:691). This type also occurred at an unnamed site in central Yuma County, Arizona, in association with Amargosa II points and a metate on the floors of rectangular, boulder-outlined house sites (Rogers 1958:21). The presence of this pottery at Snaketown on the middle Gila, and some of the associated material culture, represents either the first intrusion of the Hohokam out of Mexico (Haury 1967) or the result of influences out of Mexico on the southernmost Hakataya, who definitely were dominated by a Hohokam intrusion into the middle Gila about A.D. 500 (Schroeder 1960, 1965, 1966:table 1). Regardless of which shall prove to be correct, trade of and the later manufacture of paddle- and anvil-thinned pottery began to diffuse north and west out of the middle Gila.

North of Yuma County, about A.D. 500, Snaketown Red-on-buff and later Hohokam types appear along the Agua Fria River with another Hohokam trait—a ball court—near Humboldt, Arizona, in association with Wingfield Plain (Museum of Northern Arizona, Archaeological Survey files; Schroeder 1954), a type closely related to Gila Plain (fig. 3), which developed out of Vahki Plain on the middle Gila. To the west, in the Salton Basin of California, a preceramic level dating A.D. 370 ±260 underlies a Hakataya ceramic level dating A.D. 510 ±100 (Moriarty 1966:27). Snaketown and Gila Butte Red-on-buff are associated in the middle Verde River

U. of Ariz., Ariz. State Mus., Tucson.
Fig. 5. Elliptical ball court with basalt boulder walls, excavated at Rock Ball Court site, Maricopa Co., Ariz. (see Wasley and Johnson 1965:8-9). Court length about 48 m, width at center about 24 m; viewed facing southwest.

valley of central Arizona with Verde Brown, also similar to Gila Plain, suggesting local manufacture of a plainware near A.D. 500 (Breternitz 1966:20–21, fig. 18). Locally made paddle- and anvil-thinned pottery (Adamana Brown, fig. 4) occurs as far north as Petrified Forest prior to A.D. 600 (Wendorf 1953:74). A similar plainware, Rio de Flag Brown appears in the Flagstaff area possibly in the 600s (De Laguna 1942) and definitely by the 700s (Breternitz 1966). Diffusion of the idea of pottery making to the northeast appears to have been fairly rapid.

Its spread to the northwest seems not to have been so quick. At Bouse, Arizona, Hakataya sherds occur below intrusive Santa Cruz Red-on-buff, indicating local manufacture prior to A.D. 700 (Harner 1958:95). At Willow Beach, the uppermost preceramic level, which is dated A.D. 450 ±250 and topped by a thick flood deposit, is in turn capped by remains associated with ceramics—Lino Black-on-gray, Boulder Gray, "Utah" Gray, and Logandale Gray, all coil-scrape pottery types of the Anasazi tradition; and two Hakataya types, Verde Gray from the Prescott region and Cerbat Brown from the area within the bend of the Colorado River north of Kingman (Schroeder 1961a:42, 61). Only one of these, Lino Black-on-gray, has been suggested to date prior to A.D. 700 (A.D. 572–872, Breternitz 1966). The two Hakataya types are estimated to have been in use in the 700s, which also is the date for the appearance of Deadmans Gray in the country between Ashfork and Flagstaff (McGregor 1951:20). Catclaw Cave produced ceramic data similar to that of Willow Beach (Wright 1954).

By about A.D. 900, Pyramid Gray had become the dominant local plainware at Willow Beach (Schroeder 1961a:42) and perhaps as early in the Mojave Desert. However, both the upland Arizona (Cerbat branch or ethnic unit of the Hakataya) and riverine (Amacava branch) groups also ranged out into the Mojave Desert. Rustler Rockshelter in San Bernardino County, California, yielded a few sherds of Tizon Brown ware from northwestern Arizona alone in the four lowest six-inch levels. In the remaining four levels above, this ware had Lower Colorado Buff ware of the lower Colorado River associated, the uppermost six-inch level also containing Verde Black-on-gray (Prescott branch) and North Creek Fugitive Red (Virgin branch Anasazi of southern Nevada) intrusives. The Lower Colorado Buff ware, mostly of the Parker Series, is dominant in the upper 12 inches, suggesting that during the late use of this rockshelter (and area?) the site received more use by the Amacava branch than by the Cerbat branch. Triangular points were the most common type represented. The appearance of pottery in this Providence Mountains subarea is estimated at about A.D. 800, and the later cultural material reflects some Numic influence from the north and northwest (J.T. Davis 1962:36, 44–45, table 1).

Wallace (1962:178), who suggests that some Numic- or

103

Yuman-speaking people arrived in Death Valley while preceramic Amargosans still occupied the area, places the appearance of ceramics there about A.D. 1000. Hunt (1960:163, 169, 173) puts it about A.D. 1100. Farther west, in the Anza-Borrego Desert State Park area, the ceramics and points more or less duplicate the sequence at Rustler Rockshelter (Wallace and Taylor 1960), according to J.T. Davis (1962:47). The time of the manufacture of similar pottery farther west has not been accurately determined (Treganza 1942; McCown 1945; Harner 1957; Wallace and Taylor 1958; Meighan 1958-1959), but an A.D. 1000 date near San Diego on the west coast has been the earliest date suggested (Rogers 1941:3, 1945:195).

### Other Traits from the South

The early development and diffusion of house types generally followed the same pattern as that of ceramic influences. The rectangular surface house (jacal) with rounded corners in central Yuma County did not appear in the middle Gila Valley until late Snaketown or early Gila Butte times, about A.D. 500, at which time it also occurred in the Gila Bend area (Wasley and Johnson 1965:fig. 5). This house type, sometimes boulder-outlined, also is known in the Verde, A.D. 500 to 700 (Breternitz 1960:fig. 10); Agua Fria, A.D. 900 or earlier (Schroeder 1954); Prescott, A.D. 900 (Spicer and Caywood 1936:18, 93; Euler and Dobyns 1962:73); and Cohonina, middle 900s (McGregor 1951:20, 61) branches of the Hakataya.

Another trait that diffused from south to north after A.D. 500 into the western half of Arizona was the ball court (fig. 5), believed to be a ceremonial structure (Schroeder 1963). At Painted Rocks, a rock-outlined court associated with rectangular houses with rounded corners and a rock-outlined oval house contained Gila Butte Red-on-buff pottery and a dominant local plainware similar to, but recognizably different from, Gila Plain (Wasley and Johnson 1965:6-10, 12-13). Another court near Humboldt had intrusive Snaketown and later Red-on-buff types associated with locally made Wingfield Plain.

Courts of later date also appeared in the middle Verde Valley and as far north as Wupatki National Monument. The spread of the ball court appears to have been associated with Hohokam colonies moving north out of the middle Gila basin (McGregor 1941; Schroeder 1965:fig. 1), beginning perhaps about A.D. 500-600. These colonies exhibited a number of Hohokam-like traits, but the occupants used a plainware, different from Gila Plain, common on nearby sites lacking Hohokam traits. Inhabitants of these nearby sites either manufactured pottery prior to the arrival of a Hohokam colony in their area or picked up this trait from the intruders and used it thereafter. Hohokam-like sites without ball courts near Humboldt (Weed and Ward 1970) and in the middle Verde (Breternitz 1960:22) might have been associated with a nearby ball court as were a number of early Hohokam sites in the Gila basin.

There is little doubt that certain traits, as those above, spread north from the Hohokam on the Gila during Gila Butte times (A.D. 500-700). Probably by no coincidence, this expansion of Hohokam colonies or diffusion of ideas and sedentary sites northward, into the Agua Fria on the west and near Globe on the east, influenced localities receiving over 10 inches of rainfall annually, a factor that

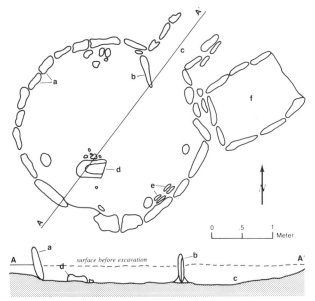

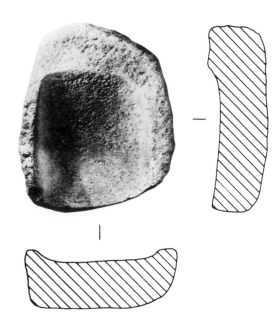

left, after Wendorf 1953:fig. 11; right, Wendorf 1953:fig. 18a.

Fig. 6. left, Plan of House H, Flattop site, Apache Co., Ariz. a, Walls of vertical sandstone slabs; b, wing wall; c, entrance; d, metate; e, manos; f, slab-lined storage cist outside house. right, Troughed sandstone metate with one end closed, excavated from Flattop site. Length about 40 cm.

would provide for the cultivation of protein-rich beans under conditions of dry farming. The appearance of indigenous paddle- and anvil-thinned pottery in the middle Verde, Petrified Forest, and Flagstaff localities prior to A.D. 600 or 700, but without any associated ceremonial structures (Wendorf 1953; Breternitz 1959a, 1960) suggests that a fully sedentary existence (Schroeder 1965:300) had not yet been adopted to the north of the Agua Fria and Globe areas. By the 900s, Hohokam expansion into the middle Verde introduced sedentary sites out of which descendants later moved among the Sinagua near Flagstaff after the A.D. 1065 eruption of Sunset Crater (McGregor 1941).

The presence of red-on-buff pottery with estimated dates prior to A.D. 500 to the north of the Gila and the general lack of excavation in and reliable dating for the more northern Hakataya sites still allows for the possibility of ceramics and other traits having diffused north prior to Gila Butte times. In addition, the rare but sloppy and simple designs of Verde Black-on-gray and Lower Colorado Buff ware, beginning dates for which are not known, have a closer affinity to Gila River basin decoration prior to Gila Butte times.

A network of trails through the Hakataya country undoubtedly played an important role in the diffusion of traits into and through their lands (Colton 1945:116–117). Shell and other material were carried north from the Gulf of California and east from the Pacific Coast to the Gila River via the Blythe-Parker area or to northwestern Arizona via the Mojave Desert. Other trails parallel the lower Colorado River and cross the Gila (Rogers 1939:13, 1941:4; Sample 1950; Breternitz 1957:12; Johnston and Johnston 1957:29–30; Schroeder 1961a:2; R.G. Vivian 1965; Hayden 1972). Abalone shell was traded across Hakataya country as far east as the Zuni area in Basketmaker times (F.H.H. Roberts 1931:160), indicating a respectable antiquity for trade along these trails, which continued to be used in historic times (Coues 1900, 1:237; Beattie 1933:62, 66–67; Schroeder 1961b:fig. 3). Obviously, traits and ideas also moved west along these routes to account for Anasazi and Hohokam items that appear in southern California (Colton 1945:115; Wauchope 1956:104–108).

*Traits from the Northeast*

Contacts with other than the Hohokam also altered the patterns of the various Hakataya branches. The earliest Sinagua developments (Colton 1946) near Flagstaff reflect the pattern of the Petrified Forest area—paddle and anvil with some scrape-finished pottery, circular house, slab-lined cists, and metate with one end closed (fig. 6). By the 700s, when all Sinagua pottery was thinned by paddle and anvil, the pit house was square to rectangular with four roof supports, more like those to the south; and possibly a ceremonial lodge was in use (Breternitz 1959a). These features continued in use, with trade pottery

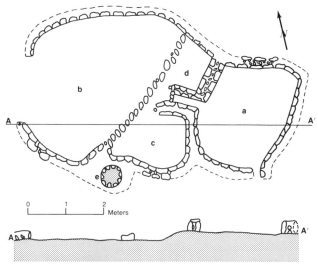

after McGregor 1951:fig. 19.

Fig. 7. Plan of Cohonina surface structure from Site NA 5142, Red Lake Wash, Coconino Co., Ariz. a, Dwelling room; b, patio work area; c-d, 2 additional rooms partitioned at a later time; e, deep circular cist outside south patio wall, probably for storage. The structure walls, constructed of limestone blocks set in double rows with smaller rock fill, were estimated to range from 1 to 2 m high (McGregor 1951:72–75).

coming in from the Kayenta Anasazi, until the eruption of Sunset Crater. Hohokam and Mogollon intrusions or influences among the Sinagua, following this volcanic upheaval, introduced new elements of culture that by the 1120s merged to form a new pattern—Pueblos without kivas, extended burials, smudged brownwares and redwares, for example. By the middle 1100s this Sinagua pattern expanded south into the Verde valley and reached the region of the Gila-Salt junction (Schroeder 1961).

To the west of the Sinagua, the Cohonina of the 700s covered many of their pottery vessels with fugitive red paint, as did the early Anasazi, and later fired their ware to a consistent light gray and used Anasazi-style decoration. The early pit houses, rectangular with rounded corners and sometimes circular or boulder-outlined, duplicated those to the south in the Prescott-Agua Fria-Gila Bend areas. The occasional square to rectangular boulder-outlined jacal in the Sinagua country west of Flagstaff, dating about A.D. 900–1000 (Ezell 1956) and perhaps derived from the Cohonina, represents the most northeastern extension of this type of structure. Later (after A.D. 1050) Cohonina sites, with massive walls of rock, rarely suggest a full-story-high structure and normally contain only a few rooms (fig. 7) (Hargrave 1938; McGregor 1951:figs. 11, 19). This type of architecture occurred as far east as the upper and middle Verde valley (C. Mindeleff 1896a; Fewkes 1912a; Shutler 1951). Those in the Cohonina area and upper Verde with considerable rock fall, suggesting a height of a full story, have been labeled "forts" (fig. 8) (Fewkes 1912a:210; Hargrave 1933:49–54, 1938:fig. 11; McGregor 1951:fig. 21). One

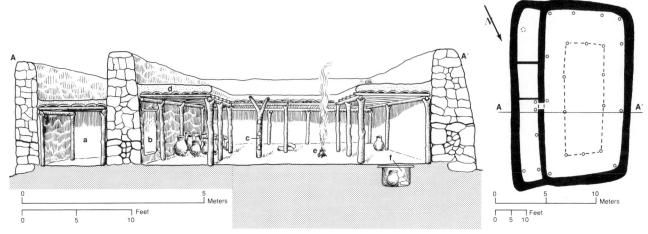

left, after Hargrave 1933:fig. 19; right, after Colton 1946:fig. 45.

Fig. 8. left, Reconstruction of Medicine Fort, Site NA 862, Coconino Co., Ariz. a, North granary room; b, doorway; c, ladder; d, timber-supported portalis with pine bark and dirt covering; e, fireplace; f, floor cache. right, Site plan indicating approximate location of roof support posts.

on the upper Verde, with rubble-filled masonry walls, contains circular rock-outlined rooms, some of which also occur outside the square fort (Fewkes 1912a: 211-212). Small Pueblos seem to have been adopted as far west as the upper Verde (Fewkes 1912a).

Early jacal structures near Prescott, like those of the early Cohonina and probably originally derived from the Agua Fria area, were replaced in the 1100s with small Pueblos lacking kivas. These Pueblos, probably borrowed from the Sinagua when they moved into the middle Verde, also diffused south into the Agua Fria drainage in the middle 1100s. This type of architecture was never adopted farther south in areas of less than 10 inches of rainfall. Massive low-walled rock structures, like those in the Agua Fria drainage (Euler 1963) and north, however, do occur near and north of the Gila with Hohokam pottery associated, mostly of the late Sedentary and Classic periods, probably post-1100. Two, near Gila

Bend and near Cave Creek, had fairly high standing walls (Schroeder 1940:60-61; Wasley and Johnson 1965:fig. 38).

Aside from a few rock-outlined structures, little is known about the early Hakataya sites in the Tonto Creek basin where a pattern with Pueblos lacking kivas, similar to that of the Sinagua of the middle Verde valley, appeared in the 1100s (Schroeder 1953).

## Cultural Influences and Hakataya Patterns

Prior to the mid-1100s, pottery, house type, and ball court, plus other elements diffused out of the middle Gila to the north and west, ceramics spreading only west of the 10-inch-plus precipitation line. Cremation seems to have been the preferred method of disposal of the dead among the Hakataya, though there is the possibility of inhumation among the Cohonina and Sinagua prior to this time (Euler 1957; Schwartz and Wetherill 1957; Turner 1958; Breternitz 1959a). In the 1100s, in upland Arizona, Pueblo architecture, redware, and extended burial expanded out of the Sinagua region to the south and west, and again none crossed to the west of the 10-inch rainfall line within the Hakataya area except redware, which reached the lower Colorado River. Much of the Sinagua pattern also reached the lower Salt-middle Gila triangle (Schroeder 1947).

The general lack of identifiable ceremonial lodges throughout the entire Hakataya region north of the Gila between A.D. 1150 and 1300 or later (except for an occasional kiva on the northeast border, see McGregor 1955) suggests that these people practiced marginal agriculture without the attendant formalized ceremony and ritual implied among the contemporary Anasazi and Mogollon. However, large Pueblo plazas or large detached rooms in the middle Verde might represent such

Hargrave 1938:fig. 12.

Fig. 9. Cohonina projectile points with serrated edges, chipped from sheet obsidian excavated from Pittsberg Village site, Coconino Co., Ariz. Length of left point 4.1 cm, rest same scale.

106

structures. General lack of excavation in the lower Colorado River valley and deserts of the Californias hampers any estimate concerning the time of the appearance of farming and other associated traits. Specific material culture inventories identifying most of the various Hakataya groups (branches) or areas are available (Treganza 1942; Colton 1939, 1946; Schroeder 1952a, 1954, 1960; Wallace 1962; Euler 1963; True 1970).

Items adopted by the upland Arizona Hakataya (Patayan) from the Hohokam, the Anasazi, and the Mogollon developed a pattern distinct from that of the riverine Hakataya (Laquish) in the lower Colorado River valley and from the Hakataya desert dwellers (not yet named) of the Californias.

A small kin group, such as a band, could have inhabited most Hakataya sites. In the case of the larger Pueblos in the eastern sector, these might represent favorable areas where several bands congregated on a more or less permanent basis for a few hundred years. The seemingly little attachment of the Hakataya to sedentary ways might have been a major factor allowing for the abandonment of the eastern Hakataya Pueblos in the 1300s and 1400s as farm plot outputs decreased, rainfall patterns shifted, or other factors of stress developed. The culture pattern of these eastern Hakataya, once they discontinued the use of Pueblos and implied sedentary aspects, differed little from that of the early historic period Yuman-speaking tribes of the same area.

## Historic Period Survivals

On the basis of the patterns of the assumed Yuman-speaking prehistoric branches so far postulated, the Roosevelt branch with Tonto Brown pottery is thought to be ancestral to the historic period Southeastern Yavapai, the Cerbat branch with Cerbat Brown to the Walapai, the La Paz branch with Needles Buff to the Halchidhoma, the Palo Verde branch with Tumco Buff to the Quechan, the Gila Bend branch with Gila Bend Beige to the Maricopa, the Salton branch with Topoc Buff possibly to the eastern Tipai, the Verde branch with Verde Brown to the Northeastern Yavapai (Schroeder 1952a, 1960), the Cohonina branch with Deadmans Gray to the Havasupai (Schroeder 1952a; Schwartz 1956; Whiting 1958), and the Amacava branch with Parker Buff to the Mojave (Schroeder 1952a; Kroeber and Harner 1955). The possible survivals of the Prescott branch with Verde Gray and the Sinagua branch with Tuzigoot Plain are in question as is that of the Lower Gila branch with Palomas Buff (to the Opa or Kavelchadom?). The pottery of the unnamed branch in the San Diego County area (Palomar Brown) and the desert west of the Colorado River seems to have survived among the Ipai-Tipai (and transmitted to the Luiseño) (Treganza 1942:159; McCown 1945:261; Clement W. Meighan, personal communication 1972).

Unfortunately, too few Hakataya sites have been excavated to provide good quantitative data for comparative studies and correlations or to demonstrate aspects of seasonal or year-round occupation. Groups surviving into historic times, if the above postulations hold, used the same trails and many of the same campsites. Since some of the prehistoric ceramic types seemingly occur in surficial association with historic-period material, the possibility of cultural continuity appears to be strong.

# Prehistory: Western Anasazi

FRED PLOG

The Anasazi (ˌänəˈsäzē) were the prehistoric inhabitants of the Four Corners area of Utah, Colorado, Arizona, and New Mexico.* Archeological data indicate considerable continuity within the area from about A.D. 1. Common features include black-on-white pottery, relatively late appearance of villages (compared to the Hohokam and the Mogollon), continued importance of hunting (in contrast with the Hohokam), the use of elaborate systems of water and erosion control devices, complex systems of communication and trade (reflected by evidence of trails or roadways in parts of the area), and

similarities in ceramic types and in domestic and ceremonial architecture.

The Western Anasazi area is the westernmost 150,000 square kilometers of this region (figs. 1–2). Material evidence of the Anasazi presence is most abundant in the drainages of the Little Colorado River, the San Juan River, and their immediate tributaries, reflecting either lengthy occupation or high population density or both. Substantial evidence of the Western Anasazi is also found in the drainages of the Animas, Dolores, Colorado, Sevier, and Virgin rivers. Their artifacts are found in sites throughout the Southwestern United States and occasionally in still more distant ones.

The distinction between Eastern and Western Anasazi in this volume is made for a number of reasons. First, material on the prehistory of the Anasazi area is abundant and difficult to synthesize in a single chapter. Second, at the eastern and western extremes of the area material culture is distinctive. Finally, as ethnologists have distinguished between the Eastern and Western Pueblos (Eggan 1950), archeologists have sought a paral-

* The term Anasazi was introduced in archeological usage by Kidder (1936:152), who based it on a Navajo word that he took to mean 'old people'. However, although Navajo *anaasází* is given in dictionaries as 'ancient people' (Young and Morgan 1943, 1:3, 2:17) and is used by the Navajo to designate the prehistoric inhabitants of their area, it is discomfiting to some modern Pueblo people that the English name now used by archeologists for these ancient Pueblo peoples comes from a Navajo term that literally means 'enemy ancestors' (Hoijer 1974:261, 270; Haile 1950-1951, 1:14; Kenneth L. Hale, Joe S. Sando, and Robert W. Young, personal communications 1973).

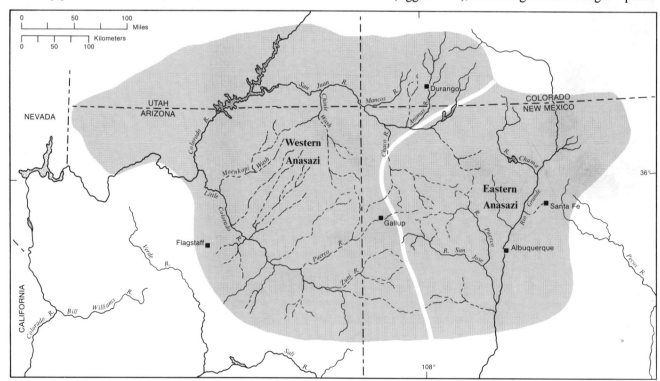

Fig. 1. Anasazi area.

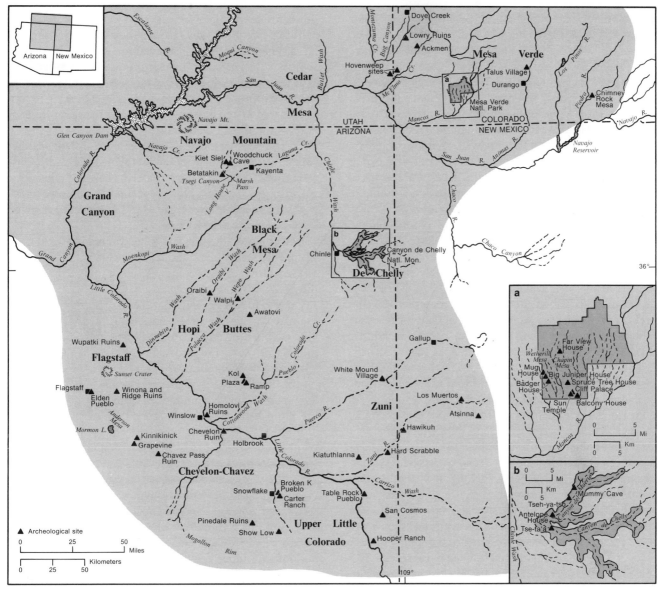

Fig. 2. Provinces of Western Anasazi and archeological sites. Insets show a, Mesa Verde and b, Canyon de Chelly site concentrations.

lel distinction for their prehistoric ancestors (see "Prehistory: Eastern Anasazi," this vol.).

Basic contrasts between the eastern and western areas as traditionally defined occur in architecture (compact and cellular in the east, rooms around plazas in the west), kivas (round in the east, rectangular in the west), pottery (graywares in the east, brownwares in the west), burial mode (flexed in the east, extended in the west), and in a variety of more detailed characteristics of artifacts (Reed 1948, 1950; Johnson 1965). Arguments concerning the boundary between the two areas are substantial; some would include southwestern Colorado and southern Utah with the Eastern Anasazi (Reed 1948), others with the Western. The nature of cultural boundaries in the Anasazi area and the ancestry of modern Puebloan groups are complex issues; it is best to view the boundary between Eastern and Western Anasazi as arbitrary, a product of

the need for a division of labor in discussing Puebloan prehistory.

Professional archeological research on the prehistory of the Western Anasazi began in the 1870s. Early surveys involving the location and description of sites as well as limited excavation were done by Bandelier (1890–1892, 1), C. Mindeleff (1895, 1897a), Fewkes (1891, 1896c, 1898b, 1911a, 1911), Hough (1903), Prudden (1903, 1914, 1918), Kidder and Guernsey (1919), Guernsey (1931), Spier (1919, 1919a), and F.H.H. Roberts (1932). Early excavation projects that contributed important information were conducted by Hewett, Kidder, and Morley (Morley and Kidder 1917), Fewkes (1911a, 1911, 1916, 1927a), Morley (1908), Guernsey (1931), Morris (1938, 1939), Judd (1930), Hodge (Smith, Woodbury, and Woodbury 1966), and F.H.H. Roberts (1931).

Much archeological research has been done in this

area, probably more than in any other area of a similar size in North America. Because of incomplete reporting of this work, it is difficult to estimate how many sites have been recorded in survey and how many have been excavated. One effort by the National Park Service to develop an inventory of previously recorded sites in the San Juan Basin alone anticipated that as many as 30,000 site records already exist even though much of this area has not been thoroughly surveyed. Wholly or partly excavated sites number in the thousands. The growing efforts of federal agencies to manage cultural resources on federal lands in the 1970s have resulted in a dramatic increase in understanding of Western Anasazi prehistory. M. Green (1978) lists several hundred reports on the prehistory of National Forests in the Western Anasazi area that have been generated within only five years. Since most of these sources are relatively inaccessible they have not been heavily cited here. Nevertheless, it is increasingly common that primary materials on the prehistory of the area are contained in cultural resource reports of agencies and contracting institutions rather than the more traditional monographs and journals.

The quantity of information available on the area creates both problems and opportunities. The primary problem is the unevenness of the data available in different areas and from different sites. For example, some areas have been "surveyed" by archeologists who asked local inhabitants to take them to sites, while others have been studied by teams of archeologists who systematically walked over an area looking at virtually every square meter. In excavation, the use of screens, of a square grid system, and of natural levels has not been characteristic. When some data recovery techniques are more sensitive than others, the kinds and quantity of data recovered on particular projects begin to reflect field methodology rather than the actual prehistory. Archeologists are only beginning to explore the problems of developing syntheses that are sensitive to both the strengths and weaknesses of available evidence (Euler and Gumerman 1978; Sullivan and Schiffer 1978). Despite these problems, the wealth of data available on the Western Anasazi allows archeologists to address questions that are difficult or impossible to study in other areas, such as many relating to subsistence practices, social organization, and exchange.

## Environment

The Western Anasazi used the resources of the Colorado Plateau to support more people than any subsequent group. Understanding the interaction of environment, subsistence strategies, and human numbers is critical to understanding the history of Western Anasazi occupation of the area.

Environments are cultural as well as natural. The manner in which the availability of plants, animals, and other resources affects the spatial variation of human culture depends on how resources are valued by particular groups, and there is immense variation in the resources that particular human groups value. Among the Western Anasazi three food-procurement strategies were employed: hunting, gathering, and agriculture. The precise degree of reliance on the three varied considerably both spatially and temporally.

Of course one must also understand differences between the environment of an area in historic and prehistoric times (see "Prehistory: Eastern Anasazi," this vol.). Nevertheless, it is possible to generalize concerning the problems that prehistoric populations would have faced in acquiring food resources.

For hunter-gatherers, spatial and temporal variations in the availability of natural resources are most important to the success of the food quest. Both are substantial in the Western Anasazi area.

Except in the broad, flat center of the Colorado Plateau, there is a recurrent gradient from a relatively flat alluvial plain through a foothill zone into high hills or mountains (see "Prehistory: Introduction," fig. 1, this vol.). This topographic variation has a significant effect on the distribution of plants and animals: when relief is high, plant-animal communities within any given locality are quite heterogeneous because they occur in distinct altitudinal zones; when relief is low the distribution of plant-animal resources is relatively homogeneous. From lowest to highest, the typical plant formations of the area are a desert grassland, a sagebrush or saltbush scrubland, a piñon-juniper or juniper-piñon woodland, ponderosa pine forest, and mixed coniferous (pine, spruce, fir) forest. However, intergradations often occur: one sometimes finds a very great area covered by a mixture of woodland and forest; similarly, while a woodland, for example, has distinctive features, it typically includes significant areas that are occupied by higher formations (like pine forest) or lower ones (like grassland). These altitudinally zoned communities are crosscut by riparian ones with quite distinctive constituents.

The distribution of animal resources is similarly complex. Some animals, elk, mountain sheep, and deer, for example, typically live at higher elevations. Others, antelope for example, are found at lower elevations. Still others, such as rabbits and mice, occur quite generally or, as in the case of water birds, only in highly specific habitats within an area.

Seasonal variation also affected the successful exploitation of wild plants and animals. Plant resources were generally available between April and October. Green plants such as chenopods and amaranths were harvested in the spring while grass seeds, roots, and nuts such as piñon, acorn, and walnut were harvested in the fall. Virtually no plant resources were available between November and April, so that prehistoric peoples were dependent on their ability to store such products. There

110

was also important variation in the annual availability of plant resources. A given stand of piñon, for example, produces a good crop only one or two years out of seven (D.H. Thomas 1973). Animal resources also vary seasonally. For example, it is easiest to harvest deer, elk, and antelope during periods when these animals are in large herds, which occurs only when they are moving from higher to lower elevations or back, and during the breeding period; thus the spring and especially the fall would have been the seasons when these animals were most easily taken. Migratory birds are another example of an animal resource that is available during a restricted period. Other animals, such as mice and rats, would have had a less restricted seasonal availability.

Topographic relief was also an important consideration for agricultural groups although for somewhat different reasons (see "Prehistory: Eastern Anasazi," this vol.; that discussion is valid for the Western Anasazi area as well).

Given the significant differences between Western and Eastern Pueblos and between Western and Eastern Anasazi, a number of anthropologists have sought environmental patterns that might correspond to the divisions. Initially, the environments of the two areas were said to be remarkably uniform (Eggan 1950). Indeed, according to most modern measures of average environmental conditions the degree of uniformity is striking. Later investigators, however, note that there is a great deal of highly localized variability in the region. Soil nutrients vary considerably within small distances, even from one field to another. Some fields may receive more rainfall during a growing season than others. Severe summer storms destroy crops in one area, but not in those only a short distance away. The dates of the last spring and first fall frost are sensitive to microenvironmental factors and, therefore, can vary greatly over a short distance. Insect and animal pests have a substantial, but capricious, effect on fields (Ford 1972a).

It is true that the average conditions over the two areas inhabited by the Anasazi are similar and that local departures from these averages are substantial. Nevertheless, there is one important difference: risk—the probability of a crop failure—is much higher in the Western Anasazi area. Precipitation is an illustrative case. In comparison with the Western Anasazi area, in the Eastern area: a higher percentage of rain falls during the crop growing season; during the growing season, there are fewer 14-day periods when no rain falls; there are fewer years in which rainfall is less than 75 percent of normal; the average dry year is wetter; in the average year, there is more rain in May and June, the two months during which moisture is critical for germination; and in dry years, there is more rainfall in May and June.

Thus, while both the Eastern and Western Anasazi areas are marginal for agriculture (Visher 1954), for these and a variety of topographic, hydrological, and geomorphic characteristics, departures from normal conditions are both more frequent and of greater magnitude in the Western Anasazi area, and the risk that prehistoric populations took in attempting to produce a crop was much greater.

## Subsistence

For most of the time that the Western Anasazi area was occupied, from about 10,000 B.C. until well after A.D. 1, hunting and gathering were the most important food-procurement strategies. Principal hunted resources included elk, deer, antelope, mountain sheep, rabbit, and turkey. Various fish, small birds, and small rodents were probably important subsistence items, although the small size of their bones results in infrequent preservation of their remains in archeological contexts. From trees were harvested walnuts, acorns, juniper berries, and especially piñon nuts. Chamiso, saltbush, and sage were the primary bushes that yielded food resources. Agave, prickly pear, cholla, and other cacti were important subsistence items. Grasses, such as Indian rice grass, roots and tubers (wild potatoes for example), and leafy greens such as chenopods and amaranths were also important resources.

Significant monitoring of the local environment was necessary to exploit such resources. Piñon is an example (D.H. Thomas 1973). Piñon nuts mature over a period of two years. At any point during this cycle rainfall or other environmental problems may destroy a crop in one locality while nuts are flourishing only a few miles away. Moreover, a variety of animals other than people rely on piñon nuts as a food resource so that if people were not present when the cones of the tree were ready for harvest, birds, rodents, and ungulates would quickly consume the crop.

While hunted and gathered resources were important throughout Western Anasazi prehistory, agricultural resources became increasingly important in some times and places. As in other parts of the Southwest region, corn, beans, and squash were the most important domesticates. The first cultigen utilized in the area was corn.

The earliest corn in the Western Anasazi area is from O'Haco Rockshelter and dates to 3000 to 2000 B.C. (Briuer 1975). Subsequently, corn is found in a number of cave deposits in the area. Early utilization of these resources was probably not very different from the historic pattern of the Mescalero Apache: crops were planted in well-watered locations in the spring, left for the summer, and harvested in the fall. If little or nothing grew in a field, the gathering activities during fall months were more intense. Beans and squash appear shortly after and before A.D. 1, respectively.

There is no evidence that corn was an important part of the diet until 3,000-4,000 years after it is first found. Direct dietary evidence (Stiger 1977) as well as secondary data (Schiffer 1972) suggest that it was not until about

A.D. 800-1000 that most of the Western Anasazi diet was derived from food production. It is also unclear whether changes in domesticates, especially corn, that made them more productive under Southwestern conditions occurred as the result of adaptation to local conditions or from the importation of new varieties from outside areas (Schroeder 1965).

Interestingly, it is at about this same time that the evidence of soil and water control devices ("Prehistory: Eastern Anasazi," fig. 9, this vol.) that would have improved the productivity of fields becomes abundant (R.G. Vivian 1974). These devices occur in a variety of different forms: irrigation ditches, terraces, linear grids, field borders, and check dams. They first appear in northeastern Arizona at about 1200, in the Mesa Verde area of southwestern Colorado at about 1100, and in the Little Colorado Valley and the Mogollon area to the south at about 1000. There are occasional references to similar features elsewhere in the area that suggest that their ultimate extent remains undefined. Where archeologists have sought such evidence it has been found, but in many areas appropriate survey techniques have still not been employed.

This evidence suggests that at about 1000 intensification of agricultural production was occurring. Previously, the most common practice was to use a field until its productivity began to decline, when a new field was then cleared and cultivated elsewhere. Reduction of the fallow period (more frequent use of fields) and the construction of water and soil control devices both involve a greater labor investment in a unit of land. There is substantial disagreement concerning the managerial skills and organizational patterns that such labor intensification required (Plog and Garrett 1972; R.G. Vivian 1974).

## Demography

Variation in the distribution of people in the Western Anasazi area has been deduced from differences in the number of sites, the number of rooms, the aggregate floor area, and the number of artifacts. Each technique has its advantages and disadvantages (Plog 1974, 1975; Orcutt 1974) since each reflects variation in human numbers but also a variety of other factors, such as length of occupation of a site.

Nevertheless, patterns of demographic change through time have been identified for several different areas within the Western Anasazi region: Mesa Verde, Colorado (Hayes 1964; Cordell 1975; Zubrow 1976; Rohn 1977), Flagstaff (Colton 1936), Hopi Buttes (Gumerman 1969, 1975), Black Mesa (Swedlund and Sessions 1976; Layhe 1977), Tsegi Canyon (Dean 1969), and Upper Little Colorado (Longacre 1970a; Plog 1974; Zubrow 1975; Orcutt 1974).

Differences in the kind of data used for reconstructing demographic change as well as in the sophistication with which the sites in each area were dated create difficulties in comparing change from area to area. Such problems are kept to a minimum when a more standardized data base can be employed. For this reason, one study of demographic change in the area used only sites for which tree-ring dates were available (S. Plog 1969). A second approach, that of the Southwestern Anthropological Research Group, involved collecting detailed data on nearly 2,000 archeological sites within the Western Anasazi area. While the site records were produced by different investigators working in different project areas, a shared research design helped insure comparability of the data (Euler and Gumerman 1978).

Drawing upon these various sources of information, the following observations concerning the paleodemography of the Western Anasazi are possible. First, for all time periods, the average Western Anasazi settlement had 6.5 rooms. It was probably occupied by a single household, a large extended family in all likelihood. Prior to about 1100, the average site had 2.9 rooms, being a farmstead occupied by a single large nuclear family or a small extended family. Between 1100 and 1400, average site size was 9.5 rooms. Such sites were occupied by more than a single family and household, perhaps by a lineage. During this period, there is also substantial variation in site size in different parts of the Western Anasazi area with averages ranging from as low as 2.5 rooms in parts of Arizona and Utah to as high as 59 rooms in the vicinity of Zuni, New Mexico. While sites are larger in some areas than in others, there is a range of site sizes in virtually every area. The larger and more aggregated of these settlements must have played important roles in the economic, religious, or political affairs of people living in the smaller surrounding sites. Nevertheless, most Western Anasazi people during most time periods lived on homestead-size sites (Plog, Effland, and Green 1978).

Second, the number of rooms per square kilometer discovered through archeological survey varies widely for the Western Anasazi region, especially during later times when very large sites exist in some areas. A good average density for all areas and all time periods is about 20 rooms to the square kilometer. It is unlikely that most small sites were occupied for more than about a generation, 30 years or so. Survey data in most areas where density data are available are best for the period about A.D. 800-1300, or about 17 generations. Thus, at any one time within this period there were about 1.2 occupied rooms in the average square kilometer. Half of these were living and half storage rooms, so that an estimate of three to six people per square kilometer is the best available average. However, small homestead-size sites were probably inhabited for even less than a generation. If this site pattern is typical, a density more on the order of one to two persons per square kilometer seems reasonable. Since not all areas were equally populated at all time periods, Western Anasazi population was probably never more than about 300,000 people and at most times was considerably less (averages are from Plog, Effland, and Green 1978 and Plog, Plog, and Wait 1978).

This homestead pattern contrasts strongly with the traditional view of the Western Anasazi, which describes a settlement pattern consisting of large central sites surrounded by "small sites" with dozens of rooms. The earlier interpretation was incorrect (Lipe 1970; Jennings 1966), since perceived variation in site density in the Southwest is mainly due to differences in archeological survey techniques rather than being a product of the behavior of prehistoric peoples (Plog, Plog, and Wait 1978).

Despite the evidence for variation, there are several patterns common to demographic change over time in the Western Anasazi area. In many but not all parts of it, there was a period of rapid population increase between about A.D. 300 and 700. In areas where this increase occurred, there was a subsequent period of population decline or dispersion. Between A.D. 900 and 1100, population grew rapidly throughout most of the area. Within two to three centuries thereafter, people disappeared from most of the previously occupied territory. The Zuni and Hopi areas, where population began to grow as it declined elsewhere, were the major exceptions. Certainly, there are many exceptions to this pattern in particular drainages within the area.

## Chronology

People first lived in the Western Anasazi area before 10,000 B.C. Evidence of their presence is the Tolchaco complex, a "preprojectile point" manifestation (K. Bartlett 1943; Krieger 1962), although the antiquity of these sites has been questioned (Keller and Wilson 1976). While the range of materials found on such sites is quite different from that on nearby sites, it is only possible to conclude that the sites are very old, not that they are certainly preprojectile point.

Paleo-Indian populations inhabited the area, although not in very great numbers (M.R. Harrington 1933; Harrington and Simpson 1961; Shutler 1965; Agenbroad 1967; Longacre and Graves 1976). Before about 3000 B.C. the inhabitants of the Western Anasazi area were peripheral to groups living outside the area ("Post-Pleistocene Archeology, 7000–2000 B.C.," this vol.). After this date, in this area and throughout the Southwest local traditions clearly developed. Evidence of these late Picosan groups is present in a number of sites (Wendorf and Thomas 1951; Martin et al. 1962; Euler and Olson 1965; Lindsay et al. 1969; Turner 1971; Fritz 1974; Briuer 1975).

The chronological framework most important for describing the bulk of the evidence in the area remains the Pecos Conference chronology (Kidder 1927, 1924) (although later research suggests a far more complex pattern) with three Basketmaker and five Pueblo stages.

Harvard U., Peabody Mus.: A-2490.

Fig. 3. Basketmaker II coiled basket for carrying water with inner surface pitched with piñon gum. Loops on either side are cord of twisted human hair, used to carry basket on back (Kidder and Guernsey 1919:168–170). Basket excavated from Cave II, Kin-Boko Canyon, Marsh Pass, Ariz. Height 43.2 cm.

Basketmaker I is defined to describe the transition between Desert and Western Anasazi culture. While some archeologists have argued for evidence of such a stage (Washburn 1975), it is generally considered to be unproved.

Thus, the first important stage in the chronology is Basketmaker II, which lasts from about 100 B.C. to about A.D. 400. Basketmaker II sites occur in the Ackmen-Lowry area of Colorado (Martin, Lloyd, and Spoehr 1938), the La Plata district near Durango, Colorado (Morris and Burgh 1954), in northeastern Arizona (E.A. Morris 1959), and in southern Utah (Lipe and Matson 1975). These sites tend to occur primarily in caves or rockshelters and on promontories with a view over the surrounding area. The large quantity of baskets (figs. 3–4) and other woven artifacts (fig. 5) recovered from early cave sites led to the naming of this and the following period. Nevertheless, the most common artifacts are chipped stone tools (fig. 6) and waste resulting from their manufacture.

Sites without pottery occur widely over the Western Anasazi area and are abundant in some places. Whether such sites are late sites at which only nonceramic artifacts were used (such as tool manufacture or butchering sites) or whether they are genuinely preceramic is not known. Similarly, it has generally been thought that Basketmaker II was primarily a northern phenomenon, but nonceramic sites or sites with limited quantities of crude pottery

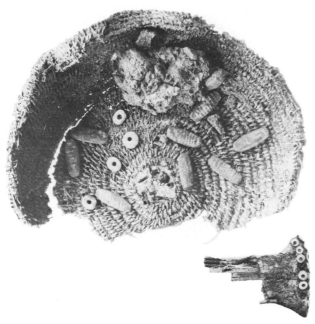

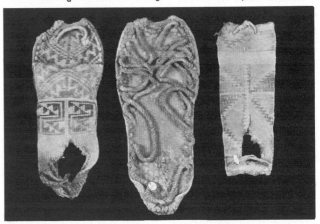

Mus. of Northern Ariz., Flagstaff: 3112/B6.25, B7.56.

Fig. 4. Basketmaker II coiled basket fragment (top) containing wooden gaming dice, shell beads, and lump of red mineral (hematite) paint. Willow wood comb (bottom) decorated with bone beads attached along handle with piñon gum. Both excavated from Woodchuck Cave, Water Lily Canyon, Navajo Co., Ariz. Diameter of top about 15.2 cm, other same scale.

Field Mus. Chicago: a, 165170; b, 165150; c, 165142; Amer. Mus. of Nat. Hist., New York: d, 29.1/1385; e, 29.1/1363; f, 29.1/1761.

Fig. 5. Basketmaker III woven artifacts. a, Yucca fiber burden strap with design painted in mineral paints on surface, excavated from Battle Canyon, San Juan Co., Utah; b, one of pair of leggings made of human hair woven in coiled netting technique; c, yucca string apron; b-c excavated from Butler Canyon, San Juan Co., Utah; d-e, crescent-toe style sandals showing (d) toe-heel tie and (e) side-loop tie from Mummy Cave; f, square-toe style with toe-heel tie from Tseh-ya-tso; d-f excavated from Canyon del Muerto, Apache Co., Ariz. (see Kidder and Guernsey 1919:pls. 40-41; Tanner 1976:60-63). Length of a 47 cm; b, d-f same scale; c estimated.

occur in the southern (Plog 1974) and central (Gumerman and Euler 1976) portions of the area. Since lithic scatters are unlikely to have been recognized given typical survey techniques, the distribution is still a major problem.

Basketmaker III lasts from A.D. 400 to 700. This is the first stage during which there is considerable evidence of occupation in almost all the Western Anasazi territory, including at least one site south of the Mogollon Rim (D.H. Morris 1970). Houses (fig. 7) of this period are typically built in deep circular pits. One to 20 houses can occur on a site although three or four are more common. The majority of ceramic vessels are a plain gray type, Lino Gray. Toward the end of this stage, a few lines of design are sometimes painted on these vessels producing Lino Black-on-gray (fig. 8); and plain redwares were produced in increasing abundance. Trough metates and rectangular one- or two-hand manos begin to replace the forms that were typical of Desert culture groups. The bow and arrow may have replaced the atlatl as the primary hunting instrument during this stage. Basketmaker III peoples were somewhat more dependent on agricultural resources than their predecessors, but hunting and gathering were still the major food procurement strategies.

The succeeding stage, Pueblo I, lasts from about A.D. 700 to about 900. The Basketmaker to Pueblo transition is marked by a number of important innovations, although there is great spatial variation in the timing and

significance of the changes (Plog 1974). Below-ground pit houses began to be replaced by above-ground masonry rooms. Plainware pottery predominated, although some vessel necks were decorated with a band of corrugations. The first hints of painted pottery other than black-on-gray appear in the form of red-on-orange and black-on-red types. Projectile points are thin and usually side notched, mostly for use with bows and arrows rather than

114

Fig. 6. Principal types of Basketmaker II stone points and drills excavated from Talus Village site, La Plata Co., Colo. a-c, Corner-notched, expanding stem points and knives; d, spindle-type drill; e, flaring-base type drill. Length of a 3.1 cm, rest same scale.

atlatls. Reliance on agriculture increased in some areas, and efforts to improve the growing conditions of particular fields by terracing, irrigation, and gridding began. Generalizations such as these are highly uncertain because this particular stage is not well known. Either sites are few in number or population was dispersed into small and widely separated sites. Moreover, the evidence from excavated sites of the period is diverse and disparate if not contradictory.

The Pueblo II and III periods last from A.D. 900 to 1100 and 1100 to 1300, respectively. Settlements are increasingly large and well planned at least in some areas. Eventually formal multistory Pueblos built around large plazas are in evidence. Pottery with surface corrugations increases in abundance relative to plainwares. Varieties of painted pottery are manufactured. The diversity of

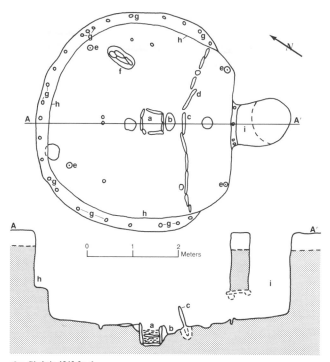

Fig. 7. Basketmaker III pit house excavated from White Mound, Apache Co., Ariz. Plan and section (A-A′) show: a, rectangular slab-lined fire pit; b, ash pit; c, deflector; d, slab partition; e, postholes for roof supports; f, slab-lined pit; g, postholes in encircling bench (h); i, ventilator shaft.

Fig. 8. Lino Black-on-gray bowl (top) excavated in northeast Ariz. bottom, Pueblo II Snowflake Black-on-white bowl from near Holbrook, Navajo Co., Ariz. Diameter of top 18.7 cm, other same scale.

black-on-white ceramics is substantial with distinctive regional styles in evidence. The increasing importance of black-on-red, black-on-orange, and especially polychrome pottery adds to the regional differentiation. Chipped stone tools are extremely casual; few well-made artifacts are found on most sites. Instead one finds easy-to-make and multipurpose flake tools. Grinding tools are typically flat slab metates and two-hand manos. While it is impossible to specify the precise proportion of the diet that was derived from agriculture, the percentage of agricultural products was certainly highest during these periods. Moreover, canals, terraces, and grid systems built during these stages indicate a substantially intensified agricultural practice. It is also during the last of these stages that the abandonment of large portions of the Western Anasazi area began.

Pueblo IV lasted from 1300 until the time of Spanish contact. During this stage people were increasingly concentrated in fewer and fewer sites within more and more limited portions of the Western Anasazi area. While small sites continued to exist, large villages of several hundreds and sometimes thousands of rooms were typical. Ceramic styles were increasingly distinctive of particular areas. Black-on-yellow pottery and red, black, white, and yellow polychrome ("Hopi Prehistory and History to 1850," fig. 2, this vol.) were typical of the area around the modern Hopi mesas while glaze polychromes of brown, cinnamon, and green were more common in the Zuni area. In some areas there was either a temporary or permanent return to a greater reliance on hunting and gathering. At the same time, in those areas where population was densest a continued reliance on agriculture and some innovation in productive strategies is evident.

While this chronology provides a useful overall framework of change in the Western Anasazi area, it is necessarily a very great simplification of complex events and spatial variation.

## Material Culture

### Variation in Pottery

Ceramic artifacts, sherds and vessels, have been fundamental to reconstructing Western Anasazi prehistory. A great many different attributes have been used in distinguishing the traditions of ceramic manufacture common at different times and in different places (Martin and Plog 1973:240-260). A very large number of different pottery types have been defined for the area, principally on the basis of design characteristics (see Oppelt 1976 for a comprehensive list of types). These types are grouped into a few dozen major wares on the basis of similarities in the raw materials and techniques of construction and firing used in their manufacture. Type and ware definitions are quite complex (L.J. Abel 1955; Colton 1955, 1956, 1958). Relatively precise dates have been assigned to some types using tree-ring determinations (Breternitz 1966).

While archeologists have long used ceramic variation for dating, the meaning of different types and styles to the people who made them has more recently become an important issue. Some archeologists have suggested that stylistic traditions may be distinctive of particular kin or residence groups (J.N. Hill 1970; Longacre 1970a). The more common and sounder argument has been that these styles were distinctive of territorial groups occupying a relatively large area.

The earliest ceramics found in the Western Anasazi area are all much alike both in style of production and design. They are brownwares, either Mogollon brownwares or the Alameda brownwares associated with the Hakataya, or some mixture (Dittert, Eddy, and Dickey 1963; Jennings 1966; "Prehistory: Mogollon" and "Prehistory: Hakataya," both this vol.). By the time ceramic vessels were being made in abundance, techniques were specific to the area. Pottery was gray, and when decorations were present, the paint was organic, except along the eastern edge of the area where paints were mineral like those of most of the Eastern Anasazi. While the first

painted ceramics in all areas are black-on-white, in short order black-on-red, red-on-orange, and black-on-orange types appeared, beginning as early as A.D. 700 for redwares made in northern Arizona and southern Utah. Similarly, unpainted pottery (probably used for cooking, storage, and other daily activities) was initially plain, but after A.D. 900 and more commonly 1100, increasingly typified by corrugated surfaces (fig. 9). Finally, black-on-white types were replaced in most areas by black-on-red, black-on-orange, and polychrome types.

It is impossible to discuss all the different wares and types that existed in the Western Anasazi area. The most important for understanding its prehistory are the black-on-white wares (fig. 10). For these wares, there were four important centers of manufacture and innovation: Mesa Verde, the Zuni area of New Mexico, the Little Colorado River valley, and the canyonlands of northern Arizona and southern Utah. Mesa Verde whitewares were manufactured with clays producing a relatively dark paste. Temper was of crushed rock and the raw materials used for paints were sometimes mineral and sometimes organic. Little Colorado whitewares had an exceptionally dark paste with crushed sherd temper, which was coated with a thin white slip. Paint was usually organic. The Cibola whitewares of the Zuni area had a white paste, variable temper, and mineral paint. The Tusayan whitewares had white paste, sand temper, and organic paint. There were accompanying gray or brownware types for each of these whitewares.

Early design styles and the general pattern of design change are common to these wares. Initially painted ceramics are characterized over all the Western Anasazi area by a relatively few thin lines. Wider lines and blockier designs follow. These are succeeded by hatched designs, then the opposition of solid and hatched designs, and more complex styles including life forms. This basic sequence of design succession is sufficiently common that it can be used for rough dating throughout the area.

left, Mus. of Northern Ariz., Flagstaff: NA 3029A.14; right, Smithsonian, Dept. of Anthr., Archeol.: 337211.

Fig. 9. Anasazi gray utility wares. left, Pueblo I Kana'a Gray pot excavated at Bonito Terrace, Coconino Co., Ariz.; right, corrugated jar excavated at Elden Pueblo, Coconino Co., Ariz. Diameter of left 24.4 cm, other same scale.

Between 1050 and 1150 distinctive regional styles specific to relatively small areas began to emerge (Colton 1953; Wasley 1959a; S. Plog 1977a). Tusayan designs, for

Field Mus., Chicago: a, 205998; b, 66772; c, 73978; d, 75114; e, 45292; f, 72991.
Fig. 10. Pottery dating from Pueblo II through Pueblo IV periods. a, Pueblo II (southwest Utah) Chaco Black-on-white ladle dating A.D. 950-1150 from Bug Canyon, San Juan Co., Utah; b, Pueblo II (Hopi Buttes) Tusayan Black-on-red seed jar dating 850-1125 from Oraibi, Navajo Co., Ariz.; c, Pueblo III (Upper Little Colorado) Tularosa Black-on-white pitcher dating 1100-1200 from San Cosmos, Apache Co., Ariz; d, Pueblo III Heshotauthla Polychrome bowl, a Zuni province glazed ceramic, dating 1275-1400 from Hard Scrabble, Apache Co., Ariz.; e, Pueblo III Mesa Verde Black-on-white mug dating 1150-1300 from Lowry Ruin, Montezuma Co., Colo.; f, Pueblo IV (Hopi Buttes) Four Mile Polychrome jar dating 1350-1400 from Homolovi, Navajo Co., Ariz. Length of a 28.2 cm, rest same scale.

example, arrange solid and hatched bands in relatively straightforward linear and circular patterns. Mesa Verde ceramics more commonly involve filling rounded spaces with dots and squiggles. The opposition of solid and hatched figures is more characteristic of the Zuni ceramics. These basic patterns are modified in a very large number of regionally and even locally distinct styles. Most of this differentiation occurs at about the time that population in the Western Anasazi area was increasing drastically, when the need for obvious social markers was probably greatest (S. Plog 1977a). Later styles, those of the Pueblo III and IV periods, are even more distinctive. Within the areas where people still lived, design traditions were more homogeneous locally and more varied regionally. Late prehistoric Zuni and Hopi pottery, for example, differs in color, paint, design, and layout.

Behaviorally, these differences must reflect the manner in which particular artisans learned to make their pottery, but the wider spatial patterns suggest that difference in learning is not the only explanation. On the one hand, the widespread distribution of particular styles represents the exchange or trading of particular vessels. On the other, ceramic traditions clearly respond to social needs such as population increases and a heightened sense of territoriality.

### Variation in Chipped Stone Tools

The factor of variation is studied in three different aspects of chipped stone tools: the raw materials from which they are made, the techniques of manufacture, and the tool forms produced.

The preferred raw material for making chipped stone tools in the Western Anasazi area was chert. Cherts vary in color and the fineness of their crystalline structure, and the finer the structure the more widely utilized the chert. Cherts occur as gravels and as nodules in some sandstone and limestone formations. Basalt and quartzite were less commonly used raw materials; the structure of both is coarser and less sharp edges can be produced. The finest material available for the manufacture of chipped stone artifacts was obsidian. This material is not available in great quantities, so its exchange was evidently highly structured. The source of obsidian raw materials can be identified on the basis of trace elements that are unique to particular flows of this volcanic glass. For example, the boundary between obsidian sources derived from the Flagstaff volcanic fields and the Red Hill deposit in New Mexico occurs at about Pinedale, Arizona. Both to the west and east of this area there are relatively exclusive trading networks. M. Green (1975, 1978) has demonstrated that exchange patterns can also be identified for chert and more common raw materials. Interestingly, the greater the distance between the source of the raw material and the locus of utilization, the greater the precision in deriving as many tools as possible from the raw material and utilizing the tools for as long and in as many different ways as possible.

Different construction techniques vary in how much they conserve the available raw material. A nodule can be smashed between two large stones (the bipolar technique), or flakes can be removed from it by striking it with another rock (hard-hammer technique), or with bone or antler (soft-hammer technique). The greatest number of artifacts can be made from a nodule when parallel-sided blades are removed by pressure flaking. All these techniques were used in the Western Anasazi area. While soft- and hard-hammer techniques were most common, rare raw materials such as obsidian were sometimes processed using a pressure technique. Exceptionally low quality materials were processed with a bipolar technique.

A relatively few limited-purpose tools were made by Western Anasazi groups. Projectile points, gravers for incising wood and bone, denticulates for shredding fibrous materials, notches for rounding wood and bone, gravers for etching, drills and punches for perforating wood, bone, and leather, and burins for chiseling wood and bone are the most common such artifacts. Flakes were sometimes removed from cobbles to create large chopping tools.

The most common chipped stone artifacts were, however, multipurpose tools. Archeologists have distinguished between knives used for slicing and scrapers for cleaning or abrading. The former have thin and acute edges; the latter, steeper and blunt edges. Edges reflecting these activities are sometimes produced by pressure flaking and sometimes by the simple act of using the tools in the activity in question. The majority of tools found on Western Anasazi sites are multipurpose scraper knives, some edges of which were used in one activity, other edges in another. Alternatively, the implement was used once or twice in a single activity and discarded. In short, generalized tools reflecting complex combinations of manufacture and use-modification in generalized cutting or scraping activities are the norm throughout the area (Decker 1976).

### Ground Stone Tools

Basalt, sandstone, and limestone were used for ground stone tools. Which raw material is typical of a particular area reflects both the local abundance and the presence of bedding planes in natural outcrops that produce manageable chunks of raw material. Manos, metates, and axes are the most commonly made ground stone artifacts. As was the case with chipped stone, artifacts made of scarcer resources were used for longer periods of time. Axes made of sillimanite schist native to the Rio Grande area that were recovered at the site of Awatovi show extensive evidence of reutilization (Woodbury 1954).

Much variation exists in the length, width, and configuration of manos and metates and is apparently due to

the length of time during which artifacts have been used; over time they become thinner and more faceted in cross-section. The actual variation in artifact form is relatively simple. There are oval, short-rectangular, and elongated rectangular manos (Mundie and Read 1976). The effective grinding surface of metates can be either an oval-shaped basin, a trough, or a flat platform. The general pattern in the Western Anasazi area involves evolution from the first to the last forms mentioned.

The most elegant ground stone tools made in the area are axes, generally polished with grooves along one or more edges to facilitate hafting. Axes are more common and of a more standardized form (three-quarter grooved) along the southern edges of the Western Anasazi area.

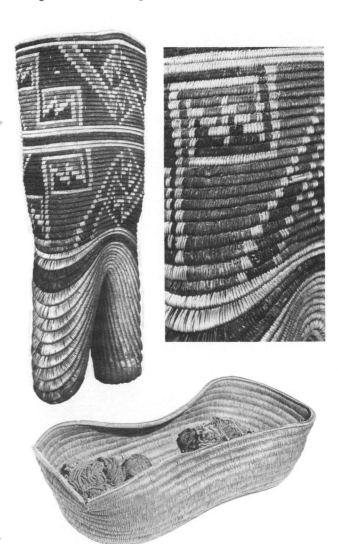

top, U. of Pa., U. Mus., Philadelphia: NA4925; bottom, Field Mus., Chicago: basket 165274, yarn 165273.

Fig. 11. Pueblo III coiled baskets. top, Bifurcated basket carried by two thongs (now missing) attached to upper section and decorated by alternating dyed coiling splints, from Moqui Canyon, San Juan Co., Utah (Farabee 1920:202–211). bottom, basket containing 5 balls of cotton yarn dyed red, yellow, and black excavated from a burial in Battle Canyon, southeast Utah. Height of top 57 cm, other same scale.

*Other Material Items*

There are a variety of other tools and features recovered from sites in the Western Anasazi area: baskets (fig. 11), prayer sticks, sandals, pouches, arrows, atlatls, storage pits, wells, and shrines. For each of these there are important patterns of variation within the area. In the case of basketry, for example, there is variation in the raw materials used—twigs, cactus, grasses—and in the manner in which baskets were made—coiling, twining, twilling (Martin and Plog 1973:239). Similarly, pits vary in shape, depth, and lining. For basketry and other perishable items, the detail of knowledge of patterns of variation reflects the pattern of preservation in different areas: basketry is both best understood and most diverse in form in areas where there are dry caves in which it is preserved. In the cases of features such as pits, the problem is somewhat different. Most excavations in the Western Anasazi area have focused on room blocks or pit houses.

## Architecture and Settlement Pattern

Architectural variation occurs in the materials used in building rooms, the kinds and configurations of rooms that occur on particular sites, and the diversity of patterns present on sites in the same and different areas. Five different construction techniques were present in the Western Anasazi area: a pit formed the lower levels of the house, while the roof and walls were made of timbers, branches, and reeds laid against a support structure and covered with earth; the pit was lined with stone or wood to form more substantial walls and wood or stone pilasters supported a roof; surface structures were built of poles lined with branches and reeds and coated with mud or clay, a technique called jacal; walls were built of stone, sometimes dry-laid and sometimes held together with mud; adobe walls were made entirely of mud mortar.

These construction techniques could be and were combined in a variety of different ways. Archeologists have sought to identify particular techniques that were characteristic of different time periods and areas (Daifuku 1961; Bullard 1962). However, the variation is great. Pit houses, for example, are generally an early form, but in some areas, people continued to live in pit houses throughout the entire occupation. A number of styles are important to understanding the prehistory of the area. The earliest of these is the White Mound style pit house (fig. 7) (Gladwin 1945). These houses were 10 to 15 square meters in area and were dug to a depth of one or two meters; they had fire pits, ventilators, partitions to separate the entrance area, deflectors (upright slabs placed between a hearth and doorway to reduce draft), and sometimes storage bins. Such houses tend to occur in groups of two or three in association with an arc of a dozen or so jacal surface rooms. Small sites are composed

U. of Ariz., Ariz. State Mus., Tucson.

Fig. 12. Spruce Tree House, Mesa Verde National Park, Montezuma Co., Colo. Ladder and roof of circular kiva D in foreground are part of 1930s reconstruction by Natl. Park Service. T-shaped dwelling room doors are characteristic of Mesa Verde and Canyon de Chelly architecture. Photograph by Helga Teiwes, 1965.

of one such cluster and large sites of a half-dozen or more. Presumably, surface rooms on such sites were used for storage, pit houses for living. Especially during Basketmaker III and Pueblo I times, this architectural style is very widely distributed over the Western Anasazi area although it often occurs side by side with other houses or sites built in locally distinctive styles.

Later Puebloan architecture is also highly variable. Three major construction styles have been defined. Mesa Verde style construction involves the use of well-shaped stone blocks. The use of thin, tabular sandstone slabs to build walls defines the Chacoan style. In Kayenta-style construction limited quantities of undressed, irregular stone are held together with large amounts of mortar. Jacal techniques are frequently used in combination with Kayenta. The Mesa Verde style is typical of Mesa Verde and surrounding areas, while Kayenta-style construction is most typical in the northwestern and central portions of the Western Anasazi area. The Chacoan style is most probably Eastern Anasazi in origin but occurs occasionally in the Western Anasazi area. Some archeologists have speculated that sites built in the Chacoan style may represent outposts of peoples who occupied Chaco Canyon ("Prehistory: Eastern Anasazi," this vol.). Again, these major styles occur along with a diversity of eclectic local traditions.

These techniques were used to construct rooms of varying sizes and shapes in which different activities occurred, although rooms, especially large ones, could have been the scene of a variety of activities, and the longer the room was occupied, the greater the probability it was used for different functions (Wilcox 1975). Three functionally different room types are generally identified: habitation or living rooms, kivas or ceremonial rooms, and storage rooms.† The numbers and associations of room types that occur on particular sites can vary widely, suggesting important differences in the organization of the groups that occupied the sites. During the Pueblo II period in northern Arizona and southern Utah, for example, two very different kinds of sites were built in the Kayenta tradition. The first of these is most common on mesa tops: a series of masonry, jacal, and pit house rooms were built around a common plaza. The rooms, and in some cases a wall, defined the plaza area. In cliff dwellings sites consisted of a living room, one to six storage chambers, and a mealing room around a common courtyard. Small sites consist of a single such complex and larger sites of several. Detailed reconstruction of building sequences at larger sites suggests that the court-yard complex was typically built at the same time, not individual rooms on the one hand or whole sites on the other (Dean 1970). Extended families probably occupied each such complex.

On Mesa Verde, rooms were also arranged around courtyards. However, sets of courtyards are themselves associated with a kiva suggesting some suprahousehold but intrasite social unit that was not present in the area just discussed. At the same time, mesa top settlements in Mesa Verde consisted of "about 8 to 15 contiguous rooms grouped nearly or partly around one kiva" (Rohn 1971:37). An even tighter association of a residence group with a ceremonial unit is suggested.

Contemporaneous sites in other Western Anasazi areas suggest still different patterns. On Black Mesa in Arizona, people were still living in villages of a few pit houses, storage rooms, and a kiva. Entire villages were the locus of organizational units equivalent to courtyard and kiva groups. At Broken K Pueblo in the Upper Little Colorado valley, habitation and storage rooms probably associated with a single household occur together with kivas more or less randomly distributed through the site. In contemporaneous sites to the west, there is little evidence of specialization in room function, and room size is highly standardized from site to site. Interestingly,

the rooms are about the same size as a habitation plus a storage room in nearby areas. Ceremonial structures rarely occur on sites, but great kivas occur in the center of site clusters.

In summary, there is considerable evidence of variation in settlement organization through the area. In some regions storage was evidently handled by families while in other areas it was communal. In some areas an architectural unit held only a single family, while in other areas it held many. The greater the evidence that is acquired from specific areas, the greater the indication of significant architectural and organizational diversity at the settlement level within each.

Quite apart from typical settlement patterns, there are important areal differences in the number of specialized types of settlements. Sites on Mesa Verde with an exceptionally high number of small kivas have a greater than usual number of storage rooms, and storage rooms are also associated with great kivas (Plog 1974; Martin and Plog 1973). It seems likely that both small kivas and great kivas were used for exchange and redistribution as well as ceremonies.

Nonhabitation sites, sites without structures at which specialized processing activities occurred, provide a second case. In some areas, such sites are more numerous than dwelling sites. In others, they are few in number (Plog, Effland, and Green 1978). Apparently in some areas living and resource processing occurred at the same site while in other areas different activities occurred at sites that were specific to particular extractive tasks. This variation probably reflects the distribution of resources in the area. When resources are homogeneously distributed, there is little justification for camping or constructing facilities away from habitation sites. When needed resources occur at discrete locations or at great distances from habitation sites, the opposite is true.

Especially problematical in this regard are sites with only one or two dwelling units. Three different interpretations of the activities carried out at such "small sites" are possible (A. Ward 1978): they were outliers of larger, central settlements; they were structurally identical to larger sites but the populations living there died or abandoned the site before it grew; or they were seasonally occupied houses such as field houses. All these patterns occur ethnographically.

The historical and organizational importance of larger sites in the area is equally problematical. While surface structures are earliest in the central provinces, a common pattern of above-ground living is earliest in the southern provinces and perhaps earlier still in the Mogollon area to the south. Large surface sites are also earlier in the south. While the inhabitants of these large sites undoubtedly played critical roles in organizing if not exploiting the products of the inhabitants of the more numerous farm-steads and homesteads that were the typical Western

† Kivas, by analogy with modern Pueblo practice, are rooms used primarily for ceremonial rather than secular purposes. However, W. Smith (1952:154-165) has noted a great deal of inconsistency in precisely what archeologists call a kiva. When the term is used consistently, it is defined by a complex of features: deflectors, fire pits, benches, ventilators, and sipapus. Unfortunately, it is sometimes used simply for rooms that are unusual when compared to others at a site. Archeologists distinguish between kivas and great kivas, the latter being larger and having features such as vaults and floor drums; but there is again inconsistency in the boundary between kivas and great kivas (Vivian and Reiter 1960).

Fig. 13. Cliff Palace Pueblo at southern end of Mesa Verde National Park, Montezuma Co., Colo. Pueblo contained 200 rooms, ranging to 3 stories, occupied from about A.D. 1100 to 1275. Photograph by Paul S. Martin, 1948.

Anasazi settlements, the precise role that these sites played as centers of trade, politics, religion, or economy has not been demonstrated.

## Spatial Organization

Major patterns of spatial variation through the Western Anasazi area have been described by a number of archeologists (Kidder 1924; McGregor 1965; Wormington 1969; Willey 1966; Martin and Plog 1973). While they have disagreed on specifics, these authors have suggested that the Western Anasazi area can be divided into a number of subregions in which artifactual remains are substantially homogeneous. Some have interpreted the spatial variation as reflecting the distribution of real social groups (Kidder 1924; Colton 1939; Gladwin and Gladwin 1934). Others have suggested that the boundaries are simply arbitrary products of the particular artifactual pattern under investigation (Bullard 1962). Still others have suggested that these apparent boundaries reflect the data recovery and analytical techniques of the different institutions that have worked in different areas (Martin and Plog 1973).

The units in question are probably best described as provinces. This term was initially used in reference to the area around Acoma Pueblo (Ruppé 1953), which is roughly hexagonal and totals a little over 10,000 square kilometers. The term was used to identify an area in which artifactual remains were sufficiently similar to suggest considerable exchange and interaction but not a singular organizational entity such as a tribe.

Anthropologists considering both ethnographic and archeological data have suggested that material cultural boundaries more likely reflect boundaries of ethnic interaction rather than simply boundaries between different social organizations (Barth 1969; Wobst 1977). Such boundaries structure the interaction between different human populations and between these populations and their environment, but there is no single organizational structure that unifies the participants. The assumption of local geographers that hexagonal packing is the most efficient form of territorial organization has been verified by the discovery that most precontact groups in North America had roughly six neighbors (Wobst 1977). Finally, research on the minimum number of individuals necessary for a group to be demographically stable, on the average distance over which changes in ceramic styles occur, and on the average distance that Western Anasazi groups could have traveled to obtain food without spending more calories than they acquired, all suggests a territorial radius of 25 to 30 kilometers (Wobst 1974; S. Plog 1977a; Lightfoot 1978). For the Western Anasazi area, assuming an average population density of about one person per square kilometer, a viable group would have occupied 200–300 square kilometers, a "nested hexagon" of seven groups 1,400 to 2,100 square kilometers, and a nested set of these groups (an effective exchange group) between 10,000 and 15,000 square kilometers. There is no evidence that proves the existence of such ethnic groups; there is only an intriguing correspondence between relatively recent theoretical descriptions of spatial behavior and relatively traditional descriptions of spatial patterning in the Western Anasazi area.

This is not to argue that identifiable and identical territorial units characterize all of Western Anasazi prehistory. In the first place, the strength of interaction within particular areas varied considerably (Dittert 1976). Furthermore, there were times when dramatic events, sometimes known and sometimes unknown, drew populations in diverse Western Anasazi areas into stronger than usual patterns of interaction. The provinces are more evident in Pueblo II and III times than in Pueblo I or IV. In fact, prior to Basketmaker III and Pueblo I stages little can be said of spatial variation in the area. Irwin-Williams ("Post-Pleistocene Archeology, 7000-2000 B.C.," this vol.) has noted the growing cultural integrity, the increasing similarity of artifactual remains within the area accompanied by increasingly great contrast with nearby areas, beginning at about 3000 B.C. While this date marks the beginning of a distinctively Southwestern tradition, it is not until well after A.D. 1 that it is useful to separate the Western Anasazi from other populations in the Plateau Southwest, on the basis of architecture, ceramics, and other material traits. Subsequently 11 major spatial units can be identified (fig. 2).

## Upper Little Colorado Province

The central portion of the Upper Little Colorado province was surveyed by Longacre and Rinaldo (Longacre 1970a, who also includes phase designations and a synthesis of the prehistory of the area). Additional surveys have covered much of the periphery (Plog 1974, 1978; S. Plog 1977; Donaldson 1975; Beeson 1966). The principal excavated sites are Show Low and Pinedale Ruins (Haury and Hargrave 1931), Kiatuthlanna (F.H.H. Roberts 1931), Table Rock Pueblo (Martin and Rinaldo 1960a), Hooper Ranch (Martin, Rinaldo, and Longacre 1961; Martin et al. 1962), Carter Ranch (Martin et al. 1964; Longacre 1970a), and Broken K (Martin, Longacre, and Hill 1967; J.N. Hill 1970).

Basketmaker architecture in the area is distinctive. Pit houses are typically quite shallow (rarely deeper than 20 to 30 centimeters) and lacking in well-developed internal features such as slab bins. The transition from below-ground to above-ground structures occurs at about A.D. 900-1000; there is some evidence that pit house sites were occupied until as late as 1250 (Harrill 1973), but it is not known whether these represent architecturally conservative and ethnically distinct populations in other parts of the drainage. Later architecture is quite diverse. One can

find contemporaneous sites built in Chacoan and Kayenta styles, blends of the two, and locally distinctive styles.

Extensive volcanic activity in the area before about 8000 B.C. disrupted the drainage pattern and created pockets of high-quality agricultural soils isolated by malpais. Sites are therefore not evenly distributed but occur in clusters in the major drainages. Early Basketmaker villages occur on high promontories and are typically quite large, including up to 100 houses (although not all were necessarily occupied contemporaneously). Late Basketmaker and early Pueblo villages are quite small, generally only a room or two. During Pueblo II and III periods there are larger central sites of 100 or more rooms. While there is great diversity in the layout of such villages, arrangement around a plaza is typical of the larger and later sites.

The ceramic tradition in the area is as eclectic as the architecture. The earliest pottery here includes Mogollon brownwares and Tusayan graywares. Early painted types include both Tusayan and Cibola whitewares, although the Cibola was predominant after about 1000.

Kivas are the main evidence for ceremonialism in the area. The excavated small kivas are generally square rooms while great kivas may be either round or square; the square are more common after 1100.

Danson (1957) labeled the area Transitional Mogollon, which is appropriate because material culture traditions here are borrowed and intermixed in a quite complex fashion.

## Chevelon-Chavez Province

Chavez Pass Ruin is the largest site in the area with at least 800 and perhaps over 2,000 rooms (Fewkes 1904; Colton 1946; Batcho 1978). Grapevine, Kinnikinick, and other large Pueblos on Anderson Mesa were described by Colton (1946). A survey of a few quite small localities is reported by Wilson (1969, who also best describes the local chronology). Extensive survey and some excavation has been done in the province (Plog, Hill, and Read 1976; S. Plog 1977a; Briuer 1975).

Basketmaker architecture in the area cannot be described because records exist for only a handful of houses and these vary widely in shape, size, depth, and manner of construction. Typical Pueblo II and Pueblo III sites are U-shaped surface structures that have been referred to as carports and patio houses because only three of the walls were of masonry and these are usually not full standing walls but only a footing between 20 centimeters and one meter high made of a dry-laid double course of roughly shaped sandstone blocks. The roof and walls of such structures were of mud-coated posts.

The topography of most of the area is a series of long ridges running from the Mogollon Rim toward the Little Colorado River. Sites are abundant and relatively evenly distributed although there is a general decline in density moving from south to north and a tendency for sites to concentrate in the vicinity of sandstone-derived soils.

Most settlements are small, being two or three U-shaped rooms arranged in a line. Larger sites do occur during the Pueblo II and III periods. In some cases 10 to 20 U-shaped structures are scattered over a site, with highly variable orientation and placement. In other cases, the rooms occur in neat lines of five or more rooms, while occasional true Pueblo units built around formal plazas are found. Circular great kivas, typically 20 to 30 meters in diameter, are abundant at the eastern edge of this province, perhaps as dense as one in every three to five square kilometers. At Chavez Pass on the western edge there is a large square great kiva.

Basketmaker pottery is a mixture of Mogollon brown-wares, Alameda brownwares, and Tusayan graywares. While corrugated types were used in this province, they were not nearly so abundant as in adjacent provinces. Tusayan whitewares were the earliest black-on-white pottery in the area. During Pueblo II and III periods, respectively, Little Colorado and Cibola whiteware types predominate. Later ceramic types are restricted to large sites on Anderson Mesa and along the Little Colorado River. While the technology and design traditions of these ceramics have scarcely been studied, they are clearly ancestral to Hopi pottery. Some Hopi clans claim that these late sites were the homes of their ancestors (Nequatewa 1967).

## Zuni Province

Surveys in the Zuni Province are reported by Spier (1917), Beeson (1966), LeBlanc (1978), and Weaver (1978). Major excavated sites are Hawikuh (Smith, Woodbury, and Woodbury 1966), Atsinna (Woodbury 1956), White Mound (Gladwin 1945), and Los Muertos (Marquardt 1974). F.H.H. Roberts (1939) excavated a number of sites in the area. Weaver (1978) provides the best synthesis of local prehistory.

Basketmaker III sites are typified by White Mound Village. Pueblo architecture varies somewhat with locally available raw materials, but the use of shaped sandstone blocks and slabs is common. The earliest above-ground sites consist of a single line of 5 to 10 rooms. In the northern part of the province, L-shaped units seem to be somewhat more common. During the Pueblo III and IV periods, immense Pueblos of sandstone were built around one or more central plazas. Round great kivas and round room kivas are typical of the area. The smaller kivas occur either inside or outside of the room block. Recesses in kiva walls occur but are not typical.

The earliest ceramics found in the area are Mogollon and Hakataya wares. During most of the Basketmaker periods and during the subsequent Pueblo periods locally made types of the Cibola whiteware predominate, although these are mixed with Tusayan whiteware types in the northern sector. This province is the center of

innovation if not actual manufacture of a set of related types for the next 300-400 years (Carlson 1970). The latest prehistoric painted types in the area are Zuni glazes (fig. 14) distinguished by their glaze paint and cinnamon and green colors.

While some of this area is typified by open valleys, much of it consists of relatively narrow canyons. Sites occur along terraces and even on the floodplains of the valleys. Mesa top sites are less typical, but do occur.

## Hopi Buttes Province

Principal excavated sites in the Hopi Buttes are Awatovi (Brew 1941; W. Smith 1952, 1971) and the Ramp, Plaza, and Kol sites (Gumerman 1969). Testing and limited excavation have occurred at the Homolovi Ruins near Winslow (Fewkes 1904) and at Walpi (C. Adams 1978). Hack (1942) and Daifuku (1961) have done survey and excavation in the area. The major survey is that of Gumerman (1969), while syntheses of local prehistory and chronology are in Gumerman (1969) and Gumerman and Skinner (1968).

The architectural pattern in the area is distinctive, if confusing. Basketmaker architecture consists of pit houses with rare surface structures. The shape, depth, and support pattern of these houses are highly variable even on a single site (Gumerman 1969). While White Mound-style pit houses occur in the area, shallower and more irregular structures are also found.

Pit houses last well into the Pueblo periods to as late as about 1200. Later pit houses are typically rectangular, three to four meters on a side, and roughly one-half meter in depth. These occur on sites with masonry surface structures of a similar size and shape. Construction is of brown clay mortar with varying quantities of tabular sandstone; a predominance of mortar is the common pattern.

Beginning at about 1200, above-ground pueblos are the typical form. In the fourteenth and fifteenth centuries sites such as Awatovi and Homolovi were quite large, ranging from a few hundred to over 1,000 rooms. Construction typically involved plazas, although their size and shape vary considerably. Walls are of sandstone slabs and blocks. The size and shape of both room and great kivas are highly variable throughout. Square and circular kivas with quite varied interior construction and furnishing are known.

Early ceramics are common Anasazi types. At about 1100, there is an increasing abundance of distinctive local Little Colorado whiteware types, which were almost certainly locally made (S. Plog 1977a). Beginning at about 1250 black-on-white pottery is replaced by black-on-orange, black-on-yellow, and then black- and red-on-yellow polychromes. These types are clearly prehistoric Hopi pottery. As is the case with Chavez Pass and Chevelon ruins, some Hopi clans trace their ancestry to sites in this area.

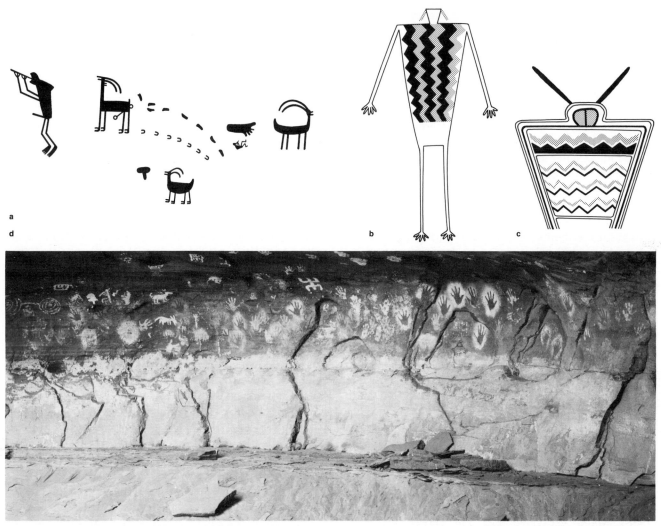

a-c, after Kidder and Guernsey 1919: figs. 96b, 100, 101; d, Smithsonian, NAA.

Fig. 14. Pictographs from northeastern Arizona. a, group of figures including a sheep and its tracks, and human sandal-prints following and coming to a stop behind the animal. Also included in the group are two humpbacked "flute-players," one reclining. Estimated date late Pueblo II–Pueblo III, location near Ruin 5, Hagoé Canyon, Navajo Co., Ariz. b-c, Human forms with headdresses or hairdressing, roughly daubed on the rocks in chalky paint, the outlined spaces representing white, black representing red, and shading yellow, estimated date early Basketmaker I, from Ruin 4, a Basketmaker cave, Navajo Co., Ariz., d, Outlines of hands, hand prints, a sitting "flute-player," and various geometric and animal forms decorating the walls of a cave in the Canyon de Chelly area, estimated date Pueblo III. Photographed between 1882 and 1893.

This area consists of broad alluvial valleys interrupted by mesas and volcanic necks. Sites tend to occur on terraces and other rises in the valley bottoms.

### Flagstaff Province

The archeological remains in the vicinity of Flagstaff, Arizona, are commonly identified as those of the "Sinagua." Although the local material culture is distinctive, the total array of items shares a great deal with surrounding groups so the area is treated as a Western Anasazi province.

There is no single survey of the whole province, although Colton (1946) and Wilson (1969) have described some survey results. The site records at the Museum of Northern Arizona, Flagstaff, include thousands of sites in the area. Wilson (1969) has provided syntheses of chro-

nology and local prehistory. Major excavated sites include Wupatki (Stanislawski 1963), Elden Pueblo (Fewkes 1927a), and Winona and Ridge Ruin (McGregor 1941; Colton 1941). Colton (1946) has described a great variety of tests and excavations at other sites in the vicinity of Flagstaff.

The earliest Basketmaker III architecture has relatively shallow pit houses (about 60 centimeters deep) of highly variable shape. After about A.D. 700 pit houses in the area are quite distinctive, generally rectangular, between one and two meters in depth, and with a ramp entryway opening to the east. The walls of the houses were contiguous upright timbers. At about 1100 sandstone masonry rather than timbers was used to form the walls of the pit houses. During this period houses following the pattern of the Hohokam of the southern desert were also built in the area; they are typically of sandstone or basalt with little or no mortar. Settlement layout varies considerably, but room blocks are usually compact with plazas generally absent.

The great kivas are typically square but sometimes round. While few have been excavated in the area, small kivas are apparently round and have wall recesses. Hohokam-type ball courts ("Prehistory: Hohokam," fig. 10, this vol.) also occur and may have been important in village ceremonialism.

Except for the very earliest centuries, plainware pottery consists of a variety of red, brown, and gray wares. Tusayan and Little Colorado whitewares are the common painted pottery. Again, Hohokam sherds are present at some sites. Black-on-red and polychrome types present near the end of the sequence are commonly ones manufactured to the north and northeast of the Flagstaff province.

A major event in the prehistory of this area was the eruption of Sunset Crater at about 1066. Not only did the eruption result in abandonments and subsequent resettlement in the area, but also local material items spread far to the south and east, probably reflecting the rapid movement of people out of the area.

## Grand Canyon Province

The prehistory of the Grand Canyon province is largely a record of Hakatayan rather than Anasazi groups ("Prehistory: Hakataya," this vol.). There is evidence of occasional Anasazi utilization of the Canyon environment from Basketmaker II (Schwartz 1970) through Pueblo IV (Schwartz 1966) periods, but the majority of Anasazi sites date to the period between 1050 and 1150 (Euler and Chandler 1978), when Anasazi sites are found both on the rim and in the bottom of the canyon, typically on the larger alluvial fans and in talus deposits. Availability of trails out of the canyon, domestic water, and shelter were the most important determinants of site location. Most settlements consist of one or two rooms, although larger sites occur both in the canyon bottom and on the rim. The style of construction and site layout are typical of the Kayenta area. Plainware, corrugated, and painted ceramics are all Tusayan types. Major surveys of the province were done by Haury (1931), Hall (1942), Taylor (1958), and Euler (Euler and Chandler 1978). Limited excavation of Anasazi sites is described by Haury (1931) and Schwartz (1970). Schwartz (1966) has summarized the chronology and prehistory.

## De Chelly Province

The center of De Chelly province is a series of high mountain ranges; deep canyon lands lie to the east and west. A number of major survey projects described sites in the area (C. Mindeleff 1897a; Mindeleff 1891; Morris 1925; DeHarport 1959; E.A. Morris 1959; Harris, Schoenwetter, and Warren 1967). Major excavated sites include Big Cave and Mummy Cave (Morris 1925, 1938), Tse ta'a (Steen 1966), and Antelope House (Rock and Morris 1975). However, these data provide only the most limited basis for characterizing the prehistory of the area; DeHarport (1959) provides the best synthesis.

Basketmaker II sites are apparently present in caves and in the higher mountain areas of the province. Basketmaker III sites, not greatly divergent from the White Mound pattern, are found throughout the area. Canyon-bottom sites are typically small, although somewhat larger sites occur on the eastern slopes of the more mountainous areas. Houses were of sufficient depth that roofs appear to have been laid across the excavated house pit. Pueblo I sites reflect a transition from subsurface to above-ground architecture. Pueblo II and III houses suggest affinities to both Mesa Verde and Chaco Canyon. Some houses are constructed of sandstone blocks, while others are of sandstone facing with a rubble core.

The ceramic pattern parallels the architectural sequence. Basketmaker and Pueblo I ceramics are typically Tusayan white and gray ware types, but Pueblo II and III ceramics are predominantly types of Mesa Verde wares. Limited evidence suggests that the area continued to be occupied well into the Pueblo IV period.

While populations living in the area seem to have been innovative in architectural style and in their reliance on agricultural products, it is unclear that the adaptive strategies they selected were viable. There is substantial evidence of more anemia among canyon-dwelling populations than in other groups living in upland areas and making more use of gathered plants (El-Najjar 1974).

## Black Mesa Province

Black Mesa province is somewhat smaller than most, being restricted to the giant depression in the top of the high Black Mesa. Because of its relative isolation the province received little attention during most of the history of archeological research in the Four Corners area (Beals, Brainerd, and Smith 1945 is an exception). During the 1960s and 1970s much work has been done there in advance of the destruction of hundreds of archeological sites by the strip mining of coal. The excavation of dozens of sites and survey records for hundreds have been described (Gumerman 1970; Gumerman, Westfall, and Weed 1972; Gumerman and Euler 1976; Layhe et al. 1976; S. Plog 1977).

The earliest pit houses in the area are irregular oval-shaped depressions between 20 centimeters and one meter deep, generally less than six per site. Later pit houses are larger and circular to subrectangular. Black Mesa peoples lived in pit houses through the entire length of their occupation of the area, which ended at about 1150. Surface architecture generally draws on the Kayenta tradition, although with perhaps somewhat more extensive use of jacal. Masonry rooms were used primarily for storage while both storage and habitation rooms were built of jacal. Pure masonry sites and sites with a mixture of masonry and jacal are both common. Round subterranean kivas usually with benches and with varying degrees of masonry finish are found on some sites.

Early Basketmaker III and Pueblo I villages are more or less of the White Mound style. Later villages are relatively uniform in layout with kivas and pit houses occurring in front of the surface rooms. At least some of the earlier villages were enclosed by fences or walls of horizontal posts. Kivas, masonry rooms, and jacal structures occur in highly variable association with one another. A strong kiva-storage room association suggests that ceremonial and economic activities were closely linked. Slightly larger upland villages may have served as centers in the area. Even the largest sites are rarely more than 10 rooms. Site locations are typically on hills and ridges along the major drainages.

The ceramic sequence in the area involves Tusayan gray and white ware types. Corrugated gray wares replace plainware types at about 1050. San Juan redwares and Tsegi orangewares also occur, probably as imports from outside the province. Siltstone baked by subterranean coal fires was the main raw material for making chipped stone artifacts. Later, some cherts were brought to the Mesa for tool manufacture from deposits far to the north.

### Mesa Verde Province

There has been more archeological work in the Mesa Verde province than any other. Important excavated sites include Spruce Tree House (fig. 12) (Fewkes 1909), Cliff Palace (fig. 13) (Fewkes 1911), Sun Temple (Fewkes 1916), the Far View sites (Fewkes 1917), Balcony House (Nusbaum 1911), Badger House Community (Hayes and Lancaster 1975), Mug House (Rohn 1971), Big Juniper House (Swannack 1969), and outside the National Park, Lowry Ruin (Martin, Roys, and von Bonin 1936), the Ackmen sites (Martin and Rinaldo 1939), and Chimney Rock (Eddy 1977). There are only unpublished descriptions of far larger sites, of hundreds of rooms in some cases, in the broad river valleys to the northwest of Mesa Verde. Surveys of Wetherill Mesa (Hayes 1964) and Chapin Mesa (Rohn 1977) provide information on site and settlement distributions. Rohn (1977) provides the best summary of local prehistory.

While there is some evidence of Basketmaker II peoples in the Mesa Verde area, major occupation seems to begin at about A.D. 600. Population increases steadily until about 1200 when the area was abandoned. The earliest settlements are pit house villages located mainly on the tops of the major mesas with typically 6 to 12 houses that are subcircular, roughly a meter in depth, usually with benches and four roof supports, and often with antechambers.

Between about A.D. 800 and 1000 enormous changes occur in local architecture. Initially, a few jacal surface structures appear on sites, but these are rapidly replaced by arcs of jacal rooms and then by surface units with jacal rooms of two different sizes, probably storage and living rooms. The only remaining subterranean structures are kivas, which evolve toward a distinctive type with stone walls, deep southern recesses, and six or more support pilasters. Construction materials also change as aboveground living becomes more common. The early jacal construction is replaced by mortar with some stone, then roughly shaped stone slabs and blocks, and eventually by the typical Mesa Verde masonry of dressed stone blocks. By about 1100, kivas were incorporated into or joined to room blocks of a dozen or more masonry rooms. Between about 1200 and 1300 both large cliff dwellings and mesa-top villages were occupied.

Individual sites (construction units) occur in clusters that represent the effective communities that occupied the area (Rohn 1977). The number of households in each cluster grows over time until Late Pueblo III when, on Chapin Mesa, for example, there were 11 clusters ranging in size from 20 to about 540 rooms.

Ceremonialism is reflected by the small kivas, occasional great kivas, and probably some of the more esoteric architectural units such as Sun Temple and a few stone towers.

Water and soil control systems, such as terraces, check dams, ditches, and reservoirs, are numerous and well described (Rohn 1977). The most impressive of these features is Mummy Lake, a circular reservoir about 30 meters in diameter contained by masonry walls. A ditch over a mile in length carried water to the reservoir from a system of collecting ditches on the mesa top. The length of occupation of particular sites and localities on the mesas correlates with the quality of soil and water resources (Cordell 1975).

Ceramic artifacts are Mesa Verde white and gray ware types that were probably manufactured within the area.

### Cedar Mesa Province

Cedar Mesa province consists of the upland areas surrounding the San Juan River as it passes through the southeastern corner of Utah. There are few reports on major excavation projects for this area (Brew 1946). The history of archeological research in the western part of the province is summarized by Adams and Adams (1959). Current understanding of the prehistory of the province is mainly based on survey research, with some limited testing of sites (Fowler et al. 1959; Lipe 1967; Jennings 1966; Lipe and Matson 1975; Matson and Lipe 1978; DeBloois and Green 1978; Winter 1976).

In almost every respect the material culture of the province reflects a complex admixture of the traditions of the Mesa Verde and Navajo Mountain provinces. Occupation begins no later than A.D. 1. Base camps associated with the Basketmaker occupation of the area were placed on the rims of the deep canyons that dissect it, apparently to maximize the access of local populations to both upland and canyon-bottom resources. Later sites occur on ridges, in canyon bottoms, and in cliff dwellings. While there are some large sites (those in Hovenweep, for example) average site size is only about two rooms for most of the area. Cliff dwellings in the larger canyons are somewhat larger, typically ranging up to 24 rooms. The abandonment and reoccupation of individual drainages is a major characteristic: in virtually every drainage that has been described in detail, very short phases separated by occupational hiatuses are evident (for example, Lipe 1970; DeBloois and Green 1978). Construction techniques are a combination of Mesa Verde style, which is more common in the east, and Kayenta style, both jacal and masonry, which is the more common style throughout the area. Kiva styles are similarly varied.

Ceramics include Mesa Verde white and gray ware types and the Tusayan wares common to the southeast. Detailed distributional studies (Adams and Adams 1959 for ceramics) indicate no sharp boundaries within the area, but rather very complex spatial and temporal patterns.

## Navajo Mountain Province

Definition of the Navajo Mountain province is difficult; ceramically and architectually it is characterized by the Kayenta style and tradition that is evident to varying degrees and at varying times in areas well to the south but is most common east of the confluence of the San Juan and Colorado rivers and north of Black Mesa. The area is one of mesas divided by canyons, some deep, others quite broad. Major excavations were conducted at Betatakin and Kiet Siel (Judd 1930; Dean 1969, 1970) while many smaller sites were excavated and large surveys undertaken in conjunction with the construction of Glen Canyon Dam (Ambler, Lindsay, and Stein 1964; Lindsay et al. 1969; Jennings 1966). The Long House Valley has been surveyed (Dean, Lindsay, and Robinson 1978).

Basketmaker architecture is generally of the White Mound style, while later architecture is predominantly Kayenta style. Common ceramic types are overwhelmingly Tusayan white and gray and San Juan redwares.

## Virgin River and Fremont Culture

The Arizona strip immediately north of the Grand Canyon and the adjacent Virgin River drainage in southwestern Utah appear to have material remains not very different from those of the Navajo Mountain area. However, archeological work has been so limited (Aikens 1963; Mueller 1974) that descriptions of material culture variation and occupational continuity are impossible. The area clearly had material culture of Kayenta affiliation, but this may simply reflect the periodic expansion of populations from the Black Mesa or Navajo Mountain provinces.

Western Anasazi artifacts are found on sites in southern Nevada and throughout most of Utah, in an admixture with non-Anasazi characteristics that has been referred to as the Fremont culture. Jennings (1966), Aikens (1966a, 1972), Winter (1973, 1976), and especially Ambler (1966) have objected to earlier descriptions of the area as the "northern periphery" of the Anasazi area. Instead, they maintain that the prehistory is locally distinct and understandable only in terms of local processes. However, there was certainly interaction between Fremont and Anasazi peoples and occasionally Anasazi people seem to have settled among Fremont people, for example, at the Coombs site (Lister et al. 1959–1961), and exchanged goods and ideas with them. Yet the evidence that Fremont has its own provinces and its own cultural developments seems undeniable.

## Perspective on the Provinces

The provinces have been treated as distinct spatial units, although there is substantial evidence of exchange and interaction among them. Probably individuals, families, and even large groups moved from one area to another. Yet, important material elements are distinctive for each.

Four of the provinces are distinguished by strong architectural and ceramic traditions, at least late in their prehistory: Hopi Buttes, Zuni, Mesa Verde, and Black Mesa. The intervening provinces drew upon the ideas and materials of these centers of production and innovation but used them to their own ends. Expansions and contractions of the areas in which the material products of the centers were exchanged is evident, especially in the case of the Kayenta tradition.

## Trade and Interaction

The rate of exchange of foodstuffs and perishable items in the Western Anasazi area was probably quite high, although there is not and probably will never be direct archeological evidence for this. However, ethnographic evidence from many parts of the world indicates reciprocal daily exchanges of foodstuffs between friends and kinsmen, periodic large-scale exchanges in association with seasonal ceremonies, and often exchanges between communities that specialize in the utilization of particular local plant and animal resources.

Prehistoric Anasazi exchange of nonperishable items is somewhat better understood. There is evidence for trade in chipped stone raw materials and in painted ceramics. Occasional sherds of pottery from quite distant regions have long been noted, but petrographic and chemical analyses of types believed to be indigenous to a particular area suggest that manufacture may have been restricted to one or a few centers and exchange widespread (S. Plog 1977:65–74).

Beyond ceramics and chipped stone, one can only speculate concerning the importance of exchange. There are provocative hints. Groups living in different room blocks at Broken K Pueblo apparently specialized in the production of bone rings and arrows (Longacre 1966). The occurrence of *Agave parryi* in relict stands along the north side of the Mogollon Rim suggests that peoples living in this area may have exchanged this foodstuff with others living south of the Rim where the plant is indigenous (Minnis and Plog 1976). Hohokam shell artifacts as well as sherds occur occasionally in Western Anasazi sites. Finally, similarities in Mogollon and Western Anasazi material culture may suggest exchange as well as continuing contact between these groups (Colton 1939).

But the magnitude of exchange cannot be estimated, nor is it yet possible to gauge the relative quantities of goods exchanged by kinsmen or trading partners from household to household or village to village as compared to movement of goods by organized trading expeditions. The pattern of spatial variation in material culture in the Western Anasazi area is probably a product of relatively higher rates of exchanges of goods, information, and mates within provinces than between them; further research is likely to confirm the importance of exchange for the structure and dynamics of Western Anasazi prehistory.

The extent to which Western Anasazi prehistory was shaped by indirect and direct contact with Mesoamerican populations is a controversial topic. It has been suggested that "all of the major Southwestern cultural developments should be considered together as peripheral manifestations of the cultural evolution of greater Mesoamerica" and that one should "refer not only to somewhat vaguely conceptualized 'influences,' but to identifiable southwestern responses to specific historic events and changes in hearthland Mesoamerica" (Kelley and Kelley 1975:178-179; Kelley 1971).

Certainly, most of the important architectural techniques, methods of ceramic manufacture, and the domesticates that underlay the survival of humans in the Western Anasazi area are of Mesoamerican origin. The design styles and coloring of painted ceramics in the area are at least inspired by Mesoamerican traditions. Occasionally the use of Mesoamerican symbols can be identified, for example, birds on late prehistoric Hopi pottery. There is also evidence for trade between Western Anasazi peoples and Mesoamericans; macaws and copper bells were certainly brought into the area from Mesoamerica; and shell trumpets, pottery stamps, and cloisonné-decorated sandstone may have been (Kelley and Kelley 1975). Finally, kiva murals such as those of Awatovi (W. Smith 1952) include elements of Mesoamerican coloring and style, leading some archeologists to conclude that a prehistoric equivalent of the modern Hopi kachina societies was a derivative of the Mesoamerican Tlaloc cult. However, the suggestions that great kivas and large towns in the Western Anasazi area were Mesoamerican trading centers (Kelley and Kelley 1975; Di Peso 1968) fails to consider the very small proportion of the material culture recovered from such sites that is of clear Mesoamerican origin and the complete absence of Mesoamerican trade items at most excavated sites in the Western Anasazi area. If Mesoamerican traders lived in the many great kivas one would expect material evidence of their presence. Such arguments also fail to consider the substantial variation in items of direct and indirect Mesoamerican origin at different times and places in the Western Anasazi area. Great kivas and large towns are easily understood as local developments, although the role of Mesoamerica in providing the technological underpinnings and stylistic overlay of local material culture was great.

## Biocultural Issues

There is some evidence of cannibalism at a number of sites in the Western Anasazi area during the Pueblo periods (Turner and Morris 1970; Flinn, Turner, and Brew 1976). Disarticulated and isolated bone fragments are reported in trash deposits at many other sites but have not been analyzed for evidence of burning, butchering marks, or splintering for marrow extraction; when they are, an estimate can be made of how widespread the practice of cannibalism may have been.

There is growing evidence of dietary problems associated with increased reliance on agriculture. Skeletal materials from Canyon de Chelly, Chaco Canyon, and Tsegi Canyon show a much higher incidence of iron deficiency anemia than for contemporaneous populations living in upland areas. The canyon dwellers evidently depended heavily on corn agriculture, but the upland dwellers subsisted on a balance of corn and gathered resources. Cavities and oral disease are more evident among groups more dependent on agriculture, and in Tsegi Canyon in the Navajo Mountain province mean age at death decreased by over 20 percent just before the abandonment of the area (El-Najjar 1974; Ryan 1977).

Analyses of genetic relationships among Western Anasazi groups support the spatial patterns described on the basis of cultural materials. Skeletons from the Upper Little Colorado and Chevelon-Chavez provinces show a high degree of similarity as do those from the De Chelly, Navajo Mountain, and Hopi Buttes provinces (El-Najjar 1974). Genetic distance is generally correlated with spatial distance.

## Social History

The prehistory of each Western Anasazi province generally ends with an indication that it was abandoned. Far from a neutral fact, the nature of the abandonment of so large an area as well as the causes for it remain one of the great unexplained events in Western Anasazi prehistory.

In the archeological record, the evidence for abandonment is the great reduction in the number of sites in most Western Anasazi areas. But what happened to the people who had once lived in them? A number of alternatives are possible: death, migration, or aggregation into larger sites. Evidence for health problems that might have resulted in death and depopulation has been mentioned. Hopi legends describe migration. And in most provinces the latest sites were typically the largest. In all probability, all three alternatives were important, although to varying degrees in different areas.

Most efforts to explain the abandonment have dealt with factors such as death, disease, invasion, warfare, and climatic change (Jett 1964 and Martin and Plog 1973 summarize alternative theories). There is some evidence for all these during the abandonment period, but they are unsatisfactory as explanations because populations living in the same area had faced such problems throughout their tenure there. Later theories (Zubrow 1975; Martin and Plog 1973; Cordell 1975; Slatter 1973; S. Plog 1977) have sought an explanation for abandonment in the dynamics of Western Anasazi subsistence and social organization, focusing on the relative marginality of most of the Western Anasazi area for agriculture and the use of increasingly unproductive lands as population grew within the area.

Domesticates first appear as potential food resources in the area at about 3000 B.C. Yet there is no evidence of widespread utilization even of corn until after A.D. 1. During the period between about A.D. 600 and 1000 there is evidence of an increasingly heavy utilization of domesticates, or more intensive agricultural strategies, or both, in most provinces.

Why did the Western Anasazi begin to modify what had been a quite satisfactory diet of some domesticated and a significant quantity of hunted and gathered resources and to work harder to obtain those resources as well? Probably they had no choice but were forced to undertake this change by the gradual filling up of all provinces in the Western Anasazi area during this period. As population grew particular resources may have become insufficient to support the number of people present in the area. Stiger (1977) notes that as corn increases in coprolites from the area, piñon decreases. In at least some areas people evidently turned to corn as a substitute for piñon because this resource was becoming scarce. As population grew, people were also forced into areas where fewer hunted and gathered resources were available—the deep canyons of De Chelly for example—and increased their dependence on agricultural products.

In the short run, greater food production and the improvement of field productivity through the use of water and soil-control devices increased the available food supply and population continued to grow. A more sedentary existence beside the fields may have resulted in the increased birth rate that is correlated with it (Binford and Chasko 1976). With more population, the need for additional agricultural intensification grew.

These changes in productive strategies had organizational consequences in the Western Anasazi region as they did to the east (see "Prehistory: Eastern Anasazi," this vol.): changes in village layout, especially in the location of storage facilities, and other changes in village organization and interaction between villages. It is during this period that distinctive regional styles in architecture and ceramics emerge, growing as the widely shared styles of the Basketmaker III and Pueblo I periods were replaced by local and regional traditions. Villages grew larger, and the organizational importance of kivas and great kivas increased. Most people continued to live in homesteads and farmsteads, but villages and kivas were probably the centers of exchange and redistribution between groups living in areas where different resources were available or engaging in slightly different productive strategies. Regional styles were the symbols of unity that bound together people with different subsistence strategies.

During periods when rainfall was abundant population expanded onto marginal lands, while during hard times of decreased effective moisture a collapse of population into areas of better land occurred (Slatter 1973). The frequency of crop failure in marginal areas was probably quite high, and soil nutrients, even with shifting cultivation, were rapidly depleted.

As soil depletion occurred, the Western Anasazi responded by building more and more water and soil control structures. Such constructions work when the availability of water is predictable; in most of the Western Anasazi area it is not. Even in a wet summer, rain may fail to fall during periods critical to germination or to the formation of fruit. A thunderstorm may water one drainage system but miss another a mile away. Variation in rainfall is simply too great in the area for intensified agriculture. The Western Anasazi would not have perceived this in these terms, although decreasing crop yields, greater disease, and shorter life spans would have been noted. Their most likely response would have been building still larger systems that would capture more water, planting more fields in a growing season, shortening the fallow cycle, and concentrating more people in those areas with good soils, which, of course, placed stress on even the better soils. As this vicious cycle continued people died or moved into larger communities in more restricted locations. Erosion, crop failure, disease, and droughts occurred to varying degrees in different areas and magnified the problem until most of the Western Anasazi area was empty. Remaining peoples concentrated in the Zuni and Hopi areas.

The distribution of agricultural patterns among modern Pueblo groups supports this reconstruction. More complex and intensive agricultural technologies are present in the Eastern Anasazi area, especially along the Rio

Grande River, where environmental variation is far less extreme. The Hopi descendants of the Western Anasazi survived using a risk-hedging strategy: planting crops in small plots and in a variety of environmentally different situations spread out over hundreds of square miles. They planted enough in any one growing season to last for three. Had the Spanish not interrupted developments in the area, most of the Colorado Plateau would probably have been repopulated by peoples using a strategy such as this one.

Which Western Anasazi provinces contributed to which modern Pueblo populations? There is no simple answer to this question. During a period of disruption as substantial as the abandonment epoch, individuals, families, groups, and communities probably moved in in-credibly complex patterns in their efforts to find a place where they could survive. Modern myths and legends describe origins for the Hopi from as far away as the Salt River valley and from nearby areas where sites with substantial quantities of early Hopi pottery indeed occur. Nor is it possible to trace the organizational differences among modern Pueblo groups to particular prehistoric areas. Nucleated villages were a relatively recent innovation prior to the abandonment, and evidence of architectural and ceremonial forms that might be associated with particular patterns is variable from area to area within the provinces. In short, peoples not cultures moved during this period and arranged their organizational practices in response to the changed circumstances in which they found themselves.

# Prehistory: Eastern Anasazi

LINDA S. CORDELL

The Eastern Anasazi area encompasses about one-third of New Mexico (fig. 1). Within this region are some of the most impressive archeological sites in the United States, including the large, multistoried ruins within Chaco Canyon, Aztec, Bandelier, and Pecos National Monuments. The area is internally heterogeneous in geologic structure, landforms, and vegetation zones. It includes portions of the Southern Rocky Mountain, Colorado Plateau, and Basin and Range geologic provinces (see "Prehistory: Introduction," fig. 1, this vol.). Elevations range from about 5,000 feet along the major river valleys and basins to slightly above 13,000 feet in the Sangre de Cristo Mountains. Semiarid grassland and piñon-juniper woodland cover much of the area with pine and spruce forests occurring in the less extensive mountain zones. The major subdivisions of the area, from the perspective of culture history, are the Rio Grande Valley, the San Juan drainage, and the Acoma-Laguna provinces. The area as a whole is the homeland of the modern Eastern Pueblo peoples—the Rio Grande Pueblos, Acoma

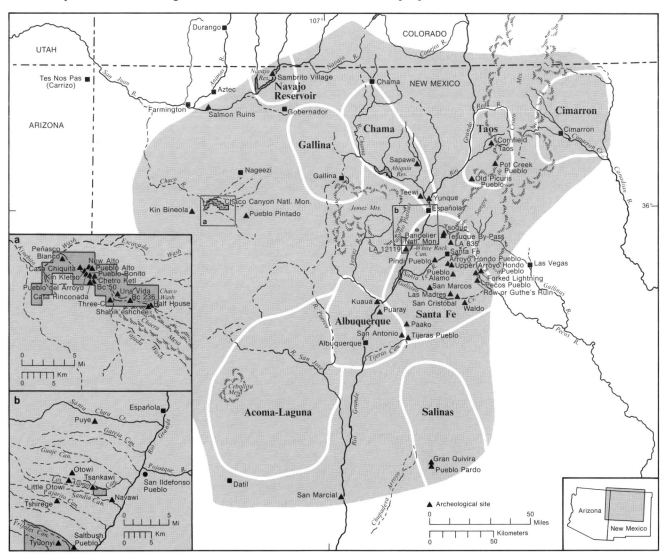

Fig. 1. Major branches of Eastern Anasazi and archeological sites. Insets show a, Chaco Canyon and b, Pajarito Plateau site concentrations.

Pueblo, and Laguna Pueblo—who share patterns of economic adaptation and social and religious organization that distinguish them from the Western Pueblo peoples of Zuni and Hopi. Archeological data indicate considerable continuity within the Eastern Anasazi area from about A.D. 1.

The prehistoric developments discussed here span more than 1,500 years and have been the subject of scholarly inquiry for more than a century. The ruins of Chaco Canyon were first described by Gregg (1954:253) in 1844. Archeological work in the Eastern Anasazi area was initiated by Bandelier (1883, 1890–1892), who was followed by the renowned figures Nelson (1914), Hewett (1906, 1938), Judd (1922, 1954), Kidder (1915, 1931–1936, 2, 1958), and Mera (1935, 1940). Historical summaries of some of this research are available (Brand et al. 1937; Bannister 1964; Vivian and Mathews 1964; Wetherington 1968). Later research in the area includes major projects in the Navajo Reservoir district (Eddy 1966), the Pajarito Plateau (J.N. Hill 1978), National Park Service survey and excavation in Chaco Canyon National Monument (Hayes 1975; Judge 1976), work by the School of American Research near Santa Fe (Schwartz and Lang 1973; Dickson 1975), by the University of New Mexico in Tijeras Canyon (Judge 1974; Cordell 1977, 1977a) and by Eastern New Mexico University at Salmon Ruin and the middle San Juan Valley (Irwin-Williams 1972).

Throughout the history of this archeological research, major questions include tracing the origins of specific cultural traits found among the modern Eastern Pueblos and isolating the cause (or causes) for the abandonment of the San Juan area prior to European contact. Especially relevant, given the barren quality of the environment of much of the area today, are considerations of the extent to which semiarid environments constrain or encourage organizational complexity among peoples who depend on agriculture. A useful framework for summarizing the vast amount of data available on the prehistory of the area is provided by examining the methods used to address these research interests. The question of the origins of specific features found among modern Pueblos has been explored through the construction of refined chronologies. Continuity in ceramic styles, architectural details, and settlement patterns has been interpreted as indicating indigenous change. Discontinuities, such as an abrupt appearance of totally new architectural styles, have been interpreted as indicating migration into the area or social interaction with different cultural groups. At this level of inquiry, archeologists have worked within very small geographic localities or cultural districts. For the Eastern Anasazi area these include the Gobernador drainage, Chaco Canyon, the middle San Juan River valley, Chacra Mesa, Cebollita Mesa, Pajarito Plateau, Galisteo Basin, and the Navajo Reservoir, Gallina, Chama, Taos, Santa Fe, Acoma-Laguna, Albuquerque, Cim-arron, and Salinas districts. Although some of these are mentioned in what follows in order to highlight points of discussion, no comprehensive view of the Eastern Anasazi can be gained by discussing each district separately. Rather, this chapter provides a chronological overview of the entire area.

Paleoclimatic reconstructions and the general problems of adaptation to a semiarid land with unpredictable rainfall patterns have been considered relevant to both the questions of development of specific cultural traits and to abandonments. For example, continuity in ceramic traditions and architecture but a change in settlement pattern, particularly from dispersed to aggregated communities, is sometimes viewed as a response to the effects of climate change on crop yields for which large investments of labor in building water and/or soil control features provide a short-term solution (Longacre 1966:97; R.G. Vivian 1974; Zubrow 1971). Abandonment of the San Juan drainage has also been ascribed by some to climate change that ultimately made a farming way of life impossible (Judd 1924; Douglass 1929; Bryan 1954). It is important to note that despite the long history of intensive archeological research in the area, not all localities have been thoroughly or systematically investigated. For this reason, most emphasis will be placed on those areas that are relatively best known through available publications.

**Environment and Paleoenvironment**

There are four widely used approaches to examining past climatic conditions. First, modern climate may be used as a general guide to the past, because much of the variability in precipitation and temperature in the Southwest is the result of latitude and topography, including elevation and exposure. Second, dendroclimatological (tree-ring) reconstructions are useful and becoming more refined. Third, palynological reconstructions (studies based on fossil pollen) are useful in reconstructing past vegetation and therefore the climatic conditions that supported the plant communities represented. Although none of these methods produces completely unambiguous results, when used in combination they are considered quite accurate.

Today, as in the past, temperature range is determined primarily though not exclusively by latitude and altitude. In New Mexico, temperature declines northward from 1.5°F. to 2.5°F. for every degree of latitude. Temperatures also generally correlate inversely with elevation, but this is conditioned by several factors related to regional topography. The direction of exposure is important to the amount of insolation received and therefore temperature. Thus, the cavate dwellings of Frijoles Canyon, Bandelier National Monument, that are restricted to the north wall of the narrow canyon are much warmer in winter than other parts of the canyon (Houghton 1959:68). Air drainage and wind shifts also cause temperature changes in narrow valleys and steep canyons. Particularly on clear, still evenings, cool heavy air drains into canyon bottoms so that temperatures at these locations may be several degrees below those on the sides of canyons (Houghton 1959:70).

Some general observations with respect to temperature are particularly important to plant germination and the length of the growing season. In New Mexico, daily temperature changes are greatest in spring, which may endanger germinating seeds (Houghton 1959:70, 71). Corn requires about 120 days to mature, even longer if there is a lack of sufficient moisture (Hack 1942:20). Variability in the length of the growing season and frost-free period is characteristic of the Eastern Anasazi area. The growing season is not reliably 120 days long in some parts of the area. This is true not only in the high elevations of the Sangre de Cristos, where a short growing season would be anticipated, but also along most of the Chama above Española and in the Red River area of Taos (Tuan 1973; Houghton 1959).

Precipitation depends on the direction of prevailing winds as well as regional topography. In general, large mountain masses act as catchment areas for rainfall, and the correspondence between elevation and precipitation is quite close. Today, about 50 percent of the annual precipitation in New Mexico falls in winter and 50 percent in summer. Summer rainstorms are of short duration and high intensity. The characteristically dry spring allows the ground surface to dry out and the soil to become compacted so that summer storms may not saturate. Runoff is high and erosion may be severe (McGehee 1963). Particularly important for agriculture is the observation that June, a relatively dry month during the growing season, is also the month of maximum evapotranspiration. The geographically spotty distribution of rainfall, especially in summer when crops are maturing, has long been noted. Variability in summer rainfall is most marked in the Gallina area, on the Pajarito Plateau, and in Tijeras Canyon (Houghton 1959). The modern climate data indicate that with respect to both the length of the growing season and precipitation, reliance on horticulture is risky, although most of the Eastern Anasazi area is more favorable for crops than the Western Anasazi area ("Prehistory: Western Anasazi," this vol.). In addition to climate, soil depth and nutrients are important for maize. In many mountain localities where rainfall is plentiful, soils may be of insufficient depth for successful planting. In other settings, inadequate drainage and high rates of evaporation create salinization problems (Fosberg and Husler 1977; Castetter and Bell 1942).

That annular ring widths in certain drought-resistant species of trees vary with the amount of available moisture has long been known (Douglass 1929). Various refinements in constructing past climate from tree rings

have been developed (Fritts 1965; Fritts, Smith, and Stokes 1965; Dean and Robinson 1977). Paleoclimatic profiles derived from tree rings indicate episodes of relatively greater moisture in Chaco Canyon from about A.D. 650 to 1150, after which there were episodes during which the climate was drier than average. The tree-ring data for the central Rio Grande area (of Santa Fe) indicate average conditions until about A.D. 970, after which there were episodes of conditions that were drier than average. The Cebollita Mesa sequence indicates relatively more moist episodes from about A.D. 680 until 1340 when average or below-average precipitation is indicated (Dean and Robinson 1977). In a study of tree-ring data from five separate areas in the Southwest, Jorde (1977) found that between A.D. 750 and 1040, most short-term droughts lasted for about two years, but that from A.D. 1050 to 1349, periods of aridity were increased from two and one-half to three years. This suggests that cultural mechanisms appropriate for adapting to short-term drought before 1050 may no longer have been adequate beyond this date (see Slatter 1973).

Studies of alluviation and palynology in the Navajo Reservoir district (Dittert, Hester, and Eddy 1961; Schoenwetter and Eddy 1964; Schoenwetter and Dittert 1968; Schoenwetter 1966) have been interpreted as indicating both changes in the seasonality of rainfall and in the amounts of rainfall annually. The studies suggest that from A.D. 200 to 700, there was abundant moisture, long winters, and a general aggradation of streams. Beginning at about A.D. 700 and lasting until 1100, there was a shift to a warmer regime with rainfall concentrated in the summer. This shift in rainfall may have produced arroyo cutting and erosion. The pattern continued through the twelfth and thirteenth centuries except for a widespread drought between 1275 and 1300. The dry period lasted into the first decades of the fourteenth century, but there was a shift in seasonality of rainfall to a winter-dominant pattern and alluviation, which lasted until 1850 when the present pattern of both short winters and summer drought began another episode of channel cutting. Similar palynological reconstructions for the Rio Grande Valley area are at present not available; however, palynological, botanical, and faunal data from archeological sites in the Gallina area (Holbrook and Mackey 1976; Mackey and Holbrook 1978) indicate locally drier conditions beginning at about 1200.

It would be imprudent to rely exclusively on the data above in order to "explain" the archeology of the Eastern Anasazi area. For one thing, methods of paleoclimatological reconstruction are relatively new and refinements are expected to continue in each field. It is undoubtedly safe to derive from the information available that there were no tremendous changes in climate in the Eastern Anasazi area since A.D. 500, but there was a great deal of variability both within any one locality through time and at any one time from one place to another. Importantly, it is this variability that affected the prehistoric population, and the paleoclimatic reconstructions provide a background against which various cultural techniques for adapting may be evaluated.

## Chronology

### Basketmaker II

Basketmaker II settlements were first known from the Durango, Colorado, area (Morris and Burgh 1954), later from the Navajo Reservoir district (Eddy 1961, 1966:471; Dittert, Eddy, and Dicky 1963:5-12), the Albuquerque area (Reinhart 1967a, 1968), and the Cimarron River area (Glassow 1972a; Kirkpatrick 1976; Kirkpatrick and Ford 1977). Radiocarbon determinations date these remains to about A.D. 1 to 500. Charred corn and a relative abundance of milling stones attest to the importance of plant foods. Faunal remains are present and particularly diverse in the Navajo Reservoir sites where they included deer, elk, and mountain sheep. Ceramics were not present at either the Albuquerque or Cimarron sites; however, an undecorated ware produced by coiling and fired in an oxydizing atmosphere was recovered in small amounts in the Navajo Reservoir sites. This ceramic type (Los Pinos Brown) is considered significant, because oxydized ceramics are characteristic of the early Mogollon and Hohokam pottery and not of Anasazi wares. Whether or not Los Pinos Brown was locally produced has not been determined (Eddy 1966:386).

House types in the three areas show considerable variability, which is also characteristic of the Mogollon, but are generally roughly circular with only slightly depressed floors. The Cimarron and Albuquerque houses lacked interior storage cists or pits and are considered to have been only seasonally occupied (Glassow 1972, 1972a; Reinhart 1967a, 1968). Basketmaker II houses in the Navajo Reservoir district contained central fire or heating pits, slab-lined storage cists or beehive-shaped mud storage areas similar to those found in the Durango sites.

The Basketmaker II villages were located on bluffs or benches away from riverbottom areas, which may indicate that proximity to diverse vegetation zones was important. Village layout is known only from the Navajo Reservoir district. There settlements consisted of from 1 to 11 irregularly placed houses. An oversized house in each village has been interpreted as an intercommunity kiva, although these structures lacked specialized features associated with later kivas (Eddy 1966:477). Kivas are ceremonial rooms used in all modern Pueblos. The term is used, somewhat loosely by archeologists, to refer to buildings that, because of their size or the presence within them of nondomestic architectural features, may have served a similar function.

Other Basketmaker II sites in the Eastern Anasazi area are known from rockshelters (Traylor 1977; Mathews and Neller 1978) and widely scattered surface deposits encountered during surveys (Lang 1977a; C.F. Schaafsma 1976; Ruppé 1966; Ruppé and Dittert 1953; Wait 1976).

### Basketmaker III

According to the developmental criteria of the Pecos Classification, Basketmaker III sites are characterized by villages of irregular, shallow pit houses, numerous interior and exterior storage pits and cists, and widespread occurrence of ceramics, all of which are interpreted as indicative of sedentism (cf. Glassow 1972, 1972a). Lithic items include small projectile points, which have been interpreted as indicating a shift from the atlatl (spear thrower) to the bow and arrow. Trough metates occur in addition to grinding slabs. Kivas have been identified on the basis of specialized architectural details. Within the San Juan drainage and the Albuquerque district, excavated Basketmaker III settlements have been dated to A.D. 500 to 700. In the Cimarron area, similar villages date between A.D. 750 and 900, on the basis of radiocarbon samples (Glassow 1972a:80). Various oxydized ceramic types occur (Sambrito Brown, Tallahogan Red), and in the Albuquerque area these include Mogollon trade wares such as Alma Plain and Alma Neck Banded (T.R. Frisbie 1967:174). Ceramic inventories also include Lino Gray, considered diagnostic of the period. Lino Gray was produced in a reducing atmosphere that is considered a distinctly Anasazi firing technique.

There is subregional variation in pit house shape and interior features. In the San Juan drainage, houses at Sambrito Village (Eddy 1966:363), Half House (R.N. Adams 1949), and Shabik'eshchee Village (fig. 2) (F.H.H. Roberts 1929) are roughly oval to subrectangular in outline. Interior features include antechambers, central often slab-lined fire pits, four roof-support posts, deflectors, and sipapus. Sipapus are small holes in the floors of modern kivas. They are symbolic representations of the sipapu that, in Pueblo cosmological myths, is the place where man first emerged into the world. Low, mud room dividers in some rooms enclose areas containing mealing bins and grinding equipment. In the Rio Grande Valley, excavated Basketmaker III houses (Reinhart 1967, 1968; T.R. Frisbie 1967; Vytlacil and Brody 1958; Vivian and Clendenen 1965) are more often circular, lack adobe or stone deflectors and room dividers, and have fire pits with raised adobe collars.

Exterior work areas containing storage cists and hearths are common features of Basketmaker III villages. At both Sambrito Village and Shabik'eshchee Village a kiva has been identified. The kiva at Shabik'eshchee was large, 38.5 feet in diameter, and had a low, stone slab-faced bench completely encircling the room. Entrance was apparently through the roof. At Sambrito Village, the kiva had a ramp entryway. In the Rio Grande Valley, specialized kiva features, such as benches, have not been

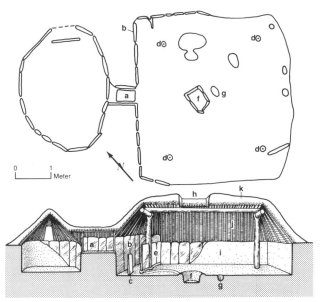

after F.H.H. Roberts 1929:fig. 1,2.

Fig. 2. Pit house of Basketmaker III type excavated at Shabik'eshchee Village site, San Juan Co., N.M. top, Plan of rectangular House A with circular antechamber. bottom, Reconstruction of cross-section of this house type showing probable construction method. a, Passage between rooms; b, slabs lining pit; c, slab deflector; d, postholes for roof supports; e, compartment wall; f, fire pit; g, sipapu; h, smoke hole; i, plastered walls; j, pole and brush framework; k, earth and plaster covering (F.H.H. Roberts 1929:10-16).

found; however, T.R. Frisbie (1967) suggests that one room that is set apart by being spatially separated from the cluster of houses making up the village may have functioned as a kiva.

Subsistence during Basketmaker III has been inferred both through the recovery of faunal and botanical remains and from the locations of villages. Plants include the three domestic staples characteristic of the Anasazi-Pueblo sequence—corn, beans, and squash. In addition, wild plant foods, such as piñon and Indian rice grass, and game animals, including cottontails and jackrabbits, deer, antelope, and Rocky Mountain bighorn sheep (F.H.H. Roberts 1929, 1935), were eaten. Sites are generally located on alluvial terraces or the first benches of rivers. Glassow (1972) suggests that these locations reflect the increased importance of cultigens in that sites are closer to arable land. Quantitative estimates of the degree of reliance on cultigens are extremely difficult, and probably varied throughout the region, but Schiffer (1972) has suggested, tentatively, that about half the diet consisted of domestic plant foods.

Trade items, in addition to the Mogollon ceramics found in the Albuquerque sites, include marine shell either in the form of whole beads or pendants. Other items of material culture found in Basketmaker III sites include baskets, sandals ("Prehistory:Western Anasazi," fig. 5, this vol.), cloud-blower pipes, and turquoise pendants (Eddy 1966:481; T.R. Frisbie 1967:17-18).

## Pueblo I

Pueblo I is generally dated to between A.D. 700 and 900. It is marked by architectural changes and ceramic variation, but it is a difficult category to apply uniformly throughout the Anasazi region, and variability in the rate of change from one local area to another would seem to be more characteristic than the "diagnostic traits" themselves. In general, Pueblo I is defined by the construction of above-ground, rectangular rooms, which were first used for storage while pit houses were retained as dwellings. Later, pit houses served as kivas and the above-ground rooms as houses. The production and use of neck-banded utility ware (Kana'a Gray) is considered a diagnostic temporal marker (fig. 3). Skeletal remains show lambdoidal flattening, deliberately produced, probably through the practice of cradleboarding.

In the Eastern Anasazi area, Pueblo I sites are best known from the Navajo Reservoir district (Eddy 1966; Schoenwetter and Dittert 1968), the Gobernador (Hall 1944), the Nageezi-Carrizo area (Hunter-Anderson 1976), and the Albuquerque district (T.R. Frisbie 1967; Schorsch 1962; Skinner 1965; Vivian and Clendenen 1965; Peckham 1957; Vytlacil and Brody 1958). Within Chaco Canyon National Monument numerous Pueblo I sites have been identified through site survey (Hayes 1975), and a few have been excavated (Judd 1924: 404-408; Truell 1976).

The ceramic assemblage of Pueblo I sites continues to include various brownwares and Lino Gray, with the addition of Kana'a Gray. Painted wares, which are more common in sites dating to the later portions of Pueblo I, include Rosa Black-on-white, Kiatuthlanna Black-on-white, Abajo Red-on-orange and La Plata Black-on-red. These wares seem to have been widely traded from one district to another. Vessel forms include jars, bowls, ollas (narrow-necked water jars), and ladles (Judd 1924:408).

Smithsonian, Dept. of Anthr., Archeol.: 340016.

Fig. 3. Banded gray utility jar excavated at Chaco Canyon, San Juan Co., N.M.; diameter 27.9 cm.

Pueblo I villages are generally located in the same kinds of topographic settings as Basketmaker III villages, but there is an expansion of settlements into the more mountainous portions of the Eastern Anasazi area (Hall 1944; Blevins and Joiner 1977; Hunter-Anderson 1976). In the Navajo Reservoir district, there is a marked increase in population, which has been attributed to both natural population increase and migration into the district from the Gobernador (Eddy 1966:485). In addition to villages consisting of surface structures and pit houses, there are campsites, which may represent seasonal activities such as late fall hunting. For example, in the Nageezi-Carrizo area, Hunter-Anderson (1976:44) noted two types of sites, pit houses associated with above-ground stone granaries and isolated sandstone hearths or pit hearths. The pit house sites were situated on ridges and mesa tops that today support a cover of grasses. The hearth sites are located in piñon-juniper forests. A lack of ground stone items at or near the hearth sites supports the interpretation that they served primarily as hunting camps.

In both the Gobernador and Navajo Reservoir districts, settlements with stockades are reported (Hall 1944; Eddy 1966) as they are elsewhere in the Four Corners area. Whether or not these were for defensive purposes has not been established. Hall (1944) suggested that they might have served either for defense or for privacy around outdoor work areas. In the late stockaded Pueblo I sites of the Navajo Reservoir district, numerous burned dwellings and human skeletons that had been burned and cannibalized are considered indicative of warfare (Eddy 1966:493).

*Pueblo II*

Pueblo II is generally dated between A.D. 900 and 1100. The period is marked by considerable shifts in population, and this is reflected, in part, by the use of specific phase sequences in local districts (Ruppé 1966; Lang 1977, 1977a; Hayes 1975; Eddy 1966). The more inclusive designation, Pueblo II, is retained here. Diagnostic ceramics include banded utility wares during the early part of Pueblo II and corrugated utility wares during the later part ("Prehistory: Western Anasazi," fig. 9, this vol.). Red Mesa Black-on-white, a distinctive type decorated with mineral-based pigment applied over a white slip, occurs widely on Pueblo II sites from the San Juan basin to Cebollita Mesa, Datil, and Albuquerque localities within the Eastern Anasazi area, as well as in the Western Anasazi area. Both pit houses and surface structures continued to be used for habitation. Masonry, rather than jacal (mud plastered over a frame of wood) became an increasingly common construction material for surface structures.

In the Navajo Reservoir district, stockaded settlements do not occur after A.D. 900. Pit houses show an increase

in floor area but do not contain elaborate floor features. Surface structures with paved floors were used both for habitation and storage. Sites are concentrated in the northern portion of the district and at higher elevations. Most of the trade items, including ceramics, seem to have derived from Mesa Verde. Artifact distributions showed a decline in frequency in milling tools and an increase in knives, choppers and hammers, and tools made of elk antler, which may imply an increase in hunting and a decline in farming. By about A.D. 1050, the Navajo Reservoir district was abandoned, and Eddy (1966: 505–506) suggests that the people moved north to Mesa Verde.

In the Chaco Canyon area, in direct contrast, Pueblo II saw a population increase and an accelerated pace of change. Early in Pueblo II, sites generally consist of linear arrangements of rooms with one or two kivas. An example is provided by the excavated Three-C site (Vivian 1965), which consisted of a double tier of nine rooms oriented north-south, with a work area to the east. Two kivas (fig. 4) were located to the east of the work area. Kiva 1 was typical of early Chaco style kivas in having a bench, subfloor ventilator shaft and slab firescreen, and irregular masonry walls. The second kiva conforms to early Mesa Verde style kivas in having a bench, four pilasters, masonry firescreen, and a ventilator that opened at floor level (Vivian 1965:11–12, 21–22). In addition to the small and variable Pueblo II sites, it

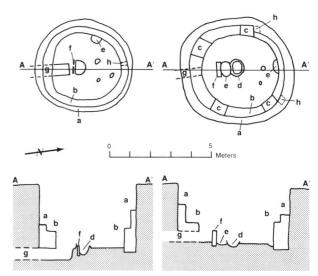

after Vivian 1965:fig. 2.

Fig. 4. Pueblo II kivas excavated from Three-C site, Chaco Canyon, San Juan Co., N.M. left, Plan and cross-section of Chaco style Kiva 1, characterized by high narrow bench around inner wall, subfloor ventilator shaft, slab firescreen, slab-lined fire pit, and absence of pilasters. right, Plan and cross-section of Mesa Verde style Kiva 2 with 4 pilasters, variable width wall bench, horizontal masonry firescreen, adobe-lined fire pit, and ventilator shaft opening in lower bench face. Horizontal masonry forms the outer walls and benches of both kivas (see Vivian 1965:14, 21–22). a, Kiva wall; b, bench; c, horizontal masonry pilasters; d, fire pit; e, floor depressions; f, firescreen; g, ventilator shaft; h, wall niches.

appears that some of the Pueblo III sites were partly constructed during Pueblo II times. Tree-ring dates indicate that initial building at Kin Bineola, Peñasco Blanco, Pueblo Bonito, and Una Vida cluster between A.D. 900 and 950. Although the re-use of wood in Chacoan sites presents a continuing problem in the dating of construction, in these cases the dates are generally confirmed by associated masonry styles (Judge 1976:6). Analysis of temper, which is nonplastic material included in potter's clay to prevent vessels from shrinking and cracking during firing, in Pueblo II ceramics from Chaco suggests that in some instances as much as 80 percent of the wares were not locally made. Decorated types seem to have been traded in from the area south of Chaco Canyon and utility wares from the Chuska area west of Chaco (A.H. Warren 1976; Judge 1976:9). Both the mixture of kiva styles at the Three-C site and the abundance of ceramic trade wares might be interpreted as an indication that the residents of Chaco were forming alliance networks with neighboring groups.

In the Cebollita Mesa area, surveys indicate a marked increase in the number of sites during Pueblo II (Ruppé 1966; Dittert 1959). Excavated sites are few, but architectural heterogeneity in wall construction has been noted. The arrangement of contiguous surface rooms, oriented north-south with a kiva depression east of the room block, as described for the Three-C site, is characteristic as well.

No abrupt changes in the Albuquerque area occurred during Pueblo II. Pit houses continued to be used. These show somewhat more standardized floor features, such as regular use of four post roof supports, ladder holes, ash pits, and sipapus. Artifact inventories include Red Mesa Black-on-white ceramics along with locally produced wares and trade wares from the Socorro and Mogollon areas. Population does seem to have expanded into the Tijeras Canyon locality, but it has been suggested that utilization of this setting was only on a seasonal basis (Blevins and Joiner 1977; Cordell 1977a).

The Galisteo Basin, Taos, Pajarito Plateau, and Chama areas seem to have been little utilized during Pueblo II (Biella and Chapman 1977:9; McNutt 1969; Lang 1977a). However, three sites in the Santa Fe district that date to Pueblo II provide evidence that the middle Rio Grande Valley was occupied and also indicate some of the interpretive problems prehistorians have been troubled by. The three sites are the Tesuque By-Pass site (McNutt 1969) and the Tsogue site (Allen 1973), both near Tesuque Pueblo, and LA 835 (Stubbs and Stallings 1953; McNutt 1969) near Santa Fe. The Tesuque By-Pass and Tsogue sites consisted of pit houses with associated surface structures. LA 835 included about 12 small surface house units, each consisting of from 10 to 20 rooms, one large kiva, and both small circular and rectangular kivas (Stubbs and Stallings 1953:155). Red Mesa Black-on-white in association with other types

occurred at all three sites. McNutt (1969) and Allen (1973) consider the ceramic assemblages found at these sites convincing evidence of a migration into the Santa Fe area from the west; however, they are troubled by the lack of San Juan architectural features, such as room partitions in pit houses or benches or pilasters in kivas. But ceramic distributions are probably more indicative of social interaction, which might include trade, than of migrations.

Finally, Red Mesa Black-on-white has been reported from the Taos area (Loose 1974; Green 1976); however, the type persisted as a trade ware after 1100 (Breternitz 1966) and no dates before 1100 have been obtained for the Taos sites.

*Pueblo III*

Pueblo III dates to A.D. 1100 to 1300 and for the Eastern Anasazi area is dominated by events in Chaco Canyon. The ceramics associated with Pueblo III are Chaco Corrugated and corrugated wares in general in the Eastern Anasazi area. Gallup Black-on-white is the diagnostic Pueblo III painted ware in Chaco Canyon, but limited amounts of Chaco Black-on-white occur as well. Mesa Verde wares, such as McElmo Black-on-white, and

a, U. of Colo. Mus., Boulder: 9421; b, Field Mus., Chicago: 81860; c, Mus. of N.M., Santa Fe: 22007/11.
Fig. 5. a-b, Chaco Black-on-white jar from La Plata Valley, La Plata Co., Colo.; pitcher from near Wingate, McKinley Co., N.M. c, Santa Fe Black-on-white bowl from Paako site, Santa Fe Co., N.M. Diameter of a 27.8 cm, rest same scale.

Chacoan copies of Mesa Verde ceramics are common throughout the San Juan drainage. In the Rio Grande Valley, both Chaco Black-on-white and a local copy referred to as Santa Fe Black-on-white are found in Pueblo III sites (fig. 5). During Pueblo III, there is generally an increase in the use of carbon paint to produce black pigment used on ceramics. Carbon or organic paints were made from plants such as the Rocky Mountain bee plant. The ceramic types, although they may be considered diagnostic "markers" for Pueblo III, for chronological purposes are not characteristic of the period in that they do not represent the full range of elaborate cultural developments. This is better appreci-ated by examining the diversity of archeological features and their complexity.

• THE CHACO AREA  Within the Chaco Canyon area, the complexity of Pueblo III is manifested by the types of villages present, the details of the great kivas, the fields and irrigation systems, the roads and trails, and the small items of material culture. The villages consist of two distinctive kinds of sites (Kluckhohn and Reuter 1939), referred to as Hosta Butte phase villages and Bonito phase towns. This terminology is awkward, because phase is a term with temporal implications. It is used here to conform to the published literature, although the two were contemporary (Hawley 1934, 1937a). Hosta Butte

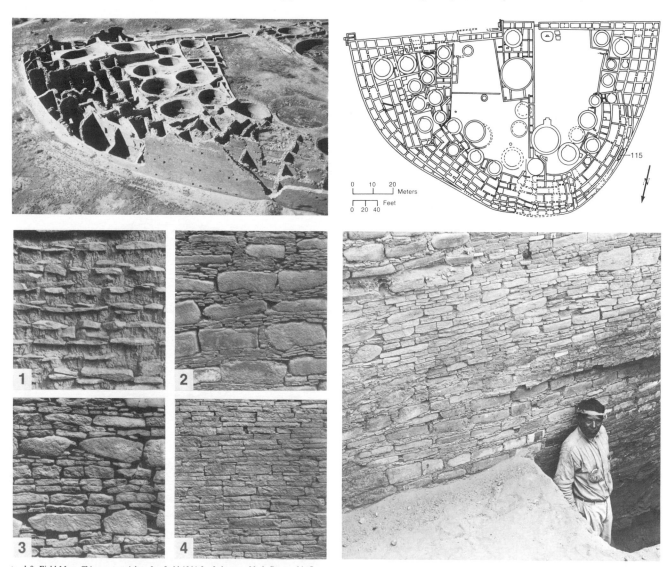

top left, Field Mus., Chicago: top right, after Judd 1964:fig. 2; bottom, Natl. Geographic Soc.
Fig. 6. Pueblo Bonito, Chaco Canyon, San Juan Co., N.M. top left, Northeastern section of Pueblo Bonito showing circular kivas and dwelling rooms with outer 4-storied wall in foreground. Photograph by Paul S. Martin, 1933. top right, Plan of Pueblo Bonito. bottom left, The 4 major types of masonry, with a 2-foot square section of each shown: "1. Spalled-sandstone slabs of wall width laid in abundant quantities of mud and often protected from the elements by closely placed stone chips. 2. Rubble veneered with casual blocks of friable sandstone dressed on the face only and chinked all around with chips of laminate sandstone. 3. Rubble veneered with matched blocks, either of laminate or dressed friable sandstone or both, alternating with bands of inch-thick tablets of laminated sandstone. 4. Rubble veneered with laminate sandstone of fairly uniform thickness laid with a minimum of mud plaster between" (Judd 1964:pl. 10). bottom right, A second addition of third-type masonry was added to second-type masonry forming the west wall of room 115. Photograph by O.C. Havens, 1926.

phase sites differ little or not at all from Pueblo II sites in Chaco Canyon. They average about 10 rooms in size and are single-story structures. Walls are masonry, but the masonry is somewhat irregular, and the arrangement of rooms is rather amorphous. Great kivas are not associated with Hosta Butte sites, although a single great kiva, such as the one at Casa Rinconada, may have served several of the small Hosta Butte communities. Hosta Butte sites are distributed on both the north and south sides of Chaco Canyon. Estimates derived from survey data suggest that about 2,900 people may have been living in Hosta Butte villages in an area of 43 square miles of Chaco Canyon National Monument (Hayes 1975:57).

The Bonito phase sites, sometimes referred to as towns, are distinctive in being large, multistoried structures with an average of 288 rooms (Hayes 1975). Pueblo Bonito (fig. 6), the largest, had an estimated 800 rooms, and parts of this site were five stories high (Judd 1964). Chetro Ketl (fig. 7) had an estimated 500 rooms and Pueblo del Arroyo an estimated 285 rooms. Sites outside Chaco Canyon proper but Bonito phase in style include Salmon

Ruin with an estimated 290 rooms (Irwin-Williams 1972) and Pueblo Pintado with perhaps 185 rooms (Judge 1976). Hayes (1975) believes that most rooms were not used as domiciles and estimates that about 2,760 people may have been living in the Bonito towns during Pueblo III. In addition to being larger, the Bonito towns are "planned" structures with interior courtyards and great kivas incorporated within the towns. Bonito phase sites are characterized by the large individual rooms and elaborate masonry walls comprised of an interior core of stones and finely fitted, often decorative, veneers of stone on both exterior and interior surfaces.

Great kivas are distinctive both in terms of their size and the elaboration of floor features. For example, the great kiva at Casa Rinconada has a diameter of about 63 feet, and a great kiva at Chetro Ketl (fig. 8), a diameter of about 55 feet (Vivian and Reiter 1960). Considering that these structures are largely subterranean, the amount of labor invested in their construction is tremendous. Antechambers are commonly associated with great kivas, and entry to the kiva was either through recessed masonry stairways from the antechamber or from the antechamber by ladder. Floor features include square raised fireboxes located on the central axis but slightly south of the center of the round room and deflectors that were either masonry or wooden wickerwork. Roof supports were either four masonry columns or four massive timbers. At Chetro Ketl, each pit for seating roof support timbers contained four sandstone disks, probably to help support the great weight of the roof. Paired masonry "vaults" are located on each side of the floor parallelling the main north-south axis. Depth of the great kivas is sometimes difficult to estimate, because the original wall height is not known, but Judd (1922:115–116) estimated that a great kiva at Pueblo Bonito had a wall height of 11 feet. Wall niches or crypts are common features of these structures, but only at Chetro Ketl II were the crypts sealed with masonry. The 10 wall niches at Chetro Ketl II were found to contain strings of stone and shell beads and pendants (Vivian and Reiter 1960).

The details of the irrigation and field systems in Chaco Canyon have been described by R.G. Vivian (1970, 1974). Importantly, these depended on water from runoff from the cliff tops bordering Chaco Canyon and not from diverting water from Chaco wash (which is now considerably entrenched). According to R.G. Vivian (1974) runoff from the exposed sandstone bedrock, which slopes toward the canyon rim, and from small side canyons, was channeled by diversion dams and canals to multiple headgates, and then by canals and ditches through bordered gardens (fig. 9). After irrigating the bordered gardens, any excess water was drained into Chaco wash. The amount of land irrigated by this method is difficult to estimate, but a bordered garden at Chetro Ketl comprised only about 11.86 acres. Although some fields may have been destroyed by historic erosion, it is unlikely that

Natl. Park Service.

Fig. 7. Chetro Ketl (top), a planned Bonito phase site in Chaco Canyon, and BC-53 (bottom), a Hosta Butte phase site on the opposite side of Chaco wash. The Chetro Ketl site is oriented south; the walled enclosure includes Great Kivas and plazas; masonry is finely finished sandstone; rooms are long and narrow and the site comprises about 500 rooms. The BC-53 site has no consistent orientation, small keyhole-shaped kivas incorporated among rooms, irregular sandstone masonry, small room size, and the site comprises about 20 rooms (see also Bannister 1964). Both sites are in San Juan Co., N.M.

Fig. 8. Chetro Ketl (San Juan Co., N.M.) great kiva, view from south. Stairway at rear of round chamber leads to the antechamber. The square firebox in the center of the photograph contained ash. It is flanked on both sides by raised rectangular features and two of the four pits that contained the massive wood timbers to support the roof. The other two round pits and the sandstone disks that helped support the timbers can be seen in the background. Some of the 29 (perhaps originally 30) crypts can be seen around the upper interior wall. The 10 sealed crypts (not visible) are in the wall just below the (later) floor level. (See also Hewett 1936.) Photograph by Ray Williamson, 1978.

irrigated land in Chaco Canyon could have supported the total population.

Complex systems of roads and trails (fig. 10) have been well documented through aerial photography and ground-checking (Lyons and Hitchcock 1977). These, like the irrigation features, are difficult to date, but their association with Bonito phase sites indicates that they were constructed during Pueblo III. The roads radiate from Chaco Canyon. They are distinctive features in being virtually straight lines, not contoured to topographic relief. When they change direction, this is accomplished by making a sharp, angular turn, rather than by curving. Some of the roads are lined with masonry curbs; others are visible as slight swales on the landscape. Although some of the roads are narrow, others are nearly 30 feet wide. Well-marked, planned, straight, wide roadways represent a great labor investment for people who did not have wheeled vehicles. It has been suggested that shrines along these roads may have served as signaling stations (Hayes 1975:75; Hayes and Windes 1975). Some of the roads lead from Chaco Canyon to outlying Chacoan Pueblos, such as Aztec and Kin Bineola. Other roads seem to lead to very small Bonito-style "outliers" of only a few rooms but apparently in close proximity to

good agricultural land. It is possible, although at present conjectural, that roads were important in bringing bulk agricultural produce into the canyon.

Items of material culture from Hosta Butte and Bonito phase sites are generally similar; however, a variety of impressive luxury items were found only at the Bonito phase sites. These include cylindrical vases (fig. 11), copper bells, quantities of turquoise, inlay pieces (fig. 12), mosaics, and macaw skeletons (Judd 1954). Both the copper bells and the macaws, which had been carefully buried, are considered evidence of trade connections with Mesoamerican cultures far to the south.

Finally, although burials have been recovered from trash deposits at the Hosta Butte phase sites, burials from the Bonito phase sites are both extremely rare and when found were in abandoned rooms or beneath floors (R.G. Vivian 1970).

Various reasons have been offered for the rapid development of Pueblo III at Chaco, as well as for the differences between Hosta Butte villages and Bonito towns. The idea that the Bonito towns represent a gradual development out of the smaller Hosta Butte phase sites is not supported by the data indicating that the two were contemporary (Hawley 1934). R.G. Vivian

CORDELL

(1970) suggested that the two kinds of sites represent the same cultural groups but two different forms of social organization. He relates the status items and elaboration present in the Bonito sites to their proximity to the irrigation system and argues that the control and maintenance of the water-control devices relate to a restructuring of portions of the society along more highly complex lines. Specifically, he suggests that the Bonito towns may have been organized similarly to the modern Eastern Pueblos in having dual divisions (moieties) that provide a more formal structure for labor organization than the clans of the Western Pueblos.

Ferdon (1955) presented the notion that the Bonito towns resulted from the presence of Mesoamerican merchant-traders, perhaps operating from a base in the Zacatecas and Durango area. This idea has since been elaborated by Di Peso (1974; "Prehistory: O'otam," this vol.) based on his work in the Casas Grandes area of northern Mexico. Various Mesoamerican states developed long-distance trade networks. Among the Aztec, a special class of people referred to as *pochteca* acted as long-distance traders, middlemen, and sometimes spies. Enjoying political immunity, they traversed Mesoamer-

ica. The Aztec, of course, ruled Mexico long after Casas Grandes and Chaco Canyon had been abandoned, but the idea of *pochteca* serves as an analogy. It is suggested that a state government in Mesoamerica may have established bases for trade operations among the Anasazi at Chaco Canyon. Presumably, few actual Mesoamerican emissaries would have been involved, but their presence, and the opportunities for trade, might have encouraged the local Anasazi populations to adopt some of the sophisticated technological, and possibly ceremonial, features available to the more highly developed Mesoamerican states. The suggested items of trade include live macaws and copper bells from Mesoamerica in exchange for turquoise from the Southwest.

In any case, the Classic Pueblo III occupation of Chaco Canyon appears to have been relatively short-lived. Although it is difficult to establish precisely when the population began to decline, or when the major ruins were abandoned, Hayes (1975) suggests a terminal date of about 1200. Following this, he suggests that there may have been an incursion of people from Mesa Verde, which is inferred from architectural features such as compound masonry of large, shaped blocks of sandstone and Mesa Verde keyhole-shaped kivas. Site Bc 236

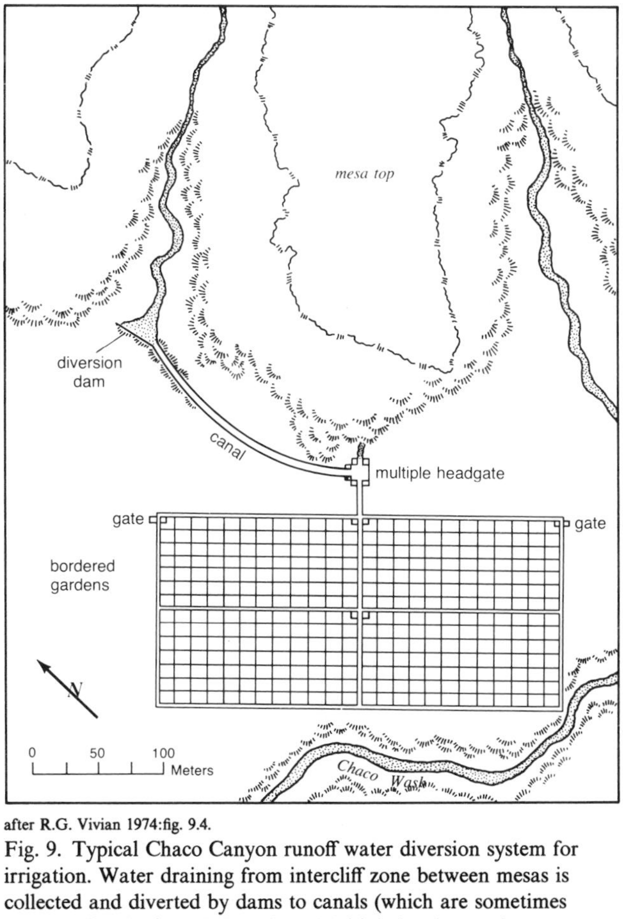

after R.G. Vivian 1974:fig. 9.4.

Fig. 9. Typical Chaco Canyon runoff water diversion system for irrigation. Water draining from intercliff zone between mesas is collected and diverted by dams to canals (which are sometimes masonry lined) about 1-2 m deep. Multiple headgates slow water flow and channel it to bordered gardens (R.G. Vivian 1974:104). Reconstruction based on aerial photographs.

Mus. of N.M.

Fig. 10. Rock cut stairway on the east side of the rincon north of Chetro Ketl, Chaco Canyon, San Juan Co., N.M. A second incomplete series of steps appears just to the right of the stairway. Photographed about 1920-1925.

*141*

Smithsonian, Dept. of Anthr., Archeol.: 336496, 336498.

Fig. 11. Painted black-on-white cylindrical vases with 4 lug handles excavated from Pueblo Bonito, San Juan Co., N.M. (see Judd 1954:pl. 68). Height of right 25.7 cm, left same scale.

phases and suggests a terminal date of 1300 for Anasazi habitation of the area. If architectural details, such as kiva form, and ceramic types represent means of communicating social alliance, it might be suggested that Mesa Verde eclipsed Chaco Canyon as a major center. Rather than representing a Mesa Verde migration into the Canyon, the material remains may indicate a shift in social affiliation.

• OUTSIDE THE CHACO AREA    Sections of the middle and northern Rio Grande Valley that showed little or no use by the Anasazi prior to 1100 were occupied for the first time during Pueblo III by Anasazi horticulturalists. In the Jemez-Nacimiento Mountains, the Gallina phase has been dated to about 1100 to 1300. There is general agreement that the Gallina phase developed out of the Pueblo I groups in the Gobernador (Dick 1976; Ford, Schroeder, and Peckham 1972), but a temporal gap separates the two. The Gallina phase has been characterized as one of relative isolation because of a lack of evidence of much trade or interaction with Mesa Verde or Chaco Canyon. Gallina ceramics consist of dense graywares, some decorated with black carbon paint (Gallina Black-on-gray), and utility wares with a variety of surface treatments that include wiping, banding, punching, and incising, but not corrugation (Hibben 1940, 1949). Gallina sites consist of numerous pit houses and small surface structures referred to as "unit houses." Both types appear to have been contemporary. The pit houses are round with an interior hearth, ventilator, and deflector, aligned north-south, four post roof supports, storage bins on the east and west side of the ventilator opening, and a bench along the wall between the bins. Unit houses are built of massive, often heterogeneous, rock masonry. A north-south orientation of interior features, U-shaped deflector, slab-lined hearth, and ventilator are standard within the rectangular room. A

(Bradley 1971) constitutes a good example of this style. The site consisted of 10 rooms and a kiva, the kiva with a keyhole modification. Previously existing sites also show some architectural renovation during this period. Thus, there was construction at New Alto, Kin Kletso, Casa Chiquita, and Pueblo del Arroyo (Vivian 1959; Hayes 1975:59). Outside of Chaco Canyon, Aztec Ruin provides an excellent example of Mesa Verde modification of a Chacoan site (Morris 1921a). At some sites where no architectural modifications are obvious, Mesa Verde Black-on-white ceramics have been found. Hayes (1975:32) does not consider the Mesa Verde occupation to have been dense or as long as any of the Chacoan

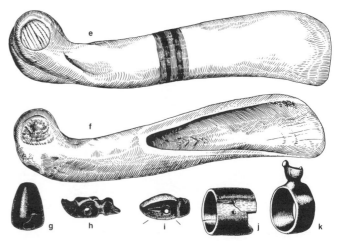

Smithsonian, Dept. of Anthr., Archeol.: a, 335743; b, 335748; c, 335701; d, 335700; e, 335157; f, 335164; g, 335608; h, 335607; i, 335573; j, 335764; k, 335761; l, 336057; m, 336052.

Fig. 12. Stone, shell, bone, and clay artifacts excavated from Pueblo Bonito, San Juan Co., N.M. a-b, Turquoise pendants; c-d, cut Haliotis shell pendants; e, scraper of deer humerus with inlay band of jet and turquoise, and Haliotis shell disk at head; f, polished plain deer humerus scraper; g, drilled lignite bead; h, lignite effigy bead; i, hematite effigy bead; j-k, lignite and turquoise finger rings; l, serpentine stone pipe; m, painted black-on-white clay pipe found in kiva (see Judd 1954). Length of m 7.1 cm, rest same scale.

142

banquette, sometimes containing storage bins, lines north, east, and west walls. The southern part of the room is set off by storage bins extending out from the walls (Dick 1976:21–27). Pit house and unit house communities occur in high densities along ridges and a few within cliffs or rock overhangs (Pattison 1968; Hibben 1938; Dick 1976). The Gallina "towers" that feature prominently in popular literature are actually quite rare and poorly understood. They are circular structures, with massive walls, and are usually located within the centers of communities. Those that have been excavated lack interior domicile features, show evidence of two successive occupations, and seem to have served as storage units before their eventual abandonment (Dick 1976:17–18; Whiteaker 1976). Agricultural features consisting of terraced gardens and rock-bordered gardens are numerous in the area, and dams and reservoirs have been reported (Pattison 1968; Hibben 1940, 1948; Dick 1976).

Particular items of material culture that have been considered diagnostic of the Gallina phase, in addition to the rather standard architectural features, are small elbow-shaped pipes with supporting knobs, an emphasis on worked antler, tri-notched axes, and pointed-bottom pots (Mera 1938; Hall 1944:60; Hibben 1938, 1940). The pots are not a characteristically Anasazi trait, and it has been suggested that they represent contact with Plains or Woodland groups (Wendorf 1953a). Seaman (1976) has noted that this vessel form occurs in the Gallina district only after 1200 and correlates with an increase in the volume of culinary vessels, perhaps indicating a functional adaptation in increased cooking or storage efficiency encouraged by climatic deterioration.

The defensive nature of excavated Gallina phase site placement (on ridge tops with difficult access) and the large number of burned sites have frequently been commented on as indicating that the Gallina were particularly warlike (Hibben 1938, 1940). Actually, the first observation seems to reflect excavation bias, in that many isolated pit house depressions exist in the foothills and valleys but have not been excavated (Seaman 1976:116). Available literature does not provide enough information to determine precisely the frequency of burned houses, or whether pit houses or unit houses are more likely to show evidence of conflagration. However, it is valuable, for perspective, to note that pit house communities far outside the Gallina area show a high incidence of burning (cf. Martin and Rinaldo 1950).

The Gallina area was abandoned by about 1300. A link between the Gallina sites and the protohistoric and historic sites of Jemez, including modern Jemez Pueblo, was first suggested by Reiter (1938, 1) on the basis of floor features and room configuration at Unshagi, and this interpretation is generally accepted (Ford, Schroeder, and Peckham 1972).

In the Taos area, pit house villages on terraces and benches adjacent to permanent streams and on alluvial terraces date to between about 1100 and 1200 (Green 1976; Loose 1974; Herold and Luebben 1968). Individual pit houses are relatively deep, usually more than eight feet, and circular to subrectangular in shape. Interior features consist of a central fire pit, ash pit and damper, and, usually, four post roof supports. Ventilators are oriented east, when found. Associated surface work areas are reported. Similar pit house villages are described for the Cimarron area. Ceramics are mineral painted. Quantitative data are not available for cultigens or wild plant and animal food, but numerous artifacts made of deer and rabbit bones indicate that these animals were hunted (Green 1976; Wetherington 1968; Blumenschein 1958; Kirkpatrick 1976).

At about 1200, Sante Fe Black-on-white, a carbon paint derivative of Chacoan ceramics, appears in the Taos district, and somewhat later, in the Cimarron district, where Anasazi affiliation is inferred from the construction of dry wall, masonry houses; the use of sandals, basketry, and matting; and the presence of corn. However, skeletons do not show cranial deformation, and the diversity of projectile point types indicates a greater emphasis on hunting than supposedly characterizes Anasazi adaptations (Lutes 1959; Kirkpatrick 1976). The Cimarron area seems to have been abandoned by groups related to the Anasazi by 1300, and subsequent use of the area was by peoples with more pronounced Plains characteristics.

With the introduction of Santa Fe Black-on-white in the Taos area, there was an abandonment of the pit house communities, and aggregation of population at multi-room surface Pueblos. Only three of these have been excavated, and Pot Creek Pueblo is probably the best known (Wetherington 1968; Vickery 1969). This site, located in a valley setting among the Tres Ritos Hills, was occupied from about 1200 to 1350. The earliest rooms were of coursed adobe, and an associated kiva had floor features similar to the earlier pit houses in the area (Wetherington 1968:81). After about 1250, Pot Creek Pueblo increased considerably in size. Coursed adobe continued to be used in room construction although multiple stories were used. In order to support the weight of second-story rooms, ground-floor rooms contained central roof support posts set in adobe basins. This rather unusual architectural feature has been documented both at Old Picuris Pueblo and at Cornfield Taos, the latter considered the ancestral village for modern Taos (cf. Ellis and Brody 1964; Wetherington 1968; Holschlag 1975).

Anasazi occupation of the Chama River area is well documented from about 1200 to the Spanish period, although the very large sites in that area date to Pueblo IV. During Pueblo III, sites are roughly quadrangular surface Pueblos, with room blocks on three sides of a plaza. The fourth side of the plaza is closed by a palisade of jacal or a line of stones. A circular kiva was located near the center of the plaza area. Of three excavated sites, 143 two were constructed primarily of adobe and one of basalt "boulder" masonry. The difference in construction material has been attributed to differential availability of materials. Kivas had central fire pits and east-oriented ventilators. Ceramics from these sites consist of Santa Fe Black-on-white, Wiyo Black-on-white, and small amounts of St. Johns Polychrome, which occurs as a trade ware. The range of site size is not well known; however, the three excavated sites consisted of 26 rooms, about 50 rooms, and more than 100 rooms (Hibben 1937; Luebben 1953; Peckham 1974).

Systems of stone grids and associated small structures, interpreted as field houses, are numerous in the Chama area. Whether they date to Pueblo III or Pueblo IV is, at present, unknown.

The vast majority of reports dealing with Pueblo III in the Santa Fe district have been concerned with tracing the origins and developments of one or more of the various ceramic types found in, and on, sites. Pueblo III is given slightly different temporal boundaries by scholars, depending on whether sites show a predominance of Kwahe'e or Santa Fe Black-on-white, or whether there are sherds of Wiyo, Galisteo, western polychromes (St. Johns or Heshotauthla) or early glazewares as well. Summaries, such as those provided by Wendorf and Reed (1955), Stubbs and Stallings (1953), and McNutt (1969) generally do indicate a considerable degree of diversity in the size, content, and location of Pueblo III sites, but the major efforts seem to have gone into trying to order this diversity along temporal lines. The fact that no such ordering is generally acceptable to everyone is probably the most instructive feature of the summaries. The only general agreement seems to be that after sparse indications of habitation during Pueblo II, population seems to have increased. Also, toward the end of the period, there is increasing aggregation of population in areas with reliable supplies of water.

Some of the better-known sites that date to Pueblo III include: Pindi Pueblo (Stubbs and Stallings 1953), Upper Arroyo Hondo, Arroyo Hondo Pueblo, Pueblo Alamo (Schwartz and Lang 1973; Allen 1973) near Santa Fe, and Row or Guthe's Ruin, Forked Lightning Ruin, the oldest part of Pecos Pueblo (Kidder 1926, 1958) in the vicinity of Pecos, and components at San Cristóbal, the Waldo site, and Las Madres Pueblo in the Galisteo Basin (Allen 1973; Kayser and Ewing 1971; Breternitz 1966).

Some of the ceramics associated with the Pueblo III sites, particularly Santa Fe Black-on-white and Kwahe'e, do resemble Chacoan types. Galisteo Black-on-white is generally considered a "cognate" or derivative of Mesa Verde types. (It is decorated with carbon paint.) The various trade wares include some wares from the west but also ceramics from the south, such as Los Padillas Polychrome. Culinary wares show a trend from sharply defined indented types to types in which indentations are smeared or partially obliterated. Increasing amounts of

mica temper occur in the culinary wares throughout the period (Stubbs and Stallings 1953:48–56).

Both adobe and masonry were used in room construction, and none of the fine stonework characteristic of Chaco Canyon is present. Kivas are variable, being round, D-shaped, or rectangular and incorporated into room blocks. Interior kiva features generally consist of an ash pit/fire pit and deflector, but benches and pilasters are lacking.

Numerous small Pueblo III sites have been located on the Pajarito Plateau, above White Rock Canyon, but very few of these sites have been excavated (Steen 1977). Two small sites, LA 12119 (Traylor et al. 1977) and Saltbush Pueblo (Snow 1974), are interesting in that each had one kiva with north-south oriented floor features and a southern recess. Both sites have been dated by tree rings and archeomagnetic dates to the early 1200s. Snow (1974:69–70) considers the kiva shape at Saltbush Pueblo sufficiently close to the Mesa Verde "keyhole" shape kivas to conclude that it constitutes "*prima facie* evidence for Mesa Verde influence on the site." It is important, for clarification, to note that Snow refers to Mesa Verde influence resulting from a migration evidenced by a population decline at Mesa Verde, which Hayes (1964) suggests occurred during Pueblo II and not as the result of the final abandonment of Mesa Verde that occurred at about 1300. Ceramics from both these small sites consisted primarily of Santa Fe Black-on-white, which has been related to Chacoan wares.

Below White Rock Canyon and in the Albuquerque district, Pueblo III sites show a movement away from upland settings to locations immediately adjacent to major drainages and arable land (T.R. Frisbie 1967; Blevins and Joiner 1977). Tijeras Canyon seems to have been utilized on a year-round basis for the first time. Although there was clearly an increase in population, as reflected by both the number of sites and the size of sites, the increase is not viewed as the result of immigration but rather as internal population growth (T.R. Frisbie 1967; Wendorf and Reed 1955).

In the Cebollita Mesa and Acoma areas, Pueblo III is characterized by the same trends seen in the Santa Fe area. Early in Pueblo III, there is the first indication that this area was inhabited on a year-round basis. Villages are found along major water courses and on mesa tops (Ruppé 1966:328). Late in Pueblo III, an increased number of sites indicates migration into the district, which continued into Pueblo IV times (Dittert 1959).

In summary, Pueblo III outside the San Juan drainage was a time of population expansion and growth. Areas that had previously not had horticultural villages were inhabited for the first time on a year-round basis. Although some of the grid bordered gardens and terrace features may date to Pueblo III times, there is no evidence that irrigation canals diverted water from the Rio Grande or any of its tributaries. Architectural features and ceramics show considerable variability throughout the area and in a general sense mimic or mirror styles produced in the San Juan basin. However, despite meticulous comparisons on the part of most investigators, there do not seem to be any sites that as a whole reflect an assemblage of San Juan features.

*Pueblo IV*

Pueblo IV, which has been referred to as the Rio Grande Classic (Wendorf and Reed 1955), dates from about 1300 to the Spanish conquest in 1540. (Some writers prefer a terminal date of 1600 to reflect the fact that in the first 60 years after Francisco Vásquez de Coronado's entrada, European influence on the Pueblos was minimal.) Very large population aggregates characterized the Rio Grande area for the first time. Population movements within the area did occur; large sites were abandoned prior to contact, and the historically known and modern Eastern Pueblos were founded.

In the Rio Grande Valley north and west of Santa Fe, the characteristic ceramic types of Pueblo IV are the Biscuit wares (Abiquiu Black-on-gray or "Biscuit A" and Bandelier Black-on-gray or "Biscuit B"), so named because their relatively friable paste resembles modern factory ceramics after the first, or biscuit, firing. In the Albuquerque area, the Galisteo Basin, Pecos, and Santa Fe areas, Rio Grande glazes were produced and widely traded. Very large sites, consisting of multiple room blocks and plazas with both large and small kivas were distributed along the Chama north of Española. Although these sites have been explored by both archeologists and collectors, there is little published information about them. Hewett's (1906) sketch maps and Hibben's (1937) descriptions are quite accurate. Probably the most outstanding characteristic of these sites is their large size. Wendorf (1953a) estimates 600 rooms for Teewi. Sapawe (Sepawi) is considered the largest adobe ruin in New Mexico, with hundreds of rooms, multiple plazas, and at least 19 kivas (Hibben 1937). Very large circular kivas have been found at Teewi (Wendorf 1953a), Paako (Lambert 1954), Pecos (Kidder 1958), and Tijeras Pueblo (Cordell 1977a). These do not contain the specialized floor features of the "great kivas" described for the San Juan drainage, including Chaco. Extensive stone gridded areas, some on the lava-topped mesa east of the Chama, may have been maize terraces (Hibben 1937:17). Some of these are filled with gravel, and Ellis (1970a) has referred to them as "gravel mulch gardens."

Wendorf (1953a:94) suggests that the large Biscuit sites of the Chama resulted from the aggregation of populations rather than migration into the area. Although the Chama Valley declined in importance as a population center shortly after 1500, at least three sites, including Yunque (the site of the first Spanish capital), were inhabited into the historic period. (For the name of Yunque, see "San Juan Pueblo," this vol.)

In the Taos area, Pot Creek Pueblo was abandoned in about 1350, and Wetherington (1968:82) suggests that the inhabitants may have moved to Old Picuris. Cornfield Taos, about one-quarter mile northwest of the modern Taos church, seems to have been founded at about 1300 or 1350. It was abandoned about 100 years later when Taos Pueblo was built (Ellis and Brody 1964).

Most of the Classic, Pueblo IV, sites of the Pajarito Plateau are inadequately dated, and it is likely that many have earlier components. Tyuonyi, and the cavate ruins of Frijoles Canyon, Tsankawi (Sankewi), and Puye may date to the late 1300s with building continuing into the mid-1400s (Robinson, Hannah, and Harrill 1972).

Steen (1977) groups the sites of the Pajarito Plateau into two basic types, Plaza sites and Big sites. The former are of masonry and consist of room blocks around a central plaza that has an entry on the east. A circular kiva is contained within the plaza and a second kiva occurs outside the Pueblo structure on the east side. The Big sites (Tshirege (Tsirege), Otowi (Potsuwi), Tyuonyi, Tsankawi, Navawi, and Little Otowi) are comprised of massive room blocks arranged around three sides of a plaza that is open to the south. The Big sites are generally at slightly lower elevations than the Plaza sites. Agricultural features consist of check dams across drainage channels and irregular terraces (Steen 1977:34).

The Classic of the Pajarito Plateau is most often interpreted as representing population immigration from the San Juan basin (Reed 1943b, 1949a; Wendorf and Reed 1955; Ellis 1967b). Steen (1977:40) suggests indigenous population growth and subsequent population aggregation. In both cases, investigators rely on a selective set of traits, emphasizing either ceramics or architecture and site placement.

Shortly after 1300, red-slipped, glaze decorated ceramics began to replace Black-on-white wares over much of the Santa Fe and Albuquerque areas. Presumably, the Rio Grande glazes were initially made in imitation of earlier western trade wares such as St. Johns and Heshotauthla Polychromes. Collectively, the Rio Grande glazes form a distinct set of ceramic types that were produced as late as about 1700 and widely traded both within the Rio Grande Valley and to groups on the Plains. Major contributions to the study of Rio Grande glazes have been made by Nelson (1914), Kidder (1931-1936, 2), Mera (1933), Shepard (1942), and A.H. Warren (1969a, 1970, 1977, 1977a). Shepard's approach, which has been continued by Warren, utilizes petrographic analysis of tempering material (or identification of temper types and sources of temper) and is particularly important to establishing suggested manufacturing and trade centers. The early glazes (A and B) seem to have been produced and traded from the Albuquerque and Cochiti areas (A.H. Warren 1970:4; Cordell 1977a). From the mid-1300s to the early 1400s, San Marcos and other Galisteo Basin Pueblos became trade centers of glazewares (C and

D). San Cristóbal Pueblo may have been a trade center from the mid-1400s to 1680, when the Galisteo Basin was abandoned. Pecos Pueblo was a particularly important trade center for the late glazes (fig. 13) and served as the location of considerable trade with Apaches and Utes during the historic period, as did Picuris and Taos. Although the glazes have been used as important chronological markers since Mera's (1933) and Kidder's (1931-1936, 2) work, the potential for studying the interaction among Pueblos through trade has not been fully explored (cf. Shepard 1942).

Throughout the Albuquerque, Santa Fe, Acoma-Laguna districts, the Galisteo Basin and the eastern frontier of the Anasazi area along the Pecos River and south to Chupadero Mesa, Pueblo IV was characterized as a time of population aggregation into a few large communities and also frequent abandonment of these settlements (Wendorf and Reed 1955; Dickson 1975; Dittert 1959;

U. of N.M., Maxwell Mus. of Anthr., Albuquerque: top, 36.12.10; bottom 36.9.22.

Fig. 13. Rio Grande Glazes. top, Rio Grande Glaze C bowl from Puaray, Sandoval Co., N.M.; bottom, Rio Grande Glaze B-Yellow from Pecos Pueblo, San Miguel Co., N.M. Diameter of top 20.3 cm, bottom 28.2 cm.

Ruppé 1966). Whereas Wendorf and Reed (1955:153) cite both warfare and a drought between 1560 and 1585 as possible motives for these abandonments, this explanation does not fit the numerous sites that were abandoned earlier in the period. Further, many sites founded during Pueblo IV were found to be occupied at the time of the Spanish entradas. These include Paako, San Antonio, Kuaua, San Marcial, Pecos, Gran Quivira, and Pueblo Pardo (Lambert 1954; Snow 1974; F.B. Parsons 1975; Kidder 1958; Toulouse and Stephenson 1960). The sites occupied into the historic period are not consistently located along sources of permanent water, which could have been used for irrigation, nor is there evidence that ditch irrigation was practiced prior to historic times. Drought, per se, explains neither the abandonments of some sites nor the continued occupation of others.

### Evaluation

With respect to the more basic Pueblo items, such as ceramics in general, domestic crops, aggregated communities, circular ceremonial structures, and some agricultural devices such as terraces, grid bordered gardens, and check dams, it is now known approximately when and where these were first used. The less tangible features of Pueblo life, such as specific ceremonies and rituals, features of political and social organization (clans, moieties, religious societies), as well as aspects of Pueblo culture that show diversity among modern groups (such as language) are not well understood, and reconstructions that attempt to trace these features into the remote past are not particularly credible. Part of the problem is that in order for such phenomena to be observable archeologically, they must have material correlates (artifacts that can be recovered through excavation). Attempts to reconstruct patterns of kinship and social organization by analyzing the distribution of ceramic design elements within archeological sites have been conducted (Longacre 1966; J.N. Hill 1970, 1978). The basic assumptions underlying these studies are that ceramics are produced by women; designs are learned by women from their mothers; and the designs are retained when the daughter marries and starts her own family. If specific design elements are found to cluster in portions of a prehistoric Pueblo, the inference made is that after marriage, women continued to live near their mothers. This pattern of matrilocal residence is a feature of some of the modern Pueblos. The first attempts in this direction of research met with productive opposition. Some considered it too simplistic (D.F. Aberle 1970), but it did serve to stimulate research among the Pueblos and nonindustrial groups as to how designs are learned and how the work of an individual potter might be observed archeologically (Stanislawski 1969a; Hill and Gunn 1977).

Attempts to determine the linguistic affiliation of various prehistoric groups have had a long history in the

Anasazi area (Mera 1935; Ford, Schroeder, and Peckham 1972) with less substantial results. There would seem to be at least two major problems in this regard. First, there are excellent ethnographic cases of two linguistically diverse groups sharing essentially the same material culture inventory, such as the Hopi and Hopi-Tewa (Tewa Village) of Arizona (Dozier 1954). Second, although the historic and contemporary distributions of related languages in the Pueblo area do show geographic patterning, the assumption that geographic patterning in ceramic types or architectural features represents linguistic patterning is both untested and probably untrue (Dozier 1970a). Despite the fact that virtually all ethnographic studies indicate that there is no relationship between language spoken and ceramics manufactured (Dozier 1970a; Brugge 1963), this line of enquiry is still being pursued (Ford, Schroeder, and Peckham 1972).

A similar problem is encountered in attempts at tracing the origins of specific ceremonial features, such as the masked dances of kachina ceremonies, and trying to relate these to architectural features. For example, the ethnographically known masked dances are most elaborately developed among the Western Pueblo groups, secondarily developed among the Rio Grande Pueblos, and do not occur at all at Taos. Masked dances are rituals involving the whole community and among modern Pueblos take place in large community buildings (Hawley 1950). Large kivas, recognized archeologically, and kivas with very elaborate features, such as the great kivas of the San Juan, including Chaco Canyon, are also more numerous west of the Rio Grande, where they additionally have considerable time depth (Vivian and Reiter 1960). On the basis of these data, archeologists have suggested that the masked dances of the kachina ceremonies originated in the west and were introduced into the Rio Grande area. Although this is logically reasonable, excavations in the Tsegi Canyon area of northeastern Arizona at sites that date 1250 to 1300 yielded no artifacts that could be associated with kachina ceremonies (Dean 1970). Studies of rock art (Schaafsma and Schaafsma 1974) showing complex masked figures and kiva murals representing kachina figures indicate that these are apparently older in the southern Rio Grande area than they are in the west, and the suggestion made is that although kachina ceremonies were first introduced into the Rio Grande Pueblos and later spread west, the long period of prohibition of the ceremonies by the Spaniards makes them appear less developed in the Rio Grande. Although this argument is not definitive, largely because rock art is notoriously difficult to date and interpret, it does highlight a major problem for the interpretation of Anasazi archeology. Put simply, the problem is to determine how appropriate the modern Pueblos are as analogies for their ancestors.

This is not meant glibly. It is well known that modern Pueblo groups are "conservative" (Ortiz 1969). However,

Fig. 14. Petroglyph from San Cristóbal, Santa Fe Co., N.M. Some characteristic design elements from the Galisteo Basin area shown here include mudheads, two-horned and one-horned masks, masks with jagged teeth, and simple stars. Though no attempt has been made to date the petroglyphs in this area, the majority probably date between the 14th and 18th centuries (Schaafsma 1975:42-44). Photograph by Ray Williamson, July 1977.

the ethnographically known Pueblo Indians have been disrupted profoundly, because they have had to cope with massive incursions of "outsiders" (other Indians, Spaniards, and Anglo-Americans) since about 1500. It has been about 400 years since options that once were available have been closed by the presence of other groups of people. For example, although migration probably features inordinately in the archeological literature of the Southwest and abandonments are documented, the degree of sedentism versus demographic mobility and long residence in one locality found among the modern Pueblos, may, in part be an artifact of centuries of preemption of Pueblo lands, by Navajo, then Spanish, then Anglo intruders. Perhaps a more productive approach toward understanding the Anasazi may be gained by examining their economic requirements, the ability of the natural environment to meet these requirements, and the various options open to the Anasazi prior to 1500.

## An Ecological Approach

Human beings have alternative courses of action that are ultimately limited by both the natural environment and the size of human populations. They can, within limits, adapt to changing conditions through various means including technological and social adjustments. The particular choice, or combination of choices, selected by groups might be evaluated in terms of "efficiency" or cost to the cultural system, perhaps measured in the amount of labor required. But the "cost" must include constraints imposed not only by the natural environment but also by the presence of other societies (cf. Steward 1955:30-42). *147*

With these considerations in mind, an examination of past adaptations in the Eastern Anasazi area must be of broad interregional scope and relate to other areas of the Southwest. An examination of the adaptive patterns among various groups is attempted here. In doing this, reliance is placed on both archeological and ethnographic examples derived from areas outside the Southwest. This approach may be considered somewhat heretical; however, the modern Pueblos do not provide adequate analogs for past adaptations, because former trade and political alliances have been disrupted and demographic mobility has been restricted by the presence of outsiders.

The very limited data about Basketmaker II adaptations are informative, in part, because they are scarce. Sites have been found only in areas where intensive surveys and excavations were undertaken for salvage purposes (the Navajo Reservoir project) or in areas where modern building activity and subsequent erosion exposed remains (the Albuquerque area). Although corn and habitation structures have been found, dependence on horticulture was probably minimal and the known sites represent seasonal occupations. This, in turn, indicates that hunting and gathering must have been critical to the economy and that local groups must have dispersed throughout much of the year. Similar interpretations have been made by others (Glassow 1972; "Post-Pleistocene Archeology, 7000–2000 B.C.," this vol.), but an alternative view is expressed by Schoenwetter and Dittert (1968:45). Although quantitative data are meager, the diversity of fauna and flora from these early sites is suggestive of a broadly based subsistence.

Basketmaker III sites have been interpreted as indicating sedentism and more dependence on horticulture, as evidenced by the shift in location of sites closer to arable land, the presence of numerous storage cists and pits, and the increase in ceramic containers (Glassow 1972). Schoenwetter and Dittert (1968) consider that the more moist climatic regime between A.D. 200 and 700 would have been favorable for this but that corn of a low yielding variety necessitated planting large fields. They suggest that general conditions of aggradation provided the land that made this possible and that the location of sites in areas of topographic variability provided access to wild plants and game. There also seems to be a relationship between the increased amount of trade goods in Basketmaker III sites and increased dependence on agriculture, but this relationship may not reflect the accumulation of quantities of surplus goods, as has been suggested (Eddy 1966:472). Rather, given the unreliable nature of crops from one year to another, increased dependence on agriculture also meant that when years of poor yields occurred, access to wild plant and animal foods may have been essential. Few societies with shaky economic bases risk maintaining exclusive territories (cf. Dyson-Hudson and Smith 1978; Flannery 1972; Waddell

1975), and one way of insuring both access to neighboring territory and information about the availability of food outside one's immediate setting is through maintaining trade relationships with several other groups of people. It might also be suggested that the kivas at Shabik'eshchee and the Navajo Reservoir sites, whatever particular ceremonies took place within them, were important places where members of different communities could meet periodically and exchange information, if not food and other goods (Athens 1977:374; Ford 1972a). There are then three basic features of Anasazi life that seem to have been established during Basketmaker III: the use of cists, pits, and ceramic containers to store immediate surpluses for periods of need; the maintenance of trade ties to other areas, perhaps as insurance against local scarcities; and the construction of special ceremonial rooms that might have been important in sustaining ties among communities. The few sites that have been found and excavated indicate that both regional and community populations were relatively small. Within each community, most of the hearths, work areas, and storage cists were outside house structures. This indicates that food preparation and storing must have been done in full view of members of the village. Hoarding individual property is virtually impossible under such circumstances, which suggests that communities were profoundly egalitarian (cf. Fried 1967:27–106). Various ethnographers (Carneiro 1967:136; Sahlins 1972) have noted that group (village) size in egalitarian societies remains relatively small and that conflicts or potential conflicts may ultimately be resolved by the fissioning off of parts of the group to form separate communities. Although the factors that condition fissioning of a local group are not entirely agreed upon, the archeological implications of such a process would be to see a gradual expansion in the distribution of small communities. This may account for the marked increase in villages seen in Pueblo I as well as the expansion of villages into the more mountainous portions of the Eastern Anasazi area.

There are three characteristics of Pueblo I that seem to be interrelated: villages expanded in number and into more mountainous settings; rectangular surface structures were built, apparently initially for storage; and there are diverse ceramic types present at each site. Schoenwetter and Dittert (1968:49) suggest that both a shift in seasonality of rainfall and a decrease in effective moisture at about this time would have lowered the water table in the Navajo Reservoir district and decreased the amount of land available for planting. Whether or not deteriorating climatic conditions are further substantiated through additional paleoclimatological research, the increased amount of storage space does indicate that people were compensating for periods of scarcity. It may be that the expansion of villages into diverse areas also limited free access to these areas. There would be more potential competition for the game and wild plant foods, because villagers had gradually moved into the elevations that support the most abundant sources of game, nut crops, and berries. Above-ground storage does more than provide additional space. One could, after all, dig larger holes in the ground. (The excavation of the large Basket-maker III kivas is good evidence that such labor would not be shirked if it were important.) Distinct storage pits in a pit-house village are in public space, but only those with access to adjoining living spaces are likely to know whether goods are hoarded in above-ground storage rooms (cf. Flannery 1972). This suggests a change in social organization from a situation of extreme egalitarianism to one in which access to produce could be limited or denied. (This does not mean to imply that certain individuals had political authority as in a ranked society.) The suggestion is that some corporate group, smaller than the entire village, existed, although it is difficult to label or define the type of group, whether clan, extended family, or some other kind of social unit (Martin and Rinaldo 1950a; Brew 1946).

The expansion of villages and the potential for limiting access to produce suggest that styles in decoration of ceramics were additional "social markers." The observation that ceramics were both widely traded and that "local varieties" of types were produced indicates that maintaining alliances and networks of communication among groups was of importance (cf. Wobst 1977; S. Plog 1977a:174–180; Flannery 1968a). The maintenance of social ties among villages, in different environmental settings, serves two advantages. First, in time of local scarcity, the potential for obtaining goods from a group that is better off is enhanced. Such exchanges would, of course, have to have been reciprocated when situations were reversed. Second, in case of a real economic disaster, such as a prolonged period of crop failure, it might be possible to move to those villages where alliances had been maintained. One may compare Waddell's (1975) account of how the Enga, a highland New Guinea group, cope with famine. In this example, although economic disaster is infrequent, when particularly severe frosts do occur in the mountains, entire villages of people abandon their homes and move in with groups at lower elevations with whom they had maintained trade ties. The homeland may lie abandoned for more than a generation. One need not look as far away as New Guinea to see this kind of mechanism operating. At a much later time, the Pecos did move to Jemez, and during the disruptions of the Spanish conquest, the Tano moved as far away as Hopi (Kidder 1958; Dozier 1954). This kind of mechanism is implied by the observations that Mesa Verde ceramics occurred in the Navajo Reservoir district during Pueblo II and that in about 1050 the population of the Navajo Reservoir district probably moved north to Mesa Verde (Eddy 1966:506). Apparently, the Mesa Verde populations could incorporate immigrants and seem to have

coped with their presence, at least in part, through the development of labor-intensive agricultural features (Hayes 1964; Rohn 1963, 1971, 1977).

The data from Chaco Canyon indicate that prior to A.D. 900 techniques for coping with uneven resource distribution and short-term droughts were the same as those in existence elsewhere in the Southwest, that is, the shift to surface storage structures and the establishment of small-scale trade networks (Judge 1976). However, after A.D. 900 the abundance of imported ceramics suggests that Chaco had developed a more formalized trade network. Judge (1976:13) proposes that during the eleventh century, Chaco may have become a center for redistribution and that turquoise, for which there is abundant evidence, might have served as a medium for exchange. The situation at Chaco is remarkable for a number of reasons, the most significant being that there are no analogs for Chaco among the modern Pueblos, and perhaps none in any contemporary society, that the tremendous growth of Chaco was so short-lived, and that the amount of labor invested in nonessentials such as beautifully decorative masonry veneers must have been enormous. The first two observations involving the lack of analogs and the short duration of the developments are striking in light of evolutionary writing in ethnological theory. For example, Fried (1960:713), in discussing the origins of social ranking and stratification, notes that contemporary ethnographic data provide "a murky mirror in which to discern the stages in the development of pristine states." Service (1971:142), commenting on the instability of chiefdoms, notes "the 'rise and fall' of chiefdoms has been such a frequent phenomenon that it seems to be part of their nature." There are important differences between Fried's conception of a ranked society and Service's notion of chiefdoms, and it is not necessary to label Chaco during Pueblo III as one or the other, because a name or label does not increase understanding of why the phenomena developed. The theoretical discussions are important, in part, because they provide direction in looking at those features of the Chaco system that might have been important to both its rise and demise. Ranked societies and chiefdoms differ from egalitarian societies in that there are a limited number of positions of status and that the economy is dominated by redistribution—the collection and dispersal of goods—both of which existed at Chaco, rather than reciprocal exchange among groups or individuals of equal status (Sahlins 1968; Fried 1960; Service 1971). It has been suggested that the development of social ranking may be related to the control of irrigation systems, general population disequilibrium within a region, and/or the control of long-distance trade (Flannery 1972; Athens 1977; see Gall and Saxe 1977). R.G. Vivian's (1974) treatment of the irrigation system at Chaco is relevant in that he argues that although each segment of the system, diverting water from one catchment, could be controlled independently, runoff from each would be unpredictable and an integrated system of apportionment would have been necessary. The integration of the system would then require some kind of central authority. The discussions of long-distance trade by Di Peso (1974) are also important in view of the effort expended in road construction, the abundance of turquoise, the debris from manufacturing items of turquoise (Judge 1976), and some of the specific similarities between Chaco Canyon and Casas Grandes.

The question of population disequilibrium must be addressed first. If Chaco were undergoing a period of climatic stress, as has been suggested, the least "expensive" (in terms of labor) solution, would probably have been to migrate. However, this option may not have been available, in part because the regions at higher elevations within the vicinity of Chaco were already densely inhabited. Those people who were closer to areas of higher elevation may have expanded into these areas, as the archeological data from the Gallina and Taos areas indicate, and perhaps the only alternatives for the Chacoan groups were the ones that required tremendous investments of labor and organization, such as for road construction and craft specialization. Perhaps the acquisition of a "valuable resource" (turquoise) enabled the population of Chaco to enhance their security by interacting with Mesoamerican states to the south, providing an item of exchange for economic support. Until necessary documentation of the extent of the redistributive network is analyzed, through determining the turquoise source locations of Mesoamerican stones, a process that has begun (Weigand, Harbottle, and Sayre 1977), and the mechanisms involved in "interregional interaction" (Flannery 1968a) are better understood, the precise nature of the Chacoan adaptation remains moot.

The archeological data do indicate that Chaco maintained ties within the Eastern Anasazi area. Some of the roads lead east to Pueblo Pintado and north to Aztec as well as south. Second, although quantitative data are not presently available, the resources present at Bonito sites indicate the acquisition of diverse fauna and flora that were not locally available but did occur in more mountainous areas (Vivian and Mathews 1964). Finally, the wide distribution of Chacoan "cognate" or derivative ceramics in the Rio Grande area indicates that at least some forms of social ties existed. An outstanding exception may be the Gallina and Taos districts, which appear to have been relatively isolated. There would seem to be two inferences with respect to these cases. The data may be biased in that no systematic investigation of early Gallina or Taos sites has been undertaken. A more reasonable alternative is the proposition that these areas, which are quite high in the mountains, were maintained as necessarily neutral "buffer zones" (in the sense that Hickerson 1965 uses this term). Game, such as elk, deer, and mountain sheep, and wild plant products, which

have been found in Chaco as well as in the Santa Fe area sites (Vivian and Mathews 1964; Traylor 1977), were still essential resources and only relative isolation could insure their continued abundance. It may be significant in this respect that after 1200, when the Gallina and Taos areas do contain evidence of dense occupation, further economic constraints seem to have been placed on the system.

Abandonment of the central San Juan during Pueblo III has been addressed from a number of perspectives (Douglass 1929; Jett 1964; O'Bryan 1951-1952, 3; F.H.H. Roberts 1935; E.L. Davis 1965; Ellis 1964a). It is useful in this regard to distinguish two varieties of abandonment and to keep them conceptually distinct. The first kind of abandonment affects individual sites or very small, local areas. This was a feature of Anasazi prehistory from its inception. Rarely did any site remain occupied for longer than about 100 years (Zubrow 1971; Cordell 1972). These abandonments probably relate to a variety of causes, from difficulties in constantly repairing houses, to local conditions of salinization, poor crop yields in any one locality, factionalism, or disease (Colton 1960; Titiev 1944; Cordell 1975). However, the abandonment of vast districts is a distinctive phenomenon, and as yet there seems to be no consensus as to its cause. The fact that Chaco Canyon and Mesa Verde were not abandoned at the same time argues against a simplistic climatic explanation. There is, as yet, no evidence to support the idea that nomadic groups were either in the area or would have posed any threat had they been (Linton 1944). It is more likely that the cause, or causes, were internal and systemic. These might include resource depletion, salinization, or the failure of the political system to maintain the necessary trade network to support the population or otherwise cope with increasing climatic variability and, perhaps, dessication (Lister 1966; Zubrow 1971; Hayes 1964). Research in the area continues to be concerned with this problem (Judge 1976; Irwin-Williams 1977; Plog et al. 1978).

Related to this question are the difficulties of trying to trace specific traits in the Rio Grande and Acoma-Laguna areas back to the San Juan populations (Wendorf and Reed 1955; Stubbs and Stallings 1953; McNutt 1969; Ellis 1964a, 1967b). Archeologists working in the Rio Grande have been troubled by the lack of a constellation of traits (ceramic types and details such as kiva orientation, lack of benches, and lack of pilasters) at Rio Grande sites, while noting the marked increase in population in the area during Pueblo IV. It is in this context that a reevaluation of the apparently long-term mechanisms of coping with minor stress is valuable. If one accepts the evidence that maintaining trade and alliance networks was a standard feature of Anasazi adaptations, then it is reasonable that when abandonment became necessary the San Juan groups, probably gradually, joined the local population to the east and southeast, integrating themselves into communities in much the same way as the highland Enga do (Waddell 1975). Thus, from the perspective of the Eastern Anasazi area, the apparent dispute over whether or not the large Pueblo IV sites are the result of local population growth or immigration may be viewed from a different perspective. Again, one need not look farther than Jemez or the Hopi-Tewa to see how difficult it would be to discern such a migration archeologically. Further indications of the adaptability with which Pueblo groups were able to integrate and incorporate others are provided by the various, defensive "refugee sites" that were founded following the Pueblo Revolt of 1680 and Diego de Vargas's reconquest of New Mexico in 1696. These sites consist of stone "pueblitos" that were occupied by various Pueblo people who had been joined by, or joined, both Apache and Navajo.

The evidence for migration into the Eastern Anasazi area, rather than consisting of specific constellations of traits, is manifest by the marked increase in population instability in the area during Pueblo IV. Numerous sites were abandoned during the Rio Grande Classic; the abandonments occurred at different times during the Classic and are not associated with any particular instances of widespread drought. The long-term stability of the Eastern Anasazi area, outside of the San Juan, which has been attributed to "marginality" with respect to the San Juan (Wendorf and Reed 1955) prior to 1400, was the result of proximity to the mountainous buffering areas. For example, within the middle Rio Grande, the time at which villages appear varies considerably. In both the Albuquerque and Cimarron districts, Basketmaker II villages have been shown to date within the appropriate temporal period for Basketmaker II elsewhere in the Southwest. However, the Taos, Chama, Pajarito, and Santa Fe areas show considerable "lag." This has been interpreted as a problem in marginality, in that much of the Rio Grande was viewed as out of the mainstream and isolated from more progressive areas. In view of the evidence from both Albuquerque and the Cimarron, which are each even more geographically isolated and distant from the San Juan than the rest of the area, the notion of marginality in this sense is untenable. Rather, it would appear that until the 1400s, the mountainous areas provided an outlet for local population increase. In essence, people could become hunters and gatherers, which requires less labor than horticulture (Lee 1968, 1969). Following the abandonment of the Chaco area, this outlet was not sufficient for the numbers of people in the eastern area. This added constraint is reflected by the large and unstable aggregated communities of Pueblo IV. The grid gardens along the Chama and in the Picuris area, the terraces and grids of the Pajarito Plateau, as well as the expansion of groups into the Plains margins in the Saline district indicate that intensive efforts were being made to support a relatively tremendous population increase. It is not surprising, given even minor climatic fluctuations, that many of these efforts would be failures, Pueblos would be abandoned, and new communities founded.

During the historic period, not only did the presence of Athapaskan speakers, Utes, Spaniards, and Anglos constrain continued migrations and relocations, but also the introduction of livestock destroyed most of the wild resources that would have been available during times of stress. The modern Pueblos display a remarkable adaptation considering that two of their former means of coping (reliance on wild food sources and migration) are no longer open.

151

# Prehistory: Southern Periphery

CHARLES C. DI PESO

Since the 1960s archeological research in northern Mexico has produced a mass of explicit data that necessitate redrawing the southern boundary of the "North American Southwest" to include all of northern Mexico as far south as the Tropic of Cancer (fig. 1). This additional expanse includes a very substantial part of what has been called, following colonial Spanish usage, the Gran Chichimeca (Di Peso 1963, 1968, 1968a)—*chichimeca* being the name applied by the Aztecs to the barbarian tribes north of the area of Mesoamerican civilizations (Wolf 1959; Di Peso 1974, 1:48–58). This vast, semiarid region of over a million square kilometers has been defined both as the northern periphery of Mesoamerica (Kelley and Abbott 1966) and as the southern periphery of the American Southwest (Di Peso 1968, 1968a). In a very real sense it was both, as on the one hand it was the homeland of Cochise-like desert dwellers, and on the other hand it was an exploitable frontier to the Mesoamericans who from time to time sponsored various mercantile ventures into this northern borderland.

About A.D. 1 this mineral-rich land was occupied by people who bore cultures sharing the simple attributes of the San Pedro stage of the Cochise culture complex (Sayles and Antevs 1941; Sayles 1945:1, 3–4; "Agricultural Beginnings, 2000 B.C.–A.D. 500," this vol.), differing considerably in temperament and lifeways from their cousins who lived south of the Tropic of Cancer (Wolf 1959). Their lands actually involved more than one-half the present republic of Mexico, which in the 1970s supported less than one-fifth of the Mexican population (with 6 persons per square kilometer as compared to 25 persons below the Tropic of Cancer). Subsequently the

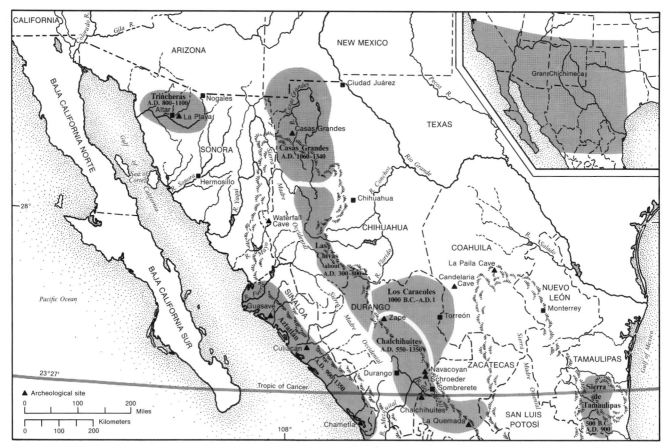

Fig. 1. Approximate areas of Mesoamerican cultural influence in the Southern Periphery. Inset shows extent of Gran Chichimeca.

peoples scattered throughout the entire area were variously stimulated at different times by diverse groups of Mesoamerican merchants, called *pochteca* by the Aztecs (Sahagún 1959; Bittman and Sullivan 1978). These merchants created trading centers represented by the Huasteca complex in the Sierra de Tamaulipas, the Chalchihuites culture in the valley of the Guadiana in Durango, the Aztatlán horizon in Sinaloa, the Medio period at Casas Grandes in Chihuahua, and possibly the Trincheras culture at Altar, Sonora (fig. 1).

This arid land is crossed by north-south running mountain ranges, which separate plateaus from several basin and range districts (see "Prehistory: Introduction," fig. 1, this vol.), some of which drain into terminal lakes. There are harsh coastal deserts, most often covered with a thorny growth that thrives only in this sun-blinding landscape (Di Peso 1963, 1974, 6). It is an expanse marked by highly localized thunderstorm activity, an extreme diurnal temperature range, and a minimal and very spotty rainfall pattern. It is crisscrossed by a few fertile, oasislike valley galleries, which these natives called home. Throughout its confines, nature gives reluctantly of her bounties, yet there are certain unique and valued items—turquoise (the prized *chalchiuitl* of the Aztecs) and the sacred peyote—that made this land a potentially rich domain in the esteem of the southern sophisticates, who went to great lengths to ferret out these luxuries.

If this area is recognized as the southern bounds of the Greater Southwest (Di Peso 1968, 1968a), it must be with the understanding that the periphery was considerably larger than the core region (Arizona and New Mexico), which was actually only a small but integral portion of the total Gran Chichimeca, amounting to some 2,700,000 square kilometers, of which the traditional Southwest constituted but 22 percent (610,400 square kilometers), the Southern Periphery 39 percent (1,044,600 square kilometers), and the remainder the outer northern portions of the Greater Southwest. This entire land block contains at least four geographical subareas (López de Llergo 1959, 1) and six, possibly seven, major biotic zones determined by altitude (Kelley 1956; Di Peso 1974, 4:1-2). As viewed from the Gulf coast in eastern Tamaulipas, this harsh, demanding Periphery comprises at least the Tamaulipas mountain forest slopes, then the drier Sierra Madre Oriental, the mesquite grasslands of the central basin and range territory, the pine-forested highlands of the Sierra Madre Occidental, and finally the desert littoral of the Gulf of California and the associated Baja California peninsula. Within this realm, the north-south trending terrain affords no real barrier to foot travel.

## The Desert Culture Base

The native Chichimecs established a static existence in this territory that has come to be recognized as the Cochise variant of the Desert culture (Jennings 1956:69-72), that is, the southern sector of the Picosa (Irwin-Williams 1967:441-450), which was in its San Pedro stage at about A.D. 1. Its eastern provincial variations in the Southern Periphery are called the Abasolo and Big Bend complexes (pre-Laguna phase) according to MacNeish, Nelken-Terner, and Johnson (1967, 2:240-244, fig. 175) or, more simply, the Coahuilan complex, a single, non-Mesoamerican, Cochise-like culture (Taylor 1966:62). In Durango, in the south-central portion of this district, lived people who bore aspects of the Los Caracoles and Las Chivas cultures described as belonging to the Cochise complex (Spence 1971:19-22). Unfortunately, little can be said of this horizon in the southwestern region in Sinaloa (Meighan 1971:759). However, the central mountains were occupied by the Rio Fuerte Basketmakers (Zingg 1940:1-4), and the north-central portion by the Cochise Forraje period folk of the Casas Grandes district (Lister 1958:15-22, 96-108, 112; Di Peso 1966:16-17). Present-day Sonora appears to have been inhabited by gleaners of the Peralta complex, acknowledged to have been still another variation of the San Pedro stage (Fay 1956, 1958; Johnson 1966:29-30). Thus this desert Cochise culture base, first defined in the American Southwest (Sayles and Antevs 1941; Sayles 1945), is now known to have extended throughout the southern section of the Gran Chichimeca (Jennings 1956:69-72).

These nonsedentary seasonal gatherers probably traveled from place to place within their territories, along with their dogs, gleaning natural foodstuffs and sleeping on bark or grass beds in caves or other unsophisticated shelters. Among other things, they harvested many different small seeds, which were prepared for immediate consumption by parching and grinding, using either a flat or basin-shaped stone metate in conjunction with a single-hand cobble handstone (mano). They were adept at weaving twined and coiled baskets (fig. 2), sewing animal skins, and shaping gourds and stones into vessels, but they made no pottery. They wove fiber sandals as well as nets and matting (fig. 3). They also hunted various local fauna to supplement their vegetal diet. This not only afforded them additional food but also became a source of skins and animal hair for clothing and bags. Killing tools included traps, curved or flat wooden clubs, and the atlatl (throwing stick), used to propel spears that had either a variety of chipped projectile points, including the San Pedro form, or wooden tips. Their family craftsmen produced a number of cutting and pulping tools, such as choppers and scrapers, by chipping chalcedony, obsidian, or other materials with conchoidal fractures. In time, their medicine men came to employ both tubular stone pipes and bone sucking tubes in performing their cures, while their patients adorned themselves with little else but brightly colored feathers, seeds, and occasional whole Oliva and olivella shells. Seemingly, many of them took

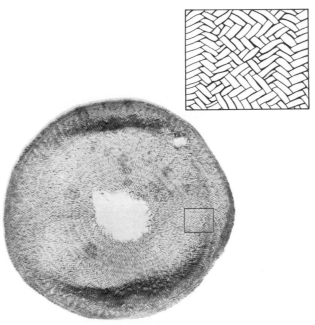

Fig. 2. Twilled yucca leaf basketry tray from a cliff dwelling (site Chihuahua H:11:3), Chuchupaste gorge, Chihuahua, from the Medio period. Detail shows 3-over, 3-under twilling in concentric rings of alternating designs (Sayles 1936). Diameter about 46 cm.

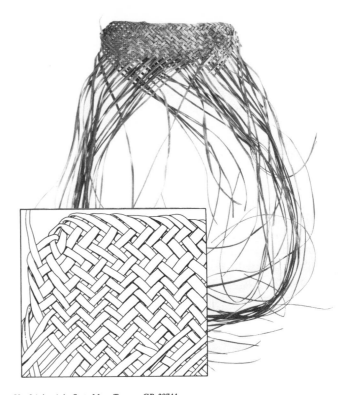

Fig. 3. Unfinished yucca leaf twilled matting from Chihuahua H:11:1. Width of completed section about 22 cm.

their evening pleasure sitting about their sleeping areas chewing various vegetable stalks, which they spit out after extracting the juices, leaving the quids scattered about for archeologists to find.

In time, and as early as 7000 B.C., some, such as the Tamaulipas cave folk (MacNeish 1958; Cutler and Whitaker 1961:483), learned to augment their basic subsistence with certain domestic plants, including the bottle gourd *(Lagenaria siceraria),* and by the birth of Christ, squash *(Cucurbita pepo).* Both corn *(Zea mays)* (according to Dick 1954:141) and beans *(Phaseolus vulgaris)* appear to have come into general use throughout the area by A.D. 500. These domesticated plants had become staple food items in Mesoamerica centuries earlier and probably reached the Southern Periphery through the eastern highlands of the Sierra Madre Occidental (Haury 1962; Kelley 1956:137). Even though these agricultural inventions first began to penetrate this zone several thousand years before the birth of Christ, their presence did not seriously alter the material culture of these people for almost two millennia, as it was only sometime after A.D. 500 that certain of the Chichimecs became serious farmers, and then at the instigation of specific Mesoamericans who brought the necessary sociotechnological knowledge of water control and irrigation. Prior to this time, those few indigenes who did cultivate crops relied on dry farming techniques that were dependent upon seasonal natural rainfall. These simple, localized tilling concepts may have been transmitted from one Chichimec group to another through the medium of a common Uto-Aztecan language (Taylor 1961; Swadesh 1959).

## The Huastecan Thrust

Prior to A.D. 1, a pre-Classic cultural conquest movement (Foster 1960:10–20) was made into the Sierra de Tamaulipas, in the southeast corner of this peripheral zone. The nonsedentary Chichimecs, who lived much like their Coahuiltecan neighbors (Taylor 1966:89) at this time, were put upon by southern entrepreneurs, either by 1500 B.C. (ibid.:88, fig. 30) or 500 B.C. (MacNeish 1958: 155–165, 167, 192, 198, fig. 48, tables 22, 30). In any event, south of the Tropic of Cancer, and sometime around A.D. 1 (± 250) north of this line (ibid.:201), this historical happening, defined as the Laguna, Eslabones, and La Salta phases, apparently caused a decided shift in the material culture inventories of the inhabitants. Several fairly large, concentrated, Mesoamerican-like villages appeared in the northern reaches of these mountains; they included ball courts and 300–400 directionally oriented domiciles built on low, stone-retained house mounds surrounding large, central, ceremonial plazas that contained truncated mounds up to 40 feet in height. These communities were serviced by some sort of city water system involving reservoirs.

The ceramists of these towns introduced orange, cream, black, red, and textured patterned pottery, as well as Mesoamerican items such as coffee bean–eyed solid figurines (fig. 4), solid legged vessels, clay beads, ladles, effigy cups, and flutes. Likewise, the stone workers were

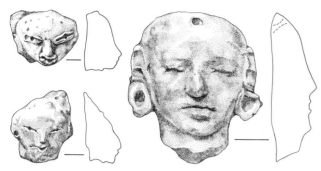

after MacNeish 1958:figs. 41-3, 41-5, 42-9.
Fig. 4. Modeled heads of clay figurines excavated in Sierra de Tamaulipas, Mexico (see MacNeish 1958:122-128). Width of top left 4 cm, rest same scale.

busied not only with specific architectural needs but also with the fabrication of products such as square-based celts and chili grinders. These town dwellers were socially structured to afford rank and status to the priesthood, the military, and perhaps to the craftsmen. As an economic unit, these intruders produced and distributed their goods for local and foreign consumption, after the *pochteca* exploitative pattern (MacNeish 1958:157-160). This event, like the subsequent ones, appears to have followed a basic culture conquest model (Foster 1960:10-20). Conceivably, the quest was one that involved certain natural products such as peyote *(Lophophora williamsii)* or, perhaps, minerals. However, most of the indigenous Abasolo population remained simple Chichimecs who, like their northern and western neighbors, continued to support themselves in the old traditional manner.

West of this initial Tamaulipas point of mix, in the land of the Los Caracoles culture in Durango, folk shifted into their Loma San Gabriel stage when some moved into small, semipermanent villages, took on a low-level farming subsistence pattern, and began to make pottery (Kelley and Abbott 1966:339; Kelley 1971:799-801; Spence 1971:19-22). These widely separated communities consisted of a dozen or so perishable rectangular houses clustered around a central compound. These part-time farmers planted some corn and a few beans to reinforce their wild food harvests, which they continued to prepare after the fashion of typical desert dwellers, using the ancient basin-shaped metates and one-hand manos. A few began to fashion a brownware that was very much like that of the northern Casas Grandes (Di Peso 1974, 6) and O'otam folk (Sayles 1945). Like them, they learned to slip some of their pottery with red paint and even took to decorating certain pieces with textured designs or with broad bands of red paint, called Chico Red-on-brown (Kelley and Kelley 1971). These were formed after the Chichimecan fashion of the time, in simple globular jars and hemispherical bowls, without any of the usual Mesoamerican embellishments such as engraving, legs, and wide flare rims.

Little is known of the Sinaloan folk who occupied the southwestern edge of the Southern Periphery, south of the Mayo River in Sonora. They may have been the predecessors of the Huatabampo and Tacuichamona cultures (Meighan 1971:759; Ekholm 1942:74-77). Unlike their southern Mesoamerican Aztatlán neighbors, they produced a Chichimecan brownware as well as a finely made redware and textured potteries that closely resembled those made by the Mogollon and O'otam potters (Ekholm 1942:136). These craftsmen also made solid-form figurines (Ekholm 1939, 1940:326), marine shell ornaments, and stone paint palettes similar to those produced by the Hohokam of Arizona (Ekholm 1942:111). In addition, they made three-quarter-grooved axheads (Ekholm 1940:326, 1942:107) not unlike those used by their eastern Loma San Gabriel neighbors, the Casas Grandians, and the Arizona O'otam and Hohokam.

North, in the Sierra Madre Occidental, the Rio Fuerte district was occupied by a group of contemporary cave dwellers whose culture has been described as being similar to that of the Anasazi Basketmakers of the American Southwest (Zingg 1940:44-48), as they, too, planted a little corn and made a crude brownware (Alma Plain), some of which was decorated in red cross patterns (Ascher and Clune 1960).

In the Coahuila portion of the Southern Periphery, there lived a widespread group of gleaners who persisted through time and were disrupted only after Spanish contact. These northern frontiersmen never learned to farm, to live in houses, or even to make rudimentary pottery (Taylor 1966), as witness the Mayran and Jora complexes (ibid.:83-84) found in the Candelaria and La Paila caves (Aveleyra et al. 1956, 1:197).

In the Casas Grandes area, the Desert culture folk took on certain elements of farming, settled in small open sites and in caves, and began making a Mogollon-like brownware pottery (Lister 1958:110; Di Peso 1963:6-7) that also resembled the ceramic products made by the Loma San Gabriel peoples. It is assumed that these Casas Grandes people remained seminomadic, even though they built small communities consisting of a dozen or so crude, shallow pit houses, which were constructed around a central community house (perhaps as winter homes). They buried their dead in graves placed at random about the village premises, sometimes covering them with stone cairns. Corn, beans, and squash were planted, but these Viejo period folk continued to hunt bison and antelope after the fashion of their ancestors. They, too, used three-quarter-grooved axes and wore marine-shell ornaments that were similar to those of their neighbors.

Across the Sierra Madre Occidental and along the Sonoran coast, bearers of the Peralta culture lived unchanged. It is not known for certain whether or not they actually took to living in villages much before A.D. 800

(Johnson 1966:31–35). Across the Sea of Cortez on the Baja California peninsula, the Comondú did not accept agriculture, or pottery, until the coming of the Spaniards (Massey 1966:50–51, fig. 9).

The bulk of the Chichimec population in the Southern Periphery remained hunters and gatherers, as only a few took up simple agriculture. Those that did take to farming also began to make a simple, non-Mesoamerican brownware pottery, which they sometimes slipped in red or black or decorated with various uncomplicated textured designs. Only a few utilized red painted patterns of decoration, and these consisted of simple straight lines that formed crosses or pendant triangles suspended from the rims of bowl interiors. Those indigenes who made any material culture advancement without direct Mesoamerican contact (in the Sierra de Tamaulipas) took on a certain provincialism. Their semipermanent villages were made up of individual jacal (mud and wattle) houses with roundish to square floor plans. Most of these folk buried their dead within the peripheries of their cave or open site dwelling areas. For the most part, they remained in their Cochise-like cultural niche.

## Subsequent Mesoamerican Donors, A.D. 500–1340

By A.D. 500, the Huasteca-inspired centers in the Sierra de Tamaulipas were well entrenched and were producing some 75 percent of their foodstuffs by farming (Mac-Neish 1958:149, fig. 48), yet by A.D. 1000 these hilltop population concentrations collapsed (ibid.: fig. 49, table 30). But while these towns were still being occupied, about A.D. 600 (± 50), there occurred a second such invasion of the Southern Periphery, this time by the Chalchihuites border guards who moved into the Guadiana Valley of southern Durango from Zacatecas. These Mesoamerican folk had for a number of generations lived on and defended this central portion of the frontier against those Chichimecs who lived north of the Súchil and Colorado river valleys. They moved through the Sombrerete Pass and built both trading and ceremonial centers in the homeland of the Loma San Gabriel people. These Ayala phase sophisticates took up residency all along the east flanks of the Sierra Madre Occidental, as far north as Zape (Kelley and Abbott 1966:339–340; Kelley 1971:787–799). They constructed the hilltop towns of the Schroeder and Navacoyan sites, which consisted of separate groups of perishable domiciles built on house platforms or terraces that surrounded a central plaza, which sometimes included round ceremonial platforms. These donors introduced a great many Mesoamerican traits, including pyramids, I-shaped ball courts, and an advanced communication road system. As in the case of the Tamaulipans, the new society became involved in the establishment of a structured class society based on priesthood, guilds, and military power. Their craft specialists included metal workers, who made copper and gold objects, and a host of other artisans who produced carved marine mollusk ornaments, pyrite mirrors, incense burners, stone paint palettes, obsidian flake knives, turquoise mosaics, and three-quarter-grooved axheads. Like so many of these frontier peoples, indigenous and otherwise, they inhumed their dead in flexed or extended positions and occasionally placed the bones of the deceased in urns.

The donor ceramists of this period were capable of making Mesoamerican-like polished red, buff, and black wares (Kelley 1971:798), as well as an assortment of textured forms. Some of these were decorated with red designs on a cream or white base, or white designs on a red base; but only occasionally did they use polychrome or red-filled engraved decorations. These craft specialists took to the production of Mesoamerican objects such as fired clay chili grinders (fig. 5), comals, modeled spindle whorls, cylindrical stamps, and effigy whistles, some of which they traded to their western Aztatlán and northern Casas Grandes neighbors, and there is a strong suggestion that they were in contact with the Hohokam (A.S. Johnson 1958) and the Mogollon of Arizona and New Mexico (Kelley and Abbott 1966:341–342; Kelley 1971:793).

Some time in the early decades of the tenth century, westward of the Sierra Madre Occidental Chalchihuites domain, down on the Sinaloan coast, a group of Mixteca-Puebla peoples came to settle north of the Tropic of

Museo Nacional de Antropología, Mexico City: 54.49/169.

Fig. 5. Brownware Morcillo chili grinder *(molcajete)* from the Chalchihuites site of LCAJ-1 near Durango, Mexico. Tripod pottery bowl with red band decoration painted around rim and grater section composed of incised lines in circle at base of interior (Kelley 1971:796; Kelley and Abbott 1966:341). Diameter 20.5 cm.

156

Cancer and introduced the Aztatlán culture. Like the Chalchihuites, they are thought to have originally been Mesoamericans who guarded the Classic period Chametla border lands against the northern barbarians, beginning around A.D. 250 or 300 (Kelley and Winters 1960:560; Meighan 1971:759-760), that is, during their Tierra del Padre (Early Chametla) phase (I.T. Kelly 1938:34). By A.D. 900, about the time the post-Classic Tula-Toltec came into power in the Valley of Mexico, and sometime after this culture had entered its Aztatlán phase (Kelley and Winters 1960:fig. 8; Meighan 1971:760-762), some of these frontiersmen moved north and settled among the Huatabampo folk of the Guasave district.

Unfortunately, very little is known of their architectural achievements, although it is suspected that they resided in large population centers in perishable abodes constructed on low mounds. They placed their dead in large artificial mounds with abundant grave goods, a practice that affords some knowledge of certain aspects of their material culture. For instance, their potters made engraved and negative painted vessels (fig. 6), and some of the most elaborately decorated potteries found anywhere in Mesoamerica, employing six colors in a single design (Meighan 1971:761). They also made Mesoamerican items such as elbow pipes (fig. 7), modeled spindle whorls, solid-form figurines with coffee-bean eyes (I.T. Kelley 1938:pl. 18; Meighan 1971:762, figs. 6, 10), legged vessels, bird-effigy whistles, clay masks, and cylinder stamps (Ekholm 1942:86, fig. 16). Some of these items were traded eastward to the Chalchihuites (Kelley and Winters 1960). The Aztatlán metalsmiths, who worked in copper, gold, and silver (Ekholm 1942:97-101; Meighan 1971:761), manufactured luxury items such as spherical copper rattles, finger rings, and beads, while their stone artisans were adept at fashioning alabaster jars (Ekholm 1942:103-105, fig. 16d-e), square-based celts, three-quarter-grooved axheads, turquoise ornaments, obsidian blades (ibid.:103-108), and overlap manos, which were similar to those used in Papagueria. Some of the Guasave

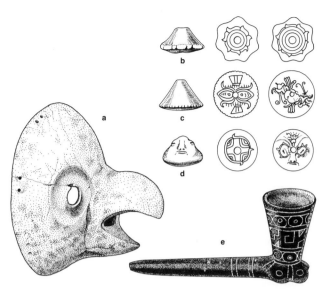

Amer. Mus. of Nat. Hist., New York: a, 30.2-4928; b, 30.2-4946; c, 30.2-4964; d, 30.2-4968; e, 30.2-4973.

Fig. 7. Aztatlán ceramic artifacts excavated at Guasave, Sinaloa, Mexico. a, Parrot mask with white-slipped exterior surface, excavated from human burial (Ekholm 1942:85-87); b-d, polished, unslipped spindle whorls with engraved designs, usually found in human burials (after Ekholm 1942:87); e, elbow type smoking pipe with incised decoration on polished red-slipped surface (Ekholm 1942:83). Length of e about 13 cm, rest same scale.

craftsmen were adept at placing paint cloisonné on gourds (fig. 8), after the fashion of the present-day Tarascan lacquer workers (ibid.: 91-96, fig. 18). It is very likely that these coastal dwellers, who utilized the sea as a food source, became involved in the marine shell extracting industry, as well as in the production of cut shell ornaments, solid bracelets, and pendants. These items for the most part involved designs that resembled those of the Arizona Hohokam (ibid.:109-111) and the Paquimé phase of Casas Grandes (Di Peso 1974, 6).

Even as the Chalchihuites and Aztatlán cultures were spreading northward, another group of donors moved into the Casas Grandes Valley (Chihuahua) and sparked

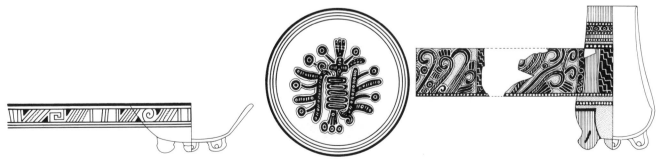

after Ekholm 1942:figs. 6f, 7g.

Fig. 6. Aztatlán pottery excavated at Guasave, Sinaloa, Mexico. left, Cerro Isabel Engraved bowl with 3 legs and brown painted decoration that has been outlined by engraving or incising on buff background. right, Sinaloa Polychrome 3-legged jar with maroon, black, and white painted decoration on buff-slipped surface (Ekholm 1942:56-62). Left diameter 26.4 cm, right same scale.

Fig. 8. Watercolor reproduction of fragment of paint cloisonné, probably from gourd vessel, excavated at Guasave, Sinaloa, Mexico. The gourd vessel no longer exists, but the two layers (interior and exterior surfaces of gourd) were preserved (for technique of manufacture see Ekholm 1942:93). Width about 19 cm.

Fig. 9. View to south of Casas Grandes, Chihuahua, Mexico, with sunken -shaped ball court to the west, multiroom dwelling complex to the east adjacent to open central marketplace, and various shaped ceremonial mounds.

the Viejo period indigenes. By A.D. 1060, the vitalized Paquimé people at Casas Grandes began cutting the timber for their fortresslike house-cluster compounds, which they cast in mud. Although these entrepreneurs came to dominate their chosen territory and overshadowed the indigenous Chichimec culture, they by no means obliterated it. In the course of several decades, the sparsely populated Casas Grandes Valley was on the upsurge, as their Medio period innovations took hold (Di Peso 1968, 1968a, 1974, 6).

The Paquimé architecture was the heritage of a sophisticated group of donor architects and engineers who, in a comparatively short time span, raised the local populace to the rank of a semicomplex hydraulic society (Wittfogel 1957). They constructed I-shaped ball courts, effigy and truncated mounds, squared-column colonnades, and roofed, atriumlike structures (fig. 9), complete with either staircases or ramps. In time, their capital had an attractive marketplace. The multistoried apartment was served with a partly subterranean system of city water ditches and a plaza cistern system, as well as a concealed underground well. Its warehouses were filled with masses of raw material, including thousands of kilograms of Gulf of California marine mollusks and many kilograms of selenite, paint pigments, specular iron crystals, copper, and turquoise. The local ceramists produced vast amounts of Casas Grandes polychrome potteries using a localized series of forms including human and zoomorphic hollow effigies (see "Prehistory: O'otam," fig. 10, this vol.). Only occasionally did these specialists resort to Mesoamerican forms such as legged vessels; and they apparently never made solid-form figurines, elbow pipes, or modeled spindle whorls. Their trading instincts carried their locally made ceramics northward to the Mesa Verde in Colorado, southward to Teotihuacán (Linné 1942: 175-178, fig. 318; Griffin and Krieger 1947:166), and

from the Gulf of Mexico to that of California. They bartered other goods, such as obsidian, modeled spindle whorls, and ceramics from Chalchihuites, ceramics and perhaps marine shell from Aztatlán, and scarlet macaws *(Ara macao)* from Tamaulipas.

Still another commercial center may have existed, which has come to be called the Trincheras, located in northwestern Sonora. This group, which occupied the lands of the historic Soba O'otam (see "Prehistory: O'otam," in this vol.), has been referred to as a Desert Hohokam culture (Haury 1950:547; Johnson 1963: 182-185, table 1). Little is known of it save that its primary population center may have been located in the Altar drainage at La Playa, or Boquillas as it is sometimes called (Sauer and Brand 1931; Woodward 1936; Johnson 1960, 1963:174-178, 1966:31-34). Here the folk built round, perishable houses, which they clustered about groups of low mounds located near several terraced hill sites (Johnson 1963:178-179). The people constructed a number of hilltop compound communities that resembled the post-thirteenth-century O'otam villages found in southwestern Arizona (Amerind Foundation Survey) and a spectacular hillside trenched defense system in this territory some distance away from La Playa, perhaps to protect its marine shell industry (fig. 11). This seems to have been a thriving concern some time between A.D. 800

158

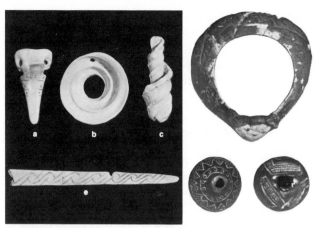

Amerind Foundation, Dragoon, Ariz.: a, CG/2574D; b, CG/2047; c, CG/7899; d, CG/8213; e, CG/6634; f, CG/2223A; g, CG/5933.

Fig. 10. Shell ornaments and bone and clay weaving implements excavated at Casas Grandes, Chihuahua, Mexico. a, Incised shell pendant; b-c, cut shell religious pendants (Di Peso 1974, 2:548–549, 6:440); d, shell armlet with pseudo-cloisonné decoration; e, incised bone plaiting tool used in mat weaving; f-g, ceramic spindle whorls imported to Casas Grandes from Chalchihuites, with incised designs filled with white paint (Di Peso 1974, 2:704). Length of a 6.6 cm, rest same scale.

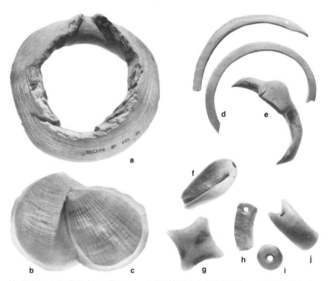

U. of Ariz., Ariz. State Mus., Tucson: a, A-21186-X-1; b, GP-50505; c, A-21188-X-3; d, A-21184-X-3; e, GP-50473; f, A-21167-X-2; g, A-36362; h, A-14978; i, A-14981; j, A-14986.

Fig. 11. Cut shell for manufacture of shell bracelets and beads, excavated at La Playa site, Sonora, Mexico (Woodward 1936; Johnson 1963:181–182). a, Glycymeris shell with center core removed to be smoothed to form bracelet; b-c, 2 cut Glycymeris shell cores; d-e, fragments of finished Glycymeris bracelets; f-j, drilled and polished shell beads of various shapes. Diameter of a 8 cm, rest same scale.

and 1100 (Johnson 1963:183), as these Trincheras people took to supplying bulk raw materials to the Hohokam shell artisans (Brand 1938:7–9; Tower 1945). In addition, their ceramists produced both a valued purple-on-red and a white-based polychrome pottery, which were used as trade items throughout northern Sonora and southern

U. of Ariz., Ariz. State Mus., Tucson: a, A-21115-X-2; b, A-21117-X-2; c, A-21141-X-4; d, A-21128-X-1; e, A-21138-X-2; f, A-21144-X-3; g, A-21125-X-3.

Fig. 12. Stone projectile points excavated at La Playa site, Sonora, Mexico (Johnson 1963:180–181). Length of a 7.8 cm, rest same scale.

Arizona and New Mexico (Sauer and Brand 1931; Di Peso 1956:356–362; Johnson 1960). In addition, the gleaner/farmer stone workers who occupied these villages made excellent raised three-quarter-grooved axes, hammers, and mauls.

In all these historic situations, save perhaps in the case of the Trincheras, these Southern Periphery centers were marked by the sudden introduction of a definable cluster of Mesoamerican traits that could have been implanted by a few *pochteca*—for example, the comparatively rapid massing of people into population centers that were dependent upon intensive agriculture, extensive trade, and artisan specialization. Certainly, the recorded architecture associated with each of these organizations cannot have been derived from the indigenous culture base, which obviously lacked the technical know-how required to produce these Mesoamerican-like designs—the I-shaped ball court complex, truncated mounds, staircases, colonnades, hydraulic farming systems, and city water systems.

Further, all these centers, with the exception of the unknown Trincheras complex but apparently including pre-Classic Tamaulipas (Stresser-Péan 1971:585–587), were strongly involved with the Mesoamerican Quetzalcoatl religious theme that seems to have been central to their stratified class systems. During the Classic period, the Chalchihuites folk utilized I-shaped ball courts and bits and pieces of this special iconography, including the cross, the morning and evening stars, the monster twin Xólotl, and the plumed serpent (Kelley and Abbott 1966:340–341; Kelley 1971:794–795). In post-Classic times the Guasave Aztatlán citizenry also used a host of Quetzalcoatl forms, including the plumed serpent and the Ehécatl wind symbols (Ekholm 1942:127), as did the Paquimé of Casas Grandes (Di Peso 1968, 1968a, 1974, 6).

Obviously, none of these frontier cultures was exactly    *159* like another in content, and it is suspected that they may actually have been economic competitors. Each zone developed its own ceramic and architectural traditions, and the various artisans used specialized tool and ornament designs. However, the religious, social, political, and economic structures were more or less alike, and each acquired a specific sphere of operation.

These various Southern Periphery trading centers flourished only because of specific Mesoamerican sponsorship, for study of their individual emplacements indicates the presence of the Mesoamerican *pochteca* exploitative strategy in terms of natural resources and available manpower. These frontier traders were probably held responsible for supplying certain amounts of luxury goods, such as turquoise and perhaps peyote, to the home merchants in return for the initial cost of their emplacement. It is well known that Mesoamerican trader families (Sahagún 1959) effected a market organization somewhat resembling certain economic aspects of the Hudson's Bay or Dutch East Indies companies. It is obvious that these leaders moved their Chichimec wards to a sociocultural level where they became capable of producing an agricultural surplus for trading, mining, and other profitable extracting industries, including slaving.

If these centers were economically motivated by Mesoamericans, then historical events in the lands south of the Tropic of Cancer would have had a decided effect upon those of the local frontiers. The Huastecan conquest was apparently inaugurated during pre-Classic times, about 500 B.C. (MacNeish 1958:166-173, 1971:578-579). This activity related to the El Prisco and subsequent three phases of the Huasteca, at a time when these Mesoamericans were in contact first with the Ticomán folk of the Mesa Central, and later with the Teotihuacán, and it is interesting that the Sierra de Tamaulipas venture ended in its La Salta phase at the same time that the Teotihuacán metropolis collapsed, and at the onset of the Tula-Mazapan movement (Piña Chan 1971; Cook de Leonard 1971:table 3). The Ayala phase Chalchihuites population, which crossed the central segment of the Tropic of Cancer about A.D. 600 (± 50), did so as the great city of Teotihuacán died (Kelley 1971:787); it grew in strength through the Toltec post-Classic but lost it when the Mexica (Aztecs) took over the Mesa Central in the first half of the fourteenth century (Kelley 1971:787-799; Kelley and Winters 1960:549). The Aztatlán movement into Guasave is reckoned to have begun about A.D. 900 (Ekholm 1958:17; Kelley and Winters 1960:549), when Tula's star was on the rise and while the Mixteca-Puebla culture was in fashion (B. Bell 1971:750). In this time segment, the Trincheras folk apparently rose to whatever economic heights they strove for. At Casas Grandes dendrochronology has indicated that this city was built during the post-Classic and while Tula was suffering internal political strife. Thus it seems that all the known

Southern Periphery population concentrations grew in strength during the time of the Toltecs' expansionist period. Consequently, it is not at all unfitting to envision these particular sites, with the exception of the Trincheras, as being active parts of this particular Mesoamerican economic endeavor.

### Changes A.D. 1340-1540

In the mid-fourteenth century, these frontier centers fell into ruin. Some, such as Casas Grandes, were wantonly burned, and many of the defending inhabitants were left where they were killed in battle in their open plazas, in defense of their temples, and in the burning collapse of their homes (Di Peso 1974, 3). It was a time when the donor groups lost their economic hold upon the Southern Periphery. In the northern sector of the Sierra de Tamaulipas, the intrusive culture appears to have been cut off at the end of its La Salta phase (MacNeish 1958:164-167, 199, fig. 49, tables 22, 30-31), when there was a sharp change into the contemporary, historic Los Angeles and San Lorenzo phases sometime between A.D. 900 and 1300 (MacNeish 1971:579-581, table 1). In the Chalchihuites, the Calera phase marked the beginning of the end of this culture, about 1350, as the cities were abandoned and allowed to fall into ruin (Kelley and Abbott 1966: 342-343; Kelley 1971:797-799). The same was true for the Aztatlán folk of Guasave, who apparently gave up their trading center about 1400 (Ekholm 1940:324, 1942:131-132; Kelley and Winters 1960:fig. 8; Meighan 1971:761), while the Casas Grandes people quit under duress about 1340 (Di Peso 1968, 1968a, 1974, 6). The little-known Trincheras culture may have declined in economic power even earlier, perhaps around 1100 if one utilizes the tentative Hohokam dating system (Johnson 1963:182-183, 1966:30).

It is clear that the mid-fourteenth century was a time of great ethnic upheaval throughout the Gran Chichimeca (Kelley and Abbott 1966:343; Di Peso 1974). In this historic hour, the Aztecs were winning their power struggle against the successors of the Toltecs. Capitals such as Tenochtitlán and Tlatelolco (both in present Mexico City) grew apace with their great politico-economic alliances (Bernal 1963:88-98, 125), and Huitzilopochtli, the Aztec sun god, came into prominence. This bit of Mesa Central history apparently had a direct bearing on the events that took place in the Gran Chichimeca. In the North American Southwest, the power of Quetzalcoatl was overshadowed by the aspect of this new god (Brew 1943:242-245; Jennings 1956: 111-115), as Aztec-sponsored traders moved northward using a new line of communication involving the Florida-Conchos-Rio Grande corridor, rather than the older Sierra Madre Occidental route. Contacts were made in New Mexico in Pueblo IV times to glean the Eastern Pueblo turquoise deposits of the Cerrillos district.

In this interim, the Southern Periphery indigenes, relieved of the older Quetzalcoatl trading posts, continued to occupy their lands. In the Sierra de Tamaulipas, after A.D. 1300, the Los Angeles phase Tamaulipans lived on in their territories until the coming of the Spaniards (MacNeish 1958:157-165, table 22, 1971:579). The Loma San Gabriel folk carried the torch of their existence in the Guadiana Valley long after the Chalchihuites collapse and became known to the Spaniards as Tepehuán (Riley and Winters 1963; Kelley and Abbott 1966:339; Kelley 1971:799-801). Similarly, the indigenous La Quinta phase Sinaloans carried on as the historic Guasave (I.T. Kelly 1945:5-6, 158-167; Sauer and Brand 1932:41-51), the Casas Grandes people as the Jova and Jocome (Di Peso 1974, 6), and the Trincheras people as the Soba O'otam. In the areas that were outside the direct influence of the pre-fourteenth-century trading centers, indigenous groups such as the Coahuiltecans and Abasolo complex Tamaulipans (MacNeish 1958:163-165) sustained themselves until visited by the Spaniards, with little change for thousands of years (Taylor 1966:61-62,

fig. 30), as did the Rio Fuerte folk, who became known as Tarahumara (Zingg 1940:4; Pennington 1963:12), the Sonorans (Johnson 1966:36), and the Comondú of Baja California (Massey 1966:50-51).

However, the vacuum left by the Quetzalcoatl centers did cause an indigenous population shift, which was still active when the Europeans entered the Southern Periphery. For example, it is believed that the Cáhita folk of southern Sonora intruded into the Yaqui River drainage in this period (Beals 1932:145), and it is recorded that the Opata were pushing the Nebome (southern O'otam) into their restricted historic area, while the Casas Grandes folk lost much of their valley lands to the Suma and others who drifted in from the east.

Historical records indicate that these indigenes sustained themselves until disrupted by the Spanish Christian lifeway, when slaving practices and European diseases such as measles and smallpox were introduced and decimated large blocks of nonimmune Southern Periphery indigenes, many of whom never laid eyes upon a Spaniard.

# Southern Athapaskan Archeology

JAMES H. GUNNERSON

This chapter deals with those archeological sites in the Southwest that have been identified, or provisionally identified, as Southern Athapaskan, excluding those identified as Navajo. Navajo archeology is treated separately in volume 10 and Apachean archeology east and north of New Mexico is dealt with in volume 13. Primary concern here is with sites in northeastern New Mexico because it is there that the most Apache archeology has been done; elsewhere in the Southwest, Apache archeology has received little attention.

## Arrival in the Southwest

The Athapaskans probably arrived in the Southwest in the early 1500s. Pedro de Castañeda, one of Francisco Vásquez de Coronado's men, learned from Pueblo Indians (probably at Pecos Pueblo) that a group called Teyas had first appeared in the area some 16 years before 1540 as marauders who had unsuccessfully attacked Pecos and other Pueblos. When their attack failed, these people made peace with the Pueblos, departed for the Plains, and became important traders of plains products to the Pueblos (Winship 1896:524; Hammond and Rey 1940:258). Coronado met Teyas and Querechos on the Plains beyond Pecos and described both groups as highly mobile dog-nomad bison-hunters who lived in sewed skin tents. The Querechos have long been accepted by scholars as Athapaskans, and D. Gunnerson (1974:17-23), on the basis of linguistic leads provided by Hodge (Mooney 1898:245) and Harrington (1940:512) plus ethnohistorical evidence, has reasoned that the Teyas were also Athapaskans. Furthermore, Bandelier (1890-1892, 2:116-120) collected at Santo Domingo a legend that matched in detail Castañeda's account of the Teyas laying seige to Pecos and destroying various other Pueblos; however, in the Santo Domingo version, it was the Kirauash (Querechos?) who were the raiders. The combined weight of history, oral tradition, and linguistic evidence, plus the fact that archeologists have failed to locate any Apachean sites that can be reliably dated earlier than 1525, or even that early, make a convincing case for an early sixteenth-century Athapaskan arrival in the Southwest. An idea that was once seriously considered and is still not ruled out by some writers (Jett 1964; "Navajo Prehistory and History to 1850," vol. 10) is that Athapaskans might have arrived in the Southwest as

early as A.D. 1000 and might have been responsible, at least in part, for the abandonment of many Pueblo sites in the 1100s and 1200s. Since there is no evidence for the presence of Athapaskans in the Southwest before the 1500s, such ideas lie in the realm of speculation.

The previous homeland of the Southern Athapaskans was almost certainly west-central Canada, where their closest linguistic relatives live. Clues to the time of split between the Northern and Southern Athapaskans and the subsequent differentiation of the Southern group are provided by lexicostatistical data presented by Hoijer (1956, 1971). He suggests that the Southern and Northern groups split well within the past 1,000 years and identifies two Southern Athapaskan linguistic groups: Kiowa Apachean, restricted to the Kiowa Apache, and Southwestern Apachean, which includes all the rest. The second he in turn divides into two groups, separating Jicarilla and Lipan from the others. He also finds that Kiowa Apachean shares with Jicarilla and Lipan some phonetic similarities that it does not share with the other Southwestern Apachean dialects. Furthermore, one of Opler's (1938:383) Jicarilla informants said of the Kiowa Apache, "They speak our language; the language is just about the same." These linguistic relationships are entirely compatible with the ethnohistorical and archeological reconstructions presented by Gunnerson and Gunnerson (1971) and D. Gunnerson (1974, but see "Historical Linguistics and Archeology," this volume, for a different view). In brief, they suggest that the Apacheans arrived in the Southwest as a more or less homogeneous group with the ancestors of the Jicarilla, Lipan, and Kiowa Apaches remaining to the east of the others, and maintaining a Plains orientation. Until the 1720s the Apacheans were all in contact (not always friendly) with one another and probably had at least tenuous contacts with the Northern Athapaskans (Gunnerson and Gunnerson 1971). In the 1720s the Kiowa Apaches, who had been the most remote since they lived on the northern edge of Plains Apacheria, were cut off from the other Apacheans by Comanches allied with Utes and by Pawnees allied with Frenchmen. As a very small group, they joined the Kiowa near the Black Hills in South Dakota. They later moved to the Southern Plains with the Kiowa who influenced them heavily. The rest of the Plains Apache bands, known to the Spaniards as Palomas, Cuartelejos, and Carlanas, were eventually all forced off the central High Plains, again mainly by pressure from Comanches, Pawnees, French, and intensified Spanish campaigns. Most of these Apacheans eventually became the Llanero or Plains band of the Jicarillas while others probably became part of the Lipans who were in central Texas by the 1730s. After the Kiowa Apaches were cut off, the remaining Apacheans retained contact among themselves with the Lipans perhaps the most peripheral. Because there is a long record of fission and fusion of Apachean bands, it is not surprising that there are inconsistencies among the split dates arrived at by lexicostatistics, but, in general, the degrees of relationship suggested by Hoijer and Opler's informant are consistent with the archeological, historical, and ethnographic evidence.

A possible reason for the Apachean migration south has been advanced by D. Gunnerson (1972, 1974), who suggested that they followed rapidly increasing herds of bison down the Plains when, according to Bryson, Baerreis, and Wendlund (1970), conditions changed for the

better after the severe droughts of the mid 1400s. This explanation is highly compatible with the idea of a rapid Apachean migration south via the High Plains just east of the Rocky Mountains. Alternative intermountain routes have been considered (Huscher and Huscher 1943; Steward 1936:62), but there is little or no evidence to support them.

On the basis of ethnohistorical evidence, the Apacheans arrived in the Southwest as bison-hunting nomads (Hammond and Rey 1940:261; D. Gunnerson 1956, 1974:17–18). Such people would not have left easily identifiable archeological sites. Perhaps eventually their early (prepottery) sites may be identified. Unfortunately, diagnostic nonceramic artifacts are both few and rare at later Apachean sites so that a direct historical approach will probably not be fruitful. Apachean sites of the 1500s may prove to be campsites with an unspecialized Plains-like stone inventory and perhaps limited amounts of Eastern Pueblo pottery, especially pottery from Pecos. On the plains of western Kansas and Nebraska and eastern Colorado and Wyoming, where one might expect to find prepottery Apachean sites, none has been identified. Sites in this area identifiable as Apachean are all assignable to the Dismal River aspect and date from the 1600s and early 1700s (Gunnerson 1959, 1968; Gunnerson and Gunnerson 1971; Schlesier 1972; D. Gunnerson 1974). Because of the geographical position of Dismal River sites on the most probable Apachean migration route, an attractive idea has been that the Dismal River aspect might represent the undifferentiated ancestors of all Southern Athapaskans. However, this suggestion can be ruled out since there is no evidence that the Dismal River aspect existed until well into the 1600s.

## Eastern Apache Archeology

### Northeastern New Mexico, 1550?–1750

Many of the Apache sites (fig. 1) in northeastern New Mexico can be attributed to the Jicarilla, or to groups known originally to the Spaniards under other names who eventually became part of the Jicarilla. Notable exceptions are a few sites provisionally attributed to the Faraon Apache who may have been assimilated by the Mescalero.

The period for which the most data exist on Apache archeology is the late 1600s and early 1700s. Good documentary evidence (Thomas 1935) including references to Apache villages existing along the eastern edge of the Sangre de Cristo Mountains in the early 1700s suggested this area as a logical starting point for Apache archeological studies (D. Gunnerson 1956; Gunnerson 1959, 1969). Also, it was in this area and during this period that the Jicarilla and related Apacheans achieved a cultural climax as semihorticulturalists.

In 1599 Juan de Oñate was told that Apaches lived in pueblos like those of the Tewas, one having 15 plazas

Fig. 1. Archeological sites.

163

(Hammond and Rey 1953, 1:484). However, there is as yet no archeological confirmation of Apache pueblos of this size. The best historical accounts are those resulting from Ulibarrí's journey of 1706 and Valverde's expedition of 1719 (Thomas 1935:62–64, 110–133, 263), which mention small Apache villages with a variety of house types and irrigated fields. Both expeditions set out from Taos Pueblo, crossed the Sangre de Cristos, and reached the Plains just south of Cimarron, New Mexico. Sometime in the mid-1700s pressure from hostile Indians, especially Comanches and Utes, forced the Apaches to abandon adobe-house villages. The Jicarilla shifted most of their farming activities westward over the mountains into the Rio Grande valley and into canyons between Taos and Picuris. However, they continued to frequent the country east of the mountain crests until they were placed on their reservation in 1887.

The remains of an Apache pueblo, the Glasscock site (fig. 2), about 22 miles southwest of Cimarron have been excavated (Gunnerson 1969:24–30). This site is located in the broad sheltered valley along Ocate Creek near its confluence with a major, dependable tributary. Although the elevation is about 7,500 feet, gardening and farming has been successful in the twentieth century in the area and was almost certainly practical when the site was occupied. Irrigation from the stream would have been easy, and the occupants had ready access to the resources of the mountains on the west and of the plains to the east. The only structure found at the site consisted of seven rectangular rooms, six forming a rectangle with the seventh attached to one side, forming an L. The overall dimensions were 24 by 32 feet. Walls about 0.8 foot thick were made of layers of adobe apparently laid wet since no evidence of adobe bricks could be detected. There was no evidence of doors or other openings through the walls, but only the wall bases remained. Charred wood and pieces of hard adobe with impressions of logs, probably vigas, were found within the structure. One room contained two partly superposed hearths, both D-shaped and built against an inside wall, and a fire pit was found in the sheltered outdoor area formed by the L of the building. Near the structure was a bell-shaped baking pit.

The predominant pottery (96%) from the Glasscock site is Ocate Micaceous (fig. 3), a very thin hard ware with deep striations on the exterior surface. Thinning was apparently accomplished with a paddle and anvil prior to scraping with a corn cob, which left the striations. The paste contains a great deal of finely divided mica and angular grit, both apparently inclusions in the clay, which was probably taken from deposits near present-day Picuris Pueblo. Decoration is very rare and appendages are absent. The two known restorable vessels of Ocate Micaceous have heights significantly greater than the maximum diameter, flat to somewhat pointed bottoms, slightly constricted necks, nearly vertical to moderately flaring rims, and simple lips. Association elsewhere with painted Pueblo pottery suggests a time span for Ocate Micaceous from perhaps the mid-1500s to about 1750.

Other pottery at the Glasscock site includes Pecos glaze ware and plain culinary ware similar to some from Pecos. Fragments of clay pipes, probably all tubular and undecorated, were also recovered. Sherds of blue and white Puebla (Mexico) majolica from the site were dated as being from the early 1700s with two sherds possibly as late as the 1740s (E. Boyd, personal communication 1967). The combined evidence for dating suggests that the Glasscock site was occupied in the first few decades of the 1700s during which time, according to Spanish documents, Apaches were living in adobe structures in the same general area. Furthermore, there are no references to Indians other than the Apaches living in the area at that time.

The chipped stone artifacts from the site are limited but varied. Projectile points, small, delicate, and well

Fig. 2. View to the west of excavated Apache pueblo at Glasscock site, Mora Co., N.M. showing 7 rooms and 2 excavated hearths in the room closest to site designation sign in background (see Gunnerson 1969:25–26). Photograph by J. Gunnerson, 1966.

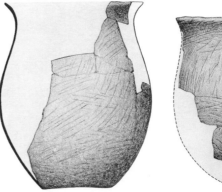

U. of Neb. State Mus., Lincoln: a, 29M020 F41-1; b, 29M020 F20-1; c, 29SM1-C F2-1.
Fig. 3. Ocate Micaceous pottery vessels. left, From Glasscock site, Mora Co., N.M.; right, from Pecos Pueblo, San Miguel Co., N.M. (see Gunnerson 1969:26–27; Gunnerson and Gunnerson 1970:4). Height of left 14 cm, other same scale. Drawings by Martha Haack.

made, are most commonly triangular and are either side notched or unnotched. Other chipped stone tools include end scrapers, knives, and small crude "double-bitted" drills (fig. 4).

Most of the metates found at the Glasscock site are of a distinctive "Jicarilla" type (fig. 5) also represented in the museum in the Jicarilla tribal headquarters building at Dulce, New Mexico, by specimens relinquished in the 1960s by Jicarillas. One complete metate from the site, representative of the type, is about 12 inches long, 5 inches wide, and 2 inches thick. Such metates are quadrilateral with rounded corners and slightly convex sides and ends. They are distinctive in that the grinding surface is slightly concave along the long axis and straight to slightly convex along the short axis. The manos are similarly shaped, but smaller and relatively thicker. Neither the metates nor manos are well finished on the nongrinding surfaces. The site also yielded shallow basin metates as well as cobble manos that could have been used with them. Other ground stone artifacts included abraders and "Plains type" sandstone arrowshaft smoothers (fig. 5).

Bone artifacts, not numerous at the Glasscock site, consisted of tubular bone beads, awls, eagle-wing bone whistles, a probable beamer (for working hide), and antler tine flakers(?).

The Sammis site, of approximately the same age as the Glasscock site but with a very different type of structure, is located about three miles north of Cimarron (Gunnerson 1969:30–31). The site is on the floor of Poñil Canyon above the reach of floods and about two miles from the Canyon mouth. Nearby farmland could be (and is) irrigated from Poñil Creek, which has permanent water. Elevation is 6,500 feet and the mountains to the north and west deflect cold winds. To the east of the Cimarron area lie the plains and to the west are passes to Taos, Picuris, and the Rio Grande valley.

At the Sammis site an ovoid pit about 10 by 12 feet and 2 feet deep had been surrounded by a ring or low wall of small rocks and roofed over with poles, bark, and probably earth, but no post holes could be found either in or around the pit. The superstructure had probably been conical and braced by the rocks, but no clue as to the nature of the entrance could be detected. A shallow basin-shaped hearth was near the center of the floor.

The fill of the pit house contained both Ocate Micaceous sherds and intrusive Pueblo sherds, presumably derived from nearby Pueblo structures dating from the 1100s or 1200s. Also in the fill was a turquoise bead, a "Plains-type snub nosed" end scraper, a drill fragment, and a broken "double-bitted" drill. From the floor of this pit structure came more Ocate Micaceous sherds, a bone awl, and a sherd of blue and white majolica dating from

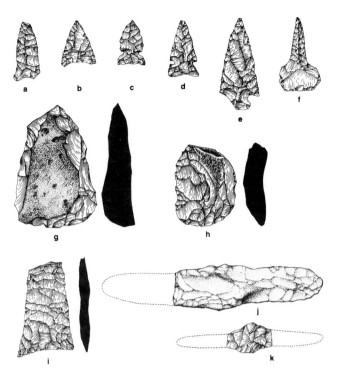

U. of Neb. State Mus., Lincoln: 29M020- a, F12-1; b, F35-1; c, F13-5; d, F10-2; e, F34-1; f, F18-1; g, F27-1; h, F27-2; i, F34-2; j, F12-3; k, 29CX68-F10-1.
Fig. 4. Chipped stone artifacts. a-e, Projectile points; f, possibly a drill; g-h, plain style snub-nosed end scrapers; i, knife (tip missing); j-k, "double-bitted" drills. a-j are from the Glasscock site, Mora Co., N.M.; k is from the Sammis site, Colfax Co., N.M. (see Gunnerson 1969). Length of g 5.6 cm, rest same scale. Drawings by Martha Haack.

the early 1700s. The scraper is especially significant since it also had a chipped graver point. No evidence for contemporaneity of the Apache and Pueblo occupations was found during the excavation of all or part of four of the nearby Pueblo structures.

Apache sites of about 1700 (as well as later) were commonly located on benches or terraces 30 to 100 feet above the floor of Poñil Canyon, but within a few hundred yards of the stream. Several of these sites were investigated in both the lower Poñil Canyon (Gunnerson 1969:32–35) and on the Philmont Scout Ranch in the Upper Poñil Canyon (Michael Glassow, personal communication 1966). Structures were amorphous, built on the surface or over shallow depressions, sometimes surrounded by a few rocks, and often showing evidence of having been destroyed by fire. Cultural remains, consisting mainly of Ocate Micaceous sherds and stone chips, are sparse at these sites.

In the mouths of other canyons near Cimarron and on the plains for a few miles out from the Sangre de Cristo Mountains are other archeological sites (D. Gunnerson 1956; Schroeder 1959:8, 33). Some with plain black pottery (and sometimes painted Pueblo pottery) are apparently all assignable to the Pueblo occupation of the area in the 1100s and 1200s. Other sites, which could be of Apache origin, are without pottery and consist of few

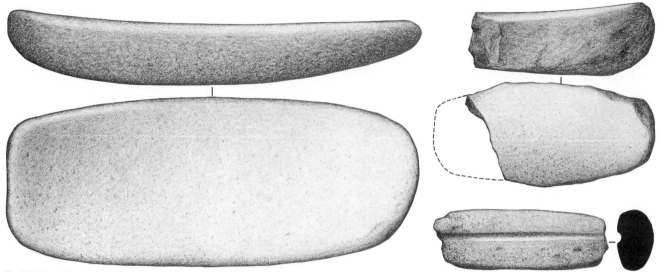

U. of Neb. State Mus., Lincoln: left, 29M020 F13–6; top right, 29M020 F19–2; bottom right, 29M020 F19–1.

Fig. 5. Ground stone artifacts. left, Jicarilla type metate and (top right) mano from Glasscock site, Mora Co., N.M.; bottom right, arrowshaft polisher made of sandstone. Length of left 29 cm, rest same scale. Drawing by Martha Haack.

to over a dozen rock rings, mostly 12 to 15 feet in diameter. It is presumed that at at least some of these sites the rocks, which are up to the size of a person's head, were used to hold down the bottoms of tepees. Other cultural materials are so sparse at these nonceramic tepee-ring sites that they can neither be dated nor given a cultural assignment.

The Faraon Apaches, so named because of their imagined resemblance to the "hordes of Pharaoh," were known under a variety of names and roamed over a large area from the Sandia Mountains east well into the Plains. Their villages, some with mud-plastered wood houses, were reported by the Spaniards in 1715 (Thomas 1935:24, 82). Precise locations were not given, but they were probably in the panhandle of Texas where at least two probable Faraon sites have been found near Canyon and Stinnett. These sites yield pottery similar to that from a large tepee-ring site on the Plains about 18 miles northeast of Las Vegas, New Mexico. This site, Ojo Perdido (Gunnerson and Gunnerson 1970:3, 1971:10), is unusual because of the large number of tepee rings (well over 200) and because pottery, although not abundant, is associated with many of the rings. The dominant pottery, Perdido Plain, is a thin undecorated ware tempered with finely crushed micaceous schist. It resembles Lovitt Plain (Dismal River Apache ware of about 1700), Ocate Micaceous, and especially Pecos Plain wares of the 1600s and 1700s, although it is thinner than the Pecos Plain. Associated glaze sherds from both Pecos and Picuris suggest a seventeenth-century date, probably pre-1680, for the site. Other artifacts were rare, considering the large size of the site. Excavation in and around rings failed to reveal any subsurface evidence of occupation, not even evidence of hearths, but the site may have been wind-eroded (fig. 6).

The function of the Ojo Perdido site is uncertain, although the presence of what had been a good spring was an obvious attraction. The paucity of cultural remains suggests temporary occupation or occupations. The most plausible explanation is that the place frequently served as a camp, perhaps only overnight, for Faraon Apaches are known to have traveled between the Plains and the Pueblos of Pecos and Picuris.

Pecos Pueblo was visited frequently not only by the Faraones but also by Carlanas, Palomas, Cuartelejos, Jicarillas, and other Apache groups. In some instances

Fig. 6. View to northwest across a tepee ring, from which the sod has been removed, at Ojo Perdido site, San Miguel Co., N.M. The sign is 1 foot long. (See Gunnerson and Gunnerson 1970:3, 1971:10.) Photograph by J. Gunnerson, 1966.

Apache visitors lived at the Pueblo for periods up to several months (Thomas 1940:124). Reconnaissance in the immediate vicinity of Pecos Pueblo disclosed that a number of areas had apparently been occupied by Apaches (Gunnerson and Gunnerson 1970). A burned pole and earth structure was excavated that had been about 12 feet in diameter and built on the surface of the ground or over a very shallow pit. Associated items were a small Ocate Micaceous pot (fig. 3), a plain black Pueblo olla, and a Pueblo redware bowl, burned corn, burned beans, a tubular clay smoking pipe (Pecos style), a copper cone, triangular stone projectile points, the tip of what had probably been an iron awl, and scraps of iron and brass. Of special interest was a sherd of blue and white Chinese porcelain probably dating from the mid-1600s (E. Boyd, personal communication 1967). A similar date is suggested by the Pueblo vessels associated with the structure.

Starting about 1550, soon after Apacheans apparently arrived in the Southwest, marked changes took place in the way of life of those settling in northeastern New Mexico. They arrived as nomadic hunters but soon adopted horticulture, permanent villages, and pottery making. The association of Ocate Micaceous with a section of a Sankawi Black-on-cream bowl (Gunnerson 1969:37), dated at 1500-1600, suggests that Ocate Micaceous might have been made by the mid-1500s. A pre-1600 date for Apache pottery is not unreasonable since in 1599 Oñate (Hammond and Rey 1953, 1:245, 484) described Apaches as "pueblo dwellers," indicating permanent settlements. Other Apache sites yielding Ocate Micaceous and Perdido Plain pottery have been dated between about 1650 and 1750. These sites include a wide variety of structures: multiroom adobe houses, rock-ringed pit structures, surface structures with brush roofs and walls (with or without encircling rocks), and tepee rings. Settlements consisted of scattered camps and farmsteads, the farmsteads situated near good irrigable farmland in the mouths of canyons. The resources of both the plains and the mountains could be exploited from such bases, and hunting may have continued to be the main subsistence activity. The artifact inventory, especially items related to hunting, strongly resembles that of the Plains (Dismal River) Apaches (Gunnerson 1960, 1968). Included are the diagnostic "double-bitted drills" and combination end scraper-gravers. These "foothills" Apaches possessed distinctive metates and manos also found archeologically at Apache sites in western Kansas and used by modern Jicarillas. Contact with the Pueblos is indicated by the presence of Pueblo pottery at most sites. Limited amounts of majolica, porcelain, and metal attest to contact with the Spaniards. The interaction of the Apaches of northeastern New Mexico with other Indians of the Plains and Southwest and with the Spaniards is also substantiated by the historical sources.

During the second quarter of the 1700s, mounting pressure from non-Apachean Plains Indians forced the abandonment of the Apachean farming villages along the eastern foothills of the Sangre de Cristos.

*Jicarilla Apache, 1750-1890*

No sites from the late 1700s or early 1800s attributed to the Jicarillas have been thoroughly investigated. By about 1750 Jicarillas had moved to the Rio Grande valley and settled mainly near Ranchos de Taos where they were reported in the mid-1700s by Bishop Tamarón (Adams 1953-1954:215) and others (D. Gunnerson 1974: 216-222, 238-239). In this area, now badly eroded, are located a number of sites yielding Cimarron Micaceous ware (Gunnerson 1969), a pottery thicker than the earlier Ocate Micaceous. Jicarilla pottery in various museums, made and collected ethnographically in the late 1800s and early 1900s, can probably also be classified as Cimarron Micaceous. Since the mid-1800s there has been a strong convergence in the pottery of the Taos, Picuris, and Jicarilla, all of whom used micaceous clay from the same deposits and influenced one another's ceramics extensively. The outer surface of the pottery of all these groups still shows striations from smoothing with corn cobs, and encircling fillets on the rims are common. One diagnostic trait of Cimarron Micaceous is a very marked thickening or splaying of the lip of many ollas such as is also found on some Plains (Dismal River) Apache pottery (Gunnerson 1960:164) of about 1675-1725. Since the Jicarillas were first joined by some of the Plains Apaches about 1730 (Adams 1953-1954:213-214; D. Gunnerson 1974:212), they could have introduced the thickened lip to the Jicarilla.

Reconnaissance along the Rio Grande in the Velarde-Pilar area has revealed sites that can be attributed to the Jicarillas after 1750 (Gunnerson 1964). Again, historical documents summarized by D. Gunnerson (1974: 240-246) indicate that there should be sites dating from the 1760s in this vicinity. Some of the known sites are situated on high benches along the river as if they had been selected with concealment or defense in mind; however, one of the largest is on a low flat near a good spring. Apache sites, probably campsites of visiting Jicarillas, have also been found near Picuris (Gunnerson 1969:35, 36).

Jicarillas were still living and hunting in the Cimarron area during the mid and late 1800s (Keleher 1964:45-65), and their sites of this period can be identified by the presence of Cimarron Micaceous. Two such sites have been excavated. At one of these, the Chase Bench site (Gunnerson 1969:32-35), which had an earlier Apache occupation, there were seven rock rings 12 to 18 feet in diameter. In the middle of each ring was a burned area or hearth. In addition to sherds of Cimarron Micaceous, the site yielded a little evidence of stone flaking and moderate amounts of metal and glass. Metal items include barrel hoop fragments (one made into a serrated fleshing tool blade), a spoon, parts of a harmonica, square nails, a conical jingle, and what was probably a tin can lid. The glass included bottle fragments and small beads. The Clinging Cactus site (Kuhman 1968), located about a mile north of Cimarron, yielded Cimarron Micaceous sherds, a glass bead, metal and glass fragments, and a U.S. military button that was too badly deteriorated for exact dating. A burned area and possible use surface were the only indications of a structure.

Surface reconnaissance has located various other sites with similar artifact inventories along the eastern foothills of the Sangre de Cristos from near Raton south to about Anton Chico. In some cases it is difficult to distinguish Jicarilla sites from those of Spanish Americans since the Jicarillas camped near Spanish villages and since the Spanish Americans traded for Jicarilla pots. At many of these Jicarilla and/or Spanish American sites of the 1800s are sherds of polished Tewa red or black pottery.

The John Alden site, an Apache community of about 1850, is located on a mesa east of San Miguel and north of Villanueva, New Mexico. The north edge of the mesa drops steeply and overlooks the old Santa Fe trail. Five crude structures were excavated out of some 100 reported to be on this 15-square-mile mesa top. Walls about three feet high, to judge by the amount of fallen rock, had been laid around slight depressions. Most structures tended to be round, about 10 feet in diameter, with evidence of a hearth in the middle. One appeared to have had three small irregular rooms. The best-preserved (fig. 7) was L-shaped with the main portion three by nine feet and the extension two by three feet. A Spanish-style corner fireplace was near the entrance at the top of the L. Trash was sparse, suggesting a brief occupation. The dominant pottery from the site, a previously unreported type, is undecorated and tempered with crushed micaceous schist. It is like Cimarron Micaceous except that it is not made from micaceous clay. Associated with this pottery, almost certainly of Apache manufacture, were sherds of Powhoge Polychrome from Nambe Pueblo, dated at 1760–1850 (Harlow 1970:8). Also of interest for dating is a U.S. Dragoon uniform button, of a type made only from 1840 until 1849, that probably did not arrive in New Mexico before 1846, when the U.S. Army took over. Thus a date of about 1850 seems certain for the site.

Considering (1) the presence of a majority ware closely resembling Jicarilla Apache pottery found elsewhere; (2) the presence of trade pottery from Nambe, a Pueblo with which the Jicarillas had much contact (Bandelier 1890a:261); (3) the date of about 1850; and (4) the site's location near the town of San Miguel, there is little doubt that it can be attributed to the Jicarilla band that James C. Calhoun (U.S. Office of Indian Affairs 1915:350) said

Fig. 7. Unusual -shaped house at John Alden site, San Miguel Co., N.M. Note extention to left in foreground, corner hearth in upper left, and entrance in upper right. Brunton compass points north, and central portion of structure is 3 feet wide. Photograph by J. Gunnerson, 1970.

was in that specific area in 1851 under the leadership of Chief Chacon. Also, no other Indian groups were mentioned in Calhoun's detailed reports as being near San Miguel at that time.

Stone artifacts and animal bones were present but not common. Items of European or American manufacture included a fine-tooth comb of bone, fragments of yellow and white English china, a steel arrowhead, part of an iron spoon, scraps of metal, and two other less easily datable buttons.

West of the Rio Grande valley proper two archeological sites thought to be Jicarilla have been investigated (Skinner 1968). These, near El Rito, New Mexico, are situated across an intermittent stream from each other and probably date, according to Skinner, from the last half of the 1800s. One consists of an irregular rock circle, perhaps a tepee ring, about 12 feet across. At the other a fire pit surrounded by a use surface was found. Both had micaceous sherds associated with them. These sites are not far from the reservation that the Jicarilla Apaches have occupied since 1887.

### Western Apache Archeology

The archeology of other Apaches who lived west of the Rio Grande is virtually unknown. There are in the Arizona State Museum, Tucson, several pots that, according to the museum's records, were identified by Grenville Goodwin as Apache, presumably on the basis of ethnographic evidence. A very similar pot, now in the collection at Western New Mexico University, Silver City, was found near Silver City. The pottery, like early Jicarilla ware (but not micaceous), is notable for its thinness, paucity of decoration and appendages, surface striations, and pointed bottoms. On the basis of similarity to the Goodwin pots, Gifford (1957) identified sherds collected archeologically from a cave in the Point of Pines area as Apache. The sherds were recent enough to be associated with a branded hide. Ron Ice (personal communication 1967) found similar pottery near Tonto National Monument. Schroeder (1960:141-142) describes an Apache plainware (Rimrock Plain) from the Verde Valley, and Brugge (1963:28) noted similarities between Western Apache pottery and Navajo utility wares. Schroeder (1960:27-28) also reports Apache pictographs showing horses.

Another site in the Point of Pines area with a component suspected of being Apache is Willow Creek Pueblo (Asch 1960). Fourteen stone rings some 10 feet in diameter were built on top of the Point of Pines phase ruins. Artifacts were rare in the rings and most could

have come from the earlier occupation. Dating could not be established more closely than post-Pueblo.

Four Apache wickiup sites are reported from the San Carlos Indian Reservation (Gerald 1958a; Tuohy 1960). Three wickiups, still standing at least in part, had been built about 1955-1958. Associated with the other one, which had been burned (Gerald 1958a), were nails, the base of a shot gun shell, and horseshoe nails, but no sherds that resemble Apache pottery. Near the burned wickiup was a camp apparently occupied until about 1940 or 1945. A probable sweat lodge, a hearth, an iron stove, a metate, and recent trash were found there.

Ethnohistorical sources indicate that Apacheans moved west into the Pueblo area soon after their arrival on the eastern border of the Southwest. It seems highly probable that intensive archeological reconnaissance in southern New Mexico and southeastern Arizona, utilizing leads from historical sources, would locate Western Apache sites. The vessels identified as Apache by Goodwin would provide the basis for a direct historical approach to the identification of earlier Western Apache pottery and hence sites.

*169*

# Historical Linguistics and Archeology

KENNETH HALE AND DAVID HARRIS

A conservative view of the aboriginal linguistic relationships within the Southwest must recognize at least seven distinct and well-established families—Uto-Aztecan, Kiowa-Tanoan, Athapaskan, Yuman, Keresan, Zuni, and Seri. If the area is understood to include southern Texas and northeastern Mexico, the picture would be complicated by the addition of the languages Swanton (1915) classified as Coahuiltecan, originally including Coahuilteco, Comecrudo, Karankawa, Cotoname, Tonkawa, Atakapa, and Maratino. These languages, largely very poorly known, will not be considered here, except to note that the status of Coahuiltecan is uncertain: Swanton (1940) himself expressed reservations, and subsequent research has cast doubt on the validity of most or all of the proposed grouping (Bright 1956; Haas 1959, 1967; Troike 1967; Voegelin and Voegelin 1965:139-145; Landar 1968; Goddard 1978). In addition, consideration of the Otopamean languages of the extreme south of the area will be omitted.

## Uto-Aztecan Family

The Southwest embraces the territories now or formerly attributed to speakers of a large number of Uto-Aztecan languages. Proceeding roughly from north to south, these include Hopi, a majority of the Piman languages (Papago, Upper and Lower Pima and Nebome, Northern Tepehuan, and Southern Tepehuan), the extant Taracahitan languages (Yaqui-Mayo or Cahitan, Tarahumara, and Guarijío), and Huichol. To this area also belong the extinct Opata, traditionally aligned with Taracahitan, and a number of other extinct languages conjecturally identified with Uto-Aztecan (Jova, Suma, Jumano, Concho, Zacatec, Lagunero, and Guachichil).

By the middle of the nineteenth century, enough data were available to enable scholars to recognize the relationships among the Uto-Aztecan languages. Buschmann (1859) proposed the Sonoran stock, which subsumed all the languages now classified as Uto-Aztecan except the southernmost; and although he did not relate Aztec to his Sonoran group, he presented evidence that would have warranted his doing so. The relationship of Aztec to its northern congeners was accepted by Gatschet (1879), and the family as a whole was given its current name by Brinton (1891), who was also responsible for an internal classification of Uto-Aztecan that recognized three branches—Shoshonean, Sonoran, and Aztec (or Nahuatl).

Although acceptance of the unity of Uto-Aztecan was delayed somewhat by the conservative stance taken in Powell's (1891) influential classification, the cohesion of the family was eventually firmly established by the work of a number of investigators (Kroeber 1907, 1934; Sapir 1913-1914; Whorf 1935, 1936b; Mason 1936, 1940; Swadesh 1954-1955, 1963; Hale 1958; Lamb 1958; Voegelin, Voegelin, and Hale 1962; Miller 1967). While the integrity of Uto-Aztecan is agreed upon, its internal classification is not. Brinton's (1891) tripartite scheme has retained a certain amount of appeal for some investigators (for example, Hale 1958; Voegelin, Voegelin, and Hale 1962), but it has been seriously questioned by others (Kroeber 1934; Whorf 1935a) who suggest a revision according to which the three recognizable subgroups of Sonoran (Piman, Taracahitan, and Cora-Huichol) and the four of Shoshonean (Plateau, Southern California, Tubatulabal, and Hopi) are viewed as roughly coordinate families within the Uto-Aztecan family. The newer classification has been accepted with enthusiasm by a number of Uto-Aztecanists, among them Lamb (1958, 1964) and Miller (1964, 1966, 1967), and certain terminological changes consistent with it have been adopted. For example, Kroeber's Plateau Shoshonean is now commonly called Numic, following Lamb (1958), and Kroeber's Southern California Shoshonean is now called Takic, following Miller (1961). This classification should, perhaps, be regarded as the more reasonable one in the light of the evidence that has so far been marshaled in support of any subclassification of Uto-Aztecan languages. But the question is still open, and serious consideration should continue to be given to the possibility that the Uto-Aztecan family has greater internal structure than is admitted by the revised classification. The unity of Sonoran (cf. Mason 1936; Hale 1964, 2), for example, cannot be said to have been definitely refuted, and the possibility that Hopi might bear some special relationship to one of the other Uto-Aztecan families, perhaps Takic (cf. Miller 1964; Hale 1964, 2), is certainly worthy of study. Heath (1977) has cited grammatical evidence for the unity of Shoshonean, now renamed Northern Uto-Aztecan.

In the absence of historical records, it is of course impossible to estimate the precise time-depth within Uto-

Aztecan, that is, the temporal distance separating the present from the beginnings of significant diversification. Nonetheless, it would be extreme to suggest that it is greater than five millennia. Glottochronological studies (Swadesh 1954–1955, 1963; Hale 1958) suggest that it is slightly less than this for the geographic extremes—Aztec as opposed to Numic—and that the more closely associated subgroups are separated by no more than 3,000 years. The subgroups themselves vary somewhat in terms of internal diversity. Piman, for example, is extremely close-knit and probably does not have a time-depth greatly in excess of half a millennium. By contrast, the time-depth within Numic may be two millennia (Lamb 1958); and the time-depth within Taracahitan, if it is a unit at all, may be considerably greater (Hale 1958; cf. also Miller 1964, in which Tarahumara is separated from Cahitan).

It has long been assumed that Uto-Aztecan is related to Kiowa-Tanoan. Sapir (1921, 1929) believed the two families to be related, giving them the name Aztec-Tanoan, and Whorf and Trager (1937) attempted to demonstrate the relationship by postulating regular sound correspondences. A careful review of this material, in an effort to arrive at a firm judgment concerning the Aztec-Tanoan relationship, leads to the conclusion that, while the case looks considerably more convincing than the comparison of randomly selected language families not believed to be related (like Uto-Aztecan and Pama-Nyungan of Australia), a cautious view must leave the question open. If Uto-Aztecan and Kiowa-Tanoan are related, then the time-depth is extremely great. For instance, of the 100 items in the revised lexicostatistical test list (Swadesh 1955), only 10 or 12 could reasonably be judged potentially cognate between the two families; in terms of glottochronological time, this approaches 10 millennia. The evidence for the even more distant relationships proposed for Uto-Aztecan, such as the Macro-Penutian hypothesis of Whorf (1935), is unconvincing.

### Kiowa-Tanoan Family

The unity of the Tanoan languages was recognized by Powell (1891), and the accepted tripartite classification of them was made by Harrington (1910a). Trager (1967) has refined Harrington's classification somewhat by suggesting that the Tiwa branch consists of a northern subgroup, comprising two languages (Taos, Picuris), and a southern subgroup, comprising two dialects (Sandia, Isleta) of a single language. The meager lexical evidence available suggests that the extinct Piro language was more closely related to Tiwa than to other Tanoan (Davis 1959); while Leap (1971) argues that it was non-Tanoan, a close examination of the material favors at least the Tanoan connection. The Tewa branch of Tanoan is probably best viewed as a single language with substantial mutual intelligibility linking even the most divergent dialects—

that is, Arizona Tewa (spoken by descendents of the Tano of the Galisteo Basin) as opposed to the Rio Grande dialects (Dozier 1954). Among the Rio Grande dialects, at least two groups (Santa Clara as distinct from San Juan, San Ildefonso, Nambe, Tesuque, and possibly Pojoaque) are recognized (Trager 1967). The Towa branch of Tanoan consists of the language of Jemez. The extinct Pecos is traditionally assigned to Towa as well (see "Pecos Pueblo," this vol.), although phrases remembered by Pecos descendents at Jemez, while unquestionably Tanoan, do not clearly identify it as Towa (Joe S. Sando, personal communication 1973).

The relationship of Kiowa to Tanoan was established quite early by Harrington (1910b, 1928) and has been amply substantiated (Hale 1962, 1967; Miller 1959a; Trager and Trager 1959). In fact, a case could perhaps be made for the view that Kiowa is coordinate with the Tanoan branches and that its apparent divergence is a result of geographic and cultural separation rather than a reflection of purely linguistic differentiation. In any event, the internal diversity within Kiowa-Tanoan as a whole is almost certainly considerably less than that within Uto-Aztecan, for example. This is shown in part by the sort of morphophonological detail that can be reconstructed for Kiowa-Tanoan, much of which was already noted by Harrington (1928; see also Hale 1967).

The time-depth within Kiowa-Tanoan is probably not greater than three millennia. Trager (1967) suspects that it is considerably less, with at most two millennia separating Kiowa from Tanoan, and he considers Davis's (1959) glottochronological figures (about 4,000 years separating Kiowa and Tanoan, and 2,000 to 2,500 years separating the Tanoan branches) excessively high. Glottochronological calculations by Hale and Harris (unpublished) are in substantial agreement with Davis's for Tanoan internally, but they indicate a lower figure for Kiowa and Tanoan (from 2,600 to 3,300 years, depending upon the degree of conservatism with which cognation is judged). It is possible that even these figures are exaggerated and that Kiowa may ultimately prove, from a strictly linguistic standpoint, to be no more distant from Tiwa, say, than is Towa. For the Tanoan group itself, it is generally agreed that Tiwa and Tewa are slightly more closely related to one another than either is to Towa or Kiowa.

### Southern Athapaskan Subgroup

The extremely close relationships that unite the Northern, Pacific Coast, and Southern Athapaskan languages have been recognized since the middle of the nineteenth century (Krauss 1964). Sapir (1931a) used Athapaskan, with representatives from the three geographic groups, as a model in his discussion of the concept of phonetic law in languages of North America, and since then his initial reconstructions have been extended and refined (Hoijer 1963; Krauss 1964). It is significant that Sapir used

Athapaskan as a paradigm for reconstruction comparable to Bloomfield's (1925, 1946) Algonquian; the precision of reconstruction that can be achieved within Athapaskan is quite comparable to what can be achieved within the rather tightly cohering Algonquian family.

As Sapir (1916) noted, the diversity within Athapaskan as a whole is no greater than that within the northern group of Athapaskan languages, and the internal diversity of the Southern Athapaskan group is considerably less. This and other linguistic considerations (for example, Sapir 1936) support the view that the north is the center of dispersal and that the Southern group reached its historically documented distribution at a time considerably later than the inception of significant Athapaskan diversity. Hoijer's (1956) glottochronological calculations indicate a time-depth of around 1,300 years for Athapaskan (Hymes 1957 proposes a somewhat greater figure), and he suggests further that the Southern group was not completely separate from the north until about 600 years ago. Within Southern Athapaskan itself (excluding Kiowa-Apache), the glottochronological calculations are consistently less than half a millennium; in fact, they are generally so low that it makes little sense on that basis alone to speak of significant divisions. In this, these languages are reminiscent of the Piman branch of Uto-Aztecan, where glottochronological calculations are likewise essentially meaningless. However, Kiowa-Apache shows a consistent lexicostatistical separation from the other Southern Athapaskan speech communities, and there is other linguistic evidence for this sharp division (Hoijer 1971:4-6). This conclusion accords with ethnohistorical evidence for the separateness of the Kiowa-Apache and with theories of their separate origin from the Fremont culture of the Great Basin (Schlesier 1972). An earlier ethnohistorical interpretation, which dated the separation of the Kiowa-Apache as recently as about 1719 (Gunnerson and Gunnerson 1971:22), was in accord with the now superseded view that Southern Athapaskan was a firm linguistic unit with two major divisions—an Eastern one embracing Jicarilla, Lipan, and Kiowa-Apache and a Western one including Navajo, Chiricahua, Mescalero, and the language commonly called Western Apache (Hoijer 1938, 1945-1949). The last term should not be confused with Western Apachean, which Hoijer used in opposition to Eastern Apachean to designate the western division of Southern Athapaskan (or Apachean, in his terminology). The Western Apache (Goodwin 1942) comprise five groups—San Carlos, White Mountain, Cibecue, Southern Tonto, Northern Tonto—speaking mutually intelligible dialects of a single language.

Of less concern here are the more remote relationships of Athapaskan to certain languages of the Northwest Coast, first to Eyak, and then to Tlingit and Haida (see Krauss 1964, 1965, 1973, 1978 for a critical review of the Na-Dene hypothesis). Limitations in knowledge prevent affirming the status of the extinct Cacaxte and Toboso of Mexico, once classified together with their Apachean neighbors to the north (Orozco y Berra 1864:387; Driver et al. 1953; Driver and Massey 1957:map in end pocket), but later put with the non-Apacheans to the east (Driver and Massey 1957:170, map 1; Driver et al. 1960).

## Yuman Family

The unity of Yuman is obvious, even upon rather superficial comparison of linguistic materials. Kroeber's (1943a) original quadripartite classification—Upland Arizona, Colorado and Gila River, Colorado Delta, and California—has been refined by Joël (1964), who separates Kiliwa from Kroeber's California subgroup, opposing it to the rest of Yuman, while classifying the two remaining members of that subgroup as coordinate to Kroeber's first three. Thus, her classification recognizes two major divisions, one containing five subdivisions, the other containing the single language Kiliwa (the southernmost extant Yuman language in Baja California). The subdivisions of the larger group are, in Joël's terminology: Arizona (Walapai, Havasupai, Yavapai), River (Mohave, Halchidhoma, Kavelchadom, Maricopa, Yuma [Quechan]), Delta (Cocopa, Halyikwamai, Kahwan), Diegueño (Ipai-Tipai), and Paipai (or Akwa'ala).

The time-depth within Yuman is in all probability extremely shallow. Cognate percentages offered by W. Winter (1957) suggest that it does not exceed two millennia (though the more divergent Kiliwa is not included in this estimate). The relationship of Paipai is rather crucial to this question. Its apparent special affinity with the geographically distant Arizona division could, as Kroeber and Joël suggest, merely reflect the continuation of a generalized ancestral Yuman tradition, the River and Delta departures from this heritage being a result of accelerated change brought about by cultural specialization. If this view is correct, then the estimated time-depth should be revised downward, in harmony with the Paipai-Arizona relationship, in order to counteract the skewing effect of the putatively specialized River and Delta traditions. If, on the other hand, W. Winter (1967) is correct in his venturesome hypothesis that the Paipai are recent migrants from Arizona (specifically from the Yavapai), then the special Paipai-Arizona affinities are irrelevant to the question of time-depth within Yuman (see D. Walker 1970 for further discussion).

It is generally accepted that Yuman belongs to the Hokan stock, first proposed by Dixon and Kroeber (1913) and later elaborated by Kroeber (1915) and Sapir (1917). The majority of languages and language families thus classified with Yuman are located in California, although two are spoken in Mexico—one (Oaxacan Chontal, or Tequistlatecan) at a considerable remove from California, the other (Seri, of coastal Sonora) geographically close to Yuman. The Hokan stock was itself related to Coahuiltecan by Sapir (1917a), and Hokan-Coahuiltecan (or Hokaltecan) was related by Sapir (1929) to the large collection of languages that he included in his (now collapsing) Hokan-Siouan phylum. In regard to these suggested relationships, a conservative position would accept as promising only a rather narrowly defined Hokan, including Yuman as a member of it. Other evaluations are even more skeptical (Campbell and Mithun 1978).

## Keresan Family

The seven varieties of Keresan are so closely related that it is commonly assumed that they are dialects of a single language, although the most separate geographically (Acoma and Cochiti) are said to exhibit considerable divergence (Miller and Davis 1963). Despite overall uniformity, Davis (1959) suggests that there is nonetheless a significant division within Keresan according to which the western varieties at Acoma and Laguna are opposed to the Rio Grande dialects of Zia, Santa Ana, San Felipe, Santo Domingo, and Cochiti. He maintains further that the time-depth within Keresan does not exceed 500 years.

In sharp contrast to the internal cohesion of Keresan, its external relationships, if any are ultimately demonstrable, are exceedingly distant. Sapir (1929) included it within his Hokan-Siouan phylum, but as yet no substantial case has been made in support of external connections for Keresan.

## Zuni Language

Like Keresan, Zuni has no close relatives. Sapir (1929) indicated his own doubt by means of a question mark when he included it in his Aztec-Tanoan phylum, and it is now generally recognized that if Zuni is in fact related to Uto-Aztecan and Tanoan, it is only indirectly and through a lengthy sequence of as yet only hypothetical connections. Swadesh (1954, 1956) suggested this indirect relationship by including Zuni in his Penutioid phylum, and Newman (1964) has explored the possible Zuni-Penutian connection to an extent that is probably as great as will ever be possible for any suggested Zuni relationship. Newman's careful comparative work (involving primarily Zuni, Yokuts, and Miwok) is extended somewhat by Swadesh (1967), who exploited the existence of consonantal ablaut, thereby admitting a class of "oblique cognates."

If Zuni and Penutian are related, and the evidence is at least suggestive, then the connection is a very remote one. Newman (1964) suggests seven millennia of separation, although the extremely low percentage of putative cognates on which that estimate is based actually corresponds to even greater glottochronological time.

## Seri Language

It is difficult to improve upon the case that Kroeber (1915) presented in support of the relationship of Seri to Hokan, since attempts to add to the small number of promising Seri-Hokan cognates (for instance, the items glossed 'water', 'tongue', 'earth', 'tail', 'eye') have been rather unrewarding. This has certainly been the experience of P.R. Turner (1967), who compared Seri to Oaxacan Chontal, and a passing remark by McLendon (1964) suggests that the other areas of Hokan (even the relatively secure northern branch) also tend to resist comparison in fully satisfying detail.

If Seri is indeed a Hokan language, it remains questionable whether its closest relative is the one suggested by geography—Yuman. Sapir (1929) classified it rather with Salinan while grouping Yuman with Esselen (see also the similar conclusion reached by Bright 1956). A review of the Seri-Hokan evidence justifies the acceptance of this relationship in much the same conservative spirit as the Aztec-Tanoan relationship. In fact, Hale and Harris's lexicostatistical comparisons of Seri to Yuman yield shared cognation percentages that are roughly equivalent to those mentioned earlier for Uto-Aztecan as compared to Kiowa-Tanoan.

## Linguistic and Cultural Associations

Of the seven language families represented in the Southwest, the one exhibiting the greatest internal diversity and presumably, therefore, the greatest time-depth is Uto-Aztecan. A period of around five millennia may be assumed to separate the present from the initial linguistic differentiation that led to the Uto-Aztecan situation as it is now known. The details of Uto-Aztecan history can never be fully recovered, since there has been extinction of both closely and distantly related languages in prehistoric as well as historic times. Nevertheless, this putative Uto-Aztecan time-depth may be used to establish a base line at about 3000 B.C. as a starting point in the presentation of a hypothesis regarding the association of linguistic groups with cultures identified archeologically in the Southwest. No attempt will be made to relate the archeological record to more ancient linguistic constructs, such as the hypothesized common ancestor of Zuni and California Penutian, the Hokan stock, or Aztec-Tanoan.

The 3000 B.C. base line is well within the Desert culture period, some four or five millennia after that culture had taken over from antecedent traditions in the area but long before the beginning of the Christian era when the Desert culture was replaced in most of the area by the distinctive Southwestern traditions (Mogollon, Hohokam, Anasazi, and Hakataya). In any attempt to associate linguistic and cultural traditions, it is necessary to rely on intelligent guesswork guided primarily by considerations of simplicity. In locating linguistic entities geographically within specific time periods, one adopts the hypothesis that involves the least complex system of migrations. Unless convincing evidence supports positing separate migrations, the most reasonable explanation for the widespread distribution of related languages is considered to be expansion, and if a language has no close relatives, or no demonstrable relatives at all, then migration is accepted as an explanation for its present or historically known location only if supported by independent evidence. This last principle excludes the postulation of homelands for Zuni, Keresan, and Seri at any great distance from the areas in which they are found in historic and late prehistoric times. In accordance with this guideline of simplicity, the center of dispersal of a geographically diffuse linguistic family or stock will be assumed to be in the area that exhibits the greatest internal diversity, according to the principle enunciated by Sapir (1916).

This consideration of the best-known prehistoric cultural traditions of the Southwest includes best guesses as to the location and cultural associations of linguistic groups at the 3000 B.C. base line and again on the eve of the introduction of ceramics and agriculture. The later traditions are briefly discussed in an order grading from least to most problematical with regard to linguistic and cultural associations: Hakataya, Hohokam, Mogollon, Anasazi. The overall results obtained here are in substantial agreement with those of other workers who have attempted to identify archeological manifestations with extant linguistic groups (Ellis 1967b; Ford, Schroeder, and Peckham 1972; Irwin-Williams 1967b; Wendorf and Reed 1955).

### Desert Culture

During the seven or eight millennia intervening between the decline of big game hunting and the beginning of agriculture in the Southwest, the dominant tradition was the Desert culture, epitomized technologically by basketry and the flat milling stone and economically by seed gathering and the hunting of desert animals (Jennings and Norbeck 1955). The tradition existed in a number of manifestations, corresponding roughly to geographic area. Certain linguistic associations with these varieties of Desert culture may be suggested by attempting to determine the geographic location of linguistic groups at the 3000 B.C. base line.

The evidence provided by the recorded languages indicates that the center of dispersal of Yuman languages is somewhere in the south of the area over which they are now distributed, since that is the area of greatest diversity in Yuman. It should perhaps be pointed out that under hunting and gathering conditions, it is possible for a single language to be spoken over a vast region. Consequently, the ancestor of the modern Yuman languages may have been spoken over an extensive circum-delta area including northern Baja California, southern California, southwestern Arizona, and northwestern Sonora.

In any event, it is reasonable to assume, with Irwin-Williams (1967b), that the ancestors of the Yumans were responsible for certain examples of southern California Desert culture, such as that of Pinto Basin (Campbell and Campbell 1935). They may also have been responsible for some materials identified with the Amargosa variety at Ventana Cave (Haury 1950) farther to the east.

It is not easy to determine the center of dispersal for the Uto-Aztecan languages. Certain regions that have been suggested for the remote Uto-Aztecan homeland, such as the northern Rockies (Taylor 1961) or the northern Great Basin (Hopkins 1965), are at considerable remove from the area of greatest diversity much farther to the south. However, the area most consistent with the methodological principles adopted here is that suggested by Lamb (1958) and accepted also by Romney (1957)—somewhere in the Southwest around the present Arizona-Sonora border and to the south of it. This is roughly central to the vast geographic spread of Uto-Aztecan languages; if it is in fact the homeland, then both northward and southward expansion must have occurred to achieve the present distribution. In 3000 B.C., it is probable that this bidirectional expansion was well underway, with a southern contingent (represented by the historic Aztecs) already somewhat distinct from a northern group that was perhaps displacing peoples ancestral to the Yumans in southern Arizona. If this is correct, then it is likely that the early Uto-Aztecans were responsible for the more westerly versions of the Cochise Desert culture (Sayles and Antevs 1941) known from southern Arizona and New Mexico.

The Kiowa-Tanoan situation is not unlike that of Uto-Aztecan. There is considerable north-south extension (discontinuous, to be sure), taking into consideration the earliest assumed location of the Kiowa (western Montana); and any hypothesis regarding a Kiowa-Tanoan center of dispersal must allow for considerable expansion, or migration, in later periods. At first, the north might seem a more reasonable suggestion than the south, since the Kiowa divergence might suggest that the north is the area of greatest diversity. But if Kiowa divergence is spurious, then the north is no more reasonable than the south, since in the absence of an area of greatest diversity, the two competing views are of roughly equal complexity. It has been suggested that the Tanoans (and therefore the Kiowa-Tanoans) were originally southern (Ellis 1967b; Irwin-Williams 1967b). This would place them either in the area of the Cochise Desert culture or in that of a distinct, as yet little known, archaic complex originating in northern Mexico and appearing in south-central New Mexico in the prehistoric period under discussion (Irwin-Williams and Haynes 1970). While it is possible that the Kiowa-Tanoans find their remotest origins in the south, it must be borne in mind that the linguistic facts are inconclusive and that most modern Tanoans have traditions placing their origins to the north. Moreover, it should be emphasized that the possible Kiowa-Tanoan connections with the Cochise tradition are not to be identified with the alleged linguistic connections to the Uto-Aztecans, who are also associated with Cochise. If Uto-Aztecan and Kiowa-Tanoan are related, their common ancestor most probably existed at a time much earlier than the base line, perhaps near the beginnings of the Desert culture development.

From the base line to about the middle of the first millennium B.C., the expansion of Uto-Aztecans, both north and south, continued with great energy. By the eve of the later agricultural traditions, about 500 B.C., the division of Uto-Aztecan into eight subfamilies (perhaps more, including languages now extinct) was at least partially complete: with Piman more or less in its historic location; Hopi somewhere to the north of the Pimans; Takic and Tubatulabal in roughly their historic locations in California; and Numic in the Death Valley region near to, and perhaps still closely associated with, Tubatulabal. This Uto-Aztecan expansion may have restricted the Yumans to the southernmost portions of their area, for a time at least, by introducing an east-west continuum of Uto-Aztecans extending from the Hopi in Arizona (probably in the area of the later Western or Kayenta Anasazi development) to Takic in California. Yuman expansion to the east would have been constrained by the Pimans.

By this time, shortly before the beginning of the Christian era, internal differentiation within Kiowa-Tanoan was well underway. Also, presumably, the considerable north-south (and perhaps eastward) extension of Kiowa-Tanoan speakers was largely achieved, thus permitting the northernmost representatives (including, presumably, the ancestors of the Kiowa) to escape participation in later developments in the Southwest—specifically, the Mogollon and Anasazi traditions. Towa, like Kiowa, was probably somewhat distinct from other Tanoan, though (unlike Kiowa) still within the same geographic sphere. The division of Tiwa-Tewa may not yet have begun to take place.

The ancestors of the Zuni and of the Keresans were in a location that permitted them to participate in the Anasazi tradition, and there is nothing to suggest that they were not in that location throughout the Desert culture period. The Keresans have been associated with the San Jose variant of Desert culture (Ellis 1967b) and have been identified more generally with the persistent, possibly western-based, Oshara tradition culminating in the early Anasazi period after some five millennia of development (Irwin-Williams 1968a, 1968b). Linguistically, the Zuni have been associated with the California Penutians, but this connection is too remote to encourage speculation that the Zuni were in a different location during part or all of the Desert culture period. It is not inconceivable that the Zuni had Penutian relatives over an extensive area to the west and northwest of them and that these were displaced as a result of the northward

expansion of the Uto-Aztecans; however, there is no evidence for this, and it is at least as speculative as is a Zuni migration from some hypothetical Penutian homeland.

It is well known that the Desert culture persisted into historic times, and it is likely that certain Yuman and Uto-Aztecan-speaking peoples continued in the Desert tradition until historic times. It should, however, be borne in mind that the historic Desert culture peoples of the Great Basin—namely speakers of Numic languages—are not to be identified with the earliest classic Desert culture sites in that area, such as Danger Cave in Utah (Jennings and Norbeck 1955; Jennings 1957a). The linguistic evidence (the center of greatest diversity) points to a Numic homeland in the southwest corner of the Great Basin (Lamb 1958; "The Numic Languages," vol. 11) and to a rather recent Numic occupation of the area as a whole; Lamb suggests the occupation was complete only by the sixteenth or seventeenth century. It seems reasonable to speculate that the rise of agriculture permitted some peoples to reduce their territorial needs, while permitting others to carry their Desert culture into more extensive areas. Dates associated with the development of agriculture in the plateau country of northern Arizona and adjacent regions are quite consistent with Numic differentiation and, presumably, expansion into parts of the Great Basin.

## Hakataya

Apparently developing out of a Pinto-Amargosa continuum of Desert culture, the Hakataya tradition (see Schroeder 1957, 1963b) centered in the Colorado River valley with bilateral extensions into southern California and Baja California and over much of western Arizona. Characterized in part by floodplain farming on the Colorado, together with a material assemblage that Schroeder aptly calls "rock oriented," the Hakataya culture has persisted into the historic period from approximately the sixth century A.D. There is no difficulty in associating the most recent phases of Hakataya with speakers of Yuman languages, and Schroeder has been able to suggest specific assignments of Hakataya branches to extant Yuman communities. However, it does not necessarily follow that all Hakataya manifestations are due to the same linguistic group, a consideration that led to the replacement of Roger's (1945) designation "Yuman" by more noncommittal terms: Patayan (Colton 1945) and then Schroeder's term Hakataya. It is conceivable, even quite likely, that Uto-Aztecans were also responsible for some sites and materials identified as Hakataya.

Linguistic differentiation among the Yuman languages known today suggests a time-depth that is, to an extent at least, in chronological harmony with the introduction and development of agriculture in the Southwest. It is possible that, as the Uto-Aztecans to the east and northeast became increasingly involved in the establishment of village agriculture, possibly thereby releasing a certain amount of territory for use by peoples still largely oriented toward the Desert culture, the Yumans were enabled to expand into areas corresponding roughly to their historic locations before they themselves became agricultural. Subsequently, Yuman linguistic differentiation became exaggerated as the River and Delta communities developed their distinctive culture oriented toward floodplain agriculture, beginning late in the first millennium A.D. If this picture is correct, then it is also possible that Yuman expansion in early agricultural times was into areas occupied much earlier by other Yuman-related peoples displaced by the preagricultural expansion of Desert culture Uto-Aztecans.

## Hohokam

Cultural sequences observed at Ventana Cave (Haury 1950), Snaketown (Haury 1976), and Red Mountain (D.H. Morris 1969) indicate that the Hohokam continuum of the Arizona-Sonora Desert region has been present there since approximately 300 B.C., although it evidently represents a migration from Mexico (Haury 1976). Schroeder (1963b) has argued that the Hohokam tradition represents a later Mesoamerican intrusion around A.D. 500–700, which achieved domination over an original Hakataya pattern in the area. And Di Peso (1956) has argued that the Hohokam were a migrant group, possibly from the northern part of the Valley of Mexico, who dominated a local Cochise-derived O'otam culture during a sojourn of two or three centuries beginning around A.D. 1000. Linguistic considerations do not settle this issue. By assuming that the small but intriguing assemblage of Aztec-derived loanwords in Piman languages (as well as in neighboring Uto-Aztecan languages and in Seri) are due to Spanish contacts, rather than to earlier migrants from Mexico, the theory of an early Hohokam presence in the region and the view that the Hohokam are ancestral to the historic Pimas and Papagos are given further support (Haury 1945, 1950; see also Ezell 1963).

While this position is not inconsistent with the linguistic facts, there is one linguistic observation that must be reconciled with the concept of Hohokam ancestry for the historic Pimans. Piman languages are now spoken in the area identified with the Hohokam, but they are spoken much farther south as well. Nonetheless, the internal diversity within Piman is minimal, suggesting a time-depth considerably less than the two millennia that separate the present from the beginnings of the Hohokam tradition. In fact, it is somewhat misleading to speak of time-depth within Piman; it is more probable that, until very recent times, Piman represented a more or less continuous chain of dialects belonging to a single language. Therefore, it cannot be assumed that the northern Pimans to whom Hohokam ancestry is attributed became completely separated from their more southerly Piman relatives in prehistoric times. A common linguistic tradition linking all the Pimans must have persisted through most of the Hohokam period, even if, as seems most likely, some Piman groups cannot be said to have participated in Hohokam culture as normally defined. Thus, contacts between Hohokam Pimans and non-Hohokam Pimans must have been of a type that could prevent radical linguistic differentiation. If this was not the case, then Hohokam antiquity and Piman homogeneity can only be reconciled by some other speculative formulation—either Hohokam ancestry for the Pimans with a late southward expansion of Piman speakers or else the Pimans now in the Hohokam culture area as recent arrivals from farther south, replacing the Hohokam.

## Mogollon

To the east of the Hohokam, in the mountains of southeastern Arizona and southwestern New Mexico, the local variety of the Cochise Desert tradition became the Mogollon culture (J.B. Wheat 1955) through the addition of ceramics and the development of village agriculture. The Mogollon beginnings are shortly before the Christian era at a period contemporaneous with the closely similar (excepting the absence of ceramics) Basketmaker antecedents of the Anasazi to the north. Probably from the beginning, the boundary between Mogollon and Anasazi, both of which were involved in the development of Pueblo life, was obscured, if not obliterated, by intensive interinfluences.

One theory of Mogollon linguistic associations identifies Tanoan as the most likely candidate (cf. Davis 1959, citing personal communication from Ellis). But since Tanoan is also identified with Anasazi, various explanations for Tanoan distributions deserve consideration. Ellis (1967b) posits migrations of Mogollon peoples into the Anasazi area, while Ford, Schroeder, and Peckham (1972) have the ancestors of the modern Tanoans in "southern Colorado and New Mexico from the Animas River east to and down the Rio Grande" in the early Anasazi era. A third possibility is that Tanoans were, in the Desert period, distributed over an area extending both north and south, and possibly east, of the Anasazi region and that they adopted the later Pueblo cultures independently at various locations. Under any of these hypotheses, it is at least conceivable that the Mogollon were Tanoan speakers, although the likelihood that they were Uto-Aztecan speakers (Ford, Schroeder, and Peckham 1972:23) is just as great, if not greater. Moreover, the Tanoan-Mogollon association is inconsistent with the view that the Mogollon pattern is continued in the historic period by the non-Tanoan Western Pueblos (Wendorf 1956) and with the suggestion offered by Cynthia Irwin-Williams (personal communication 1972) that the ultimate origins of Tanoan are to be found in the archaic tradition to the east of, and distinct from, that of the Cochise antecedents of Mogollon (Irwin-Williams and Haynes 1970). Alternative proposals for the earliest Tanoan associations, among them the less favored, but highly intriguing, Plains derivation of Hawley (1937) and Trager (1967), deserve careful consideration. In any event, it is relatively clear that many of the Tanoans were intimately involved in the Anasazi tradition and had associations to the north of their present location.

## Anasazi

To the north of the Mogollon, in the territory drained by the Rio Grande and by the rivers of the Four Corners region, the local varieties of Desert culture developed into the Basketmaker (or pre-Pueblo) stage of Anasazi.

At least four groups, representing four of the seven linguistic stocks found in the Southwest, are directly involved in the Anasazi development. In discussing the linguistic associations of the Anasazi, the problem has been (and will continue to be) the precise identification of historic with prehistoric communities. The Uto-Aztecan increment of the Hopi community may have arrived in the mesa and Four Corners area with the earliest northward expansion of Uto-Aztecans at a time early enough to permit their participation in the Basketmaker-Anasazi transformation of the Desert culture. This is consistent with the identification of the Hopi with Kayenta Anasazi (Wendorf and Reed 1955; Ellis 1967b; Irwin-Williams 1967b). The cultural sequence in the Zuni area includes an Anasazi period, but it has been suggested that the language now spoken at Zuni, together with the predominant cultural complex there, was brought in by a people who moved into the area from eastern Arizona (Wendorf and Reed 1955) and replaced the local Anasazi, who Ellis (1967b) intimates were Keresan. Peckham has suggested Chacoan ancestry for the Zuni, while Ford and Schroeder accept an in-place development for them (Ford, Schroeder, and Peckham 1972).

There is little disagreement about associating Keresan and Tanoan with Anasazi, but there is considerable disagreement about their location prior to Pueblo abandonment of the San Juan Anasazi (San Juan–Chaco) area. San Juan Anasazi is variously assigned to the Tanoans (Reed 1949a), to the Keresans (Fox 1967; Mera

1935; Wendorf and Reed 1955), or partly to one and partly to the other (Ford, Schroeder, and Peckham 1972; Hawley 1950; Wendorf 1954). Irwin-Williams (1968b) argues that the modern Keresans derive from the Oshara antecedents of the central Anasazi. Whether or not some San Juan Anasazi were Tanoans, there is widespread agreement that Rio Grande Anasazi was developed by Tanoans. Linguistic knowledge of the area is not sensitive enough to permit any firm assertion with regard to this matter, but the linguistic facts appear to be consistent with San Juan ancestry for the Keresans and with a scheme of the following sort for the Tanoans: the Rio Grande Anasazi were ancestral to the historic Tiwa and Tewa, already differentiated from the Towa, who developed the Anasazi variety distinguished in the Largo-Gallina area (Reiter 1938; Hawley 1950; Reed 1950). Linguistic considerations suggest an early Towa differentiation from Tiwa-Tewa, but only archeological considerations can suggest a pre-Gallina origin in the upper San Juan for Towa (Eddy 1966).

## Summary

The concern here has been to suggest an identification of Southwestern linguistic groups with certain major cultural traditions known from the archeological record of the area. There has been no attempt to provide a detailed account of the manner in which various groups achieved their historic distributions or to extend the discussion into chronologically recent periods that can be studied by historical and ethnological means as well as by means of partially, or wholly, hypothetical models. Thus, this account ends prior to the Pueblo abandonment of the San Juan area and prior to the entrance of Athapaskan-speaking peoples into the Southwest. From a linguistic perspective, there is little to add with regard to the prehistoric cultural associations of certain historic groups, such as the Seri, or with regard to the linguistic associations of certain less central archeological patterns, such as Sinagua and Salado. Also not considered is the possibility that some Numic-speaking peoples arrived in the Four Corners area early enough to participate in the Anasazi tradition there (Gunnerson 1962; see also Goss 1965, in which this view is criticized on linguistic grounds).

# History of Pueblo-Spanish Relations to 1821

MARC SIMMONS

## Conquest and Colonization

The first information Europeans had regarding the Pueblo people was obtained by Alvar Nuñez Cabeza de Vaca and three companions shipwrecked on the Texas coast in 1528. South of present El Paso this party learned of wealthy agriculturists who resided on the upper Rio Grande in large towns and who wove cotton blankets. In 1539 Fray Marcos de Niza, accompanied by Indian servants and a Negro, Esteban, who had been with Cabeza de Vaca, traveled north from New Spain as far as the legendary Seven Cities of Cíbola (actually the villages of the Zuni). Esteban in advance entered the southernmost of these Pueblos, Hawikuh, and was slain by the Indians. Fray Marcos, fearing for his safety, halted on a hilltop, viewed the villages from afar, claimed possession of the region for the king, and then hastened homeward. On the basis of his enthusiastic if exaggerated report to the viceroy, an expedition under Francisco Vásquez de Coronado (see "Pueblos Abandoned in Historic Times," fig. 1, this vol.) was outfitted in the following year for the conquest of Cíbola and other kingdoms of which the friar had heard, including Acus (Acoma) and Totonteac (Hopi).

Departing from Compostela February 23, 1540, Coronado moved up the west coast of New Spain. His glittering company was composed of 300 men, divided among cavalry, infantry, and artillery; 1,000 horses and 600 pack animals; and a contingent of six Franciscan friars who intended to begin missionary work among the Pueblos and see that "the conquest might be Christian and apostolic and not a butchery."

The Zuni area, devoid of gold, silver, or other treasure, proved a disappointment. Hawikuh, reached on July 7, resisted the Spanish army but was captured by storm and converted into Coronado's headquarters. A party sent north under Pedro de Tovar discovered the Hopi Pueblos, which were revealed equally barren of wealth.

Spanish hopes received a lift when a delegation of Indians under Chief Bigotes ('Whiskers') reached Zuni and spoke of a populous country to the east. They told of a province called Tiguex astride a great river, of their own Pueblo of Cicuye (Pecos), and of an endless plain over which woolly cattle roamed. The river spoken of by Bigotes proved to be the Rio Grande, and Tiguex, a cluster of 12 Southern Tiwa Pueblos near modern Berna-

lillo. Here Coronado quartered his army during the rigorous winter of 1540-1541. When levies of food and blankets were made upon the Tiwa and several women were molested, the Indians resisted. The Pueblos of Arenal and Moho were assaulted by the Spaniards, and their occupants, not slain in battle were burned at the stake. This so terrorized the Tiwa that many abandoned their homes in mid-winter, resulting in virtual depopulation of that province.

After a fruitless journey to the plains in search of a golden kingdom called Quivira during the spring and early summer of 1541, Coronado gave up his quest and returned to New Spain. Two friars he left behind were martyred by the Indians. Formal charges were subsequently brought against Coronado for unnecessarily waging war against the Tiwa, but upon investigation these were dropped.

No other formal expedition visited the Pueblos for almost 40 years following Coronado's venture. But interest in the area revived during the period 1581 to 1591 when three parties of Spaniards undertook a new series of explorations. From the frontier settlements of southern Chihuahua, Father Agustín Rodríguez with two missionary companions and nine soldiers commanded by Francisco Sánchez Chamuscado blazed a trail up the Rio Grande to the Pueblos in 1581. One of the friars was slain by the Tano and the other two, who remained at the Pueblo of Puaray (near Bernalillo) when Chamuscado returned to New Spain the next year, were martyred by the Tiwa. Antonio de Espejo in 1582 led a small force to New Mexico, ostensibly to rescue the two friars left by Chamuscado. But upon learning of their deaths, he prospected for mineral deposits as far west as the Hopi villages, finding promising signs in the Verde Valley of central Arizona. In 1590-1591 an expedition commanded by Gaspar Castaño de Sosa entered the region by ascending the Pecos Valley. At Pecos, one of the most populous Pueblos, mustering 500 warriors, Castaño encountered a hostile reception and felt obliged to battle the Indians into submission. Moving westward he visited the Tewa and eventually stopped at the Keresan village of Santo Domingo where he hoped to plant a permanent settlement. But a troop of soldiers arrived suddenly from New Spain, arrested Castaño and his followers for launching a colonizing expedition without royal license, and the entire company was carried back in disgrace.

The sixteenth-century expeditions, from Coronado to Castaño, set the pattern for Spanish-Indian relations that prevailed during the first half of the colonial era. Although the native people initially showed a desire to deal peacefully with the intruders, contact inevitably led to conflict. Espejo recorded that as he entered the Piro villages "the people came out to receive us, taking us to their pueblos and giving us a great quantity of turkeys, maize, beans, tortillas, and other kinds of bread" (Bolton 1916:177). However, the Spaniards could sustain themselves for extended periods only by making forced levies of food and clothing upon the slender reserves of the Indians. When these demands became oppressive and a Pueblo revolted, it was drummed into submission to enforce obedience and to serve as an example to others. Requirements that the Indians submit to the civil authority of the king and suffer the blandishments of the friars grew to be serious irritants only with the spread of colonization and intensification of the missionary program in the seventeenth century.

Chroniclers with the earliest expeditions presented the first descriptions of Pueblo life and culture. These writings indicate that in the beginning the Spaniards' view of the Indians was strongly influenced by previous experiences with the Moors of Spain and the Aztecs and warlike Chichimecs of central and northern Mexico. On the frontiers of New Spain the Spanish soldier easily drew a parallel between the infidel Moors vanquished by his forefathers and the non-Christian native people that he proposed to subdue by force, even after Spanish law had given full theoretical recognition to the obvious differences between Moslems and Indians. Thus the first New Mexican narratives of Spanish activity include reference to the similarities of Moorish and Pueblo custom and unhesitatingly speak of the ceremonial kivas of the Indians as mosques. In a like manner comparisons were noted with the Mexican Indians, the Spaniards calling the Pueblo dances mitotes, the same term they applied to the frenzied war dances of the Chichimecs.

Notwithstanding, the stability of Pueblo society and culture, together with visible achievements in architecture, agriculture, and crafts, aroused the admiration of the Spaniards and gradually led them to abandon superficial comparisons with other peoples. The following comments from Hernán Gallegos's journal of the Chamuscado-Rodríguez expedition convey something of the respect the explorers came to hold for Pueblo ways:

> We found the houses very well planned and built in blocks, with mud walls, whitewashed inside and well decorated with monsters, other animals, and human figures. . . . The inhabitants have a great deal of crockery . . . all decorated and of better quality than the pottery of New Spain. . . . There is not an Indian who does not have a corral for his turkeys, each of which holds a flock of one hundred birds. . . . They have large cotton fields. . . . They use shoes. . . . These people are handsome and fair-skinned. They are very industrious

and the best craftsmen found in New Spain. . . . For a barbarous people the neatness they observe in everything is very remarkable (Hammond and Rey 1966:82-86, 102).

In spite of such praise, the Spaniards perceived much in Pueblo culture that appeared repugnant, particularly in native religion. Especially offensive to them were the snake dances, once widespread among the villagers but today confined to the Hopi, in which rattlesnakes and other serpents were treated ritually and released to carry messages to the gods. In fact, attempted suppression of this and other religious practice soon emerged as the chief point of friction between Spaniard and Indian.

In one sense Coronado was responsible for the "conquest" of the Southwest since his exploration resulted in establishing Spain's permanent claim to the area. But in spite of his fights with the Zuni and Tiwa, his adventurism was not of the same character as Hernando Cortés's conquest of the Aztecs or Francisco Pizarro's of the Incas. Along the Rio Grande there occurred no toppling of native states, no burial of Indian culture. This might have ensued had the Pueblos possessed storehouses of treasure or if Coronado had initiated settlement. But by the time Spain was prepared to colonize, 60 years after Coronado, the term conquest had been legally banished.

Under the prodding of churchmen and leading jurists, Phillip II promulgated the Royal Ordinances of 1573 (Pacheco and de Cárdenas 1864-1884:142-187) that imposed severe restrictions and established strict regulations upon the extension of Spanish settlement and treatment of the Indians. Significantly, those entrusted with the discovery and colonization of new lands were forbidden to engage in "conquests" and instead were enjoined to pacify the native people by resort to all benevolent means. The humanitarian principles contained in these detailed ordinances explicitly applied to the program of colonization undertaken in the country of the Pueblos, but in practice the Indians there came to suffer many of the abuses common to a conquered people.

Early in 1598 Juan de Oñate, scion of a wealthy mining family, led a body of 400 soldiers, colonists, friars, and Mexican Indian servants northward to occupy the upper Rio Grande Valley (fig. 1). The motive behind Spanish expansion into this area was primarily a missionary one, based upon the desire to bring Christianity to one of the last large bodies of sedentary, agricultural Indians remaining unconverted in the viceroyalty of New Spain. At Santo Domingo Pueblo on July 7, Oñate assembled leaders from neighboring villages and, after subjecting them to a stern lecture on Spanish politics and religion, received their "spontaneously" rendered declaration of vassalage to the king. Moving north, the settlers took up residence among the Tewa at San Juan, and the Indians began to feel the full weight of European rule. On September 8 New Mexico was declared a missionary province of the Franciscan Order, and Pueblos were assigned to individual friars who were divided, for administrative purposes, among seven districts. Oñate initiated a series of exploratory expeditions from his seat at San Juan in a vain effort to discover precious metals that might form an economic base for his colony. That such riches did not materialize meant the Indians increasingly bore the burden of supporting the Spaniards, for as the viceroy noted caustically in observing conditions in the fledgling colony, "no one comes to the Indies to plow and sow, but only to eat and loaf" (Hammond and Rey 1953, 2:1068). One of Oñate's captains reported that the system used to support the settlers has been "to send people out every month in various directions to bring maize from the pueblos. The feelings of the natives against supplying it cannot be exaggerated . . . for they weep and cry out as if they and all their descendants were being killed. The Spaniards seize their blankets by force, leaving the poor Indian women stark naked, holding their babies to their breasts" (Hammond and Rey 1953, 2:608–610).

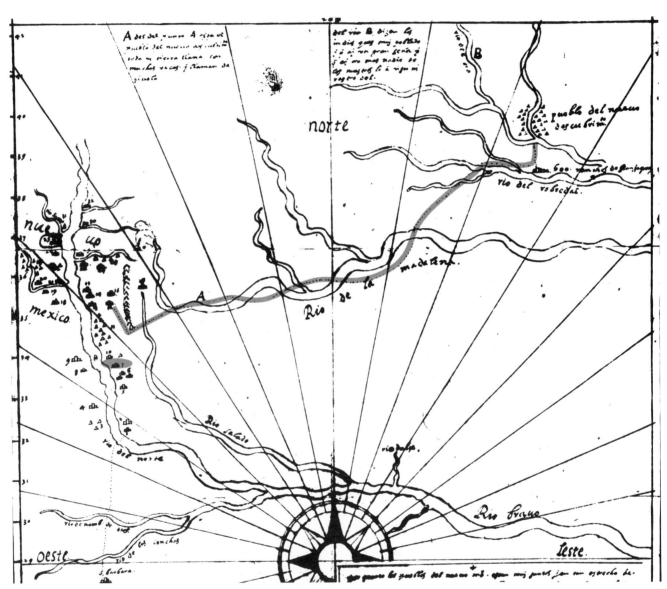

Archivo General de Indias, Seville: Mapas y Planos, Mexico, 49.

Fig. 1. Section of sketch map of Juan de Oñate's route (dotted lines, tone added) from Mexico City to the Rio Grande Pueblos in 1598, and the route followed by his 1601 Quivira expedition. Between expeditions, Oñate was headquartered at the Pueblo of San Juan, here indicated by the cluster of buildings labeled 7 (tone added) on the Rio Grande *(rio del norte)*. The 1598 route (only partly shown) starts at Mexico City and proceeds through San Juan del Río, Zacatecas, and Santa Barbara. (See Hammond and Rey 1966:endpapers.) The 1601 Quivira route starts at San Cristóbal, proceeds across the Pecos River *(Rio salado)*, the Canadian River *(Rio de la madalena)*, and the Arkansas River *(rio del robredal)* and ends at the "pueblo del nuevo descubrimiento," probably a Wichita Indian village on the banks of the Walnut River, which did not contain the hoped-for riches ascribed to Quivira (Wheat 1957–1963, 1:29–31). Drawn in 1602 by Henrico (or Enrique) Martínez, the king's Mexican cosmographer, on the basis of information provided by Juan Rodríguez, a member of Oñate's party, this is the earliest known extant map of the area.

These harsh measures provoked rebellion among the Tiwa and Tompiro villages and at Acoma. Acoma, where 15 soldiers including Oñate's nephew were killed in December 1598, was destroyed, and 500 captives were enslaved. Within a few years most of the Acomas escaped and returned to rebuild their village.

Discontent among the colonists and friars over Oñate's policies and failure to find mineral wealth prompted complaints to the viceroy and king, which brought about Oñate's removal from the governorship in 1607. His successor, Pedro de Peralta, did not reach New Mexico until late in 1609. Early the following year, Peralta founded the city of Santa Fe to serve as the new capital of the province and conscripted large numbers of Indians to construct the governor's palace and other public buildings. For the next 70 years, the Pueblos toiled under an oppressive yoke, rendering tribute and performing personal service, while laws designed for their protection were generally disregarded.

## The Missionary Program

The colonization of New Mexico had been a private endeavor, financed by Juan de Oñate under license of the king. With Oñate's failure, the crown briefly considered abandoning the province because of its poverty, but the large Pueblo population, offering a potentially rich field for the Church, led to the maintenance of New Mexico as a royal colony supported almost wholly by the treasury. In the years following 1610, friar reinforcements and supplies arrived to bolster and expand the faltering missions begun during the Oñate period.

In 1626 the energetic Fray Alonso de Benavides became custos, or chief prelate, of the New Mexican missions, and his memorials, detailing the progress of evangelization, resulted in the recruitment of 30 additional friars and extension of activity to Pueblos previously neglected by the churchmen. Up to 30,000 Indian baptisms were claimed for this period, but the figure may have been inflated to impress superiors and gain more support.

The Pueblo of Santo Domingo was designated as ecclesiastical capital, and imposing churches were raised with Indian labor at Pecos, Acoma, the Hopi village of Awatovi, at sites among the Tompiros, Southern Tiwa, Jemez, and elsewhere. Because there was never sufficient missionary personnel to staff all Pueblos, chapels, known as *visitas*, were placed in the lesser towns and were served regularly by clergy from the nearest mission center where one or more friars maintained residence. With baptism of the people and building of a church or chapel, each Pueblo became a *doctrina* or Indian parish. The missionaries selected *fiscales de doctrina*, Indian lay assistants, to serve as teachers and interpreters, and native *alguaciles* to enforce religious discipline. One tireless clergyman, Fray

Gerónimo de Zárate Salmerón, baptized 6,566 persons in the Jemez district during the early 1620s, learned the Jemez language, and in it prepared a theological treatise (Zárate Salmerón 1966:26). His linguistic proficiency was unusual, since most missionaries throughout colonial times ignored repeated viceregal orders to learn the language of their Indian parishioners.

As a corollary to the missionary program, the friars introduced economic changes meant to wean the Pueblo people away from native life and incorporate them into provincial society. Schools and shops, teaching mechanical arts as well as religion, became important adjuncts of the mission. Native smiths made and repaired iron tools, improved methods of agriculture and new crops were introduced, and development of animal husbandry allowed use of extensive rangelands adjacent to the Indian communities.

While the friars to some degree shielded the Pueblos from abuse by the Spanish colonists, their own strict demands and meting out of corporal punishment for infractions of ecclesiastical rules aroused hostility. The missionaries, with support from the governor and soldiers, waged relentless war upon what they considered idolatrous practice. Masked kachina dances were eventually prohibited, and periodic raids upon places of worship resulted in confiscation and public burning of sacred paraphernalia. Such attacks on religion disturbed the entire web of Pueblo life. The native priesthood became implacable foes of the Spaniards and to avoid persecution conducted traditional rites in secret. Thus while a veneer of Spanish Catholicism was imposed upon the Pueblos, they remained wedded to their own rich ceremonialism and ancestral religious heritage.

Implicit in the conduct of the Franciscans and in their treatment of the Pueblos was a corpus of law and theory relating to the Indians that formed both the basis and the rationale for Spanish activity in the New World. Beginning with Ferdinand and Isabella the guiding principles of Spain's governmental policy were grounded in a steadfast belief in Roman Catholic orthodoxy and royal absolutism. Thus in the "conquest" of New Mexico, as in other areas of America, religious and political motives were intermingled, with propagation of the faith, at least in theory, taking precedence. The Crown in fact unequivocally declared that conversion of the indigenous population was the primary aim of colonial enterprise, and this position received its justification and legality from ecclesiastical and lay scholars who asserted the rights of dominion of Christian, civilized peoples over natives of other lands. Since it was thought the aborigines would benefit by introduction to higher levels of human reason and exposure to a superior form of religion, their submission to Spanish law and the Church, it was held, might legitimately be established by force if necessary. This principle was not fully abandoned until codification of the Laws of the Indies in 1680, which provided "that war cannot and shall not be made on the Indians of any province to the end that they may receive the Holy Catholic faith, or yield obedience to us, or for any other reason" (Zavala 1943:46).

Far more than any other European, the Spaniard was acutely concerned with the legal and moral aspects of his treatment of the Indians. Theory put forward by remote scholars might satisfy needs for a general statement of policy, but the realities of direct Spaniard-Indian confrontation produced problems that admitted of no easy solution. The Church, for instance, upheld equality of the Indians and argued for their unrestricted admission to colonial society once they passed from neophytes to full membership in the ecclesiastical body. The Crown, in accepting the native people as its vassals, acceded to the same view. Yet the conquistador-colonist class could only regard such a canon as inimical to its own fortunes, since maintenance of permanent political dominance and social privilege depended upon relegation of the Indians to a subservient role that implied natural inequality. This conflict of motives—the play of private economic interests opposed to the maximum development of the missions—led to open rivalry between the clergy and the civil population and provoked struggles for supremacy that weak and ill-supported provinces such as New Mexico could scarcely afford. The kings, attempting to reconcile differences and at the same time to protect the Indians, passed endless legislation that was inevitably confused and contradictory, so that the rift between clergy and colonist remained unhealed and the native people suffered from lack of consistent administration.

By the time the missionary program began among the Pueblos, the Franciscans had learned from previous experience in central Mexico not to expect rapid conversion of the Indians, but to prepare for a long civilizing guardianship. Their simplified methods of indoctrination stressed veneration of the Cross, respect for the clergy, instruction concerning the sacraments, the teaching of elementary prayers, and regular attendance at religious services (Scholes 1936-1937:21). Since the Crown was committed to the expenditure of large sums on the missions and an ample Indian population was available as a labor force, New Mexican friars often built churches and convents far more sumptuous than the simple needs of their program required. Moreover, at each mission agricultural and grazing lands worked by the Pueblos were designated for support of the clergy, but these usually exceeded the actual physical needs of the priests, allowing them to convert surpluses to their own profit. Therefore, the missionaries developed strong vested interests whose preservation depended upon retention of the Indians in a state of tutelage. Thus natural resistance of the Pueblos to evangelization and weaknesses inherent in ecclesiastical goals and procedures led to failure of the missionary performance in seventeenth-century New Mexico.

## The Pueblos Under the Colonial System

When the Spaniards settled New Mexico in 1598, the largest concentration of Pueblo Indians was situated along the upper Rio Grande and its tributaries, where there was sufficient land to meet their agricultural needs. Although population density was relatively heavy, the numerous communities were scattered and small, few containing more than 800 to 1,000 persons. Spanish law forbade encroachment upon tilled Indian domain, but during the first decades of the seventeenth century the number of settlers was few, no more than 2,000, so that enough marginal lands existed apart from Pueblo fields to satisfy the requirements of the colonists. The transfer of Spaniards from the vicinity of San Juan Pueblo to unoccupied lands along the Santa Fe River in 1610 was undertaken partly to fulfill the law protecting Indian property. By the late eighteenth century, when Spanish population reached 20,000-25,000, the number of Pueblos had significantly declined, leaving large agricultural tracts vacant and subject to reassignment to colonists. Since the Pueblos accepted vassalage to the crown, they were recognized as hereditary possessors of the land they tilled and used. During the first century of Spanish rule, each Pueblo was tacitly allowed a minimum of four square surrounding leagues. But only after 1700, and then at different times for individual villages, were formal grants issued (fig. 2). The Hopi, free from Spanish domination in later colonial times, never received a royal grant, and the legal status of their lands under the United States government was not defined until 1882.

The first Spaniards, with their aristocratic pretensions and dislike for manual toil, developed various devices to extract labor and service from the Indians. The encomienda, introduced into New Mexico by Oñate, was a privilege extended to certain favored subjects to collect an annual tribute from a specified town or number of Indians. The proprietor of such a grant, the *encomendero,* was expected to exercise a trusteeship over his tributary subjects, providing material aid to their church and offering military protection. Although the amount of tribute he was allowed to collect from the Pueblo in the form of maize and cotton blankets was strictly limited by law, the system here, as elsewhere in New Spain, cloaked all manner of abuses.

The encomienda functioned in New Mexico from 1600 to 1680, its tribute exactions causing much discontent among the Indians. Of greater economic importance was the repartimiento, a system of forced labor designed to provide workers for Spanish farms and haciendas. Indians conscripted for such labor were supposed to be paid a fixed wage—half a *real* a day until 1659, at which time the amount was increased to a full *real* by Gov. Bernardo

López de Mendizábal. But even this nominal sum was not always rendered, the colonists preferring to squeeze labor from the Indians without compensating them. During the first two-thirds of the seventeenth century, the ratio of Spaniard to Indian was such that the number of potential workers exceeded the labor demands of the settlers. However, after 1665, famine, pestilence, and raids by nomadic tribes so reduced the Pueblo people that they were hard pressed to meet these labor obligations. One of their chief complaints at the time of the Pueblo Revolt in 1680 was that the Spaniards so burdened them with tasks, they had little time left to care for their own fields.

While the Church claimed the Pueblo Indian's soul and the colonist his tribute and labor, the provincial government demanded his civil allegiance. When Oñate accepted the submission of individual villages, he acknowledged their status as *repúblicas,* which, in the Spanish sense, referred to semiautonomous municipalities with certain inherent rights of self-government. It was recognized that a form of native administration already existed under a system of caciques, but to fit more smoothly into the Spanish scheme, a new set of officers was soon created to deal directly with the governor in Santa Fe. Among the Pueblos, these officials usually included a governor (called *gobernadorcillo* or 'little governor' to distinguish him from the provincial head), a lieutenant governor *(teniente),* war captains *(capitanes de guerra,* present only after 1700), sheriff *(alguacil), mayordomos* (irrigation ditch bosses), and church wardens *(sacristanes).* A viceregal order of 1620 (Bloom 1928:363) provided for the free election of these functionaries on January 1 to serve a one-year term and forbade interference in their selection by government officials or clergy. Once elected, the Pueblo officers traveled to Santa Fe and were confirmed in their positions, the Spanish governor presenting the *gobernadorcillo* a black cane trimmed with silver and silk tassels as a symbol of authority. Within their own village, ex-Pueblo governors formed a group of

elders (called *principales* or *justicias*) serving as advisers to the incumbent governor and dispensing justice for misdemeanors. Nevertheless, it is clear that the Pueblo caciques continued to exercise their old authority as before and sub rosa to control the activities of men holding office under the Spanish system.

As a function of his office, the Spanish governor in Santa Fe was required to oversee the temporal and spiritual welfare of the Pueblo Indians, but, as legal proceedings reveal, several officeholders in the mid-seventeenth century were guilty not only of slighting this trust, but also of actively exploiting their charges for personal advantage. Indians were confined in sweatshops in the governor's palace weaving blankets, stockings, and other articles without pay, and native women were violated. The priests, natural protectors of the Indians, protested such conduct, but their own record was not without blemish. Capt. Nicolás de Aguilar, a Spanish soldier, charged in 1662 that "the friars are not content with a few helpers. They want . . . the Indians of the entire pueblo, for gathering piñon nuts, weaving, painting, and making stockings, and for other forms of service. And in all this they greatly abuse the Indians, men and women" (Scholes 1942:59). A civil officer, known as Protector of the Indians, functioned in New Mexico intermittently

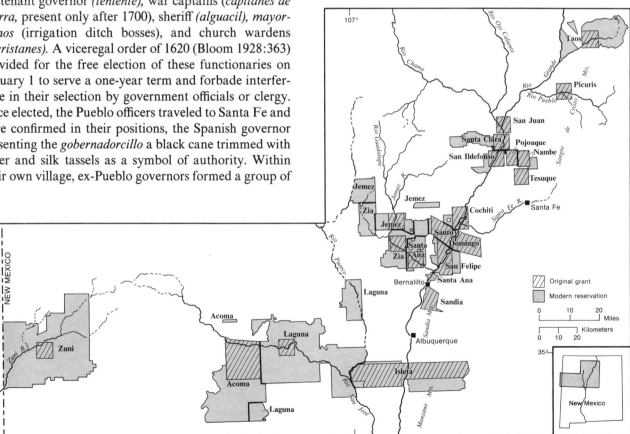

Fig. 2. Original land grants and modern reservation areas. There was no Hopi grant. See Aberle (1948) for a description of subsequent grants and purchases. For a more detailed map of modern reservations see "Pueblos: Introduction," fig. 1, this vol.

during the seventeenth and eighteenth centuries, his duty being to defend Indian rights, in court if necessary; free them from all oppressors; and make certain they received proper religious instruction. Although beneficently conceived by the royal authorities, the office proved impotent in preserving the Pueblo people from mistreatment.

The peaceful inclinations of the Pueblo people were severely tested during the mid-seventeenth century, not only by the painful exactions of Spanish church and state but also by the increasing hostility of their nomadic neighbors, the Apache and Navajo. Friars made several feeble attempts in the 1620s and 1630s to convert small Apache bands, but unprincipled Spanish slavers, who seized Indians to be sold in the Chihuahua mining towns, nullified this work by their actions and made of the Apache a formidable enemy. In preconquest times, the nomads and Pueblos had maintained a cordial commercial relationship, but this amity was sundered soon after arrival of the Spaniards. The Apache, as they developed an equestrian hunting economy and gained in strength and numbers, became more predatory in their habits. The Pueblos, cast in the unwilling role of allies of the Spaniards, bore the brunt of nomadic raids, since many of their villages lay exposed on the frontier. Superiority in firearms was denied them by restrictive Spanish laws that forbade sale of guns to Indians. The first large-scale Apache attack upon New Mexico occurred in 1640 during which they burned 20,000 fanegas of corn. Another damaging blow fell on the Pueblos in 1647. Raids upon the mission churches of the Tompiro east of the Manzano Mountains resulted in profaning of the places of worship and considerable other damage in 1653 and 1670. A powerful Apache force assailed the Zuni Pueblo of Hawikuh in 1673, killing Fray Pedro de Avila y Ayala and 200 Zunis, taking 1,000 captives and all livestock, and burning the village (Forbes 1960:150–151; Adams and Chavez in Domínguez 1956:197).

The misery of the Pueblos was further aggravated by a series of severe droughts. Lack of rain in 1640 combined with the destructive Apache raid of that year produced widespread famine and 3,000 Indian fatalities throughout the province. Other thousands perished in the drought and famine of 1663–1669 when Pueblo people were seen "lying dead along the roads, in the ravines, and in their huts" (Vivian 1964a:153). Fearful of working in their fields because of marauders, under growing pressure to tend the crops of the Spaniards leaving their own unfenced plots to be ravaged by livestock, and plagued by years of scant rainfall, the Pueblos steadily succumbed to starvation. European disease, often appearing as epidemics during famine years when the native population was weakest, took a further toll (see table 1).

To the Pueblo mind the root cause of all this misfortune lay with the Spaniards who not only had imposed alien rule but also through interference with native ritual had upset the delicate balance between man and the forces of nature, thereby precipitating cosmic disaster. The seventeenth century, from the days of Oñate's first settlement to the upheaval of 1680, was characterized by a growing antagonism between Pueblo and Spaniard and punctuated increasingly by instances of violence. On February 22, 1632, the Zuni murdered and scalped their priest Fray Francisco Letrado and five days later slew another, Fray Martín de Arvide, and two soldiers. Fearing punishment, they abandoned their villages and fled to a nearby mesa top where they remained until 1635. Fray Pedro de Miranda met death at Taos Pueblo in 1639, and authorities in Santa Fe learned that his vestments were worn in tribal dances. In 1650 the Tewa plotted to kill the friars and soldiers in their district on Thursday evening of Passion Week, but their intentions were discovered and the massacre prevented. At about the same time, the Jemez people revolted, killing a Spaniard, and when the disturbance was quelled, 29 of their number were hanged.

Acts of brutality were committed as regularly by the Spanish colonists, and on occasion even by members of the clergy. A delegation of Hopi appeared in Santa Fe in 1655 to denounce their priest Fray Salvador de Guerra who had whipped an Indian for practicing idolatry, then doused him with turpentine and set him afire. An equally sordid story derived from Taos Pueblo in the early 1660s where the resident priest struck and killed an Indian woman because she had failed to spin some cotton he had given her. For several years both civil and church officials punished Indians for minor offenses by shearing their hair. The viceroy ordered this practice halted in 1620 since the Pueblos took great offense to such treatment and "some fled to the Rock of Acoma, reverting to idolatry" (Bloom 1928:366).

The Spanish hold on the province of New Mexico was seriously weakened beginning in the 1640s by a bitter rivalry between several of the Spanish governors and the Franciscan clergy. At issue was the fine line dividing the jurisdiction of government and ecclesiastical officers over the Pueblo people. In theory the governors held supremacy in temporal matters, the clergy in the spiritual realm, but in practice each claimed and actively asserted final authority. At the heart of the matter was the desire of both governors and friars to manage and exploit the Pueblos without interference. The conflict of church and state resulted in acrimonious public debate, prolonged litigation in the court of the Holy Office of the Inquisition, occasional incidents of violence, and polarization of sentiment within the Spanish community, as well as increased confusion among the Pueblos, who could not comprehend antagonism between secular and religious spheres of life since these were closely integrated in their own culture.

The assortment of stresses weighing upon Pueblo society after 1650 gave ample cause for discouragement and dislocation across the province. The inroads of

# Table 1. Pueblo Population, 1630–1821

| Pueblos | 1630[a] | 1680[h] | 1706[l] | 1744[m] | 1749[p] | 1752[q] Families | Total | 1760[r] Families | Total | 1776[t] Families | Total | 1789[u] Warriors | Total | 1793[v] | 1797–1798[x] | 1805[y] | 1810[z] | 1821[a'] |
|---|---|---|---|---|---|---|---|---|---|---|---|---|---|---|---|---|---|---|
| Acoma | 2,000 | 2,000[i] | 760 | 110 | 960 | 283 | 890 | 308 | 1,502 | 135 | 530 | 150 | 783 | 820 | 757 | 731 | 818 | 477 |
| Cochiti | [b] | 300 | 520 | 80+ | 521 | 80 | 309 | 105 | 450 | 116 | 486 | 120 | 527 | 720 | 505 | 656 | 701 | 339 |
| Galisteo | [c] | 800 | 150 | 50 | 350 | 66 | 195 | 80 | 255 | 41 | 152 | — | — | 152[w] | — | — | — | — |
| Isleta | [d] | 2,000 | — | 80[n] | 500 | 85 | 318 | 107 | 304 | 114 | 454 | 75 | 383 | 410 | 479 | 419 | 498 | 511 |
| Jemez | 3,000 | 5,000 | 300 | 100 | 574 | 127 | 207 | 109 | 373 | 102 | 345 | 75 | 265 | 485 | 272 | 264 | 299 | 330 |
| Laguna | — | — | 330 | 60 | 228 | 130 | 415 | 174 | 600 | 178 | 699 | 100 | 653 | 668 | 802 | 940 | 1,016 | 779 |
| Nambe | [e] | 600[j] | 300 | 50 | 350 | 41 | 144 | 49 | 204 | 50 | 183 | — | — | 155 | 178 | 143 | 196 | 231 |
| Pecos | 2,000+ | 2,000 | 1,000 | 125 | 1,000 | 127 | 318 | 168 | 344 | 100 | 269 | 40 | 138 | 152[w] | 189 | 104 | 135 | 54 |
| Picuris | 2,000 | 3,000 | 300 | 80 | 400 | 65 | 239 | 51 | 328 | 64 | 223 | 41 | 213 | 254 | 251 | 250 | 226 | 320 |
| Pojoaque | [e] | — | — | 30 | — | 22 | 79 | 31 | 99 | 27 | 98 | 8 | 77 | 53 | 79 | 100 | 48 | 93 |
| Sandia | [d] | 3,000 | — | — | 440 | 65 | 219 | 51[s] | 196 | 92 | 257 | 55 | 252 | 304 | 236 | 314 | 372 | 405 |
| San Felipe | [b] | 600[k] | 500 | 60+ | 400 | 74 | 224 | 89 | 458 | 95 | 406 | 56 | 260 | 532 | 282 | 289 | 331 | 310 |
| San Ildefonso | [e] | 800 | 300 | 100[o] | 354 | 83 | 262 | 90 | 484 | 111 | 387 | 74 | 317 | 240 | 251 | 175 | 283 | 525 |
| San Juan | [e] | 300 | 340 | 60 | 500 | 69 | 217 | 50 | 316 | 61 | 201 | 44 | 205 | 260 | 202 | 194 | 199 | 232 |
| Santa Ana | [b] | 600[k] | 340 | 50+ | 600 | 68 | 211 | 104 | 404 | 102 | 384 | 80 | 399 | 356 | 634 | 450 | 511 | 471 |
| Santa Clara | [e] | 300 | 210 | 100[o] | 272 | 56 | 163 | 70 | 257 | 67 | 229 | 48 | 201 | 139 | 193 | 186 | 216 | 180 |
| Santo Domingo | [b] | 150 | 240 | 40 | 300 | 64 | 214 | 67 | 424 | 136 | 528 | 120 | 493 | 650 | 1,483 | 333 | 726 | 726 |
| Taos | 2,500 | 2,000[i] | 700 | 170 | 540 | 141 | 451 | 159 | 505 | 112 | 427 | 120 | 479 | 518 | 531 | 508 | 537 | 753 |
| Tesuque | [e] | 200+ | 500 | 50 | 171 | 53 | 147 | 31 | 232 | 45 | 194 | 45 | 152 | 138 | 155 | 131 | 162 | 187 |
| Zia | [b] | — | 500 | 80+ | 600 | — | — | 150 | 568 | 125 | 416 | 45 | 222 | 275 | 262 | 254 | 290 | 196 |
| Zuni | 10,000 | 1,500 | 1,500 | 150 | 2,000 | 251 | 745 | 182 | 664 | 396 | 1,617 | 450 | 2,437 | 1,935 | 2,716 | 1,470 | 1,602 | 1,597 |
| *El Paso Pueblos:* | | | | | | | | | | | | | | | | | | |
| Ysleta del Sur | — | — | — | 90 | 500 | 108 | 353 | 80 | 429 | — | — | 96 | 398 | — | — | — | — | — |
| Senecú del Sur | [f] | — | — | 70 | 389 | 84 | 297 | 111 | 425 | — | — | 80 | 382 | — | — | — | — | — |
| Socorro del Sur | [g] | — | — | 60 | 250 | 39 | 135 | 46 | 182 | — | — | 70 | 495 | — | — | — | — | — |

[a] Figures of Fray Alonso de Benavides (1916).
[b] One of 7 Keresan Pueblos with total population given as 4,000.
[c] One of 5 Tano Pueblos with total population given as 4,000.
[d] One of 15–16 Southern Tiwa Pueblos with total population given as 7,000.
[e] One of 8 Tewa Pueblos with total population given as 6,000.
[f] Piro refugee Pueblo founded after 1680, but Benavides gives 1,400 for Piro population in 1630 with 6 Pueblos.
[g] Tompiro refugee Pueblo founded after 1680, but Benavides gives 10,000 for Tompiro population in 1630 with 14–15 Pueblos.
[h] Figures of Fray Agustín de Vetancurt (1960).
[i] Includes some Spaniards.
[j] Figure includes neighboring Pueblos of Jacona and Cuyamungue.
[k] Aggregate figure for San Felipe and Santa Ana.
[l] Figures of Fray Juan Alvarez (Hackett 1923–1937, 3:373–377).
[m] Figures of Fray Miguel de Menchero (Hackett 1923–1937, 3:402–407).
[n] Includes some Hopi.
[o] Aggregate figure for San Ildefonso and Santa Clara.
[p] Figures of Fray Andrés Varo (Ocaranza 1934:145–146).
[q] General Census of New Mexico (Archivo General de la Nacion, Mexico Provincias Internas, 102).
[r] Figures of Bishop Pedro Tamarón y Romeral (1954).
[s] Figures represent Tiwas; 95 Hopis in 16 families also lived there.
[t] Figures of Fray Francisco Atanasio Domínguez (1956).
[u] Census of Gov. Fernando de la Concha (Ritch Papers, Huntington Library, San Marino, Calif.).
[v] Figures after Bancroft (1889:279).
[w] Aggregate figure for Pecos and Galisteo.
[x] Figures of Fray Francisco de Hezio (Meline 1966:208–209).
[y] Figures of Gov. Real Alencaster (Meline 1966:212).
[z] New Mexico Census (Ritch Papers, Huntington Library, San Marino, Calif.).
[a'] Figures of Fr. José Pedro Rubín de Celís, Dec. 31, 1821 (Mexican Archives of N. M., Santa Fe).

Apache raiders and decline of the economic base owing to drought prompted most of the Tompiro and Tiwa villagers beyond the Manzano Mountains to abandon their homes in the 1670s and join relatives living in the Rio Grande Valley. Abandonment of Pueblos with consolidation of survivors into larger villages occurred among the Jemez, Zuni, and to a lesser extent other groups. Spanish military campaigns against the Faraon Apache on the eastern border and the Navajo on the west in 1675 did little to alleviate pressure on the Pueblos. In that same year a serious episode involving the Tewa called attention to growing Indian resentment and a deterioration of the Spanish position. According to official reports, native priests bewitched several friars and citizens causing their deaths. Other missionaries complained of a resurgence of idolatry and the old faith, so that evangelization was gravely jeopardized. Gov. Juan Francisco Treviño responded by arresting Indian leaders, confiscating religious paraphernalia, and burning kivas. Three Tewas were hanged and a fourth hanged himself, while 43 others were lashed and condemned to slavery. When a belligerent party of Tewas entered Santa Fe and demanded the release of the prisoners, Governor Treviño acquiesced, an act indicative of the weakening Spanish grip on provincial affairs. By 1680 Pueblo Indians totaled approximately 17,000 with 6,000 warriors, while the non-Indian population had reached only 2,500–3,000, including Spaniards, mixed-bloods, and Negro or mulatto servants.

*Revolt and Reconquest*

Pueblo enmity toward their oppressors culminated in a general revolt that broke out on August 10, 1680. An Indian of San Juan Pueblo, Popé, one of those flogged by Governor Treviño for witchcraft in 1675, laid the careful plans and directed the diplomacy that forged an alliance among the majority of villages. Twenty-one missionaries and some 400 colonists were slaughtered at once. Warriors from Pecos and the Tano and Tewa villages spearheaded a siege of Santa Fe that lasted nine days and ended with the flight of surviving Spaniards southward to the El Paso district. Gov. Antonio de Otermín attributed this "lamentable tragedy, such as never before happened in the world" to his own "grievous sins" (Hackett 1923-1937, 3:327), but it is clear that 80 years of misdirected policies on the part of Spanish administrators led to the bloody debacle. For the Pueblos, success of the Revolt meant a return to political and religious freedom and, in a larger sense, represented fruition of a nativistic movement—the rejection of foreign domination and the revival and reaffirmation of traditional culture. From a historical view, the Revolt delivered a severe blow to the prestige of the Spanish empire and stands as the most spectacular victory achieved by Indian arms within the present limits of the United States.

The Pueblos held firm to their independence for 12 years, but ingrained particularism and strong traditions of village autonomy led to dissolution of the unity that had crested briefly in the summer of 1680. However, the spirit of cooperation was still strong enough in the winter of 1681-1682 to turn back an attempted reconquest by Governor Otermín, who managed to sack and burn most of the Pueblos south of Cochiti. The definitive reconquest was initiated in 1692 by a new governor, Diego de Vargas. His plan to pacify the Indians, where possible by resort to peaceful persuasion, at first met with some success, largely because the Pueblos had split into warring factions among themselves. With a troop of soldiers, Vargas visited Pueblos as far north as Taos and westward to Zuni and Hopi, receiving at each at least token submission, then returned to El Paso. In 1693 he launched a more formidable invasion but found most of the Indians, except those of Pecos and some of the Keresans, newly committed to resistance. Tanos and Tewas who had settled in the ruins of Santa Fe after 1680 were forcibly expelled. A campaign was directed against hostile Tewas and their allies at San Ildefonso. The Keresans gathered at Cieneguilla on Horn Mesa were subdued and the men captured there executed. Taos was sacked, though its population escaped to the mountains. In the summer of 1694 the Jemez district was ravaged and its people forced to surrender.

The year 1695 passed in relative tranquillity as the Indians concentrated upon repairing their Pueblos and bringing in crops to replenish depleted food supplies. The Rio Grande villages lay under nominal Spanish control, but the western Pueblos of Acoma, Zuni, and Hopi remained free and a source of concern for Vargas. By year's end rumors appeared in Santa Fe and the new settlements of Bernalillo and Santa Cruz that another revolt was brewing. Reports indicated that the Apache and Navajo, cooperating with the Pueblos against the common enemy, were instrumental in constructing plans for a resumption of hostilities. In June 1696 the Northern Tiwa, the Tewa, and some Tano and Keresans rebelled, killing five missionaries and 21 settlers and soldiers. By vigorous campaigning Vargas compelled the majority to sue for peace, but some diehards refused to submit and fled to the western Pueblos or to refuge with the nomads. Spanish victory rested in large measure upon assistance given by villages that remained friendly and supplied substantial numbers of warriors as auxiliary soldiers.

The two decades of turmoil beginning in 1680 wrought profound changes in the Pueblo world. Population, on the wane before the Revolt, suffered a sharp decrease, to about 14,000, as a result of battle deaths, starvation, and enslavement of Indian prisoners sent south to be sold in the mines. The extent and magnitude of the fighting caused a permanent reduction in the number of villages, relocation of most of the remaining ones, and shift of some surviving populations to new areas. The Piro, who had remained loyal to the Spaniards in 1680 and retreated south with them, were resettled in the communities of Socorro del Sur and Senecú del Sur on the Rio Grande below El Paso (fig. 3). Governor Otermín, during his abortive reconquest of 1681, overcame Isleta and carried 385 captives downriver where they were placed in a new community near the Piro. They never returned to New Mexico, but the original Isleta was reoccupied in 1706 by scattered Tiwa who gathered there. The other Southern Tiwa Pueblo, Sandia, was abandoned upon the approach of Vargas in 1692, its inhabitants receiving asylum among the Hopi where they built a new village on Second Mesa. In 1748, 350 of these Tiwa, who had returned to the Rio Grande valley, refounded Sandia.

During the tumult the Tano in the Galisteo Basin suffered total ruin. Refugees from that district housed themselves in Santa Fe after 1680, but upon expulsion by Vargas late in 1693, some moved to temporary sites in the Santa Cruz Valley, and thence in 1696 to the Hopi country where they established Tewa Village on First Mesa. Subsequently other Tanos were resettled by the Spaniards in their old homeland, but they failed to prosper, and the last village, Galisteo, was abandoned by 1793, the handful of survivors going to the Keresan Pueblo of Santo Domingo. Many of the Pecos and Jemez sought refuge among the Plains Apache and Navajo, respectively. Some Jemez people remained with the Navajo as late as 1705. The Keresan villages also experienced severe dislocation with all but three of their Rio Grande Pueblos meeting with permanent destruction. Homeless Keresans received temporary shelter at Acoma, but about 1697 these moved northeast to a large lake and established the Pueblo of Laguna, whose formal founding dates from July 4, 1699, when submission was made to the Spanish governor.

The ravages of war also shattered the provinces of the Tewa and the Northern Tiwa above Santa Fe. In 1696 the Tewa of San Juan remained in their village, but neighboring Santa Clara was virtually untenanted as most of its inhabitants fled temporarily to the Hopi and Navajo. Smaller Pueblos in the same district, like Jacona and Cuyamungue, simply disintegrated. The people of Taos left their village briefly but reoccupied it upon assurances of pardon by Vargas. The Picuris, one of whose number, Luis Tupatú, had served as leader among the northern Pueblos, refused reconciliation and took refuge among the Apache at El Cuartelejo in western Kansas. But the Apache enslaved them and they remained in bondage until 1706 when a Spanish expedition under Juan de Ulibarrí came to escort them back to their Pueblo. The commander reported, "I brought back sixty-two persons, small and grown, of the Picuríes who were living as apostates, slaves of the devil, and as captives of the barbarity of the Apache" (Thomas 1935:21).

Another consequence of the Pueblo Revolt and reconquest was the development of serious internal factionalism within many villages. Throughout the period 1692–1696 an increasing number of Pueblos joined the Spanish in warring upon those villagers remaining hostile, and their decision to desert the Indian cause promoted much discord and bitterness. At Pecos the majority of the population adopted a pro-Spanish attitude, but in 1696, 20 dissenters fled to Acoma. Others of similar persuasion who remained in the Pueblo attempted to foment rebellion, and of these, five were executed by the village governor. Another effort to spark an uprising in 1700 was similarly crushed, and members of the hostile faction fled to the Jicarilla Apache. Another serious instance of factionalism appeared the same year among the Hopi when the Pueblo of Awatovi permitted Franciscans to resume work interrupted in 1680. The remaining Hopi towns, infuriated by this concession to the Spaniards, fell upon Awatovi, massacred its male citizens, and carried off the women and children as captives. The village was never repeopled.

In sum, the Pueblo Revolt provided the Indians a brief interlude of independence, but at enormous cost when weighed against population and territorial losses and social disruptions.

## A New Era

By the opening of the eighteenth century the Indians of the Rio Grande Valley were again firmly under Spanish sovereignty (fig. 4) and the western Pueblos of Acoma and Zuni had also offered their submission. Two decades of strife and woe had not been borne in vain, for the royal government and colonists drew grim lessons from their own disastrous experience. The encomienda system of tribute, so abrasive to the Pueblos in the pre-Revolt period, was not reestablished. The missionary program, while reintroduced (fig. 5), was tempered by a new spirit of moderation on the part of the Franciscans, whose ranks had been badly depleted. The Church in fact never regained the influence it held during the seventeenth century, partly because interest and support of the government declined and partly owing to a vastly reduced Indian population. The new generation of Spanish colonists, many of them drawn from the north Mexican provinces, soon surpassed the Pueblos in numbers, yet developed cordial relations with them. The earlier predominant large haciendas, with their constant demands for native labor, became overshadowed by the growth of small farms whose proprietors and their sons, accomplished agriculturists and stock raisers, were usually content to perform their own work. District officers, the *alcaldes mayores,* who had ruthlessly exploited the Indians during the previous century, were returned to power, but although instances of flagrant misconduct continued, the Pueblos discovered that the governors in Santa Fe listened to their complaints with greater sympathy and provided redress. By the early eighteenth century new Spanish governors as a matter of policy made a tour of

the Pueblos upon assumption of office to acquaint themselves with affairs of each village and provide residents the opportunity to present charges against alcaldes, friars, or Spanish citizens who had infringed upon their rights.

The drawing together of Pueblo and Spaniard after 1700 was facilitated by an outside threat that imperiled both. The Apache and Navajo, who had bedeviled the New Mexican frontier from 1640 onward, grew progressively troublesome toward the end of the century, but even more foreboding was the appearance along the northern border of two new enemies—the Ute and Comanche. The Comanche expanded rapidly southward, displacing the Plains Apache, and by 1725 became the principal foe of New Mexican residents. In their own defense, the Pueblos organized militia companies under war captains and joined Spanish troops in pursuit of Comanche and other raiders. The old government prohibition against providing Indian allies with firearms was gradually relaxed, and the Pueblos added guns to their arsenal of native weapons.

In the summer of 1726 Inspector General Pedro de Rivera, visiting New Mexico to examine its military defenses, commented favorably upon the performance of Pueblo auxiliary soldiers. He was impressed to learn that they readily joined campaigns when called out by the governor, that their conduct in battle was exemplary, and that for all their service to the Crown, they never submitted a bill to the royal treasury for their time or expenses. A priest, Fray Manuel de Trigo, echoed these sentiments in 1754, declaring "the mission Indians are so brave and warlike that the enemy always is defeated," and speaking of Galisteo Pueblo, "its Indians are so courageous that on the occasion of an attack . . . boys of fifteen scaled the walls, the gates being shut, so as to be able to give the enemy a warm welcome with arrows and slings" (Hackett 1923–1937, 3:465–466).

These statements suggest that the stereotype of the Pueblo Indian as nonaggressive and essentially peaceful lacks validity. In fact, the historical record furnishes ample evidence of assertive personality characteristics and warlike propensities of the Pueblos (Dozier 1970:78–80). The first Spanish explorers refer to intervillage conflict, particularly among the Piro and between

Pecos and its neighbors, that indicates war was an accepted feature of Pueblo life. Instances of Indian resistance to Spanish domination, culminating in the Revolt of 1680, as well as the Awatovi massacre by the Hopi, further aid in dispelling the image of the Pueblos as a passive and docile people. A thorough documentation of their military activity after 1700 (Jones 1966) bears out the opinions of General Rivera and Father Trigo that the Pueblo Indians were meritorious and worthy allies.

Under pressure of nomad assault, the defensive arrangement of the Indian villages was improved during the eighteenth century. The traditional terraced Pueblo structure, with removable ladders giving access to upper stories and devoid of doors and windows at ground level, was in itself a highly effective fortress. To this many Pueblos added protective walls with heavy gates, bastions, and fortified towers in imitation of defensive techniques used in the Spanish haciendas. Taos Pueblo, strengthened in this manner, became practically invulnerable to Comanche and Ute attack, with the result that nearby Spanish colonists in times of danger took up residence in the village as a safety measure.

At fixed periods during the late summer and fall, the Pueblos and surrounding tribes submitted to truces so that trading fairs might be held. The largest and best known of these was conducted in Taos with the Comanche, but lesser fairs took place at Picuris and Pecos, initially for Plains Apache and later for Comanche, and at Santa Clara, Jemez, and Acoma for the Navajo and occasional bands of Western Apache. The Piro and Southern Tiwa, who remained at El Paso after the Pueblo Revolt, also held a fair for the Mescalero Apache. During the truce periods, the nomads pitched their camps adjacent to the Pueblos and exchanged slaves, buffalo hides, buckskins, jerked meat, and horses for the agricultural and manufactured products of the villagers.

Initially the Spaniards opposed such contacts with the enemy, but a desire to share in the profits caused them to put aside their objections and enter wholeheartedly into this commerce. The royal government even extended official sanction to the Pueblo fairs in the hope that communication could be opened with the hostile nomads during the truce periods, to lead to a permanent peace. In 1723 the Taos fair was placed under the jurisdiction of

Staatsbibliothek, W. Berlin: Kart. R 9085.

Fig. 3. Map of New Mexico by Visitor General Juan Miguel Menchero, based on his tours of inspection of the province in the 1740s. Missions are indicated at 34 of the 64 entries in the key, including the Rio Grande *(Rio del Norte)* Pueblos of Santo Domingo (28), Pecos (30), Tesuque (32), San Ildefonso (33), Pojoaque (34), Nambe (35), San Juan (37), Picuris (40), Taos (41), Santa Clara (43), Cochiti (44), San Felipe (45), Santa Ana (47), Zia (48), Jemez (49), and Isleta (51); the Pueblos of Laguna (53), Acoma (54), and Zuni (55); and the resettlements at San Lorenzo (16), Senecú del Sur (17), Ysleta del Sur (18), and Socorro del Sur (19) along the lower Rio Grande. Named towns and villages include the Spanish towns of Chihuahua *(Chiguagua)* (9), Albuquerque (27), and Santa Fe (31), and the Hopi area *(Provinsia de Moqui)* settlements of Walpi *(Gualpi)* (57), Tewa Village *(Tanos)* (58), Mishongnovi *(Moxonaui)* (59), Shongopavi *(Manxopaui)* (60), Oraibi *(Oraibe)* (63); mesas occupied by the Tiwas, which they settled during and after the reconquest *(Mesas de los tiguas)* (62), and what is probably the old settlement of Shongopavi *(Pueblo Antiguo de Moxi⁺ xong⁺* 'Old Pueblo of the Xongopavi Moquis') (61). Presidios, including the presidio at El Paso *(Presidio del Paso del Norte)* (15), and privately owned haciendas and ranches (with owners identified by name) are also indicated. Map undated, probably drawn 1746 or later (based on dedication); place-names modified in caption to conform to modern usage.

*189*

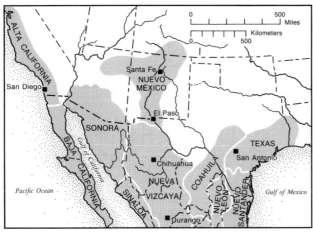

after Simmons 1968:following p. xv.

Fig. 4. Northern provinces of New Spain, originally administered by the viceroy of Nueva España. In 1776 to improve administration and defense, all these provinces except the Californias were grouped as the *Provincias Internas,* under the administration of a commandant-general. Nuevo Santander and Nuevo León were detached from the *Provincias Internas* and again placed directly under the viceroy of Nueva España in 1793. The rest remained under the commandant-general until they became part of an independent Mexico in 1821. Alta California was added to the United States in 1848 (see Henige 1970; Simmons 1968:25-32, 42-50).

the district alcalde, but when serious quarrels or brawls developed, he summoned soldiers from Santa Fe to impose order. This fair became such an important adjunct to the colonial economy that in the late eighteenth century its date was fixed in the fall to immediately precede the departure of the annual trading caravan to Chihuahua, by which New Mexico maintained its mercantile relations with the outside world.

Although some of the smaller Pueblos experienced privations after 1700, the majority began to recover a measure of prosperity. Agriculture flourished, particularly the raising of maize, wheat, and vegetables, and Santo Domingo and Cochiti regularly supplied lettuce, chili, garlic, and other garden crops to the Spanish towns. Gov. Pedro Fermín de Mendinueta (1965:16) wrote in 1773 that "the pueblos are the storehouses of all kinds of grain, especially corn. Thither come the Spanish citizens to make purchases, as well as the governor when grain is needed . . . for the troops." His description of orderly dealings with the Indians contrasts sharply with the rapacious conduct of Oñate's first colonists. The western Pueblos of Acoma, Laguna, and Zuni bred large flocks of sheep, using their wool in the production of fine blankets. The Rio Grande villagers, having abundant water available for irrigation, concentrated on raising cotton, and their textile products were bartered for goods not produced at home. Since little fencing was done, Pueblo fields suffered constant damage from untended livestock. The governor repeatedly warned Spaniards to keep cattle

and horses at least three leagues from Indian farmland, but the rule was generally violated, and court records show owners often obliged to pay damages to the Pueblos. The improved economic condition of the Indians was confirmed by Domínguez (1956), who made a thorough inspection of the province in 1776 (fig. 6), visiting the 22 Pueblos that remained north of the El Paso district.

During the last quarter of the eighteenth century, relief from nomad depredations was granted both Pueblo and Spanish citizens when four tribes—Comanche, Ute, Navajo, and Jicarilla Apache—agreed to peace. This coup was engineered by Gov. Juan Bautista de Anza (in office 1777-1787) who combined energetic military campaigning with artful diplomacy in cementing, by the late 1780s, a firm alliance with these tribes, known henceforward as the Allied Nations. This left the remaining Apache as the only enemies of New Mexico, and against them to the end of colonial times marched armies composed of Spaniards, Pueblos, and warriors of the Allied Nations. The alliance with the Comanche was the one most prized by the Spanish government and it was scrupulously maintained to 1821, the year of independence.

A frustrating problem confronting New Mexico officials in this later period was that of the reconversion of the Hopi, who, because of their isolation, had managed to remain independent since the Revolt of 1680. Frequent expeditions mounted by both missionaries and soldiers failed to bring the Indians under Spanish control, although in 1742 Fray Francisco Delgado with several companions succeeded in convincing 350 Tiwa and Hopi to leave their homes and resettle at Jemez and Isleta. At this time Delgado reported the total Hopi population to be 10,846 divided among six villages (Hackett 1923-1937, 3:31). Beginning in 1777 severe drought affected the Hopi country for several summers, occasioning widespread famine. Governor Anza informed the Indians he was willing to provide material relief and expressed the hope they would now submit to the authority of the friars. About 150 entered the New Mexican settlements, accepted Christianity, and were fed. In late summer Anza started west with food supplies. At Zuni he observed deplorable conditions as a result of the drought, most of the people having abandoned their village and moved eastward to join other Pueblos. The Hopi towns he found almost depopulated, but although the survivors readily accepted his gifts of food, they refused to bow to Spanish rule. When the rains returned, so did much of the refugee population, yet smallpox epidemics and constant warfare with the Navajo, Ute, and Apache nibbled away at Hopi numbers for another century. Periodic aid furnished by the Spaniards, much of it in the form of voluntary contributions from private citizens, did much to sustain both Hopi and Zuni in periods of extreme distress.

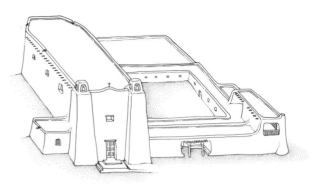

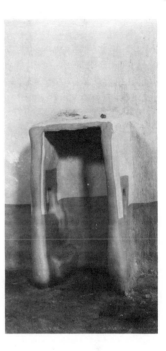

Calif. Histl. Soc., Los Angeles: Title Insurance Coll.; drawing after Domínguez 1956:191.

Fig. 5. Church and mission of St. Stephen (San Esteban) at Acoma, as it was rebuilt, probably in the 17th century. top left, Exterior view of the church and adjacent convent photographed from the southwest. top right, Diagrammatic view of the church and convent structure (baptistry on the left) as it might have appeared in the 18th century, when it was described by Domínguez (1956:188-193; for diagrammatic interior view of a similar church and mission complex at Awatovi, see "Hopi Prehistory and History to 1850," fig. 8, this vol.). bottom left, Interior view of the church, facing west toward the sanctuary: carved niche at center of first tier above altar holds a statue of St. Stephen, adobe walls are plastered and painted, floor is of dirt. bottom right, Adobe confessional at Acoma; an identical or similar confessional was noted by Domínguez (1956:191) over a century earlier. Photographs probably by G. Wharton James or C.C. Pierce in the 1890s.

## End of the Spanish Era

By 1800 the Pueblo Indians had gained a secure and comfortable place in provincial New Mexican society. Throughout the previous 50 years the number of Franciscan missionaries had declined, and those remaining at their posts performed a minimum of ecclesiastical duties in a perfunctory manner. As long as the Indians conformed superficially to a few outward practices of Christianity, the friars seldom meddled with other aspects of village life. The industry and productivity of the Pueblos lent them prestige, and their long acceptance of and cooperation with the Spanish system gave them a social position superior to that of either the *genízaros,* acculturated nomads who formed Hispanicized settlements, or members of the Allied Nations.

For more than 200 years under the Spanish regime, the Pueblo Indians were held to be of minority status, entitled to the protection of the Crown and exemption from certain tax and tithe obligations imposed upon ordinary citizenry. But in 1812 a liberal constitution promulgated in Spain provided the basis for a revision in the status of New Mexico's Indians. Article 5 of this document defined Spaniards as all free men born within Spanish dominions, the inference being that race was not a qualification for full citizenship. Further, Article 309 declared that all *pueblos* must be allowed to elect ayuntamientos or legal municipal governments. The framers of

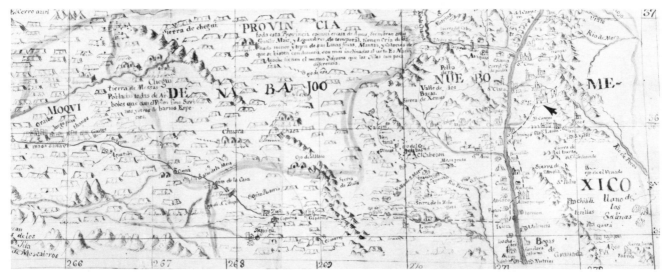

Fig. 6. Section (southeast portion) of map by Bernardo de Miera y Pacheco, the cartographer-engineer who accompanied Fray Francisco Atanasio Domínguez, Fray Silvestre Vélez de Escalante (a missionary residing at Zuni) and 7 others on an exploratory expedition through territories north, northwest, and west of the Spanish province of New Mexico, ostensibly in search of a passable overland route to Monterey, Calif. (Domínguez 1956; Bolton 1950). The thick lines define rough boundaries of tribes; narrower line (extended on basis of British Lib. Additional Ms. 17661-C) shows the route taken. The expedition started from Santa Fe (right center, see arrow) on July 29, 1776, proceeding northwest in an ultimately circular route that returned to Santa Fe from the southwest at the end of the year, passing through the area shown here: the 5 Hopi (Moqui) villages of Oraibi (Oraibe), Shongopavi (Jongopavi), Mishongnovi (Masa sanavi), Walpi (Gualpe), and Awatovi (Aguatubi), Tewa Village (Thanos), and the Pueblos of Zuni, Acoma, and Laguna. This map, one of several manuscript copies (Wheat 1957-1963, 1:94-116), is either the original or a contemporary copy of a signed and dated map drawn by Miera y Pacheco at Chihuahua in 1778. Entire map reproduced in Wheat (1957-1963, 1:opp. 108) and in color in Josephy (1961:130-131). According to a scale bar elsewhere on the map, the section reproduced is about 150 by 48 leagues (actual area about 600 by 250 km).

the constitution by *pueblo* meant simply a Spanish town, but in New Mexico Gov. Facundo Melgares in 1820 chose to interpret the law regarding the creation of municipalities as extending especially to the Pueblo Indians. Although native towns elsewhere in New Spain had long maintained ayuntamientos with mayors and councilmen, the practice had not been carried to the Indian communities of New Mexico. Since Governor Melgares understood Article 5 regarding citizenship as also applying to the Pueblos, he announced that the "minority of the Indians was ended and, henceforth, they should be regarded as Spaniards in all things, exercising especially their right to vote and to stand as candidates for office" (Simmons 1968:213). Consequently, by late 1820 most of the Pueblos had installed formal municipal governments around freely elected ayuntamientos. Thus in the year before independence and the deliverance of New Mexicans from colonial magistracy, the Pueblo Indians gained full citizenship and legal equality.

## Population

The earliest and certainly the best population figures for any Indian group within the United States recorded during colonial times are those compiled by the Spaniards for the Pueblos (see table 1). Even so, calculations made by explorers during the sixteenth century were sometimes grossly exaggerated in a deliberate bid to impress royal authorities with the importance of new discoveries. Clerical estimates in the following century were similarly inflated, especially when the friar felt that by magnifying the number of baptisms and of heathen still unconverted he could gain added support from the government. Yet because of the relative abundance of figures, cautious comparison and allowance for error permit drawing of a fairly reliable picture of Pueblo numbers.

The keeping of accurate census records was a comparatively late development of the eighteenth century, but Vetancurt (1960) speaks of a general census made in New Mexico as early as 1660. Most of the available population records were compiled by clergymen, although increasingly after 1750 censuses were assembled by civil authorities.

Miscegenation began with the first appearance of Spaniards among the Pueblos, and racial mixing was not uniformly taken into account in many census reports. If the union was a formal one sanctioned by the Church, the offspring became a part of the father's community and merged with the Hispano population, but if, as was commonly the case, the children were born out of wedlock, they might enter Pueblo society. The Spanish practice of engaging Pueblo women as servants provided abundant opportunity for mingling of the races, and the number of mestizos grew steadily throughout the colonial era. At the time of the Revolt of 1680, mixed-bloods raised in the Pueblos generally gave allegiance to the Indian cause, while those in the Spanish communities cast their lot with the colonists. Negro servants brought from New Spain by the settlers also intermarried with the Indians. Likewise the presence of Tlaxcalans, Aztecs, Tarascans, and Chichimecs from the south, again as retainers of the Spaniards, introduced still another element into the racial picture. While outsiders, whatever their origin, did occasionally win acceptance in Pueblo society, in most instances marriage beyond the village meant exclusion from community life. Within larger Spanish towns could be found a sizable number of *castas,* or mixed-bloods of varying origin, and Indians—*genízaros,* Mexican Indians, or Pueblos—who had voluntarily or under compulsion left their native villages. A 1749 census shows 570 Indians living in Santa Fe and 200 in Albuquerque (Ocaranza 1934:145-146). An undetermined portion of these were Pueblos in the process of assimilating Spanish ways.

It is apparent from observing population figures that the advent of the Spaniards in 1540 precipitated demographic disaster among the Pueblos. The greatest losses, both in population and number of villages, were sustained during the years 1650-1700, although the nadir was not reached until about 1750. The rapid decrease in villages in the early contact period was owing partially to diminution of population, but also to voluntary consolidation of Indians in larger communities for defense.

Population decline was the result of multiple causes: drought and famine, warfare with Spaniards and nomads, and epidemic disease, but the last of these was the most important. While the history of epidemics among the Pueblos lacks meticulous study, it cannot be questioned that imported diseases such as smallpox, measles, typhus, and influenza spread havoc through Indian ranks. In the terrible plague of smallpox that visited New Mexico in the years 1780-1781, 5,025 Pueblo Indians died, the heaviest losses occurring at Pecos and among the Hopi. The villagers were particularly susceptible to contagious European diseases, living crowded together in closed airless rooms and lacking any natural immunity, but the high mortality rate during all epidemics paralleled the experience of other groups in Indian America.

After 1750 a gradual recovery and increase of Pueblo population began, and steady if unspectacular growth was noted for the area as a whole until the twentieth century, when population growth accelerated.

## Sources

The literature on the early history of the Pueblos is thin. Concise overviews are provided by Dozier (1961, 1970) who was both an anthropologist and a member of Santa Clara Pueblo. Sando (1976) also treats the Pueblos in colonial times from an Indian perspective. A detailed and well-documented narrative is given by Forbes (1960), including new material on the relationship of the Pueblos and Apaches in pre-Spanish times. His work shows a strong anti-Spanish bias. Spicer (1962) provides a detailed authropologically oriented history of all Southwestern Indians from the colonial period onward.

Bandelier's documentary history (in Bandelier and Hewett 1937:115-241) was an early, and still useful, attempt to synthesize from existing Spanish materials the Pueblo story during the sixteenth century.

The first and most complete look at Pueblo culture by a European can be found in the report of Coronado's chief chronicler, Pedro de Castañeda (Winship 1896; Hammond and Rey 1940:191-283). Added material on Pueblo life and history appears in the documents related to the governorship of Juan de Oñate during the late sixteenth and early seventeenth centuries (Hammond and Rey 1953). A primary source for the early seventeenth century is Benavides's (1916, 1945) descriptions of each of the Pueblo groups and their response to the missionary program.

Several collections of translated documents offer a valuable look at conditions among the Pueblos in the eighteenth century (Thomas 1932, 1935; Hackett 1923-1937, 3).

Jones (1966) presents a thoughtful and well-researched account of Spanish and Pueblo military cooperation during the second half of the colonial period. Some understanding of Indian domestic affairs in these same years can be drawn from Domínguez's (1956) careful description of the New Mexico missions. Pino's report to the Spanish government in 1812 on reforms needed in New Mexico (Carroll and Haggard 1942) contains some reference to the state of the Pueblos at the very end of the colonial era.

*193*

# The Pueblo Revolt

JOE S. SANDO

Strange people from another world made their initial contact with the Pueblo Indian people in the year 1539. The cast of characters included the greeters, the Zuni Pueblo people of Hawikuh, and the ones being greeted, an assortment of native people from what is now Mexico. These straggly and worn-out adventurers were led by a person darker than any of the greeters and also the dark one's fellow travelers. The dark one was a Black from Azamore, Morocco, who had been in the service of the Spaniards for some time. The actual leader of this initial group of explorers was a religious, Fray Marcos de Niza. He had dispatched the Black with a few Mexican natives to go ahead to scout, when they came upon the Pueblo people for the first time. The Black was killed by the Zunis for his brazen behavior and threats during this first meeting. The friar did not make contact with the Zunis but observed from a distance. His party returned home to make a questionable report of his findings. Nevertheless, the following year another larger and well-armed party returned to verify the report of the initial explorers. Thus in 1540, the young governor of the north Mexican province of New Galicia, Francisco Vásquez de Coronado, was detailed with 230 mounted troops, 62 foot soldiers, a company of priests and assistants, and again almost 1,000 natives from Mexico, to explore and seize the new territory.

This group toured and contacted the majority of the Pueblo Indians in their villages—the first time for all of the Pueblos to see Europeans. This first meeting was not exactly cordial as the Europeans took advantage of the innocent native hospitality.

## Colonization by Spain

An assortment of smaller groups went to reconnoiter the Pueblo area until 1598, when a larger party arrived with the idea of colonizing. This initial group of colonizers was led by Juan de Oñate, son of a governor and husband of a granddaughter of Hernando Cortés, the conqueror of Mexico.

These new arrivals were guided by the principles of Francisco de Victoria and the writings of Bishop Bartolomé de las Casas (Spicer 1969:172; Wagner 1967). They were to be more apostolic and less military than their people were during the conquest of Mexico and Peru. From the very beginning the Spaniards found the

natives usually cooperative and docile, as compared to other tribes the Spaniards had encountered in the New World. As community dwellers and farmers, the natives were called *Indios de los pueblos* and recognized as peaceful and civilized, as compared to other tribes that were nomadic and whom the Spaniards called *Indios bárbaros*.

Subsequently the Spaniards attempted to dominate the patient and peaceful Pueblos by forcing their Christian religion on them and persuading the Pueblos to sacrifice their own religion, which was an integral part of their lives. The Pueblos were a people who had practiced their own religion, the way their ancestors had passed it on to them, for many centuries before the Spaniards arrived in the area. Even in the late twentieth century, the Pueblo religion is not a once-a-week activity. The various societies and the sacred priests in these societies have a commitment to pray for the world, and in order for their prayers to be answered they must fast and sacrifice. The entire year is crowded with religious activities, some of which are dances that are open to the public, while other dances are for tribal members only, and still others are seen only by the members of the societies.

It was this religious system that kept the Pueblos content and peaceful. Nevertheless, the Spaniards wanted to displace the native religion and force a new one on the Pueblos. War chiefs and war captains, who were entrusted by the Pueblo government systems with the protection of the religion, were persecuted and harassed. Some kivas in which the religiously oriented dances were performed were filled with sand and destroyed by the Spaniards.

And as if religious persecution were not enough, the Spaniards had another strange custom they imposed upon the industrious Pueblo people. From the very beginning, when only small groups arrived, the Indians had given them food when the Spaniards asked for it. Now, under their own custom, the intruders asked for set amounts of corn for the corncrib of the governor in Santa Fe, as well as for the local padre. Once a year after the harvest the ox-drawn two-wheeled cart went through the streets of the villages to collect so many fanegas of wheat or shelled corn. It was rumored that every governor who took office wasted no time in collecting or amassing a personal fortune before he was removed by the viceroy. When families did not have corn or wheat they brought wood on their backs for the padre, or worked around his household. The Spaniards called this practice *repartimiento*.

To add to the Pueblos' bewilderment, the lay government in Santa Fe constantly fought with the Franciscans over who had ultimate authority over the Pueblos and who could collect while there was something to collect. This divided the Spaniards into two camps and rocked the Pueblo country with turmoil that grew worse as the years went on and more Spaniards settled in it.

During dry or drought years the problems of the Pueblo people were doubled by the marauding nomadic tribes. With food scarce on the open plains to the east and other areas to the west and southwest, the hungry nomadic tribes launched desperate raids against the agricultural settlements. The raiding tribes made no distinction between Spanish and Pueblo Indian property.

The times were really challenging the soul and the heart of the peaceful Pueblo leaders. What was to be done? Which group presented the darkest threat? The raiders historically came during dry years, but the Spaniards were trying to take two things, the Pueblos' religion and also what the raiding tribes were after, food.

**Planning the Rebellion**

After over 80 years of frustration and fruitless efforts to compromise, some Tewa and Northern Tiwa leaders began to meet to plan for a solution. One of the planners was Popé of San Juan Pueblo. Popé is the best known of the Tewa leaders, and the Spaniards gave him all the credit for inciting and leading the revolution. Another leader was probably the war chief from San Ildefonso Pueblo, Francisco El Ollita. The Tewa area was the most closely patrolled, so the leaders began to meet secretly to discuss a possible solution, or to plan an ultimatum. In the beginning it was mostly war chiefs and war captains who met secretly.

The initial plan was to decide on the manner of approaching the Spaniards in order to exchange views on their ultimatum. As the problem grew in scope, more Pueblo men who understood the Spanish mentality were invited to participate. Thus, some of the mixed bloods and others who spoke Spanish entered the scene, among them being Domingo Naranjo, a half-Black from Santa Clara (Chavez 1967), Nicolás Jonva from San Ildefonso, and Domingo Romero from Tesuque.

And as more Pueblos joined the planning and discussion meetings, suggestions began to be cast about that they should go all-out and evict the Spaniards entirely. The men who understood and could speak some Spanish were most persistent that the Spaniards must go. Obviously they knew and understood the Spaniards' stratagems to do away with Pueblo religious practices that the Spaniards thought were a deterrent to Spanish religion.

As the plan was considered and accepted over the

larger Pueblo area, more men of stature and knowledge of the Spaniards entered the scene. These included a Taos Pueblo man called El Jaca by the Spaniards; the great leader of the Picuris, Luis Tupatu; the Tanos' spokesman, Antonio Bolsas; Cristóbal Yope of San Lázaro; Don Felipe de Ye of Pecos; Juan of Galisteo, often referred to by the Spaniards as Juan el Tano (in the same manner, Luis Tupatú was often referred to as Luis el Picurí); Alonzo Catití of Santo Domingo; Luis Cunixu or Coniju of Jemez; and of course the great leader and interpreter of the Keresans, Antonio Malacate (Espinosa 1942).

These were some of the many leaders. Tupatú of Picuris for the north and Malacate from the south were two of the important multilingual leaders. Each spoke for his tribe as well as for the grand council. Even in modern times Pueblo Indian leadership has called for unified efforts and cooperation, and a meeting is not over until everyone understands the issues and is totally aware of the decision sought. Then the council can vote with no dissenting voices.

Meetings were held after midnight in the homes of the war chiefs, usually on the feast days of the patron saint of a particular village. This way the Pueblo leaders could come to a fiesta, join with some of the Spanish during the day at the fiesta, and stay late for the meeting. The delegates generally left before the break of dawn, and no one ever saw them as they traveled on foot, trotting all the way home.

As the time approached, at one of the secret meetings, two young men from Tesuque were detailed to take a message to the participating villages so all would act in unison on the same day. The two were Nicolás Catua and Pedro Omtua.

By then the plan had been carefully worked out. First, they would cut off the capital, Santa Fe, from the outlying Spanish settlements and farms, thus leaving these without leadership and, therefore, easy to overcome. Second, the other messengers from the planning group would send word to the settlements south of Santa Fe that the capital had fallen, and to the settlements north of Santa Fe that the Pueblo people were in control of the south. This would confuse the Spaniards and weaken their confidence. They would post guards along the trails to keep the Spaniards from sending for help, escaping, or communicating with each other.

The third element of this ingenious plan was the timing. Every three years a caravan came from the far south to replenish the Spaniards' supplies. If the people hit just before the caravan was due, the Spaniards would be low on weapons, horses, and ammunition with which to fend off the attack. This particular year, unknown to the Spaniards but predicted by both Popé and Malacate, the caravan was to be late due to adverse weather conditions. This gave the people time to plan and execute the uprising very carefully.

## The Revolt

As careful as the planners had been, word of the two messengers reached the Spanish governor, Antonio de Otermín, in Santa Fe. Consequently, the governor dispatched his *maestro de campo,* Francisco Gómez Robledo to Tesuque, where they arrested the two messengers. The youths were taken to Santa Fe and brought before the governor for interrogation and imprisonment.

By the evening of the day of the arrest, August 9, the fact became generally known throughout the Pueblo country. Tension became high. It was so high that a Spaniard, Cristóbal de Herrera, was killed at Tesuque, the home of the two messengers. As a result, that evening, Padre Juan Pío, the resident padre of Tesuque, decided to go to Santa Fe overnight for his safety.

The following morning, August 10, Padre Pío, in the company of a soldier named Pedro Hidalgo, started out for Tesuque to say mass for his people. When they reached Tesuque they found it deserted. Eventually Padre Pío found the Indians in the hills a short way from the village. The men were all armed with bows and arrows, lances, and shields; they had red paint on their faces. Padre Pío approached them and asked, "What is this, children; are you mad? Do not disturb yourselves; I will help you and die a thousand deaths for you" (Hackett 1942, 1:6). He then asked them to return to the village where he might say mass for them. The padre entered a ravine to meet with the main body of men who were armed. Meanwhile, the soldier, Hidalgo, was stationed on a knoll to intercept any who might pass that way. While waiting there Hidalgo saw the man known to be the war chief of Tesuque come out of the ravine with a shield that the padre had carried. Also a little later he saw the interpreter of the village, named Nicolás, come out of the same place bespattered with blood, which looked different from the red paint on his face. Other men then approached the soldier and caught his horse by the bridle. They took his sword and hat away. But fearing injury or death, the soldier spurred his horse and was able to escape. He even dragged for some distance those who held onto him. Many arrows were shot at him but with no effect. He returned to Santa Fe safely.

Thus began perhaps the most successful revolt by natives of the New World. The pent-up hatred for the Spanish soldiery, suppressed for so long throughout the Pueblos, was released; loosed by the unfortunate capture of the two young messengers from Tesuque it was being generated throughout Río Arriba, the land of the Tewas. Soon it was to reach the rest of the Pueblos.

The agreement was to inform the Spaniards, both clergy and laymen, that they must leave. And if they refused to abide by the orders of the people and their leaders, then they must suffer the consequences. Of particular interest to the Pueblo leaders were three Spaniards who had been harassing ceremonial leaders,

war chiefs, and war captains. One was the secretary to Governor Otermín, Francisco Xavier, and the others were his two henchmen, Diego López Sombrano and Luis de Quintana.

Once the news of the beginning of the struggle reached each of the Pueblos, the action was similar. The padres were ordered to leave, but the most dedicated ones who had hoped to remain to save souls refused to leave and were martyred. In all, 21 of the 33 Franciscan friars in the territory were killed. With them, some 400 of the more stubborn Spaniards also were killed.

Hence the prophecy of Fray Juan de Escalona of nearly a decade earlier had come true. During the time when Juan de Oñate was collecting volunteers and preparing for the initial colonization, at a convent in the frontier of Nueva Vizcaya, during the angelus a few religious fell on their knees. After short prayers most of them arose, except for one who remained on his knees and appeared to be in a trance, and he was heard to murmur a few words in Latin. The other religious asked the friar why he said what he did. The Friar would not reveal his vision. Finally they agreed to ask his father confessor to question him in the confines of the confessional. Even there the friar refused to reveal his reasons unless he was promised that nothing would be said until he was gone from this world. The priest to whom the friar went to confess finally convinced him to tell. The friar said:

> I will tell you, my dear Father, that yesterday afternoon, when we were praying the Ave Maria, God our Lord revealed to me all the riches and world possessions that he is keeping in the interior land (of New Mexico) to the north. It was also revealed to me that some religious of my father, Saint Francis, are to explore it. And as the first ones who will enter there, they are to be martyred. These religious appeared before me and I saw them being martyred in spirit, and because I was joyful to see them suffer martyrdom with so much spirit and courage, I said, "Beati primi, Beati primi."
>
> It was also revealed to me that when this happens, and after the land is sprinkled with the blood of these martyrs, the Spaniards will go in there to enjoy the many riches that are there (Zárate Salmerón 1966:99).

Despite much written by Spanish chroniclers and Anglo romanticists, it is questionable that the otherwise peace-loving Pueblo Indians sprang the revolt with outright killing as the prime motive. It has been emphasized that the Pueblos' reasons were to rid themselves of the Spaniards due to the repartimiento system and the forcing on them of a new religion while the indigenous one was suppressed. Thus their hope was to have the Spaniards depart from the Pueblo country, and only if they refused to leave would they be killed. So, from most areas the Spaniards left to go to Isleta Pueblo, where Lt. Gov. Alonso García was waiting for the newly dispossessed Spaniards.

Meanwhile, in Santa Fe, Governor Otermín chose to

battle the native emancipators. Frightened Spanish families rode into Santa Fe from the outlying districts to report their shocks and tragedies. After the Pueblo warriors completed their mission in their home areas, they concentrated on the forces of Governor Otermín. Knowing the power of the Spanish arms, the Pueblos could not storm the Spanish citadel. But, knowing that the Spanish and their animals had to have water, the Pueblos concentrated on cutting off the source of their water supply, the stream of the Agua Fría as it is called today.

Once the Pueblos accomplished this feat, Governor Otermín was placed in the position of having to order his people to leave. Hence, on August 21, the Spaniards began an exodus to the south. If the Pueblos had been warlike, they could have attacked helpless, thirsty, and bedraggled Spaniards. But as their purpose appeared to become a reality, the Pueblos only observed the Spaniards moving out. And once the Spaniards were gone, every object and relic of the Spanish era was destroyed.

Subsequently, with the hated Spaniards gone, the leadership of the conquering Pueblos and the warriors assembled to say prayers and to give thanks to the Twin War Gods, who are known by different terms in each of the Pueblo languages. The leaders in their prayers told the supreme deity their reasons for the recent action. They also reminded the warriors that, after arriving home, as a priority, they must go to the river the next morning before sunrise to cleanse their minds and bodies symbolically and practically, before they could return to normal life with their families.

## Sources

Hackett (1942:xix-liii, chapters 1-3) is the principal source on the Pueblo Revolt. Other useful references include Hackett (1923-1937, 3), Espinosa (1942), and Vargas Zapata Luxán y Ponze de Léon (1914). This chapter has also used Pueblo oral traditions collected by Joe S. Sando in 1970.

# Genízaros

FRAY ANGELICO CHAVEZ

## Definition

*Genízaro* was a specialized ethnic term current in New Mexico during the eighteenth and early nineteenth centuries. It was used by the local Hispanic folk to designate North American Indians of mixed tribal derivation living among them in Spanish fashion—that is, having Spanish surnames from their former masters, Christian names through baptism in the Roman Catholic faith, speaking a simple form of Spanish, and living together in special communities or sprinkled among the Hispanic towns and ranchos.

Fray Agustín Morfi, referring to the *genízaros* of Analco in Santa Fe in 1779, gave a precise and correct definition of them: "This name is given to the children of the captives of different [Indian] nations who have married in the province" (Thomas 1932:92). Yet, many writers have wrongly translated the word as 'half-breed', which is more applicable to *mestizo,* meaning a mixture of Indian and non-Indian. Morfi was careful to say "nations" instead of "races." With the ultimate amalgamation of the New Mexico *genízaros* into Pueblo Indian life and into the lower social or economic strata of the Hispanic population, the term disappeared in common usage, to be found only in the civil and ecclesiastical documentation of the times. (Still, in the early twentieth century, a Hispanic father would playfully call his child, if he or she happened to be extra swarthy, his little *genízaro* or *genízara.*)

The derivation of the term itself has been obscure but is not insoluble. Also used for aboriginal mixtures in the rest of Spanish America, it there varied in its applications. Sometimes it was synonymous with *mestizo,* as when Carlos de Sigüenza y Góngora in 1692 stated that Gov. Diego de Vargas employed a *genízaro* as a guide and also had rescued many *mestizos* and *genízaros* during his reconquest of New Mexico in that same year (Sigüenza y Góngora 1932:18). This author blended the two terms, for most of the people he referred to were an admixture of Indian and Spanish, and even African in some cases (Vargas Zapata y Luxán Ponze de Léon 1940:143-144, 184-185; Chavez 1954:5, 50, 53-54, 64, 66, 68, 81, 170-171, 1957a:180-181, 1967:95-111).

Actually, the use of the word *genízaro* as an ethnic term goes further back, to Spain, where it first designated a Spaniard having foreign European blood, like French or Italian or Greek. It is now generally spelled *jenízaro,* and its primary meaning has come to be 'one begotten by parents of different nations', or 'composed of different species'. It is derived ultimately from Turkish *yeniçeri,* 'select guard', 'janissary', a term applied to auxiliary troops.

This older meaning misled early and succeeding historians to state that the New Mexico *genízaros* were thus called because they served as auxiliaries to the Spanish militia. Thomas (1940), for example, wrote that the *genízaros* were Indian captives sold to the Spaniards by the Comanches and "were under the obligation to explore and pursue frontier enemies." Then he says in a footnote, quoting his previous book, that Morfi had another definition, the one cited above (Thomas 1940:18ff.). Thomas was more or less correct in the first part of his statement, but the second part is his own assumption; in fact, the Morfi definition is the only correct one—a purely ethnic designation with no military connotations when it was first applied to the *genízaros* of New Mexico.

It is true that much later, in widely scattered instances, small groups of *genízaros* were martially employed, as in the example that Thomas cites, and a few other occasions in the years 1777, 1800, 1808, and 1809 (Twitchell 1914, 1:258, 413, 526, 539); but this was decades after the ethnic designation had been firmly established. Throughout the Spanish colonial period, 1598-1820, the indigenous auxiliary troops were composed of Pueblo Indians under their own village chiefs. At one period, 1700-1720, all the Pueblo auxiliary forces did have a single designated leader, the noted José López Naranjo, who was of Negroid, Hispanic, and Tlaxcalan ancestry (Chavez 1967:95-114). Naranjo certainly did not fit the term *genízaro* as this was accepted by Morfi and his contemporaries and confirmed by extensive documentary evidence.

## Origin

The *genízaros* of New Mexico had their origin in women and children, and rarely male adults, of Plains Indian nations who had been captured in intertribal raids, and whose captors then sold them to the Spanish inhabitants of the Rio Grande Valley. Spaniards "ransomed" them with the alleged pious purpose of rearing them as Christians, which did not exclude the more mundane motive of acquiring unpaid household servants and herders for their livestock. Some also were captured by the Spanish militia during a retaliatory campaign, but these were in the minority during the first century. Whatever the manner of their acquisition, the mixed progeny of these people lost their tribal identity, customs, and language after having been reared in a Hispanic milieu. American writers have referred to this practice as a form of slavery, which it was in a broad sense, except that it was benevolent and the servitude lasted only into early adulthood, usually at marriage time. The children of such mixed unions, the actual *genízaros,* were born free. Naturally, because of the strictly limited pastoral economy of a backward and completely isolated region, a goodly number of these people did continue in peonage to their former owners, but this happened also with the poorer Hispanic folk with regard to their own *patrones.* There was no other employment to speak of. So many were the free *genízaros* leading a shiftless and poverty-stricken existence before the mid-1700s that the colonial authorities tried to remedy the situation by gathering them into villages with grants of land and livestock.

In church registers of baptism and marriage as well as in civil papers the original ransomed captives were designated by tribal origin as Kiowa *(Caigua),* Pawnee *(Panana),* Ute *(Yuta),* Apache *(Apache),* Comanche *(Cumanche),* and so forth. Occasionally they might be called *genízaros* as a whole, but this was in association with their mixed progeny to whom the term properly belonged. For these latter were a new people, even if genuinely Indian, who were generated from diversified Indian parents; since they neither spoke the language nor observed the tribal customs of either parent but followed the local Hispanic life patterns—and yet were not Spanish, *mestizo,* or Pueblo Indian—the word was ready-made for them. Hence the former practice of rendering *genízaro* as half-breed is historically as well as ethnically unsound.

For as long as this type of intermarriage and procreation continued, the designation persisted for those concerned. But if any individual *genízaros* married into resident Pueblo families, they and their progeny were considered Pueblo Indians thereafter. If any intermarried within the lower scale of Hispanic folk, or if a *genízaro* girl had a natural child by a European, their children and further descendants were variously designated as *coyotes, lobos, mestizos,* and *mulatos,* depending on the registrar's fancy as to their degree of racial admixture.

The use of *genízaro* and the other ethnic designations was more or less strictly observed during the Spanish colonial period. In the year following Mexico's independence from Spain, the Mexican democratic Plan of Iguala of 1822 decreed that all peoples in the future, of whatsoever racial origin or admixture, were to be designated in both civil and church documents only as *"Ciudadanos Mexicanos"*—Mexican citizens pure and simple. This order was punctiliously carried out in official papers, and it helped end the use of the term *genízaro* among the Spanish-speaking people of New Mexico. Likewise, as a people, the *genízaros* themselves were absorbed either into the Indian Pueblos or into the newly created status of universal Mexican citizenship among the Spanish-speaking folk.

What has been said thus far may be gathered from a thorough perusal of the extant church and civil records of the period, available in film at the State Record Center and Archives in Santa Fe. There the smaller number of civil references may be found by means of the index in Twitchell's (1914) calendar. References in the loose documents of the church archives have been indexed (Chavez 1957); but the hundreds of references within their bound mission registers of baptisms, marriages, and burials must be sought out page by page. No previous in-depth study had been made on the subject, chiefly because the *genízaros* had been thought to be part of the general run of mixed breeds and not a distinct body of true Native Americans, even though they were of mixed tribal origin and no longer observed tribal ways.

## Some Statistics

Contemporary with Morfi's happy definition of *genízaros,* the first overall statistics on them were compiled in the famous report of his Franciscan confrere, Fray Francisco Atanasio Domínguez (1956:42, 119-126, 208). In 1776 there were three main *genízaro* settlements (fig. 1): Analco in Santa Fe with 42 families and 297 persons; Abiquiú (Tewa *ávéšúʔ*) to the north with 46 families and 136 persons (the small number of persons could be an error); and Los Jarales to the south, near Belén, with 49 families and 209 persons. Just north of Santa Clara Pueblo there were also nine families living among some scattered Hispanic ranchos. Domínguez did not mention that other families and individuals were employed as household servants and livestock herders in the many other settlements and ranchos throughout the region, but the mission registers give ample testimony to the fact.

Previous to this, *genízaros* had been stationed at the posts of Valencia and Cerro de Tomé since 1740 (Thomas 1940:18), but these could well have been transferred by Domínguez's time to Los Jarales just across the Rio Grande. It is to be noted also that the *genízaros* of Analco in Santa Fe were moved as a body to the new military post of San Miguel del Vado around the years 1794-1798, and they also founded the nearby town of San José del Vado. Occasional Comanches joined them at these two places, and perhaps also some of the last survivors of Pecos Pueblo; gradually Hispanic people moved in also (Chavez 1957:68-69, 74, 205, 232.) Since these were buffer towns next to a military post on the Comanche frontier, it could be said that the *genízaro* male inhabitants were employed as auxiliary troops whenever the need arose; in fact, they must have been settled there for

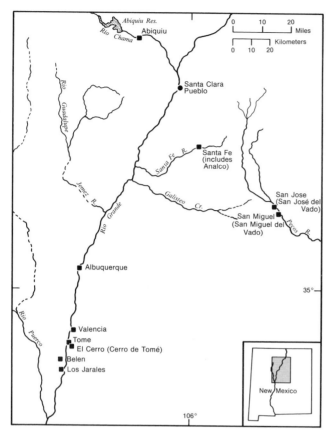

Fig. 1. *Genízaro* area.

the purpose. But their ethnic designation had been established long, long before.

While the New Mexico *genízaros,* like most of the other common folk, whether Hispanic or Indian, remain nameless in published historical annals, there was one individual who did make a name for himself in the region's colorful history as the only "Indian governor of New Mexico." He was José Gonzales, who led a successful but short-lived revolt against Mexican rule in 1837 (Chavez 1955). And once in a while there is a record of a "Mexican" joining some Plains Indian tribe and there becoming a noted war chief; no doubt he was either an Indian boy old enough when captured and ransomed to have remembered his people or else a true *genízaro* who, having learned of his tribal origin from either of his parents, felt the pull of ancestral ties strongly enough to make him seek out his father's or his mother's people.

During the short Mexican period of New Mexico, 1821–1846, which preceded the American occupation, there was a very serious flare-up of mutual retaliatory raids between the Hispanic (Mexican) people of the Rio Grande Valley and the Apache, Navajo, and Ute nations surrounding them. On the Mexican side, women and children were impounded and hispanicized, as had happened with the ransomed ones of other tribes in former times. But the term *genízaro* no longer appears in the records as a rule, thanks to the Plan of Iguala of 1822. At baptism they were still designated as Indian "servants," or "captured" and "bought" Indians, and sometimes the tribe was mentioned. But within a relatively short time, those who were assimilated along with the former *genízaros* into the Spanish-speaking community, whether through some Hispanic intermarriage or none at all, became "Mexicans."

On the other hand, the ones who were integrated with the Pueblo communities became Indians of their particular adopted Pueblo. For the Plan of Iguala had failed to make the tag of "Mexican citizens" stick to the centuries-old and firmly fixed identities of the various types of Pueblo Indians and their respective communities.

# Relations of the Southwest with the Plains and Great Basin

CHARLES H. LANGE

This chapter focuses upon the three centuries between 1540 and 1850, beginning with accounts from the time of initial Spanish explorations and continuing on into records of the early years of American influence, emphasizing interaction and interrelationships between Southwestern tribes and those of the Plains and Great Basin.

With the advent of the first explorations, significant European influence, represented by Spanish, French, Mexican, or American people and policies, clearly became an increasingly important ingredient in many tribal cultures of the area. Source materials, in fact, have come almost exclusively from the records, notes, and observations of these European-American representatives—civil officials, military personnel, traders, missionaries, settlers, and others. Firsthand native insights have been virtually nonexistent regarding these three centuries, even though European influence may often be viewed as having been filtered through one Indian culture in the process of reaching that of yet another tribe.

Richness and reliability of information vary with both time and place, reflecting the interests of the writers, their attitudes toward the tribes, and, reciprocally, the amount of contact tolerated by the tribes. The greatest amount of information (sketchy as it is) concerns various Puebloan tribes and their relations with Plains tribes. Relations between the Hopi Pueblos and either the Plains or Basin tribes and, similarly, relations between non-Puebloan Southwesterners and peoples of the Plains or Basin have not been so well documented (for detailed discussions, see Schroeder 1968, 1972).

A considerable body of evidence from archeological investigations affirms longstanding contacts or relations between Puebloan tribes and those to the east and north. Such materials range through the historic period and extend well back into Puebloan and other forms of prehistoric cultures.

From the time of the first Spaniards in the area, the Puebloan tribes demonstrated appreciable knowledge of adjacent regions, especially to the northeast and east, and of the tribes who lived there. Contacts and interaction between Puebloan peoples and the more nomadic Plains tribes appear to have been well established at the time of European arrival in the northern Rio Grande area. Wedel (1959:19-98, 536-641) in his synthesis of Kansas archeology and culture history has provided a valuable summary and appraisal, critically evaluating the numerous contributions of archeologists, historians, and ethnohistorians (including Bolton 1916; Champe 1949; D. Gunnerson 1956; Gunnerson 1956, 1960; Hammond and Rey 1940; Kidder 1932, 1958; Krieger 1946, 1947; Scholes and Mera 1940; Thomas 1935; Winship 1896). There have been subsequent archeological discussions on Apachean aspects of the problem of Plains-Southwest relations (Gunnerson 1969; Gunnerson and Gunnerson 1970), and Brugge (1965) has presented documentation of Plains Indians in Spanish missions.

A summary of the archeological evidence (Jennings 1956:114-115) noted that "eastward contacts with or across the Plains appear to have increased markedly after 1300, at least for the Rio Grande pueblos," although

> Comparatively few actual Plains traits were accepted and incorporated in the Southwest culture . . . and trade pottery rather than acculturation from the Southwest is found in the Plains in most cases (Krieger 1946; Wendorf 1953a). The stone and bone artifacts of Plains types from Pecos (Krieger 1946:62) could well represent actual presence of visitors from eastward, camping and trading, rather than "influence" on the Pueblo, and Southwestern artifacts in the Plains mark the passage of Pueblo hunting parties as well as trade. . . . To the north, and even in the San Juan, the record is missing for this period—a gap (no doubt more apparent than real) of almost five centuries between the archaeological complexes and the historic tribes.

In using data from historical and ethnohistorical sources unresolved problems persist in establishing tribal identities and delineating the Southwestern culture area at given points in time. The Puebloans, their several villages, and their adjacent lands present no great quandary insofar as recognition and chronology are concerned; however, for their nomadic, or at least less sedentary, neighbors, the situation is frequently less clear.

It appears sufficient to assume that on the eastern and northern Puebloan peripheries were various Apache bands and tribes (Carlanas, Cuartelejos, Faraones, Jicarillas, Lipans, Palomas, Vaqueros), the Comanches, the Kiowas, the Utes and Southern Paiutes, and the Navajos. Assignment of at least some of these groups, if not all, to the Southwest, to the Plains, or to the Basin, depends very much on the time horizon under consideration. The Puebloan tribes retained distinctive qualities and continued to be recognized as such even in outposts beyond the core area, which extended from the Hopi towns in the west, through Zuni, Acoma, and Laguna, to the Rio Grande villages, from Taos in the northeast, Pecos in the middle, and on to the Saline Pueblos in the southeast.

Since the arrival of the Spaniards in the Southwest, the non-Puebloans, in contrast, moved in and out of the Puebloan area, hovered along its fringes, and periodically swung away, often to more distant regions as hunting, gathering, and trading opportunities changed. This non-sedentary, fluid pattern of life, at times approaching Taylor's (1964) "tethered nomadism," often resulted in recurring contacts that, over a period of time, cumulatively enhanced the chances for intercultural exchanges.

When Francisco Vásquez de Coronado left the Eastern Pueblo villages and ventured eastward into the Plains in 1541 he found the Indians there were friendly. But this initial situation changed: as the Spanish occupied New Mexico they became involved in the old antagonism between raiders from the Plains and the Pueblo settlements then within the colonial periphery. The Plains Indians and the Apaches, used to attacking the Pueblos for food, could add to their take the Spanish-introduced grains, cattle, sheep, pigs, chickens, and especially the horses that were quickly adopted for use in war and buffalo hunting and as prestige items (Thomas 1940:1).

With the establishment in the seventeenth and eighteenth centuries of Spanish settlements in the Puebloan region, trade with the Plains tribes was encouraged by the governors and alcaldes. Perhaps of special importance was the annual summer fair at Taos; Pecos and Picuris likewise were important points of contact between the Pueblos and the Plains Indians. In addition to the items listed above, buffalo hides, antelope and deer skins, meat, tallow, and salt were offered in return for Puebloan

Smithsonian, NAA.
Fig. 1. Apache men photographed at Taos in 1871, while visiting the Pueblo during the Feast of San Geronimo. (See "Taos Pueblo," fig. 3 top, this vol. for Taos woman photographed on the same occasion.) Photographs by Orloff R. Westmann, Sept. 30, 1871.

cotton blankets, pottery, maize, breadstuff, and turquoise; and Indian and Spanish prisoners were exchanged and ransomed. From European and Mexican origins came a variety of hardware (axes, hoes, awls, arrow and spear heads, and assorted knives), glass beads, gunpowder, and firearms. These fairs and trading sessions, while valuable to the Spaniards and their Puebloan charges, often had a debilitating effect on the Spanish missionary effort and on their general control, or influence, in the region (Thomas 1940; Kelly 1941:171–183; Bandelier 1890–1892; Hackett 1923–1937; Espinosa 1942:368).

As early as 1598 some of the Tompiro Pueblos east of the Manzano Mountains were called Humanas by the Spaniards because Jumano Indians from the Plains traded there (see "Pueblos Abandoned in Historic Times," this vol.). Jumano hunters and traders are mentioned between 1623 and 1629 as living east of the Tompiro Pueblo now known as Gran Quivira on the margin of buffalo country, and as trading not only with the eastern Tompiro Pueblos but also in 1629 visiting Tesuque near Albuquerque and settling temporarily near Gran Quivira (Kelley 1955:991). The abandonment between 1672 and 1675 of these Pueblos east of the Manzano Mountains, such as Abó and others of the so-called Saline Pueblos and missions, has been attributed to attacks by the Apaches and Comanches and to fear of such attacks (J.H. Toulouse 1949:1). However, there is said to be no historical evidence for Comanche harassment of the New Mexico missions until the eighteenth century, although earlier Apache depredations are certain (Brew and Montgomery 1951:328). In addition to the hostilities, drought and epidemics seem to have persuaded the Tompiro or Saline Pueblos to join their kinsmen in the more protected Rio Grande valley (Walter 1931:23).

In the eighteenth century competition between the Spanish and the French inevitably enmeshed tribes of the southern Plains. In the middle 1700s the French actively supplied the Comanches with firearms and encouraged their hostilities against the Spanish and their Puebloan allies. Their activities became an increasing problem as Comanches gathered strength and pushed the Apaches into more intensive confrontations with the Puebloans and the Spaniards (Espinosa 1942:369). Bernardo de Gálvez in the late 1700s issued instructions to his Spanish frontier authorities to increase the trade of firearms and powder to the Comanches, a sharp reversal in traditional Spanish policy. He intended thereby to retain the friendship of these Indians and to increase their dependence upon the Spaniards. By involving them increasingly in a degree of technology that they could not maintain at their native level, and at the same time weakening their efficacy with the bow and arrow, Gálvez saw a means of reducing the threat of the Comanches and other Plains tribes. His policy was only partially successful (Gálvez 1951:5-8, 22-24, 47-49).

Between 1727 and 1786, the Comanches and Utes fought continually except for brief, localized truces. It was during this period that the Jicarillas, moving or pushed westward, ceased to serve as a buffer between the two tribes. The Utes then formed an alliance with the Spaniards against the Comanches, but in 1786 the Spaniards made a separate peace with the Comanches. Consequently, the Utes and Jicarillas entered into an alliance against the Comanches and Kiowas. Thomas (1940:29-30) gave an earlier date, about 1750, for this alliance. On the Plains the Comanches held the advantage, but in the hills and mountains the advantage went to the Apaches (Wallace and Hoebel 1952:286-291; see also Forbes 1960).

During the mid-eighteenth century the Comanches vacillated between war and peace with the New Mexicans as prospective rewards of raiding or trading were perceived to be more advantageous at any given moment. Jones (1962:86-97) traced the shift that occurred prior to and following the 1786 treaty concerning Comanche relations with the New Mexico Spaniards and Puebloan tribes. From the earlier state of rather constant hostilities, the Spaniards successfully recruited Comanches to serve alongside the Puebloans and the new allies—Utes, Navajos, and Jicarillas—as auxiliaries against the Gila Apaches. Of four "divisions" of 84-86 Indian auxiliaries, the 1st Division listed 30 mounted Comanches out of a total of 85.

The New Mexico Spaniards also realized the strategic value of the Comanches as a barrier between themselves and the French and Indian allies such as the Pawnee; accordingly, they were inclined to defer to the Comanches rather than risk offending them. In the late 1700s this resulted in the Comanches directing their hostilities toward the south—against the Spaniards, Mexicans, and Texans. In the south, despite the policy announced by Gálvez, the Spanish authorities of Texas were quite reluctant to trade guns and ammunition with hostile Indians. Consequently, the Comanches raided Texas and even into Mexico for horses and other items that could be traded to the New Mexicans for guns, ammunition, and other desired goods. Again, traffic in prisoners and captives, Spanish and Indian, was an important aspect of this trade (see L.R. Bailey 1966).

For more than a century, up to about 1875, an important ingredient in Southwest-Plains trading relations was the activity of a sizable group who came to be known as the Comancheros. They have been characterized as being primarily of two groups; one consisted of indigent and rough elements of the frontier villages and the second, the Pueblo Indians. As time passed the group acquired a generally unsavory reputation; their valuable knowledge and proven ability to deal effectively with the Comanches and other hostile Indians were often compro-

mised by their known and alleged duplicity and lack of commonly recognized moral and ethical standards. Kenner (1969) has provided an extensive treatment of the Comancheros, who were effective in procuring or retrieving stolen cattle and other property and also in the handling of slaves, captives, and prisoners.

The repeated references to prisoner exchanges, bartering of slaves, extended periods of captivity, and various forms of adoption all suggest a considerable opportunity for admixtures of the populations involved. The physical features of numerous northern Pueblo Indians, such as those of Taos and some of the Tewas, show distinctive qualities that are much more basic than the superficial Plains traits in costuming and hair styling. Plains genetic contributions are certain; however, the calculation of degree or amount is highly tenuous at best.

At Cochiti Pueblo there was an elderly woman in the late 1940s who was the daughter of a Comanche woman who had been raised by a Spanish family in that Pueblo. She had married into the Cochiti tribe and had gained both clan and moiety affiliations; her daughter and other children had become fully accepted Cochitis (Lange 1959:513). Bandelier (1890-1892, 1:262-263) noted several such instances from various Pueblos. Stating that Jemez was more than half Navajo, he claimed one of the leading men, "whom unsophisticated American Indian-worshippers are wont to admire as a typical and genuine Pueblo, the famous Nazlé, was Navajo by birth, education, and inclination." Toya, the well-known Pecos chief, was identified by Bandelier as "a full-blooded Comanche." He added: "Such mixtures should be taken into

Smithsonian, NAA.

Fig. 2. Casemiro Tafoya, a San Ildefonso man dressed in Plains-style beaded buckskin shirt, leggings and moccasins, and wearing hair braided in Plains fashion. Trappings for the horse are also reminiscent of the Plains. Photograph by Adam C. Vroman at San Ildefonso, 1899.

203

account by anthropological investigators. They have had their influence upon language, and, in a certain sense, upon customs." Bandelier also observed that the Tewa "Sar-it-ye Jia-re, or dance of the French" was of Kiowa origin while the eagle dance performed at Santa Clara was borrowed from the Utes of Colorado.

Another example of contacts between Pueblo and Plains Indians was found somewhat unexpectedly by Bourke (1892) in the Hopi villages, most remote from the Plains tribes, where he was told of a sizable group of Comanche traders who had remained two years on First Mesa, at Walpi. At a Hopi snake dance in 1881 he saw a possible Ute buffalo robe. The Rio Grande Pueblos also told him of regular trading visits to the Staked Plains where they exchanged cornmeal for buffalo hides and meat; he understood that these relationships had been extant at least as early as 1598, the date of Juan de Oñate's arrival in the northern Rio Grande. Actually, a report from the Coronado expedition of 1540–1541 provides evidence for trade between the Apaches and Picuris even that early (Hammond and Rey 1940:292–293).

Citing Vetancurt for the period between 1630 and 1680, Bourke (1892:529–530) noted that the Apaches came into Pecos with "dog trains," packing the barter of "more than five hundred traders arriving each year." Eickemeyer and Eickemeyer (1895:45) at San Ildefonso

in the 1890s met a young man, well traveled among the Pueblos, who had spent a year with the Utes and still followed the Ute manner of dress, including the parted and braided hair style.

Dozier (1958:443) commented upon small-group dances that were supervised by secret societies but that the Pueblos opened to the public:

These consist primarily of animal and war dances, and preparations and costuming take place in society houses or in the home of the society leader. The dances and accompanying songs are frequently similar to those of the Plains Indians. Both Pueblo and Plains Indians have animal and war dances and the two groups have long been in contact, so it is reasonable that considerable similarities are apparent. It would be erroneous, however, to claim a Plains provenience for these dances, for concepts of animal fertility and warfare ceremonies appear old among the Rio Grande Pueblo Indians. One might argue with equal probability that influences went from the Pueblos to the Plains.

Particular similarities between the Pawnee and the Pueblos have been noted. The Pawnee, who had traditions of once living in the Southwest, had four Corn groups (as does Isleta), a Mother Corn (like the Keresan Iyatiko), and divided their sacred bundle groups into summer and winter moieties (a parallel to the Eastern Pueblo system) (Underhill 1954:650–651). Parsons

Smithsonian, NAA.

Fig. 3. Zuni pack train, such as might have been used for a trading expedition. The people are carrying burdens of goods wrapped in Pueblo blankets, and the burros are also laden with goods (including, or just wrapped in, blankets) and gourds that probably contain water for their journey. Photograph by John K. Hillers, 1879.

204

Smithsonian, NAA.

Fig. 4. Arikara Buffalo dancers, members of the Buffalo order of the Medicine Fraternity dancing in a 1908 reenactment of a Medicine ceremony. They wear buffalo headdresses and perform dance steps that imitate the animal's movements (Curtis 1907-1930, 5:64, 70-76). For dance impersonations of buffalo and other animals among the Pueblos, see "San Ildefonso Pueblo," figs. 10-12, "San Juan Pueblo," figs. 6-7, and "Tesuque Pueblo," fig. 6, all this vol. Photograph by Edward S. Curtis, Beaver Creek, Fort Berthold Reservation, N.D.

(1929a, 1933a, 1939, 2:1029-1037) discussed Pawnee-Southwest-Mexican ties, concluding that the Plains and Pueblo tribes shared an appreciable number of cultural traits and patterns with other areas of western North America.

The broad distribution of such similarities across the Pueblos, Plains, and Great Basin has long been noted (Spinden 1912:155; Underhill 1954:651). The presence of such similarities specifically between the Eastern Pueblos and the adjacent Plains must be interpreted in this context (Lange 1953b, 1957a). While there was an appreciable amount of contact between the Pueblo tribes and their eastern and northern neighbors of the Plains and Great Basin respectively (particularly the Plains), extending over a long span of historic and prehistoric times, these contacts must be viewed as repeated examples of diffusion and cultural influence, often reciprocal, but nonetheless falling short of the intensity associated with valid instances of acculturation between, or among, the several cultures of the Plains and Basin tribes.

This general situation remained little, if any, changed through the decades of the nineteenth century under the government of the United States.

# History of the Pueblos Since 1821

MARC SIMMONS

## The Pueblos Under the Mexican Republic

With the independence of Mexico in 1821, the Pueblo Indians became subjects of a national regime that was to govern their affairs for 25 years. Some trends evident in Pueblo-Spanish relations during colonial times continued and were intensified while others were reversed. The Indians no longer shouted *Viva!* at public celebrations for the king, nor was his paternalistic and remotely benevolent image replaced by any of the inept and colorless figures who occupied in rapid succession the Mexican presidency. Under the new order the office of provincial governor was filled, with only a few exceptions, by native New Mexicans. Colonial governors invariably had been outsiders and usually members of Spain's New World aristocracy, possessed of education and endowed with an aloofness that allowed a measure of impartiality in their administration, but withal deficient in understanding and knowledge of local affairs. Because of endemic turmoil in the national capital, Mexican governors in Santa Fe ruled their province with minimal interference, so that when they were men of sound character, the Pueblos and neighboring tribes received justice, but when they were not, the Indians fared badly and had little recourse to higher authority.

The Treaty of Córdoba, consummating Mexican independence and proclaimed on August 24, 1821, guaranteed racial equality, preservation of private property, and personal rights. By it all Indians were granted Mexican citizenship and protection of lands held under the Spanish regime. But little was done in years following to implement specific legislation to safeguard Indian rights and ensure equitable treatment. In the absence of detailed laws or even guidelines from Mexico City, governors in Santa Fe generally followed custom and precedent established by colonial predecessors in dealing with the Pueblos, although on the whole they evinced less direct concern.

With the opening of the Mexican period, Pueblo population totaled 9,034 (4,498 male, 4,536 female), exclusive of the Hopi and the largely acculturated Piro-Tiwa settlements in the vicinity of El Paso (Bloom 1913–1914:28). The number of villages subordinate to provincial authority was 20. The Hopi, although within the territorial jurisdiction of New Mexico, continued their isolationism and remained free from Mexican sovereignty. In fact ruling officials, beset by other problems, showed no interest in their activities or welfare.

During Independence Day festivities celebrated annually after 1821, Pueblos surrounding Santa Fe sent contingents of dancers to participate in the commemorative events. For the Indians the change in government meant relief from outside interference, both in their religious practices and in management of village affairs, so that the shift from presumptuous Spanish paternalism to indifferent Mexican neglect was greeted with genuine enthusiasm.

At the beginning of 1822, 20 missionaries were serving New Mexico, the majority of them resident in Pueblo missions. Ten years later only five remained among the Indians. In the interval the Franciscan Order had failed to fill vacancies created by retirements or deaths, and mission establishments had been closed. Friars who remained attempted to minister to neighboring villages, but, spread so thin, their labors were ineffectual. In 1830, for example, Father Sánchez Vergara from his seat at Cochiti attended the missions of Santo Domingo, Jemez, and Zia, the circle of his ministry necessitating periodic trips of almost 100 miles. Bishop José Antonio de Zubiría of Durango, whose jurisdiction included New Mexico, inspected the condition of the Church during an official visitation in 1833 and found the state of the missionary program, from his view, deplorable. Mission structures everywhere were shabby and in despair, vessels and vestments were worn out, and the friars were unable or unwilling to enforce ecclesiastical discipline so that many Pueblos had relapsed into idolatry.

Rather than simply reverting to ancient religious practice, as Bishop Zubiría interpreted it, the Pueblos by the decade of the 1830s had begun to relax policies of secrecy and present publicly rituals that had continued, hidden but uninterrupted, throughout the period of Spanish censure. Once again ceremonies were given in the plazas and open to observation by non-Indians, making clear that the rich and active religious life of the Pueblos, far from having been extirpated, retained a vital and pervasive role in native culture.

Actual civil administration of the Pueblos was scarcely affected by transfer of rule from Spain to Mexico. The elective municipal councils or ayuntamientos, introduced in the waning years of the colonial era, disappeared from many Pueblos after 1821, and even where they continued at places such as Jemez, Cochiti, Sandia, San Juan, Isleta, and Laguna, they displayed little vitality. This experiment in liberal home rule ended in 1837 with abolition of all municipal councils in New Mexico and establishment of the prefecture system that divided the province into administrative districts governed by appointed prefects.

These changes in no way influenced internal Pueblo government, the caciques and *gobernadorcillos* continuing to exercise their functions along traditional patterns. Trader Josiah Gregg, who observed Indian custom during these years, noted that as in times past the Pueblos selected from among the elders their *gobernadorcillos* who traveled to Santa Fe to be confirmed by the Mexican governor. Of the cacique he wrote: "When any public business is to be transacted, he collects together the principal chiefs of the Pueblo in an estufa, or cell, usually underground, and there lays before them the subjects of debate, which are generally settled by the opinion of the majority. No Mexican is admitted to these councils, nor do the subjects of discussion ever transpire beyond the precincts of the cavern [kiva]. The council has also charge of the interior police and tranquility of the village" (Gregg 1954:190).

In one important area the new Mexican regime proved detrimental to Pueblo welfare—that of protection of Indian land and water rights. Grants of land conceded to the Pueblos by the Spanish Crown were still recognized, but their preservation from encroachment by non-Indians had always been dependent upon the willingness of government officials in Santa Fe to support the villagers' title. Not only were the laws of the republic much less strict in their guarantees to the Indians, but also an expanding Mexican population put greater pressure on available farmland and with growing frequency trespassed on Pueblo grants. More and more the Indians were drawn into litigation in an effort to preserve their claims, a circumstance that persisted well into the Anglo period.

The land problems of the Pueblo of Laguna were representative of those suffered by other Pueblos during the interval of Mexican administration. Encroachment by Spanish-speaking settlers upon Indian domain had begun in late colonial times but increased during the years following independence. In 1826 a delegation of Lagunas composed of the *gobernadorcillo,* cacique, and war captain appeared in Santa Fe, confronted Gov. Antonio Narbona with grant papers, and asked that he confirm their holdings and exclude trespassers. Convinced of the justice of this request, Narbona wrote at the bottom of their petition: "Let it be done as is asked, returning all to the interested parties for their use and convenience" (Jenkins 1961:60). However, in less than a year, the Lagunas returned with additional complaints against the settlers, but a new governor, Manuel Armijo, cared little for Indian justice and took no action. The district alcalde, Marcos Baca, was one of the principal offenders appropriating Laguna land, and when the Indians received no aid from Santa Fe in curbing his abuses, they sent one of their tribesmen to Mexico City in 1830 with instructions to hire a lawyer and prosecute their case. Shortly afterward Baca either resigned or was removed from office.

Other Pueblos experienced similar difficulties, particularly Taos, which fought for exclusive rights over the waters of the Rio Lucero needed to irrigate its cultivated fields. The same village lost some of its sacred mountain land in 1843 when Governor Armijo granted a huge tract to two Mexican citizens over protests of the Indians.

Another consequence of independence that served to the disadvantage of the Pueblos was the disintegration of the once fruitful alliance between New Mexico and the four Allied Nations—Comanche, Ute, Navajo, and Jicarilla Apache. The friendship of these nomad tribes, carefully cultivated during the final 50 years of Spanish administration, had been possible only because of the maintenance of a well-coordinated and consistent Indian policy. The last colonial governors treated the allies with scrupulous rectitude and cemented their amity with liberal distribution of rations and gifts. After 1821 neither the funds nor the will remained to preserve the loose bonds of this alliance, and the fidelity of the nomads was lost. The Navajo, growing and gaining new muscle as warriors, posed a particularly ominous threat to both Mexican settlements and Pueblos. Gregg (1954) asserts that the root of difficulties lay in the faithlessness of the provincial government. In one instance it summoned a delegation of Navajo chiefs to Cochiti, ostensibly to discuss peace terms, then permitted irate New Mexicans, who had suffered in recent raids, to massacre them (Gregg 1954:99). Also promoting discord were slaving raids carried out by Mexican citizens against isolated Navajo rancherias. Although slaving was illegal, the authorities seldom intervened, and the vicious practice invited indiscriminate retribution upon both Spanish and Pueblo communities.

In late summer of 1837 a tumultuous political upheaval with strong social overtones shook the foundations of New Mexican civil government and demonstrated how closely the Pueblos had come to share common interests with the poorer segment of the Hispano population. In 1835 Col. Albino Pérez of the Mexican army was appointed governor of New Mexico, his selection coming at a time when a trend toward centralist rule was developing in the national capital. Arrogant and brassy in manner, Pérez allied himself with a handful of the social elite in Santa Fe and let it be known that Mexico City, henceforward, would exercise more direct control over provincial affairs. When a rumor spread in August 1837 that direct taxes, heretofore unknown, would soon be imposed upon local produce, resentment flared among the rural folk. Discontent in the Santa Cruz Valley north of Santa Fe exploded into open rebellion, and Governor Pérez with a small force of his supporters and a few Pueblo militiamen hastened out to restore order. Misjudging the strength of his opposition, he fought a brief engagement near San Ildefonso Pueblo on August 8. Here most of the Indian militia deserted to the rebels, and the remainder of the army was routed and retreated to the capital.

Although the insurgent movement was composed largely of Hispano poor, Indians of San Juan, San Felipe, Santo Domingo, and Cochiti joined and contributed warriors. When Pérez attempted to flee Santa Fe, he was overtaken by Santo Domingos, captured, and decapitated. Approximately 2,000 of the rebel force, including many Pueblos, set up camp on the outskirts of the city and elected one of their number, José González, as the new governor. González, son of an acculturated Plains Indian *(genízaro)* and a Taos mother, possessed qualities of leadership and probity but was untutored in the realities of Mexican politics, as his abortive effort to establish government on a popular base soon demonstrated. Invitations to send representatives to a People's Assembly were dispatched to all village leaders, Hispano and Pueblo alike. González's message to the *gobernadorcillo* of Cochiti, asking him to attend the assembly and report on conditions among his people, concluded with the words: "Let us as compatriots and good Mexicans purify our native land so that we can live in peace and quiet" (Reno 1965:205).

When the Assembly convened with Pueblo delegations in attendance, action was taken on only one substantive matter. A commission was appointed to go to Mexico City and present assurances of loyalty and a summary of grievances that had inspired the revolution. González specifically asked the Pueblos to offer their views to the emissaries going to the capital so they might be represented. But even as these measures to secure a popular government went forward, a counterrevolution took form in the settlements south of Albuquerque.

Ex-governor Manuel Armijo, an opportunist and man of slight principle, marshaled support among the landed gentry of the Rio Abajo and marched north to quell the uprising. He warned the Pueblo Indians to take no part in the struggle and suggested they govern themselves until reestablishment of an administration sanctioned by the Mexican government. In the face of Armijo's advance, the insurgent movement crumbled, and in a skirmish near Santa Cruz on January 8, 1838, González was captured and subsequently executed. His pleas of loyalty and appeals for reform had gone unnoticed in Mexico City, and Armijo, who had taken pains to exaggerate the dimensions of his own patriotism, was confirmed as the new civil and military governor. Although members of several Pueblos in the vicinity of Santa Fe did participate in events surrounding the revolution, effects on village life were minimal. However, the affair showed that the Indians held strong resentment for corrupt and highhanded practices of the provincial government and that a potential for violence persisted.

Instances of friction between Mexican and Pueblo notwithstanding, interests of the two peoples continued to converge during the quarter-century the Republic of Mexico held possession of the Southwest. Throughout the period, formally enrolled militia units commanded by native officers could be found in practically all Pueblos, the Indians continuing the practice begun under the Spanish system of contributing auxiliary soldiers to regular provincial forces. Expeditions against hostile Apache or Navajo counted heavily upon such support; a campaign against the Navajo in 1839, for example, included a contingent of 71 San Juans and 55 Santa Claras. When troop escorts were organized to protect merchant caravans from attack by Plains Indians along the Santa Fe Trail, Pueblos provided a share of the men. Maj. Bennet Riley encountered such a force on the Trail in 1829 and observed that "the Pueblo auxiliaries from Taos were probably the bravest and most efficient fighting men in the Mexican escort" (Young 1952:149).

## The American Period

With the outbreak of the Mexican War in 1846, Gen. Stephen Watts Kearny and his Army of the West occupied New Mexico in a virtually bloodless conquest. The Pueblos, content to offer formal allegiance to whomever filled the governor's chair in Santa Fe, sent their *gobernadorcillos* and other officers to the capital to have them reconfirmed and to announce adherence to the new powers. Lt. W.H. Emory, one of Kearny's officers, recorded that

> Their interview was long and interesting. They narrated what is a tradition with them, that the white man would come from the far east and release them from the bonds and shackles which the Spaniards had imposed, not in the name, but in a worse form than slavery. They and the numerous half-breeds are our fast friends now and forever. Three hundred years of oppression and injustice have failed to extinguish in this race the recollection that they were once the peaceable and inoffensive masters of the country (U.S. Army. Corps of Topographical Engineers 1951:58).

Emory's reference to the Pueblos as "fast friends now and forever" was not only premature, but in one instance, that of Taos, grossly misplaced. Soon after creating the semblance of a civil administration, with prominent Santa Fe trader Charles Bent as governor, General Kearny marched west to participate in the conquest of California, leaving a token force to garrison New Mexico. In January 1847 a mixed mob of Pueblos and Mexicans massacred and scalped Governor Bent and several municipal officials in Taos. Kearny's successor, Gen. Sterling Price, led troops northward from Santa Fe and surrounded the rebels, who took refuge in the Taos Pueblo church. After heavy fighting and sustaining great loss of life, the Indians surrendered. Their war chieftain, Tomasito, was captured wearing a shirt of the late Governor Bent; shortly after being imprisoned he was killed by a guard. Other leaders, mainly Mexican, were tried and executed. This rebellion, as that of 1837, united certain discontented elements among the Pueblo and Mexican population and led to a brief but bloody assault on established authority. As motive for their actions, the Taos rebels made vague appeals to patriotism, but the tragic outburst appears to have been rooted more in local problems and frustrations growing out of land grant and other conflicts of long standing.

When Anglo-Americans assumed control of the Southwest, they discovered in the upper Rio Grande Valley two distinct village culture types: one, an archaic Spanish rural culture, heavily overlaid with Indian elements; the other, the Pueblo, preserving the underpinnings of its indigenous culture, yet showing to a significant degree the assimilation of Hispanic folkways. This situation required an adjustment in Anglo thinking, which then was firmly attached to stereotypes drawn from contact with Indians in the eastern United States and the Mississippi Valley. Already formed was the policy of isolating Indians on government reservations so that Anglo expansion might proceed unimpeded in remaining areas. Wholly foreign was the idea underlying Spanish and Mexican administration of the Indians—that the native people when ready should be incorporated as full citizens and allowed unrestricted participation in provincial life. Almost at once those responsible for Indian affairs in New Mexico realized that relations with the Pueblos would have to be founded, not upon any civilizing mission, but rather upon a program of government protection that extended them aid in maintaining their self-sufficiency and peaceful habits.

In April 1849 James S. Calhoun was appointed first Indian agent in New Mexico, his jurisdiction encompassing some 40,000 members of the Pueblos and Apache, Navajo, and Ute tribes. His initial task was to convince Washington officials that sharp distinction should be made between the relatively advanced village Indians and the often hostile nomads. He drew attention to Mexican law under which the Pueblos had been recognized as citizens and expressed the belief that they were entitled "to the early and special consideration of the government of the United States." In reporting to the commissioner of Indian affairs, he wrote: "They are the only tribe in perfect amity with the government, and are an industrious, agricultural, and pastoral people. . . . These Indians are anxious to have schools established among them and to receive agricultural information, which if granted on a liberal scale, could not fail to produce marked and beneficial results" (Keleher 1952:44–45).

Calhoun worked diligently for confirmation of Pueblo property rights and urged that Pueblos be extended the voting privilege. Their eligibility to participate in elections at this time was a subject of much confusion, as was the entire spectacle of New Mexican politics. Since 1846 the province had been under military administration, but in 1850 a convention of citizens met in Santa Fe, agreed to apply for statehood, and framed a constitution. A majority of the Hispano population favored admission as a state since this course promised home rule through exercise of the ballot. They were opposed by a minority party composed mainly of recent Anglo immigrants who hoped to see New Mexico organized as a territory with all official appointments made by Washington. After much acrimonious public debate, the proposed state constitution came up for ratification in June 1850 and was overwhelmingly accepted by the people. Before the election military governor Col. John Monroe had issued a proclamation allowing the Pueblos to cast votes, as a result of which the Indians suffered much badgering from both the statehood and territorial parties. Unscrupulous individuals cajoled and intimidated in an effort to win ballots, while some Indians were threatened with loss of their possessions if they voted at all. In the end the constitutional election was without meaning since Congress ignored it and created a territorial government for New Mexico. Shortly afterward the Pueblos were formally denied the right to vote, but their brief participation in the new political structure had already soured them on the democratic process.

Soon after assuming his duties as Indian agent, Calhoun received delegations from the western Pueblos, including the Hopi, who came to learn of the policies and views of the new government. Already there had been friction growing out of unwarranted demands made by California gold seekers on Pueblo larders, and Calhoun was seriously disturbed by the litany of outrages recounted by the emissaries. In one instance a party of emigrants kidnapped the governor of Laguna when he refused to give them sheep and carried him tied to the Pueblo of Zuni.

The delegations also complained bitterly of the depredations of the Navajo and pleaded for adequate military protection. From the beginning of Anglo occupation of New Mexico, firm promises had been made to both Pueblos and Hispanos to guard them against the damaging inroads of hostile tribes; however, the harsh realities of frontier warfare prevented ready fulfillment of this commitment. The civil population was strictly prohibited from taking reprisals against enemy raiders as had often happened in Spanish and Mexican times, for now the government wished to exert close supervision over all military activity. The Pueblos continued their practice of supplying auxiliary soldiers for campaign duty; and as early as 1849, 55 Indians from the villages of Santo Domingo, Santa Ana, Zia, and Jemez joined a major expedition against the Navajo. Until defeat of the nomads later in the nineteenth century, Pueblos held the war problem to be of overriding concern.

In the area of land grants, Agent Calhoun's advocacy on behalf of the Indians bore fruit. The commissioner of Indian affairs in his report for 1850 warned that intervention of the government was imperative to secure the Pueblos "against violations of their rights of person and property by unprincipled white men, from whose cupidity and lawlessness they are continually subject to grievous annoyances and oppression" (Keleher 1952:75–76). The Pueblos were particularly vulnerable to encroachment upon their agricultural tracts, even more so than during the Mexican period, as land-hungry settlers moved into the Rio Grande Valley. Fortunately original Indian grants were confirmed by the territorial government in 1854 and reaffirmed by the United States Supreme Court in the 1890s; nevertheless, the Pueblos were forced to exercise constant vigilance to exclude squatters. The duty of the federal government to actively intervene on behalf of Pueblo Indian land claims was not recognized until 1913.

In the years following 1850 Anglo officials made little effort to intrude upon Pueblo internal affairs, although village problems were frequently brought to the attention of the Indian agent in Santa Fe by the Indians themselves, who recognized him as heir to the paternal authority formerly wielded by Spanish and Mexican governors. Entries in the journal of John Griener, Calhoun's successor, indicate the nature of some of the external annoyances affecting village life:

April 16, 1852. Four Santa Clara Indians today came to complain that their water was being taken by a Mr. Rudolph, an American, who is settling upon pueblo lands.

April 17. Santa Clara Indians went home today. Told them I would be at the pueblo on Tuesday next to settle claims to the water between them and Rudolph.

May 15. Pueblo Indians came in today to complain that the Mexicans were taking the water from the acequias [ditches] of San Ildefonso near the pueblo. Told them to pursue the same course they always used to do before an agent was appointed for them, which was to drive the Mexicans away. [They] appeared satisfied.

Learned today from Mr. Rudolph that he had given up the piece of land belonging to Santa Clara Pueblo. Also learned from Rudolph that some of the mischievous Mexicans around Pojoaque were trying to excite the Indians by telling them that the Americans were sending more troops here for the purpose of destroying the pueblos. Wrote a letter to the governor of Pojoaque requesting to see him on this business.

May 17. The governor of Pojoaque . . . came in and said that the Mexicans had told that the Americans were sending troops to this country for the purpose of destroying the pueblos, he had inquired into the matter and placed but little confidence in the report.

After advising him to come here whenever he heard such report in future and learn the truth, I paid him for his trouble in coming and he went away satisfied (Abel 1916:209).

Until the late 1870s official Anglo attention was riveted upon military campaigns being waged against marauding plains and desert tribes, so that Pueblo interests received only peripheral notice. Management of Indian affairs, transferred from the War Department to the Department of the Interior in 1849, was in the hands of civilians who not only lacked coherent policy to guide them but also faced repeated conflicts with the military establishment over methods for subjugation of hostile groups and policing of new reservations. Occasionally special inspectors were sent to New Mexico Territory to gather firsthand information for the Bureau of Indian Affairs, but even when their recommendations were beneficently formulated, little could be done to rectify the harm caused by uninterested or dishonest agents, corrupt territorial officials, thieving supply contractors, and arrogant, land-hungry settlers.

In March 1870 Interior Secretary Jack D. Cox named William F. Arny, a knowledgeable and unprejudiced service officer, as "Special Agent for the Indians of New Mexico" with instructions to visit every Pueblo, take a census, examine land titles, and investigate the need for schools. In fulfilling this directive, Arny, motivated by a healthy bias in favor of the Indians, prepared a series of thorough reports containing precise and accurate statistics and laying stress on fundamental problems with suggestions for their alleviation. During his tour of the Pueblos he observed firsthand the critical need for formal education and emphasized the desire for it among the Indians. At Santa Clara the people had engaged a teacher at their own expense, with the result that 11 children could read and write a little Spanish. But if government assistance could be obtained they offered to donate land for a school and build a residence for the teacher. Elsewhere the agent found almost total illiteracy to be the rule. At Picuris, "not an Indian can read or write in this village." At Taos, "not one can read and write. They want a school for 159 children winter and summer." At Santo Domingo, "this pueblo last winter had a school of 36 scholars, a native Indian teacher who taught in Spanish." At Santa Ana, "one person can read and write. Have had no school." At Jemez, "they want a school and will do all they can to have their children taught to read and write" (Arny 1967).

Everywhere Arny found hordes of outsiders, mostly Hispanos, residing on Pueblo grants. Many had been ensconced there for long periods, and the Indians seemed willing to allow them to remain providing the government aided in preventing further trespass. In village councils Arny learned that some Pueblos had not seen an agent for 10 years and that official neglect was the rule. The Zuni spoke of sending a delegation to Santa Fe to seek assistance that returned empty-handed. They told him that because they did not steal, the government refused to give them anything, but if they stole like the Navajo they would get something.

Unfortunately proposals submitted by Agent Arny for an improved policy toward the Pueblos were shelved by the Indian Bureau. Incompetent and venal officials and perennial insufficiency of funds precluded, at least for the moment, effective assault on the massive problem of illiteracy, resolution of the land problem, or offers of technological assistance.

## Acculturation and Change in the Pueblo World

Throughout the second half of the nineteenth century, the Pueblo lifeway underwent modifications as it absorbed elements of expanding Anglo-American culture. Beginning in 1821 with development of the Santa Fe trade, manufactured goods from the United States flooded New Mexican markets, influencing the tastes and habits of Hispano and Indian alike. Expanding freight business after 1846 increased the flow of tools, household articles, and foodstuffs so that by the coming of the railroad in 1880, the Pueblos were dependent upon numerous American-made products. In some cases the manufacture of native goods was almost totally displaced. Weaving, for example, with the exception of belts and sashes, died out among the eastern Pueblos who had ready access to cheap cotton and woolen cloth, but the

Pueblo One—Indian Arts, Scottsdale, Ariz.

Fig. 1. Pueblo women, possibly from Acoma, displaying their wares (large pottery water jars and a coiled basket containing smaller pottery items) at one of the stations along the Atchison, Topeka, and Santa Fe Railway line, about 1900. Photographer unknown.

craft survived among the Hopi who remained isolated from the principal commercial centers ("Hopi Economy and Subsistence," fig. 6, this vol.). Pottery making declined in importance with the spread of inexpensive metal, crockery, and china containers but did not disappear, since New Mexicans preferred native wares in some culinary practices.

Architectural innovations became evident as new building materials and tools were accepted by the Indians. Milled lumber and iron hardware appeared in Pueblo doors, and panes of glass replaced small mica panels that served as windows in colonial times. As the threat of war receded, both doors and windows were opened at ground level in village structures; heretofore security had required that the only entry be through a hole in the roof from the second story (fig. 2). Imposition of peace also allowed some dispersal of population, since it became safe for individual farmers and their families to reside permanently near distant fields, returning to the main Pueblo only on ceremonial occasions. The majority of the inhabitants of Santa Ana eventually moved to irrigable lands along the Rio Grande, leaving the Pueblo to elderly caretakers, while dispersal of a growing Laguna population resulted in establishment of seven satellite villages.

By 1880 the military arm of Pueblo organization that had defended the village against nomad invaders was no longer needed and began to wither away. Participation of Pueblos as auxiliary soldiers had steadily declined after 1850 since United States cavalry units shouldered the burden of final campaigns against the Apache (fig. 3), Navajo, Comanche, and Ute. As late as 1872, a party of hunters from San Juan Pueblo seeking buffalo on the plains beat off an attack by 300 hostile Kiowas, probably the last major engagement fought by any Tewas. The office of war captain, present in all villages except those of the Hopi (who apparently never accepted the Spanish-imposed duties), was not abolished, but its duties rapidly changed to assume religious or civil functions. New responsibilities of this official varied but included maintenance of kivas, guarding dances in progress, assuming charge of ceremonial hunts, announcing religious events, and recruiting labor for communal projects (Aberle 1948:39).

As Anglo influence became more pervasive and signs of disintegration of Indian culture appeared, the Pueblos hastened to define boundaries of their traditional lifestyle by way of preserving it from total erosion. In the process many Spanish elements, since they were rooted in the past, not only persisted but also were identified as part of the Pueblo cultural framework (fig. 4). In dress the Spanish rebozo equated with the Indian woman's shawl, the serape with the Indian robe, and Pueblo men clung tenaciously to loose cotton trousers split at the ankles, the common garment of the Mexican peon ("Isleta Pueblo," fig. 3, "Santa Clara Pueblo," fig. 10, this vol.). Even in the

Fig. 2. Row of houses at Laguna, showing old method of access (ladders leading to second stories) and newer method (doors at ground level). The ladders could be withdrawn in the event of attack. Photographer unknown, photograph undated (possibly taken about 1900).

1970s many Rio Grande Pueblos conserve these same articles of clothing, especially on ceremonial occasions, as manifestations of "native" raiment.

Even the Catholic Church, so long the foe of Indian religion, emerged as a bulwark against the aggressive inroads of Protestant missionaries. Instances are recorded of Pueblo leaders denouncing as traitors to the Indian way those few villagers who succumbed to the blandishments of non-Catholic ministers. Amalgamation of Spanish religious practice with traditional ceremonies, already well underway, was speeded by the appearance of these alien pressures. All villages except those of the western Zuni and Hopi showed and still show a mingling of Pueblo and Spanish religious elements on Catholic feast days (see "Acoma Pueblo," fig. 16, this vol.), while

performance of the Matachine Dance ("The Mythological Triangle: Poseyemu, Montezuma, and Jesus in the Pueblos," fig. 2, this vol.), the Horse Dance, and Jemez Corn Dance reveal explicit examples of syncretism in Indian ritual.

## Protestantism: The New Missionaries

In 1850 the Bishop of Durango, Mexico, José Antonio de Zubiría, exercised ecclesiastical jurisdiction over New Mexico even though the territory had been under the political control of the United States since 1846. In mid-century he made a final inspection tour of the upper Rio Grande churches and missions, exhorting Hispanos and Pueblos to remain loyal to the faith even while the quality

left, Mus. of N.M., Santa Fe; right, Austin N. Leiby, Scottsdale, Ariz.

Fig. 3. Laguna's response to the Apache campaigns of the 1880s. left, Call to arms during an Apache scare, at the residence of the governor, Aug. 1881. right, Troop F, one of 4 units of Company I, the Third Batallion of the New Mexico Volunteer militia, a cavalry unit composed almost entirely of Pueblo Indians (Leiby 1973:217), in 1882. Under the command of Walter G. Marmon (far right), an Anglo who married a Laguna woman and took up residence there (see "Laguna Pueblo," this vol.), the "Marmon Batallion" was mustered in response to the danger posed by marauding Apaches. Photographs by Ben Wittick (left) and unidentified photographer (right).

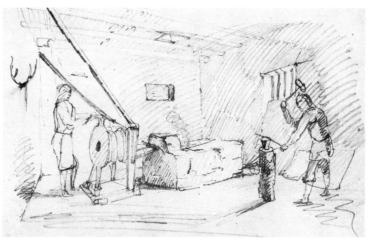

Fig. 4. Spanish-style blacksmithing at Zuni Pueblo, 1851, possibly by Mexican smiths living at Zuni (Simmons 1973). left, Detail sketches showing Spanish-style "concertina" bellows (a double-bellows with each side operated by one hand), and "block" anvil (probably locally made of wrought iron) with no horn. right, Sketch of shop showing arrangement of anvil, bellows, and forge (constructed of adobe bricks lined with stones), with an opening above the forge to allow the smoke to escape. Sketches by Richard H. Kern, cartographer and artist for the Sitgreaves Expedition, which was at Zuni Sept. 1–24, 1851. These undated sketches, presumably drawn at that time, were evidently the basis for the lithograph entitled "Indian Blacksmith Shop (Pueblo Zuni)" published by Sitgreaves (1853:pl. 5). Sketches in private collection.

of local ministry continued to decline. Shortly afterward the New Mexico Territory was elevated to episcopal rank and in 1851 French-born John Baptist Lamy arrived in Santa Fe to assume office as New Mexico's first resident bishop. His formal entry into the capital was attended by elaborate ceremony and wild displays of horsemanship by some of the 8,000 Pueblos who gathered to greet him. One of Lamy's assistants recorded that in the background "filled with rage and envy were four Protestant missionaries who had been losing their time for the past two or three years among the Mexicans of Santa Fé" (Howlett 1908:166).

Bishop Lamy found ecclesiastical discipline among clergy and laity almost nonexistent, and the apostolic spirit, which had sustained the church during colonial times, wholly gone. When he instituted a program of reform, some priests quit and departed for Mexico, but he was able to recruit replacements in 1854 from France. Although he acknowledged 9,000 Catholic Pueblos, Lamy gave them only minimal attention, concentrating his zeal instead upon the Spanish-speaking population in urban centers. The few priests who ministered to Indian villages were hamstrung by lack of funds and by their inability to interest the bishop in the problems of remote missions. As late as the end of the century when the church counted a Catholic membership of 18,000 Indians, mostly Pueblos, only two day schools and two boarding schools were maintained for the native population.

Protestant missionaries of several denominations entered the Southwest soon after American occupation, but for the first several years they made practically no converts among Hispano Catholics or Indians. In 1852 a Baptist preacher, Samuel Gorman, settled at Laguna Pueblo, won some respectful listeners, but found no parents willing to send children to the school he opened. He was followed by the Reverend John Menaul, a Presbyterian, whose efforts at education met with more success. Menaul obtained a printing press and produced a reader in both English and his own version of the Laguna language. Later, Presbyterians expanded their work with establishment of a mission school at Zuni, but in 1871 there were only 11 representatives of Protestant churches serving in New Mexico. Among the Hopis of northern Arizona, Mormon missionaries led by Jacob Hamlin began proselyting in the 1860s, yet within six years they gave up in despair, their success no greater than that of the colonial Franciscans.

Beginning in 1869 the Indian Bureau initiated a policy of encouraging religious denominations to found schools on Indian reservations. Nevertheless, not until the 1890s did churches enter the Pueblo field to a significant degree. By 1915 eight Christian sects had set up schools, limited medical facilities, and charity programs. The Christian Reformed Church, which had supplanted the Presbyterians at Zuni, sponsored the translation of prayers and hymns into the native language, but other denominations evinced little or no interest in adjusting their traditional approach to Indian speech or custom. In fact Protestant indoctrination after 1900 was characterized by growing intolerance and by vituperative sermons that condemned out of hand Pueblo religion and much social practice. Assuming an uncompromising attitude, ministers insisted that new converts reject entirely all participation in native rites and spared no opportunity to disparage ceremonial dances. This assault on the traditional fabric of Pueblo life complemented the policy pursued by administrators in the Indian Bureau who saw their mission as one of speeding assimilation by imposing upon their untutored charges the regenerative fruits of civilization. The nurturing of Christian sectarianism among the Pueblos thus appeared as a useful device for promoting dissolution of their close-knit communities.

After World War I older denominations somewhat tempered the militancy of their approach and placed greater emphasis on social and medical services. But this trend toward moderation was offset by the entry of new evangelical Protestant sects that, with asperity of voice, preached no compromise with Indian religion. Both the attitude of the missionaries and the inhospitable nature of the culture they represented stiffened resistance among traditionalist elements within the Pueblos, but serious cleavages also occurred as individuals or small groups occasionally yielded to Protestant entreaties. Yet no major conquests were made by the missionaries, nor did there emerge any noticeable fusion of the old religion with the new as had happened with Roman Catholicism.

## Legal Status and the Land Problem

Difficulties surrounding preservation of Pueblo Indian lands increased toward the twilight of the nineteenth century as instances of encroachment upon village soil arose with alarming frequency. Under obligations imposed by the Treaty of Guadalupe Hidalgo ending the Mexican War, Congress confirmed 35 distinct Spanish grants made to the Pueblos, totaling 700,000 acres. These grants, since they were not then reservations in the accepted sense, were considered by territorial officials to be disposable property and subject to purchase by non-Indians. This position was upheld by local courts in a series of decisions between 1848 and 1876 under the assumption that the Pueblos, not being "tribal" Indians and hence not wards of the government, were excluded from protection by the federal Indian department. Further weight to this view was added by a decision of the United States Supreme Court in 1876 (*United States* v. *Joseph*), which declared that the Pueblos had complete title to their lands, could dispose of them at will, and that in effect federal Indian laws were not applicable to them. This decision clearly threw the Pueblos on their own meager defenses and opened the way for spoliation of their proprietary holdings.

Throughout, the Indian Bureau and government attorneys resisted this interpretation of Pueblo status and sought to have Pueblos included under existing protective legislation. Then in 1913 in *United States* v. *Sandoval* the Supreme Court reversed its 1876 decision, claiming that it had been based on "opinions of the territorial court, . . . which are at variance with other recognized sources of information now available," and ruled that the Pueblos were entitled to the same protection as other Indian tribes in the United States (see fig. 5). Although this action was to be instrumental in the preservation of Pueblo territory,

Smithsonian, NAA.
Fig. 5. Pueblo delegation, representing the All-Pueblo Council, in Washington, D.C., Feb. 1913, probably in connection with the Sandoval case. The All-Pueblo Council, which had been functioning for an indeterminate length of time in 1913, was reorganized in 1922; a formal constitution was drafted and signed in 1965 (Sando 1976:227–231). Standing, left to right: Francisco Montoya, Cochiti; Juan Sarracino, Acoma; Francisco Naranjo, Santa Clara; Ambrosio Martinez, San Juan; Jose Martin, Acoma; and Victoriano Sisneros, Santa Clara. Sitting, left to right: Antonio Romero, Taos; J.M. Abeita, Isleta; Pablo Abeita, Isleta; Juan Naranjo, Santa Clara; and Santiago Quintano, Cochiti. Group portrait by DeLancey Gill, Bureau of American Ethnology photographer.

214

the goodwill that it might have engendered was diminished by the court's graceless assertion that federal protection was necessary because the Indians "are essentially a simple, uninformed, and inferior people . . . adhering to primitive modes of life and largely influenced by superstition and fetishism" (Brayer 1938:25).

The *Sandoval* decision meant that the federal government at last had full control over Pueblo lands and could move to reclaim not only parcels appropriated by squatters but also even tracts legally deeded in fair sale after the 1876 ruling. This fact spread consternation among the ranks of those persons who had purchased Pueblo property in good faith and whose only recourse was to seek an act of Congress granting them compensation. Investigation revealed that approximately 3,000 non-Indians representing families aggregating 12,000 persons maintained claims within the boundaries of Pueblo grants. Actually the disputed acreage comprised no more than 10 percent of the total area of Indian land, but it posed a threat as most was choice irrigable ground. For 11 stormy years, until resolution of the problem by the Pueblo Lands Act of 1924, there was serious friction between Indians and non-Indian claimants with the latter, aided by friends in territorial offices, resorting to diverse means of obstructionism in an effort to evade the consequences of the *Sandoval* decision. The situation was rendered more tense by the fact that even though some Hispano settlers had lived on Pueblo grants for several generations, they were unable to invoke a statute of limitations against the government since it was exempt from such provision as a guardian of dependent wards.

Secretary of the Interior Albert B. Fall, hoping to resolve the controversy, asked Sen. Holm O. Bursum of New Mexico to introduce a bill in Congress that would settle ownership conflicts. In July 1922 Bursum submitted to the Senate "An Act to Quiet Title to Lands Within Pueblo Indian Land Grants," a measure that, far from providing justice for the Indians, in practice would have benefited trespassers by confirming all non-Pueblo claims of title held for more than 10 years prior to 1912, the year of statehood. It also proposed that Indian water rights and contested land be placed under the jurisdiction of hostile state courts (Philp 1970:242). That an act so inimical to the genuine interests of the Indians should have been proposed may be traced to the personal leanings of Bursum and Secretary Fall, also a New Mexican, who had close ties with political machines in the state that cared little for Pueblo welfare but coveted votes of non-Indians.

When it became apparent that the Bursum bill would work to the serious detriment of the Pueblos and could deprive them of as much as 60,000 acres, a strong coalition of sympathetic Anglo forces—individuals and groups—formed to oppose it. This included intellectuals and artists in New Mexico who knew and appreciated Pueblo culture, Indian rights organizations, and the powerful General Federation of Women's Clubs, under the leadership of Stella M. Atwood, which engaged the polemical services of John Collier. These all worked with ardent zeal under the banner "Let's Save the Pueblos" to create a public furor, bring pressure on Congress and the secretary of the interior, and defeat the onerous bill. The campaign on behalf of the Indians, although attended by much emotionalism, proceeded with grim determination and the development of an effective lobby. As the growing clamor began to be felt in Washington, the Bursum bill was recalled from the House of Representatives by unanimous consent and sent back to the Senate Committee on Public Lands and Survey.

The Pueblos themselves, who had been slow to recognize the serious implications of Senator Bursum's legislation, began to rally and coalesce in a united front. Under the urging of John Collier, they met in an All-Pueblo Council at Santo Domingo on November 5, 1922, and with several Franciscans present as advisers, drafted a protest against the bill that would destroy their "common life and will rob us of everything we hold dear" (Philp 1970:248). Moreover they voted to raise $3,500 to send a delegation to Washington to appear at hearings of the Senate Committee on Public Lands.

Although the Bursum bill received the backing of President Warren G. Harding's administration, this was insufficient to offset the attack mounted by the pro-Indian opposition, and it was defeated in Congress. Senator Bursum then introduced a new measure calling for creation of a commission to investigate and settle land titles, and this bill, known as the Pueblo Lands Act, was approved in 1924. It effected something of a compromise in that the minority of non-Indian claimants who could prove legitimacy of title by satisfying a strict list of requirements might receive government patents for their lands, but in all such cases the United States, acknowledging that loss to the Indians resulted from negligence on its part, agreed to provide monetary compensation. However, since it was anticipated that the majority of claims would not be confirmed, Congress offered reimbursement for lands surrendered to the Pueblos.

In 1925 suits to quiet title were initiated by the attorney general and hearings were conducted in 19 Pueblos, passing individually on title to each of the private claims (Aberle 1948:9). By 1938 the complicated adjudication of Pueblo titles was completed, non-Indians without patents had been evicted, and the Indians for the first time were free from serious land controversy. The heated debate over the Bursum bill had aroused national interest in Indian rights, prepared the way for fundamental reforms in government policy toward the Indians, and at the same time showed the Pueblos the need for mutual assistance and unified action in facing shared problems.

*215*

## Land Acquisition

With Pueblo boundaries clearly and safely defined and subject to federal protection, attention could be turned to extension of farming and pasture lands needed for a growing population. Much Indian land suffered from overgrazing and soil depletion so that government aid beginning in the late 1930s centered on technical assistance, especially to control erosion and increase irrigated acreage. Equally significant, a land acquisition program was instituted to serve the expanding Pueblo economy. In some instances villages raised funds from among their own members to buy adjacent lands, as occurred with Laguna's purchase of the Paguate Tract; but when compensation money provided by Congress for lands lost in 1924 became available, Pueblos used it to acquire a total of 47,054 acres (Aberle 1948:12). Further, the federal government proceeded to purchase some of the tracts confirmed to non-Indians under the Pueblo Lands Act and reintegrate these within the original Indian domain. Finally, many Pueblos were able to enlarge their grazing capacity by obtaining permits or leases on neighboring federal or state land.

Thus by 1944 the acquisition program had added 667,479 acres to Pueblo use, or roughly half again as much land as was owned prior to 1933 (Aberle 1948:16). In this way all Pueblos, except Cochiti, Picuris, Pojoaque, and San Juan, extended their holdings beyond the original Spanish grants and the long-abiding problem of land was virtually eliminated.

Since World War II interest in Pueblo lands has focused upon their management and development in an effort to diversify the economic base of village life. Laguna profited from discovery of uranium deposits in the early 1950s and used some of its funds to invest in an electronics plant established on the reservation by the Burnell Company. Jemez, and to a lesser degree several other Pueblos, possess and exploit commercial timber resources. As the importance of agriculture and stock raising declines, some villages have developed recreational facilities or have sold concessions to Anglos to do so. On its own initiative Santa Clara created highly lucrative fishing and camping facilities in the mountainous section of its lands, while Cochiti, with BIA approval, leased sections of its holdings to commercial enterprises for recreational or residential development. Remembering the long struggle to win confirmation of territorial boundaries, most Pueblos remain hesitant about admitting outsiders to their lands, even under legal contract, and in those villages where concessions have been sold, the decision was not always unanimous and dissension has ensued.

A single but remarkable case involving land acquisition drew to a head in the late 1960s and was resolved when President Richard M. Nixon on December 15, 1970, signed a congressional bill deeding 48,000 acres of Carson National Forest, including sacred Blue Lake, to Taos Pueblo. Basing its claim on aboriginal use and ownership, Taos for more than a half-century had sought exclusive title to the mountain land, its efforts becoming more urgent as instances of vandalism and forest misuse threatened the Blue Lake shrine. In 1965 the United States Indian Claims Commission decreed that the Pueblo had established legitimate claim to the disputed area, but appropriate action by Congress was delayed for almost five years by New Mexico's Sen. Clinton Anderson. In the interval vast public support rose in defense of the Indians' cause, which proved as effective as that called forth to protest the Bursum bill in the 1920s. Return of the land to Taos not only reaffirmed basic principles of justice but also demonstrated a strong sentiment among the Anglo community for the preservation of a divergent cultural and religious enclave within its otherwise homogeneous midst.

## The Pueblos and the Federal Government

Consistently the eastern Pueblos have experienced greater exposure to Anglo culture than have the western villages, particularly Zuni and Hopi. However, since the 1880s the fundamental pattern of all Pueblo life has undergone varying degrees of alteration. The federal program of administration adopted a progressively more active interest in Pueblo welfare and problems and encouraged adjustment of community organization to changing political and economic conditions. During some periods, especially from about 1920 to 1930, this took the form of iron-handed paternalism, the Bureau of Indian Affairs deciding almost unilaterally what course Pueblo development should take. In these years the BIA pressed for rapid cultural assimilation, assuming that problems would dissolve once the Pueblos completely fused with the surrounding Anglo-Hispano community. Briefly it pushed enforcement of a Religious Crimes Code directed against practices and rituals deemed immoral or contrary to accepted Anglo custom. But the injustice of such a policy produced an outcry and attempts to apply the code were abandoned.

Although church-sponsored schools continued to serve a minority of Pueblo students, increasingly the government assumed the burden of education. By 1922, 8,000 children were receiving classroom instruction, some in off-reservation boarding institutions and others at nearby day schools. Nevertheless, opposition was voiced by Indian parents and village leaders on occasions when the BIA used schools as vehicles for indoctrination—to wean children from their ancestral heritage and traditions. Official handling of Pueblo education, as well as other facets of government activity, came under meticulous review in the Merriam report presented to Congress in 1928. Instances of mismanagement and corruption within the Indian Bureau were documented, leading to

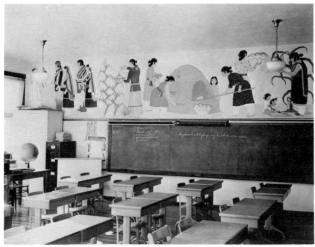

N.M. Dept. of Development, Santa Fe.
Fig. 6. Santa Fe Indian School classroom, probably in the 1940s or 1950s. The school, founded in 1890 and renamed the Institute of American Indian Arts in 1962, was instrumental in promoting painting by Pueblo and other Indian artists starting in the 1930s (Brody 1971:126–158), largely under the direction of Dorothy Dunn (1968:243–312). The murals shown here, extant in 1978, were painted by Cochiti artists Joe Herrera (See-Ru) (left) and Ben Quintana (right) and Taos artist Eva Mirabal (center). Photographer unidentified.

basic administrative reforms in the following decade. Further, the Pueblos' hand was significantly strengthened when their staunch friend and former champion in the fight over the Bursum bill, John Collier, was appointed by President Franklin D. Roosevelt in 1933 as commissioner of Indian affairs.

Indicative of a new and progressive orientation in the conduct of Indian affairs was the passage in 1934 of the Indian Reorganization Act, designed to give tribes greater autonomy over external matters and to hinder assaults from outside on their cultural integrity. Besides prohibiting alienation of Indian lands, establishing a system of agricultural and industrial credit, and providing funds for college and technical training, the act proclaimed the right of native groups to organize their own government under a freely adopted constitution and bylaws. Since its professed intent was to allow Indians a measure of democracy, this law stipulated that each tribe must accept or reject its terms in a referendum held by secret ballot. Among the Pueblos, only Jemez failed to vote its approval.

Prior to 1934, a system of self-government, based upon the hierarchy of officials originally created by the Spaniards, functioned within rather vague and ill-defined limits everywhere except among the Hopi. But the new legislation offered an opportunity both to strengthen the machinery of local government and to clarify its legal status and prerogatives. Notwithstanding, the majority of Pueblos still have not adopted written constitutions, partly because of innate conservatism that continues to

resist separation of religion and politics, but also because a consensus of approval, as demanded by tradition, cannot be achieved. Indeed, the prospect of political innovation has prompted much disharmony and is one of the multiple causes that have promoted internal feuds in the twentieth century.

In 1935 federal administration of all New Mexico Pueblos was centralized under the United Pueblos Agency with offices in Albuquerque, and branches or subagencies directed by assistant superintendents at Santa Fe for the northern villages and at Zuni. The Hopi of Arizona remained subject to an independent agency. The purposes and functions of the Pueblo agencies as delineated by the Indian Reorganization Act are: (1) to encourage and assist the Indians to become self-supporting within the context of the progressive shift from subsistence economies to outward orientation and wage labor; (2) to coordinate educational programs and provide scholarships; (3) to administer a revolving credit fund for the benefit of Indian business; and (4) to vest power in Pueblo governors and councils so that villages may operate legally as municipalities (Aberle 1948:57). Originally health programs were included within the agencies' jurisdiction, but with support of the Bureau of Indian Affairs, this responsibility was transferred by act of Congress in 1955 to the United States Health Service. The United Pueblos Agency was dissolved in 1969 with creation of separate agencies for the northern and southern villages.

The most important principle underscored by federal reorganization in the mid-1930s was one giving the Pueblos greater voice in management of their own external affairs. The authority of local governors and councils to assist in formulation of plans and programs and ultimately to approve or reject these received affirmation, and the United Pueblos Agency acknowledged that matters of purely internal nature were the exclusive jurisdiction of Pueblo officials. This policy emphasized that while the Indians remained technically "wards" of the government, such status entailed only certain legal protection, economic assistance, and administrative aid, and that fundamentally the Pueblos exercised full control over personal concerns. This concept has been continually enlarged and reaffirmed since 1940, resulting in expanded autonomy and responsibility for all Pueblos.

In May 1970 Zuni took a unique and significant step toward full self-determination when it reached agreement with the federal government to assume charge of and directly supervise all Bureau of Indian Affairs personnel and activities at the Pueblo. Under this system the governor and Pueblo council, functioning within a constitution accepted on July 9 of the same year, directly administer village affairs and promote an expanding program of economic development (the Zuni Comprehensive Development Plan).

During the 1950s and 1960s the All-Pueblo Council—

the forum to which the eastern villages send delegates to discuss mutual interests—became increasingly vocal in asserting rights and publicizing problems, especially as these related to federal and state policies toward the Indians. Through its elected chairman it endorses or opposes government actions affecting the Pueblos and speaks out on political, social, and economic issues. Tighter organization was given the council when 19 Pueblo governors meeting at Santo Domingo on October 16, 1965, adopted a constitution giving the body power to employ legal counsel; negotiate with all governments, persons, and firms; contract for and accept loans and grants; conduct educational and health campaigns; and raise revenue for its operations. Concession to even this loose union by villages proverbially jealous of their independence suggested that a pan-Pueblo spirit, in abeyance since the Revolt of 1680, might yet experience a new resurgence.

## Factionalism

Historical evidence reveals that divisive particularism was endemic among the Pueblos throughout Spanish colonial times and, by inference, was equally prevalent in the precontact period. The traditional mechanism for handling deviant individuals or groups involved the threat or actual use of force to compel conformity. Refusal to acquiesce inevitably led to expulsion from the community and loss of tribal membership, a penalty that until recent decades brought severe physical hardship upon the exiles. In some cases a controversial issue split villages apart, so that one faction voluntarily withdrew to found a new Pueblo or received asylum in another community. Much of the disruptive factionalism discernible among the Pueblos in the late nineteenth and twentieth centuries may be linked directly to the intensification of pressures accompanying enlarged contact with aggressive Anglo culture.

Serious factional disputes have caused temporary or permanent schisms at San Juan, San Ildefonso, Santa Clara, Isleta, Cochiti, Zia, San Felipe, Acoma, Laguna, Zuni, and among the Hopi. Several of the smaller Pueblos have avoided major dissension as have some of the larger, such as Santo Domingo, because the conservative religious hierarchy retains sufficient vigor to enforce a measure of unanimity. Where serious factionalism has occurred, acculturation in one form or another may be shown to have weakened the grip of those men whose traditional prestige once allowed them to wield unquestioned authority.

Several of the earliest documented instances of factionalism grew out of conflicts precipitated by Protestant missionaries or advocates. At Laguna in the 1870s Walter G. Marmon, a government schoolteacher and militant Presbyterian, won some prominent converts, married an Indian woman, and gained enough influence to be elected

Pueblo governor. Such a conquest by an Anglo would have been unimaginable in any other village; but Laguna, founded in the mid-colonial period, lacked homogeneity and the structural cohesiveness evident elsewhere. Marmon worked to discredit the old religion and customs, and when his proselytes destroyed two kivas, about 40 orthodox persons led by the cacique departed and established the village of Mesita to the southeast. The following year the cacique and his family moved to Isleta, were given land, and formed their own conservative enclave within that Pueblo. Laguna itself remained subject to friction between traditionalists and progressives but continued to function under the one Spanish-Pueblo type of community organization (Spicer 1962:177–178). Similar difficulties were experienced by the Hopi after Mennonite missionaries, who commenced work in 1893, caused a split in the village of Oraibi.

In most cases factionalism has grown out of internal conflicts directly related to acculturative distress. At Isleta beginning in the late 1880s, a movement developed to limit the traditional village theocracy and implement political techniques more suited to modern conditions. The struggle to achieve secularization, lasting until 1949 when the Pueblo adopted a constitution and a tribal council form of government, seriously rent the once well-integrated community and produced an example of political pathology (French 1948).

Taos Pueblo experienced a comparable upheaval when returning veterans of World War II formed a progressive faction, challenged the old guard in an effort to segregate religion and village government, and attempted to introduce electrification and a modern water system (Fenton 1957). Here the conservative element, encouraged by Anglo artists and writers, has been more successful in resisting change (although it yielded to underground electric cables in 1971), but periodic attacks upon its sovereignty breed tension and debilitate the spirit of cooperation fundamental to the preservation of the social fabric.

Since land is now strictly limited, serious division within Isleta, Taos, and other Pueblos in the twentieth century could not be solved in the traditional way—by expulsion or voluntary withdrawal of the dissident faction—and hence it has become necessary to search for new methods of accommodation and compromise, which in itself places stress on the traditional framework of government. As a Cochiti summed up the problem in the late 1950s: "Anyone who thinks that everything in an Indian Pueblo is all calm and cooperation, just simply doesn't know anything about Pueblo politics" (Lange 1959:194).

## Pueblos, Anthropologists, and "Yearners"

The earliest contact of the Pueblos with Anglo culture came largely through dealings with government officials and missionaries. But by 1880 anthropologists began to take an interest in the native people of the Southwest and to initiate fieldwork requiring prolonged association with the Indians. Some were able to break down the Pueblos' defensive barriers and record useful data on traditional culture as well as on the processes of culture change. Yet many met passive hostility and a few, through a lack of diplomacy or meddling in village affairs, provoked serious controversy and occasionally brought censure by Pueblo leaders upon persons serving as informants.

Among the first to pursue serious scientific investigation was ethnologist Frank H. Cushing, who worked at Zuni from 1879 to 1884. For several months he was regarded with distrust, but by adopting Zuni dress and customs and learning the language, Cushing was able to ingratiate himself with prominent persons, finally gaining membership in the secret Bow Priesthood and becoming a war chief (see "History of Ethnological Research," fig. 1, this vol.). In 1882 he accompanied village leaders on a tour of the East, highlighted by a meeting with President Chester A. Arthur. The purpose of the journey was to broaden the Zunis' perspective and arouse interest in education (see "Zuni History, 1850-1970," fig. 4, this vol.). Subsequently Cushing performed valuable service in helping the Pueblo resist encroachment upon its lands by Navajos and Anglos. Yet on repeated occasions he antagonized the Indians by the violation of taboos and in the end alienated them by publishing extensively on their sacred legends and ritual practice. The pattern of Cushing's activity—overcoming suspicion, winning acceptance, assisting in solution of village problems, serving as an agent of acculturation, and eventually betraying this trust—was one repeated often by anthropologists and writers.

Pioneer archeologist-historian Adolph F. Bandelier worked briefly at conservative Santo Domingo in 1881, but his tactless prying and photographing aroused such resentment that he moved to neighboring Cochiti, where his inquiries met with more tolerance. A Bandelier protégé, Charles F. Lummis, who lived at Isleta during the 1890s, compiled a body of Pueblo folk tales and became persona non grata when these were published. Later Elsie Clews Parsons ("History of Ethnological Research," fig. 6, this vol.) wrote an anthropological report on Taos that infuriated the Indians and caused reprisals against her informants. These and similar incidents reinforced Pueblo mistrust of Anglo ways and led to a resurgence of the kind of protective secrecy once used to guard native ceremonialism and custom from Spanish interference.

Notwithstanding, anthropologists sometimes made positive contributions (as in the example of Cushing) that assisted the Pueblos or improved their economies. At San Ildefonso, north of Santa Fe, with the encouragement of archeologists Edgar L. Hewett and Kenneth Chapman, potters returned about 1911 to prehistoric designs and techniques and produced a black polished ware that gained an immediate market. By 1920 one-third of the families of San Ildefonso derived their income from manufacture and sale of ceramics, and the profitable revival had spread to neighboring Santa Clara. Hewett also helped spark the birth of the Pueblo school of watercolorists.

In other ways the work of and the information recorded by anthropologists proved useful to the Pueblos in their struggle to preserve ancestral forms or to meet current problems. For example, the testimony of archeologists in legal cases during the 1960s was instrumental in establishing the extent and length of Indian occupancy upon lands surrounding Laguna and Acoma. And the archeological recovery undertaken by Herbert Dick at Picuris Pueblo in the same period, which revealed a wealth of data on the prehistory and early history of the village, stimulated interest and pride of the people in their past.

Besides anthropologists, the Pueblos have had to contend with another category of intrusive Anglos—the escapists, sometimes referred to as "yearners" or aficionados. Cushing and Lummis (fig. 7) were precursors of this phenomenon, which first became noticeable after World War I. Whether intellectuals, scholars, writers, or artists, the yearners in varying degrees identified with Pueblo life and affected styles of Indian dress. Attendance at numerous public ceremonials allowed them to participate vicariously in the intensity of village life, the more so since Pueblos felt that anyone who watched with sympathy and respect contributed to the efficacy of the rite. One observer of such people in the 1930s noted that for them "it was obligatory to go to every Pueblo dance. Failure to appear on a sunny roof on every saint's day marked one as soulless and without taste" (Philp 1970:243-244).

For several decades the artist and writer colonies in Taos and Santa Fe have been yearner seedbeds, and interest has focused on Pueblos nearby, individuals selecting favorite villages upon which to bestow their affection. Mabel Dodge Stern, who moved to Taos from New York City in 1917 and married a Pueblo, attracted other yearners, among them D.H. Lawrence, John Collier, and poet Witter Bynner, forming the basis for a long line of Indian enthusiasts. Their ranks in Taos and elsewhere were augmented in the late 1960s by an influx of hippies who found some solace in taking up the yearner tradition.

For the most part such persons have been quietly tolerated by the Pueblos, and some have established close and helpful relationships with individual families. On rare occasions in a few less restrictive villages like Cochiti, they or their children have taken part in dances and other communal activities. Yearner allegiance to the Pueblos has been most productive in periods of crises, such as the fight over the Bursum bill or the effort to secure Blue Lake for Taos, when they formed the

Fig. 7. Charles F. Lummis, Indian aficionado and publicist. left, Lummis in 1887, posing in Apache garb. center, "El Alisal," Lummis's Los Angeles home, built in 1897 (with the help of several Isletans from N.M.) and bequeathed to the Southwest Museum (founded by Lummis in 1913) upon his death in 1919; Pueblo pottery (displayed on the shelf directly under the roof) and Navajo rugs were among the many artifacts collected by Lummis. right, Lummis's daughter Turbese who was born at Isleta in 1892 and named (allegedly from a Southern Tiwa term for 'Rainbow of the Sun') by an Isletan godmother, dressed in Pueblo costume (with a Zuni water jar) in 1898. Lummis (1916, 1925, 1925a) photographed and wrote about the Pueblos and was known for his lobbying activities on behalf of the Indians (see Lummis 1968; Fiske and Lummis 1975; Simmons 1968a).

vanguard of Anglo support for the Indians. Yet at times their overweening patronization of native ways and, as at Taos, their self-portrayal as custodians of ancient tradition have constituted a distinct nuisance.

## Pueblo Population

Pueblo numbers did not begin to show a marked increase until the opening of the twentieth century. Although warfare took a progressively smaller toll after 1850, health conditions and sanitation practices improved slowly, with the result that fatalities from epidemics and infant mortality remained high. Early hostility toward Anglo culture contributed to a rejection of modern medicine, necessitating in recent times a long and carefully framed program of health education. As late as 1898-1899, a severe smallpox epidemic afflicted the western Pueblos even though the Spaniards had introduced vaccination into the Southwest almost 100 years before. At Zuni, where the disease appeared most virulently, government efforts to vaccinate the people were stoutly resisted and there was great loss of life.

During the course of the colonial period, the total number of villages steadily declined, but this trend was halted and finally reversed in the nineteenth century. Pecos, the last major Pueblo to become extinct, dwindled in population until in 1838 the 17 survivors sought refuge at kindred Towa-speaking Jemez. After 1900 several smaller villages, notably Nambe, Pojoaque, and Picuris, maintained a measure of Indian identity but in fact became largely hispanicized, losing many ceremonial features and most of their arts and crafts. Yet by the early 1970s, the most acculturated Pueblo, Pojoaque, had

experienced something of a native revival as an outgrowth of both the new prestige accorded Indian culture and government housing and community action programs that spurred a renewed sense of identity among village members.

A similar phenomenon appeared unexpectedly among the Tigua remnants living at Ysleta, Texas, 12 miles below El Paso. Descendants of Indians who moved south at the time of the Revolt of 1680, these people were long thought to have been fully assimilated by the surrounding Mexican community. But in 1968 the United States Congress granted formal recognition to 167 tribesmen and gave trust responsibility to the state of Texas, which provided administration under a Commission for Indian Affairs. Near Las Cruces, New Mexico, exists another small body of Indians known as Tortugas (Turtles) whose origin is obscure but who exhibit traces of the Tiwa language and Pueblo ceremonialism. Although constituting a distinct social and ethnic entity, the Tortugas possess no separate legal status and their numbers are unknown.

The majority of Pueblos experienced spectacular population growth after 1930 (table 1). Since that year many villages have doubled the number of inhabitants, even while some tribal members were moving to large urban centers searching for economic betterment. Laguna, for example, has sizable colonies in Albuquerque, Winslow, and Los Angeles, which continue to maintain close ties with the Pueblo. Census figures generally reflect the number of enrolled members for each village rather than the total of actual residents. In some Pueblos live Hispano families—at Cochiti these participate in communal activities and contribute players to the village baseball

**Table 1. Pueblo Population, 1860–1970**

| | 1860–1861 | 1900–1905 | 1930–1932 | 1940–1942 | 1948–1950 | 1964 | 1970 |
|---|---|---|---|---|---|---|---|
| Taos | 363 | 425 | 723 | 830 | 907 | 1,457 | 1,623 |
| Picuris | 143 | 125 | 112 | 115 | 130 | 181 | 183 |
| San Juan | 341 | 425 | 530 | 702 | 768 | 1,259 | 1,487 |
| Santa Clara | 179 | 325 | 382 | 528 | 573 | 908 | 1,119 |
| San Ildefonso | 154 | 250 | 123 | 147 | 170 | 296 | 358 |
| Nambe | 103 | 100 | 129 | 144 | 155 | 249 | 328 |
| Pojoaque | 37 | —[b] | 7 | 25 | —[b] | 85 | 107 |
| Tesuque | 97 | 100 | 120 | 147 | 160 | 222 | 259 |
| Sandia | 217 | 74 | 115 | 139 | 139 | 236 | 261 |
| Isleta | 440 | 989 | 1,077 | 1,304 | 1,470 | 2,331 | 2,527 |
| Cochiti | 172 | 300 | 295 | 346 | 497 | 652 | 779 |
| Santo Domingo | 261 | 1,000 | 862 | 1,017 | 1,106 | 1,905 | 2,311 |
| San Felipe | 360 | 475 | 555 | 697 | 784 | 1,327 | 1,632 |
| Santa Ana | 316 | 226 | 236 | 273 | 288 | 431 | 472 |
| Zia | 117 | 125 | 183 | 235 | 267 | 468 | 534 |
| Jemez | 650 | 450 | 641 | 767 | 883 | 1,566 | 1,765 |
| Laguna | 927 | 1,384 | 2,192 | 2,686 | 2,894 | 4,834 | 5,086 |
| Acoma | 523 | 739 | 1,073 | 1,322 | 1,447 | 2,415 | 2,861 |
| Zuni | 1,150 | 1,514 | 1,991 | 2,319 | 2,671 | 5,176 | 5,020 |
| Hopi | 2,500[a] | 2,100[a] | 2,842[a] | 3,444[a] | 4,000 | 4,500 | 4,857 |
| Tewa Village | [a] | [a] | [a] | [a] | 405 | 450 | |
| Totals | 9,050 | 11,126 | 14,188 | 17,187 | 19,714 | 30,948 | 33,569 |

SOURCES: 1970 data from Bureau of Indian Affairs; all other from Dozier 1970:122.
[a] Hopi and Tewa Village combined.
[b] Unknown.

## Pueblos and American Society

From the beginning of historic times to 1900, Pueblo assimilation of Western culture proceeded at a leisurely pace and was cast in a Hispanic mold, at least among the New Mexican communities. The Spanish language served as a lingua franca, Roman Catholic feast days promoted intervillage social contact, and the system of political officials under a governor inherited from the colonial era stood as an efficient buffer between the traditional structure of Pueblo society and government and a foreign culture that urged change. At the opening of the twentieth century, however, the shift from Hispanicizing to Anglicizing of Pueblo ways had become clearly apparent. By 1950 English had replaced Spanish as the major second language, and indeed, many children in less conservative Pueblos spoke only English and understood the Indian languages imperfectly or not at all. Horse and wagon transportation rapidly gave way to motor vehicles, allowing village residents to commute to city jobs; cash income brought radio, television, and telephones to a majority of families; and greater reliance on public utilities and wage labor promoted community dependency, inexorably shattering Pueblo insularity.

A period of accelerated change commenced among the Rio Grande Tewa with opening of the nearby Los Alamos Scientific Laboratory in 1943. Pueblo men, many of them returning war veterans, obtained unskilled or semiskilled jobs, and women gained employment as household domestics. Since these persons lived within commuting distance of their work, they could remain as residents of their village and at the same time secure income sufficient to allow larger participation in a consumer economy. Ready acceptance of the Tewa by Los Alamos residents created an atmosphere of mutual respect and led many Indians to adopt Anglo tastes in house styles and furnishings and attitudes of thrift and hard work. In 1964 the Los Alamos Junior Chamber of Commerce nominated James Hena, a lithograph operator and governor of Tesuque Pueblo, as its candidate for one of the 10 outstanding men in the United States.

The greatest force moving the Indians toward integration with Anglo and Hispano neighbors has been education. In spite of a strong disposition to preserve the core of their native heritage, the Pueblos continue to manifest the same deep-seated desire for quality schools that Agent William Arny reported in 1870. A firm boost to education was given by the Johnson-O'Malley Act of 1934, which provided funds to states wishing to assist in instruction of Indian children. This financing made possible the enrollment of Indian pupils in public schools, whereas before their opportunities had been limited to Bureau of Indian Affairs, mission, and private schools.

team—while many towns contain outsiders, Indian or non-Indian, who have married into the community.

Because the poverty of many local districts prevented construction of new buildings to handle a sudden influx of Pueblo students, New Mexico was unable to take advantage of the Johnson-O'Malley Act until 1951. But in that year a program was undertaken at the request of the Pueblos themselves, and every village voted to enter its children in the public schools. By the late 1960s, Indians were showing a growing interest in the activities and policies of local school boards and were actively campaigning for and winning places on these boards, so that the needs of their students might be represented. In fact participation in politics at all levels has steadily expanded since 1948 when New Mexico finally granted Indians full voting rights.

On the basis of general trends evident in Pueblo history during the first three-quarters of the twentieth century, it appears safe to predict that the transformation of this Indian culture will continue as it seeks to accommodate itself to the exigencies of modern American life. But while many traditional practices will disappear, others will be reworked and adjusted to fit a changing scene, permitting each of the Pueblos to retain its identity and maintain pride in a lifeway that is distinctly its own. Already a portion of the ceremonial dances, whose function was once strictly religious, has evolved into social and trading events that serve to reinforce community spirit and remind outsiders that tribal members still give allegiance to their "Indianness."

The revival of native crafts, which by the mid-1960s had flowered into a renaissance, offers a specific example of the way an old pattern may profitably be fitted to contemporary need. A sudden demand for American Indian art and handicrafts gave native artisans the opportunity to receive premium prices for their work and encouraged them to improve the quality of their production. Although a government-sponsored Indian Arts and Crafts Board had long sought to build a nationwide market for Pueblo products, public demand for such goods outside the Southwest remained small. But by 1970 Pueblo potters, silversmiths, painters, and weavers attending the annual Indian market in Santa Fe or the native craft fairs promoted in Albuquerque, Gallup, Flagstaff, and elsewhere discovered that their wares in some cases had doubled or tripled in value. This occurrence, while further stimulating craftsmanship and significantly bolstering income, also served to inform the Pueblos that their inherited talents and the mature fruits of their old culture were at last gaining merited recognition from their fellow countrymen (see fig. 8).

This is not to say that the prolonged period of transition ahead will be a road without thorns. Instances of serious factionalism will surface periodically as they have in the past, and the Pueblos, individually or collectively, will rise to challenge the actions of government, private business, or even other tribes whenever these may conflict with the course the villages have charted for

Ind. Pueblo Cultural Center, Inc., Albuquerque, N.M.

Fig. 8. Logo of the Indian Pueblo Cultural Center, a nonprofit corporation jointly owned by 19 Pueblos, by Santa Clara artist Pablita Velarde (see Wilks 1976), 1976. Planning for the Center, which opened in 1976, was begun in 1967. Among the Center's goals (as outlined in an undated pamphlet distributed by them in 1978) were the creation of a facility that would celebrate the heritage of the Pueblo people, that would serve as a central location for the All-Pueblo Council, and that would encourage the production and sale of quality Pueblo arts and crafts. Construction of the facilities, which include a museum and sales shop, was financed by a grant from the Economic Development Administration of the Department of Commerce and contributions from the community.

themselves. As traditional social controls inevitably weaken and as more families move to cities, problems such as alcoholism, juvenile delinquency, and crime will have to be confronted and resolved by new means. And at last the Pueblos will find it necessary to define a fresh framework of reference that will reconcile that part of their ancient legacy they wish to keep with the strict demands imposed by the present and future. Only if this is done will they find comfort in remaining American Indians.

## Sources

The literature on the subject of the Pueblo Indians is vast, but much of it deals only with cultural description and analysis. The history of these people under American rule has been neglected, and beyond the sources already cited in the text only a few printed works may be considered useful to the serious reader.

Dale's (1949) work contains an informative but sketchy summary of recent Pueblo history. Crane (1928, 1929), who served as Indian agent to the Pueblos, recounts his personal observations and calls attention to some of the major problems the Indians faced in the early twentieth century.

Valuable history as well as statistical data for the 1890s are provided in U.S. Census Office. 11th Census (1893, 1894).

Marriott's (1948) biography of Maria Martinez also reveals much of historical interest for San Ildefonso. Many of the scientific monographs prepared by anthropologists for individual villages include authoritative historical summaries derived from published and manuscript sources and from Indian informants. Representative of these are Dozier (1954) on the Hopi-Tewa and Lange (1959) on Cochiti.

An unusual book is Stubbs's (1950) on the Pueblos, which presents aerial photographs and scale drawings of all villages prior to modification of their urban pattern by government housing projects.

# Pueblos: Introduction

FRED EGGAN

The Pueblo Indians of the American Southwest have been known since Francisco Vásquez de Coronado's expedition in 1540-1542. They reside in a number of Pueblos or towns, compact permanent settlements on the semiarid Colorado plateau of northern Arizona and New Mexico, where they practice intensive agriculture, create distinctive arts and crafts, and maintain a comprehensive ceremonial system and world view (fig. 1). Here, surrounded by the ruins of ancestral communities, they have preserved a portion of their lands and much of their complex and colorful culture. Much of their distinctiveness derives from their participation in the Desert culture and from early cultural influences emanating from Mexico. Their relations with the Spanish intruders and their adjustments to Spanish colonists, and later, to American control, have been important factors in shaping their development. With their neighbors, the Navajo and Apache groups, the Yumans, and the Pima and Papago, the Pueblo Indians have been the subject of intensive investigation for several decades.

These two volumes on the Southwest summarize what has been learned about the Pueblos and their neighbors, but there is much that remains unknown, particularly with regard to the inner world of the Pueblos and the meaning and significance of various aspects of ritual and ceremony. The unremitting efforts of the Spanish missions to stamp out native religious practices were largely responsible for the patterns of secrecy that developed during the seventeenth century and persist in most of the Pueblos. The archeological backgrounds for the modern Pueblos have been worked out in considerable detail and the integration of archeology with social anthropology is well underway. The increasing contributions of Pueblo Indian scholars to knowledge of Southwestern cultures are particularly important and promise more satisfying and comprehensive accounts of the Pueblos than have yet appeared.

## Culture and Early History

The Pueblos form a unit in comparison with neighboring groups. Pueblo culture is both highly distinctive and uniform in its externals. According to Benedict (1934), the Pueblo Indians have a distinct ethos and world view, as well. Pueblo subsistence is centered on agriculture and the cultivation of corn, beans, and squash. The Pueblos'

ancestors occupied the greater Southwest as hunters and food gatherers for thousands of years, but the gradual introduction of agriculture from the south led to sedentary life in hamlets and later villages, with compact stone and adobe houses centered around plazas and rising for several stories. Along with cultigens, such as corn, beans, squash, and cotton, came pottery and other crafts, knowledge of irrigation techniques, and a growing trade in shell and copper ornaments, turquoise, macaw feathers, and other objects.

The sixteenth-century Spanish expeditions of exploration were followed by the first colonists under Juan de Oñate in 1598, who established their headquarters first near the Tewa Pueblo of San Juan and later at Santa Fe, from which they began the systematic reduction and christianization of the Pueblo populations. New domestic animals and crops were introduced, political institutions to mediate Pueblo-Spanish relations were instituted, and the friars set to work to root out all aspects of native religion that were not consonant with Christianity. The Rio Grande Pueblos felt the brunt of these efforts, which were directed particularly at the native priests and medicine men, and which involved whippings, torture, and public executions. Under the leadership of Popé, a Tewa medicine man from San Juan, the Pueblos were organized for a determined effort to get rid of the Spaniards. The Pueblo Revolt of 1680 took the Spaniards by surprise and resulted in the killing of most of the Catholic priests and the driving of the colonists and soldiers out of New Mexico. The reconquest was not completed until 1692, when Diego de Vargas received the submission of all the Pueblos, sometimes after bloody assaults. A further rebellion of the Tewa villagers occurred in 1696, supported by other communities, but the New Mexico Pueblos were again forced to submit—all except the group of Tanos (Southern Tewas) who fled to the Hopi country and were given sanctuary on First Mesa, where they still reside in the 1970s.

With the end of the rebellion a better accommodation was gradually achieved between the settlers and the Pueblos, and political and religious pressures were considerably reduced. The Navajo and Apache—Southern Athapaskan-speaking groups who had entered the Southwest a short time before the Spaniards—secured horses and sheep and expanded considerably in population and wealth. During the eighteenth century they increased

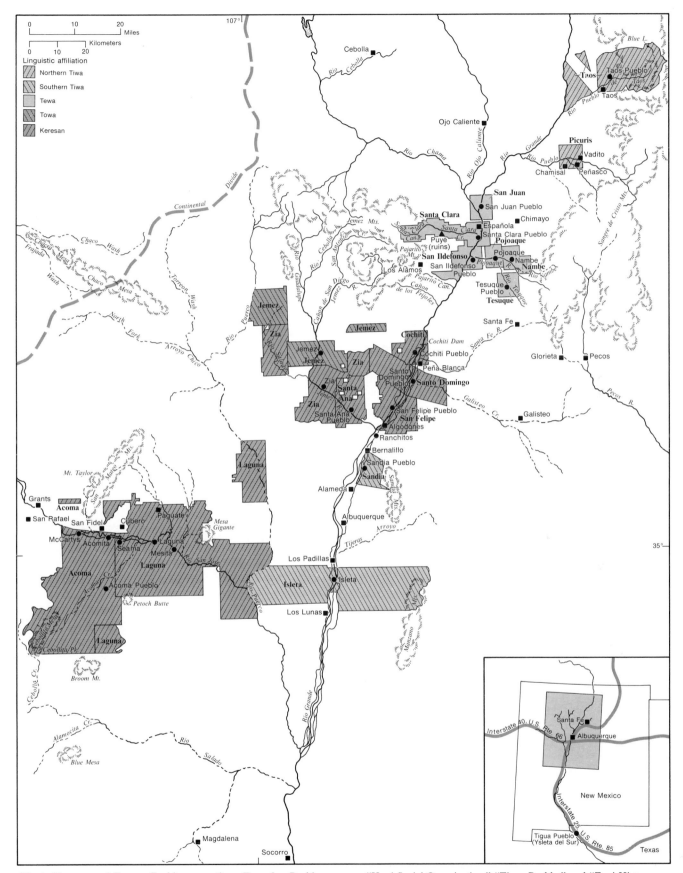

Fig. 1. Keresan and Tanoan Pueblo reservations. For other Pueblo areas see "Hopi Social Organization," "Tigua Pueblo," and "Zuni History, 1850-1970," this vol.

their raiding of Spanish and Pueblo communities, and the Spaniards enlisted the Pueblos in mutual defense and retaliation. During the same period, mounted Comanche warriors appeared in the southern Plains and took over control of trade, driving out Apache groups, reducing Pueblos such as Pecos, and attacking Spanish settlements and herds.

The revolt of Mexico against Spain was successful in 1821 and New Mexico became a part of the Republic of Mexico. During the Mexican period, which lasted for 25 years, civil and religious affairs were largely neglected so far as the Pueblos were concerned, and Navajo raids and depredations were no longer checked. During the eighteenth century Hispano communities in the Rio Grande received large infusions of Indian population, both through intermarriage with Pueblo populations and through settlement of *genízaros,* Indian captives redeemed from the Comanche and other Plains tribes and resettled in strategic places. During the Mexican period Indians were made citizens of Mexico, and it is estimated that perhaps one-third of the population of New Mexico was of Indian origin.

With the end of the Mexican War, United States rule was extended over New Mexico and Arizona in 1846 by the Treaty of Guadalupe Hidalgo. During the American period trade over the Sante Fe trail greatly increased. Anglo administrators established law and order and broke the hold of the Hispano communities on Pueblo lands and the power of the Roman Catholic Church. The U.S. Army was used to stop raiding and warfare; the Navajo were rounded up by Col. Christopher Carson and interned at Fort Sumner from 1864 to 1868, after which they were allowed to return to their old reservation on the promise of good behavior.

## Regional Variations

While the Pueblos form a unit in comparison with neighboring groups in the Southwest, closer examination makes it possible to establish various divisions based upon differences in location and in ecology, language, and social institutions. There is a basic cultural division between the Eastern Pueblos of the Rio Grande and its tributaries and the Western Pueblos of the mesa and canyon country, but the line of cleavage is not a sharp one. Parsons (1924a) pointed out that there is a gradual shift in many aspects of Pueblo social institutions as one moves from the Hopi in the west to Taos in the east, and Fox (1967) has argued that the Keresans in the central portions of the Pueblo crescent were distinctive enough to be considered as a third basic division.

Despite the general Pueblo cultural unity, there are four linguistic stocks represented in the Pueblo populations. The Hopi villages in the west speak a language of the Uto-Aztecan family that is closely related to the Numic languages of the Great Basin, but their close cultural neighbor, Zuni, belongs to a different stock, perhaps distantly related to California Penutian. The Keresans, partly in the west (Acoma and Laguna) and partly in the Rio Grande valley, have no known linguistic

Calif. Histl. Soc., Los Angeles: Title Insurance Coll.

Fig. 2. Hopi Second Mesa. View of Mishongnovi, looking northwest, with the town of Shipaulovi in the distance, about 1900 or before. For general views of the Hopi villages in 1977, see "Hopi Social Organization," fig. 2 (First Mesa), figs. 5-7 (Second Mesa), and figs. 9-11 (Third Mesa), this vol. Photograph probably by G. Wharton James or F.H. Maude.

Fig. 3. Winter street scene in one of the Rio Grande Pueblos, probably Jemez, around 1920. (General views of most of the Rio Grande Pueblos appear with the individual Pueblo chapters, this vol.) Photograph by T. Harmon Parkhurst.

affiliations. The Kiowa-Tanoan family is represented in the Rio Grande valley by the three Tanoan subgroups—Tiwa in the north and the south, and Tewa and Towa in the center. The Southern Tewa, or Tano, who fled to the Hopi country, occupy the Hopi-Tewa Pueblo called Tewa Village, which is adjacent to Walpi and Sichomovi on First Mesa. The Tanoans are close linguistic relatives of the Kiowa, a Plains Indian tribe. These linguistic differences suggest different historical origins for Pueblo populations, and the groupings are relevant for more recent historical comparisons. The patterns of secrecy that were established to preserve native religion have also been extended to the study of the individual languages, so that knowledge of Pueblo languages is in many ways not adequate by modern standards.

With regard to Pueblo social organization, the situation is more complicated, and the social institutions cut across the linguistic divisions. The Western Pueblos—Hopi, Tewa Village, Zuni, Acoma, and Laguna—conform to a general pattern based upon matrilineal exogamous clans, matrilocal households, and a Crow or matrilineal lineage type of kinship system. The Eastern Pueblos of the Rio Grande region, particularly the Tewa villages, have essentially patrilineal but nonexogamous dual divisions, or moieties, associated with summer and winter, a bilateral extended family structure, and a kinship system of Eskimo type that emphasizes seniority and reciprocal relations. The Keresans of the Rio Grande—Zia, Santa Ana, San Felipe, Santo Domingo, and Cochiti—have matrilineal exogamous clans and a variant Crow type kinship system, along with a dual

ceremonial division based on two large kivas for dancing and other purposes. The membership of the dual divisions is essentially patrilineal, with wives joining their husbands' kivas if they belong to the opposite side. The Tanoans of the Rio Grande, other than the Tewa and the Hopi-Tewa, show still other patterns. The Southern Tiwa—Isleta and Sandia—are divided into "Corn" groups for which recruitment is matrilineal. These are associated with colors and directions but are not exogamous. There is also a dual organization associated with summer and winter and with the kiva system, children being assigned alternately if the parents belong to different sides. The Northern Tiwa—Taos and Picuris—have a dual organization based on northside and southside divisions, with three kivas on each side. There are no clan groups, so far as is known, and the kinship system is similar to that for the Tewa. The Towa-speaking Pueblo of Jemez, on the other hand, has a social structure that partly approximates the Western Pueblos, with matrilineal exogamous clans, plus two kivas with generally patrilineal affiliation, and a ceremonial dual division expressed in terms of the Clown societies. The kinship system is incompletely recorded but appears to have both eastern and western elements, with some terms being used in both lineage fashion and bilaterally. Pecos, the easternmost Towa Pueblo, was abandoned in 1838; the survivors settled in Jemez, for the most part, but few details of their social institutions have survived.

The ritual or ceremonial organizations take a variety of structural forms and provide other possible groupings. The kachina cult is strong in the Western Pueblos but

Fig. 4. Street scene in the Hopi First Mesa Village of Walpi, looking northeast. The ladder just to the right of distinctive Dance Rock (tall rock formation in middle foreground) is the entrance to the Middle kiva (Nashabki) associated with the Snake Society. Photograph by Frederick Monsen, probably 1896 or later.

Fig. 5. Hopi children playing in a large mud puddle after a summer rainstorm at Oraibi, probably in the large plaza to the west of the old town center. Photograph probably by G. Wharton James, about 1898.

join the kachina cult, and individuals are affiliated with particular multiple kivas in terms of selected "ceremonial fathers," though only males dance. Among the eastern Tewas, the kachinas are associated with the moiety divisions, and moiety initiation is a prerequisite for dancing with masks. In the Keresan Pueblos the situation varies, with Acoma and Laguna following the western model and the Rio Grande communities apparently utilizing the dual kiva groups, though few details are known for certain.

The medicine societies have their major development among the Keresans and have apparently diffused both to the west and to the east, particularly to the Tewa of the Rio Grande. Emphasis on curing disease is marginal among the Hopi, though each ceremonial society controls a particular "disease," and individual medicine men formed societies in the past. The central role of medicine societies among the Keresans is indicated in their control of priestly appointments, including the cacique or town chief. The Tewa medicine societies are a partial reflection of the Keresan societies, with similar curing activities but without the central control functions. For the Northern and Southern Tiwa, there are few data available.

## Ceremonial and Political Organization

Despite the differences in organization and cultural purpose between the kachina cults and the medicine

fades out in Taos and Picuris. It may have been absent in Isleta before the migration of traditionalists from Laguna, who introduced kachina masks and dances in recent times. In the Western Pueblos everybody is expected to

Fig. 6. Hopi girls at the Second Mesa village of Shongopavi, about 1900. They wear woven woolen mantas tied with woven belts, shawls of commercial cloth and of native-woven wool, turquoise and shell earrings and necklaces. All wear their hair in the side-whorled style of postpubescent girls. Photograph by Charles C. Pierce or G. Wharton James.

societies, both are concerned with the production of rain for the crops and with community integration and welfare. Archeological evidence and tradition suggest that the cult of the kachinas was a relatively late introduction to the Southwest from Mexico and had its greatest development among Zuni and Hopi. The medicine societies may well have grown out of the earlier shamanistic activities and the control of witchcraft, the belief in which was intensified by parallel beliefs among the Spanish settlers. The dual organization of society and ceremony has its most comprehensive development among the Rio Grande Tewa, where Ortiz (1969) has outlined the relations of the social, political, and economic activities to the summer and winter divisions for the Pueblo of San Juan, all of these operating within a four-dimensional universe. Various aspects of dualism are found throughout the Pueblo regions but are less developed in the west.

Among the Western Pueblos, who escaped from strongly imposed Spanish controls after 1700, a series of societies performs calendric rituals throughout the year, along with kachina dances and other activities. The private rituals of the societies are held in the kivas, with altars and other ritual activities (or in the household of the clan that "owns" or controls the ceremony), and a public performance dramatizing tradition or symbolizing ceremonial roles is presented in the plaza or elsewhere. Among the Hopi, the Soyal ceremony, held at the winter solstice, involves all the major groups under the leadership of the village chief. At Zuni, where there are both ceremonial and medicine societies, the Shalako ceremony held in December is the major event (see "Zuni Religion and World View," fig. 1). In the Keresan and Tanoan Pueblos, the saint's day celebrations share the stage with native rituals, and the older patterns are not yet clear. In most Eastern Pueblos there are rituals and public dances at Christmastime, celebrating both the solstice and Catholic sacred periods.

Within these social and ceremonial patterns, hunting, war, and clowning are all represented, though in differing contexts and ways. Hunting was more important in the Rio Grande region, and animal dances and rituals are frequently performed (see "San Ildefonso Pueblo," figs. 10-12, and "San Juan Pueblo," figs. 7-8, this vol.). War was important up to about the 1870s, and scalps were often in the charge of a women's scalp society, but ritual activities are now largely gone. Clowns, in addition to fun-making, had a sacred character everywhere. In the west they often appeared with kachina dancers, or with Shalako, as at Zuni. In the east there were dual organiza-

Smithsonian, NAA.

Fig. 7. Rain Dance at Zuni, 1899, performed by the Good kachinas (*kokkʔokši*, sg.), who are here shown in the plaza following a pilgrimage to the Sacred Lake. Rain Dances occur throughout the summer months at Zuni. The Hopi Long-Haired kachinas (Angakchina, sg.) are similar to the *korkokshi* and are thought to have been borrowed from the Zuni. Photograph by Adam C. Vroman.

229

PUEBLOS: INTRODUCTION

Fig. 8. Corn or tablita dance, a generalized dance to insure fertility, as performed at the Tewa Pueblo of San Ildefonso, Sept. 9, 1970 as part of a Harvest ceremony. right, Line of dancers, alternating male and female, perform in plaza near the (temporary) saints' bower. A Koshare clown stands in front of them and another behind them, obscuring the banner carrier. left, Koshare (Tewa *ḱohsa·*) clown is offered food during an intermission. Photographs by Helga Teiwes.

tions of clowns, the Koshare (Santa Ana Keresan *ḱi̧ṣáirí*, Tewa *ḱohsa·*) and Quirana (Santa Ana *kúiṙainá*, Tewa *kʷíráná*), associated with the two seasons or with the kiva groups.

The political organization and social control systems also vary widely. In the west government is essentially theocratic, and public opinion, expressed through gossip or "enforced" by special kachinas, was a major means of control until the 1950s. In the east political control is apparently strong and centralized; the cacique and the council decide on the allocation of land and can revoke permission to live in the Pueblo. The governor and his assistants, a Spanish-instituted system dating from 1620, continue in all the Pueblos except the Hopi villages and are traditionally appointed by the religious hierarchy. Since the Indian Reorganization Act of 1934, it has been possible for Pueblos to elect their secular officials. At Zuni, and in other villages, this change has begun to take place. In 1970 Zuni took over control of reservation affairs from the Bureau of Indian Affairs, and tribal councils are taking a more active role in all but the most conservative villages.

The Roman Catholic Church continues to play an important role in all the Pueblos, except for the Hopi and Hopi-Tewa villages, but the Catholic priests are often in residence only on feast days and special occasions and are content to let the Pueblos work out their own versions of Catholicism. The pressures in the past led Dozier (1961) to argue that the Rio Grande Pueblos have utilized a process of compartmentalization with regard to religion,

keeping the native rituals and activities uncontaminated by Catholicism or Spanish terms and practices. The *fiscales* and other officials designated to take care of the church and its activities continue to serve, but few if any natives have become Catholic priests. However, the saint's day activities involve both Catholic and Pueblo elements, and it may be more difficult to keep them apart, now that pressures for conformity are relaxed on the part of the Church.

With the beginning of the American period in the 1850s, Protestant missionaries and secular schooling introduced new factors. Factions, divisions of long standing among the Pueblos, often became associated with Catholic and Protestant converts or, alternatively, with "traditionalists" who wished to continue ancestral ways and "progressives" who wished to take advantage of the new opportunities. Factions sometimes represent a means of reaching village-wide decisions but may also result in the splitting of Pueblos into new units, as among the Hopi in 1906 and later. They may also destroy village unity, as at San Ildefonso and Santa Clara in the early twentieth century, without actual separation.

## History Since 1850

The large number of Pueblos discovered by the Spanish explorers during the sixteenth century—90 or more— were greatly reduced by the conflicts attending the Pueblo Revolt of 1680 and its aftermath, and the initially large Pueblo population suffered a considerable reduc-

Smithsonian, NAA.
Fig. 9. Zuni man, presumably the governor, posing with the Pueblo's Lincoln cane of office (in his right hand) and a Spanish cane and rifle (in his left) in 1873. He was identified as Match'olth tōne in 1935 (by Lorenzo Chavez of Zuni). Photograph by Timothy H. O'Sullivan, photographer for the Wheeler Expedition of the U.S. Geological Survey.

tion. The Rio Grande communities were particularly hard hit; some groups, such as the Piro, became extinct, while others, such as the Southern Tewa and Southern Tiwa, were scattered and disorganized. In the Rio Grande region, where 18 Pueblos survive, the population doubled from 1942 to 1968, and the patterns of acculturation and interethnic relations have taken a variety of forms, which makes any generalization premature. Since World War II, there has been a considerable revival of social and ceremonial life in the Rio Grande region, centered in part on new economic resources, more support from U.S. governmental agencies, and greater cooperation in the All-Pueblo Council.

For the Northern Tiwa communities, recent archeological research suggests a longer period of in situ development than formerly thought. Kenneth Hale believes the breakup of Tanoan into constituent languages occurred around a millennium ago and that the separation of Kiowa was not much earlier. The linguistic studies of George L. and Felicia H. Trager have added considerably to knowledge of the relations of Taos and Picuris, and the work of Herbert Dick in the reconstruction of Picuris kivas has assisted in the renaissance of this isolated village. At Taos, the return of Blue Lake, their

most sacred shrine, to Pueblo ownership and control has climaxed a long and bitter struggle.

The Southern Tiwa were greatly disturbed by the Pueblo Revolt and its aftermath and more recently by their urban locations. Acculturation is further advanced at Sandia than at Isleta and English is the primary language of Sandia, but the Sandians also retain much of their organization, values, and identity. After the Pueblo Revolt many of the Southern Tiwas fled to the Hopi country where they built the Pueblo of Payupki on Second Mesa, before returning in 1741, but Hopi influence apparently survives only in a few loanwords. The Tigua community of Ysleta del Sur, founded by Southern Tiwas who fled with the Spanish colonists to El Paso during the Pueblo Revolt, has remained as an urban enclave and in the 1970s revived from its status of apparent extinction. A small group of traditionalists has retained a number of indigenous beliefs and practices despite overwhelming acculturation.

For the Tewa Pueblos of the Rio Grande, Ortiz's (1969) monograph on San Juan provides a model that will allow the more fragmentary data on the other Tewas to be put in clearer perspective. In San Ildefonso and Santa Clara factional disputes in the early twentieth century and the influenza epidemic of 1918 had devastating effects on village organization and moiety balance. During the 1920s the development of pottery and painting for the tourist trade strongly affected the economic conditions of these Pueblos and led to further internal changes. The Hopi-Tewa are a group of Southern Tewa who fled from Spanish retribution after the rebellion of 1696 and were given a village site and farm lands by the Hopi. Their adjustments to Hopi society and culture provide a basis for evaluating the amount and character of acculturation taking place between two Pueblo groups over a period of two and one-half centuries. The Hopi-Tewa have established a basis for psychological superiority and through the efforts of Nampeyo took the lead in the renaissance of Hopi-Tewa pottery making. In the Rio Grande region both Nambe and Pojoaque have experienced a marked cultural renaissance since the 1960s. In the 1970s Nambe presented at least four religious dances during its saint's day celebration, and Pojoaque began to celebrate its saint's day with a dance.

The Keresan Pueblos of the Rio Grande region retain much of their conservatism, though Santo Domingo has allowed the installation of both plumbing and electricity, and Cochiti, the beneficiary of a new dam and lake, has leased reservation lands for a large-scale condominium and resort project. Zia and Santa Ana, on the Jemez River, a western tributary of the Rio Grande, are more isolated, and Zia retains its traditional forms. Much of Zia organization and belief is reminiscent of Western Pueblo culture, and Hoebel (1968) notes that for the Pueblos generally there is no private law; legal power is centralized in the bureaucracy and all procedure must move through it.

For Acoma and Laguna the situation is similar, though there is new information on the development of Laguna in both Spanish and more recent times. The presence after the Civil War of a strong group of American Protestant missionaries who married into Laguna, wrote a constitution, and even provided the governor for a period, transformed the Pueblo in many ways. Farming communities were established, the "traditionalists" migrated to Isleta, the Catholic Church was threatened with destruction, and secularism flourished. The land base was also greatly enlarged, and the later discovery of uranium provided both jobs and royalties for the Pueblo. Old Laguna is now used mainly on ceremonial occasions. It stands in the 1970s as the wealthiest and probably the most acculturated of all the New Mexico tribes.

The far western Pueblos of Zuni and Hopi are more open, and research of various kinds continues. The Zunis have published a series of self-portrayals (Quam 1972) with the sponsorship of Zuni Gov. Robert E. Lewis and a grant from the Office of Economic Opportunity. In addition, native scholars such as Edmund Ladd for the Zuni and Emory Sekaquaptewa, LaVerne Masayesva Jeanne, and Charles Loloma for the Hopi are providing an authoritative view on various subjects. When the Spaniards arrived in the Southwest both Zuni and Hopi comprised some six Pueblos each. Modern Zuni was established in 1692 when the six Pueblos, who had fled to the top of Dowa Yalanne mesa at the time of the Pueblo Revolt, returned and built a single village on the site of Halona. It was during this period that the integration of the social and ceremonial system in terms of the six directions and the "center," as described in Cushing (1896), took place, providing Zuni with the most complex ritual organization of any of the Pueblos. The Hopi villages, more isolated, moved to the mesa tops during the same period and never developed a centralized structure. In 1977 the Hopi had 12 villages as a result of population pressures and factional disputes.

As Tedlock (1972:xv–xvi) characterizes the Zuni: "Their social structure is exceedingly complex, involving twelve matrilineal clans, thirteen medicine societies (organizations with secret curing powers), a masked dance society into which all males are initiated, a series of hereditary rain-bringing priesthoods whose highest-ranking members form the religious government of the village, a secular government of elected officials, four mission churches, three public schools, a crafts cooperative, and a small factory." The major developments since the 1960s have involved the great expansion of Zuni silver and turquoise jewelry manufacture, with 90 percent of the population participating, and the gradual secularization of the government, with election of the governor and other officials rather than their appointment by the religious hierarchy. Zuni has gone further; the governor

and council have taken over the administration of the Zuni reservation from the Bureau of Indian Affairs, and the agency superintendent has become technically an advisor rather than the administrator.

For the Hopi, village organization is based on a "mother" village, a "colony" village, and a "guard" village. Within the village there is a clan-phratry grouping, with each clan ideally divided into a "prime" matrilineage controlling the clan house and the sacred objects relating to clan deities and "reserve" lineages who take over if something happens to the "prime" matrilineage. The economy no longer is subsistence-based but has shifted almost entirely to a cash basis. In the postwar period the tribal council began to function as the spokesman for the reservation as a whole, despite opposition from conservative villages, and has been active in obtaining government funds for various projects. This has led to greatly increased opportunities for jobs on the reservation and to an increase in the number of college students and graduates.

Since the 1950s the Hopi have been locked in struggle with the Navajo tribe over ownership of the 1882 executive order reservation, originally set up to protect the Hopi communities from being overrun by Whites and other Indians. Since 1868, when the Navajo were allowed to return from captivity in Fort Sumner, they have increased their numbers tenfold. Their reservation lands completely surround the Hopi reservation, and much of its area has been occupied by Navajo families and their herds of sheep and cattle. In 1962 a federal court divided the Hopi reservation into a Hopi portion and a joint-use portion, and the Hopi have attempted to gain control of their half of the joint area through appeal to Congress and the courts.

Hopi traditionalists were active in the 1970s, boycotting the tribal council, tearing up water lines and electrical installations, and even working with the Navajo against Hopi interests with regard to land claims. In 1906 the traditionalists were strong enough to split Oraibi and found Hotevilla a few miles away, but Hotevilla itself is no longer united in the face of new economic opportunities, and the tribal council is increasingly effective in matters affecting the reservation as a whole.

## Questions of Prehistory

It might be useful to consider the relevance of new developments in the continuing search for solutions to the classic problems of Pueblo culture, namely the origins of different linguistic groups, the influences from Mexico and other regions, and interaction and migration within the Pueblo regions. The discovery of the Desert culture by Jennings (1956:59–89) and his associates and the increasing knowledge of its time-depth, wide distribution, and local diversity provided the material basis for Basketmaker I, the earliest hypothetical unit in the Basketmaker-Pueblo sequences proposed by Kidder (1927). The Hopi are the closest Pueblo representatives of the Great Basin Desert culture, and linguistic research places them with the Numic-speaking groups, as part of the northern Uto-Aztecan peoples in the western Mojave Desert and the southern Sierra Nevada foothills. Around 1000 B.C. by lexicostatistic dating, the Uto-Aztecan populations began to break up, and the Hopi ancestors moved eastward into the deserts to the Grand Canyon region, where Schwartz (1970a) has documented their residence over a considerable period of time. The Peabody Museum Awatovi Expedition found evidence of occupation of the Hopi country since around A.D. 500–700, and Oraibi has been continuously occupied since around A.D. 1100.

The ancestors of modern Zuni very likely came even earlier from the California region and made up part of the Mogollon populations of central New Mexico, who had had a long period of development on a Desert culture base, known as Cochise, farther to the south. The discovery by MacNeish (1978) of the long period of agricultural development in the Tehuacán valley of Mexico beginning around 6500 B.C. has clarified some of the problems as to the introduction of cultivation into the Southwest and its gradual dominance of subsistence. By the middle of the thirteenth century Pueblo culture had reached its greatest expansion, but the great drought of A.D. 1276–1299 and probably incursions of Apachean and other groups led to a withdrawal and consolidation in most areas. The Keresans moved south, toward the Rio Grande, and the Tanoans moved from the upper San Juan and the Mesa Verde to the Rio Grande valley. Ultimately it should be possible to trace the modern communities back into the past but archeological research is difficult on most reservations, except as it has been allowed in order to document claims against the government.

The basic differences between the Western and Eastern Pueblos were originally considered by Eggan (1950) as developing from a common Western Pueblo archeological base and differentiating in the east on the basis of the disruptions involved in forced migrations, the possible influences of Spanish contacts, and developments in irrigation techniques. Fox (1967) has reexamined the evidence in terms of his fieldwork at Cochiti and concludes that a diversity of origins for Pueblo social structures is more probable. Following some of Lévi-Strauss's (1949, 1965) suggestions, he proposed that the earlier system was an "elementary structure" that was in the process of shifting to a Crow system but never went all the way. The Keresan system in the San Juan, he believes, was characterized by a patrilineal, exogamous moiety system, with a later development of matrilineal clans, with exogamy being lost during the migrations, so far as the moieties were concerned. With the appearance of Ortiz's (1969) authoritative view of the Tewa dual

organization as nonexogamous, Fox has modified his views to a considerable extent, though maintaining his general position. Of relevance here is Ellis's (1964) reconstruction of the basic Jemez patterns of social organization, which shows that Jemez combines matrilineal clans with a moiety system that has various dualities, reflecting both Tanoan and Keresan patterns. It seems clear that the social structures of the Eastern Pueblos are considerably more complex than was originally thought.

A seminar convened by the School of American Research produced a dozen papers (Ortiz 1972) devoted to recent developments and new results on a variety of problems, both old and new. Ford (1972a) utilizes an ecological perspective for the Eastern Pueblos, and specifically for San Juan. He attempts "to test the hypothesis that in an egalitarian society living in an effective environment with unpredictable and potentially disastrous fluctuations of biotic and abiotic variables, reciprocity and ritual will regulate the circulation of nutrients for the survival of the human population." Using 1890 as a baseline and considering San Juan as an ecosystem, Ford calculates a small surplus of about 15 percent, which formerly was saved for lean years or used for trade. In times of famine the Pueblos were less egalitarian, attempting to save the ritually more important households at the expense of marginal families and groups.

The nature of reality and man's place in the universe are of fundamental importance in the Southwest. Ortiz (1969) considers particularly the concepts of space and time, which differ in important ways from Anglo Americans', as well as the symbolism of the solstices and the equinoxes, and the behavior of clowns. The pioneer studies of Cushing (1896) provided a world view in mytho-sociological terms that was far ahead of its time.

## World View and the Future

Pueblo religion is of central importance in Pueblo life but despite Parsons's (1939) monumental work there is still much to be learned. This is particularly true for those Pueblos with a strong commitment to secrecy, both within the village and with regard to outsiders. The rituals of initiation into ceremonial organizations are normally held in secret, though the general procedures are more widely known. In the west the public performances are open to everybody, but in the central and eastern Pueblos outsiders are not welcome, and the village is closed and guarded during the ceremonial periods.

Taos, the northernmost of the Tiwa-speaking Pueblos, is probably the most secretive of the Rio Grande villages, and what happens in its six kivas is well guarded. However, in the effort to regain full control of Blue Lake, their most sacred region, the Taos elders were ultimately persuaded to disclose some aspects of their religious practices, particularly with reference to initiations, and their successful results may allay some of their anxieties with regard to possible suppression of their rituals. Taos Indians allowed limited archeological work within the Pueblo in order to document their claims case against the U.S. government.

The Keresan Pueblos along the Rio Grande are likewise noted for their secrecy, particularly Santo Domingo and San Felipe, along with Zia and Santa Ana. But Cochiti is more open, and their experiment with the development of a residence and resort area in connection with Cochiti Lake may encourage changed attitudes on the part of their neighbors. There is no longer the danger of suppression for their ceremonial activities, such as occurred in the early decades of the twentieth century, and greater openness will lead to a better understanding of Pueblo problems.

Farther west the economic success of Laguna has had some influence on Acoma, where the population spends much of their time at farming villages, with Acoma itself becoming a tourist attraction and a steady source of income. Zuni, the best known of the Western Pueblos, has resolved its factional differences to the extent that it has filed a land claim against the U.S. government. There has also been considerable debate over the possibility of establishing Hawikuh, the village first discovered by the Spaniards, as a national monument. The Hopi, more isolated, have maintained much of their social and ceremonial life and are beginning to organize a tribal unity from the independent village communities by means of the tribal council and through their efforts to save their lands from Navajo and White encroachment. A Hopi-run newspaper has become an important factor in this process, as younger educated Hopis begin to play a major role in determining their future.

The Pueblo Indians conceive of their society as in a "steady state," unfolding according to a preordained pattern or plan and continuing in a "timeless" existence. The proper procedures are established in the origin myths and embodied in tradition, as interpreted by the priests and leaders. Proposals for change are tested against past experience and frequently rejected, at least initially. Here the factions have an important role in their questioning of the innovations, and the religious leaders are often forced to take political positions. Social and cultural changes are occurring continuously, but their impact has been slowed, in part by isolation, but more important by the wall of secrecy and conservatism that most Pueblos make use of. But American technology, individualism, and the cash economy have a strong appeal, and the Pueblos face the crucial problem of absorbing these without destroying the communal fabric that has served them so well.

Since the 1940s there has been a considerable revitalization in the whole Pueblo region, from Taos in the east to the Hopi villages in the west, involving population expansion, better health, the revival of ceremonies and dances, and a more aggressive attitude with regard to Pueblo rights and Pueblo land. The return of Blue Lake to the Taos Indians had an important psychological effect on all the Pueblos, and the settlement of the claims cases against the U.S. government provides large sums of money for individual Pueblos. How these resources are utilized will have important effects on Pueblo society and culture, and it is necessary that their members have an adequate knowledge, both of their own history and traditions and of the ways of the White American world.

## Synonymy*

In this synonymy are discussed the names of the linguistic groups among the Pueblo Indians that encompass more than a single Pueblo or tribal unit.

Keresan ($^{1}$kĕrəsən, kə$^{1}$rēsən). This name was coined by Powell (1891:10, 83) by adding the termination -an to the earlier name Keres, used by William W. Turner as early as 1856. Keres, in turn, was an adaptation to English of Spanish Queres, a term in general use since 1598 (Oñate, in Hammond and Rey 1953, 1:461; Domínguez 1956) and appearing in earlier recordings as Quirix (Castañeda, in Hammond and Rey 1940:254, 259) and Quires (Espejo, in Pérez de Luxán 1929:117). The Oñate documents also have Cheres and Cherechos (Hammond and Rey 1953, 1:345, 342). A Cochiti Indian who worked with Bandelier gave ḱeɾes as the Keresan source of this name, but subsequent investigators have failed to confirm the existence of such a name in Keresan (Powell 1891:83; Curtis 1907–1930, 16:262; Harrington 1916:574). Perhaps Jemez kíȋiš (pl.) is the origin (Curtis 1907–1930, 16:261–262, phonemicized).

The Tewa name for the Keresans is témá; this word has no etymology and cannot be derived from te 'cart, wagon', as suggested by Curtis (1907–1930, 16:262), or from te 'house, structure'. The Taos name is miǽlɛnæmǫ̈ (Curtis 1907–1930, 16:261, normalized). The Zuni name given as wehka 'Eastern Keresan' (Newman 1958:45, 75) is apparently specifically wehkʔana 'Santo Domingo Pueblo' (Dennis Tedlock, personal communication 1977); Cushing (in Hodge 1907i) translated the traditional Zuni name as 'Drinkers of the Dew'. Hodge (1907i) obtained Isleta pabierniʼn and Sandia bierniʼn as names for the Keresans generally, but C.T. Harrington (1920:42) has Isleta bíernin 'Laguna Indians', with the comment that this name, though properly referring to Laguna, might be applied to Cochiti and possibly to other Keresans except Zia and San Felipe.

Tanoan (tə$^{1}$nōən). This name was coined by Powell (1891:121), in the spelling Tañoan, for the linguistic family he had early referred to as Taño (1878). Powell (1880) had also called the family Téwan in a classification that used the name Taño for Southern Tiwa. Tagno and Tahano, though including Jemez and Pecos (Gregg 1844,

* This synonymy was written by Ives Goddard.

1:269; Pimentel 1874-1875, 2:92), appear to be variants of Tano (for which see the synonymy in "Hopi-Tewa," this vol.); they are of uncertain origin, though Hodge (1910k) obtained taháno as the Sandia name and this may be the source of the form Tahanos he cites from Zárate Salmerón. The spelling Tanoan has been standard since Hodge (1896:345, 1910k:687); Harrington (1910a:12) wrote Tánoan.

Tewa (ˈtāwu). Téwa appeared as early as 1865 (Ward in Hodge 1910i:738) as an anglicization of Spanish Tegua (Oñate in Hammond and Rey 1953, 1:342; Tamarón y Romeral 1937:341, 348; Domínguez 1956:51) or an independent rendering of the Tewa self-designation téwa. Among the spellings given by Hodge (1910i) are (Spanish) Teoas, Tehua, Tevas, Theguas, and (English) Taowa, Tawas, Tay-wah, Tay-waugh. The name téwa has nothing to do with Spanish tegua 'moccasin' and has no meaning in Tewa except as a linguistic and ethnic label; an ultimate relationship with the sources of the names Tiwa and Towa has not been demonstrated. In some sources Spanish Tegua and Tigua are confused, Tegua, Tehuas, or Teoas being used for both (Tamarón y Romeral 1937:334; Villagrá 1900:97; Benavides 1630:21[19], 31[29]).

Names for the Tewa in other Indian languages are Taos tǫ́banǫ (pl., Trager 1960); Picuris tǝpíanę̆ (pl.), used specifically for the San Juan people (Trager in Parsons 1939a:214); Jemez tǽwa (pl. tǽwiš) (Joe Sando, personal communication 1978); Cochiti Keresan tʸìwa and tʸíwatsa (locative) (Harrington 1916:576; Curtis 1907-1930, 16:260, normalized); Zuni te·wa (Dennis Tedlock, personal communication 1977; Kroeber 1916:275).

Tiwa (ˈtēwu). The term Tiwa was introduced by Hodge (1896:345) to replace the Spanish form Tigua, but Tigua continued in use in English for some years (Hodge 1910n). A specialized use is described in "Tigua Pueblo," this volume. Spanish Tigua appears to have been used only for the Southern Tiwa, although the linguistic affinity of the Southern and Northern Tiwa was recognized as early as Benavides (1630:31[29]). Spanish spellings listed by Hodge (1910n:749) include Tigüex, first applied by Coronado to Puaray Pueblo in 1540, Tiguas (1554), Cheguas, Chiguas, Tigües, Tigüez, Tihuex, Tioas, and (incorrectly) Téoas. According to Schroeder (1964:244-247) the Tihues of Benavides (1945:47) are not the Tiwa but the Piro, also called Atziqui, Tziquis, and Atzigues; late seventeenth- and eighteenth-century Spanish writers confused the two sets of names. Bandelier (1890-1892, 2:223) claimed that Tigüex represented tiguesh ([tiweš]), heard from one speaker as the plural of the Isletan self-designation otherwise given as ti-guan. Tiguan is Isleta tíwan 'Southern Tiwas' (sg. tiwáde) (William Leap, personal communication 1977); Harrington (1916:577) gave the singular as tiwa and said it was "sometimes" applied to Taos and Picuris Indians. Similar names for the Southern Tiwa in other languages are Taos tǽwanǽnæ (Harrington 1918), Picuris tewě'lǐně 'Isleta people' (Spinden in Harrington 1916:577), Jemez téwa 'Isletan' (Joe Sando, personal communication 1978) but téwa-łæ̃ʔš 'Isleta and Sandia Indians' (Harrington 1916:577, phonemicized), Santa Ana Keresan tî̀·wA 'Tiwa Indian' and tí·wá·cé 'Tiwa Pueblo' (Davis 1964:121), and Acoma ṭî̀·wa 'Isletan' (Miller 1965:202) and ṭî̀·waʔáné 'Isleta Pueblo'. Tewa has pocą́·nû· (łowa) for Isleta and Sandia Indians (Harrington 1916:577, phonemicized).

Towa (ˈtōwu). This name was coined by Harrington (1909a:594) on the basis of what he took to be the Jemez word tôwa 'home'; this is tí·wa 'at Jemez Pueblo (to the north)' (Kenneth L. Hale, personal communication 1977).

# Pueblos Abandoned in Historic Times

ALBERT H. SCHROEDER

This chapter summarizes the names, locations, and cultural traits of Pueblos reported by the Spanish expeditions of the 1500s and some additional sources for the 1600s (fig. 1). Not summarized here is cultural information that cannot be assigned to specific Pueblos—from the Francisco Vásquez de Coronado materials of 1540-1542 (Hammond and Rey 1940:254-256), the 1581-1582 Agustín Rodríguez-Francisco Sánchez Chamuscado expedition (Gallegos Lamero 1927a:42-44), from the documents pertaining to the Juan de Oñate colonization of 1598 and after (Hammond and Rey 1953, 1:483-484, 2:610, 625-637, 644-648, 653-656, 658-664, 680, 687, 698, 710, 851, 862-863), and from Benavides (1945:42-45) for the 1620s.

Noncontemporary spellings and misprints of Pueblo names are not usually included in the text. The equations of the Spanish names for Pueblos with native or modern names are tentative in many cases (fig. 2); they do not always agree with those in the previous literature, and further investigations may make other alterations. (In addition to the sources cited in the following sections, see Schroeder 1968, 1972.) The spellings of the names of the Pueblos in the early Spanish documents are problematical, and scholars have differed on the correct reading of the manuscripts in many cases. In this chapter an attempt has been made to follow the spellings of the most recent or most authoritative editions, but inconsistencies and inaccuracies doubtless remain.

The following sections are organized according to Pueblo language groups and the "provinces" named by the Spanish sources.

## Piros

While at Zuni in 1540 Coronado learned of a province of eight Pueblos, which he reached in eight days. This was Tutahaco, where the terraced Pueblos and the people's dress were like those of Tiguex (Southern Tiwa), which lay up the Rio Grande. Later, four more Pueblos were found downstream (Hammond and Rey 1940:220, 245, 259).

The records of the entradas of 1581-1582 and 1582-1583 say this southernmost province, which can be identified as that of the Piros, had mud-walled houses, square with square windows, tau-shaped doorways, and whitewashed interiors decorated with painted monsters, animals, and human figures. Their settlements (12 according to Obregón in Hammond and Rey 1928:290) were on both banks and away from the river, built two to four stories high with many rooms in each house. Walls were one-half vara (16 inches) wide, and movable ladders provided access. The lower part contained kitchens, pantries, and granaries, the last having four to eight mills (metates and manos) at one end of the room in a bin enclosed with whitewashed stones. In the center of the plaza, with ladders in the hatchways, were two large kivas, two and one-half estados (4.6 yards) deep, with whitewashed walls and a stone bench encircling the interior. Games and dances took place there, and visitors gathered in them. Sweatbaths stood to one side (inside the kiva?). Each Pueblo had a house containing small stone idols to which food was carried. Small shrines of stone were located between Pueblos in which they placed painted sticks and feathers.

These people raised corn, beans, squash, and cotton, in fields either dependent on rain or irrigated with good diversion ditches. The farmers, all day in the fields, ate food brought to them in a ramada where they also took siestas. They made tortillas and atoles (corn flour gruel), had buffalo and turkey meat, used picietes (medicinal herbs), and drank pinole (made from toasted ground maize). They had decorated jars, pots, and griddles, and water jars held in earthen stands.

Cotton and campeche-type cotton blankets and buffalo hides, dressed deerskins, and mantas tied around the waist with a sash like those of Mexican Indians provided warmth. Men wore colored cotton loincloths or went naked, with the prepuce tied with a cord, and used deerskin jackets. Women, whose hair was put up in "moulds," one on each side, had color-embroidered cotton skirts and shoes or boots with buffalo-hide soles and deerskin uppers. They used cotton blankets, tanned deerskins, and feather-quilt cloaks, which also were used for sleeping. Domesticated turkeys, kept in pens that would hold 100 birds, provided feathers. Small shaggy dogs were kept in underground huts.

Each Pueblo had its cacique, the number varying according to the Pueblo's size, as well as tequitatos, under-caciques, who performed like alguaciles and executed the cacique's orders by crying them out to the people. These people were at war with the nation upstream (identifiable as the Southern Tiwa), and for weapons used a few poor Turkish-style bows, arrows with fire-hardened shafts and flint points, wooden clubs like a mace *(macanas)* 16 inches long with thick heads and stones strapped on, buffalo-hide shields, clubs, and bludgeons. They respected their boundaries (Gallegos Lamero 1927:262-263, 348-350; Pérez de Luxán 1929:69-74; Espejo 1916:176-179).

The only details added by the colonizing venture of 1598 were the mention of gods of water, mountain, hunt, and crops and that unmarried young women had the status of common property but were faithful after marriage (Villagrá 1933:140-141).

By the 1620s the Piros, under pressures by other Indians (Apaches de Perrillos), had been reduced to 14 Pueblos of 6,000 people. The church established three missions—San Luis Obispo de Sevilleta at Seelocú, Nuestra Señora de Socorro at Pilabó, and San Antonio at Senecú, the last the southernmost Pueblo in 1680. Seelocú, along with others burned during Apache raids, was refounded, and another mission was set up at Alamillo, about 12 miles north of Pilabó (Benavides 1945; Sigüenza y Góngora 1932:87; Hackett 1942, 1:62; Scholes 1936-1937:323). By 1626, grapes planted by the missionaries at Senecú produced wine (Villagrá 1933:146).

Pilabó had a population of 400 in 1641 and 600 in 1680 (Benavides 1945:248). The governor in 1659 moved the people of Sevilleta, whom the previous governor in 1656 congregated into the Pueblo of Alamillo, to their former location where they took up their rituals on the nearby Rio Puerco. Two years later, kachina masks were taken from Alamillo in an attempt to curb the dances (Hackett 1923-1937, 3:186, 206, 220). Also in 1661, Pilabó, Senecú, and Alamillo put in a claim to the Spaniards for payment for transporting piñon nuts to a warehouse at Senecú and for the manufacture of stockings, as did Pilabó for carrying salt from the east side of the Rio Grande to the Pueblo (Scholes 1936-1937:394-395).

Later in the 1660s, some at Senecú were hanged as traitors and sorcerers by the Spaniards (Hackett 1942, 2:266). By 1670 only four Pueblos remained. Apache attacks caused Senecú to join Pilabó in 1675, but two years later Senecú was reoccupied. Most of the Piros of these Pueblos, in fear of retaliation by other Pueblos for not joining the Revolt of 1680, about which they had not been informed, joined the Spaniards in their retreat to El Paso del Norte and formed two Pueblos, Socorro del Sur and Senecú del Sur (Hackett 1942, 1:70, 1923-1937, 3:288, 292, 297-298; Twitchell 1914, 2:53; see also "History of Pueblo-Spanish Relations to 1821" and "Tigua Pueblo," both this vol.). The N. de Fer map of 1695 (Sigüenza y Góngora 1932) shows the original Socorro and Senecú on the west bank and Alamillo and Sevilleta on the east.

When Gov. Antonio de Otermín made an exploratory probe into Pueblo country in 1681, he noted that of the Piros who had remained behind, those of Senecú had planted crops but fled to the high mountain on his approach (Hackett 1923-1937, 3:398). Senecú, Pilabó, and Alamillo, all located on a plain of the river, had been attacked by Apaches who set fire to parts of these towns. Those of Sevilleta had joined other Pueblos to the north, and at their abandoned town a new underground kiva and deep subterranean chambers "in four parts" contained spoiled maize, calabashes, and pottery. On top was a clay vessel with a toad carved on it having the face of an Indian. Inside it were powdered herbs, feathers, two pieces of human flesh, and other things that had been offered to protect the maize. Those of Pilabó, which had been attacked twice, took refuge at Isleta, some going farther north to join other Pueblos at Cieneguilla (near Santa Cruz) and to Acoma where they received bad treatment (Hackett 1942, 2:203-207, 243, 329, 339).

A few Piros were noted at Taos in 1692, and four years later at Cochiti and also with some Tiwas and Tanos of San Lázaro and San Cristóbal, taking refuge in the Sangre de Cristo Mountains (Espinosa 1942:80, 234, 252). The 1696 rebellion by some of the northern Pueblos reportedly took place because a Piro informed the Cochitis that the Spaniards planned to kill all the men and that the Piros and Tiwas of El Paso del Norte would assist in attacking the Spaniards (Twitchell 1916:361; Hackett 1923-1937, 3:352).

In 1760, 111 Piro families of 425 persons lived at Senecú del Sur, but none at Socorro del Sur, whose former Piro inhabitants evidently joined Ysleta del Sur where 80 Piro families of 429 people were recorded this same year (Tamarón y Romeral 1954:38-39). After the 1850s the Tortugas settlement south of Las Cruces is reported to have contained some Piros from these southern Pueblos, and in 1923, *el barrio del pueblo,* a suburb of Ciudad Juárez, contained 55 Piro descendants with a tribal organization and ceremonies (Bloom 1933-1938, 13:206-207; "Tigua Pueblo," this vol.).

The names applied to the individual Piro Pueblos during the early Spanish expeditions are difficult to correlate. A rough correlation of the Spanish names applied by the Rodríguez-Chamuscado and Antonio de Espejo entradas (Gallegos Lamero 1927; Pérez de Luxán 1929) is attempted in table 1. Records of the Oñate entrada list considerably more sites on the east and west sides (not banks) of the river by their native names (Hammond and Rey 1953, 1:318, 346, 2:633; Hodge 1935) as shown in table 2.

## Tompiros

The Rodríguez-Chamuscado party visited five Pueblos near the Salines on the east side of the Sierra Morena (Manzanos), 14 leagues* from Puaray (of the Southern Tiwas), probably by way of Tijeras Canyon. The records

* The league used by the Spaniards in New Mexico varied between 2.6 and 4 miles.

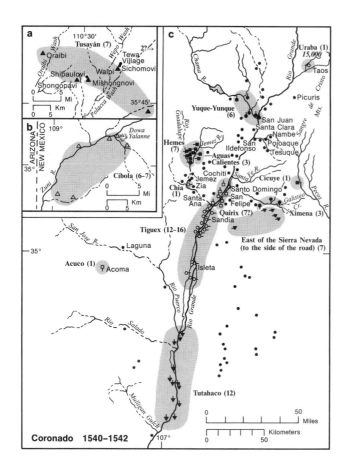

**a**

110°30'

*Tusayán (7)*

▲Oraibi    Tewa
          Village
Shipaulovi  Sichomovi
          ▲Walpi
Shongopavi  Mishongnovi

0    Mi
0    Km
                    35°45'

**b**

ARIZONA
NEW MEXICO

109°

*Dowa
Yalanne*

*Cíbola (6–7)*

Zuni

0    5 Mi
0    5 Km

**c**

Uraba (1)
*15,000*
• Taos

Chama R.

• Picuris

Yuque-Yunque
(6)

San Juan
Santa Clara
Nambe
Pojoaque
Tesuque

Hemes
(7)
Aguas
Calientes (3)
San
Ildefonso

Jemez
Chia
(1)
Santa
Ana
Zia
Santo Domingo
San Felipe
Cochiti
Cicuye (1)

Ximena (3)
Quirix (7?)
Sandia

Tiguex (12–16)

East of the Sierra Nevada
(to the side of the road) (7)

San Jose R.
• Laguna

Acuco (1)   Acoma

35°

Rio Puerco

Isleta

Rio Grande

Rio Salado

Tutahaco (12)

Mulligan Gulch

0         50
         Miles

0         50
         Kilometers

107°

**Coronado   1540–1542**

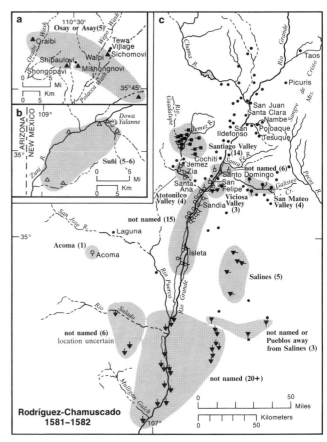

**a**

110°30'

*Osay or Asay(5)*

▲Oraibi    Tewa
          Village
Shipaulovi  Sichomovi
          ▲Walpi
Shongopavi  Mishongnovi

0    Mi
0    Km
                    35°45'

**b**

ARIZONA
NEW MEXICO

109°

*Dowa
Yalanne*

*Suñi (5–6)*

Zuni

0    5 Mi
0    5 Km

**c**

Chama R.

• Taos

• Picuris

San Juan
Santa Clara
Nambe
Cochiti
Pojoaque
Tesuque
San
Ildefonso

Santiago Valley (14)

not named (6)

Jemez
Santo Domingo
Zia
Santa
Ana
San
Felipe
San Mateo
Valley (4)

Atotonilco
Valley (4)
Viciosa
Valley
(3)
Sandia

not named (15)

San Jose R.
• Laguna

Acoma (1)   Acoma

35°

Rio Puerco

Isleta

Rio Grande

Salines (5)

Rio Salado

not named (6)
location uncertain

not named or
Pueblos away
from Salines (3)

not named (20+)

Mulligan Gulch

0         50
         Miles

0         50
         Kilometers

107°

**Rodríguez-Chamuscado
1581–1582**

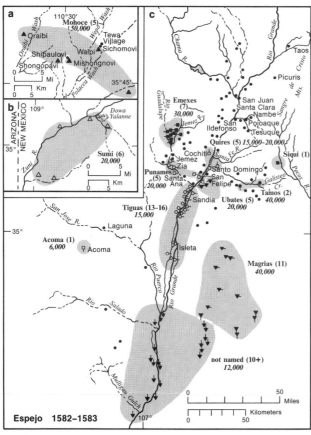

**a**

110°30'

*Mohoce (5)*
*50,000*

▲Oraibi    Tewa
          Village
Shipaulovi  Sichomovi
          ▲Walpi
Shongopavi  Mishongnovi

0    Mi
0    Km
                    35°45'

**b**

ARIZONA
NEW MEXICO

109°

*Dowa
Yalanne*

*Sumi (6)*
*20,000*

Zuni

0    5 Mi
0    5 Km

**c**

Chama R.

• Taos

• Picuris

Emexes
(7)
*30,000*

San Juan
Santa Clara
Nambe
Pojoaque
Tesuque
San
Ildefonso

Quires (7?) *15,000–20,000*

Siqui (1)

Punames
(5)
*20,000*
Cochiti
Zia
Santa
Ana
Santo Domingo
San
Felipe

Jemez

Tamos (2)
*40,000*

Tiguas (13–16)
*15,000*
Sandia
Ubates (5)
*20,000*

San Jose R.
• Laguna

Acoma (1)
*6,000*   Acoma

35°

Rio Puerco

Isleta

Rio Grande

Magrias (11)
*40,000*

Rio Salado

not named (10+)
*12,000*

Mulligan Gulch

0         50
         Miles

0         50
         Kilometers

107°

**Espejo   1582–1583**

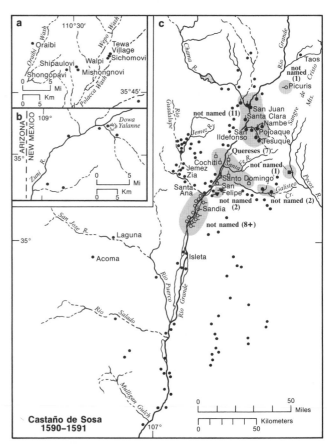

**a**

110°30'

• Oraibi    Tewa
            Village
• Shipaulovi  Sichomovi
            • Walpi
Shongopavi  Mishongnovi

0    Mi
0    Km
                    35°45'

**b**

ARIZONA
NEW MEXICO

109°

*Dowa
Yalanne*

Zuni

0    5 Mi
0    5 Km

**c**

Chama R.

• Taos

not
named
(1)
• Picuris

not named (11)

San Juan
Santa Clara
Nambe
Pojoaque
Tesuque
San
Ildefonso

Quereses (7)

Cochiti
Zia
Santa
Ana
Jemez
not named
(1)
Santo Domingo
San
Felipe
not named
(2)
not named (2)

Sandia
not named (8+)

San Jose R.
• Laguna

• Acoma

35°

Rio Puerco

Isleta

Rio Grande

Rio Salado

Mulligan Gulch

0         50
         Miles

0         50
         Kilometers

107°

**Castaño de Sosa
1590–1591**

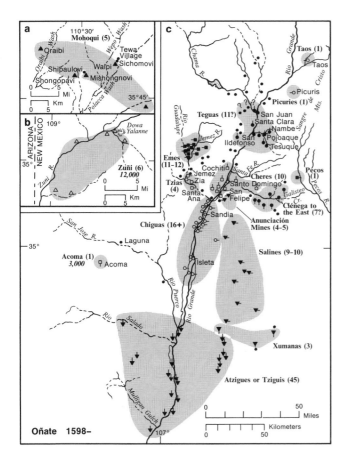

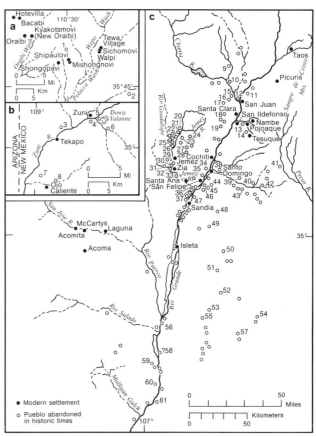

Fig. 2. Pueblos abandoned in historic times (numbered) and modern settlements. 1, Payupki; 2, Awatovi; 3, Kwakina; 4, Halona; 5, Matsaki; 6, Kiakima; 7, Hawikuh; 8, Kianawa (Kechipauan); 9, Sapawe; 10, Tsama; 11, Pioge; 12, Yunque; 13, Jacona; 14, Cuyamungue; 15, Teewi; 16, Ku-Owinge; 17, Pesere; 18, Puye; 19, Tsirege; 20, Unshagi; 21, Nonyishagi; 22, Amushungkwa; 23, Giusewa; 24, Seshiuqua; 25, Astialakwa; 26, Patoqua; 27, Kiatsukwa; 28, Quiashidshi?; 29, LA 499; 30, LA 241; 31, LA 924; 32, Old Zia (LA 384); 33, LA 374; 34, LA 922; 35, Old Santa Ana; 36, LA 2049; 37, Kuaua; 38, Gipuy; 39, San Marcos; 40, Galisteo; 41, Pecos; 42, San Cristóbal; 43, San Lázaro; 44, Tunque; 45, LA 1779; 46, Old San Felipe; 47, Puaray; 48, Paako; 49, Portezuelo; 50, Chililí; 51, Tajique; 52, Quarái; 53, Abó; 54, Tabirá; 55, Tenabó; 56, Seelocú; 57, Gran Quivira (Humanas); 58, Alamillo; 59, Pilabó; 60, Senecú; 61, Qualacu. The names of the abandoned Pueblos are in some cases those recorded in the early Spanish period and in other cases renderings of names applied to Pueblo ruins by Indians in the modern period. Some ruins occupied in historic times and probably noted by the Spaniards are indicated by the number assigned to them by the Laboratory of Anthropology, the Museum of New Mexico, Santa Fe.

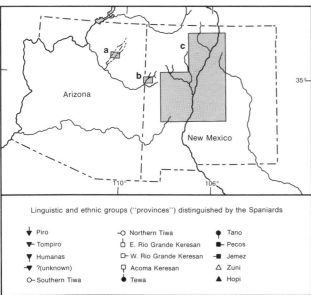

Fig. 1. Pueblo language groups or "provinces" as reported by Spanish entradas. The number of Pueblos in each group is in parentheses; population figures, when given, are italicized. Modern settlements are named. See key map for the location of areas shown on the maps.

give only the names bestowed by the Spaniards: Zacatula—125 houses, 2-3 stories; Ruiseco—200 houses, 2-3 stories; La Mesa—90 houses, 3 stories; La Hoya (La Joya)—95 houses, 2-3 stories; and Franca Vila—65 houses, 2-3 stories. Here they learned of, but did not visit, three large Pueblos (Humanas). These eight seem to have been referred to in another statement. After reaching the Pueblos of Buena Vista and La Barranca on a north-flowing stream in Valley Vicioso (Tonque Arroyo) on the north end of the Sandia Mountains, they were told that up this stream and to the south were 11 or 13 Pueblos in three days' travel whose people spoke a different language (Hammond and Rey 1966:107, 119; Espejo 1916).

239

**Table 1. Possible Correlation of Piro Pueblo Names**

| Rodríguez-Chamuscado Party, 1581–1582 | | Espejo, 1582–1583 |
|---|---|---|
| *West bank* | *East bank* | *Location not given* |
| Taxumulco 123 houses, 2–3 stories | Tomatlán, 70 houses, 2–3 stories (in 2 sections) | El Termino de Puala, 60 houses, 20 houses (2 stone Pueblos) |
| | Mexicalcingo, 40 houses, 2 stories | (3 leagues) |
| Piquinaguatengo (Chiquinagua) 100 houses, 2 stories | Caxtole, 15 houses, 2 stories | Juevas de las Camadres (a place?) |
| | Pueblo Nuevo[a], 25 houses, 2 stories | |
| | Ponsitlán[a], 25 houses, 2 stories | |
| | La Pedrosa, 14 houses, 2 stories | within 5 leagues, 4 Pueblos in ruins and 1 small one |
| | El Hosso (El Osso), 50 houses, 2 stories | |
| | Elota, 14 houses, 2 stories | |
| Piña, 85 houses, 2 stories (2 plazas) Piastla, 35 houses, 2 stories Santiago, 25 houses, 2 stories | San Juan, 40 houses, 2 stories San Miguel, 47 houses, 2 stories | El Gallo, 100 houses, 800 people 50 houses, 400 people 50 houses, 400 people 50 houses, 400 people 50 houses, 400 people |
| | (2 leagues) | (3 leagues to 5 Pueblos close together) |
| | San Felipe (San Phelipe), 45 houses, 2–3 stories | First pueblo, 50 houses, 400 people |

NOTE: The Pueblos are listed in the order encountered from south (bottom) to north (top). West bank and east bank Pueblos given on the same line are described as opposite each other.

[a] In reverse order on Pedrosa's list.

Espejo, two days east of the Rio Grande, via Abó Pass, reached the Magrias or Maguas (Manguas of Obregón in Hammond and Rey 1928) with 11 stone Pueblos located in a waterless region with pine nuts that bordered on the buffalo. They clothed themselves in buffalo hide, cotton, and deerskin. These were warlike people, governed as in other provinces, and had idols and ores in their houses. The first Pueblo had two plazas with four kivas (Tenabó) where they danced and bathed. These also served as community centers and lodging for strangers. In front of each stood a black stone "four fingers" thick, two feet wide, and about five and one-half feet high, on which an Indian with a flaming crown was painted. Each of the two Pueblos (the second Pueblo was Abó) housed 800 people. The Magrias were those who killed Fray Juan de Santa María on his way to Mexico to report on the discoveries of 1581–1582 (Pérez de Luxán 1929:77–78; Espejo 1916:180–181).

The Oñate records (Hammond and Rey 1953, 1:345, 351, 393, 482, 2:705) report 9 to 10 Pueblos of the Salines (or Gallinas): Acoli (Tenabó?), Abó or Abbó, Apona (his last Pueblo of the Salines?), Axauti (Tajique?), Amaxa, Cohuna, Chiu and Alle (Chililí?), Atuya, Máchein or Nyachien (first Pueblo of the Salines?).

In going south from the first Pueblo behind the sierra (Sandia Mountains), "the last pueblo of Puaray," Oñate went five leagues to the first Pueblo of the Salines and another five leagues brought him to the last of the Salines.

Three leagues more brought him to Abó, which in two documents is included with the Humanas and in others is given separately. A second Pueblo of Abó (perhaps Tenabó, or possibly Montezuma Ruin) was one and one-half leagues from the Pueblo of the Humanas (Gran Quivira). The latter Humanas and the Indians of Abó spoke the same language, Tompiro. The Tompiro language of the Humanas was also referred to as Atzigui, to be compared with the name Tziguis or Atzigues used for the Piro (Scholes 1937–1938:401; Schroeder 1964).

From Abó, where Chili was the captain, Oñate traveled four leagues to the province of the Humanas (Hammond and Rey 1953, 1:345, 351, 428, 2:650). They were called Humanas (Xumanas, Jumanas, Jumanes), meaning 'striped Indians' *(indios rayados)* because of a stripe painted across the nose and because the Jumanos of the Plains often came to them to trade (Benavides 1945:66). Only some Humanas painted themselves; other Pueblos did not. These people lived in three terraced Pueblos with plazas and streets, one being very large and the other two small. The Pueblo of Cueloze, Cuelóce, Quellotezei, or Coloze (Gran Quivira) had as its captain Yohla; Genobey or Xenopue (Tenabó?) had Pocaetaqui; Pataotzei or Patasci (Tabirá?) had Haye.

The Humanas (of Abó in one report) killed two of five Spaniards escaping from the colony, drawing Spanish retaliation. Though the Humanas ambushed the Spaniards en route to Abó at the Pueblo of Agualagu or

**Table 2. Native Names for Piro Pueblos, 1598**

| West side of Rio Grande | East side of Rio Grande |
|---|---|
| Pencoana | Preguey (from where Abó |
| Quiomaqui | Pueblos were visited? also |
| Peixoloe | Nueva Sevilla?) |
| Cumaque | Tuzahe |
| Teeytzaan | Aponitze |
| Peeguey | Vumaheyn |
| Canocan | Quiapo |
| Geydol | Cunquili |
| Quiu-Baco | Pinoe |
| Tohol | Calziati |
| Cantemachuc | Aquiabo |
| Tercao | Emxa |
| Poloaca | Quiaguacalca |
| Tzeyey | Quialpo |
| Quelquelu | Tzelaqui |
| Ategua | Peequias (Puquias) |
| Tzula | Ayqui |
| Tzegual | Yanamo |
| Tecahan | Teyaxa |
| Qualahamo | Qualacú or Cuelaqu [b] |
| Pilogue (Pilabó) [a] | Texa |
| Penjeacu (Senecú?) | Amo [c] |
| Teypama or Teypana | |
| (first Socorro) | |
| Tzenaquel de la Mesilla | |

NOTE: The Pueblos are listed in order from north to south.
[a] Second Socorro.
[b] Calicu on 1602 map (Hammond and Rey 1966:endpapers, errata slip).
[c] Earlier called San Felipe?

Acoloco, the Spaniards killed more than 900 and took 400 prisoners (Hammond and Rey 1953). The locale of the battle seems to be east of the Sandia Mountains.

In the 1620s Benavides reported that the Tompiro (or *la nación Tompira*) lived in 14 or 15 Pueblos (?), totaling some 10,000 people. Chililí (La Navidad de Nuestra Señora), with a population of 500, was the first Pueblo. Tajique (San Miguel), a Pueblo built of stone, had 300 people. Included in this group was a large Pueblo, Humanas, the site of the mission of San Isidro, later called San Buenaventura, and identified with the modern ruins known as Gran Quivira. It had 3,000 people, who were very cruel (Benavides 1945:65-66). The buffalo in dry years roamed as far as the Salines belonging to the Tompiro Indian nation (Zárate Salmerón 1966:88). Near Cuarac (Quarái) were fields where three of the neighboring Pueblos raised corn and cotton (Hackett 1923-1937, 3:131).

Apaches (of the Sierra Blanca or Siete Ríos) attacked the Humanas Pueblo (Cueloze) east of Abó (San Gregorio) in 1653 (Scholes 1937-1938:150). The Spaniards in 1659 had the Indians of the six remaining Pueblos of the Salines carry salt 30 leagues without pay (Hackett 1923-1937, 3:188). In the 1660s these people traded with the Apaches de los Siete Ríos near Carlsbad (Scholes 1937-1938:396) in between raids on their Pueblos and held kachina dances (Hackett 1923-1937, 3:143, 408). The friars claimed that the missions lost a large number of cattle at Chililí, Tajique, Abó, and Humanas because the Indians no longer could work without pay as they had in the past (Scholes 1937-1938:67). This appears to be an exaggeration since water was so scarce at Humanas that the Indians had to depend on 32 wells (Hackett 1923-1937, 3:205).

In 1661 Tabirá put in a claim for transporting salt to the Rio Grande, as did Abó for carrying corn from Tabirá and Humanas to the house of the *alcalde mayor* of the Saline district, and Humanas for labor. Tabirá (San Diego) at this time was a *visita* of Humanas in the Saline province (Hackett 1923-1937, 3:135, 188, 203). Apache attacks, one by those of the Siete Ríos in 1670 (Scholes and Mera 1940:283), plus the droughts and famines of the late 1660s from which 450 died at Humanas in 1668, weakened these Pueblos, and in the early 1670s they abandoned their homes, four specifically in 1672: Humanas with more than 500, Abó with more than 300, Chililí with more than 100, and another called Las Salinas (Tajique) with more than 300 (Hackett 1923-1937, 3:271-272, 298). The Tabirá and Quarái abandonment dates are not specifically known. The N. de Fer map of 1695 shows, from north to south, six sites—Chilili, Tayip (Tajique), Cuana, Abo, Humanas, and to the east, Tavira (Sigüenza y Góngora 1932).

Most of these people joined their Piro relatives along the Rio Grande, only to leave New Mexico permanently in 1680. According to Bandelier (1890-1892, 2:273), Indians at Senecú in Chihuahua claimed to be descendants of those of Abó.

One Pueblo of the Saline area, Quarái (Cuarac, Querac, Nuestra Señora de la Concepción), appears not to have been mentioned in the 1500s, unless it was Oñate's "last pueblo" of the Salines. Ceramic material at the site suggests that the Pueblo (LA 95) possibly was abandoned in late prehistoric times and reoccupied in historic times (Museum of New Mexico archeological survey files). Some would identify the language of this Pueblo as Southern Tiwa on the basis of a report that occupants spoke Tiwa to a woman near Isleta (Hackett 1923-1937, 3:178). Yet when Quarái was abandoned, its 600 people joined those of Tajique (Bandelier 1890-1892, 2:258-259, 262), according to a 1696 statement by a Piro (Tompiro), formerly resident at Tajique (Twitchell 1916:343, 361, 363). It is possible that the friars brought Tiwas to Quarái and established a Pueblo there to assist in missionizing the Tompiros. Bandelier (1890-1892, 2:234) reported that some of the Indians at Ysleta del Sur claimed to have come from Quarái, which might indicate they were Tiwas. However, 80 Piro families also were recorded at Ysleta del Sur in 1760 (Tamarón y Romeral 1954:38-39).

Quarái provided labor to transport piñon nuts from

Humanas Pueblo to the Rio Grande in the middle 1660s (Scholes 1936-1937:298-299, 1937-1938:394). Also in this decade, a plot hatched by Esteban Clemente of Quarái to overthrow the Spaniards was discovered, resulting in his death (Bandelier 1890-1892, 2:265).

For information obtained from excavations within the Tompiro area and for this period, see Vivian (1964) and J.H. Toulouse (1949).

## Southern Tiwas

The province of Tiguex served as the base for Coronado's explorations. On both banks of the river stood 12 Pueblos close together or 15 within 20 leagues. According to Obregón (Hammond and Rey 1928:17, 322) there were 16 within 20 leagues, some with 600 people, two of the Pueblos with 100 each being six leagues to the southeast of the 12 (perhaps one in Tijeras Canyon and one at the east end). The Pueblos, enclosed by a palisade, were two stories high with wooden galleries and kivas (estufas). The houses, narrow with a small entrance, lacked doors at ground level. Governed by old men, these people raised maize, beans, squashes, and some turkeys (the feathers of which were used to make blankets), but they had no markets. Dressed in cotton, feather cloaks, and buffalo skins, they wore shoes of hide. Food and clothing were found in the Pueblos but no jewelry. Also seen were flutes, bows and arrows, and maces. The people of Cicuique (Pecos) were enemies of Tiguex.

These people evacuated the Pueblo of Coofor or Alcanfor on the west bank for Coronado's use. During the Spanish siege of the Pueblos of Moho, also referred to as Tiguex and located three to four leagues from Coofor, and Arenal, one-half league from Coofor, both fortified Pueblos, the Indians at Arenal dug a well to obtain water. One-half league from Moho stood the strongest (unnamed) Pueblo of all. The Pueblo of Alameda stood between Coofor and Arenal, all on the west bank. The last Pueblo (south) on the east bank was small. Following the siege, the Indians deserted the 12 Pueblos located within one-quarter to three leagues of Coofor, which the Spaniards burned in part (Hammond and Rey 1940).

Records of the Rodríguez-Chamuscado entry of 1581-1582 report that this nation, with speech and dress different from their southern neighbors the Piros, lived in three to five story Pueblos, some with 300 to 400 houses with corridors and rooms 24 by 13 varas, whitewashed and painted inside, and with good plazas connected by streets.

They built their houses square, baking (sun-drying?) the clay, making narrow walls, using adobes for the doorways and willow timbers 10 to 12 feet long. Ladders provided access and were taken up at night. Men cut their hair to form a sort of skull cap on their head; others wore it long. Painted cotton cloth 24 inches long and about 6 inches wide covered their privy parts. Blankets painted with figures of various colors, fastened at the shoulders, hung to their knees. Most wore hand-painted and embroidered cotton shirts and shoes. Women had colored and embroidered skirts and over them a blanket like those of the men with a cotton sash with tassels. Their long hair was combed and parted.

Men carried burdens and worked the fields of maize, going out at daybreak with their hoes, and women prepared the food and made and painted their pottery and griddles in which they baked bread. Large water jars were covered with clay lids. Women with daughters had them do the grinding. Water jars were carried on the head, resting on a palm (yucca) cushion. These people were well provisioned with maize, beans, gourds, turkeys, tortillas, and corn flour gruel. Girls were not allowed to go outside without their parents' permission; they married at about 17 years of age. Men had only one wife. Women spun, wove, and painted (Gallegos Lamero 1927:263-266, 350-352).

Tomatlán, built in two sections on the east bank of the Rio Grande, seems to be the most northern of the Piro Pueblos visited by these Spanish observers. Assuming that it correlates with El Termino de Puala (table 1), said to be two Pueblos two harquebus shots apart and the last Pueblo of the Piros seen by Espejo, who followed in 1582-1583, the Pueblos recorded for the Tiwas by these two parties might roughly correlate as shown in table 3.

One-half league, according to Espejo, or four leagues or more, according to Lujan, to the north of the Piros Espejo came to the Tiguas. There some of the Pueblos and whitewashed houses were larger than those of the previous province (Piros) and contained maize, beans, squash, green and sun-dried vegetables, potatoes (wild tubers?), turkeys, many ores of different colors, numerous masks for dances and ceremonies, good crockery, and an instrument like a flageolet. Some 7,000 to 8,000 Indians (near Puaray) took refuge in the sierra (Sandia Mountains). Here it was learned that two friars who had stayed behind from the previous entrada were martyred at the large Pueblo of Puaray (Pérez de Luxán 1929:76, 80; Espejo 1916:179).

Gaspar Castaño de Sosa in 1591, coming south from the Keresan country by way of the north end of the Sandia Mountains, arrived at a cluster of three Pueblos on the Rio Grande, one on the east bank (Campos of 1581-1582?) and two one-quarter league apart on the west side (Medina de la Torre and Palomares of 1581-1582?). Traveling south on the east bank, he visited four more, perhaps Caseres, Malpais (close to *malpaís* 'badlands'), Nompe, and Zenpoala. He crossed to the west bank visiting others (number not given, possibly La Palma, Villarasa, Culiacán, and Analco) and slept at a small Pueblo (San Pedro?). The next day he went to the last Pueblo on the east side, which was large (Puaray of 1581-1582?), before turning back upstream to Santo Domingo (Castaño de Sosa 1965:167-175).

**Table 3. Possible Correlation of Southern Tiwa Pueblo Names**

| Rodríguez-Chamuscado Party, 1581–1582 | | Espejo, 1582–1583 |
|---|---|---|
| *West bank of Rio Grande* | *East bank of Rio Grande* | |
| Medina de la Torre, 232 houses, 2–3 stories | | Poguana or Puaguana |
| Palomares, 80 houses, 2–3 stories | Campos, 60 houses, 2–3 stories | Comise<br>Achine or Aychini |
| | Cáseres, 60 houses, 2–3 stories | Guagua |
| | Malpaís, 123 houses, 2–3 stories | Gagose |
| | Nompe, 77 houses, 2–3 stories | Simassa |
| | Cempoala or Cempoalla, 20 houses, 2 stories | Suyte |
| La Palma, 134 houses, 2–3 stories | | Nocoche |
| Villarrasa or Villarasa, 100 houses, 2–3 stories | | Hacala |
| Culiacán, 84 houses, 2–3 stories | | Tiara |
| Analco, 40 houses, 2–3 stories | | Taycios |
| San Pedro, 62 houses, 2–3 stories | | Casa |
| | Puaray, Puari, or Puarai, 112–123 houses, 2–3 stories | Puala, 400 houses, 3 stories (2 leagues) |
| | San Mateo, 50 houses, 2 stories | Los Guajolotes on east bank; passed one Pueblo (5 leagues) |
| | | Los Despoblados (2 deserted Pueblos, 1 with 250 houses) on east bank; (4 leagues) passed a deserted Pueblo |
| Santa Catalina, 100 houses, 2–3 stories | | El Corvillo on east bank; 4 leagues from opposite Abó Pass, past some small pueblos and many deserted ones |

NOTE: The Pueblos are listed in order from north to south except the top 13 named by Espejo (Poguana through Puala). These are described as all within 1 league, but their order and bank location are unknown.

Oñate's itinerary from the Abó Pass area (Hammond and Rey 1953, 1:319) recorded four leagues to the Pueblo of San Juan Bautista, with many painted idols (El Corvillo of 1582–1583?), six leagues passing many Pueblos on both sides, and another 10 leagues to Puaray, named San Antonio de Padua. Poquia was listed as captain of the Chiguas (Tiwas) and the "pueblos of the west" (west bank?). Paquia, probably the same, is referred to again as captain of Tziati and Pequen (perhaps Tziymatsi and Piaque, on the west bank). Atequite is named as captain of the Tzios (?) and of the Pueblos of Comitze and Ayquin (Comise and Achine of 1582–1583) (Hammond and Rey 1953, 1:338).

Poquia's "pueblos of the west" (Hammond and Rey 1953, 1:337) include: Piaque—(Isleta, perhaps the Mesilla of Martínez's 1602 map) (Hammond and Rey 1966: endpapers); Axoytze (perhaps Suyte of 1582–1583) (Pérez de Luxán 1929:115); Piamato; Quioyoco; Camitze (perhaps the Comise of 1582–1583). Another listing of the Chiguas or Tiguas (Hammond and Rey 1953, 1:346) contains other Pueblo names without repetition: Napeya (perhaps Sandia); Tuchiamas (perhaps the Taycios of 1582–1583); Pura, together with the next four in order downstream; Popen; Puarai (perhaps the Puala of 1582–1583); Tziymatzi (Simassa of 1582–1583); Guayotzi (Gagose of 1582–1583); Acacagui (Guagua of 1582–1583); Henicohio (Nocoche of 1582–1583); Viareato (perhaps the Tiara of 1582–1583). These listings do not contain Ayquin or one other possible Tiwa site that Oñate noted after leaving the northern Pueblo of the Salines as he turned west to the Rio Grande. This was Portezuelo ('little door or opening', at the east end of Tijeras Canyon, site LA 24 of the Museum of New Mexico files) from where he proceeded seven leagues to the Pueblo where Father Juan Claros was stationed, Isleta (Hammond and Rey 1953, 1:394).

Oñate's documents do not provide much specific information that can be identified with the Tiwas. At Puaray, however, underneath a fresh coat of whitewash, the Spaniards discerned a wall painting depicting the martyrdom of the two Spanish priests of the 1581-1582 entrada (Bandelier 1890-1892, 2:229).

In the 1620s the 15 or 16 Pueblos within 12 or 13 leagues along the river contained some 7,000 people with churches at San Francisco de Sandia and San Antonio de Isleta (Benavides 1945:64). The missionization program seemingly reduced the number of Pueblos, population figures for only three being listed in 1626 or 1641—Sandia with 640, Alameda with 400, and Isleta with 750. However, in 1680, four were noted—Puaray with 200, Sandia with 3,000, Isleta with 2,000, and Alameda with 300 (Hodge in Benavides 1945:253-258). It would appear by these figures that Isleta absorbed the populations of the Pueblos near Albuquerque and Sandia those in the Bernalillo area.

The people of these Pueblos, except at Isleta, fled prior to the arrival of Governor Otermín's probe into Pueblo country in 1681. The stone Pueblo of Alameda exhibited a new kiva with idols, masks, figures of the devil with herbs, and feathers. A good supply of maize and beans and birds of the country was found in the Pueblo as well as at Puaray on the east bank where two new kivas with masks of baize and idols were found along with a supply of maize, beans, and salt. At Sandia, three leagues from Puaray, two new kivas with masks and other articles also were noted along with maize, beans, and vessels. The Pueblos and kivas with their contents were put to the torch (Hackett 1942, 2:220-230, 258-260, 267-268).

Of 500 Isletans, 385 accompanied Otermín to El Paso del Norte after he set fire to the Pueblo and the large kiva in the main plaza (Hackett 1942, 2:357-358; "Isleta Pueblo," this vol.). In the 1660s an underground kiva was near the *convento,* close to the west side of the church.

Isleta, Puaray, and Sandia do not appear on the 1706 population list, but Alameda does with 50 Tiwas at this new mission. More were expected from other Pueblos where they had taken refuge (Hackett 1923-1937, 3:209, 361, 367, 373-377). Since 441 Tiwas and Hopis came to the Rio Grande in 1742, many of those of Puaray, Sandia, and Alameda must have gone to Hopi country. Of those who returned, 350 resettled Sandia in 1748 (Kelly 1941:44, 47-48; "Sandia Pueblo," this vol.) where 12 years later there were 196 Tiwas and 95 Hopis (Tamarón y Romeral 1954:44). As for the Isletans, some had returned to their Pueblo by 1715 or 1718, but from where is not definitely known (Chavez 1957:12, 158, 202).

For information obtained from excavations within the Southern Tiwa area and for this period see Vivian (1934) and Dutton (1963).

### Keresans

The early Spanish explorers seem to have divided the Keresans into several groups: the Zia Pueblos west of the Rio Grande, the Keresans along the Rio Grande (whom they especially called *Queres,* here called Eastern Rio Grande Keresans), Acoma ("with its surrounding and adjoining pueblos" in 1598, though only Acoma is named), and those of the Galisteo Basin, which are not clearly distinguished (table 4).

In Coronado's day all four groups are referred to. Only Chia (Old Zia), "a fine pueblo with a large population" west of the river (Rio Grande), is mentioned in the Zia group (Hammond and Rey 1940:233). There quilts, skins, and blankets were obtained. Among the Eastern Rio Grande group only "the first pueblo" of seven (San Felipe, the southernmost), with 100 people, is recorded. Aside from the possible inclusion of a Keresan Pueblo in the Galisteo Basin in a statement referring to seven Pueblos by the side of the road from Pecos to the Keresans (Hammond and Rey 1940:258), no identifiable Keresan Pueblo is mentioned. (For Coronado's visit to Acoma see "Acoma Pueblo," this vol.)

In 1581-1582, aside from Spanish names applied to the Pueblos, the number of houses, and the height of each, specific information on any one group is slight and restricted to the Galisteo Basin area with only the mention that at Malpartida (San Marcos) they learned of mineral deposits a league away. One of the friars who left from there in advance of the party's return to Mexico was killed three days to the south (by the Magrias according to the Espejo accounts) on the east side of the mountains (Gallegos Lamero 1927:341-342, 351-352).

The Espejo party, which did not visit any Keresan Pueblo in the Galisteo Basin, named five on the Rio Grande. At Cachiti, Catiete, or La Tiete (San Felipe), named Los Confiados, most houses were three stories high. A cacique governed, having authority only at his own Pueblo, and in dress and other respects these people were like those of the Puala (Southern Tiwa). They had a parrot in a cage and had "sunflowers like those of China, decorated with the sun, moon, and stars." Obtaining maize, turkeys, tortillas, and pinole, the party traveled one and one-half leagues west to La Milpa Llana (Old Santa Ana) where they bartered for similar items (Pérez de Luxán 1929:82-83, 117; Espejo 1916:181).

At Ziaquebos or Sia (the Queraque of Obregón in Hammond and Rey 1928:323), in the province of the Punames (see the synonymy in "Zia Pueblo," this vol.), three caciques, Quasquito, Quchir, and Quatho, ruled. The houses were whitewashed and painted with colors and pictures like those of the Mexicans. Men were dressed in blankets, cloaks, shawls, cotton loincloths, and leather boot-shaped shoes. Women wore blankets over their shoulders tied at the waist with a sash and had feather-blanket cloaks. Hair, cut in front, was plaited into two braids. This Pueblo, located five leagues west of La Milpa Llana on a south-flowing river (the Jemez), was the chief and largest of the five Pueblos of this province. The people provided cotton mantas, maize, turkeys, tortillas,

244

**Table 4. Tentative Correlation of Keresan Pueblo Names**

| | Coronado, 1540 | Rodríguez-Chamuscado, 1581 | Espejo, 1582 | Castaño de Sosa, 1590 | Oñate, 1598 |
|---|---|---|---|---|---|
| • Acoma | Acoma<br>Acuco<br>Acus | Acoma<br>500 houses, 3-4 stories | Acoma | | Acoma<br>500 houses |
| • Western Rio Grande Keresans | | Atotonilco Valley | Punames<br>(5 Pueblos) | | Tzias |
|    LA 241 | | La Rinconada<br>60 houses, 3-4 stories | | | Pelcheu |
|    Old Zia (LA 384) | Chia | Valladolid<br>200 houses, 3-4 stories | Ziaquebos<br>1,000 houses,<br>3-4 stories<br>Sia<br>Queraque[a] | | Tzia |
|    Zia (LA 28) | | La Guarda<br>100 houses, 2-4 stories | | | Acotziya<br>Yacco |
|    LA 374 | | Guatitlán<br>Guaxitlan<br>76 houses, 2-3 stories | | | Toxogua |
| • Eastern Rio Grande Keresans | Quirix<br>(7 Pueblos) | | Quites<br>Quires | Quereses | Cheres<br>Cherechos |
|    Old Santa Ana | | | La Milpa Llana<br>(may be<br>included in<br>Punames) | | Tamaya<br>Tamy (included<br>in Tzias) |
|    LA 2049 | | Castilleja<br>40 houses, 2-3 stories | | | |
|    San Felipe | | Castildabid<br>Castil de avid<br>200 houses, 3-4 stories | Cachiti<br>Catiete<br>La Tiete<br>Los Confiados | | Cachichi<br>Castixe<br>San Felipe |
|    Old San Felipe | | Castilblanco<br>200 houses, 3-4 stories | Sieharan | perhaps passed<br>but not named | Comitze |
|    LA 922 | | Suchipila<br>90 houses, 2-3 stories | | | |
|    Gipuy (LA 182) | | La Nueva Tlascala<br>500 houses, 1-7 stories | Tipolti | visited but<br>not named | Olipoti<br>Tipoti<br>Tipotin[b] |
|    Santo Domingo (before 1886 flood) | | Talaván<br>Talabán<br>80 houses, 2-3 stories | Gigue | Santo Domingo | Quigui<br>Santo Domingo |
|    La Ciénega | | | | | Ciénega de<br>Carabajal |
|    Cochiti | | | Cochita | 4 Pueblos | Cochiti<br>La Cañada? |
|    San Marcos | | Malpartida<br>100-500 houses, 2-3 stories | | San Marcos | Yatez<br>Yates<br>San Marcos |

[a] Obregón in Hammond and Rey 1928.

[b] 1602 map in Hammond and Rey 1966:endpapers, errata slip.

and vegetables (Pérez de Luxán 1929:83-84; Espejo 1916:181-182).

The identification of Ziaquebos as LA 384 (Old Zia) in table 4 is based on the names applied to the four Pueblos in the Atotonilco Valley by the Rodríguez-Chamuscado expedition and their apparent correspondence to four sites known to have been occupied in historic times. Named from east to west, the first was Guatitlán (LA 374); the second was La Guarda 'the guard', which aptly describes the site locale of Zia (LA 28) on the tip of a mesa overlooking the valley; the third was Valladolid (LA 384), the largest site; and the fourth, La Rinconada 'the corner' (LA 241) "because it is in a turn of the valley," where it turns more to the north toward present Jemez Pueblo (Gallegos Lamero 1927:352). A fifth Pueblo, noted by Espejo, may have been LA 924 or LA 499.

Acoma, with 6,000 people, was said (erroneously) to have been built on a mesa because of a war with the Querechos (Apaches). Four stairways led to the top where water was caught in cisterns. House doors resembled trap doors (see "Acoma Pueblo," this vol.). Obregón refers to shacks (ramadas) in fields away from the Pueblo and also in fields below the mesa and says 400 Indians took part in the dances, which lasted all day and night (Hammond and Rey 1928:325). Perhaps the irrigated fields, some distance from the Pueblo and seasonally occupied, represent the "surrounding and adjoining pueblos" of Acoma referred to in 1598 (Hammond and Rey 1953, 1:346).

Castaño de Sosa saw four Pueblos in the immediate Cochiti vicinity and went to another of their language, which he named San Marcos; a league farther on he examined mineral deposits. Later, he passed through a deserted Pueblo (Gipuy, where a few days later he obtained the obedience of the occupants) and went on to Santo Domingo (Oñate's Quigui, flooded out in 1886), which he named (Castaño de Sosa 1965:140-145, 157-160; synonymy in "Santo Domingo Pueblo," this vol.).

Records of Oñate's colonization of 1598 provide native names for almost all Keresan Pueblos (Hammond and Rey 1953, 1:337, 345), but unfortunately little detail on the Pueblos except those relating to the battle at Acoma, in which women also took part. There were several plazas and narrow streets and "fortified" estufas with underground passages in the rock through which imprisoned Acomas escaped to the houses, which also were connected by tunnels and passageways. The Indians dug deep pitfalls at the base of the cliffs to snare horses; used bows and arrows, stones, war clubs, and wooden spears and sticks in defending themselves; and hurled insults and pulled ladders up to the roofs to prevent access. The Acomas also threatened to punish the Eastern Rio Grande Keresans, Southern Tiwas, and Zias for not opposing the Spaniards. Of the occupants of the 500 houses, 800 died and 330 to 500 women and children plus 70 to 80 men were taken prisoner, a total of about 600. The Spaniards burned and destroyed the Pueblo. As in other Pueblos, they noted maize, flour, tortillas, turkeys, and blankets. Chiefs or captains of the "wards" of the Pueblo were Cooma, Chaamo, and Ancua. Acoma witnesses at the trial included Cat-ticate, Taxio, Xunusta, Excasi, and Caucachi.

As for the Keresans on the Rio Grande (those Oñate called Cheres), Cali is given as the captain of Cachichi (San Felipe). Comitze (Old San Felipe) and Castixe (San Felipe) are linked together in the listings of friars' assignments (Hammond and Rey 1953, 1:345), suggesting the above identifications. This Comitze should not be confused with the Camitze of the Southern Tiwas. It should be noted that in the Oñate documents, reference often is made to a captain of several Pueblos, suggesting political groupings.

By the 1620s Benavides lumped the Keresans into one group under the name Queres, with the exception of Acoma, with a population of more than 1,000, and San Marcos, which he erroneously included among the Tanos (Benavides 1945:65, 67; Castaño de Sosa 1965:144-145).

As for the Keresan Pueblos abandoned in the 1600s, the four reported in 1591 as being within sight of one another, including Cochiti, are not mentioned again, aside from Cochiti, unless the other three are those not listed in table 4, Oñate's Ojana, Quipacha, and El Puerto, also called El Pueblo Quemado 'the burned Pueblo' (Hammond and Rey 1953, 1:345) and Messillas (Martínez's 1602 map in Hammond and Rey 1966:endpapers and errata slip), which may well have been absorbed by Cochiti in the missionization process of the early 1600s.

Old San Felipe (Comitze), probably absorbed by San Felipe in the same period, seems not to have been mentioned after Oñate's day. It is shown on the east side of the Rio Grande on the N. de Fer map of 1695, but the San Felipe on the west side is not (Sigüenza y Góngora 1932). When the Spaniards passed from Santo Domingo to Sandia on the east bank in 1680, no reference was made to Old San Felipe on that side. The same was true in 1681 (Hackett 1942, 1:xci-xciii, 2:259).

Old Santa Ana, referred to in 1582-1583 as La Milpa Llana, one and one-half leagues from San Felipe (Pérez de Luxán 1929:83), must have been on the mesa above the present Pueblo as the distance was not enough to reach present Santa Ana nor is the river at Santa Ana mentioned. In 1680 the population of Old Santa Ana was included with that of San Felipe (Hackett 1942, 1:xliii; "Santa Ana Pueblo," this vol.). In 1692 Santa Ana Pueblo was said to be deserted. Since there seems to be no mention of Santa Ana in its present locale by the river in the documents of the early explorers, only of Old Santa Ana near San Felipe, perhaps present Santa Ana was built after 1687 and was the deserted Pueblo of 1692 and the one with a few people in it in 1693 (Espinosa 1942:141).

Four Zia Pueblos were mentioned in 1581–1582 and five by the chroniclers of the next two entradas that visited this group. These seem to have been absorbed into present Zia during the missionization of the 1620s and later. Old Zia (the Chia, Valladolid, Ziaquebos, Sia, and Tsia Pueblo of early days) appears to have been the large Pueblo sacked in 1689 by Gov. Domingo Jironza Petriz de Cruzate, resulting in the death of some 600 (Bandelier 1890–1892, 2:198). It was in ruins in 1692 when the Zias were at Cerro Colorado with the Santa Anas four leagues to the west. Diego de Vargas suggested to the Zias that they return to their Pueblo, stating the walls were still good, as were the nave and choir of the church. In 1693, the Zias still were at La Alameda del Cerro Colorado de Sia, five long leagues from Santa Ana, and he again urged them to reoccupy their Pueblo three leagues away (Espinosa 1942:84, 139–141).

San Marcos and La Ciénega, the latter shown between Santo Domingo and Jacona near the Rio Grande on the N. de Fer 1695 map (Sigüenza y Góngora 1932), were abandoned in 1680 and their people joined the Tanos and others in the attack on Santa Fe in the 1680 Revolt. San Marcos, known as 'turquoise pueblo ruin' in Tewa (Harrington 1916:551), and others mined the turquoise as well as lead for making glaze paint in the nearby Cerrillos Hills, both activities ceasing at about the time of the Revolt (Snow 1973). Pueblos also used the gypsum deposits in the Galisteo Basin for making whitewash (Harrington 1916:494). La Ciénega was vacant in 1694 (Espinosa 1942:179), and efforts to resettle it in 1695 failed (Bandelier 1890–1892, 2:91). In the following year, some Keresans from La Ciénega, Santo Domingo, and Cochiti were reported at Acoma (Espinosa 1942:342), some of whom probably joined in the founding of Laguna in the late 1690s. Vargas in 1692 found San Marcos in ruins and the people living with the Cochitis on Horn Mesa, where Vargas attacked them in 1694 (Espinosa 1942:83, 137, 140, 180; "San Felipe Pueblo," this vol.). Shortly after, Cochiti was reoccupied.

The people of San Felipe had taken refuge in a stone Pueblo of about 58 rooms on the mesa above their Pueblo during the Revolt and remained there until at least 1696. A church built there saw brief use before these people reoccupied their Pueblo below (Espinosa 1942:136; Bandelier 1890–1892, 1:190).

## Tanos

In 1540–1542 two Pueblos were recorded in the Galisteo Basin between Quirix (Rio Grande Keresans) and Cicuye (Pecos), one a small strong Pueblo with 35 houses called Ximena (San Lázaro) and the other not named (Galisteo), only one section of which was occupied (Hammond and Rey 1940:257).

The Rodríguez-Chamuscado party, five leagues from the river in the Valle de San Mattheo or Mateo, saw four Pueblos, one of which was Malpartida (San Marcos), a Keresan Pueblo. The other three appear to be Tano (table 5). Corridors, plazas, and streets were noted at Malagón (Gallegos Lamero 1927:342–343, 354).

Espejo, traveling east from the province of the Ubates (north end of the Sandia Mountains), reached the Tamos or Atamues (Tanos) three leagues away. They were more warlike than the others. Their well-built houses, three to four stories high, had movable ladders and flat roofs with drainage troughs. At Jumea (San Lázaro), they wore their hair like a skull cap. Women dressed as in other provinces and hired themselves out to men. Turkeys and pinole were found there. Pocos or Pocoje (San Cristóbal), referred to as Los Pozos in 1626 (Zárate Salmerón 1966:56), two leagues away, had 1,500 warriors. This very large Pueblo with wooden corridors was entered by ladders (Pérez de Luxán 1929:119–120; Espejo 1916:189; Castaño de Sosa 1965:139–140).

Castaño de Sosa, who also entered from the west (after visiting San Marcos, which he specifically referred to as Keresan), named two Pueblos, San Cristóbal and San Lucas (Galisteo), and obtained maize, flour, beans, and turkeys as he did at other Pueblos. The identification of San Cristóbal as San Lázaro (Schroeder in Castaño de Sosa 1965:155) is unlikely.

Oñate, again entering Galisteo Basin—"the ciénaga to the east"—from the west, visited San Cristóbal and Galisteo (named by him Santa Ana). Only the first seven Pueblos on one of Oñate's lists (combined with those of the Salines) can be correlated with the "seven pueblos of the ciénaga to the east" (Hammond and Rey 1953, 1:321, 345). All other Pueblo lists are accounted for. Included in the list of seven is Xaimela, similar to Espejo's Jumea, Obregón's Xameca, and Coronado's Ximena (table 5).

Judging from the records of previous entries, no more than three Tano Pueblos were reported prior to Oñate's day. There are other archeological sites known with late glaze-decorated pottery that may represent those included in Oñate's list. However, Benavides (1945:67) in the 1620s recorded five Pueblos among the Tanos, erroneously including the Keresan San Marcos (and La Ciénega?), which would reduce the number to four (or three) Tano Pueblos. It does appear that Oñate included a few Pueblos other than Tanos, possibly some of those Coronado's chroniclers referred to as to the side of the road through Galisteo Basin or some of those in the province of the Ubates.

These three Tano Pueblos, occupied up to the 1680 Revolt, were among the first whose warriors reached Santa Fe to attack the Spaniards (Hackett 1942,1:xxxvii). After the departure of the Spaniards, those from Santa Cruz de Galisteo, with a population of 800, converted the Palace of the Governors into a Pueblo for their own use. The people from San Lázaro and San Cristóbal settled

**Table 5. Tentative Correlation of Tano Pueblo Names**

| | Coronado, 1540 | Rodríguez-Chamuscado, 1581 | Espejo, 1582 | Castaño de Sosa, 1590 | Oñate, 1598 |
|---|---|---|---|---|---|
| | | *Valley of San Mateo* | *Tamos or Atamues Tamones* [a] | | *"ciénaga to the east"* |
| San Lázaro | Ximena 35 houses, small and strong | Malagón, 80 houses, 3–4 stories, 1,000 people Porno or Porue [a] | Jumea, 3–4 stories Xameca [a] | | Xaimela |
| San Cristóbal | | Piedra Alta Piedra Quita Piedra Hita 300 houses, 5 stories, stone, 5–6 stories [a] | Pocos Pocoje, 4–5 stories Tepocoty [a] Tepotra [a] | San Cristóbal [b] | San Cristóbal |
| Galisteo | only one section was occupied | Galisteo Galisto 140 houses, 3–4 stories | | San Lucas [b] | Galisteo Santa Ana Calisteo [c] |
| | | | | | Quauquiz [d] Yhohota [d] Yonalu [d] Xotre [d] Aggei [d] Cutzalitzontegi [d] |

[a] Obregón in Hammond and Rey 1928.
[b] Revised from the identifications of Schroeder in Castaño de Sosa 1965:155.
[c] 1602 map in Hammond and Rey 1966:endpapers, errata slip.
[d] Listed with Xaimela; 2 of these may be San Cristóbal and Galisteo.

along the Santa Cruz drainage north of Santa Fe. When the Spaniards returned in 1692, the Galisteos were evicted and took refuge among some of the Tewas. Two years later, San Lázaro and San Cristóbal joined the Tewas in an unsuccessful revolt. The following year, the people of these two Pueblos were dispossessed so that colonists from Mexico could have a home, and these Tanos moved into Tewa Pueblos. After another minor revolt in 1696, the Tanos took refuge in the mountains. In the following year, Galisteo Pueblo was reestablished with some of the people of San Cristóbal and San Lázaro, but this was short-lived.

At about this time, a number of Tanos took refuge among the Hopis, establishing the Pueblo later called Hano (see synonymy in "Hopi-Tewa," this vol.). In 1706 Galisteo (Santa María de Galisteo or Nuestra Señora de los Remedios) was reestablished by 18 Tano families living at Tesuque Pueblo. As the lone Pueblo in the basin, it suffered Comanche attacks and epidemics until weakened to the point that the occupants abandoned it, between 1782 and 1794, the remaining 52 Tanos joining Santo Domingo (Bandelier 1890–1892, 2:102–105; Espinosa 1942; Reed 1943b; "History of Pueblo-Spanish Relations to 1821," this vol.).

For information obtained from excavations within the Keresan area and for this period see Nelson (1914).

## "Ubates"

There are several Pueblos (table 6) mentioned in the documents of the late 1500s that seem not to fit into the usual categories of language groups or the provinces devised by the Spaniards. The Pueblos referred to seem to be those in the general region of the north end of the Sandia Mountains.

In 1540–1542, two Pueblos in the Galisteo Basin are mentioned (Galisteo and San Lázaro), and another one beyond them that had been completely destroyed and leveled (probably to the west or southwest of San Lázaro since no site occupied in historic times is known between Galisteo and Pecos by way of Glorieta Pass) by the Teyas (a tribe on the Plains). Then reference is made to seven other Pueblos by the side of the route through the basin in the direction of the snowy mountain (south toward the Sandia Mountains) (Hammond and Rey 1940:257–258). Names for Pueblos east of the Sandias or any reference to them are lacking in the Coronado documents. The same applies to sites on the north end of the Sandias.

In 1581–1582 the Rodríguez-Chamuscado party, while in the Galisteo Basin, was informed of two Pueblos on the slopes of the Sierra Morena (Sandia Mountains) but did not visit them. Later, on a north-flowing stream (Tunque Arroyo) in Valle Visiosa, three Pueblos were seen—

Castilblanco (Old San Felipe), Buena Vista (Tunque), and La Barranca (a nearby site?). Here it was learned that to the south, up this stream and beyond, were 13 Pueblos in three days' travel (Gallegos Lamero 1927:353). This would include sites on the east side of the Sandia Mountains from Paako south through the Saline Pueblos, including the Humanas.

Espejo's party left the Keresans on a route that was to take them through the Galisteo Basin. Before reaching the basin, he traveled seven leagues to the Pueblo of Santa Catalina and nearby mines. This was Tunque, occupied into historic times and near several mineral deposits, including lead mined by the Indians (A.H. Warren 1969). The mines were not those of the San Marcos area as has been previously supposed. The journal (Pérez de Luxán 1929:117) indicates that the mines of Santa Catalina were named by members of the previous expedition, though the name was not recorded by them. Moreover, Obregón (Hammond and Rey 1928:301) points out that mineral deposits were found both one league from Malpartida (San Marcos) and at Santa Catalina, five leagues from Malpartida. Five Pueblos were recorded in this province of Ubates, as it was named. These people had much maize, turkeys, and other food and dressed in white and colored mantas and tanned deer and buffalo hides. They governed themselves like the others, lacked rivers, but had springs and marshes (Espejo 1916:188-189; Castaño de Sosa 1965).

Castaño de Sosa left San Marcos to visit a Pueblo two leagues away (near Ortiz Mountains?). Later, from Santo Domingo, he set out in search of some mineral deposits and a Pueblo in the mountains (Sandias) that he had not seen (Tunque?). Two Pueblos, with much maize and beans, deserted a few days before because of a war with others according to the Indian guides, showed signs of many deaths. From there he went to the Southern Tiwas on the Rio Grande (Castaño de Sosa 1965; Hammond and Rey 1966).

Oñate's records refer to the mines of Anunciación near which 9 or 10 Pueblos and some salines of white salt were discovered. These mines are mentioned as separate from those of San Marcos or San Mateo. The itinerary indicates the deposits were six leagues from San Marcos at the Pueblo of El Tuerto (apparently Tunque or a site in the Ortiz or San Pedro Mountains). From there Oñate went two leagues to the first Pueblo behind the mountain and proceeded to the Saline Pueblos. This Pueblo is probably the ruin Bandelier called Paako (its Tano name), a site occupied into early historic times (Hammond and Rey 1953, 1:393, 2:641-642; Bandelier 1890-1892, 2:112; Lambert 1954).

All the lists of Pueblo groups given in Oñate's acts of vassalage are accounted for except for two containing nine names in all: Poloco was captain of the Pueblos Cuchin, Baguacatxuti, Yncohocpi, Acacagua, and Tzijaatica; in the province of Chealo, Xay was captain of Paaco, Acilici of Cuzaya, Tegualpa of Junetre (perhaps San Antonio), and Ayquian and Aguim of Acolocu.

Table 6. Tentative Correlation of Names for the Pueblos of the Ubates

| | Coronado, 1540 | Rodríguez-Chamuscado, 1581 | Espejo, 1583 | Castaño de Sosa, 1590 | Oñate, 1598 |
|---|---|---|---|---|---|
| | Toward the Snowy Sierra | Valle Visiosa | Ubates | | |
| | (7 Pueblos) | | (5 Pueblos) | | (9-10 Pueblos) |
| Tunque (LA 240) | | Buena Vista 200 houses, 3-4 stories | Santa Catalina mines nearby (5 leagues from San Marcos) | visited? | El Tuerto? Anunciación Mines (6 leagues from San Marcos) |
| LA 1779 | | La Barranca 60-70 houses, 3 stories | | | |
| unknown | 1 destroyed by Teyas | | | Pueblo in Ortiz Mts.? (2 leagues from San Marcos) | (Poloco, captain) Cuchin Baguacatxuti Yncohocpi Acacagua Tzijaatica |
| | | | | 2 Pueblos abandoned due to war | (Chealo, captain) Paaco Cuzaya Junetre Acolocu or Agualagu |

Perhaps these represent Oñate's 9 or 10 Pueblos near the mines of Anunciación (Hammond and Rey 1953, 1:338, 348, 2:813, 820). Since the province of Chealo appears to be the Pueblos behind the Sandia Mountains, given the inclusion of Paaco (Paako), Poloco's Pueblos probably were on the north end of the Sandias.

Poloco gave his vassalage and obedience at Santo Domingo along with other southern Pueblos, and Oñate obtained that of the province of Chealo three months later en route to the Tompiros via the east side of the Sandia Mountains. The nature of the areas involved, the distances or relation to other provinces, the number of Pueblos, and the mineral deposits mentioned by the journals of the various entradas all appear to place these sites in the same general region. Moreover, in 1626, Gerónimo de Zárate Salmerón (1966:56) referred to minerals in the mountains of Puaray and in the Tunque area in addition to San Marcos and other places.

The language groups to which these Pueblos belong have not been established with any certainty. On the basis of the names assigned by Tano refugees at Santo Domingo, Bandelier believed Tunque and Paako to have been Tano but also remarked that Paako (which he confused with Portezuelo, considerably to the south) was Tiwa according to the documents (1890-1892, 2:109, 112, 114). Traditions of San Felipe refer to Tunque as Tano (Harrington 1916:501), Reed (1943b) suggests Keresan, and Schroeder favors Tiwa (Castaño de Sosa 1965:162) since the Oñate documents imply a language change south of Paako in referring to the first Pueblo behind the Sandia Mountains (Paako) as the last Pueblo of Puaray. El Tuerto cannot be identified in any of the lists in Oñate's acts of vassalage (Hammond and Rey 1953, 1:393).

To add to the confusion, Oñate's Paaco is included in the list that also contains Acolocu, which appears to be the same as Agualagu, where the Tompiros ambushed the Spaniards (Hammond and Rey 1953, 2:705). Bandelier (1890-1892, 2:109) applied two of Oñate's Keresan Pueblo names, Ojana and Quipacha (Hammond and Rey 1953, 1:345), to two unidentified ruins (which he suggested were Tano but did not visit) south of Tejon on the north end of the Sandia Mountains on the basis of the Tano names Ojana and Kipanna he obtained for these ruins. Until more data are available, little more can be said about these sites and their linguistic affiliation.

For information obtained from excavations within this area and period see Lambert (1954) and Barnett (1969).

### Tewas

In 1540-1542, the province of Yuque-Yunque, with two Pueblos (Yunque and San Juan) on opposite sides of the Rio Grande and four other strong ones in the craggy mountains, is mentioned. These four were possibly Sapawe (Sepawi), Pesere, Teewi, Ku-Owinge, and Tsama, or four of these (Castaño de Sosa 1965:131). One is shown as Sama, between the Chama and Rio Grande, on Martínez's 1602 map (Hammond and Rey 1966:endpapers). Glazed (decorated) pottery of many shapes and a shiny metal (galena) from which the paint was made were noted in the first two Pueblos (Hammond and Rey 1940:244).

Castaño de Sosa, the next to visit the Tewas, stopped at a small Pueblo (Tesuque), where he noted tortillas, maize, and turkeys. Four other Pueblos, one league apart and two to three stories high, were heavily populated (Cuyamungue, Nambe, Pojoaque, and Jacona). Maize, flour, beans, squash, tortillas, turkeys, and bows and arrows were seen at the second one. Two leagues beyond was a large Pueblo (San Ildefonso) with four houseblocks of adobes (apparently coursed adobe), two to three stories high, well whitewashed, with ovens and a very large plaza with exits at each corner. In its center was a big round house (kiva), half above and half below ground, containing many idols as in the previous Pueblos, wherein the people gathered on certain occasions to perform ceremonies. A large area was under irrigation, as in the previous Pueblos, and the people dressed the same as at Pecos. Upriver were two more Pueblos (San Juan and Pioge), across the river another (Yunque), one league from which was another (Teewi), and downstream the last of these Pueblos was Santa Clara (Castaño de Sosa 1965:110-121, 129-133).

Oñate's colony in 1598 settled among these people in a Pueblo of 400 houses, which were adapted to Spanish needs (Yunque). The place was named San Gabriel and some of the Indians remained in the Pueblo (see "San Juan Pueblo," this vol.). The itinerary erroneously gives the Tewa name Caypa (Santa Clara) for San Juan Bautista, which was so named by Oñate (Schroeder in Wendorf 1953a). Bove is given correctly for San Ildefonso, where Antonio Gutiérrez de Umaña had spent a year in 1595. Oñate's list for the Pueblos of the Teguas (Tewa) does not appear to be complete (Hammond and Rey 1953, 1:320, 337, 346, 416): Tziatzi, which may be Tesuque; Tziaque, which may be Tsirege, a ruin with a tree-ring date in the late 1500s; Bove, San Yldefonso (San Ildefonso); Caypa (Santa Clara); San Juan Bautista (San Juan, Tewa *ohke·*); San Gabriel (Yunque, Tewa *yúngé*); Tzooma (Tsama); and five Pueblos with names similar to those of five given on another list as Chigua (Southern Tiwa): Xiaquimo, Xiomato, Axol, Camitza, and Quiotzaco (compare the Chigua names Piaque, Piamato, Axoytze, Camitze, Quioyoco).

By the 1620s, only eight Tewa Pueblos, with 6,000 people, are recorded (Benavides 1945:68), those of the Chama drainage apparently having joined their kin on the Rio Grande between 1598 and 1620 (Schroeder in Castaño de Sosa 1965:132). Of the eight Pueblos, two, Jacona and Cuyamungue, about which little is known, were abandoned in the northern Pueblo revolt of 1696.

For information obtained from excavations within the Tewa area and for this period see Jeançon (1923) and Wendorf (1953a). Work accomplished at Cuyamungue, Yunque, and Sapawe has not been published, but see Tichy (1944) on Yunque.

## Northern Tiwas

In 1540-1542, Braba, Yuraba, or Uraba, named Valladolid (Taos), with three stories of mud and three of wood, had wooden corridors on each story and was divided by a stream spanned by a bridge. The largest and finest estufas in all the land seen there had 12 pillars two arm lengths around and two estados high. These people worshiped the sun and water, wore buffalo and deer skins, lacked turkeys and cotton, and buried their dead in dirt mounds outside the Pueblo (Hammond and Rey 1940:244, 259, 288, 300).

Oñate's records refer to this Pueblo as Tayberon (or Tayberin), Taos, and San Miguel. Picuríes and the province of Taos "with its neighboring pueblos and those that border upon it and those of that cordillera on the bank of the Río del Norte" were assigned to one friar (Hammond and Rey 1953, 1:321, 345, 371). These "neighboring pueblos" may have been those on the Chama and Ojo Caliente drainages.

First reported by Castaño de Sosa, though the name was first used by Oñate, Picuris had several house blocks and stood seven to nine stories high with breastworks the height of a man on the roof, to which boys carried stones. Nearby huts served as quarters for foreign Indians (Apaches) who went there for refuge (in the winter). Much turquoise was seen as well as an amulet with "rich stones" (Castaño de Sosa 1965:123-128). In 1601 this Pueblo was called Picuries or San Francisco del Monte (Hammond and Rey 1953, 1:321, 2:631), and it appears as Picurines on Martínez's 1602 map (Hammond and Rey 1966:endpapers).

## Towas

In 1540 the "province of Hemes" (Jemez) contained seven Pueblos, and the province of Aguas Calientes (San Diego canyon) had three (Hammond and Rey 1940:244, 259). In the Valle de Santiago in 1581-1582, a Pueblo the Spaniards called Baños ('baths') had 100 houses, two to three stories high, above which there were 13 more that were not visited (Gallegos Lamero 1927:355). Espejo (1916:182) reported that the province of Emexes contained seven Pueblos with 30,000 people, one very large one in the mountains, and that idols, bows and arrows, and other arms were seen there.

Oñate described the approach to the great Pueblo of Emes as a difficult hill. Below it were 11 others, of which he saw eight, plus the last Pueblo of the province, which was near hot waters (Giusewa). Pestaca was the captain

of the Emmes and of the Pueblos named (in addition to the "great pueblo"?) on two lists with different spellings (Hammond and Rey 1953, 1:322, 337-338, 345): Yxcaguayo or Yjar Guayo, Quiameca or Guiamecá, Tzia, Quiusta or Guiusta (Giusewa?), Lecca or Ceca, Potze, Tziaguatzi or Tzea, Tzyiti or Gautitzilti (Quiashidshi?), Caatzo or Catzoho (Kiatsukwa?). The great Pueblo, if not named on the above list, may have been Astialakwa.

Benavides (1945:69-70) stated that these people, about 6,000, in their mountain Pueblos had been induced to settle in a new Pueblo in the valley below, but it burned in 1623 and the Indians returned to the mountains. In 1626 or 1628 the valley Pueblo was reestablished with a church dedicated to San Diego. The mission San José at Giusewa was established in 1621 (Scholes 1936-1937:160).

During this decade, Zárate Salmerón (1966:93) mentioned two Jemez Pueblos by name—Amoxunqua (Amushungkwa) and Quiumziqua (Giusewa, with tree-ring dates in the early 1600s), the former yielding historic-period objects and the latter containing a church. Other Jemez sites of the historic period are Seshiuqua (single tree-ring date of 1597), Nonyishagi (dates up to 1570), unnamed site (1609 and later), unnamed site (dates in the 1680s), Kiatsukwa (dates from one test, 1615-1616), and Unshagi (late 1500s to after 1605), making eight historic-period Pueblos (Robinson, Hannah, and Harrill 1972). Add to these Patoqua, which has a church (Hewett 1906:46), and Astialakwa for a total of 10.†

The Jemez as early as 1614 were allied with Apaches and continued so throughout the 1600s (Schroeder 1963a:10; Sigüenza y Góngora 1932:75). In the late 1600s Navajos were hostile to the Jemez (Scholes 1937-1938:150), who remained in their mountain Pueblos as late as 1695 (Espinosa 1942:199, 224). That many, if any, Jemez took refuge in Navajo country during the rebellion period is doubtful. See Hodge in Benavides (1945:274-279) and Bandelier (1890-1892, 2:205-216) for mission names at these Pueblos and the complications of the identification of the Pueblos involved. For information obtained from excavations within this area and period see Reiter (1938). For early historical data on Pecos, see "Pecos Pueblo," and for later information on Jemez see "Jemez Pueblo," both this volume.

## Zunis

Esteban, who was killed at Zuni in 1540, had been held in a large house outside the Pueblo (Hawikuh). Known as

† There is considerable confusion among historians and archeologists over which Jemez names apply to which Pueblo ruins. The identifications assumed in this chapter, with which the tree-ring dates are correlated, are those commonly used by archeologists (for example, Robinson, Hannah, and Harrill 1972), with the spellings those of Hodge (1907-1910), where available. Different identifications for some names are given by Harrington (1916:map 27) and Sando ("Jemez Pueblo," this vol.), on the basis of traditional Jemez knowledge.

Cíbola or Granada to Coronado, this Pueblo was the only one of the seven (six according to Juan Jaramillo, who accompanied Coronado) surrounded by a wall, which had a gate that led through a winding entrance. House walls were a span thick, timbers were thick as a wrist, and roofs were covered with small reeds with leaves and dirt on top. It stood three to four stories with one plaza and had 200 rooms, as did another, a third Pueblo nearby (Matsaki) with 300 rooms being larger, four to seven stories high, and equipped with loopholes for defense. The other Pueblos were small with 50 to 100 rooms. In all there were 500 hearths (houses), the Pueblos standing three to seven stories with corridors reached by rung ladders, and without doorways in the lower part. Some were of mud, most of stone, either in clusters or in two or three sections (house blocks). Rooms exhibited good wall paintings. Underground rooms (kivas) in the plazas were paved with flagstones, those in the plazas being used in the winter and those outside in the summer. These were used for meetings by all, but women could not sleep in them. The largest Pueblo, Maçaque, had no streets, and the corridors projected like balconies supported by pillars.

These people had skin, painted cotton, and henequen (yucca) blankets; dressed skins; buffalo robes; and feather or rabbitskin cloaks. Women, who gathered their hair over the ears in two wheels like coil puffs, wore skirts that hung to the feet, open in front, and a blanket over the left shoulder, the right arm being over it, tied with a cotton sash at the waist. Others were naked except for a cloth covering with fringes and a tassel at each corner covering the privy parts. They used cloaks of dressed skins. Boots of skin reached to above the knees.

Crops included maize, which the women ground, squashes, and beans. Seeds were planted in holes. Though the maize was not tall, three or four large ears produced 800 kernels. Though they did not raise cotton, cotton thread was seen. They gathered piñon nuts and obtained salt from a nearby lake (Zuni Salt Lake). Deer, hares, and rabbits were hunted, and some fowl (turkeys) were kept, more for their feathers than for food. Fish were not used. Other items seen at Matsaki were turquoise earrings, a blanket of many pieces, boards decorated with turquoise, many baskets, rolls to wear on the head to carry water containers, pottery, and combs. Two points of emerald (?) and broken stones the color of garnet (jasper?), the latter found in a paper, were seen at another Pueblo. Firewood was obtained four leagues from Granada.

The lord of the Pueblos (at Matsaki) and other chiefs of the country governed these people and the people worked in common, according to Coronado, yet Pedro de Castañeda states there was no ruler, only a council of eldest men at each Pueblo. Priests preached like town criers and told them how to live. They worshiped water, because of crops and life sustenance, to which they offered painted sticks, plumes, and powder of a yellow flower, usually at springs. They also held rituals before some idols. The dead were cremated with the tools of their occupation. Hostile to those of Tusayán (Hopis), their weapons were bows and arrows with bone arrow points, stones cast from the roofs, and mallets. They had shields and sounded a trumpet (conch shell) on retreat. They attacked the Spaniards at midnight and took refuge in the hills (Hammond and Rey 1940).

The Rodríguez-Chamuscado party reported that the six Suñi Pueblos of stone, with their plazas, streets, and corridors, windows, doorways, and stairways of wood (ladders), were two to three story houses, each with eight rooms or more, plastered and painted inside and out. Sleeping mats of light palm (yucca) were noted. One report mentioned only five Pueblos (Gallegos Lamero 1927:355–356; Hammond and Rey 1966:120), names for which are compared with those of the Espejo journals in table 7.

Records of the Espejo journey, which also refer to this province as Amí or Cami, described the stone Pueblos of Suny, Basumi, Zuñi, Somy, Sumi, Sibula, or Cíbola as being three to four stories high with estufas for every 15 or 20 people, built underground with heavy timbers and lined with slabs. Easter was their planting time. At Aguico, waterholes provided water to irrigate maize by means of two canals. Though they gathered little cotton, they obtained some from Mohose (Hopi), which they spun and wove into mantas and blankets. They also had coarse linen or agave blankets. These people shared in common whether experiencing famine or abundant returns. They offered pinole and vegetables in jars and bowls at small prayer houses (shrines). There was no polygamy. Women wore their hair in large puffs (Pérez de Luxán 1929:85, 89–94; Espejo 1916:184).

Names in the Oñate documents applied to the six Pueblos of Comi or Zuni, also referred to as Xala, Tzuñi, or Quini, closely resemble those of the previous records— Aquima, Mazaqui, Holonagu, Aguicobi, Canabi, and Coaquina. Four of the six were almost in ruins. "Nagua homi" and "Atiz oha" were chiefs of the six Pueblos. They raised maize, beans, and squash, hunted rabbits and hares, made tortillas, and obtained salt from a lake. Blankets were made of istle (perhaps yucca). Flour, painted sticks, and feathers were offered to their idols (Hammond and Rey 1953, 1:327, 346, 357). The Spaniards joined 800 Zunis in a rabbit hunt, forming a semicircle one league long, and closed in on the game (Villagrá 1933:168).

Fray Francisco de Escobar reported in 1604 that four of the six stone Pueblos with very good estufas for the cold winter were almost completely in ruins. The largest was called Scíbola, or Hauico by the Indians. In all the Pueblos there was a total of 300 inhabited houses. The people dressed in buckskin and in the winter with buffalo skins, but most commonly in blankets made from a small

**Table 7. Correlation of Zuni Pueblo Names**

| | Rodríguez-Chamuscado Party, 1581–1582 | | Espejo Party, 1582–1583 |
|---|---|---|---|
| Kiakima | Aquima<br>75 houses,<br>3 stories | Aquiman<br>75 houses,<br>2–3 stories | Quequema<br>Zaquema |
| Matsaki | Maça<br>100 houses,<br>4–5 stories | Maça<br>100 houses,<br>4–5 stories | Mazaque<br>Malaque<br>Masaque |
| Halona | Alonagua<br>44 houses,<br>3–4 stories | Aconagua<br>44 houses,<br>3–4 stories | Alona |
| Hawikuh | Aguico<br>125 houses,<br>2–3 stories | Allico<br>118 houses,<br>3–4 stories | Aguico<br>Acinco |
| Kianawa | Not named<br>44 houses,<br>3–4 stories | Acana<br>40 houses,<br>3–4 stories | Cana |
| Kwakina | No mention | Coaquina<br>60 houses,<br>3–4 stories | Quaquina<br>Quequina |

palm, like istle or hemp (Hammond and Rey 1953, 2:1013–1014).

Benavides (1945:73–75) in the 1620s mentioned 11 or 12 Pueblos with 10,000 people (clearly exaggerations), who had a perpetual fire worshiped with great ceremonies in an estufa. They performed rituals with snakes enclosed in a corral of sticks one span apart and four to five high, whipping them so they bit pieces of liver that were used to poison arrows. A house purchased for the friars (at Hawikuh) became the first church (La Purísima Concepción, which was followed by Nuestra Sênora de Candelaria at Halona), which the Indian priests opposed.

Fray Esteban de Perea (in Benavides 1945:213–216) in 1629 stated the Pueblos had streets and houses in rows and that one cacique with several chiefs headed an orderly government. Women wore cotton clothing, and men dressed in deerskins and furs. Captive snakes provided venom for arrows, and in their temples, which only their priests entered, they had stone and profusely painted wooden idols. They had gods of the mountains, rivers, fields, and houses.

After murdering two friars in 1632, the Zunis moved to Dowa Yalanne (Corn Mountain), remaining there until 1635. Sometime later the missions were reestablished, but Hawikuh was again abandoned after being attacked by Apaches in 1672 or 1673. Hawikuh may have been reoccupied briefly, but the Zunis abandoned all their Pueblos in the 1680 Revolt, once again settling on Dowa Yalanne where Vargas found them in 1692 (Hodge 1937:93–95, 98–102; Adams and Chavez in Domínguez 1956:197). By 1705, 1,500 Zunis were living at the site of Halona, which is present Zuni (Hackett 1923–1937, 3:376–377).

For information obtained from sites or excavations within this area and period see Smith, Woodbury, and Woodbury (1966) and Mindeleff (1891). For this and later periods see "Zuni Prehistory and History to 1850" and "Zuni History, 1850–1970," this volume.

## Hopis

In 1540 the people of Tusayán (also Tuçayan, Tucano, and Tuzán), living in seven terraced Pueblos (possibly including two Jeddito Valley Pueblos that might have been abandoned prior to the 1580s) larger than those of Cíbola (Zuni), approached the Spaniards in wing formation armed with arrows, shields, and wooden maces. They drew lines (ceremonial closing of the trail?), and after a brief scuffle the people came out of the Pueblos (perhaps being inside because of the summer fire ceremony) and offered cotton clothes, dressed hides, flour, piñon nuts, maize, native fowl, and turquoise. They also had buffalo hides and raised cotton. They were governed like Zuni by elders with a governor and captains (Hammond and Rey 1940:175, 213–215).

Though not visited by the Rodríguez-Chamuscado party, it was learned from the Zunis that to the west were five Pueblos among the Asay or Osay (Hopis) and also a mineral deposit (Hammond and Rey 1966:108, 131, 137). Espejo reached Maxosa, Mohoce, Mohose, Mojose, or Moje where many Chichimecos (nomadic tribes) also were present. While camped near the great Pueblo of Aguato (Awatovi), which had a main plaza, the Indians brought maize, ears of green corn, venison, dried rabbits, pinole, tamales, small and large white and painted blankets, blue and green ores to color the mantas, and firewood.

As the Spaniards approached Gaspe, Xoalpe, Alpe, or Oalpes (Walpi), two leagues away, "a very high and rocky pueblo" with a main plaza and estufas like those of Zuni, the people scattered pinole, carried in a bag and bowl, on the road. The Spaniards also noted jars of water and food along the way. More than 1,000 met them at the Pueblo with fine water jars, rabbits, cooked venison, tortillas, atole, beans, cooked squash, much maize, and pinole as well as white and painted blankets. Water was obtained from very deep wells, and crops were grown in sandy places. Painted cotton kilts with tassels, plus cotton blankets, clothed the men, and the well-dressed women had their hair in puffs.

Two leagues beyond, on two stony sierras separated by one-half league, were Majanani, Mahanami, Moxanamy, or Moxonami (Mishongnovi) and the larger Pueblo of Comupaui or Xomupa (Shongopavi). These people provided water in large "jars and barrels," squash, maize, and cooked vegetables along with small and large blankets. Three leagues away, at the foot of Olalla or Olayyola (Oraibi), the largest Pueblo, the well to which they descended by stone steps went dry, and water in jars was brought from other wells. Raw and prepared food, blankets, and spun and raw cotton also were provided. Each Pueblo had three or four caciques who had as little power as the commoner. Along the roads were shrines, and in their Pueblos houses of worship like those of Zuni (Pérez de Luxán 1929:95–104; Espejo 1916:185–186).

In 1598, at Mohoqui, Mohuqui, Moze, Mooqui, Mohoce, Mohoze, or Mochoqui, Oñate provided a confused list that includes the Pueblo names Aguatuyba, Xumupami, and Oraybi, and six others that are apparently chieftains' names (Hammond and Rey 1953, 1:360). In 1604 four of the five Pueblos were half in ruins, totaling 500 occupied houses, though not so good as those at Zuni. These people had more maize than Zuni and also grew beans, squash, and cotton from which they made heavy blankets, the best in the land, and well colored. They dressed in these as well as buckskin and in buffalo hides in winter. A small amount of wood provided warmth in the estufas in winter (Hammond and Rey 1953, 2: 1013–1014).

Benavides (1945:75) added little, describing the Moqui (Hopi) as similar to the Zunis except in language, with a population of 10,000—clearly an exaggeration.

Of the Hopi Pueblos of 1680, Awatovi was the only one that did not survive. Hopi traditions refer to their hostilities in late prehistoric times with other Pueblos of the Jeddito Valley that led to the destruction of those Pueblos, which may have been the reason for the final attack on Awatovi.

For information obtained from sites and excavations within the Hopi area and for this period see Mindeleff (1891), W. Smith (1952), Montgomery, Smith, and Brew (1949), and "Hopi Prehistory and History to 1850," this volume.

## Conclusion

The number of Pueblos reported by the journals and documents of the 1500s is considerable. The Coronado, Rodríguez-Chamuscado, and Espejo records mention 70 to 75, not including several language groups they did not visit. Castaño de Sosa, who visited only a few groups, recorded 35, and Oñate named more than 134. Population figures range from a total of 20,000 men to 130,000 to 248,000 people. The last is Espejo's exaggerated estimate, Oñate's 16,000 to 60,000 "conservatively" being the lowest. In the 1620s Benavides estimated 69,000 in a minimum of 64 Pueblos. In 1638, 40,000 or less were estimated with the added statement that prior to the smallpox epidemic the number probably was more than 60,000 (Hackett 1923–1937, 3:108). In 1679, 46 Pueblos with 17,000 Christian Indians are mentioned. Two years later, the Tanos, Teguas, Queres, Jemez, and Acoma accounted for 26 Pueblos (Hackett 1923–1937, 3:218, 255). Vetancurt's list of 1695 has 18,600, but it does not include the Piros, Tompiros, or Tanos who had abandoned their homes in the 1670s and 1680. By 1706, 18 Pueblos, not including the Hopis, contained 6,440 people (Hackett 1923–1937, 3:373–377).

# Taos Pueblo

JOHN J. BODINE

Taos (ˈtäˌ ōs) (figs. 1–2) is the northernmost of the Eastern Pueblos, located 70 miles north of Santa Fe, New Mexico (see "Pueblos: Introduction," fig. 1, this vol.). The term Taos is also applied to the Anglo and Spanish-American town 2.8 miles south of the Pueblo and to the predominantly Spanish-American settlement of Ranchos de Taos that is three miles farther south.

Taos Pueblo is a single community effectively separated both socially and culturally from the Anglo and Spanish-American communities in Taos valley. Many of the Indians are in frequent, often daily, contact with their non-Indian neighbors as a consequence of the major economic shift from subsistence agriculture to wage work, but the social and cultural isolation that is maintained is profound. Obviously massive changes have been wrought since the arrival of the Spanish and, ultimately, the Anglo-Americans. Reorientations of certain values and attitudes have occurred, yet clear cultural boundaries still obtain between the Taos and their non-Indian neighbors and between themselves and other Indians. Relations of long standing with other Pueblos, particularly those along the Rio Grande, can be documented. The same is true of friendships many Taos have with Oklahoma Indians and somewhat less so with Utes, Apaches, and Navajos. However, these interactions are individual or familial, not truly institutional. This is true in spite of the fact that Taos has borrowed freely from the cultures of others in the course of the centuries of contact.

Cultural isolation has been maintained for reasons internal and intrinsic to Taos culture. It is also the result of external forces over which the Taos had little control. The ethnocentrism of the Pueblos, which is very marked at Taos, is an important factor. That this has contributed to cultural isolation from other Indians is a fact to appreciate in comprehending how much more it affects their separate identification from Anglos and Spanish-Americans. The gulf is easily crossed for the practical purposes necessary for interaction and adaptation to changing circumstances, but it is nevertheless maintained very rigidly. Endogamy is the rule. While it has often been ignored and many exogamous marriages have occurred, these have, in most cases, led to residence off the reservation and normally many miles distant. As a result, exogamous unions have not constituted a real threat to the way of life of those Taos Indians who remain at the Pueblo or even for those who return after a number of years away, although the latter often face serious problems of readjustment. Equally important in the matter of boundary maintenance are the attitudes held by Anglos, Spanish, and other Indians toward the Taos. (Bodine 1967, 1968).

## Language and Environment

Taos is a Tiwa-speaking Pueblo of the Kiowa-Tanoan language family. The language is most closely related to that of Picuris, a smaller Pueblo 25 miles south and west. The Taos and Picuris languages constitute the Northern Tiwa subgroup of Tiwa and are somewhat more distantly related to the Southern Tiwa dialects spoken at Isleta and Sandia in the Albuquerque area.*

Taos is the primary language of the majority of Taos Indians. In the first six decades of the twentieth century, Spanish declined significantly as a second language of communication, while the use of English steadily increased. There is no evidence that the Taos language is in danger of extinction (Bodine 1968a:27). The Taos have successfully preserved their language, in part by the same dictum used to maintain secrecy about many other aspects of their culture: no Taos Indian should reveal anything intrinsic to Taos life, which includes the language.

Taos Pueblo is situated on a broad, well-watered intermontane plateau at the base of the Sangre de Cristo mountain range. Until rather recent times, it was a highly productive area for the Taos. The mountains afforded easy access to hunting opportunities. Around 1840 they were well stocked with deer, elk, bear, turkey, grouse, and squirrel. The Taos frequently crossed the pass located near their Pueblo to hunt buffalo on the plains. The feathers of birds, such as eagles, hawks, and ducks were of importance ceremonially. On sagebrush lands to the

* Taos words in this Handbook are written in the phonemic system of Trager (1948a), except that the glottal stop is written with ʔ rather than with the apostrophe. The glottalized obstruents are interpreted as clusters (pʔ, tʔ, cʔ, kʔ, kwʔ), as are the aspirated stops (ph, th) and labialized obstruents (kw, xw, kwʔ). The affricates c and cʔ are more often pronounced [č] and [čʔ] than [c] and [čʔ]. There are three degrees of stress (loud, medial, and weak) and three tones (normal, high, and low). The combinations of stress and tone are indicated with accents as follows: á (loud normal), à (medial normal), ã (loud high), ǎ (medial high), â (loud low), ä (medial low), a (weak, which has no tonal contrasts).

west of the Pueblo and across the canyon of the Rio Grande, the Taos formerly hunted antelope and rabbits. Antelope have disappeared, but rabbits are still hunted and are important in ritual activity. Native trout were obtained in the numerous streams and rivers of the area, although not traditionally taken from the high mountain lakes, most of which are considered sacred. Many species of wild plants were and are gathered, including wild onions, many kinds of berries, pine nuts, osha (wild celery), and sage. Innumerable wild flowers figure importantly in ceremonial observance.

The total resources of the area were basically very beneficial in spite of the fact that Taos Pueblo is at an altitude of 7,098 feet. This, plus its northern position, provides a frost-free growing season of about 140 days. This is too short for cotton; hence the Taos relied on other Pueblos for woven goods. Even other crops were frequently endangered by adverse climatic conditions. As

a result, the Taos relied on hunting and gathering to a greater extent than did the more southerly Pueblos (see Ford 1968). Drought or flood do not appear to have been known. Domínguez (1956:112) wrote in 1776: "With the exception of frijol and chile, everything yields such an abundant harvest that when (as happened in the year '74) there is scarcity in most of the kingdom, everyone goes to Taos and leaves there well supplied, not just once, but many times."

## External Relations

Taos is designated a Pueblo, which connotes not only a permanent settlement but also certain cultural features shared with the other Pueblo communities in New Mexico and Arizona. It is apparent that Taos differs considerably from the rest, which is not to deny the cultural similarities with the other Tanoan, Keresan,

256 Fig. 1. Taos Pueblo. Photograph by Peter Dechert, June 1977.

Zuni, and Hopi towns. The uniqueness of Taos requires a consideration of those elements that have shaped and molded Taos culture and that continue to affect change to the extent that Taos emerges differently from other Indian populations. The relationships with other Indian groups, notably the Pueblos and the southern Plains tribes, such as the Comanche in the 1700s and other Oklahoma groups, have been important. Previous researchers speculated on the influence of the more nomadic peoples on Taos culture. "Taos does reveal pictures of an early culture, but to what extent they are Pueblo is problematical" (Parsons 1936:5). It is true that Taos has been in more continuous contact with Plains people than most of the other Pueblos. Moreover, it survived the more hostile periods of contact, unlike Pecos. While it is not possible to measure accurately all the effects these relations have had on Taos culture, one thing is certain. In spite of the many Plains influences—

such as Peyotism, dress styles (fig. 3), secular dances and music—Taos is most definitely Puebloid in basic characteristics. Some of what appears to be Plains-derived may well have been elaborated independently or borrowed in response to ecological adaptation. For example, the reliance on hunting, including frequent buffalo hunts, fostered major dependence on horses with all the material culture that requires.

## Prehistory

Nearly 300 archeological sites are known in the Taos area. The earliest settlements date from A.D. 1000–1200 and are primarily pithouses with some small surface units of coursed adobe construction (Blumenschein 1956, 1958, 1963; Herold and Luebben 1968; Peckham 1963; Green 1963). None of these early settlements is on the site of present Taos Pueblo, but then, with one notable excep-

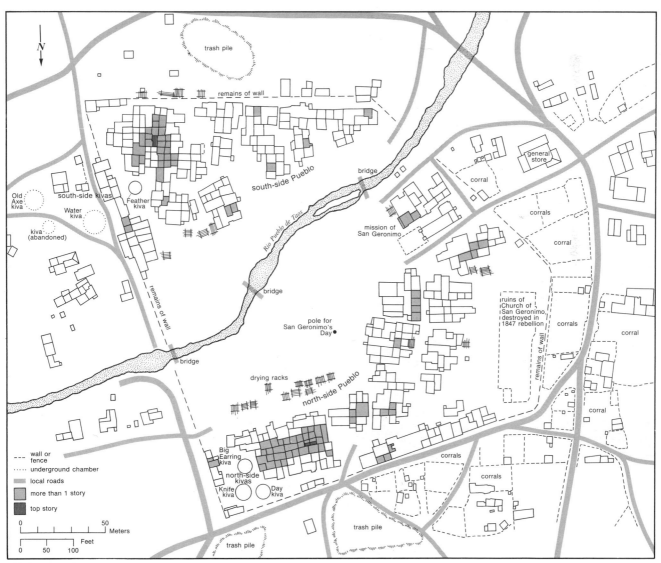

revised from Historic Amer. Buildings Survey, Natl. Park Service, map for 1973.

Fig. 2. Taos Pueblo.

TAOS PUEBLO

Fig. 3. Plains and hunting influence in hide clothing. top, Woman in old-style deerskin dress, holding child. Photograph probably by Orloff R. Westmann at the Feast of San Geronimo, Sept. 30, 1871. bottom, Juan Jesús Leo (b. about 1830), governor of Taos. Carrying his Lincoln cane, he is wearing a Plains-style fringed and beaded buckskin shirt, Navajo blanket, and shell gorget. Studio portrait by unknown photographer, 1863–1877, probably in Washington, D.C.

tion (Ellis and Brody 1964), the Taos have not permitted excavation in close proximity to their village.

As population increased, larger, multi-family surface Pueblos dating A.D. 1200–1250 appeared. Settlement was primarily along the Rio Grande de Ranchos in the Llano-Ranchos-Pot Creek area, which is a few miles south of Taos Pueblo. Ceremonial growth is reflected archeologically in the appearance of the kiva (Jeançon 1929; Wendorf and Reed 1955; Ellis and Brody 1964). Contact with the Santa Fe district was established and continues on into the next phase dated A.D. 1250–1350. However, this northern area around Taos, due to its relative isolation, began the crystallization of its socio-cultural pattern without significant participation in the cultural development occurring in the south (Wetherington 1968:82). At this time, there were two major centers of population, one at Pot Creek on the Rio Grande de Ranchos about 12 miles south of Taos Pueblo and the other adjacent to the modern Pueblo at Picuris. Pot Creek was abandoned around A.D. 1350, and the first known settlement at Taos Pueblo, actually "Cornfield Taos," which is one-quarter mile northeast of the present village, was begun (Ellis and Brody 1964). "Cornfield Taos" was abandoned between 1450 and 1500 and, while there may have been overlap in construction with the present buildings, it is certain that the Taos have resided in the general vicinity of their present location for over 600 years. The impressive multistoried Pueblos on the north and south sides of the Rio Pueblo de Taos were well established when the Francisco Vásquez de Coronado expedition came north in 1540.

Previous homes of the Taos and their Kiowa-Tanoan linguistic relatives can only be speculated about. Archeological opinion, as well as the legends of the Taos, agree to a northern derivation. While certainly cultural influences and perhaps increments of population may have come from the west and south at certain periods of Taos prehistory, the Taos appear definitely to have come from the north. Some archeologists have speculated that the Chimney Rock-Piedra district east of Durango, Colorado, is their previous home and are even willing, albeit cautiously, to suggest that the great Anasazi Pueblo of Chaco in northwestern New Mexico is the ancestral home of the Taos and other Tanoans (Ellis and Brody 1964:326–327). A more conservative opinion may be concluded from similar pottery types, which indicate that "Chaco influences were well established in the Northern Rio Grande Region by the beginning of the 11th century, probably earlier" (Wetherington 1968:77).

Chaco influences do not necessarily mean purposeful migration of peoples. Trager (1967) feels that the Kiowa-Tanoans originated in the northern Plains and moved southward to eastern Colorado or eastern New Mexico. The Kiowa went east to Oklahoma, while the Tanoans moved west across the mountains and into the northern Rio Grande area. Subsequently, they separated and most moved south. Only the Northern Tiwa remained in their relatively isolated position in the area of Taos valley. In the process, they all adopted the pre-Pueblo and developing Pueblo culture. Of importance, the dates for linguistic separation proposed by Trager correlate well with the archeological evidence. There is disagreement between certain of the dates arrived at by Trager through comparison of linguistic structure and those of Davis (1959) using lexicostatistics. However, the dates for the separation of Tiwa and Tewa, as well as for the Northern Tiwa languages, Taos and Picuris, are the same. The latter is well in line with the abandonment of Pot Creek, the settlement at Picuris, and the subsequent establishment of Taos Pueblo (Trager 1969).

## Culture

The following description of Taos culture represents an amalgamation of data ranging in time from around 1840 to 1970. A complete portrayal of strictly aboriginal life is not possible due to the general lack of archeological and ethnohistorical information. Where the data are good, indications of change since 1840 are noted.

### Subsistence

Approximately 300,000 acres of mountain and valley land were habitually used for traditional economic pur-

suits, with agriculture restricted mainly to the lands adjacent to the Pueblo, although some Taos raised crops several miles distant. The heavy reliance on hunting and gathering was complemented by an equally important preoccupation with cattle and horses. Both have decreased markedly with increased Spanish and Anglo settlement. Federal and state controls and the creation of the Carson National Forest in 1906 further restricted these traditional Taos activities. However, the Taos gained a reputation for the production of animal hides convertible into clothing, drum heads (figs. 4–5), and other items. Burros and oxen, once used for transporting firewood and tilling the soil, respectively, are no longer used. Pigs and chickens were and are raised by some. The Taos never kept sheep and goats; they look with disdain on the herding of these animals. The dog was ubiquitous, but the most important animal for both practical and prestige purposes was the horse. Horses figure prominently in myth and legend and, while their number has declined greatly, they are highly valued animals.

### Technology

Ceramic ware never reached the excellence it did elsewhere. Since 1600 the dominant type of pottery, and in the twentieth century the only kind, is a utilitarian ware of micaceous clay (Ellis and Brody 1964:316). Crafts partially reflect reliance on the products of the hunt. The Taos make hard-soled moccasins and the folded deerskin "boots" (fig. 6) worn by mature women for ceremonial

Fig. 4. Taos man beginning to core a log for a drum. The turban-wrapped commercial blanket around his head serves as protection from the sun. Photograph by Joseph C. Farber, summer 1970.

Mus. of N.M., Santa Fe: 42231/12ab.

Fig. 5. Modern drum and beater. Hollowed wooden body with cowhide heads and lashing. Height about 27.5 cm, collected in 1958.

259

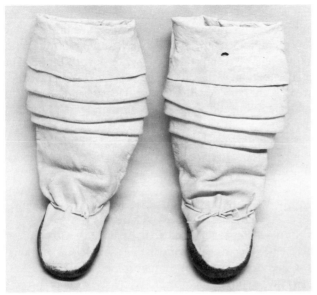

Fig. 6. Married woman's whitened deerskin boots. Although these boots are modern (with soles constructed of black, commercial shoe leather), they have the traditional folded uppers that could be unfolded and attached to the thighs for protection when horseback riding. Height about 43 cm (as folded), collected in 1958.

performance or special occasions. Buckskin leggings and shirts, buffalo robes, and rabbitskin blankets were made formerly. The art of weaving rabbitskin blankets was revived by Taos Pueblo women in 1970 with the establishment of an arts and crafts center at the Pueblo.

### Structures

The Taos consciously and purposefully preserved much of their traditional architecture within the confines of the village proper (fig. 7). The four- and five-storied Pueblos of Taos, replete with outside ladders to reach the upper rooms, are justly famous and have become the most important visual symbol of Taos culture, in addition to being somewhat synonymous with Pueblo culture generally. Untold thousands of visitors have come to Taos to see the ancient buildings. Tourism in the area is based significantly on Taos Indian culture. It is an important source of communal revenue at the Pueblo through parking and camera fees. Individuals profit through arts and crafts production. More important is wage work in the Anglo and Spanish towns, whose sole industry is tourism (Bodine 1964).

Additions have been made to the old buildings as the population has increased. Windows have been cut in the lower stories and glass, not allowed in the 1930s, is now used (Parsons 1936:17). Doorways are also permitted. Very few were seen on the first floor at the turn of the twentieth century (M. L. Miller 1898:19).

Much of the recent settlement has been outside the village proper; however, most of it is in the immediate environs of the Pueblo. These homes are outside the wall constructed around the village for defense. The wall served as a valuable bastion during the Comanche raids in the 1700s. The remains of this wall are still visible and constitute an important boundary in Taos thought. Anything inside the wall is sacred; most of that which is outside is not, except for the four trash piles immediately adjacent to the walled area. Two of the six active kivas and a seventh, which is abandoned, are outside the wall and also sacred. In recent decades, the old village area could not accommodate the increased population. Parsons (1936:17) counted 175 house units within the wall and simply mentioned several summer or ranch houses "south or southeast of town, with a few out in the sage to the west." In 1971 there were only 109 house units consistently used in the village, while 192 were outside the wall (Bodine 1971:6). Clearly there has been a change in settlement pattern. It reflects not only population growth but also the desire of many to have a separate dwelling away from the Pueblo. Changing attitudes are apparent in the construction of these newer homes. Fenced yards, flower beds, and the incorporation of more and more commercial building materials are increasingly evident. Electricity was permitted outside the wall by the Pueblo Council in 1971. There are very few indoor bathrooms but an increasing number of gas and electrically operated appliances. Furnishings, overwhelmingly of commercial American manufacture, are usually simple and almost always utilitarian. This is not only a result of the low per capita income but also a reflection of the egalitarianism of Taos society. A high value placed on generosity and reciprocity is not matched by an ostentatious display of material wealth.

### Clothing

Certain dress styles mirror those of a previous era but are habitually worn only by older individuals. Braids, blankets, moccasins or heelless shoes (figs. 9–10), and simulated leggings effected by cutting the seat from store-bought pants are distinctive items of dress for older men. All adult women wear brightly colored shawls and normally moccasins or heelless shoes. Only the older ones wear the chignon hair style. Younger Taos prefer Anglo-style clothing, which is generally characterized by being inexpensive and durable. During male initiation periods and on special occasions, younger Taos will conform to more traditional styles either because these are required or out of respect for their elders (Bodine 1967; Trager 1948).

### Social Organization

Knowledge of Taos social organization is somewhat muddled, since this is generally the area of Taos culture about which the people have been most secretive. The kinship system is completely bilateral and there is no evidence that it was ever anything else. There are no clans. Moiety is expressed at Taos, but it does not appear

top, Smithsonian, NAA; bottom, Farber and Dorris 1975:168.
Fig. 7. North side house cluster (see fig. 2), looking northeast in 1899 and in 1970. Taos Peak, the sacred mountain of the Taos, is barely visible at extreme right of 1899 view. Top photograph by Adam C. Vroman; bottom by Joseph C. Farber.

house sites. This has partially restricted agricultural endeavors.

There is a very strong sense of communality at Taos, which is expressed most often in terms of community duties, which every able-bodied adult must perform. They include both secular work projects, such as cleaning irrigation ditches, repairing fences, and plastering the church, as well as dance obligations and other ceremonially linked activities. Many Taos fear losing the rights and responsibilities stemming from communality; they believe such a loss would endanger the continued stability of the Pueblo.

### Life Cycle

Rituals surrounding birth, death, and marriage generally reflect Roman Catholic practice. A native naming ceremony is held separately but often coincides with the time of an infant's baptism. The illegitimate child is usually not discriminated against in any way and, because of the extended family, formal adoption is largely unnecessary. The onset of the menses is recognized but no longer ritualized. No puberty ritual is held for boys. Marriage may be purely secular and/or consummated by Catholic ritual. Divorce is more frequent than formerly. Many instances of interpersonal conflict, like paternity suits and child-support claims, which were formerly taken to the Pueblo governor for resolution, are increasingly handled by the courts and other agencies of social control outside the Pueblo. The dead are interred in the courtyard of the church destroyed in 1847. The cemetery has had to be expanded and gravestones are replacing simple wooden crosses.

to be so important an organizing principle as it is among the Tewa (Ortiz 1969). While individuals belong to either the north- or south-side Pueblos and there is alternative jurisdiction ceremonially by north- and south-side kiva groups, residence is not determined by moiety nor is kiva membership so affected. Nuclear family residence is most common, although the bilaterally extended family is of great importance for the individual. This group of relatives constitutes the primary nexus for socialization as well as a source of continual security throughout life. Relative age and sex are reflected in kinship terminology. Older males are accorded somewhat more respect than females; otherwise, the two sexes are generally equal, and inheritance of land, houses, and other property can occur from either. With respect to the land, equal inheritance has resulted in fractionization to the extent that many inherited plots are too small for anything other than

261

Fig. 8. Woman wearing whitened deerskin boots (fig. 6), a cotton dress worn over the right shoulder and under the left arm in the same manner as woolen dresses, woolen shawl, and a kerchief fastened in front and hanging down the back. The side-whorled hair is a borrowing from the Western Pueblos. Photograph by Adam C. Vroman, 1899.

### Religion

Kiva initiation, which usually begins for males between 7 and 10, is very elaborate. Depending on the society, a boy can undergo 6, 12, or 18 months of initiation. The periods are timed so as to be completed and publicly validated in August at the tribal ceremonial pilgrimage to Blue Lake. Only a select few endure these initiation rites and this was probably always the case, though prior to the periods of increased population, more males relative to the total male population were involved in the kiva religion. The kiva societies are small and the positions of authority few. Uninitiated boys are often given some religious training, but they are forever excluded from the more esoteric aspects of Taos religion and they cannot hold important positions in secular government. The uninitiated, regardless of age, are referred to as "boys," while the term "elder" is applied to any initiated male. There is some

Fig. 9. Joseph Concha, Taos farmer, preparing corn for drying. His hair is braided in the traditional way, wrapped and worn behind the ears, and his shoes have been modified by removing the heels and substituting a flat sole, moccasin-style. Behind him are a bread paddle and a beehive oven. Photograph by Charlotte Trego, Oct. 1973.

indication that the relatively small cadre of the initiated reflects the distinction Ortiz (1969) makes between ordinary people and the religious leaders among the Tewa—Dry Food People and the Made People.

The religious qualification for secular leadership has been an increasingly important conflict point. Many of the "boys" are potentially able leaders and yet thoroughly frustrated in their attempts to exercise their talents. Much of the literature on Taos deals with the problem of factionalism and has employed the vague and cloudy terms progressive and conservative, which have confused the issue unnecessarily (Fenton 1957; Lasswell 1935; Siegel 1949, 1952; Siegel and Beals 1960). The studies of Taos governing by M.E. Smith (1967, 1969) have clarified this problem considerably.

The Taos would not approve of an exposition of their religious system and, until they want the total fabric of their religious belief revealed, it would be improper to delve into the complex esotericism so characteristic of this aspect of Taos culture. Certain published materials

Fig. 10. Group of Taos councilmen. Their dress includes moccasins and blankets draped in characteristically Taos style. Photograph by Don Blair, late 1960s.

(Parsons 1936, 1939) can be consulted but need to be interpreted very cautiously.

The six kivas, together with their constituent societies, are quite active. Big Earring People, Day People, and Knife People are the kivas of the north side. Water People, Old Axe People, and Feather People are on the south. The seventh kiva may have been primarily for ceremonial activities related to war, hence its abandonment. The office of cacique is hereditary at Taos, but he is not all-powerful or even the most important religious leader. The cacique has both secular and religious duties. However, his role is more symbolic and titular than is the case with other religious and secular positions. The leaders of Big Earring People and Water People are two of the most important. Taos religion can be compared to a mosaic. Each kiva and each kiva society has its special functions to perform. Ritual knowledge is not pooled, but held separately; therefore, no one person could provide detailed description of all the facets of Taos religion. In concert, ritual activity performs the functions for which religion is necessary. Strength lies in maintaining the integrity of each kiva and each role assigned to it. Were there to be widespread knowledge of these special activities, then the strength and efficacy of religion would be sapped and ultimately destroyed.

The aboriginal Taos use area contains many sacred sites to which individuals must go to perform certain rituals at specified times of the year. Important are the high mountain lakes, most particularly Blue Lake from which the water supply of the village originates, natural springs, certain mountain peaks, and other places at which something unusual happened in the past. Certain of these sites are in heavily settled non-Indian areas, which makes correct ritual performance difficult. The Taos held tenaciously to the rituals they could perform more or less undisturbed in the mountains and in a certain sense used Blue Lake, their most important "shrine," as the symbol for their struggle to regain control of this land. The battle began in 1906 when the area was designated a national forest and continued until 1970 when Congress finally returned 48,000 acres, including Blue Lake, to the Taos (fig. 11).

The ceremonial calendar, with public performances as integral parts, has been described more or less adequately by Parsons (1936) and continues relatively unchanged. It is noteworthy that the so-called corn dances staged in the summer are no match, in terms of participation and overall enthusiastic performance, for the "animal dances" held in the winter. One factor may help to explain this. Rites of intensification directed toward game animals may well have been more important to the Taos in the past due to their emphasis on the hunt. Certainly a comparison with a Keresan "corn dance" such as that of Santo Domingo in August is no comparison at all.

The Taos are considered and consider themselves to be Roman Catholics. Catholicism has not gained added strength, as Parsons (1936:120) predicted, but there is no evidence that it has weakened either. It is an important focus for religious belief and even the staunchest member of the kiva religion does not find participation in Catholic

Fig. 11. Celebration of the return of Blue Lake attended by people of Taos and representatives of other tribes, most notably from Okla. Ben Marcus leads the procession of dignitaries and dancers (dressed in pan-Indian style), past the Pueblo church of San Geronimo into the plaza for the festivities. Photograph by Charlotte Trego, Aug. 14 or 15, 1971.

ritual incompatible. A few Taos have converted to Protestantism, but most of the people and the Catholic Church have steadfastly opposed Protestant proselytizing.

The highly individualistic, and, at Taos, male-dominated, Peyote religion was introduced in 1907 from contacts with Oklahoma Indians. It caused controversy and considerable problems but survived the organized opposition of the Taos Council and remains active. Membership appeared to be declining in the 1970s. Taos

is the only Pueblo to adopt Peyotism to any group extent. Only individuals in other Pueblos are adherents. Collins (1968:448) believes that Peyote activities occupy a sort of intermediate position, offering individuals without other religious affiliations an opportunity to participate together in a meaningful manner. This really does not explain the appeal of Peyotism for those who are also active in both Catholicism and the native kiva religion, but then the notion of collective autism put forth by Lasswell (1935), which he attributed to the influence of Plains individualism, is not totally satisfactory either. The problem is complex and its psychodynamics intriguing, if not completely clear. The atomized nature of Taos religion may help to clarify the question. Catholicism and Peyotism may operate as legitimate alternatives to problem solving and hence are no more antithetical in a total scheme of religious belief and ritual than are the six kivas with their separate functioning societies. The special problems posed by culture contact processes at Taos obviously contributed as well.

## Political Organization

Secular government is strong at Taos. Annually the Taos Pueblo council elects 22 civil officers. They include the governor, lieutenant governor, and eight members of the governor's staff: a sheriff, two assistant sheriffs, a *fiscal,* an assistant *fiscal,* and three deputy *fiscales.* Generally the *fiscales* are responsible for matters dealing with the Catholic mission of San Geronimo. The sheriffs assist the governor with the civil affairs of the Pueblo. The chase officers number 12 and include the chase officer leader, or

left, Smithsonian, NAA; right, Mus. of N.M., Santa Fe.

Fig. 12. Raising and climbing the pole at the harvest festival of San Geronimo, held annually Sept. 29-30. The pole is climbed by members of the clown society, the Black Eyes, who share the freshly butchered sheep and bags of other edibles secured to the top. Photograph at left by Charles F. Saunders, 1920-1930s; photograph at right by unidentified photographer, possibly at about the same time.

war captain as he is usually called, assistant war captain, and 10 deputy war captains. The chase officers are responsible for problems and activities that may arise outside the village but generally on Pueblo land, for example, the organization of rabbit hunts, repair of range fences, rotation of stock, and patrol of the forest areas for fires and unauthorized trespassers in the Blue Lake area.

Matters of great importance to the Pueblo at large, such as the long battle for Blue Lake, are usually discussed in the Pueblo council, which numbers around 50. The governor, lieutenant governor, war captain, lieutenant war captain, and any person who has previously held these offices are members. To be eligible for office one must have been initiated. Two leaders and two assistant leaders from each of the six kivas, plus the cacique, round out the membership. It is in the council where the panorama of Taos politics is so well portrayed. Much of what has been described as the conservatism of Taos is dramatized in the actions and the personalities that make up the council. M.E. Smith's (1969:39) analysis of Taos governing concluded that "it is this dance with time—two steps forward, one step back—which allows the Taos to gradually adapt to the new while retaining (or even inventing when necessary) the past."

## History

Taos was one of the most isolated of the Eastern Pueblos. Taos was not so remote as Zuni and the Hopi towns, yet, relative to most of the other Rio Grande Pueblos, an analogy can be drawn. In the early period of Spanish settlement, 1598-1680, Taos was farthest removed from the intensive centers of Spanish influence on the Rio Grande. Of the 2,800 Spanish who were in New Mexico at the time of the Pueblo Revolt of 1680, only 70 were in the Taos area (Hackett 1942, 1:xx, xxx). The leaders of the rebellion plotted against the Spanish from the kivas of Taos. In 1776 Domínguez (1956:258-259) documented the retention of native habits and the degree of acceptance of Christianity: "The Indians of Picuris and Taos outdo all the rest in all the general customs. On their way to church, whether they be old or young, they go mincing along one by one, but when they leave, first comes first, because they fall over one another like sheep leaving the corral for pasture."

The Taos figure prominently in every attempt to expel Europeans from their territory. Charles Bent, first United States territorial governor of New Mexico, was a resident of Taos at the time of the 1847 revolt and hence a logical target for a successful overthrow of the Americans, but it is probably not coincidental that Mexican agitation, coupled with the willing cooperation of many Taos Indians, resulted in the plots being hatched at Taos. Bent and others were scalped, and the ruins of the old mission at the Pueblo are mute testimony to the punishment the United States Army meted out.

The suggestion formulated here is that some of the so-called conservatism ascribed to Taos and the opinion of Parsons (1936:6) that the Taos have a "strain of Plains Indian self-assertiveness" may be due in part to the relatively unsuccessful effects of Spanish and Anglo acculturative processes at this Pueblo. This does not explain the "conservatism" of Pueblos like Tesuque or Santo Domingo, but it could be argued that conservatism, whatever that term really means, can be achieved in different ways even given similar circumstances. Dozier (1961, 1970) applied the concept of compartmentalization to explain the mode of accommodation of the Pueblos to the pressures of acculturation. Perhaps it is more applicable to other Pueblos than to Taos. As far as Parsons is concerned it is stretching diffusion a bit far to explain all this simply as Plains influence and, in any case, much more valuable to do so in terms of the uniqueness and integrity of Taos culture itself.

Although certain major changes have taken place, it is also apparent that much cultural integrity remains. Many things constituting changes at Taos are actually accretions. This is particularly true in the material realm. The Taos eagerly adopted items from the contact cultures. They firmly resisted anything they felt would compromise those values that are intrinsic to their way of life. This has led to impeding material change as well, even when clamored for by Pueblo residents. Taos was the last New Mexico Pueblo to permit electricity and then only outside the old village. The road to the Pueblo was finally paved in 1956, but not before a long struggle in which it was argued that an ancient race track would be permanently marred and hence desecrated. Indeed, religion has often been the powerfully persuasive force used to block change. Younger Taos and those not active in the kiva religion protest but are often silenced when they ask why a certain change would be against the religion. The answer is that no reason can be given, because it is necessarily secret knowledge. Frequently the protest is weakened out of respect for the "old folks." However, change has occurred at Taos and more appears imminent. The problem, so frequently encountered elsewhere, is how to evaluate change and to predict the ultimate ramifications a given change might have.

Several factors have been pointed to by many observers as crucial to the continued stability of Taos culture. Of importance is the retention of a governmental system heavily influenced by religion and religious leaders, though the system itself is secular and cannot be labeled a pure theocracy. The ceremonial system has remained intact and it appears that the socialization process for many is largely undisturbed. A marked tendency toward endogamy and both overt and covert attempts to discourage on-reservation residence of outsiders who have married Taos are additional evidence of their conscious

**Table 1. Population, 1864–1970**

|      | Population | Source                  |
|------|------------|-------------------------|
| 1864 | 361        | U.S. Census Office 1893 |
| 1890 | 401        | U.S. Census Office 1893 |
| 1910 | 515        | Hodge 1910a             |
| 1927 | 656        | Parsons 1936            |
| 1930 | 694        | Parsons 1936            |
| 1942 | 830        | Aberle 1948             |
| 1950 | 938        | Tax and Stanley 1950    |
| 1964 | 1,457      | Smith 1966              |
| 1970 | 1,463      | Bodine 1971             |

efforts to maintain cultural integrity and separatism. Blocking the incorporation of certain material items into the Taos life-style, such as electricity and plumbing, are really only symptomatic of the kind of resistance the Taos have mounted against wholesale acceptance of Anglo and Spanish-American values and attitudes.

It is helpful to consider these changes in the light of available demographic data. Doing so permits a more accurate picture of change or the lack of it (Bodine 1971). Table 1 clearly shows that there was a rather gradual increase in the Taos population through time until the dramatic changes that occurred after World War II. This period of increased involvement with the Anglo world brought about significantly greater understanding of what that world meant to Taos Pueblo.

The increase this reflects, particularly in the later periods, has had definite effects on Taos culture. As the population increased, so did the number of non-residents on the reservation. While out-migration from the Pueblos is an old phenomenon, economic pressures combined with the expanding opportunities for jobs in the urban centers of the west and elsewhere lured more and more Taos away from their reservation. In 1970, 39 percent or 464 Taos were not resident out of the total roll population of 1,463. These persons had been away at least three years, meaning that the percentage is not due to seasonal fluctuation. The 999 Taos who remained may well represent an approximate maximum that the reservation and surrounding communities could support, given the fact that the traditional occupations of agriculture and stock raising have been greatly reduced. Wage work in the Spanish and Anglo town of Taos, certain federal work projects, some revenue from tourism, and increases in the numbers of persons receiving welfare, old age assistance, unemployment compensation, and government pensions became the chief economic resources of Taos in the 1960s. These offset the losses in traditional economic pursuits to a considerable extent but could not fail to have their effects on Taos culture.

Welfare and other forms of governmental assistance were slow to be accepted. Fear on the part of the aged

that the government would some day request that these funds be repaid and the general dislike by the Taos to accept government "handouts" on an individual basis were important in impeding acceptance. While these forms of support improved the lot of many, it meant a relative weakening in two very crucial areas of Taos life. The sense of community suffered, while individualism increased. No longer would relatives and friends donate their labor or reciprocate with goods and services as freely. The aged parent who formerly took the role of family patriarch or matriarch, living with and presiding over the family and its affairs, now very often resides alone in order to receive the maximum amount of old age benefits. The community and the family were two of the most vital structures of Taos life and many Taos looked upon welfare as a serious threat to their cultural integrity.

The majority who have left their reservation are young adults and their offspring. This is not surprising, for they are in the most favored age group for urban employment. Of those remaining on the reservation, over half were either under 19 or over 60 (40% and 18%, respectively). This is important to note, since a common pattern of child care was to leave young children with their grandparents, who thereby naturally had significant influence over their socialization. This pattern increased as more young adults sought wage work in the surrounding communities. For a considerable number of Taos, the processes of socialization that effectively produce individuals loyal to the system have therefore not been destroyed.

In 1970 only 24 outside adults were resident on the reservation, which is low compared to 66 for San Juan and 85 for Isleta. All outsiders were Indians, except for one young Spanish-American female. Indeed, only seven of the 24 outsiders were males. The Taos state that an outsider is ignorant of community obligations and frequently reluctant to perform them. Community duties are more important for males than females and the Taos have consistently discouraged non-Taos male residents. The degree of endogamy that this reflects can be measured, as well, by calculating the degree of Indian "blood" recorded for each individual by the Bureau of Indian Affairs. Compared to the other Eastern Pueblos, Taos was very high, with a mean percent of Indian blood of 95 (Bodine 1972).

In spite of the many problems the Taos have faced, there is no indication that the cultural system they have maintained for so long is doomed. It would be as foolish to predict extinction as it is impossible to know the direction future change will take. One thing is certain. The Taos possess a strong and resilient culture. They have withstood the vicissitudes of over 400 years of European contact, adapting selectively as change was necessary. Surely they can withstand future forces of change.

## Synonymy†

The Spanish and later English name Taos is an adaptation of Taos tôotho 'in the village', the usual term of reference for the Pueblo (Trager 1960). The -s was originally the Spanish plural ending, but the name is now invariable in both Spanish and English. The native self-designations are t’óynemą 'the people' (t’óyna, sg.) and tháwílana 'Taos Indian' (Harrington 1918, normalized). The name of the Pueblo is ʔìałopháymų-p’öhą́othąolbo 'at red-willow canyon mouth' (Trager 1960) or for short ʔìałopháybo 'at the red willows' (Harrington 1916:180, phonemicized), from which comes the designation Red Willow Indians (ARCIA 1872:382).

Recorded as Picuris names are a cognate of the alternate Taos term tôobo 'to or toward the village' and the name kwapíhałki 'chief village'; there is also Picuris thą́-wélene 'Taos Indian' (F.H. Trager 1968:51). Southern Tiwa has Isleta thúhwir tą̀aʔi 'sun-bow village' and thùhwíride 'Taos Indian' (thûhwírnin, pl.) (William Leap, personal communication 1977) or forms with a stem thəwir- or thəawir- (C.T. Harrington 1920:43, 50), and similar designations in Sandia. In Tewa both p̣insôʔ ówînge 'large-mountain pueblo' (a reference to the Taos mountains or Pueblo Peak) and θaˑwíʔ ówînge are attested. Jemez yíla 'Taos Indian' (pl. yíłæš) or a locative form such as yíláta 'Taos Pueblo' may be the source of Spanish Yuraba and Uraba, 1542; Curtis (1907–1930, 16:261) gives the Jemez as gyuláta. In Keresan, beside borrowings of the Spanish name, there is Cochiti tʸetʸšóḱocæ 'north corner place' (normalized). The Zuni name topoliana 'place of cottonwood trees' (Cushing in Hodge 1910a:691) is of uncertain interpretation. Navajo Tówoł 'murmuring water' (Robert W. Young, personal communication 1977), also written Tóghoł (Haile 1950–1951, 2:295, phonemicized), and Jicarilla kóhoˑhlté (Hodge 1910a:690), which may be a cognate of this, resemble the Southern Tiwa names.

Early Spanish names include Braba and Valladolid, 1541 (Castañeda, in Hammond and Rey 1940:244) and Oñate's Tayberon or Tayberin, beside Taos, 1598 (Hammond and Rey 1953, 1:321, 371). As the seat of a mission Taos has been referred to as San Miguel and, most commonly, San Gerónimo de (los) Taos.

## Sources

The only standard ethnography of the Taos, by Parsons (1936), is very out of date with respect to contemporary Taos culture, but it remains a valuable source book if used very cautiously. Parsons was unsure of much of her data and said so; other errors were inadvertently made and are well known to the Taos, who view her work with considerable hostility. Trager (1971) lists Trager's publications on the Taos language. Some manuscript materials are held in the National Anthropological Archives at the Smithsonian Institution, and extensive photographic collections are maintained in a number of the more prominent museums. Very few Taos artifacts have been placed in museum collections, and most of them are examples of Taos micaceous pottery. Much more of Taos culture could be known, but that knowledge must await the decision of the Taos to reveal it to the world and to preserve it for the edification of future generations of Taos Indians.

† This synonymy was written by Ives Goddard. Unless otherwise credited, forms cited or referred to are from Harrington (1916:179–183) or anonymous sources.

# Picuris Pueblo

DONALD N. BROWN

## Language, Territory, and Environment

Picuris (ˌpĭkə¹rēs) Pueblo (figs. 1-2) is located in the mountains of northern New Mexico. A Northern Tiwa language is spoken within the Pueblo.* It is closely related to the other Northern Tiwa language spoken at Taos, and to the Southern Tiwa languages spoken at Sandia and Isleta. The residents of Picuris Pueblo are also fluent in English, and the older residents speak Spanish as well.

The Picuris Pueblo Grant is located on the western slopes of the Sangre de Cristo Mountains in southern Taos County (see "Pueblos: Introduction," fig. 1, this vol.). The boundaries of the original grant from the Spanish Crown in recognition of the Picuris occupation of this land at the time of the initial European contact were one league in each direction from the mission church (Twitchell 1914, 1:477). In 1864 a patent for 17,468 acres was issued to Picuris Pueblo by the U.S. government. However, rulings by the Pueblo Lands Board and the U.S. District Court in 1930 found that 2,507 acres within the grant boundaries, mostly irrigated farmlands, were in non-Indian title (Aberle 1948:76). Through subsequent purchases and exchanges the land in Picuris title in 1977 totaled 14,960 acres. However, only 260 acres of irrigated land remained in Picuris ownership (Pueblo of Picuris 1962:8).

The northern half of the grant is mountainous, with steep rocky slopes that are occasionally broken by narrow canyons with small streams. The southern half of the grant includes three irrigated valleys separated by rocky ridges and low mesas. The Pueblo and the remaining Picuris farmlands are located in the northernmost valley through which the Rio Pueblo flows. The other two valleys are occupied primarily by Spanish-Americans. The elevation of the grant ranges from 7,000 feet at the western border to 9,700 feet at the northeastern corner. The Pueblo and surrounding farmlands have an elevation of about 7,300 feet.

Summers are generally cool because of the elevation, and the average growing season is only 128 days (Ford 1977:142). The short growing season not only limits the plants that can be grown successfully but also results occasionally in the loss of the entire crop of those plants that can be grown. Winters are moderately cold and heavy snow accumulations are not unusual. The average annual precipitation is about 15 inches (Ford 1977:142).

Forms characteristic of three life-zones are found within the grant boundaries. Stands of ponderosa pine, Douglas fir, white fir, limber pine, spruce, and aspen occur in the higher elevations. The large variety of useful plants includes numerous food plants and seasonings as well as medicinal and ceremonial plants.

The animal life is also varied. Large game animals such as deer, elk, and bear and many small animals such as rabbits, squirrels, and chipmunks are native to this area. Trout were found in the mountain streams and many forms of birds lived in the mountains. Occasionally, grasshoppers were a menace to crops.

## External Relations

The remote location of Picuris Pueblo limited the interaction of Picuris residents with other groups. Relations with the Jicarilla Apache, who camped and hunted in the mountains north and east of the Pueblo, were generally friendly. Even after their reservation was established in 1878, Jicarilla families visited the Pueblo during the summer months and participated in the annual Picuris feast day activities (Brown 1973:69).

Taos Pueblo is the nearest Indian Pueblo, only about 18 miles north by trail, and the dialects of the Tiwa language spoken in the two Pueblos are mutually intelligible. However, relations were frequently strained and marriages between these Pueblos were rare. The primary contact between the residents of these two Pueblos was on feast days. There was also a limited trade into Taos of various mountain plants, an activity that continued in the 1970s (Brown 1973:69–71).

---

* Picuris words written in italics are in the phonemic system of F.H. Trager (1971), with the substitution of č for her c and ʔ for her apostrophe, to accord with the standard technical alphabet of the *Handbook*. The glottalized stops (pʔ, tʔ, kʔ, kʔw), aspirated stops (ph, th), and labiovelars (kw, kʔw, xw) are analyzed as clusters. There are three degrees of stress and three tones. With middle tone the stresses are primary (v́), medial (v̆), and weak (v), the last occurring only with this tone. The other tones are indicated by an accent to the right of the stress mark, acute for high tone (v̆, v́) and grave for low tone (v̂, v̀). The words cited are from George L. Trager (in Parsons 1939a), F.H. Trager (1968), and Amy Zaharlick (personal communication 1977). The linguistic editor is responsible for selecting from among the variant forms recorded for some words and for phonemicizing the author's form for Women's Group on the basis of the formation of other group names.

Fig. 1. Picuris Pueblo, partial view. Photograph by Peter Dechert, June 1977.

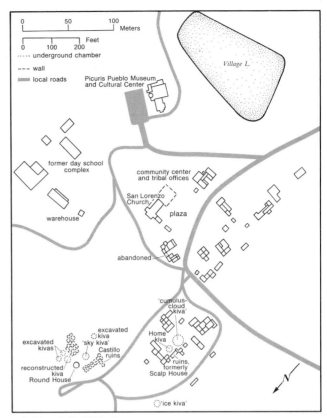

revised from Stubbs 1950:fig. 5.
Fig. 2. Picuris Pueblo.

Relations with the Tewa-speaking Pueblos to the south, especially San Juan Pueblo, were more cordial. In 1881 several individuals from San Juan Pueblo were reported to be married into Picuris (Bloom 1933-1938, 10:278), and marriages between these two Pueblos were not uncommon in the 1970s. Visits were exchanged on feast days and pottery from San Juan was traded for mountain plants from Picuris (Ford 1972). Residents of Picuris are occasionally treated for illnesses by the Indian doctors at San Juan (Brown 1973:71).

Since the eighteenth century Picuris Pueblo has been surrounded by Spanish-Americans. Except for the problem of land encroachment, relations with these Spanish-American neighbors were generally friendly. Pottery from Picuris was traded for food products, and surplus Picuris crops were sold to merchants in neighboring communities. Occasionally, Picuris men would work in the fields of Spanish-Americans for wages. The closest ties were those through the Roman Catholic Church. The mission church at Picuris also served the Spanish-Americans in the region until the late 1800s, when a church was built in Peñasco and the residence of the priest was moved from Picuris to Peñasco. Spanish-Americans served as godparents for Picuris children and as sponsors at Picuris marriages. However, marriages with Spanish-Americans were rare. A few Picuris men were members of the Penitente Brotherhood in the Spanish-American

villages of Vadito and Chamisal. Since the late 1920s this friendly relationship has deteriorated, and in the 1970s few formal ties were maintained with Spanish-Americans (Brown 1973:71-74).

The establishment of an Anglo-American government in New Mexico in the mid-nineteenth century had little immediate influence on Picuris Pueblo. Generally, relations with Anglo-American residents of the area have been friendly. Since the first decade of the twentieth century Picuris men have accepted wage work away from the Pueblo, and Picuris men have participated in the armed forces since World War I. Most adult men and many women have worked in the Anglo-American world away from the Pueblo. They have chosen to return to Picuris Pueblo because they feel comfortable there in this mountainous location.

## Prehistory

Archeological investigations conducted in the 1960s indicate that the initial settlement of this site (fig. 3) took place in the last half of the twelfth century. By the mid-thirteenth century small coursed adobe structures replaced the original pithouses. Late in the fourteenth century work was begun on two large multistoried structures and a third multiroomed structure, which indicates an increasing population. Prehistoric Picuris reached its climax in the sixteenth century when addi-

Fig. 3. Original site of Picuris, located at northern edge of the present Pueblo: a, excavated kivas; b, excavated rooms of prehistoric structures, including c, the multistory complex known as the Castillo; d, round house, used for summer rain ceremonials; e, restored kiva (fig. 4); f, current Sky kiva, associated with the Southside People. Photograph by Peter Dechert, 1977.

Fig. 4. Restored prehistoric underground kiva. top, Interior view showing ladder to roof, south wall, and firebox or hearth with stepped (deflector) back, which is directly under the roof opening. The wall paintings follow the original designs. bottom, Exterior view, from the northeast, showing entrance to restored kiva (ladder at center), Sky kiva entrance (ladder barely visible to the left), and excavated kiva (foreground), part of the "Castillo ruins" (background) and the round house (right). Part of the modern Pueblo is also visible (buildings at extreme left). Photographs by Helga Teiwes, Aug. 1970.

tions were made to these large structures. By the following century parts of these structures began to collapse through disuse (Herbert W. Dick, personal communication 1969). This decline was likely a response to the arrival of Athapaskans into the area in the sixteenth century.

## History

### Contact and Missionization, 1541-1680

Although the earliest Spanish exploration into the region, that of Francisco Vásquez de Coronado in 1540-1541, may not have contacted Picuris Pueblo, the expedition of Gaspar Castaño de Sosa visited the Pueblo in 1591 (Jenkins 1966; Reed 1943; Castaño de Sosa 1965:124). Seven years later Juan de Oñate was welcomed into the Pueblo (Hammond and Rey 1953, 1:320).

During this initial period of European contact additions were made to the Picuris cultural inventory, but few changes took place within the Picuris cultural system. New crops and the raising of livestock were added. The collection of revenue for the *encomiendo* removed Picuris products from the community (Hackett 1923-1937, 3:247-249). The activities of the Catholic Church were introduced, but the influence of the Church appears to have been minor at this time. A new form of civil government was imposed on all Pueblo communities during the seventeenth century; however, these new offices did not replace the traditional political groups composed of the ceremonial headmen. The most impor-

tant addition was a new language, Spanish. Although it did not replace the original language of the Pueblo, Spanish facilitated communication among the many Pueblo communities along the Rio Grande and became a lingua franca throughout the area.

### Rebellion, 1680-1706

By the mid-seventeenth century, demands by the Spanish missionaries and civil authorities for labor and revenue resulted in a deep resentment toward them by the residents of the Pueblo. Attempts to abolish the traditional ceremonial activities cut at the heart of the community. The resentment and hostility finally erupted in 1680 as the residents of Picuris Pueblo joined the other Pueblo communities in a revolt against the Spaniards.

For the next 12 years Picuris Pueblo remained free from Spanish contact. During this period a Picuris man, Tupatu or Luis Picuri, became an influential leader among the northern Pueblos (Twitchell 1914, 1:54). In 1692 Spanish domination returned to the area, but two years later the northern Pueblos again revolted (Espinosa 1936:182). During the summer of 1696, the third revolt erupted and in October of that year Picuris Pueblo was abandoned (Thomas 1935:54). For the next decade most of the Picuris remained among Apache groups on the plains at a place referred to as Cuartelejo. In August 1706 the last of the Picuris exiles were returned to the Pueblo (Thomas 1935:76).

The period of rebellion lasted only 26 years, yet the changes that occurred significantly altered the community and cultural system. The most dramatic change was in the size of the Pueblo. From a population listed as 3,000 in 1680 (Vetancurt 1960:273), the largest population listed for all the northern Pueblos, the population decreased to less than 300 in 1706 (Hackett 1923–1937, 3:374). No doubt the 1680 estimate was an exaggeration, but Picuris Pueblo changed from a sizable community into a small village. A second significant change was the Picuris attitude toward the Spaniards. The Picuris appear to have accepted the Spanish presence as inevitable, and revolts against Spanish authority were never attempted again.

## Reconstitution, 1706–1796

In the early 1700s the residents of Picuris Pueblo became active allies of the Spaniards in an attempt to control and contain the nomadic Indian groups that raided both Spanish and Indian communities in New Mexico. Picuris men participated as auxiliaries in campaigns against various Apache groups, Utes, and Comanches (Thomas 1935:23–26, 28, 93, 103, 111; Jones 1966:71).

Because of its location on the eastern frontier of Spanish New Mexico, Picuris Pueblo played an important role in Spanish-French relations in the eighteenth century. As early as 1659 Apache Indians trading at the Pueblo reported French traders on the plains (Hodge 1929). The first French traders entered the Rio Grande region when the trading party of Pierre and Paul Mallet reached Picuris Pueblo in 1739 (Thomas 1940:15).

By the mid-1780s peace was made with the Comanches and the threat of raids was reduced. Population within the Spanish settlements grew rapidly, and with the possession of the Santa Barbara Grant in 1796, Picuris Pueblo became surrounded by Spanish settlers (Pearce 1965:148).

**Table 1. Population, 1630–1972**

| Date | Population | Source |
|------|-----------|--------|
| 1630 | 2,000 | Benavides 1916:25 |
| 1680 | 3,000 | Vetancurt 1960:273 |
| 1706 | 300 | Hackett 1923–1937, 3:374 |
| 1717 | 464 | Jones 1966:85 |
| 1744 | 80 families | Hackett 1923–1937, 3:403 |
| 1776 | 223 | Domínguez 1956:98 |
| 1790 | 254 | ARCIA 1868:213 |
| 1808 | 309 | ARCIA 1868:213 |
| 1809 | 313 | ARCIA 1868:213 |
| 1850 | 222 | ARCIA 1868:213 |
| 1860 | 143 | ARCIA 1868:213 |
| 1864 | 122 | ARCIA 1868:213 |
| 1870 | 127 | Arny 1967:44 |
| 1890 | 91 | ARCIA 1890:260 |
| 1890 | 108 | U.S. Census Office. 11th Census 1893:92 |
| 1899 | 96 | ARCIA 1899, 1:245 |
| 1900 | 125 | Hodge 1910h:245 |
| 1939 | 97 | Parsons 1939a:206 |
| 1972 | 167[a] | U.S. Department of Commerce 1974:368 |

[a] Enrolled, not resident, population.

## Encroachment, 1796–1890

The struggle against encroachment upon Picuris lands was the dominant theme of the 1800s. A second theme was the erosion of political autonomy within the Pueblo by non-Indian civil authorities. As the Spanish population increased in the region, the Picuris population declined (see table 1).

Picuris farmlands in the Peñasco and Chamisal valleys were occupied by Spanish settlers. Several Spanish families lived within the Pueblo and farmed lands in the Rio Pueblo valley. One Spanish family operated a store within the Pueblo in the late nineteenth century (Brown 1973:74).

The residents of the Pueblo successfully sought the aid of non-Indian civil authorities to remove Spanish settlers from some Picuris land (Twitchell 1914, 1:444–445; Abel 1916:199, 241). As first Spanish authorities, then Mexican authorities, and finally United States authorities actively intervened in the affairs of the Pueblo, the authority of the traditional Picuris government diminished.

## Anglo-American Dominance, 1890–present

The isolated location of Picuris Pueblo delayed the impact of the arrival of Anglo-Americans into New Mexico by almost a half-century. However, in the last decade of the nineteenth century Anglo-American influence began to permeate the Picuris cultural system. With the opening of the government day school in 1899 (fig. 5)

Smithsonian, NAA.

Fig. 5. Picuris in 1899, facing north toward the Sangre de Cristo Mountains. Government day school (flagpole in front) at center, church at extreme right, cornfields in foreground. Photograph by Adam C. Vroman.

(ARCIA 1899, 1:247), Anglo-American values and orientations were taught to Picuris children. Adult men were encouraged to leave the Pueblo for seasonal wage work (ARCIA 1906:273), and several families moved away permanently. Timber and tie operations on Picuris lands damaged the irrigation system and resulted in the destruction of a religious shrine (U.S. Congress. Senate 1932:10322; Harrington 1916:191).

In the 1920s attitudes toward the Spanish neighbors began to shift to hostility as disputes over land ownership were taken to the federal courts through the Pueblo Lands Board. By the 1930s the authority of the council was challenged as traditional ceremonies and other activities began to be ignored. Several governors appointed by the council were impeached, usually at the request of officials of the Bureau of Indian Affairs (Brown 1973:202–203). Subsistence farming and hunting were being replaced by wage work sponsored through federal relief programs. Rations of food and clothing were distributed within the Pueblo by government agents and the Red Cross (Brown 1973:196–197).

Symbolic of the many changes, in the summer of 1947 the adult men of Picuris Pueblo voted to change the name of the Pueblo to San Lorenzo in honor of the patron saint of the community. The name change lasted only until 1955 when the name was officially changed back to Picuris Pueblo (Brown 1973:212, 221). Finally, in 1950 the governor and the other civil officers were elected by a vote of the male residents for the first time (Brown 1973:213), and the governor replaced the cacique as the leader of the Pueblo. With the closing of the day school in 1953, Picuris children began attending the public schools of Peñasco (Brown 1973:215).

## Culture in 1880

In 1880 Picuris Pueblo remained a relatively self-contained traditional community. Through subsistence farming, gathering wild plants, and hunting large and small game animals, the residents of the Pueblo were able to provide for most of their needs. Surplus farm products were sold to merchants in Peñasco (U.S. Census Office. 11th Census 1893:118). The Pueblo conducted a limited trade with other Spanish and Indian communities, exporting mountain plants and the pottery manufactured at Picuris (Ford 1972). Visitors to the Pueblo at this time remarked about the poverty. "The Picuris impress me as an extremely poor people," wrote one visitor in 1881 (Bloom 1933–1938, 10:277), and another stated in 1891, "the Picuris people are about the same in all respects as those at Taos, only they are poorer in worldly goods" (U.S. Census Office. 11th Census 1893:119).

### Life Cycle

The Picuris life cycle of this time reflects the integration of elements from the Spanish-Catholic cultural system with traditional Picuris elements. After birth the child was placed with the mother who remained in bed for 30 days. An ear of corn was laid next to the child to act as its "corn mother." At the end of the 30 days, the mother took corn meal to a shrine and prayed. "If the child is a girl, the mother prays that she may grind, cook, and do well the other kinds of work that women do. And if the

272

Fig. 6. Winnowing (probably wheat) using a pitchfork and colonial Spanish-style sieve, probably with a perforated rawhide bottom. There would normally be a blanket or cloth underneath the sieve to catch the kernels of wheat as they fall. Round house, used for ceremonials, is at right; tribal cemetery is in the hills at left. Photograph by T. Harmon Parkhurst, probably 1930s.

child is a boy, she prays that he may be brave, a hunter, a runner, and do well the other kinds of work that men do" (Harrington and Roberts 1928:389). The child was named soon after birth. Favorite names for females included references to plants, flowers, and leaves, while male names referred to animals, mountains, and running. This name was generally used within the Pueblo (Brown 1973:111).

Before the child was one month old, it was taken to the church for christening. Two adults, chosen by the parents to act as sponsors, provided a Spanish-Catholic name that was recorded in the church records. When the child was between 6 and 12 years of age, it was confirmed in the church. Confirmation required another sponsor, a male for a boy and a female for a girl (Brown 1973:112–113).

As the child matured it was expected to participate in adult activities as soon as it was physically able and had acquired the needed skills. Skills were learned through participation in the various activities.

Church records and census data indicate that marriage generally occurred when girls reached their late teens or early twenties. Husbands tended to be about four years older than their wives (Brown 1973:114). Marriage was strictly monogamous and followed the rules of the Catholic Church. A married couple was chosen to act as sponsors for the wedding, which was held at the church. The newly married couple was expected to establish a new household, although initially they might live with the parents of either the bride or the groom.

At death the deceased was dressed in traditional Picuris clothing. A stripe of black mica was placed on the face, and a prayer feather was placed in the hands. Special death songs were then sung. Throughout the

night a wake was held and Christian hymns were sung. In the morning, when the body was taken out for burial, a bag of food was tied at the waist of the body. Cedar sprigs were used to sweep the area. Burial took place in the grounds north of the Pueblo. Family members and friends remained at the house of the deceased for four days after the burial (Harrington and Roberts 1928:389–393).

### Ceremonial Organization

The traditional ceremonial organization remained a central part of Picuris Pueblo in 1880. The entire population of the Pueblo was divided into two ceremonial groups, *hù?ótha* 'Northside People' and *hùkwétha* 'Southside People'. Affiliation with these groups was based on patrilineal descent; however, women generally changed membership into their husband's group if it was different from their own. The annual relay race on San Lorenzo's Day was a competition between these groups, and the long-distance races that were part of the summer rain ceremonials included representatives from these groups. The kiva associated with the Southside People was *p?äpǝ́k?ǝma* 'sky kiva' (fig. 3) while *mìasíakèma* 'cumulus-cloud kiva' was that of the Northside People (Brown 1973:97–98).

Affiliation with the ceremonial associations was through selection by the membership, volunteering, or trespassing into a restricted area during a ritual. The Spring People (*tǫ̀wǫnt?áy?enę̌*) conducted the first of three summer rain ceremonials in June. The second was directed by the Summer People (*pèlt?áy?enę̌*) in August. The Fall People (*p?àčot?áy?enę̌*) were in charge of the third ceremonial, in September. All three groups used the

273

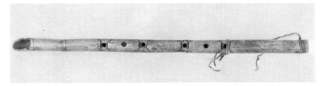

Mus. of N.M. Santa Fe: 31926/12.

Fig. 7. End-blown flute of bamboo with hatched surface decorations and 6 holes, one of which has been plugged. End is wrapped with rawhide strips. Flutes are played by men to accompany ceremonies. Length 48 cm, collected before 1958.

Bureau of Ind. Affairs, Northern Pueblos Agency Land Operations, Santa Fe, N.M.

Fig. 8. Virginia Duran, Picuris potter, with an undecorated micaceous pot typical of Picuris ware. She is seated on the ledge of a beehive oven. Photograph by Elmer J. Kingsolver, 1977.

Round House (*tolíwene*) located north of the Pueblo for these ceremonials. The Winter People (*tòwiatʔáyʔenę̀*) held ceremonies for weather control and animal increase during the winter months in *pʔäčíkʔəma* 'ice kiva'.

Other ceremonial associations included the Water Clowns (*pʔäwayénę̀*), who held a pole climb on San Lorenzo's Day and also took part in the winter deer dance; the Mountain Group (tianapu, i.e., *pʔįntʔáyʔenę̀?*), which was headed by the hunt chief (*čə̀tʔǫ̀néne*) and sponsored the Mountain Dance in late September; the cacique's group (*ʔahàyénę̀*), which sponsored the annual Spring Picnic ceremonial (*pʔäkéne*) and used Home kiva (*pʔähə́pa* 'at the canyon'), and the Women's Group (*ɫìwtʔáyʔenę̀*), which assisted the other groups in ceremonial activities and in the maintenance of the kivas (Brown 1973:98–103).

The council of *principales,* composed of the headmen of the ceremonial groups and other elderly men respected for their knowledge and judgment, was the heart of Picuris Pueblo. The cacique (*thə̀-ɫapíane*), the ceremonial leader of the Pueblo, acted as the leader of the council, which met in *pʔähə́pa*. The council formulated policy for the Pueblo and acted as a court for trying any offenses within the Pueblo. Another important activity of the council was the annual appointment of the civil officers. These officers were responsible for executing the policies and decisions of the council and for maintaining order within the Pueblo and protecting it from outside threats. Two sets of civil officers were appointed, a governor (*tàpóne, ɫàwĭane*) with a staff of four and a war captain (*xò(m)-ɫàwĭane*) with three assistants (Brown 1973:105–110).

## Sociocultural Situation in the 1960s

Picuris Pueblo in the 1960s was only a dim reflection of the traditional community. Paved roads, electricity, television sets, and telephones linked the Pueblo to the outside world on which the residents had become dependent. Most of the ceremonial associations had disappeared. The cacique had been replaced by the governor as the leader of the Pueblo, and the community building constructed in 1964 and the museum completed in 1968 had replaced *pʔähə́pa* as the center of community activi-

ties. The Pueblo had shifted from a ceremonial to a more secular orientation.

The economic activities were dominated by various federal programs and state assistance programs. Less than 20 acres were planted in 1967, and only 24 animals were kept (Brown 1973:251–253). Both hunting and gathering continued but on a much reduced level. Pottery making continued to be an important economic activity

Bureau of Ind. Affairs, Northern Pueblos Agency Land Operations, Santa Fe, N.M.

Fig. 9. Tribal officers in 1977. left to right, Joe D. Martinez, sheriff; Pat Martinez, first war chief; Joe I. Quanchello, governor; Donna Mermejo, secretary-treasurer, Jess Mermejo, Jr., lieutenant governor; Benny Lopez, third war chief; and Manual Archuleta, second war chief. All but the secretary-treasurer, which is the most recently established position, carry canes that are traditionally symbolic of their offices. Photograph taken in the tribal community building by Elmer J. Kingsolver.

(fig. 8). The entire region was economically depressed and few jobs were available. In 1962 only two families were reported to have received income from wages, while 14 families received income from assistance programs (Pueblo of Picuris 1962:13). In 1967 it was estimated that 51 percent of the cash income for the entire Pueblo was from federal programs, 37 percent from assistance programs, 11 percent from wages, and 1 percent from craftwork (Brown 1973:262). Fighting forest fires as a member of a U.S. Forest Service organized team is the primary source of wages.

The annual election of officers takes place in the community building on New Year's Day, and the new officers were installed on January 6. All men over 18 years of age are eligible to vote and hold office, and collectively they form a community council. The officers (fig. 9), headed by the governor, continue to be responsible for maintaining order within the Pueblo. They must also manage the many programs available through the federal government. Since the late 1960s the government has stabilized, and the impeachments that characterized the Picuris government in the 1950s and early 1960s have become rare.

The annual celebration of San Lorenzo's Day on August 10 includes the Sunset Dance on the evening before, either vespers that evening or mass the next morning at the Pueblo church, the relay race the morning of August 10 (fig. 10), and a dance in the afternoon (fig. 11). The division between Northside People and South-

*Albuquerque Journal*, N.M.

Fig. 11. San Lorenzo's Day Corn Dance. The women carry spruce boughs and wear colorful mantas, woven belts, and Tiwa-style moccasins (see "Taos Pueblo," fig. 6, this vol.). The Picuris, like the Taos, do not wear tablitas for this dance. Photograph by Bill Hume, Aug. 10, 1970.

side People is largely ignored, and an attempt is made to have good runners at each end of the race track. The race track was shortened in 1965 when a new road into the Pueblo cut across the western third of the track.

In the late 1960s the Water Clown association was revived. After a quarter-century the pole climb was reinstituted as a part of the annual feast day. This revival appears to signal a renewed interest in traditional Picuris activities among the residents.

The Mountain Dance held annually in late September is under the direction of the war captain. It is scheduled on a weekend so that school children can participate. Dances are also held on New Year's Day and January 6, as well as on other significant occasions. Occasionally social dances are held in the evening. The war captain is responsible for all dances and his permission must be obtained before a dance can be held. Only *mìasíakèma* kiva is used for ceremonial activities.

The population figures for Picuris Pueblo can be misleading because the enrolled population includes all individuals enrolled with the Bureau of Indian Affairs as members of Picuris Pueblo. The resident population, or those individuals who actually live at Picuris Pueblo, is only about half the enrolled population and varies as individuals move in and out of the community seeking jobs in the Anglo-American world or returning to the Pueblo after retirement.

### Synonymy†

The name Picuris is Spanish Picurís, originally a plural, first recorded by Oñate as Picuríes, 1598 (Hammond and

Fig. 10. San Lorenzo's Day footracers, before the race, holding poplar branches. The races were traditionally by moiety with Northside dancers led by their Northside headman on north side of the track and similar Southside contingent on south side. Photograph by Donald N. Brown, Aug. 10, 1974.

† This synonymy was written by Ives Goddard incorporating some material supplied by the author. Uncredited forms are from Harrington (1916:192–193), who gives additional variants, or anonymous sources.

Fig. 12. Basket dancers. The Basket Dance is performed by male and female dancers, who dance in parallel lines. The women then kneel, placing their baskets face down on the ground, and accompany the men's singing by scraping notched rasps held against the baskets, which act as resonators. Photograph by Richard Erdoes, Aug. 1975.

Rey 1953, 1:320). It is most likely a borrowing from Jemez *pè·kwile* 'Picuris Indian' (pl. *pè·kwileš*); compare *pè·kwiletá* 'Picuris Pueblo'; literally 'at the mountain gap' (Harrington 1916:192, phonemicized). Alternate spellings and misprints include Pecuri and Pecures in the Spanish period and, in nineteenth-century sources, Pecora, Pecucio, Pecucis, Pecuris, Picaris, Piccuries, Picoris, Pictoris, Picuni, Picuri, Picuria, Picux, Ticori, and Vicuris (Hodge 1910h; Harrington 1916:193). Hodge (1910h:245) derived the Spanish name from Keresan *pĭkuría* (or *pĭkuría*), but the Keresan name (also recorded as Cochiti *pikurí* and *pikulí*) is more likely a borrowing from Spanish (Harrington 1916:192–193; Curtis 1907–1930, 16:260, 264).

The Picuris call themselves *pʔĭnwélʔenę* (sg. *pʔĭnwélene*) and their Pueblo *pʔĭnwéltha*; literally 'mountain *wel*-people' and 'mountain *wel*- place'. One Picuris interpreted the element *wel*- as from an obsolete word for 'warrior' (hence 'mountain warrior people' and 'place'; F.H. Trager 1968:51), but Curtis (1907–1930, 16:264)

records the meaning 'mountain pass place' and translates Taos *wílatho* 'Picuris Pueblo' (F.H. Trager 1968:51) as 'at the pass'. It seems likely, then, that the Jemez and Picuris names, as well as Taos *pʔian-wílanǫ* 'Picuris people' (F.H. Trager 1968:51), beside *wílanǫ* (Harrington 1918, phonemicized), and Tewa *pinwî̂* (*ówînge*) 'Picuris Pueblo' (literally 'mountain-gap (Pueblo)') contain cognate elements with the same original meanings, referring to the location of the Pueblo at the west end of a pass leading to the Great Plains.

Other names are the alternate Taos hiūtuta and Jemez ota, perhaps related; Isleta samnai and *šą́mnǫk* 'Picuris Pueblo' and *šą́mnǫhúde* 'Picuris Indian' (C.T. Harrington 1920:45), beside the apparent loanword *napikerénu* (William L. Leap, personal communication 1977); Sandia samnán 'Picuris people(?)'; and Jicarilla Apache *tókelé*.

As the seat of a Spanish mission the Pueblo has been called San Lorenzo, San Lorenzo de los Picurís, and San Lorenzo de Picurís (Domínguez 1956:92). From 1947 to

1955 the official name was San Lorenzo Pueblo, but this has never been in common use. Oñate named it San Buenaventura in 1598.

## Sources

Relatively few published sources are available that deal specifically with Picuris Pueblo. Anthropological studies include Parsons's (1939a) brief notes collected in 1935, a study of Tiwa kinship systems that includes a section on Picuris kinship terminology (Trager 1943), two studies of social organization (Siegel 1959, 1965), a study of architectural units (Brown 1974), and a study of irrigation at Picuris (Ford 1977). A study of Tewa trade includes some data on Picuris (Ford 1972), and Harrington's (1916) study of Tewa ethnogeography includes useful Picuris data. There is also a study of Picuris social structure using an ethnohistorical approach (Brown 1973).

The first extensive linguistic study of the Picuris language was conducted by Harrington using children's stories primarily (Harrington and Roberts 1928). Felicia H. Trager (1968, 1971, 1971a) and George Trager (1935-1971, 1942, 1946) have also written on the Picuris language, and there is a doctoral dissertation on syntax by Zaharlick (1977).

A description of Picuris Pueblo in 1776 by Domínguez (1956) is the most complete historical account of the Pueblo. The two versions of Benavides's *Memorial* provide not only excellent accounts of seventeenth-century Picuris Pueblo but also useful annotations (Benavides 1916, 1945). The journal of Gaspar Castaño de Sosa's expedition includes a description of Picuris Pueblo in 1591, the earliest generally accepted historical account of the Pueblo (Castaño de Sosa 1965). Several brief historical sketches are also available (Prince 1915; Coan 1925, 1; Stanley 1962).

Three reports of visits in the late nineteenth century are also most useful (Arny 1967; Bloom 1933-1938, 10; U.S. Census Office. 11th Census 1893). Two reports of congressional hearings include basic data on Picuris Pueblo in the early decades of the twentieth century (U.S. Congress. House of Representatives 1932; U.S. Congress. Senate 1932). Information about the Pueblo in the 1930s is contained in three brief articles written by a day school teacher (McGilberry 1934, 1935, 1935a). Finally, a report on the status of New Mexico Indians in the 1960s includes a description of the Pueblo (Smith 1966).

Herbert W. Dick (1965a) directed extensive archeological excavations at Picuris Pueblo in the 1960s.

*277*

# San Juan Pueblo

ALFONSO ORTIZ

San Juan (ˌsăn'hwän) is the largest and northernmost of the six Tewa-speaking Pueblos.*

## Territory and Environment

The country of the Tewa consists of that portion of the Rio Grande valley stretching from just north of the confluence of the Rio Grande and Rio Chama to just north of present-day Santa Fe, or a distance of 20 miles (see "Pueblos: Introduction," fig. 1, this vol.). San Juan is situated on the east bank of the Rio Grande, just south of the canyon country from which the two great rivers burst out of the mountains, and just northeast of where they merge. The large wedge of land lying between the two rivers just before they converge comprises a rich alluvial floodplain that has always been fertile and bountiful. San Juan truly has a favored location, for despite the small size of the communal land base of just over 13,000 acres, nearly half, or 6,000 acres, are arable. Although the people cultivated very little of this acreage in the 1970s, water to cultivate that sufficient for their needs is guaranteed them from the two rivers by a law of 1908.

Ranging out to the east, north, and west, there are two additional environments comprising the traditional homeland. The first begins just a few hundred yards from the river bottomlands, and it consists of rolling, slowly rising hills punctuated by gullies. These hills, so apparently barren, actually yield an impressive array of floral and faunal resources to human use, and the women and children of San Juan, especially, have roamed over it each spring and summer to gather in the floral largesse, while the men and boys hunted in the hills during the autumn and winter for small game. This micro-environment comprises a wedge between the farmlands at the 6,000-feet elevation and the higher mountain country, which begins at approximately 6,500 feet. The mountain region, a country of pine nuts and larger game, rises sharply from the low foothills and culminates in peaks that tower 11,000–13,000 feet above sea level.

This higher and larger environment is also a land of mystery and visions, for the San Juan people consider the mountains of their world to be sacred, in good part because they are the sources of water, the most precious element of life in this dry land. Hence, only those men and boys who have been initiated into their Tewa meanings may wander therein. At that, there is always some form of ritual preparation required before one ventures out into these higher places. The most frequently visited of these mountains is *cikumu* 'obsidian covered', in the west (Chicoma Mountain on maps), and so sacred is it that on its slopes there may be no violence if men of enemy nations encounter one another there. The Tewa and Navajo, though long-time enemies, are said never to have fought on *cikumu* because they shared a common reverence for sacred mountains. No human blood must ever be shed there because, as one San Juan described *cikumu*: "It is the chief of all the mountains, the most sacred thing we see each day." This quest for and tradition of peace has imbued the lives of the San Juan people with a sense of ultimate sanctuary, with a belief that there are places so sacred that one can be safe from harm while there. This sense is deeply embedded in the Tewa consciousness.

The special relationship with the land that the people of San Juan and, indeed, of all the Pueblos, have is also reflected in the way in which the villages, as architectural entities, are distributed upon that land. These villages of adobe blend in so well with their surroundings that it is impossible to spot them on the ground from more than a few hundred feet away. This is so despite the fact that they are all built on level ground elevated slightly from the nearby watercourses, and it is as true for Taos, with its twin five-story apartment buildings, and for the large Keresan Pueblos, as it is for the smaller and more dispersed Tewa Pueblos. Obviously this camouflaging, brought about as much through the use of natural building materials as it was through careful site selection,

---

* Tewa words cited in italics in the *Handbook* are in the orthography described by Hoijer and Dozier (1949), except that (1) their ʋ, hʷ, and mid tone are dispensed with as unnecessary, and (2) the vowel system is enlarged to include vowels of six qualities (*i, e, æ* [their ɛ], *a, o, u*) occurring short, long (*i·*, etc.), and nasalized short (*i̜*, etc.), and four nasalized long vowels (*i̜·, æ̜·, q̜·, y̜·*). The high tone is marked by the acute accent (*á*), contrasting with the low tone (unmarked). The circumflex accent (*â·*) marks the falling (high-low) tone. Initial vowels are preceded by a [ʔ], which may be phonemic. *r* is a voiced apico-alveolar flap. *f* and *v* vary between bilabial and labiodental pronunciations, and *xʷ* varies from [xʷ] to [hʷ]. *n* assimilates in position to a following obstruent and is [ŋ] before a pause. The fricatives *f, θ,* and *x* are pronounced by some Tewa speakers, especially in some Pueblos, as affricated or heavily aspirated stops, and if these pronunciations are taken as the norm they could be written pʰ, tʰ, and kʰ, equivalent to Harrington's (1916) p', t', and k'. Some cited Tewa forms are from sources that prefer to remain anonymous.

Southwest Foundation For Audio-Visual Resources, Santa Fe, N.M.
Fig. 1. San Juan Pueblo. Photograph by Peter Dechert, June 1977.

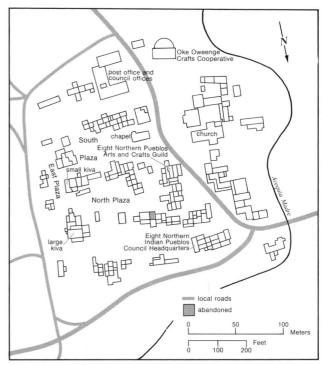

revised from Stubbs 1950:fig. 8.
Fig. 2. San Juan Pueblo.

was necessary when the Pueblos were engaged in intermittent defensive warfare with the Navajo, Apache, and some southern Plains nations. But still in the 1970s this building pattern conveys a sense of being a part of the earth itself, and, therefore, of fading into the landscape. The only buildings that do not fit this pattern are some churches and structures erected of nontraditional materials in nontraditional ways since the mid-nineteenth century (figs. 1–2).

## External Relations

The people of San Juan have interacted most closely and most frequently with members of the other Tewa Pueblos through mutual visitations during festival and religious occasions. They have also long assisted one another during initiation rituals for young people and priests, and they have traded and intermarried with one another. Relations are less close, but still common, with Taos and Picuris, the Jicarilla Apache, Cochiti, and Jemez. San Juan also trades, shares home-grown produce, and maintains a complex irrigation system in common with its immediate Spanish-American neighbors. Individual families from each group often forge friendships so close that they invite one another to be sponsors for their children's initiation rites within the Roman Catholic Church. It is not even unusual for a Hispanic brotherhood, drawn from several villages, to conduct prayer services in Spanish at the home of a prominent deceased resident of San Juan. Trade for locally unobtainable food and

religious and medicinal goods is also conducted with more distant Pueblos, Spanish-American villages, and other Indian groups.

Since the end of World War II, when automobile travel became common, San Juan's network of wider relations has expanded to include regular, if infrequent, visits to ceremonial-festival occasions as far away as the Hopi mesas, and even into the Plains states. San Juan people also visit with relatives in the large cities of the West and Midwest. With relocation and the increasing option of going to college or vocational school far from home has also come, since the 1950s, increasing intermarriage, not only with Indians of distant tribes, but also with Anglos and Spanish-Americans. In the majority of such cases the couples live away from San Juan, but a steadily increasing number who have vocational skills and can find employment nearby are making their homes at San Juan.

## Prehistory

According to sacred narrative traditions of their origin, the San Juan people began life within the earth "at *si·p̂ô·fe·næ*" (the Tewa Sipapu), beneath a lake somewhere to the north. Thinking that *si·p̂ô·fe·næ* actually exists in a single place, scholars have sought it in the mountains and rolling hills of southern Colorado because, when pressed, Tewa exegetes have always posited the lake of emergence in that area. The most frequently mentioned site has been a brackish lake that formerly existed within the present Great Sand Dunes National

Monument near Alamosa, Colorado. This lake was called *oxángé po·kʷíngé* 'lake at sandy place' in Tewa. However, it is unlikely that *si·pô·fe·næ* exists in a single time and place because it is a generic term denoting not only the place of Tewa origin and emergence, but also any symbolic representation thereof. Hence, the referents of the name *si·pô·fe·næ* are more metaphorical than literal in the historical sense. Those who really know of the power and usage of metaphor never really claim that a particular group of ancestors actually came up through a lake onto this world at one point in time. Rather, they are making the more subtle and everlastingly true point that all life—human, plant, and animal—ultimately derives from within the earth (Ortiz 1977). There was once an *oxángé po·kʷíngé*, which has since dried up, but *si·pô·fe·næ* lives on in Tewa belief and ritual, and it is in this sense that it must be understood.

Tewa tradition holds that after emergence from *si·pô·fe·næ* the people migrated south down both sides of the Rio Grande, establishing 10 different villages on each side along the way before rejoining at *posiʔówíngé* 'village at the hot springs' near present-day Ojo Caliente, 18 miles northwest of San Juan. From there they eventually broke off into, and dispersed as, the seven separate communities known in historic times. The one no longer surviving, Jacona (*sakǫ́ʔnæ* 'tobacco arroyo'), was located near an area of barren hills and washes on the Nambe River between present-day Pojoaque and San Ildefonso (Harrington 1916:330-331). Other villages occupied only a short time, or before history intruded, are also remembered and mentioned in traditional narratives. Remains of many of these remembered villages are, indeed, visible up both the Rio Grande and the Rio Chama to the north and northwest. These the Tewa cite as proof, to anyone who would dispute them, that the original migration did occur. The Tano (Tewa *θanu* or *θannúʔ* 'near the sun' or freely, 'other Tewa who live nearer the sun than we') of the Galisteo Basin to the south of modern-day Tewa country are also accounted for in San Juan traditional history.

Each group that established its own village along the Rio Grande contained within it both those who migrated down the west side to *posiʔ* and those who migrated down the east side of the Rio Grande, these forming the basis of the present-day summer and winter moieties, respectively (Ortiz 1969:13-28; Parsons 1929; Bandelier 1890-1892).

Archeological evidence purporting to explain which historic Pueblo group came from where in terms of prehistoric migrations is sketchy at best (Ford 1972). But just from what is known for sure the Tewa-speaking Pueblos can lay claim to numerous ancestral village sites on both sides of the Rio Grande and the Rio Chama. Most of these sites are west of the Rio Grande, and they reflect a general Tewa concern and familiarity with the country to the north and west of them (Harrington 1916).

The belief that these sites are almost certainly Tewa is based on three kinds of evidence. First, they are known by Tewa names and have been claimed as ancestral homes by Tewa since Bandelier's (1890-1892) pioneering investigations. Second, they usually have associated with them specific events of Tewa traditional history. Third, they have associated with them particular items of material culture known to be Tewa. Especially persuasive in this regard is the impressive continuity in stylistic traditions in pottery making from some of these prehistoric communities to historic Tewa Pueblos.

One very important question that remains unanswered is that having to do with what historic Tewa group occupied which prehistoric village. All that can be said is that the Tewa in late prehistoric times were generally to the north and west of their present location; how far north and west depends on how far back one goes into prehistory. It would not yet be safe to speculate as to whether the Tewa once occupied any of the impressive cliff-dwelling structures of the Mesa Verde area in Classic Pueblo times, A.D. 900-1300 (see "Prehistory: Eastern Anasazi," this vol.).

## History

The first European intrusion into San Juan and into the Tewa country generally was by a food-seeking party of men from the Francisco Vásquez de Coronado expedition of 1541 (Hammond and Rey 1940:244, 259). News of the expedition's rapacious plunder and murder to the south had apparently preceded them, for when the exploring party was setting up camp near San Juan the people fled to four well-protected villages they had in the mountains, presumably to the northwest and west (Winship 1896; Schroeder in Castaño de Sosa 1965:131). At this time the San Juan people were living both in San Juan Pueblo and in the Pueblo called in Tewa *yúngé* 'mockingbird place', directly across the Rio Grande to the west on a low promontory overlooking the confluence of the rivers. *yúngé* was then, and remains, a beautiful place, with a commanding view for many miles in all directions but north, which is blocked off by Black Mesa. To this "province" of six Pueblos the Spaniards gave the name Yuque-Yunque, a rendering of *yúngé ówînge* 'yúngé Pueblo'. The party plundered the two deserted villages and moved on, leaving behind for the San Juan people shock and the sure knowledge that their heretofore sacred world would not remain dependably their own.

Fifty years passed before the Spaniards again visited San Juan. It was once thought that the Agustín Rodríguez-Francisco Sánchez Chamuscado expedition reached San Juan and *yúngé* in 1581 (Mecham 1926:281-282; Gallegos Lamero 1927: 252-253), but scholars now agree that this expedition got no farther north than Galisteo Creek (Schroeder in Castaño de Sosa 1965:162, 164; Hammond and Rey 1966:58-59). However, in 1591 the expedition of Gaspar Castaño de Sosa, the lieutenant governor and captain general of Nuevo León, did visit San Juan and *yúngé*. In both Pueblos, as was his practice everywhere, Castaño erected a cross, received the obedience of the Indians to the king of Spain, and appointed a governor, alcaldes, and an *alguacil* (Castaño de Sosa 1965:121, 129). These ceremonies appear to have had no practical effect at the time, but they foreshadowed events that soon followed.

In 1598 the colonizing expedition of Juan de Oñate arrived at San Juan and *yúngé*. These people meant to stay, and so they established the first permanent Spanish settlement in New Mexico, proclaiming it at the same time the capital of the province. The people of *yúngé* are reported to have willingly given up their houses there and to have joined their relatives across the river in present-day San Juan. It was at this time that the village acquired the Spanish name, *San Juan de los Caballeros* 'San Juan of the horsemen (gentlemen)', the compliment being appended to the village's new Christian name by Oñate because of the *yúngé* people's alleged hospitality (Harrington 1916:213). Since their side of this historical encounter has never been told, one wonders how many Spanish harquebuses the San Juan people were staring at when the request was made.

*yúngé* was renamed San Gabriel after it passed into Spanish possession, and a church dedicated to this saint was constructed at the southern end of the village. The Moorish-derived Matachine Dance, which the Spaniards brought with them to the New World, was performed for the first time in New Mexico at the dedication of this church in September 1598. This dance has continued to be performed at San Juan each Christmas Eve and Christmas Day into the 1970s (see "The Mythological Triangle: Poseyemu, Montezuma, and Jesus in the Pueblos," fig. 2, this vol.).

The Spanish colony at *yúngé* got into trouble almost immediately, in good part because of Oñate's poor administration and his preference for using his men to explore the Southwest in quest of riches rather than to settle in and make the colony self-sufficient and self-sustaining. Hence, the colony did not last out the first decade of the seventeenth century. The capital and primary base of operations was moved to Santa Fe by 1610 (see Hammond and Rey 1953).

From 1600–1680 San Juan suffered under a succession of inconsistent but usually repressive Spanish civil and ecclesiastical rulers, being often persecuted and overworked by both. Especially galling was the religious persecution, which the people endured until they arose in revolution in 1680. During these decades the San Juan people and their Pueblo neighbors were routinely thrown into jail or trooped off in work gangs, usually on trumped-up charges of witchcraft. Their kivas, houses of worship, were frequently burned, and sacred objects contained therein destroyed.

In 1676, in what may have been the single most important event to fan revolutionary fervor, 47 traditional Pueblo religious leaders were jailed and flogged in Santa Fe for their "idolatrous" vocations. Among them was Popé (probably *po ʔpe·* 'ripe cultigens'), a man of San Juan, under whose leadership the Pueblo Revolt was subsequently planned and carried out, and the Spanish driven out of New Mexico ("The Pueblo Revolt," this vol.; Hackett 1942).

The Spaniards returned to stay in 1692, but they were not to turn again to the sustained harshness that characterized their earlier rule. The next century and a quarter were relatively uneventful years for San Juan. The one important exception was the occurrence, in 1781, of a smallpox epidemic, which took the lives of approximately one-third of the population (Aberle, Watkins, and Pitney 1940:167). Raiding at the hands of the Navajo and other groups continued, but this did not prove seriously disruptive. The village emerged, during this long period, as a Roman Catholic parish center, with the resident priest also serving four neighboring Spanish hamlets. San Juan also became a center of trade for the same reason it became a parish center: its favorable location, which resulted in the convergence there of several major travel routes. San Juan has continued as a parish center into the 1970s, and it remained a trade and commerce center until mid-twentieth century, when paved roads and automobile transportation made it possible for people in the area to journey, first to Española five miles to the south, and then eventually to Santa Fe, 28 miles to the south, for their trade. Accordingly, the Tewa trails-turned-wagon-routes that once converged at San Juan had evolved by the 1970s into three major interstate highways running north and south.

In the generation between Mexican independence in 1821 and the establishment of American sovereignty over

Fig. 3. The church at San Juan, from the east. Perhaps an 18th-century structure, this was destroyed sometime after 1900 (Kubler 1940:122–123, pl. 201) and was replaced by a new church in 1913. Photograph about 1880, probably by William H. Jackson.

the Tewa world in 1848 the San Juan people continued to reconsolidate their cultural integrity. They enjoyed considerable freedom of expression and action because they and the other Pueblos were endowed with full rights as Mexican citizens. These rights were recognized and assured again by the United States, at least on paper, in the Treaty of Guadalupe Hidalgo, which ended the Mexican-American War. Initially, American dominion and presence had no serious effect on life at San Juan, except for the fact that French priests replaced the Spanish and Mexican ones after 1862. The third French pastor, Camilo Seux, who came to San Juan in 1868, remained until his death in 1922. His successor, Joseph Pajot, also French, was pastor at San Juan until 1948. These facts assume significance when it is noted that the people regarded their French pastors, especially Seux, as much more tolerant of Tewa cultural expression than their Spanish predecessors. Hence they aided, even if only inadvertently, in the reconstitution and perpetuation of Tewa culture.

In 1863 another significant event occurred. Samuel Eldodt, a trader, took up residence in San Juan and opened a small general store. This grew in time to a very significant business, which served several communities in the area and lasted, through a succession of owners, until 1973, when it burned down. By this time it had become the oldest continuously operated general store in New Mexico, and it was this business, more than any other single institution, that maintained San Juan's standing as a major center of trade until after World War II.

By 1881, the Atchison, Topeka, and Santa Fe Railway and the narrow gauge Denver and Rio Grande entered the country of the Pueblos, and with them came increased numbers of Anglo tourists and other newcomers (Dozier 1970: 114–115). A little later colonies of artists sprouted in nearby Santa Fe and Taos. These events did little to alter life at San Juan. However, beginning in the 1930s the artists and tourists participated in a revival of traditional arts and crafts at San Juan by making them widely known through their purchases and thereby rendering them in wider demand. The artists and touring public also contributed to the less fortunate emergence of an image of the San Juan and other Pueblo Indians as primarily artists, an image that was firmly established in the 1970s.

A final, ubiquitous, presence in San Juan life since mid-nineteenth century was the United States government. This factor is neatly, if too generously, summarized in the following terms:

(1) The pueblos were recognized essentially as reservations with a distinguishing feature that pueblo lands were held communally; no individual allotments were ever made. (2) The Indian educational program, inaugurated in the latter part of the nineteenth century, was extended to San Juan in 1874. (3) The Pueblo Lands Board and later court rulings determined the validity of private claims to property located within the pueblo grant; provision was made to compensate Indians for titles to land within the grant where the decision was made in favor of private claimants. (4) With the passage of the Reorganization Act of 1934, which was accepted by San Juan, a new policy in the administration of Indian Affairs was brought into existence. Its most significant features are its recognition of the Indian tribal councils as governing bodies of the pueblos, promotion of an enlightened educational policy, an extension of improved medical services, and most important a concerted effort to better the Indians' economic condition (Aberle, Watkins, and Pitney 1940:147).

The nation's involvement in World War II resulted in the abandonment of the grand hopes of the Indian Reorganization Act of 1934. For comprehensive surveys of the history of the whole Rio Grande Pueblo area, see Schroeder (1972) for the Spanish and Mexican periods and Dozier (1970) for the American period.

## Social and Symbolic Classification

The people of San Juan classify human society along what may be termed three vertical dimensions. The lowest dimension is that of the ordinary, earth surface,

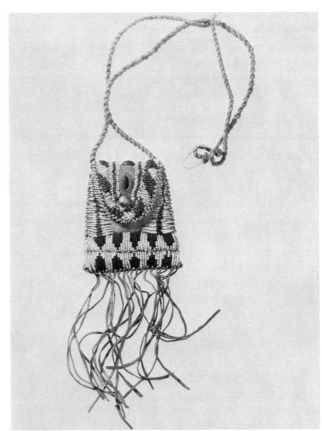

Smithsonian, Dept. of Anthr.: 47815.

Fig. 4. Buckskin medicine bag, decorated with red, white, and blue glass seed beads and cast silver buttons, worn by men over shoulder to carry cornmeal or herbs for ceremonies and curing. Bag has shoulder strap of two twisted buckskin cords and contains folded paper packets of cornmeal. Bag length 9 cm, collected in 1880.

sæ·ía· people. In the middle, as mediators between the top and the bottom dimensions, are the íowaʔê· 'youths', who are chosen by the pa· íowa 'Made People', or priests to serve as their assistants, seconds, and executive officers for repeatable one-year terms. These íowaʔê·, who come from and return to the sæ·ía· after their terms are up, are temporarily "placed upon cloudblossoms" by being given authority by the pa· íowa, who consist of eight separate priesthoods organized around winter and summer, curing, clowning, hunting, and defense (Ortiz 1969). The pa· íowa are all-powerful, for they coordinate not only the religious life of San Juan but also its political and subsistence activities. Of the eight societies of Made People, the Winter moiety society is restricted to members of the Winter moiety, while the Summer moiety society is restricted to members of the Summer moiety. The other six societies draw their members freely from both moieties. These six are a strongly cohesive force for

San Juan society, because they mediate the sharp distinctions represented by the moiety societies.

Long ago, when first informing their world with meaning, the San Juan people took their three-tiered social order and projected it outward and upward to encompass the whole of their physical world as well by imbuing that world with a three-tiered spiritual meaning, one both reflecting and reinforcing their social order. The fit among their ideas of order in society, in the physical world, and in the spiritual realm is ingenious, for these three orders interlock and render order into everything within the Tewa world.

The Tewa classify their physical world into three micro-environments. The first of these, at the center, consists of the village, the farmlands, and other lowlands near the village. It is given its spiritual dimension by four shrines at the outer periphery of the village, one in each cardinal direction. These shrines are dedicated to the no-

Fig. 5. Four kohsa· clowns, mugging for the photographer (see Parsons 1929:pl. 22 for such clowns with a line of Turtle dancers). Photograph by T. Harmon Parkhurst, about 1935.

longer-*sǽ·ía·* spirits of departed ancestors, who are spiritual counterparts to the living *sǽ·ía* people of the village. The shrines and this innermost circle are most accessible to the ordinary *sǽ·ía·* people, as, indeed, they must be. In religious terms anyone Tewa may go to the shrines to pray to the departed ancestors and leave an offering of cornmeal or feathers. In subsistence and other social terms, the farms and other lowland areas may be wandered over freely and used by all *sǽ·ía·* people as well. Since all farming, most gathering, and some hunting is carried out within this environment, it is the crucial one for subsistence, and easily the most *sǽ·ía·* of the three.

This innermost realm is also the women's domain much more than that of the men, for it has both the homes and the major subsistence areas. Although the Tewa have for long been characterized by a loose form of patrilineal descent and an even looser form of patrilocal residence, beneath this Spanish-introduced and American-reinforced tradition there is implicit a matrilineal ideology. Women have always been deferred to as knowing the most about the things of home, family, and society. A standard admonition to Tewa of all ages is to "listen to the women, for they are of the home."

Mus. of N.M., Santa Fe.

Fig. 6. Two women dancers wearing squash blossom headpieces and hair visors before their eyes for the Hopi buffalo dance, borrowed from the Hopi in the past. There is also a Tewa buffalo dance for which the costuming is different. Both buffalo dances were formerly performed mostly in autumn and winter, but in the 1970s they may be performed at any time during the year. Photograph by T. Harmon Parkhurst, about 1935.

The second circle, that of hills, mesas, and washes, is a mediating environment in every important sense. First, it is an area in which both men and women may be, but one into which women and children did not usually go unless accompanied by men. This environment is in the charge of men but does not exclude women. Both hunting and gathering are done there, by both sexes. In a spiritual sense, it is an area defined by four sacred mesas, or flat-topped buttes, one in each direction. Each of these mesas is believed to have a cave or labyrinth that permits entry into the *o·pá· nunæ*, or underworld; so the ritually unprepared, women and children both, may not venture too close, to avoid being drawn into the cave or labyrinth. The mesas are in the spiritual charge of the *towa ʔê·*, who are spiritual counterparts of the *towa ʔê·* of San Juan society. These original *towa ʔê·* were in the underworld at the beginning, but they came up with the people at emergence. Indeed, they led the way out, so they are both pre-*sǽ·ía·*, and post-*sǽ·ía·*. Their human counterparts are called *ahkónu ʔin* 'those of the barren hills.' The spiritual *towa ʔê·* are both temporal and spatial mediators, in the sense that, on the one hand, they mediate the transition from the metaphorical time of emergence to the historic one of earth-surface existence, as well as the spatial one between the extreme circles of the Tewa world, on the other. The human *towa ʔê·*, in turn, are social mediators between the two most extreme categories of Tewa social existence, as well as spatial ones because they are assigned the middle place between the spatial, hence, cultural, extremes. Spatially, socially, sexually, spiritually, and even in subsistence terms, then, this middle space is an ambivalent, mediating area.

The third concentric circle is the clearcut domain of men, as contrasted with the innermost circle, the domain of women. This is an area of purely male hunting and gathering, and the destination of purely male religious pilgrimages. Made People who are women may go on pilgrimages as well, but they go only as far as a shrine in the foothills of the middle space, which they have for their own ritual use. At that, they are accompanied by male *towa ʔê·* who stand watch for them nearby to protect them from possible surprise intrusion by enemy peoples. Spiritually, the realm of the higher mountain fastnesses is in the keeping of the most non-*sǽ·ía·* order of spirits, those that never became *sǽ·ía·*, because they never left the sacred underworld.

Complementing this tripartite social and spatial classification by cutting across it and dividing it approximately in half is another social classification, that of the Winter and Summer moieties. Every San Juan person is either a Summer person or a Winter person and becomes so through undergoing the Water-giving and Water-pouring rites, both of which are moiety-specific childhood initiation rituals. Each moiety society conducts separate versions of these rituals for its members' children, the Summer society in the spring, and the Winter society in

Fig. 7. Deer Dance, a game propitiation ceremony performed in Jan. or Feb. by young men and boys dancing in a line, with youngest at the end. The headdress consists of antlers with turkey feather tied to each tine, visor of blue and yellow painted split cane, and cotton renewed yearly. The faces of dancers are painted red with a white border. The costumes, which include white shirts, embroidered kilts, sashes, leggings, decorated armbands, ties of red woolen yarn at knees, are common items of Tewa men's dress. left, Dancer, photograph by T. Harmon Parkhurst, about 1935; right, line of dancers, by unknown photographer, 1920s.

the fall. With rare exception, one is initiated into one's father's moiety. Brides whose husbands are of the opposite moiety are also newly initiated into that moiety.

Just as the tripartite social classification is projected out onto the spatial world and reflected there, so also is the dual social classification represented by the moieties projected out onto the temporal cycle represented by the year and reflected there. The Winter and Summer moieties represent social agents of temporal ordering for Tewa society and culture, based as they are on the major seasonal alternation, that between summer and winter. They order the annual round of activities by season in a number of ways in addition to the moiety-specific initiation rituals. In the first place, the head of the Winter moiety society rules the village during the autumn and winter, which is regarded as the winter half of the year, and the Summer moiety chief rules during the spring and summer, the summer half of the year. The annual calendar of religious dances and other activities is also planned and divided in accordance with this fundamental alternation, for winter-associated rituals are not scheduled during the reign of the Summer chief, and vice versa. Subsistence activities also follow this alternation, with hunting and trade expeditions to distant places, both male activities, not being permitted until after the Winter chief takes over rule of the village. The summer cycle is of course that of farming and gathering from the plant world, activities symbolically more closely associated with women.

Fig. 8. Men representing caricatures of Apache hunters, who shoot sunflower stalk arrows into the air just over the antlers of the dancers and generally pretend to hunt them. They also "sell" 6–8 of the youngest dancers to respected senior women. This small income is their reward for serving as "Apaches." Photograph by T. Harmon Parkhurst, about 1935.

*285*

SAN JUAN PUEBLO

Fig. 9. Basket dance, performed in the winter or early spring for agricultural and general well-being; traditional religious elder in foreground, ritual clown at right, line of men dancers, line of women dancers (each holding notched rasp, rasping stick, and basket resonator). Photograph by T. Harmon Parkhurst, about 1935.

The moiety chiefs also alternate in appointing the nonpermanent ritual and secular officials of the Pueblo, who all serve for one-year terms, which may be repeated on a nonconcurrent basis. These include the governor, his two lieutenants, the sheriff, the four *fiscales,* and the six *ȼowaʔêˑ*. Because the two moiety chiefs alternate right down the list in selecting these 12 officials at the end of each year, the whole process works out in such a way that on the year when one moiety chief selects the governor, who is in charge of primarily secular affairs, the other moiety chief selects the head of the *ȼowaʔêˑ*, who coordinates native ritual activities for the Made People in general. Hence, each moiety chief selects half the officials from each group, the secular and the ritual, during any given year. Each chief appoints only men from his own moiety. Thus there is a splendid and continuing system of checks and balances between the moieties, one that pervades all important institutions and activities at San Juan and one that is in operation at all times. The difference from the tripartite system of social and spatial ordering and mediation lies in the fact that the ordering and mediation represented by the moieties is all temporally based. The two systems together do not leave much room for enduring sharp cleavages in San Juan society.

Fig. 10. Cloud Dance, also called Dance of the Corn Maidens, a winter-spring fertility ceremony related to the agricultural cycle. The eagle feather fans worn by two women are cloud symbols; the women dancers are usually the wives or daughters of the year's village officials. Like the men and boys, they volunteer to dance. Photographer unknown, probably 1880s–1890s.

286

One final problem of classification should also be addressed. The original givers of life within the primordial lake of emergence were mothers (Ortiz 1969:13). Thus, the summer moiety chiℰf of earth surface existence, a man, is regarded as the mother of San Juan. Hence, the question may be posed: How can deities of the male domain be mothers, and how can a man within the female domain also be regarded as a mother? The answer to the first part of the question has to do with the simple fact that those spirits that never became sæ·ìa· are not only of beyond, but within and around the world as well. They transcend spatial boundaries even as they are thought of as belonging most purely to the domain of the mountains by earth-surface Tewa. A concluding phrase in Tewa prayers addressed to these deities sums up how they are regarded: *nan fo· nunæ, cin fo· nunæ, p̄in fo· nunæ, unbí tu̧· únwé·bunmæn; wé·mû·, wé·gín, po·win, yó·næn* 'Within and around the earth, within and around the mesas, within and around the mountains, your authority returns to you, one time, two times, three times, four times'. The answer to the second part of the question applies with equal force to the first. It is, simply, that spiritual mothering must be distinguished from social mothering. The Summer moiety chief who, as the earth-surface representative of the primordial mothers, embodies the female principle in life, is a spiritual mother, and, like the primordial mothers, "she" can be anywhere. Further, "her" existence does not detract in the least from the existence of "real" Tewa mothers of real Tewa children, whether considered as social, cultural, or biological entities. Beyond all this, men represent the unmarked sexual category in Tewa culture (Ortiz 1969:146-147). That is to say, they are regarded as embodying qualities of both sexes and may be thought of in either sense. Women are regarded as having only female characteristics. Tewa men confine their femaleness to spiritual and other ritual contexts.

The Tewa world is, then, not only a well-centered and well-bounded world but also a well-ordered world, one informed by many explicit ideas for proper conduct even under constantly changing circumstances.

## Becoming and Remaining Tewa

The two most meaningful things one can say about the Tewa life cycle are, first, that one is not born a Tewa but rather one is made a Tewa and second, once made, one has to work hard continuously throughout one's life to remain a Tewa. A child born to the Tewa is made a Tewa through a long process of socialization and enculturation, which begins when the child is presented to the sun and given a name four days after birth. This process (described in detail in Ortiz 1969:30-43) continues through the moiety-incorporating Water-giving rite in the child's first year of life, the societal-incorporating Water-pouring rite between the ages of six and nine, and on through the

finishing rite of initiation into Tewa religion in adolescence or middle teenage years.

Through these rites of passage, undergone by all Tewa children through their father's moiety, and later ones distinctive to each sex, to marriage, to office as a *ìowa ʔê·*, or to initiation into permanent membership into one of the eight societies of Made People, Tewa people consolidate their Tewa consciousness and identity. They also participate in a complex annual cycle of communal activities ranging from the maintenance of an intricate network of irrigation canals during the growing season to the performance of religious dances, which occur overwhelmingly in the fall and winter. From the songs, prayers, and traditions that surround these dances Tewa learn of the order in their world, and of the most important ideas guiding their relationship to it. From the dance paraphernalia and other accoutrements, many of which have to be made anew or redecorated by each dancer every year, they learn of the many ways Tewa culture has evolved to represent and embody aspects of the physical and spiritual realms into these dances. Through their traditional crafts, principally pottery making and embroidery for the women and weaving, carving, and leatherwork for the men, they learn how to express the beauty of their cultural heritage and the perceived

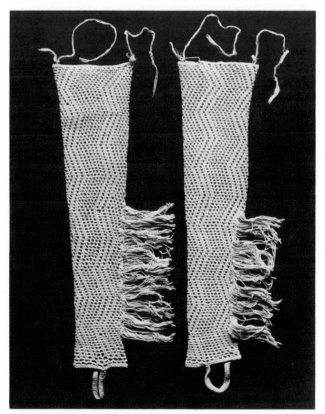

Fig. 11. Crocheted cotton leggings worn by men (see fig. 7) at ceremonial dances. Made by Eloisa A. Povijua for the 1923 Santa Fe Indian Fair. Length 57 cm.

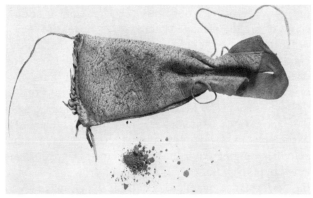

Fig. 12. Buckskin pouch containing red ocher pigment used for ceremonial body painting. This pigment was formerly obtained directly from mountains 40-50 miles northwest of San Juan Pueblo, but since the 1940s it has been traded from Hispanic ranchers and herders who live close to the ocher source. Length 24.3 cm, collected in 1904.

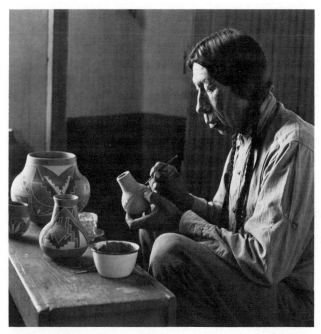

Fig. 13. Demecio Cata, painting pottery, probably made by Flora Cata, his wife. This style, developed in the 1930s but based on a prehistoric type found in the area, has incised designs painted with red and white clay; the large jars represent a variant of one traditional shape. Photograph by J. Baylor Roberts, 1934-1940.

world in ways that ensure that they will be surrounded by reminders of their traditions in their everyday life.

All these activities require sustained commitment, and a man who never occupies office as a *íowa⁷ê·* or as another, more purely political official, never becomes a Made Person, never dances, and does not also work well with his hands in a variety of ways is not really regarded as living a Tewa life. For women childraising and maintenance of a Tewa home is the equivalent of serving

as *íowa⁷ê·* or as political officials. Women participate as full partners in four of the societies of Made People, and as assistants in two of the others. As Tewa elders never tire of saying: "It is hard work being a Tewa." This is why remaining a Tewa is just as important to a consideration of the life cycle as becoming one.

If one lives as a Tewa, when his time comes to return to *si·pô·fe·næ* to the beginning and continuing source of all Tewa identity, it will be the community as a whole that will give him back to the earth and to the on-going cycle of creation. In the Tewa hereafter, *íowa⁷ê·* and *sæ·ʔa·* people become spirits of the category no longer *sæ·ʔa·*, while Made People join the spirits of the category *sæ·ʔa·* who never were, their spiritual patrons and counterparts. This is their reward for serving as Made People (Ortiz 1969:50-56). It may have been that in pre-Spanish times the office of *íowa⁷ê·* was permanent, and *íowa⁷ê·* souls also joined their spiritual counterparts in the middle realm, but this is no longer so.

## Culture in 1940

### Subsistence

The San Juan subsistence pattern in 1940 was over-whelmingly an agricultural one. Most of the 2,000 acres that were cleared and within reach of their irrigation

Fig. 14. Two styles of San Juan pottery. left, Plain bowl typical of the period 1880s-1920s with polished red slip around neck; diameter about 43 cm; collected in 1880. right, Bowl with micaceous slip in incised designs made by Luteria Atencio for 1961 Indian Crafts Show in contemporary style based on 15th-century incised pottery designs (G.P. Schroeder 1964; Toulouse 1977:57-58); diameter about 30 cm.

Fig. 15. Corn husking after the harvest, in the village plaza, a scene typical through the 1950s when enormous quantities of corn were grown. The different colors of ears, not grown in separate fields, were sorted and then husked: blue, for the cornmeal most desired as food; white, ground for ceremonial purposes; and mixed yellow and red, used mainly as cattle feed. The most perfect blue and white ears were selected, their husks braided together, and hung on a special rack (right, with strings of chili peppers). left, Photograph by T. Harmon Parkhurst, about 1935; right, photographer unknown, Oct. 1940.

system were under cultivation. The traditional crops were, principally, corn, wheat, beans, squash, chili, and, secondarily, a whole host of other garden vegetables. Alfalfa and hay were also grown for the horses and other stock, which each family had. Rare was the family that did not have a few cattle, some pigs, and, less frequently, chickens. Sheep and goats were also obtained on a regular basis in trade from the Jicarilla Apache and from Hispanic neighbors from the mountains, but these were usually butchered a short time thereafter. San Juan never developed a taste for herding; there was the added problem in the summer months of the sheep and goats getting into gardens. During the agricultural cycle horses and cattle grazed on their own fenced communal grazing lands. When the crops were all harvested, the farmlands were open to them for forage as well.

Most families also had at least a few fruit trees on their land, with apples, peaches, pears, apricots, and plums being most common. Indeed, fruit and vegetables constituted important trade items for San Juan, especially in trade with the Jicarilla Apache. In addition, all wild plant foods, such as asparagus, amaranth, chenopodium, mint, and the Colorado bee plant, could be picked by anyone who found them and needed them, no matter where they grew. The idea is that anything that the earth yields forth without benefit of human effort cannot be owned, even if it grows wild on an otherwise cultivated field. This same principle was applied as well to wild plum and berry bushes growing along the banks of the communal irrigation canals.

Fig. 16. Corn drying on roof, with plaza of San Juan in background; view looking west. Photograph by William H. Jackson, 1879.

SAN JUAN PUEBLO

289

Fig. 17. Women washing and winnowing wheat. Photographs by Edward S. Curtis, 1905 or earlier.

All land within the reservation was and is owned by the community, with individuals and families enjoying use rights only to particular plots of farmland, to house sites, and to the communal grazing area. The San Juan governing council, consisting of the governor, two lieutenants, the sheriff, all living former governors, and male heads of the societies of Made People, administer the lands for the people, and they have the authority to take away a family's land if there is serious and sustained misconduct on the part of that family. However, in practice, the council has rarely done this, so most farmland has passed patrilineally through particular families for generations beyond the reach of memory. The same had been true of homes and most other material property. The patrilineal, patrilocal tendency was just a tendency, for San Juan women owned and inherited material property almost as often as men. The ideal, often stated in lukewarm fashion, was that a groom should provide a home for his bride and have farmland so that he could support her, but if this were not possible all needed adjustments could be made without serious stigma attaching to the groom.

Religious property, on the other hand, was more sex-specific, and it was inherited more dependently along sex lines. The exceptions were religious property owned by the societies of Made People, which remained within the society in question, and that owned by the moieties, which stayed within the two moiety societies, or in the kiva, to be used only during rituals.

San Juan farming technology by 1940 consisted of then-modern farming implements distributed by the federal government, or purchased or traded for in the nearby general store. Cumbersome but still efficient Spanish hoes, shovels, plowshares, and other metal tools had long since supplanted the aboriginal digging stick and other stone and wooden tools, so the transition to still more efficient metal tools was not a difficult one. For gathering, metal containers and gunny sacks from the store had replaced the earlier skin bags and baskets, just as, for hunting, the gun had replaced the bow. Household wares consisted mostly of metal, glass, and commercial crockery, instead of the traditional pottery, gourds, and baskets. The use of traditional handmade items designed for household use was confined to ritual occasions. New Deal support for Indian communities to retain their cultural integrity, augmented by increasing tourism, led to a revival in several areas of traditional craftwork, especially pottery, weaving, and embroidery, but it was interrupted by the outbreak of World War II.

*Social and Political Organization*

Seven of the eight traditional societies of Made People were still active in 1940, with only the priest in charge of defending the Pueblo and his group having become extinct. There were the most important social groups in San Juan, because they coordinated religious, economic and political activities. The six *ʔowaʔê·* worked closely with the Made People and carried out their instructions on all three fronts, especially that of maintaining order within the community. The council conducted relations with all external agencies and with the Catholic church. The governor and his staff, which included two lieutenants and an *aguacil,* or sheriff, conducted these activities on a day to day basis. There were also four *fiscales,* who

290

Fig. 18. Antonio José Atencio, *nana qʔyæn* 'swaying aspen', traditional elder, of San Juan, wearing quilled, fringed buckskin shirt, fur mantle, and abalone shell gorget. Studio portrait, probably by C.M. Bell or other Washington photographer, before 1870.

Fig. 19. Sotero Ortiz (b. ca. 1877, d. 1963), interpreter when younger for meetings of the All Pueblo Council. During Pueblo reorganization to meet the threat of the Bursum bill in 1922 he was chosen as the first elected leader of the modern 19 Pueblos; in 1923 he accompanied John Collier to speak against the bill in Washington, D.C., where this photograph was taken by DeLancey Gill.

Fig. 20. Eliseo Trujillo, governor of San Juan, with his wife Margarita and grandson Pedro. He holds canes of office. Photograph by T. Harmon Parkhurst, about 1935.

acted as church wardens, and who had, in addition, primary responsibility for burying the dead. A ditch boss and a *sacristán,* the *sacristán* charged with heating the church and otherwise assisting the parish priest in discharging his pastoral duties, rounded out the roster of office-holders. The annual ceremonial cycle, which involved all these organizations and office-holders at one time or another, was still well intact in 1940 (Ortiz 1969:79–119).

The basic household unit at San Juan in 1940 was, most commonly, patrilineal—at least as regards property—and patrilocal, and had three generations living under one roof; however, nuclear families and others built around a female nucleus were by no means uncommon, especially for those families in which the husband was not from San Juan. For important work projects such as harvesting and housebuilding, these household units were expanded into *ma·tuʔin,* bilaterally extended kin, who assisted one another. For example, a poor man who had a harvest to get in but no sons to assist him would simply "borrow" a son or two from a sister or cousin within his *ma·tuʔin.*

## Education and Health

There was a federal day school at San Juan in 1940, and its graduates, after finishing the sixth grade, went on to

291

boarding school in either Santa Fe or Albuquerque. A few had gone as far as the Carlisle Institute in Pennsylvania while that institution operated early in the twentieth century, and others continued to go to the Haskell Institute in Kansas. Many of the early Haskell and Carlisle graduates went to work for the Bureau of Indian Affairs or elsewhere in the world outside San Juan, since they could not use their education to obtain gainful employment within the village.

The health care that the people could not provide for themselves through traditional means was provided by the BIA-operated Indian hospital in Santa Fe. There were also regular visits to the community by nurses from the hospital. Generally speaking, at that time the hospital was regarded as an option of last resort, even as a place in which to die, rather than as a place in which to get well.

On the day in 1945 when the news of Japan's surrender came over the radio, the first person to hear it ran out into the plaza shouting, "The war is over," in Tewa, over and over again. People of all ages came pouring out of homes and onto the plazas, shouting, jumping for joy, or weeping. The young man who originally made the announcement kept right on running into the church, and, once inside, started ringing the bell, to signal those in the fields and woods away from the village that a momentous event had taken place. People were either relieved and happy, or saddened anew if they had lost a loved one to the war. No one was unmoved by the news, for a great many sons and even some daughters of San Juan were involved in the war effort. San Juan was at this time already, in many important respects, and for better or for worse, of the nation and of the wider world.

**Sociocultural Situation in the 1970s**

The San Juan of the 1970s was almost like two separate sociocultural entities. On the one hand, most of the traditional social and cultural institutions of 1940, save, most notably, the subsistence economy, survived. On the other hand, an almost bewildering plethora of federally funded programs was set into motion starting in the mid-1960s, and buildings constructed to house them. These are programs so extensive in their reach throughout San Juan life as to almost conceal, except on ritual occasions, the traditional soul of the Pueblo.

The old economy, based on a combination of subsistence and trade, and supplemented by wage work, had been all but totally supplanted by a cash economy. Few residents of San Juan raised even a substantial fraction of their food. Even fewer owned livestock. Most of the agricultural lands lay fallow, and some were rented by individual families to Hispanic farmers. Even a portion of the communal grazing land had been leased by the council to a Hispanic stockman on a nonexclusive use basis. Whereas the major source of wage work from the end of World War II until about 1970 was the atomic

research facility of Los Alamos, 19 miles away, in the 1970s the federal programs provided many more jobs. The shift from an overwhelming dependence on external wage work to one of working within the community, or at least in another nearby Pueblo, began to take place after the passage of the Economic Opportunity Act of 1964, and it gained progressive momentum in the 1970s.

Whereas in 1940 only the Department of the Interior, through the BIA, operated programs at San Juan, in the 1970s the Departments of Commerce, Health, Education, and Welfare, Housing and Urban Development, and Labor were also involved in the lives of the people. The once streamlined San Juan Council had a planning committee, a full-time secretary, a business manager, a treasurer and community director, a law and order branch independent of the *ȋowa'ê·*, health and Headstart programs, Comprehensive Employment Training Act and Tribal Work Experience Program employment assistance, and even a grants program. There were also separate land resource and community education programs. The council also operated a general store through a board of directors and a manager.

The little day school housed a bilingual, bicultural education program that operated with council guidance. There was also an independent, self-sustaining arts and

ACTION, N.M. VISTA Program, Washington.
Fig. 21. Marie T. Moquino of San Juan, VISTA volunteer and former local school teacher, supervising children at play in the Pueblo as part of VISTA program. Photograph by Paul Conklin, Oct. 1971.

crafts cooperative, and a crafts guild shop run for all the eight Pueblos north of Santa Fe by the Eight Northern Pueblos Indian Council, which also had its headquarters in San Juan and employed a number of San Juan people. Clearly, San Juan had become a very complex community, one that, if not fully dependent on the federal government for its economic viability, could no longer be fully understood without reference to happenings in Washington.

The basic family unit in the 1970s had become a nuclear one, with the limited patrilineal, patrilocal ideal further eroded. Old people were sometimes left to live alone, a practice almost unthinkable in 1940. Intermarriages, especially those involving non-Indians, also increased markedly, a fact that reinforced the tendency toward nuclear family life. Most families in the 1970s lived in federally funded low-income houses, most of which are set out in rows away from the adobe houseblocks. In the 1970s most of those families who had moved into new housing retained their old adobe ones in the village, and returned there for ritual and festive occasions.

San Juan Pueblo Tewa Bilingual Program, N.M.

Fig. 22. San Juan Pueblo Bilingual Program activities. top, Day School students depicting the nativity scene, entirely in the Tewa language, during an annual Christmas play directed and produced by the program's staff. bottom, Day School staff and students playing shinny, an Indian game that is similar to field hockey. Photographs by Harry Berendzen, Dec. and Feb. 1974.

**Table 1. Population, 1680–1977**

| Year | Population | Year | Population |
|------|-----------|------|-----------|
| 1680 | 300 | 1916 | 431 |
| 1707 | 400 | 1917 | 435 |
| 1749 | 404 | 1918 | 449 |
| 1760 | 316 | 1919 | 430 |
| 1790 | 203 | 1920 | 422 |
| 1793 | 260 | 1921 | 439 |
| 1799 | 202 | 1922 | 441 |
| 1805 | 210 | 1923 | 450 |
| 1808 | 201 | 1924 | 458 |
| 1809 | 208 | 1925 | 483 |
| 1821 | 232 | 1926 | 497 |
| 1851 | 568[a] | 1927 | 505 |
| 1860 | 341 | 1928 | 500 |
| 1863 | 385 | 1929 | 503 |
| 1871 | 426 | 1930 | 505 |
| 1879 | 500 | 1931 | 510 |
| 1881 | 408 | 1932 | 530 |
| 1888 | 381 | 1933 | 546 |
| 1889 | 373 | 1934 | 561 |
| 1890 | 406 | 1935 | 578 |
| 1901 | 425 | 1936 | 586 |
| 1903 | 402 | 1942 | 702 |
| 1904 | 419 | 1950 | 821 |
| 1906 | 419 | 1964 | 1,259 |
| 1910 | 387 | 1968 | 1,255 |
| 1911 | 377 | 1972 | 1,586 |
| 1912 | 376 | 1973 | 1,627 |
| 1913 | 416 | 1974 | 1,663 |
| 1914 | 425 | 1976 | 1,713 |
| 1915 | 428 | 1977 | 1,721 |

SOURCES: for 1680 through 1936, Aberle, Watkins, and Pitney 1940; for 1942 to 1968, the old United Pueblos Agency of the Bureau of Indian Affairs in Albuquerque; for 1972 to 1977, the census records of the Northern Pueblos Agency in Santa Fe.

[a] Submitted by first Indian Agent to New Mexico James S. Calhoun; may be regarded as wildly exaggerated.

Demographically, there were more San Juan people living away from than in San Juan. The dramatic increase since the 1960s in the population enrolled as San Juan community members (table 1) should be viewed with this fact in mind. The pattern of out-migration, set into motion primarily by the BIA's relocation program, which was begun in 1952, has resulted in large San Juan colonies living in California, and small ones in cities of the Midwest. A large number of those relocated have returned to San Juan since 1970, after they learned through relatives that there were jobs to be had implementing the new federal programs. Whereas in 1940 educated people from San Juan could not find employment within the village, in the 1970s there were not enough college graduates and others with technical skills to fill even most of the available jobs. This was still so despite the fact that at least a quarter of San Juan high school graduates went to college, and more than the same number went to some other form of advanced training.

The health care available to San Juan also improved vastly in the 1970s, an improvement that actually began after 1955, when responsibility for administering Indian health programs throughout the nation was transferred from the BIA to the U.S. Public Health Service. A San Juan person was employed full time to deliver patients to and from doctor's offices and to and from the Indian hospital. A clinic on the day school grounds was staffed by a doctor and nurse for one day each week, and someone from San Juan was employed as a community mental health representative. In general, non-Indian health professionals dealing with San Juan were more culturally sensitive and personally solicitous in the 1970s than their counterparts were in 1940.

Perhaps the most dramatic change to come to San Juan in the 1960s and 1970s is one that occurred quite independently of Washington: a tremendous increase in the demand for traditional arts and crafts, and others such as silver jewelry making that were not traditional to San Juan but have been taken up because of the tourist and local non-Indian market demand. This increased sharply the number of people who are involved in crafts work, at least on a part-time basis. The O ke Owinge Arts and Crafts Cooperative, which began with little more than a dozen members in 1968, had about 80 in 1977. Most of this increase has come since the dedication, in 1973, of a beautiful building that has both work areas and a display area for members' art and wares. So pervasive has this return to crafts work been, in fact, that it has also had repercussions in the area of ceremonial attire for dances, and in other items used for ritual. These became, in the 1970s, better made, better decorated, and more authentically Tewa.

The continuing challenge for the San Juan people, as always in the past, ever since the Spaniards first entered their world, is to maintain their mature vision of order and meaning in that world, while also evolving a stable, self-sustaining economy, this time one based on cash. If the macadamization of their portion of the great river valley with wider and wider roadways, and the increasing appearance of other obtrusive monuments to human haste and waste does not distract them from their original vision, the people of San Juan should retain their cultural integrity, and eventually becalm even the materialist effects of the new federal programs.

## Synonymy

The Pueblo has had its Spanish name, originally and in full San Juan Bautista, since it was bestowed in 1598 by Oñate, who used the older spelling Sant Joan Baptista (Benavides 1945:232). A number of Indian languages, including at least Jemez, the Keresan dialects, and Isleta, use borrowings of the Spanish.

The Tewa name for San Juan is *ohke·,* the etymological meaning of which is unknown. It is definitely not the same as *óhkê·* 'hard metate', as some have claimed (Harrington 1916:211–212; Folsom 1973). A person or people from San Juan is *ohken.*

The Tiwa names for San Juan refer to its location where the Rio Grande flows out of a gorge onto a plain: Taos p̓akǽp'al'ayą̄, pǫkáfalayą̄ 'water-course end' (Harrington 1918; Curtis 1907–1930, 16:261, 263, normalized), Picuris pákupala, Isleta (older name) pakų́parai (Harrington 1916:212). Navajo uses both *Kin Łichíí* 'red house' and *Kin Łigaaí* 'white house' (Robert W. Young, personal communication 1977), though older sources give only the former (Curtis 1907–1930, 1:138; Franciscan Fathers 1910:128, 138; Haile 1950–1951, 2:254). Hopi has yúmpaka téwa 'last (i.e., northernmost) Tewa' (Harrington 1916:213, normalized).

The San Juan people also designate their Pueblo by a sacred metaphorical phrase, used only in religious oratory, the significance of which has been overlooked by earlier investigators. This is *xų́· očú te²i ówînge* (*xų́·* 'corn'; *očú* 'of fresh appearance, dewy'; *te²i* 'structure; kiva'; *ówînge* 'village'), or freely in English, 'village of the dew-bedecked corn structure'. It is clear from the sacred narratives of San Juan origins and migrations that at any given time in the remembered past this phrase was used to designate the particular village that the people who are the San Juan of historic times then occupied. It is appended to any ritual mention of any of the villages preceding the present one. A discussion of the names of San Juan Pueblo would be incomplete without an account of this metaphorical reality. For one thing, the recurrent use of this name reflects the way the San Juan people think of their village, and hence their lives as well, as having had a number of beginnings, each with separate significance. Second, their view of the events of the past is metaphorical rather than empirical, and the metaphorical aspect of their sacred narratives has the same significance for them that traditional history has for White Americans. Third, this notion of *xų́· očú te²i* gives yet further insight into how the San Juan people have never lost their ties to the sacred throughout the long epochs during which they have moved about on the land. Throughout their past as a people every place where they have lived has been an ever-youthful structure based on young, fresh corn, with plenty of moisture about. *xų́· očú te²i* speaks and recalls endless times and places, ever on the edge of an equally endless dawn.

## Sources

The most comprehensive ethnographic treatise available based primarily on work at San Juan is by Ortiz (1969); it focuses primarily on world view and ritual and social structure. A good short ethnographic profile is by Curtis (1907–1930, 17), while Parsons (1929, 1939) also records useful ethnographic detail. Adolph Bandelier's Southwestern journals for the years 1885–1888, as edited and annotated by Lange, Riley, and Lange (1966–1976), have some historical and ethnographic information on San Juan as well. The most detailed description of a major ritual is by Laski (1959), although the Jungian analysis she presents of it falls far short of revealing the rich texture of meanings to be found in that ritual, which is a masterwork of Tewa drama. Parsons (1926) presents a collection of Tewa traditional narratives, with most of the best texts coming from San Juan, while Spinden (1933) provides sensitive translations of many songs from San Juan and other Tewa Pueblos. Kurath with Garcia (1969) provide detailed ethnomusicological analyses of most of the major dances still performed at San Juan into the 1960s, as well as analyses of other dances from some other Tewa Pueblos.

Ford (1968, 1972) provides much valuable trade and subsistence data for San Juan, data that are interpreted through, and informed by, a mature grounding in ecological theory. Robbins, Harrington, and Freire-Marreco (1916) and Henderson and Harrington (1914) supplement Ford's work with dated but still useful specialized studies on the ethnobotany and ethnozoology of the Tewa, respectively. Aberle, Watkins, and Pitney (1940) provide a vital history of the population of San Juan, something quite rare in the literature on North American Indian groups because of the usual paucity of data. Even more rare is the extremely detailed ethnogeography by Harrington (1916). This work is one of the most comprehensive treatises ever assembled for the geographical terminology of any non-Western society.

The data presented here for 1940 and the 1970s come from Ortiz's (1963–1977) unpublished field notes for each period. Aside from these two periods, there is no other historical period for which sufficiently balanced ethnographic information exists to make further comparisons meaningful and worthwhile.

# Santa Clara Pueblo

NANCY S. ARNON AND W.W. HILL

Santa Clara ('săntə 'klärə) (figs. 1-2), third largest of the six Northern Tewa-speaking Pueblos,* is located on the west bank of the Rio Grande between Santa Fe and Taos in northern New Mexico (see "Pueblos: Introduction," fig.1, this vol.). The other five Tewa villages are San Juan, San Ildefonso, Nambe, Pojoaque, and Tesuque.

The total land grant of the Pueblo is 45,742 acres, of which only 700 acres are irrigated. Range land and forest extend over 44,818 acres (Smith 1966:135).

## Prehistory

It is generally accepted that the present Pueblo peoples are cultural descendants of the Anasazi tradition, with marked Mogollon characteristics (Dozier 1970:36).

The sites of the prehistoric Pueblos cover a vast area extending over much of New Mexico, Arizona, Colorado, and Utah. Here, late prehistoric Mogollon and Anasazi farmers developed large communities that reached their cultural peak in the thirteenth century. The end of this century brought drought and climatic changes that probably forced the Pueblo population to relocate in the areas occupied when the Spanish first entered the Southwest in 1540-1541 (Dozier 1970:39).

The Santa Clarans themselves tell of the Tewa emergence from a lake in southern Colorado, from which they migrated south. After stopping at Ojo Caliente they passed through the Rio Grande valley to the village of Pecos, only to retrace their steps to the Rio Grande valley, where they built their towns (Jeançon 1931:5). They also say that their ancestors lived in the abandoned Pueblos of Puye and Shufinne, clusters of artificial caves dug into cliffs of pumice stone west of the Rio Grande, but other Tewas probably occupied these cliff-lodges as well (Hodge 1910b:456).

## History

The present-day Pueblo of Santa Clara occupies almost the same site as that viewed by the Spaniards when they first arrived. According to local tradition, the Pueblo occupied two earlier sites, the first northwest of the present Pueblo and the second (after the first was abandoned) northeast of the present Santa Clara (Harrington 1916:242).

The Santa Clarans have been affected by three Euro-American cultures: Spanish, Mexican, and Anglo-American. The Tewa first saw Whites in 1540-1541 with the arrival of Francisco Vásquez de Coronado's expedition. Following on his heels in 1598 to colonize New Mexico came Juan de Oñate, whose vigorous program of "civilizing" and Christianizing the aborigines included dividing the Rio Grande Pueblos into missionary districts and forcing labor from the Indians. Santa Clara itself was made the seat of a Spanish mission, with a church and monastery erected between 1622 and 1629, and then became an outpost of the mission at San Ildefonso until 1782, when it was again made a mission with San Ildefonso as its outpost (Hodge 1910b).

In the Pueblo Revolt of 1680 the Pueblos united and drove the Spaniards out of New Mexico, but the Spaniards returned 12 years later under Diego de Vargas and reestablished Spanish rule. This time the policy was different; former coercive and repressive measures were relaxed.

In 1821 New Mexico became part of the Republic of Mexico and in 1846, following the Mexican-American War, New Mexico became part of the United States. These changes did not seriously affect the Pueblos until after the 1850s, when Americans reintroduced religious suppression. Anglo-American missionaries and United States Indian Service officials criticized "obscene" and "immoral" practices of the Indians, forcibly removing Indian children to boarding schools and stopping ceremonial practices judged to be un-Christian. Finally, after much protest in the courts and press, a more humane policy for Indians was formulated at the end of the 1920s (Dozier 1970:5).

Between a recorded population of 134 persons in 1790 (U.S. Bureau of Indian Affairs 1854-1871) and a population of 1,204 persons recorded in 1974 (Northern Pueblos Agency) lies a myriad of events, both tragic and fortunate, that affected population numbers (table 1). Although most of these events are unrecorded, it is known that recurrent epidemic diseases have swept the Pueblos; for example, Bandelier (1890-1892, 2:23) claimed that a smallpox epidemic in 1782 killed over 500 Indians in the Santa Clara and San Juan vicinity in just two months.

---

* For the spelling of Tewa words in the *Handbook,* see the orthographic footnote in "San Juan Pueblo," this vol.

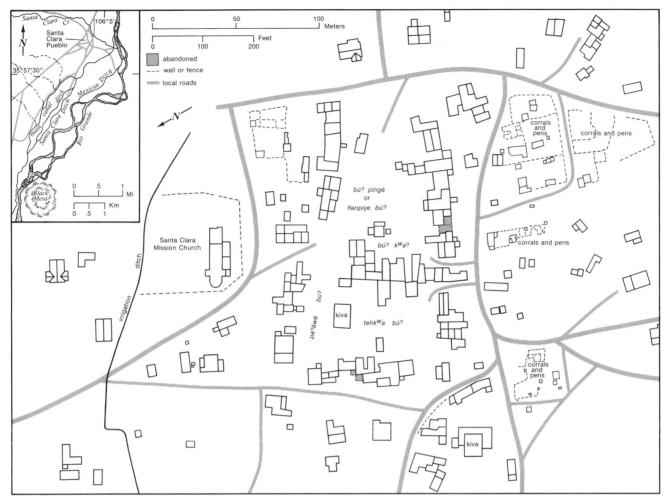

revised from Historic Amer. Buildings Survey, Natl. Park Service, map for 1972.

Fig. 1. Santa Clara Pueblo. Plazas are located by Tewa names.

Southwest Foundation for Audio-Visual Resources, Santa Fe, N.M.

Fig. 2. Santa Clara plazas. Photograph by Peter Dechert, June 1977.

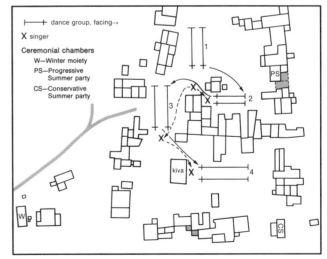

after Kurath with Garcia 1969:fig. 9.

Fig. 3. Circuit pattern for dances. Ceremonial chambers for each moiety are indicated; dances begin and end at these chambers and therefore entrances and exits depend on the moiety affiliation of the dancers. See fig. 1 for scale and general key.

297

**Table 1. Population, 1790–1974**

| Year | Population | Source |
|------|-----------|--------|
| 1790 | 134 | U.S. Bureau of Indian Affairs 1854–1871 Records |
| 1809 | 220 | U.S. Bureau of Indian Affairs 1854–1871 Records |
| 1850 | 279 | U.S. Bureau of Indian Affairs 1854–1871 Records |
| 1860 | 179 | U.S. Bureau of Indian Affairs 1854–1871 Records |
| 1864 | 144 | U.S. Bureau of Indian Affairs 1854–1871 Records |
| 1870 | 189 | U.S. Bureau of Indian Affairs 1854–1871 Records |
| 1910 | 277 | Hodge 1910b |
| 1934 | 440 | |
| 1974 | 1,204 | U.S. Bureau of Indian Affairs |

## Culture

### Social and Ceremonial Organization

Important units of social and ceremonial organization among the Tewa are dual subdivisions, usually called moieties, that are mirror images of each other and serve as governmental divisions for the management and conduct of practical tasks and ceremonial activities (figs. 4–6). The basis for these subdivisions or moieties is the two-part agriculture cycle of the Pueblos, which is comprised of "summer" and "winter" activities.

Every Pueblo member belongs to either the Summer moiety (*xayé*) or Winter moiety (*kʷ·ǽri*), inheriting his moiety association from his father. A woman marrying a man of opposite affiliation must join her husband's moiety, "shaking off her blossom petals and replacing them with icicles" if she is a Summer moiety member, or shaking off her icicles if she is of the Winter moiety (Ortiz 1969:123).

Tewa society has both vertical and horizontal divisions. In addition to the moiety (or vertical) divisions, six horizontal divisions or "levels of being" organize all human and spiritual existence. The first three levels are human, the next three supernatural, as shown in table 2.

Each human category is associated with a supernatural category; and at death, the soul of a human becomes a spirit in its linked supernatural category.

**Table 2. Levels of Being of Tewa Society**

| | |
|---|---|
| Supernatural Categories | 6. Dry Food Who Never Did Become<br>5. *towaʔê·*<br>4. Dry Food Who Are No Longer |
| Social Categories | 3. Made People<br>2. *towaʔê·*<br>1. Dry Food People |

SOURCE: Ortiz 1969:17.

Each level of being has a distinct function. Ordinary people, who hold no political offices, comprise the first level (linked to level 4) and are called Dry Food People. The *towaʔê·* make up the second level (linked to level 5) and act as government officials. Finally, the Made People, or Priests, stand at the apex of the Tewa social order as level 3 (and represent the deities of level 6). To carry out successfully their crucial functions of ensuring the normal progression of seasons and promoting peace and social harmony, the Made People must not show anger or interfere directly in the affairs of ordinary men.

The Made People also comprise the membership of the ceremonial organizations, of which there are three kinds: two moiety associations that have governmental and religious functions; medicine associations, which are responsible for healing and exorcising; and "specialty associations," such as those concerned with war, hunting, and clowning.

Households are units of organizations smaller than the associations. They are partially extended to include relatives on either parent's side and are usually headed by prestigious and influential older males. Tewa kinship terms are descriptive and bilateral.

### Political Organization

Although politically autonomous, Tewa villages share the same fundamental pattern of political organization. The following description of this pattern, although still applicable to San Juan and Tesuque in 1975, would apply most accurately to Santa Clara before 1890, the year in which began a major political schism that wrought significant changes in the political structure.

Tewa political organization blends two systems—one native, the other Spanish-imposed—so thoroughly that no one has yet satisfactorily disentangled them (Ortiz 1969:61). Political organization comprises three groups: the Spanish officials (governor, lieutenant governors, and sheriff), church wardens (*fiscales*), and war captains (*towaʔê·*). The first two groups were imposed by Spanish civil and church officials around the early seventeenth century to facilitate civil administration and missionary programs; the *towaʔê·* were added after 1693.

The *towaʔê·*, or war captains, have confused many an observer of the Pueblos. With bewildering inconsistency these officials have been variously referred to as "outside chiefs," "twin war gods," or "war captains." In all probability, when required to choose their own military leaders after the Spanish Reconquest in 1693, the Pueblos filled these positions from offices already existing, namely, from the traditional assistants of the moiety chiefs who were named after the Twin War Gods of mythology. They may have added more assistants up to the number of war captains required to carry out the necessary ritual tasks in each Pueblo. The Tewa refer most often to these war captains as *towaʔê·* 'little people', and they are identified with the *towaʔê·* who, as the Twin

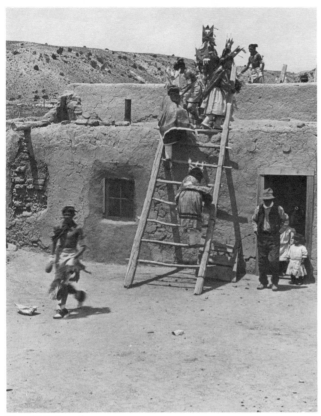

Fig. 5. Dance steps and formations used in the Corn Dance include the single line weaving formation shown here by which the dancers thread their way between dance stations (fig. 3). Women hold spruce boughs in both hands and wear flat tablitas with painted and cutout designs and eagle down. Men wear white dance kilts, white paint, skunk-skin anklets, fox skins suspended from their belts (extreme right), and eagle feathers on their heads; they carry gourd rattles in their right hands and spruce boughs in their left hands. Photograph by Edward Kemp, late 1920s or early 1930s.

Fig. 4. Corn dancers emerging from Summer People's kiva. The Corn Dance *(xóhé?yé)*, also called Tablita Dance from the distinctive headdress worn by the women, is danced by members of both moieties on various occasions (see Lange 1957). Photograph by unknown photographer, about 1920.

Fig. 6. Corn dancers, on the same occasion as fig. 5, in the plaza in front of the kiva and saint's bower. They are in two lines facing in opposite directions. A drummer and a few members of the chorus are at left. Photograph by Edward Kemp, late 1920s or early 1930s.

SANTA CLARA PUEBLO

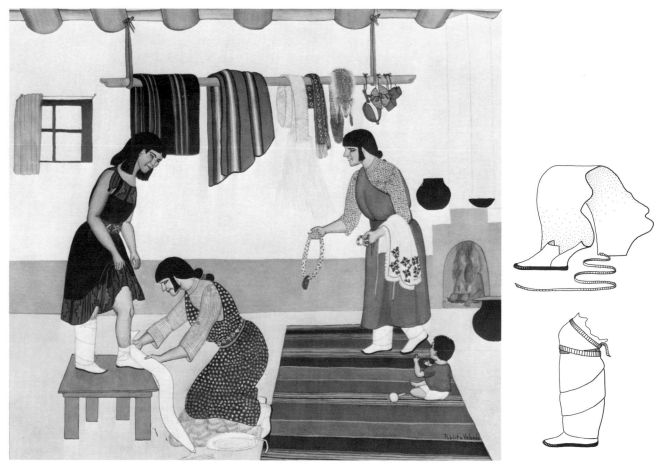

Fig. 7. *Her First Dance,* tempera painting by Pablita Velarde, a Santa Clara artist, painted in 1953. The dance could be several different ones for which the basic costume is a black manta, woven belt, and high wrapped white moccasins. Another version of these wrapped moccasins, made of whole deerskins with kaolin-whitened uppers, is shown at right (after Roediger 1941:fig. 17). The woman at right brings a turquoise and shell necklace, a bracelet, and an apron to be tied over the shoulders and hung down the back. Two blankets and several items of a man's dance outfit are hung on the suspended storage bar, including a white "rain sash," a fox skin, gourd rattle, tortoise-shell rattles with dangling claws (worn behind the knees), and leather armbands. The room, a typical interior, has a corner fireplace and whitewashed walls with the lower portion painted. Slightly cropped.

War Gods, occupy the middle level of being in the supernatural world.

The officials were all chosen from ordinary or Dry Food People, and all began office on January 1 for one year, subject to reappointment. The moiety heads appointed officials in consultation with the other male heads of the Made People's societies. In Santa Clara the moiety heads annually rotated nominations for governor and the head *łowaʔê·*; one year the Summer moiety head appointed the governor and the Winter moiety head appointed the head *łowaʔê·*; the next year these appointments were reversed. Moiety heads would take turns nominating officials; first the Summer chief would call a name, then the Winter chief, until all the officials had been nominated. Appointees did not learn of their appointment until the first day of office lest their wariness of time-consuming positions with no recompense cause them to flee town altogether. But any protest was futile, and officials would assume duties January 1 after being sworn in at the governor's house with dignitaries and priests in attendance.

Each group of officials had distinct functions. The Spanish officials—governor (figs. 8-9), two lieutenant governors (known as the governor's "right and left hands"), and sheriff (Spanish *alguacil,* Tewa *awasî·*)—conducted business with the outside world, including maintenance of an elaborate system of irrigation canals, in cooperation with neighboring Spanish-American farmers; control of stock and grazing rights on village land; and rental of land and other village property to outsiders. The governor served a limited role as judge of more serious lawbreakers; minor offenders could be punished by the sheriff. Since Santa Clara apparently appointed neither a town crier nor a ditch boss (positions found in other Pueblos), the governor may also have performed their duties of making daily announcements from his rooftop and overseeing maintenance of the irrigation system.

Fig. 8. José Leandro Tofoya, with grandchildren. He was governor of Santa Clara in 1899, when this photograph was taken by Adam C. Vroman.

Fig. 9. Juan Gutierrez, governor of Santa Clara in 1960, with silver-headed canes of office. These are the Spanish cane incised with a cross and the Lincoln cane more elaborately engraved and bearing the inscription: "A. Lincoln Pres.: U.S. à Santa Clara 1863." Each governor may add a ribbon to the cane when he is elected. The canes are kept in the governor's house and used on ceremonial occasions in the kiva and elsewhere (Anonymous 1960:7).

Four *fiscales* had responsibility for church-related affairs, including driving people to church at the point of a whip! A related Spanish official, the *sacristán,* served as assistant to the resident priest.

Six *íowaʔê·* guarded religion and custom. Before 1860 their principal function was to guard the village from outside attack by maintaining sentries to warn the village of marauding bands. This guard duty was extended in the 1860s and 1870s to include vigilance against outside liaisons or internal ideological deviations that might jeopardize the village's well-being. The *íowaʔê·* also carried out the policies and wishes of the moiety chiefs and served generally as the protectors and agents of the Made People, who were prohibited from interfering directly in mundane affairs. At the same time, they provided a check on the authority of the Made People through their impersonations of masked supernatural whippers (the *cáveyó*), in the guise of whom they could punish anyone, including a Made Person, who had refused to participate in rituals. They also punished women and children derelict in their responsibilities.

A check on the authority of the secular officials, in turn, was provided by the council of *principales* (distinct from the Council of Ceremonial Priests). The moiety chief could request the governor to convene this council, which acted in effect as a jury to ascertain guilt in cases of serious charges and to mete out punishments such as confiscation of property, beatings, whippings, tying up in public and, in extreme cases, banishment. Council membership included the governor, two lieutenant governors, sheriff, war captains, *fiscales,* and all ex-governors, all of whose decisions had to be unanimous.

As important as the Spanish officials came to be, the native government system—religious rather than secular—was the structure beneath the entire political organization. Supreme village authority lay not with the governor but with the two moiety heads, equal in status and authority, who traded responsibility for village control approximately every six months. The Summer chief ruled from spring to fall and the Winter chief ruled the rest of the time, paralleling the seasonal transfer of authority between the two moiety associations. The moiety priests held themselves aloof from affairs of ordinary men but selected the secular officials and had final authority in all matters, sacred and profane.

Despite the intentions of Spanish authorities to supplant the native governmental and ceremonial system with new officers, this displacement never occurred. Ironically, the Spanish only strengthened the native officials by giving them a useful tool—the Spanish officials—to handle new roles demanded by external events and to mask their own activities.

• FACTIONALISM The traditional pattern of Tewa political organization broke down in Santa Clara from 1894 to 1935 when the village suffered a major schism, which ended in adoption of an elective form of government.

Santa Clara is not unique among the Pueblos in having experienced factional disputes; in fact, factionalism in the Pueblos has interested many observers, who have formulated various hypotheses to explain this phenomenon. For example, Edward P. Dozier, an anthropologist native to Santa Clara, suggests: "It is opposition to the compulsory dictates of the Pueblo authorities which has brought about dissatisfaction and discord in the past as well as at present. Forced participation in all communal activities and the prohibition of all deviant behavior, though designed to discourage the rise of dissident groups, have often had the opposite effect and have resulted in frequent factional disputes" (Dozier 1966:175).

Throughout most of the nineteenth century and the early part of the twentieth, a number of Santa Clara families who opposed the dictates of the Pueblo authorities formed a "core" group within the more progressive moiety, the Winter moiety. Advocating a separation of religious from secular activities, this dissident group argued that families and not officials should designate planting and harvesting dates, that work on irrigation canals should be compulsory only for families owning land irrigated by the canals, and that ceremonial participation should be voluntary rather than required (Dozier 1966).

By the end of the nineteenth century, the dissidents comprised almost the entire Winter moiety. But it should be pointed out that each side made similar claims: each professed to observe traditional ways; each accused the other of nonconformity; each, when in seasonal control of government, forced all members of the opposite moiety to participate in ceremonials.

The year 1894 marked the beginning of a 30-year schism. At this time the canes symbolizing authority passed to Summer moiety officials. The Summer moiety and a handful of Winter moiety members applied for, and obtained, recognition from the Indian agency in Santa Fe as the de facto governing body of the Pueblo. For the next 30 years the Summer moiety elected all the secular officials (except the lieutenant governor, a Winter member) and tried in every conceivable way to force Winter moiety members to participate in public works and ceremonies. Though in the minority, the dissident Winter moiety members were determined enough to successfully resist and to openly defy the group in power.

New disputes arose in the early 1930s. Curiously enough, similar and almost simultaneous disputes within each moiety over the election of officials split each moiety in half, each along progressive and conservative lines.

Thus four factions formed: a progressive and conservative faction within each moiety. Two alliances were drawn up: one between the two progressive factions, the other between the conservative factions.

The alliances worked well during 1934, but fresh problems arose at the end of the year when the governor (a Summer progressive) refused to return his cane of authority to the moiety priest (a Summer conservative) as was customary, the two having quarreled. All sides requested arbitration by the Indian Service in Santa Fe, which proposed an elective form of government under terms of the Indian Reorganization Act of 1934. After Pueblo approval of this proposal, a constitutional committee, composed of members of all four factions and Indian Bureau lawyers and advisors, drew up a constitution. When this document was ratified by the Pueblo late in 1935 and approved by the secretary of the interior, Santa Clara became the first Pueblo community to incorporate under the Indian Reorganization Act.

While the constitution of 1935 did not end all disputes, at least religious and secular affairs became divorced and ceremonial participation was made voluntary. The constitution set forth guidelines for an initial nomination of officers: each of the four parties was to submit nominations for governor, lieutenant governor, secretary, treasurer, interpreter, and sheriff. Each party was also to elect two representatives to the council. However, in practice, the Pueblo has never submitted four complete lists of candidates. A ballot containing two full lists of candidates has become customary, and factions that do not submit candidates support candidates of other factions. The village council was given authority to designate election procedures. In fact, the constitution vests the entire governing power of the Pueblo in this council, consisting of all the officers and representatives mentioned, including the eight representatives. The council has both legislative and judicial powers.

This example of the major schism in Santa Clara history not only illustrates types of arguments that can give rise to factional disputes but also, more importantly, demonstrates the solidarity of Pueblo villages. Rarely have factional disputes dissolved a Pueblo. This continuity is perhaps explained in part by the practice of "skimming off malcontents," that is, elimination of nonconformists through forced eviction or voluntary moves. Most significant, the perpetuation of Pueblo societies attests to an intricate system of balances and interlocking organizations that blend together to form a harmonious whole.

## Subsistence

While agriculture and hunting were the most important means of livelihood before the Spanish appeared, farming gained and hunting declined in importance after the Spanish arrival. Less important economic pursuits that have contributed to the economy in varying degrees at

Fig. 10. Santa Clara woman wearing a traditional belt of Pueblo manufacture, a cotton manta, and a Spanish-type shawl with brightly colored paisley pattern. Purchased shawls and pieces of commercial fabric replaced native-woven shawls. Photograph by H.T. Cory, 1916.

different times including gathering, fishing, raiding, animal husbandry, trade, handicrafts, and wage work.

Not only did the Spaniards influence the relative importance of farming and hunting, but also they introduced a number of material changes. Most important was the introduction of new crops and domesticated animals (Dozier 1970:65). To the aboriginal crops of Santa Clara—maize, beans, squash, cotton, gourds, and tobacco—the Spaniards introduced a variety of new crops—wheat, barley, chili, tomatoes, onions, peaches, apricots, apples, and melons. Wheat became the most important of these new crops and soon rivaled maize as a staple and surpassed it in trade. Equally significant for agriculture was the introduction of new mechanical techniques and draft animals, although the scarcity of these resources in the seventeenth century contributed to the practice of forcing Indians to labor to benefit Spanish officials. Technological innovations included the metal hoe, fork, and shovel, and wooden rake and plow. Introduced draft animals included oxen, horses, and burros. These additions increased the amount of land that could be cultivated and lightened the load of the farmer who, in prehistoric times, had to move dirt and debris with wooden shovels and hoes, stone axes, and woven fiber baskets.

Irrigation systems of considerable mechanical ingenuity existed in prehistoric times. By diverting waters from the Rio Grande and its tributaries to fields planted at a lower elevation, the Indians were freed from sole dependence on rainfall for crops. The consequences of such a sophisticated irrigation system are far-reaching: it is claimed that the development of irrigation led simultaneously to the formation of the highly centralized Pueblo political organization, which was needed to maintain the complex water systems (Dozier 1970:131).

Farming was done mostly by men, with women assisting in communal tasks. Otherwise, women performed duties within the household: caring for children, preparing meals, and making pottery. The extended family, or even larger units, which were usually bilateral descent groups, owned house sites and garden plots. Work in the fields was usually a task of these kinship units, although friends and distant relatives might share weeding, planting, and harvesting. An individual's needs, equipment, and ability to enlist help from relatives and friends would determine the amount of land under cultivation. Often a man would farm three plots: one in a river bottom, another in the mountains near Santa Clara Creek valley, and the third a small garden plot near the Pueblo.

The dual subsistence cycle of the Tewa (which forms the basis of the moiety organizations) is divided into agricultural activities approximately from the vernal to the autumnal equinox and into nonagricultural activities the other half of the year. Underpinning this subsistence cycle are annual "works" or day-long retreats and prayer sessions performed by each of the ceremonial societies to influence the basic rhythms of nature for the good of the Tewa. For example, the springtime work known as Of Moderation or To Lessen the Cold is conducted to melt the snow, thaw the ground, and prevent further extreme weather (Ortiz 1969:99).

Game once contributed substantially to subsistence. Deer, buffalo, antelope, and rabbits were the most important animals hunted, the first three furnishing the bulk of the meat supply and hides for clothing.

Lengthy buffalo hunts occurred in the fall, when the animal was said to be in its prime. The Hunters' Society head or a war captain would lead a hunting party of 6 to 10 men, frequently augmented by Spanish-Americans and men from neighboring Pueblos, to the plains, where bands of Kiowa and Comanche might join the party. Hunters on horseback would ride close to the animal and shoot with bow and arrow, or, more rarely, with a lance. Meat was jerked, packed in skin sacks, and carried back to the villages in carts or on horseback. Antelope hunts were similarly organized; a successful hunt would yield 30 to 50 animals out of a herd.

Single families often hunted deer in the foothills. Rabbits were hunted or trapped nearby; they were a relatively unimportant food source but were distributed as gifts by clowns and kachinas at dances.

Fig. 11. Santa Clara in 1879 (top) and 1899 (bottom), facing southeast, showing flexibility of Pueblo architecture (see also fig. 12). Both views show the rectangular kiva at center, animal pens and threshing floors behind the last row houses, and the Sangre de Cristo Mountains in the background. In addition to architectural modifications, corrals and garden enclosures (foreground) replaced open garden plots. Photographs by John K. Hillers (top) and Adam C. Vroman.

Fish probably contributed substantially to the Tewa food supply. They were caught in large quantities with sharp-pointed sticks and with seines made of yucca fiber weighted down with rocks and floated at the top by gourds.

Bear, mountain sheep, several species of cats and rodents, and various birds were less important game. Bears were eaten and used for ritual paraphernalia. Mountain lion hides were highly prized for robes and quivers. Many small animals and birds were procured for ceremonial use.

The Santa Clarans used to augment agricultural produce with the native plants they gathered, which included yucca, prickly pear, beeweed, amaranth, chenopodium, and piñon nuts. Gathering was a seasonal, somewhat desultory activity that never took full advantage of existing natural foods, since agricultural methods were so successful.

Animal husbandry was unpopular. Domesticated animals introduced by the Spaniards were scarce and usually profited the newcomers at the expense of increased labor by the Indians. Domesticated animals included chickens,

304

sheep, goats, donkeys, mules, horses, and cattle. Some livestock was obtained in trade from the Apache, Navajo, and other tribes marginal to the Plains.

## Technology

With the arrival of the Spaniards, new crafts were established—wool weaving, blacksmithing, and woodworking—which brought with them a complex assortment of tools and equipment such as saddles, bridles, harnesses, metal knives, sickles, needles, and axes.

Architectural practices were little changed by contact. Adobe bricks and wooden ovens were in use aboriginally.

## Trade

Trading at Santa Clara was sporadic and contributed little to the overall economy. Not only did neighboring Indian and European villages produce similar commodities, but also they lacked surpluses; usually only food was exchanged. However, Santa Clara did obtain the following products in trade with other Pueblos: baskets, woven items, Navajo blankets, dance paraphernalia, turquoise beads, and terraced pottery bowls for ceremonial use. Inter-Pueblo trade patterns varied.

During the seventeenth and early eighteenth centuries, a somewhat formalized trade flourished with the Comanche and to a lesser extent with the Kiowa and the marginal Plains groups, the Southern Ute and the Jicarilla Apache. Exchanging cornmeal, wheat flour, bread, and woven materials, the Santa Clarans received jerked meat pemmican, buffalo robes, pipe pouches, tortoise shells, parfleches (rawhide articles), lances, and osage orange wood for bow-making. The balance of trade favored the Tewa. They also gained livestock from the Comanche who were anxious to dispose quickly of livestock secured from raids as far south as Texas.

Due to their northern location, Santa Clarans acted as middlemen for the more southern Pueblo villages by disseminating desirable Plains goods such as buffalo robes and deer hides. Santa Clara also manufactured many of the items valued by Plains traders. For example, Santa Clara wove fabrics until forced to stop in protest over the Spanish habit of confiscating the fabrics for "tribute."

## Warfare

Since economic factors formerly determined most offensive actions, warfare may be considered an "economic" pursuit. Most raids were conducted against the Navajo, traditional enemies of the Tewa, and these military efforts probably yielded many goods, including horses and equine equipment, livestock, and jewelry and other easily transportable contraband.

U. of Ariz., Ariz. State Mus., Tucson.

Fig. 12. Adobe houses of traditional Pueblo construction in 1970. Nontraditional modifications include the addition of television aerials, electrical poles, a water tank, and a basketball backboard and basket. Photograph by Helga Teiwes, Aug. 29, 1970.

## Socioeconomic Situation in the 1970s

Though not among the largest of the Pueblos in population, Santa Clara does have a large and resource-rich land base. In this regard it may be viewed as one of the wealthiest of the Pueblos. The most extensive uses made of reservation land are for tourist recreation, and these range from tours through the spectacular cliff dwellings of Puye to hunting, fishing, camping, and picnicking in Santa Clara Canyon, just above Puye. Each year during the last weekend in July the Pueblo hosts a program of Indian dances at Puye. Tourists are invited to these; in return for a modest admission charge, they may take photographs to their hearts' content, sample native cuisine, and purchase local crafts. Ruins restoration work done by archeologists and the erection of service buildings by the Works Progress Administration during the Depression years have made Puye conveniently accessible and a popular tourist attraction. Santa Clara Canyon, in turn, is one of the most attractive and carefully developed outdoor recreation areas in northern New Mexico. Both areas are important not only for generating tribal revenue but also for providing employment opportunities.

Santa Clara also owns extensive pumice deposits, timber, and commercial properties, which are leased to business concerns in the nearby town of Española. These produce tribal revenue but not much in the way of employment for community members. On the other hand, the Pueblo's proximity to the nearby atomic research facility of Los Alamos has provided further employment opportunities for those not employed by the Pueblo, by Española businesses, by federal programs, or in full-time crafts work for themselves. The total employed in Los Alamos has decreased slightly from a high of approximately 30 in the 1960s, but Los Alamos and

Fig. 13. Santa Clara woman using a small stone to polish a leather-hard pot, prior to firing. At left is a similar completed pot, fired black. The incised bear claw on each is distinctively Santa Clara (LeFree 1975:74). Photograph by Edward S. Curtis, 1905 or before.

Fig. 14. Pottery jar with deer dancer and wedding vase in modern Santa Clara style, made for sale by Flora Naranjo, combining the traditional polished black surface (see fig. 13) with incised and carved designs (see LeFree 1975). Height of left about 23 cm, right about 34 cm; both collected in 1975.

other federal employment opportunities, both within the Pueblo and out, remain the largest sources of wage income for Pueblo residents.

The traditional crafts of Santa Clara, especially the black pottery (figs. 13-14), are among the most prized by tourists and collectors alike. As a result a significant number of Santa Clara people derive a comfortable income from the sale of pottery, although very few have ever made their living exclusively from pottery for any length of time. A few who have begun to innovate and build upon the traditional polychrome and black-on-black designs are especially successful in marketing their wares for high prices. These and all other Pueblo craftspeople have been assisted considerably by the proliferation of artists' and craftmen's shows throughout the Southwest, as well as by the increasing popularity of Indian arts and crafts nationwide.

Santa Clara has long been gifted with aggressive and effective political leadership. The careful development of tribal resources for the widest possible benefit to Pueblo residents attests to this, as do innovations in customs that generate tribal revenues and jobs without simultaneously proving socially disruptive. The introduction in 1962 of the annual Puye Cliffs Ceremonials, a weekend program of traditional Tewa dances, is an example of this. Since the passage of the Economic Opportunity Act in 1964, Santa Clara has also enjoyed considerable success in attracting federal grants for local construction and economic development. Chief among these has been a neighborhood multiple-use building, erected with the aid of funds from the Economic Development Administration. This houses everything from tribal offices to recreational facilities. Santa Clara's long experience with a constitutional form of government has undoubtedly been the major factor in its people's ability to manage change so that it is not disruptive, as well as to seize genuine opportunities to improve their lives.

This same experience has also made the Santa Clara people more conscious of the value of a Western education for their children. In the early 1960s the Pueblo ran a Montessori school, and local parents have long taken a firm and positive role in all matters pertaining not only to their local educational facilities but also to the nearby Española public high school. As a consequence of this concern for and valuation of school-taught knowledge, a large number of local students continue to college, with a success rate of more than 50 percent.

In summary, Santa Clara has been favored both by its resource base and by its form of government, for nearly three decades, which, by the fact of having separated civil and religious matters, has been very responsive to modern challenges. Economic opportunities, especially, have been seized, and the broad-scale participation of Pueblo members in Pueblo affairs has been consistently maintained during the post–World War II decades. In view of these several factors it is not surprising that the Pueblo has lost fewer people through out-migration to distant cities during these same decades than most other Pueblos along the Rio Grande and its tributaries.

## Synonymy†

Santa Clara Pueblo received its Spanish name in 1598 from the colonizer Juan de Oñate. The Tewa name is now

† This synonymy was compiled by Ives Goddard. Uncredited forms and interpretations are from Harrington (1916:240–242) or anonymous sources.

pronounced *xaʔpoˑ* (as if *xaʔ* 'wild rose' and *poˑ* 'water'), perhaps a folk etymology based on the earlier attested but uninterpretable form *xaˑpôˑ* (*xaˑ*, no meaning; *pôˑ* 'trail'). The first syllable has also been interpreted as if identical with one of several other slightly differing words or word-elements meaning 'corral, fence', 'weight, heavy', and 'spherical', and the second syllable has also been taken to be the word for 'moon'. The resulting translations, such as 'rose trail', 'spherical moon', 'heavy water', 'rose water (or dew)', and so forth are probably just guesses. In any event, the name probably does not refer to a feature of the present Pueblo, as it is said to have earlier been borne by two successive ancestral Pueblos. Spellings in the historical literature include Capo, Capoo, and Ca-po.

The recorded Tiwa names are all similar: Taos háipâái, Picuris haiphahá, Isleta k'haibhai', and variants with different final syllables showing different locatives; a Picuris form kaipāā is translated 'in the river there are wet cornstalks'. Cochiti káipa (normalized) and Acoma kaíïpa may be borrowings from Tiwa; a similar form was recorded in 1598 by Oñate as Caypa. Zia has tinyitityame (normalized), and San Felipe has ḱówame (White 1932:62, normalized). Jemez *šǽˑpæ* 'Santa Clara Indian', whence *šǽˑpǽˑgʸiʔ* for the Pueblo, may be related to the Tewa name. Pecos has ákeji and giowaka-ā. The Hopi name nasaveʔ-tewa (normalized) 'middle Tewa' refers to the location of Santa Clara between San Ildefonso and San Juan. The Navajo name *'Anaashashí* 'bear aliens' is explained as a reference to the bear sand paintings the Santa Clarans make (Robert W. Young, personal communication 1977) or to "their skunk-skin moccasins which at first were thought to be of bear skin" (Curtis 1907–1930, 1:138); this name and the variant *Naashashí* are also applied to the Arizona Tewa (Robert W. Young, personal communication 1977; Haile 1950–1951, 2:146, 297).

## Sources

This article is based primarily on a manuscript by the late W.W. Hill (1940–1941), who carried out long-term studies of the village, primarily during the early 1940s, and on work by Jeançon (1931).

Published studies of Santa Clara are few. Among these are two accounts of factionalism that should be read in conjunction, Dozier (1966), who reviews causes and effects of the village's major schism, and Barbara Aitken (1930). A detailed review of Santa Clara synonymy may be found in Harrington (1916). Parsons (1929) contains an appreciable amount of detail on Santa Clara social organization.

Several sources provide excellent description and analysis of Pueblo culture and history. Dozier (1970) contains a wealth of detail on Pueblo history, religion, and culture, both past and present. Tewa world view is set forth brilliantly by Ortiz (1969), while Parsons (1929) describes Pueblo religion, social organization, and cultural changes in a fascinating encyclopedic work. Eggan (1950) provides a superb analysis of social organization in the Western Pueblos, where comparison is made to social organization in the Eastern or Rio Grande Pueblos. A special study of Pueblo economy and civil organization is given by Aberle (1948).

# San Ildefonso Pueblo

SANDRA A. EDELMAN

## Language and Territory

San Ildefonso ('săn ĭldə'fän₁sō) (figs. 1-2) is one of six extant Rio Grande Tewa-speaking Pueblos.* Tewa is a division of the Tanoan branch of the Kiowa-Tanoan language family. The village is 22 miles northwest of Santa Fe, New Mexico. Its nearest Tewa neighbors are Santa Clara Pueblo, with which it shares a common boundary (the northern limit of San Ildefonso land), and, directly east, the tiny Pueblo of Pojoaque (see "Pueblos: Introduction," fig. 1, this vol.). San Ildefonso owns or uses 28,136 acres, of which 15,413.40 are from the original Spanish grant confirmed by Congress in 1958 and 4,430.72 are in reservation from a 1929 act of Congress. In addition, the Pueblo uses 5,913.66 acres of government land.

## Culture

The aboriginal social structure of San Ildefonso was disrupted early in the twentieth century by demographic-economic factors and by a factional schism. Since nearly all descriptions of the Pueblo are based on postschism data, some reconstruction of the earlier organization is necessary. The following reconstruction describes pre-schism organization (Curtis 1907-1930, 17; Dozier 1961, 1970; Ortiz 1969; Parsons 1929, 1939; Whitman 1940, 1947).

The Pueblo had a dual organization expressed in Summer and Winter moieties that functioned alternately and reciprocally, uniting at life crisis rites and for purposes of community welfare (like maintenance of fields, harvesting, cleaning of irrigation ditches, transitions of authority). Moiety chiefs were appointed for life and were assisted by a Right-hand Man and a Left-hand Man as well as by a council comprised of the heads of the societies. Moiety affiliation was patrilineal, but recruitment did not follow a rigid pattern (for example, a bride could become a member of her husband's moiety), and the usual exogamous marriage function of the moiety structure was absent. The typical Tewa tendency to moietal endogamy was more marked, at least in theory, at San Ildefonso than at other Tewa villages, according to Parsons (1929:97); however, this finding derives from the

period immediately following the schism, when endogamy may have been pronounced because of intense factionalism, so intense at one time that a resident of one plaza would refuse to speak to a resident of the other.

Kinship is reckoned bilaterally. Kinship rules are flexible, with moiety affiliation being patrilineal, name-giving matrilineal, and clan affiliation variously matrilineal or patrilineal (however, it was most frequently matrilineal). Dozier (1961:105) found no indication that clans were kinship units, stating that clan names are merely sacred terms inherited variously from either parent. Parsons (1929:91) found in the social consciousness no alignment between moiety and clan.

Tewa kinship terms have been to a great degree displaced by the use of Spanish Christian names, and two Tewa terms, those for aunt and uncle older than mother and father, were generally discontinued altogether by the late 1930s (Whitman 1940:406).

San Ildefonso wives typically take their husbands' clans. Societies included the Winter and Summer moiety societies, the Winter and Summer clown societies, two medicine societies, a Warriors' Society, two Women's societies (Blue Corn Girls), and the Hunters' Society. Property is inherited from either parent or grandparent equally by offspring of either gender; this equality of inheritance rights is a relatively recent development and may have been the result of Keresan influence. It fosters a growing tendency to equal female ownership. Land is owned by the Pueblo, at least in theory, and only land-use rights are inherited.

The kachina cult is thought to be marginal among the Tewa. Parsons (1929:162-163) noted the appearance of Seeds and Rain-bird kachinas. While it is true that kachinas do not appear in San Ildefonso plaza dance rituals, figures representative of the kachinas are part of the kiva paraphernalia.

Secular government (the "Spanish officials" imposed by the colonials and continued by the United States) consisted of the governor, his two lieutenants, five *fiscales* (church caretakers; Tewa *pihkâ·*), and the sheriff. These officials were elected by the moiety chiefs and the *iowaʔê·*. The latter are the earthly representatives of the mythological Twin War Gods, from whom they take their names. Their head, the War (or Hunt) chief, occupied a position both religious and civil and was therefore unique among the Tewa officials. Ortiz (1969:36, 62-63, 74)

---

* For the spelling of Tewa words in the *Handbook*, see the orthographic footnote in "San Juan Pueblo," this vol.

Southwest Foundation for Audio-Visual Resources, Santa Fe, N.M.
Fig. 1. San Ildefonso Pueblo. Photograph by Peter Dechert, June 1977.

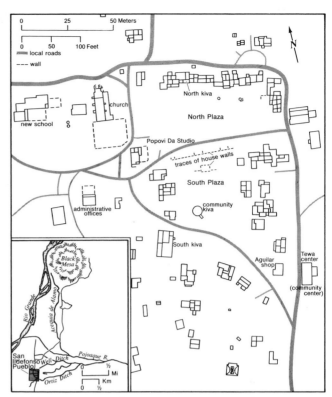

revised from Historic Amer. Buildings Survey, Natl. Park Service, map for 1973.
Fig. 2. Central portion of San Ildefonso Pueblo.

describes him as a mediator between the moieties, a middle level in the political organization, and, with the other officials, as a mediator or link between categories of being, that is, between the Made People (society members) and the Dry Food People, villagers neither officials nor society members.

Generally speaking, the preschism organization of San Ildefonso was fundamentally identical to that of other Rio Grande Tewa Pueblos. Relatively minor deviations may be noted: the Koshare (fig. 3) and Quirana clown societies (Tewa *ǩohsa·* and *ǩʷíráná*) are associated with winter and summer, respectively, which is a reversal of the usual Tewa pattern (here following the Keresan practice); the three-kiva pattern contrasted with the usual two-kiva one noted by Dozier (1961:99, cf. Dozier 1970:167); the tendency to equality of female ownership rights and the pronounced endogamy.

The factionalism and demographic-economic changes that disrupted the traditional moietal duality may be summarized as follows. Causes of the dispute were several and informants described as secretive, but most accounts agree that the dominant factor, or at least the one that became the focal point, was a disagreement, apparently along family lines, over the placement of the plaza. In the late nineteenth century, the village had been moved north of its old location, making it still a single-plaza Pueblo surrounding what is now North Plaza, the southernmost houserow being just north of the old round kiva (fig. 4), leaving that kiva outside the plaza. High

mortality rates and declining prosperity caused some of the people to look upon the northward movement as having been the result of bad counsel; migrations, for cosmological-mythic reasons, ought always to be southward, and a northward one is contrary to Tewa tradition. About 1910 some of the people began to urge moving the village south, returning it to surround once again the old plaza and round kiva. In 1923 the move was physically initiated, with the Summer chief and six families relocating and building a new village. The date of the move is elsewhere given as 1910, 1918, or 1921 (Hewett 1930; Whitman 1940; U.S. Office of Indian Affairs. Indian Land Research Unit 1935, 1). The majority of the people, however, preferred to remain where they were, in what came to be called North Plaza. By this time, the Winter moiety had been reduced to two families by the influenza epidemic of 1918 (Whitman 1940:432) and was unable to continue performing its moietal duties. Thus the dual organization came to be expressed not in moiety-seasonal terms but in residential terms: the Summer people divided into North and South people and absorbed the Winter families. Ortiz (1969:135) holds that the division by residence was a purposive sustaining of duality in the face of Winter moiety depopulation. However, the reciprocity characteristic of moietal relationship did not obtain between the two factions until about 1943 and then only in matters of civil authority. But the Summer-Winter frame of reference persisted in the mental set of the people, and for many years after the schism they seem

Fig. 3. Two male and three female Koshare at a fall Harvest Dance (*tenbí šare*). They are painted with characteristic black and white stripes and either wear two-horned caps or have their hair bound in two horns with corn husks. Female Koshare (who may participate only in the nonsacred dances) as well as the more usual male Koshare were reported in San Ildefonso in the 1920s (Parsons 1929:130) and in the late 1930s (Whitman 1947:16-17). In the foreground are braids of dried corn and baskets of squash and other foods. Photograph by M.C. Stevenson, probably in 1904.

to have continued thinking of themselves in the old moietal terms: one of Parsons's (1929:100, 122) informants identified round kiva (figs. 4-5) as a Winter kiva; Whitman (1947:6) was told, no doubt by a South Plaza Summer man, that the south rectangular kiva belonged to Summer people only, in spite of the fact that the majority of Summer people had remained in North Plaza. This persistence of the old moietal frame of reference, together with the reluctance of residents to discuss internal affairs, no doubt accounts for many of the contradictions and inconsistencies in descriptive accounts of the 1920s and 1930s. This summary is based primarily on Spicer (1962); there are other, somewhat divergent accounts (Hewett 1930; Whitman 1940, 1947; U.S. Office of Indian Affairs. Indian Land Research Unit 1935, 1). The Spicer account, with the exception of the date of relocation—1923 or 1910 (Spicer 1962:179, 497)—is cohesive, does not conflict with Harrington's (1916:305) 1910 diagram of the Pueblo, conforms to demographic residential patterns still apparent until 1973-1974, and corresponds in the 1923 date to the recollections of Maria Martinez of San Ildefonso (Marriott 1948) as well as to information provided by other residents of San Ildefonso.

The disruption of moietal organization and the intensity of factionalism greatly affected both the ritual and the civil organization of the Pueblo. What had been a single ritual organization became two, each plaza becoming an autonomous ceremonial unit, but neither complete. Postschism observations reveal the diminution or disappearance of certain officials and societies: by the

late 1930s, the Hunters' Society was nearly extinct, though there was still a Hunt chief (war captain); the Warriors' Society had disappeared, as had the Winter chief, the Winter chief society, the Quirana clown society, and both Blue Corn Girls societies. Curtis (1907-1930, 17:50) reported that in 1924 the medicine society—he did not specify which—had only two members and was no longer active. Of the 24 clans recorded by Hodge in 1895, Parsons (1929:87) could identify only seven in 1923, and of those only three were still specifically represented (Red Stone, Sun, and Grass); in 1936-1937 Whitman (1940:453) located the Sun, Red Stone, and Turquoise clans but was unable to find the Grass clan. Parsons (1939, 2:1140) surmised that kachina dances were no longer performed; however, Whitman (1947:140) implies that they were, and the Tewa Basin Study reported 25 kachinas (U.S. Office of Indian Affairs. Indian Land Research Unit 1935, 1). The Summer chief society had been weakened and much of the ritual forgotten. The Tewa Basin Study (ibid.: 85, 95) noted a general decline of ceremonialism, the loss of appointive powers of the Summer chief, the breaking down of the governmental system, and the weakness of the societies. There were only three male Koshare. In September 1973 the plazas held separate Corn Dances on different dates, both with small numbers of dancers, dancing out of their respective kivas, in contrast to the traditional single dance out of the communal (round) kiva. It was evident that the once-communal kiva was in use; it had been maintained and

310

Fig. 4. Church and round kiva in 1898. Access to kiva is through ladder at top of stairs. Photograph by C.C. Pierce or unknown photographer, facing northwest.

Fig. 5. Round kiva, traditionally used for communal religious events, in the 1960s. View of southside plaza, facing southeast. Photograph by Dick Kent.

electricity brought in, but it was apparently being used by South Plaza only. No clowns attended either ritual.

Secular authority was for many years in the hands of the North side. In 1930 the factional dispute took the form of physical violence when some North Plaza men raided South Plaza kiva to reclaim ceremonial objects removed to the South at the time of the schism; South Plaza men retaliated for the raid some two years later by burning North Plaza kiva. But factionalism had already reached its peak in 1930, when the governor was a North Plaza man (South Plaza, for many years, had been unable to elect a governor because it was a minority). The incumbent governor subsequently refused to relinquish his cane (a gift of Abraham Lincoln), symbol of the governor's authority, to any South Plaza man. North Plaza had not only numerical superiority (extrapolating from a division of new land made in 1935, approximately two-thirds of the residents were in North Plaza) but also economic superiority, since it included the then more prosperous families of potters. Its people were more acculturated and for many years the North Plaza governor was recognized by the Bureau of Indian Affairs as the official civil head of the entire Pueblo. In 1935 the governor, his two lieutenants, and the Hunt chief and two assistants were all North Plaza men (U.S. Office of Indian Affairs. Indian Land Research Unit 1935, 1:95). In 1943 an agreement was reached whereby governors were nominated and elected from the two plazas in alternate years. Under this agreement, the governing body con-

*311*

sisted of: the governor, one assistant, a head *fiscal* and four assistants, a Hunt chief and four assistants (not mentioned in the agreement), and four councilmen, two from each plaza; this agreement expired in 1945 (Aberle 1948:49, 91), and for a few years the governorship was once again a North Plaza office. A 1953 House Report (U.S. Congress. House. Committee on Interior and Insular Affairs 1953:49, 1228) showed no general council, no elected administrative body, no administrative board subcommittee, no constitution and bylaws, no charter, and, as of 1951, no governor for the Pueblo. In the late 1950s the Pueblo adopted a resolution reinstating alternation and providing for a stable form of civil government. This procedure obtained in 1974, facilitated by attainment of numerical and economic equality by South Plaza. The governor is elected for a two-year term; he is assisted by a lieutenant and by a 12-member council whose membership is staggered: six are elected with the governor, six are previous members. In addition, former governors serve as an advisory committee.

Smith (1966:128) reported that the factional schism had been reconciled by the mid-1960s, an observation probably based on the removal of the houserow separating North and South plazas, but this is true only with regard to civil authority; in 1974, the aboriginal ceremonial organization was still divided and vestigial, especially in South Plaza, although within each faction certain of the traditional practices still obtain, such as inheritance customs, kinship rules, and religious observances. While religious affairs are nominally in the hands of the men, they are dominated sub rosa by a few of the older women, who exert influence through male family members.

## Subsistence

Once characterized by the typical Pueblo susbsistence economy based on agriculture, San Ildefonso beginning in the mid-1920s experienced a shift to an economy centered around a cash nexus and based in large part on its arts and crafts. Some accounts (for example, Parsons 1939, 2:1082) imply that the shift was optative, farming abandoned in favor of commerce in pottery, but the more accurate understanding of cause and effect is that commerce was a solution to an already weakened agricultural economy. Farming as a means of livelihood became increasingly unrewarding in the late nineteenth century and first third of the twentieth because of population decrease and Anglo- and Spanish-American disregard for Pueblo land rights. The 1900 Annual Report of the Department of the Interior records that only 99 acres were under cultivation (ARCIA 1900, 1:293); in 1919 the Board of Indian Commissioners reported that San Ildefonso had probably suffered greater land loss through squatters than had any other Pueblo. In addition, commercial (non-Indian) timber removal on the hills above the Pueblo drastically affected the terrain and watershed.

Nearly 10 percent of Tewa deaths around the turn of the nineteenth century were from malnutrition (U.S. Office of Indian Affairs. Indian Land Research Unit 1935, 1:17). In the late 1930s Whitman (1940:440) found that only six farmers raised enough produce to support their families; earlier, the Tewa Basin Study indicated that probably not one farm produced enough food for its family.

Arts and crafts did not become a source of income until about 1925; Whitman (1940:404) states that the Pueblo around the turn of the century had come to rely so heavily on exchange with outside groups that some native crafts, especially basketry and weaving, had fallen into disuse; pottery at that time was made only for internal household or ceremonial use. But in the 1930s, because of the unusual number of women who were potters (figs. 6–7) and men who were painters (fig. 9) the Pueblo became known as a center of Indian arts and the source of their revival. In 1936 half the employed adult residents were artists (20 potters, 11 other artists, 22 farmers, 3 cattlemen, 7 lumbermen), and two-thirds of total annual income derived from arts and crafts ($12,825 compared to $6,246 for other employment). Without income from the arts, the Pueblo would have had the lowest family income of all Pueblos. The unemployment rate was only 5 percent (Burton 1936:34, 39).

Following World War II, the availability of stable employment at Los Alamos led to a decline in art activity among the males; in addition, a few returned to farming, and some who had been in the armed forces attended college on their veterans' benefits (Forbes 1950:237–239). In the 1950s some Pueblo income was produced through sale of land and gravel resources and leasing of 30 acres of land to a Los Alamos construction firm (U.S. Congress. House. Committee on Interior and Insular Affairs 1953:546–547). By the mid-1960s, unemployment had risen to as high as 53 percent; of a total labor force of 83 men, 39 had permanent jobs away from the Pueblo, 14 of them at Los Alamos. In addition, tribal funds made it possible to employ some men for temporary work on Pueblo projects. Farming as a means of livelihood had almost disappeared. Arts and crafts, predominantly pottery, and wage work continued in the 1970s to be virtually the only sources of income (Dozier 1970:13). There were two shops in the Pueblo, one in each plaza, both selling artwork from other Pueblos as well as that produced by San Ildefonsans, some of whom sold from their homes as well as through retail outlets outside the Pueblo.

## History

The San Ildefonsans trace their ancestry to north of Mesa Verde; their tradition holds that they migrated south to the Pajarito Plateau, establishing the villages of Potsuwi (Otowi) and Tsankawi before settling in approximately the present site, possibly around A.D. 1300.

Fig. 6. Rose Gonzales (*sǽ·povi* 'prickly-pear-cactus flower'), a South Plaza potter, who was known for blackware pots with carved designs. Some of these, in an unfired state, are on the shelf behind her. This style was popular in the 1970s in Santa Clara. The basket in foreground probably contains dry, sifted clay to which water was added to produce the clay she is working. The base was molded into a plate, and the sides were built up by the progressive addition of coils, which were then smoothed. Photograph by Fred K. Hinchman, 1936.

Fig. 8. San Ildefonso pottery styles. a, Polychrome water vessel in style of 1880s-1920s, painted with black and red stylized plant forms and geometric motifs on white-slipped background (see Guthe 1925), made about 1920 by Maria Martinez; b, black-on-black jar made by Maria and Julian Martinez in 1928, collected in 1942; c, contemporary jar of polished polychrome design made for sale by Crucita Calabaza (Blue Corn) in 1976, diameter about 24 cm, rest same scale.

Fig. 7. Maria Montoya Martinez (*póvi ka·* 'flower leaf'), probably the most famous Pueblo potter, has been since the 1920s the most active North Plaza potter. She was an innovator of the black-on-black style consisting of dull black paint on a polished black surface, a style that was followed by several members of her family and for which San Ildefonso became known (see Maxwell Museum of Anthropology 1974). She is shown here with a great-grandchild. Photograph by William H. Regan, Apr. 1964.

Fig. 9. Julian Martinez (*pokanu* 'sky trail(?)'), removing black-on-black painted ware from the ashes and partly burned cakes of manure in which it was fired. The pottery was made by his wife (fig. 7), and probably painted by him, which was a common division of labor. Julian Martinez was one of several San Ildefonso artists who went from painting on pottery to watercolor painting on paper as early as 1920 (Tanner 1973:98-101). Photograph taken Nov. 1937.

The date of first Spanish contact is uncertain, but the Pueblo seems to have been the headquarters of an expedition in 1593, and it was visited by Juan de Oñate in 1598. San Ildefonso played a leading role in the Pueblo Revolt of 1680, at which time it was the largest of the Tewa villages. One of its chiefs, Francisco, was with Popé, El Taqu (San Juan Pueblo), and Saca (Taos), a leader of the revolution (Hackett 1942, 1:xxxix, 2:239). The most resistant of the Tewa Pueblos in defiance of Diego de Vargas's reconquest, erroneously referred to as "bloodless," San Ildefonsans, along with people from other villages, fortified themselves atop Black Mesa and held out against the Spanish until 1694, two years longer than most other Pueblos. Yet another uprising occurred in 1696, when the San Ildefonsans killed two priests and once more took refuge on Black Mesa; this was the last of Pueblo armed resistance (Spicer 1962:165), but in 1793 a "suspicious meeting" at the Pueblo led to arrests, floggings, and the detention in chains of several men, although nothing was proved against them (Bancroft 1889:268).

## Religious Acculturation

San Ildefonso was of the Tewa Pueblos one of the least receptive to Christianity, and it was not until well into the nineteenth century that Roman Catholic practices were accepted and began to merge with aboriginal ceremonialism (Dozier 1961:150). The first mission at the Pueblo was built in 1617, destroyed in 1680 when its two religious were killed in the revolt (Hackett 1942, 1:109), rebuilt about 1694, destroyed again in the attempted revolt of 1696, and rebuilt again in 1717 (fig. 4) (Whitman 1947:4). The present church was built about 1905. Friction between the Church and the Pueblo continued through the eighteenth century. In the twentieth century, Catholic practices have merged with aboriginal ceremonialism: for example, the Pueblo feast day, January 23, in honor of the saint by whose name the Pueblo is known is celebrated with the Buffalo-Deer Dance (North Plaza) (figs. 10–12) and the *kʷítara* or Comanche Dance (South Plaza) (fig. 13).

## Education

The first government day school was opened in 1897 (U.S. Congress. House. Committee on Interior and Insular Affairs 1953:1580), but a contract school for which no opening date was recorded had been operating for about a decade before. Attendance was termed phenomenal by the 1899 Annual Report (ARCIA 1899, 1:247): with a capacity of 21, the average attendance was 17.34 in 1898 and 36.69 in 1899. By 1903, 24 percent of all residents spoke English, and of 45 school-age children, 43 were enrolled (ARCIA 1904:504). In 1910, 76 percent of school-age children were enrolled (compare San Juan, 69.5% and Santa Clara 54.3%); and 52 percent of the residents were English-speaking, compared to Santa

Smithsonian, NAA.

Fig. 10. Participants in the San Ildefonso's Day Buffalo-Deer Dance, also called Game-Animal Dance, 1908 or 1909. At left is a buffalo impersonator in buffalo headdress with eagle feathers and dance kilt (probably of hide), which is painted with a snake design and edged with metal tinklers. His face and chest are darkened and marked with white Xs. A gourd rattle is traditionally carried in one hand, and bow, arrows, and evergreen in the other. At center is a deer dancer in characteristic stance. At the right is a male side dancer in headdress consisting of a painted buffalo horn on one side and a fan of eagle feathers on the other. Costumes and position of dancers seem consistent with those in photographs taken as early as 1893 (Spinden 1915:113–114) and as late as 1968 (fig. 11). See Parsons (1929:197–198) and Kurath with Garcia (1969:199–217) for descriptions of the dance and dancers. Photograph by M.C. Stevenson.

Fig. 11. Buffalo-Deer Dance, San Ildefonso's Day 1968. (See Scully 1972:147–151 for other photographs in this series.) Photograph by Vincent Scully.

Mus. of N.M., Santa Fe: School of Amer. Research Coll.

Fig. 12. Detail of *Eleven Figures of the Animal Dancers* by Crescencio Martinez (Ta-e), sometimes credited along with other San Ildefonso artists as the founder of the modern school of American Indian painting (Dunn 1968:198-217). left to right, Deer dancer (shirt retouched), male buffalo dancer, female buffalo dancer. The woman's headdress, although in the shape of a buffalo head, is constructed of turkey feathers. One of a series of watercolor paintings of San Ildefonso dance figures commissioned by Edgar L. Hewett of the School of American Research in 1918 (Hewett 1918:67-69).

Mus. of N.M., Santa Fe.

Fig. 13. Comanche Dance (*kʷítara*). This dance, one of several borrowed ones, is generally performed immediately after the Buffalo-Deer Dance on San Ildefonso's Day. The men's dance steps, songs, and costumes, which include feather bonnets and feathered standards, show more of the western Oklahoma derivation than do those of women. See Kurath with Garcia (1969:233-235). Photograph by T. Harmon Parkhurst, probably around 1935.

Clara, 54 percent, and San Juan, 46 percent (U.S. Bureau of the Census 1915:241). By 1936, 73 percent were English-speaking (Burton 1936:34). By the 1960s English was the common second language of the Pueblo, in

**Table 1. Population, 1680-1973**

| Year | Total | Source |
|------|-------|--------|
| 1680 | 800 (estimate) | Hackett 1942, 1:xxxi |
| 1760 | 484 | Bancroft 1889:279 |
| 1790 | 240 | Burton 1936:46 |
| 1860 | 154 | U.S. Bureau of the Census 1915:105 |
| 1900 | 138 | U.S. Bureau of the Census 1915:105 |
| 1922 | 91 | Crane 1928:225 |
| 1937 | 131 | Parsons 1939, 1:frontispiece |
| 1948 | 170 | Stubbs 1950:47 |
| 1963 | 224 | U.S. Bureau of Indian Affairs 1963:22 |
| 1973 | 413 | Northern Pueblos Agency 1973 |

greater use than Spanish. In 1966, 53 pupils were attending the government day school (grades 1-6), 10 were in training beyond high school, and three were in college on Bureau of Indian Affairs scholarships (Smith 1966:129).

### Population

The notable population decrease after 1680 was due to deaths from warfare in the Pueblo Revolt and from post-revolution migrations. The smallpox epidemics of 1780-1781 and 1788-1789 had killed half the population of San Ildefonso by 1793 (Spicer 1962:166). In 1918 an influenza epidemic resulted in a large population loss (table 1).

### Synonymy†

San Ildefonso retains the name of the Spanish mission founded at the Pueblo in the sixteenth century. Variant spellings include San(t) Ilefonso, San Ildephonso, and San Yldefonzo.

The Rio Grande Tewa name of the Pueblo is *ṗoxʷoge* 'where the water runs through or cuts down through'; there is also an irregular derivative *ṗoxʷore* (normalized) for 'San Ildefonso Indian'. Early ethnographic sources show many attempts to write these forms, such as Powhoge, Pojuoge, and Ojoque, the last showing a failure to hear the initial *ṗ*.

A number of other languages use names that resemble the Rio Grande Tewa name to varying degrees and may be borrowings or partially cognate translations: Arizona Tewa posówe and pokwádi, Taos pähwâ″líta, said to mean 'where the river enters a canyon', Isleta p'áhwia'hlíap, Jemez *ṗæ̀·šogʸíʔ* (phonemicized; from *ṗæ̀·šó* 'San Ildefonso Indian'), Cochiti ṗákʰwetE (normalized), Santa Ana pákwiti. The Hopi call San Ildefonso sɨstavana-tewa (normalized) 'first Tewa', because it is the first Tewa Pueblo reached in traveling up the Rio

† This synonymy was compiled by Ives Goddard. Uncredited forms are from Harrington (1916:303-306), who has further alternants, or anonymous sources.

Grande. Navajo has *Tséta'kin* 'house between the rocks' (Robert W. Young, personal communication 1977). Oñate's 1598 form Bove is of uncertain explanation.

## Sources

Whitman's (1947) study is the major source of data on the Pueblo and the only one of book length. For information on the factional schism, Spicer (1962:496–498), though brief, is recommended. Marriott (1948) provides a novelistic but insightful and generally accurate picture of Pueblo life, 1890–1943. Parsons's (1929) study of social organization is valuable but by her own admission flawed by secrecy on the part of her informants and by her consequent failure to recognize and delineate structural changes resulting from factionalism. Bunzel (1929) provides a sound treatment of pottery aesthetic and technique.

# Nambe Pueblo

RANDALL H. SPEIRS

## Territory and Environment

Nambe (ˌnämˈbā) (figs. 1–2) is a small Pueblo located in Santa Fe County, 15 miles due north of Santa Fe, New Mexico, and 20 miles by road from there (see "Pueblos: Introduction," fig. 1, this vol.). The people of Nambe speak a dialect of Tewa, a Kiowa-Tanoan language also used in six other Pueblos.*

Figures on the area of land held by the Pueblo vary according to the source but agree that an official land grant, undoubtedly reflecting informally recognized boundaries (Twitchell 1914, 1:23–24, 481) of some 13,000 acres made in the mid-nineteenth century, was supplemented at the turn of the twentieth century with reservation land of about 6,500 acres. A couple of smaller land parcels acquired since then bring the total to some 20,000 acres. Claims to an additional 45,000 acres near the Santa Fe ski basin were brought by the Pueblo. In December 1976 the Pueblo rejected the government's offer of a cash payment in favor of further efforts to obtain the land. Some 300 acres of Pueblo land are suitable for farming, with the rest almost evenly divided between open grazing land and noncommercial timber and grazing land. In addition, the Pueblo leases another 2,000 acres from various government agencies for grazing purposes.

## Subsistence

Economic assets of the Pueblo are few, with the exception of Nambe Falls, a tourist attraction. However, plans are being drafted and submitted to various agencies for economic development, such as expansion of tourist facilities and augmenting irrigable land acreage, both to be accomplished by building a dam above Nambe Falls, and the building of a trailer park.

In the early 1970s a few families still grew gardens, about 10 families raised alfalfa, and a cattlemen's association numbered 10 members. A few Nambes were employed in Los Alamos or worked for local businesses, and several found employment in federal government programs. There were in 1972 virtually no native crafts. The Pueblo as a whole received interest from the United States treasury on monies held there in deposit for land claim compensation.

* For the spelling of Tewa words in the *Handbook,* see the orthographic footnote in "San Juan Pueblo," this vol.

## Culture

### Political Organization

Village business is conducted in a manner combining old and new ways. Although there is no written constitution, a governor and four other officials have been elected annually since 1960. These officials and past governors meet for business, but actual voting is restricted to the group of governors. Speaking to an issue is done in order of seniority. Meetings are opened in Tewa, but actual business may be discussed in either Tewa or English.

### Religion

Most Nambe inhabitants are, at least nominally, Roman Catholics, though several are of Protestant persuasion. The only Pueblo ceremony, apart from a tourist-oriented one held each July 4 at Nambe Falls, is that held on October 4 to honor Saint Francis with Catholic mass and traditional Indian dances.

Curtis (1907–1930, 17:61) noted at the turn of the century that many of the ceremonial functions of the village were "painfully decadent" and that religious practitioners were sought from outside, particularly Tesuque. The last cacique is said to have died in 1970 (Hume 1970), and there were no medicine or other societies in the 1970s, though one writer claimed that one ceremonial clown still functioned in the 1960s (Smith 1966:115). There was some interest in reviving portions of the Indian culture (Hume 1970).

### Social Organization

The moiety system was in the 1970s virtually nonfunctional, and though older records list many clans (for example, Hodge 1910c:15; Curtis 1907–1930, 17:64 gives 68, 34 extant and 34 extinct in 1924) no trace of these remains. The basic social unit is becoming more and more the nuclear family, and some kinship terms have virtually passed out of existence (true to a lesser extent in all Tewa Pueblos).

## History

Although one writer claims that "what this pueblo lacks in size it makes up in history" (Crocchiola 1966:2), historical data on Nambe are relatively meager, and little

Southwest Foundation for Audio-Visual Resources, Santa Fe, N.M.
Fig. 1. Nambe plaza area. Photograph by Peter Dechert, June 1977.

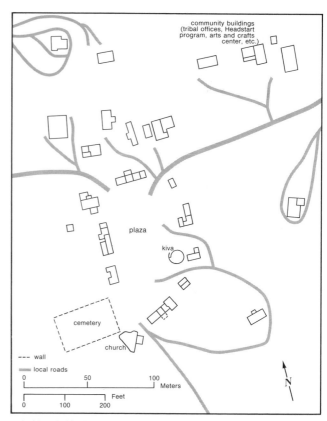

revised from Stubbs 1950:fig. 11.
Fig. 2. Nambe Pueblo.

archeological research has been done in the area. Older sources are either church records that make brief mention of the Pueblo (for example, Benavides 1916; Domínguez 1956; Tamarón y Romeral 1954) or military accounts that incorporate the name in a list of places visited (see Bailey 1940).

The first church was established in Nambe by the Franciscans in the early 1600s (Domínguez 1956:52). The most complete account is that given in 1776 by Domínguez (1956:51–60) during his inspection tour of missions and churches of the area, included in which are incidental accounts of Pueblo life. The church then extant had been built about 1729 to replace another that had been gutted in the Pueblo uprisings of 1680 and 1696, during which the assigned priests had been killed. This church stood until 1909, when it was destroyed in a storm. A more recent structure stood there till the 1960s, and a new building was dedicated in 1975.

There are ruins of a former Pueblo near the current site, and Hodge (1910c:15) mentions the names of several Pueblos that the inhabitants claim to have formerly inhabited. Bandelier states that "Tezuque [Tesuque], Nambé, and Pozuaque [Pojoaque] were formed after 1598 by people of San Ildefonso, Santa Clara, and San Juan settling there," and, though he does not document his claim, that "this is very important" (Bandelier 1966–1976, 2:172).

*Population*

Population figures vary with the source, statistics coming from those with vested interests being particularly unreliable (Bandelier and Hewett 1937:112, 125, 132). All indications are, however, that since the 1600s the number of inhabitants has never exceeded about 350 (Kelly 1940:362). All Pueblo population figures in Hodge (1910c:325) are disproportionately high for 1680 and 1856.

A steady decline in population has been attributed variously to infanticide or abortion (Bandelier 1966–1976, 2:173), outmigration and intermarriage with outsiders (Dorsey 1903:43), and executions for witchcraft (for example, Bandelier 1966–1976, 2:173; Benavides 1916:240; Hodge 1910c:15). By 1881 Lt. John G. Bourke was led to call Nambe "an inconsiderable pueblo of six or seven families" (Bloom 1933–1938, 12:72), and other writers (for example, Bandelier and Hewett 1937:94; Dorsey 1903:43; Smith 1966:116) have made dire predictions about the Pueblo's demise. However, a 1972 census counted a population of 356 (table 1). In 1970, with slightly fewer enrolled, a governor stated that about 80 percent were actually resident in the village area and that 25 percent of the enrollees were of pure Indian ancestry (Hume 1970). Compare this to 1963–1964 figures that showed total enrollment of 280 but only 48 percent in

318

Smithsonian, NAA.
Fig. 3. View of Nambe in 1879, facing northeast, taken from the roof of the church. The round kiva and a few additional buildings are out of frame to the right. Photograph by John K. Hillers.

residence (Smith 1966:115) and, in regard to ethnic composition, figures for 1956 that counted 45 percent as full-blood (Northern Pueblos Agency census figures). In 1972 children of male members were automatically enrolled, but children of female members married outside the Pueblo were not enrolled unless voted so by the Pueblo council.

The upsurge in both total and resident population is probably a result of a combination of several factors: increased health facilities, new government housing (fig. 7), more job opportunities (particularly government-financed or related), and a general participation in the

**Table 1. Population, 1972**

| Age | Male | Female | Total |
|---|---|---|---|
| 0–4 | 11 | 12 | 23 |
| 5–14 | 34 | 44 | 78 |
| 15–19 | 12 | 16 | 28 |
| 20–34 | 51 | 47 | 98 |
| 35–54 | 40 | 47 | 87 |
| 55–64 | 8 | 5 | 13 |
| 65 and over | 14 | 15 | 29 |
| Total | 170 | 186 | 356 |

SOURCE: Northern Pueblos Agency 1971.

"nationalistic" spirit moving among many Indian groups that provided an increasing feeling of and desire for group cohesiveness.

*Linguistic Acculturation*

Linguistic acculturation can be viewed from either of two viewpoints. The first involves the replacement of the native language by another language or languages either completely, or a certain percentage of the time in general, or within specific social contexts. The second involves the modification of the native language by the incorporation into it of elements—phonological, lexical, grammatical, perhaps stylistic—of any other language. Nambe shares with its neighbors both types.

In regard to attrition in the use of Tewa, general use of Spanish and a marked increase in the use of English are more prevalent in Nambe than in any of the other Pueblos (save Pojoaque, which because of its history has no dialect of its own). As early as 1776 Spanish was more entrenched in Nambe than in many other Pueblos, to the point that confession was made without the aid of an interpreter (Domínguez 1956:59). In the 1970s most of the older residents were trilingual; many of the younger were bilingual in Spanish and English but spoke little or no Tewa. The trend in the 1970s was toward monolinguality in English. In 1972, all at the Pueblo spoke

Fig. 4. Musical instruments: a, pair of gourd rattles; b, rattle made of bear claws; c, tortoise-shell drum; d, flute; e, bull-roarer. Length of d 37 cm, rest same scale; collected in 1964.

English. A large percentage of those over 20 and a few under 20 spoke Spanish. Most of those over 30, a half-dozen between 20 and 30, and none under 20 spoke Tewa. Total number of Tewa speakers was 70, 10 of these originally from other villages.

Reasons for this move away from Tewa include, doubtless, generalized culture contact factors involving mass media, greater mobility, and schooling patterns (children are now bused out to public school; virtually 100 percent complete high school, in which they participate in a wide range of social activities with non-Indians; some are taking post-high school training). But it is probably the case that, since these forces are operative to a large extent in all the other Pueblos and yet Tewa retention is far higher in the others, the greatest single factor in the loss of the language in Nambe is marriage patterns.

Using round figures, of some 90 Nambe marriages, 70 are with non-Indians, 10 are with non-Tewa Indians, and only 10 are with Tewas from Nambe or elsewhere. Since this has made Spanish or (increasingly) English the language of the home in at least 80 out of 90 instances (a certain percentage of even Tewa-Tewa marriages involve English a good portion of the time in the home), and since there are no monolingual grandparents to force youngsters to learn the language, the results are inevitable.

Lack of strong ceremonial life has also undoubtedly contributed its toll. Apart from the amount of Tewa used in council meetings, it can be fairly said that all communication in Tewa is among adults, seldom with and never among children; and even adult communication involves the use of Spanish or English more often than Tewa.

The only foreseeable forces that could reverse this trend would be a conscious inclusion of the language in a general cultural revival, or adoption of a bilingual program of education for Indian children in the schools, such as is increasingly being carried on among many Indian groups including neighboring San Juan Pueblo.

The grammatical and lexical command that Tewa speakers have of either Spanish or English is a function of many factors, and abilities vary from near native command to various nonstandard levels. Regarding phonology, those who are fluent in Spanish conform closely to the Spanish of the area. However, the English spoken by the majority of Tewas, even many who are monolingual in English but have been raised in the Pueblo, is generally with a marked accent involving vowel modification, devoicing of syllable-final voiced obstruents, frequent substitution of glottal stop for syllable-final dental stop, use of dental stop for initial dental spirant, and a few other phonological shifts.

Fig. 5. Pabla Tafolla (possibly Tafoya), carrying a blackware water jar. She is wearing a blue or black woolen manta of twilled weave with extensive embroidery at the edges. Stevenson (1911:118, pl. 8) identified her as a Nambe girl wearing a dress from Tesuque, noting only that the Tesuque claimed in 1879 that the elaborately embroidered dresses of blue and red were of their manufacture. However, since weaving had not stopped in Nambe until around 1870, it is possible that this embroidered garment was woven there (Douglas 1939a:159). Her belt is also woven. Photograph by John K. Hillers, 1880.

SPEIRS

The second type of linguistic acculturation, modification of the native tongue by borrowing from another, has been dealt with for the Tewa in part by Dozier (1956), whose thesis is, in summary, that (1) Tewa has been resistant to wholesale borrowing from Spanish because of general resistance to acculturation, a result of attempts at enforced change in early days of contact; (2) borrowings such as there have been are restricted primarily to nominal designations for items of Spanish or Mexican introduction, and these have retained much of their Spanish phonology, with Tewa phonology, morphology, and syntax little affected; (3) English loanwords are much more acceptable than Spanish, especially with younger speakers; and (4) each speaker is aware at any given point that a given item is borrowed, and in a social situation involving the presence of a speaker of Spanish or English, Tewa forms can replace the non-Tewa forms. This last mentioned is a function of the fact that Tewa has devices for coinage of new descriptive expressions and extension of meaning of old Tewa words. Dozier draws examples from various categories: persons and domesticated animals, domesticated plants, religious designations, government terms, and material items.

Some modifications and additions must be made to this thesis. While younger speakers do freely borrow from English, many Spanish nouns are firmly entrenched, and when asked for a Tewa word for a given object that is customarily named in Spanish, the reply is usually, "We say that in Spanish." In these cases the Spanish word is presumably felt to be more "Tewa" than the English equivalent, probably because of its long history of use.

Verbs are quite frequently expressed by compounding a non-Tewa (usually English) word with the Tewa verb $?o?$ 'to do', this type of compound already being a productive pattern in the language. Thus, $dé·$-work-$?o?$ 'I work' might be heard instead of $dé·tô·?o?$ (from $tô·$ 'work'). This pattern is used even when the Tewa verb is built on a different pattern, for example, $dó$-spank-$?o?$ 'I spank him' for $dóx^wæ?$. Some Spanish verbs, however, are used with Tewa tense-mode suffixes to form what sounds like a native Tewa verb, for example, $dóresíbínde?$ 'I receive him' from $recibir$ 'to receive'.

Apart from nominal and verbal elements, outside influence on the language is negligible. An exception, particularly in Nambe, is the use of $poke$ (Spanish $porque$) 'because' as a conjunction, usually with resultant modification of clause structure.

In normal conversation mixed constructions can be heard in the speech of the old as well as the young. While, as Dozier (1956) points out, choice of a pure Tewa form

Smithsonian, NAA.

Fig. 6. Nambe officials in 1880. left, War captain, also identified as Nambe's chief hunter, carries a rifle and wears a bear-claw necklace, a powder horn, and a pouch. right, Antonio José Vigil, the governor, appears to be wearing leggings over cotton trousers. Both posed sitting on a Pueblo rabbitskin blanket or robe. Rabbitskin blankets, woven from thin strips of skin, predate woolen blankets in the Pueblo region (Hough 1918:262). Photographs by John K. Hillers, 1880.

*321*

NAMBE PUEBLO

may be deliberate when non-Tewas are present, it is difficult to discover the sociolinguistic factors that determine choice of form at other times.

In general, English words used in a Tewa matrix retain the pronunciation that the speaker would use if he were speaking English, no effort being made to "Tewa-ize" them. However, Spanish words have undergone various degrees of modification: some are radically altered so that the result conforms completely to Tewa phonological structure; some are partially altered, retaining some non-Tewa element, be it a specific phoneme or an atypical combination of phonemes; and some are taken over intact. Of these last, some may happen to conform to Tewa patterns, others may not. Usually, though not always, Tewa high or glide tone coincides with Spanish stress.

Reasons for the various levels of modification, as well as reasons for various types of anomalies, might be found through a knowledge of the exact dialect of the early Spanish contacts or the details of Tewa historical phonology. (There is little actually recorded of Tewa prior to 1910 that is of any linguistic value, and general proto-Tanoan reconstructions leave many questions unanswered.) Perhaps some words came not directly from Spanish but were filtered through another Indian language. Likely there has been some temporal layering of borrowings, as has been suggested for Yaqui (Spicer 1943:420-422) and Taos (Trager 1944).

Differences among Tewa dialects mainly involve certain elements of phonology, such as vowel length and nasalization, use of syllable-final *n* before *d*, occasional substitution of phonemes including tones, and (most noticeable to the Tewa themselves and the subject of much good-natured joking) the presence in the Santa Clara dialect of a ʒ phoneme, which substitutes in many instances for the *y* of the other Pueblos. There are also some vocabulary items peculiar to each Pueblo, and some that undergo a semantic shift. Finally, a few differences exist in verbal tense-mode suffixes and pronominal prefixes. As isoglosses are drawn involving the foregoing, various dialect patterns emerge, some coterminous with Pueblo boundaries, some grouping Pueblos together in various ways, and some revealing intra-Pueblo divisions.

## Synonymy†

The name Nambe is from Spanish Nambé, a rendition of the Tewa name *nanbeʔ* (pronounced [nambeʔ]). This is uniformly etymologized as *nan* 'earth' and *beʔ* 'roundness', though the specific referent of the roundness is variously interpreted. Round hill or valley (Hodge 1910c:15), the numerous round sandstone and clay columns and cones nearby (Curtis 1907-1930, 16:263, 17:61), roundish earth (Harrington 1916:381), circle of land (former governor, personal communication 1972), and earth enclosed with hills have all been suggested. Early variant spellings include Namba, Nampé, Nambi, and others.

Jemez and the Keresan languages generally use borrowings of the Tewa (or Spanish) name. The Tiwa names appear to be loan translations with cognate elements: Taos námmúluva 'earth round-object' (Curtis 1907-1930, 16:261), Picuris nammóʼloʼna 'little mound of earth', Isleta namburuap. Jemez has páshiukwa (Curtis 1907-1930, 16:261). A Hopi name for Nambe and Tesuque is tiˑkwiveʔ-teˑwa 'Tewa near the mountains' (normalized).

As the seat of a mission the Pueblo was referred to as San Francisco de Nambé.

## Sources

There are few whose transcriptions of the Tewa language can be relied on; these include (in chronological order) Harrington, Hoijer, Dozier, Yegerlehner, and Speirs (1966). Harrington's works (1910, 1912, 1916, 1947; Henderson and Harrington 1914; Robbins, Harrington, and Freire-Marreco 1916) suffer chiefly from frequent (and admitted) failure to record tone and vowel length but on the other hand overmeticulously record other facets of phonetic detail. Besides providing a voluminous vocabulary, Harrington usually attempts to break polymorphemic words into their constituent morphemes and sketches some phases of the grammar (1910). Hoijer and Dozier's (1949) phonemic inventory has been checked by Speirs (1966), whose analysis differs in positing one less tone and in recognizing stress. Dozier's (1953) description of the Tewa verb is sketchy, its chief value lying in

*Albuquerque Journal*, N.M.

Fig. 7. Nambe housing. Nambe was the first Pueblo to accept federal government housing. In 1967-1968 the first low-cost Department of Housing and Urban Development houses, of the type at left, were built. Subsequent houses, of the type at right, are more Pueblo in character (Hume 1970). Photograph by Bill Hume, 1970.

† This synonymy was prepared by Randall H. Speirs and Ives Goddard. Uncredited forms cited or referred to are from Harrington (1916:358-361).

voluminous exemplification; but it is marred by frequent misspellings and typographical errors. Yegerlehner (1959, 1959a) deals with Hopi-Tewa, geographically separated from Rio Grande Tewa for nearly three centuries but retaining a high degree of similarity to it. Speirs's publications include some of cultural and pedagogical nature (1968, 1968a, 1969, 1969a, 1970, 1971) and translations of Bible portions and hymns (1969b, 1971a, 1971b). Speirs (1966) deals with Tewa phonology, morphology, and number categories. He provides a lengthy bibliography of both published and unpublished materials and one chapter devoted to describing and evaluating all works that incorporate any reasonable amount of Tewa.

In addition, Hale (1967), in a comparative study, uses Tewa examples elicited by himself (in contrast to Whorf and Trager 1937, whose Tewa examples are taken from Harrington), but he differs from both Hoijer and Dozier (1949) and Speirs (1966) in respect to phonemic inventory.

Sources mentioning land boundaries include Twitchell (1914, 1), in which old Spanish records are quoted, and Kappler (1904–1941, 2), which gives the delineation about 1900. Description of the present status is found at the Northern Pueblos Agency in Santa Fe.

Ethnographic material from the hands of anthropologists is confined mainly to scattered references in Parsons (1929, 1939) and brief mention by Bandelier (1966–1976; Bandelier and Hewett 1937). Curtis (1907–1930, 17) gives a fairly lengthy ethnographic sketch, but his strength lay mainly in his remarkable ability as a photographer.

Lieutenant Bourke in the nineteenth century (Bloom 1933–1938, 12) and travelers in the early part of the twentieth century (Dorsey 1903; Forrest 1929) make brief mention of the Pueblo.

References to the situation in the mid-twentieth century are found in Smith (1966), a volume written for the New Mexico State Planning Office; and Hume's (1970) newspaper article.

Without question the most complete overall account of the Pueblo is a popularized one by Crocchiola (1966), which draws on a wide variety of sources ranging from archival records to newspaper accounts but is marred by lack of adequate documentation.

# Pojoaque Pueblo

MARJORIE F. LAMBERT

Pojoaque (ˌpōˈhwäkē) is a small Indian settlement located 16 miles north of Santa Fe at the junction of U.S. 285, the main highway to Taos, and New Mexico Route 4, which leads to San Ildefonso, Santa Clara, and Los Alamos. It is the smallest of the six Tewa villages.* Its name rarely appears on published lists of New Mexico Pueblos, much to Pojoaque's resentment.

The village conducts no ceremonies, nor is there a cacique. Nevertheless, the Pojoaque people treasure their kinship with other Tewa-speaking Indians in the northern Rio Grande valley, especially those of Nambe and Santa Clara. Cultural identity is maintained through their participation in religious rites and other communal events in related Indian Pueblos. They also attend a Pojoaque valley Roman Catholic church along with Anglo and Spanish-American parishioners.

In the late nineteenth century, although greatly reduced in population, Pojoaque was still governed by a cacique (the governor), his two lieutenants, a war chief, two war captains (preservers of the peace), and a *sacristán*. This body of officials looked after communal affairs and the Pueblo land. The last cacique died around 1900. The two war captains had died shortly before the turn of the century, with no one to replace them, and after 1910 the position of *sacristán* was no longer filled.

Since the early 1930s the Pueblo has become primarily a land-holding entity that administers tribal funds and conducts communal business affairs. Once a year a new governor is chosen. The council is comprised of the governor, lieutenant governor, past tribal officials, a secretary, and a treasurer. It is not uncommon for a woman to hold one of the last two offices, and one woman has served five times. In January 1974 Pojoaque elected a woman to serve as governor, and the council then consisted entirely of women with the exception of the sheriff, whose position is honorary. Council meetings are held every two weeks, or oftener.

## Territory

In 1940 the gross area of the Pojoaque grant was 13,438.15 acres, but through rulings of the United States District Court and the Pueblo Lands Board, 1,856.95 acres were determined to be of non-Indian title; in the 1970s there was still some bitterness within the Pueblo regarding this decision. Subsequently the Pueblo has bought up a few private claims and also relinquished several acres of land.

From the 1680 Pueblo Revolt onward, Pojoaque suffered serious losses of some of its most fertile land. In the Spanish contact period choice land was usurped by non-Indians. From time to time, land was also given to Spanish neighbors for favors extended, especially while owners were away. But the governors and council of elders have become good business managers, and the use of any of their land, other than by the tribe, is now by lease only.

The Pueblo owns land of considerable commercial value fronting U.S. 285. The tribal council has drafted and executed a long-term program for commercial development. They have built and leased La Mesita Restaurant, Nambe Mills (pottery), and an attractive pueblo-style shopping center, Pojoaque Pueblo Plaza (fig. 1), which houses Northern Pueblo Enterprises, Inc., a bank, beauty parlor, auto parts store, cleaning establishment, arts and crafts shop, and 10 office units. Other income-producing ventures have been planned. The main function of the governor has become that of "developer" of the industrial area (Gov. Alvin Duran, personal commu-

*Albuquerque Journal,* N.M.
Fig. 1. Pojoaque Pueblo plaza, looking east. Photograph by Bill Hume, Oct. 1970.

---

* For the spelling of Tewa words in the *Handbook,* see the orthographic footnote in "San Juan Pueblo," this vol.

nication 1972). Income derived from these enterprises is divided among all tribal members, resident and nonresident. In spite of the resulting prosperity, some of the people question the value of so much commercial activity coming to the reservation, and leases are given only for a 10-year period. The council also insists that Indians have top job priority.

## Culture

In 1972 only one Pojoaque man farmed, and alfalfa was the sole crop (table 1). A water shortage partly accounted for the lack of farming activity. Fruit trees were abundant, but the tribe was no longer dependent on yield from these. A few families had small vegetable gardens, but many bought their produce outside the Pueblo. Some livestock was raised, usually one animal for each family member up to five.

A Santa Clara woman married into the Pueblo was a potter in 1972, but Pojoaque had no active arts and crafts program. Unemployment was not a problem, since some of the Indians worked in Nambe Mills, and others were employed in various capacities in Santa Fe, Española, and elsewhere. With income derived from commercial and forestry leases, as well as from their jobs, the people were very well off when compared to many other Rio Grande valley Indians.

The people live in individual homes, some of which are on the west side of the highway toward Española and Taos. A pueblo-style community building and additional houses are located to the east of the highway. Most of the homes are attractive and prosperous looking, and the majority are indistinguishable in style from similar dwellings throughout Spanish and Anglo New Mexico.

In the eighteenth century Domínguez (1956:63) described "the little pueblo of Pojoaque and its church. . . . The pueblo forms a plaza in front of the church. . . . The four sides of the plaza consist of four tenements, which leave a larger space in the middle, with three passageways. . . . The church is outside the plaza that faces southwest." Although potsherds and outlines of earlier dwellings are noticeable, none of this old Pueblo is now visible except a fragmentary section of the old church (fig. 2).

## Table 1. Pueblo Land Use, 1971

| Type of Land | Acreage |
|---|---|
| Open grazing land and forest | 11,101 |
| Irrigated farm land | 36 |
| Other, including commercial | 463 |
| Total | 11,600 |

SOURCE: U.S. Bureau of Indian Affairs 1971a.

## History

Anasazi antecedents of Pojoaque were in the general area about A.D. 900, and possibly earlier. Indian occupation of this region has since been constant. The more immediate ancestors of the Pojoaque Indians are Tewas whose settlements became numerous in the northern Rio Grande valley in the late thirteenth and early fourteenth centuries. Archeological investigations conducted on the Pojoaque reservation have revealed substantial evidence of a large prehistoric population, particularly from A.D. 1300 into protohistoric times. The only ditch supplying Pojoaque is a remnant of a more elaborate irrigation system operated by farmers supplying crops for the inhabitants during the prehistoric period (Ellis 1967a:16-27).

No serious trouble seems to have befallen Pojoaque until the arrival of the Spaniards in the mid-sixteenth century. A map depicting Indian Pueblos of 1598, when Juan de Oñate arrived in New Mexico, shows Pojoaque as being in its twentieth-century locale (Hammond and Rey 1953,1: opp. p. 584; Jenkins 1972:117).

There are two major causes of the socioreligious, economic, and subsequent physical decline of Pojoaque, the first being effects of the 1680 Pueblo Revolt. Pojoaque, along with Tesuque and other Tewa-speaking villages, took an active part. Among other acts of resistance, for which eventually they suffered, "they have killed, in the pueblo of Pojoaque, Captain Francisco Ximenes; Don Joseph de Goitia, and the wife and family of Francisco Ximenes; and there was no sign of Doña Petronila de Salas, and eight or ten children whom she has" (Hackett 1942, 1:10).

Spanish colonization, which took place after Diego de Vargas's reconquest of New Mexico in 1692-1694, also took a serious toll. As a consequence the Pojoaque tribe was greatly decimated and scattered; however, in 1706 Pojoaque was reestablished by Gov. Francisco Cuerbo y Valdes, with five families being settled there. By 1749 it was a *visita* of Nambe. In 1782 it again had a resident priest, who also ministered to Nambe and Tesuque (Benavides 1945:236).

The Pueblo population numbered 79 in 1712, but by the latter part of the eighteenth century only 53 Indians were living there. The resident population was reduced to 32 in 1870. Forty inhabitants are listed for the year 1890. During the nineteenth century the population became so small that ceremonies, so important to the tribe, could no longer be conducted, nor could secular affairs be administered. The steady encroachment on the best farming and grazing land by non-Indians contributed further to lowering the morale and to economic loss. In order to survive, the people gradually left to join relatives in other Pueblos or to seek a livelihood in the Anglo world.

In the early twentieth century Pojoaque was described as abandoned by Indians (Hodge 1910f:274). Harrington

Smithsonian, NAA.

Fig. 2. Two views of Pojoaque in 1899, showing the old church, now in ruins. top, One wall and the roof of the building at right are deteriorating, perhaps indicating that the building has been abandoned. A falling ceiling beam has been braced with a log where part of the roof has fallen in, revealing its construction: round beams extending the width of the room and anchored into the wall are crossed with poles, then with willow rods of brush, and finally covered over with layers of moistened and dry earth (Mindeleff 1891:148-151). bottom, View showing the plaza in front of the church. Photographs by Adam C. Vroman.

(1916) found no one living there in 1909, although he located two Pojoaque families living in Santa Fe, and still another in Nambe. But there is reason to believe that five houses north of the old church were occupied in 1909-1910 (Ellis 1967a:8). An Indian born in the Pueblo in 1910 stated that there were three families in residence in that year. He grew up in Santa Clara, where an uncle lived who periodically went to Pojoaque to check the land belonging to his wife and nephew. For many years there were also others who returned from Nambe, Santa Clara, and elsewhere to inspect their holdings.

Pojoaque people recognize that they are of "mixed blood," even though they insist on a Tewa identity. They attribute their mixed ancestry to the tribe's forced dispersal in bygone times and to their small numbers, so few that marriage within the village was not feasible. Much of the seventeenth- and eighteenth-century population was lost or absorbed by other Pueblos. Those who have lived in the Pueblo since the resettlement in the early 1930s are an admixture of Tewas, Tiwas, and some Spanish-Americans.

When Pojoaque Indians departed from their homes to join kinfolk in related Pueblos or to work in the White society, they assumed that their land and affairs would be cared for by relatives and friends. Valuable tribal documents said to have been placed for safekeeping with trusted persons, including those pertaining to water rights and the original land grant from Spain, have disappeared.

The governor, war chief, and another tribal officer appeared before the surveyor general of the United States on June 28, 1856, and claimed title to their land on the basis of the original land grants to all the Pueblos. They stated that 40 years previously a land suit occurred between a Mexican and the Pueblo, during which the deed was presented to the alcalde of Chimayo as evidence in the case; this deed was never seen again. Further proof given was that their church bell was dated 1710. On September 30, 1856, the surveyor general made a favorable report regarding Pojoaque (Surveyor General's Report 1856:2-3). The grant was subsequently confirmed by an act of Congress, December 22, 1858. On November 1,

NAA, Smithsonian.

Fig. 3. Jesús Medina (top) and Bautista Talache (or Talaché), photographed while visiting Washington in 1905. Medina wears silver hoop earrings and has a silk kerchief around his forehead; his hair is wrapped *chongo*-style, probably with a traditional woven band, red with a green and white pattern. Talache wears a commercial blanket; his hair is braided and wrapped with yarn. Photographs by T.W. Smillie.

1864, it was patented by the United States. The Pueblo governors, Pojoaque's included, traveled to Washington to receive the patents, and, with these, President Abraham Lincoln presented each with a silver-headed cane. There are several versions of the disappearance of the original Pojoaque cane. It has since been replaced and hangs in a place of honor in the governor's house, until it is taken down and carried to meetings.

It is generally agreed that Pojoaque was not occupied by Indians between about 1912 and about 1934, although some of its people were constantly in the vicinity. However, Hewett's (1930:92) statement that he watched the Pueblo dwindle from about 20 Indians in 1897 to final extinction in 1922 may mean that someone was living in the village as late as the early 1920s.

Antonio José Tapia is credited with Pojoaque's resettlement. After living in Colorado where he had gone to work in 1912, he returned to New Mexico in the early 1930s, and his efforts from then on were, with the assistance of five or six other Pojoaque Indians, directed toward making a "new Pojoaque." Landgrabbers and interlopers were evicted from what had turned into a Spanish-American settlement. Livestock owners were ordered to remove their animals from the land, and by 1934 the Pojoaque grant was fenced (Lambert 1942-1970).

Pojoaque Indians, in the 1930s numbering 14, were reimbursed for losses they had suffered. These payments acted as an incentive to other Indians to return to the reservation. No more individuals are said to have been accepted after a 1957 deadline (see table 2).

*Education*

An excellent public school complex is built on land leased from the Pueblo for 99 years. Included among the students are children from Nambe, San Ildefonso, and Tesuque, and from Spanish, Anglo, and Black American families in the area. Pojoaque was compensated for the lease of this land, but in spite of the large Indian enrollment, it had no Indian representative on the school board until the 1960s. Representation came through the Pueblo's insistence. The governor, or a member of the council, attends meetings concerning school affairs.

The tribe has scholarships for students who wish an education beyond the high school. Youths attend trade schools, secretarial and business colleges, the police academy, and institutions of higher learning.

Because of the Pueblo's business acumen, as well as its pride in its accomplishments, Pojoaque's future seems assured. Despite a lack of cultural attributes usually associated with Rio Grande Pueblos, the village concentrates on keeping its Tewa identity. Traditionally Pojoaque was once the center for all the surrounding Tewa

Table 2. Population Distribution in 1970

| Age Group | Male | Female | Total | Family Groups[a] | Single Heads[b] |
|---|---|---|---|---|---|
| 0-4 | 4 | 6 | 10 | | |
| 5-14 | 14 | 22 | 36 | | |
| 15-19 | 3 | 4 | 7 | | |
| 20-34 | 12 | 18 | 30 | | |
| 35-54 | 7 | 4 | 11 | | |
| 55-64 | 2 | 3 | 5 | | |
| over 65 | 4 | 1 | 5 | | |
| Total | 46 | 58 | 104 | 20 | 14 |

SOURCE: U.S. Bureau of Indian Affairs 1971.
[a] Household head and family (one or two parents with children).
[b] One-person head (unmarried).

Fig. 4. Pojoaque in 1949, facing north toward the Jemez Mountains. Road in foreground is probably N.M. Route 4. Photographer unidentified.

Fig. 5. Pojoaque community center (top left), used for council meetings and other functions. The three buildings at bottom are dwellings, one with pitched roof and the others of more traditional adobe construction. Photograph by Peter Dechert, facing east, June 1977.

Pueblos. The people feel that Pojoaque is again becoming the major Tewa center.

## Synonymy†

The Spanish name of Pojoaque appears to be a borrowing of the Tewa name, which is *posuwǽge* 'drink-water place', though the borrowing of *s* as Spanish j (phonetically [x]) is unusual (Harrington 1916:336). Variant spellings in Spanish include Pojuaque, Pujuaque, Pajagüe, Pusuaque, Pasúque, and (showing failure to hear the initial *p̓*) Ojuaque and Ohuaqui. Tewa pokwádi, given as a synonym by Hodge (1910f), with variants, is a name for the people of San Ildenfonso.

Recorded names in other languages are probable borrowings from Tewa, like Picuris ásoná and Isleta p'asuiáp, and borrowings from Spanish, such as Cochiti pohwáke.

† This synonymy was prepared by Ives Goddard. Uncredited forms are from Harrington (1916:334–336), who gives additional spelling variants, or anonymous sources.

As a Spanish mission the Pueblo is referred to as Nuestra Señora de Guadalupe de Pojoaque (Domínguez 1956:60). A 1749 census refers to it as San Francisco Pajagüe (Villagrá 1900, 1:96).

## Sources

Several standard publications on the Pueblos as a whole provide material pertinent to Pojoaque: Domínguez (1956) on the missions, Hackett (1942) on the Pueblo Revolt and reconquest, Hammond and Rey (1953) on Juan de Oñate and Spanish colonization, Harrington (1916) on ethnography, Hewett (1930) on prehistory, and Jenkins (1972) on Spanish land grants.

Ellis (1967a) is an important study of the water rights of four Pueblos, prepared for the Bureau of Indian Affairs. Much information pertaining to Pojoaque vital statistics and economy, especially for 1970–1972, is to be found in the files of the Bureau of Indian Affairs, Eight Northern Pueblos Office, Santa Fe.

# Tesuque Pueblo

SANDRA A. EDELMAN AND ALFONSO ORTIZ

## Language and Territory

Tesuque (te$^{l}$sōōkē) (figs. 1–2) is the southernmost of six extant Rio Grande Tewa Pueblos and the closest to Santa Fe, New Mexico, which is nine miles south (see "Pueblos: Introduction," fig. 1, this vol.). The language is Tewa, a member of the Kiowa-Tanoan language family.* The village is situated on the Tesuque River in the approximate center of Tesuque land holdings, which consist of 17,024.41 acres—16,706.36 from the original Spanish grant, confirmed in 1858 by the United States Congress, plus the 318.05-acre "Aspen Ranch," a compensation purchase made in 1937 (Aberle 1948:81). The nearest Tewa neighbors are those at Nambe Pueblo, with whom Tesuque has traditionally had a notably close relationship. The nearest non-Tewa Indian neighbors are those at Keres-speaking Cochiti Pueblo, some 30 miles southwest of Santa Fe.

## Culture

Tesuque has remained, in spite of its proximity first to Spanish, then to Anglo-American influence, the least-known and most conservative of the Tewa villages. Harrington (1916:385) reported that his work there on place-names was first made difficult and then forbidden altogether. Bandelier and Hewett (1937:94) described the Pueblo as being recalcitrant to acculturation, still hostile to White visitors. In the mid-1960s, it was found to be a "small, close-knit community. . . . dedicated to its old ways" (Smith 1966:150). The contrast between these reports and Lt. John G. Bourke's account of his friendly reception in 1881 (Bloom 1933–1938, 7:311–315) would indicate an increasing reluctance to accept Anglo-Americans.

With minor exceptions, Tesuque is culturally identical to the other Tewa Pueblos. The society is dual, divided into Winter and Summer moieties that function reciprocally, uniting at certain times critical for the life of the individual (life crisis rites) and for the general welfare of the community (maintenance of fields, harvesting, transitions of authority). Moiety affiliation is patrilineal, but recruitment is ambiguous (that is, does not follow a rigid

Southwest Foundation for Audio-Visual Resources, Santa Fe, N.M.
Fig. 1. Central portion of Tesuque Pueblo. Photograph by Peter Dechert, June 1977.

revised from Historic Amer. Buildings Survey, Natl. Park Service, map for 1973.
Fig. 2. Central portion of Tesuque Pueblo.

---

* For the spelling of Tewa words in the *Handbook,* see the orthographic footnote in "San Juan Pueblo," this vol.

pattern), and the usual exogamous marriage function of the moiety structure is absent (Ortiz 1969:44-46). Parsons (1929:91) noted a tendency for the moieties to be endogamous.

Parsons's (1929:82) informant identified Cloud People, Red Stone, Weasel, and Sun clans in addition, erroneously, to Turquoise and Squash, which are not clans but alternate names for the Winter and Summer moieties respectively. Spinden (1933:120) remarked upon a clan similar to the San Juan Corn Silk Women, but Jocano (1963:11) found no evidence of a clan structure during his month's residence at the Pueblo. Dozier (1970:165-166) holds that clan names among the Tewa represent an imperfect diffusion of the clan concept borrowed from the Keresans and that a clan system as such does not figure in the religious, governmental, or social structure. In his view, clan names among the Tewa are merely terms with some religious significance that are inherited variously from either parent (Dozier 1961:105). Kinship is reckoned bilaterally; kinship rules are flexible, certain things being patrilineal, such as moiety affiliation, and others matrilineal, such as name giving.

Property inheritance does not depend on gender, offspring of either sex inheriting equally (Parsons 1929:38). Dozier (1970:134, 174) specifies the existence of a kachina organization at Tesuque but defines it as weak. Parsons (1929:163) listed as kachinas in a 1927 dance the Corn, Squash Flower, and Yellow Flower kachinas. There is an annual outdoor kachina dance in October, when the Pueblo is sealed off to outsiders.

Sociopolitical organization follows the basic Tewa pattern: Winter and Summer chiefs are attended by heads of what Dozier (1970:133) calls "sodalities," and Ortiz (1969:61 ff.) calls societies of "Made People." Some deviation from the pattern may be noted for Tesuque. Ortiz (1969:81) indicates for San Juan the Bear Medicine, Winter and Summer clown, Hunt, Scalp, and Women's societies. Parsons listed for Tesuque two medicine societies: Flint and Fire, or *témá ke·* 'Keres bear' and *téwa ke·* 'Tewa bear' (1929:122); three clown societies: the Quirana *(kʷíráná),* composed of both sexes and the ultimate chief of which is in Cochiti, considered by the Tesuque to be the source (lake or spring) of the Quirana (1929:126), and the *témá ǩohsa·* and *téwa ǩohsa·,* corresponding to the Keresan Koshare (1929:123); a Snake (curing) society peculiar to Tesuque; and the customary Hunters', Warriors' (Scalp), and Women's societies.

The rest of the village population is comprised either of Dry Food People or of those not yet initiated into the community (usually children). Depending on age, sex, and religious status, the individual may be a Made Person at one time and a Dry Food Person at another.

To this indigenous structure is added what was originally a Spanish institution, continued in slightly altered form by the United States government, and now thoroughly integrated with the aboriginal organization. These "Spanish officials" are elected by the moiety heads and the *ťowa?ê·* and consist of: a governor, two lieutenant governors, two *fiscales* (church caretakers), and a treasurer (an appointive office and the only one instituted by

Natl. Arch., Washington.

Fig. 3. View of plaza facing southwest (from northeast entrance) showing corn (probably just harvested) on ground and roof-tops, beehive ovens also at both levels, and the use of pots as chimney tops. Wooden plough in foreground. Photograph by John K. Hillers, probably Sept. or early Oct. 1879 or 1880.

TESUQUE PUEBLO

the U.S. government) (Aberle 1948:91). The usual term of office is one year, elections being held in December and installation in January. Tesuque follows the unique practice of rotating the governorship among four men; and the *fiscales,* whose duties in other Pueblos are usually only church-connected, have added responsibilities as administrative assistants to the governor and of helping with work on the irrigation ditches. Tesuque is the only Tewa Pueblo that does not regularly elect a sheriff, those duties being assumed by one of the lieutenant govenors (Aberle 1948:35, 38, 41). These officers, together with former governors and the war chief, comprise the council, which acts as liaison between the Pueblo and outside contacts.

The position of the War chief (who has, at Tesuque, a lieutenant and two helpers) is unique among the officials in that his duties, although primarily religious, encompass civil ones as well: a seat on the council, with concomitant supervision of work on the irrigation ditches, and certain police functions (Aberle 1948:39). The ambiguity of his position, and that of the group he heads, the *íowa?ê·* (see Ortiz 1969), led Dozier (1961) to assign the office to Spanish derivation. However, Parsons (1939, 2:1125–1126) and Aberle (1948:61, 91) hold the position to be indigenous. So does Ortiz, who described the War (Hunt) chief as a mediator between the moieties (1969:36), the *íowa?ê·* as the earthly representatives of the mythological Twin War Gods (1969:162), as a third and middle level in the political organization (1969:62–63), and, with the other officials, as a mediator or link between categories of being (1969:74).

### Subsistence

Tesuque, like all Pueblos, was a sedentary society with a subsistence economy traditionally based on an agricultural-hunting cycle. Precontact crops included corn, squash, beans, and some cotton and tobacco. The Spanish introduced in the sixteenth century wheat, chili, peaches, and melons (including watermelons), along with horses, sheep, and pigs; but as late as 1912, Robbins, Harrington, and Freire-Marreco (1916:85) reported that at Tesuque anyone who planted nontraditional crops would be punished. The govenor at Tesuque told Lieutenant Bourke in 1881 that the Pueblo had commercial relations with the Navajos, Apaches, and several Plains tribes (Bloom 1933–1938, 7:313). Census reports around 1900 imply that the Tesuque were lacking in refined agricultural techniques, their corn growing too close together and not in regular rows, but this method insured cross-pollenization. It is notable that in 1910–1911, yellow corn, which was not raised at all at Santa Clara (considered one of the more "advanced" of the Pueblos), had been developed into a "fine strain" at Tesuque (Robbins, Harrington, and Freire-Marreco 1916:82).

Smithsonian, NAA.

Fig. 4. Tesuque men with oxcart at outskirts of the Pueblo. The wooden structures on either side of them are pens with storage platforms and drying racks on top. Photograph by John K. Hillers, about 1880.

In the late 1960s farming was still of the subsistence type, the primary crops being corn, chili, and beans. Irrigation remained a problem (Smith 1966:149) in spite of a storage dam constructed in the early 1920s, which was thought to have solved the problem (ARCIA 1924:17), or at least to have improved the condition (Bandelier and Hewett 1937:94). Smith (1966:148) indicated that Tesuque's lands were used as follows: 600 acres, farm lands; 392, open grazing; 350, commercial timber; 15,547, noncommercial timber.

### History

The Pueblo first came under Roman Catholic influence in 1598 with the appointment of Fray Cristóbal de Salazar, a Franciscan, to the Tewa province (Crane 1928: 111–112). The Tesuque mission was known as San Lorenzo prior to the 1680 Pueblo Revolt (Coan 1925, 1:66). The burning of church paraphernalia and the murder of Fray Juan Bautista Pío, the priest assigned to Tesuque, on the eve of the 1680 Pueblo Revolt indicate the extent of resistance to conversion. Eventual relaxation of church sanctions against indigenous religious practices permitted a gradual assimilation of Catholicism, and by the early twentieth century, Catholic religious practices had been incorporated with Tewa ceremonialism. Thus, Tesuque's feast day (November 12) in honor of its patron saint, San Diego, is celebrated with a native dance as well as with the usual church services. The Tesuque people are nearly without exception Roman Catholic, and proselytizing by other churches is met with polite indifference.

Efforts to establish a school, begun in 1886 (U.S. Department of the Interior 1886), failed repeatedly until about 1923, at which time the day school had a capacity of 30, a total enrollment of 27, and an average attendance

Fig. 5. Woman grinding corn with a stone metate and mano. To her right is a pottery bowl in which the ground corn is probably being mixed with water (from the iron pot); the woman at left appears to be making and stacking corn tortillas from this mixture. Both women wear their hair in traditional style, cut in a fringe at front and sides and tied in back with yarn or string. Photograph by Warren Dickerson, before 1934.

of 26. These figures are nearly identical to those provided by Smith (1966:149), for 1966, who states that many pupils go on to public high schools in Santa Fe. Brant (1950:257) observes that in 1871 only three persons out of a population of 98 were able to read and write. It is important to understand these figures in the perspective of the statewide situation in that period: in 1880, 60 percent of New Mexicans were unable to read, 65 percent unable to write (Bancroft 1889:774).

The original village site (location uncertain) was abandoned sometime after the 1680 revolution, the present site having been occupied since its establishment in 1694. Tesuque, under Spanish domination one of the most revolutionary of the Tewa Pueblos, figured prominently in the revolt. Two of its men, Nicolás Catua and Pedro Omtua, had been sent as runners to the other Pueblos to alert their chiefs to the date for first strike, probably August 13. Betrayed to the Spanish governor, Antonio de Otermín, by the Tano, San Marcos, and La Ciénega chiefs, Catua and Omtua were arrested (Hackett 1942, 1:xxvii, 3). Fearful of disclosure, the Tesuque chiefs sounded the alarm to the allies, and the date was moved up to August 10. It is probable that the first blood of the revolt was shed at Tesuque on August 9 with the killing

of a Spaniard, Cristóbal de Herrera (Hackett 1942, 1:xxxii, 7; see also Folsom 1973).

Notable population decreases followed the 1680 Revolt and the smallpox epidemics of the late eighteenth century (table 1).

In the 1930s, an investigator for the Tewa Basin Study (U.S. Office of Indian Affairs. Indian Land Research Unit 1935) reported that many Tesuque families lived from day to day, the next day's food often depending upon the sale of pottery by the women. In the early 1950s, the only source of tribal income was from interest on

Table 1. Population, 1680–1973

| Year | Total | Source |
|------|-------|--------|
| 1680 | 200 | Bancroft 1889:172, citing Vetancurt |
| 1790 | 138 | U.S. Bureau of the Census 1915:106 |
| 1821 | 187 | Bloom 1913–1914:28 |
| 1850 | 119 | U.S. Bureau of the Census 1915:106 |
| 1889 | 94 | U.S. Bureau of the Census 1915:106 |
| 1910 | 77 | U.S. Bureau of the Census 1915:120 |
| 1935 | 124 | Bandelier and Hewett 1937:94 |
| 1942 | 147 | Aberle 1948:90 |
| 1963 | 142 | Smith 1966:149, citing BIA |
| 1973 | 281 | Northern Pueblos Agency |

top, Atchison, Topeka, and Santa Fe Railway, Chicago; bottom, N.M. Dept. of Development, Sante Fe.

Fig. 6. Eagle Dance (*ce šare*), one of several animal dances involving animal impersonation and mimicry, as performed in 1938 (top) and in 1941 (bottom). The dancers are painted and dressed in feather headpieces with gourd beaks, tail feathers, and imitation wings. top, Drummers, wearing typical Pueblo dress, carry a variety of drums; bottom, drummers wear Plains-type feather bonnets (the one on the right has a headdress constructed from a leather aviator's helmet) and beaded vests and leggings. Top photograph probably by Gabriel Moulin; bottom by an unknown photographer.

Mus. of N. M., Santa Fe: 44869/12, 25260/12; Smithsonian, Dept. of Anthr.: 35407.

Fig. 7. "Rain god" figurines of the type made for sale at Tesuque, especially beginning in the late 1890s when they were widely sold by the Gunther Candy Company of Chicago. left to right, Figure with buff slip of the type dating about 1890-1930, figure decorated with poster paints of the type popular since the 1930s, and unpainted figure of micaceous clay collected before 1879 (Cole 1955; Gratz 1976). Height of right 25 cm, rest same scale.

Smithsonian, Dept. of Anthr.: 23180, 39744.

Fig. 8. Domestic and tourist pottery. left, Water vessel with complicated floral motifs in black on cream; diameter about 28 cm; collected before 1876. right, Flower pot made for sale with simplified traditional design elements; height about 18 cm; collected in 1879.

funds on deposit (U.S. Congress. House. Committee on Interior and Insular Affairs 1954:125). The recurrent unemployment rate in the late 1960s was 48 percent, somewhat lower than that of other Tewa villages (compare Nambe, 64%; San Ildefonso, 53%; Pojoaque, 81%) (Smith 1966:5–6). Many Tesuque males are employed in Santa Fe or at the Los Alamos laboratories (Jocano 1963:9).

Bandelier and Hewett (1937:94) saw the commercial development of pottery (figs. 7–8) becoming an important source of income. However, the craft at Tesuque declined aesthetically since about 1935 and had not, as of the early 1970s, commanded the viable market for pottery from other Pueblos, such as San Ildefonso. Pottery observed in

1973 evinced the interest of a few potters in returning to traditional colors and design.

Factors such as undeveloped crafts, small proportion of arable or timber-producing land, small population, failure or lack of desire to attract industry, and the absence of a potential tourist attraction such as Santa Clara's Puye camping facilities—all led to the decision of Pueblo officials to lease part of the land for residential development.

334

In 1964, in the hope of providing employment opportunities for tribal members, as well as of generating tribal revenues, the Tesuque council requested permission of the secretary of the interior to enter into 99-year leases with external non-Indian interests, for the development of tribal lands and other resources. This request was approved in 1968. During this same year a group of prominent New Mexico Democrats incorporated the Sangre de Cristo Development Company in Santa Fe, nine miles south of Tesuque, and three of their number approached the Tesuque council about entering into a land-development lease.

After two years of negotiations an agreement was signed by Tesuque officials and Sangre de Cristo and approved by the Bureau of Indian Affairs in spring 1970, permitting Sangre de Cristo to lease 1,345 acres of Tesuque land, with an option on an additional 3,700 acres, for recreational, commercial, and economic development. Included in the planned development were an 18-hole golf course, stables, tennis courts, skeet-shooting facilities, restaurants, hotels, and enough residential lots to house as many as 15,000 persons. In addition to the land, Tesuque officials signed over rights to 450 acre-feet a year of the Pueblo's water, to be obtained from wells drilled on the leased land. As planned, the entire development would take 15 years to complete and cost approximately 75 million dollars.

Although careful provisions were made in the lease to compensate the tribe as a corporate entity from these various ventures, as well as to generate some employment for tribal members, the agreement very quickly became caught up in a swirl of legal controversy. Squared off in opposition to the parties to the lease were the city and county of Santa Fe, the state of New Mexico, local environmental groups, and, eventually, a group of 60 Tesuque Pueblo residents. The maze of legal issues raised by this cluster of groups was complex, ranging from questions of city and state jurisdiction and environmental impact considerations to the conduct of internal tribal affairs. There were several points of enduring significance in the lease itself. First, Tesuque was the only Tewa Pueblo and only the second New Mexico Pueblo to enter into a 99-year lease (the other is Cochiti), for extensive development of tribal lands. Hence, its experience with the developers would be significant for other Southwestern tribes, and not alone the Pueblos. Second, the development would have decidedly altered Tesuque economically, politically, and ecologically. In the end the question for the Pueblo of Tesuque was: Was the 99-year lease truly a new opportunity for economic prosperity and self-determination, or was it just the latest in a long series of artful devices to separate Indian people from their land and resources? In 1976 the Tesuque people had the lease canceled after they uncovered evidence of deception and bad faith on the part of non-Indian signatories.

Tesuque is a member of the Eight Northern Indian Pueblos Council formed in 1965 as part of the Office of Economic Opportunity program. It is one of the least active members (Nambe informant, personal communication 1973).

## Synonymy†

The English name of the Pueblo is from Spanish Tesuque, also spelled, for example, Tezuque, Tesuqui, Tezuqui, Thezuque, and in English sources Tesuke and Tesuki. This is taken to be a rendering of the Tewa name tečúgé 'structure at a narrow place', originally applied to the kiva but symbolically extended to the Pueblo as a whole. A more complicated explanation was given by Harrington (1916:387), who interpreted Tewa tecuge (normalized), which he recorded without glottalization, as a reborrowing from Spanish and the Spanish name as "probably a corruption" of "the old Tewa name" ła·θį̂·ge 'down at the dry spotted place' (phonemicized) or of a Keresan borrowing from this.

Most names for Tesuque in other languages resemble the Tewa names and are probably borrowings or folk etymologies: Taos túts'uíba (Harrington 1918), given as meaning 'small pueblo', Picuris tâtsürma and tōtsēma, Isleta tucheaáp, Jemez and Pecos tsótâ, Cochiti tyúcuko (normalized), and Santa Ana tiótsokoma. Hopi has tɨkwive'-tewa 'Tewa near the mountains' (normalized) for both Tesuque and Nambe. Navajo has Tł'oh Łikizhí 'spotted grass' (Robert W. Young, personal communication 1977). Some languages also use direct borrowings of the Spanish name.

As the seat of a mission the Pueblo has been called San Lorenzo de Tesuque, 1696, and San Diego de Tesuque.

## Sources

There is no single major study of the Pueblo. Bourke's eyewitness account of his 1881 visit (Bloom 1933–1938, 7:311–315) provides the earliest English-language description of life at the village. Parsons's (1929) study of the Tewa, with its entries on Tesuque, is a reliable source of data on certain fundamental aspects of social organization and kinship terms, as is Jocano's (1963) paper. Aberle's (1948) report is the most comprehensive treatment of the history of land grants and land usage, the economic situation, and the specifics of civil organization; certain of those figures related to land use and economic factors are updated by Smith's (1966) study of New Mexico's Indian population. The Tewa Basin Study (U.S. Office of Indian Affairs. Indian Land Research Unit 1935) provides a detailed description of the efforts to establish a craft center and reasons for its failure.

† This synonymy was compiled by Alfonso Ortiz and Ives Goddard. Uncredited forms are from Harrington (1916:387–388), who provides minor variants, or from anonymous sources.

# Tigua Pueblo

NICHOLAS P. HOUSER

Ysleta del Sur Pueblo, inhabited by Tigua ('tēwu) Indians descended from refugees of the 1680s, is located within the southern boundary of El Paso, Texas (figs. 1-2). Formerly, the inhabitants of this Texas Pueblo spoke a language of the Southern Tiwa subgroup of the Kiowa-Tanoan language family (Trager 1967:336-338). Since the early 1900s, Spanish has replaced the indigenous language, which has persisted in the form of numerous words, phrases, and songs. The Tigua have accepted English as a second language (Houser 1970:34).

## The Community

When it was founded in the 1680s, Ysleta was a compact Pueblo with Indian houses arranged in a rectangular pattern about the church plaza (Fewkes 1902:61). Since the early 1900s Indian settlement has shifted several blocks east of the old mission church that previously had been the center of both the Indian Pueblo and original land grant. The Indian community has been commonly called 'the Neighborhood of the Indians' *(el Barrio de los Indios)* because it contains the largest concentration of Indian families in the general area (fig. 3). This neighborhood is shared by many Mexican-American and Anglo families, both of whom the Indians have referred to as *vecinos* or neighbors. The relationship between the Tigua and *vecinos* has been congenial. The tusla, or tribal building (cf. Southern Tiwa *túłag*), has been incorporated within the home of a tribal officer. The tribal drum, dance rattles, masks, and other ceremonial paraphernalia are stored and protected in the tusla. Here tribal meetings and celebrations are held.

Most Tigua families are closely related. The Indians comprise a close-knit community united by consanguineal bonds as well as ceremonial ties that are both Indian and Mexican. These bonds include the mutual obligations associated with the principal feast day of the tribe's patron, Saint Anthony, and other related tribal activities. In many respects, the highly acculturated Tigua differ little from their Mexican neighbors. For the past two centuries, the Ysleta Indians have intermarried with other Indians, Mexicans, and in some cases, with Anglos. Social distance is closer in relation to Mexican people than to Anglos because the Tigua share the language, religion, and customs of the Mexicans. Anglos represent the dominant political and economic power structure and are sometimes viewed with suspicion.

The Tigua recognize a special affinity with Isleta Pueblo in New Mexico. Some state that it is their ancestral home, while others at least acknowledge that they are closely related. Although the two Pueblos are separated by a distance of some 250 miles, throughout the centuries they have maintained a sporadic but warm relationship with each other. The Texas Pueblo is associ-

Real Academia de la Historia, Madrid: Col. Boturini t. 25, between ff. 332 and 333.

Fig. 2. Section of a map of the lower Rio Grande (the *Rio del Norte* from San Elizario to San Pascual), drawn by Bernardo de Miera y Pacheco. Senecú, Ysleta, and Socorro, and the Spanish settlements of San Lorenzo and El Paso (*Passo del Rio del Norte*) all appear here on the west bank of the Rio Grande. However, there were numerous shifts in the river during the years 1680-1852, resulting in land disputes among these Pueblos. This undated map, which accompanied a 1773 document, was prepared as an aid in selecting a site for a presidio in which to garrison Spanish troops. According to a scale bar elsewhere on the map, the section reproduced is about 17 by 27.5 leagues (actual area about 75 by 125 km). See Wheat 1957-1963, 1:89-90, 222-223.

Fig. 1. Ysleta Grant in the 1970s.

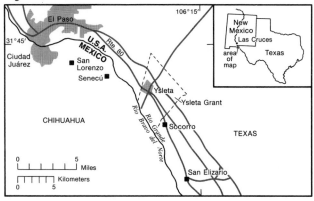

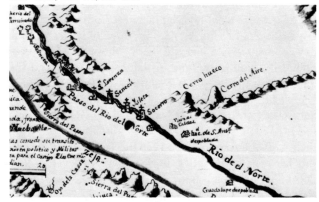

Fig. 3. Family of Enrique and Tomasa Paiz. Their home, constructed of adobe bricks, is within the barrio. Photograph by James S. Griffith, 1968.

ated with the nearby Tigua community of Tortugas in Las Cruces, New Mexico. This Indian community is a daughter colony of Ysleta del Sur. It evolved some time between 1850 and 1900 from a composite of Tigua, Piro, and Manso Indians and was formally incorporated in 1914. Those individuals identifying as Tortugas Indians are divided between those who retain active membership in the corporation and those who claim to represent the traditional Indians. The latter, through legal action, have sought to require the federal government to extend the benefits of the Snyder Act (42 Stat. 208) to them as Indians. This legislation allows the expenditure of appropriated funds for Indians without regard to degree of Indian blood, membership in a federally recognized tribe, or residence, as long as it is in the United States.

The Ysleta Indians have relatives across the river in Mexico, from the former Piro Pueblo of Senecú near Juarez. In fact, many Tiguas are descendants of Piros who married into the Ysleta Pueblo. The Piro tribe of Senecú ceased to exist as an organization around the first decade of the twentieth century; the Piro tribe of Socorro became assimilated at an earlier date. Descendants of both tribes, including the Manso, can still be identified within the El Paso-Juarez area.

The Tigua possess the form of civil government received from the Spaniards centuries ago. The tribal positions include the following: cacique or chief; cacique *teniente* or lieutenant chief, synonymous with *gobernador* or governor; *alguacil* or sergeant-at-arms; and *capitán de guerra* or war captain (fig. 4), who also is the first captain. The other officers include four subordinate captains. With the exceptions of the lifetime positions of chief and war captain, these offices are subject to reelection each New Year's Eve at the midnight tribal meeting.

The Roman Catholic religion has been an important integrative force favoring Tigua cultural persistence. The

Fig. 4. Trinidad Granillo, war captain, holding the tribal drum in one hand and a drumstick in the other. Behind him is the tribal beehive oven, located at his residence within the barrio. At the time this photo was taken, his residence also served as the tusla. Photograph by James S. Griffith, 1968.

surviving indigenous religious elements blend harmoniously with folk Catholicism. The Tigua regard the old church in Ysleta as belonging exclusively to the tribe, though shared with others. The church is dedicated to our Our Lady of Mount Carmel. However, the patron of the tribe is Saint Anthony who was the original patron of old Isleta Pueblo prior to the 1680 Pueblo Revolt. Although the patron has been changed several times by ecclesiastical authority, the Indians have always recognized Saint Anthony as the true patron of the church and tribe. The main feast day is June 13, the day of Saint Anthony (fig. 5).

A small core of traditionalists, particularly associated with the tribal officials and their families, honor a number of indigenous beliefs. They respect the kachinalike manifestation known as the awelo (Spanish *abuelo*) or grandfather (fig. 6) who is the tribal protector embodying the tribal essence. He is said to dwell in nearby Cerro Alto in New Mexico. He monitors all tribal behavior and punishes transgressors. The tribe possesses the buffalo awelo masks (grandfather and grandmother), which are periodically fed with smoke as is the tribal drum. The aboriginal kinship system has been abandoned although pioneer American ethnologists John G. Bourke (Bloom

Fig. 5. Celebrants at the Feast of Saint Anthony, grouped at the door of the old Ysleta church. At center (in front of door) is Mariano Colmenero, governor of the Pueblo, who, with other Tigua men, had been an Indian scout for the U.S. Army and the Texas Rangers during the Apache campaigns. The numerous decorations worn by the men on their jackets are medals, probably received during military service. The two men at the front of each line are Piro Indians from Senecú and Socorro; the man at right holds a bow and arrow and wears a feather headdress decorated with what may be small carriage mirrors. The tribal drum is held by the man just in front of Colmenero. Photograph by an unknown photographer, June 13, about 1898.

1933–1938, 13:208) and J. Walter Fewkes (Fewkes 1902:70) both reported the remnants of a clan system.

Pottery was made until the 1930s when the last female potter died. Until the early 1900s men wove blankets and braided rope, and women made baskets from willows and plants gathered along the riverbanks. Most of these crafts were sold in the El Paso-Juarez area, although on occasion the Indians would go on a trading expedition to Chihuahua City to sell their goods. Some use is made of medicinal plants and herbs, which are either purchased from herbalist shops in Mexico or gathered in the neighboring deserts and mountains. During the spring and summer months, the nearby Hueco Mountains are visited by the Tigua families for this purpose.

### History, 1680 to 1900

On August 10, 1680, the Pueblo Indians from the northern Rio Grande Pueblos to the Hopi mesas rebelled against the injustices of Spanish rule. The Indians of the Tiwa Pueblo of Isleta near Albuquerque and the Piro Pueblos to the south did not become actively involved in the revolt. During the uprising, over 2,000 Spanish colonists congregated at two locations for shelter and defense. The settlers in the vicinity of the capitol assembled at Santa Fe under the command of Antonio de Otermín, governor and captain-general of New Mexico (Hughes 1914:301). The Spanish settlers in the southern district, known as the Rio Abajo, organized under the leadership of Alonzo García, lieutenant-governor and captain-general, and received temporary asylum at Isleta Pueblo (Hackett 1942, 1:1). However, on August 14, the 1,500 Rio Abajo refugees were forced to abandon Isleta when their "hosts" became hostile. They received a similar reception at Socorro Pueblo and retreated southward to Fray Cristóbal, about 60 leagues from El Paso (Hackett 1942, 1:lxxvi), where they were united with Otermín's contingent. At Isleta, Sevilleta, and Socorro, García's division was augmented by 317 Indians composed of Tiwas from Isleta and Piros from Sevilleta, Socorro, Alamillo, and Senecú (Hughes, 1914:315). It may be that many of these Indians joined the Spanish retreat not from loyalty to Spanish authority but from fear of reprisal by the northern revolutionaries (Hackett 1942,1:lxxiii). An undetermined number of the Indian refugees were from Pueblos that had been abandoned before 1680. Prior to the revolt, especially during the 1670s, several Rio Grande Tiwa and Piro Pueblos had

HOUSER

Fig. 6. Awelo dancers with 2 Tigua girls. Until some time before 1920 the Awelo Dance, also called the Turtle Dance (*Baile de Tortuga*), was danced by two masked men on Christmas afternoon. The buffalo hide masks shown here were still in the tribal kiva or tusla in the 1970s. Photograph by an unknown photographer, probably Dec. 25, about 1912. The girls are Juanita Holguín (left) and Ramona Paiz.

received accessions from the eastern Tiwa, Tompiro, and Jumano Pueblos of the Saline Province, as well as from the Piro Pueblo of Senecú. By mid-October, the refugees were relocated at Guadalupe del Paso in the general area of the Manso Indian mission by that name. During the fall of 1680, the refugees established three camps below the El Paso mission (Walz 1951:36).

In November 1681 Governor Otermín launched an expedition to reconquer New Mexico. In December his forces attacked Isleta Pueblo, which offered little resistance and soon surrendered. The Spaniards approached within 10 leagues of Santa Fe, but the Indians were determined to preserve their independence and Otermín's troops departed for El Paso. As they withdrew, they arrived at Isleta Pueblo. Here they discovered that of the 511 Indians captured during the assault on that Pueblo, only 385 remained. The rest had escaped to join the rebels. The remainder were placed under guard and forced to march to El Paso (Hackett 1942, 2:393–394). The expedition returned to El Paso in February 1682. Presumably, most of the 385 captives were resettled that year at the new Pueblo of Sacramento de la Ysleta, later called Corpus Christi de la Ysleta.

In February 1682 Otermín realized that the unsuccessful reconquest necessitated the organization of permanent settlement to accommodate the exiled Spanish colonists, the Indian refugees of 1680, and the newly arrived Isleta captives. He desired that both races share the same settlement, but the clerics opposed this plan for several reasons. They did not wish to disturb the conversions of the Manso and Suma Indians of the El Paso region (Walz 1951:73). Indians were separated from Europeans on the insistence of Fray Francisco de Ayeta, the *procurador general* and custodian of the New Mexico missions. This was done to maintain the policy of ethnic separation practiced in New Mexico, to prevent arguments arising over land and livestock, and to protect Spanish settlers from an epidemic among the Indians (Hughes 1914:321). Spanish colonists were established at San Lorenzo, appropriately named for Saint Lawrence on whose feast day the Pueblo Revolt had begun. Tigua Indians were settled at Corpus Christi de la Ysleta located between Senecú and Socorro (Hughes 1914:323). The names of the former New Mexican pueblos of Isleta, Senecú, and Socorro were merely transferred to the new settlements in the El Paso region (fig. 2).

Following the reconquest of New Mexico in 1692, Gov. Diego de Vargas had planned to return refugee Tiguas and Piros to their homeland in New Mexico (Vargas Zapata y Luxán Ponze de León 1940:287). But the "temporary villages" of Ysleta del Sur, Socorro del Sur, and Senecú del Sur were never deserted. It is possible that the aboriginal inhabitants of those newly founded Pueblos desired to remain in the El Paso area rather than return to their conservative cousins who they feared would regard them as traitors. In the years after the reconquest, the El Paso settlements developed and prospered. During the eighteenth century, numerous civil and ecclesiastical reports mentioned the prosperity of the El Paso missions and the industry of the Indians.

From 1681 to 1881, during the Spanish, Mexican, and American periods, Tigua scouts defended the El Paso settlements against hostile Comanche and Apache bands. Pueblo Indian auxiliaries from the El Paso Pueblos took part in the reconquest of New Mexico (Vargas Zapata y Luxán Ponze de León 1940:51). During the 1684–1686 Manso and Suma revolt in the El Paso region, Pueblo Indians from these Pueblos assisted the Spanish troops in suppressing that uprising (Hughes 1914:355). During the 1700s (Daniel 1956:262–270) and the 1800s (Campbell 1950, 2:5, 15, 61), Pueblo scouts of the El Paso communities were deployed against Apache and Comanche raiders.

The occupation of the El Paso area by American troops in 1846 initiated the beginning of the Anglo-American era. The 1848 Treaty of Guadalupe Hidalgo fixed the boundary between the United States and Mexico in the middle of the Rio Grande channel. This officially placed Ysleta, Socorro, and San Elizario within the jurisdiction of the United States (West 1924:438). From its inception as a Spanish presidio in 1774 until 1780 San Elizario was located 37 miles downriver from its present location. It was never a mission settlement (Gerald 1968:25-27).

On occasion during the early American period, 1848-1900, the federal government recognized the Ysleta tribe. In 1850 James S. Calhoun, Indian agent in Santa Fe, wrote to his superior in Washington recommending that a federal commission be sent to the Texas Pueblos to learn more about the Indians, protect Indian land grants, and give them additional lands if necessary (U.S. Office of Indian Affairs 1915:173). He also suggested that a representative of the Indian Service be stationed at every Pueblo (Calhoun 1849-1850:218-219).

Tigua scouts soldiered with the Texas Rangers (Gillett 1925:202) and the United States cavalry during the Apache campaigns in Texas (U.S. National Archives 1880). Between 1894 and 1907, over 20 Indian children from Ysleta del Sur were enrolled at the Albuquerque Indian School (Samuel Rosenberg, personal communication 1966).

After the advent of Anglo-Americans in the El Paso area, there were a number of land transactions and schemes, the legitimacy of which is highly suspect. Much of the story concerning the nature of land transactions in the El Paso region is shrouded behind the mysterious maneuvers of Anglo opportunists who, after 1848, assumed powerful positions in local and state government. Therefore, they could prejudice and manipulate laws and surveys and influence legalistic interpretation for personal gain. During this period the Indian and Mexican residents were subjected to frequent abuses by the newcomers who attempted to deprive the former inhabitants of much of their land.

It was reported that the prefect at El Paso del Norte, just prior to Col. Alexander Doniphan's arrival in El Paso in 1846, was engaged in disposing of lands in that area for his own benefit and preparing fraudulent deeds for sale (U.S. Department of the Interior 1872:68). In 1852 the people of Ysleta petitioned the governor of Texas for protection from the injuries suffered from Americans who lived there and ignored law and order and attempted to divest the people of their land (Winfrey et al. 1960, 3:166-168). Even as late as 1881, when John G. Bourke visited Ysleta, the old Indian governor complained "that the American and Mexican were crowding into their beautiful valley taking up, without recompense land belonging to the people of the pueblo" (Bloom 1933-1938, 13:208).

*The Ysleta Grant*

As was the case of several New Mexico Indian Pueblos, the Ysleta Indians received a grant from the king of Spain. Although the original grant has not been located, numerous references exist. It is alleged that it was deeded by royal decree to the Pueblo of San Antonio de Ysleta on March 13, 1751 (West 1924:435, 437). Indian title to this land was recognized by the State of Chihuahua in adjudicating land disputes between the contiguous Indian Pueblos of Ysleta and Senecú (El Paso County Deed Records 1825, Book B:24, Book D:392; Campbell 1950, 2:18-20, 61-68). Indian possession was mentioned in the land disputes between these two Pueblos following American annexation (El Paso County Deed Records 1825, Book D:392-396).

Examination of the historical record supports the oral tradition among the Tigua Indians that they were divested of their lands by the town of Ysleta. On February 1, 1854, the Texas legislature approved a special act that relinquished the town tract of Ysleta to the inhabitants of the town, authorized issuance of a patent, and recognized the original Spanish grant of 1751 (Texas. Laws, Statutes, etc. 1898, 3:1027, 1094, 4:42, 53). On May 9, 1871, the Texas legislature approved a special act incorporating the town of Ysleta. This bill became law without local election as then specified by law. It provided the mechanism to tax and sell lands within the grant (El Paso County Deed Records 1825, Book I:184).

During the 15-year existence of this allegedly illegal incorporation, land speculators divested the Indians of most of the tribal lands. This was accomplished by deeding certain tracts to non-Indians without recompense or by confiscating land from Indians who were unable to pay the realty tax imposed by the incorporation or were heavily encumbered by debt. In some instances, the land was merely purchased from the Indians for a small sum of money or traded for cheap goods. On May 2, 1874, the Texas legislature passed a special act that provided for the dissolution of the town by election and authorized the commissioners' court to sell and dispose of all assets of the abolished incorporation (Texas. Laws, Statutes, etc. 1898, 8:348). On October 14, 1895, the county judge abolished the incorporation (El Paso County Deed Records 1825, Book IV:42). The many repetitions of the same conveyances to quiet title, from 1880 when the county judge approved the town's incorporation to 1895 when the town was dissolved, even after this date, suggest unusual concern to legitimize title.

## Sociocultural Situation in the 1960s

On May 23, 1967, the state of Texas recognized the Ysleta Indian Community and accepted all trust responsibilities pending recognition by the federal government (Texas. Laws, Statutes, etc. 1962:91). On April 12, 1968, the federal government officially recognized the Ysleta Indians as a surviving tribe of American Indians and transferred all trust responsibilities to the state of Texas (82 Stat. 93). The trust responsibilities are administered by the Texas Commission for Indian Affairs. The state of

Texas is trustee of approximately 60 acres of land obtained by the state since 1969. Some 23 acres, located in four different tracts within the Ysleta vicinity, are designated for Indian housing, a tribal museum, a tusla or ceremonial center, and an administrative office. Two other tracts, situated 26 miles northeast of Ysleta, comprise 20 acres at Sabinas archeological site and 16 acres at nearby Hueco Tanks State Park. These two tracts are for recreational development.

During the 1960s as a result of favorable publicity, tribal recognition, and a land claims case, there was a revitalistic spirit to retain and reinterpret Indian identity (Houser 1966). This new interest included the revival of dances and songs as well as some motivation to learn the Tiwa language. This activity also emphasized the reinstitution of former tribal celebrations and communal hunts. Some families have been engaged in producing beadwork such as bolo ties, pendants, and headbands (see fig. 4). Some rather coarse pottery has been made in an attempt to resurrect that craft. It has been the policy of the Texas Commission for Indian Affairs to sponsor the instruction of "Indian culture," which includes craft work and dance courses. The objective of the commission is to promote the Indian community as a tourist attraction. This economic development plan is analogous to that of the Alabama-Coushatta Reservation, which is the only other Indian community in Texas for which the state has assumed trust responsibilities. The economic program for the Tigua Community is exemplified in the establishment of the Tigua Tribal Museum and Gift Shop, located before the old Ysleta Mission, and by the tourist-oriented projects for the Hueco Tanks region.

Many individuals, over the years, disassociated themselves from the tribe, denying Tigua ancestry; however, as a result of the newly instilled pride in Indian heritage and the introduction of a land claims case, many new "members" have been added to the tribal rolls by the Commission. Recruitment has taken place without consultation and approval of the tribal council. A tribal census compiled (Houser 1966a) for a study funded by the Office of Economic Opportunity recorded 166 persons who were active members of the tribe. In contrast, the 1971 census compiled by the superintendent for the Tigua Indian Community, an employee of the Texas Commission for Indian Affairs, recognized 348 tribal members (U.S. Department of Commerce. Economic Development Agency 1971:350). Despite the attempts of that agency to introduce a formal constitution, the tribe has rejected this form of tribal government in order to preserve the old system.

In 1966 and 1971 it was reported by federal and state officials that the economic level of most Tigua families was within the poverty income as then defined by the federal government. Until the industrialization of agri-culture since the 1940s, many families were engaged in field labor and often left Ysleta as migrant workers. Some families have retained this type of labor, but more individuals have become unskilled wage laborers. Some five to six men are employed by the Texas Commission for Indian Affairs in the maintenance of the Hueco Tanks Park.

## Synonymy

Ysleta del Sur received its Spanish name, meaning 'Isleta of the South', from Isleta Pueblo in New Mexico, from which it was settled. The old alternate spelling Ysleta has been arbitrarily used here for the Texas Pueblo simply in order to avoid confusion with the parent Pueblo. Similarly Tigua, the Spanish spelling of Tiwa, has been retained for the designation of the Ysleta people (see the synonymies in "Isleta Pueblo" and "Pueblos: Introduction," this vol.).

Ysleta del Sur has also been refered to in the historical literature by the names of patron saints associated with the mission church. The name of Saint Anthony of Padua, the original patron of Isleta Pueblo, New Mexico, was transferred during the latter part of the seventeenth century to Ysleta del Sur. Since the early 1700s Ysleta Pueblo has been most frequently known as San Antonio de la Ysleta, since Saint Anthony was and is the patron of the Tigua tribe, though the church is dedicated to Our Lady of Mount Carmel. Some historical sources indicate that Ysleta del Sur was first dedicated to El Santísimo Sacramento, for example, Lopez, 1685 (in Hughes 1914:328; Walz 1951:36). Apparently by the late 1690s the church was dedicated to Corpus Christi de la Ysleta (Hughes 1914:369; Chavez 1957:8; McConville 1966:342; Walz 1951:145).

Ysleta was known occasionally by the combined name of Corpus Christi de San Antonio de la Ysleta: about 1682 (Walz 1951:76), 1760 (Tamarón y Romeral 1954:38). During the 1700s Ysleta was frequently known as San Antonio de la Ysleta: 1744 (Hackett 1923–1937, 3:406), 1766 (Lafora 1958:83), 1801 (Chavez 1957:61). Other references to Ysleta are: Islettas, 1854 (Wilson in U.S. Department of the Interior 1872:69; Calhoun 1849–1850:206); Isletta, 1854 (Pope in U.S. Army. Corps of Topographical Engineers 1855:6); and Isleta del Paso, 1882 (Ten Kate 1885; Gatschet 1882).

The historical record, when referring to the inhabitants of Ysleta in both the Spanish and English languages, sometimes makes a distinction between the *indígena* 'Indian, native' and the *vecino* 'neighbor, citizen' meaning non-Indian (El Paso County Deed Records 1825:Book B; Campbell 1950). The term Pueblos was often applied by Anglo-Americans, during the early American period (1846–1900), to the Indians of Ysleta (Baylor 1900–1906;

Gillett 1925). The term Ysleteños also has been given to this tribe (Fewkes 1902).

## Sources

Major historical sources for Ysleta during the Spanish period include the publications of Hackett (1923-1937, 1942) and Hughes (1914). Historical theses on this region include those by Bowden (1952), Campbell (1950), Hankins (1962), McConville (1966), Walz (1951), and K.H. White (1961). Historical studies of Ysleta and the other El Paso Pueblos were written by Decorme (1950) and Calleros (1952, 1953, 1953a).

Early ethnological investigations of Ysleta and the neighboring Pueblos were made by Bartlett (1852, 1854, 1, 1909), Bourke (Bloom 1933-1938, 13), Ten Kate (1885), Bandelier (1890-1892, 1966-1976; Burrus 1966), Mooney (1897; Bartlett and Mooney 1897; Powell 1900), Fewkes (1902), Harrington (1909a), and Hodge (1907-1910, 1:622-624, 2:747-749). More recent historical and anthropological studies of Ysleta include those by Diamond (1966) and Houser (1966, 1970).

Most linguistic investigation, though of a cursory nature, concerns the Piro dialect of Senecú with brief attention given to the Tigua dialect of Ysleta. For brief references to both dialects see Gatschet (1882:259), Hodge (1896:346), and Fewkes (1902:69-71). For additional references with accompanying vocabulary lists, primarily in Piro, see Bartlett (1852, 1854, 1:149, 1909:429-433), Bartlett and Mooney (1897), and Harrington (1909a).

# Sandia Pueblo

ELIZABETH A. BRANDT

Sandia (ˌsănˈdēu) is a small community (figs. 1–2) located 15 miles north of Albuquerque, New Mexico, on U.S. Highway 85 and 2.5 miles south of the Spanish-American town of Bernalillo (see "Pueblos: Introduction," fig. 1, this vol.).

## Language

The people of Sandia speak one of the two Southern Tiwa languages, the other being that of Isleta Pueblo.* Southern Tiwa and the two Northern Tiwa languages, spoken at Taos and Picuris, make up the Tiwa branch of the Kiowa-Tanoan language family. The Northern Tiwa languages are said to be intelligible to some Sandia speakers even though the separation of Northern and Southern Tiwa occurred about 800 to 900 years ago (Trager 1967; see also "Historical Linguistics and Archeology," this vol.). The languages of Sandia and Isleta are mutually intelligible but show very divergent morphological and syntactic structures. Trager (1967), noting their close similarity, considered them to be dialects of a single language rather than two separate languages, but Brandt (1970a) and Leap (1970) have called this conclusion into question. Not only do the structural differences between the two forms of speech reduce their mutual intelligibility, but rapid linguistic change has recently affected both and increased their divergence. For example, in the 1960s Sandia speakers used three different sets of pronominal verb prefixes depending on their age level. Sandia was then used in religion and governing, but in other, nontraditional contexts the use of English predominated, with older people generally knowing Sandia, Spanish, and English, but over 50 percent of the resident population, mostly young people, speaking no Sandia. There were two monolingual Sandia speakers (Brandt 1969). In 1930 Sandia children entering school knew Sandia but no English, though a few knew some Spanish (Ferguson 1931:72). The decline in the use of Sandia

---

* The orthography used in the *Handbook* for Sandia words printed in italics is that of Brandt (1970, 1970a), with the substitution of ʔ for the apostrophe to indicate the glottal stop. The aspirated stops *(ph, th, kh)*, glottalized stops *(pʔ, tʔ, kʔ)*, and labialized segments *(hw, kw, kʔw)* are interpreted as clusters, but *ph, th,* and *kh* are also pronounced as fricatives, [f], [θ], and [x], especially by younger speakers.

since then and the replacement of it and Spanish by English has been brought about by the increasing use of English in school and employment, especially in nearby Albuquerque, and with the children of the many marriages to non-Sandia speakers.

## Territory and Environment

Sandia is separated geographically from the predominantly Anglo town of Albuquerque and the Spanish-American town of Bernalillo by an open area of the reservation. The Pueblo itself occupies approximately 26 acres within a total reservation area of 24,034 acres (New Mexico State Planning Office 1972:1). The Pueblo is situated near the center of the reservation with a clear view of the mountains.

The natural environment of the Sandia ranges in altitude from 5,000 feet up to 10,670 feet at Sandia crest. The farmlands lying in the alluvial valley of the Rio Grande are fertile, well-watered, and abundant with birds. The Pueblo itself is situated on a sandy plain. To the east is a region of sand hills rising to the foothills of the Sandias. This area is abundant in game, such as rabbit and deer, and has many useful plants. The foothills are important for piñon, which is still harvested. Communal rabbit hunts are carried out and plants are collected from all environments for medicinal and ceremonial use. The hunting of deer is important and provides a reserve of meat over the winter. Although the Rio Grande is near, fish were rarely consumed. The idea of consuming fish or shellfish is repellent to most Sandias.

Before the Middle Rio Grande Conservancy district was established, flooding of fields and flood damage to homes were frequent. The Pueblo has been severely damaged at least three times by flood waters coming down the arroyos from the mountains. This danger has been controlled by irrigation and diversion dams in the waters, and marshy land near the river is again suitable for cultivation. The reservation contains 1,760 acres of farmland, 19,000 acres of grazing land, and 2,525 acres of noncommercial timber land (New Mexico State Planning Office 1972:13–14). The only mineral deposits are sand and gravel pits, which are being mined by a company that leases the land from Sandia. Clay for pottery making was formerly obtained in the foothills.

Southwest Foundation for Audio-Visual Resources, Santa Fe, N.M.
Fig. 1. Sandia Pueblo. Photograph by Peter Dechert, June 1977.

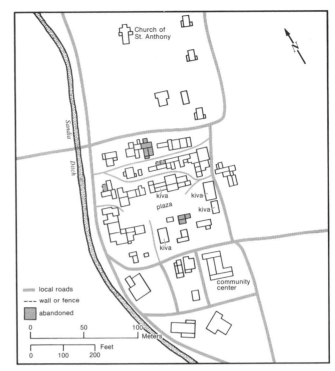

revised from Stubbs 1950:fig. 6.
Fig. 2. Sandia Pueblo.

## External Relations

Sandia retains the basic social organization of the Tano-an Rio Grande Pueblos but differs from them in the extent to which the Pueblo has been exposed to other cultural influences. In general culture and organization it is most like Isleta, its sister Pueblo to the south; however, it would be mistaken to equate the two as has been frequently done in the past. Sandia has possibly more Keresan influence than other Rio Grande Pueblos, though this might be due to a period of residence at Jemez (Colee 1969) rather than direct Keresan influence. Sandia has close ties with the Pueblos of Zia, Santa Ana, San Felipe, and Laguna. There are also frequent interactions with Isleta, at both a community and an individual level. Sandia should show Hopi influence as the Sandias were supposed to have fled to Arizona after the Pueblo Revolt (Hodge 1910d:429), and indeed there are some possible Hopi loanwords in the language, including the word for 'rattlesnake' and that for 'blanket' (although the latter is common in other Pueblos as well).

The Sandias were often raided by the Navajo, the Apache, and the Comanche in the past. Navajos are still considered enemies, but there is at least one case of intermarriage and Navajos are frequent visitors to Sandia fiestas. Strong relationships of mutual aid and support were developed between individual Sandias and Spanish-Americans in Bernalillo. Many personal friendships as well as business relationships exist with Anglos.

Socially and culturally Sandias are a distinct group from the surrounding Spanish-Americans and the nearby Pueblos of Zia, Santa Ana, and Isleta. Strong ties bind Sandias to individuals in all these communities, but anyone who is not a Sandia is considered an outsider. Formal incorporation procedures exist for the acceptance of other Indians into the community (Brandt 1969; Simons 1969). Non-Indians are allowed to reside in the community but are denied membership and participation in many affairs, though it is sometimes possible for young non-Indian children to become Sandia members if they come to the community before they have been enculturated in any other society.

## Prehistory and History

Potsherds found on refuse mounds at present-day Sandia show a continuous series from 1300 to the present with no great gaps in occupation of the site (Stubbs 1950:31). The location of the Pueblo at the time of first Spanish contact by the Francisco Vásquez de Coronado expedition in 1540 is in doubt. The Tiguex province, as it was later known, contained from 12 to 20 Pueblos. Fisher (1931) lists 18 sites that may have been historic Southern Tiwa Pueblos. There are also a number of prehistoric sites in the area. Sandia has been identified with the Pueblo known as Arenal by the Coronado expedition, but this is probably a mistake (Bolton 1964:206) since the distances among identifiable Pueblos do not fit. The "napeya" of

344

Juan de Oñate in 1598 is probably a corruption of the native name of Sandia (Hammond and Rey 1953; Hodge 1910d:430). Sandia is identified by name and in its present location for the first time in 1617 when it was established as the seat of the mission of San Francisco (Bandelier 1890–1892, 3:220).

Sandias participated in the Pueblo Revolt. After the Revolt Sandia was burned by Antonio de Otermín, governor of New Mexico (Hackett 1942). The Pueblo was then reoccupied. In 1681 Otermín, attempting reconquest, passed Sandia and burned it again. Other attempts at reconquest were made in 1688, 1689, and 1692 (Vargas Zapata y Luxán Ponze de León 1940:17). Sandia was found abandoned during each of these entries and in ruins in 1692. Therefore the Pueblo must have been abandoned some time after 1682 and before 1688. Tradition states that the Sandias fled to Hopi, where with other refugees from the Rio Grande they built the Pueblo of Payupki (Hopi *payípki*) on Second Mesa (Hodge 1910d:429, 1910e:218); this Hopi name is also used for Sandia Pueblo (Fewkes 1894:397). However, this tradition is difficult to confirm, and there is some evidence against it. Oral tradition at Sandia denies that they ever left the Pueblo and asserts that the Hopi came to live with the Sandia (Brandt 1969). De Vargas, who visited Hopi in 1692, gave the names of five Hopi Pueblos and listed refugee groups of Indians living there, but no mention is made of Payupki, Tewa, or Tiwa in the records of this expedition (Vargas Zapata y Luxán Ponze de León 1940:216). This omission suggests that the Sandia had not yet arrived at Hopi, if they did go there. Mindeleff (1891:40–41) relates a Hopi legend of Payupki that states that the people "returned to San Felipe from whence they came." A Tiwa Indian captured by Otermín told him that the inhabitants of the Pueblos of Alameda, Puaray, and Sandia were thinking of settling among the "Sima" in the jurisdiction of La Cañada near the modern-day Pueblos of San Juan and Santa Clara (Hackett 1942, 2:361). A Harrington (1909) manuscript refers to a "Sima dialect of Sandia," words of which were collected at Ysleta del Sur, but no other information is available on this tantalizing Sima reference.

In any case some explanation must be postulated for the severe population decrease of Sandias from 3,000 in 1680 to 350 in 1748 (Meline 1966:214–215). Some Sandias may have been absorbed in other populated Pueblos, some may have gone to Sima, and some to Hopi.

Sandia was abandoned until 1748. In 1733 an unidentified group at Isleta requested permission to resettle the still-abandoned site of Sandia, but permission was denied (Colee 1969). In 1742 Fathers Delgado and Pino went to Hopi, brought back 441 Indians to the Rio Grande valley, and promised that they would be allowed to return to their homes, which they identified as Sandia, Alameda, and Pajarito (Puaray?) (Hackett 1923–1937, 3:389–390). The governor of New Mexico refused and they were

settled at Isleta and Jemez (Hackett 1923–1937, 3:472; Colee 1969:8). In 1748 Father Menchero petitioned the governor of New Mexico to allow settlement at Sandia of 350 converted Indians from Hopi and a Hopi cacique. These Indians are probably not the group who were settled at Jemez, though it is possible that some Indians had returned to Hopi. This group was permitted to settle (Meline 1966:214, 217–220). By 1760 there is evidence of two different settlements at Sandia, one Hopi and one Sandia (Tamarón y Romeral 1954:44). No sources have been found to determine what happened to the Hopi settlement. It is certain that when Sandia was resettled, it was by a mixed group of refugees from various Pueblos. This must have given the Pueblo a very different character from that before the Revolt, and may account for differences between Sandia and other Rio Grande Pueblos.

*Culture Change*

Prior to the Pueblo Revolt, Sandia was in an area heavily settled by the Spanish. After the resettlement, the area was also a focal point for Spanish influence, as population figures show:

|  | Sandias | Spaniards | Source |
|---|---|---|---|
| 1777 | 304 | 810 | Bancroft 1889:278 |
| 1789 | 236 | 384 | Bancroft 1889:278 |
| 1799 | 1,513 | 1,490 | Bancroft 1889:278 |
| 1827 | 1,328 | —— | Carroll and Haggard 1942:88 |
| 1860 | 217 | —— | Carroll and Haggard 1942:88 |

The wide fluctuation in these figures implies that those for 1799 and 1827 might be in error, although the 1827 census is considered the first accurate one. It included figures for each occupation: farmers, 265; craftsmen, 97; merchants, 4; day laborers, 99. Even at this time, the Sandia did not rely totally upon a farming economy. Almost no information is available on any other aspects of Sandia culture. Bandelier noted in 1882 that the Sandias made excellent willow baskets and pottery (Bandelier 1966–1976). Both crafts are no longer practiced. Hewett (1930) noted that Sandia was "much Mexicanized" and headed for extinction. The first ethnography of Sandia by Ferguson (1931) shares that opinion on acculturation but notes that American influence at this time was almost nonexistent and that the Spanish language was used by only a few speakers and only for conversation with outsiders. Ferguson's work contains little data that enable any discussion of culture change to be undertaken. Pottery making was still practiced by one woman at this time. Houses were one-story, and horses as well as automobiles were in use. American education for Sandia children was just beginning with the establish-

Smithsonian, NAA.
Fig. 3. Sandia in 1879, viewed facing east toward the Sandia Mountains. At extreme right is a rectangular kiva, extant in 1978 though no longer in use. In the background, right and center, are animal pens with hay stored in overhead racks, and to their left are communal threshing floors. The building at left has old-style windows with wooden strut supports; next to it is a structure (either abandoned or being built) that shows adobe brick walls in an unplastered state. Photograph by John K. Hillers.

ment of a day school at the Pueblo. Clans no longer existed, though they were presumed to have existed in the past. Two basic divisions cross-cut the Pueblo, the Summer people and the Winter people. Descent was matrilineal and only one kiva was in use. Two curing societies are mentioned, but it is unclear if these are different from the Summer people and Winter people (Ferguson 1931:31–32). Ferguson stresses the conservatism of the Sandia and their reticence to discuss any aspect of their culture; this may account for the general lack of information on social organization at Sandia. American influence was not extensive at Sandia until the Second World War.

Sandia is a visibly acculturated Pueblo. Electricity came into the community in the early 1920s. Gas and running water, indoor plumbing, and hot water heaters are found in almost all homes. Radio, television, automobiles, trucks, and a wide range of electric appliances are used by most Sandias. Traditional dress was worn by only three women at Sandia in 1972. Only a few older men wear distinctive hair styles, though younger males are once again wearing their hair longer as a visible sign of their Indian heritage. Cultural distinctiveness is maintained by a strong emphasis on the community, religion, language, and a very strong Indian identity. The Sandia have been able to acculturate and take advantage of the things they desired from the wider world and still retain their Pueblo organization, their values, and their identity.

## Sociocultural Situation in the 1960s

Of the 265 enrolled tribal members in 1971 (table 1), 174 were resident at Sandia (Southern Pueblos Agency 1971). This represents a dramatic increase in the population during the twentieth century. The population fluctuations must have had great impact upon the social organization of the village. Sandias recognize that some loss of information on ethnohistory, ritual, and religion has occurred due to death of important individuals.

Religion is tremendously important to the Sandias and is a major means of retaining their identity. The major feast day of the Pueblo, the feast of Saint Anthony on

Table 1. Population, 1900–1971

| Year | Population | Year | Population |
|------|-----------|------|-----------|
| 1900 | 74 | 1950 | 155 |
| 1910 | 73 | 1955 | 175 |
| 1920 | 114 | 1960 | 188 |
| 1925 | 99 | 1965 | 211 |
| 1930 | 115 | 1967 | 227 |
| 1935 | 121 | 1969 | 253 |
| 1940 | 131 | 1970 | 261 |
| 1945 | 136 | 1971 | 265 |

Source: United Pueblos Agency 1900–1970; Southern Pueblos Agency 1971.

Note: Figures are not all of equal value. Some indicate resident population for the earlier years; others, total tribal enrollment.

June 13, is celebrated by a Corn Dance. Another major feast is the Feast of the Three Kings on January 6, normally celebrated by either Eagle or Buffalo Dances. Many other dances occur during the year, particularly at the change of seasons. Sandia is considered by its members to be a "complete" village, ceremonially having retained its complete religious heritage. Some sacred shrines are located in the Sandia Mountains, where recreational development and commercial use make it difficult to perform all ritual obligations. There is cooperation in ritual with nearby Pueblos. In respect for the wishes of the tribe, nothing further can be said about traditional religion, nor have the Sandias revealed any information on religion to outsiders. The Roman Catholic religion is also an important part of life and no conflict is perceived between the two religions. There are a few Protestants at Sandia, but Protestantism plays no major role.

The village is divided into two groups, Turquoise and Pumpkin, to which children are assigned at birth. These two groupings have permanent leaders and are responsible for Eagle and Buffalo Dances. Membership in these two groups is determined ambilineally. In addition there are the kiva organization; corn groups, which are matrilineal in recruitment; and curing groups (Simons 1969a:125, 127, 128, 208). Detailed information on these groupings, their membership, their activities, and their interrelationships has not been divulged by the Sandia. Their importance lies in the interlocking net of ceremonial as well as kin relationships that provide a secure web of constant interactions for a Sandia from birth to death. Further information on some of the social structure that is known can be found in Simons (1969a).

The *t'áy-kabéde* (often known as the cacique) is considered the spiritual and true leader of the village. He is often referred to as "the mother of his people." This position is not hereditary as in some other Pueblos. He has several assistants, one of whom will eventually succeed him in office (Brandt 1969:17; Simons 1969a:203). He and his assistants choose the governor, though the opinions of outgoing officers are also considered.

### Political Organization

Governing officials at Sandia are chosen for one-year terms annually. If the Pueblo is involved in complex litigation, a governor may be asked to stay on for an additional period of time because of his familiarity with the matter. The following is a list of Pueblo officials: governor, lieutenant governor, war captain, lieutenant war captain, governor's staff, war captain's staff, and members of the council (Brandt 1970a:67-69). Other nontraditional appointive positions are sheriff, treasurer, sacristan, and water boss. The governor also has an administrative aide. Liaison officials are also maintained with other governing bodies. There is a representative to

Smithsonian, NAA.

Fig. 4. Juan Avila, carrying governor's cane of office and wearing a Pendleton blanket. Blankets of this type were adopted by the Pueblo men and worn in the same manner as the more traditional blankets of Pueblo and Navajo manufacture. Photograph by DeLancey Gill, Washington, D.C., 1923.

the All-Pueblo Council, a chairman for the All Indian Pueblo Housing Authority, and a legal counsel. As Sandia becomes increasingly involved in the modern world the need for more appointive officials to deal with specific problems becomes greater.

The secular authority of the governor and the war captain is essentially equal but operates in different spheres both territorially and culturally. The governor has control over the aspects of Sandia life that relate to the outside world. He serves as liaison officer between the Pueblo and all outside agencies and individuals. He acts in a judicial capacity to settle minor disputes in the Pueblo. If a problem is of concern to the whole community, the council and other officials are brought in. His territorial authority extends from the Sandia ditch west to the river. This land is outside the Pueblo and is primarily farming land.

The war captain has authority at ceremonial functions, such as dances, and assists at funerals. He and his staff and also the governor's staff police the Pueblo when it is closed to outsiders. His territorial authority extends from the Sandia ditch to the boundaries of Sandia land to the east. This is primarily grazing and hunting land. His permission must be obtained to hunt in this territory.

The council is an advisory judicial body of 15. Governing is in traditional form with modern positions added as necessary. Disputes are settled within the community

*Albuquerque Journal,* N.M.
Fig. 5. Domingo Montoya, governor in 1970, standing in front of the first segment of new homes in Sandia, built under a Department of Housing and Urban Development program; tank for Pueblo's water system in background. Photograph by Bill Hume, Aug. 1970.

except for crimes that come under federal or state jurisdiction with Pueblo consent to bring in outside agencies. Women do not have the right to vote in Pueblo elections, but a matter of concern to the whole community such as housing or community-action programs will be discussed both in the council and in a community-wide meeting that women attend. Votes are sometimes taken in these situations and the force of public opinion is strong.

### Subsistence

Farming and herding were practiced by 30 people in 1972, but the majority of Sandias are employed outside the community. Both farming and herding are underutilized (New Mexco State Planning Office 1972:13-14), though some individuals are part-time farmers. Both males and females normally work, and it is not unusual for unmarried children of both sexes to work. Most Sandias are employed in skilled labor such as surveying, construction, and jewelry making, or in white-collar jobs with various corporations or state, federal, and local organizations. Simons (1969a:243-244) estimated income per household at approximately $5,000 with over one-half of all households receiving incomes ranging from $4,500 to $11,000. Unemployment is negligible, ranging from 5 to 8.5%, and many unemployed individuals are part-time farmers (New Mexico State Planning Office

1972:11). Public financial assistance is utilized in time of need and by the elderly or handicapped. Simons (1969a:243) states that only 2 percent of Sandia residents used public assistance at any given period. Industrial development at the Pueblo will provide new jobs for residents. In 1972 Sandia Indian Industries had a contract to manufacture metal post office boxes for the federal government. Plans are being developed to utilize some land as an industrial park. Albuquerque is expanding to the north, and Sandia has excellent land and is developing facilities to attract industry. Increase in local job opportunities will make it possible for nonresident Sandias, many of whom are in California, to return to this area.

### Education

The average education level for the Pueblo is twelfth grade. In 1973 five individuals had received college degrees, two were working toward a master's degree, and many students were beginning college. Students were strongly encouraged to complete high school and to go on for further education either in colleges or vocational and technical schools. At least six students have completed courses in vocational and technical schools. The educational level of the community is rising rapidly, and the Pueblo supports a commitment to higher education through a scholarship loan fund. Sandias with advanced education are being given greater authority and positions of responsibility in the Pueblo's governing structure.

### Kinship

The basic unit of Sandia social structure is the household, which is generally coterminous with the nuclear family. The kinship system is bilateral (Brandt 1969; Simons 1969a:129). Membership in corn groups is matrilineal (Simons 1969a:125). These groups are endogamous and have no lineage organization. They are similar to but not identical with corn groups at Isleta. Patrilineal descent is the rule for kiva group membership. Membership in the Pumpkin and Turquoise groups is ambilateral. Children are usually assigned alternately by birth order. Thus, various principles of descent cross-cut the whole social fabric of Sandia. Males and females inherit equally from both parents. Extended families occur rarely and generally only in cases of illness or incapacity of an aged parent. Most Sandias live in single-family homes, though there is an old tendency for married offspring to live in contiguous houses near their parents. This former pattern is being obliterated by a total change in settlement pattern brought about by the construction of single-family modern homes on the sand hills behind the Pueblo. The majority of the community now lives in the new homes leaving only a few people in the old village. These homes were constructed by the All Indian Pueblo Housing Authority in cooperation with the Department of Housing and Urban Development (Brandt 1971).

Exogamy has become the prevailing pattern of marriage at Sandia, although endogamy is the preferred form. In 1970, 66.6% of all marriages were contracted with non-Sandias (Brandt 1970a:64). An equal number of marriages was contracted with Spanish-Americans and with Isletas (Brandt 1969). Other exogamous marriages were with nearby Keresan Pueblos and with Anglos. Although exogamy occurs at this high rate, most participants in exogamous marriages continue to reside at Sandia; the few that do not generally live in other states or at some distance from Sandia. The Indian spouses of Sandias may become corporate members of the community, so that Sandia has an overall gain in population rather than a loss due to exogamy.

Exogamy stems from a number of sources. In 1900, the resident population was only 74 individuals (table 1). Marriage restrictions and the age structure of the population may have increased the probability of marriage outside the village. The ease of travel and increasing contact with the outside world through schools, the armed forces, and employment in other communities account for this trend.

## Synonymy†

The name of the Pueblo is from Spanish *sandía* 'watermelon', said to have been first applied to the Sandia mountains to the east because of their shape and color at sunset. Variant spellings include: Çandia, Zandia, and corruptions in non-Spanish sources such as St. Dies, Deis, San-Diaz, Sandea, and Sandilla.

The native name of the community is *napʰiʔad* 'at the dusty place', a locative derivative of *napʰi* 'dust'. Cognate and with the same meaning is Isleta *nafi̧ʔat*; the derived form for 'Sandia Indian' is *nafi̧húde* (C.T. Harrington 1920:47, 50) or *nafi̧ʔathúde* (William Leap, personal communication 1977). Variant spellings of this Southern Tiwa name are in Harrington (1916:525), of which the name Napeya, recorded by Oñate in 1598, is probably the earliest. The Taos name *na̧phȩtho* has been explained as 'place of the cloud hills'—*ná(nema̧)* 'hill', *phé(na)* 'cloud', *-tho* 'at (the place of)'—a presumed reference to the sand dunes in the area; it probably reflects a Taos folk etymology of the Sandia name (George L. Trager, personal communication 1973).

As the seat of a mission the Pueblo was known as San Francisco de Sandía in 1630, Nuestra Señora de los Dolores de Sandía, Nuestra Señora de los Dolores y San Antonio de Sandía, and perhaps Asunción, spelled Asumpcion, about 1760.

The Jemez name (*sa̧déyag̯ʸiʔ*, also used for a Sandia Indian) and one Tewa name are borrowings from Span-

ish. Another Tewa name is *pocá·nû·*, of obscure etymology, also said to be used for all Southern Tiwas (Harrington 1916:577). Santa Ana has *wá·ṣú·ce*, and the recorded forms in other Keresan languages are similar. Zuni *we·ɬuwalʔa* 'foot village' (Cushing in Hodge 1910d:430; Dennis Tedlock, personal communication 1977) may be a folk etymology from this rather than a reference to "the large feet of the inhabitants." The Hopi name is given as payopi 'at the river' (Harrington 1916:526) and *payɨpki*, with *-ki* 'house, pueblo' (Fewkes 1894:397, phonemicized), the latter also (or especially) being the name of the ruined pueblo on Second Mesa in which the Sandia are said to have lived (Hodge 1910e; Stephen 1936, 2:1163). Navaho has *Kin Łigaaí* 'white building', apparently a reference to the old church (Robert W. Young, personal communication 1977; Haile 1950-1951, 2:253; Franciscan Fathers 1910:135). The Navajo name meaning 'striped houses' given by Curtis (1907-1930, 1:138) is apparently the name of Bernalillo, a nearby town (Franciscan Fathers 1910:135).

## Sources

Fewer data are available on Sandia than almost any other Pueblo. It has been ignored by historians, anthro-

Smithsonian, NAA.

Fig. 6. Mariano Carpintero, governor of Sandia, in Washington, D.C., as part of a Pueblo delegation protesting the proposed construction of a canal through their lands by a private company (Anonymous 1899). On this occasion he visited the Bureau of American Ethnology, where he served as consultant for the first recorded Sandia vocabulary (Gatschet 1899, 1899a). Photograph by DeLancey Gill, Nov. 1899.

† This synonymy was prepared by Ives Goddard incorporating materials from Elizabeth A. Brandt. Uncredited forms cited or referred to are from Harrington (1916:525-527) or anonymous sources.

pologists, and tourists. The only easily accessible source is Simons (1969), an article dealing with the survival of Sandia as a Pueblo community in the face of extensive pressure toward acculturation. The other major sources are Ferguson (1931), which contains an extensive section on history but deals little with ethnography; Simons (1969a), the most complete source for ethnography and ethnology; and Brandt (1970), the major source for linguistics, which also contains some information on history and ethnography.

Other published sources include Hodge's (1910d) article on Sandia and White (1945), containing eight pages of field notes on Sandia. Hodge's own field notes for 1885, 1895, and 1899 on Sandia do not appear to be extant. Few of the major historical sources for the Southwest contain any mention of Sandia. Colee (1969) has the best historical summary for this area. Applegate (1930) contains a romanticized version of Sandia history but cites no sources. Meline (1966) contains copies of the documents on the resettlement of Sandia.

The principal linguistic source is Brandt (1970a), which contains an outline grammar of the language. Brandt (1970) details general differences in Sandia speech. The earliest Sandia vocabulary is Gatschet (1899) (fig. 6), and the earliest language classification is Gatschet (1876). Harrington's (1909) manuscript of Piro with "words in the Sima dialect of Sandia added" may provide additional evidence on the history of Sandia if Sima can be located. Trager (1938) also collected a vocabulary and did the first phonemic analysis of Sandia. The first published source on the language is Trager (1942).

There are no sources for archeology or physical anthropology. Some unpublished material is available in the Bureau of Indian Affairs archives and the Pueblo archives. An unpublished practical orthography is available from Brandt (1971); copies are also in the Pueblo archives. Some language tapes are available in the Library of the American Philosophical Society, Philadelphia.

350

# Isleta Pueblo

FLORENCE HAWLEY ELLIS

## Language and Territory

Isleta (is'letu) is a Pueblo whose people speak a Southern Tiwa language.*

Tiwa, Tewa, and Towa are the three Tanoan branches of the Kiowa-Tanoan language family. Within Tiwa three subgroups are recognized, Northern Tiwa, Southern Tiwa, and Piro, though there is uncertainty about the last (Leap 1971). Isletan Tiwa is one of the two languages in Southern Tiwa, the other being that spoken at Sandia.

The Pueblo (figs. 1-2) consists of a main village on the west bank of the Rio Grande (see "Pueblos: Introduction," fig. 1, this vol.), known as *šiehwíb-àg* to the townspeople and San Agustín to its Spanish-speaking neighbors (from its current patron saint), and two farm villages three miles below on the east side of the river. These farm villages are *šì- łá ʔag* (Chikal) and *t ʔày-kabéde* 'town chief', taking its name from the fact that the fields and summer residence of Isleta's town chief or cacique were there. The old community of *berhwín tðaʔi* 'rainbow village', five miles south, had been almost entirely taken over by Spanish-Americans by the 1920s. Tradition states that a small settlement, *nàm č ʔùrt ʔáynin* 'yellow earth', formerly stood on the bluff just across the river from Isleta and that directly below it was *napáthð tðaʔi* 'white village' (Ranchito), whose people spoke a dialect slightly different from that of the people of *šiehwíb-àg* and were reputed to be mean. Parsons (1932:208, 386, 388) was told that the group that accompanied the Spaniards south

---

* The italicized Isleta words cited in the *Handbook* are in the phonemic system described by Trager (1942:1-2), with substitutions made to conform to the standard technical alphabet. The consonantal phonemes are: (plain stops) *p, t, c, k, kw;* (glottalized stops) *p ʔ, t ʔ, c ʔ, k ʔ;* (fricatives) *f, th* [θ], *x, ł, s, š, hw;* (voiced stops initially, fricatives medially, and voiceless lenis affricates or fricatives finally) *b, d, g;* (resonants) *m, n, r* (alveolar tap), *l, w, y;* (glottals) *h, ʔ.* The vowels are *i, e* [ɛ], *a* (low, back), *ð* (lower high, central), *u,* and their nasalized counterparts *i̧,* etc. The stresses are primary stress (v́), secondary stress (v̀), and unstressed (v). Tone, the analysis of which is incomplete, is unmarked. The writing of the glottalized stops, the fricatives *f, th,* and *x,* and the labialized consonants (*kw* and *hw*) conforms to Trager's later analysis (1948a) and the current practice of Tanoan scholars, motivated by the change of the aspirated stops [pʰ], [tʰ], and [kʰ] (Trager 1942) to fricatives in contemporary speech and by practical orthographic considerations. The Isleta words in this orthography have been phonemicized by William Leap. Words cited from C.T. Harrington (1920) have been mechanically converted into this orthography; they are phonemically transcribed, though only one degree of stress (v́) is indicated.

to El Paso without protest in early 1682 came largely from the hamlets on the east side of the Rio Grande. *nàm č ʔùrt ʔáynin* and *napáthð tðaʔi* may have housed some of the refugees who in the 1600s left their villages in and along the eastern foothills of the Manzano Mountains (Chililí, Tajique, two small Pueblos near Torreon, Tabirá or Gran Quivira, Abó, and Tenabó) to join the Southern Tiwa on the Rio Grande because increased Apache depredations made further occupation of their own territory impossible. Some believe that those Pueblos spoke Tiwa (Wilson 1973:15) or Piro (Bandelier 1890-1892, 2:254), but Schroeder (1964) has combined archeological and historical evidence to argue that all were Tompiro, close relatives of the Piro Pueblos who extended from just below Isleta to the present location of Socorro.

## Prehistory

Isleta itself quite certainly grew from an amalgamation of several related early villages in the Isleta area and possibly up Tijeras Canyon. Isletans claim as immediately ancestral the small site known as Puré Tuay (LA 489), the ruins of which can be seen on top of and at the northern base of Mesa de los Padillas, an isolated lava-topped "island" in front of the big volcanic mesa that at this point forms the western edge of the Rio Grande Valley. Sherds go back to Casa Colorado Black-on-white (ca. A.D. 1200, a local outgrowth of Socorro Black-on-white, commonly accompanied by Los Lunas Smudged, a Mogollon Red ware derivative) and extend up through Rio Grande Glazes E and F or to approximately A.D. 1700, a proof of occupation there in early Spanish times. Bandelier (1890-1892, 2:233) noted six ruins on the two sides of the Rio Grande in this general vicinity. Surface examination of the present site of Isleta Pueblo shows little of pre-1700 Glaze ware sherds (Ellis 1945-1953). This may place it as an early eighteenth-century settlement that had started as a cluster of seasonally occupied field houses, a common arrangement for Pueblo farmers of late prehistoric and historic times. Isletans have no memory (and there is no evidence) of any decorated pottery having been made between the early 1700s, when glaze paint was dropped, and the late 1800s, when an adaptation of Laguna Matte Paint Polychrome (fig. 3) was introduced by Laguna immigrants. Isleta did con-

Southwest Foundation for Audio-Visual Resources, Santa Fe, N.M.
Fig. 1. Isleta Pueblo plaza areas. Photograph by Peter Dechert, June 1977.

revised from Stubbs 1950:fig. 7.
Fig. 2. Isleta Pueblo.

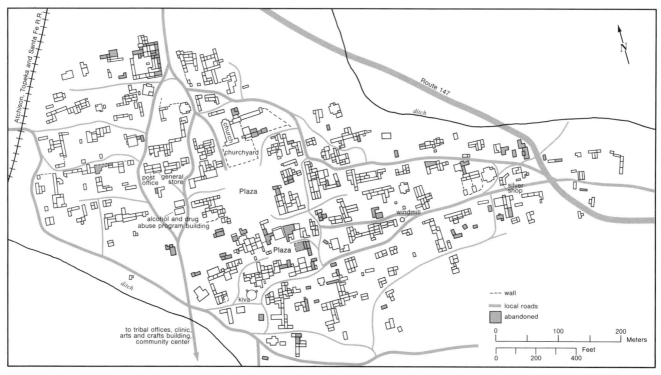

tinue to produce red and possibly gray paste cooking vessels and plain red "service" ware reminiscent of the old Mogollon Red ware though commonly with a wide band of polished slip just outside or below the rim. Red clay was easily available in a deposit near the railroad one-half mile from the Pueblo.

Isleta legend (Ellis 1945–1953) refers to one group of ancestors having come from the north and one from the south. The claim to northern ancestry may have resulted from the spread of Anasazi peoples out of the general San Juan River area in numerous waves between Basket-maker times and A.D. 1300. There is no Southwestern

Fig. 3. Isleta residents in 1900. The woman is carrying a polychrome jar of the type introduced by Laguna immigrants. Her hair is worn without bangs and swept across the forehead, in imitation of the Laguna style. The man's outfit, typical of the time, incorporates several items of Spanish derivation: flat-brimmed felt hat, white cotton pants (which he wears tucked into leggings), and cotton shirt with pleated (and probably crocheted) front. Photograph by Sumner W. Matteson.

Pueblo that does not claim northern ancestry in whole or part. Isleta's tradition of partial southern derivation could refer to a movement of ancestral groups from the old Mogollon area of southern New Mexico or to the late seventeenth-century addition of peoples from the Manzano foothills whose ancestors probably were from the Rio Bonito area near Carrizozo (old Jornada branch of Mogollon culture).

## History

The early Spanish explorers reported numerous occupied sites in Tiguex (compare Spanish *Tigua* 'Tiwa'), the Southern Tiwa area that extended from the present location of Bernalillo on the north to Los Lunas on the south. The great majority were east of the Rio Grande. On the west the Rio Puerco separated the lands of the Tiwa from those of Keresan-speaking Acoma and Laguna. The Manzano and the Sandia mountains marked the eastern border of the province and provided plant and animal foods to supplement the native agricultural staples.

Fig. 4. Man's shirt set: a white cotton overblouse with crocheted front and a red cotton underblouse. Length of overblouse 80 cm. Made by Gertrude Jojola before 1958.

Missionaries and churchmen carried Europe's late fifteenth-century beliefs about heretics and witches into the New World, and by 1650 Spanish friars were blaming their slow success in New Mexico on Pueblo ceremonialists accused of hexing the padres and otherwise using black magic. Troops raided Pueblo religious chambers and brought masks, fetishes, and other ritual paraphernalia into the plazas for burning. Pueblo religious leaders were beaten, condemned to slavery or imprisonment, or hanged (Simmons 1974). The result was that in 1680 the Pueblos joined ranks to initiate the Pueblo Revolt, which effectively removed all Spanish settlers from the province of New Mexico until forces for a reconquest were acquired by Diego de Vargas in 1692. Isleta did not participate in the initial massacre. Whether this was because of sympathy with the Spaniards, fear of retaliation, or hesitation in the unusual step of allying themselves with other Pueblos is unknown. Certainly the quick move of 1,500 settlers from the Bernalillo area into Isleta Pueblo, whose own population was only 2,000, prevented any second thoughts on the matter. When Gov. Antonio de Otermín and his refugees from stricken Santa Fe managed to reach this Pueblo, they found it largely deserted. Thinking that all Spaniards to the north had been killed and being aware of increasing hostility from their unwilling Isletan hosts, the local settlers and 317 Tiwa, Piro, and Tompiro Indians had started for El Paso.

A year later when Governor Otermín made a dash into New Mexico, he found Isleta reoccupied, but leaders from the northern Pueblos had burned the church. The Isletans made little resistance when the Spaniards attacked, took 511 captives (of whom 126 escaped) to be escorted to El Paso, and burned the Pueblo. The Piros (and Tompiros?) in this native group later were resettled in two new Pueblos, Senecú and Socorro, with the Isletans between them at Corpus Christi de la Isleta, later to be known as Ysleta del Sur, only a few miles south of the center of present El Paso (Hackett 1942, 1:xx, 2:104, 201, 393-394; Hughes 1914; Houser 1970). The blood and culture of their descendants has been largely diluted through close Mexican contacts, but relationship to the original Isleta still is recognized (see "Tigua Pueblo," this vol.).

Some of the Southern Tiwa who did not go south with the Spaniards moved to Hopi territory in northern Arizona for a time, Isletans perhaps traveling and living with the people of Sandia who established the village of Payupki on Second Mesa (Bandelier 1890-1892, 2:234). Morfi (Thomas 1932:102) reported 80 families there in 1744 and spoke of 441 Tiwa having been escorted back from Hopi by two Spanish friars in 1742. The first full-time occupation of Isleta's present site may date from after that year. Sometime in this period churchmen attempted to settle some converted Hopi in the area, but secular authorities objected and the Hopi gradually deserted. Isleta tradition mentions a party having been led by their great snake to the Rio Grande. They remained longer at San Felipe than elsewhere but the snake (Pueblo-style designation for a leader representing or carrying a snake fetish) decided he did not like the country and took his people homeward. Some appreciable cultural borrowings that reflect the "Western" variant of Pueblo culture in Isleta probably resulted from early eighteenth-century Hopi contacts, and the low hill known as Oraibi may have been named at this time.

A new page in the history of Isleta acculturation was turned in the last quarter of the nineteenth century (Parsons 1932:348-357; Ellis 1945-1953). The geographic location of Laguna Pueblo long had subjected its people to painful stresses through non-Indian contacts, a problem eventually enlarged by the presence of a Protestant minister-school teacher and three other Protestant Whites who married Laguna women and lived in the Pueblo. Like most Pueblo tribes, Laguna had two major factions. Collaboration grew between certain aspiring "Progressive" native religious officials from Old Laguna and Paguate, another Laguna town, and the non-Indian residents who were convinced that tribal welfare would be best served by breaking with tradition and native government, a religious hierarchy that for three centuries had been associated with the local type of Catholicism. Pressure built up increasingly until in 1879 or 1880 Laguna's top officials (Conservatives) decided that they no longer could stand the ever-increasing strife, which even included accusations of witchcraft. Packing ritual

354

Fig. 5. San Antonio de Padua Mission church and convent in 1867. The padre stands at right. The two men standing on the roof may have been there to toll the bell, which was at that time beaten rather than pulled. The two men at center who appear to be dressed in buckskin robes may be Pueblo officials, possibly Grandfathers. Photograph by William A. Bell.

paraphernalia on their backs, they started for Mesita, at that time a sparsely settled farm center three miles east. The elderly town chief, Humika, was followed and beaten. Too frail to go on, he died there, leaving no successor, but 30 or 40 of the others decided to put more space between themselves and Old Laguna by moving to Sandia Pueblo on the Rio Grande. The war or outside chief had died earlier, without successor. The migrants, including heads of the Giant or Ant, the Fire, and the Flint societies (all the major religious organizations except for the Shikami, whose leader spearheaded the opposition) were led by Francisco Correo (Kaiuti or Kaituri), the kachina chief.

Since the 1700s Isleta Pueblo had been closely surrounded with Spanish neighbors. A monastery under patronage of San Antonio had been erected as early as 1629 (fig. 5). The villagers were without kachina masks but some of the old cults still existed. When the displaced Lagunas made their labored way into the Rio Grande valley in 1881, the officials of Isleta saw an opportunity to augment their own ceremonial program. If they would agree to live by Isleta's unwritten laws and promise never to remove their power-imbued masks and corn mothers (the fetish whereby each member of a religious society symbolizes his ties to Earth Mother), the refugees would be provided with land for homes and agriculture. They need not go on to Sandia.

The weary Lagunas accepted the offer. Their kachina chief became town chief for the Laguna colony, which was given the hill of Oraibi as a center. A house was provided for their ceremonial activities. The immigrants

N.M. Dept. of Development, Santa Fe.
Fig. 6. Dominga Chewiwi, an Isleta woman of Laguna descent, seated on a ledge between two beehive ovens. Photograph by unidentified photographer, May 17, 1954.

were taken into whichever of Isleta's Corn groups were closest to their own matrilineal clans. Residence would be matrilocal, as at home. Their religious society heads banded together to form a single esoteric curing organization, the Laguna Fathers, which would parallel Isleta's Town Fathers but also double as their own characteristic religious council and would appoint their own governor and war captains. Most of this conservative Laguna group returned within a few years to Mesita, but the kachina chief was constrained to stay and was succeeded by son and then by grandson, for the masks promised to remain forever in Isleta would become dangerous if not correctly tended with rituals.

## Population

There seems to have been little change in Isleta's population during the nineteenth century. In 1790 it was recorded as 410; in 1808, 471; in 1809, 487; in 1850, 751; in 1860, 440 (probably incomplete); in 1864, 786; in 1870, 768 (Arny 1967:39). Ward (U.S. Census Office. 11th Census 1893:92) gives 1,059 for the carefully handled 1890 census, an increase that included the Laguna influx (fig. 6).

## Culture

### Subsistence

Isleta's economic basis differed little from the general Pueblo pattern. The people were primarily dependent on agriculture, largely sustained by four ditches that took water from the Rio Grande even before the Spaniards reached the Southwest. There was no need for dry farming. Technically the irrigated farmlands belonged to the Pueblo as a whole. Through assignment by the Isleta governor, an individual usually obtained a single acre of land, but if the governor or war captains found that the assignee left the land within a year or did not farm it, the plot and accompanying water rights were returned to Pueblo possession and reassigned. Land and rights, if used, customarily passed from father to son. In the 1940s the few large landowners had some 30 acres apiece, but the average was no more than 10. As in other Pueblos, land farmed for a year or more could be sold to other Isletans, though never to outsiders. Wheat, corn, beans, pumpkins, chile, a small amount of vegetables, and a little cotton were grown. Some families had fruit trees (fig. 7). More raised grapes (fig. 8). Fruits, including the grapes, were packed in native-made crates to be carried on burro back to Laguna Pueblo for trade or sale. More of the grapes were made into wine, which found easy sale among the Indians and the Spanish-American neighbors. Isleta-owned lands outside the irrigated valley bottom were used by all the community for gathering wood and wild plant foods, dyes, and medicinal herbs. Isletans kept a few horses, a few sheep and goats, and a slightly larger number of cattle (Euler 1954).

Rabbit hunting was common, but much of the meat (never plentiful) was obtained by hunting in the Manzano Mountains east of the village. The people also fished in the Rio Grande and mountain streams.

### Clothing

Deer hides (fig. 9) were tanned and colored a red-brown with plant dye for making men's moccasins and leggings. The women's thick white wrapped leggings and attached moccasins were of white buckskin. Buckskin also was used to a small extent for items of men's clothing and in assorted small home and ceremonial uses.

### Trade

As local basketmaking died out, Jicarilla Apache baskets and others became important in trade. Trade brought decorated pottery from other Pueblos, especially Acoma, Zia, and Santo Domingo, and religious pictures framed in ornately decorated tin work came from the Spanish-Americans. Social and economic contact between Isletans and Spanish-Americans was close and apparently usually happy.

Fig. 7. Woman laying peaches out to dry. In 1890 Isleta had 60 acres of fruit trees, primarily yielding peaches, plums, and apricots (U.S. Census Office. 11th Census 1893:113), which were sold, eaten, or dried and stored for winter usage. A string of chili peppers, also drying, hangs on the wall. Photograph by Sumner W. Matteson, Sept. 30, 1900.

## Social Organization

Throughout the Tanoan Pueblos there is a social system in which both patrilineal and matrilineal relationships are officially recognized, but emphasis is somewhat stronger on the patrilineal side. Isleta males but not females, for example, usually inherit farmlands. The Isleta child is born into a bilateral extended family and introduced to a host of relatives among whom marriage is believed to be incestuous and hence dangerous unless beyond the degree of fourth or fifth cousins, limits far more extended than those set by the Roman Catholic church. The kinship system makes no differentiation in terminology between relatives on the patrilineal and matrilineal sides in ascending generations, nor are age distinctions within a category of kin indicated. In descending generations, members of ego's direct line are distinguished from all other relatives except that an older brother's children are sometimes given the same terminology as one's own. One of his father's sisters or Corn group sisters serves as a male's ceremonial sponsor (Parsons 1932:230–233).

The most basic organization other than the family into which a child receives membership is the Corn group or one of its parts (Parsons 1932:210, 269–274; Ellis 1945–1953). The five directionally oriented Corn groups and their components are White Corn (east), also known as Day people; Black Corn (north) with Poplar and Magpie components; Yellow Corn (west); Blue Corn (south) with Water bubbling and Cane components; All-colors Corn (above-middle-down direction) with Corn, Eagle, Buzzard or Goose, and *šíču* components. A Corn group with components has no single leader, but as the chiefs of those components are in charge of the fetishes and alternate in handling the ceremonies of the group each is spoken of as a Corn chief or Father. Every Corn group leader is expected to have at least three assistants, men who have vowed that if they are cured of some malady they will agree to take over the leader's position. A women's auxiliary known as the *keʔíde* 'mothers' exists in each Corn group to participate in dancing and to perform certain other specific duties, but it never sings.

Fig. 8. Farm house on the outskirts of Isleta, possibly used to manufacture wine from grapes growing in vineyard (foreground). The shaded area at top was often used for summer work and sleeping and for drying corn and fruit. A peach tree stands at right. Photograph by Sumner W. Matteson, 1900.

Isleta's Corn groups or their components often are incorrectly referred to as clans. They are neither patrilineal nor matrilineal, endogamous nor exogamous. Parents "give one" to a chosen group, characteristically that of one or of both parents. Corn groups are ritual units that function in personal crisis rites but also in solstice rituals of importance to the entire Pueblo. They can be likened to Taos kiva groups with their components, and it seems quite possible that before the period of Spanish domination and influence, the Isleta Corn groups had their own "small" or "religious society" kivas. Except for use of a special ceremonial house by White Corn, in the 1970s the meetings were held in the household of a component's leader. The Corn groups have five major responsibilities: (1) Baptism of a child with ritually blessed water during the first solstice ceremony after his birth, the conferring of a name selected by father's sister, and presentation to him of a perfect ear of corn to protect him against harm during his first year. (2) Provision of "medicine" water for each member, and those of other groups if they wish, to sip for purification and new strength. (3) A Corn Father as escort to a member of a curing society when he goes to society meetings. (4) Holding a four-day retreat in the home of their leader for officers and a few members during the full moon before the summer and winter solstices (June 1–15; December 1–16). These retreats, which occur in specified sequence, include two to four days of complete fasting, the placing of fetishes on floor altars, and dancing to invite Sun's descent through a hatchway in the roof to accept the prayer plume laid out for him (Parsons 1932:288–301). The rituals are intended to remind Sun that when he reaches his summer or winter home a few days later, he should not tarry but promptly resume his movement to the north or the south. Prayer plumes are placed on a Sun shrine east of the Pueblo to be delivered by Sun to Moon, who is responsible for rains. The actual winter solstice date when Sun reaches his most southern point opens the new year, further divided by solar and lunar observations. (5) Performance of rituals by Corn Father to insure that the spirit of the dead reaches that specific locality of the afterworld where his own group centers. The leaders of father's and of mother's group bring a prayer feather to be tied into the hair of the corpse (fig. 11).

The other organization of which each infant is made a member is the moiety (Parsons 1932:261–263, 317–320, 332–336; Ellis 1945–1953). When he is but four days old he is introduced to the leader. Membership in the *šúde* (Red Eyes, Summer) or the *šífun* (Black Eyes, Winter) reflects the Tanoan principle of emphasis on the bilateral family. The first child goes into father's moiety, the second into mother's, and the third into father's, the sponsor being a ceremonial father from that moiety. In the 1970s there was no initiation. For dances the color identifying each group is painted around the eyes of members. The child receives his moiety name at the

*357*

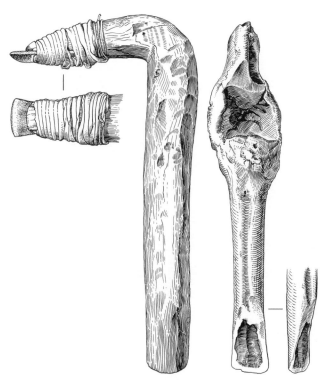

Smithsonian, Dept. of Anthr.: 31317, 31316.

Fig. 9. Tools used by men in tanning hides. left, Adz-shaped scraper with wooden haft and sharp steel blade attached with buckskin thong, used to remove flesh and to thin by paring; length 28.3 cm. right, Tool made from horse tibia with sharpened posterior end, used to remove hair or perhaps to thin hide; length 29.5 cm. Both collected in 1873.

spring ceremony for opening the irrigation ditches or when he is carried to the moiety house on the leader's shoulders during one of the semiannual retreats and purification rituals, an emasculated parallel to initiation into the kachina cult in the more western Pueblos.

*Religious Organization*

Each moiety is in charge of ritual requirements for the Pueblo as a whole during its own season, and ceremonies marking transfer of this responsibility from one to the other moiety are held in late March and late October. At this time the leader of each moiety and his three assistants go into retreat in their isolated moiety house, marked with a stepped facade over the doorway. Parsons (1932:209) erred in referring to these as kivas but later corrected herself (1962:6); Isleta has always had only one kiva or round house. Each moiety has a war captain (hwiławéde) with two assistants for one year and three the next (Ellis 1945-1953), authoritative groups that handle the ritual permission required for presentation of every ceremony. Four men of each moiety serve for life as téʔen, the čàpiuʔúde or Grandfathers, kachinalike exorcisors and disciplinarians closely related to units of the same name and function in the Tewa Pueblos, the Chapeyecam of a number of north Mexican tribes, the suyukʔi and

ʔaˑtošle of Zuni, and the Hopi ogre family, which regularly comes to threaten unruly children in February (Parsons 1916).

Each moiety is responsible for one major dance a year. The łíwa fɔ̀ar (Grandfathers', land turtle, or preplanting spring dance) of the Black Eyes is intended as a prayer for rain, good crops, and general fertility. The Red Eyes are requested to participate so that two dance companies can perform alternately. Headdresses are cotton plaques edged with small feathers, symbolizing clouds and prayers for rain, and carry two horizontal eagle feathers. Turtle-shell rattles are attached under the knee. The Grandfathers who toss live rabbits to the audience as a symbol of plenty also wield yucca whips to keep onlookers in order. During the evening the women of šíču Corn group perform a dance for precipitation. The Red Eyes have charge of the *pínitu,* or water turtle fall dance, in which men wear on their heads a stepped tablita with projecting arrows, symbolizing rain clouds and lightning. Accompanying them are the *kápiwʔùn.* One of Isleta's losses to Spanish religious zeal was her Quirana (fertility) and Koshare (representatives of the Sun, dedicated to fertility and therapeutic clowning) organizations. As substitutes, the Black Eye chief annually appoints *kápiwʔùn* representatives who go to the round house (kiva) to receive body paint in the black and white horizontal stripes and encircled eyes and mouth typical of the Koshare. Their hair is in two side buns. Quirana representatives receive an all-over body coat of red, white, or yellow coloring and face stripes. Their hair is pulled into a single high tuft. The *kápiwʔùn* put on a long amusing skit against a background of piled harvest products to be distributed after the dance.

Parsons (1939, 1:129, 349, 1962:7) has pointed out that these moiety performances are in reality the old kachina dances from which masks were deleted. It is significant that the local Laguna Kachina Father has taken charge of both.

*Curing*

During his youth or later an Isletan may be dedicated to one of two medicine societies. In old Pueblo belief, illness results either from some type of misbehavior in relation to Pueblo standards or from witchcraft. Symptoms are both psychological and physical. The leader of the society is told that if the patient recovers he may join that group, though this move is not required. If the illness is no more than recurrent bad dreams or malaise, the leader may decide that treatment by one medicine man is sufficient. A more serious illness requires the work of several or all medicine men of the society. To locate the foreign object "shot into his body" by a witch, the men gaze into a bowl of water or use the crystal hanging from a necklace of bear claws worn by each. Removing such objects (mice, red ants, rags, balls of cordage) is a matter of combining imitative magic and sleight of hand. Should evidence of

Fig. 10. Plastering the adobe walls is traditionally the responsibility of women. left, Mixing the adobe plaster. right, Applying a thin coat of the plaster to the exterior wall. The ledge along the base of the house, used for sitting outdoors, was popular in the 1920s and 1930s. Photograph by Fred K. Hinchman, 1937.

witchcraft appear to be considerable, as when masses of people were dying in the influenza epidemic of World War I, the curers work themselves into a state of high excitement and at night dash through the village seeking the witch, which may be transformed into a bird or a dog at their approach. The representation of a witch finally brought into the ceremonial house in the form of a rag

Fig. 11. Isleta funeral, about 1915. After the corpse has been washed and ritually prepared for travel to the afterworld, it is laid out on a house ladder and carried first to the church and then to the graveyard. The body is wrapped in a black manta and buried with the head to the south, with a ritually "killed" bowl placed on the grave. A hole for food, personally owned ceremonial gear, and other objects is traditionally dug some distance away, thus equipping the individual (buried in Christian graveyard) for the native afterworld (Ellis 1968). Photographer unknown.

doll with a black kernel of corn for its heart is "killed" and burned (Parsons 1939, 1:339–340; Ellis 1970).

After recovery the patient may be required to wait two or three years before the society accepts him in the presence of his relatives. His new "medicine man's heart" is symbolized by a grain of corn, which he swallows. Days or years later he takes the final step, which requires fasting, four days of instruction in secret curing techniques, preparation of a corn "mother" to be set on the altar with those of other members, and a final night in which he practices some of his new techniques on family members present. At dawn he carries his corn mother outside for prayers to the sun.

Until the advent of the Lagunas, Isleta apparently had but one curing society, the Town Fathers, as in basic Tanoan social structure (Ellis 1964). The Laguna Fathers medicine society differed from the local organization of Town Fathers only in their number of specialists: Rattlesnake Father, Ant Father, one who aided hunters, one who ritually dedicated new houses, and a female doctor for childbirth. Each society included a man who could find lost objects and track thieves. Both societies were equally open to Isleta and to Laguna-descendant members. The Town Fathers used their leader's home for meetings. The Laguna Fathers eventually constructed a new ceremonial house and painted its interior walls with important supernatural beings: sun, moon, Orion's belt, the Sky deity, xúmpa who is his guard, triangular cloud symbols with lightning, the rainbow, the horned serpent who is the deity of irrigation, and the bear and mountain lion who carry power for curing and killing. One is reminded of murals on walls of Pueblo IV religious chambers in the ruin known as Pottery Mound on the Rio Puerco, quite certainly an old Acoma or Laguna site.

Fig. 12. Feast of the Dead, held on All Souls' Day (Nov. 2). Bowls, lined with upright ears of corn and the favorite foods of the dead, are taken by women to the unmarked graves of their relatives, which are in the churchyard (shown here) and within the church itself. These offerings for the dead are placed on their graves; candles are placed around the periphery of the graves and lit. Painting (slightly cropped) by an Isleta man dated Nov. 29, 1939 (see Goldfrank 1962). Photograph by Charles F. Lummis, probably in 1884 when he witnessed this event (Lummis 1916:144–153).

Cures for which the medicine societies were responsible included the preplanting ceremony (šún?ab), which ritually cleansed fields and domesticated animals. In this the two organizations always cooperated except during a period of quarrels when the Laguna Fathers were intentionally overlooked. Later illnesses and deaths among the Town Fathers engendered suspicion that the neglected medicine men had indulged in witchery, a good example of native belief that persons who have learned the secrets of curing can, if they choose, misuse their "power" to cause sickness. Known "witches" may be paid for secrets and equipment whereby others may damage enemies or raise themselves above their fellows. Fear of witchcraft persisted in Isleta until the mid-twentieth century or later, though since the 1930s ailments introduced by non-Indians had been taken to non-Indian medical facilities for treatment.

Meetings of medicine societies always were guarded by members of the xúmpa, the old Warriors' or Scalp Society. The real xúmpas were men who had taken a Navajo scalp and then been cleansed by the society of danger inherent in that act. The personal "power" thus acquired was for tribal benefit. When warfare and scalping were prohibited by the United States government, the society was continued by men who vowed to become xúmpas if they survived some potentially dire calamity. The xúmpa group, like town chief and kápiw?ùn, was closely associated with the round house or great kiva, as elsewhere, and all scalps taken were sealed into niches within its interior wall. Only members of the mà-fúrnin, the women's war society or branch of the xúmpa, with their own leader and her assistants, were permitted to clean the round house, the town chief's "business" or ceremonial house, and the track where ritual races for the Sun were run (fig. 13). These women sang xúmpa songs

and in initiation years were expected to chew the Navajo scalps removed for the time from the sealed niches and spit the resulting "blood" into fine white clay. The men then patted the mixture into cakes from which a morsel could be broken as medicine for men complaining of loneliness or a weak heart. In the war dance the xúmpa men formed two lines between which two of the mà-fúrnin performed, each with a scalp on a pole.

## Structures

Isleta's single round house (Parsons 1962:6; Ellis 1945–1953) or great kiva (šiehwíb?àb) is said to symbolize the world. Like prehistoric Rio Grande kivas, it has no bench. Horns of deer, buffalo, antelope, and mountain sheep are set into the walls for hanging garments or other things. The fireplace, backed by a deflector with stepped top, is in the center under the hatchway through which the ladder descends. In the floor is a covered stone-lined box into which bits of the flesh of all animals of their world were placed. The special fuel for kiva fires comes from a shrub growing in the western hills. The fire must be laid by the chief of Yellow Earth people and lighted with a cedar bark torch kindled at the blaze in the town chief's house. With song, the kiva fire is offered to the five directions. The kiva roof represents the sky, held up by four stout pillars of wood, which the Grandfathers and medicine men periodically purify with their eagle feathers. Outside entrance steps are on the south side. In late times the kiva was used on the first night of the spring preplanting dance (łíwa-fəar) and as an assemblage and starting point in ritual races for the sun. Secular meetings were not permitted in this kiva lest it be profaned by loud or unseemly talk, and other uses declined as the ceremonial system broke down.

Fig. 13. Races for the sun. These relay races were performed on three or four consecutive Sundays every year, beginning with a race by small boys on Easter Sunday afternoon. Run on a prescribed east-west course, the races were organized by the war chief, town chief, and *xúmpa*, as part of a series of related ceremonial events (Lummis 1925:111–130; Parsons 1932:324–330). Photograph by Charles F. Lummis, Apr. 19, 1896.

## Political Organization

The native political structure of Isleta was entirely an extension of the religious structure (Parsons 1932:254–261; Ellis 1945–1953). It followed the general Tanoan pattern but with variations (Ellis 1964). Isleta, like its Keresan neighbors, had one town chief or cacique (*t?ày-kabéde*). As representative of Earth or Corn Mother, he must be a gentle person who would harm neither men nor animals. Never permitted to leave the confines of the Pueblo, each morning he emerged through a hatchway in his roof to toss a cornmeal offering to the rising sun. Every year he renewed the "salt circle," 18 or 20 inches across in cornmeal in one corner of his ceremonial house (Parsons 1962:10; Goldfrank 1962:78; Ellis 1945–1953). This circle, crossed with directional lines to form the sun design, symbolized the Pueblo, and all religious leaders must toss an offering of cornmeal onto it as their request to present a ceremony. Small rituals occupied him throughout the year. Because all his time was spent in his ceremonial house "working" for his people, he and his family were publicly supported. The field set aside for him was planted and harvested under direction of the war priest, and one or more great jars buried in front of his fireplace kept filled with seed corn for which the poor could apply. The war priest went through the village collecting meat, wood, and other necessities for the cacique's family. His ceremonial dress, similarly provided, consisted of buckskin shirt and pants and a little black cap edged with cotton, symbolic of clouds, with prayer feathers attached on one side. His face was painted black, and a white stripe edged his chin. At the time of appointment he received a new name symbolic of his new role. His corn mother was believed to be the most powerful in the Pueblo (Ellis 1945–1953).

The town chief appointed or at least installed the war or bow priest (*kàbe-hwíride*) representative of Sun, who carried a bow rather than a cane to symbolize his office. This man, who must come from the *xúmpa* groups, worked with the cacique and was of approximately equal importance (the Parsons 1962:4 account is somewhat confused about this group of officers, some of whom have not existed for several generations). The leader of the *xúmpa* or Warriors' Society was referred to simply as *xúmpa, pà?ị-hwì- ławéde,* or *pá?ịde*(?); he represented the older of the supernatural twin war gods. His assistant, representative of the younger of those twins, was known as the *tị̀-hwì- ławéde.* The war or bow priest and the head *xúmpa,* who would have been the war chief, were responsible for village security in relation to law and order and for control of witches inside the Pueblo, as well as for security of the outer boundaries of lands used and claimed by the Pueblo. After dangers from invaders disappeared, the war chief sent his assistants on horseback to check Isleta's lands for trespass by foreign herds

*361*

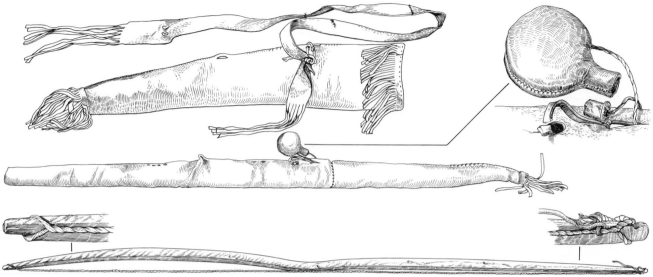

Fig. 14. Quiver, bow case, powder flask, and bow. The narrow buckskin case for the bow and the fringed buckskin quiver were said to be "five generations old" in 1913. Attached to the bow case is a rawhide powder flask, using a brass 30-30 cartridge case as a stopper. The bow stave is of wood and the bow string of twisted sinew. Length of bow 132 cm, rest same scale; collected in 1913.

of sheep or cattle. The bow priest's functions lay in the line of planning and direction, combined with prayer and ritual, and he could take administrative action. The head *xúmpa* who gave him aid, and the *xúmpa*'s assistant, could go into the field of battle, though a major concern of the *xúmpa* group lay in socioreligious matters.

A hunt chief or *humúhu* completed the roster of officials. His responsibilities were ritually assuring reproduction of wild animals, providing good luck for individual hunters by means of a ceremony and the loan of small animal fetishes, and making prayer sticks to be buried in the mountains with an offering of cornmeal, turquoise, and coral beads for game animals. He also directed periodic communal hunts in which an area was surrounded except for one open side through which beaters drove game into the circle. His assistant, pledged into that position by being cured from some ailment, became his successor through appointment by the town chief.

The existence of a secular government in Isleta, as in other Pueblos, had been decreed by Spain in 1620, but the Pueblos implemented this decree by having the religious hierarchy appoint secular representatives to deal with non-Indians. At a public meeting opened with prayer, the Isleta town chief customarily announced that he and the council of *principales* (all religious officers, heads of organizations and first assistants) had met in his ceremonial house to discuss the best possible candidates for next governor. Others could be nominated from the floor. After a standing vote, the elected man was expected to repeatedly assert that he was unworthy, too busy, and did not want the office. Long arguments followed until he would agree to accept this unpaid public duty. Then, while he knelt, the town chief prayed over him, touched

his body with the governor's cane of office (presented by Abraham Lincoln), which was believed to carry "power" like that of native fetishes, and explained that in his cupped hands he would hold all the ceremonies and business of the village. After the governor had been "completed," he appointed his own two lieutenant governors (fig. 15) and two sheriffs. The first lieutenant received the cane given by the Spanish king, but the second lieutenant and the war captains, nominated from each moiety by the Corn group leaders and then chosen by vote, had native-made shorter canes, some of which were decorated with beads. The majordomo in charge of irrigation ditches had no cane. The important town crier and a sacristan added since Spanish times both served for life, unpaid and caneless.

According to the native plan of succession, when the town chief died, the war or bow priest would take over his duties until a new town chief could be selected by the Corn group leaders. If the war priest died, the *xúmpa* picked up that office on a temporary basis. This planning sounds adequate. But just after Laguna was wracked by its social breakup, Isleta found itself in almost equally deep problems of religio-political organization.

The last real and correctly installed town chief was Rafael Huipi (*thúr- łùa*), who died in 1896. He had come from Blue Corn group, as had his father, the preceding town chief, who died before 1880. The bow or war priest took over the town chief's duties for the expected interim and the Corn chiefs made their selection for a successor, but the man chosen emphasized his initial refusal by moving out of the Pueblo. Acculturation had made the rules of caciqueship appear too personally restrictive. Then—or before—the war priest died. Dolores Jojola,

Milwaukee Public Mus., Wis.
Fig. 15. Governor of Isleta (center) and his lieutenant governors, all with canes of office, in 1900. The man at right is Pablo Abeita. Photograph by Sumner W. Matteson.

the head *xúmpa,* then had to take over the duties of town chief. He served for all his remaining years but never could actually become town chief because only a war priest could have "power" to conduct his ceremony of installation. Similarly, it was impossible to "make" a new war priest because only a properly installed town chief had "power" to install a war priest. Isleta had reached a thorough impasse. Jojola was followed as acting town chief by three other head *xúmpa*s in succession (Ellis 1945-1953).

The characteristically conservative Pueblos cherish a strong and tenacious belief that no person has the right to handle a ceremony of office until he has gone through the technically correct training and rituals administered by designated officers whose own positions came as the result of equally correct training and installation by constituted officers. Knowledge of a ceremony or ability in governing men does not give any right to manage such matters because without the ritually acquired "power" the would-be leader cannot expect the supernatural backing necessary to success.

The outcome of this substitution, which the Corn chiefs saw as an attempt of the *xúmpa* group to take over the

Pueblo, was a local revolution, which raged between 1940 and 1942 and continued to wrack social relations for another five or more years (Ellis 1945-1953; French 1948). Accounts vary. According to one, on New Year's Day when Juan Trinidad Zuni, the last *xúmpa* to act as town chief, was about to hand the canes of office to his secular appointees, the crowd in the plaza erupted into noisy disturbance. The head of one of the medicine societies, claiming that he was leader of a new party, proclaimed that the *xúmpa* could not appoint officers unless he first had the consent of all the Corn groups. One of the young men snatched the bundle of officers' canes from the *xúmpa*'s hands and ran. A melee followed with knots of men pommeling each other. All the canes were retrieved shortly thereafter except for that of the governor. The distressed *xúmpa* obliterated the cornmeal ring known as the "salt ring," which had existed since time immemorial in the town chief's office, took the town chief's cane, which thereby gave him continued power, had a new lock put on the door, and retired. After this, leaders requiring permission to put on a ceremony could only toss the cornmeal required as a gift in supplication at the closed door.

According to another version, the retiring Radical party governor refused to turn in his cane of office because the new governor-to-be was a Conservative. Instead, he gave the cane to a medicine man of his own party. As it was believed that the power of office actually lay in the cane and thereby was available to its holder, Isleta technically had two governors, one appointed but without cane and one with cane but not appointed. When the Radical refused to hand over the "archives" (the suitcase full of Pueblo papers) the appointed governor had him jailed. Meanwhile, the Indian office, hearing comments that the fight concerned the possibility of someone appropriating Pueblo funds to his personal use, froze those funds and left them thus for five years. Jealousy seems to have concentrated most strongly between the conservative Laguna Fathers and the *xúmpa*s on one side and all the Corn groups, termed Progressives, on the other. The Progressive leader, as would be expected, was the head of White Corn, Pablo Abeita (fig. 15), half-Spanish, educated, acculturated, and a very dynamic person who long had served as official interpreter. After this Isleta broke into three major and an ever-changing number of minor factions, including the Veterans party, all so mistrustful of one another that nothing could be accomplished.

Late in 1945 a Neutral party was organized to postpone 1946 elections until some intraparty agreements should be made. In 1946 interested officials of the United Pueblos Agency called a Sunday meeting of all Isleta voters and proposed that a constitution be drawn up by the Pueblo. This seemed finally to offer a solution, and three men from each of the three major parties acted as a people's committee to draft the document in a series of work sessions, aided by the Bureau of Indian Affairs superintendent or his representative. In 1950 when the superintendent was requested to install the new officers after the first election, the governor's cane reappeared.

The transition to this more democratic form of government has not been free of problems. War captains were forgotten in the constitution, and as no one felt he had the "power" to install those religious functionaries, for several years no dances could be held. Grave doubts existed about the novel concept of separating the judicial branch of native government from the administrative, especially when the new judge raised fines. Realization that registration was necessary before a party's candidate could run did not come at once. It took considerably longer to understand that a party's not voting at all did not automatically eliminate an unfavored candidate and that an elected governor carries authority even if his moves are disapproved. As might be expected, Isleta's constitution has suffered considerable renovation since first formulated (Ellis 1945-1953).

## Sociocultural Situation in the 1970s

In the 1970s Isleta was flourishing economically. A few good silversmiths worked at jewelry. Some pottery was made for tourist sale, unfortunately often decorated in bright synthetic colors or of commercial clay, wheel turned, with Indian designs painted in commercial glazes and fired in a commercial kiln. The majority of men commuted to work for the Bureau of Indian Affairs, at Kirtland Air Force Base, Sandia Base, or in other urban businesses. A successful cattle range operation was being conducted on the reservation, which contained some 210,948 acres of all types of land. About 5,000 acres of farmland were under irrigation. Most of the main canals were concrete-lined, which put this Pueblo ahead of the surrounding non-Indian communities. Approximately 202,073 acres (open and timber) were grazed.

As local jobs also were available, unemployment was low. Government funds permitted preparation of 20 acres as a recreation area, including fish ponds. An electronic company and a welding supply company established themselves in the Pueblo in 1974. An industrial complex growing at the interchange where Highway I 25 crosses the reservation assures further tribal income and employment possibilities. Almost all of Isleta's land had been leased for extensive oil testing.

With a 1974 population of 2,710, Isleta stood fourth among all the Pueblos. Several hundred new homes were erected with government aid. Education was being emphasized. Serious difficulties with one nonsympathetic Catholic priest led to his being escorted from the village in 1965 (Olguin and Olguin 1976), but the townspeople are proud of the fact that the first ordained—in 1977— Roman Catholic priest of Pueblo lineage is an Isletan.

## Synonymy†

Isleta Pueblo has its name from that of the Spanish mission, called San Antonio de la Isleta in the seventeenth century and San Agustín de la Isleta 'Saint Augustine of the little island' since its refounding in 1710 following the Pueblo Revolt. The name San Antonio de la Isleta was transferred to the Pueblo founded near El Paso for the Indian converts from Isleta who fled there in 1681; this Pueblo is now referred to as Ysleta del Sur, using an obsolete alternative spelling of the word for 'little island' that is also found in early Spanish references to Isleta (Domínguez 1956:203). According to Bandelier (1890-1892, 2:234) the Pueblo abandoned in 1681 stood very near the site of present Isleta "on a delta or island between the bed of a mountain torrent and the Rio Grande," and Domínguez (1956:207) wrote in 1776 that the rise on which the Pueblo stood (and still stands) was sometimes cut off by the waters of the Rio Grande, which split into two branches at flood stage. This accounts for the Spanish name, which was in use as early as 1630 (Benavides 1916:20, 1945:64). Garbled spellings and misprints include Llieta, Ilet, Iseta, Islella, Usleta, and Yslete.

The name for the Pueblo in the Isleta dialect of Southern Tiwa is šiehwíb-àg 'flint kick-stick place', said to be a reference to the shape of the height of land on which it is built (Lummis in Harrington 1916:528; cf. Curtis 1907-1930, 14:261, 264). Names with the same meaning and using cognate elements are Taos čiæ-hwíp-ta (Curtis 1907-1930, 14:261, 264, normalized), Picuris chīwhetha, and Tewa ci· xʷeve ówînge. Borrowings from Tiwa are Acoma siwhipa and Hopi čiyahwipa and čiyawihpa (normalized). Other names are Jemez téwákʷa or téwagʸíʔ (locatives of téŵa 'Tiwa Indian', pl. téŵiš), San Felipe kohernak, Acoma ṭîŵaʔáné, Laguna hanichina 'eastern river', Zuni kʔaššita·kʷe 'people of the fish' (Dennis Tedlock, personal communication 1977), and Navajo Naatoohó (Robert W. Young, personal communication 1977; Haile 1950-1951, 1:140, 2:172; Franciscan Fathers 1910:136).

## Sources

A problem with which all Pueblo ethnographers have struggled is the strong rule of secrecy, which evolved during Spanish oppressions. Available informants are few and reliability varies. Parsons's (1932) description of Isleta, together with her short papers and a very few by others on special topics (such as Euler 1954; Harvey 1963; Lummis's 1894 collection of tales) for years provided the only relatively reliable source on Isleta; how-

† This synonymy was prepared by Ives Goddard; uncredited forms are from Harrington (1916:527-530), who has additional spelling variants, or from anonymous sources.

ever, errors did exist. Parsons (1962) gives a very brief summary of Isleta history and social organization as introduction to 140 watercolors by an Isleta townsman who sent them to her with written explanations in the 1930s. He felt that she had been incorrectly informed on various details and a few major points and also that her illustrations were very insufficient. Goldfrank (1967) unfortunately revealed his identity only 10 years after his death, which brought the agony of public and private accusations to his extended family. Several generations may pass before the importance—to that sincere informant and eventually to other Isletans—of an accurate record of the traditional culture of their people may be realized by the townsmen.

# Cochiti Pueblo

CHARLES H. LANGE

The Indians of Cochiti ('kōchĭ₁tē) Pueblo (figs. 1-2), on the west bank of the Rio Grande in north-central New Mexico (see "Pueblos: Introduction," fig. 1, this vol.), belong to the Keresan-speaking group of tribes. Cochiti and other Puebloan tribes have shared an appreciable assemblage of culture traits and patterns, serving to distinguish this cultural group from adjacent non-Puebloan tribes. At the same time, the Cochiti, along with other Puebloan tribes, have maintained distinctive features and nuances of cultural traits that have served to provide a unique character to their tribal culture.

## Language, Territory, and Environment

Although Sapir (1925) conjectured an affiliation of Keresan with a number of other North American language families, most linguists have been inclined to consider Keresan as an isolated language, having no close linguistic relatives. The seven Keresan languages, or dialects, spoken at seven Pueblos, are closely related, having a time depth of only an estimated 500 years (Miller and Davis 1963:310). The least mutually intelligible varieties are spoken at the geographical extremes, Acoma and Cochiti, and the Cochiti variety is most readily understood by its nearest Keresan neighbors, the people of Santo Domingo and San Felipe Pueblos.*

In the quarter-century following World War II, Keresan at Cochiti lost eminence to English. Spanish similarly declined in common usage. Where formerly numerous adults were trilingual, or spoke both Keresan and Spanish if not English, young people of the 1970s had relatively little interest in Spanish, and even Keresan, preferring English instead. With increasing intermarriage with non-Cochitis, the household reinforcement of Keresan, especially among absentee families, had become difficult to maintain. Education, travel, military service, radio, and, perhaps most important, television had also contributed to these changes.

The Cochiti Indians have occupied their present village, about 25 miles southwest of Santa Fe, from some point in time prior to the earliest historic contacts, well over four centuries ago. Aside from possible additional

Cochiti villages reported as inhabited in 1591 (Castaño de Sosa 1965:140) and scattered family ranchitos, or farmhouses, occupied only seasonally for the most part in more recent times, the present Pueblo site has been the prime residence of most Cochiti Indians throughout the historic period. Since early in the twentieth century and increasingly since World War II, absentees have varied in residence from nearby Santa Fe and Albuquerque to communities throughout the United States and, particularly during military service, in a number of other countries as well.

Kinship and other cultural ties continue to attract absentees and their families back to the Pueblo for the major Roman Catholic feast of San Buenaventura's Day on July 14, as well as for Christmas, Easter, and other important occasions. However, with the passing of time, absentees grow in numbers, actually and proportionately; their return visits to the home Pueblo become less frequent.

Bodine (1972:272, 273, 275) presented data showing that there had been a population increase at Cochiti from 346 persons in 1942 to 799 in 1968. Further, he showed that between 1950 and 1968 the percentage increase was 93 percent, and from 1964 to 1968, the percentage increase was 23 percent. Between 1960 and 1968, Cochiti had an increase in nonresident population of 15 percent, which gave the Pueblo an absentee total in 1968 of 53 percent.

From a somewhat different perspective, restated, the 1968 data gave Cochiti a resident population of 376 out of 799 for regular cultural participation and interaction in contrast to the much larger Pueblo of Santo Domingo where the figures gave 1,943 as residents, out of the total of 2,206.

In the period since World War II, the rising number and percentage of absentee tribal members has served to place very real strains on the traditional patterns of culture. These patterns have rested on premises of widely based cooperation and reciprocity among family members and also among other population components. Their disruption has created problems, aggravated with the passage of time and the continuing trend away from traditional values (Lange 1960).

The single village, or Pueblo, of Cochiti is near the center of a rectangular reservation of over 26,000 acres, approximately divided by the Rio Grande flowing south-

---

* No phonemic analysis of the Cochiti dialect of Keresan is available, but the sound system is very similar to that of Santo Domingo (see "Santo Domingo Pueblo," this vol.; Miller and Davis 1963).

Southwest Foundation for Audio-Visual Resources, Santa Fe, N.M.
Fig. 1. Central portion of Cochiti Pueblo. Photograph by Peter Dechert, June 1977.

revised from Stubbs 1950:fig. 14.
Fig. 2. Central portion of Cochiti Pueblo.

ward. Bordering the river, there have been well over 600 acres under irrigation; however, the total acreage being farmed has steadily declined since the end of World War II. While accurate statistics are difficult if not impossible to obtain, it is reasonable to assume that as much as half, or more, of the potential irrigated acreage is no longer cultivated as more remunerative economic opportunities have become available in nonagricultural pursuits, commonly away from the immediate vicinity of the village.

The remaining reservation acreage consists of sandy alluvial fans and gravel hills covered, in part, by thin deposits of brown soils. The vegetation includes a scattering of piñon and juniper, and a variety of sparse grasses and cacti. Along the river and irrigation canals are cottonwoods and a greater abundance of willows and tall grasses.

## Subsistence

The Cochiti Indians have been agriculturists for a very long time. Based on maize (figs. 4–5), beans, and squash, the level of farming practices remained rather primitive until the advent of Spanish missionaries and colonists who introduced a number of agricultural improvements among the Pueblo Indians. In addition to major introductions such as wheat and other cereal grains, alfalfa, sheep, cattle, and horses, as well as various garden vegetables, improved irrigation systems were also made possible through the use of metal tools and implements, often crude and clumsy but nonetheless definite advances over the native wooden forms.

Mus. of the Amer. Ind., Heye Foundation, New York.
Fig. 3. Man making a plaited basket from lengths of yucca leaves, which have first been soaked in water. He is using his feet to anchor the horizontal elements as he weaves in the vertical elements. Photograph by Frederick Starr, about 1897.

Whether or not actual ditch irrigation was practiced in the area prehistorically remains a somewhat obscure point, although it seems probable that it was. However, the major effort was in terms of floodwater farming in fields located on or near the alluvial fans at the arroyo mouths. These fields, as contrasted with those used as dry-farming tracts, continued to be used in the early decades of the twentieth century.

The reliability of the irrigation system at Cochiti was greatly improved in the 1930s when the Middle Rio Grande Conservancy district completed a concrete dam about three miles north of the Pueblo and included a major canal on each side of the river. Cochiti, being the first community below the dam, has benefited slightly from this location although district allocation of available water has prevented this position from becoming significantly more advantageous than those of the downstream communities of Peña Blanca, Santo Domingo, San Felipe, or Algodones. Following activation of the dam and canals, a near maximum in irrigation farming and a corresponding demise of floodwater farming resulted, a situation that continued up to the period of World War II.

Paralleling these changes, there has been a gradual abandonment of ceremonialism in association with agriculture. While vestiges persist, much has disappeared from this phase of Cochiti life.

In the early 1960s, work was begun on a new dam, approximately midway between the 1930 dam and the Pueblo. This was a vastly larger dam, originally intended for irrigation and also flood control. In time, recreational uses were also authorized, and the permanent pool area was expanded accordingly. In 1975 construction of this tremendous earth and concrete structure was completed. While a certain amount of irrigated acreage has been obliterated in the course of the construction, the loss cannot be viewed as seriously damaging in the overall Cochiti agricultural effort because of the steady decline in agricultural activity. The new dam should assure a more reliable supply of irrigation waters for the remaining acreage than the old dam.

As one sequel to the construction of this new dam, the Cochiti tribe has entered into a 99-year lease agreement with a private, non-Indian development company; the agreement involves the 7,500 acres north of the Pueblo on each side of the river and along the northern boundary of the reservation. This area is to be developed as a retirement community, with business services, schools,

Mus. of N.M., Santa Fe.

Fig. 4. Women grinding corn in fixed wooden bins containing graded metates, probably of sandstone. They use two-handed manos. Three grades of metates are traditionally used to break, crush, and finally pulverize the corn. Corn ground in this way is used to make tortillas and paper bread and is added to stews and gruels. Photograph by T. Harmon Parkhurst, about 1920.

368

Mus. of N.M., Santa Fe.

Fig. 5. Woman removing fancy breads, probably for a feast day, from a beehive oven with a wooden bread paddle (on her right). Beehive ovens, found in a variety of forms in all the Pueblos, were introduced by the Spanish. At left is visible a portion of the swab (wooden pole with rag attached) that is used to clean out the oven once it is heated and the embers have been removed. Photograph by T. Harmon Parkhurst, about 1935.

and the usual utility and security installations and agencies. Plans for the new community anticipate a resident population (estimates ranging as high as 30,000), including not only retired persons but also individuals who will commute regularly to employment in Los Alamos, Santa Fe, and even Albuquerque.

The Cochiti leadership entered into this venture in consultation with the United Pueblos Agency officials as well as with those from other federal and state agencies. The intent has been to provide expanded, nonagricultural opportunities to the Cochiti, primarily, but also to other neighboring communities, both Indian and non-Indian, as the new community grows and recreational and other facilities associated with the new lake become operational. The decision to embark upon this venture has been a most difficult one, and the Cochiti leaders have entered into the arrangement accompanied by bitter protests from some tribal members. In terms of culture dynamics and change, there is bound to be a strong impact, impossible to calculate in its intensity or to anticipate fully in its ramifications.

## Culture

### Structures

On the northern periphery and a little on the western edge of the Pueblo itself, there has appeared, during the 1960s and 1970s, a small housing project of 10 or 12 single-family dwellings for the Cochiti themselves. These have been built cooperatively by the eventual residents; architectural styles vary from conventional "Santa Fe pueblo" forms to pitched-roof ranch types. The houses are of concrete block and frame construction, and they are scattered at intervals of 100 yards or more, a pronounced break from the traditional pattern of contiguous houses tightly clustered around the plaza or arranged in rows along several village streets, but a pattern that has been evident at Cochiti for several decades. This dispersed pattern of residence, while present in neighboring Pueblos, seems to have been accentuated earlier at Cochiti than elsewhere. A factor in this difference may be influences from the several resident Spanish families at Cochiti, in itself a break from traditional Puebloan patterns.

The great majority of Cochiti houses conform outwardly to traditional Puebloan architecture. Floors range from packed earth to wooden planking, both frequently covered by linoleum, rugs, or carpeting. Walls are of adobe bricks, most commonly plastered with adobe to prevent or retard weathering and to look better; ceilings and roofs have shifted from peeled log vigas, transverse poles, twigs or rushes, and adobe construction to sawed beams, boards, and tar paper covering under the adobe

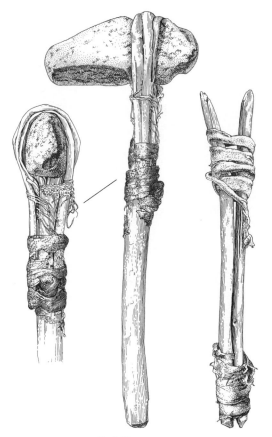

Smithsonian, Dept. of Anthr.: 47470, 47471.
Fig. 6. Stone mauls with wooden hafts secured by cloth and buckskin wrappings. left, Stone head is attached by a wood splint wrapped around the groove in the stone and lashed with cloth strips; length 29.5 cm. right, Entire haft is split to hold the maul head (which is missing) and held together by cloth and buckskin; length 24 cm. Both collected in 1880.

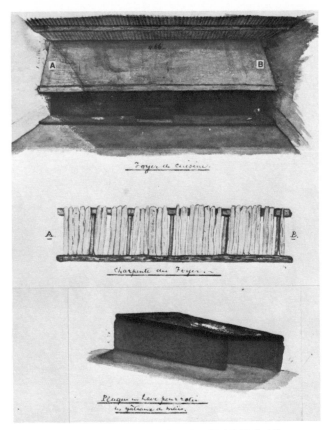

Biblioteca Apostolica Vaticana, Vatican City, Bandelier 1887, f.33: VI. V. #17.
Fig. 7. Architectural sketches of a Cochiti kitchen. top, Sketch of hearth, which extends across entire wall of kitchen, with hood that comes down from ceiling and is attached to the side walls (labeled A and B). middle, Sketch showing structure of the hood, which is apparently constructed of transverse poles covered with twigs and plastered over with adobe; (A and B correspond to top sketch). bottom, Lava stone, which is shown at the center of the hearth (top), used for making corn tortillas or piki bread. Colored sketches (page cropped and slightly rearranged) by Bandelier (1969) as part of a 1,400-page illustrated history of the missions and the colonization of the area that had been New Spain commissioned as a gift for the Pope and presented to him in 1887.

topping. Doors and windows are increasingly of commercial millwork and even metal frames, casements, and jambs.

During the late 1960s, a community-wide project under the sponsorship of the United States Public Health Service brought running water and sewer lines to virtually every house, permitting the installation of modern kitchen and bathroom facilities throughout the village. Telephones and a variety of electrical appliances are in more and more Cochiti houses; of great significance among these appliances is television, which introduces outside culture, ideas, values, potentialities, and wants, to the residents of Cochiti. Many houses still have only two or three rooms although newer ones are more likely to include additional rooms in more conventional American norms. Multiple-storied houses have not been seen at Cochiti for several decades; Goldfrank (1927:7) commented upon the atypical gabled roofs of corrugated iron she found in the early 1920s, a few of which continue to exist.

### Clothing

Clothing has similarly come closer to American norms; older women are more likely to continue with traditional dresses, woven belts, and even moccasins. However, these items are ever fewer, and it is primarily on ceremonial or festive occasions that traditional garb is worn, in some instances by the men (fig. 9) as well as the women.

### Education

In the late 1960s, a new day school with homes for the teachers was built near Peña Blanca, across the Rio Grande from Cochiti; the children come and go each day by bus. In addition to the Cochiti children, there are those from neighboring Spanish-American communities as well. With this change, the former homogeneity of the day school in the village has been altered. The Cochiti people have rather consistently been among the Pueblos

Fig. 8. Construction of a modern home in Cochiti, using the traditional bricks of sun-baked adobe. Photograph by Charles H. Lange, 1951.

Fig. 10. Man weaving a sash on a waist or belt loom, using a continuous warp, which is looped around the stake at left and the bar worn at his waist. Vertical looms (see "Hopi Economy and Subsistence," fig. 6, this vol.) can also be used. Photograph by Frederick Starr, about 1897.

most interested in fostering formal education for their children. For decades, many Cochitis have gone from the day school to high school, usually in Santa Fe; in more recent times, they have attended high school in Bernalillo. From high school, forms of vocational training have been pursued, and in a few cases, college courses have proved an attraction. Although relatively few have completed a college or university education, the interest is growing. Within the Pueblo itself, there has been a federally sponsored Headstart program; interest has been expressed in using this facility not only to strengthen English and other basics but also to teach Cochiti children their native Keresan. Not much progress in this last regard has been achieved.

## Social Organization

In social structure, the simple family prevails; family units have been, in turn, bound together in a kinship system based on the clan. The Cochiti clans are matrilineal and, ideally, exogamous. Residence has tended to be matrilocal—especially in the early months after marriage. The clans are named after plants, animals, and natural phenomena such as the sun, turquoise, and water. No ideas of "totemic" relationships are involved, and no taboos of food or other usages are observed (or even remembered). There appear to be, or have been, few clan

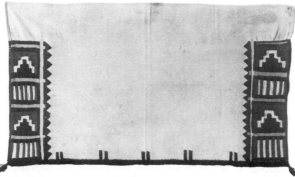

Fig. 9. Embroidered kilt of cotton worn by male dancers so that the design runs vertically over the right thigh (see fig. 17) and secured at waist by belt. Designs of red, green, and black commercial yarns represent rain symbols (Roediger 1941:116). Length about 104 cm, width about 60 cm; collected in 1964.

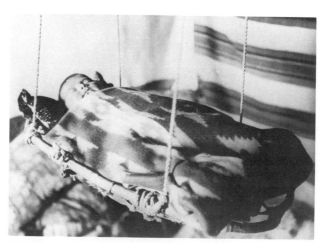

Fig. 11. Baby, wrapped in a Pendleton blanket, in a swinging cradle that is suspended from the ceiling beams. Cradles of this type and of a variant form (2 parallel pieces of wood inserted within a blanket or piece of sheepskin) were used, along with a variety of cradleboards, by the Rio Grande Pueblos (Dennis and Dennis 1940:107–115). Photograph by Simeon Schwemberger, 1906 or earlier.

rituals or officers in special capacities dependent upon clan affiliation. An occasional clan adoption or clan curing rite is still held, and it is customary to refer to the oldest woman of the clan as its "head." This "headship" is virtually nonfunctional aside from a certain degree of prestige accorded the person concerned; this attitude exists both within the clan and outside among the villagers.

Lange (1959:374-377, 515) summarized the clan rosters listed by several earlier authors; his informants could add a number of clans that had disappeared from Cochiti and several more that had come into the tribe either through intermarriage or immigration from other Pueblos in the twentieth century. With data from 1881 through 1948, informants in 1948 indicated the presence of 13 clans: Antelope, Bear, Corn, Cottonwood, Coyote (or Fox), Ivy, Oak, Pumpkin, Red Shell, Sage, Shipewe, Turquoise, and Water. In addition, they acknowledged the one-time presence of three additional clans; eight clans, reported by one or more earlier investigators, were denied as ever present at Cochiti. In two instances, these denials referred to clans noted by John G. Bourke in 1881 (Bloom 1933-1938, 11:235).

Clan exogamy has been the rule, but it has also been rather consistently violated in a small number of in-stances back through the years. Seemingly, this deviation has occurred primarily in clans that were strong numerically at the particular period. In such circumstances, the man and the woman have been outside the kinship taboos normally observed by Catholics and European-Americans even though they belonged to the same clan.

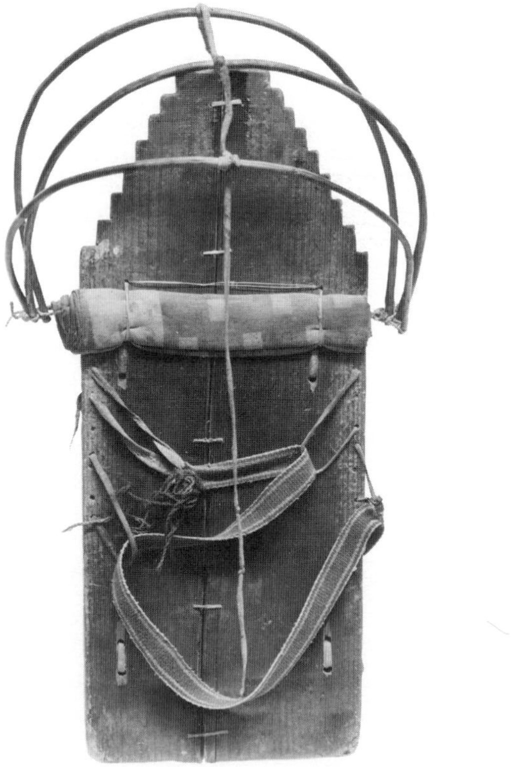

Counterposed with the matrilineal clan system has been the patrilineal moiety, or dual kiva, organization. Taking this affiliation, either Turquoise or Pumpkin, from one's father, the wife has traditionally transferred to that of her husband upon marriage, if it was an exogamous marriage in the moiety sense. (Either exogamy or endogamy may be followed in this regard, seemingly for the past century, more or less; earlier, there may have been a rule of endogamy, but this is by no means certain.)

The principal contrasts between the clans and the kiva groups, beyond this matrilineal or patrilineal basis, respectively, lie in several additional features. There is an inescapable affiliation with a clan at the time of birth although this may subsequently be changed through specific rituals of adoption; moiety affiliation may be changed by means of a formal request made to the respective kiva leaderships. This request is invariably granted, both by the former and the new groups. The kiva affiliation may also be dropped in a way and to a degree quite inconceivable in the case of a clan membership.

Accordingly, moieties, or kiva groups, may be considered as nonkin associations. The two kiva groups assume prominence in many ceremonials, the "sides" complementing each other's activities, as they alternate as dance teams. These may be dressed similarly and may perform similarly as in the Corn Dances, sometimes called Tablita Dances (Lange 1957, 1959:324, 365-366) (fig. 13), or they may present completely different ceremonial dances (fig. 14).

*Political Organization*

It is from the two kiva groups that the headmen of the three medicine societies (Flint, Giant, and Shikami) have traditionally selected the principal officials of the tribe each calendar year. The war captain and lieutenant war captain were named by the Flint headman, or cacique; the governor and lieutenant governor were designated by the Giant headman; and the *fiscal* and lieutenant *fiscal*, by the Shikami headman. Each year, the senior officer of the pair and his lieutenant were named from opposite kivas; also, the senior war captain and his lieutenant should come from the kiva opposite that of the governor and the *fiscal* and their lieutenants, respectively. In other words, the senior war captain, the lieutenant governor, and the lieutenant *fiscal* should be of one kiva, and their counterparts, from the other kiva. This alternation has evolved into the more simple pattern of having all senior officers from one kiva and all lieutenant officers from the other each year. In either pattern, the objective has

Mus. of N.M., Santa Fe: School of Amer. Research Coll. 14254/12.
Fig. 12. Hard-backed cradleboard for newborn, with terraced top, wooden hoops for protective flexible canopy, cloth head rest, and woven band for securing the child to the board (Lange 1959:74; Dennis and Dennis 1940:113); length about 58 cm; collected in 1936.

Southwest Mus., Los Angeles.

Fig. 13. San Buenaventura's Day Corn Dance, performed by the two moieties, first the Turquoise, then the Pumpkin, in front of the church and campo santo (Lummis 1925:253-270; Lange 1959:343-347). The men wear either red or dull blue body paint and have armbands of green and white; the women wear black mantas and bright green tablitas. From the pattern of the tablitas, the dancers appear to be of the Turquoise moiety. Two of the three Koshare clowns who were present can be seen just in front of the chorus; they are covered with bluish-white clay with black markings and have their hair drawn out in top knots. Photograph by Charles F. Lummis, July 14, 1888.

consistently been to maintain balance between the two kivas in this dualistic system.

About 1960 the Giant headman, sole surviving member of that society, died, and the society passed out of existence. The cacique, or Flint headman, assumed the additional duty of naming governors as well as war captains. The apparent ease with which this adjustment was made may well be characteristic of other accommodating shifts to compensate for cultural losses over the years.

It is difficult to assess accurately the prestige or importance of the cacique at Cochiti Pueblo in the early 1970s. The incumbent, who became cacique in December 1946, has failed to retain the prestige and respect generally accorded this official. The cacique has been traditionally considered to be the foremost medicine man; as such, deference is paid him by many. There is genuine concern that he continue to perform his official duties as the "mother" of his people, serving as their spiritual leader faithfully and consistently. Although there is increasing doubt expressed that this is, in fact, the case, there has been no concerted effort to initiate action or any inclination to take remedial steps.

Traditionally, when the cacique's role was deemed much more essential in the overall well-being of the tribe, he could be, and was, brought to trial by the war captains in response to charges of negligence or wrongdoing. The cacique could, on decision of the council of *principales,* be punished, deposed, or even executed. As acculturation progresses, even the least harsh of these measures begins to seem of small likelihood. This is not to discount the office of cacique completely, but it does indicate that the status of this once all-important official has steadily declined (see Lange 1952, 1958a).

Other similar adjustments in societies and offices can be hypothesized for times past; however, with the absence of written records, it is simply impossible to determine these shifts outside of very unusual circumstances. A clue, but no real proof, may be found through careful analysis of other Puebloan tribes, but over the years too many variables have entered the picture to make such parallel reconstructions anything more than hypotheses.

### Religion

Medicine societies form the base for much of the tribal political and ceremonial organization. In addition to the theocratic function of naming the officials each year, thereby assuring leadership compatible with traditional patterns and values of the tribe, the societies collectively and individually have concerned themselves with matters

Fig. 14. Navajo Dance performed by members of the Pumpkin moiety, probably as one of several Christmas dances. The dancers mimic the dress and dance movements of a neighboring group, as in Zuni or Comanche Dances (which can also be performed at Christmas). The men wear Navajo blankets as dance kilts (which at least one dancer has belted with a Navajo concho belt), dark paint over their bodies, and feather headdresses that include silverwork. Photograph by T. Harmon Parkhurst, about 1920.

such as curing, weather control, and the general well-being of all tribal members (see White 1930).

As time passes and the degree of acculturation progresses, there is increasing resort to modern physicians, dentists, clinics, and hospitals. An ever larger percentage of births occurs in hospitals rather than at home. Paralleling this trend is the declining interest in and reliance upon native medicine; the societies find ever fewer candidates for their ranks. However, among the older people and in specific contexts, the medicine man, or the society, is still called upon to function on behalf of an individual, group, or the entire tribe. Even in this last category, United States Public Health Service personnel and programs are making inroads.

In addition to the medicine societies there are other societies; two deserve special mention. These are the Koshare and the Quirana societies; these were termed "managing societies" by Goldfrank (1927:37ff.) because of their prominence in the supervision of numerous ceremonies throughout the course of a year. At other Pueblos, corresponding societies may assume leadership seasonally or in regard to specific ceremonies in the

course of the annual ceremonial calendar. At Cochiti, supervision alternates between the two on an annual basis.

The Koshare are affiliated with the Turquoise kiva and with the Flint medicine society, and the Quirana are similarly identified with the Pumpkin kiva and the Shikami medicine society (see Lange 1959:227–316 for details of Cochiti ceremonial organization). It appears reasonable to expect that the two managing societies may well endure long after the demise of the several medicine societies. These latter appear to be steadily losing ground under the constant pressure of acculturative processes; belief in the efficacy of the societies has waned, and interest in continuing their existence, either through patronage of services or actual membership affiliation, has declined. In contrast the managing societies, which have played only a small role in curing in the past, will presumably continue to have supervisory responsibility for assorted ceremonies as long as the ceremonies themselves persist. These ceremonies may be expected to be continued for their religious significance and ultimately, perhaps, solely for their intrinsic value as explicit manifestations of tribal tradition or folklore.

*Community Life*

The following is a description of the events and activities of a typical year in the late nineteenth century and early twentieth century. With the advent of the new year, the recently designated new officers (war captains, governors, *fiscales*, and younger assistants, *alguacilitos* and *fiscalitos*) assume their responsibilities. Major decisions are arrived at through discussion among these six major officials as long as reasonably applicable precedent exists.

Failing this, or if some new consideration is perceived, the matter is taken to the tribal council for discussion and decision. This council of *principales* has traditionally been composed of the six major officers and all who have previously held any of these positions. Formerly, questions were ultimately handled with essentially unanimous stances; since the end of World War II, there has been a discernible trend toward majority votes. This change and a tendency among the *principales* to avail themselves of the knowledge and experience of younger, more educated individuals, not technically qualified to sit on the council, have characterized prevailing attitudes among the tribal leaders in recent years.

Economically, winter activities have stressed hunting, wood gathering, and indoor occupations, generally; ceremonially, this is a relatively active period. Momentary release from the rigorous demands of the agricultural cycle has allowed this elaboration. Traditionally, these rituals and the associated public performances (open to outsiders for most nonkachina events and closed to outsiders and nonbelieving insiders for kachina and medicine society activities) have been deemed essential in contributing to the ongoing good or the improvement of the tribe's condition, such as its health, weather, food supply, and freedom from natural catastrophic forces.

While a substantial core of such feelings unquestionably persists, there is a growing tendency to consider these performances less as religious essentials and more as valuable traditions and as entertainment. It can hardly be ignored that the continuation of various celebrations, rendered in faithful adherence to traditional forms, brings outside visitors (as well as absentee kinsmen) to the village, with direct benefits in sales of assorted arts and crafts aimed at the general tourist trade. On the other hand, as numbers of absentees increase, it is ever more difficult to stage these ceremonies or celebrations properly or effectively.

Solstice rituals and ceremonies are portents of the new growing season—blended with the events and ideas of the Christian Easter time. From an essentially nonmechanized pursuit of agriculture, the Cochiti have moved to tractors in place of horses and oxen and adopted first the threshing machine and then the combine harvester, hay baler, and other farm machinery. With the help of Indian Service personnel and heavy equipment, irrigation canals were deepened and improved, and fields were graded and consolidated to allow more effective utilization of machinery in planting, cultivation, and harvesting.

Increasingly, the summer means a greater number of tourists and other outside visitors to the village; coupled with this direct impact within the Pueblo itself are more numerous fairs and exhibits away from the Pueblo for all tribes to show their arts and crafts products. The Santa Fe Arts and Crafts Show, the Gallup Intertribal Ceremonials, the Santa Fe Fiesta, the New Mexico State Fair, as well as feast days at various Pueblos—all provide opportunity to profit economically and to engage in activities that seem to have the dual effects of "homogenizing" various aspects of intertribal, or pan-Indian, culture and of reinforcing individual tribal pride.

As a tribe, the Cochiti have perhaps received the greatest acclaim for their drums; these range from large, essentially ceremonial, drums to rather small ones made for toys and the tourist trade. These are two-headed cylindrical drums, fashioned out of hollowed sections of cottonwood logs; they may be as large as 18–24 inches in diameter and 30–36 inches high. The regular lacings, over natural or painted sides, give an overall appearance that is widely recognized as having been made at Cochiti. Recognition has also been accorded the pottery makers at Cochiti; their products (fig. 15) range from bowls and ollas to a variety of figurines, including turtles, frogs, birds, and even dinosaurs. Cochiti pottery pieces are typically black-on-grey, with brick-red bases and interiors. Since the mid-1960s, there has been a resurgence of large figurine manufacture, repeating but not duplicating a practice of the early 1900s. The most common form is that of a woman sitting, with as many as a dozen small

Smithsonian, Dept. of Anthr.: 39575; Mus. of N.M., Sante Fe: 47653/12.
Fig. 15. Two styles of Cochiti pottery. left, Animal-shaped water vessel of type common in the 1880s–1890s, with black painted designs associated with ceremonial symbolism (Frank and Harlow 1974:77); diameter 25 cm; collected in 1879. right, "Storyteller" figure, which has been a popular tourist item; height about 22 cm; made by Aurelia Suina about 1975.

child figures arranged on her (fig. 16). This innovation has been remarkably successful. In addition, lapel pins of beadwork on leather or cloth or wood and a variety of dyed corn necklaces are commonly produced for sale to tourists and to curio shops.

Over the years, a number of the Cochiti, almost exclusively the men, have produced quantities of silver rings, bracelets, pins, and necklaces. These are most frequently decorated with turquoise and other stones,

Fig. 16. Helen Cordero, innovator of the storyteller figure, with a very elaborate version, dried but not yet fired. Finished figures are generally white (from an overall white slip), with details appearing in black and brick-red. Photograph by Richard Erdoes, 1976.

often petrified wood. Still others among the Cochiti have achieved considerable prominence for their paintings, watercolors, and to a lesser extent, oils. Others have done ink sketches. Subject matter ranges from dance figures, permissible for outsiders to see (fig. 17), through a variety of normal daily activities, to a range of animals, either in realistic colors or in unnatural shades, such as blue horses. There has been increased experimentation by Cochiti artists in both media and subject matter.

Aside from the summer agricultural activities, arts and crafts, and various forms of wage earning both near and away from the village, there are a series of ceremonial events scattered through these months. The principal event is the celebration of the tribe's major feast day, July 14, San Buenaventura's Day. This is celebrated with morning mass and a day-long Corn Dance, with the two moieties, or kiva groups, alternating—first in front of the church and campo santo and then in the plaza. This is not only a time of homecoming for the Cochiti but also an occasion that brings many Indians from surrounding Pueblos and innumerable visitors both from the area and also from great distances. This is particularly true when the date falls on a weekend.

While lacking the spectacle aspects of the much larger feast day performance at Santo Domingo Pueblo exactly three weeks later (August 4), the Cochiti ceremony is generally popular. It is valued for the faithfulness with which the traditional ceremonies and the costumes are

maintained; there is an intimacy that the smaller numbers make possible; and, over the years, the Cochiti people have developed and maintained a widespread reputation for friendship and hospitality.

In addition to the major feast day at home and others in the neighboring Pueblos, there are lesser celebrations of several other saints' days. These include San Antonio's Day (June 13), San Juan's Day (June 24), San Pedro's and San Pablo's Day (June 29), San Lorenzo's Day (August 10), and Santiago's Day and Santa Ana's Day (July 25). Santa Ana's Day should actually be celebrated July 26, but that is the day of the major feast at neighboring Santa Ana Pueblo, and many of the Cochiti prefer to be free to attend that occasion (see Lange 1952a for details on the San Juan Day celebrations in 1894 and 1947).

In the autumn, ceremonial occasions to which the general public is admitted decline. However, masked kachina dances continue at this time, although much of the village energy is still diverted to activities of the harvest season. To an even greater extent in former times, late summer and autumn have been the period of gathering wild nuts, berries, seeds, broom grass, and other vegetable items in the hills and mountains above Cochiti. Simultaneous with these activities are hunting trips, primarily into the mountains for deer.

Hunting activities are no longer so significant as formerly in Cochiti culture. Several factors have contrib-

Mus. of N.M., Santa Fe.

Fig. 17. Corn dancers. left, *Green Corn Dance* by Tonita Peña (Quah Ah) a prominent Cochiti artist, showing costumed dancers, drummer with chorus (at right), banner carrier, and Koshare clowns. The female dancers are barefoot, as was customary, and are apparently of the Turquoise moiety (as indicated by their tablitas). Watercolor about 1925. right, Paul Trujillo in dance costume similar to that worn by the male dancers at left: eagle feather headdress, buckskin armbands with spruce boughs, embroidered kilt, rain sash, yarn wristlet, shell or turquoise necklace, and body paint. Photograph by T. Harmon Parkhurst about 1935.

376

uted to this change. There are simply fewer animals, and more outside hunters in the national forests of the vicinity. Consequently, competition has increased, the prospect of successful hunts has diminished, and with these changes, interest has also waned. Among the Cochiti, the hunting of bears, mountain lions, and eagles was ceremonially important, and much ritual was required. With diminished interest in native medicinal practices in which these three animals play important roles, many prefer not to become involved in the hunting of these medicine animals (Lange 1953).

## Synonymy†

The name of Cochiti Pueblo is a Spanish rendering (Cochití) of the Keresan name, recorded in the Santa Ana dialect as *ǩúv̓îˑv̓I*. The Cochiti form, which is not available in phonemic transcription, has been recorded as *ǩótʸitI* (Harrington 1916:439, normalized) and ko-tyīt′ (Lange 1959:3), and the forms in the other varieties of Keresan are similar. A person from the Pueblo is called in Cochiti *ǩotʸitime* (Harrington 1916:439, normalized), with the Keresan suffix -*me* 'person of'. This name has no etymology, but the Acoma name *ǩúˑv̓iˑme, ǩúˑv̓iˑv̓amé* 'Cochiti Indian' has the shape of a derivative from the stem of *ǩúˑv̓ʰi* 'mountain' (Miller 1965:41, 88). Variant spellings, from the sixteenth to the twentieth centuries, include Cochita, 1583 (Hammond and Rey 1966:204), Cocheti, Cocheto, Cochit, Cochite, Cochito, Cochitti, Cochity, Cotchiti, Gotchti, Ko-cke, Chochité, and Chochiti (Hodge 1907:318). The Spanish tribal names Cochiteños and Cochitinos are found only in late nineteenth-century sources. Hodge's Cuchin is a misreading of Cuchiti on an 1846–1847 map (Abert 1966). Other errors and misprints are listed by Hodge (1907:318).

Borrowings or folk-etymologized distortions of the Keresan name appear in several languages: Taos koatöava (Curtis 1907–1930, 16:261, normalized); Tewa *ǩuˑteˀge,* literally 'stone kiva'; Jemez *kʸǽˑtɨˑge,* literally 'mountain-sheep home'; Zuni kochutikwe (Kroeber 1916:275); Hopi kwičiti (normalized). Jemez has *kʸǽˑtɨˀ* 'Cochiti Indian'.

Tewa also uses *témá* 'Keresan' especially for a Cochiti Indian (Harrington 1916:438; Bandelier 1966–1976, 3:57). Isleta has *pˀä ɫáˀi,* literally 'water-foam (place)' (William Leap, personal communication 1977), also translated as 'soapweed place' (Hodge 1907:318). Picuris páthaïtá may be related to this. Navajo has *Tó Gah* or *Tó Gad* (Franciscan Fathers 1910:128, 135; Haile 1950–1951, 2:55; Curtis 1907–1930, 1:138, phonemicized), the last translated 'cedar water', a Cochiti Indian being *Tó Gahnii.*

† This synonymy was prepared by Ives Goddard incorporating material supplied by the author. Uncredited forms are from Hodge (1907) or Harrington (1916:438–441), who give additional variants, or from anonymous sources.

As the seat of a Spanish mission the Pueblo has been called San Buenaventura de Cochití (Domínguez 1956:486). The designation San Bartolomeo, or St. Bartholomew, is an error.

A 1581 designation as Suchipila has been suggested, without etymology (Hammond and Rey 1966:59, 105); the same source gives Medina de la Torre as the name for Kuaua (LA 187) correcting an earlier identification of it as a name for Cochiti (Gallegos Lamero 1927:352). For other suggested identifications of these Pueblos see "Pueblos Abandoned in Historic Times," this volume.

## Sources

Anthropological and historical sources pertaining to the Indians of Cochiti Pueblo have appeared sporadically since the onset of history (mid-sixteenth century) but have become increasingly numerous during the twentieth century. Even yet, the literature often proves to be disappointingly limited. Nonetheless, it may be said that the total bibliography on Cochiti amounts to relatively complete coverage, in terms of both synchronic and diachronic interests, considering the total literature on Southwestern Puebloan cultures and tribes.

Cochiti Pueblo welcomed Spanish settlers, often as comrades in arms against the Navajo raids, at an early date, and it has remained one of the more open Pueblos in the sense of hospitality and receptivity to strangers. Despite this feature, there has been a general and persistent reticence to discuss or reveal tribal life, and there are innumerable facets and details of Cochiti culture that remain uninvestigated or only minimally described.

It is hoped that continued research will remedy some of these lacunae; realistically, however, informants are often no longer knowledgeable regarding traditional data (even when they want to collaborate), and documentary evidence has frequently been lost forever, if indeed it ever existed. This means that many significant details will never be recovered or learned.

Lange's (1959) general monograph on Cochiti culture and history contains appendices on Cochiti language by Robin Fox and on Cochiti dance by Gertrude Kurath. For Cochiti culture history see Lange (1952, 1953a, 1958a, 1960, 1967). Lange (1968) recounts the Cochiti Dam archeological salvage project.

Noteworthy earlier sources on Cochiti include Benedict's (1931) tales; Goldfrank (1927) on social and ceremonial organization; Curtis (1907–1930, 16), Dumarest (1919), and Starr's (1897–1899) study of a census. Finally, special attention should be directed to the article on Cochiti by Hodge (1907), which contained considerable ethnographic data and a useful listing of early historical sources.

Other sources valuable for widened perspectives on

Cochiti include a number of more general syntheses; while focused on subjects broader than Cochiti alone, there are ample data presented in comparative statements, and Cochiti examples are often cited. One example of such syntheses would be Fox's (1967) analyses of Keresan social structure and culture history. Similar syntheses of Keresan culture may be found in Lange (1958) and White (1930).

Bloom (1933-1938) edited the diary of Capt. John G. Bourke, covering the late decades of the nineteenth century in the Southwest. During that same period, a brief trip was described by Eickemeyer and Eickemeyer (1895). More intensive and extensive in its coverage, Bandelier's (1890-1892) two-volume report discussed his archeological and ethnological investigations in the area between 1880 and 1885.

These data are significantly augmented by Bandelier's journals (1966-1976, 1-3), which reveal many insights on late nineteenth-century Cochiti. His novel, *The Delight Makers* (Bandelier 1890), is a remarkably authentic portrayal of prehistoric life among the people of the Rito de los Frijoles, now a portion of Bandelier National Monument. Bandelier's characterizations and descriptions were based upon his own experiences among the Keresans of Cochiti and the Tewas of San Juan and Santa Clara Pueblos.

# Santo Domingo Pueblo

CHARLES H. LANGE

The Indians of Santo Domingo ('săntō dō'mĭŋgō) Pueblo, New Mexico, are among the best-known tribes, Puebloan or non-Puebloan, of the American Southwest. Located on the east bank of the Rio Grande, 30–35 miles southwest of Santa Fe (see "Pueblos: Introduction," fig. 1, this vol.), the Pueblo (figs. 1–2) and its inhabitants have long held a prominent position among the Rio Grande Puebloan peoples. White (1935:21) wrote that Santo Domingo was "the most important of the Keresan pueblos."

## Language

Santo Domingo Indians speak Keresan;* in this, they are linguistic relatives of their neighbors immediately to the south and north, San Felipe and Cochiti Pueblos, respectively. These tribes, together with Santa Ana and Zia, to the west, comprise the so-called Eastern Keresans. Still farther to the west and rather different in dialect are Acoma and Laguna Pueblos, the Western Keresans. Mutual intelligibility among these Keresans varies directly with the geographical distances separating the tribal villages. Each one of these seven Pueblos speaks a different variety of Keresan, but the languages, or dialects, are closely related. The time depth of the language divergence is about 500 years (Miller and Davis 1963:310). The more distant linguistic relationships of Keresan are uncertain.

As in the case of other Pueblo Indians, many of the Santo Domingos also speak Spanish and English. Of these two languages, English is steadily becoming more

and more dominant. For Keresan itself, Santo Domingo Indians are sufficiently numerous and conservative that the native language persists to a much higher degree than at other villages, such as Cochiti, for example.

## Territory

Physically, the Pueblo has retained a relatively compact format; there are a number of multistoried (no more than two levels for at least the present century) houses arranged in contiguous fashion along a series of streets, primarily arranged on an east-west axis, with north-south transverse streets at either end. A number of houses lie beyond this pattern on the western edge of the village. On the eastern edge, separated from the Pueblo by an irrigation canal, there is the Roman Catholic mission church of Santo Domingo (Saint Dominic). It is a typical, mission-style church with service rooms (newly renovated as of 1972) along the south side and a campo santo in the front, or on the west. Nearby is a relatively recent addition, a community center, and 100 yards farther east are a few homes, including former residences of Indian Service day-school teachers.

From the time following the emergence upon earth at Sipapu, somewhere in the north, the Santo Domingo lived at White House, also to the north of their present location. It was during this period that many of the Indians divided into their present tribal units, Santo Domingo included. Somewhat more tangibly, tradition also has it that the Keresans (and perhaps others) remained together as recently as their joint occupancy of Frijoles Canyon. There, some centuries before the Spaniards entered the area, the tribes broke into their present composition: San Felipe, Cochiti, Santo Domingo, and others.

## Culture

The longstanding general prestige of Santo Domingo may be attributed to a number of factors. Situated on the east side of the river, the Pueblo was directly on or near the established roads, from the Camino Real of early Spanish times to the modern state and federal highways. The Santo Domingo Indians have rather consistently been among the numerically larger tribes. In 1807 the Pueblo held an estimated 1,000 persons (White 1935:17).

* Words in the Santo Domingo dialect of Keresan in italics are in the orthography used by Miller and Davis (1963), with substitutions made to bring it in line with the standard technical alphabet of the *Handbook*. These are from this source and from a consultant who prefers to be anonymous. Voiceless unaspirated stops are *p, t* (alveolar), *t^y* (alveopalatal), *k* (Miller and Davis's b, d, d^y, g); the voiceless aspirates *p^h, t^h, č^h, k^h* (their p, t, č, k); the alveolar affricates *c, c^h* (their z, c); and the retroflex affricates *ç, ç^h* (their z̧, ç). Other symbols are the same as theirs: the consonants are *p̓, t̓, c̓, ç̓, č̓, k̓; s, ş, š; ś, ṣ̌, ṣ́; m, n, r, w, y; m̓, n̓, r̓, w̓, y̓; h, ʔ*, the vowels are *i, e, a, ɨ* (central to back, unrounded), *u* (mid to high, back, rounded), also occurring long (*i·*, etc.) and voiceless (*I, E, A, Ɨ, U*). The accents are v́ (high level), v̂ (falling), v̌ (glottal), v (unaccented). There is a rare voiced stop *d* (Miller and Davis's ᴅ) and some additional uncommon phonemes in loanwords. Santo Domingo words not in italics are approximate spellings based on sources that fail to distinguish many significant phonological features; in these o is used for Keresan u and u for ɨ.

Southwest Foundation for Audio-Visual Resources, Santa Fe, N.M.
Fig. 1. Santo Domingo Pueblo. Photograph by Peter Dechert, June 1977.

revised from Stubbs 1950:fig. 15.

Fig. 2. Santo Domingo Pueblo.

In 1970 it had a population of 2,311 in 485 families (Dutton 1970:62). Collectively, and with few nonconformists amongst their numbers, the Santo Domingos have maintained a conservative and rigid position in reference to innovation and change.

While unable to sustain a completely unchanging stance, the Indians of this Pueblo have come to serve as a cultural model, or ideal, for many other tribes. While Santo Domingo's conservatism has been increasingly, over recent years, a target of ridicule among some younger Puebloan tribesmen, or among those who were for some other reason noncompliant, this very conservatism and its diverse manifestations have also been admired, sometimes grudgingly but yet very genuinely, by many Pueblo people who still value the traditional ways and patterns.

The sheer size of Santo Domingo and its conservative bent have combined to perpetuate a tribal pride and élan that in turn have served to maintain high standards of ceremonial costuming and performance—dancing, singing, and drumming. These manifestations are important aspects of the tribe's relatively united front in confronting, and eliminating, if need be, unsanctioned deviations or innovations from within or disruptive intrusions from without in the less religious aspects of the culture.

Economically, Santo Domingo has been relatively prosperous; the reservation comprises 74,192 acres, more than twice the size of that of any other eastern Keresan tribe (White 1935:25). Smith (1966:140) provided some-what different data on land; her total was 69,262 acres, comprising 686 acres of home sites, roads, and community buildings, 3,611 acres of farmlands, and 64,965 acres of open grazing lands. In any case, its rangelands are relatively extensive; its fields, under irrigation, are similarly extensive (fig. 5) and respond well to generally conscientious care (fig. 6). The men and women are well known for their craft products: pottery (fig. 7), jewelry, woven belts, and leather moccasins and leggings. The men frequently range far afield, to Arizona, Colorado, Oklahoma, or California, trading Santo Domingo products as well as serving as middlemen for Navajo blankets and other items not produced locally.

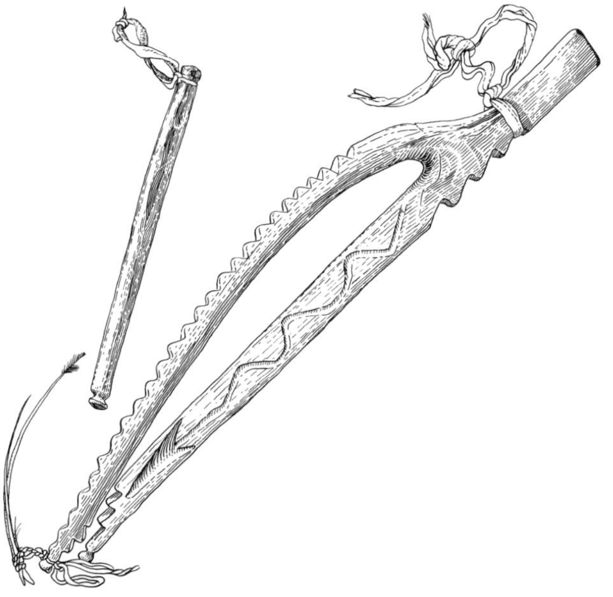

Constant contacts with the outside world, traveling afar or manning roadside shelters on the reservation or booths along the Pueblo streets or in the homes on ceremonial occasions, either in Santo Domingo or elsewhere, have provided Santo Domingo Indians with numerous insights into the "other way of life." Choosing selectively, these Indians have maintained their core, or basic, values to an almost unparalleled degree at the same time they have slowly and somewhat reluctantly integrated a number of new objects and patterns with the old.

With the confidence emanating from tribal pride and the prestige accorded Santo Domingo leaders, it is rather common to find the men of this tribe assuming leadership roles in inter-Puebloan affairs, such as the All-Pueblo Council, or in sporadic delegations sent to Washington to present a Puebloan case to Congress or to other national agencies and leaders.

## Political Organization

Santo Domingo culture may be characterized as a hierarchy, or perhaps more accurately as a theocracy; tribal tradition, extending back to an earlier life within the earth rather than on it, contains an explanation of the whys and hows underlying much of the cultural content as well as the supernatural authentication and authorization for the continuing tribal leadership and the rationale for daily interpersonal relationships and individual values.

The cacique is at the head of the tribal hierarchy, or theocracy. Sometimes referred to as yaya 'mother', the cacique may be considered as representing the Corn Mother Iyatiko; he is the ceremonial leader of the tribe—the chief (hochanyi). As head of the Flint Medicine Society, he is the principal medicine man. While commonly referred to as an election, there is an annual designation, or selection, by the medicine men of a number of tribal officers, a procedure assuring a traditional and conservative leadership.

The cacique designates the war priests, or captains, and their 10 helpers, or guards (gowachanyi). These were considered by White (1935:32-33, 73) to have been indigenous, with primary roles in the preservation and protection of the tribal theocracy and overall culture.

Smithsonian, Dept. of Anthr.: 176376 (2).

Fig. 3. Musical rasp of carved wood. Rubbing the straight stick across the notches of the curved stick produces the sound, which is often amplified by placing the lower end of the notched stick on a drum, gourd, or basket that acts as a resonator (Jeançon and Douglas 1931). Length, 36.5 cm; collected before 1897.

Fig. 4. Summer brush arbor near Santo Domingo. Shelters of this type were constructed at the edge of the more distant fields in summer. Photograph by Philip E. Harroun, Sept. 1897.

Fig. 6. Governor (at right?) with part of crew of irrigators on Irrigation Day. As described by White (1935:141–142) the irrigation ditch is ceremonially opened each year, with the burial of prayer sticks by the supervisor of the ditch system and the war chief. The actual clearing of the ditches, which takes about two weeks, is accomplished under the supervision of the governor and *fiscales*. Irrigation Day usually occurs in late March or early April. Photograph by unknown photographer, 1900–1930.

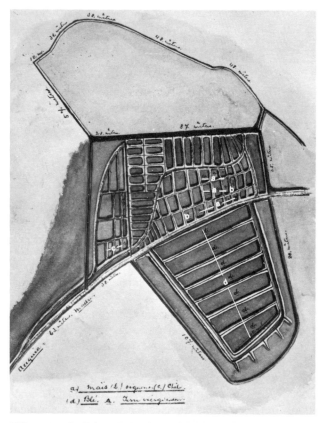

Fig. 5. Irrigated fields at Santo Domingo in the 1880s. Water is supplied by a main ditch (labeled *acequia madre*), the largest ditch shown here, which was also a source of drinking water before wells were installed (White 1935:23). Identified crops on the cultivated fields are as follows: a, maize; b, onions; c, chili; d, wheat. Colored diagrammatic sketch (letters replaced by modern type) by Adolph F. Bandelier, 1887 or before (see Bandelier 1969; "Cochiti Pueblo," fig. 7, this vol.).

Conforming to a basic pattern of dualism, repeatedly manifested in the culture, the other annual appointments are by the Shikami medicine society headman to offices created by the early Spaniards and of a more secular nature. These officers include the governor, the chief representative of the tribe vis-a-vis the outside world (dabopo), his lieutenant (dabopo tenyente), their six assistants (*capitanes*), and the six *fiscales* (bishgari)—senior *fiscal,* lieutenant *fiscal,* and four helpers—whose prime concern is the care and operation of the physical facilities and furnishings of the Roman Catholic mission church of Saint Dominic.

Through the years, young men have been selected for service in one of three tracks of officialdom: one leads to the war captaincy; a second, to the governorship; and the third, to the office of *fiscal*. Once within any of the three lines, an individual rarely, if ever, is diverted to another line; however, he may serve repeatedly within a line first at the junior, or helper, level and later, upon proving himself, in either of the two top positions, senior (Spanish *mayor*) or lieutenant (*teniente*).

The tribal *principales* include all who have served in one of the six major appointed offices. White (1935:45) noted this status as coming automatically upon assuming a major office; a *principal* serves for life. His role consists primarily of advising and collaborating with the tribal officials. White characterized the *principales* as not constituting an organization because they have no head;

Fig. 7. Pottery water vessel in style distinctive of Santo Domingo during 1880-1920. The type is generally characterized by black-on-cream designs in horizontal bands of repeated geometric elements (see Chapman 1936). Diameter 22 cm, collected in 1915.

however, this may be largely a matter of semantics. The group, serving as a council of elders, may be convened by a major officer, normally the war captain or governor, for purposes of consultation and setting, or soliciting broad support for, the policies and acts of the leadership. In this capacity, the body is accorded prestige, respect, and, in a very real sense, power, or, perhaps better, influence.

Smith (1966:140-141) provided data on the government of Santo Domingo that are at some variance with White's account. Discrepancies may be attributable to different informants, the interval of 30 years between the accounts, or to a combination of the two. Smith (1966:140-141) shows to what extent the Pueblo government is involved in detail:

> The government of the pueblo is in the hands of the religious leaders. Former governors are lifetime members of the council and choose the governor, lieutenant governor, mayor, and lieutenant mayor [*fiscales* ?] who serve one-year terms. They also appoint thirty-four officers and the treasurer, who serve indefinite terms. The council appoints thirteen councilmen for one-year terms.

> Control over individuals by the religious hierarchy and tribal government is certainly more extensive in Santo Domingo than in any other pueblo. For example, the 1957 Long Range Planning Program states that, "The pueblo committee on credit (should be) advised of all credit matters pertaining to the Pueblo or to *individual members* of the Pueblo." The pueblo requests the BIA branch of Law and Order "to use its good offices with Probation Officers of the Courts so that the Governor may be informed on paroles and parole releases of their youth; that the BIA Relocation office inform the Governor and Council when a member of the Tribe applies for relocation, and the new adress [sic] of the relocatee;" and the Council requests "that all assistance cases, both State and Federal, be reported to the Governor so that he may act as liaison person in making the proper referral."

## Social Organization

Somewhat surprisingly, White (1935:70-71) found it more difficult to obtain data from informants on the subjects of clans and kinship than on some of the more overt aspects of the religious and ceremonial life. His explanation was that the latter "were pueblo (and hence, to the native, public) matters. But kin and clan are personal, private." Also, White noted, divulgence of these data could easily have led to detection and harsh consequences for the informant involved. Nonetheless, some features were learned in regard to clan and kinship.

In 1933 White was given the names of 21 clans for Santo Domingo; nine of these are correspondences to the list of 18 compiled by Bourke (1884:50) in 1881.

Despite the general reticence in discussing these matters, White (1935:72) found that clans were exogamous but moieties (or phratries) were not. Clans did not control offices, memberships in societies, or ceremonies; and there was no clan house, head, paraphernalia, ceremony, or land.

From the presence at neighboring Cochiti Pueblo of matrilineal clans, limited ceremonial functions, and titular clan headship accorded the oldest female member, certain correspondences to practices at Santo Domingo may be inferred; however, it is not safe to conclude parallels. At Santo Domingo, the issue is somewhat clouded by the fact that the father-child relationship appears to be stronger than at Cochiti—stronger than the kiva affiliations would readily explain. For further insights, consult Dozier (1970:144-162) and Fox (1967:3-47).

In reference to the individual life cycle, the processes of acculturation have had their impact on the life of Santo Domingo relative to birth, naming, childhood, puberty, marriage, and death. White's (1935:80-87) limited data revealed a strong representation of native customs and practices prevailing as late as the 1930s. As in the case of most other Rio Grande Pueblos, the general situation remained essentially unchanged until the end of World War II.

## Mythology

Santo Domingo lore has the Indians, while inside the earth, associated with Iyatiko, their mother and one of the most important supernatural beings. Somewhat ephemerally conceived, Iyatiko remains still at Sipapu and is ritually represented by the perfect corn ear fetish of the medicine men (iyariko). The sun is also highly venerated and is considered the father of the twin war gods, elder and younger brothers, Masewi and Oyoyewi, respectively, culture heroes who are credited with numerous innovations and gifts to the Indian ancestors. Much of this learning occurred at White House, where life closely resembled that of the nineteenth century, still remembered at least in part by the old people. At White

House, the people were already agricultural, and the kachinas (shiwana) came to the village and danced for rain. The kachinas are said to live at Wenima, to the west; they are anthropomorphic and are effective in bringing rain and good crops. Since the tribes left White House, the kachinas themselves no longer appear; they are impersonated in masked ceremonies, or dances, by the initiated men of Santo Domingo.

Similarly, the Koshare and Quirana, also human in form, came from their homes in the east to help the crops. Again, the actual deities no longer come to perform in the village, but members of these two societies carry on their activities, often assisting the kachinas and other ceremonial performers.

Numerous other deities or supernatural beings persist in the world of the Santo Domingo Indians. Witches also abound, and to counteract their doings, medicine men act. Such activities are normally carried on as distinct societies rather than as individuals; the memberships of the four medicine societies are recognized as having special powers and capabilities. These groups also protect against both tribal and individual enemies; they cure the sick and help the infirm. They also bring rain, and they control the movements of the sun, causing the seasons to change in regular order.

The chief of the Hunters' Society (shayaka) has similar control over the game, having charge of communal and other hunting activities—rituals, dances, and the organization of the hunts.

Supernatural beings are also associated with the six directions, the four cardinal points and also zenith and nadir. Sacred animals and plants, as well as particular colors, are similarly affiliated with the six ritual directions. Thus, the present-day roster of ceremonial personages at Santo Domingo can accordingly be viewed as a close approximation of the supernatural originals of long ago.

### Religion

The longstanding, though sometimes tenuous, presence of Roman Catholicism is another interesting example, repeated elsewhere in the Rio Grande Indian Pueblos, of the acculturative phenomenon wherein the native religion has simply expanded to integrate the alien religion introduced at the time of the earliest Spanish expeditions. Some of the doctrines and teachings, much of the paraphernalia, and a large part of the calendar of Catholicism have been incorporated within the native religion. The annual calendar of activities and events repeatedly demonstrates the blending of the two religious traditions.

New Year's Day is observed with a mass and public dances by the two kiva groups, Turquoise and Squash or Pumpkin, honoring the newly appointed officers. January 6, the feast of the Epiphany (in Spanish *día de los Reyes* 'day of the kings'), is similarly celebrated, with small dance groups visiting the homes of the new officers and of persons bearing the name of Rey or Reyes (Lange 1951).

In late January or early February, there is commonly the Sandaro ceremony, depicting the coming of the Spaniards. A Matachine Dance, of Mexican origin, frequently comes at this time of the year. On the native side, February is the time for the Koshare's special dance; the Hanyidyidya ceremony is also held, honoring the sun and observing the sun's return to the north.

Late winter or early spring is when the curing, or medicine, societies cleanse the entire village of evil spirits and "cure everyone." This is the prelude to the cleaning and opening of the irrigation ditches and the beginning of spring planting. These events are accompanied by ceremonies and the "planting" of prayer sticks, with a variety of dances performed by several different groups.

At Easter, there is a four-day period of corn, or tablita (fig. 8), dances (Lange 1957). This is followed by a series of retreats, in set sequence, by the medicine societies; retiring to their houses for four days of fasting and prayers, they are considered to be returning to Sipapu to secure the vital rains for successful crops. Masked kachina dances should follow each of these retreats—further assurance of agricultural success; however, White (1935:33) reported occasional omissions of these ceremonies as the men were too busy in the fields to be so diverted.

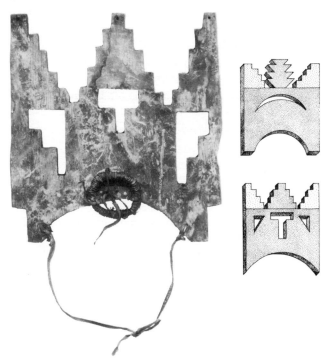

left, Mus. of the Amer. Ind., Heye Foundation, New York: 7/711; right, after Bourke 1884:pl. 4.

Fig. 8. Tablita headdresses. left, Rear view of flat, painted wood headdress showing protective head pad; worn by women participating in the Corn or Tablita Dance; width about 28 cm, collected before 1917. right, Headdresses with different styles of center peaks and cutout designs; both are painted green except for the outer peaks, which are orange, top, and yellow, bottom.

Mus. of N.M., Santa Fe.

Fig. 9. Corn or Tablita Dance, Aug. 4, 1918. Photographed in the central plaza, facing west. At right, a Koshare clown; at left, chorus, gathered around a lone drummer. The banner or decorated pole, held by a special carrier, is made of a long sash, foxskins, feathers, bells, and a carved and painted ball; it has been explained as a corn plant or kachina figure (see Lange 1957:70-71). Bourke (1884:19-53), describing saint's day festivities that included tablita dances, illustrated the banner, drum, and tablitas (fig. 8). Photograph by Nathan Kendall.

The summer months are observed with a series of saint's day celebrations: San Juan's Day (June 25), San Pedro's Day (June 29), Santiago's Day (July 26), San Lorenzo's Day (August 10), and others. These generally include rooster pulls and present throwing (both called *gallo* in Spanish), footraces, and occasional ceremonial dances. On such days, there is also a pattern for many of the people to travel to neighboring Pueblos for the celebration of that village's major feast day and also for socializing and trading with other Indians and with the inevitable tourists and other outsiders. At times, individual Santo Domingo Indians will actually participate in these ceremonies, just as members of other Pueblo tribes will occasionally "dance for Santo Domingo."

August 4 is the celebrated Corn Dance, presented by both kivas in full strength (fig. 9). In size, careful costuming, and in conscientiously executed performance, this is a genuinely spectacular event that has long been an attraction to the Santo Domingo Indians, residents and absentees, Indians from neighboring villages, and non-Indians as well.

In the autumn, harvest time (fig. 10), the Squash and Turquoise kiva groups present masked dances; the Quirana Society also has its special dance, sometimes including initiation rites, in which case the event is held in September.

In November, there is the feast of the dead in conjunction with All Souls' Day. Later, Hanyiko is held, again honoring the sun; this is the counterpart of the Hanyidyidya ceremony in the spring. Again, this is a ceremonial

high point in the year, involving the participation of the four curing societies as well as the ordinary people (sishti).

Christmas is a period of festive celebration, both in terms of Catholicism and also in terms of a series of dances, starting in the church itself following the Christmas Eve midnight mass and continuing in the plaza with a variety of performances during the next four days.

On the final days of December, a series of meetings occurs as most of the people pause to rest between these Christmas dances and New Year's. It is in these meetings that selections are announced of the officers for the coming year. Their installation occurs on December 31, and the celebrations begin again on January 1.

*Ceremonial Organization*

In addition to the *principales,* there is the dual kiva organization. Everyone belongs either to the Turquoise or the Squash; a wife joins the kiva of her husband, and the children belong to the father's kiva. A widow may return to the kiva of her father.

There is a headman for each kiva who supervises its ceremonial activities, among which the organization of masked kachina dances is most important. With a number of assistants and helpers, primarily men, he is responsible for proper preparation of the dancers, including the paraphernalia required for the performance. The masked kachina dances are exclusively male; in theory, the uninitiated (women and children) do not know that the kachina dancers are men. To perpetuate such impres-

385

Fig. 10. Woman husking and stacking corn. Dried chilies, strung on yucca strips or cotton cord, are hanging under the portico behind the corn. Drying and storing of the corn is generally done by women, husking by men and women, and harvesting and working the fields by men. Photograph by T. Harmon Parkhurst, probably Oct., around 1940.

sions, the uninitiated are actively discouraged from attending masked ceremonies such as the Shalako at Zuni Pueblo, where the dancers pause in the course of the all-night ceremonies and may be observed resting and unmasked.

A series of secret societies, of more restricted membership, completes the roster of ceremonial groups at Santo Domingo. These include the Koshare (k̂î·ṣari) and Quirana societies (fig. 11), the Warriors' Society (ʔú·pʰi), four major curing societies (Flint, Shikami, Boyakya, and Giant), four minor curing societies (Kapina, Beraka, Ant, and Snake), and the Hunters' Society.

These societies are highly important in the life of Santo Domingo, individually and collectively; they lead in the active resistance to any threat upon the traditional ways or any intrusion that may serve to erode the base of established values. The numerical size of the Pueblo and the ultraconservative bent of this tribe combine to maintain the vitality of these organizations to a greater extent than is true of most Puebloan tribes. More information is needed in regard to the interaction of these societies with their counterparts in other villages. Assistance is requested and granted from time to time in the performance of rituals and ceremonies; enduring relationships are established between societies in different Pueblos because of joint or visiting sponsorship in initiations, cures, and other functions.

Inevitably, a particular society may lose members and fail to enlist recruits to the extent that its proper functions are impaired. In such cases, these functions either become lost to the culture, or other societies absorb these additional functions, or a new membership must be mustered—in extreme cases by starting over again with the aid of a society from another Pueblo. More often than not, it has been Santo Domingo that has been the customary source of strength and resuscitation in perpetuating these facets of the native religion and values among the various Puebloan cultures.

Finally, mention should be made of a basic feature of Santo Domingo ceremonial organization. This is the close affiliation of the various secret societies, one with another as well as with specific officers, all of which serves to emphasize the importance of the concept of dualism in Santo Domingo and Eastern Keresan socioreligious structures. The Flint Society head, the cacique, appoints the war chiefs, or captains, and the gowatcanyi; the Shikami Society headman appoints the governor, his lieutenant, their assistants, and the *fiscales*. The Flint Society is affiliated with the Koshare, and both belong with the Turquoise kiva; the Shikami Society is linked to the Quirana, and both identify with the Squash kiva. The Flint headman initiates men into the Turquoise kiva group, while the Shikami headman performs in similar fashion for the Squash kiva group.

Masewi and Oyoyewi, the war priests, are chosen from the two kivas, never from the same one; White (1935:79) was uncertain whether the senior and junior positions alternated annually between the two kivas or whether the Masewi, the elder brother, or senior officer, always was chosen from the Turquoise kiva membership. Throughout the year, the normal pattern is for each kiva, or "side," to present a dance in the course of a particular ceremonial observation; in instances when both kivas perform, the Turquoise kiva group performs first. The day's festivities may conclude with a performance by the Squash kiva dancers, or the two groups may combine in "a grand finale."

## Sociocultural Situation in the 1960s

The World War II years undoubtedly had some impact on Santo Domingo lifeways; however, the events centering around the return of the veterans with their collective world-wide experience, their greater sophistication from additional formal and informal education, enhanced by the variety of veterans' benefits, contributed even more to an understanding and appreciation of, and diminished fear and distrust of government medical personnel, services, and facilities. Home births and the services of midwives and medicine men have slowly yielded to the utilization of hospital services and modern medical practices. Sanitation at home in the Pueblo has also improved since the end of World War II; many homes have

Smithsonian, NAA.
Fig. 11. Koshare (left) and Quirana (right) clown society members. Koshare belongs to the Turquoise kiva or moiety, Quirana to Squash. Each group is, in addition, associated with one of the two medicine societies (White 1935:52-59). The Koshare grouped at left are wearing the characteristic white paint with black horizontal stripes and black rings around mouth and eyes, hair done up in corn husks and covered with mud, black breechclouts, rabbit fur bandoliers, hoof rattles, and bare feet; they have additional painted designs on their backs and legs. The man at far right has been identified as a Quirana clown based on the sparrow hawk feathers, an insigne that he wears on his head. Like the Koshare, he wears a dark breechclout and is painted with horizontal stripes; he has a darkened face and wears evergreen boughs around his body, wrists, and ankles. Both photographs by Adam C. Vroman, 1899.

running water and electricity, and the number with inside plumbing steadily increased during the 1960s.

The rites of marriage and death have been at least shared with the practices of the Roman Catholic Church to an ever-increasing degree; however, native customs frequently assert themselves to the point of dominance if not exclusion. Records concerned with the usual vital statistics have improved insofar as Santo Domingo is concerned, but they are still rather far from complete, partly in deference to native values and partly from a suspicion as to the possible use of such information. Except for stillborn babies, who are buried under the floor of the mother's house, all are buried in the church cemetery. Males are buried to the north, or left when facing the altar; females are buried to the south.

For some years, the children of Santo Domingo have been bussed several miles to a new school, complete with classrooms, lunch facilities, gymnasium, and separate homes for teaching and administrative personnel and their families. These buildings are on the high ground east of the Pueblo, one-half mile from the highway between Santa Fe and Albuquerque. While this practice is less frequent than in the past, the children are from time to time restrained from going to school or are returned to the Pueblo early in order to observe or participate in special religious ceremonies. On other occasions, tribal leaders avail themselves of the school's public address system in order to make certain announcements (invariably in Keresan) or to issue words of warning or caution or to advise particular behavior in relation to some threat or possible danger that has been so perceived by the officials of Santo Domingo. While these actions are commonly taken by the governor or some other secular official, the threat is most often of a religious nature, prompted by the cacique or other members of the theocratic hierarchy.

An increasing appreciation of education has developed among the Santo Domingos, particularly for English and arithmetic. Nonetheless, elementary preparation is still often inadequate or unvalued; many drop out of high school, and very few continue with their education beyond high school. "The council has opposed higher education on the ground that it will encourage the young to leave the pueblo, or will change the old order of things

387

at the pueblo, and 'there might be women doing men's jobs, or even wanting to sit on the council'" (Smith 1966:142–143).

The population of Santo Domingo increased from 1,017 persons in 1942 to 2,206 in 1968; from 1950 to 1968, the increase was 91 percent, and from 1964 to 1968, the increase was 12 percent. Comparable data for all tribes under the United Pueblos Agency showed a 42 percent increase between 1950 and 1968, and a 7 percent increase between 1964 and 1968 (Bodine 1972:272–273). The nonresident population of Santo Domingo increased 3 percent from 1960 to 1968, at which time 21 percent of the population was nonresident (Bodine 1972:275).

While an important consideration would involve the precise cultural identities (statuses and roles) of the absentees, even the gross figures have significance—the fact that 1,743 of the 2,206 total population are available for daily cultural participation and interaction. By comparison, the much smaller Pueblo of Cochiti regularly carried on with only 376 of its 799 total.

In 1964, males were more numerous than females (467 to 421) in the 1–17 year old age group and the same predominance was shown in age groups 36–55, 56–65, and over 65 (304 to 206). Only in the age group 18–35 were females more numerous, 258 to 249 (Smith 1966:140).

## Synonymy†

Santo Domingo Pueblo has its name from that of the Spanish mission within it. It has also been referred to as Santo Domingo de Cuevas and Santo Domingo de Cochití. Misspellings and other erroneous forms include Santo Demingo, San Domingo, Saint Domingo, and Santa Dominga.

In the Santo Domingo dialect of Keresan the Pueblo is called ťî·wa, similar if not identical forms being also recorded at Cochiti (Lange 1959:3) and San Felipe. This name is also attested—with a different final vowel—as Santa Ana ťî·wi· (Davis 1964:121), Acoma ťî·wi, and similar forms in Zia and Laguna. A person from Santo Domingo is called in Santa Ana ťî·wi·ṁE (Davis 1964:121) and in Acoma ťî·wiṁé (Miller 1965:41); the Santo Domingo form, which would be similar except for having a in the second syllable (Harrington 1916:448; White 1935:20), is not available in phonemic transcription. In nonphonemic recordings by English speakers the initial ť in these names (a voiceless unaspirated alveopalatal stop) has been variously rendered as k, k', g, t, t'w, and dj; Harrington (1916:448) used symbols for both [tʸ] and [kʸ]. Early examples are the Ki'-o-wummi and variants of Whipple (1854–1855:9, 90). The "old word" was said to be špémoç (White 1935:205, normalized).

† This synonymy was prepared by Ives Goddard incorporating material supplied by Charles H. Lange. Uncredited forms are from Harrington (1916:447–451), who has additional variants, or anonymous sources.

Many non-Keresan languages have names for Santo Domingo that appear to be borrowings of the Keresan name, often with a native locative suffix added. Tiwa has Taos tŭwita (translated 'haliotis place', no doubt by folk etymology), Picuris tŭ-wit-ha', Isleta tewíʔai (C.T. Harrington 1920:44) or tüwi'-ai beside tɔ́ʔu kwihun ag 'at the northern place' (William Leap, personal communication 1977), and Sandia tewíai. Tewa has téwige; an apparently folk-etymologized te· xʷevege ówînge 'move trees Pueblo' has also been recorded. Jemez has tǽwigʸíʔ for the Pueblo or a person from it, and Hopi has töwíʔi for the Pueblo.

Zuni has wehkʔana for the Pueblo and wehkʔa·kʷe for a person or people from it (Dennis Tedlock, personal communication 1977). A variant has been recorded as wehka 'Eastern Keresan' (Newman 1958:45, 75), and Curtis (1907–1930, 16:261–262, phonemicized) gives we·ɫuwala 'puppy town'. The Navajo name for the Pueblo is Tó Hajiiloh, literally 'people draw up water with a rope'; the people are Tó Hajiilohnii (Robert W. Young, personal communication 1977; Haile 1950–1951, 1:111, 2:254; Franciscan Fathers 1910:128, 135). The Navajo name given by Curtis (1907–1930, 1:138), meaning 'white houses', is actually that of Sandia; this may call into question the identification of the Castilblanco of a 1581 Spanish expedition with Santo Domingo (Hammond and Rey 1966:59, 106).

An eighteenth-century source (Domínguez 1956:138) says that the inhabitants of Santo Domingo were commonly called Chachiscos in Spanish, a nickname based on their word for 'I don't understand you'.

Santo Domingo is referred to in the earliest Spanish records as Gigue, 1583 (Pérez de Luxán in Hammond and Rey 1966:204), and Quigui, 1598 (Oñate in Hammond and Rey 1953, 1:337), which appear to be renderings of the Keresan name. An earlier reading of the Oñate document as having Guipui (Pacheco and Cárdenas 1864–1884, 16:102) is not correct (Hodge 1935:41). Still, it is curious that Bandelier (1890–1892, 2:185–187) recorded Gi-pu-y as the name used by the Santo Domingo Indians for an abandoned protohistoric Pueblo about four miles east of Santo Domingo on Galisteo Creek (Harrington 1916:452); he called this "old Gi-pu-y" (also Schroeder in Castaño de Sosa 1965:162) to differentiate it from "historical Gi-pu-y," which was Oñate's Santo Domingo. The latter was very near the site of the present Pueblo, which has been relocated several times after floods. The explanation for Bandelier's name Gi-pu-y is uncertain, but it is not correct to refer to "Oñate's Gipuy" (Hammond and Rey 1966:204).

## Sources

White's (1935) monograph remains the best single source on this tribe. In addition, the size, location, and overall importance of this village have resulted in frequent references to it in the historical source materials (see Hodge 1910:462).

Several historical sources contribute significant commentary on Santo Domingo (Castaño de Sosa 1965; Dale 1949; Bloom 1933-1938; Curtis 1907-1930, 16; Eickemeyer and Eickemeyer 1895; Bourke 1884). Bandelier's final report (1890-1892) and his journals (Bandelier 1966-1976) reveal additional historical data on this Pueblo.

Comparative data involving Santo Domingo and other Pueblos have also appeared steadily (Ortiz 1972; Dozier 1970; Fox 1967; Smith 1966; Lange 1957, 1958; Parsons 1923, 1939; White 1930).

Specific aspects of Santo Domingo culture that have been discussed are the Kings' Day ceremony (Lange 1951) and music (Densmore 1938).

# San Felipe Pueblo

PAULINE TURNER STRONG

San Felipe Pueblo (ˌsăn fəˈlēpē) (figs. 1–2) is the central village of the five Eastern Keresan-speaking Pueblos* located in the Rio Grande valley of New Mexico. The Spaniards assigned the patron saint San Felipe Apóstol to the Pueblo in 1598 (Domínguez 1956:161).

The Eastern Keresan Pueblos share many cultural characteristics, and ceremonial, economic, and social relationships are close among them, although each Pueblo is autonomous. San Felipe holds a special relationship to Cochiti, as tradition states that the ancestors of these two Pueblos were one people in former times. The five Eastern Keresan Pueblos are bounded to the north and south by the Tanoan-speaking Pueblos, and there has been considerable borrowing between the Keresans and the three Tanoan language groups. However, the Eastern Keresans differ significantly from the Tanoans, as well as from their Western Keresan linguistic relatives. These cultural similarities and differences among Eastern Keresans, Western Keresans, and Tanoans have been the focus of a long-standing discussion by anthropologists on the relationship between the social organization of the Eastern and Western Pueblos (Eggan 1950; Fox 1967, 1972; Dozier 1970).

## Territory

San Felipe lies at the foot of Santa Ana Mesa, on the west bank of the Rio Grande, six miles north of its junction with the Jemez River (see "Pueblos: Introduction," fig. 1, this vol.). The San Felipe reservation consists of 48,930 acres, including Spanish grant land, much of it on the east side of the Rio Grande. Of this land, 1,670 acres are farmland, 30,126 are open grazing, and 16,964 are noncommercial timber (Smith 1966:125). The region surrounding San Felipe is primarily an arid one but ranges from the fertile valley of the Rio Grande, to the surrounding plains and volcanic mesas with their juniper and piñon trees, to the nearby Jemez and Sandia mountain ranges with their coniferous forest and game animals.

*No separate study specifically of the San Felipe dialect of Keresan is available, but as it is virtually identical with that of Santo Domingo the same transcription may be used ("Santo Domingo Pueblo," this vol.). The San Felipe words in italics are phonemic transcriptions provided by an anonymous consultant; words not in italics are approximate spellings based on sources that fail to distinguish many significant phonological features.

The modern city of Albuquerque is 25 miles to the south of San Felipe.

## Prehistory

Keresan traditions and archeological evidence agree in tracing the ancestors of the San Felipe people to the north of the present Pueblo. The traditional history of San Felipe Pueblo was recorded by the tribal council in a document protesting the attempt to impose the Civil Rights Bill of 1968 upon the Pueblos. This unique and valuable document was written by Pueblo elders well versed in Keresan traditions but with little formal American schooling. The traditional history can best be understood as a metaphorical rendering of the experience of the San Felipe people, rather than as literal history (Ortiz 1977). The Spirit referred to in the document is the Corn Mother, who bore and nourished the Pueblo people (White 1960).

> The Council in telling the spiritual legend of the ancient people remember them telling of the fortunes of the spirit world, the egress or emergence into the world, and the ingress or returning to the hereafter, whence we came. They remember too, that the emergence into the world was a great act of the Spirit for it came about with reverence and love for what was left behind in the spirit world, and of fear and respect for what was found above, on earth and in the sky. So it came to reality long ago that all life came forth from the womb of the earth, said the Council.
>
> With them came the Spirit, and the Spirit guided the ancient people through all sorts of arduous tasks of everyday life. Age after age the Spirit, the guardian and leader of the Pueblo Indians, took the ancient people across this great continent southward, until they came to settle temporarily in the places of today's National Parks and National Monuments. Everything they planted was harvested and was eaten along the route. Maybe to preserve the human race from total annihilation of any attack which may befall them, the Spirit caused the people to migrate in groups in separate directions from these places of historic settlements. He continued to guide each group on their trek until he brought them to a region where they can readily be safe and begin their tribal settlement.
>
> So said the Council. This was how it came about that the ancestral people of San Felipe Pueblo were guided into the region of the valley of the Rio del Norte [the Rio Grande]. . . .
>
> [T]hroughout the entire region of pueblo settlement, the Spirit began to give final instructions to the people. They

Southwest Foundation for Audio-Visual Resources, Santa Fe, N.M.
Fig. 1. San Felipe Pueblo. top, Detail showing plaza, which is several feet below ground level. Photographs by Peter Dechert, June 1977.

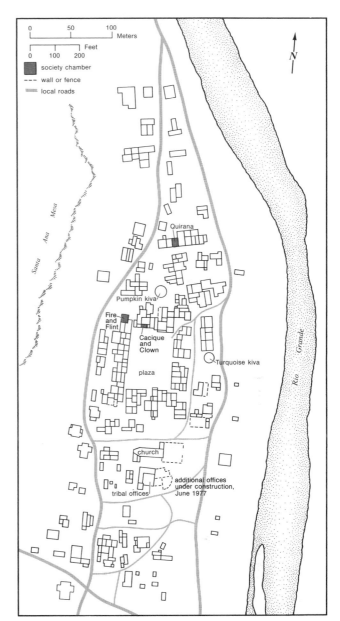

revised from Stubbs 1950:fig. 16.
Fig. 2. San Felipe Pueblo.

were reminded of the past trials and dangers they had endured; the sorrows and joys they experienced together; the unity they showed each other at working and living together in a community, and the necessity of planting and farming crops for survival. The ancient people remembered these experiences well and began to show great concern. Now the Spirit was telling of another plan, he pointed out indigenous plants that grew wild and abundantly which the people can use as food; teaching the people to respect and obey the laws of nature and the orders of its chief, the Cacique ... Thus, the plan was revealed to the ancient people and it was truly a way of life and living.

However, the people were not without dangers. They were warned of the dangers to come as more people inhabit the

new continent. Here again, the Spirit reminded her people of their past experiences of building dwelling places in fortress style. "This you must do," said the Spirit. Then before secluding, the Spirit promised the people protection from the dangers of war when the time was near (Deloria 1971:222-223).

In summary, the migration of the San Felipe people began with the emergence from the spirit world below this one, and proceeded through separations and hardships under spiritual guidance. Central aspects of life in San Felipe—religion, government, agriculture, architecture, the preeminence of community concerns—were established during the migration. This native history, ritualistically repeated for centuries in San Felipe, pro-

391

vides the meaning of the prehistory documented in more factual detail by archeologists.

Scholars consider the four language groups that comprise the Rio Grande Pueblos as cultural descendants of the people bearing the archeological Anasazi culture, with some influence from the Mogollon peoples as well. Although it is generally agreed that the Keresans and Tanoans derive from separate prehistoric groups, there is disagreement over the source areas, movements, and dates of arrival in the Rio Grande valley of these groups. The Keresans have been traced to an area centering around Chaco Canyon and extending north to the Aztec and Mesa Verde regions and, perhaps, southeast to Acoma and the middle Puerco River. Because of a severe drought and other climatic changes, the Keresans moved to the southeast in the late thirteenth century. They were certainly inhabiting the Rio Grande valley by the end of the fourteenth century (Ford, Schroeder, and Peckham 1972:34–36).

When the Keresans reached the Rio Grande valley, there were subsequent separations and relocations. Traditional history attributes these to the guidance of the Spirit in avoiding "imminent dangers of disasters" and the leadership of the twin war gods, Masewi and Oyoyewi, in "seeking out better land for cultivation and for permanent settlement" (Deloria 1971:223). San Felipe and Cochiti traditions, as recorded and interpreted by Bandelier (1890–1892, 2:166, 188), stated that the ancestors of San Felipe and Cochiti were one people who lived together at various successive villages. The last village inhabited jointly was Kuapa, which was destroyed by the Pinini, a diminutive but strong people, who killed nearly all the inhabitants of Kuapa. A woman and a boy who had hidden from the Pinini traveled south in search of a new home. They were received coldly by the people of Sandia and went to live among the Tanos to the east, where the woman had five children. When her sons learned they were not Tanos, however, they were told by their mother that they would find their future home on the east bank of the Rio Grande, at the foot of the small round black mesa now called La Mesita. There they raised abundant crops for two years and carried the harvests home to their mother, for the Tanos were in the midst of a famine. Finally the ancestors of the San Felipe people left the Tanos and established a village on the west bank of the Rio Grande, at Cubero. When this was abandoned a second village (Old San Felipe) was built at the foot of La Mesita.

The ruins of Kuapa lie five miles north of Cochiti in Cochiti Canyon (Bandelier 1890–1892, 2:162–166). Bandelier believed that it was conflict with the Tewa that forced the people of Kuapa to abandon the village and that the Tano village that took them in was Tunque. Prior to Spanish exploration of the Keresan country in the sixteenth century, the Pueblo was located at various times on Santa Ana Mesa and on both sides of the Rio Grande near its present location. The site of the present village was probably occupied from prehistoric times (Schroeder 1970).

## History

When Francisco Vásquez de Coronado passed through Pueblo country in 1540, he found a Pueblo at the foot of La Mesita (White 1932:8). The Spanish expedition of 1581–1582 noted a three- to four-storied Pueblo with 200 houses, the "Castil de Avid," on the west side of the Rio Grande. It stood across the Rio Grande from a Pueblo of the same size they called Castilblanco. These two Pueblos, probably the two villages of the San Felipe people on either side of the river, seem to have thrived contemporaneously (Pérez de Luxán 1929:82–83; Schroeder in Castaño de Sosa 1965:162). In 1598 Juan de Oñate noted one Pueblo on each side of the river (Hammond and Rey 1953, 1:345).

A church was built at Old San Felipe, the village on the east side of the river, and its builder, Fray Cristóbal de Quiñones, was buried there in 1607 (Bandelier 1890–1892, 2:188–189). However, after 1643 Old San Felipe was usually referred to as a *visita* of Santo Domingo (Benavides 1945:260). There appears to be no mention of the Pueblo on the west side of the river, the present site of San Felipe, in the seventeenth century (Schroeder 1970).

San Felipe people took an active part in the Pueblo Revolt of 1680, killing and driving out Spanish missionaries and settlers. Two San Felipe men who were captured in 1681 reported that some members of the Pueblo were killed because they refused to participate in the uprising. The men reported that the Pueblo joined the revolt because the Spanish officials "would not let them alone, and burned their estufas [kivas]." After the uprising, they said that the leader of the rebellion, Popé:

came down to the pueblo of San Felipe accompanied by many captains from the pueblos and by other Indians and ordered the churches burned and the holy images broken up and burned. They took possession of everything in the sacristy pertaining to divine worship, and said that they were weary of putting in order, sweeping, heating, and adorning the church; and that they proclaimed both in the said pueblo and in the others that he who should utter the name of Jesus would be killed immediately; . . . and that thereupon they could live contentedly, happy in their freedom, living according to their ancient custom . . . .

They declared further that by order of the said Popé and Alonso Catití, governor and head of the Queres nation, they were commanded to place in the pueblo and its environs piles of stones on which they could offer corn and other cereals and tobacco, they saying that the stones were their God, and that they were to observe this, even to the children, giving them to understand that thereby they would have everything they might desire . . . as soon as the señor governor and the rest of the Spaniards had left, the Indians erected many estufas in the pueblos and danced the dances of the cazina and of losse [kachina and Koshare dances] (Hackett 1942, 2:250-251).

The San Felipe people abandoned their Pueblo in 1681, when Antonio de Otermín attempted to reconquer the Pueblo country. They fled to the top of Horn Mesa (the Potrero Viejo of Bandelier 1890-1892, 2:169) southwest of Cochiti Canyon along with people from Cochiti, Santo Domingo, San Marcos, Taos, and Picuris. The Spaniards found Old San Felipe abandoned except for one old man; the church was unroofed, the convent destroyed. Many masks "such as are employed by the Indians in their ceremonies" were found in the houses, and a stone shrine stood in the plaza. The Spaniards sacked the Pueblo and burned the kivas, which they called "houses of idolatry" (Hackett 1942, 2:258-260; White 1932:8-9).

Diego de Vargas arrived at Horn Mesa with 60 soldiers in 1692. The people taking refuge there agreed to return to their homes and presented over 100 children for baptism. Though some of the refugees remained at Horn Mesa, the San Felipe people returned to their own country, and established themselves on top of Santa Ana Mesa, where a church was built in 1694. The people of San Felipe remained friendly to the Spaniards after the reconquest, and they suffered from the attacks of other Pueblos because of this. The Spanish people and soldiers of Bernalillo gathered on top of the mesa with the people of San Felipe during the uprising of 1696 (Domínguez 1956:161; White 1932:9-10).

After the 1696 revolt the people descended from the mesa and established themselves at the present site of San Felipe on the west bank of the Rio Grande. A church and a new Pueblo were being built there in 1706 (Domínguez 1956:161).

The Rio Grande was crossed by rafts in the late 1600s, and by canoes in the 1700s, to reach San Felipe. In 1776 San Felipe consisted of two plazas surrounded by houseblocks, with a few scattered houses nearby and a church to the south of the Pueblo. Farmlands extended upstream and downstream on each side of the river, yielding crops of good quality and quantity. A small settlement of Spanish-speaking people to the south of the Pueblo was assigned to the mission (Domínguez 1956:161-165; Schroeder 1977).

There are few other accounts of San Felipe in the eighteenth century, and nineteenth-century reports are scant as well, attesting to the isolation of the Pueblo. In 1849 an observer noted that San Felipe had two stories and was not built in as purely "Indian" style as the other Rio Grande Pueblos; he found it "rather a neat looking village" (Simpson 1964:156). An 1881 visitor noted the Pueblo was two-storied (fig. 3), with two plazas and circular kivas that extended above the ground. Entry was gained to the houses by ladders, and most homes had

Smithsonian, NAA.
Fig. 3. San Felipe, in 1879, from the south. This view of the main plaza, circumscribed on all sides by two-story buildings, was probably taken from the roof of the church. Santa Ana Mesa at left; the Rio Grande in the background (with bridge spanning it barely visible at left). Photograph by John K. Hillers.

Fig. 4. East and west bank San Felipe settlements in 1899, from the top of Santa Ana Mesa, facing south. The east bank settlement (at left) includes numerous cultivated fields at the very edge of the river, dwellings, and round threshing floors. The railroad tracks (barely visible at upper left) are part of the Atchison, Topeka, and Santa Fe Railway between Lamy and Albuquerque, which opened in 1880. San Felipe Pueblo (at upper right) is linked to the outlying east bank farmlands by a bridge, part of which is visible at center. Photograph by Adam C. Vroman.

Fig. 5. Section of native-built bridge spanning the Rio Grande just north of San Felipe, in 1899. A bridge existed in approximately this spot in 1879, but it may not have been the same bridge. An 1885 visitor described a native system for crossing the river by means of a canoe that was alternately paddled and hauled by rope (Bandelier 1966-1976, 3). According to an eyewitness to the building of a similar bridge at Cochiti in 1897 (Lange 1959:57-60), wicker-woven basketry cribs of the type shown here were placed over wooden braces that had been sunk into the river bed; the cribs were then filled with rocks. Photograph by Adam C. Vroman, facing west.

selenite windows (Bloom 1933-1938, 12:70, 13:210-214). An observer for the 1890 census reported that:

> In proportion to the population, San Felipe has more land available for agriculture than any other pueblo. It has, therefore, become wasteful of its privileges. The town, of recent construction, is laid out with the precision of a military camp, surrounding a plaza 250 by 175 feet. The houses facing this have been whitened for the first story, the second, when

**Table 1. Population, 1680-1970**

| Year | Population | Source |
|------|-----------|--------|
| 1680 | 600 | Dozier 1970 |
| 1730 | 234 | Dozier 1970 |
| 1750 | 453 | Dozier 1970 |
| 1776 | 406 | Domínguez 1956 |
| 1805 | 289 | Dozier 1970 |
| 1860 | 360 | Dozier 1970 |
| 1905 | 475 | Dozier 1970 |
| 1930 | 555 | Dozier 1970 |
| 1942 | 697 | Dozier 1970; Bodine 1972 |
| 1950 | 815 | Bodine 1972 |
|  | 784 | Stubbs 1950 |
| 1964 | 1,327 | Smith 1966 |
| 1968 | 1,575 | Bodine 1972 |
|  | 1,542 | Dozier 1970 |
| 1970 | 1,811 | Southern Pueblos Agency |

there is one, being left in its original color. The effect is striking. At the corners of the plaza are openings wide enough for a horse to pass through, and on the north and south sides are gates for wagons. To the south stands the church, a large building of greater architectural pretensions than any other among the pueblos . . . . The whole town is shadowed on the west by a high volcanic mesa, which rises abruptly to a height of 650 feet. On the top of this, half a mile above, are the ruins of the old pueblo from which the inhabitants moved.

He also noted burros and cattle grazing on the mesa, and horses, on the bottomlands. There were a few orchards and, in general, food to spare. Of the 168 children between 5 and 18, four were in the Albuquerque government school and two were at the Carlisle Indian School (U.S. Census Office. 11th Census 1894:433, 424). See table 1 for population figures for San Felipe.

## Culture

### Political and Ceremonial Organization

The people of San Felipe place great emphasis upon traditional community values and social and religious responsibilities, which are always superordinate to individual interests. San Felipe is one of the most culturally conservative Pueblos; it follows the governmental and ceremonial structures said to have been established by the Spirit before returning to the world below this one. The traditional history set down by the council explains:

The Cacique, said the Spirit, will guide you henceforth, and as the head of the tribe he will be concerned with your spiritual lives as well as with your government when the need for it arises. With these revelations, the Spirit empowered the Cacique with spiritual properties and with jurisdictional powers by which to make laws and govern his people. Hitherto, said the Spirit, it is the only way you and your children can live and give protection to each other. . . .

From the time the Spirit had secluded, the people have lived everafter under the guidance of the Cacique, and obeyed his orders for they all knew he was empowered by the Spirit. Everything went according to the prophecy of the Great Spirit. . . .

However, as the population increased and civilization took roots many problems begin to burden the Cacique. Naturally, more and more this took the attention of the Cacique away from his primary duties of devotion to prayers for spiritual livelihood of his people. Constant prompting of the Spirit to exercise the power vested in him, the Cacique began on a plan to formulate a sovereign government by which his people can be governed. Calling upon the assistance of the Great Spirit, for he did no important act without the ritual, he began to work on a momentous plan for his people and his community (Deloria 1971:223–224).

The cacique called forth the "first office," that of the war chiefs, to aid him in his ceremonial and secular duties. Traditional history records that the Spaniards suggested the creation of the "second office," the governorship, and the "third office," the *fiscales*. The office of governor was assigned to two men to handle the external affairs of the Pueblo, and the office of *fiscales* to two men to assist the Catholic priests. Concludes the council:

Today the setup of the tribal government of San Felipe Pueblo is still the same and its function, in nature, is similar to the olden times except with minor changes made by the people where feasible . . . One then can see at this point that the idea of sovereignty and self-government are deep rooted in the history of the Pueblo people (Deloria 1971:223–224).

Consistent with this statement, White (1932:14) found that the cacique "is the center of the ceremonial configuration of the pueblo, the custodian of their most sacred customs and traditions, the fountainhead of the power by which the village lives." The term cacique was imposed by the Spaniards and is used in English; his native title is *hù·cʰani*. He holds office for life and is succeeded by a man previously designated by the first war chief. The people provide him with food to free his time for meditation, governing, and his preeminent role in the kachina and medicine societies. Though his clan affiliation is not significant, he must be the head of the Flint and Koshare societies (White 1932:12–14).

The war captains, tsiyakiya and lieutenant tsiyakiya, are also called Masewi and Oyoyewi, respectively, after the twin war gods they represent. Chosen yearly, they actually exercise and administer the power of the cacique. One war captain is chosen from each kiva group. They

Smithsonian, NAA.

Fig. 6. A governor of San Felipe, quite possibly Pedro José Quivera ("Ah-fit-che in his own idiom"), who was reportedly the governor in Nov. 1881 (Bloom 1933–1938, 13:211). He is demonstrating the use of a pump drill, a device used to drill holes in flat turquoise and shell beads (see "Zia Pueblo," fig. 3, this vol.). Photograph by John K. Hillers, about 1881–1882.

have eight assistants, the gowachanyi (White 1932:14-15).

The officers created to deal with the Spanish government continue to deal with the world outside the Pueblo. These include the governor (tâ·pupʰU), his lieutenant, eight captains, and six *fiscales*. They are appointed yearly by the cacique (White 1932:19-20). The *principales* are a group of men who have held the offices of war captains, governor, or *fiscales*. They are an advisory council who confer with the cacique and other officers over important issues. This group of elders remains closed and influential, a fact that makes San Felipe one of the most conservative of the Pueblos (White 1932:16; Smith 1966:126).

Office is not sought out but is thrust upon an individual as a communal responsibility and obligation. Annual appointments are made by the cacique in concert with the heads of the Giant Society and the Shikami Society. The candidates must be physically present to be invested, during the period between Christmas and January 6, the feast of the Epiphany ('kings' day' in Spanish). The offices alternate between kachina groups; for example, if the governor is Turquoise, his lieutenant is Squash, and the next year the reverse; the same applies to the war captains (Martin Murphy, personal communication 1977).

The various societies are essential for the well-being and functioning of San Felipe. They are closely related to the officers, for the cacique is the head of the Flint and Koshare societies, and the heads of the Giant and Shikami societies aid the cacique in the selection of officers. There are four curing or medicine societies: Flint, Giant, Shikami, and Snake. They are concerned both with the curing of individuals, especially the purging of witches who cause disease, and the public welfare. They are prominent in kachina ceremonies, and go into retreat at the summer solstice to bring rain (White 1932:16, 40-50). Other societies include the Koshare and Quirana, complementary groups; the Shayaka (Hunters' Society); and the Opi (Warriors' Society, now extinct). The Koshare are related to the Flint curing society, and function at kachina dances and as clowns; the Quirana are related to the Shikami Society and appear at dances. The Shayaka are involved in the communal hunts, in the Buffalo Dance, and in performing other rituals to assist hunters in the taking of game. The Opi Society was formerly composed of men who had killed an enemy in battle and performed certain rituals with the scalp (White 1932:16-19, 53-60).

The kachina organization represents the kachina spirits in masked dances to bring rain. Tradition states that the kachinas formerly visited the Pueblo in person, and rain always followed their visit, for they are shiwana, or rainmakers. There are three kachina groups in San Felipe: the Turquoise, Squash, and Yashcha. The first two belong to the kivas of the same name, while the last, the smallest, has a house where masks are kept, but no kiva (White 1932:24-40). The Yashcha separated from the Turquoise kiva group around 1900, along a traditionalist (conservative, "hostiles") versus modernist (progressive, "friendlies") cleavage. For certain purposes, such as the annual feast day, Yashcha combines with Turquoise; for other purposes, such as Christmas dances, it operates separately (Martin Murphy, personal communication 1977). Each kiva group is headed by a nawai and his assistant; they are appointed by the Masewi. An important officer, the nawai supervises the dances and preparations for them. All men and mature boys belong to a kachina group (White 1932:24-40).

White (1932:50-52) gives the ceremonial calendar of San Felipe. San Felipe's Day, May 1, is celebrated with a corn dance (fig. 7). In general, the dances at San Felipe are among the finest of the Rio Grande Pueblos.

## Social Organization

Every member of the Pueblo belongs to a matrilineal, exogamous clan. In 1928 White noted the Corn, Tobacco, Wolf, Ant, Eagle, Fire Water, Antelope, Sun, Toad, Turkey, Dove, and Yashcha ("all kinds beads") clans but did not note any special clan functions (White 1932:21).

Denver Public Lib., Western Hist. Dept.

Fig. 7. Corn Dance, probably on the occasion of San Felipe's Day or possibly Kings' Day (Jan. 6). The women wear the customary tablita headdresses and carry evergreen boughs. The men wear embroidered dance kilts, sashes, headdresses composed of feathers, and skunkskins tied around both ankles. Photograph by J. A. Jeançon, 1915.

396

There are several treatments of Keresan kinship (Eggan 1950; Fox 1967, 1972; Dozier 1970).

## Sociocultural Situation in the 1960s and 1970s

In the 1970s only one plaza was obvious at San Felipe. Other houses surrounded the plaza, but the village was less compact than formerly, with houses scattered on the east side of the river. Some of these were built with funds from the U.S. Department of Housing and Urban Development.

The people of San Felipe, like those of other Pueblos, were farmers, gatherers, and hunters until the twentieth century. Wage work in Albuquerque has increasingly replaced farming as a means of subsistence. In 1966 permanent jobs were held by 23.6% of the labor force, 64% had temporary or seasonal work, and 12.4% were unemployed. Recurring unemployment was estimated at 76.4%. Children attended the day school in the Pueblo, and high school students attended public school in Bernalillo (Smith 1966:126–127).

San Felipe is not noted among the Pueblos for crafts. However, in the late 1960s there were some traditional crafts being pursued by a few individuals in the village. Small quantities of yucca-ring baskets and of men's and women's woven woolen sashes or belts were being made. The traditional Pueblo moccasins with deerskin uppers and cowhide soles continued to be made. All these crafts, of good quality workmanship, were conducted almost solely for internal consumption. Items for ceremonial use were likewise being made for the village. As part of a summer program at the village day school, children of both sexes were being instructed in these traditional crafts by adults of the village. No pottery was manufactured in the 1960s nor does one find in museum collections much ceramics attributed to San Felipe. Of the few examples of pottery apparently collected at San Felipe, there is no unequivocal documentation to indicate it was actually manufactured there, and indeed much of it appears to be Santo Domingo ware. If San Felipe has not manufactured pottery in recent times it must have acquired these necessary items by regular trade with adjacent Pueblos. In the early and mid-1970s with the increased national interest in Indian artifacts, especially jewelry, many San Felipe men took up the manufacture of shell necklaces, which allowed them to remain in the village at a time when the house-building industry in Albuquerque was no longer expanding. Later the importation of cheap shell jewelry from Taiwan and the Philippines depressed the market.†

Keresan remained the preferred language in 1977, and marriage was generally maintained within the Pueblo. With Santo Domingo, San Felipe had in 1968 the lowest percentage (21%) of the Rio Grande Pueblos of nonresidence of Pueblo members (Bodine 1972:275). These factors, along with the strong ceremonial and other social structures maintained by the Pueblo, indicate that San Felipe will remain a vital and distinctive community.

## Synonymy§

The Pueblo of San Felipe takes its name from that of the Spanish mission there. The earliest spelling is Oñate's Sant Phelipe, 1598. It has also, wrongly, been called San Felipe de Jesús (Domínguez 1956:161).

In the San Felipe dialect of Keresan the Pueblo is called ká·tʰĪšᵗʼa, a name of no known etymology also borne by other Pueblos earlier inhabited by the San Felipeans, notably at Cubero and Old San Felipe. An attempt to spell this may be seen in Castixe, Oñate's name for the village on the west bank of the Rio Grande opposite what he called Comitze (Hammond and Rey 1953, 1:345). The Santa Ana form is kátʰĪšᵗʼá.

The diverse names in other languages include Taos pɔ̀tɔ́ata (Curtis 1907–1930, 16:261, normalized), Picuris thoxtlawīamã́, Isleta pʼatśak, literally 'the water is way down (under high cliffs)' (C.T. Harrington 1920:43), Tewa nan kʷǽrige 'sticky-earth place' (Harrington 1916:498 and Curtis 1907–1930, 16:260, 262, phonemicized), Jemez kwilegi'i or kʷílìgʸíʔ 'at the pass' (also 'San Felipe Indian') and Zuni wehkʔana cʔana 'little Santo Domingo' (Dennis Tedlock, personal communication 1977) and wepłapatsa (Curtis 1907–1930, 16:261, normalized). Hopi has the borrowing katisča (normalized). Navajo has Dibé Łizhiní 'black sheep' (Robert W. Young, personal communication 1977) and Séí Bee Hooghan 'dwellings of sand' (Franciscan Fathers 1910:135 and Haile 1950–1951, 1:223, phonemicized), the former apparently extended from the name of the San Felipe clan among the Navajo; the name given by Curtis (1907–1930, 1:138) is actually that of Santo Domingo. The information that the Navajos call San Felipe Tsédahkin 'house(s) on the edge of the rocks' or Tséta'kin 'house(s) between the rocks' (Richard Van Valkenburgh in Simpson 1964:157) is in disagreement with other information that the latter is the name of San Ildefonso (Robert W. Young, personal communication 1977).

## Sources

White (1932) is the only source specifically on San Felipe Pueblo. White (1930) also wrote on Keresan medicine societies and Keresan world view (1960). Fox (1967) deals with Keresan kinship.

† This paragraph was prepared by Martin Murphy.

§ This synonymy was prepared by Ives Goddard. Uncredited forms are from Harrington (1916:498–500), who gives additional variants, or from anonymous sources.

# Santa Ana Pueblo

PAULINE TURNER STRONG

Santa Ana Pueblo (ˌsăntuˈănu) (figs. 1-2) is one of five Keresan-speaking Pueblos located in the Rio Grande valley of New Mexico.* The closely grouped Eastern Keresans have many cultural characteristics in common, which, in turn, are often distinct from those of their Western Keresan linguistic relatives, Acoma and Laguna. The Eastern Keresan Pueblos form a wedge in the midst of the Tanoan-speaking Rio Grande Pueblos and differ significantly from the Tanoans in many respects, though there has been considerable borrowing between the Keresans and the three Tanoan language groups (Eggan 1950; Fox 1967, 1972; Dozier 1970).

Relations have traditionally been closest between Santa Ana and the Pueblos of Zia and San Felipe. Interaction with these and other Pueblos includes visiting at dances and ceremonies, trading, assisting each other in rituals, helping in irrigation work, and occasional intermarriage. Relations with non-Pueblo Indian groups, such as the Navajo, Apache, Ute, and Comanche, have been traditionally distant, even hostile at times, though there is also a history of trade and cultural exchange with the nomadic tribes.

## Territory and Environment

The old Santa Ana Pueblo is on the north bank of the Jemez River eight miles northwest of its junction with the Rio Grande and 27 miles northwest of Albuquerque, in a semiarid area of volcanic mesas and sandy plains (see "Pueblos: Introduction," fig. 1, this vol.). The ecosystem varies from the cactus, juniper, and piñon area of the surrounding hills to mountains with pine, spruce, and fir, and river valleys with cottonwoods. The mean annual rainfall is only a bit over eight inches, with a mean temperature of 54° F. The mean temperature in the summer months is in the 70s; in the winter months, the 30s. These data on climate are significant because the culture of Santa Ana is based upon intensive agriculture, the ceremonialism is concerned primarily with rainmaking, and cloud and lightning symbols are profuse. These are "a people whose conception of beauty in a landscape is a cloudy day" (White 1942:32).

The original Pueblo, *támáyá*, is about 5,400 feet above sea level. The Jemez Mountains lie 15-20 miles to the northwest, while the Sandia range is about an equal distance to the southeast. The village is enclosed by the Jemez River on one side and "almost leans against the craggy wall of the extensive mesa of San Felipe" (Bandelier in White 1942:35). This setting has provided good protection against enemies and considerable isolation. Santa Ana was visited by non-Indians less frequently than almost any other Pueblo in New Mexico, for it was not encountered either by travelers on the Rio Grande or by those going westward. This isolation has contributed to the conservatism and cultural tenacity of the Santa Ana people (White 1942:30, 35).

In historic times, the land immediately surrounding *támáyá* was poor for farming. Early in the eighteenth century the Santa Anans began to purchase from the Spanish settlers tracts for farming located on the Rio Grande about 10 miles southeast of *támáyá* and just north of the Spanish town of Bernalillo. Gradually the Santa Anans began to live seasonally in this region of small ranchos—Ranchitos—and they eventually abandoned the old Pueblo except for ceremonial use. The land base includes 17,360 acres surrounding *támáyá* confirmed by the Spanish and United States governments, and 4,945 acres at Ranchitos confirmed by the U.S. Court of Private Land Claims (White 1942:39-40). The Santa Ana people have acquired land in addition to these grants, and in 1966 they owned 42,085 acres, including grant land, of which 1,150 acres were irrigable, 1,307 noncommercial open timber, and 39,540 open grazing (Smith 1966).

---

\* Words in the Santa Ana dialect of Keresan that are cited in italics are written according to the phonemic system of Davis (1964:59-66), with substitutions made to bring it in line with the standard technical alphabet of the *Handbook:* the voiceless unaspirated stops are *p, t* (alveolar), *tʸ* (alveopalatal), *k* (Davis's b, d, dʸ, g); the voiceless aspirates *pʰ, tʰ, čʰ, kʰ* (his p, t, č, k); the alveolar affricates *c, cʰ* (his z, c); and the retroflex affricates *ç, çʰ* (his z̧, ç). Other consonant symbols are the same as his: *p̓, ḽ, c̓, c̣̓, č̓, k̓; s, ṣ, ṣ̌; š, ṣ̌, š̓; m, n, r* (alveolar flap), *w, y; m̓, n̓, r̓, w̓, y̓; h, ʔ*. The vowels are *i* (high front), *e* (mid to low front), *a* (low central, *ɨ* (high, central to back, unrounded; Davis's ə), *u* (mid to high, back, rounded); they also occur long (*i·*, etc.) and voiceless (*I*, etc.; Davis's small capitals). The accents are *v́* (level, normally stressed and high-pitched), *v̂* (falling), *v̀* (breathy), *v̌* (glottal), and v (unaccented). Sounds introduced through loanwords are *č* (alveopalatal affricate; Davis's ž), the voiced stops *b, d,* and *g* (his B, D, G), and *l* (alveolar lateral). *tʸ* is aspirated [tʸʰ] before a voiceless vowel. These italicized words are from published sources and a consultant who prefers to be anonymous; words not in italics are approximate spellings based on sources that fail to distinguish many significant phonological features.

Southwest Foundation for Audio-Visual Resources, Sante Fe, N.M.
Fig. 1. Santa Ana Pueblo. Photograph by Peter Dechert, June 1977.

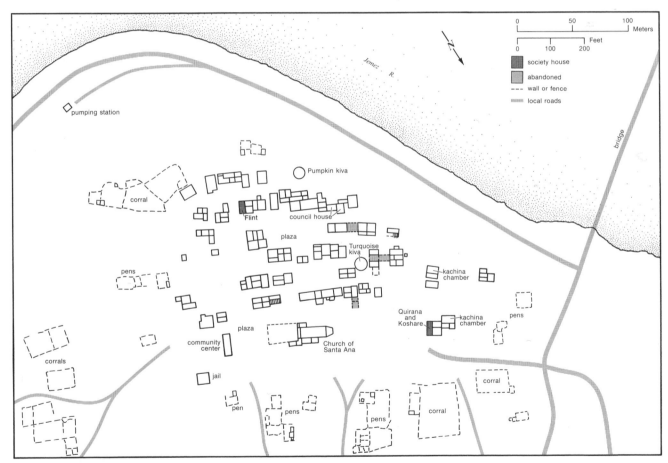

revised from Historic Amer. Buildings Survey, Natl. Park Service, map for 1975.
Fig. 2. Santa Ana Pueblo.

399

## Culture

### Structures

The old Pueblo is set out in parallel rows of houses, with several plazas, the largest being the principal dancing area for ceremonies. Early descriptions of the Pueblo indicate that Santa Ana was not always constructed in parallel rows, for it was arranged around a central plaza in 1776 and went through several subsequent changes (Domínguez 1956:170; U.S. Census Office. 11th Census 1894:431; Bloom 1933–1938, 13:216–218). The house blocks were formerly of two and three stories (fig. 3), entered by ladders, but now have only one story. The Pueblo is constructed of adobe, and there are no modern utilities. There are two circular kivas, or ceremonial structures, partly above and partly below the ground. Other ceremonial houses are scattered among the residences. The church, built in 1706 and rebuilt in 1734, with an added convent, lies on the north edge of the Pueblo. The convent no longer stands. Corrals, sheds, and refuse heaps are on the outskirts of the village. Though *támáyá* is reserved for ceremonial use, most families maintain a home there as well as one in Ranchitos.

Ranchitos (fig. 4) outwardly resembles many New Mexican rural villages. The homes are similar in construction to those at *támáyá* but usually stand independently of one another and have modern conveniences. There is a church, erected in the early twentieth century, but no kivas or other native religious objects in Ranchitos (White 1942:35–41; Domínguez 1956:166–171; Stubbs 1950:76–77).

### Social and Religious Organization

The life of each individual in Santa Ana is connected with that of the entire community through social and ceremonial relationships and obligations. Each individual, of course, has his or her own kinship ties and life cycle (see White 1942:157–179; Eggan 1950; Fox 1967), but the greatest emphasis in the Pueblo is placed upon the common welfare. The people of Santa Ana are divided into clans that are matrilineal, exogamous kinship groups. A person is usually born into a clan but can be formally adopted into one as well. White noted the Eagle, Dove, Coyote, Turkey, Siyana (*síyañł* 'mouse'), Corn, Water, Sun, Fire, Badger, and Yashcha clans at Santa Ana, and several others may have become extinct by his time. Many of these are related to other Keresan clans, and several have been imported from other Pueblos. Clan affiliation determines kiva membership and regulates marriage, but it is not known to structure other matters (White 1942:144–157).

Smithsonian, NAA.

Fig. 3. Santa Ana, viewed from the northwest, in 1879. North Plaza is at center, the church is at left, and the Jemez River is out of frame to the right. Cattle are in the corral at foreground, constructed of wooden stakes that are lashed (probably with strips of rawhide) to a horizontal support. Hay is stored just behind the wooden carts at far right. Photograph by John K. Hillers.

400

Fig. 4. Street scene in Ranchitos. Photograph by Bill Hume, Jan. 1971.

Each member of Santa Ana belongs to either the Squash or the Turquoise ceremonial group, each of which has its own kiva. It appears to be unique to Santa Ana to derive kiva membership from clan affiliation. The kiva groups are in charge of the medicine societies and certain dances, but this dual organization does not serve nonceremonial functions (White 1942:142–144).

The Keresan tradition that the gods left religious officers and societies to take their places when the gods themselves left the people is the basis for the most important governing structures of Santa Ana society. The native officers consist of a cacique (çáiḱá·čI or líyaṁini), the chief official; his assistant and successor (gowiye); two war priests, Masewi and Oyoyewi; their four assistants (káučʰáni, sg.); and a ditch boss.

The cacique is the most sacred, thus the most important, official. He is primarily a priest, charged with keeping all things in order and taking care of the people. He authorizes all communal rituals and makes the yearly appointments of officials. Holding office for life, he is succeeded by the gowiye, who is selected by the war priests. White's (1942) report that the last cacique died before 1910 was contradicted by a native consultant in 1978, who observed that there has always been a cacique.

The war chiefs are selected annually by the cacique and formerly dealt mainly with external relations and warfare. In the 1970s they administered the ceremonial and political life of Santa Ana for the more withdrawn, contemplative cacique. The ditch boss, selected annually by the cacique, ensures the proper operation of the irrigation system by ritual and the organization of duties. A council (fig. 5), formerly composed only of old men but now composed of all male heads of families, can be convened by certain officials to discuss and reach agreement upon matters of common concern.

With the coming of the Spaniards, a new group of officers was set up to handle Pueblo-Spanish relations. These officers continue to deal with American society for the Pueblo: a governor, his lieutenant, four or five captains, six *fiscales,* a *sacristán,* and a *kahé·ra.* The governor is the principal intermediary between the Pueblo and the outside world. The captains and *fiscales* watch over the Pueblo or Ranchitos while the people are absent. The *fiscales,* with the *sacristán,* chiefly serve the Catholic church, and the *kahé·ra* rolls his drum in certain ceremonies of Spanish derivation. These officers are appointed yearly by the cacique, except for the *sacristán* and *kahé·ra,* who serve for life (White 1942:95–115).

The medicine, clown, warrior, hunter, and kachina societies are likewise essential for the well-being of Santa Ana. The principal function of the various medicine societies is to bring rain through retreats, fasts, and ceremonies. They also have charge of the solstice ceremonies, the installation of caciques, the purging of witches, and the treatment of diseases. Each head of a Shikami medicine society (šíˑḱami) has charge of a kiva group. Women may affiliate themselves with the medicine societies, but only men are said to cure.

The Koshare (ḱïṣáirí) and Quirana (kúiŕáiná) are two distinct, but closely related, societies concerned chiefly with fertility and the growth of crops. They accompany the kachinas (ḱâ·cina, sg.), masked representations of gods, in dances and have charge of certain ceremonies. In addition, the Koshare often function as sacred clowns. The šáyàikʰA, or Hunters' Society, is concerned with the proper rituals to ensure the securing of game, such as the game animal dances and the communal hunts. The ʔùˑpʰI, or Warriors' Society, was formerly composed of men who had killed and scalped an enemy in battle. By the ritual use of scalps they were said to bring good to the Pueblo. In modern times this has been modified to a society of men who have killed a bear, mountain lion, or eagle.

Fig. 5. Members of the tribal council in session in 1940. Photograph by an unidentified photographer.

Fig. 6. Jesus Antonio Moya, governor of Santa Ana, in 1899. Studio portrait by DeLancey Gill, Washington, D.C.

The kachina organization is concerned with impersonating kachinas in dances in order to bring rain and general well-being to the Pueblo. There are five groups, each of which is controlled by a medicine society. Membership is open to both sexes and is usually voluntary, in contrast to the other societies, which generally gain members by a vow, in return for a cure, by a trespass upon sacred ground, or by some other circumstance.

There are several features of Santa Ana religion that are unique among the Keresans. It is the only Pueblo with two šĭˈk̇ami societies and with masked dances involving women. Also unique among the Keresans, initiation to the kachina organization is voluntary and the member keeps his or her own mask. Finally, unlike other Eastern Keresans except for Zia, the kachina organizations are associated with medicine societies instead of kiva groups. White (1942:115–142) attributes these factors to the small size of Santa Ana and its partial loss of ceremonial life, but this explanation is not completely satisfying.

### Seasonal and Ceremonial Cycle

The yearly cycle of Santa Ana life is based upon the movements of the sun and the agricultural and hunting seasons. Several traditional rituals have been moved to Spanish holy days in accommodation to Catholicism. Also, because of the movement to Ranchitos, ceremonies

402

at támáyá, the old Pueblo, have been concentrated into certain periods of the year.

The medicine societies observe the winter solstice at támáyá, and shortly thereafter (in mid-December) the Santa Ana people go there for the winter ceremonial events. Christmas dances are held there, as are the installation of officers on January 1 and a dance in their honor on January 6. These winter dances are generally buffalo or other game dances (fig. 8). A number of masked dances, a communal rabbit hunt, and the Aowe 'to help in making a crop' are held in January and early February, after which the people return to Ranchitos.

On June 13 the people go to Sandia Pueblo to the south, to participate in their festivities in honor of San Antonio, who is also the patron saint of Ranchitos. The medicine societies observe the summer solstice at támáyá and the people follow them for about a week in late June. San Juan's Day (June 24) is celebrated with a dance, a rooster pull (Spanish gallo), and the distribution of presents from the rooftops of homes where a person named Juan resides. The gallo is a Spanish-derived custom in which horsemen attempt to pull buried roosters from the ground while riding by at a full gallop and then

Fig. 7. Bandolier and rattle worn by dancer of the Warriors' Society (see White 1942:307–308, 345). top, Bandolier made of concentric loops of braided buckskin strips with two hoof shells and bone flute attached; the section wrapped with buckskin lies over the right shoulder as the loops are worn across the chest and under the left arm; length about 61 cm. bottom, Rattle worn at dancer's waist, of petrified wood chips suspended from a wooden rod by buckskin thongs; length of rod about 15 cm. Both collected in 1932.

may fight with the roosters until they are torn to pieces. At this time the medicine societies go into retreat to fast and perform rituals to bring rain.

Santiago's Day (July 25) is celebrated at *támáyá* with a *gallo* and a dance. On Santa Ana's Day (July 26) a mass and a corn dance (*pá·skʰU* 'feast day') are held, as well as much feasting and visiting. Santiago and Boshayanyi (*púšáyâ·ni*) may appear on these two days to bless the people and livestock of the Pueblo. The former is a saint who appears on a makeshift horse and shows other strong Spanish influences, while the latter is a traditional culture hero.

There is usually a masked dance in the autumn to celebrate the harvest, as well as a rabbit hunt in honor of the women. The deer hunting season begins about mid-November, and soon the observance of the winter solstice renews the cycle (White 1942:92-94).

## Subsistence

The Rio Grande Pueblos practiced extensive agriculture by irrigation when the Spaniards arrived, chiefly growing corn, beans, and squash. Their diet was rounded out by hunting and gathering. The importance of corn to the Pueblos is underscored by the fact that corn is considered their mother and nourisher; it is sacred and used ceremonially in many ways. Since the coming of the Spaniards, the people of Santa Ana have raised wheat, alfalfa, chili, and melons and various fruits and other vegetables in addition to the aboriginal crops. Deer, elk, antelope, and rabbits were the most important game animals, and regular expeditions were made to the plains for buffalo. The Santa Ana people have also raised horses, cattle, and oxen since the Spaniards brought these animals to the area (White 1942:42-47, 280-282). With the increase in wage work in the mid-twentieth century, store-bought foods have come to supplement and partially supplant the native diet. Hunting has declined in importance, though cattle continue to be raised. Farming had almost completely died out in the 1960s, but fields were again being cultivated in the 1970s.

## Technology

Traditionally, cotton was grown for the weaving of textiles, for both daily and ceremonial use. The people of Santa Ana made baskets, pottery (fig. 9), and leather items (fig. 10) and, with the arrival of the Spaniards, filigree jewelry and straw-inlay work (fig. 11) as well. They traded with Pueblo and non-Pueblo Indians for other items and, later, with the Spaniards and Americans (White 1942:48-49). In 1881 an observer of Santa Ana noted drums, tortoise rattles, buffalo robes, abalone shell jewelry, bows, arrows and quivers, large fine pottery jars and bowls, and Navajo blankets (Bloom 1933-1938, 13:216-218). By the 1940s most of these arts were discontinued, but there was a revival of pottery-making and belt weaving in the 1970s. However, in general wage work in Albuquerque was much more important to the

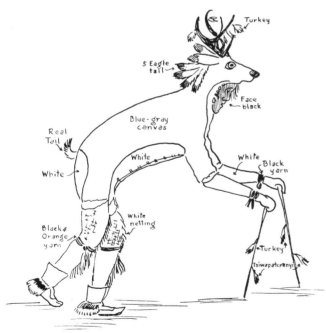

Amer. Anthropological Assoc., Washington: White 1942:fig. 31.

Fig. 8. Deer dancer as he would appear in a Buffalo Dance, a dance that generally includes 2 bison, 4 or 5 deer, and 12 or more antelope (White 1942:296-302). Compare with San Juan deer dancer, "San Juan Pueblo," fig. 7, this vol. Drawing by an anonymous Santa Ana artist, between 1928 and 1941.

School of Amer. Research, Santa Fe, N.M.: Ind. Arts Fund Coll. IAF426; Smithsonian, Dept. of Anthr.: 409805.

Fig. 9. Santa Ana pottery, characterized by fine sand temper and blocky red designs (partly edged in black) painted on a cream slip (Frank and Harlow 1974:102). left, Water jar of the type common from 1800 until the 1940s, when pottery traded from Zia became more popular (Toulouse 1977:38); diameter 28 cm; in use when collected in 1925. right, Contemporary jar made by Eudora Montoya, who alone preserved the pottery tradition at Santa Ana for some 40 years until a revival project in 1972; diameter 16 cm; collected in 1967.

*403*

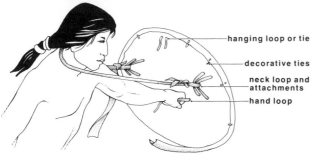

top, Heard Mus., Phoenix, Ariz.: Fred Harvey Coll. 1605CI, 1619CI (Northland Press); bottom, after Wright 1976:14.

Fig. 10. Santa Ana shields. top, Two shields, each of two hide thicknesses sewed together: left, painted design with central circle of white, a pair of black horns, and lower portion of multicolored rays, collected before 1908; right, back side of Spanish shield with design of leather thong stitching and bilobed shape, which has been slightly modified to circular Indian shape, collected in 1907; both diameters about 53 cm. bottom, Neck loop permits the shield to be swung to the back when not in use. See Wright 1976:66–69.

U. of Ariz., Ariz. State Mus., Tucson: E4883.

Fig. 11. Wooden cross with straw mosaic inlay. Height 20.5 cm; made by Porfirio Montoya before 1961.

economy of Santa Ana in the last third of the twentieth century than either agriculture or crafts.

## Mythology and Prehistory

Like other Keresans, the people of Santa Ana trace their ancestry to the north. They believe that they originated inside the earth, where their mother Iyatiko resides. Priests, officers, medicine men, gods, witches, birds, animals, and insects were in the underworld as well. When the proper time came, various birds, animals, and insects assisted the people to climb up trees and ascend through four worlds below this one—the white, red, blue, and yellow worlds. When they emerged onto this, the fifth world, at Sipapu (Santa Ana *šípá·pʰɨ*) in the north, the gods hardened the earth and set the sun, moon, and stars in their places. The people soon had to leave the place of emergence because it was too sacred for human habitation, but before they left Iyatiko gave them corn to take her place as the nourisher. Also, a priest named *íiyaṁɨni*, also called *čáiḱá·čI* 'cacique', was given the duty of caring for the people as a mother would.

The people moved south to a place called White House, where they lived for a long time with the gods, who taught them all they needed to know about living on this earth. After a time a quarrel arose between the people and the kachinas, the gods primarily in control of rain, and the kachinas refused to come to White House. Instead, they promised to send their spirits to be with masked dancers impersonating them in ceremonies. The people continued to quarrel, and Iyatiko also became angry with them. One night she altered the people's language, causing each quarreling faction to speak a different tongue. The gods appointed societies of priests to take their places and returned to their homes at various places on the earth. (See White 1942:80–86 for a map and description of the homes of the gods and the world surrounding Santa Ana in native cosmology.) The people abandoned White House, with the various factions eventually settling in different places. One faction moved south, finally settling at the present site of Santa Ana (White 1942:86–91, 1960).

What scholars know about the prehistory of the Keresan people is consistent with this tradition. The four language groups that comprise the Rio Grande Pueblos are cultural descendants of the Anasazi tradition, with some influence from the Mogollon peoples as well. Scholars generally derive the Eastern Keresans and the Tanoans from two distinct prehistoric groups, but there is some disagreement as to the source areas and movements of these groups. The Keresans have been traced to an area centering around Chaco Canyon, extending north to the Aztec and Mesa Verde regions, and, perhaps, southeast to Acoma and the middle Puerco River. Migration from these areas was necessary because of a severe drought and other climatic changes. In the late thirteenth century the Keresans moved to the southeast, and they were certainly inhabiting the Rio Grande Valley by the end of the fourteenth century (Ford, Schroeder, and Peckham 1972:34-36).

## History

Santa Ana has occupied approximately its present site since at least the late 1500s, according to documentary and archeological evidence. The first Spaniards to explore Pueblo country, Francisco Vásquez de Coronado and his men, entered the lands of the Keresans in 1540. There are a few records of early Spanish visits to Pueblos that may have been Santa Ana prior to Juan de Oñate's colonization of New Mexico in 1598 (Gallegos Lamero 1927:352; Pérez de Luxán 1929:82-84).

In July 1598 Santa Ana submitted with other Pueblos to the king of Spain at Santo Domingo. The patron saint Ana was assigned to the Pueblo that same year (Hammond and Rey 1953). During the seventeenth century, Santa Ana was usually referred to as a *visita* of the mission at Zia, though there may have been a church and convent in Santa Ana prior to 1680 (Benavides 1945:65; Scholes 1938a:66-67; Bandelier 1890-1892, 2:194).

The Santa Anans joined the other Pueblos in revolt against Spanish oppression in 1680. A Spanish official reported that the Pueblo was deserted by the men at the time of the revolt and "the women there said with much impudence that their husbands had gone to kill all the Spaniards" (quoted in White 1942:25). After driving out the Spaniards the leader of the revolt, Popé from San Juan Pueblo, took a tour of the Pueblos. A contemporary Spaniard reported that at Santa Ana Popé

> caused to be prepared an invitation feast of the viands which the priests and governors were wont to use; and a great table according to the fashion of the Spaniards. He seated himself at the head, and in the opposite place he had Alonso Catití sit, seating the rest in the remaining places. He caused to be brought two chalices, one for himself and the other for the said Alonso, and both began to drink toasts in scoff at the Spaniards and the Christian religion. And Popé, taking his chalice, said to Alonso (as if he were the Father Custodian): "To your Paternal Reverence's health." Alonso took his chalice, and rising said to Popé: "Here is to your Lordship's, Sir Governor." In fine, there remained in all the kingdom no vestige of the Christian religion; all was profaned and destroyed (White 1942:25).

The revolt and its aftermath caused repeated dislocations of the people from Santa Ana. When Gov. Antonio de Otermín attempted to reconquer the Pueblo country in 1681, he heard that the inhabitants had abandoned Santa Ana and were taking refuge in the Jemez Mountains with members of other Pueblos (Bandelier 1890-1892, 2:54). Otermín burned and sacked many Pueblos but left Santa Ana alone. Archeological evidence suggests that some Santa Ana people may have returned to Black Mesa near the present Pueblo after Otermín's departure in 1682 (Schroeder 1970a).

In 1687 Gov. Pedro Reñeros de Posada invaded the Pueblo, probably located on Black Mesa at the time, and burned it. Zia was destroyed in like manner the following year (Bandelier 1890-1892, 2:195). The Santa Ana and Zia peoples joined together to build a new Pueblo farther up the Jemez River, where Gov. Diego de Vargas found them in 1692. By the next year the Santa Ana people were settled in the present Pueblo location on the plain below Black Mesa. They consistently joined with the Spaniards against Pueblo and other Indian groups opposing them after this (White 1942:26-27; Bandelier 1890-1892, 2:173, 195; Bloom and Mitchell 1938:100-101; Bloom 1931:175).

In the eighteenth century the Santa Ana people began buying and cultivating the fields at Ranchitos, and a church and convent were built at the old Pueblo. They crossed the Rio Grande in what a priest described as "canoes" to get to their fields. The population rose steadily in the eighteenth century until it was reduced by a smallpox epidemic in 1789-1781. Santa Ana was again made a *visita* of Zia in 1782 (White 1942:27-28; Bancroft 1889:274).

In the nineteenth century the Santa Anans spent an increasing amount of time, finally the entire growing season, at Ranchitos. The Pueblo was relatively prosperous. There were a few American visits to Santa Ana after the United States won control of New Mexico in 1846, but it remained isolated. In 1890 an agent of the Bureau of Indian Affairs reported that the Pueblo was inhabited only in autumn and winter. In the summer, while the rest of the people were farming on the Rio Grande, two men, at the direction of the governor, guarded the Pueblo, occupying their time by making thread and moccasins. He further described the Pueblo:

> On the outskirts are numerous cedar corrals, and near these a guest house, the most comfortable lodge in the village. Here strangers are entertained and, on the occasion of private feasts or dances, imprisoned. . . . A complete removal is made in March. . . . The cats alone remain, prowling like gaunt specters over the roofs and through the deserted street.
>
> At the ranches of Santa Ana are two small villages half a mile apart. Each is surrounded by orchards of peach, apple, and plum trees and small vineyards. The corn crop is one of the finest to be seen on the Rio Grande (U.S. Census Office. 11th Census 1894:431-432).

In 1890 the people of Santa Ana owned about 600 horses, 2,000 cattle, 30 yoke of oxen, and 150 burros. Only one inhabitant could speak English, while almost all could speak Spanish in addition to Keresan. All those for whom an occupation was given in the census were farmers; of the 75 children between the ages of 5 and 18, 11 attended boarding school in Albuquerque (U.S. Census Office. 11th Census 1894:431-432). In the early 1900s a day school was established at Ranchitos (White 1942:56). Reports of Indian agents of the late nineteenth century speak of epidemics of smallpox, diphtheria, and

**Table 1. Population, 1707-1977**

| Year | Population | Source |
|------|-----------|--------|
| 1707 | 340 | Bancroft 1889: 274 |
| 1730 | 209 | Dozier 1970:122 |
| 1750 | 353 | Dozier 1970:122 |
| 1776 | 384 | Domínguez 1956 |
| 1805 | 450 | Dozier 1970:122 |
| 1809 | 550 | White 1942:54 |
| 1850 | 399 | White 1942:54 |
| 1864 | 298 | White 1942:54 |
| 1879 | 342 | White 1942:54 |
| 1890 | 253 | White 1942:54 |
| 1900 | 226 | Dozier 1970:122 |
| 1930 | 236 | Dozier 1970:122 |
| 1950 | 300 | Bodine 1972:273 |
| 1964 | 431 | Smith 1966 |
| 1968 | 456 | Bodine 1972:273 |
| 1977 | 498 | Santa Ana Governor's Office |

tuberculosis; trachoma and influenza ravaged the village as well (White 1942:54–55), as is reflected in population figures for Santa Ana (table 1).

The life of the people of Santa Ana in the mid-twentieth century, like that of other Pueblos, is a blend of the traditional and the contemporary. The proximity of Albuquerque has modified Santa Ana life, as have certain U.S. government programs. The population increased 52 percent from 1950 to 1968, with 76 percent of the 1968 population residing in Santa Ana. The remaining percentage lived away from Santa Ana but often returned for ceremonies and usually returned to live eventually. There was a strong tendency toward marriage within the Pueblo (Bodine 1972:282). In 1966 Bureau of Indian Affairs figures showed a 12 percent unemployment rate, with 57.4% temporary and seasonal employment and 69.5% recurring unemployment (Smith 1966). Unemployment was most severe among the older members of the Pueblo.

Children attend the Bernalillo Consolidated Schools, which increases interaction with the predominantly Hispanic people of Bernalillo. Higher education was attracting more young people of Santa Ana in the 1970s.

In the 1970s there were many federal programs serving the people of Santa Ana, almost entirely staffed by natives of the Pueblo. Many of these programs were under the auspices of the Community Action Program and dealt with matters such as employment, consumer education, home economics, recreation, alcoholism, drug use, and problems of the elderly and youth. There was also a Headstart program. The Public Health Service clinic reduced the health problems previously reported in the Pueblo. Through the Department of Housing and Urban Development program, some 30 single-family dwellings were built, and more were planned.

Both because of programs such as these and adherence to traditional values, Santa Ana is a proud, vigorous, and cohesive community.

## Synonymy†

The English name of Santa Ana Pueblo is from that of the Spanish mission there; the Spanish pronunciation is *santána*.

In the Santa Ana and Acoma dialects of Keresan the name of the Pueblo is *támáyá;* in Santo Domingo it is *tâ·maya* (Miller and Davis 1963:321). This name has sometimes been used as Tamaya in English (White 1942:17) and was recorded in Spanish as Tamaya and Tamy as early as 1598 (Hammond and Rey 1953, 1:371). It was earlier applied to Pueblos previously inhabited by the Santa Anans. A person from Santa Ana is *támáyâ·ṁE* (Davis 1964:121).

Borrowed names are Hopi tamaya, Zuni tamaiya (Curtis 1907–1930, 16:261), and perhaps Navajo *Dahmi* (Robert W. Young, personal communication 1977). Tewa has *šarege ówînge* 'dancing place Pueblo'. The names in other languages are of obscure origin: Picuris has pátuthấ, Isleta hwerói or hwewrói (Curtis 1907–1930, 16:261), and Jemez *tįdæ gʸíʔ*, beside *tįdæ* 'Santa Ana Indian' (pl. *tįdæcóš*).

Possibly referring to Santa Ana Pueblo in the period before 1598 are the names Guatitlan and La Milpa Llana (Gallegos Lamero 1927:352; Pérez de Luxán 1929: 82–84; Albert H. Schroeder, personal communication 1977).

## Sources

Apart from general histories of the Southwest and ethnographic accounts of the Pueblos, the only major source on Santa Ana is the monograph by White (1942), who earlier attempted a comparative statement on Keresan medicine societies (1930) and later wrote a general sketch of eastern Keresan world view (1960). Fox (1967) dealt with comparative Keresan kinship systems, emphasizing the east. Davis (1964) is a grammar of Santa Ana Keresan. For the present chapter, the author acknowledges valuable assistance from Donna Pino on contemporary affairs and from Albert H. Schroeder on historical data.

† This synonymy was prepared by Ives Goddard incorporating references supplied by the author. Uncredited forms are from Harrington (1916:519–521) or anonymous sources.

# Zia Pueblo

E. ADAMSON HOEBEL

## Language, Territory, and Environment

Zia ($^1$zēu, $^1$sēu) is a Keresan-speaking Pueblo (figs. 1–2) on Jemez River, a tributary of the Rio Grande, approximately 30 miles north of Albuquerque, New Mexico (see "Pueblos: Introduction," fig. 1, this vol.).

Zian is a dialect of Keresan, a family of closely similar languages or dialects also spoken at Santa Ana, Santo Domingo, San Felipe, Cochiti, Laguna, and Acoma.* Most adults speak Spanish, a few speak some Navajo, and almost all Zians are literate in English.

Prior to World War II the social boundaries of Zia were sharply defined and limited. Almost all Zians lived in the Pueblo. Formal permission to live or work outside the Pueblo had to be obtained from the governor and renewed annually. All adult members of the Pueblo were required to be present for the performance of the communal services of maintaining irrigation ditches, cleaning the plaza for ceremonies, plastering and whitewashing the mission church, participating in communal hunts, and cultivating the cacique's fields. The practice of allowing money payments to the Pueblo in lieu of mandatory labor was instituted during World War II when members were drawn into war production or the armed forces. The Pueblo needed all its human resources for survival. As late as 1957 (aside from a dozen or so Pentecostal converts) only two or three Zians had married outside the Pueblo and gone elsewhere to live (White 1962:213–214). The pattern was for Zians to be born, live, marry, and die within the Pueblo.

The few Mexicans and Anglos who have married into the Pueblo are barred from all secret rituals for some time. They and non-Zia Indians can receive full rights in the Pueblo only on approval of the entire Pueblo council.

The influence of the Bureau of Indian Affairs agency in Albuquerque, with its agricultural and home extension services, its local primary day school, and the secondary

---

* There is no phonemic analysis available for the Zia dialect of Keresan, but it is very similar to that of Santa Ana (Davis 1964; "Santa Ana Pueblo," this vol.). The Zia words cited in the *Handbook* have been respelled on the basis of available transcriptions, especially those of White (1962), in an English-based orthography that gives only an approximation of the correct pronunciation. The consonants and digraphs should be pronounced as in English and the vowels should be given their continental values. An r after an affricate indicates retroflexion; o is used for Keresan *u* and u for *i*.

---

school at Santa Fe increasingly opened up the social boundaries of Zia after 1930. Improved medical services, after the United States Department of Public Health took over in this field in 1955, have increasingly involved Zians in modern medical treatment. The effect of military service in World War II was definitely unsettling to old ways. After 1960, new jobs in Zia, Albuquerque, and elsewhere have been opened up through programs of the Departments of Labor and Commerce, while the Department of Health, Education, and Welfare has intensified the educational experience of Zia children and provided significant housing developments outside the old Pueblo. In 1975, numbers of Zians no longer live lives centered in the old Pueblo or focused on the traditional core culture.

Zia is located in a high-altitude subdesert. It rests on a low mesa on the east bank of the Jemez River at 35° 30′ north latitude, a few miles west of 106° 30′ west longitude and one mile above sea level. Nearby mountains are pine-covered. Junipers and piñons are scattered over the foothills, while sagebrush, cactus, yucca, sparse grasses, and other Sonoran desert-type vegetation thinly cover the sandy plains. The climate is arid, moderately hot in the summer (72°F. mean) and not extremely cold in the winter (35°F. mean). Extremes of 102°F. and −18°F. are recorded.

It is not known whether the Rio Grande Pueblos claimed territorial boundaries in pre-Spanish times. In 1689, Zia was "presented" an arbitrarily defined royal grant of land one league square in the name of the king of Spain. The grant, comprising 16,282 acres, continues to this day as an inalienable holding of the Pueblo. In 1938, through the land acquisition programs of the New Deal for Indians, 40,585 additional acres of land were granted by the United States to Zia and Santa Ana jointly. Permits issued by the United States Soil Conservation Service and the United States Grazing Service plus a lease from the New Mexico State Land Office added another 57,807 acres to Zian use (Aberle 1948:83). The total acreage held by Zia in 1973 was 112,510. Rights of use to garden and grazing lands are held by individual Zia families, but title or leasehold of all land is vested in the Pueblo. There is no individual ownership of land.

## Prehistory and History

The early ancestors of Zia are provisionally identifiable as Eastern Anasazi who lived in the Chaco Canyon area

Southwest Foundation for Audio-Visual Resources, Santa Fe, N.M.
Fig. 1. Zia Pueblo. Photograph by Peter Dechert, June 1977.

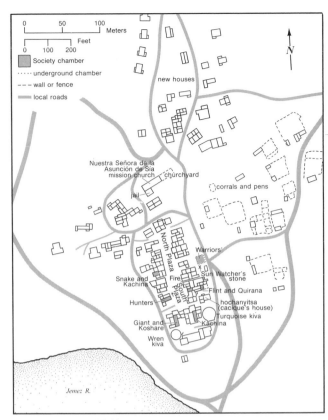

revised from Stubbs 1950:fig.18.
Fig. 2. Zia Pueblo.

of western New Mexico prior to A.D. 400. Between A.D. 400 and 700, the distribution of Keresan-type pottery spread northward to include Mesa Verde. At the end of the twelfth century, there was a strong southeastward shift that established protohistoric Keresan-speaking peoples in their present area (Ford, Schroeder, and Peckham 1972:24-35). Zian belief agrees with archeology on a northwestern origin, and Zians claim both Pueblo Bonito and Mesa Verde as ancestral homes.

There are six Pueblo archeological sites in the Jemez valley that are certainly associated with modern Zia. All date from the thirteenth century, and five were actively occupied into the sixteenth to eighteenth centuries. These would probably be the five Zian Pueblos collectively called the Punames by Antonio de Espejo, who visited them in 1583 (Pérez de Luxán 1929:83-85) and claimed the Pueblos for Spain. The first Spanish contact with Zia was made by Capt. Juan Jaramillo of the Francisco Vásquez de Coronado expedition in 1541. The Zians, who were well aware of the destruction that had just been wreaked on the nearby Pueblo of Tiguex by Coronado, received Jaramillo peaceably. He, in turn, reported Zia especially as one of three New Mexican Pueblos "well worth seeing" (Winship 1896, 1:587). Espejo (1916: 181-182) described Zia as a large city with eight plazas and over 1,000 well-kept, two- and three-storied houses in which lived more than 4,000 adult males in addition to

women and children (Pérez de Luxán 1929:83-85). This large Pueblo was Old Zia ("Pueblos Abandoned in Historic Times," this vol.). Espejo estimated the population of the five Zian Pueblos at more than 20,000 but some scholars consider this figure exaggerated.

After the founding of the Spanish colony at San Gabriel by Juan de Oñate in 1598, a mission and convent were introduced at Zia about 1610-1612. Interference with the religious life of Zia led Zians to join the Pueblo Revolt of 1680, but they offered no resistance to Antonio de Otermín's efforts to reestablish Spanish rule in 1681. Zia successfully resisted Pedro Reñeras de Posada's invasion of 1688, and the following year the new governor of the province, Domingo Jironza Petriz de Cruzate, reduced Zia in a bloody assult. Seventy Zians were carried off to 10 years of captivity at El Paso del Norte. The remaining Zians built a new town near Jemez but returned to the ruins of Zia after being directed to do so by Gen. Diego de Vargas in 1692. Zia collaborated with the Spaniards in their campaigns against other Pueblos from 1692 through 1696. In 1692 the Zians accepted mass baptism and became nominal Roman Catholics (White 1962:23).

*Population*

From a population of at least 5,000 (and possibly 20,000 in the five Zian towns together) in A.D. 1540 to less than

408

300 in 1690 is the story of Spain's impact in its first 150 years of rule over Zia. By 1890 only 100 Zians survived (see White 1962:36 for a detailed population table). Outsiders freely predicted the extinction of Zia. How wrong they were! The downward trend of Zia's population was arrested by 1910. In the next decade it increased 30 percent to 140. By 1960 it had quadrupled to 400. In 1972, Zia registered 555 members and was still growing. Zia has apparently won its battle for survival.

## World View and Cultural Survival

To understand the outlook and character of Zia, it must never be forgotten that here is a people whose ancestors had steadily built up over a millennium an elaborate culture designed to make the difficult life of gardening in a marginal desert a meaningful and successful undertaking.

Zia shares the general Pueblo view of:

the universe as an orderly phenomenon. People or things are not merely "good" or "bad." "Evil" is a disturbance in the equilibrium that exists between man and the universe, while "good" is a positive frame of mind or action that maintains harmonious balance.

To keep man and the universe in harmonious balance, all must work together and with "good" thoughts. Unanimous effort of body and mind is not only a key value, but it is also enforced. . . . The cacique and the War Captains exert strict control over the activities of village members and see that all physically able members participate in a rigid calendric series of ceremonies. Among the members of a village there is serious concern over a neighbor's behavior and a perpetual watch is maintained over his or her activities. Any action, whether physical or verbal, which is construed by Pueblo authorities to be contrary to group concerns and unanimous will of the village is promptly and severely punished.

Rio Grande Pueblo culture thus makes rigorous demands on the individual and fills him with deep anxiety and suspicion toward his fellow men. Not only is his personal behavior and social interaction strictly circumscribed, but his thoughts as well are rigidly harnessed. He is constantly plagued by an apprehension that he or his fellow man may break the harmonious balance of the universe and bring illness, famine, or some other form of dreaded disaster (Dozier 1961:122).

Expressed more simply by a Zian, "Yes, it's like the Hopi. If I would refuse the request to drum in the Fiesta, it would delay the answers to the people's prayers. There would be no rain. Or else too much rain would come and flood everything. It wouldn't come just right. It is a hard world that requires correct treatment" (Hoebel 1969:97).

To achieve and maintain the goals of good crops, internal peace and cooperation, and harmony with the universe, Zia, like other Pueblos, developed between A.D. 300 and 1200 an elaborate religious and ceremonial system, operated by a complex bureaucracy of priests, who were the heads of powerful secret religious orders, or medicine societies. Innovation was then slowed down,

Smithsonian, Dept. of Anthr.: 134170.
Fig. 3. Zia pump drill with wooden shaft, crossbar, disk flywheel, and metal point. Used by men to drill turquoise beads by pushing down on the crossbar, which untwists the skin thongs wrapped around the upper shaft and spins the drill. The flywheel keeps the shaft spinning as the thongs retwist around the shaft. (Underhill 1944:121). Length of shaft 38 cm, collected in 1887.

Smithsonian, Dept. of Anthr.: 134430.
Fig. 4. Double-headed drum made from Euro-American metal kettle by cutting out the bottom and stretching rawhide across both ends. Diameter 25 cm, collected in 1887.

and later, in the face of Spanish devastation, the marauding pressures of the Navajos, Apaches, Utes, and Comanches, as well as American interference, the Pueblos dug in their heels with dogged conservatism.

Above all, they never lost faith in their own view of man and the universe and in the extreme importance of man's individual responsibility and collective ceremonial responsibility to keep the orderly operation of the universe on an even footing. Since the fifteenth century Zia has maintained the elaborate superstructure of ceremonial organization, priestly personnel, and centralized coercive power originally designed to organize and manage a much larger population than now struggles to carry the load.

If Zia today, like other Keresan Pueblos, is secretly protective of its mystic ways, tolerates little individualistic deviation from the set mold, and strives to hold to its time-tested values and lifeways, it is because by so doing it has survived and maintained its cultural integrity in the face of 500 years of Spanish and American domination—something few other Indian peoples have managed.

## Culture

### Subsistence

At one time, the Zians cultivated floodwater gardens along the river and in side canyons above and below the Pueblo. In the 1970s they rely mostly on irrigated fields concentrated on both sides of the river immediately above the town. These are served by a modern irrigation system installed by the Bureau of Indian Affairs. However, the total acreage under irrigation was less than 300, or only 0.5 of an acre per tribal member in 1970. Major crops are corn, wheat, alfalfa, oats, beans, chili peppers, melons, and some fruit. More than half the Zia crop harvest is sold on the cash market.

Although it is customary to think of all Puebloans as horticulturists, the fact is that the Zians have become predominantly sedentary pastoralists. Their traditional ideology and ceremonial social organization are still focused on ritual control of the weather and the fertility of their crops, but their major economic production comes from sheep and cattle, first introduced by the Spaniards. By mid-twentieth century, Zia was tending about 1,500 sheep, 500 cattle, 200 goats, 100 horses, 30 hogs, 200 chickens, and a few turkeys and dogs. More meat, hides, and wool are sold than consumed directly, and the cash income from livestock exceeds that from crops by 3 to 1 (White 1962:87–96).

Stock raising is a joint enterprise conducted by cattle and sheep groups, each such group being made up of clan members and each concentrating either on cattle or sheep (fig. 6). In 1943, for example, there were 24 cattlemen (fig. 7), organized in four groups holding 330 cattle. There were 16 sheepmen, organized in four groups holding

2,100 head of sheep and 210 goats. Each group selects a head, who hires Zia herders and cowboys, deals with the BIA extension agents, supervises the roundups and shearings, and is the agent for government loans and sale of produce (Hoebel 1943–1950).

### Settlement Pattern

Zia forms a north-to-south oriented rectangle (figs. 1–2). A two-room house in the very center of the rectangle once divided the village into a north and south plaza. Two round kivas stand out at the southern edge of the village. To the east of the village off the mesa are a number of stock corrals belonging to individual households. North of the pueblo is the Franciscan mission church and churchyard, flanked by scattered houses that form a suburb.

Since 1950, additional houses have been built along the river below the old Pueblo and on the San Ysidro grant between Zia and Jemez. In the late 1960s an entirely new satellite suburb of 14 modern houses was built by the

Smithsonian, Dept. of Anthr.: 134189, 134191, 134207.
Fig. 5. Rattles and water bottle made from dried gourds. Wooden handles are attached to gourds containing pebbles, which are carried by male dancers. The water bottle, carried by a cotton strap secured to rawhide lashings, has a dried corncob inserted in the mouth as a stopper. Water bottle length 41 cm, rest same scale; collected in 1887.

federal Housing and Urban Development Authority across the Jemez River from Zia proper.

## Social Organization

The household is the basic unit of Zia society. It consists of a head (male or female), who "owns" the house, plus sons and daughters (married or unmarried), their children, and perhaps surviving elderly parents, grandparents, and unmarried siblings.

The Zia household included in 1972 an unusually large number of young people, a consequence of its population explosion. There was also a significant surplus of males over females; the ratio has varied between 106 and 132 males per 100 females since 1870 (White 1962:43).

Zia adheres to strict monogamy. This, combined with the surplus of males, contributes to the very high proportion (54% in 1957) of unmarried adult males in the

Fig. 6. Sheep grazing on the Zia range, with Santa Ana Mesa in background. Despite the poor quality of this range land, stockraising has been an important economic enterprise with traditional emphasis on sheep and wool production, which by 1978 had been largely shifted to cattle. Photograph by an unknown photographer, 1943.

Fig. 7. Zia cattlemen. Bridge over Jemez River, which is generally dry after the spring run-off. Photograph by unknown photographer, probably 1940s or 1950s.

population. Over a third (39%) of Zian women were also recorded as "unmarried" (White 1962:44); however, these data may be deceptive for Zians draw an important distinction between "Indian marriages" and "Catholic marriages." The former are formed through cohabitation without benefit of clergy or Pueblo ritual. They are readily dissolved at the wish of either spouse. "Catholic marriages" are sanctified by the Franciscan priest. They are for life, and Zians become very emotional over possible divorces in such marriages. It may be that both White and the U.S. Bureau of the Census report only Catholic marriages. If so, the real marriage rate in Zia households would be much higher than is indicated.

Within the household all resources are shared. The unit is tight and self-centered. Household matters are not subject to outside gossip. The village governor does not normally interfere in its affairs. Outsiders must not peer in through its windows; to do so is the mark of a witch (Hoebel 1943–1950).

Traditional houses are constructed of undressed stone walls, heavily plastered, with beamed ceilings and flat earthen roofs. Most have three rooms: a living-sleeping room, a kitchen-dining room, and a small storeroom. Although prehistoric houses were entered through the ceiling by means of a ladder, all Zia homes now have ground-level doors and glass windows. Floors are packed earth, covered with linoleum. Interior walls are whitewashed and decorated with snapshots, calendars, and occasional artifacts. Tables, chairs, beds, stoves, and trunks are universal. Some houses have indoor fireplaces, and each household owns an outdoor beehive baking oven. In the 1970s the majority of the old homes were served with electricity; many had running water, but no indoor toilets. Outhouses were first added in the 1930s.

The 30 or more modern homes built in the suburban extensions of Zia are modest American-type, four- to six-room bungalows, complete with toilets, baths, refrigerators, electric stoves, radios, and television. Houses may be inherited bilaterally, by either a male or female. Marital residence is bilocal, depending on whether the husband or wife owns a house or is likely to inherit one.

• MOIETIES AND CLANS   Residents of the North Plaza area are usually associated with the Wren kiva for ceremonial activities, while the Turquoise kiva group lives in the southern half of the town. The resulting north-south moiety arrangement is spatial and ceremonial only. The moieties are neither exogamous nor linked to medicine-society membership.

Clans are ideologically important in Zia but not functionally of great significance. Clan membership is matrilineal, although children may shift identity through adoption. Clan exogamy is preferential, representing 90 percent of all marriages in 1957 (White 1962:189), but not prescriptive. Zia clans do not act as corporate entities in legal matters. They own no common property, rituals, masks, or medicine bundles. Clan membership is not

411

linked to membership in the religious societies or in the moieties and kivas. In the modern development of stock raising, sheep and cattle group membership does run along clan lines.

The six clans of Zia are the Coyote, Saltbush, Corn, Bear, Tobacco, Water. Coyote had almost half of Zia as its members, while the Bear clan had only two male survivors in 1952. Although "Acoma Corn" and "Zia Corn" are often referred to as separate clans, they appear to be subclan divisions. The same is true of Antelope Saltbush and Zia Saltbush.

*Religion*

• STRUCTURES Hidden within certain private homes are eight secret-society rooms. One house, the hochanyitsa, belongs to the town head (cacique). It has a large room used for meetings of the Zia councils and a connecting room used to store corn and dried rabbit and deer meat to be given to the needy and for ceremonial feasts. A secret room, beyond the food storeroom, holds the sacred paraphernalia of the cacique (fig. 8).

The two round kivas at Zia are conspicuously visible at the south edge of the Pueblo. The southeast kiva belongs to the Turquoise moiety, the southwest one to the Wren moiety.

The Warriors' Society chamber is built inconspicuously into the eastern face of the mesa at the very edge of the village, its entrance covered with a flat stone. At the southwest edge of the chamber area is a flagstone on which the Sun Watcher stands each morning to pray and observe the position of the rising sun relative to the skyline of Santa Ana Mesa. As the sun shifts its position along the horizon, he determines the time for various rituals in the annual ceremonial cycle and for the plant-ing and harvesting of corn (Hoebel 1943–1950). The Snake Society ceremonial house is near the society's shrine in a canyon about a mile and one-half from the Pueblo.

Since 1692 a conspicuous wooden cross, marking the spot of the mass conversion of Zia to Catholicism, has stood on the west edge of the South Plaza. The South Plaza also contains two small boulders near its northern edge (fig. 9). The one to the west is called Mountain Lion. It is the focus of certain hunting rituals and helps protect the Pueblo from disease. Its companion stone, Aiwana, is associated with the Twin War Gods; it also embodies all the ancestral spirits of Zia. Yet another stone in the North Plaza marks the dwelling place of a beneficent spirit called White Man. Until 1950 White Man was visible above ground, but then a decision was made to hide it from the view of the ever-increasing visitors to the Pueblo.

• MYTHOLOGY In essence, the Zian universe at its beginning consisted of four stratified worlds. At the bottom was the Yellow World, then Blue-green, then Red, and at the top the White. Tsityostinako, the original mother, lived with two daughters in the Yellow World. They were Uchtsiti and Naotsiti. The two sisters had powers of creation. One after the other, Uchtsiti created first a tiyamunyi (supreme priest of Zia), then a corn-ear fetish (iyariko) for a Flint Society, then all the other societies (originally in the form of a man or woman). Songs, dances, and rituals for each were specified. The two sisters then created pairs of animals, some of which had medicine powers to help the priests of the societies cure sickness. After four years in the Yellow World, the goddess mother and her two daughters grew a tree by which the people could climb up to the Blue-green World. After four more years, they ascended to the Red World, which they abandoned after four years to reach the White World. On the White World they wandered south, building temporary Pueblos until they came to White House. Here they settled, and Uchtsiti gave them seeds to grow plants and begin gardening; later animals were added to help feed the growing population. At White House, men and women quarreled and the women boasted that they could do without men. To test them, the men crossed a river to live alone. Some women "couldn't stand it" and stole across at night to have intercourse. Their offspring were born monsters who terrified all mankind. A virgin daughter of the tiyamunyi, impregnated by the Sun, then gave birth to Masewi and Oyoyewi, the Twin War Gods, who journeyed about destroying the monsters and serving as protectors of the people ever since (Stevenson 1894:26–73).

And so the Zians "know how everything came into being and what its purpose and function are. And, knowing this, they know how to behave with reference to the gods, spirits, plants, and animals, and so on; they know what to do in all kinds of situations . . . the social

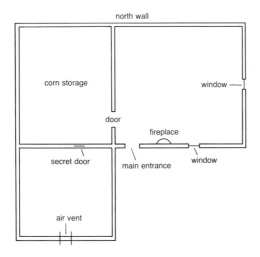

after White 1962:fig. 9.
Fig. 8. Floorplan of the hochanyitsa, the meeting place that is under the jurisdiction of the cacique and maintained by the war captain. During the 1950s, it adjoined the residence of the man who had been cacique since 1917.

Fig. 9. South Plaza in 1879, facing north. The cross commemorating Zia's conversion to Christianity is at left (the cross bar is difficult to see). The boulder on which a man is resting, center, is Mountain Lion, said to represent all the animals of the 6 directions (White 1962:49). To the right, also being used as a seat, is the boulder called Aiwana, which represents the Twin War Gods and their helpers. The house block at right, which previously served to divide the plazas, was not extant in 1977. The rocks and stake in foreground remain from a previous structure, which was rebuilt. Photograph by John K. Hillers.

and ceremonial world of the Sia themselves is accounted for also. . . . The creation myth tells how the Sia got their societies and how the medicinemen got their powers. . . . Even their clan organization is accounted for" (White 1962:121–122).

After abandoning White House, the Zians moved to their present location, taking with them the social structure that Uchtsiti had bestowed upon them.

*Ceremonial Organization*

The religious societies (chayanyi) of Zia are comprised of medicine (curing) and nonmedicine societies. They are central to the social structure of the Pueblo, for on them rests the responsibility of ceremonial control of fertility of crops and people, the bringing of rain to grow the crops, the control of pestilence to ward off epidemics, the combatting of witches who would destroy all human life, the recovery of "lost hearts" of very sick people, the curing of wounds and snake bites, the treatment of warriors who are spiritually contaminated by the enemies they have killed, the magic of successful hunting, and the relations of all living Zians to their ancestors and mythological spirit-creators of the Pueblo world.

In 1950 Zia had three major curing societies and four minor ones. The major societies are the Flint (hishtiyanyi), Giant (shkoyo) (fig. 10), and Fire (hakanyi). They have full honawai'aiti, mystic supernatural power of ineffable sacredness in Zian thought and feeling. With such power, expressed through their rituals and dances, these societies can control communal diseases, cure illness caused by "lost hearts," participate in winter and summer rain-making and fertilization activities, and perform funeral rites. Fire Society members "swallow" hot coals and Giant Society members push 18-inch digging sticks down their throats "to prepare the soil for spring planting." The highest priests of the three major societies are called honaite 'those who know the deepest mysteries of honawai'aiti'. Stevenson (1894) errs in calling officers of other societies hó-na-aite.

Zia has two pairs of minor curing societies that have qualities of honawai'aiti. The Quirana and Koshare societies are linked together and possess full honawai'aiti. However, they wear none of the ceremonial badges of the major curing societies. In their original creation they obtained their powers from the sun (and moon); hence, they are directly concerned with the fertility of living things and have nothing to do with the burial of the dead. The Koshare are messengers between the people and their ancestors. They are important guardians of Zian morality in that they can "capture" wrongdoers, who must then join the society or be bought off through public distribution of gifts by their relatives. In their clowning at

Fig. 10. Priests of the Giant Society, in their society chamber evoking the power of the bear to cure a boy of a sore throat said to have been caused by angry ants who entered his body when he urinated on their ant hill (Stevenson 1894:97-101). The priests are barefoot, wear breechclouts and bear-claw necklaces, and hold eagle wing plumes. The highest priest of the society is at center. A cornmeal line separates the patient from the sacred area. The religious objects at center have been placed on a sandpainting executed earlier in the day; just behind them are skins of bears' forelegs, used in the 4-night curing ceremony. The slat structure at left, not in use, is the altar of the Giant Society. Photograph by M.C. Stevenson, 1888-1889.

dances they hold deviants up to public ridicule. The Koshare or Quirana supervise the annual Saint's Day Dance (August 15).

The Kapina Society is notable for its miraculous feats in the kiva, where corn is grown in a single night and bears, cougar, and deer are conjured up out of seemingly nothing. It works with the Snake Society in the latter's handling of live snakes in rain-making ceremonies. Neither society performs major curing ceremonies.

Zia has two weather-control and fertility societies of masked dancers who represent ancestral spirits and specific rain gods. They do no curing and are probably not endowed with honawai'aiti. Their special effect resides in their many masks, representing the spirits whom they enact. The Kachina Society dances only in the summer, and the impending arrival of its masked spirit impersonators is announced by the Gomayawish Society members, who are Kachina messengers. Gomayawish can perform in winter weather and communal

curing ceremonies. These societies had only one or two surviving members in 1950, and it is not known whether or not they still existed in the 1970s. Possibly, they have been wholly replaced by the hoaine, a large group of masked dancers who are not accounted for in the creation myth, have absolutely no honawai'aiti or curing powers, and no sacred paraphernalia other than a few masks. Hoaine are modern mummers who portray the empty roles of those who once had mastered the discipline of true mystic belief and power.

Traditionally, if a Zian killed an enemy or touched anything belonging to him, he was required to scalp the corpse and bring the scalp to the Warriors' Society (opi) priests for purification. He, himself, was initiated as a member. This society had one old member in 1945 "who did not know the rituals." However, Opi priests from another Pueblo were called upon to "cure" several disturbed World War II veterans by initiating them into Opi. A variant form of Opi services exists for slayers of mountain lions and bears. Up to 1700 the Warriors' Society was undoubtedly extremely important. In the 1970s it has only minor significance.

The Hunters' Society (shayek) traditionally performed hunting rituals and supervised communal hunts to obtain deer and rabbit meat for the cacique's storehouse. Early in the twentieth century, its leader named young men to serve as herders for the Pueblo horses. He also supervised the communal horse corral. These activities have dropped into disuse and the society was nearly defunct, if not actually extinct, in 1978.

When one thinks of the structural and ideological power of the religious societies of Zia, it comes as a shock to learn how few members are involved. In 1960 the all-powerful Flints had but 8 members, the Giants 9, and the Fire Society 10. Except for the Koshare, all others had less, the Warriors', Hunters', Kachina, and Gomayawish being all but extinct (White 1962:146-182). Their state as of 1970 is not known. More and more Zians are becoming sishti, laymen who belong to no religious society.

*Political Organization*

Uchtsiti created the tiyamunyi to be the chief of all Zia in the Yellow World. So he was through all the ages of Zia until around 1900. Since then, no tiyamunyi has been installed or is likely to be in the future, for the necessary installation rituals have been forgotten. A substitute for the tiyamunyi was found in the office of his first assistant (chraikatsi) who fills the general role of the original tiyamunyi as head priest-chief of Zia and is therefore identified as the town chief, or cacique. No modern cacique has the ritual knowledge to possess the full medicine power once held by a tiyamunyi; therefore, he is less sacred and, probably, less influential. Nonetheless, the cacique is the object of much reverence, is freed from physical labor, and is supported by the produce of certain fields that are communally cultivated on his behalf under the orders of the first war captain. Communal deer and rabbit hunts provide him with meat. He holds surpluses for ceremonial feasts and for dispersal to the needy. He invests the "annual officers," who in the modern situation are his executive officers. He is thus not ordinarily directly involved in the administration of legal or governmental affairs, for he should concentrate all his thoughts in a positive way, "willing" the well-being of Zia. Quarrels and mundane affairs spoil his good thoughts. Such matters are for the war captain and the governor and their staffs to handle, in conjunction with the heads of the medicine societies. The caciqueship is rotated among the four lineages of the Saltbush and Corn clans.

The purely sacerdotal executive arm of Zia administration is headed by two officers appointed annually by the cacique. They are the first and second war captains, named Masewi and Oyoyewi, the two brothers who were fathered by the Sun and who rid the world of monsters. Once these posts seem to have been filled by priests of the Warriors' Society, but this is no longer so. Their prime requisite is that they be "brave, clean-hearted men," for they must patrol the town at night on the lookout for witches. With their four assistants (gowachanyi) and sacred bows and arrows, they guard the entrances to ceremonial chambers when societies are in retreat. They are the watch and ward who search out heresy, ceremonial derelictions, and individual deviants of any type—all of whom they may denounce and bring to trial as witches.

The governor's branch of Zia political structure was established by the Spanish as a body of Pueblo officials through whom they could rule. The governor (dabopo), lieutenant governor (dabopo tenyenti), and four assistants (*capitanes*) are annual appointees who function as intermediaries between the Pueblo and the outside world. The governor has two silverheaded canes (one from the king of Spain and one from President Abraham Lincoln) and a Spanish cat-o'-nine-tails as symbols of office. The power of the governor in Pueblo matters has steadily increased at the expense of the war captains as culture change moves more and more in the direction of secularization. Former governors, known as *principales,* constitute an informal advisory panel to each incumbent governor.

The adobe mission church stands apart from the main village. It was built before 1613, badly damaged in the revolt of 1680, then rebuilt and refurbished. During the nineteenth century it fell into serious decay, but it is now maintained in good condition. In 1973 the mission was plastered to eliminate the women's annual task of whitewashing the old adobe. The enclosed yard in front of the church contains the Pueblo burial ground, while the outbuilding next to the church is the Pueblo "jail," a sacred detention room for malefactors. Zians view the custodian of the mission church as a public official, albeit a minor one. As the collector of church revenues, he is called the *fiscal;* his assistant carries the title of *fiscal minor.* Both attend the priest when he visits Zia for the Christmas, Easter, and Saint's Day services.

Zia has two types of councils. One, which deals with secular matters, such as proposals advanced by government agencies, is a democratic town meeting open to all males but rarely, if ever, attended by the cacique. Known as owadyami, it is usually covened and presided over by the governor. The sacerdotal council (hotsenyi), which is made up of the medicine society heads, the war captains, and the cacique, is much more important. Its meetings are exclusive and secret and deal with matters of ritual participation, appointment of annual officers, serious moral delict, and heresy. Its jurisdiction supersedes that of the secular council in all matters in which it wishes to intervene.

Zia retains its traditional forms of governmental organization and has steadfastly rejected tribal reorganization under the Indian Reorganization Act of 1934.

• LAW   The most distinctive feature of Pueblo law as it

operates in the twentieth century is that within the sphere of its jurisdiction there is no private law. All legal power is centralized in the bureaucracy and all procedure must move through it. People with small complaints go first to one of the governor's assistants to seek redress. If satisfaction is not obtained, or if the issue is quite serious, the matter may be taken to the governor, who then makes his own investigation and issues a judgment. In yet more serious cases, the governor, after consulting other *principales* and the heads of the major medicine societies, may convene the secular council to decide the case. Or, if the religious tinge is highly colored, the governor may give way for the war captain to put the matter before the Sacred Council. The object of the trial is to obtain a confession and recantation called tsaitsi tsawia 'totally, myself I blame'. Supression of deviationism and heresy are primary legal concerns, but enforcement of the duty to perform community work is the focal concern of contemporary Zian law. Apart from participation in the dances, which is also a universal obligation, all able-bodied men are required to cultivate the head priest's field, to join in the deer and rabbit hunts to fill the head priest's larder, to sweep the village plaza for ceremonies, to join in cleaning and repairing the irrigation ditches each spring or at any additional times determined by the governor, and until 1973 to help the women in the annual whitewashing of the mission church.

## Sociocultural Situation in the 1970s

The social structure of Zia as it has been described to this point expresses the nuclear core of the Pueblo's lifeway. It is still its vital, sustaining force. Yet there have been many external changes that have a highly pervasive effect. Zians have entered the money economy from which they derive much of their material goods. Men still weave wool kilts for ceremonial wear. Women still produce the fine, waterproof orange-on-white Zia pottery (fig. 11) for their own artistic satisfaction and for an ever-growing market. Yet, half the Zian population lives outside the Pueblo, engaged in wage work on ranches and in towns. The 1972 per capita income was estimated to surpass $1,000. The cash flow provides normal Western American-type clothing and shoes for men, women, and

Smithsonian, Dept. of Anthr.: 133759, 133708.

Fig. 11. Two styles of Zia pottery water jars. top, Trios Polychrome, common during the period 1800–1850, recognizable by the black-on-cream volute motifs. bottom, Zia Polychrome, popular since the 1870s, characterized by red-orange and black floral motifs and the distinctive small-headed bird (road runner) with outspread wings. Zia clay is unique in having temper of powdered black basaltic lava (Frank and Harlow 1974:97). Diameter of top 35 cm, of bottom 28.5 cm; collected in 1887.

Mr. and Mrs. Joe Bowman, Denver, Colo.

Fig. 12. *Initiation of the Spruce Society.* Idealized version of a ceremonial initiation rite by Zia artist Rafael Medina. Watercolor, 1970.

children, although traditionalists wear deerskin moccasins. Homes are equipped with conventional American cooking utensils and dishes. Radios are common and some households have television. Autos and pickup trucks are owned by a third of the males. A dozen or more tractors are used to prepare the fields, and wheat is machine thrashed. Hay is mowed and baled in contemporary farm fashion. The primitive hand-hoe culture that prevailed to 1930 is wholly a thing of the past.

Zia protects itself as best it can from all non-Catholic missionizing efforts, but its devotion to Catholicism is largely external and a protection against other European religions. Nor is there any known use of peyote in the Pueblo. Drunkenness is a problem of concern, and the Pueblo has its own prohibition ordinance. Although there are conflicts of interest between sheep and cattle groups, Zia has remained largely free of the factional divisions that have torn at the vitals of many other contemporary Pueblos.

Its unity reflects the cultural pride and motivation that have distinguished Zia through the middle half of the twentieth century. "We are the best dancers," they say. "Our people raise their knees higher and stamp harder than any other Pueblo." It is no idle boast. Zians want the earth and its spirits to know that it is Zia dancing.

## Synonymy†

The name of Zia Pueblo is from the Spanish spelling of its Keresan name. The Zia dialect form is not available in phonemic transcription but is similar to Acoma and Santa Ana *čí·y̓á* and Santo Domingo *čí·y̓a* (Miller and Davis 1963:321); the addition of the suffix *-ṙhe* forms the word for a person from Zia: tsi·yame (Hoebel 1943-1950, normalized). In modern New Mexican Spanish *Zia* is pronounced [síya], but in the late sixteenth and early seventeenth centuries this spelling could have represented [tsíya]. Variants in the early Spanish sources include Chia, Cia, Sia, Siay, Tria, Trios, Tzia, and Ziá. The English spelling Sia has been widely used, especially by ethnographers (for example, Hodge 1910g).

Borrowings of the Keresan name are Taos síya-va, Jemez *sæ̨yák^wa,* Hopi tsiya⁷, and Zuni tsia⁷a (Curtis 1907-1930, 16:261, normalized and phonemicized), a person from Zia being in Jemez *sæ̨y̓a* (pl. *sæ̨y̓iš*) and in Zuni ts'i'a'akwe (Kroeber 1916:275). Other names are Picuris ël-ke-ai', Isleta *ṫśanǫbák* (C.T. Harrington

† This synonymy was prepared by Ives Goddard incorporating material supplied by the author. Uncredited forms and etymologies are from Harrington (1916:517-519), who has additional minor variants, or from anonymous sources.

1920:42) or t⁷önavák (Curtis 1907-1930, 16:261, normalized), Tewa *okú warege ówîŋge* 'Pueblo of the place of scattered hills', and Navajo *Tł'ógí* (Robert W. Young, personal communication 1977). The explanations of the Keresan and Tewa names given by Curtis (1907-1930, 16:262) appear to be folk etymologies.

As the seat of a Spanish mission the Pueblo has been called Nuestra Señora de la Asunción de Zia and, in the years 1692 to 1700, Nuestra Señora de la Purísima Concepción (Domínguez 1956:171-172).

The name Punames, which Espejo appears to use for the five Zian Pueblos of 1583 (Pérez de Luxán 1929:83-85; Espejo 1916:181), has been interpreted as a Keresan term meaning 'people of the west'. Cuame and Cuname appear to be corruptions of this rather than a different term for 'people of the south'.

## Sources

Published materials on Zia are meager. For nearly 70 years Stevenson (1894) was the sole significant source on the Pueblo. Based on fieldwork initiated in 1879-1880 and resumed in 1887 and 1890, the period when Zia was at its lowest ebb, this monograph is not well balanced or comprehensive, or always comprehensible; however, it offers a quite detailed version of the Zia creation myth, plus descriptions of several medicine-society rituals, birth practices, and funerary rites. Information on subsistence techniques and social structure is conspicuously lacking. The monograph is notable for its numerous full-page colored lithographs of Zia ceremonial objects and sketches redrawn from photos of Zia medicine societies with their altars and paraphernalia in their secret chambers. Stevenson's invasion of secret rituals caused her ultimately to be driven from the Pueblo, and her field studies were never completed.

The most useful source on Zia is the monograph by White (1962), which presents a comprehensive overview of virtually all aspects of the material and social culture of the Pueblo. Since Stevenson's time, direct observational fieldwork in Zia has been all but impossible, except on limited subjects of research and under tightly circumscribed conditions. Under the circumstances, White's monograph, based on field studies carried out intermittently from 1928 through 1957, is an impressive achievement and valuable resource.

Hoebel (1969) contains details on Keresan law, drawn mostly from fieldwork in Zia from 1943 to 1950. Unpublished field notes (Hoebel 1943-1950) from the Zia law study have been extensively drawn on in the preparation of this article.

*417*

# Jemez Pueblo

JOE S. SANDO

Jemez (ˈhāmĭs) Pueblo (figs. 1–2) is a Towa-speaking village* whose population, in 1970, was approximately 1,940. The village is located on the east bank of the Jemez River, 25 miles northwest of Bernalillo, New Mexico, in Sandoval County (see "Pueblos: Introduction," fig. 1, this vol.).

Towa is a branch of the Kiowa-Tanoan language family consisting of Jemez and, traditionally, the now extinct language of Pecos Pueblo, whose surviving members joined the Jemez in the nineteenth century (see "Historical Linguistics and Archeology" and "Pecos Pueblo," this vol.).

## Territory and Early Missions

According to oral history, the Jemez people had their origin at *wáˑvɨnatɨˑtá*, a lagoon in the north apparently to be identified with Stone Lake on the Jicarilla Apache reservation, south of Dulce, New Mexico, in Rio Arriba County. This was the general area in which the Jemez lived beginning about A.D. 1. That the Jemez lived in this territory, east of the Keresans of Mesa Verde and Chaco Canyon and south of the Tewas, at that time, is authenticated by the abundance of Jemez place-names today in those areas.

Maps of prehistoric Pueblos based partly on the distribution of pottery types (Ortiz 1972:26) serve to augment tribal oral history. Additionally, oral history discusses the ancients' acceptance of a nomadic race that arrived upon their land at one time. This nomadic race is

identifiable as the Athapaskans, who arrived in the Southwest probably after A.D. 950 and adopted much of the Pueblo culture.

Following the arrival of the Athapaskans the Jemez vacated the northwest quadrant of their homeland and spread southward (Ortiz 1972:28). By A.D. 1300 the Jemez had arrived in the area of their next home in the mountains and mesas above present Jemez Pueblo (according to archeological evidence).

About this time also, a segment is shown to have occupied an area in the Galisteo region, south of Santa Fe and extending into the Pecos and Glorieta area. It was in these areas that the Spaniards found the Jemez in 1540–1541. The first mention of the Jemez is by Pedro de Castañeda, the chronicler of Francisco Vásquez de Coronado's expedition of 1541. He wrote of seven Jemez Pueblos and three others in the province of Aguas Calientes, identified with the Jemez hot springs. Antonio de Espejo in 1583 also reported seven villages. Juan de Oñate in 1598 heard of 11 towns but saw only eight (Benavides 1945:275). One of the friars who entered New Mexico with Oñate's colonizers was Fray Alonso de Lugo, who was assigned to the Province of Jemez where he stayed until 1601 (Scholes 1938:61–71; Scholes and Bloom 1944–1945:328). He began his missionary work by founding the San José church at Giusewa Pueblo (*gʸísewa* 'boiling water place'), near the Jemez hot springs, for the Jemez living in the San Diego canyon-Guadalupe canyon area (Bloom 1946). A *visita* to minister to the people of the eastern province was probably at Walatowa, present Jemez Pueblo.

Fray Gerónimo de Zárate Salmerón was the next missionary at Giusewa. It is sometimes said that he arrived in New Mexico in 1618, but he is listed among six friars who came to New Mexico with the supply caravan of 1621 (Zárate Salmerón 1966:13; Scholes and Bloom 1944–1945:62). He started his missionary labor in the Jemez area in the winter of 1621. Soon after he founded the mission at the Pueblo de la Congregación (the present Jemez Pueblo), for the benefit of the more numerous Jemez living to the east, away from the San Diego canyon-Guadalupe canyon area. This church was temporarily abandoned in 1623, following a disastrous fire. Zárate Salmerón was a good minister and linguist, who served the Jemez until 1626. He was regarded by Fray Alonso de Benavides as the real founder of the mission of

---

* Italicized Jemez words in the *Handbook* are cited in the orthography of Kenneth L. Hale, which uses symbols in their standard *Handbook* values. The inventory is: voiceless unaspirated stops *p, t* (lamino-alveolar), *ṭ* (centro-domal), *kʷ;* voiceless aspirated stops and affricates *c* [ts ~ tʰ], *č, kʸ* (fronted velar), *k;* voiced stops and affricate *b, d, ȝ, gʸ, g;* glottalized stops and affricates *p̓, t̓* [t̓ ~ c̓], *c̓, k̓ʸ, k̓;* fricatives *φ* [φʷ], *s* [s ~ θ], *š, v* [v ~ β], *z* [z ~ δ]; resonants and glides *m, n, l, w, y, h, ʔ;* glottalized resonants *m̓, n̓, l̓, w̓, y̓;* oral vowels *i, ɨ* (back unrounded), *e* [eⁱ], *o* [oᵘ] ([u] after rounded consonants, lamino-alveolars, fronted velars and the centro-domal), *æ, a* (low back, slightly rounded), and the long counterparts of these (*iˑ,* and so forth); nasal vowels *į, ɨ̨, ǫ, æ̨, ą,* and the long counterparts of these. The tones are tentatively analyzed as high (v́), stressed low (v̀), and nonhigh (unmarked; realized as low or mid-level). Initial vowel with plain onset contrasts with initial glottal stop plus vowel. This transcription differs from that of Hale (1962) in writing *ṭʸ* for earlier *kʸ,* and *kʸ* for earlier *kʰʸ.* A number of the segments recognized in this transcription arise from certain morphophonemic processes (Hale 1967, 1970).

418

San José as well as that of San Diego de la Congregación. Jemez historians relate that to build these churches, slave laborers were brought in from the Jemez communities in the province. The ruins of the San José church at Giusewa Pueblo are maintained as a state monument to Zárate Salmerón (Domínguez 1956; Scholes 1938:64; Jemez tradition).

Two years after Zárate Salmerón left, Benavides, who was the custos, assigned Fray Martín de Arvide to the Jemez mission field with orders to revive the two churches and bring the scattered communities into one area. Arvide came from Picuris Pueblo, where he had served since 1621. He probably settled at Jemez Pueblo at the mission of San Diego de la Congregación since San José of Giusewa was abandoned some time between 1628 and 1638. In his new assignment Arvide cultivated lands for the Jemez to plant and saw the Pueblo grow to 300 houses. Arvide later suffered martyrdom at Zuni in 1632 (Bloom and Mitchell 1938:92, 96; Benavides 1945:79–80, 252, 277).

"More than any other Pueblo people, the Jémez were the 'highlanders' of New Mexico," building "most of their pueblos on lofty mesas, among the yellow pine and usually protected on one or more sides by sheer cliffs" (Bloom and Mitchell 1938:94). There were also a few dwellings in the vicinity of the mission church of San Diego. There were settlements along *gʸíꞏlawimį* 'value-ridge', north of Jemez; at *séꞏtɨkʷa* 'eagle-cage place', south of Jemez (Setoqua in Hodge 1907a:629); and *kʸǽꞏtʸásɨꞏkʷá* 'manure-pile place', past the government day school of 1970 (Kiatsukwa).

At the time of the Pueblo Revolt of 1680, the following are some of the communities in which Jemez lived. *pàtɨkʷá* 'Turquoise-moiety place' (Patoqua) was located at the base and southern tip of San Diego mesa. At the direction of Gen. Diego de Vargas a small church named San Diego del Monte was built there in 1694 (Bloom and Mitchell 1938:103). *ʔǽꞏtʸòlékʷa* 'grinding-stone lowering place' (Astialakwa) was located atop San Diego mesa (*mà̀tʸàsɨꞏkʸoꞏkʷa* 'big-thumb hilltop place'). Here another church, San Juan de los Jémez, was built in summer 1694, but it was abandoned in less than two years. Fray Miguel Tirzio was the religious representative, and he probably supervised the construction (Benavides 1945:278; Bloom and Mitchell 1938:104).

Other villages occupied about that time were *hǽnæꞏkʷa* 'horned-toad place' (Hanakwa), above Giusewa; *ɨ́šæꞏgʸi* 'cedar growing place' (Unshagi), farther north; and *nǫ́ꞏníšæꞏgʸi* 'aspen growing place' (Nonyishagi), across a creek south of *ɨ́šæꞏgʸi*. On the west side of the San Diego mesa is the Guadalupe Canyon. Near the mouth of the canyon was *pébɨlekʷá* 'shell place' (Pebulikwa), while *ʔǽmɨ́šɨꞏkʷá* 'ant hill place' (Amushungkwa) was farther up the canyon. Other places of significance where the Jemez lived were: *bɨ́lécekʷá* 'shell eye place' (Bulitzequa), also known as *wǽhǽčꞏa·nɨkʷá* 'Squash moiety place';

*tʸǽꞏšɨꞏkʷá* 'cactus hill place'; *séꞏšòkʷa* 'eagle lived place' (Seshiuqua); and *nòkʸɨ́célékʷa* 'light or white place' (Nokyuntseleta), all on the east side of the Jemez province. It was for these people that the mission of San Diego de la Congregación was established at Jemez (Scholes 1938:69; Jemez tradition).

## History

The Jemez people clung to their native religion tenaciously and rejected any Spanish demands for taking on a strange other religion. During the tenure of Gov. Luis Argüello, 1644–1647, the Jemez allied themselves with the Navajos and killed a Spaniard, Diego Martínez Naranjo. For this deed the Spanish governor hanged 29 Jemez leaders (Bandelier 1890–1892, 2; Scholes 1938:95).

Fray Diego de San Lucas, to whom the present church at Jemez Pueblo was dedicated, was serving at San Diego de la Congregación in 1639 when an arrow killed him during a Navajo attack (Bloom and Mitchell 1938:109; Scholes 1938:94). He was succeeded by Fray Juan del Campo in 1640 (Scholes 1938:94), who was listed as *padre guardián* of the Jemez. Fray Nicolás de Chaves may have succeeded del Campo by 1660. In that year the vice-custos sent Chaves to Mexico City as a messenger with reports for the civil and ecclesiastical authorities in the capital (Scholes 1938:96).

In 1661, records indicate that the distraught pastor, Fray Miguel Sacristán, hanged himself on the day before the Feast of Corpus Christi while stationed at San Diego de la Congregación. His assistant Diego de Pliego, a lay brother, journeyed to the convent at Santo Domingo Pueblo to inform other religious of the tragedy (Scholes 1938:97).

Jemez Pueblo, after its refounding in 1628, became an important center for missionary activity among the Jemez. By 1672, it was the residence of the custos, where the missionaries of all New Mexico gathered for chapter elections and appointments (Bloom and Mitchell 1938). Fray Tomás de Torres was assigned to San Diego de la Congregación in 1672 and served until 1675.

During the Pueblo Revolt of 1680, Fray Juan de Jesús Morador was killed at Jemez and buried close to the wall of the kiva.

Gov. Antonio Otermín attempted to regain possession of New Mexico in 1681. At this time the Jemez were probably at Jemez Pueblo and *pàtɨkʷá,* or even at *ʔǽmɨ́šɨꞏkʷá,* but with Otermín's arrival they retreated to *ʔǽꞏtʸòlékʷa* or other sites on the San Diego mesa. Upon the departure of the Spaniards, the people returned to the lower villages. Here they probably remained until 1689 when Gov. Domingo Jironza Petriz de Cruzate returned, causing them to return to the top of the mesa. When de Vargas returned three years later, in 1692 (Espinosa 1940:178), the Jemez were found on the mesa in a large

Southwest Foundation for Audio-Visual Resources, Santa Fe, N.M.
Fig. 1. Jemez Pueblo. Photograph by Peter Dechert, June 1977.

Pueblo, probably ʔǽ·t̯òlékʷa. At this time they were induced to descend to pátɨ́kʷá and probably to Jemez Pueblo.

When the Spaniards returned in 1692 it had been upon an invitation, with an understanding that the Jemez would give them their support. The invitation was extended by Pueblo Indians under the leadership of a mixed-blood Indian from Zia Pueblo who is listed as Bartolomé de Ojeda. Among the Keresans were Jemez men, one who oral historians say was of the Sun clan (Sando 1976).

The majority of the Jemez failed to support the Spaniards. Hence, there was much misunderstanding between the Jemez and their Keresan neighbors, Zia and Santa Ana, during 1693 and 1694. In 1693 General de Vargas visited Jemez to show his support of the Keresans. During this visit the padres baptized 117 children.

Despite this visit the Jemez continued to disagree with the Keresans and raided their livestock. After four Zia men and one Jemez man were killed, de Vargas detailed a punitive expedition. On July 21, 1694, 120 Spaniards with Zia, San Felipe, and Santa Ana auxiliaries arrived in the Jemez country and camped at the confluence of the two canyons, the San Diego and the Guadalupe, below pàtɨ́kʷá. On July 24 they stormed the San Diego mesa with brother Eusebio de Vargas in charge of 20 Spanish soldiers and some of the Keresan warriors. They were to go up the San Diego gorge and climb the mesa on a steep trail in the rear of the highest plateau. Meanwhile, Governor de Vargas, with a similar size military group, was to climb from the southwest, the Guadalupe Canyon side, near pébɨlekʷá. This strategy, plus their firearms, eventually succeeded after a desperate engagement. Three hundred sixty-one women and children were captured, and 84 Jemez were killed, of whom five were burned to death and seven were lost down the cliffs (Bloom and Mitchell 1938).

According to Jemez legend, during the course of the battle some people jumped over the cliffs to avoid capture. Soon a likeness of San Diego appeared on the

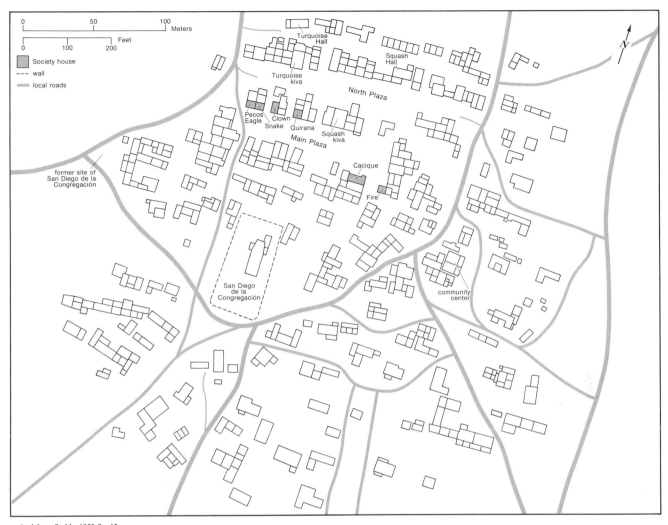

revised from Stubbs 1950:fig. 13.
Fig. 2. Jemez Pueblo.

cliff. After that the people who jumped landed on their feet and did not die. The likeness of San Diego is visible today on the red rock cliffs on San Diego mesa, facing east at the midpoint between Jemez Springs and the south point of the high mesa. It is especially visible from about mid-morning until near noon.

The conquerors camped at ʔǽ·v̓òlékʷa and remained on the mesa for 16 days, to remove the stores or booty and the 361 women and children. After destroying the villages on the top, de Vargas and his troops descended to pàtɨkʷá, then to Jemez, and eventually returned to Santa Fe.

Of the booty collected at Jemez the majority of nearly 500 bushels of corn was given to the friendly Keresans who helped de Vargas. Most of the 175 head of cattle were given to Fray Juan de Alpuente for his use at the Zia mission. Loaded mule trains of booty went to San Felipe Pueblo from where it was relayed in ox carts to Santa Fe.

On August 8 the prisoners were taken to Santa Fe. Six days later a few Jemez leaders came to Santa Fe to beg for their families. They were told to return to their old Pueblo, Jemez, and rebuild their church. And to prove their good faith the Jemez were asked to assist the Spaniards in their battle with the Tewas and Tanos. After helping to conquer the Tewas at Black Mesa, north of San Ildefonso, the prisoners were pardoned. On September 11, 1694, the former prisoners returned to their home at ʔǽ·v̓òlékʷa.

The people who survived the burning probably scattered to the other villages, with most of them returning to Jemez. This village was then occupied, with Fray Francisco de Jesús as the representative of the church. In 1695, the residents of ʔǽ·v̓òlékʷa may have completed their move to Jemez again (Bloom and Mitchell 1938).

This traumatizing experience was a prelude to additional bloodshed and intrigue. On June 4, 1696, Fray Francisco de Jesús was killed (Bloom and Mitchell 1938). Anticipating another punitive expedition by the Spaniards, the people returned to the mesa from which they sent for help to the west, from Acoma and Zuni Pueblos and the Navajos.

A few days later Luís Cunixu arrived at Pecos Pueblo carrying a reliquary, the property of the slain priest. Thereupon, the Pecos governor took Cunixu to Santa Fe where he described the killing. He was summarily sentenced to death and killed by a shot from a harquebus (Bloom and Mitchell 1938:105–106).

On June 29 there was a fight in San Diego canyon and the Spaniards destroyed the village of *pàt̯kʷá*. The Spaniards were led by Capt. Miguel de Lara of Zia and the *alcalde mayor* of Bernalillo. Twenty-eight to 40 Indians were reported killed; among them were eight Acomas but no Zunis or Navajos. The assisting Indian warriors returned home after this and the Jemez dispersed. In August Captain de Lara reconnoitered and found the area deserted.

At this time some of the Jemez returned to their ancestral homeland in the northwest, Canyon Largo or Stone Canyon (*k̯à·wá·m̯*). Others went to *ʔǽy̯kʷin̯* 'lion standing place' (Anyukwinu in Hodge 1907a:629), to the west of Jemez in Navajo country. These people lived among the Navajos for many years before they returned. Many never returned from the Navajo country but became a part of the Navajo, preserving Jemez traditions. Many also fled to the Hopi country but were returned a few years later, many of them by the individual efforts of dedicated missionaries who wanted the Jemez to be nearer to a Christian mission (Chavez 1967:108).

Upon their return from exile the Jemez people began to settle at Jemez Pueblo, 12 miles south of their former mesa and mountain top homes. This movement was accomplished between 1703 and 1706. The first church at Jemez, here described (from Jemez tradition) as San Diego de la Congregación, was located on the way to the mission school and post office of the 1970s.

Since the history of the missions in the Jemez district is obscure, it is not known when San Diego de la Congregación was abandoned. The new church, San Diego de los Jémez, was built 300 yards east of the old one. It was visited and inspected by Fray Francisco Atanasio Domínguez on May 15, 1776 (Domínguez 1956). By 1887–1888 this church was in ruins, and the present one was built on the same site.

With regard to Indian land, it is an accepted statement, often made without serious evaluation by both Indian and non-Indian alike, that the "king of Spain gave the land to the Indians" and that the ownership of the lands dates from the time that Spain held the area. The Pueblo Indians are the oldest known inhabitants of a given area of land in the United States and northern Mexico, so it would be impossible for the king of Spain to give these people land that they already occupied and had occupied long before the Spaniards came to the New World. The Spaniards did recognize the rights of the Pueblos to the lands upon which they were living. But like other European invaders, they did not bother to ask the Pueblos how much land they were using and why. Thus,

the sites of many sacred shrines and centers of religious activities were absorbed within non-Indian holdings. Nevertheless, land grants by the Spaniards did serve to help preserve the Pueblo Indian culture and religion, to an extent greater than that allowed by other European powers.

The original grant of 17,331 acres was recognized by the Spanish Crown and officially granted through Governor Cruzate on September 20, 1689. Earlier that year Cruzate had toured the Pueblos prior to his assignment of land grants to the Pueblo Indians (Bloom and Mitchell 1938:98). This was nearly a century after Juan de Oñate and the initial Spanish settlers arrived in the general area and asked for permission to settle. It also was nine years after the Spanish had been expelled from the province by the Pueblo Revolt of 1680. Nevertheless, Cruzate granted the land to 10 Pueblos on that date while his government was out of favor and based nearly 300 miles to the south at Guadalupe del Paso. The distances for the grants were measured from the front of each Pueblo church and so many *varas* in each cardinal direction.

The administration of the Spanish grants and other lands taken over by the United States from Mexico stems from the Treaty of Guadalupe Hidalgo of 1848, which in articles 8 and 9 provided that the United States should recognize and protect the rights to private property established under the Spanish and Mexican regimes. To administer those provisions in the treaty, the United States Congress by the act of July 22, 1854, established the office of the surveyor general for the Territory of New Mexico. Section 8 of that law provided that the surveyor general, under instructions given by the secretary of the interior, should investigate and make recommendations with a view to confirming all bona fide land claims within the newly ceded territory. Upon the recommendation of the surveyor general in his report dated September 30, 1856, Congress confirmed the grant to Jemez Pueblo by the act of December 22, 1858. A patent covering this grant was issued to the Pueblo by the United States and signed by President Abraham Lincoln on November 1, 1864.

The original Spanish land grant began to be whittled away early in the twentieth century. By the decisions of the Pueblo Lands Board (created by act of June 7, 1924) the Pueblo's title to 19.18 acres within the Jemez Pueblo grant was extinguished, and the Pueblo received compensation for the lands and water rights lost in this grant (Bureau of Indian Affairs, Southern Pueblos Agency). Subsequently, through various acts, executive orders, deeds, and purchases, Jemez Pueblo trust land expanded to 88,867.22 acres by 1975. Counting grazing leases from the state of New Mexico and other small tracts in use by federal agencies, the total of tribal trust land and use areas is 90,262.99 acres.

The violent history of the people during the early years of their encounter with the Spaniards fairly explains the

422

vicissitudes of the Jemez people, and therefore, the fluctuation of the population. Zárate Salmerón (1966) explains that he baptized 6,566 during five years from 1621 to 1626, without counting Zia, Santa Ana, and Sandia, his other responsibilities at that time. A round figure of 3,000 is given by other historians as the number of Jemez people in 1630. In the reports of these historians the figure rose to 5,000 by the time of the Revolt in 1680. However, after the Revolt only a handful were left. By 1706, when the present village was refounded, with the majority of the returnees included, the figure was 300. These figures are from somewhat doubtful military and missionary reports. The conditions of the era dictated a drastic population decrease. The greatest number was congregated a few years after the Spaniards returned in 1692. The continuing conflict caused the Jemez people to move about for the next decade. Following those years, the figures available indicate a struggle for survival (table 1).

In 1835, there was an instant increase by 17 or 20, the number of new citizens who came from Pecos Pueblo (Parsons 1925). Besides the Pecos, who brought much mixture of blood—Spanish, Comanche, and *genízaro*— there was much mixture of Navajo and Hopi blood with Jemez in the past. The last was due to their taking refuge among these people.

Intertribal marriage was rare before World War II, though there were a few women from Santa Clara, San Ildefonso, San Felipe, Cochiti, Laguna, and Zia Pueblos and one Spanish-American from Jemez Springs who married in. Soldiers returning from World War II and from college thereafter brought a few non-Indian wives to the Pueblo.

**Table 1. Population, 1744–1970**

| Year | Population |
| --- | --- |
| 1744 | 100 |
| 1752 | 207 |
| 1760 | 373 |
| 1776 | 345 |
| 1790 | 485 |
| 1810 | 297 |
| 1850 | 365 |
| 1860 | 650 |
| 1870 | 344 |
| 1890 | 474 |
| 1900 | 498 |
| 1910 | 566 |
| 1920 | 547 (following an epidemic) |
| 1930 | 634 |
| 1940 | 719 |
| 1950 | 952 |
| 1960 | 1,329 |
| 1970 | 1,939 |

Source: BIA reports, Southern Pueblos Agency.

The Bureau of Indian Affairs initiated a relocation program in 1952. With this program both boys and girls went out in every direction to metropolitan areas, and they met and married people from just about every tribe and from other ethnic groups. This situation will cause some problems for the tribal leaders. Some of the progressive leaders say that only a tribal constitution with all its specific ordinances can control the heterogeneous population of the Jemez of the future. Other conservatives question adopting a constitution and tell themselves that the traditional system of the past can be applied to all.

## Culture

### Political Organization

The Pueblo form of government in the 1970s was simultaneously native and European, having been influenced by the Spaniards in colonial times. The titular head of the Pueblo is the cacique, the theocratic leader "from the time of the emergence from the underworld." Under the cacique and his staff are the war chief and his assistants. They are the functioning arm of the hierarchy that enforces the rules, regulations, and ordinances of the theocratic system (fig. 3). All of these are lifetime positions and there are no successions. Occasionally, an assistant may be acting in the temporary absence or death of the head, but he never takes a position or title that was not given him.

Another branch of government under the war chief includes the positions of war captains and their aides. These positions are filled yearly by the cacique, his staff, and the war chief. A war captain with five aides is selected from either of the two moieties of the Pueblo in alternating years. The lieutenant war captain also has five aides. These men are responsible for policing, conducting, and supervising the social activities of the two moieties, the Turquoise and the Squash. The social activities range from ceremonial and social dances to recreational rabbit hunts, competitive footraces, and hunts for other game animals.

The Spanish-introduced government was in the 1970s the civil government. Under the cacique, the governor is responsible for all other tribal business of the modern world. As such he is the liaison with the outside business world and its activities. The governor has an official staff composed of the first lieutenant governor, second lieutenant governor, a sheriff, and five aides who serve as messengers and chauffeurs. Other members of the governor's official staff are the *fiscales,* or the church officers. The *fiscal* has a lieutenant and five aides. They are concerned with and responsible for the activities involving the Catholic church, such as burials and maintenance of church property.

All these officials are selected annually by the cacique and his staff. All Pueblo officials serve without salary and consider the year's service as a duty to their people and their Pueblo.

Fig. 3. *Easter Ceremonial, Jemez.* Masked guards (*hilé·yɨ* sg.), who served under war captains to exclude non-Indians from Holy Week dances, are received by the cacique and religious society leaders on first entering the Pueblo. Man second from right, with smaller mask and a whip for naughty children, has the duty of catching any loose chickens in the area. The women are carrying baskets of bread to offer to the guards. Tempera painting by the Jemez artist José Rey Toledo, dated 1936—a reconstruction, as such guards ceased to function about 1900.

When the Pueblo was provided these officials by the Spanish Crown, a cane was given them as a sign of authority. It was the various holders of the cane with their authority that the Spaniards turned to for consultation. These canes have a silver head with a Christian cross engraved on it. This cross indicates that the cane also had the blessing and support of the Roman Catholic Church. By tradition, all the canes of the higher civil officials are blessed on January 6, the feast day of the Three Kings.

According to Chester E. Faris, a former Indian Bureau employee who had much charisma among the Pueblo people, the king of Spain in the 1620s issued a royal decree requiring each Pueblo, with the close of the calendar year, to choose by popular vote the civil officials. This came about because even after 80 years had passed since Coronado wintered with the Pueblos on the Rio Grande in 1540, the military as well as the missionaries had little understanding of the peaceful Pueblo organization and government. The Pueblos were silent people, and even in the 1940s the Bureau of Indian Affairs did not know of the Pueblo hierarchy system.

When Mexico won independence from Spain, sovereignty was successfully established, and new staffs, silver thimbled, were presented to the Pueblos. They were again authorized and commissioned to function in line with their long custom. These canes as well as Spanish ones are now kept by the lieutenants.

In addition to his Spanish cane the governor has an Abraham Lincoln cane. This cane was presented to each Pueblo governor by Lincoln in recognition of the peaceful attitude of the Pueblos during the beginning of the American administration in the territory. During the Civil War the Navajos and the Apaches suffered the war fever by attacking indiscriminately, but the Pueblos manifested definite neutrality and even assisted in their way.

The majority of the people of Jemez are registered to vote. The school board election for the local school district is of great interest to the people. In 1974 there were three Jemez men on the school board, one of which was the president. Interest in other elections is not so

Academy of Nat. Sciences, Philadelphia.

Fig. 4. Francisco Hosta (*hóv̓i* 'lightning'), Jemez governor who served as guide and informant to members of an 1849 government expedition. He is dressed "in his war costume" in this watercolor portrait on which was based a lithograph in the expedition's official report (Simpson 1850:69, pl. 4). He is wearing moccasins and tied buckskin leggings (wrapped incorrectly), red breeches (which would not have been typical), a red and black striped upper garment over a white shirt, a red bandana, and a shell gorget. He is carrying a shield similar to that shown in fig. 5 (possibly the same shield inaccurately rendered), bow and arrows, and a lance with attached eagle feather. His face is painted with black lines. Inaccurate or improbable details in this and other paintings in this series suggest that the painting was not done directly from life. Painted by Richard H. Kern, allegedly Aug. 19, 1849.

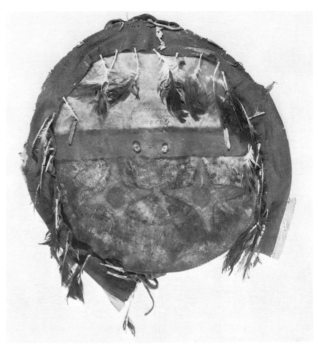

Smithsonian, Dept. of Anthr.: 17352.

Fig. 5. Buffalo hide war shield with buckskin cover, once owned by Francisco Hosta. The upper half is painted yellow, the central band is red, and the lower portion is blue with yellow-green stars. It is edged with red flannel with eagle feathers. Diameter 60 cm; collected in 1873 (Putnam 1879:374–390).

great, as they have not benefited by county or state politics.

## Social and Ceremonial Organization

Jemez clans are matrilineal and exogamous; they have ceremonial functions, and membership in specific clans is required for appointment to some leading ceremonial-political offices. But Jemez families also have a patrilineal emphasis, which may come from the teachings of mis-sionaries that the man is the head of the household. Members of a nuclear family take the surname of the male head of the household.

Membership in the two kiva moieties, Squash and Turquoise (see fig. 6), is also basically patrilineal, and each moiety tends to be endogamous. In the 1970s these groups continue to provide entertainment for the people. They compete in kick-stick races held each spring during the irrigation ditch cleaning season, and they also put on dances. These ceremonial dances are usually closed, limited to Indian people who understand the religion and its meaning; they went underground after the return of the Spaniards in 1693, following the eviction during the Pueblo Revolt of 1680. Other religious dances are often merged with Roman Catholic rites introduced by the Spaniards, being performed on a saint's name day and during the Christmas holiday season; these are open to public viewing.

Every Jemez man belongs to one of two societies, Eagle and Arrow, that have traditional functions dealing with defense and war. Affiliation follows the male line (although sons of the same father may divide in member-ship). Ellis (1964:15) reported that there were in addition 21 religious societies, with affiliation determined on various nonhereditary bases, that form the basic social and political units of Jemez society. Actually there were 23 societies when she wrote, and even then the Flute society was extinct (its last member having died in the

Mus. of N.M., Santa Fe.

Fig. 6. Main plaza in winter, looking west toward Jemez Mountains. The Squash kiva is the building, second from right, with double ladders, one to climb to the roof and the other to descend into the kiva. Squash and Turquoise kivas are almost identical in exterior appearance and orientation (see figs. 1–2), leading Parsons (1925:pl. 1b) to an erroneous labeling of the Turquoise kiva. Parsons (1925:13, pls. 3–4) reported that the interior painted designs of the kivas were also almost identical. The windmill, center background, supplied power to the community well. Photograph by T. Harmon Parkhurst, about 1925.

1940s). The last male member of the Tovahesh society (*tovahéš*) died in 1976, leaving three women auxiliaries. This society was responsible for the pit-house ceremony, held every 20 years or so to renovate and rededicate the kivas. The last such ceremony was held in 1940, and another may never be held. Otherwise, and despite all the obstacles in recent years, the religious calendar is still full and there are enough new and young society members. There is no room for anything new, the religion of the Peyote Way for one example.

*Subsistence in the Eighteenth and Nineteenth Centuries*

The Jemez economy improved somewhat in the eighteenth and nineteenth centuries with settlement in their present home area. Before then they lived in mountainous country where large areas for farming did not exist and the weather was not so favorable. Very likely through the efforts of Franciscan padres the Jemez people began to grow a greater variety of crops: chili, wheat (figs. 7–8), fruit, grapes, and melons were added to their traditional corn, squash, beans, tobacco, and cotton. Grapes did very well in the Jemez valley until World War II when the shortage of manpower prevented the special care grapevines require, and many either froze or withered away. Only a few families had vineyards in the 1970s, but cotton and tobacco were still grown by a few families for ceremonial use.

Horses, donkeys, oxen, cattle, sheep, and goats were also introduced to Jemez by the Spaniards. A donkey was owned by an average household. Some owned horses, which were more a sign of wealth with an occasional use in the fall for threshing wheat. Horses were also used to tend cattle and for transportation. Oxen were used more than horses to pull two-wheeled carts. Cattle were popular because they could take care of themselves with occasional special attention during calving, when they were brought to the village corrals for milking and protection of young calves from predators. Sheep and goats were not so numerous because they demanded constant care, with which religious commitments at times interfered. But at any time one could work for or trade with neighboring Spanish communities.

Some years wild resources were plentiful. Then the people had piñon seeds, fruits from the yucca plant called Spanish dagger, as well as from cacti, berries from the salt bush, and thumb-size sweet wild potatoes. The practice of digging this wild potato lasted until World War II.

Existence in what may be considered as harsh circumstances was accepted as a fact of life. The community was very responsive to group activity, for example, work on irrigation canals, an activity that continued in the 1970s. During droughts the civil officials supervised irrigation of farmlands. During flooding of irrigation canals, the community was called upon to repair the damages. Farm work was a cooperative affair of the extended family.

To supplement their diet of mutton, venison, and beef, the Jemez people journeyed east to the Plains in quest of buffalo and antelope. At this time they also took goods to trade with the Apaches, Comanches, and Kiowas. Buffalo were hunted at least twice a year. After the corn and

426

SANDO

Fig. 7. Woman washing wheat, a task performed in tubs of water, as shown here, in main irrigation ditch (pictured in Hewett and Dutton 1945:96), or in the river (see "San Juan Pueblo" fig. 17, this vol.). The sieve, blurred by motion, is probably a twilled ring basket of the type shown behind the tub and in fig. 8. The coiled basket at left is of a tighter weave. Photograph by T. Harmon Parkhurst, about 1935.

Fig. 8. Basket of twilled yucca leaves attached at rim to sumac rod ring. Used in Rio Grande Pueblos to store food and to wash wheat. For construction techniques see Underhill (1944:26) and Tanner (1968:11). Diameter about 42 cm; collected in 1936.

other crops were planted hunting parties left during June. At this time the male buffalo was fat although the hide was not good. After the harvest was in, by October, there was another hunting party. By then the female was fat and with grown calves, but the bulls were poor; however, the hide had become woolly and valuable for trade and domestic use. Old timers who spoke of these events were enthusiastic about the delicacy of the tongue and the usefulness of the fat buffalo grease.

*Technology*

What the dominant society calls arts and crafts were for practical purposes entirely. Although some mantas and rabbit fur blankets were sold to Spaniards and Mexicans, handwoven and embroidered kilts, shirts (fig. 10), rain sashes, and belts (fig. 11) were for ceremonial use. The arts were mainly visible on the kiva walls and in other objects of ceremonial use.

Pottery was created for dry storage and sometimes for trade for waterproof Keresan ollas. Decorative pottery was made in the 1940s by a family whose mother came to Jemez as a bride from Zia Pueblo. As it became commercially useful, more Jemez women began to learn the art of pottery making. At first this pottery was garishly decorated with showcard colors that easily rubbed off, but with the beginning of the commercial arts and crafts revival in the late 1950s, Jemez women developed another type of pottery that resembles the traditional San Juan Tewa red ware. The Jemez variety is identifiable by its distinct black designs and an occasional highlight of turquoise. A few pieces are painted with natural earth

colors. Wedding vases seem the most popular with a few figurines of animals and "grandma with her grandchildren" hanging all about her. In 1977 Pecos pottery with its own designs and colors began to be produced and was popular as a novelty (fig. 12).

Jemez women also make the yucca ring basket (fig. 8). It is mostly for utilitarian purposes; however, non-Indians have also discovered it as another novelty and it is in great demand by the tourists. For ceremonial uses, and to hold cornmeal, a Jicarilla Apache type of small basket is also made by a few men; it is not sold.

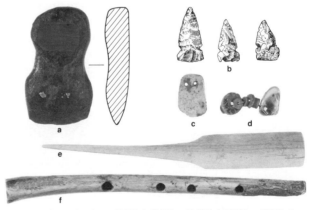

Fig. 9. Stone and bone objects. a, Ground stone ax head; b, arrow points; c-d, beads of stone (including turquoise) and shell used in earrings and necklaces; e, polished and sharpened bone awl with wide end used for creasing leather; f, flute of eagle bone. Length of awl 15.3 cm, rest same scale; collected in 1904.

Denver Art Mus: RJ-3.
Fig. 10. Man's cotton shirt. Men weave the cloth in three sections: the two sleeves and the body (folded at the shoulders with hole cut for the head). The designs in red and indigo wool are embroidered by women (see Mera 1943). Shoulder to hem length about 58 cm, collected in 1916.

Fig. 12. Lucy Chavez Toledo painting contemporary Jemez pottery. Photograph by E.S. Scholer, Dec. 1977.

## Sociocultural Situation in the 1970s

In the 1970s many families produced consumable garden crops with chili as the main product. Some raised corn and wheat. Alfalfa was high on the list of crops that stock owners fed to their cows and horses. Very few owned work horses to pull their plows and do other related work. Otherwise, the tractor has taken over and it has decreased the horse population. This decrease affects other former recreational activities, such as the "chicken pull" during the feast days during the summer, horse races, and rabbit hunts on horseback.

Since World War II the land-based or agricultural economy of Jemez has been shifting to a wage economy. Land-use figures best tell the story. Of 1,828 acres of irrigable land in 1972, 1,260 acres, or 68.9%, was idle. In 1973, 1,217 acres, or 66.5%, was idle. There are several reasons for the lack of farming. New Mexico has experienced a drought except for the winter of 1972. Second, the older men whose livelihood was farming have reached the seventies and eighties in age and are no

Mus. of N.M., Santa Fe: 48031/12.
Fig. 11. Woman's woolen waist belt (see "Santa Clara Pueblo," fig. 10, this vol.). This example, by Eutemia B. Loretto, won a prize in a 1976 crafts show. The Indian Service introduced weaving by women (rather than by men) at Jemez in the 1920s (Parsons 1925:16).
Woven on a horizontal loom (see "Cochiti Pueblo," fig. 10, this vol.). Length including fringe, about 120 cm.

longer capable physically. Third, the soil bank program of the government takes land out of production. Fourth, the war veterans returned with some skills that they could use in nearby towns. Fifth, these veterans became the models of younger men who also went to the cities for jobs. Sixth, welfare payments are available to Pueblo people. Seventh, newcomers to New Mexico bought land near Indian land, drilled wells, and usurped the already small stream.

For a while there were three sawmills in the Jemez mountains where many men were employed. Unfortunately, high prices eventually caused the sawmills to discontinue operations around 1970. In 1974 the men were employed in Albuquerque with the construction industries as carpenters, welders, painters, plasterers, and dry-wall installers. Some are employed by the state highway department, and a few have federal government jobs, including some within the community.

Education begins at age four in the community Headstart program. All the teacher aides and some of the teachers are from the community. From Headstart the six-year-olds go to the Bureau of Indian Affairs day school, the San Diego Mission school, or the Jemez Valley public school. The day school has classes from kindergarten to the sixth grade, the mission school goes to eighth grade, and the public school to twelfth grade. Some attend Saint Catherine's or the Institute of American Indian Arts, both in Santa Fe.

In the late 1940s there were four college graduates at Jemez. The number has grown considerably since then, due in large part to the veterans' education payments, especially after World War II, and to financial aid given by the scholarship division of the All-Pueblo Council, which has contracted with the Bureau of Indian Affairs to engage in this activity. In 1974 there were five students in graduate schools for advanced degrees. Some of these were assisted by the American Indian Graduate Scholarship program (from its office at Taos Pueblo).

Unlike the inability of many American Indians to elect people into political offices or onto local school boards, the Jemez people are able rather freely to vote members of the tribe onto the school board. In the school district in which the children of Jemez and Zia Pueblos are educated, the school board usually includes Indian or pro-Indian members. The Sandoval County Commission even has a Jemez man among its members; in 1977 he was the chairman of the Commission.

The majority of the people in the 1970s still speak Jemez. A few children from mixed marriages and those reared in urban areas do not speak the language. Usually when their mother is the Indian in a mixed marriage, the children understand and often speak the mother tongue. Half a dozen Jemez couples who experienced the relocation program of the Bureau of Indian Affairs did not speak the language to their children while they were away. Many of them have returned and some are learning to speak the language. Others seem lost in the cold air of fragmentary existence through not knowing the language of the people and therefore the religion and culture. Whereas Jemez people used to learn the Spanish language of their neighbors, the Headstart generation is learning English, and this is changing the image of the traditional shy and quiet Indian student. From the Headstart classes as well as television, the children pick up English as a peer language and are growing up bilingual in English and Jemez. An earlier generation was multilingual in various Indian languages, Spanish, and English.

As the younger generation masters White culture and adapts to its ways, they also appear to want to learn and to understand more of their own heritage. Thus, the proverbial American melting pot does not seem to affect the Jemez. They want to maintain and live their culture but use the tools of the technological society of their neighbors. It would be safe to predict that the Jemez will remain tribal people for a few more generations, judging from their respect for traditional ways, the living language, and their choice of the best from two viable cultures, the Pueblo and the general American.

## Synonymy†

The name Jemez is from Spanish Jémez, the name for the Jemez Indians, spelled many ways in the historical sources. For the first segment J-, G-, H-, X-, and nothing have been used, and for the last segment -z, -s, and -x. More divergent are Emexes, Emeges, Amejes, and

† This synonymy was prepared by Ives Goddard. The Jemez forms were supplied by Kenneth L. Hale (personal communication 1975) and Joe Sando (personal communication 1978), except for *hį́·wa*. This and other uncredited forms are from Harrington (1916:399–403), who has additional variants, or from anonymous sources.

Ameges. The name is ultimately from the Jemez self-designation *hį́·míš* (pl.; Kenneth L. Hale, personal communication 1975), perhaps via a Keresan borrowing of this.

The name of Jemez Pueblo is *wàlatɨ·wa* 'at the Pueblo in the cañada', English Walatowa, in which the first element is not to be identified with *ɸǽlá* 'bear', as some sources suggest. It is commonly referred to simply as *tɨ́·wa* 'at the Pueblo', rarely as *hį́·wa* 'at Jemez-Indian place'.

Borrowed forms of the name in other Kiowa-Tanoan languages are Taos híemma (Curtis 1907–1930, 16:261), Picuris hemimá, and Isleta *hįemíde* 'Jemez Indian' and *hįemʔai* '(at) Jemez Pueblo' (C.T. Harrington 1920:43; omitted *m* in first form supplied from Harrington 1916:400). Keresan has for 'a Jemez Indian': Santa Ana *hê·mišI* (Davis 1964:121), Acoma *hê·miši* (Miller 1965:170); for 'Jemez Pueblo': Santa Ana *hé·míší·cé*, Santo Domingo *hé·mišice*, Acoma *hé·míší·cʰi* (Miller and Davis 1963:322). Other borrowings are Zuni *he·muši·kʷe* (Dennis Tedlock, personal communication 1977), Hopi hemisi, and Southern Ute emasi.

Of unknown origin is Tewa *wán* 'Jemez Indian', whence *wángé ówînge* '(at) Jemez Pueblo'. Navajo has *Mą'ii Deeshgiizh* 'coyote pass' as the name of the Pueblo and *Mą'ii Deeshgiizhnii* for the Jemez people (Robert W. Young, personal communication 1977). The Jemez relate this name to a tradition that when they returned from living among the Navajo after the Pueblo Revolt many members of the Coyote clan stayed behind and married Navajos.

The Spanish mission at Jemez Pueblo was known as San Diego de la Congregación and later as San Diego de los Jémez.

## Sources§

Parsons's (1925) ethnography is thin and badly outdated. As is characteristic of so much of her work, she conveys very little sense of how Jemez holds together, how the various aspects of the society and culture she describes separately contribute to form an operational whole. Hers is the best general account available on Jemez, but it consists of a series of kaleidoscopic glimpses of many aspects of Jemez reality of the first quarter of the twentieth century, rather than an in-depth look at a few critical institutions. Ellis (1952, 1953) fills important gaps in knowledge of some of the oldest religious practices and beliefs of the Jemez people, while her monograph (1964) provides a much more systematic statement of the general outlines of Jemez social structure with comparisons made with other Tanoan Pueblos. Aside from many brief discussions of Jemez scattered through the historical literature, these are the key sources.

§ This section was prepared by Alfonso Ortiz.

# Pecos Pueblo

ALBERT H. SCHROEDER

## Language and Territory

Pecos (¹pākōs), a Pueblo formerly occupied by sedentary farming Indians, is located about 18 miles southeast of Santa Fe, New Mexico. The inhabitants, and the Jemez in the 1600s, spoke dialects of Towa, a member of the Kiowa-Tanoan language family* (Tamarón y Romeral 1954:66; Domínguez 1956:181; Simpson 1850:68; U.S. Office of Indian Affairs 1915:496). The Jemez tradition that their present dialect grew out of a combination of the original dialects of Pecos and Jemez suggests that a sizable number joined Jemez prior to the 1838 exodus of the few individuals remaining at Pecos (fig. 1) (Hewett 1904).

Pecos Pueblo is situated on a small mesa in the upper Pecos Valley near the northern edge of the Upper Sonoran life-zone, 6,950 feet high. Separated from other Pueblos along the Rio Grande on the west by the southern foothills of the Sangre de Cristo range and from the Plains Indians on the east by the Tecolote Mountains, these Indians claimed the width of this valley from north of their Pueblo south to Anton Chico (Hewett 1904).

## Prehistory

Traditionally, Tonchun Pueblo, five miles southeast of Pecos, and others nearby came from the west and were of Jemez stock. Others in the south end of Pecos territory had come from the south. However, the first Pecos settlers claimed a northern origin. Tonchun was the last of the seven or eight outlying villages to be abandoned during merging at Pecos (Hewett 1904).

Archeological surveys reveal a number of small ruins in the upper Pecos Valley occupied in the 1100s. By the 1200s these people began to concentrate into larger, coursed adobe, one-story dwellings with rare exterior doorways and with kivas contiguous to the rooms, such as Forked Lightning across the arroyo from Pecos Pueblo. By the 1300s, construction started on the Pecos mesa with circular kivas detached from the dwellings. Not until about 1450 did these people build the large, multistoried, rectangular Pueblo enclosing a plaza with circular kivas. The architecture and contents excavated from this Pueblo and other structures are the subjects of several reports (Kidder 1931–1936, 1, 1932, 1958).

The early occupants conformed to the widespread Southwest Plateau physical type. The more recent inhabitants (see photographs in Hewett 1904; Twitchell 1911–1917, 1:192) exhibited the addition of physical traits more commonly found to the north and northeast, but these late influences are not thought to be responsible for skeletal changes that did occur in late prehistoric times (Seltzer 1944:25, 30–32). Both the archeological and physical anthropological evidence support oral traditions that Pecos represented a basic native population unit that received accretions from late prehistoric times on. During this period, these people traded for a variety of material from other Pueblos and Plains Indians, such as pipes (fig. 2), alibates flint artifacts, Biscuit ware from the Tewas (fig. 3), glazed-paint ware from the Tiwas and Tanos, and obsidian from the Jemez (Kidder 1932; Wendorf and Reed 1955).

Smithsonian, NAA.

Fig. 1. Agustín Pecos (sésǽɸi·ya). From 1902 until his death in 1919 he was the last survivor of the 1838 emigration from Pecos to Jemez. In 1904 he provided a list of the 17 individuals who had emigrated; he believed himself to have been about 12 to 15 years old at the time (Hewett 1904:439, 429). The list of emigrants was subsequently expanded to include 3 more individuals (Parsons 1925:130–131), based on church records and information obtained at Jemez. Photograph by Adam C. Vroman, 1902.

* There are no phonemic recordings of the Pecos language. Pecos words cited in the *Handbook* follow the spellings of the sources.

Fig. 2. Clay tubular pipe characteristic of Plains and Southwest Indians. Excavated from convento at Pecos, New Mexico (see Kidder 1932:156). Length 14 cm.

## History

Members of the Francisco Vásquez de Coronado expedition in 1540, who approached Pecos from the west via Glorieta Pass, learned that they traversed the route that provided a natural gateway to the plains. Antonio de Espejo's small party stopped briefly in 1583 (Pérez de Luxán 1929) as did Gaspar Castaño de Sosa in 1590-1591 (Castaño de Sosa 1965). All were treated with suspicion by the occupants, who boasted of their strength, although capitulating to Castaño de Sosa. Following the arrival of the first Spanish colonists in 1598, Juan de Oñate visited Pecos and assigned missionaries (Hammond and Rey 1953).

With the establishment of a church and convento, Pecos served as a base for missionary activities in the plains and for trade with Plains Indians. Pecos converts learned new crafts, and the entire Pueblo paid tribute in the form of labor and goods. In 1680 these people joined other Pueblos in an attack on Santa Fe, forcing the Spaniards out of New Mexico. On their return 12 years later, the Pecos aided them in the reconquest and minor rebellions of the 1690s.

In the early 1700s, with the appearance of the mounted Comanches along New Mexico's eastern border, the Pecos suffered many attacks and saw their Apache allies forced off the plains into the mountains of New Mexico and into west Texas. During the middle 1700s, some Frenchmen, allies of the Comanches, reached Pecos in an endeavor to open up trade (Folmer 1941:265, 270). At about the same time, Jicarillas and other Apaches who took up residence near the Pueblo and Spanish troops occasionally garrisoned there assisted in repulsing Comanche attacks, though not always with success (Thomas 1940:68, 179; Hackett 1923-1937, 3:465; Kelly 1941:174). Similar pressures, smallpox epidemics, and other diseases in the late 1700s decimated Pecos to the extent that the mission there became only a *visita* without

Fig. 3. Matte and glaze paint pottery found at Pecos. a, Biscuit ware bowl with characteristic black banded patterns painted on white slipped exterior and interior surfaces; b, biscuit ware "salt dish" bowl with cuplike appendage on rim and lug on opposite side of rim for attachment of carrying handle (Kidder 1931-1936, 2:105); c, modern painted ware olla (Tewa Polychrome) with polished red slip; d-e, distinctive polychrome glaze decorated ollas. Diameter of a about 43 cm, rest same scale.

**Table 1. Population, 1540-1838**

| Year | Population | Remarks | Sources |
|------|-----------|---------|---------|
| 1540 | 500 warriors | | Hammond and Rey 1940 |
| 1583 | 2,000 warriors | Total population? | Pérez de Luxán 1929 |
| 1620s | 2,000 | | Benavides 1945 |
| 1641 | 1,189 | | Benavides 1945 |
| 1680 | 2,000 | Secondary source drawing on earlier figures | Benavides 1945 |
| 1692 | 1,500 | | Vargas Zapata y Luxán Ponze de León 1940:158-159 |
| 1694 | 736 | | Espinosa 1942:216 |
| 1706 | 1,000 | | Hackett 1923-1937, 3:373 |
| 1707 | 1,000 | | Thomas 1932:93 |
| 1730 | 521 (98 families) | | Tamarón y Romeral 1954:97 |
| 1738 | | Smallpox epidemic | Chavez 1957:234 |
| 1744 | (125 families) | | Hackett 1923-1937, 3:403 |
| 1748 | | Epidemic in August | Chavez 1957:234 |
| 1750 | ca. 300 | | Tamarón y Romeral 1954:48 |
| 1760 | 344 (168 families) | | Tamarón y Romeral 1954:48 |
| 1765 | 344 (178 families) | | Thomas 1932:93 |
| 1776 | 269 (100 families) | Epidemics in 1770s | Domínguez 1956:214 |
| 1782 | 84 | Enemy attacks | Thomas 1932:93 |
| 1790 | 154 | Peace with Comanches from 1786 | Kidder 1958:327 |
| 1797 | 189 | | Benavides 1945:273 |
| 1812 | (30 families) | Pecos Indians moving to San Miguel | Chavez 1957:74-75 |
| 1815 | 40 | | Chavez 1957:75; Domínguez 1956:214 |
| 1820 | 50 | | Twitchell 1911-1917, 1:474 |
| 1826 | 40 (9 families) | | Ellis 1964:59-61 |
| 1838 | 17 | | Hewett 1904:439; Parsons 1925:130-131 |

a friar in residence. Spanish soldiers camped here as late as 1808 (Loomis and Nasatir 1967; Bolton 1917:392).

As nearby towns, such as San Jose and San Miguel del Vado, developed in the Pecos Valley in the late 1700s and early 1800s, some of the Pecos trained in Spanish crafts moved into the new villages, their names being on record in local non-Pueblo churches. The last baptism at Pecos took place in June 1828 (Chavez 1957:205). The few remaining Pecos Indians occupied the north end of the Pueblo until the time of its abandonment in 1838 (Kidder 1958:68; Bandelier 1883:42, 48, 125, 133). The varying population of Pecos Pueblo is shown in table 1.

Briefly exposed to the Coronado expedition of 1540-1542 and to a lay missionary who remained with some sheep and a few tools, Pecos received little influence from the Spaniards until the early 1600s when missionaries took up residence here. By the 1620s, under instruction of the Spaniards, these people became known for their carpentry (Benavides 1945:67). They also learned to make adobe bricks by assisting in the construction of the church; adopted vegetables, grains, and domestic animals introduced by the Spaniards; paid tribute to the state; and provided the church with staff assistance. Before the end of the 1600s, the Pecos had resigned themselves to having the Spaniards appoint their Pueblo officials (Vargas Zapata y Luxán Ponze de León 1940:169). By the middle 1700s, Spaniards were garri-

soned in their own buildings at Pecos to help defend against Comanches (Thomas 1932:60), and the Pecos needed a permit to hunt buffalo (Kelly 1941:181).

According to tradition, when the Pecos left they turned their Pueblo and land over to Mariano Ruiz who had been adopted into the tribe (Curtis 1907-1930, 17:20-21). Eight years after abandonment, the Pueblo stood in a fair state of preservation (Emory 1848:37); however, vandalism by Mexican soldiers, using structural wood for making fires, contributed to the rapid decay of the Pueblo (Falconer 1844:216). By about 1858 the roof of the church had been removed (Bandelier 1883:42). Traditions about a giant snake, an eternal fire, and Montezuma arose after the abandonment of the Pueblo (Curtis 1907-1930, 17:20-21; Roberts 1932; U.S. Army. Corps of Topographical Engineers 1962:42; Emory 1848:30; U.S. Office of Indian Affairs 1915:496; Gregg 1844:188ff.; Bell 1965:191-193; Bandelier 1883:112).

Gross, Kelly, and Company acquired the Pueblo and surrounding land in 1902. In 1920, 67 acres encompassing the Pueblo ruins and mission were deeded to the Archdiocese of Santa Fe, which in turn donated the parcel to the School of American Research. Designated a state monument in 1935, Congress established it as a national monument by an act of 1965, after the state donated the land to the federal government. Research in and stabilization of the ruins was followed by development of the

Mus. of N.M., Santa Fe: Kidder 1958:fig. 22.

Fig. 4. View of Pecos about 1700, seen from the north. The three clusters of buildings, north to south, are: the Quadrangle (with 4- to 5-story houseblocks and round kivas), South Pueblo, and church with convento. (See Kidder 1958.) Reconstruction drawing by Singleton P. Moorehead, based on archeological investigation.

monument, in the process of which the foundations of the church built in the 1620s were discovered as well as some of the structures that housed the Spanish garrison.

## Culture

### Structures

In the last half of the 1500s and early 1600s, this rectangular masonry Pueblo had four houseblocks. It stood four to five stories high, arranged around a central plaza with staggered entrances, and lacked ground-floor doorways. It was completely surrounded by a low wall and had ladders that could be drawn up to the upper stories through hatchways in the ceilings of the porchlike galleries fronting on the rooms on each level. Gallery roofs provided walkways to various parts of the Pueblo and to the five to eight plazas on the upper floor levels. A labyrinth of cellars and passageways in the lower floors connected houseblocks, and in one known case, a circular subterranean kiva. At the sides of the Pueblo were two bathing areas (Hammond and Rey 1940; Castaño de Sosa 1965:101; Benavides 1945; Kidder 1958).

Each house, with three or four apartments, totaling 15 or 16 rooms, was terraced on the plaza side and backed up against a similar house facing the exterior of the Pueblo. Several rooms in each served for storage of crops, another for grinding food (Castaño de Sosa 1965:98), and the remainder for sleeping and the daily living activities of the nuclear family and younger married kin of the household (Kidder 1958:122–123). Each of the 16 active circular kivas (Castaño de Sosa 1965) served an estimated average of four or more households or about 34 adults (Kidder 1958:101–104), which compares to 20 people to one kiva at Zuni in 1583 (Pérez de Luxán 1929). Large amounts of timber were stockpiled for future construction (Castaño de Sosa 1965:101).

Prior to the 1620s, a Spanish missionary constructed a small adobe church to the east of the Pueblo. This church was replaced in the 1620s by a large one with a convento attached built near the south end of the mesa (Benavides 1945; Stubbs, Ellis, and Dittert 1957). At an unknown date, but perhaps not much later, the Christianized Pecos Indians erected a large houseblock without any kivas just north of the church, utilizing adobes in the upper stories (Kidder 1958).

At the time of the Pueblo Revolt of 1680–1692, the Indians razed the church, using adobes from it in places in the large north Pueblo that then stood three stories

Pecos Natl. Monument, Pecos, N.M.: 4AB.
Fig. 5. Wooden cross excavated from 18th-century church, Pecos, N.M. These were often associated with burials in the church floor (Kidder 1932:296). Length 10 cm.

high and had one entrance. A kiva built in the convento during this period may have been the "new" kiva ordered suppressed by the Spanish governor in 1714 (Vargas Zapata y Luxán Ponze de León 1940:121-122, 169; Bancroft 1889:232). Two years after the reconquest of 1692, a small chapel was in use at Pecos. It was in the process of being enlarged in 1696 and was replaced 10 years later (Hackett 1923-1937, 3:373).

In 1776 a full description of the existing church and convento and the small chapel, with less detail on the Pueblo, also mentions the south Pueblo (which lacks kivas, suggesting construction by converts) (fig. 4) but not the buildings used by the Spanish garrison. The wall surrounding the Pueblo was said to be of adobe. As in 1692, only one entry, reportedly on the north, provided access into the Pueblo, and in contrast to the situation in 1591, only nine kivas remained in use (Domínguez 1956:208-214, 256).

In 1821 the Pueblo, entered through a gate, still stood three stories high, had six-foot-wide wooden galleries on the upper stories with ladders between each level, and exhibited selenite windows. It was floored with adobes laid on pole, bark, and mud ceilings of rooms below (James 1962:80-81).

Four to eight years after abandonment, a few people were reported living at the Pueblo. Although it already had suffered from vandalism (Falconer 1844:216; Gregg 1844:188), it still stood three stories high in places and showed evidence of four kivas (Cutts 1965:51).

### Subsistence

Like other Pueblos, the Pecos farmers raised maize and beans of several colors, greens, and squash (Hammond and Rey 1940; Castaño de Sosa 1965), but they did not plant cotton. Some "chickens" were reported in 1540 (Hammond and Rey 1940:310). Women made pinole and bread and gathered a variety of herbs and piñon (Hackett 1923-1937, 3:463), and the men hunted bison, deer, and turkey (Kidder 1958:123).

Land surrounding the Pueblo was farmed (Thomas 1940:171). Irrigated plots to the northeast of the Pueblo (Domínguez 1956:213) and along the banks of the Pecos River (Vargas Zapata y Luxán Ponze de León 1940:122; Tamarón y Romeral 1954:51) also provided crops.

### Clothing

These people dressed in skins, had feather blankets, and wore headpieces, though children and unmarried girls went "unclothed" (Hammond and Rey 1940:257). In winter, men, who wore a highly decorated loincloth, covered themselves with a cotton blanket with a buffalo hide over it. The women used a blanket drawn in a knot on the shoulder and open on one side with a sash around the waist. Over this they had a gaily worked blanket or turkey-feather robe and "many curious things" (Castaño de Sosa 1965:100).

### Technology

Pecos had turquoise ornaments (Hammond and Rey 1940) and made a variety of pottery (red, black, plain, and some glaze decorated) in the form of dishes, bowls, salt containers, basins, and cups (fig. 3). They also made religious objects (Castaño de Sosa 1965:100). Items furnished to the Spaniards included dressed antelope and buffalo hides and cloth (Sigüenza y Góngora 1932:69; Hackett 1923-1937, 3:260). Pecos fashioned baskets and matting for various uses (Kidder 1958:123) as well as headpieces and shields (Hammond and Rey 1940:217) in addition to other items (Kidder 1932). Stone and bone artifacts provided the necessary tools for the manufacture of these items.

### Religion

With 16 kivas in 1590-1591, "many" in 1692 (Vargas Zapata y Luxán Ponze de León 1940:133-134), 9 in 1776, and evidence of 4 still visible in the 1840s, ritual obviously played an important part in the calendar of activities at Pecos. Oriented to the east, kivas served as council rooms to discuss matters of government, planting, work arrangements, or election of new officials and to rehearse dances or do other things (Domínguez 1956:256). One kiva reportedly contained a consecrated fire in the basin of a small altar (Gregg 1844:270-272). A surface kiva to the north of the Pueblo was used in late prehistoric and early historic times (Kidder 1958:176).

The Eagle Hunt Society, after the move to Jemez in 1838, kept the mask of the Pecos bull as well as the image of Porciúncula used during the August 2 fiesta of the same name, at which time female participants wore tablitas. A rabbit hunt preceded the fiesta by a day or two. The bull also appeared in a Squash kiva burlesque in December (Parsons 1925:14, 79-81, 96, fig. 10, pl. 10).

Fig. 6. *Pecos Bull Dance at Jemez,* Fiesta of Porciúncula. In 1922 (Parsons 1925:96–100), the bull mask was worn by a man dressed in dance kilt, belt, crocheted stockings, and dance moccasins with skunk-skin anklets, in the manner of a kachina impersonator. The mask consisted of a large wooden frame covered by pieces of dark cloth that were patched together and spotted with white rings, with a somewhat stylized head from which a red tongue protruded and to which flicker feathers and a piece of sheepskin were attached. The bull was followed by bull-baiters, members of the Eagle Watchers' Society dressed in burlesque of Whites, who attempted to lasso the bull. Tempera painting by Jemez artist José Rey Toledo, 1940.

Burlesque (fig. 6) also provided amusement. One of the principal men of the Pueblo, with two assistants in September 1760, imitated a Spanish bishop's visit and attendant ceremony, the entire activity lasting four days (Tamarón y Romeral 1954:50–51). Drums and flageolets (fig. 7) accompanied various activities and dances (Hammond and Rey 1940; Tamarón y Romeral 1954:50).

Ceremonial gear also included gourd and tortoise-shell rattles, terraced ceramic pipes (fig. 8), small canteens like those associated with the water serpent among the Tewas, conus shell parts, stone idols, depictions of the guardian of permanent water sources (the Tewa *avanʸu* serpent) on pottery, wooden "lightning arrow" and little bow, and reference to an eternal fire (Kidder 1958:123, 229–234). Two shrines north of the Pueblo, which Pecos Indians and their descendants visited as late as the twentieth century, and a sacred cave also formed a part of their ceremonial structure (Hewett 1904:437, 439). Religious customs differed to some degree from those of Jemez (Simpson 1850:68; Parsons 1925:135).

### Sociopolitical Organization

In addition to the Pecos Cloud and Sun clans to which eight survivors belonged (Parsons 1925:26), the following are said to have once existed at Pecos: Badger, Calabash, Corn, Coyote, Crow, Eagle, Earth, Pine, Turquoise, Ant, Bear, Buffalo, Deer, Fire, Mountain Lion, Oak, and Turkey. The last eight clans are not recorded at Jemez (Hodge 1896).

In the 1500s, Pecos had a cacique and war captain, and "old men" who opposed Christianity (Hammond and Rey 1940:217, 233–234). Another village reportedly was subject to Pecos at that time (Hammond and Rey 1940:258), perhaps Tonchun. The cacique seldom left the Pueblo, from which it may be inferred that he took care of local matters. It was the war captain who dealt with outsiders, and there was a Spanish-appointed governor, who was also a warrior (Bandelier 1883:127). Weapons included bows and arrows, sling shots, stones, and the throwing of ashes at enemies (Castaño de Sosa 1965; James 1962:80–81). Young men formed the major body of warriors (Vargas Zapata y Luxán Ponze de León 1940:125), and when on guard at the Pueblo, they maintained contact with "bugles" and calls to one another (Hammond and Rey 1940:258).

Communal organization played an important part in life at Pecos as indicated by the planning that went into

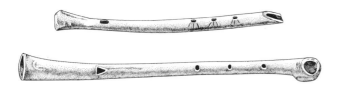

Robert S. Peabody Foundation for Archaeol., Andover, Mass: after Kidder 1932:fig. 209.

Fig. 7. Bone flageolets excavated from Pecos Pueblo, N.M. top, Made from ulna of bird, probably a hawk, with incising about the finger holes; length about 14 cm. bottom, Made from golden eagle ulna; length about 20 cm.

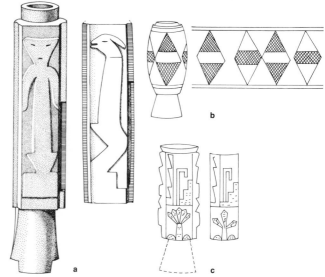

Robert S. Peabody Foundation for Archaeol., Andover, Mass: after Kidder 1932:figs. 141, 146, 154.

Fig. 8. Clay pipes with "fishtail" mouthpiece excavated from Pecos, N.M. a, Terraced pipe from ceremonial cache, of polished black clay with anthropomorphic figure and horned serpent carved in relief; b-c, barrel-shaped and rectangular pipes with incised line designs. Length of a 18 cm, rest about same scale.

the construction of the rectangular Pueblo and the total action exhibited against Castaño de Sosa. The average family had 4 to 5 people (Domínguez 1956), suggesting that a single household, including married children, might range as high as 9 or 10.

The prehistoric Pecos usually buried their dead in a shallow oval pit in a flexed position, face down, less often on the side, and rarely on the back. No orientation toward the cardinal points was favored. In later (historic) times, inhumation in an extended position was common (Kidder 1958:285-286, 301, 304).

## External Relations

Pecos resembled many other Rio Grande Pueblos during the Spanish period in being a multistoried, terraced, plaza-type town of sedentary, dry, and irrigation farmers. It differed primarily from its close neighbors in being one of the few that used circular little kivas rather than big kivas alone, in having considerable contact and trade with Plains Indians, and in speaking a language understandable only to distant Jemez Pueblo.

Pecos was no stranger to warfare. They were attacked in 1526 by the "Teyas," probably a Caddoan-speaking Plains group, who by 1540 conducted trade at Pecos, as did Plains Apaches with meat, hides, and tallow, but under a vigilant night watch during their stay. In their midst the Pecos held slaves from the Plains. At this time, reportedly because of the need for more lands, Pecos was warring against the Tiwas (Hammond and Rey 1940:219, 235, 258).

Fifty years later, Pecos was reported at war with unidentified tribes (Castaño de Sosa 1965) and in 1609 specifically with Tewas, being friendly then with the Taos, Picuris, and Apaches (Hammond and Rey 1953, 2:1094), the last being friendly with Pecos throughout historic times. During the Pueblo Revolt of 1680-1692, Pecos had difficulties with Tewas as well as Tanos (Benavides 1945:284) and Picuris but continued friendly with the Taos, Jemez, Keresans, and Apaches (Vargas Zapata y Luxán Ponze de León 1940:80, 106, 110, 117, 132-134).

In the 1700s Comanches moved onto the plains and began raiding Pecos (Kelly 1941:174), French traders crossed the plains to the Pueblo, and Jicarilla Apaches took up residence near Pecos, where they left their women when they hunted on the plains (Thomas 1940:82, 90, 124). Following the Spanish defeat of the Comanches in 1786, Comanches attended fairs and carried on free trade at Pecos (Thomas 1932:303, 314, 330-331). However, former Comanche raids and widespread epidemics had taken such a heavy toll on the Pueblo population that Pecos no longer had a resident priest.

This decline so affected membership in various Pueblo societies, clans, and ceremonies that customs, observances, kivas, and the entire fabric of their way of life no longer could function or cope with the daily needs. Although the Santa Fe Trail opened in 1821, it came too late to have any beneficial effect on the economy of this frontier Pueblo "trading post," and after an outbreak of mountain fever (Parsons 1925:3), the remaining occupants abandoned it in 1838.

## Synonymy†

The name Pecos appears as Pecos and Peccos in the account by Oñate, 1598 (Hammond and Rey 1953). It is a Spanish adaptation (originally a Spanish plural) either of the Keresan name, recorded as (Cochiti) p̌eyok$^h$ona (normalized) and p'éaku', or of the Jemez name p̌ǽ·k$^y$o 'Pecos Indian' (pl. p̌ǽ·k$^y$oš; p̌ǽ·k$^y$óla 'at Pecos'), also spelled p'atyulá and (with failure to hear initial [p̌]) aculah and âqiu.

† This synonymy was prepared by Ives Goddard; uncredited forms are from Harrington (1916:472-477), who gives additional variants, or from anonymous sources.

Pecos names for Pecos Pueblo recorded after its abandonment are k̓ak̓ora 'place down where the stone is on top' (normalized) and tshiquite or tziquite. This last seems to be a form of the name that appears in the early Spanish records as Cicuique—and the misread variant Acuique—Coronado, 1541 (Hammond and Rey 1940) and variants: Cicuyé, Cicuic, and Cicuio (Benavides 1945).

Other names for Pecos are Taos pˀǽiba (Harrington 1918); Picuris hiuqūā; Isleta hyóquahoon, hiokŭöˊk, and the loan form sikuyé; and Tewa c̓úngé, supposed to refer to an unidentified type of bush.

As a Spanish mission Pecos was referred to as Nuestra Señora de los Ángeles de Pecos and Nuestra Señora de los Ángeles de Porciúncula de Pecos. Oñate named it Santiago in 1598.

## Sources

There is no single major source for the ethnohistory of Pecos. Data are scattered through a variety of Spanish documents or in a few articles concerned with Pecos (Hewett 1904). The best description of the early historic period Pecos culture is contained in the 1590-1591 journal of Castaño de Sosa (1965:79-105).

In the 1880s, Bandelier (1883) visited and described the remains of Pecos Pueblo, reporting the surrounding wall to be six feet, six inches high.

The best treatment of the material culture, both historic and prehistoric, is by Kidder (1931-1936, 1932, 1958), who excavated at Pecos Pueblo from 1915 to 1929.

Materials from the site went into the collections of the Museum of New Mexico, Santa Fe, and Phillips Academy, Andover, Massachusetts.

# Laguna Pueblo

FLORENCE HAWLEY ELLIS

## Territory and Environment

The Laguna (lə'gōōnu) people of central New Mexico live in six major villages (fig. 1) of which the political center is Old Laguna (Kawaika) (figs. 2–3) on the knoll of Chichkawaika above the San Jose River 42 miles west of Albuquerque on U.S. Route 66 (see "Pueblos: Introduction," fig. 1, this vol.). The 1972 census figure of 5,400 makes Laguna largest of all the 19 Pueblo tribes of New Mexico except for Zuni.

Laguna speaks Keresan, in a form very similar to that of Acoma.* Acoma-Laguna Keresan is more similar to the Keresan of Zia and Santa Ana than it is to the more easterly dialects of San Felipe, Santo Domingo, and Cochiti, which Lagunas can understand only with great difficulty.

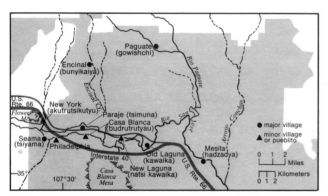

Fig. 1. Laguna towns and part of Laguna Reservation. Laguna names for towns are in parentheses.

## History

Historians usually give 1697, 1698, or 1699 as the date of Laguna's founding (Vélez de Escalante 1856:172; Bancroft 1889:221; Bandelier 1890–1892, 2:294; Twitchell 1911–1917, 1:417, 1914, 1:478; Jenkins 1961:51). In 1680

* No phonemic orthography has been developed specifically for the Laguna dialect of Keresan, but that described for the Acoma dialect ("Acoma," this vol.) is probably very close to what would be needed. Laguna words cited in the *Handbook* are in a normalized nontechnical orthography that omits the many significant features of the language not distinguished in the available imperfect recordings; Boas (1925–1928) has been used as a guide for these transcriptions.

the Pueblo Indians had united long enough to drive the Spaniards from New Mexico. At the reoccupation in 1692, the Pueblos of Cochiti, Cieneguilla, Santo Domingo, and Jemez rebelled against Spanish control, and something over 100 of their people fled to seek haven with the sympathetic Acoma in the Pueblo on their isolated mesa. Some went on to Zuni, but in 1697 the remainder are reported to have left the mesa with some disgruntled Acomas and moved northeast 14 miles to establish Laguna Pueblo a cannon shot from the old lake held by a beaver dam on the San Jose. In 1698 Laguna offered to make peace with the Spaniards, and in 1699 New Mexico's new governor, Pedro Rodríguez Cubero, came with the Franciscan vice-custos to take possession of that Pueblo, Acoma, and Zuni and to confer their patron saints. The date does not pertain to the founding of any of these Pueblos. Laguna's population of 330 in 1707 (table 1) was only half that of Acoma, so a small church was built as a *visita* of Acoma where a massive church had stood since about 1644. By 1782 Laguna population almost equaled that of Acoma, and as the clergy appreciated Laguna's position on the main road across New Mexico, Acoma then was made a *visita* of Laguna (Kubler 1940).

According to references in two genuine documents pertaining to other matters, Laguna apparently received an official grant of land from the Spanish Crown after Domingo Jironza Petriz de Cruzate became governor of New Mexico in 1684, but the paper, like those of all but one of the other New Mexico Pueblos, has been lost

### Table 1. Population, 1707–1870

| | Number | Source |
|---|---|---|
| 1707 | 330 | Thomas 1932 |
| 1744 | 60 families | Thomas 1932 |
| 1765 | 174 families, 600 people | Thomas 1932 |
| | 20 families, 80 people—"settlers" | |
| 1790 | 668 | Arny 1967 |
| 1799 | 116 Indian families | Thomas 1932 |
| | 184 Spanish families | |
| 1808 | 1,007 | Arny 1967 |
| 1809 | 1,022 | Arny 1967 |
| 1850 | 749 | Arny 1967 |
| 1860 | 927 | Arny 1967 |
| 1870 | 927 | Arny 1967 |

(Jenkins 1961). The grant commonly is said to have measured one league out from the church in each direction, but this is not certain. Four square leagues would not have approximated the area Laguna was accustomed to use for farming, hunting, and gathering. A royal decree promised that native peoples who required more land should receive it, and José Aragón, chief justice and war captain for the area, stated that Governors Fernando Chacón, Joaquín del Real Alancaster, Alberto Maynez, and José Manrique authorized the Lagunas to plant as far from the Pueblo as necessary to provide food for their families. In 1872, 26 years after the United States took over New Mexico, Laguna's "grant" was approved by the surveyor general but not by Congress. Laguna filed for confirmation in the U.S. Court of Private Land Claims in 1891 and gained title, but Will N. Tipton demonstrated that their "grant paper" had been composed after 1832 (publication date of a book in Spanish from which some plagiarized sentences were recognized) but before 1856–1859 when it was translated in the surveyor general's office in Santa Fe. These and the other so-called Cruzate grant papers probably had been sold to the frightened Pueblos as substitutes for originals they could not find, so well had they been hidden away generations earlier.

The problem of the precise boundary between Acoma and Laguna brought litigation and even one battle and a legacy of hard feelings. In 1884 a line was made official through the Cañada de la Cruz where north and south drainages meet in the east-west valley of the San Jose River near Seama (Pueblito) and Casa Blanca. At least since the 1500s Lagunas have been using an area that ran east to the Rio Puerco and from Mount Taylor south to Pakwenima Mesa just north of the Rio Salado. The outline was made by shrines on high spots tended by the outside chief and war captains. Laguna's present reservation composed of "grant" and other lands, though one of the two largest held by the Pueblos of New Mexico, covers only a fraction of the old area.

## Prehistory

It is impossible to discuss the prehistory and legendary history of Laguna without considering that of Acoma. The pre-1400 Acoma-Laguna area as defined by tradition, distribution of characteristic pottery types, and historic use reached from Mount Taylor on the north to Alamocita Creek and the Salado on the south, and from the Rio Puerco on the east to the Zuni Mountains on the west. Here a continuous culture succession has been traced back as far as 3000 B.C. when heavy J points were being made by hunters. At about 2000 B.C. little bands characterized by San José culture, a relative of the Pinto or Amargosa segment of western Archaic (Bryan and Toulouse 1943), subsisted in the wide valleys by a combination of widespread plant gathering, hunting, and cultivating some little plots of domesticated but still primitive and miniature-cobbed maize. Succeeding developments ran through the prehistoric Basketmaker and Pueblo periods. Chacoan neighbors inhabited sites in an arc around the northern edges of Mount Taylor and the upper slopes of Mesa Gigante. Mogollon sites lay just to the south and southwest. Until the thirteenth century culture in the Acoma area was reminiscent of that of contemporary Chaco Canyon but also of that of the Pinelawn Valley in the Reserve area of the Upper Gila. In other words, culture in the Acoma area was peripheral to that of both the nearby Anasazi and the Mogollon.

A number of late thirteenth- or early fourteenth-century small Mesa Verde sites can be spotted along both sides of Mount Taylor and in the valley of the Rio Puerco (Davis and Winkler 1959), as well as farther to the east on Jemez Creek and in the Rio Grande valley. Mesa Verde sherds also are found in a small concentration in that portion of the Acoma trash mound or "ash pile" dating from the fourteenth century, and a large Mesa Verde site existed in the drainage of the Salado Wash a few miles northwest of Magdalena on the southern edge of Acoma-Laguna territory. A scattering of Pueblo IV Hopi-type sherds also is found in sites around Mount Taylor, and the heavy proportion of Hopi sherds and the heavy Hopi influence evident in kiva murals at Pottery Mound on the Puerco are evidence of trade or a small influx from the Hopi-Jeddito (also Jadito) district in northern Arizona.

Mera (1935) posed the question of whether the Keresan language and Mesa Verde pottery could be considered to represent parts of one culture, which is not to say that Keresan culture originated in the Mesa Verde (the more likely origin being the San José culture) or that Keresans may not have shared the Mesa Verde with Tanoan neighbors, as has been true in the historic Rio Grande. When the Four Corners area was abandoned in the thirteenth century, the displaced Mesa Verdeans spread and merged with other Pueblo peoples. Pottery proves that some went into the Rio Grande and some into Acoma territory. Hopi tradition derives a portion of their ancestors from the Mesa Verde and some from Canyon de Chelly, a Mesa Verde colony in Pueblo III. When the Pueblo IV site of Kawaika in the Jeddito was abandoned, say the Hopi, its people migrated to Acoma country. Possibly they went to Pottery Mound to merge with Keresans there. Laguna, its native name duplicating that of the Jeddito town (Stephen 1936, 2:1157), had a Hopi Sun clan, but that could have grown from no more than one female Hopi migrant.

That Mesa Verde had been the home of a portion of the ancestors of both Acoma and Laguna is stated in the traditions of both Pueblos. In considering the possibility that Pueblo oral history is a more or less specific account of past movements of a people, it is necessary to look past most of the heavy embroidery resulting from native preoccupation with religion, except as explanations after the fact. Laguna tradition tells of the ancestors, after the

*439*

Southwest Foundation for Audio-Visual Resources, Santa Fe, N.M.
Fig. 2. Laguna Pueblo. Photograph by Peter Dechert, June 1977.

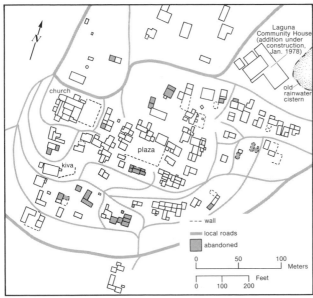

revised from Stubbs 1950:fig. 19.
Fig. 3. Laguna Pueblo.

mythological exit from the underworld home (womb) of Earth Mother, settling on the Mesa Verde. Earth Mother had directed them to go farther south, but a wizard residing on the Mesa promised the people that if they settled on his fertile lands they could expect ample crops because rain dripped whenever he shook his rattle. Forgetting "Our Mother's" orders, the people settled and planted fields. For some time all went so well that the young men neglected their religion and spent their time in gaming. Incensed, "Our Mother" removed the wizard's power to produce rain. Crops wilted from drought. Birds and game animals disappeared; not even a cornhusk or a feather could be found. When a few of the older men attempted some ceremonies they could bring only a small cloud or two into the sky. The people were starving. Earth Mother sent a messenger offering enough food for survival if her children would make prayer offerings, leave the mesa, and go south to the home she had intended.

Packs on their backs and carrying a basket full of ceremonial items, the chastened ancestors started southward. They went along the east slope of Mount Taylor, and at the cliff area called Kwischi they camped. The village of Paguate now marks this spot. When the people saw the lake on the San Jose they did not recognize it as their designated home and so continued southward until they were within a few miles of present U.S. Route 60. Here they stopped for a time (perhaps at the Mesa Verdean site near Magdalena?), one leader deciding he

ELLIS

should take his followers back to the lake but his son preferring to go on southward (Boas 1925-1928; Ellis 1959a).

When the northbound party came in sight of Acoma Mesa and saw smoke rising, one of the head men took his party to see who lived there. He found the Pueblo of Acoma and remained for some time with its people, using his "power" to close cracks in the mesa and remove the too-abundant snakes to a distance. In the meantime the other party of Lagunas-to-be established the fourteenth-century village of Punyana on the western edge of the lake on the San Jose, where the contingent that had stopped at Acoma later joined them. Population was under 300. Some Rio Grande families came seeking new homes, and it was decided to move the village to the knoll of rock above the river on the east side of the lake. Thus Laguna was born. The new two-story houses of stone set in clay mortar made a hollow square with a southwestern entrance where they buried their basketful of sacred objects to make a shrine at the opening into the plaza. A few sherds of late Pinnawa Polychrome variants and affinis Hawikuh glaze-on-white weathering from an unexcavated trash mound on Laguna's south side indicates some fifteenth-century occupation. Later, when Acoma took in some refugees from the Rio Grande, dissensions arose and the refugees moved northward onto Laguna lands, to settle at the hamlet of Seama. By then the Lagunas were establishing summer farm villages, which later became pueblitos occupied year-round.

Acoma claims that their original nucleus was a local people whose culture had developed within the area but that eventually they accepted a party that had come from Mesa Verde after being devastated by illness. This group had stopped for some years in the Chaco to grow corn and then came on via the west side of Mount Taylor. The name and clan of the leader of the party said to have joined Acoma differs from that given by Laguna, but Acoma credits one of their own men with the miracle of the snakes and the mesa cracks. The village of Punyana was established, says Acoma, by one of their dissident leaders whose views on details of the important subject of religious practice led to altercation, so he was given permission to move his family up to the lake. The Rio Grande people who came to borrow Acoma land, they say, were well received and given Acoma land in the Seama district to cultivate.

The site of Punyana, the original Pueblo by the lake, measures 150 by 200 feet and had something over 100 ground-floor rooms. It certainly housed more than one family, even if extended, but whether established by an Acoma-becoming-Laguna leader or a Mesa Verde-becoming-Laguna leader who had lived for a time at Acoma may be a matter of definition.

Only in a very limited area of the Rio Grande and Eastern Periphery area did the Black-on-white pottery characteristic of the thirteenth century last into the fourteenth. The concept of Red ware decorated in black glaze, sometimes with an addition of matte paint, rapidly spread through the White Mountain-Little Colorado and Zuni-Acoma areas and eastward. Tradition gives the only indication of whether sites marked by Laguna-Acoma Glaze types belonged to one Pueblo or the other, but an enumeration of Laguna habitation sites (table 2) identified by matte paint sherds of the eighteenth and early nineteenth centuries shows the spread of farm and ranch locations by single families or groups of families until danger from the Navajo necessitated withdrawal toward the center. New expansion followed termination of raids in the late nineteenth century.

## Culture

### Subsistence

Laguna and Acoma both used dry farming and ditch irrigation during pre- and post-Spanish periods, Laguna specializing in ditch irrigation near Cubero and at Santa Ana (approximately the location of New Laguna) above the Pueblo but also taking some water from the stream below near Mesita. Paraje and Mesita were the sites of dry farms planted before 1850 by men who daily went out to their fields of corn, beans, squash, and wheat from Old Laguna or stayed overnight in dugouts nearby. Permanent villages grew up at both locations between 1880 and 1890 after raids subsided. In the eighteenth century the Apache made the southern Acoma and Laguna areas too dangerous for occupation or herding. The Laguna herding area was further reduced after 1753 when Spanish ranchers settled between the confluence of the Puerco and the San Jose and the upper end of the Montano Grant. The Navajo raided both Spaniards and Pueblos for sheep and horses between 1700 and 1716 but concen-

**Table 2. Approximate Numbers of Laguna Ranch Sites, Pueblitos, and Pueblos known by Pottery Types after A.D. 1700**

|  | 1700s | early 1800s | late 1800s |
|---|---|---|---|
| Central Laguna area | 6 | 6 | 12 |
| Encinal area | 1 | 1 | 1 |
| Mesa Gigante | 2 | 3 | 7 |
| Cañoncito area | 3 | 3 | 8 |
| Paguate area | 6 | 7 | 6 |
| Cebollita and Agua Salado | 12 | 3 | 1 |
| Montano Grant area | 3 | 1 | 2 |
| Puerco area | 15 | 2 | 5 |

SOURCE: Ellis 1959.

Fig. 4. Winnowing wheat at Paguate, one of Laguna's outlying farm villages. Animals trampled the grain on hard-packed adobe threshing floors about 30 feet in diameter and surrounded by stakes or a wooden fence. In preliminary winnowing with pitchforks, as here, the straw and chaff were blown off while the kernels of grain fell to the floor. Photograph probably by G. Wharton James, late 1890s.

trated on repelling the Ute between 1716 and 1768 and did not return to general raiding until 1769. In 1748 the Spanish government ordered Laguna to establish a village at Cebollita (now Seboyeta), a few miles from Paguate, for defense against the Navajo. Sometime before 1769 Pascual Pajarito, Vicente Pajarito, Antonio Paguate, and perhaps Miguel Moquino (of Hopi descent?) apparently bought land on which to farm and herd in the Paguate area (though this earlier had belonged to Laguna by use). Laguna later paid those individuals for the tract, which thus became the Paguate Purchase. In 1779 Lagunas were farming as far north as Cebollita. Raids led to desertion of this northern area in 1782, but by 1800 Spanish families were moving in. The second occupation of Paguate dates from 1816, after Laguna had lost her El Rito land near Mesita to Juan Pino. In 1813, with Spanish encroachments pinching on all sides, a Pueblo officer referred to by the Spaniards as the Laguna cacique but who quite certainly would have been their outside chief, had gone to the retiring alcalde of the area to request a statement listing Laguna holdings. He himself presented papers covering the El Rito, Santa Ana, Gigante, and San Juan areas, all small Laguna settlements. In 1830 Kiyé, a Laguna leader, made a trip to Mexico to protest the granting of Laguna lands to Pino and to complain of the local alcalde who had been preying upon the Indians. Both were removed from

Laguna's doorstep, but Spanish families who offered to aid the Pueblos in fighting off Navajos in return for use of certain pieces of land soon were claiming the "borrowed" lands as their own, a tactic rather common in New Mexico (Jenkins 1961).

Until 1864 night raids stemming from the Navajo stronghold at Big Bead Mesa (dated by tree rings to between 1768 and 1822, Keur 1941) on the northeastern slope of Mount Taylor, from Chacra Mesa at the head of Chaco Canyon, from the San Juan and, eventually, from Canyon de Chelly made life hazardous for herders and cut into the numbers of Laguna sheep, horses, and burros. Occasional Ute raids from the Chama Valley northwest of Santa Fe added to the perils. Spanish settlements of the Montano Grant and the Rio Puerco were abandoned about 1775, occupation of the latter not to be resumed until about 1870 (Thomas 1932:100, 106; Domínguez 1956:254).

Few of the animals stolen were recaptured. Finally, after all of Acoma's animals had been run off in 1861 or 1862 by a large party said to have come down from the San Juan, Col. Kit Carson was ordered to round up all Navajos for removal to Bosque Redondo on the Pecos. Relieved, the Pueblo herders again spread out. Herding areas were assigned by the Laguna governor for each year's use, a conservation measure designed to preserve the grass. The majority of Laguna's herders were men of the Pueblo, but some families hired Navajos or Spanish-Americans and some used Navajo "slaves," children offered by their parents when more were born than could be fed. "Slave" children were raised with children of the Laguna family, worked beside them, and were accorded freedom as adults. Some married into Laguna. Payment to herders, as for cutting corn on Laguna farms, commonly was providing food and giving a sheep to the herder (Ellis 1959).

Four types of herding shelters were used. Available caves could be walled almost to the overhang, thus allowing escape of smoke from a fire. For lambing and when flocks were to be kept in one area for the winter, a small rectangular house was built near a cliff or on a talus slope, which reflected warmth. The most typical herding shelter duplicated the type often used by piñon pickers in late fall expeditions, logs being laid horizontally into a rough horseshoe shape to hold brush or branches upright. The back sometimes was a dry-laid stone wall, which threw out heat all night after a fire was built against it. During periods of frequent raids, herders slept in dugouts and lighted fires only for daytime cooking. A low cone-shaped sweathouse constructed over a shallow pit or dug into a bank of earth was a common adjunct to central herding camps and is still used in the 1970s. Concept and structure may have been borrowed by the Navajo from the Pueblos.

By 1935 Laguna had 52,000 sheep and had become far more pastoral in orientation than any other Pueblo. The once grass-covered land was sadly denuded. As part of a widespread government program to control dangerous erosion, in the next decade the numbers of sheep and cattle permitted were drastically limited, Laguna being allowed only 15,000 sheep and about 1,400 head of cattle.

Early Laguna made considerable use of wild plant foods. The small wild potato, the wild onion, and the yucca fruit referred to as "wild bananas" and gathered far south of the Pueblo were important. Piñon nuts, a staple, were collected in great quantities in late fall of those years when the trees produced and several bushels would be sealed into a large niche in a house wall to use in time of famine. As harness and other necessities became available through traders, the nuts served as a medium of exchange.

## Technology

When times were hard black woolen manta dresses woven by men and decorated with a yellow cord near the bottom were taken to trade to Pueblos in the northern Rio Grande. Small rodlike fetishes supposed to ward off illness were cut from travertine deposits southeast of Laguna and traded. Mica was quarried for window lights. Fine white clay a short distance west of Old Laguna permitted production of excellent pottery. When glaze-paint was dropped, the new matte-paint ware, like the

Smithsonian, NAA.

Fig. 5. Laguna woman carrying a water jar. Though similar in design to an Acoma vessel, it was probably made in Laguna (see Ellis 1966; Frank and Harlow 1974:123). Store-bought shoes here replace the more traditional leggings attached to buckskin moccasins (see fig. 6). Photograph by an unknown photographer, probably 1910-1920.

Zuni-Acoma Ashiwi Polychrome (eighteenth and early nineteenth century) of which it was a variant, was decorated in black manganese paint and yellow ocher, which fired to red. Designs on late Laguna Polychrome (fig. 5) averaged coarser than those of contemporary Acoma. The tempering material that Laguna added in mixing the paste for heavy sturdy vessels was a distinctive crushed diabase from a volcanic dike running just east of the Pueblo and up onto the slopes of Mount Taylor. Temper for more delicate pieces was of crushed sherds, as at Acoma (Ellis 1966). Little Laguna pottery has been produced since the 1940s, but a project in teaching ceramics was subsidized in 1972. A few wicker baskets of red willow shoots were still being made in Paraje in the 1970s.

## Social Organization

In structure the native social organization of Laguna (Boas 1925-1928; Parsons 1920, 1923a, 1939; Ellis 1959a) was much like that of Acoma. The matrilineal clan with a recognized head was important in marriage control and also carried several largely secular functions. The seven original Laguna clans grouped as the Kawashihash, which have been explained as having come from Mesa Verde, are Water, Lizard and Snake together referred to

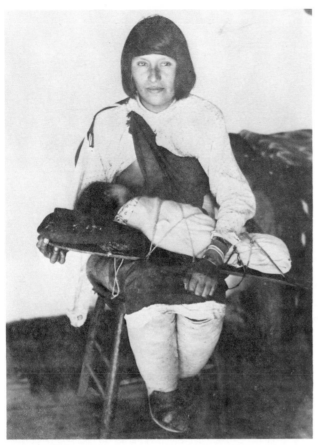

Fig. 6. Laguna woman nursing a baby who is fastened to a flat wooden cradleboard. Babies are placed in a cradleboard within a few days of birth and use the board for about a year; it is placed in a swing at night (Dennis and Dennis 1940:112). Photograph by F.H. Maude, before 1898.

as Earth People, Turkey, Eagle, Antelope, and Sun. Clans introduced by families remembered to have later joined the Laguna nucleus are the Hopi, Navajo, Zuni, and Jemez subgroups of Sun, the Roadrunner and Badger from Zuni, the Bear from Hopi, the Parrot from Zia or Acoma, the Corn, Coyote, and Oak from Acoma, and the Turquoise, sometimes given as from Jemez. These all were represented in a list made in 1939, but deaths, migrations, and intermarriages change such lists through time. Parsons (1923a:234) cautions against implicit faith in statements of clan derivation, some of which conflict, because a clan often is represented in several Pueblos and may have been introduced more than once. The Laguna joking relationship between "sister clans" (not mutually exogamous) is a type of phratry linkage not reported for other Pueblos. The requirement of specific clanship for certain heads of the chayanyi and religious officers of the Pueblo sometimes led to a man's being initiated into a clan that had disappeared, though he still retained membership in the clan of his birth. As in Acoma (contrary to some statements) farmlands were owned by clans. Houseblocks were largely clan oriented in the late nineteenth century (Bloom 1933–1938, 12). In the 1970s Laguna fields are individually owned and houses may be inherited through mother or father but also can be bought and sold like farmland to other citizens of the Pueblo. The maternal family still is important and a feeling of close personal relationship to clan relatives and to "children of the clan," persons whose fathers are of that clan, is obvious. Economic aid, the control of deportment, and certain ceremonial responsibilities were clan duties (Ellis 1959, 1959a).

One of the most important possessions of each clan was its fetish or tsamahiya, the custodianship of which is passed through the matrilineal line of the leading family of the clan. This image is a smooth more or less rodlike stone about a foot long, fashioned by nature except where a groove may be pecked in to demark the head. Face and body are simply painted, the whole being reminiscent of the cylindrical type of Rio Grande kachina images. The female custodian guards the tsamahiya in her storeroom but brings it out for symbolic feeding and rocks it like a baby in her arms. Tsamahiyas and the corn mother fetishes (yapaishe or iyatiko) owned by members of Laguna's formerly existing religious societies and now in the custody of their descendants are lent to existent ceremonialists for periods of prayer (Ellis 1967).

### Religious Organization

Laguna ceremonialism was primarily in the hands of the chayanyi ('shamans'), the religious societies or sodalities often loosely referred to as medicine societies. Each was known for a specialty though all took part in the major events of the ceremonial calendar. Following the typical Keresan pattern, the four principal societies responsible for curing and for insuring regular succession of the seasons were the Flint, Fire, Shahaye (Giant and Ant together), and Shikami, the last so closely bound to the Quirana priestly group that Parsons (1939) links them as the Quirana-Shikami Society. This unit was responsible for the important winter solstice ceremonial. The Koshare, primarily concerned with fertility, as in all Pueblos was important in general village control. As among the Rio Grande Keresans, it cheered the people by clowning and ridiculed the evil spirits to insure general health. The Mountain Lion society was responsible for continuing reproduction of game animals, for the success of Laguna hunters, and for selecting areas in which hunting was permitted in any given year. The Kapina Society, which at Acoma was concerned with warfare, may have been present. The Scalp Takers (opi) were men who had been warriors and in the acts of taking a scalp and the subsequent required purification had become priests whose new "power" was important in gaining supernatural aid for the active warriors and also in helping to insure

Fig. 7. Christmas Dance, 1895–1897. Probably a Comanche Dance, a borrowed dance sometimes performed in conjunction with a maskless Corn Dance during the 4-day period beginning with Christmas Day (Parsons 1939, 1:537). The dancers have painted faces, wear buckskin kilts and eagle feather headdresses, and carry bows and arrows (cf. Lummis 1916:161–165 on an 1884 Christmas Day dance). The blanketed men at right form the chorus. Photograph by Elizabeth Snyder.

precipitation. If, as some informants state, a Snake Society once existed, its functions probably were concentrated on weather control and curing, as elsewhere. The leader of a specific religious society, as at Hopi, Acoma, and Zia, must come from a given clan or at least be a "child of the clan." If males in those categories were lacking, the officers could arrange clan adoption.

Persons who had been struck by lightning were known as Shiwana, a designation also used for spirits of the dead who were believed to have become supernatural cloud beings. The lightning Shiwana used their new "power" for curing but, like the Hopi "doctors" of the twentieth century, were not organized.

Every young person of Laguna was initiated into the kachina cult. Laguna's original kachina group, the gowapiyautsi, danced hemish and kaiya (mixed kachina). Later, copying Zuni, the wayush was organized to dance duck kachina. The shtoroga also apparently came from Zuni, though when is unknown. In the late nineteenth century the Chakwena kachina cult was introduced by a Zuni migrant, but under sponsorship of a local faction. A definite line between the chayanyi and the kachina groups was recognized at Laguna, as in all the Pueblos, though each of the chayanyi groups owned two masks to be worn in initiations and sometimes in dances.

Parsons (1939) was told that the kachina dancers formerly had several houses, these probably being rooms in which masks were kept. She also learned of six structures with mural-decorated walls used by the chayanyi societies, and Ellis (1959a, 1974) was told of six small kivas. The Fire Society, which cured by fire, and the Shahaye, which cured by use of heated stones, shared one. Two big kivas were the centers for emergence of alternating dance groups, as in the Rio Grande Pueblos.

*Political Organization*

The original officers of the Laguna, according to legend, were Hadjamunyi Kayokai 'holding (i.e., remembering) the prayer stick' (or a variant 'broken prayer stick'; Boas 1925–1928, 1:288) and Kamagashe 'white hands', who led the people down from the northwest. The title and position of Hadjamunyi Kayokai were conferred on a series of successive town chiefs who served for life as the overall leader and head of all native religion, including kachina affairs. As the tiyamunyi hochanyi 'leader chief' (who led the people out of the underworld) and representative of Earth or Corn Mother, he neither went to war nor could be selected from the ranks of the Scalp Society (Ellis 1959, 1974, 1974a). He acted as Father to the kachinas when they danced but his major function was offering prayers for his people and for general fertility. The leader of the closely associated Flint and Koshare societies and the leader of the Quirana-Shikami, together, conducted the installation of this chief priest whom anthropologists commonly refer to as cacique, though Laguna itself has continued the older Spanish use of this originally Arawakan term to cover all native leaders. Less commonly he has been spoken of as the house chief. His office was a second floor room on the north side of the Old Laguna plaza.

Some say that the original Hadjamunyi Kayokai was of the Water clan and that officers succeeding him must be from that clan, the position going to the brother or to the sister's son of the last incumbent. Others believe that the first choice for replacement should have been his own son, "a child of" his father's clan into which he could be initiated if clanship were that important. Second choice then would be the sister's son. The idea of succession to office through the paternal line could have resulted from acculturation.

Kamagashe was the prototype for the dzatyau hochanyi 'outside chief', who was nominated by the council without regard to clan or family but probably came from the Scalp Takers. He must be strong, swift, and brave, for he was responsible for the security of all the Laguna area and for placing offerings on the boundary shrines and certain others such as the top of Mount Taylor. His first and second assistants represented and were known respectively by the names of the Older and the Younger of the Twin War Gods, though in the historic period these assistants came to be designated war captains. The outside chief and assistants made up the outside chief's unit, whose duties were guarding ceremonial societies in retreat, punishing witches, and seeing to general protection and peace within the Pueblo.

The hunt chief (shayaika), responsible for reproduction of game animals, fashioned small animal images of pollen and "planted" them in the mountains even as corn is planted in fields. He was leader of the Mountain Lion Society.

The secular offices (governor, two lieutenants, *capitanes, fiscales*) imposed in 1620 by Spanish decree for all native peoples in their colonies were filled through appointments by the religious hierarchy. Such officers were primarily front men for the priests and served unpaid terms of one year as a citizen's duty.

## The Laguna Break

Disruption from a combination of acculturation and inner stresses led to the Laguna break, which reached its climax in the late 1870s. Laguna's position on a highway and within an area being settled by Spanish ranchers in the 1700s and by Anglos after 1850, plus the immediate presence of several progress-minded Protestant Whites who moved into the Pueblo itself, provided tinder for an explosion further fed by personal ambitions and factional

Mus. of N.M., Santa Fe.
Fig. 8. Laguna group portrait, taken in a New Mexico photographic studio in the 1880s. The pottery and the various weapons were probably studio props, but the dress is typical of the time. The men wear bandanas, wrapped buckskin leggings belted at the top with narrow woven bands, cotton shirts and trousers, shell and silver jewelry, and at least one wears a decorated leather bandolier. The women wear dark mantas over cotton blouses, woven belts, and back aprons or blankets. Silver ornaments worn down the side of the manta, often consisting of silver quarters looped together, were in vogue (woman at far left). Photograph by Ben Wittick.

446

competition. The Rev. Samuel Gorman had taken residence in Laguna as a missionary in 1851 and stayed approximately 10 years. In 1868 Walter G. Marmon came to work on a boundary survey for Laguna Pueblo and in 1871 was appointed government school teacher to supplant the Spanish-American teacher whose school was private, requiring pay by the parents. Robert G. Marmon, Walter's brother, arrived in 1872 as surveyor and trader, and George H. Pratt (Pradt), also a surveyor, at about the same time. The Marmons' cousins—John, Elgin, and Kenneth Gunn—then settled at Laguna, John establishing a flour mill. Pratt, the Gunns, and the Marmons all married Laguna women, their families forming a small colony on the northeastern edge of the village. Walter's wife later attended Carlisle while Ohio relatives by marriage cared for their children. Dr. John Menaul moved into Laguna as missionary and successor to Marmon as teacher when the Presbyterian church took over the school in 1875; he remained until 1887 (Bloom 1933-1938, 12:359, 373-376; Parsons 1939, 2:888; Ellis 1959, 1974, 1974a). These men all were sincerely dedicated to progress for Laguna. From their Protestant viewpoint the long-standing combination of old Pueblo beliefs and Roman Catholicism, supported by the native religious-governmental hierarchy, was stultifying. The Marmons set themselves to writing a constitution, the first to be adopted by any Pueblo, its text modeled after that of the United States. By 1872 Laguna was voting for its governor. Respect for the Marmons is seen in each being elected to serve one term as Laguna governor, an unprecedented arrangement. Pratt was initiated into the Chakwena religious society, which he explained to Bourke as having been organized for mutual assistance and such Pueblo improvements as better ventilation of houses and the building of water closets, a new touch in the traditional beneficence of kachinas!

The rapid changes inflamed the insecurity and factionalism smoldering since early in the century with charges, countercharges, and accusations of witchcraft. According to the Water clansman who still ritually "feeds" and cares for the sacred canes of office once belonging to the hunt and the town chiefs (each cane with an equal-armed cross cut into the head, the town chief's shortened in length by scrapings from the tip being taken for "medicine"), Guwesiwa of the Water clan was the last real town chief. Old, unmarried, and increasingly distressed by the growing disturbances, which he attributed to witchery, before 1850 he "gave himself as a sacrifice to the witches," permitting himself to die because in native belief this should appease their hunger and save his people. The subsequent confusion did not allow the choice of a successor, so the outside chief took over certain of town chief's duties. That outside chief probably was Miguel Correo (Korio) who began acting as Kachina Father at this time (Ellis 1959a). He was old and soon his eldest son,

Lorenzo (Kayotiye or Gaiyuwe of Lizard clan) learned his songs and took his place. Although Parsons (1923a:255, 271) states that Taiowityue or Taiyuwaidyu (or Meyo—Boas 1925-1928, 1:188) of Lizard clan was the last town chief, her informant being his daughter aged over 70 years, Ellis (1959) could find no one, not even an elderly Lizard clansman occupying the houseblock indicated as that of Taiowityue, who recognized this name, their opinion being that it was a mistake for Kayotiye. As a member of the Flint Society as well as a Scalp Taker, he actually was ineligible for the position of town chief but could have served as outside chief. Like his father, he apparently combined some of the duties of the two offices, a concession to exigency. In the census of 1851 his younger brother, Francisco (Keunai or Kakaiye) then 60 and a member of Fire Society, signed himself "first cacique." Lagunas remember him as a Kachina Father.

Laguna's progressive or pro-White faction was led by Kwimé (Luis Serracino), an energetic individual with ambitions enlarged after trips outside the Pueblo, including seven years of education by priests in Durango, Mexico. His position as leader of the powerful Quirana-Shikami combination was topped only by that of the town and outside chiefs. In 1860 or 1870 Kwimé sponsored introduction of the Chakwena cult through an emigrant from Zuni, "stealing the masks" (probably copying them without ritually arranged rights) because Zuni did not want to part with a set. Many Lagunas ridiculed these masks as ugly, spat upon them, and whispered of their power for witching. Influenced by Walter G. Marmon, his daughter's husband, and noting the accelerated shift away from the old power structure, in the 1870s Kwimé embraced Protestantism, though without giving up his Quirana-Shikami or Chakwena affiliations. The Chakwena cult and Protestantism are said to have been major factors in the final break.

While Robert G. Marmon was governor, the two big kivas were torn down. At the threat that the Roman Catholic church also was about to be demolished, Hamí, a Shahaye shaman and a Shiwana and at the same time official *sacristán*, ritually cleansed himself, prayed, and planted himself in its doorway, daring the crowd to pull the structure down over him. Then, having won his point, he set himself to its repair, for some say burros had been kept in it. Later, as governor, he made several trips to Washington and received the Abraham Lincoln cane for his Pueblo. By the late 1870s the conservative and larger faction decided it could bear no more. Weeping, the Korio brothers and the other ceremonialists packed their ritual equipment and the old image of the patron saint, temporarily cached them at a shrine on Mount Taylor, and later carried them to the new homes they established in Mesita. Under Governor Marmon's orders, the image and some of the altars later were retrieved, the image to go back into the church but the altars to be destroyed.   *447*

Kwimé was left with what some still speak of as "the stolen leadership of Laguna."

In 1878 or 1879 approximately 40 of the displaced Lagunas decided to attempt a move to Tiwa-speaking Sandia Pueblo just north of Albuquerque on the Rio Grande. But Isleta, also Tiwa-speaking and just south of Albuquerque, offered them land in exchange for the benefits of Laguna masked dances (Chakwena, duck, and "dark kachina"), the presence of its religious societies, and the "power" believed to emanate from the associated religious equipment (Parsons 1928). Since the Spanish period, Isleta's kachina dances had been unmasked (Harvey 1963). Whether Isleta ever had had more than the single religious society known as the Town Fathers is debatable.

The displaced Lagunas accepted Isleta's offer, but stress was inevitable, and within a few years a majority of the migrants had returned to Mesita. The Laguna Flint, Fire, and Shahaye societies, with only a few members each, combined forces in a sodality that came to be known as the Laguna Fathers and has continued to exist. Francisco Korio had to remain in Isleta to care for the masks, which they had promised never to take away. As a result, he and his successors have acted as Kachina Father for the now intermarried remnant of the Laguna colonists (about 70 in 1928) in Isleta and at the same time for the returnees in Mesita. Isleta pottery long had been plain red-brown, but a few Isleta women learned to make the Laguna-like black, white, and red pottery that was sold from Isleta until the 1940s.

Within a few years after the break, the Chakwena chief at Old Laguna realized that a ceremonial vacuum existed and introduced the Zuni Koyemshi as a sacred clown (mud-head) substitute for the missing Koshare. An Antelope clansman was selected to serve as Kachina Father, as in Acoma, and went to Acoma for installation rituals.

Interest in the revival of ceremonials has increased, although the religious hierarchy never was replaced and Laguna has made a point of adapting to the contemporary scene. The old constitution was revised and then replaced in 1949, and that one was revised in 1958. In the 1970s the paid, annually elected secular officials met in a handsome community house set near the old walled surface reservoir where the feet of women bearing water jars once wore deep trails in the rock. After uranium was discovered on the reservation in the early 1950s, two mines were opened. In 1972, 350 Pueblo residents were employed in mining operations, and approximately 160 others had work with Ominetec, a firm that opened a plant for manufacturing electronic products on the reservation. Other sources of employment in the 1970s included the Laguna Rock Enterprise, the Community Action Program of the Department of Health, Education, and Welfare, with its various components, the Laguna Housing Program, and a number of tribally funded programs.

Many of Laguna's old structures still exist in the 1970s, and the overall view of this Pueblo set on a hill crowned with a small church remains beautiful. Through the Housing Program (financed by the Department of Housing and Urban Development) a number of existing homes have been renovated or remodeled and 205 new houses were constructed by 1975. An elementary school operated by the Bureau of Indian Affairs, a public junior-senior high school, an out-patient clinic operated by the Division of Indian Health of the Department of Health, Education, and Welfare, an outdoor swimming pool, and several commercial facilities are located on the reservation. Many high school graduates have taken advantage of the full college scholarships funded by the tribe (Smith 1966:11-114). More than half (2,900 in 1975) of Laguna's members live in the six major villages of the 420,000-acre reservation; 2,500 live elsewhere. Less than one-fourth depend on agriculture, cattle, or sheep and the transition to wage economy is alleviated in part by the public works program provided by tribal funds. Laguna has close-knit colonies in Albuquerque, Holbrook, Los Angeles, and Richmond, California, as well as on the reservation.

Thanks primarily to the energy of its leaders and to its mineral wealth, all but a small proportion of which is set aside for investment and improvements rather than being distributed to individuals, Laguna in the 1970s stands as the wealthiest and probably the most acculturated of all the New Mexico Pueblo tribes.

## Synonymy†

The name of Laguna Pueblo is from that of the Spanish mission, San José de la Laguna 'Saint Joseph of the Lake' and was conferred after the formal submission of the Pueblo to Governor Cubero on July 4, 1699 (Domínguez 1956:183). The name refers to the beaver pond that was on the San Jose River to the west of the Pueblo until the dam was washed out in 1855 (Harrington 1916:541). According to Bandelier (1890-1892, 1:189) the shortened name Laguna was in use as early as 1702. Garbled forms in non-Spanish nineteenth-century sources include Lagouna, La Laguna, Layma, Saguna, and Seguna.

The Keresan name for the Pueblo has not been recorded phonemically in the Laguna dialect, but it is similar if not identical to Acoma ḱáwàikʰa 'Laguna Pueblo' (Miller 1965:210, 226); cf. Santa Ana ḱáwàikʰA. Acoma also has ḱáwàikaṁé 'Laguna Indian(s)' (Miller 1965:202). The alleged Laguna self-designations ko-stété, for the Pueblo (Loew 1879:339), and sitsimé, for the people (Gatschet 1882:263), are obscure.

Names in other languages that appear to be borrowings of the Keresan name are Jemez ḱeowe'egi'i or

---

† This synonymy was prepared by Ives Goddard; uncredited forms are from Harrington (1916:539-541), who gives additional variants, or from anonymous sources.

*kʸówegʸíʔ* (Curtis 1907–1930, 14:261, phonemicized) and Hopi Kawaika (Stephen 1936, 2:1157); Jemez has *kʸówe* 'Laguna Indian' (pl. *kʸóweš*). Names with reference to the beaver pond or lake are Taos pɔ-xwíæ-ba 'water stand-up at' (Curtis 1907–1930, 14:261–262, normalized), Tewa *ṗo·kʷîn diwe* 'at the lake' and *ṗo·to iwe* 'where water is in (something), i.e., dammed up', Zuni *kʔana łanʔa* 'big lake' (Dennis Tedlock, personal communication 1977), and Navajo *Tó Łáanii* 'much water people' (Robert W. Young, personal communication 1977; Hoijer 1974:258; Haile 1950–1951, 2:176; Franciscan Fathers 1910:128). A Navajo name *Naatoohó* or *Naatoohí* sometimes given as 'Laguna Indian' (Hoijer 1974:261; Haile 1950–1951, 2:176) is properly the name of the Isleta people (Robert W. Young, personal communication 1977; Haile 1950–1951, 1:140, 2:172; Franciscan Fathers 1910:128). Other names are Tewa *kunkʷa·ge ówînge* 'skunk-bush bank Pueblo' and perhaps tunkʷage (Curtis 1907–1930, 14:260, normalized) and Isleta kö̱hweaí (Curtis 1907–1930, 14:261, normalized), or kŭhkweaí, and *bíerʔai* (C.T. Harrington 1920:42), beside *bieríde* 'Laguna Indian' (William Leap, personal communication 1977).

## Sources

Sources to be consulted on Laguna are few. Boas (1925–1928, 1:276–300) summarized several aspects of Laguna ceremonial organization and religion as an appendix to a volume of English translations of mythological and other texts collected at Laguna in 1919–1921; the Keresan texts are given by Boas (1925–1928). Parsons (1920, 1923a) fortunately captured in her notes much of what information remained on religious observances still existent in Laguna and on family and group relationships about 1920. Parsons (1928) also wrote on the Laguna break, and her two-volume work on Pueblo religion (1939) puts the whole into a comparative frame of reference. The most extensive historic and overall coverage for Laguna and its colonies is found in the papers by Ellis (1959, 1959a, 1974, 1974a) and Jenkins (1961) written in support of Laguna's land claim. These also cover almost all the extant data on hunting, gathering wild plant foods, and collecting minerals and other substances that formerly figured in their economics, as well as the great dependence of this people on sheep during the historic period. Archeology, recurrent Navajo raids, and disputes between Acoma and Laguna, and the increasing encroachments of Spaniards and then of Anglos are summarized. Further archeological work on Laguna's old ash piles is very much needed to improve historical knowledge of the controversial date of first occupation of the knoll and the origins and early trade contacts of this tribe.

# Acoma Pueblo

VELMA GARCIA-MASON

## Language

Acoma (ˈăkəmu) is one of two Western Keresan dialects; it is mutually intelligible with Laguna Keresan but is relatively slower, phonetically longer, and morphophonemically different from the Laguna dialect in some important items of vocabulary.* Acoma Keresan (ʔáˑk̓ùˑ́mé cê·ni) is spoken as the first language by about 95 percent of the population resident on the reservation. Nearly all the inhabitants also speak English. Most elders speak Spanish as a third language and can also comprehend other Keresan languages.

Two varieties of Acoma Keresan can be distinguished. Archaic Keresan is more sophisticated and grammatically more complex; it is used in songs, prayers, oratory, philosophical discussions, and legends and mythology. Contemporary Keresan shows more influence from other languages and permits code-switching with English and the use of Spanish loanwords. English, Spanish, and other Keresan languages are used for communication with non-Acomas.

## Territory

The Acoma tribe resides in its aboriginal location 60 miles west of Albuquerque, New Mexico (see "Pueblos: Introduction," fig. 1, this vol.). The reservation is composed of three primary residential communities—ʔáˑk̓u (Acoma, the old village on the mesa, figs. 1-2), tíˑč̓híná (a

* Italicized Acoma words in the *Handbook* have been rewritten by Ives Goddard to conform to the standard technical alphabet. The values of the symbols correspond to the phonemic system of Miller (1965:7-20) as follows. The consonants are: plain stops *p, t* (dental), *t̓* (lamino-palatal), *k* (for Miller's b, d, dʸ, g); aspirated stops *pʰ, tʰ, t̓ʰ, kʰ* (for p, t, t̓, k); plain affricates *c* (dental), *č* (palatal), *ç* (retroflex) (for z, ž, z); aspirated affricates *cʰ, čʰ, çʰ* (for c, č, ç); other plain consonants *s* [sθ], *š, ṣ; m, n; r* (alveolar flap); *w, y, h, ʔ;* glottalized consonants *p̓, t̓, t̓ʸ, k̓; c̓, č̓, ç̓; š̓* [sθ̓], *š̓, ṣ̓; m̓, n̓; r̓; w̓, y̓*. The vowels are *i, e, a* (low front), *u, ɨ* (high to higher-mid central or back unrounded; Miller's ə); all also occur long (*i·*, etc.). The tonal accents are high (v́), falling (v̂), glottal (v̌) and unaccented (v). Acoma forms are from Wick R. Miller (personal communication 1977) or from published or anonymous sources; some dialect differences are represented, and the tones have probably not been recorded consistently. Where complete information on tone, length, glottalization, and vowel quality was not available the Acoma words are not italicized but written in an approximate nontechnical orthography. In 1977 the Acoma tribe was developing a standard orthography for general practical use by the community.

farming village in 'north valley', which was renamed Acomita by the Spanish), and tíˑč̓iyâ·ma (a farming village in 'north pass', which was renamed McCartys by the Atchison, Topeka, and Santa Fe Railway). While ʔáˑk̓u was the original permanent village of the tribe, it has become more of a ceremonial home in the twentieth century. However, there are a handful of families who by official appointment or on a voluntary basis annually alternate in residence on the mesa. Almost every family on the reservation maintains an individual house or clan home at ʔáˑk̓u.

At an early time there were several farming camp sites along the valleys in the hills within about 15 miles of ʔáˑk̓u (Arizona State Museum 1968). Ruins along the dry riverbeds indicate that some of these were abandoned; only those along the San Jose River have survived to the present. Since the late sixteenth century these camps gradually acquired more permanent residential structures, perhaps in reaction to the encroachment of early Spanish colonizers upon the village of ʔáˑk̓u. By 1700 these were obviously home sites, for the Spanish missionaries divided them by an arbitrary boundary line into two farming villages, a division later followed by the U.S. Geological Survey and the American school authorities. Acomita and McCartys, therefore, each has a Catholic church with adjoining parish hall, and until 1975 each had a Bureau of Indian Affairs school.

Within these two villages there are 16 primary reference points that identify subvillage areas (fig. 3), nine within Acomita and seven within McCartys. Several further subdivisions with the subvillages labeled tíˑč̓híná and tíˑč̓iyâ·ma are identified by descriptive terms that are directional and depend on the location of the speaker. All the subvillages except kanípa, ʔáˑš̓íʔíˑni, and Sky-Line village are thought of as traditionally founded horticultural settlements. All these are residential only. They share a common government housed in a single tribal administrative office, one Bureau of Indian Affairs elementary–junior high school (since 1975), a U.S. post office (since 1977), a cooperative food store, a community recreation facility, and a community library. All these are centrally located to encourage the preservation of a single reservation community. In 1977 there were no trading posts, gas stations, motels, hotels, or restaurants on the reservation. In 1978 the tribe planned to operate a museum and a Public Health Service hospital on the

Fig. 1. Acoma Mesa and Pueblo. Photograph by Dick Kent, Sept. 1967.

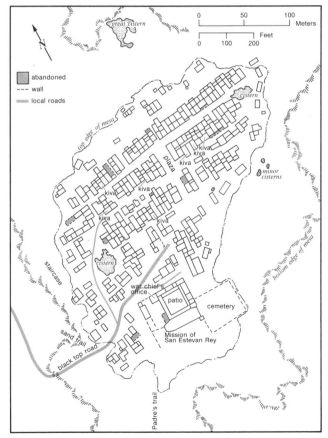

revised from Historic Amer. Buildings Survey, Natl. Park Service, map for 1965.
Fig. 2. Acoma Pueblo.

reservation. The tribal administration provides four main types of services for the community: education (Community Education, library, Parent-Child Development, Headstart); social services (Human Services Delivery, Alcohol Treatment and Education, Health Management Program, Community Health Representative Program); community services (Consumer Education, Public Works, Home Improvement, Postal Services, Census, Client Services); and economic development (Visitor's Center, Food Cooperative, Vendors, Game Warden). There are also legal and law enforcement services provided within the community.

Traditionally and legally, only the tribal members hold residency or property claims to the Acoma land held in trust by the federal government. Ninety-nine percent of the enrolled population lives on the reservation. One percent are known to have married off-reservation or to have moved to other states, particularly California and Oklahoma. Some of these individuals were participants in the federal government relocation program of the 1950s. Interracial marriages are permitted but discouraged; for example, members of other races are barred from participating in or observing religious and ceremonial events. Intertribal marriages have been permitted and practiced, and the non-Acoma Indian in-law may be given rights to participate in and observe ceremonial events. Such a person may be accepted as an honorary member of the tribe, but not as an enrolled member.

There is daily open social contact with the non-Indian peripheral communities. The cities of Grants and Albuquerque serve the reservation with their shopping conveniences. Approximately 30 miles west of the reservation are Anaconda Uranium and Kerr-McGee Mining industries, which serve as the tribe's major sources of labor employment. In the more immediate vicinity are several Mexican-American communities, chiefly San Fidel, Cubero, Chief Rancho, and Los Cerritos, which provide gasoline service stations, grocery stores, trading-post operations, and postal services. Frequent interactions also take place with several non-Indian employees and non-Indian missionaries on the reservation, and with visiting non-Indian tourists.

Traditionally and culturally, Acoma like all other Keresan groups remains a closed system and maintains the right to keep the knowledge of the culture within.

The Acoma Reservation consists of 245,672.03 acres, which includes 94,196 acres of the original Spanish land grant patented by the United States in November 1877 and its surrounding aboriginal land, which was restored by U.S. executive order and established by public law in May 1928 (45 Stat. 717); 320 acres of allotted land; and 5.79 acres of the federally owned school site. Within the boundaries, there are 467.27 acres that are not owned by or in trust for the tribe—258.60 acres belonging to the Atchison, Topeka, and Santa Fe Railway Company and 208.67 acres in the Santa Ana grant.

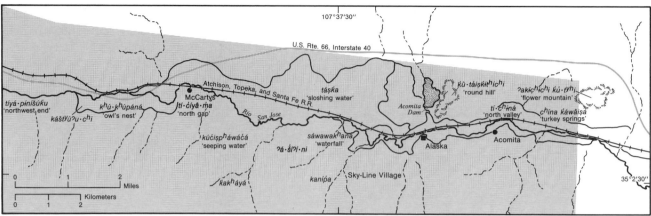

Fig. 3. Part of Acoma Reservation and named Acoma subvillage areas with English translations where known.

## Environment

Topographically, the reservation is characterized by mesas, deep-rimmed valleys, stark escarpments, arroyos, and rolling hills. The northwest portion rises toward Mount Taylor, one of the highest peaks in New Mexico. The northern landscape consists of basaltic lava flows.

The altitude ranges from 6,000 to 8,000 feet. Precipitation is only about 10 inches during the average year; July, August, and September provide more than 50 percent of the rainfall. The annual mean temperature is 51.5°F., with the highest recorded temperature 103° (in August) and the lowest 20° (in December). The growing season averages 118 days of frost-free weather from May 15 to September 15.

In land use, proportionately, there are 17,000 acres of dry farmlands; 2,000 acres of irrigated farmlands (a total of 145,000 acres has been determined as irrigable land from low intensity soil surveys); 3,000 acres of timberland; and approximately 250,000 acres of open grazing land. In 1970 the grazing capacity was estimated to be 21,052 animal-unit months. In 1969 actual animal-unit months grazed was 24,382. The principal commercial species on the timberland is ponderosa pine, with Douglas fir also important. The main noncommercial species are piñon and juniper. There are also sparse oak trees, and aspen grow in the wooded pine areas. Sparse grasses consist of blue grass, Indian rice grass, galleta, sand drop, and mesa drop seed grass. Within the San Jose valley are tamarisk, willow, and cottonwood. The dry farmland produces crops primarily of corn, squash, and melons. The irrigable lands on the reservation are generally located on the laterals of the San Jose River. Water for irrigation is obtained from three diversion dams on the river and from Acomita Lake, a reservoir of an estimated 650 acre-feet storage from the San Jose River flow. With a growing season of approximately 160 days, this valley produces alfalfa, oats, wheat, corn, chili, melon, squash, vegetables; and less extensively, fruits—mainly apples, peaches, plums, pears, cherries, and apricots. Because of the limited basin, residents depend primarily on surface water for agricultural needs. Domestic water supplies are from wells drilled into the San Jose River basin. Water quality is exceedingly hard with a high concentration of iron sulfate and other minerals. On the range, several wells have been drilled for watering livestock. The economic uses of the environment include the tourist industry, the recreation potential on the lake, farming, and to a lesser extent, commercial timber. There are also known deposits of pottery clay, obsidian, coal, building stones, lava rock, and limestone on the reservation.

## Culture

Acoma Pueblo, traditionally classified as one of the 19 Pueblo tribes in New Mexico, shares with other Pueblos the basic architectural (fig. 4) and art designs, food preparation, dress style (fig. 5), music, and dances. With the other Keresan-speaking groups it shares a language and a basic religious system, political system (fig. 6), and kinship (clan) system. The differences occur in variations of these and in dialect difference. In terms of social structure, the differences are more pronounced. Acoma emphasizes clanship (while the Eastern Keresans stress the moiety system) and follows a matrilineal extended family kinship system. The architectural style of the kiva among the Eastern Keresans is circular, while Acoma uses the rectangular design (fig. 7). The physical locale of the original village is also unique because it sits fortresslike atop the high mesa. Acoma lacks certain Spanish influences present among the Eastern Pueblos, a difference attributable to its southwesternmost location and its unique historical experiences.

The Pueblo vies with Hopi in claiming to be the oldest continuously inhabited village in the United States. This occupation of at least 1,000 years has been confirmed archeologically largely through pottery-sherd analysis (Ruppé 1953). Unique among Pueblos, the physical

452

Fig. 4. Interior of Acoma house about 1900. Pottery (*vû·ni*) includes several named types: water jars (*vû·ni* in narrower usage) of various sizes holding up to several gallons, vase-shaped bottles and canteens (*spú·ná*), and bowls and plates (*ẃáišĺâ·ṅi*). Several pots, the largest of which is painted with a parrot design typical of Acoma, are displayed on the floor in various stages of completion. Bowl at left contains implements (probably gourd chips) used for shaping the pottery, trimming the necks, and making indentations. Pictures and utensils hang from walls and are stored on shelves; bowl at extreme right probably contains cornmeal. Photograph by William H. Jackson.

location of *ʔá·ǩu* has contributed to the theory that it forms a cultural bridge between the Western Pueblos and the Eastern or Rio Grande Pueblos; for example, it is considered an important agent affecting the character of differences in social structure between the Eastern and the Western Pueblos (Eggan 1950:247; Fox 1967).

## External Relations

Adhering to the philosophy of tribal sovereignty, the tribe has its own system of government with complete tribal jurisdiction over the entire reservation. Because of the trust land status, technically, the secretary of the interior reserves the right to approve any sale or leasing of land. Except for the tribally contracted programs, the federal government maintains control over all other federal programs. There is no state jurisdiction over the reservation.

Under its intertribal activities, Acoma has been a recognized participating member of the All-Pueblo Council since 1680. Beyond its major political lobbying activities, the All-Pueblo Council has full control over the

Fig. 5. Woman's embroidered woolen dress (see "Nambe Pueblo," fig. 5, this vol.). bottom, Detail from lower left corner showing diamond twill weave of black cloth woven by men and embroidery applied by the women in blue homespun wool and red yarn ravelings of commercial bayeta cloth (Douglas 1939a:156). With the exception of Acoma, Pueblo men also did the embroidery (Douglas 1939a:154; Tanner 1968:52). Length about 120 cm, width about 36 cm; collected before 1939.

453

Calif. Histl. Soc., Los Angeles: Title Insurance Coll.
Fig. 6. Governor Eusebius (third from left) and staff, probably the 2 lieutenants and 3 sheriffs at door of church. The governing structure is described in fig. 18. Photograph probably by G. Wharton James, about or just before 1900.

Mus. of N.M., Santa Fe.
Fig. 7. Roof-top entrance (ladder at left) to an Acoma kiva. Unlike the detached circular kivas that are the common type among the Eastern Pueblos, the Acoma kivas are incorporated into the houseblocks. (See Kidder 1958:266-278 for comparative discussion of modern Pueblo kivas.) Roofs of lower floors of houseblocks serve as work and storage areas. Window at right is of selenite. Photograph by Ben Wittick, 1880s or possibly early 1890s.

administration of several federally contracted programs offered to Acoma, for example, impact aid and Johnson-O'Malley Act programs for school systems, higher education assistance, consumer education, and administration grants from Administration for Native Americans in the Department of Health, Education, and Welfare. With its immediately neighboring tribe, Laguna Pueblo, Acoma has shared two major joint ventures, the development of a junior and senior high school and of local hospital facilities. Although historically there were sensitivities that grew out of land boundary and land-lease disputes, these two Pueblo tribes maintain a good working relationship.

## Prehistory

The Acoma ancestors comprise four groups of people, one of which had inhabited the Pueblo since early prehistoric times and another who came in around A.D. 1300 from the Mesa Verde area. The other two are believed to have migrated from the Cebollita region (Ruppé 1953). Prehistorically, Acoma province included the occupations within a broad area from the Rio Grande west to the El Morro area. There is evidence that during the thirteenth century, including the period of the Great Drought, 1276-1299, the province received a number of migrations. Many ruins of villages formerly inhabited by the Acoma tribe are found in the Los Vetedos and Los Pilares areas.

The sequence derived from the Cebollita excavations at the Los Pilares and Los Vetedos sites extends from a Pre-Pueblo I horizon to an Early Pueblo IV horizon (Dittert and Ruppé 1951:122-123). The earliest horizon in the region was discovered below the floors of a small Pueblo built in a cave shelter. Materials recovered included a seated, full-flexed burial, basin metate, and some brownware sherds (Dittert and Ruppé 1951:119). This fits into the Basketmaker III period, about A.D. 400-700 (Daifuku 1952:191; G.R. Willey 1966:202).

Pueblo I sites, about A.D. 700-900, tend to be on slopes and benches, and more or less on "mouths of tributary canyons." They generally are single-room structures located singularly or scattered in groups. During the transition period from Pueblo I to II, there was a pattern of movements to mesa tops and valleys with changes from single house to contiguous rooms. From before Pueblo III until its end, sites were located around the edges of canyon floors. Sherd contents showed the usual Northern Gray Corrugated, Tularosa Black-on-white, and Saint John's Polychrome assemblage, plus approximately 30 percent of brownwares. The transition from Pueblo III to IV, about A.D. 1300-1700, is indicated by the appearance of Pinedale and Four Mile Polychrome in the upper levels. Masonry was adobe (Dittert and Ruppé 1951:121). By correlating the features in the transition of Pueblo II to III to the present Acoma Pueblo, one can conclude that the first migration of these people took place at this time. Then also, by a correlation of the features of the late Pueblo III with those of modern Acoma Pueblo, there is reason to believe that the second set of peoples migrated at this time. Acoma pottery corresponds to this second migration. The defensive tactics of the Pueblo also correspond to this period. In late Pueblo III, there was also a characteristic use of stones for construction in contrast to the predominant use of adobe in mid-Pueblo III.

Around A.D. 1200 Acoma pottery became distinctive from that made by Zuni in its use of volcanic stone temper. Evidence of dry farming indicates the use of Paradise Valley with occupations in Acoma Pueblo, Cebollita Mesa, and what is now Seama village (Laguna Reservation). There were several main villages identified—Acomita, McCartys, Locomotive Rock, Spider Spring, Cebolla, and Questa. These were primarily farming and herding camps since the old Pueblo village was used as the home area.

## History

The earliest documented history of ʔá·ku begins in 1539, when Fray Marcos de Niza returned from his expedition to report a "Kingdom of Hacus" to the viceroy of New Spain (Mexico). Although de Niza had not visited ʔá·ku himself, he heard about it through a message sent to him by Estevan, a Negro servant who was probably the first non-Indian to set foot in the village. His message indicated that besides the Seven Cities of Cibola, there were other territories called Marata, Acus, and Totonteac, describing Acus as an independent kingdom and province. Its people he called *encaconados,* meaning they had turquoise hanging from their noses and ears (Wagner 1934:205–207; Villagrá 1933).

In 1540 Francisco Vásquez Coronado sent Capt. Hernando de Alvarado eastward to ʔá·ku for exploration. Alvarado's account indicated that within five days he "arrived at a town called Acuco," which was described as "a very strange place built upon solid rock": "These

people were robbers, feared by the whole country round about. The village was very strong, because it was up on a rock out of reach, having steep sides in every direction. . . . There was only one entrance by a stairway built by hand. . . . There was a broad stairway of about 200 steps, then a stretch of about 100 narrower steps and at the top they had to go up about three times as high as a man by means of holes in the rock, in which they put the points of their feet, holding on at the same time by their hands. There was a wall of large and small stones at the top, which they could roll down without showing themselves, so that no army could possibly be strong enough to capture the village. On the top they had room to sow and store a large amount of corn, and cisterns to collect snow and water" (Winship 1896:490–491).

A further account of Alvarado's first meeting with the inhabitants indicates that there was both natural fear and curiosity among the people. These inhabitants drew boundary lines on the ground to prohibit the expeditioners from crossing it. Alvarado claims that he tried to persuade Acoma guards to allow the Spaniards' entry but failed, and then when he indicated attack, the guards were willing to make peace. As a few Acoma individuals recognized that the foreigners' horses were sweating and overridden and that these strange visitors were tired, they welcomed Alvarado's soldiers by a traditional and common sign of welcome—crossing the second fingers of each hand to indicate 'our meeting' and crossing hands on each other to indicate 'we are friends and will not harm

Mus. of N.M., Santa Fe.

Fig. 8. Southern entrance to the mesa top, referred to as the Burro trail or Padre's trail in early accounts of Acoma. Women transport water from the southern cistern up the trail in pottery carried on their heads (cistern is south of the area shown in fig. 2). This trail, used by the Spaniards, was the least used trail in the 1970s. Photograph by Ben Wittick, 1880s or possibly early 1890s.

Smithsonian, Dept. of Anthr.: 127692 a-c.
Fig. 9. Plaited yucca rings used by women to support water jars carried on their heads. Diameter of left 11.5 cm, height 8 cm; rest same scale. Collected in 1884.

each other'. They presented the strangers with basic food and clothing provisions. Alvarado describes his interpretation of this gesture: "They went through their forms of making peace, which is to touch the horses and take their sweat and rub themselves with it, and to make crosses with the fingers of the hands. But to make the most secure peace they put their hands across each other. . . . They made a present of a large number of [turkey-]cocks with very big wattles, much bread, tanned deerskins, pine [piñon] nuts, flour [cornmeal] and corn" (Winship 1896:491).

Such is a picture of the Pueblo around 1540: a village of about 200 men, situated on an almost inaccessible mesa about 400 feet high, with cisterns on the summit, evidence of woven cotton, deerskin, buffalo-hide garments, corn, domesticated turkeys and turquoise jewelry. Castaneda also tells of some prayersticks he found in an area near a spring (Bolton 1949).

In 1581 Fray Agustín Rodríguez and Francisco Sánchez Chamuscado visited ?áˑk̓u with 28 others, including 12 soldiers, 3 friars, and Indian servants, for the purpose of converting the Pueblo. There were reports of a little opposition and fear toward these invaders initially, which were probably natural reactions inspired by the capture of Indian servants for silver mines that the Spanish were beginning to establish within the region. Rodríguez asked for food in exchange for merchandise they had brought along. The inhabitants welcomed the Spaniards atop the mesa, which is described as having 500 houses of three and four stories.

In the following year, 1582, Antonio de Espejo arrived at Acoma and spent three days. He describes clothing and staple foods: "mantas, deerskins, and strips of buffalo-hide, tanned as they tan them in Flanders, and many provisions consisting of maize and turkeys." He further mentions the existence of the San Jose River irrigation fields in the North Valley (Acomita). "These people have their fields two leagues from the pueblo on a river of medium size, whose waters they intercept for irrigation purposes, as they water their fields with many partitions of the water near this river, in a marsh" (Bolton 1916:183). Espejo observed rose bushes and wild onion plants near the fields and referred to possible intertribal trade relations. Mountain people called Querechos, thought to be of Apachean origin (Villagrá 1933), were observed to "come down to these settlements to trade for salt, and game such as deer, rabbits, hares, and tanned deerskins" (Wagner 1934). Acoma oral history does not verify such relations; however, it does refer to frequent messengers from the mesa village to the farming camps in the North Valley area: Acomita, Seama, and McCartys.

Espejo's narratives also indicate observations of some native ceremony. "They performed a very ceremonious 'mitote' and dance, the people coming out in fine array. They performed many juggling feats, some of them very clever with live snakes" (Bolton 1916:182-183). The Snake Dance, which is no longer practiced by the tribe, apparently existed during the sixteenth century.

From 1595, when Juan de Oñate contracted to colonize New Mexico, through April 1598, when he took formal possession of the territory, he claimed it necessary to force the submission and obedience of the natives. An Acoma warrior historically called Zutacapan had heard about this plan and returned to the mesa to warn the tribe. He immediately had a band of warriors prepared for defense, but his son, called Zutancalpo, spoke of the widespread belief that the Spanish soldiers were immortal. Thereupon an elder, historically referred to as Chumpo, decided to disarm to prevent war and bloodshed. When Oñate arrived at Acoma on October 27, 1598, he was received cordially and presented with corn, turkey, and sufficient quantities of water, including food for the horses. According to the usual custom, surrender and obedience to Spanish rule was demanded. "On reaching the top, the soldiers fired a salute, to the wonder and terror of all the savages" (Villagrá 1933:166-167). No resistance was reported. Zutacapan, described as a highly intelligent and keen man, offered to lead Oñate to descend into the kiva, where pledges and sacred oaths of obedience are known to be traditionally made. The appearance of the roof-laddered hatchway into the religious chambers of silent darkness frightened Oñate, and he refused the honor. With inadequate communication and fear of the unknown, he had suspicions that the Acoma warriors were plotting his death, so he left with his army. The fourth Acoma mentioned in this historical period was Purguapo, apparently one of four individuals elected to negotiate with the Spaniards.

Shortly after Oñate's departure, Gaspar de Villagrá, the *procurador general,* reached Acoma Pueblo with only his horse and a dog. He was met with friendly entreaty as he asked Zutacapan for provisions and water. He was urged to dismount but suspiciously refused and left for Oñate's trail. Zutacapan and others called for him to return. In need of provisions, he turned back and found Zutacapan inquisitive, asking him if more Spaniards were following and how long before they would arrive. Villagrá informed him of 103 well-armed men at two days' journey away, at which time he was then asked to leave.

On December 1, 1598, Juan de Zaldívar, a nephew of Oñate, arrived at the Pueblo with 20-30 men and was met by Zutacapan in the friendliest guise. Zaldívar brought hatchets and other tools to trade for food and blankets, but he was told it would take a few corn-grinding days to fill their needs. Three days later, Zaldívar left his camp nearby with 16 men clad from head to foot in shining steel armor to climb atop the village. They were met by Zutacapan who informed them that the food was ready and directed him to the homes that prepared it. Zaldívar divided his Spanish force to collect the food. Inferences from oral history indicate that these soldiers who went into the homes may have attacked some of the women, which drew an attack on them by the tribal warriors. Spanish records do not document this incident as such. Their narratives say that Zaldívar's dispersion of his forces was a response to Zutacapan's conspiracy to attack and kill them (Villagrá 1933; Hall-Quest 1969:79). Using warclubs, darts, spears, and stones for weapons, the Acoma warriors killed Zaldívar and all but five of his troops. Of the five, one met death as he leaped over the citadel and the other four fell on sandy slopes at the base and escaped with the waiting soldiers.

On December 20, 1598, Oñate received word of Zaldívar's death and decided that the Acomas should be punished. He sought the advice of the friars, who concurred that "as the purpose of war is to establish peace, then it is even justifiable to exterminate and destroy those who stand in the way of that peace" (Villagrá 1933:208). Vicente de Zaldívar, a brother of Juan, was dispatched to carry out the punishment. Not only was revenge in order, but other Pueblos must not see Acoma remain victorious (Villagrá 1933:207-209; Hall-Quest 1969:80).

Within this period, Acomas sought the assistance of other tribes to help defend the village. Several leaders are mentioned as war captains: Gicombo, Popempol, Chumpo, Calpo, Buzcoico, and Ezmicaio. Bempol, an Apache war captain, joined the Acoma tribe for preparation for the battle. Zutacapan and two other warriors, Cotumbo, Tempal, and a medicine man, Amulco, participated in consultation. Some leaders urged the removal of women and children from the village, but at the confidence of Zutacapan, everyone remained on the mesa.

On January 21, 1599, Vicente de Zaldívar arrived at the Pueblo with 70 men, including Villagrá. On January 22, the fight began and lasted three days. Zaldívar sent most of his men to engage at the trail. Unnoticed by the Acoma guards, on January 23, 12 men stealthily ascended the south mesa, and gained the summit. The Spaniards lost only one man when they finally gained the village and attacked house by house. The cannon was dragged through the streets, the adobe walls crumbled, and the homes were burned down. Acoma finally yielded to the Spaniards around noon January 24, when they felt defeated by a supernatural power.

Of the approximately 6,000 Acoma population, 800 were killed. Zaldívar carried away eight Acoma girls to Mexico. In February 1599, a trial for those who had been taken prisoner announced "sentences" in accordance with sixteenth-century Spanish law. All Acoma males over 25 years of age were condemned to have one foot cut off and to give 20 years of personal service; all males between the ages of 12 and 25 were to give 20 years of personal service. All females above the age of 12 were to give 20 years of personal service. Two Indian men who had been captured while visiting Acoma were sentenced to have their right hands cut off and to be sent back to their own Pueblos as a warning of what could be expected if Spanish authority was flaunted. What was called personal service was really slavery, and the Indians were distributed among government officials and missions (Hall-Quest 1969:84).

In the period 1599-1620, the Pueblo village was rebuilt and repopulated while not being threatened by the Spaniards. Fray Andrés Corchado was assigned to minister to Acoma, Zia, Zuni, and Hopi. Since the distances among these villages are enormous, there is little probability that Fray Corchado was able to have any significant influence on Acoma. In 1620 Father Gerónimo de Zárate Salmerón visited Acoma during a period of great hostility, and he records that he succeeded in pacifying the tribe for a season. Around July 1629 Fray Juan Ramírez went to Acoma, where historians have recorded two miracles performed by the friar that gained him acceptance by the tribe. He restored health to an unconscious eight-year-old girl who had fallen off the cliff and, through baptism, to a year-old infant who was near death. About this time, Ramírez began building a church on top of the mesa, which he decorated with imports from New Spain. The construction of the church bears an interesting symbolism of dedication that Acoma expressed toward the friar. High timbers for the vigas were transported from the San Mateo Mountains, and bags of sand and large quantities of water were hauled to the top of the mesa by foot. The vigas were intricately carved during many hours of labor.

Ramírez remained at Acoma for 20 years, sharing his knowledge and assisting the tribe in developing their natural resources. It is said that he introduced fruit trees—pear, plum, peach, apricot, cherry, fig, and date—as well as herds of horses, cows, sheep, and burros. After his departure, Acoma does not receive historical mention until the era of the Pueblo Revolt.

About 1645-1675 Acoma and the other Pueblos began to feel the Spanish oppression, particularly the suppression of their native religious beliefs and practice. Consequently, they participated in the Pueblo Revolt of 1680, during which they burned all Christian emblems and put to death their Franciscan padre, Lucas Maldonado, and possibly two others. (There is some evidence that this priest was thrown over the mesa.)

During the Spanish reconquest of the new territory, Diego de Vargas visited Acoma on November 3, 1692. Acomas had barricaded the entrance to the mesa and would not allow him into the village. On November 4, he met the chief named Matthew, who is historically referred to as the "educated Indian," and agreed to a peaceful mission. A Christian cross was planted in their midst and Acoma was yielded to the Crown of Spain. Records show that 87 children were baptized at this time (Bancroft 1889:200-201). All through 1693, though some Keresan villages aided Vargas, Acoma was insubordinate, and early in 1695 the Pueblo made an alliance with Hopi, Zuni, and certain Apaches (Sedgwick 1926:122). In 1696, when missionaries were once more appointed to the tribes, Acoma does not appear to have been included.

On June 4, 1696, Acoma took in refugees from five of the Rio Grande Pueblos who had killed their resident priests and 21 other Spaniards. These refugees had abandoned their homes and fled toward the mountains. Spanish confirmatory intelligence observed that "there was a multitude of people and a trail of women going toward Acoma." Four days later, a meeting was held with expectation of reinforcements from Hopi, Zuni, and the Utes. On June 12, Vargas received word of a "general revolt" that was instigated by the provinces of Acoma, Zuni, Hopi, and Apaches. More refugees from San Cristóbal, a village taken by Vargas, arrived at Acoma and Zuni. Acoma and other Pueblo warriors in the meantime had fortified themselves at Chimayo, a steep mountainous ridge. However, on June 13, an Indian prisoner confessed to Vargas the strategic plans, and the native alliances were broken. In spite of this loss, the Pueblos threatened that they would unite and return in 100 days. To quiet the Acomas, Vargas marched to the Pueblo. On August 15, 1696, he attacked the village, capturing five prisoners, one of whom was a chief, but did not succeed in entering it. When his attempt to persuade Acoma to submit through the captives failed, Vargas shot the captives, destroyed the cornfields, and finally retreated.

Oral history implies that around 1697-1699 the refugees who had escaped to Acoma Pueblo left to begin settlement at a nearby lake vicinity. The settlement has since become known as Laguna. Oral history also indicates that the Acoma farming camps in Acomita and McCartys were also reestablished as temporary seasonal settlements around this time. Adobe homes were increased in size and moved closer to the fields.

Pedro Rodríguez Cubero, successor to Vargas, returned once again to Acoma on July 6, 1699. The Acoma tribe, seeing all the other Pueblos submitting to Spanish rule, finally yielded submission to the general. Thereafter, the mission was reestablished and the church was brought back to power.

The eighteenth century found Acoma in peaceful relations with the Spaniards, although history mentions some suspicious incidents. In 1702 Cubero ordered an investigation of Acoma on grounds of a rumored conspiracy. In 1703 Zuni and Hopi called on Acoma for a revolt coordinated in Zuni, but the alliance again was subdued. In 1713 the people of both Acoma and Laguna are known to have threatened their resident priest with death because of his interference with the native religions. However, in 1710 the mission at Acoma was restored and reopened again. In 1744 a report by Father Miguel Menchero indicates that Acoma had 110 families and that there was a process of catechizing the Indians. By 1752 Acoma, Zuni, Taos, and Laguna showed the largest population concentration of the 22 Pueblos. Until 1780 Acoma was recognized by other Pueblos to be a mother settlement. However, after the smallpox epidemic of 1780-1781, the mission headquarters was transferred to Laguna. This epidemic is known to have caused a tremendous decrease in the Acoma population (see table 1).

For the nineteenth century, there is more descriptive historical detail. About 1800 Laguna asked to borrow from the Acoma mission a painting of Saint Joseph that was a gift from King Charles II of Spain in 1629. This oil painting was believed to have had miraculous powers that kept Acomas in peace and prosperity, and those at Laguna wanted to improve their own situation after the epidemic, drought, and other misfortunes. The loan was

**Table 1. Population, 1630-1966**

| Year | Population | Year | Population |
|------|-----------|------|-----------|
| 1630 | 2,000 | 1900 | 739 |
| 1680 | 2,000 | 1910 | 820 |
| 1700 | 760 | 1920 | 1,013 |
| 1740 | 110 | 1930 | 1,025 |
| 1750 | 960 | 1935 | 1,150 |
| 1760 | 890 | 1940 | 1,225 |
| 1790 | 1,052 | 1945 | 1,375 |
| 1810 | 816 | 1950 | 1,576 |
| 1850 | 350 | 1955 | 1,839 |
| 1860 | 523 | 1960 | 2,133 |
| 1870 | 436 | 1965 | 2,417 |
| 1890 | 582 | 1966 | 2,512 |

SOURCES: U.S. Census Office; U.S. Bureau of Indian Affairs.

Fig. 10. Acoma runners, identified by photographer's son as, left to right: Catarino Victorino, John Sanchez, Santiago Sanchez, and Lorenzo Abeyta. Like all catholicized Pueblos, Acoma celebrates the feast days of four saints. An Acoma celebration typically includes foot races in the morning followed by a game similar to field hockey (*tú·kímu·č*ʰ*i*), and highlighted by a rooster pull on foot; in the afternoon another rooster-pull (on horseback) takes place, followed by brief equitation exercises. This culminates in social gatherings outside the homes of all those named after the saint, where individuals dispense donations of goods from the rooftops. Photograph by Emil Bibo, about 1905.

Fig. 11. Faustín or Faustino, identified as war captain of Acoma (Lummis 1925:73, 1925a:opp. 256), in an irrigated wheat field. Photograph by Charles F. Lummis, 1892.

refused, but the painting was taken anyway. After several years, Acomas asked to have the painting returned. At the refusal of Laguna, the two tribes fought a court battle in 1852. In 1857 the U.S. Supreme Court settled the dispute in favor of Acoma (De Huff 1943; Forrest 1929). In 1863 the governors of seven Pueblos, including Acoma, went to Washington, D.C., to settle land-boundary disputes. At this time, President Abraham Lincoln presented each governor with an engraved silver-headed cane. To each Pueblo this represents United States recognition of each tribe as an independent seat of Pueblo traditional government.

About this time, oral history indicates the encroachment of Navajos into the territory. Navajos were caught stealing livestock and other domestic possessions of families so that Acoma proclaimed a campaign against Navajo encroachment.

On July 6, 1857, the determination of Acoma and Laguna land boundaries was made. For Acoma, the territory was to include the area recognized in 1848, when the United States acquired sovereignty over New Mexico

under the Treaty of Guadalupe Hidalgo. In 1858 Congress confirmed the land claims of Acoma as well as other Pueblos, which had been surveyed and reported in 1856 to the Department of the Interior (11 Stat. 374).

In 1864 Acoma was described in the same manner as it was in 1540, with houses in parallel rows, ladders used for ingress and egress to the dwellings, low arch formation for doorway passages, and window plates of crystallized gypsum (selenite). There are also descriptions of a variety of fruits and vegetables, blue corn foods, herds of sheep and cattle, weaving, pottery and basketry, and evidence of Spanish silver (Gwyther 1871).

Oral history describes the maintenance of Acoma traditional food sources and practices. The favorites include blue corn drink, corn mush, pudding, wheat cake, corn balls, paper bread, peach bark drink, flour bread, wild berries, wild banana, and prickly pear fruit. A socialist economy was observed to be present as a tribal practice. Tribal policy called for the community to share work—planting, harvesting, building irrigation ditches, and hunting. The community provided the labor and the chief distributed the produce equally among the community (fig. 12). There were also several corn-grinding teams. Up until 1850, lands were dry-farmed as well as irrigated north of Grants and eastward along the San Jose River, south of Grants around Ojo del Gallo and San Rafael, somewhat farther south at Cerro Carnero, just west of the lava flow, along the northern boundary of the

459

Fig. 12. View of the church courtyard showing convento gardens no longer in existence in the 1970s similar to the waffle gardens of the Zunis (see "Zuni Economy," fig. 12, this vol.) in right foreground and communally used corrals (to the left) in existence in 1978. Mt. Taylor in the background (left), Enchanted Mesa at right. Photograph by Charles Saunders or W.H. Cobb, facing north (from church) probably in 1880s.

Acoma grant, Cebollita Spring and Pilares area, Cebollita Mesa and Blue Meadow area, and the Petoche region south between ʔáˑ·ku and Broom-Brush Mountain (Acoma Land Claims Records 1967).

The people in general were highly philosophical, religious, and aesthetic, in that most activities involved native prayer and songs. Some individuals were also creative and industrious in various arts and crafts. They made pottery (figs. 13-14), blankets, woven belts, dresses, capes, socks, skirts, moccasins, baskets (fig. 15), and carvings. Highly poetic, they also continued to create a variety of songs and dances. There was also traditional native drama, depicting both comedy and tragedy. Indian medicine was a highly sophisticated and organized system. The tribe also had a formal education system with kiva headmen as the traditionally recognized professional teachers. Their native school curriculum consisted of lectures on care of human behavior, human spirit, and the human body, ethics, astrology, child psychology, oratory, history, music, and dancing. Theology was not only taught but also practiced as the most crucial substance of existence.

Statistics collected by the military in 1870 show Acoma with a population of 435 in 124 families. Livestock included 58 horses, 860 cattle, 92 oxen, 1,600 sheep, 503 goats, 82 swine, 68 asses, and 10 mules (Arny 1967:53). Oral history describes Acoma irrigation and dry farming fields as prosperous with corn, melons, squash, beans, chili, onions, turnips, and orchards—peach, plum, pear, apple, apricot, and cherry.

Fig. 13. Woman, identified only as "Acoma Mary," painting polychrome designs. Black paint, yucca brushes, and minerals from which paint is made are in the stone metate at her side; the bowls probably contain yellowish-orange and reddish-orange mineral paint. Guide lines have been drawn on both pots first, with areas of color filled in (see Bunzel 1972:29-38). Behind her are two water jars of the same type: one, covered and with a gourd dipper resting on it, probably contains water for mixing with paint; the other is possibly being used as a design model. Photograph by Adam C. Vroman, 1902.

GARCIA-MASON

a-b, Smithsonian, Dept. of Anthr.: 109970, 110024; c, School of Amer. Research, Santa Fe, N.M.: IAF Coll. 2780; d, Mus. of N.M., Santa Fe: 25831/12.

Fig. 14. Acoma pottery. a-b, Water vessels of the style dating from 1880s, with characteristic thin walls, undefined neck, orange and black geometric and parrotlike bird designs painted on a stark white slip; collected in 1884. c-d, Modern pottery styles of Lucy Lewis and Marie Z. Chino (see Maxwell Museum of Anthropology 1974); designs of black hatched lines (called *sámúmú*, fine line design) and geometric elements are based on prehistoric patterns (Toulouse 1977:80; Maxwell Museum of Anthropology 1974:9); c, collected in 1959, d, collected in 1961. Diameter of b 23 cm, rest same scale.

Mus. of N.M., Santa Fe: School of Amer. Research Coll. 1122/12.

Fig. 15. Twined burden basket, probably of yucca, with wooden hoop ring bound with wood splints, and leather and cloth carrying strap. Used for carrying piñons, acorns, and seeds. Height about 33 cm, collected before 1930.

Sometime after 1879, the Atchison, Topeka, and Santa Fe Railway was constructed through the villages Acomita and McCartys. These villages were observed to be somewhat permanent settlements with a church and adjacent school hall in sight.

Bandelier (1966-1976, 2) provides some historical data on Acoma. During his observations in 1883-1884 there was a dance performed called Chakᵘuya. He also mentions nine clans that are no longer in existence—Snake, Lizard, Shiahut, Turquoise, Coyote, Mountain lion, Badger, Cricket, and Purple corn. He mentions 14 clans that still existed in 1978—Water, Sky, Sun, Turkey, Eagle, Roadrunner, Oak, Ivy, Red corn, Yellow corn, White corn, Pumpkin, Bear, and Antelope.

In October 1884 Acoma Pueblo sued the Cleland Cattle Company and Solomon Bibo for having fraudulently obtained a lease to the Pueblo. The tribe asked for a vacating of lease and ejection of the defendants from Pueblo lands on grounds of fraud. Gov. Martin Valle, who could not read or write, had understood that the lands around Gallo Springs were to be leased for three years, whereas the actual contract, which had not been read to him, provided for a 30-year lease of the entire Pueblo grant. The suit was dismissed in 1887 on grounds that the U.S. government had brought it rather than the Pueblo itself (Valencia County District Court Records, New Mexico State Records Center and Archives, Case 574, 575).

In 1897 an "Indian Agency" reported 55 children living on the mesa, but no school was available. In 1917 the agent reported that of 150 children of school age, only 19 were in attendance at Acomita and that "Acomas were very backward and almost resentful of anything being done to assist them." The agent's remedy was to increase permanent school facilities at Acomita and exert proper pressure for attendance. In 1922 all the children

Fig. 16. Feast of San Esteban (*saništê·wa*), patron saint of Acoma. top left, Procession leaving the church after mass, carrying the image of the saint. The governor, Governor Eusebius, is at extreme right; the priest, G.J. Juilliard (standing at doorway) does not join in the procession. top right, Saint's bower of cottonwood boughs and corn plants, lined with native embroidered cotton mantas and Athapaskan blankets; following the procession, the saint is placed within this shrine with candles and offerings of food. middle left, Gathering in front of the shrine includes: Santiago (impersonated by the figure on costume dancing horse in foreground) and his companion (*čʰapʰiyú*), holding whip, and their leader; in the 1970s these figures made an appearance every 7-10 years. Drummer appears at extreme right; men in blankets (at center) are probably the war chiefs, who are the last to enter the shrine. middle right, Feast dance (*tá·ławá·yá*), one of several performed by members of each kiva in alternation and together, traditionally held in the afternoon. bottom, Random dispensing of goods, which takes place at the *ǩá·kʰa·łi* (plaza), to dancers (left), chorus (men at center), and onlookers by maternal relations of those named after the saint whose day is being celebrated. Photographs by G. Wharton James and F.H. Maude, Sept. 2, about 1898.

Fig. 17. Children playing on porch of building in the old village. Structure in background is the church with attached convent. Photograph by Helga Teiwes, Sept. 1970.

who were not in Acomita were sent to Albuquerque or Santa Fe (Sedgwick 1926:139–140).

In the entire history of Acoma the intertribal and governmental disputes over land boundaries had the most significant impact on the tribe. Although the recorded effect of the Dawes Severalty Act of 1887 on Acoma reservation is not immediately accessible, it has been concluded (Spicer 1961) that the Pueblos, in general, were not affected by this statute, at least by evidence of nonallotted lands. However, there are 320 acres of individually owned land on the reservation, which were bought under the Homestead Act provisions on surplus lands. In 1922 Senate Bill 3855, the Bursum bill, was passed; as it seemed a threat to land ownership, the tribe of Acoma opposed it. On March 23, 1928, Congress, based on the need for additional pasture lands, set aside for the tribe all vacant lands within a certain area (Public Law 481).

After the Indian Reorganization Act of 1934, Acoma chose to retain the traditional government system with no written constitution. Acoma traditional government remained the honored system in 1978. Other legislative acts, specifically, H.R. 108 and Public Law 280, were observed to be threatening to the tribe. Although Acomas in the 1950s totally rejected Public Law 280 and although they opposed the Civil Rights Act and Indian Bill of Rights in the 1960s, there were subtle gestures in the 1970s that allowed the state authorities to assist the tribal law and order system. Tribal law enforcement in the 1970s received its primary source of funding from the state's Law Enforcement Assistance Agency program. The implications of this tendency remain unclear for many tribal members. Because of political and economic

needs, there are pressures on the tribe for cultural adjustment, and Acoma's social and cultural changes cannot be denied. Nonetheless, traditional culture is strong and is perpetuating itself, particularly within the religious sphere. However, because of its historical experiences, Acoma as a tribe prefers not to reveal information about the sacred aspects of their culture.

## Sociocultural Situation in the 1970s

The theocratic government system serves as the principal instrument for promoting policies for either social change or cultural maintenance. The office of cacique (fig. 18), through theological appointment, consists of the Antelope matrilineal clan brothers who are recognized as having the duly respected and vested authority over government and land allocations. The tribal council members are elected by the cacique for indefinite terms; the governor and his staff are elected by the cacique yearly. These appointments are announced to the community in the last week of December, and formal inauguration takes place soon thereafter.

The social organization can best be described in terms of the kinship system and the kiva system, which prescribe the roles of its members. The kinship system (fig. 19) is of the Crow type. There are 19 clans (*hánuc$^h$a, háňuc$^h$a*) that are organized by social functions as follows:

| Functions | Clans |
|---|---|
| A | Antelope (*k$^h$ɨ·c$^h$i*) |
| B | Water (*čic$^h$i*) |
| | Sky (*hûwáḱa*) |
| C | Oak (*hà·p$^h$ani*) |
| | Tansy Mustard (*ʔɨsé*) |
| D | Squash (*aittâ·ni*) |
| | Parrot (*šâ·wiv$^h$a*) |
| E | Turkey (*c$^h$íňa*) |
| F | Bear (*k$^h$uháya*) (two): Acoma and Zuni-related |
| G | Eagle (*t$^y$á·mí*) (two): Acoma and Zuni-related |
| H | Roadrunner (*šà·ṣḱa*) (two): Acoma and Laguna-related |
| I | Corn (*yá·ḱa*) (two): Red (*k$^h$ɨ·káňiši*) and Yellow (*ḱú·č$^h$íňiši*) |
| J | Sun (*ʔuṣâ·c$^h$a*) (three): Acoma, Zia-related, and Zuni-related |

There are two main kivas that could be considered comparable to the Eastern Pueblos' moieties, with two kiva groups in one moiety and three kivas in the other. There is one other kiva that remains independent. Since the kiva system has intricate religious implications, its social organizational implication will not be further discussed here.

Marriage ceremonies are conducted through the Roman Catholic Church; few Indian-custom marriages exist. Divorce is uncommon. Only exogamous marriages

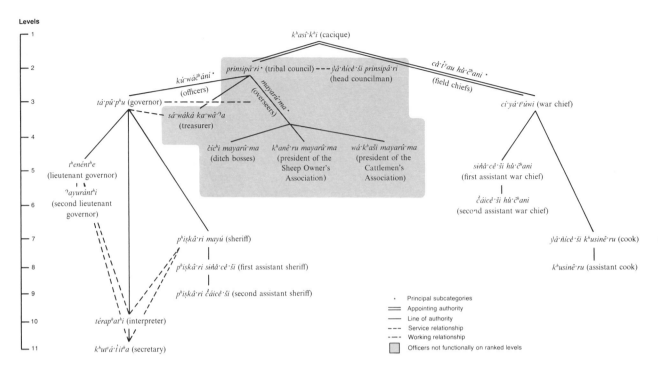

Fig. 18. Governing structure. Except for those indicated, all officers are functionally on 11 ranked levels, as for example at the Governor's Feast Day (Inaugural Feast). All official tribal documents require the signatures of the governor and the head councilman. This structure is derived from traditional Acoma, early Spanish, and American bureaucratic forms. It may vary with interpretations by different incumbents of the governor's position. Efforts to develop a written constitutional government were underway in 1978. The cacique has only appointing authority, not a working relationship with the officers. He appoints all these officers for terms of one calendar year, except that the tribal councilmen serve indefinitely, the treasurer is appointed by the council for an indefinite term, and the presidents of the Cattlemen's Association and the Sheep Owners' Association are elected annually by their associations.

occur. Acoma households generally follow the matrilocal residence rule. However, this rule is becoming violated in the villages of Acomita and McCartys as changes are made through construction of federal housing projects for nuclear families. Total households and population continue to grow (table 2).

Chili-spiced stew preparation remains the primary traditional dish. In addition, New Mexico state extension programs have influenced preparation of meals to include non-Indian food planning. According to their horticultural production, individual families also use and prefer certain varieties of fruits and vegetables.

Although many maintain the totally traditional adobe-masonry architecture, federal housing projects have introduced the cement-block ranch-style and frame houses with exterior adobelike stucco. However, outside ovens are still maintained. The high rate of American mobility and the auto industry have influenced the culture quite extensively to allow an average of two automobiles per household. The federal government's tendency toward tribal contracting for services has allowed the tribe to provide employment for both females and males on the reservation. Employment of females has substantially influenced the return of traditional practices of grandmother child-care patterns.

In terms of educational status, in 1976 there were 20

college graduates from the tribe, 30 undergraduate students, and 3 individuals who had completed master's degrees. Several federal programs on the reservation were providing in-service training programs for Acoma employees toward some accreditation. The elementary school under Title VII of the Elementary and Secondary Education Act (Public Law 93-380) was planning a bicultural and bilingual program. This initiative has reinforced the community's interest in revitalizing the traditional Acoma culture.

Indian dancing, both religious and nonreligious, songs, legends, mythologies, philosophies, religion, medicine, drama, and adolescence rites are actively maintained. For detailed descriptions see White (1932a), Sedgwick (1926), and Minge (1976), keeping in mind the limitations of non-Indian interpretations.

### Synonymy†

The English name Acoma is from Spanish Ácoma, 1583 (and Acóma, 1598), a borrowing from Acoma *ʔá·k̇ù·ṁé*. Although English and Spanish apply the name to both Acoma Pueblo and its people, the Acoma word means only 'a person from Acoma Pueblo (*ʔá·k̇u*)', the plural

† This synonymy was prepared by Ives Goddard; uncredited forms are from Harrington (1916:541-545), who gives additional spelling variants, or from anonymous sources.

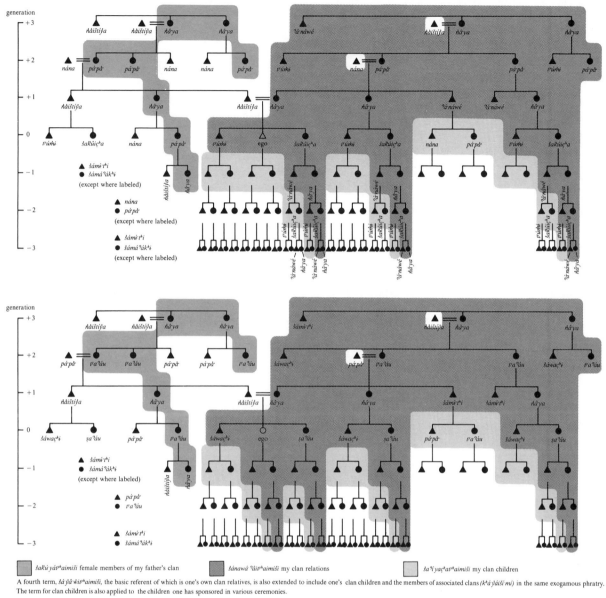

Fig. 19. Kinship terminology and clan relationships. top, Male ego; bottom, female ego.

A fourth term, *šá·yâ·ẁitʰaimiši*, the basic referent of which is one's own clan relatives, is also extended to include one's clan children and the members of associated clans *(kʰá·yáiší mí)* in the same exogamous phratry. The term for clan children is also applied to the children one has sponsored in various ceremonies.

Legend:
- *šaRú·yátʰaimiši* female members of my father's clan
- *šánawá·ʔáitʰaimiši* my clan relations
- *šaʔí·yaçʰatʰaimiši* my clan children

## Table 2. Population, 1967–1974

| | | 1967 | | 1968 | | 1969 | | 1970 | | 1971 | | 1972 | | 1973 | | 1974 | |
| | | Female | Male | Female | Male | Female | Male | Female | Male | Female | Male | Female | Male | Female | Male | Female | Male |
|---|---|---|---|---|---|---|---|---|---|---|---|---|---|---|---|---|---|
| Age | 0–4 | 153 | 120 | 148 | 126 | 169 | 154 | 157 | 161 | 140 | 155 | 147 | 162 | 146 | 160 | 171 | 172 |
| | 5–14 | 326 | 369 | 367 | 387 | 371 | 403 | 401 | 409 | 415 | 402 | 402 | 421 | 404 | 407 | 436 | 396 |
| | 15–19 | 136 | 134 | 144 | 147 | 145 | 148 | 146 | 169 | 167 | 159 | 171 | 163 | 186 | 181 | 190 | 189 |
| | 20–34 | 333 | 262 | 345 | 276 | 344 | 274 | 366 | 297 | 311 | 359 | 321 | 369 | 325 | 367 | 345 | 367 |
| | 35–54 | 279 | 241 | 253 | 209 | 246 | 218 | 257 | 216 | 217 | 269 | 220 | 275 | 222 | 301 | 221 | 313 |
| | 55–64 | 58 | 66 | 74 | 66 | 71 | 66 | 77 | 70 | 75 | 81 | 67 | 77 | 74 | 75 | 72 | 77 |
| | 65+ | 26 | 52 | 57 | 89 | 57 | 84 | 60 | 77 | 88 | 62 | 89 | 67 | 94 | 77 | 98 | 80 |
| Total | | 1,311 | 1,244 | 1,388 | 1,300 | 1,403 | 1,347 | 1,464 | 1,397 | 1,413 | 1,487 | 1,417 | 1,534 | 1,451 | 1,568 | 1,533 | 1,594 |
| Family Groups | | 576 | | 571 | | 584 | | 617 | | 539 | | 912 | | 909 | | 866 | |

SOURCE: U.S. Bureau of Indian Affairs, Southern Pueblos Agency.

being ʔaˑƙùˑm̀èˑc̣ʰa (Miller 1965:164, 212, 228). Borrowed or adapted forms of this name in other languages include: Santa Ana Keresan ʔáˑƙú, Tewa aƙo (from Keresan) and ákuma and ákomage from Spanish (Curtis 1907–1930, 16:260), Zuni hakuˑka 'Acoma Pueblo' and hakuˑkaˑkʷe 'Acoma Indian(s)' (Dennis Tedlock, personal communication 1977), Hopi ákokavi, and Navajo Haak'oh 'Acoma Pueblo' and Haak'ohnii 'Acoma people' (Robert W. Young, personal communication 1977). Among the spellings in the early Spanish sources, generally from the Keresan or Zuni name, are: Acus, Acux, Aacus, Hacús (whence Vacus, Vsacus), Yacco (for y Acco), Acuca, Acogiya, Acuco (whence Coco, Suco).

The name ʔáˑƙu does not mean 'Sky City', as it is sometimes called for the convenience of non-Acomas. It has no meaning in the contemporary Acoma language, but some tribal authorities compare the similar word háˑƙu 'preparedness, place of preparedness' as having an appropriate meaning and perhaps being the origin of the name.

Other names are Isleta tʔóławéi (Curtis 1907–1930, 16:261, normalized), Jemez tóv̓agʸíʔ (from tóv̓á 'Acoma Indian', pl. tóv̓éš), and Navajo Tsekízthohi (Stephen 1936, 2:1153).

As the seat of a Spanish mission the Pueblo is called San Esteban de Acoma; the original patron saint appears to have been the Protomartyr Saint Stephen, but the Pueblo's saint's day is now celebrated on September 2, the feast of Saint Stephen, King of Hungary (Domínguez 1956:188–191).

### Sources

Gunn (1917) was the first to attempt a complete ethnography of Acoma and Laguna. The social and cultural situation of Acoma in the 1920s was surveyed by Sedgwick (1926) and White (1932a). Folklore and mythology have also been well treated (Paytiamo 1932; Stirling 1942; Benedict 1930). Miller (1959), Mickey (1956), Eggan (1950), Bandelier (1966–1976, 2), and Minge (1976) have contributed to knowledge on Acoma social organization and kinship.

# Zuni Prehistory and History to 1850

RICHARD B. WOODBURY

The region in which the present town of Zuni is situated lies just west of the continental divide in western New Mexico. The town is on the banks of the Zuni River (fig. 1), a tributary of the Little Colorado. The area traditionally used by the Zunis extends 35 miles east and northeast to the Zuni Mountains, which rise to elevations of 8,000-9,000 feet, and about 50 miles west and south into lower, drier country.

## Prehistory

Few comprehensive archeological results have come from nearly a century of intermittent survey and excavation. In the 1880s Victor Mindeleff mapped some of the larger ruins of the area while preparing a plan of Zuni Pueblo. In 1888-1889 the Hemenway Southwestern Archaeological Expedition excavated briefly in the ruins of Halona, the prehistoric and historic village that is now Zuni, and at the prehistoric site of Heshotauthla (Fewkes 1891).

Significant archeological work in the Zuni area began with Kroeber's (1916a) study of the chronological meaning of the varieties of potsherds he found on sites near Zuni, during his ethnographic research. Spier (1917, 1917a) systematically surveyed ruins in a wider area, following Kroeber's lead in determining their sequence by seriation, a technique based on the assumption (proved correct) that any particular style of pottery decoration began as an infrequent minority, increased to a maximum frequency, and then declined and went out of use. Spier concluded that "the Zuñi valley has been occupied continuously from an early period . . . [with] no site being occupied for any considerable period" (Spier 1917a:282). He also recognized the gradual change from "single houses," that is, ruins of a half-dozen rooms, to "communal dwellings of the well-known Pueblo type" and commented on the relative geographic isolation of Zuni that resulted in the "specifically Zuñian character" of the pottery. Spier's contribution was important not only to understand Zuni prehistory but also to demonstrate the utility of seriation as a chronological device for sites lacking in stratigraphic data.

From 1917 to 1923 Hodge (1937; Smith, Woodbury, and Woodbury 1966) carried out the most extensive excavation ever in the Zuni area at the historic village of Hawikuh (figs. 2-3), which lies about 15 miles southwest of Zuni and was occupied from about A.D. 1300 to 1680 by the ancestors of the modern Zunis. Hodge's interest was in studying the village as it existed from the first Spanish contact in 1540 through the next century and one-half. Although he cleared some 370 rooms of the

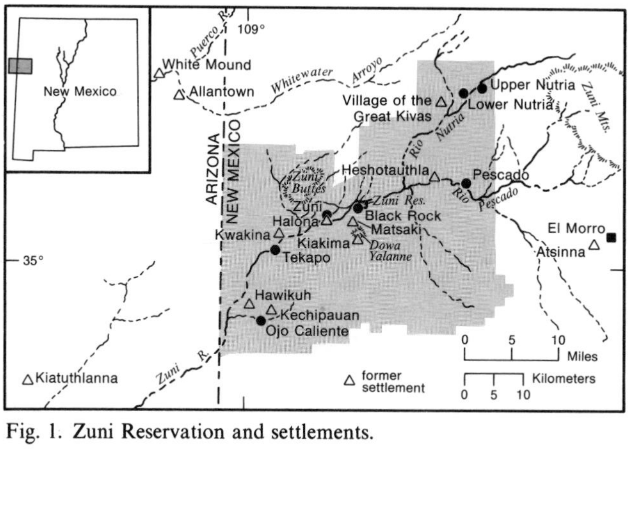

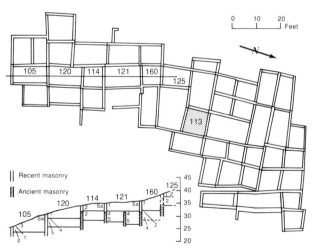

after Smith, Woodbury, and Woodbury 1966:figs. 17-18.

Fig. 2. House Group E, one of 6 house blocks (labeled A-E by Hodge) excavated at Hawikuh, N.M. (see Smith, Woodbury, and Woodbury 1966:fig. 1 for diagram of the entire site). top, Plan of rooms (upper levels); room 113 (fig. 3) is shown in tone. bottom left, Partial cross-sectional view showing ancient and recent masonry and indicating presence of Spanish artifacts (Sa) and type of native pottery (1, Recent Glaze; 2, Late Polychrome; 3, Sikyatki; 4, Ancient Glaze; 5, Early Polychrome) at each level.

Fig. 1. Zuni Reservation and settlements.

467

village, dug up nearly 1,000 graves (both cremations and inhumations), exposed much of the mission and friary, and secured some 1,500 whole or restorable pottery vessels for the museum, he failed to achieve any real understanding of Hawikuh's place in Zuni prehistory.

Details of the prehistory of the Zuni region as a whole began with comprehensive reports on Kiatuthlanna, a ruin nearby in Arizona that proved to have been occupied in Pueblo I and Pueblo III times (F.H.H. Roberts 1931); the Village of the Great Kivas, a Pueblo III site in the Nutria Valley about 15 miles northeast of Zuni (F.H.H. Roberts 1932); and the Allantown ruins 25 miles northwest of Zuni, occupied in Basketmaker III and Pueblo I and II times (F.H.H. Roberts 1939, 1940). Although Roberts was not primarily concerned with linking historic Zuni culture to its prehistoric origins, he provided a record of continual cultural development from small pit-house settlements to the large accretionary masonry villages of the late prehistoric period and identified details of architecture and ceramics that linked the Zuni area to the Chaco Canyon cultural centers to the northeast. He also noted the possibility of later influences from the south, possibly from the Upper Gila area. Further work has supported this idea that Zuni lay on the periphery of both the Chacoan and the Upper Gila regions, by which it was successively influenced. It is perhaps important in this connection that the Zuni language, in contrast to those of other Pueblo peoples, has no close relatives in surrounding regions.* An affiliation with California Penutian has been proposed, but it is too distant to be measured accurately by glottochronology (Newman 1964), if indeed, it exists.

Although the continuity of the modern Zunis with the past occupants of the area cannot be proved for more than the final two or three centuries prior to the conquest by Spaniards, there is a relatively unbroken development from Basketmaker times onward. The record begins about A.D. 700 or 800, with sherds of Basketmaker III age at Allantown (although no traces of houses were found) and with remains at White Mound (Gladwin 1945) of two small groups of pit houses and adjacent storerooms at ground level. Each pit house, about 10 to 12 feet across, was probably occupied by a single family, and the clusters of four or five pit houses reflect larger kin groups.

* The Zuni words cited in italics in the *Handbook* are written in the phonemic system of Newman ("Sketch of the Zuni Language," vol. 17). The values of the letters and symbols used are those of the standard technical alphabet of the *Handbook*, except that *k* is pronounced [kʸ] before *a, e,* or *i,* or before a ʔ followed by any one of these vowels; the plain [k] appearing before *a* in certain loanwords is written *q.* The first syllable of each word bears the main stress. Specialists are not in complete agreement on how to indicate word boundaries and the phonetic modifications (such as the dropping of final vowels) that occur when words come together in the phrase, and *Handbook* spellings are not entirely consistent on these points. In the rewriting of Zuni words the editors have had the valuable assistance of Dennis Tedlock.

Mus. of the Amer. Ind., Heye Foundation, New York.
Fig. 3. Room 113, a room in House Group E of Hawikuh (fig. 2), lower level, looking through doorway into room 124. Architectural features include 2 slab-lined fireplaces with stones thought to have been used as supports for cooking pots, a large corner storage bin, and a doorway. Photograph by Jesse L. Nusbaum, 1919.

The settlement lay in the valley of the Rio Puerco of the West, probably not deeply trenched by erosion then as it is now, and ample farmland would have been available close by. The rows of small storerooms would have kept the corn harvest secure against rodents, when sealed with mud plaster. It can be safely assumed that similar small farming settlements of a few families each occurred widely scattered throughout the Zuni area at this time.

Kiatuthlanna is a slightly larger village of about a century later where four groups of pit houses (fig. 4) were found within a few hundred feet of one another, totaling 18 homes and suggesting a population of perhaps 75 people. By the beginning of the eleventh century, at Allantown, each pit house had near it a compact cluster of five or six masonry rooms large enough to have been lived in, and the pit house was probably serving mainly as a meeting place for ritual purposes—a kiva. Large trash mounds associated with these clusters of kivas and surface rooms suggest greater permanence of occupation. In many parts of the Anasazi region at this time population was apparently increasing, villages growing in both size and complexity, and associated with this can be assumed an increasing effectiveness of farming technology.

The rapidity of this change is well illustrated by the Village of the Great Kivas, occupied about A.D. 1100-1200, which included: three masonry structures containing 6, 20, and 60 ground-floor rooms; three kivas incorporated within the room blocks; four more kivas outside them, more closely resembling pit houses of a century earlier; and two "great kivas" standing in front of the village (figs. 5-6). Instead of a settlement of a few families, this was a community of considerable size with ceremonies requiring not only seven of the traditional house-size kivas but also two much larger structures.

WOODBURY

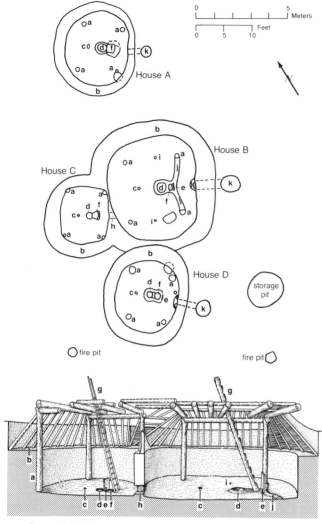

top to bottom, after F.H.H. Roberts 1931:figs. 1, 3.

Fig. 4. Group No. 1 dwellings of Kiatuthlanna, Ariz. top, Plan of pit houses A–D with adjacent storage pit and surface fire pits; bottom, reconstruction of pit houses B and C. a, Post holes for main support posts; b, earth bench; c, sipapu; d, fire pit; e, deflector; f, ladder pit; g, ladder; h, ventilator opening between pit houses; i, holes for loom posts; j, plaster ridge connecting fire and ladder pits with support posts; k, ventilator shaft (see F.H.H. Roberts 1931:19, 25-26).

These were 51 and 78 feet in diameter and the one excavated had an encircling bench and a pair of subfloor vaults that probably served as drums, sounded by the stamping feet of dancers.

Rinaldo (1964) has pointed out that strong relationships with the Chaco area are shown not only by details of kiva architecture, such as foot drums, but also by the pottery types of the prehistoric Zuni sites—types of the ninth to eleventh centuries including Kiatuthlanna, Red Mesa, and Puerco Black-on-white, followed by Wingate Black-on-red and Chaco Black-on-white, and by the thirteenth-century Tularosa Black-on-white, Saint Johns Polychrome (fig. 7), and Wingate Polychrome (formerly Querino and Houck Polychrome).

Although other settlements in the Zuni area contempo-

rary with the Village of the Great Kivas have not been excavated, F.H.H. Roberts (1932) published a sketch plan of a similar one at Allantown, one block of 30 or more rooms with three kivas enclosed within it, a small block of rooms with one enclosed and one adjacent kiva, and one great kiva. These twelfth-century villages are often located in the small valleys of tributaries of the Zuni River, partly protected from the wind and from winter storms by nearby cliffs, and perhaps with fields in these small canyons rather than along the river itself.

By the thirteenth century villages had greatly increased in size and at least some were built on mesa tops or high benches, where a commanding view of approaches on all sides was possible. Atsinna, on Inscription Rock, is one such village, built in a rectangle about 215 by 330 feet, with about 1,000 rooms including many at the second and third floor levels (Woodbury 1956). The rooms faced inward on a large central plaza, and the outer wall had few or no openings at ground level. By the late 1300s Atsinna had been abandoned, as had other large villages in the vicinity, so that the higher, eastern end of the Zuni Valley was deserted, while villages to the west, including Zuni itself, were probably growing in size. At Hawikuh Hodge (1937) found traces of earlier occupation under the later rooms, but not enough was exposed to determine the extent of the older village. In Zuni (the Halona of early Spanish accounts) Caywood in 1966 found sherds at eight to nine feet below the church floor of types datable to the 1300s: Heshotauthla Black-on-red and Polychrome (fig. 8), Gila Polychrome, and Kwakina Polychrome. These and four additional towns comprised Zuni settlement at the beginning of the historic period in 1540: Kiakima and Matsaki at the foot of Dowa Yalanne, a precipitous mesa a few miles east of Zuni and the people's traditional refuge, as well as the location of important shrines (popularly called Corn Mountain); Kwakina, a few miles downstream from Zuni; and Kechipauan, just a little farther, close to Hawikuh. Thus all were concentrated in a 25-mile stretch of the Zuni River, where it provided broad level areas of farmland that could be irrigated easily from the permanent flow in the river.

## History

Zuni contact with Europeans began in violence. In 1536 Álvar Núñez Cabeza de Vaca and three companions reached Mexico City, survivors of shipwreck on the Gulf Coast eight years earlier, with reports of impressive cities far to the north. The viceroy sent a Franciscan priest, Marcos de Niza, to verify this, guided by one of the survivors, Estevan, a black slave from the Barbary Coast. Estevan, reaching Hawikuh a few days ahead of Fray Marcos, was killed by the Zunis, probably because of his demands or threats. Fray Marcos glimpsed Hawikuh from a distant mesa and returned south, but his report was sufficient reason for a large-scale exploring expedi-

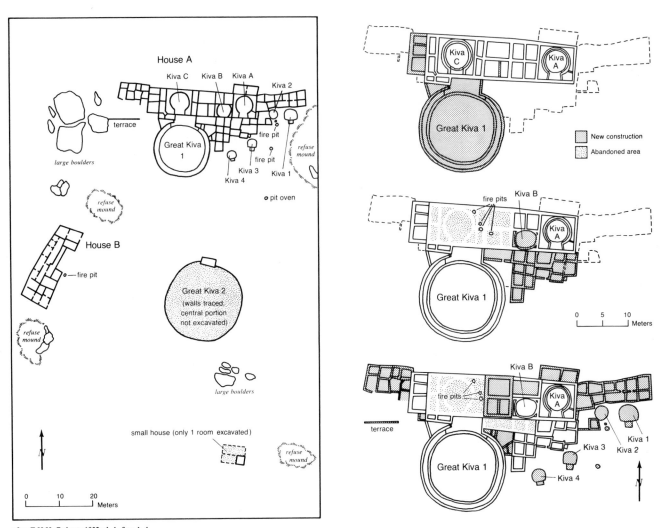

after F.H.H. Roberts 1932:pl. 1, figs. 1-4.

Fig. 5. Village of the Great Kivas. left, Plan of the entire site showing house blocks, large kivas (Great Kivas 1 and 2), kivas enclosed within rectangular walls in the house blocks (Kivas A-C), and 4 small subterranean or dirt kivas (Kivas 1-4). right, Plans of the largest of the house blocks showing probable stages of development. Abandoned areas indicated in stipple, new construction in tone; dotted line indicates outline of completed structure. See F.H.H. Roberts 1932:28-47.

tion the next year, under Francisco Vásquez de Coronado. He "captured" Hawikuh on July 7, 1540, after a fierce battle (Hammond and Rey 1940). Soon after, he continued his explorations toward the Rio Grande Pueblos and eventually as far as the plains of Kansas, finding neither gold and riches nor the fabled "Seven Cities of Cíbola." Nevertheless, the name Cíbola became attached to the Zuni towns and region thenceforth. When Coronado passed through Zuni in 1542 on his way back to Mexico he left behind him several Mexican Indians from his party. They were still there when Antonio de Espejo visited the Zunis 40 years later. What effects this extended contact with partly acculturated Indians may have had is not known, but it may have been partly responsible for the cordial reception received in the Zuni villages by the explorers Francisco Sánchez Chamuscado in 1581, Espejo in 1583, and Juan de Oñate in 1598.

These sporadic contacts were followed in the early 1600s by Spanish efforts to establish missions through the Pueblo country. The first mission to the Zuni began at Hawikuh in 1629, and by 1632 a church and friary were completed as well as a mission in Halona (present-day Zuni). The Hawikuh church proved to be part of a substantial group of structures. The church itself measured 103 by 20 feet inside the nave, its entrance flanked by square towers. Adjacent to the church was a group of 16 rooms around an open hearth, including kitchen, refectory, sacristy, chapel, schoolrooms, and workrooms. For a town of perhaps 600 to 800 people this was an impressive three years' work. But in spite of the apparent willingness of the Zunis to build this church and friary, hostility continued and climaxed in February 1632 when Fray Francisco    Letrado and a fellow priest were killed by the Zunis of Hawikuh. The people reportedly fled to

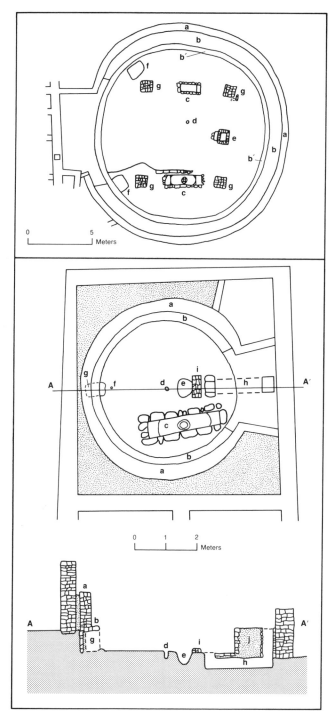

after F.H.H. Roberts 1932:figs. 7, 15.

Fig. 6. "Great Kiva" (Great Kiva 1) and traditional house-sized enclosed kiva (Kiva A) from the Village of the Great Kivas. top, Plan of Great Kiva 1, showing: a, outer walls; b and b', upper and lower benches; c, subfloor vaults possibly used as drums; d, circular hole believed to be a sipapu (symbolic earth navel); e, fire pit; f, adobe lined holes of unknown function; g, four masonry support pillars (F.H.H. Roberts 1932:86–98). bottom, Plan of Kiva A, showing: a-e, as above; f, hole for prayer stick; g, kachina niche; h, subfloor ventilator passage; i, deflector (protecting fire from draft from ventilator); j, fill above ventilator passage (F.H.H. Roberts 1932:52–64). Diameter of Great Kiva, about 16.6 m at widest; of Kiva A about 6.6 m.

Field Mus., Chicago: 74157, 74080.

Fig. 7. Painted prehistoric ceramic bowls from Zuni area. top, Tularosa Black-on-white; bottom, St. Johns Polychrome. Diameter of top, 22.3 cm, other same scale.

Dowa Yalanne, and it is uncertain whether any missionary efforts were recommenced among the Zunis until after 1660 (Hodge 1937:91–93).

Apaches killed the priest at the rebuilt Hawikuh mission in 1672, and it was finally destroyed in the widespread uprising of 1680 when Spanish priests and settlers throughout New Mexico fled or were killed (Hackett 1942). It is reported that when Diego de Vargas established Spanish control again in 1692, he found that the Zunis on Dowa Yalanne had preserved with care the ritual objects taken from the churches, the only instance where these were not destroyed during the Revolt (Vargas Zapata y Luxán Ponze de Léon 1940).

There is no reliable information on Zuni population prior to 1680, although in 1536 Chamuscado reported the number of "houses" in each town, with 118 at Hawikuh and others with 100, 75, 60, 44, and 40, a total of 437. If "house" meant "household," this would suggest a population of possibly 4,000 to 6,000, a great contrast to the 2,500 reported by Vetancurt (1960) in 1680. Even if population had not declined sharply before 1680, it almost certainly did soon after. Fearing the Spanish

471

after Smith, Woodbury, and Woodbury 1966:figs. 39f, 41c.

Fig. 8. Interiors of prehistoric Zuni ceramic bowls excavated from Hawikuh, N.M. top, Heshotauthla Polychrome characterized by red slip with black or green glaze decoration on interior surface and white line decoration on red-slipped exterior (Smith, Woodbury, and Woodbury 1966:304-308). bottom, Reconstruction from fragment of Kwakina Polychrome with black glaze paint on white-slipped interior surface and black glaze and white painted decoration on red-slipped exterior (Smith, Woodbury, and Woodbury 1966:311-313). Diameter of top about 28 cm.

return the Zunis took refuge on defensible mesa tops, including Dowa Yalanne, where hardships would have been great. These refuge settlements consisted of flimsy clusters of 5 to 50 rooms, interspersed with corrals for the sheep that the Spanish had introduced. Water and firewood must have been hard to secure, and crops harvested in the fall would have been brought to store-rooms with difficulty.

In 1692 the Zunis returned to only a single town, Zuni, leaving empty their other five towns. Some of the complexity of modern Zuni social and ritual organization may be due to this amalgamation of previously independent towns as well as to the possibility of accretions in prehistoric times from the Mogollon area to the south (see J.M. Roberts 1961; Rinaldo 1964).

Until the 1700s there had been no secular Spanish settlement among the Zunis, in contrast to the Rio Grande valley. But three Spanish "exiles" came from Santa Fe to Zuni with the priests and soldiers sent to reestablish the mission after 1692. In 1703 these three were killed by the Zunis, reportedly for their overbearing and aggressive behavior. This is the first and last recorded Spanish settlement in the Zuni area until Spanish-speaking communities grew up in the 1860s some 30 miles to the east.

In 1820 the Franciscan mission efforts at Zuni ended, the withdrawal caused partly by continued Zuni resistance to conversion and partly by increasingly serious risks of raids by Apaches and Navajos. The heritage of nearly three centuries of Spanish contact included a few metal tools; significant agricultural crops, especially wheat, oats, and peaches; sheep and burros, the burros permitting harvests from more distant farmlands to be brought back to the village; and a variety of concepts and practices that were incorporated into the beliefs and rituals of the Zunis, including the system of secular government for contact with the outside world, paralleling the religious leadership.

Zuni population was reported as 1,600 and 1,900 in the late 1700s, as 1,600 in 1820, and as 1,300 in 1850. Nevertheless, the pattern of Zuni settlement began to undergo expansion in the nineteenth century, with the establishment of "summer villages," first at Ojo Caliente 15 miles to the south, and later at Nutria (see "Zuni History, 1850–1970," fig. 3, this vol.) 25 miles to the northeast and Pescado closer to Zuni. These outliers were adjacent to farmlands that could not be reached on a daily basis from Zuni. However, the summer homes were deserted each winter as families returned to Zuni. This pattern of dispersed settlement eventually extended over an area greater than that occupied by the Zuni towns of the fifteenth to seventeenth centuries. In the 1880s these summer farming villages became year-round settlements, and a fourth village, Tekapo, was established in 1912 or 1914 (Hodge in Benavides 1945:294).

## Sources

This section† refers to all the chapters on Zuni. It is limited almost entirely to works that meet the following qualifications: the author did actual fieldwork at Zuni; the work is of monograph or book length; and the work contains historical or ethnographic information not previously published. Articles are included only where they provide major corrections to previous work or are considered classics in their fields. A more extensive (but unannotated) bibliography is in Murdock and O'Leary (1975, 5:370-380).

The only comprehensive account of Zuni history (and

† This sources section was written by Dennis Tedlock and Barbara Tedlock.

the only detailed treatment of the entire post-Hispanic period) is that of Crampton (1977). The source of choice for the early Hispanic period is Bandelier (1892a); Hodge's (1937) treatment of this period was copied verbatim from Bandelier. Smith and Roberts (1954) give a detailed political and legal history, especially of the American period.

The only attempt at a general ethnography of Zuni is that of Stevenson (1904). Various aspects of ceremonialism have been detailed by Cushing (1883), Parsons (1917, 1924), and Bunzel (1932, 1932a), while Adair (1948) is the major source on witchcraft. The fundamental source on Zuni kinship remains Kroeber (1919), with Schneider and Roberts (1956) providing clarification. J.M. Roberts (1956) has published four scenarios of everyday interaction in Zuni households. Socialization is the subject of works by Stevenson (1887) and Leighton and Adair (1966). The most widely read piece on Zuni is Chapter 4 in Benedict's (1934:52-119) *Patterns of Culture;* her description of Zuni personality drew counterstatements from Li (1937) and Goldfrank (1945), while J.W. Bennett (1946) attempted to resolve the controversy.

Newman has provided the only dictionary of the Zuni language (1958) and the only full treatment of Zuni grammar (1965). The grammar should be used together with Walker's (1966a, 1972) amplifications. Pioneering contributions to what would later become the field of sociolinguistics were Kroeber's (1916b) "The Speech of a Zuni Child" and Newman's (1955) "Vocabulary Levels: Zuni Sacred and Slang Usage."

Zuni narrative is the subject of a sociolinguistic treatise by Tedlock (1968). Collections of narratives have been published by Bunzel (1932b, 1933), Benedict (1935), and Tedlock (1972). There are other narrative collections, those of Cushing (1896, 1901) and the Zuni people (Quam 1972), but these should be read with great caution, the former because of Cushing's elaborations and the latter because of oversimplification. Bunzel (1932c) has published a collection of spoken and chanted ritual oratory. The serious collection of Zuni song began with Fewkes (1890), whose sound recordings at Zuni were the first ever made of a non-Western music. The only lengthy anthropological treatment of Zuni music is that of B. Tedlock (1973).

The literature on Zuni technology and plastic arts is unusually rich. Stevenson (1915) surveys the uses of more than 100 species of plants, while Cushing (1920) focuses on agriculture and food preparation. Ladd (1963) details the trapping of birds and the care and use of their feathers. Bunzel (1929) presents the art of the potter; Adair (1944) is the basic source on silversmithing, corrected on historical matters by Walker (1974). Architecture and settlement patterns are described by Mindeleff (1891).

473

# Zuni History, 1850–1970

FRED EGGAN AND T.N. PANDEY

With the successful revolt of Mexico against Spain in 1821, the withdrawal of Spanish troops and missions left the Spanish-Mexican settlements and the Indian Pueblos exposed to raids by Navajos and Apaches, as well as the Comanches and other Plains tribes. The newly established Mexican government lacked the resources to staff the posts and missions on the northern frontier. In the same year William Becknell inaugurated the Santa Fe trade, which gradually reoriented New Mexico toward the United States; and a quarter-century later Gen. Stephen W. Kearny and his Army of the West conquered the region without opposition, before continuing to California. In the Treaty of Guadalupe Hidalgo in 1848, New Mexico was acquired by the United States and two years later established as the Territory of New Mexico (Lamar 1970; Duffus 1930).

As Spicer (1962) has noted, the Southwest has been a region in which one society did not really conquer another, but the groups remained fragmented in separate cultural enclaves. By 1850 the heterogeneous populations had built up walls of resistance to one another—and to intruders—that were not easily breached. The new owners were soon to discover this as they set out to explore and pacify their new lands and assimilate the peoples and cultures to the expanding nation.

## 1850–1900

In 1850 Zuni was still self-sufficient after three centuries of Spanish contacts, but the next half-century brought about changes in almost all aspects of Zuni life. During the Mexican period, 1821–1846, the Pueblo was visited only at intervals and had no foreign residents, but Zuni was on several important trade routes and continued as an important center. In addition to periodic Navajo and Apache raids, the discovery of gold in California brought an increasing number of travelers, who often took whatever they needed from Zuni flocks and crops.

James S. Calhoun, the first superintendent of Indian affairs and later the first territorial governor of New Mexico, visited Zuni in 1849 as part of Col. John M. Washington's expedition against the Navajo. He noted the presence of Mexican traders, who provided firearms and firewater in exchange for stolen horses and captives and who traveled freely throughout the region (McNitt

1962). The following year Navajo raids on Zuni led to a military expedition against the Navajo and the loan of firearms to the Zuni, but the raids were not checked until the establishment of Fort Wingate in the early 1870s.

Zuni was visited by various survey parties in the 1850s (fig. 1), and the first American resident, A.F. Banta, arrived in 1865. Banta had become ill while passing through Zuni and, after his recovery, remained to learn the language. He was adopted by the Zuni war chief and invited to join the Bow Society, an honor he declined. In 1873 he became a guide for the George M. Wheeler Expedition and returned to Zuni in 1880, where he met Lt. John G. Bourke. Catholic missionaries made new attempts to establish themselves at Zuni but were unsuccessful. The Atlantic and Pacific Railroad had reached Gallup, some 40 miles to the north, in 1881, and opened the way for an influx of outsiders—traders, missionaries, and settlers. Gallup, initially a railroad center, has continued to be a central community for both Zunis and Navajos.

In 1879 the population was still concentrated in a single village (fig. 2), though they had begun to spread out into farming communities during the summer (fig. 3). After the Navajo were incarcerated at Fort Sumner from 1864 to 1868, they were less of a problem, but the Apaches were not fully controlled for another decade. John Wesley Powell, director of the Bureau of Ethnology under the auspices of the Smithsonian Institution, sent the first anthropological expedition to Zuni in 1879. Under the leadership of James Stevenson, this group included Stevenson's wife, Matilda, and a young ethnologist named Frank H. Cushing, both of whom made important contributions to the knowledge of Zuni. When the expedition moved on, Cushing remained behind to learn the language and to make an ethnological study of the community. To facilitate his researches Cushing moved into the governor's house and after some initial difficulties was accepted by the Zuni and admitted to the Bow Society (see fig. 4). His membership in the Bow Society gave him access to the political and ceremonial system of Zuni. When Cushing incurred the enmity of Sen. John A. Logan of Illinois by opposing the attempt of a group of Whites, including the senator's son-in-law, an army officer from Fort Wingate, and a civilian, to take over Zuni land for their cattle ranch, he was forced to leave Zuni in 1884. However, he later was able to return

Smithsonian, NAA: Sitgreaves 1853:pl. 1 (bottom).

Fig. 1. Buffalo Dance at Zuni, as recorded by Richard Kern, official artist and cartographer for the Sitgreaves expedition down the Zuni and Colorado rivers. top, Sketches of male and female dancers on facing pages of the artist's sketchbook are among the earliest surviving depictions of Zuni. Details of the woman's wrist band and headdress, with colors indicated, are shown. bottom, Published lithograph of the dance from the expedition's official report shows the dancers and chorus in front of the church, with multistoried dwellings in background. The costumes, choreography, and banner are similar to those of an Eastern Pueblo corn dance (see "Santo Domingo Pueblo," fig. 9, this vol.). The headdress worn by the woman in the sketch (and one of the women in the lithograph) corresponds to those worn in Eastern Pueblo Buffalo Dances (see "San Ildefonso Pueblo," fig. 10, this vol.). Sketches by Richard Kern, Sept. 1851, in private collection.

to central Arizona as director of the Hemenway Expedition (Cushing 1941; Mark 1976).

Matilda Stevenson continued to work with her husband until his death in 1888, when she was appointed to a position in the Bureau of Ethnology and was able to continue her research on Zuni ceremonies (fig. 6) (Stevenson 1904). While the contributions of Cushing and Stevenson were quite different, and even contradictory at times, together they provide an important baseline for understanding Zuni society and culture in the 1880s and 1890s that is unrivaled for the Pueblo region.

Zuni had been provided with a land grant of 17,635 acres by the Spanish Crown in 1689, and the grant was recognized in the treaty of 1848 and later confirmed by the U.S. government. Subsequent additions greatly increased the Zuni reservation and brought the total to 406,967 acres.

In 1876 Mormon missionaries visited Zuni. The following year the first Presbyterian missionary arrived at Zuni and a mission was built north of the village and a school was started. Attendance was low until the mission brought in two women as teachers, who doubled the enrollment by providing clothing and a noon meal to the children. In 1896 the government purchased the school and the Presbyterian mission was discontinued, though one of the teachers remained as a matron-teacher.

In 1890 the population of Zuni was 1,547, but a severe smallpox epidemic in 1898–1899 is reported to have caused 282 deaths. The high mortality from epidemics was gradually decreased around the turn of the century by improved sanitation and better medical services, with a consequent rise in population over the next decades. In 1897 the Christian Reformed Mission sent the Rev. Andrew Vanderwagen to Zuni, and his wife, a trained

Fig. 2. Zuni Pueblo in 1879, looking south, showing food drying on the rooftops, chimneys of masonry often surmounted by one or more pots, at least one terrace cooking pit (center foreground), skylight openings, and beehive ovens. Terraced houses reached to a height of 5 stories (see Mindeleff 1891:97-99, pl. 86 for a description and plan of the Pueblo in 1881). Photograph by John K. Hillers, the Bureau of Ethnology photographer who accompanied the expedition led by James Stevenson.

Fig. 3. Village of Nutria. In 1881 this was the smallest of three farming villages of Zuni occupied during the planting and harvesting season (Mindeleff 1891:94-95; "Zuni Prehistory and History to 1850," this vol.). Photograph probably by John K. Hillers, 1879.

nurse, aided the Zunis throughout the smallpox epidemic. As a result, the Zunis provided them with land for a chapel, but Vanderwagen later resigned and turned his attention to trading.

During the 1870s Anglo traders had begun to replace itinerant Mexicans and during the period 1880-1900 Zuni supported three Anglo and two Indian traders. At that time the Zuni economy was mainly agrarian, but the traders gradually shifted the emphasis toward sheep and cattle after the construction of the railroad opened new markets. By the 1890s there was a considerable number of resident Anglos in Zuni: teachers, missionaries, traders, and a few government officials. They began to have an important influence on the internal affairs of the Pueblo, both by increasing the dependence of the Zuni on the traders and the government and by calling in U.S. troops from Fort Wingate to halt trials for witchcraft.

## 1900–1950

In the 1880s control of Zuni was in the hands of a hierarchy of six or seven senior priests, who were assisted by the Elder and Younger Brother Bow Priests acting as the executive arm of the council of priests. The Bow Priesthood (fig. 6), composed of warriors who had taken scalps from the enemy, was responsible for protecting the

Fig. 4. Studio portrait of 6 Zunis who accompanied Cushing on an 1882 expedition East, which included a meeting with President Chester Arthur, a presentation at the National Academy of Sciences in Washington, and a visit to the Iroquois reservation at Tonawanda (Baxter 1882; Brandes 1965:82–93). left to right, (back row) Naiyutchi, senior member of the Bow Priesthood; Nanahe, a Hopi who had been adopted by the Zuni; Kiasiwa, a junior member of the Bow Priesthood; (front row) Laiyuahtsailunkya; Laiyuaitsailu (Pedro Pino), a former governor of Zuni; Palowahtiwa (Patricio Pino), governor with whom Cushing stayed and member of the Bow Priesthood. Photograph by John K. Hillers, 1882.

Pueblo against both external and internal enemies, but with the decline in warfare, its numbers and prestige also declined, and its primary concern came to be warfare against Zuni witches, who were believed to cause drought, sickness, and death. The procedure of the Bow Priests was to force witches to confess their misdeeds by hanging them from a bar and beating them; once they had confessed, their powers for evil were believed to be lost.

The turn of the century found Zuni in turmoil. The Agency for Indian affairs was at Santa Fe and the teachers and traders who represented the Bureau of Indian Affairs in Washington began to call in troops to suppress witchcraft trials and maintain law and order. The Agency for Zuni was moved to nearby Black Rock in 1902, with Douglas Graham, a long-time trader, as first superintendent. Smith and Roberts (1954) collected some 18 cases of witchcraft accusations, 14 of which occurred between 1880 and 1900. When the troops arrested the Bow Priests their authority was destroyed and on their release the Elder Brother Bow Priest refused to serve any longer.

An interesting case involved a Zuni, Nick Tumaka, one of the most powerful men in the Pueblo. He challenged the authority of the Bow Priests, who were trying to force him to confess to witchcraft, by sending his father to bring the troops from Fort Wingate. They arrested four Zunis, and later a troop of soldiers remained at Zuni for over a year. The case of Nick Tumaka marked the end of the Bow Priests' powers since the witches had been saved by the Whites. The senior priests, who were not supposed to be directly concerned with secular affairs, were forced to take a greater interest in political matters and in the selection of the appointed officials (Smith and Roberts 1954).

The tribal council in the nineteenth century was composed of the governor and a number of assistants who were annually selected by the Bow Priests and

Fig. 5. Zuni ceramic canteen and water jars, part of the extensive Zuni collection made by James Stevenson, characterized by black and red stylized plant, bird, and deer motifs with repeated geometric units painted on a white slipped background. The deer with red "heart line" from the mouth to the animal's interior is distinctively Zuni. Diameter of left 28 cm, rest same scale. Canteen collected 1879, jars collected 1884.

Fig. 6. Choir of the Bow Priesthood, on the ninth day of a ceremonial of initiation into the Society. They are seated on the ledge of a house, resting and smoking between dances. The drum (made by covering a large pot) and hooped drumstick were used in dances. Photograph by Matilda C. Stevenson, probably in Oct. 1891 when she witnessed the ceremony (Stevenson 1904:578–608).

installed by the council of priests. During the twentieth century the council gradually increased in size and importance and came to achieve a dominant position in the political life of Zuni. Though Kroeber (1919) thought the tribal council to be a native institution, it originated in a Spanish edict of 1620 that was apparently not applied to Zuni until after the Pueblo Revolt of 1680. During the nineteenth century the council played a minor role, but the new outside contacts and pressures that were developing, and the new problems resulting from factional divisions, put the tribal council in the forefront (Pandey 1967, 1977).

In 1916 a proposal for the establishment of a new Roman Catholic mission aroused strong opposition, and a general meeting was "unanimously" against the suggestion. But the Catholic group persisted, and, with the aid of a sympathetic agent, the Bureau of Indian Affairs was persuaded to grant a plot of Pueblo land for the construction of Saint Anthony's Mission Church in 1922. The Zuni were sharply divided on this issue, with two senior priests favoring the Catholics and three or four opposing, the division gradually hardening into permanent factions. During the period 1920–1927 three sets of tribal council officers alternated between pro- and anti-Catholic groups. In 1928 an anti-Catholic governor was appointed and served for seven years, since the senior priests could not agree on a successor (Trotter 1955).

Frederick W. Hodge had carried out archeological excavations at Hawikuh, an abandoned Zuni village, from 1917 to 1923, and in 1923 he received permission to photograph the Shalako ceremony from the anti-Catholic or "progressive" faction. However, the Catholic "conservative" faction objected to the photographers and their cameras were smashed and Hodge was forced to leave. The following year, when two anthropologists arrived at Zuni to carry out linguistic and ethnological research, they found the village in an upheaval and the "progressives," who were supported by the Protestant sympathizers, in disgrace. From 1924 to 1934 the two factions gradually solidified into political groups and became a permanent part of the election system. The Zuni council of priests attempted to restore the old system by which they had selected the secular officials, but with the acceptance of the Indian Reorganization Act of 1934, the Indian Service preferred to keep church and state separate. It should be noted that despite the use of "Catholic" and "Protestant" appellations, there were relatively few converts, and the bulk of the population continued to support the Zuni religion (Benedict 1934, 1935; Bunzel 1938, 1952).

In 1934 the Zuni accepted the provisions of the Indian Reorganization Act, which provided, among other things, for the election of a tribal council by secret ballot. The Zuni agent appointed a nominating committee, divided equally between the two factions, to select candidates for governor, lieutenant-governor, and five (later six) *tenientes* representing the farming villages and Zuni proper. The resulting tribal council was elected by popular vote and installed by the council of priests. The insignia of office are canes—one set originally from the Spanish Crown and the second presented by President Abraham Lincoln in 1863. Since the 1940s only the Lincoln canes have been used. The authority of the office resides in the cane; when it is taken away the official has no power (Pandey 1968, 1977).

The tribal council is responsible for the health, safety, morals, and welfare of the Zuni community and has the power to negotiate with the federal and state governments with regard to tribal resources and activities. Through the years 1905–1909 the government had built the first of several dams at Black Rock to provide for more adequate irrigation from the Zuni River, though dry farming remained the major agricultural practice. Initially the tribal council set up farm and stock committees, but in the 1930s soil erosion, brought about by overgrazing, became a major problem and ultimately resulted in stock-reduction programs in the early 1940s, which caused a great deal of friction with traders and Zuni alike (Leighton and Adair 1966).

World War II was an important turning point in the history of Zuni. Over 200 Zuni men were involved in the war effort and many others left the Pueblo to engage in war-related activities, while governmental programs were

478

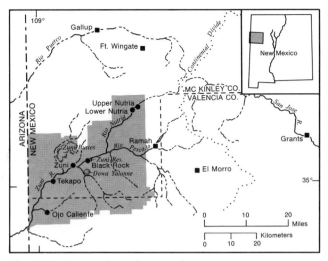

Fig. 7. Zuni Reservation and surrounding area.

sharply curtailed. After the war there was a concerted effort to re-integrate Zuni veterans into ceremonial activities, but the returning soldiers had a difficult time adjusting to the restrictions of Zuni life and did not begin to exert their full influence until the 1950s (Adair and Vogt 1949; Bunker 1956).

## 1950–1970

The major changes in the postwar period were the continuing shift in political power from priests to politicians; the growth of the factions into political "parties;" the increasing importance of the tribal council ("Zuni Social and Political Organization," fig. 7, this vol.) in the process of gaining control over reservation resources and activities, for example, the development of crafts centering around silver jewelry into a major source of income for the community; attempts to attract industry to the reservation; and the expansion of the educational system to approximate that of local White communities. With increasing prosperity and mobility have come the problems of law and order that affect most American communities.

The tribal council expanded its jurisdiction during the 1950s and 1960s with regard to community services, including a water system, sewage disposal, electricity, and paved roads, as well as new housing. Committees concerned with agriculture, education, firefighting, legal aid, economic development, and recreation were in operation, and a water board, police department, housing authority, and utility authority regulated these concerns. In 1965 women were given the privilege of voting in this matrilineal society. The Craftsmen's Cooperative Association was established in the 1960s to facilitate the manufacture and sale of Zuni silver jewelry, in which 90 percent of the men and women were involved to some degree. In 1977 Zuni had a Lions Club, an American Legion Post, a Women's Home Extension Club, and

other associations that shared common interests, but with all these new activities Zuni managed to remain determinedly Zuni.

In the 1970s there was a considerable expansion of federal grants and projects, which enabled the tribal council to expand the employment of Zunis on the reservation. Because the annual tribal income from trader's taxes, from industrial enterprises, and from fines and leases was not large, Zuni has been dependent on federal support. However, in 1970 the Indian Service agreed to turn over control of the reservation to the tribal council, with the agent occupying the status of advisor to the tribe. The veterans have been instrumental in getting a modern school system run by McKinley County under contract with the tribe, and some 2,000 children were in school in 1970. About 200 students from Zuni were in institutions of higher learning; most of them did not return to the reservation after school. The problems of law and order centered around drinking, with the tribal council handling all offenses except those that required federal action.

Despite the multitude of changes, Zuni has managed to maintain its ceremonial system and world view, even if its dominant values were changing under the pressures of modern life. Zuni has grown from 1,500 to over 6,000 in 100 years and is the largest Pueblo by far. While its outward appearance is vastly different ("Zuni Religion and World View," fig. 2, this vol.), its central integrative pattern of cross-cutting systems is still strong, and as long as the priests carry out their ritual duties the bulk of the population can remain as spectators (Kluckhohn and Strodtbeck 1961; Vogt and Albert 1966).

Kroeber once said (1919:203): "I have never heard from a Zuñi the least reference to a historic event," but the modern Zuni have begun to think of both their past and their future. One expression is seen in their cooperation in an account of their narrative poetry and its significance (Tedlock 1972). More central is a book of self-portrayals, which provides an inside view of their thinking:

> With the ways of the white man entering into our lives, perhaps it will not be long before our people become a wandering tribe, aimlessly roving the path of self-deterioration and destruction. But it is for our children to decide and work for. We cannot tell them of the way our people survived, for they would not believe us. We must just hope they, too, can survive what lies before them (Quam 1972:38).

## Synonymy*

The English tribal name Zuni ('zōōnē) is adapted from Spanish (and earlier English) Zuñi ([sunʸi]), itself a

* This synonymy was prepared by Albert H. Schroeder and Ives Goddard. The phonemic Zuni forms were furnished by Dennis Tedlock (personal communication 1978). Additional spellings are listed by Hodge (1937:128–134).

Fig. 8. Salesroom of the Craftsmen's Cooperative Association. The display case at left contains jewelry and 3 female dolls dressed in traditional Zuni costume and carrying pots on their heads; the case at right contains a variety of items including beaded dolls (far right) and a modern version of a clay ceremonial prayer-meal basket (see J. Stevenson 1883:figs. 448–453 for terraced baskets of this type collected in 1879). Albert Peywa Sr. (right) and Fred Bowannie stand behind counter. (See B. Bell 1975 for a photographic record of contemporary Zuni craftsmen and their products.) Photographer unidentified, 1968.

rendering of a form of the Keresan name like Acoma *sɨ́·ni* ([sθɨ́·nʸi]) 'Zuni Indian(s); Zuni Pueblo' (Miller 1965:164, 170, 202) or Santa Ana *sɨ́·ni* 'a Zuni Indian' (Davis 1964:121). The Spanish name first appears, as Suñi and Zuñi (also with plain n), in the reports of the Rodríguez-Chamuscado entrada of 1581–1582 (Gallegos Lamero 1927a:51, 67; Hammond and Rey 1966:137). Later spellings, and corruptions, in the Spanish sources include Tzuñi, Quini, Cuñi (Çuñi?), Somi, Comi, Ami, Sumi, Sumy (Bolton 1916:184; Hammond and Rey 1953, 1:346, 426, 2:1013; Pérez de Luxán 1929:86, 93, 95; Zárate Salmerón 1966:31). The Spanish mission was called Nuestra Señora de Guadalupe de Zuñi.

Derivatives of the Keresan name include Acoma *sɨ́·nɨ́·cʰi* and Santa Ana *sɨ́·nicé* for 'Zuni Pueblo' (Miller 1965:170, 216; Davis 1964:121). Similar forms in other languages are Jemez *sɨ́·ní* (pl. *sɨ́·niš; sɨ́·nígʸiˀ* 'at Zuni') (Joe Sando, personal communication 1978), Tewa *súⁿyûⁿ* (Curtis 1907–1930, 16:260), and Hopi (Mishongnovi) *síyo*

(pl. *siyótɨˀ*) (Whorf 1936:1294) and (Third Mesa) *siˀo* (Harrington 1916:569; Voegelin and Voegelin 1957:49). Tewa *sunʸi* (Harrington 1916:569) and Taos *súnyiˀínæ* (Harrington 1918) appear to be loans from Spanish. Isleta has *saráde* (pl. *sáran; sarái* 'Zuni Pueblo') (C.T. Harrington 1920:47) and Navajo has *Naasht'ézhí* (Robert W. Young, personal communication 1977), literally 'charcoal-blackened enemies' (Hoijer 1974:261; Kenneth L. Hale, personal communication 1973).

The Zuni call themselves *šiwi* (pl. *ˀa·šiwi*) and their Pueblo *šiwinˀa* 'Zuni place'. The name is unanalyzable and is not derived from *ši-* 'meat, flesh'. These forms may be the source of the similar names in other languages, none of which has any meaning except as a name. Other names used by the Zuni for their Pueblo are *ˀitiwanˀa* 'middle place' and *halona·wa*, the name of Halona Pueblo.

The first reference to the Zuni by the Spaniards was in 1539, when Fray Marcos de Niza, in northern Mexico near the present Arizona border, mentioned the province

EGGAN AND PANDEY

of Cíbola or of the Seven Cities, and Cíbola continued in use during Francisco Vásquez de Coronado's explorations of 1540–1542 (Hammond and Rey 1940:69, 157, 170, 298, 308). Spelling variants include Cevola, Tzibola, and Zíbola, sometimes applied to specific Zuni Pueblos. Bandelier's conjecture that Cíbola reflects Zuni *šiwin ʔa* (Hodge 1910j) has not been demonstrated, and the origin of the name is uncertain.

*Pueblos of the Early Spanish Period*

The following is a synonymy for the names of the Zuni Pueblos of the early Spanish period, of which all except Halona were abandoned in the middle to late seventeenth century.

Halona. The Zuni name is *halona·wa* 'red ant place'. Spanish spellings are Alonagua or Aconagua, 1581–1582 (Gallegos Lamero 1927a:51, 65), Alona, 1582–1583 (Pérez de Luxán 1929:89), and Holonagu, 1598 (Hammond and Rey 1953, 1:357). The Zuni name is now used for the present Pueblo of Zuni, built on the site of Halona, and is specifically the name of a certain shrine on the south side of the river (Dennis Tedlock, personal communication 1978).

Hawikuh. Zuni *hawikku* has no clear etymology. The name appears in Spanish reports as Aguico and Allico, 1581–1582 (Gallegos Lamero 1927a:51, 65), Aguico and Aquico, 1582–1583 (Pérez de Luxán 1929:89; Bolton 1916:185), and Aguicobi, Aguiocobi, Aguiuocobi, and Hauico, 1598–1605 (Hammond and Rey 1953, 1:357, 363, 2:1014). Names earlier used by the Spaniards and sometimes appearing in later sources were Granada and variants of Cíbola, such as Scíbola (Hammond and Rey 1940:66, 170, 208, 308, 1953, 1:394, 2:1014). Zárate Salmerón (1966:31, 65) used both Zíbola and Havico. Further variants are listed by Hodge (1907c).

Kechipauan. The modern Zuni name *kečipa·wa* 'gypsum place' is attested from the late nineteenth century on. An earlier name rendered by Cushing as Kiá-na-wa and K'yá-na-we (Hodge 1907d), appears in early Spanish accounts as Acana, 1581–1582; Cana, 1582–1583; and Canabi, after 1598 (Gallegos Lamero 1927a:65; Hammond and Rey 1953, 1:357; Pérez de Luxán 1929:89).

Kiakima. The current Zuni name is *kaki·ma,* also rendered Kyakiima (Tedlock 1972:viii). An earlier or alternate form with *k ʔa-* for *ka-* is suggested by the recordings of Mindeleff (1891:85), k'iakima; Cushing, for example, k'iákime; and Powell (Hodge 1907e), and by the failure of some Spanish recorders to hear the initial *k,* as in Aquima and Aquiman, 1581–1582 (Gallegos Lamero 1927a:51, 65). Later spellings include Quaquima (Pérez de Luxán 1929:89) and Caquima (Hodge 1907e). Cush-

ing's interpretation 'house of eagles' assumes a connection with *k ʔak ʔali* 'eagle'.

Kwakina. The Zuni name *kʷa ʔkinna* or *kʷakkinna* has no definite translation, though Cushing rendered it 'town of the entrance place' (Hodge 1907–1910, 1:744). Spanish sources have Coaquina, 1581–1582, and Quaquina, 1582–1583 (Gallegos Lamero 1927a:65; Pérez de Luxán 1929:89).

Matsaki. The Zuni name *mac ʔa·ka* makes no reference to salt, as Hodge (1907f) claimed. Spanish renderings include Maçaque and Mazaque, 1540–1542; Maça, 1581–1582; Mazaque, Masa, and Malaque, 1582–1583; and Mazaqui, 1598 (Hammond and Rey 1940:174, 222, 252, 324, 1953, 1:357; Gallegos Lamero 1927a:51, 65; Pérez de Luxán 1929:89, 108). Perea applied the name Zíbola (a variant of Cibola) to the "largest" Zuni Pueblo, which contemporary reports imply was Matsaki, though Hodge took it to be Hawikuh (Benavides 1945:214–215, 290–291). Similarly, Ahacus (1539), though with a name that resembles renderings of Hawikuh, was described as the "principal" Pueblo and is therefore likely also to have been Matsaki (Hammond and Rey 1940:72–73, 222).

*Farming Villages*

The seasonal farming villages became year-round settlements only in the early 1880s, and their names do not appear in the early sources.

Nutria. Referred to in English by the Spanish name Nutria 'otter' or Las Nutrias (Hodge 1907–1910, 2:100). The Zuni name *to ʔya* has no known meaning.

Ojo Caliente. The Spanish name is Ojo Caliente 'hot spring' or Ojos Calientes (Hodge 1907–1910, 2:112). Zuni has *k ʔapkʷayina* 'water comes up from the depths'.

Pescado. The name is from Spanish Ojo (del) Pescado 'fish spring' (Hodge 1907–1910, 2:234–235; Cushing 1920:363). The Zuni name is *hešota c ʔina* 'marked house', a reference to the pictographs in the ruined Pueblo at the site.

Tekapo. The Zuni name *tekappowa* 'full of hills, hilly' has also been rendered Tekyapoawa (Hodge, in Benavides 1945:294).

**Sources**

Materials for the history of Zuni during the American period are widely scattered. The most comprehensive coverage is Pandey's (1967) dissertation on factionalism, and Crampton (1977) gives a useful general account of Zuni history. Of great importance are the letter books and the annual reports of the Zuni Agency, generally not published in full in the Annual Reports of the Commissioner of Indian Affairs (ARCIA) but available at Zuni and the National Archives.

# Zuni Social and Political Organization

EDMUND J. LADD

The Zuni social, religious, and political system, with its strong interconnections to the ceremonial and religious cycles and to the kin and clan system, is a complex structure that has occupied scholars and defied interpretation by them since the 1890s. Kroeber's (1919) and Eggan's (1950) are perhaps the outstanding works on the subject. Earlier studies of Zuni life by Cushing (1896) and Stevenson (1904) add historical perspective. More recent studies have added some new data and some reinterpretation of old data. What follows is a brief resumé of these sources from my own perspective as a Zuni.

When contacted by Francisco Vásquez de Coronado in 1540, the Zunis occupied six villages along the Zuni River and its tributaries. Events after 1680, the year of the Pueblo Revolt, and the Spanish "reconquest" in 1692 led to their consolidation into a single village at *halona·wa*.* In the 1970s there were also four outlying farming villages, which were occupied during the spring and summer growing season.

The basic economic activities in order of their importance are: arts and crafts, especially silversmithing; wage work both on and off reservation; stock raising, mainly sheep and cattle; and agriculture.

The mother's household is the social, religious, and economic unit. Normally, it is composed of a maternal lineage segment: an older woman, her sisters, and the married and unmarried daughters to which from time to time are added various male relatives and in-laws.

In the 1970s the maternal household was still the social and religious center of the family. However, the economic base and the makeup of the household have changed. Male members who join the household bring into it well-developed skills and knowledge by which they gain immediate status. In most cases, husband and wife have skills (usually silversmithing) by which they can support their family and become independent of the household early in life—something that took years of planning and preparation under the old system. And, because heads of families gain more and better assistance from the state and federal social services, there is a tendency toward separation from the maternal household. Although young people move away from their maternal household early, they maintain strong ties with their respective households to which they return for all major social and religious occasions.

## Socioreligious Organization

The Zuni socioreligious system is composed of four interlocking subsystems, each operating independently yet synchronically to provide for the physical and psychological needs of the users. Superimposed one upon the other are the clans (*ʔannoti·we*), the kiva groups (*ʔupa·we*, which together make up the *kotikanne* 'Kachina Society'), the curing societies (*tika·we;* sg. *tikanne*), which include the eight Societies of the Completed Path (*ʔona· ya·naka tika·we),* and the priesthoods (*ʔa·šiwani* 'Rain Priests' and *ʔa·piʔɬa ʔa·šiwani* 'Bow Priests') (tables 1–2). Of the Rain Priests, 6 are Daylight Priests and 10 are Night Priests; counted as Daylight Priests are the Head Bow Priest, as the priest of the nadir, and the *pekʷinne šiwani* 'spokesman priest', the priest of the zenith and generally referred to in English as the Sun Priest. In 1978 the office of *pekʷinne* had been vacant since the 1940s and there were only two Bow Priests. Underlying, welded, and cross-tied to these four systems is the kinship system.

A child is born into the system. At birth its position is established within the kin-clan group (fig. 1). What it is called, how it will call others, and who it cannot or can marry are established. Position at birth determines future behavior and how others will behave toward the child. It belongs to its mother's household where its greatest responsibilities and loyalties will lie, and it belongs to its mother's clan, which immediately establishes certain behavior patterns and also, to some degree, determines what positions of responsibility it will hold in the religious system. It is a 'child of' its father's clan, a relationship that determines future behavior and responsibilities toward the members of its father's household and father's clan, who will provide support in various religious and life crises.

Within the limits of the foregoing framework is the nucleus of a system (fig. 1) that is well understood by the users. The "irregularities" and "inconsistencies" in the system noted by students (Schneider and Roberts 1956:3, 4) are in the areas of "extended usage" beyond the limiting boundaries of the nucleus (they are also due to a

---

* The translations and interpretations from Zuni to English in this chapter are my own as a native speaker. The orthography used is that of Newman (1965:12–15; "Sketch of the Zuni Language," vol. 17).

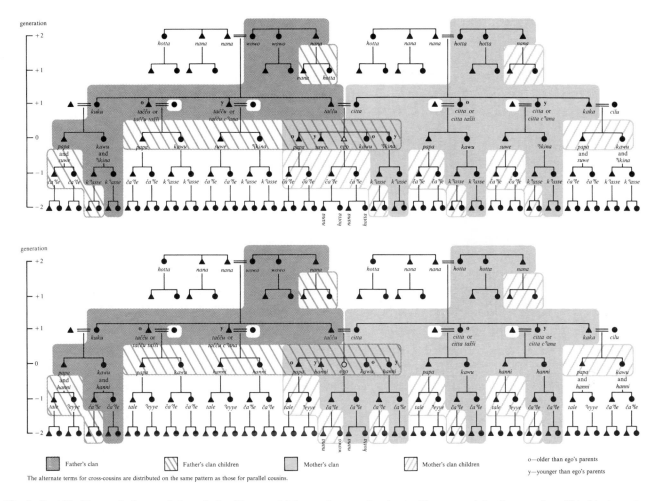

Fig. 1. Zuni kinship terminology and clan relationships. top, Male ego; bottom, female ego. The text explains the extension of kinship terms to relatives here unlabeled. See also Eggan 1950:figs. 11–12.

degree to faults in data collecting and interpretations). To the users of the system, there are no "wrong," "incorrect," "irregular," or "inconsistent" usages. Standing at the center of his universe, which is determined at birth, the individual is keenly aware of his relationships. Although he does not separate them overtly with separate terms of identification, he is never confused among blood kin, clan kin, and ceremonial or religious relationships (Kroeber 1919:73). He is aware of the broad outlines of the total system that includes the entire village. He relates to this broader universe by reference to the basic system. And, perhaps because of the short life expectancy—prehistorically perhaps 40 to 50 years—there was never any real need to classify or identify beyond the mother's mother and father's mother.

### Kinship Terms

The Zuni kinship terms are used to designate not only blood kin and relatives by marriage but also clan kin and ceremonial relatives.

The basic applications of the 16 terms used for blood

kin are given on the kinship charts (fig. 1) (compare Kroeber 1919:178–179); superimposed here are boundaries for the mother's and father's clan and for the "children of the (mother's) clan" and "father's clan children," which may bring into sharper focus the terminology applied to certain categories of relatives. Of these terms all but *wowo* 'father's mother' are also used to designate clan kin; the specific usages depend on the relative ages and personal closeness of the individuals concerned. The terms for relatives by marriage are *ʔulani* 'daughter-in-law', *taˑlakʔi* 'son-in-law', *cilu* 'mother's brother's wife', and *ʔinniha* 'step-mother'. There are also extended uses of *ʔulani* and *cilu*, and there is a term *hašši* applied to women older than one's mother of relatively distant blood or clan relationship.

Ten of the kinship terms are used to designate ceremonial relatives: *taččū, citta, kaka, hotta, nana, kawu, papa, suwe, hanni,* and *tale.* Five of these together with three terms not otherwise in use occur with a suffix *-mo* in a series of reciprocal terms of address used by the two participants in a certain smoking ritual: *taččumo, talemo;*

Fig. 2. Young Zuni girl carrying a small child, probably her younger brother. The boy is held on her back with a wrapped shawl, the usual way of carrying very young children. Photograph by Jesse L. Nusbaum, 1911.

*papamo, suwemo; kakamo, kʔassemo; nanamo, tošlemo; ʔalemo, ʔuwakamo* (Newman 1965:62-63; Kroeber 1919:70-71; Bunzel 1930:762).

There are some questions concerning the type of kinship system the Zuni have. Eggan (1950:182) says "there is a marked structural resemblance to the Crow type in general and the Hopi system in particular"; Murdock (1949:247, 346) has called Zuni kinship "Normal Crow"; and Schneider and Roberts (1956:22) say the Zuni system "can best be described as 'modified Crow.'" Clarification awaits additional field study.

In the center of the system are the true blood kin; peripheral to this are the close clan kin of mother's and father's lineages. As observed by Kroeber (1919), true blood relationship and clan relationship are never confused. Because of this recognition, there are no wrong or incorrect uses of terms. In actual usage, then, the relationship term selected by the user depends on this recognition but it also depends on how close the speaker wishes to bring the person into the circle of kin—blood or clan. "Irregularities" center in the third to fifth degree of remoteness—"that is to say, these irregularities do not center primarily on distant members of Ego's own clan, or Ego's mother's father's clan, but instead seem to occur randomly among all tertiary or more remote relatives" (Schneider and Roberts 1956:12). The rules for selection of available alternate terms for these secondary relatives are entirely dependent on the user's knowledge of the system and the situation. There are no explicit rules or laws but rather broad general guidelines that are implicit in the selection of the "proper" term.

*Special Kin Terms*

Kinship terms and their application to the various kin categories have been documented in detail (Kroeber 1919; Eggan 1950; Schneider and Roberts 1956). A few applications still need special attention. It will be noted that there are no special terms for son and daughter. However, there are a number of descriptive terms that apply.

In kinship usage (whether male or female speaking) a child in general reference is called *čaʔle* 'child' (pl. *čawe*). If asked specifically "what do you call your son? your daughter?" the most likely reply would be *hom ʔakcekʔi* and *hom kacikʔi* 'my male child' and 'my female child'. These two terms, *ʔakcekʔi* 'boy' and *kacikʔi* 'girl', are probably the only ones that come near to designating 'son' and 'daughter' in the English sense. If the son and daughter are teenagers or the son has undergone his final initiation into the kiva group, the reply would be *hom cawakʔi* and *hom ʔeʔle* 'my young male child', and 'my young female child'. After the *ʔeʔle* has had a child of her own, she then becomes *makkʔi* 'young woman'. In a very general way a Zuni might say *hom ʔa·cʔan ʔa·či* 'my two small children' or *hom čaw ʔa·či* 'my two children'.

If the terms *čaʔle, ʔakcekʔi, kacikʔi, cawakʔi, ʔeʔle,* and *makkʔi* are modified by *hom* 'my', the speaker brings the person spoken of into individual (personal) kin or ceremonial relationship. If the terms are modified by *hoʔnʔa·wan* 'our', collectively speaking for the clan, or household, it puts the person spoken of in the distant general clan or ceremonial relationship with the speaker.

Children of ego's male clanmates (whether ego is male or female) at, above, and below ego's generation are ego's clan children, called *čawe* 'children'. The children of the men of ego's father's clan, including ego and ego's brothers and sisters, are the clan children of ego's father. The members of ego's father's clan call ego, their clan child, *čaʔle* 'child' and have a special joking relationship with him; ego calls them *tačču* and *kuku,* the terms used for father's brother and sister. Ego and all others that are clan children of the same clan (except brothers and sisters) are *čawe* to each other and call each other *čaʔle.* With his father's clanmates that are also blood kin ego has a closer relationship than with those that are not, and with these kin he may use ordinary kinship terms as well as the terms with clan-relationship meanings.

## Religious Organizations

The backbone of Zuni ritual life is the religious and ceremonial organizations. Membership in them cuts across kinship and clan boundaries and is based on individual choice, accident (trespass or illness), and clan affiliation. All male members at age 8 to 12 undergo their final initiation into one of the six mens' groups or kivas (sg. *kotikanne*) (table 1). The original choice is made by the father or mother at the child's birth, but in future years, for personal or social reasons, a member can change membership to another kiva; membership in one kiva is not binding for life. Women are generally excluded (there was only one female member of the *heʔi·kʷe* kiva in the 1930s). Membership in any one of the 12 curing societies (*tika·we*) (table 1) sometimes called "the cult of the Beast Gods" (Bunzel 1932a:476), is by choice through illness or trespass, and is open to men and women. Although some individuals "quit," membership is usually for life. The *ʔa·šiwani*, the Rain Priesthoods (called by Bunzel the cult of the *ʔuwanammi*, which is the ritual term for the rain-bringing beings), of which there are 16, is also open to men and women but is limited by clan affiliation. Membership in the *ʔa·piʔɫa ʔa·šiwani*, the Bow Priesthood (cult of the Gods of War), is limited to male members who have taken an enemy scalp. Each of these organizations performs various ritual and ceremonial rites, both public and secret, throughout the year to assure the spiritual well-being of the tribe (see also "Zuni Religion and World View," this vol.).

When a young man joins the kiva he acquires a new set of "older and younger brothers." The kiva leaders he calls 'father', the older men 'grandfather'. He calls his sponsors 'father' and 'mother', and they call him *čaʔle* 'child'. This relationship is only between the young man and his fellow kiva members and sponsors and does not include any other members of his household, the sponsors' household, or the households of his fellow kiva members. The same pattern is true for membership in any of the other religious or ceremonial organizations (Kroeber 1919:186).

## Clan System

The Zuni clan system overlaps and interlocks with the kinship and religious systems to enforce, regulate, and, to a degree, control the socioreligious behavior patterns.

Every Zuni is born into a clan and is the child of its father's clan. Cushing (1896) recorded 16 active clans in the early 1880s; Kroeber (1919) listed 15 active clans. In 1977 there were 14 matrilineal, totemically named, exogamous clans (table 2) (Kroeber 1919:table 2).

The Zuni clan system is in a continual state of flux. Since 1896 there have been nine clans that have become extinct or inactive. Stevenson (1904) reported only one male member in the Antelope clan in 1904. By 1916 when Kroeber was working in the area, it had become extinct. Kroeber (1919) reported only one household for the Yellowwood clan *(taɫupcʔi·kʷe);* it became extinct in 1975 when its last member died. Both of these were not subclans but separate and distinct units.

Subclans are recognized more frequently in the larger clans. This may have been forced by circumstances as discussed by Kroeber (1919:101), but it may also provide a mechanism for the "creation" of new clans as some die off. Those clans reported as being extinct by Cushing (1896:368) and Stevenson (1904:292) were actually subclans that became inactive or ignored as the clan of which they were a subdivision became smaller and there was no longer any need for them.

It is explicit in Zuni teaching that one does not marry anyone from one's own clan, even if the individual is from another lineage segment. This does not mean it has never happened, as Kroeber (1919) records a situation in which the people involved didn't realize their relationship, married, and later found out they were from the same clan. This is an exception rather than the rule.

Marriage with members of one's father's clan or their children is severely condemned but does occur. Marriage with members of one's father's household is absolutely forbidden, since such people are blood kin, not merely clan kin. Marriage between subclans, such as Macaw and Crow of the *picči·kʷe* clan, is condemned but does occur.

Marriage is an agreement between two people. When a woman welcomes the advances of a man, after a few preliminary meetings, she consults with her mother to make sure the young man is acceptable to the household.

**Table 1. Zuni Religious Organizations, 1977**

*Kiva Groups*

1. *heʔi·kʷe*
2. *heʔkʔapa·kʷe (sa·pi·pi·kʷe)*
3. *čupa·kʷe*
4. *muhe·kʷe*
5. *ʔohe·kʷe*
6. *ʔupcʔana·kʷe*

*Curing or Medicine Societies*

*Societies of the Completed Path*

1. *makkʔe ɫana·kʷe*
2. *makkʔe cʔana·kʷe*
3. *šiwana·kʷe*
4. *čikkʔali·kʷe*
5. *ʔuhuhu·kʷe*
6. *pešacilo·kʷe* (3 male members)
7. *halo·kʷe*
8. *newe·kʷe*

*Other Societies*

9. *saniyaka·kʷe (sutikanne)*
10. *šuma·kʷe*
11. *kʔo·ši·kʷe* (2 inactive members in the 1960s)
12. *ɫewe·kʷe* (2 members)

*Priesthoods*

1. *ʔa·šiwani* (16 priesthoods): 6 Daylight Priests, including the Bow Priest (nadir) and the *pekʷinne* (zenith), a position vacant since the 1940s; and 10 Night Priests
2. *ʔa·piʔɫa ʔa·šiwani* (2 members)

Fig. 3. Zuni house interiors about 1900. top, General living room, usually the largest room of a Zuni house, in which the family spends most of its time and guests are entertained; it can also function as a ceremonial room (Stevenson 1904:292). Typical features include a ledge, used for seating or as shelving, against one wall; mealing bins (see "Hopi Economy and Subsistence," fig. 16, this vol.), placed against the back wall; pole, on which blankets are hung, suspended from ceiling rafters at left; large hooded fireplace at right. Skylight (at center) and oil lamp (on right wall) provide light. bottom, Narrower room with skylights and dirt rather than stone floor; storage niches; ladder (at back) probably providing access to rooftop; fireplace (mid-way along the right wall, seen here from the back). Zuni houses consisted of as many as 8 and as few as 2 rooms, the usual number being 4 to 6 (Stevenson 1904:292). Photographs by (top) Adam C. Vroman, 1897, and Ben Wittick, 1890s.

After this she invites him to her bed "in secret." He leaves the bride's home very early each morning and takes care not to be seen by the neighbors. During this period of cohabitation, either partner can call off the marriage. If she calls it off, there are no major complications; however, if he calls it off, he has to "pay a bride price" or the woman can force him into the arrangement by making public her intentions. She does this by going to his mother's home at noon, so everyone will see, with a gift (a large basket of corn or wheat flour); there is a special verb for this act, ʔulaˑwaˑne. The man's mother then returns her gift by presenting her with the traditional black dress, moccasins, shawl, and beads, and the girl takes the man back to her home. After this, if the man still refuses to stay in the woman's home, she can move into his household until she "becomes ashamed" (yacati), at which time she returns to her own home and all is forgotten.

If the couple finds they are compatible during the period of cohabitation the woman will grind corn as a gift to her mother-in-law. At an appointed time the man presents his wife to his mother, who returns the gift in the same manner discussed above. The couple returns to the bride's home; the man leaves the bride's house the next day after sunrise and it is no longer a "secret" as to whom the woman has married. The man returns to his new home near the evening mealtime and eats with the rest of the family for the first time. The marriage is confirmed.

Another form of marriage was called ʔipela ('to make a request for marriage without courtship'). In this pattern, the first step is eliminated. When the man desires a certain woman, he collects a gift to be presented to her.

Fig. 4. Men laying roofbeams for a house, standing on the roofs of the two adjacent houses. Housebuilding follows the standard Pueblo division of labor with women performing the less heavy chores, such as plastering (see "Isleta Pueblo," fig. 10, this vol.). Few individual houses were over 2 stories high, though the dwellings were layered to as many as 5 stories with different families living above one another. Photograph by Matilda C. Stevenson, before 1898.

Without the previous knowledge of the prospective bride, he presents himself and his gifts at the woman's home early one evening. His bundle is placed in the center of the room and he is fed, after which the father asks him to state his business. The man asks for the daughter's hand in marriage, and the formal reply is "it is up to my daughter." Usually, the woman makes a "conditional" acceptance after which the two retire. Again the woman can reject the suitor at this point (the gifts are hers to keep) or they can enter a period of cohabitation. A large number of the winter stories *(telapna·we)* incorporate this theme in which the woman continues to reject suitors until the gods get involved to settle the matter.

In the 1970s young people courted in much the same manner as do the Anglos. They are married in a church or by the justice of the peace. Divorce, very simple and easy in the older system, has become complicated by non-Zuni values of ownership. However, it is interesting to note that, except in mixed marriages, there have been no alimony payments between tribal members, and the young people usually remarry in the older common law pattern. Record of marriage is by a tribal "marriage license." Since the children belong to mother's clan and

Table 2. Zuni Clans and Subclans, 1916 and 1976-1977

| Zuni Name 1976-1977 | Approximate English Translation | Families or Lineages in 1916 (Kroeber 1919:table 2) |
|---|---|---|
| 1. *picči·kʷe*, 500 members | Dogwood (Stevenson 1904) | 59 |
| *ła?picči·kʷe* | Twig dogwood | |
| *mula·kʷe* | Macaw | |
| *kʷ?alaši·kʷe* | Crow[a] | |
| 2. *k?ak?ali·kʷe* | Eagle | 28 |
| *poškʷa·kʷe* | Golden Eagle | |
| *pa?k?oha·kʷe* | Bald Eagle | |
| 3. *yatokka·kʷe* | Sun | 20 |
| 4. *tonaši·kʷe* | Badger | 21 |
| 5. *tona·kʷe* | Turkey | 20 |
| *tona k?ohanna·kʷe* | White Turkey | |
| *tona kʷ?inna·kʷe* | Black Turkey | |
| 6. *towa·kʷe* | Corn | 15 |
| *towa k?ohanna·kʷe* | White Corn | |
| *towa kʷ?inna·kʷe* | Black Corn | |
| 7. *tekka·kʷe* | Frog | 11 |
| 8. *k?olokta·kʷe* | Crane | 18 |
| 9. *suski·kʷe* | Coyote | 10 |
| 10. *?anše·kʷe* | Bear | 5 |
| 11. *?ana·kʷe* | Tobacco | 6 |
| 12. *?ayaho·kʷe* | Tansy mustard | 7 |
| 13. *šohhita·kʷe* | Deer | 3 |
| 14. *poyyi·kʷe*, 10 members | Chaparral Cock (Roadrunner) | 1 |
| 15. *tałupc?i·kʷe* (extinct) | Yellowwood | 1 |

[a] Incorrectly translated by some scholars (Eggan 1950:199-201) as 'raven'.
NOTE: The clans are listed in order of their size in 1977.

Fig. 5. Living room of a Zuni household in 1978. left, Francine Laate getting ready to make bread, while G. Owaleon and Tom Awalate converse on the sofa behind her. right, Alda Martea works on silver jewelry (at left) as Phylis Laate grinds turquoise to shape. Photographs by Helga Teiwes, March 1978.

family, there are no "illegitimate" children in the Western sense.

At birth it is the *hotta* 'mother's mother' (or, if complications ensue, a midwife) who attends the delivery. The birth of a child is a household and clan matter. After the birth it is the *wowo* and sometimes the *kuku* (father's sister) who attend the new mother and child for four days. Throughout life the *wowo* and *kuku* will "remove the shame" (*ʔi·yacannaha*) for this child (provide support through the various social and religious crises) and, upon death, prepare the body for burial.

### The Political System

In general, the whole political system revolved around the religious leaders, who acted as a unit rather than as individuals. The *pekʷinne* was responsible for the overall ceremonial and religious cycles; the *ʔa·šiwani* took their turn in retreat during the spring and summer in prayer for rain; the *ʔupa·we* (kivas) performed various winter and summer series of public dances; the *ʔa·piʔla ʔa·šiwani*, in conjunction with the *šohhita·kʷe* (Deer) and *ʔanše·kʷe* (Bear) clans, performed public ceremonies for the *ʔahayu·ta*, the War Gods. Any irregularities in the performance of these rituals, queer behavior by anybody, or "national crises" such as an epidemic or drought were cause for suspicion of witchcraft. The *ʔa·piʔla ʔa·šiwani* would search out and remove these people with "two hearts." Because of these obvious actions by the *ʔa·piʔla ʔa·šiwani*, most Zunis agree that during precontact times, the people were governed by them, acting under the direction of the priestly council. In this sense it was a theocratic system of government.

488    In the past all matters relating to divorce, death,

marriage, and birth were matters of family. All property acquired during marriage belonged to the woman; children belonged to the woman; and agricultural lands were "owned" by the woman. Therefore, any division of property under any circumstances was effected only by the families concerned without outside intervention.

According to tradition, in the old days, "before we became mixed with other races," there was no need for a council such as now exists. All disputes were settled privately between the individuals concerned. Offenses against the gods by individuals were punished by the gods. Offenses against the people, usually by witchcraft, were punished by the *ʔa·piʔla ʔa·šiwani* in public trial. The last public witch trials in Zuni were in 1925 (Smith and Roberts 1954:48). Belief in witchcraft remained very strong in Zuni in the 1970s. The punishment for a witch caught practicing his art against an individual or a family is settled privately between the witch and the person who caught him in the act. However, how much or how many of these stories are in fact true is hard to say, because the people who catch these witches and extract confessions from them never reveal the name of the person except by innuendo.

The Rain Priests, officers of the medicine societies (*tika· ʔa·mossi*), kiva officials (*kokko ʔa·mossi*), and the sun chief were in no way supposed to deal in violence. They were to remain "pure of heart." Therefore, the enforcement of tribal affairs fell to the *ʔa·piʔla ʔa·šiwani*, whose position and rank was rooted in violence (they had to take a scalp in war) and leadership in war against all evil. On the one hand, they stood between the religious council, for whom they were the speakers, and the people to enforce the religious laws; and on the other hand they stood between the "outside forces" and the people as protectors. It would be logical to assume that such an organization would have been founded and formed prior to contact when the Zunis lived separately in six or more villages, and this is probably what Kroeber (1919:97) and Cushing (1896:332) allude to as being reflected in the present civil government.

Nothing is positively known concerning the origin of the council. However, based in part on traditional knowledge, there was probably a supreme council of ʔaˑpiʔɫa ʔaˑšiwani among the Zunis, instituted by them for their mutual protection when they lived in segregated towns. Their center of activities was probably one of the larger villages, perhaps Hawikuh or Kechipauan, until after 1692 when the Zuni consolidated into a single village at Halona, where the council of Bow Priests continued to function as an arm of the priestly council. Because it was the Head Bow Priest who was the most obvious leader, it was likely he who was appointed as the governor by the Spaniards. A tribal organization was already there in the form of the council of Bow Priests. Certainly this institution has continually undergone change from its original introduction when it probably functioned in its purely native form. The changes instituted by the forces of the Roman Catholic Church and by the Pueblo Revolt in 1680 (Smith and Roberts 1954:28, 29) probably influenced most strongly the formation of the tribal council in its present form. Most observers, both Zuni and non-Zuni, agree that the present form of civil government was instituted by the Spaniards no earlier than the late 1500s and maybe not until as late as 1692 (Smith and Roberts 1954:29). Nevertheless, it is rooted in the native system.

There seems to be a fair amount of evidence to suggest that during the mid-nineteenth century the offices of governor and council had become appointive positions. However, Cushing's (1896) accounts suggest that the Bow Priests still had a great influence in civil matters (Smith and Roberts 1954:30-32, 86-89) during this period.

There is no doubt that during the 1800s and early 1900s, the interactions with outside cultural forces were increasing; earlier, perhaps under stress from the Spanish administrators, the priestly council had developed a secular government parallel to the existing religious system. In the precontact system, which continues to exist, the priestly council appointed and installed various religious officials at the beginning of each year. The symbol of office was a special feather staff called a teɫnanne. The appointing priest placed the feather staff in the hands of each appointee, said a prayer, and breathed on the feather staff four times. By this ceremonial installation (yehčukʔa, literally 'to cause to inhale') the priestly council charged the appointees with religious and ceremonial responsibilities for the year. They became the yanʔuɫʔona 'those who have the responsibility of an office'.

When the secular government was instituted, the religious installation ceremony was taken over and used to install the governor and his council, with the substitution of the Spanish governor's cane for the feather staff. This cane was later replaced by the Lincoln cane, given by President Abraham Lincoln, which is still used (fig. 6). The tribal council is called yanʔuɫʔona, originally the term for the appointed religious officials, and the governor is sometimes called ʔanʔuɫɫa mossʔona 'the head (boss) of the yanʔuɫʔona'. The governor is also called taˑpuˑpu 'he who blows on wood', an apparent allusion to the blowing on the cane during the oath-taking ceremonies. When the governor is installed, the kʔakʷe mossi 'House Chief', the head Rain Priest, charges the governor with the responsibility of taking care of his people, whether rich or poor, clean or dirty. He gives him the oath of office (yehčukʔa) to discharge his duties to the best of his abilities.

Until about 1692, or after the "reconquest," the priestly council and the ʔaˑpiʔɫa ʔaˑšiwani controlled both religious and civil affairs. Some time after this period an individual who could cope with outside matters was selected by the priestly council and installed as governor, probably at first for one year, the same as the various appointed ceremonial officials, and later for more extended periods of time up to four years.

This system was changed in 1934 when Zuni Subagent Andrew Trotter of the Bureau of Indian Affairs persuaded the Zunis to accept a new system of selecting the tribal council. At this period there was only a handful of Zunis who could speak English and there was little or no interaction with the Spanish-speaking community. All

Smithsonian, NAA.

Fig. 6. Wayhusiwa, governor of Zuni in 1923, with cane of office. Photograph by DeLancey Gill, Washington, D.C.

outside business had to be conducted through an interpreter. Trotter's plan was to appoint six members, three from each of two contending factions, to a "nominating committee" who would hold office for two years, after which others would be elected every two years. Trotter's system worked well, except the original six members of the nominating committee were in office for over eight years, during which period their members varied from six to two in 1940.

The committee consulted with the nominees for their approval, whereupon they informed the kʔakʷe mossi of their selection. Two names were submitted for governor at a public meeting where the "men stood up" (women, although not officially excluded, did not participate) for the nominee of their choice for governor. The one getting the most standup votes became governor and the other became lieutenant governor. Members of the three outlying villages were consulted for two names each—a total of six—who would become the council. The governor and lieutenant governor had some influence on the choice of their council. The terms of office have varied among one year, two years, and four years. The kʔakʷe mossi installed them ceremonially, and they became the yanʔuɬʔona. The job of governor and councilman was unpaid, except that when "the governor's word was broken," a fine was imposed on the offending individual that was split among the council.

In 1958, under the direction of the Bureau of Indian Affairs agent, a salary of $6,000 was established for the governor. The funds came out of the "Tribal Fund," a fund collected from various fines and fees.

In 1965 women fully participated for the first time in the election of the tribal council. Voting was by secret ballot, for the first time. The governor's position was salaried, but only on paper for there was no money in the Tribal Fund.

A number of major changes occurred in 1970. The Zuni Constitution was ratified, establishing the terms of office of the governor and council at four years and setting a salary for the governor equal to that of the Indian agent. Funds for the salaries, including salaries for the councilmen, were allotted annually to the tribe through the Bureau of Indian Affairs. On July 1, 1970, as part of the overall Zuni comprehensive development plan, the tribal government, based on a federal law passed in 1834 (25 U.S.C. 48), applied for and received the right to control the reservation and all functions of the tribal council with an Indian agent representing the secretary of the interior in the status of tribal programs advisor.

It was not until these major changes in salaries that the position of governor and lieutenant governor became actively sought. The changes that started in 1958 when a salary was established culminated in the 1974 elections

Pueblo of Zuni, Zuni Archeol. Program, N.M.

Fig. 7. Zuni Pueblo Council in the governor's chambers. Members are (left to right): Chester Mahooty, councilman; Dorson Zunie, lt. governor; Edison Laselute, governor; Fred Bowannie, councilman; Quincy Panteah, councilman; Chauncey Simplicio, councilman; and Virgil Wyaco, councilman; (Councilman Lowell Panteah not present). Hanging on the wall directly behind them are photographs of Palowahtiwa (taken on the same occasion as "Zuni History, 1850-1970," fig. 4, this vol.) (left) and of Wayhusiwa (fig. 6). Photograph by Barbara J. Mills, Oct. 4, 1978.

490

when there was a lively campaign launched by a number of office seekers. Although the original, or older, nominating committee was functioning during the 1974 elections, their role was reduced by the office seekers acting on their own and not at the invitation of the committee.

In the 1974 elections, the village was given a slate of officers. The governor and the lieutenant governor ran as a team with the councilmen "running at large" at the invitation of the nominating committee. The elected officers are still installed by the *kʔak*e mossi*.

491

# Zuni Economy

EDMUND J. LADD

The Zuni Reservation, established by executive order on March 16, 1877, is situated in western New Mexico in McKinley and Valencia counties, in the heartland of the aboriginal Zuni territory. Gallup, New Mexico, 39 miles to the northeast, is the principal modern off-reservation trading, transportation, and communications center.

The population of Zuni has been variously estimated by visitors from an exaggerated 20,000 to a low of 1,597 (table 1). Epidemics of smallpox, measles, and whooping cough in the 1820s to 1890s brought the population to its lowest levels, but since 1910 there has been a steady increase.

The land base, the reservation, consists of about 400,000 acres; 375,293 acres are used for livestock grazing and 4,967 acres are croplands irrigated by the federally constructed reservoir at Black Rock, three miles east of the main village. About 20,333 acres are in dryland farming and other uses.

The Zunis, since World War II, have become dependent upon a modern industrial cash economy for most of their needs. Most households have some means of high-speed transportation, mainly pickup trucks, that provide a ready access to all the modern trading centers in New Mexico. The Zunis, like the rest of America, are in constant contact with the world at large via telephone, television, and radio. Most are bilingual in Zuni and English.

A large number of Zunis trade regularly in Gallup where they sell their arts and crafts and cash their wage checks. Many have established credit at the various business establishments. All buy a variety of goods from the local trading posts, but most of the grocery shopping is done in the supermarkets in Gallup. Purchases such as appliances, furniture, and motor vehicles are made in Gallup, Grants, or Albuquerque.

In 1973 there were six major educational institutions in operation in Zuni ranging from the preschool Head Start program through high school. Since about 1950 many young people have gone on to attend a variety of institutions of higher learning. As Zuni men and women become trained in a variety of income-producing specialties, there is a decreasing emphasis on the strict division of labor and more and more of a breakdown and blending of the responsibilities. Generally, men raise cattle and sheep, do some farming for home use, hire out for wages, and do some silversmithing on the side.

Women are still mainly responsible for the household chores. In addition they may work as silversmiths. A number of women were employed in 1973 at an electronics plant near Black Rock.

## The Economic Base

The economic patterns are geared to the agricultural and ceremonial cycles; however, the emphasis has been shifted, from a farming-hunting-gathering pattern to the modern industrial cash economy. The rounds of social and religious activities remain definitely linked to the older patterns. Bunzel (1938:352) captured the essence of Zuni economic attitudes: "The outstanding characteristics of the economic system are the strong development of cooperative attitudes and techniques, the corresponding absence of competition and aggressive behavior in general, the dominant role of women in economic affairs, the fluidity of wealth, which implies the absence of acquisitiveness, and a thoroughly realistic attitude toward property, which is valued for direct use and not as an instrument for power and prestige." Even after contact with Whites and adoption of Western means of earning, such as sheep herding, Zunis confined their use of the

Table 1. Population, 1583-1972

| Date | Population | Remarks |
|------|-----------|---------|
| 1583 | 20,000 | 6 villages |
| 1680 | 2,500 | Year of Pueblo Revolt |
| 1788–1799 | 1,617–2,716 | Range of estimates |
| 1820 | 1,597 | |
| 1880 | 1,650 | |
| 1910 | 1,640 | |
| 1920 | 1,813 | |
| 1930 | 1,952 | |
| 1940 | 2,205 | |
| 1950 | 2,922 | 535 tribal members lived off reservation |
| 1960 | 4,190 | Age under 1 year, 146; 1–19 years, 2,122; 20-64 years, 1,702; 65 and over, 220 |
| 1970 | 4,952 | |
| 1972 | 5,760 | |

SOURCES: Hodge 1910j:1017-1018 for 1583 to 1910; Bureau of Indian Affairs records, Zuni, N.M. for 1920-1972.

492

Fig. 1. Panoramic view of Zuni in 1899, from the south, showing enclosed gardens and Zuni River in foreground. Photograph by Adam C. Vroman.

profit motive to dealings with the American economic system and with Whites. "Within the tribe the older attitude and value still ruled." But more frequent litigation over inheritance, especially after 1929, was "an indication of increasing interest in acquisition and retention of property" after realizing its possibilities in relation to Whites. Quarrels over land were rarer, perhaps because "male ownership and inheritance, taken over from the Whites, cut across the main stem of economic structure, the solidarity of the female line" (Bunzel 1938:356–357).

It is during the American period (since 1848) that the greatest technological and economic changes have taken place. The introduction of sheep, cattle, and pigs during the Spanish period, for example, paved the way for a shift from a purely subsistence economy to that of a cash economy. Perhaps the one individual who bears the most responsibility for this shift is the Indian trader. It was the Indian trader who established the value of livestock and who introduced the concept of credit buying. He also made the Zunis aware of the fact that certain objects had value and that by placing these objects in his custody they could enjoy the same buying power as a person with sheep. Pawn became a way to secure material goods provided by the trader.

With the advent and development of cross-country railroad travel a demand for "Indian curios" increased. Painted wooden tomahawks, pottery owls (fig. 2), ashtrays, candle holders, and anything else that would strike the fancy of an Eastern tourist were sold by the carload at the railroad stations in Albuquerque and Gallup.

## The Economic Unit

The household, the basic economic unit in the older pattern, was built around the maternal lineage. The men of the household were those who married into the wife's clan. They joined the unmarried, widowed, and divorced male members of the household to support the group. The children belonged to the mother's clan and home unit with minor and secondary obligations to the father's clan.

The basic economic unit in the 1970s was still the household; and it was still, although very loosely, built

Fig. 2. Zuni ceramic owl with reddish-brown painted feather details on white slip, made for tourist sale. Height 23.5 cm, collected 1879.

around the maternal lineage. The men of the household, as in the older pattern, are those who have married into the clan. Some of the marriages continue to follow the old pattern of a simple agreement of partnership between two people as in common law, but more and more young people are getting married in the church. Divorce is common and very emotional; quarrels over ownership of property, including land litigations, are a normal part of the pattern. It is interesting to note that when the young people remarry they generally return to the older pattern of common law marriage. Children, regardless of the type of marriage, belong to the mother's family; there are no "illegitimate" children. Except in extreme cases, the property accumulated during the marriage is considered to belong to the female and her household. Confrontations occur over property such as sheep, cattle, automobiles, silversmithing tools and the like when claimed by the male. With the exception of intertribal or mixed marriages, there have been no alimony payments between tribal members.

Unlike the old pattern of simply bringing in another hand to till the soil, the men who join a household bring an assortment of already established properties and skills that give them immediate status in the household. Young people no longer have to depend entirely on the wife's household for their support and soon move out to establish their own homes—something that took years of preparation and planning under the old system. Both husband and wife still maintain their ties with their respective mother's households, returning for all major ceremonial occasions. The women dominate in all economic affairs of the household.

## Economic Activities

Modern Zuni suffers from the economic ills of underemployment and unemployment. Lack of adequate education and substandard living conditions aggravate the situation with the increasing population. The elected administrative body and the Zuni people have attempted to change this, to bring the standard of living up to that enjoyed by other Americans. In July 1969 Robert Lewis, the governor of the Pueblo, launched the Zuni five-year comprehensive development plan (fig. 3), stating:

> We live in accord with Zuni Pueblo concepts and, in the past, have asked or expected little of those not of our pueblo. Now we want to achieve a level of living such as other Americans enjoy. We have a long way to go in a short period of time.
>
> Zunis want to retain their identity—not the mocassin and feather image—but the cultural and historical identification any man uses to reflect pride of his forefathers and of their accomplishments and contributions to society (Anonymous 1969).

On July 1, 1970, as part of this overall development and improvement package the tribal government, based on a federal law passed in 1834 (25 U.S.C. 48), applied for

Bureau of Ind. Affairs, Washington.

Fig. 3. Presentation of the Zuni 24-Projects/24-Months Plan (forerunner of the 1969 development concept plan) by Gov. Lewis (left) and Clifford Mahooty, a Zuni tribal employee in the Bureau of Indian Affairs auditorium. Under the heading "community improvement," the presentation sheet lists: sewer lagoons, street improvement, land use, park development, improved sanitation, tribal safety program, junior high school, and community center. Photographer unidentified, 1967.

and received the right to take over its own administrative and management responsibilities. This task was formerly delegated by the secretary of the interior to the Bureau of Indian Affairs. The Bureau administered Zuni affairs through a superintendent of the Zuni Agency at the Pueblo.

## Sources of Income

Income statistics for the various activities are either nonexistent or unreliable at best (table 2). For the years when figures are available they show a steady increase in dollar income, but per capita income is still well below the national level. Listed by order of dollar value the principal income sources are: wage labor including federal, tribal, local industry, and off-reservation employment; arts and crafts; livestock; and agriculture.

### Wage Labor

Total income from wage employment has continued to show an increase due to the development of on-site industry fostered by the new policies and the Zunis' own development of a number of tribal enterprises that provide new jobs and new skills. However, the number employed remained relatively low compared to the available labor resource, which continued to grow in the 1970s. Fire fighting is seasonal (fig. 4) and has lost its importance as a wage-earning activity since more permanent job opportunities have become available. A large

**Table 2. Reservation Income**

| Source of Income | 1962 | 1964 | 1967 |
|---|---|---|---|
| Federal government salaries and wages | $ 800,000 | $1,104,606 | $1,547,431 |
| Zuni Tribe | | 42,899 | 70,529 |
| Schools | | 572,309 | 639,784 |
| Business | 6,300 | 117,480 | 243,731 |
| Employment wages in Gallup | | 297,000 | 363,868 |
| Fire fighting | 375,000 | 170,666 | 267,992 |
| Livestock and wool sales | 171,718 | 227,459 | 176,589 |
| Arts and crafts | 700,000 | 625,872 | 854,100 |
| Unearned income | | 57,175 | 449,382 |
| Agriculture | 76,770 | | 66,000[a] |
| Total | $2,129,788 | $3,215,466 | $4,332,290 |

SOURCE: Bureau of Indian Affairs records, Zuni, N.M.

[a] 1969 figure, not included in 1967 total.

Fig. 5. Drilling (right) and shaping (left) turquoise or shell beads. The drilling, with a pump drill (see "Zia Pueblo," fig. 3, this vol.), preceeds the final shaping, which is accomplished by stringing drilled rough blanks of shell or turquoise, knocking the rough edges off, and rolling the resultant string of beads on a wet slab of sandstone (Underhill 1944:121). Photographer unknown, probably 1890s.

number of young people find employment in Gallup as nurses, waitresses, and construction workers.

## Crafts

Silversmithing, a craft introduced during the Spanish period, began to be exploited in the late 1920s and reached a peak of development in quantity and quality in the 1970s. It produced the second highest income and involved the largest portion of the Zuni population. In 1965 it was estimated that 900 individuals were producing silver and turquoise jewelry, 344 of whom did so on a full-time basis. Practically every household was involved. Men generally tended their livestock (if not working for wages) and worked with their wives as

silversmiths in the evening. Silversmithing started out as a man's activity (fig. 6); however, women soon became expert in certain aspects of the art such as stone cutting. The men work out the pattern and cut the silver and the women cut and mount the stones. Certain households and individuals became known and recognized for their special styles and forms, which are jealously guarded

Fig. 4. Men signing up to work as firefighters. Building at left is the old tribal council building and jail. Photograph by Richard Erdoes, 1964.

Fig. 6. Zuni silversmith of the 1880s or 1890s, standing at his anvil, just in front of a forge. The earliest recorded Zuni silversmith learned the art from a Navajo who came to the Pueblo in 1872 (Adair 1944:121-128), although there is earlier evidence of blacksmithing at Zuni (see "History of the Pueblos Since 1821," fig. 4, this vol.). For history and detailed discussion of Zuni silvermaking, see Adair 1944:121-171; Bedinger 1973:130-152.

*495*

from all others. "Needle point" is a distinctive Zuni style (fig. 8) in which bits of turquoise no larger than two by four centimeters are cut and mounted in various patterns (fig. 9). The most distinctive Zuni jewelry is that formed by the inlay method. The most popular and distinctive design is the Knife-Wing Bird (fig. 10) (ʔačiya latapa). The inlay style is produced by cutting and piecing together in various forms and patterns shell, coral, jet (a black mineral similar to coal that takes a fine polish), and turquoise. These are then mounted in silver.

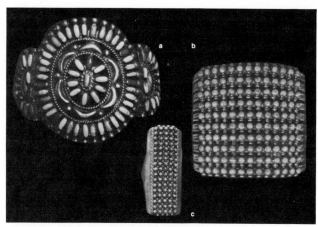

Fig. 9. Zuni silver and turquoise jewelry with multiple turquoise settings in the "needle point" style. a–b, Bracelets with medallion and row settings, collected 1965 and 1961; c, ring with one mm diameter hand-polished turquoise stones set in 17 rows, collected 1971. Diameter of medallion setting 5.1 cm, rest same scale.

Fig. 7. Negative mold of sand (with an iron frame) for casting a silver buckle, probably part of the set of silver-making tools purchased by Matilda C. Stevenson in 1902 from Lanyade, the first Zuni to learn silversmithing (Adair 1944:122,126). As described by Lanyade, sand made from soft rock was placed in a shallow wooden or metal box, sugar water was poured over it, and a piece of silver (in this case a belt buckle of the desired shape) was pressed into the sand to produce the negative mold; a groove leading to the depressed section (into which the silver could later be poured) was also made (Adair 1944:149–150). Length 13 cm.

Fig. 10. Zuni pin with mythical Knife-Wing Bird in turquoise, pink agate, channel and inlay jet, and mother of pearl shell on silver base. Width 7.6 cm; collected before 1954.

Lapidary arts and silversmithing have come a long way from the blowtube, sheepskin bellows, and potsherd crucible era. One reason that so many are involved in silversmithing or can very readily become involved is that a minimum of tools is required to produce good silver; however, those involved full-time can invest as much as $1,000 in their tools.

Minor crafts include production of beaded rabbit feet, dolls, and stone fetishes. Some good pottery was being made, but weaving was extinct in 1973 and basketmaking nearly so.

Most of the salable crafts find their way into the hands of various traders in Gallup. Some craftsmen purchase the raw material and make up different objects in the hope of selling these to the Gallup traders. Some of the crafts are produced for the traders on a piece basis.

Fig. 8. Della Casi setting stones, probably turquoise, in one section of a silver belt. She is wearing a squash blossom necklace, probably with cast ornaments, two large brooches, bracelets, and rings, all of which appear to be set with turquoise. A distinguishing characteristic of Zuni silver, as opposed to that made by the Navajo, is the preponderance of turquoise sets (Adair 1944:151). Photographer unknown, probably 1930s.

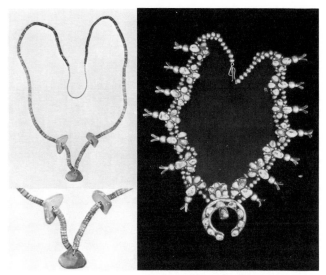

left, Smithsonian, Dept. of Anthr.: 381661; right, U. of Colo. Mus., Boulder.
Fig. 11. Zuni necklaces. left, Green turquoise drilled and polished stones with 3 turquoise pendants, collected before 1941; right, squash blossom necklace set with large turquoise stones, collected about 1925 (see Tanner 1978). Length of left 43.2 cm, other same scale.

Depending on the type of jewelry currently popular, the trader farms out the work to various craftsmen, providing all the necessary raw material. The craftsmen make the jewelry and the trader pays the craftsmen by the piece in cash or in trade goods.

Some craftsmen make road trips to Albuquerque, Santa Fe, Flagstaff, and elsewhere to find new outlets. The Zuni Craftsmen's Cooperative Association was formed to provide marketing and merchandising services and a ready outlet for the craftsmen at a competitive price ("Zuni History, 1850-1970," fig. 8, this vol.). There were 440 paid members in the coop in 1971. The coop showed an activity of $445,584.64 for a nine-month period ending December 31, 1971.

*Livestock*

The raising of livestock, although producing important income, involved only a few men in the 1970s. This is controlled directly by the carrying capacity of the reservation and available grazing land. Although there has been improvement of range land management since 1962, the authorized carrying capacity at that time was 4,699 animal units—including sheep, cattle, and horses. There were, in 1972, 256 individual sheep owners and 44 cattlemen.

Sheep are generally owned and tended by men. A number of individuals, usually related, join to form one large flock and each owner takes his turn tending the flock during the year. Sheep owned by women are tended by their brothers or husbands.

Grazing land is used by the sheepmen on "use rights" and "traditional" bases. Separate areas are designated and fenced as cattle pastures.

Since the ownership of livestock is controlled by a percentage of the total carrying capacity of the range land, owners must sell those animals that are in excess of their quota each year. There is a very delicate balance between what a man must butcher as a part of his regular ceremonial obligations for the great winter ceremonies, what he needs for his own table, and what he must remove by sale. During 1969 the Zuni stockmen realized $219,166.67 in cash income.

The reservation can be looked upon as a single cattle ranch with a single herd, the herd being made up of individually owned animals. All the business concerning the herd—assessing the owners for inoculation, feed purchasing, and the like—is conducted through the

top, Mus. of N.M., Santa Fe; bottom, Natl. Arch., Washington: Bureau of Ind. Affairs RG-75-G.
Fig. 12. "Waffle gardens" at Zuni. The rectangular compartments, enclosed by ridges of clay earth, retain water. Traditionally, fruits and vegetables such as melons, herbs, chili, and onions were grown in these small garden plots, which were enclosed with sticks or adobe walls and irrigated from the river (Underhill 1946:33-35; Stevenson 1904:353). top, Group of women, probably of the same household, planting or tending a garden. bottom, A young girl watering a garden; a metal bowl and bucket are used instead of the more traditional gourd dipper and large clay pot. Photographer unknown, about 1915 (top); United Pueblos Agency photographer, 1940 (bottom).

cattlemen's association. In 1972 there were 46 members. The care of the herd, range land, water stations (windmills), fence mending, and transfer of the stock from one pasture to another is conducted by the cattlemen. Cattle ranching is strictly a cash business and home butchering seldom occurs. If a cattleman is ceremonially obligated he will usually purchase sheep for the occasion.

*Agriculture*

When measured by the dollar income, agriculture is a very minor source of revenue, due, perhaps, to the fact that only marketable forage and grain products are reported. In 1962 The Zuni Subagency, Bureau of Indian Affairs, reported a valuation of crops including corn, pinto beans, wheat, horticultural produce, and forage plants produced on 2,837 acres at $76,770. A variety of garden vegetables such as chili, cabbage, onions, and beets were produced in quantity for home use in the four outlying farming villages. Crops such as blue corn and white corn were still produced for the traditional foods and for use in certain ceremonies in the 1970s. Unfortunately the peach orchards, traditionally tended by men, have been neglected since the 1940s. Around the main village women have traditionally tended the "waffle" gardens, so called because the planting areas, outlined by clay ridges, form patterns resembling the texture of waffles (fig. 12). The *latekʷinne* 'enclosed with sticks' (referring to the juniper-stick palisade surrounding the plots) slowly fall into decay as the older women who maintained them die.

## Sociocultural Situation in the 1970s

In the 1970s young married couples are no longer economically tied to the bride's household. They can, with relative ease, establish their own homes through the

Bureau of Ind. Affairs, Washington.

Fig. 13. Modern Zuni construction. Zuni men learning stone masonry as part of a mutual help and housing improvement training program. Photographer unidentified, 1969.

tribal government. Modern subdivisions, single-family type homes (fig. 13) including paved streets, streetlights, sidewalks, grassy lawns, central heating, gas and electricity, and completely equipped kitchens are already developed. These subdivisions are located away from the old or central village complex. Plans are to maintain the old village as a nucleus for an exhibit and demonstration area as part of the living "Zuni cultural park."

As per capita income and leisure time increases and, as new business developments are attracted to the reservation, there will undoubtedly be many more changes. With all the changes that have already taken place, Zuni is the first language in the home. There remain strong emotional ties to the family of the mother's household, a strong respect for the elders, and recognition of the ceremonial and religious observations. Modern Zuni, as in the past, is in a position to select and choose those outside cultural elements that will best meet the needs of the people to insure and maintain cultural identity.

# Zuni Religion and World View

DENNIS TEDLOCK

## The World and the Raw People

There are six points of orientation in the Zuni world, each with its own color and its own hierarchical position: the yellow north, the blue west, the red south, the white east, the multicolored zenith, and the black nadir. Toward the nadir are a black mountain and the four underworlds: on the fourth story down is the Sulphur Room, totally dark, where the ponderosa pine, tree of the north, first grew; on the third is the Soot or Moss Room, with the Douglas fir of the west; on the second is the Gray or Mud Room, with the aspen of the south; and on the story just beneath our own world is the Wing (sunray) Room, with the cottonwood of the east (Stevenson 1904:25; Bunzel 1932b: 560–562). Toward the zenith, beyond the inverted stone bowl of the sky, are a multicolored mountain and the four upper worlds, the first the home of crows, the second of Cooper's hawks, the third of nighthawks, and the fourth of eagles* (Benedict 1935, 1:131). In all, then, there are nine stories, with the familiar world in the middle.

Toward the north, west, south, and east are the oceans, which together bound the earth with a circular coastline (Bunzel 1932a:487). In the oceans are four mountains, each with the color of its direction (Cushing 1883:17). The oceans are connected by underground passages with all the seeps, springs, ponds, and caves of the earth to form a single water system; the Zunis compare this system with the hidden roots and runners that connect willow shoots into a single plant (Bunzel 1932c:710). At the water outlets and on mountaintops are the *teɫašṣina·we* 'sacred old places', or shrines, of the world.†

The people who inhabit the world are of two kinds: *kʔapin ʔa·hoʔʔi* 'raw people' and *ʔakna ʔa·hoʔʔi* or *tekʔohannan ʔa·hoʔʔi* 'cooked people' or 'daylight people'. The cooked or daylight people depend on cooked food, while the raw people eat food that is either raw or has been sacrificed to them by daylight people (Bunzel 1932a:498). Raw people can change their forms (Cushing 1896:439); they are "people" in the sense that one of their potential forms is anthropomorphic, and in the sense that

they and daylight people (humans) should behave as kinsmen toward one another.

The earth itself is a raw person, *ʔawitelin citta* 'Earth Mother'; trees and bushes are her arms and hands (Tedlock and Tedlock 1971–1972:D), and she wears a robe of yellow flowers (pollen grains) in the summer and white flowers (snowflakes) in the winter (Bunzel 1932a:484). But foremost among the raw people are *hoʔnʔa·wona·willapʔona* 'The Ones Who Hold Our Roads', especially *yatokka taččᵘ* 'Sun Father' and *yaʔonakka citta* 'Moonlight-Giving Mother', the ultimate givers of light and life.‡ The Sun Father has two houses, one in the eastern ocean and the other in the western; in the western house lives *kʔohak ʔoka* 'White Shell Woman', who is his mother or maternal grandmother (Stevenson 1904:169; Benedict 1935, 2:63–64). The Moon Mother is his wife, but she is always separated from him (Tedlock 1965–1966:H–2). His sister is *maʔlokaccikʔi* 'Old Lady Salt', who lives in a lake to the south (Stevenson 1904:169).

In the oceans live the yellow, blue, red, and white *kolo·wisi*, four giant feathered serpents who are capable of causing a world flood (Bunzel 1932a:515–516; Edmund J. Ladd, personal communication 1973). Along the shores of the oceans and in springs live the *ʔuwanammi* (or *ʔuwanam ʔa·šiwani* 'rain priests') of the six directions, who take the form of clouds, rainstorms, fog, and dew when they leave their homes (Bunzel 1932a:513). Their *ʔa·piʔɫa ʔa·šiwani* 'bow priests' (warriors), also of the six directions, make lightning and thunder (Stevenson 1904:22); and their *pekʷi·we* 'spokesmen' (sg. *pekʷinne*) are the six *kʔašima wowe* 'water-bringing birds': oriole (north), Steller's jay (west), macaw (south), magpie (east), purple martin (zenith), and rough-winged swallow (na-

---

* The identification of biological species has been cross-checked with Newman (1958) and Ladd (1963). In many instances it is corrected from that given in the older ethnographic sources.

† The orthography used for Zuni words is that described by Newman (1965:12–15; "Sketch of the Zuni Language," vol. 17).

‡ It has been variously claimed that *ʔa·wona·wilʔona* 'The One Who Holds the Roads' is: an epithet for the Sun Father (Cushing 1883:13, 1896:379), the name of a bisexual creator separate from the Sun Father (Stevenson 1904:25), or any supernatural who influences human affairs (Bunzel 1932a:486). The term is used as an epithet for the Sun Father, but it can also be used for the Moon Mother; in its plural form, *ʔa·wona·willapʔona* 'The Ones Who Hold the Roads', it has the meaning Bunzel gave the singular form (Edmund J. Ladd, personal communication 1973). As Bunzel (1932a:486) has suggested, Stevenson probably assumed a bisexual deity because, taking the epithet to be the name of a deity, she asked whether it was male or female, and the correct answer was "both" (or "either"), since she did not specify which deity she had in mind.

dir) (Stevenson 1915:89). The *ʔuwanammi* usually come to Zuni on winds from the southwest or southeast; their winter counterparts are the *suniyaˑšiwani* 'snow priests', who come from the northeast and northwest (Stevenson 1904:21, 445; Tedlock 1965-1966:H-1).

To the east of Zuni, somewhere in the vicinity of the Sandia Mountains, is *šipaˑpuliʔma,* the home of the *ʔonaˑ yaˑnaka ʔaˑšiwani* 'priests of the completed path', who possess healing herbs. At their head is *pošayaˑnkʔi;* his bow priests or *wemaˑ ʔaˑšiwani* 'beast priests' are the mountain lion (north), bear (west), badger (south), wolf (east), eagle (zenith), and mole (nadir) (Cushing 1883:16). Sometimes *ʔačiya latapa* 'Knife Wing', with flint-blade feathers, is assigned to the zenith instead of the eagle (Bunzel 1932c:784); the morning star is his head and the evening star is his heart (Benedict 1935, 2:97). Other priests of the completed path include the rattlesnakes and ants of the six directions (Bunzel 1932c:829; Stevenson 1904:529). When these animals or the beast priests die they go to *šipaˑpuliʔma,* where they are restored to life (Benedict 1935, 2:34).

The *kokkoˑkʷe* 'kachinas' (sg. *kokko*) are raw people who wear masks and dance all the time. A few of them come from *šipaˑpuliʔma,* including *šicuˑka* and *kʷelele,* who bring new fire at the new year, and the six *šumeˑkuli,* whose masks are in the six directional colors (Stevenson 1904:407, 531; Bunzel 1932:923-924). These eastern kachinas, like the priests of the completed path, possess

medicines. Most of the other kachinas live in the west at Kachina Village, at the bottom of a lake at a two days' walk from Zuni; there they sing and pray for rain and the growth of crops. The *komossʔona* 'kachina chief' of their village is the tall and stately *pawtiwa;* his spokesmen are the stubborn cripple *kaklo* and the young fire god *šulaˑwici* (Bunzel 1932:845, 909, 958). The *kʔakʷaˑmossi* 'house chiefs' of Kachina Village are the 10 koyemshi (*koyemši,* popularly called mudheads), who are at one and the same time the silliest and most dangerous of the kachinas (ibid.:947, 951). The kachina bow priests include *saya taša* 'Long Horn', who speaks of the winter; *huˑtutu,* who speaks of the summer; the 12 *salimopiya* (two for each direction) and four *sayaɬiʔʔa* 'Blue Horns', all of whom carry yucca whips; and the six Shalakos (*šaʔlako*), who are 10-foot-high couriers (fig. 1) (Bunzel 1932c:719, 1932:920-922, 937, 989). The ordinary people of the village range from the kindly *kokkʔokši* 'good kachina' and *kokkʷeʔle* 'kachina girl' to the clumsy *heheʔa* and the lazy *yaʔʔana* (Bunzel 1932:1012-1041).

Kachina Village is also a home for the *nawe* 'hoofed game animals'. At least some kachinas become *nawe* when they die, and when *nawe* themselves die they go to Kachina Village and are restored there (Benedict 1935, 1:72, 77, 2:70-71; Tedlock 1972:32), just as the beast priests are restored at *šipaˑpuliʔma.* And like the beast priests, the *nawe* have directional assignments: mule deer (north), mountain sheep (west), antelope (south), and

left, Mus. of Northern Ariz., Flagstaff; right, Mus. of N.M., Santa Fe.

Fig. 1. Shalakos, couriers for the priests of Kachina Village. left, *Zuni Shalako and Man,* by Theodore Edaakie, Zuni artist. right, Shalakos crossing the Zuni River to the ceremonial grounds south of the old part of town. Each Shalako is accompanied by an alternate impersonator and by members of the particular curing society to whose music it danced throughout the previous night (the upright object carried by the man in the lead is the badge of membership in a curing society). When all 6 Shalakos and their alternates have reached the ceremonial grounds, they will run back and forth over a race course, planting feathered offering-sticks (such as those held by the second man) for the general well-being and fecundity of the villagers and their animals and crops. This ceremony takes place in late Nov. or early Dec. of each year. Photograph by Ben Wittick, probably in 1896.

TEDLOCK

whitetail deer (east), with two other game animals, the jackrabbit (zenith) and cottontail (nadir), added to make six (Stevenson 1904:441). These six game animals are hunted by the prey animals of the six directions, who are the same species as the beast priests except that coyote is west, bobcat is south, and the zenith is represented not only by the eagle but also by the red-tailed hawk (Cushing 1883:20-30).

At one time all the game animals were corralled by the *kanʔa·kʷe* kachinas, who live to the south of Zuni and are the enemies of the people of Kachina Village proper (Bunzel 1932:1009-1010). The principal warrior of the *kanʔa·kʷe* is *čaʔkʷen ʔoka*, whose legs are covered with rabbit blood; she is the mother of the game animals, responsible for their increase (Stevenson 1904:89-94).

Living much closer to Zuni than the raw people discussed so far are the *ʔahayu·ta* twins and *payatamu*, the sons of the Sun Father, most of whose shrines are within a 10-mile radius. The *ʔahayu·ta* "sprouted" when the Sun's rays struck the alkaline foam of a waterfall§ (Tedlock 1972:227). They are warriors, hunters, athletes, and gamblers. They are also diviners and the creators of a medicine for divination (Stevenson 1915:46). They guard Zuni from six hilltop shrines representing the directions (Stevenson 1904:580) and possess six different kinds of violent wind (Cushing 1896:421-422); their maternal grandmother lives just north of Zuni itself and comes to the aid of barren women (Tedlock 1965-1966:I-6). Whereas the *ʔahayu·ta* are active primarily in winter, *payatamu* belongs to the summer; instead of carrying weapons and hunting, as they do, he carries a flute and produces flowers and butterflies (Stevenson 1904:48-57). In his *nepayatamu* (clown) form, he wears his hair knot on his forehead and says the opposite of what he means (Tedlock 1972:118). Like the *ʔahayu·ta,* he possesses medicine for divination (Stevenson 1904:569).

Equidistant from the four oceans is Zuni itself, also called *ʔitiwanʔa* 'the middle place'. Nearby are the raw people who are under the direct care of the daylight people, especially the corn plants, whose tassels are their heads and whose children are the maturing corn ears they hold in their arms (Bunzel 1932c:645, 658). On the northern edge of the village, even closer in than the *ʔahayu·ta* grandmother, is a shrine containing the "Navajo Priests," enemy scalps converted into bringers of water and seeds (ibid.:674-685). In the village itself, in the storerooms of the houses, are the *towa ʔa·citta* 'corn mothers', the harvested corn ears of the six directional colors (Benedict 1935, 1:41, 2:26). In the innermost rooms of some of the houses are the *ʔetto·we* 'sacred bundles', many of them brought all the way from the

fourth underworld when the Zunis migrated eastward to their present village (Kroeber 1919:165-174). In the various bundles are water and seeds belonging to the *ʔuwanammi* (Stevenson 1904:163), stone images of the beast priests and prey animals (Cushing 1883:19, 24-32), and the masks used to impersonate the kachina priests (Bunzel 1932:880-885). Taken together, the contents of the sacred bundles constitute a microcosm. At the center of the bundles, at the center of Zuni, there rests a stone on a permanent altar (Bunzel 1932a:514), and inside this stone beats the heart of the world.

## Religion and the Daylight People

In the beginning the Sun Father had no one to give him offerings, so he asked his twin sons, the *ʔahayu·ta,* to bring the daylight people out of the fourth underworld (Bunzel 1932b:584). In return for the prayers and offerings the daylight people now give him, he grants blessings, including daylight itself. The daylight people have a similar relationship with all the other raw people, be they rainstorms, bears, deer, kachinas, or corn plants; this is *tewusu* 'religion'.

The offerings made to the raw people consist of food and clothing. The food is tobacco smoke, cornmeal (plain or mixed with crushed turquoise, shell, and coral), or small portions of cooked food (Bunzel 1932a:498-499). The "clothing" consists of *telikina·we,* willow sticks given life by the cutting of a face and the addition of feathers and paint; these sticks are not merely offerings but sacrifices, lives given up to the raw people as a surrogate for the self (B. Tedlock 1971). The daylight person making such a sacrifice prays that the raw people will grant breath, a completed path (a life not shortened by an untimely death), old age, waters, seeds, riches (clothing and jewelry), fecundity (children, domestic animals, and game), power, strength of will, good fortune, and daylight (Bunzel 1932c:754-756). After making the sacrifice he abstains from sexual relations and quarrels for four days; on some occasions the abstinence extends to food (or specific foods) and commerce (Bunzel 1932a:501).

Even the Zuni who is *tewukoʔliya* 'poor, without religion' must make personal stick sacrifices at the solstices; other Zunis may make these sacrifices as many as 20 times a year (Ladd 1963:28). Only men make the sticks, but both sexes sacrifice them, men to the Sun Father and the kachinas, women to the Moon Mother, and both sexes to the *ʔa·łaššina·we* 'ancestors' in general (Parsons 1917:162). During the time when many women were potters, the painting of feather designs on vessels (see "Pueblo Fine Arts," fig. 4, this vol.) was held to be equivalent to the making of offering-sticks by the men (Bunzel 1929:106). Other personal religious acts include prayer and sacrifice on daily occasions such as the rising of the Sun Father (Parsons 1917:163) and the eating of a meal, and on special occasions such as the presentation of

§ Sometimes there is talk of two different sets of twins: *watuci* and *yanaluha,* who were active in "The Beginning," and the *ʔahayu·ta* proper, who came into being later (Bunzel 1932b:584, 597).

an eight-day-old infant to the Sun Father or a death in the family (Bunzel 1932c:632-635).

Sometimes the purpose of religious acts is to ʔelekkʔa 'make good' or šuwaha 'purify' (literally 'make circular motions') when something has already gone wrong, but often the main purpose is to ʔiʔcuʔma 'do something now that will come to fruition in the future', even reaching all the way into the afterlife. The performance of such acts, or even the mere knowledge of how to perform them, helps to make a person tehya 'valuable, protected'. Females are tehya, to a degree, by their very nature (Tedlock 1968:134-135, 147), but all boys must be initiated into the kotikanne 'Kachina Society' in order to "save them" or "make them valuable" (Bunzel 1932:975). This is done in two stages, the first when they are 5 to 9 years old, the second when they are 10 to 14. In the second initiation the boys are whipped by the Blue Horn kachinas and then trade places with them, putting on their masks and whipping them back, thus learning that they themselves can become kachinas (Stevenson 1904:103-104; Leighton and Adair 1966:69-70). At first the new initiate borrows a mask when he joins dances, but sooner or later he will want to have a mask of his own; this, like his first wearing of a mask, comes to him with a severe purificatory whipping (Bunzel 1932: 849-853).

Formerly women were occasionally initiated into the Kachina Society in order to cure them of having been badly frightened by kachinas (Stevenson 1904:65; Parsons 1917:162; Bunzel 1932:875). Otherwise women have participated in the affairs of this society primarily in their capacity as wives of the male members, preparing feasts for kachina impersonators (Bunzel 1933:11-14), helping with costumes, and providing an admiring audience.

One of the primary purposes of the dances put on by the Kachina Society is revealed by the story of its origin, in which the Zunis ask, "How shall we enjoy ourselves?" (Bunzel 1932b:605). Many kachina dances are not so ʔattanni 'sacred' as they are coʔya 'beautiful, novel'. The most beautiful performances are asked for encore after encore, so that 20 or 30 separate productions can expand to fill as many as 85 days of the year, as in 1916 (Parsons 1933:85-90), or even 100 or more, as in 1971. The performers hope especially to attract the favorable attention of women; indeed, tales depict kachinas as lovers (Benedict 1935, 2:153-158), and it is said that when the kachinas came in person, before impersonation began, they always took a woman away with them (Kroeber 1916:277). It is as if the kachinas were trying to lure women to Kachina Village, but if a woman were to be so attracted as to follow a dancer, death would be the result (B. Tedlock 1973:71-74).

Some kachinas sing or pray for rain and the growth of crops, while others sing about hunting. The Blue Horns who whip initiates may on other occasions whip spectators, in order to purify them or cure them of bad dreams (Parsons 1922:188; Bunzel 1932:875). A dancer may give a kachina doll to a woman who has had a miscarriage so that she may have a normal pregnancy (Parsons 1919:281); sometimes dances are performed outside the house of a sick person to help the recovery (B. Tedlock 1973:70). Thus, in addition to being seductively beautiful, the dancers may bring fertility and health.

The Kachina Society is headed by the komossʔona 'kachina chief' and the kopekʷinne 'kachina spokesman', each with his own kopiʔɬa šiwani 'kachina bow priest' (Parsons 1917:162). The membership is divided among six kivas (ceremonial rooms entered through the roof), each with its own ʔotakka mossʔona 'dance chief' (Bunzel 1932:876). The kivas are hierarchically arranged according to a counterclockwise circuit of the village, beginning with the Wall kiva on the main plaza and continuing west to the Blackwall kiva, south to the Parched Corn kiva, up a blind alley to the Dung kiva, east to the Brain kiva, and then north to the Little Group kiva (figs. 2-3) (B. Tedlock 1973:41). This arrangement, with various permutations, determines the sequence in which the kivas perform dances during a given season. In the course of a typical year each kiva puts on dances at four different times: during the summer, during the harvest, just before the winter solstice, and during the winter itself (B. Tedlock 1973:39). During the spring, at least formerly, the kivas competed in kick-stick races (Stevenson 1904:318); by 1972 the winter dance series had become so long that it extended right through the former racing season.

The impersonation of some of the kachina priests, including Long Horn, the six šaʔlako (one for each kiva) (fig. 1), and the 10 koyemši (fig. 4), involves year-long duties. Only men of good character are eligible; while in office, they must say daily prayers and attend nightly or weekly meetings and rehearsals, keeping their minds away from mundane matters as much as possible (Bunzel 1932c:702, 1932:962-963). The impersonation of the kanʔaˑkʷe, who are the ghosts of a defeated enemy people, falls to an organization housed in the Parched Corn kiva. Only members of the Corn clan, said to be descendants of the kanʔaˑkʷe, are eligible for initiation into this group. Every fourth year the kanʔaˑkʷe bring tribute to the other villagers (Stevenson 1904:217-226).

In addition to the Kachina Society, which constantly enters the life of every Zuni, there are 14 smaller tikaˑwe 'societies' of a more esoteric nature. Closely allied to the Kachina Society itself is the sutikanne 'Coyote Society'. These two societies jointly conduct a quadrennial pilgrimage to Kachina Village (Tedlock 1972:283), and formerly they collaborated in running communal rabbit hunts (Stevenson 1904:89-94). The principal patrons of the Coyote Society are the prey and game animals of the six directions; the members are experts in hunting and able to cure illness caused by deer. It is an all-male society, and normally a vacancy opens up only on the

Fig. 2. top, Zuni Pueblo; bottom, detail of central portion of Zuni Pueblo. Photographs by Peter Dechert, June 1977.

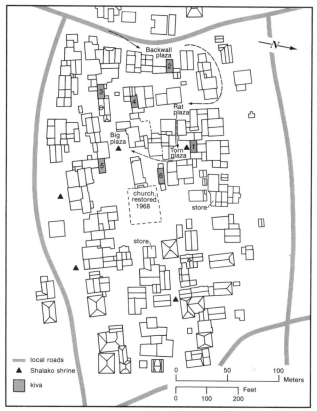

revised from Natl. Park Service, Histl. Amer. Buildings Survey: map for 1972.
Fig. 3. Central (original) portion of Zuni Pueblo. Kivas are numbered: 1, Wall kiva; 2, Backwall kiva; 3, Parched Corn kiva; 4, Dung kiva; 5, Brain kiva; 6, Little Group kiva. Arrows show route taken by kachina dancers.

čikkʔaliˑkʷe 'Snake Medicine People'; the makkʔe cʔanaˑkʷe 'Little Fire People' and their offshoot, the pešaciloˑkʷe 'Bedbug People'; and the haloˑkʷe 'Red Ant People' and the makkʔe łanaˑkʷe 'Big Fire People'. Two other societies, though not counted as part of the Completed Path group, are associated with šipaˑpuliʔma. These are the łeweˑkʷe 'Sword People' or 'Ice People', whose patrons include the beast priests, and the šumaˑkʷe 'Helix People', whose patrons are eastern kachinas.

These 10 societies of šipaˑpuliʔma and the specialized orders within them have the knowledge of physical and mental powers that exceed ordinary human capacities. The Clowns, founded by the opposite-talking nepayatamu, know how to drink what is not potable (including urine) and eat what is not edible (including dung), and with great relish at that (Stevenson 1904:437). They have medicine that takes away the sense of shame, and with occasional help from the Priestly People they present public parodies of everything from kachina dances to lunar space probes (fig. 5). The Priestly, Uhuhu, Snake Medicine, Little Fire, Bedbug, and Helix People all have orders whose members know the mastery of fire, bathing in it, swallowing it, and (in the case of Little Fire and Bedbug) dancing on a bed of hot coals, all without getting burned (ibid.:503, 506, 566). The Sword People,

death of a member, passing to whichever of his kinsmen is interested.

Eight of the societies are composed of people who once came close to death through illness, accident, or taboo violation and had to place themselves under the protection of the beast priests of šipaˑpuliʔma in order to complete their lives. These are the ʔonaˑ yaˑnaka tikaˑwe 'Societies of the Completed Path': the šiwanaˑkʷe 'Priestly People' and their "younger brothers," the neweˑkʷe 'Clowns'; the ʔuhuhuˑkʷe 'Uhuhu People' (probably named after a cry they use) and their offshoot, the

503

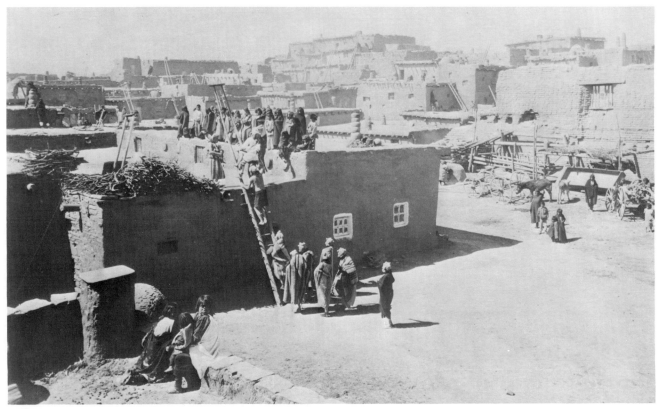

Fig. 4. Koyemshi, here wrapped in blankets though normally attired only in pinkish clay that covers their bodies, and their distinctive masks (with bulbous protuberances at top and mouth), a ragged kilt, and a piece of dark fabric tied round the base of the neck, ascending a ladder to a rooftop kiva. Koyemshi accompany kachina dancers from their kivas to public outdoor performances, where they provide cues for dancers and clown for the audience during intermissions. Photograph by Ben Wittick, probably 1890s.

Fig. 5. A member of the *newe·kʷe* 'Clown People', dressed and painted for a public performance. Clown People, in contrast with Koyemshi (fig. 4), use face paint rather than masks and favor tattered non-Indian clothing. Photograph by Matilda C. Stevenson, probably Jan. 8, 1909.

on the other hand, know the mastery of cold, breaking the ice to bathe in the river during the winter (ibid.:452). Both the Sword and the Big Fire People have orders whose members are able to swallow long wooden swords or the trunks of Douglas firs cut to the same shape as the swords (fig. 6); in addition, the Big Fire People have an arrow-swallowing order (Stevenson 1904:466–485, 504–520).

Knowledge of the kinds so far discussed is available to the society member either at the time of his first initiation into a society or as a first step beyond that initiation. At a higher level are orders with powerful curing knowledge. In three societies the power of these curing orders comes through the impersonation of eastern kachinas: Big Kachina and *mito taša* for the Clowns; Big Kachina (not the same as that of the Clowns), *šicu·ka,* and *kʷelele* for Big Fire; and the *šume·kuli* and Horned Ones for Helix (Stevenson 1904:429, 485, 530). The Uhuhu, Snake Medicine, and Red Ant People each have an order whose curing powers come through red ants, horned toads, and rattlesnakes. When a patient has a sore throat or skin troubles caused by ants, members of this order are able to see the bits of gravel in his body, bring them to the

Fig. 6. Members of the Great Fire order of the Big Fire People, swallowing swords (center foreground) on the fifth day of an initiation ceremony (Stevenson 1904:504–511). They are distinguishable from the Sword People, who also swallow swords, on the basis of their dance kilts and characteristic markings—black face paint streaked with white, and blackened upper arms with white crosses (Stevenson 1904:509, pls. 114, 118). A drummer stands near the doorway at right, while spectators watch from roofs. The seated men at left are musicians for the Sword People, who dance in the plaza in alternation with the Big Fire People; notched sticks with which they will accompany their own dancers rest on the boxes in front of them. Photograph by Matilda C. Stevenson, Jan. or Feb., possibly 1897.

surface, and brush them off with bunches of grass (ibid.:529).

The most dangerous and difficult of all the curing orders is that of *ʔicepčo* 'magicianship', found among the Priestly, Uhuhu, Little Fire, Bedbug, and Red Ant People. The magician, possessed by the bear or mountain lion, is able to see into the body of his patient, and when he locates the foreign object that is the cause of the illness, he draws it to the surface with an eagle feather or by sucking, finally catching with the hand or in the mouth (Bunzel 1932a:528; Stevenson 1904:415, 494–501). Other abilities of magicians, sometimes displayed before large crowds, include lifting heavy objects with feathers, turning balls of mush into stones and back again, restoring burnt feathers, and slicing a man in half without hurting him (Stevenson 1904:270–271, 429, 522–527).

The remaining specialized orders in the societies of *šipa·puliʔma* include the Navajo Dance order in Big Fire,

which performs a Navajo-style dance for the public, and the *payatamu* order in Little Fire and Bedbug, which performs on long flutes (Stevenson 1904:485, 549). And finally, there is the Knife order of the Red Ant People, consisting of warriors and counting the *ʔahayu·ta* twins and the roadrunner among its patrons (ibid.:528; Benedict 1935, 1:67–68).

Each of the 10 societies of *šipa·puliʔma* has four officers: *tika mossi* 'society chief', *pekʷinne* 'spokesman', *ʔakʷʔa mossi* 'medicine chief', and *piʔła šiwani* 'bow priest' (Parsons 1917:161). These positions are open only to men, but otherwise all 10 societies are open to women, except for the arrow-swallowing order in Big Fire, the *payatamu* orders in Little Fire and Bedbug, and the Knife order in Red Ant.

All the societies remaining to be discussed are associated with war, and all are exclusively male. The principal war society, whose patrons are the *ʔahayu·ta* twins, is the

Smithsonian, NAA.

Fig. 7. Dance of the *pakokko* 'Navajo kachina'; this is a Zuni rendition of the Navajo Yeibichai, complete with the appropriate Navajo songs. It is performed just before and during Shalako. The participants are members of the Kachina Society but are organized independently of the kiva groups. They are always accompanied by members of the Clown Society (the 2 unmasked men at left); Navajos always join the audience (the men in hats on the rooftops). Photograph by Matilda C. Stevenson, before 1898.

*ʔaˑpiʔɬa ʔaˑšiwani ʔaˑwan tikanne* 'Society of Bow Priests', sometimes called *patikanne* 'Navajo Society' (Kroeber 1916:275) after the enemies its members once fought. Formerly any man who had killed an enemy had to join this society in order to save his life from the ghost, unless he was already a member of the Coyote Society or one of the two war societies mentioned below (Bunzel 1932c:674). The returning veterans of World War II had to be purified before entering the village, but this was done by societies with curing orders rather than by the Bow Priests (Adair 1948:109–110). The Scalp Dance, sponsored by the Bow Priests and the Knife order of Red Ant (Stevenson 1904:579–585; Parsons 1924), was held as recently as 1971, but by that time it had become a regular fall ceremony and was no longer a victory celebration over a new scalp.

Two war societies are defunct. One of these, a close ally of the Helix People, is *cʔuʔɬana* 'Big Shell' (Parsons 1933:80); its members cured bloating and caused enemies to fall dead by blowing on a conch shell trumpet (Benedict 1935, 2:159, 206–207). The other is the *košiˑkʷe* 'Cactus People', who whipped one another with cactus for pleasure and cured puncture wounds (Stevenson 1904:570–575).

In ancient times the *ʔaˑhaɬikʷi* 'witches', people whose nature it is to plot the deaths of those who arouse their jealousy or resentment, had a clandestine society of their own, the *hatikanne* 'Witch Society' (Tedlock 1972:189). Today they work as individuals, making their victims ill by working on bits of hair, nails, excrement, or clothing, or by shooting foreign objects into their bodies (Adair 1948:47–74). "Poor" Zunis, those without religious knowledge beyond that of the Kachina Society, often suspect "valuable" Zunis of witchcraft, that is, of using religious knowledge for private ends (Parsons 1917:234; Benedict 1935, 2:86, 153, 160). But these same lay people have the benefit of an annual winter solstice ceremony called "The Good Night," in which all the Societies of the Completed Path hold open meetings and perform free cures for all comers (Bunzel 1932a:531–532).

The Zuni rain priesthoods, dedicated primarily to the *ʔuwanammi,* are much smaller bodies than the societies, but their concerns are much broader. Their "children," the people under their care, include all the Zunis, even the witches, and they pray for all the other village-dwelling peoples and for all the raw people as well, even "every dirty bug" (Bunzel 1932c:666–667; Tedlock 1972:32, 142, 152). Their conduct in everyday life sets an example for all the people: it is said that "a really good Zuni will not fight and argue—he is just like a priest" (Smith and Roberts 1954:127).

During the summer the rain priests go into seclusion with their sacred bundles to establish direct contact with the *ʔuwanammi* (Stevenson 1904:173–178, 386). When there are questions to settle that affect all the people, they may go into seclusion to divine the answers: it was they who discovered, with the help of the *ʔahayuˑta,* the location of the middle of the world (Tedlock 1972:277–280), and with the help of *nepayatamu* they divined the hiding place of the Corn Mothers during a famine (Benedict 1935, 1:24–43). On lesser occasions they accept private clients who wish to divine the location of lost or stolen objects, and formerly they had clients who wished to know the outcome of gambling games (Stevenson 1904:334, 386–387).

The summer retreats of the rain priests, four or eight days apiece, run consecutively from the summer solstice into September. The first six retreats are those of the *tekʔohannan ʔaˑšiwani* 'Daylight Priests', representing the six directions, and these are followed by eight retreats of the *tehkʷinan ʔaˑšiwani* 'Night Priests' (Kroeber 1919:176). The first four Daylight Priests, representing a clockwise circuit of the four horizontal directions, are the *kʔakʷaˑmossi* 'House Chiefs': the *kʔakʷemossi* 'House Chief' proper, whose sacred bundle is kept in a house north of the main plaza; the End Priest, whose house is at the east end of the village; the Road Priest, beside a road on the south side; and the Backwall Priest, beside the kiva of that name, on the western edge of the village (Parsons 1933:80–81; Kroeber 1919:175, map 8).

The fifth Daylight Priest to go into seclusion, representing the zenith, is the *pekʷinne* 'Spokesman' of the House Chiefs, also called *kʔašima wowe* 'Water-Bringing

Birds', after the spokesmen of the ʔuwanammi (Bunzel 1932c:639, 695), and yatokka šiwani 'Sun Priest', because he is the keeper of the calendar and the spokesman of the Sun Father himself (Kroeber 1916:274-275). In the sixth position, representing the nadir, is the Bow Priest of the House Chiefs; he is a member of the Society of Bow Priests and is called tekʔohannan piʔɫa šiwani 'Daylight Bow Priest' to distinguish him from other members. The Sun Priest and the Daylight Bow Priest do not have sacred bundles like those of other rain priests; instead, the Sun Priest goes into retreat "to try himself" rather than relying on a bundle, and the Daylight Bow Priest,[#] instead of secluding himself in a house, wanders among his fields and goes to mountaintops to pray to the bow priests of the ʔuwanammi (Bunzel 1932c:663-664, 1933:19, 24). Taken together, the retreats of the six Daylight Priests span 40 days. The office of Sun Priest has been vacant since 1952, but his retreat days are still counted and he is still mentioned in prayers. His duties (other than those of retreat) have been taken over by the House Chief.

The Night Priests go into retreat as follows: first, Eagle clan's Priest; second, Little Group Priest, whose bundle is kept in a house adjacent to the kiva of that name; third, Corn clan's Priest; fourth, koloˑwisi Priest, named after the feathered serpent effigy his bundle is kept with; fifth, Helix People's Priest, who is the head of the Helix Society; sixth, Sun clan's Priest; seventh, Priest of the kanʔaˑkʷe, head of the kanʔaˑkʷe group in the Parched Corn kiva; eighth, Red Door Priest, whose bundle is kept in a house with a red door (Kroeber 1919:171, 175; Parsons 1933:80-89). The Big Shell Society head, although the society itself has long since ceased to function as such, is also a rain priest; he goes into seclusion during the latter half of the fourth Night Priest's retreat. (A different enumeration of the rain priests is in "Zuni Social and Political Organization," this vol.).

Each of the Daylight and Night Priests, except for the Sun Priest and the Daylight Bow Priest, has anywhere from two to five ranked male assistants, the first among whom is usually his successor; several priests have one or two female assistants as well, but they are not potential successors (Kroeber 1919:169-170; Parsons 1933:80-83). The House Chief and the Sun Priest must be members of the pičči·kʷe clan or the sons of men who are; some of the other priesthoods are associated with particular clans, but only because their sacred bundles are kept in houses belonging to members of these clans (Kroeber 1919:166-167). In no case is there any automatic inher-

itance of priestly office within particular lineages; suitability of temperament counts for more than kinship.

## Death and the End of the World

Death was introduced among daylight people by the first witch, who was allowed to live among them because he brought the first yellow corn (Tedlock 1972:258-261). Witchcraft is still one of the major causes of death, but there are others: a man who does not believe in the kachinas may be choked by his mask, and deaths may also result when a kachina dance goes on for too many days; the dead themselves may appear in dreams and try to take the living with them (Bunzel 1932c:634).

Every living person carries with him an invisible road, long or short, which determines the proper time for his death (Benedict 1935, 2:51, 65). If a person dies prematurely, through suicide or because of excessive grief, he is barred from the afterworld until he comes to the end of his appointed road (Ladd 1963:25-26). All deaths are portended, most commonly in dreams; the deaths of rain priests are forecast by the cosmos itself in events such as landslides (Bunzel 1933:54) and unseasonable thunderstorms.

Burial of the body takes place within a day after death, but the pinanne 'spirit' (literally 'wind') of the dead person remains in his home until four days after his death. A deceased rain priest then joins the ʔuwanammi priests in the waters of the world (Bunzel 1932a:482). A member of the Society of Bow Priests becomes one of the lightning-makers, who are the bow priests of the ʔuwanammi (Stevenson 1904:20, 110). Members of the Societies of the Completed Path join their raw counterparts in the east at šipaˑpuliʔma (Bunzel 1932a:517).

Among the remaining people, any initiate of the Kachina Society goes west to Kachina Village. If a man owned a mask during life he may both join the constant dancing at Kachina Village and come invisibly to Zuni to "stand before" the living kachina impersonators (Bunzel 1932b:607; Ladd 1963:27). A woman, unless she is one of the rare female initiates, goes to Kachina Village by virtue of marriage (a reversal of the uxorilocal residence of life), being reunited with her first husband (Benedict 1935, 1:130). She does the same thing there that she did in life, preparing feasts for the dancers. Any person of Kachina Village may return among the living as a cloud, most happily in a whole group of rainclouds, but a person who never went to see the dancers in life will be alone in the sky, and a person who was not "straight" in life will be a "lying" cloud (Bunzel 1929:94-102). Girls and uninitiated boys become turtles or watersnakes when they die, and they try to return to their living kin (Tedlock and Tedlock 1971-1972:A7, 1).

When a person has been separated from his former daylight existence by four deaths, he finds himself all the

---

[#] As Kroeber points out (1919:176), both this office and that of Eagle clan's Priest (who follows the Daylight Bow Priest in the retreat sequence) were apparently held by the same man in Stevenson's time, resulting in her description of the nadir priest as going into retreat with a bundle (1904:173-178) when in fact no bundle attaches to that office per se.

way back at the hole where the Zunis emerged from the earth, which is even farther west than Kachina Village (Tedlock and Tedlock 1971–1972:A7, 1), or else he has descended, death by death, to the lowest of the four underworlds, where the Zunis originated (Edmund J. Ladd, personal communication 1973). At this point he may return among the living as an animal, the species depending on the knowledge he acquired in life. A member of a Society of the Complete Path might become a mountain lion, bear, badger, wolf, eagle, mole, rattlesnake, or red ant; a witch might become a coyote, lizard, bullsnake, or owl; a member of the Kachina Society might become a deer (Ladd 1963:26; Tedlock and Tedlock 1971–1972:A7, 1).

Even the first death brings about a loss of personal individual identity. When a person dies, he ceases to be mentioned by name, though he does receive personal prayers and offerings when he is first sent away from Zuni (Bunzel 1932c:632–634). Once he is gone he is addressed only in the sense that he is a member of one or more of the groups of dead people mentioned in prayers: ancestors in general, kachinas, or, more specifically, the dead of one of the smaller societies (Stevenson 1904:570; Benedict 1935, 2:17), or, still more specifically, the deceased officers of a society (Benedict 1935, 1:39). The only exceptions to this loss of individual identity are the deceased rain priests, whose successors invoke them by name, going as far back as the names are known (Bunzel 1932c:656).

There is some talk at Zuni about the death of the world itself. At the beginning the earth was soft and wet (Tedlock 1972:226); the fathers and grandfathers of the present-day elders began to wonder whether it was getting old and dry (Tedlock 1965–1966:H–38). They prophesied a famine, and some now say that the famine is already here but has been made invisible by the supermarket. At the end, they said, all man-made things would rise against us, and a hot rain would fall.

# Zuni Semantic Categories

WILLARD WALKER

Though the semantic domains and categories of Zuni are still little known, a number of them have been explored and reported upon. Many, of course, are explicit in the grammar of Zuni, a sketch of which may be found in volume 17. Others have been described by Lenneberg and Roberts (1956), Schneider and Roberts (1956), Walker (1966, 1966a), and Walker and Roberts (1965).

## Color Categories

The color categories of Zuni have been treated by Lenneberg and Roberts (1956), who identified the "highly codable" color categories of Zuni and described them in terms of their range and location on the dimensions of hue and brightness, the range and location of their foci, the degree to which the categories "fill" the color space, and the distribution of the categories, relative to one another, along the various dimensions. The color categories cannot be described here; but it is worth noting that there is evidence of change in the color classification, evidently as a consequence of contact with English speakers and with Anglo color categories. Thus monolingual Zunis use the term *łupc̓ina* for colors that might be called "yellow" or "orange" by English speakers, while bilingual Zunis tend to approximate the English categories, using *łupc̓ina* for "yellow" and *ʔolenčinanne* (apparently derived from the English term *orange*) for "orange."

It is also noteworthy, perhaps, that some Zuni color terms relate to other terms not specifically identified with color but consisting, in part at least, of the same linguistic components. Thus one can best comprehend the semantic value of *łiʔʔana* 'blue' if one knows that *łiʔʔakʷa* is the standard term for turquoise; and the term *k̓eˑkʷʔina* "purple" offers little difficulty when one knows that the stem *k̓e-* refers to cornstalks after the harvest, by which time they often take on a purplish cast, and that *kʷʔina* is a word meaning 'black' or 'dark'.

## Kinship

The Zuni kinship categories, unlike the color classification, seem highly resistant to change. Schneider and Roberts (1956:18) understate their case, perhaps, when they write that "the fact that our data, collected in 1953, are so closely similar to Kroeber's data, collected almost forty years earlier, suggests that the rate of change in the terminological system is not extraordinarily rapid."

At any rate, the kinship terminology equates mother with mother's sister, both of which are called *citta*, but not with father's sister, called *kuku*. Likewise, it equates father with father's brother, both of which are called *taččú*, but not with mother's brother, called *kaka*. In this and in other respects the system tends to equate members of a single lineage and to differentiate members of different lineages; on the other hand, the system sometimes equates members of a single generation regardless of lineage affiliation, as in the case of father's father and mother's father, both called *nana*. The lineage and generational principles are often represented by alternative terms for the same category of kinsmen, as in the case of father's sister's daughter, for example, who may be called either *kuku*, thus equating her with father's sister, or *kawu*, which equates her with elder sister. Irregularities in the application of kinship terms, which are frequent at Zuni (Schneider and Roberts 1956), provide additional evidence for the coexistence of the lineage and generational principles in the Zuni system, as when a maternal uncle (a member of the speaker's lineage, normally called *kaka*) is referred to as *taččú*, a term that equates him with the speaker's father and hence with the speaker's father's lineage.

Schneider and Roberts (1956:18) account for the widespread occurrence of pairs of alternative terms and of apparent irregularities in the usage of terms by suggesting

> that genealogical position alone does not determine what a particular kinsman will be called or what role will be played toward him, but rather that genealogical position is one among a group of determinants and its strength as a determinant depends on the situation. Relative age, affiliation through ceremonial extension, clan affiliations, considerations of courtesy, personal relationship, and the value of extending kinship as widely as possible all go along with genealogical position to determine the kinship term applied and the role played.

They conclude that "in Zuni the dominant value of kinship terms is the adequate representation of roles played and not the classification of genealogical positions." This interpretation may serve to explain, not only the kinship system per se, but also a number of terms that serve both as kin terms and as terms for a variety of age-sex categories. Thus,

> Ego's own children may be designated "child" *[čaʔle]* regardless of sex, or distinguished on the basis of age and sex by being called "boy" *[ʔakcekʔi]* or "young man" *[cawakʔi]*, "little girl" *[ʔeʔle]*, "girl" *[kacikʔi]*, or "young woman" *[maʔkʔi]*. These terms are also applied by a woman to her sister's children, and by a man to his brother's children. They do not necessarily imply kinship and may be used simply as age-sex designations (Schneider and Roberts 1956:11).

According to this view, the Zuni kinship terminology is not, strictly speaking, a kinship terminology at all. Rather, the Zunis have a set of terms for types of social relationships, most of which are, to varying degrees, identified with genealogically definable classes of kinsmen. This pattern of identifying social roles in terms of genealogical categories is not unrelated, perhaps, to the fact that Zunis identify certain colors by association with items outside the color domain, for example, purple with mature cornstalks.

## Beings

The term *ʔaˑhoʔʔi* may be used either as a verb meaning 'they are alive' or as a noun meaning 'beings, living things'. In the second sense the term is generic, there being subcategories of *ʔaˑhoʔʔi*, and serves to define a large segment of the universe as perceived by Zunis, a semantic domain that embraces mammals, reptiles, birds, insects, deities, ghosts, certain natural phenomena (earth, moon), and also plants.

Animals and human beings are both classed as *ʔaˑhoʔʔi* 'beings' by monolingual Zuni speakers; however, there is no generic term in Zuni denoting either the class of animals or the class of humans. Likewise, certain subcategories of the *ʔaˑhoʔʔi* include both human and nonhuman beings. Thus the *wemaˑwe* include all paw-footed mammals, "beast fetishes," and the ritual impersonators of the "beast deities"; and the *wowe* include any and all valuable, animate possessions, for example, cattle, horses, mules, burros, sheep, goats, slaves, captives, and various servants of the gods in the Zuni dance-drama, such as the retainers, or *wowe*, of the Shalakos. At various key points in the native Zuni classification of the 'being' domain, then, human and nonhuman beings are equated by the terminology. Given this situation, it is extremely unlikely that any Zuni prior to European contact could have conceptualized humans as opposed to animals, or that he could ever have conceived of the exploitation of nature by man; for the categories *human, animal, nature,* and *man* are all alien to the native Zuni classification of the universe insofar as this is known to linguists.

The *ʔaˑhoʔʔi* 'beings' subsume two major subcategories: *wowe* 'creatures' and *lenaˑwe* 'plants' (fig. 1; see also Walker 1964, 1965, 1966, 1966a). There are, of course,

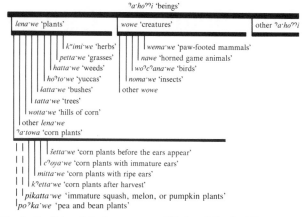

Fig. 1. Traditional Zuni taxonomy of "beings." Dashed lines indicate classifications that are acceptable to some but not all native speakers.

*ʔaˑhoʔʔi* that are neither *wowe* nor *lenaˑwe,* for example, the earth, moon, clouds, and stars. Bilingual, high-school-educated Zunis, though not their monolingual parents, were using the term *ʔaˑhoʔʔi* in the 1960s in two senses: 'beings' and 'people'. The first was consistent with the usage of their parents and presumably with that of pre-Columbian Zunis; the second is an innovation resulting apparently from the acquisition of a European concept by English-speaking Zunis with considerable experience in English-speaking schools. For these Zunis, there are two homonymous terms: *ʔaˑhoʔʔi* 'beings', on the topmost level of the 'being' hierarchy, and *ʔaˑhoʔʔi* 'human beings', on the next level of the hierarchy.

The term *wowe* 'creatures' has had a similar history. Originally, it evidently subsumed four subcategories: *wemaˑwe* 'paw-footed mammals', *nawe* 'horned game animals', *woʔcʔanaˑwe* 'birds', and *nomaˑwe* 'insects'. It subsumed also, of course, sundry small categories such as *takka* 'frogs' and *čittola* 'rattlesnakes', which are not included in any of the four subcategories of *wowe.* The old structure changed as a consequence of contacts with the Spaniards and specifically the acquisition of European livestock in the sixteenth and seventeenth centuries. The term *wowe* came to be used in two senses: 'creatures' and 'valuable, animate possessions'. As with the two semantic values of *ʔaˑhoʔʔi,* the first was presumably consistent with the usage of pre-Columbian Zunis; the second resulted from the Zunis' acquisition of livestock and their increasing familiarity with the institutions of slavery and peonage.

The old Zuni plant terminology evidently consisted of the generic term *lenaˑwe* 'plants' and eight subordinate terms: *kʷimiˑwe* 'herbs, roots', *pettaˑwe* 'grasses', *hattaˑwe* 'weeds', *hoʔtoˑwe* 'yuccas', *łattaˑwe* 'bushes', *tattaˑwe* 'trees', *wottaˑwe* 'hills of corn' (or other plants, usually garden plants), and *ʔaˑtowa* 'corn plants, garden plants'. As in the case of the 'being' and 'creature' categories, there are types of *lenaˑwe* 'plants' that are not members of any of the subcategories of *lena·we,* for instance, *ʔopo·cisiʔa* 'puffball' and *heʔkʷitola* 'cornsmut'.

There was a difference of opinion among native speakers of Zuni in the 1960s as to whether the *ʔa·towa* 'corn plants' include other garden plants such as *pikatta·we* 'immature squash, melon, or pumpkin plants' and *poʔka·we* 'pea or bean plants'. However, all agreed that the *ʔa·towa* include the four codable types of maize plants: *šetta·we* 'corn plants before the ears appear', *cʔoya·we* 'corn plants with immature ears', *mitta·we* 'corn plants with ripe ears', and *kʔetta·we* 'corn plants after harvest'.

The category of *wotta·we* 'hills of corn' overlaps with the *ʔa·towa* and perhaps with certain other categories. Two middle-aged Zunis who were brothers brought up in the same household disagreed in the 1960s as to whether the *wotta·we* include leafless bushes and also as to whether they are limited exclusively to domestic plants; however, they agreed that *wotta·we* invariably have several stems or stalks, hence the gloss 'hills of corn'.

The *ɬatta·we* 'bushes' include all perennial plants that grow in clumps and have no foliage, hence any bush in winter. The *kʔapuʔli* 'tomatillos', since their foliage is very sparse, may be referred to as *ɬatta·we* even in summer.

The *hatta·we* 'weeds' include all plants or bushes having *hawe* or 'leaves'. This definition excludes the *hoʔto·we,* a category that includes all plants having *howe* or 'yucca leaves'.

Just as the old Zuni terms *ʔa·hoʔʔi* and *wowe* came to refer to pairs of discrete categories (people as well as beings and animate possessions as well as creatures, respectively), the generic term for plants, *lena·we,* came to be used in two senses also. It continued to be used for plants in general but also came to have a more restricted meaning, 'crop plants'. In this sense, it overlaps with *ʔa·towa* 'corn plants' and *wotta·we* 'hills of corn'; but, unlike these other two terms, it may refer to plants introduced by Europeans and plants that do not grow in clumps. Therefore, it seems probable that *lena·we* in its more restricted sense of 'crop plants' came into use as a result of European contacts and the acquisition of new crop plants from the Spaniards. Thus each of the three generic terms at the apex of the old Zuni being taxonomy has come to function on two discrete levels of the taxonomic hierarchy. In them there is evidence of a patterned semantic shift affecting the most basic categories of the being taxonomy due, it would seem, to the impact of alien concepts, such as 'human being', and alien categories, such as European livestock, in postcontact times.

## Goods and Chattels

A Zuni household inventory made in 1951 was translated into Zuni and tape recorded eight years later by a Zuni World War II veteran long familiar with the household and the objects it contained. "A Zuni Material Inventory Code" (Walker and Roberts 1965) is based on this tape recording and has served as the basis for what follows.

A few loanwords from English and Spanish appear in the Zuni version of the inventory; and these, of course, imply the acquisition of corresponding semantic categories. The Spanish or probable Spanish loans are *wa·kaši* 'cattle', *kane·lu* 'sheep', *čiwa·tu* 'goat', *meliqa* 'White man', *mansana* 'apple', *ma·kinanne* 'machine', *maččɛ·tanne* 'sword, bayonet', *pistolʔanne* 'pistol', *se·la* 'silk, nylon, gabardine', and *sontalu* 'soldier'. With one or two exceptions, all these words have been reworked to conform to the phonological patterns of Zuni. In *kane·lu* (Spanish *carnero*), for example, stress has moved to the first syllable, Spanish [k] before [a] has become palatalized [kʸ], and Spanish [r] has been deleted in one case and in the other has been replaced by [l], all in accordance with Zuni phonological practice. Most of these loans seem to have entered the vocabulary of Zuni three centuries or more ago; very few, certainly, have entered the vocabulary since that time. The word for 'soldier', *sontalu,* is so completely naturalized that it occurs in abbreviated form as the first component of such compounds as *so·teʔle* 'cast-iron kettle' (soldier-pot) and *sole·wanne* 'army uniform coat' (soldier-coat).

English loans are more numerous in the inventory; and many of them, being more recently acquired, are less completely adapted to Zuni phonological rules. Thus English [r], which has no analogue in Zuni, occurs in *treylo* 'trailer' and *poreks* 'borax', though not in *ʔeplanne* 'apron' or *kʷismas* 'Christmas'. Likewise, English [v], which is quite alien to Zuni, occurs in *vasali·n* 'vaseline'. Other English loans that appear in the inventory are *hankeči* 'handkerchief', *pu·cinne* 'boot', *su·ci* or *su·cinne* 'suit', *li·p* (lady's) 'slip', *li·pos* 'shoe' (from English *slippers*), *pa·y* 'pie', *kek* 'cake', *ʔotmi·l* 'oatmeal', *kapičči* 'cabbage', *qa·po* 'cowboy', *to·lettonne* 'outhouse', and *wašinton* 'Washington, federal government'. Most interesting, perhaps, from the standpoint of semantics, is *piččoh,* denoting both 'picture(s)' and 'pitcher(s)'.

In addition to the loanwords there are a very few words that might be considered loan translations, for example, *ɬe·tu·ši* 'sawhorse' (boards-horse); but the great majority of items in the inventory are named by words or phrases made up of native Zuni components combined in accordance with what appear to be native Zuni principles of classification.

Some items are identified in terms of their taste, sound, smell, color, size, or shape. Thus peaches are called *mo·čikʷa* (spherical-sweet), a well pulley is referred to as *kʔewunan ʔan wicicinanne* (well its squeaking-thing), talc is called *ʔitečikʔanaka* (for-making-oneself-stink), a blue cotton dress is called *ɬiʔʔana piccen ʔuččunne* (blue cotton shirt/dress), an apricot is called *mo·čikʷa cʔana* (spherical-sweet small or peach small), a spatula is called he?k?apa (metal-wide). Four categories of shape and/or consistency can perhaps be inferred from the terms mu·čikʷa 'candy' (loaf-shaped-sweet, cf. muwe 'loaves of bread, solid substance'), mo·čikʷa 'peach' (spherical-sweet, cf. mowe 'beads, fruit, squashes, spherical objects'), ma·čikʷa 'sugar' (granular-sweet, cf. mawe 'rock salt, granular substance') and k?ačikʷa 'soda pop' (liquid-sweet, cf. k?awe 'liquid, water').

Many items are identified in terms of the materials of which they are composed. Thus a leather belt appears in the Zuni inventory as kemmekʷinne (leather-thing-that-encircles), a workbench as ?i·kʷanikanaka ɬempowanne (for-working board-platform), some bushel baskets as ta·sawe (wood-bowls), some roofing paper as he?šo po?yanne (gum/rubber/plastic thing-that-fits-over-the-top-of-an-erect-object, as in the case of a hat, roof, or lampshade), a mirror as ?i·yunaka ?a?le (for-looking-at-oneself glass/stone), a can of lard as ?iššana·we wop?e (grease/oil deep-container-of-nonliquid), a stovelid handle as heɬemotinan ?aɬtišnaka he?le (stove for-repeatedly-doing-the-converse-of-causing-a-three-dimensional-enclosure-to-be-sealed-up piece-of-metal), a canvas coat as kotaton le·wanne (canvas coat/jacket), some burlap as hopa· pissenne (burlap cloth), and a blue wool skirt as kane·l ?uwe ?uččunne ɬi??ana (sheep wool shirt/dress blue).

Many of the items in the inventory are coded in terms of their functional attributes. Kerosene, for example, is called tohapiya· k?awe (native-lamps liquid, old-fashioned-lights liquid, or the like), a reference to the use of kerosene in tohapiya·we, old-fashioned (kerosene) lamps, prior to the advent of (wilo??a) hapiya·we, (electric) lights. The functional criterion is crucial in coding corn kernels in the inventory, for those meant to be eaten are called čuwe (corn-kernels), but those to be planted as seed are called mi?le to·šo·we (ear-of-corn seeds).

Many items are identified by phrases consisting of a word indicating some very general function qualified by other words that further specify the item. Thus the word matto·we 'fasteners' appears in phrases such as hepiculliya· matto·we 'washers' (metal-rings fasteners), heyaɬaka matto·we 'staples' (for-wire fasteners), kew ?a·wan matto·we 'rivets' (leather-pieces their fasteners), ɬewe ?a·wan matto·we 'wood screws' (boards their fasteners), tatepololon ?an matto·we 'wagon nuts' (wagon its fasteners), and yallupna· matto·we 'bolts' (things-that-engage-by-turning fasteners).

An explicitly functional suffix -ka 'for' (the purpose of) is of common occurrence in the inventory, as in tek?oskʷišnaka 'beer-can opener' (rigid-container-for-repeatedly-doing-the-converse-of-causing-it-to-stick-out). Another suffix, -kowa or -?kowa, can often be translated 'formerly used for' (the purpose of) and is also of very high frequency. Phrases containing this suffix are ma·čikʷa woppokowa c?ina·wahtanne 'sugar sack' (granular-sweet formerly-used-for-enveloping-nonliquid-items

paper sack) and tummokʷkʷ?a· woppo?kowa ɬelonne 'hosiery box' (stockings formerly-used-for-enveloping-nonliquid-items box). These two contrasting suffixes, -ka and -kowa, are used to specify the potential or former functions of items such as the beer-can opener that has yet to be applied and the hosiery box that has long since ceased to contain hosiery.

## Spatial Relationships

Zuni grammar provides mechanisms for discriminating among many types of spatial relationships. Newman's (1958:109–117) affix dictionary gives words and phrases illustrating the use of suffixes such as -lo 'buried', -paɬa 'wrapped in a bundle', -p(a) and -ppo 'enclosed in a deep container' (but not necessarily covered at the top), -pi 'remove from a deep container', -?annan or -(an)nan 'inside' (but not necessarily sealed in), -ɬ or, with plural inflection, -la 'shallow container of', -li 'in/on a shallow container', -limo 'dispersed over a (three-dimensional) surface', -na 'occupying an area on a (three-dimensional) surface', -ya 'a (growing) mass of', -la 'a group growing or projecting out of the ground', -tta 'a growing bunch', -to 'an object resting on a surface', -ti (a pile) 'resting on a horizontal surface', -ɬɬi 'stacked up', and -ɬpo 'an arrangement of'. The glosses given here may be quite unreliable. They are intended only to suggest the general dimensions of the Zuni affix system as it relates to space and spatial relationships. For a lengthier and, no doubt, more accurate analysis, see Newman (1958, or 1965).

The affixes listed above appear in some striking idioms, for example, pep?e 'broom' (deep-container-of-grass-stems), ?op?e 'cartridge' (deep-container-of-powder), ponne· wollika 'ashtray' (cigarettes shallow-thing-for-containing-nonliquids), k?ali·we 'honeycomb' (Newman 1958:22, 113, liquid-in-shallow-containers), tattekʷinne 'corral' (pieces-of-wood-growing-together-in-the-form-of-a-circle), saɬɬinne 'cupboard' (Newman 1958:113, dishes-stacked-up-thing), ?ohepponne 'witch' (Newman 1958:15, deep-container-of-brains).

Other types of spatial relationships are indicated, not by affixes, but by words, for example, po?yanne 'hat, roof, lampshade' (cover-for-the-top-of-an-erect-object), ?aɬtinne 'plug, lid, door' (cover-for-an-aperture-in-a-three-dimensional-object), and yaɬtonne 'cover' (for a horizontal surface, as in pewin?an yaɬtonne 'sheet, bedspread').

## Containers

There are several Zuni terms for specific types of containers dating from pre-Columbian times: c?i?le 'wicker basket', ho??inne (a type of large, compactly woven basket made by Apaches), hu?čiponne (a type of round-bottomed, wicker pack basket), ɬalinne 'plaque basket', and mehhe?to 'pottery canteen'. Other terms are more general: *łelonne* 'box', *pehanne* 'bundle', *wahtanne* 'sack'. Two words, *saʔle* and *teʔle,* have very extensive and overlapping reference categories and are used with appropriate qualifiers to denote a wide variety of containers that have come into use at Zuni only in the twentieth century. Both *saʔle* (plural *sawe)* and *teʔle* (plural *tewe)* are used in the household inventory to designate a variety of containers from cooking pots to drinking glasses, thus *woleya·ka saʔle* 'cooking pot' (for-boiling *saʔle*), *woleya·ka teʔle* 'cooking pot' (for-boiling *teʔle*), *saʔwalolon tutunaka* 'drinking glass' (*saʔle*-shiny for-drinking), and *ʔaʔwalolon teʔle* 'drinking glass' (glass/ stone-shiny *teʔle*). Both terms even occur together in the same phrase, as when an earthenware jug was identified in the inventory as *saʔto· teʔle, saʔto·* being a compound evidently composed of *saʔle* and *towa* 'native, old-fashioned' applied to any sort of pottery, earthenware or chinaware.

Though the reference categories of *saʔle* and *teʔle* overlap, they are not coextensive. The term *saʔle* is likely to be applied to items such as cups, bowls, dishes, saucers, plates, and platters. It may also be used for other items, for example, *šiʔalekʷika saʔle* 'frying pan' (meat-for-frying *saʔle*), *ta·sawe* 'bushel baskets' (wood-*sawe*). The term *teʔle* is used less often for containers from which people eat or drink and tends to be reserved for buckets, kettles, bottles, jars, and cans; however, it may be used for mugs or drinking glasses. Thus *helippo·tewe* 'cans of paint' (paint-deep-container-*tewe*), *kʔewunanʔan teʔle* 'well bucket' (well-its *teʔle*), *luppoka teʔle,* 'ash can' (deep-container-for-ashes *teʔle*) are used. When containers for food or drink are called *tewe,* they tend to be bulk containers, rather than those from which one eats or drinks directly, for instance, *so·teʔle* 'cast-iron kettle' (soldier-*teʔle*), *nočapi· kʔappoka teʔle* 'thermos bottle' (coffee deep-container-for-liquids *teʔle*), *kʷika· ʔa·wan tewe* 'milk bottles' (milk their *tewe*).

## Summary

The Zuni classifications of beings and household artifacts suggest that changes have occurred as a result of contacts with alien concepts and the acquisition of new categories of beings and of things. New reference categories have been acquired and old ones realigned. While many pre-Columbian items are specified with a single word, the more recently acquired products associated with industrialized societies tend to be identified by relatively complex words and phrases. In acquiring the material benefits of the industrial age and in casting about for names for them, the Zunis have retained old forms such as *wowe* 'creatures', *matto·we* 'fasteners', and *tewe* 'bulk containers'; but they have found it convenient to qualify these old terms in intricate and manifold ways. No doubt this strategy is well calculated to preserve the viability of their language in the context of a consumer economy. In general, it seems that the language has adapted to changes in its environment not so much by adding new vocabulary as by utilizing its syntactic devices to create myriad phrases for new things and by developing new semantic values for old linguistic forms.

# Hopi Prehistory and History to 1850

J.O. BREW

Although most scholars are now prepared to admit that man has probably occupied the region of the Hopi towns for at least 10,000 years, the first identifiable remains date from the early centuries of the Christian era (Euler and Dobyns 1971:1–8). Sites representing the late Basket-maker and early Pueblo phases of the prehistoric culture are to be found throughout the Hopi country (fig. 1), and one of them has been thoroughly excavated (Daifuku 1961). That the villages of 1,500 and 1,600 years ago were occupied by direct ancestors of the modern Hopis is a matter for discussion, but the cultural remains present a clear, uninterrupted, logical development culminating in the life, general technology, architecture, and agricultural and ceremonial practices to be seen on the three Hopi mesas today (Brew 1941).

Until the mid-thirteenth century the major cultural affiliation seems to have been with the villages at the other end of Black Mesa in Marsh Pass and vicinity to the north, the people known as the Kayenta Anasazi. Until that time the Hopi area was characterized by hamlets, small pueblos, and isolated farmsteads. From the middle of the thirteenth century, for 100 years, the population on the Hopi mesas grew and grew as the populous centers in Marsh Pass, the Flagstaff area, and the Little Colorado valley were abandoned, presumably because of drought, with the attendant loss of fields through arroyo cutting,

and the increased aggressiveness of the so-called wild tribes—the Navajos, Apaches, and Utes.

Consequently, during the last half of the thirteenth century and the first half of the fourteenth a striking change is noted not only in the size of sites but also in their contents. Traits previously foreign to the area became integral parts of the culture. Influence from the Little Colorado River valley was particularly noticeable in pottery (W. Smith 1971). The Hopi country became one of the three major centers of Pueblo life during the fourteenth, fifteenth, and sixteenth centuries, along with Zuni-Acoma and the Rio Grande Pueblos.

The influx of immigrant population at that time brought into being sizable towns of 500 to 1,000 people throughout the Hopi country. Scholars have argued as to whether or not the large towns on Antelope Mesa, east of First Mesa, were indeed Hopi. These towns were Awatovi, Kawaika (Kawaika-a), Chakpahu, Nesuftonga, Kokopnyama, and Lululongturque.* They have been called

* The Hopi language is a member of the Uto-Aztecan family; Hopi, Takic, Tubatulabal, and Numic make up the Northern Uto-Aztecan branch of the family (Heath 1977:27), earlier known as Shoshonean (Powell 1891:108–110; Kroeber 1907:97). The differences and correspondences among the various Hopi dialects have not been studied in detail, but it appears that there are at least four major varieties: First Mesa (called Polacca by Whorf 1946:158), Mishongnovi (Whorf's Toreva [tô'rēva]), Shipaulovi (Whorf's Sipaulovi), and Third Mesa (Whorf's Oraibi). Hopi forms written in italics in the *Handbook* are in the Mishongnovi dialect or, where so labeled, the Third Mesa dialect.

The phonemes of the Mishongnovi dialect, as described by Whorf (1936:1198–1201, 1946:159–161), are as follows: (unaspirated stops) *p, t* (alveolar), *c* (alveolar affricate, [tsʸ]), *k* (palatal), *kʷ, q* (velar); (preaspirated stops) ʰ*p* (Whorf's 'p), ʰ*t*, ʰ*c*, ʰ*k*, ʰ*kʷ*, ʰ*q*; (nasals) *m, n, ŋʸ* (Whorf's ɲ), *ŋʷ, ŋ*; (fricatives and resonants) *s, l, v, r* (untrilled, retroflex, and slightly spirantal), *w, y*; (voiceless continuants) *M, N, Ṇ, L, W, Y*; (laryngeals) *h, ʔ*; (vowels) *i, e* ([ε]), *a, o* [oᵘ], *ɨ* (Whorf's e), *ö. k* is [kʸ] before *a, e,* or *i*; in syllable-final position *c* is [ts], *k* is [k], and *v* and *r* are devoiced to [f] and [ɽ], respectively. *v* is bilabial [β], varying to labiodental. Plain [k] before *a* (in loanwords from Spanish) is written *ḳ*. Vowels have three lengths: long (*i·*, etc.), medium (*i*, etc.), and clipped (*i̧*). Medium vowels are half-long with a decline of force before a following consonant; clipped vowels are short and staccato, being interrupted at full force by the closure of the following consonant. There are three levels of force-and-pitch stress: high (v́), middle (v̇), and low (v̧). Long and clipped vowels always have high or middle stress; only medium-length vowels may have low stress.

The Third Mesa dialect differs from the Mishongnovi dialect in lacking the preaspirated stops, the voiceless continuants, and the distinction between medium and clipped vowels. Where Mishongnovi

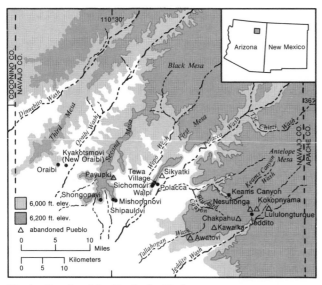

Fig. 1. Abandoned Pueblos in the Hopi area.

Keresan by some. Keresans may very well have been present, particularly after the Pueblo Revolt of 1680, and representatives of other Pueblo groups were likely to be found in them as well. Archeological excavations at Awatovi, however, show that the town was well established in the twelfth or early thirteenth century, and the remains are similar to those found in contemporary sites elsewhere in the Hopi country. In any case, by the time the Spaniards arrived in the Hopi country assimilation had been achieved and most of the Antelope Mesa towns abandoned. Present Hopi clans on both First and Second Mesas claim rights in Awatovi and to the still-cultivated farmlands in Tallahogan and Bluebird canyons, on the western escarpment of Antelope Mesa, by direct descent. The legitimacy of these claims is attested by clan and family names (Montgomery, Smith, and Brew 1949:7).

The picture of Hopi life and achievements during the three centuries preceding European contact presents three outstanding facets: their highly specialized agriculture; their extraordinary artistic talents as shown in mural and pottery painting; and their mining and using coal at a time when a royal edict proscribed its use in the city of London as injurious to health.

## Agriculture

The basis of Hopi life and the reason that the tribe could persist in their harsh, dry environment and attract others

has a vowel followed by a preaspirated stop, Third Mesa has a long vowel with falling pitch (written v̂·) followed by a plain stop. These lengthened vowels with falling pitch, which also arise from sequences of vowel plus glottal stop, have been analyzed by Masayesva Jeanne (1978) as underlying v + ʔ, in contrast to the long vowels with level high pitch analyzed as v + v: e.g., Mishongnovi wíhti 'woman', Third Mesa wî·ti (analyzed as wɨʔti); Mishongnovi and Third Mesa só·hɨ 'star' (analyzed as soohɨ). There are other patterns of correspondence between the vowel nuclei of the two dialects. Stress is assigned to the first vowel of a word if the vowel is long, followed by a consonant cluster, or in a disyllabic word; otherwise it is assigned to the second vowel. Suffixed verb forms keep the stress of the simplex: máqa 'gives', hence máqani 'will give'; some loanwords make up another class of exceptions. Because the stress is regarded as basically predictable it is not written on Third Mesa words, except when sources that mark stress are quoted; the patterns of secondary stress in compounds and other complex forms have not been described. Third Mesa and First Mesa Hopi retain p before a consonant and finally, where Mishongnovi and Shongopavi have [f] (phonemically v). Some other differences among the dialects are mentioned by Whorf (1946:160). His statement that Third Mesa has preaspiration agrees with Harrington's (1913) data against the later information used here; his statement that First Mesa lacks preaspiration disagrees with the evidence of the forms in Stephen (1936), which seem to have it regularly. A Third Mesa dialect lexicon, organized by semantic field, is Voegelin and Voegelin (1957); Kalectaca (1978) is an introductory pedagogical grammar by a Shongopavi speaker.

Hopi words not available in phonemic transcription are cited in a normalized spelling in roman. In these forms u often represents ɨ (and sometimes ö) and rz or zr sometimes appears for r.

to them in periods of serious drought was the skill with which Hopis developed especially adapted plants and their ability to coax them into high yields. To view the region today and to see the meager corn plants and stunted fruit trees struggling for survival in dunes of shifting sand brings expressions of pity from tourists familiar with the lush fields of Nebraska or Illinois. The yield from those "poor" plants is phenomenal (Hack 1942:19–38, 71–80).

The Hopi country lies on the southern escarpment of Black Mesa, a dissected highland about 60 miles wide, underlain by highly resistant Upper Cretaceous sandstone. The ephemeral streams of the Tusayan washes, which separate the fingering prongs of the escarpment upon which the Hopi towns are built, bring sand and silt from Black Mesa to the barren lower plains leading toward the Little Colorado River. The prevailing southwest winds separate the sand from the silt and carry it back northward to bank it against the escarpments. Because of the relatively large quantities of dune sand resulting from this process, the Hopi country has a lower runoff after rain and more permanent springs than areas of similar climate nearby. As the moisture content of these sand-dune fields is relatively high, the crops are not affected by epicycles of erosion or by the dissection of floodplains as are flood-water fields. Because of the high winds, which produced this type of field in the first place, the crops have to be protected from the shifting sand. For this purpose windbreaks are constructed of brush held in place by large stones. The ancient fields, where the sand has now blown away and the brush has decayed, are marked for archeologists by parallel lines of stone running at right angles to the contours of the escarpment terraces. To utilize such fields, plants with deep roots must be grown, such as beans and maize and, since contact with Europeans, peaches and apricots. Specialized strains have been developed. A maize plant not many times higher than the length of its abundant ears may have roots reaching 15 to 20 or more feet into the sand aquifer.

The Hopis practiced three other types of farming (as they do today) and the records of all these are found by the archeologist (Hack 1942:19–38). Two of these are types of flood-water farming: the standard type where fields are planted in the valleys of major streams that overflow their banks during high water caused by rapid snow melting or summer cloudbursts; and the akchin type (a Papago term) wherein crops are planted in the area where water spreads out at the mouth of an arroyo (Bryan 1929). This is the most common type used by the Hopi now and in prehistoric times. Irrigation is the fourth type of agriculture that goes back to ancient times. Crops are grown in artificial terraces irrigated by ditch or by

515

hand (see "Hopi Economy and Subsistence," fig. 1, this vol.).

## Mural and Pottery Painting

The beauty of Hopi painted pottery is known throughout the modern world; so also was it known and highly valued in the aboriginal world of the North American West. Until approximately A.D. 1300 pottery in the Hopi country was simply a regional variation on the wares of other parts of the Pueblo area. Then, with the advent of the fourteenth century, came an artistic explosion. The black-on-white designs, beloved of archeologists but relatively undistinguished, were superseded by brilliant

black-on-orange designs and orange polychromes (fig. 2) (W. Smith 1971:352–473). These in turn were superseded by black-on-yellow types quite different in design layout and execution from any other Pueblo ware. By the addition of red to this, a polychrome was produced. Its modern counterpart is in constant demand in shops throughout the country. It is called Sikyatki Polychrome (fig. 3) after the first major archeological excavation in the Hopi country. Fewkes (1898) assigned the name in honor of the large prehistoric town he dug during the 1890s on the eastern terraces of First Mesa.

In contrast to the almost exclusively geometric nature of other Pueblo wares, the late prehistoric Hopi yellows and polychromes are characterized by startling sweeping

after Smith 1971: figs. 185f, 226a, 228a, 269b.
Fig. 2. Awatovi pottery. a–b, Jeddito Black-on-orange jar and bowl with black curvilinear and angular design elements painted on unslipped orange surface; c, Jeddito Polychrome jar, distinguished from Jeddito Black-on-orange by the addition of white paint in the decoration; d, Awatovi Black-on-yellow bowl with characteristic black symmetrical designs painted on unslipped yellow surface. Diameter of a about 17 cm, rest same scale.

Smithsonian, Dept. of Anthr., Archeol.: left to right, 155498, 155545, 155681.
Fig. 3. Sikyatki Polychrome pottery with characteristic painting of highly stylized life forms on yellow ware bowls and jars. left and center, Shallow food bowls with designs on interior surface representing birds; right, storage jar with wide, horizontal shoulder decorated with butterflies, possibly indicating the 6 cardinal points (Fewkes 1919:254), and geometric elements derived from abstracted bird and feather forms around the mid-body. Diameter of right 36.2 cm, rest same scale.

curvilinear motifs; bird, animal, floral, and human representations; and religious masks and ceremonial scenes. Their freedom of rendition is completely at variance with the canons of all other prehistoric Pueblo schools of pottery design, except for the contemporary Mimbres ware in western New Mexico, which shared some, but far from all, of its freedom from established tradition.

The Sikyatki and black-on-yellow wares have an interesting history. The painted pottery being turned out on First Mesa in the 1970s is a modern manifestation. The tradition is not continuous. With the coming of the Spaniards in the early seventeenth century, Hopi pottery went into an artistic decline. During the nineteenth century, although curvilinear designs persisted, they became highly formalized and stereotyped. The untutored eye is unable to distinguish them from the products of Zuni to the east. Then came Fewkes to dig at Sikyatki. The Hopis then, as they are now, were vitally interested in their own history. One of the more avid observers was a young girl from Tewa Village (Hano) named Nampeyo. Fascinated by the ancient designs, she instituted a neo-classical revival that took hold immediately.

Paintings on kiva walls have been found in a number of Pueblo sites back to at least as early as the eleventh century (Brew 1946:fig. 87). The early Pueblo II and III examples are mostly geometric in design. The largest number known are the 180 found at Awatovi and Kawaika in the Hopi country (W. Smith 1952). These date from the fifteenth, sixteenth, and seventeenth centuries and are splendid examples of Hopi painting. The

Harvard U., Peabody Mus.

Fig. 4. Mural paintings from excavated kivas at Awatovi (W. Smith 1952:figs. 45a, 48a), similar in design to pottery decoration. top, Geometric pattern in red, yellow, black, and white, reminiscent of Anasazi textile and black-on-white pottery designs; one of over 100 plaster layers, 27 of which were painted (from room 218, front wall, design 3). bottom, Red, orange, blue, gray, black, and white design on yellow ground (from Test 14, Room 3, right wall, design 12) similar in type to designs painted on Sikyatki Polychrome pottery. Stylized feathers, wings, cloud symbols, and scrolls are characteristic of Sikyatki patterns. Length of each approximately 265 cm. Slightly reconstructed copy of original murals made by the Peabody Museum Awatovi Expedition, 1935-1939.

relationship with Hopi pottery painting is clear, but the murals are more varied and often more elaborate (fig. 4). Designs are both geometric and naturalistic (fig. 5). The animal, bird, and human figures are often stylized (fig. 6) and frequently masked. The murals are not decorations; they are part of the religious ceremonies performed in the kivas. Some of the figures can be identified with modern Hopi ritual.

The reason so many were found is that, when they had fulfilled their function in the ceremonies, they were covered with a layer of plain, unpainted plaster so as not to be seen by unauthorized persons. (In modern Hopi kivas with more stable wall surfaces the paintings are washed off.) Archeologists carefully scraped the layers off, one by one, and revealed the paintings. At Awatovi chunks of fallen wall plaster were found with over 100 layers, 20 to 30 of them painted. Many of the recorded Hopi murals may well be grouped among the finest examples known of indigenous American art.

## Coal Mining

Although coal crops out extensively throughout the Pueblo area, no evidence has been presented for its industrial or domestic use in prehistoric times except by the Hopis. They used it for cooking, for heating, for firing pottery, and for pigment. They used the flaky, resilient ash as a bed for the flagstones on their kiva floors (Hack 1942a; W. Smith 1952:6, 20, 27).

Throughout the Hopi country coal beds crop out on a wide bench beneath the mesa rim. It is mined in the 1970s and was mined in Pueblo III and IV times, the thirteenth through the seventeenth centuries. Coal was used to heat the houses and kivas. Since fuel has ritualistic significance among the Hopis, coal ash and wood ash occur in separate fireplaces in the kivas. Pottery was fired in ash heaps conveniently near the coal outcrops. The simple technique of prehistoric Hopi coal mining consisted of removing the overburden and digging out the coal—strip mining, that is. The waste was piled behind the mining face. The result, which can readily be observed in air photographs, is an area stripped of coal and overlying rock, piled high with heaps of waste material. Such heaps occur on the appropriate bench on all Hopi mesas. When the overburden became too thick for easy removal, that particular face was abandoned. Underground mining was also practiced, and the few occurrences found indicate a primitive combination of the longwall and the room-and-pillar methods (Hack 1942a:8-9). It is estimated that some 30,000 tons of coal were mined in prehistoric times near Awatovi. The amount mined along the Jeddito Valley escarpment of Antelope Mesa probably exceeded 100,000 tons. The tools used were simple: elongated picks, approximately 10 to 30 centimeters (4 to 12 inches) long; hammerstones (one found at a Jeddito

Fig. 5. Mural painting from Kawaika (Test 4, Room 4, front, right and back walls, design 8) (W. Smith 1952:fig. 60). Lower band is of dark blue, over which frogs, lizards, a large fish with red snout and white teeth, and ears of corn in variegated colors have been painted, joined by what appear to be bolts of lightning. Several rectangles, composed of bands of yellow, dark blue, and maroon, possibly symbolize rainbows. Polychrome ceremonial bowls filled with ears of corn arranged vertically alternate with bowls stacked with round flower "blossoms" (W. Smith 1952:234–237, 249–261). Length of section shown approximately 380 cm. Slightly reconstructed copy of original mural made by the Peabody Museum Awatovi Expedition, 1935–1939.

mine was of heavy quartzitic sandstone); and large reused potsherds. Some of the potsherds at the old Jeddito coal faces and in trenches through mining waste showed evidence of having been used as scraping tools. They were probably also used on the face for prying chunks of coal loose by working along the vertical joints (Hack 1942a:11–12; Woodbury 1954:180–181).

Fig. 6. Section of painted mural from an Awatovi kiva (Room 529, right wall, design 1). Warrior figure at right holds a bow and white shield or banner and wears a quiver, lavender shirt, white necklace and bandoleer, gray kilt, and feathered headdress. A squash-woman, composed of yellow squash with tendril arms and human head (with side-whorled hairdo), appears to his left. Above her is a cloud-terrace symbol, and the posterior end of an unidentified figure (see W. Smith 1952:figs. 38c, 61b). Height of squash-woman almost 60 cm. Slightly reconstructed copy of original mural made by the Peabody Museum Awatovi Expedition, 1935–1939.

During the 300 years of Hopi coal mining near Awatovi the daily output is estimated at about 450 pounds (Hack 1942a:18). With primitive methods used in mining, this implies great activity, since Awatovi probably had a population of only a few hundred persons at a time. From the waste heaps on the terraces it is assumed that a similar consumption characterized the other contemporary Hopi Pueblos. The use of so great a quantity implies that coal must have largely, if not entirely, supplanted wood as fuel. In any case coal was an important natural resource to the Hopis from the thirteenth to the seventeenth centuries.

There is no real evidence as to why coal came to be used as a fuel by the Hopis or why it was abandoned. The location of the Hopi towns is in a border zone between desert scrub-type vegetation and the piñon-juniper forest. Since coal crops out so widely near the towns it may have been discovered accidentally and have come into use after the forest border had been pushed back by cutting or had retreated because of a slight climatic change. Perhaps when the properties of coal became known, it was easier to use coal than to cut wood with the stone axes then in use, even though the burning of coal must have been more unpleasant. The recognition of the relatively more noxious nature of coal fires seems indicated in crude stoves with chimneys found in Pueblo IV sites.

The reason for dropping the use of coal is also a puzzling problem. After the arrival of the Spaniards, wood came to be used again for fuel in the houses, and sheep dung for firing pottery. Perhaps the supply of easily available coal by stripping had become exhausted. The possibility of this at Awatovi is suggested by the dangerous undermining resorted to at the western end of the mining area. More important is the change in culture resulting from contact with the Franciscans. The priests built their church and friary along one side of the main plaza of the seventeenth-century town. Perhaps the friars disliked the fumes from the coal. Also when the Spaniards came they brought sheep, burros, carts, and iron tools. With donkeys and iron axes the work of gathering wood would have been much less and the area around the towns from which wood could be easily gathered greatly increased. Furthermore, the shoveling up of dried dung from the sheep corrals would have been simpler than knocking coal from the seams below the village and hauling it up. Quite probably the combination of the new technology with the dwindling of the easily mined coal supply brought about the change.

## History

### Franciscan Awatovi

The Spaniards were never numerous in the Hopi country. The extent of European contact was limited to sporadic, widely spaced military exploring expeditions, followed by a few resident Franciscan friars. The records of Spanish activity in the region are sparse and no actual document has come to light that originated in the Hopi country. All information comes from reports of military men, political officers, and priests, written mostly in Santa Fe or Mexico and found all the way from New Mexican to Spanish and other European archives (Montgomery, Smith, and Brew 1949:3-43, 113-176).

It is fairly well established that Awatovi was the first town in the Hopi country to be visited by Spaniards. In 1540 Gen. Francisco Vásquez de Coronado dispatched Pedro de Tovar with 17 horsemen and three or four footmen from Cíbola (Zuni) to seek the province of Tusayán (Hopi), described by the Zuni as a group of "seven villages of the same sort as theirs." A Franciscan friar, Juan de Padilla, accompanied them (Pedro de Castañeda in Winship 1896:488). A brief skirmish was followed by present giving and Tovar moved on to other Hopi towns. During his visit Tovar learned of a large river farther to the west. Since the main purpose of the exploration was to discover a route from New Mexico to the "South Sea," when Tovar reported to Coronado a new expedition was soon organized to investigate the river. The leader was García López de Cárdenas. He was well received when he reached Tusayán and was entertained by the natives, who gave him guides for his journey (Winship 1896:489). Again, the town or towns visited are not mentioned by name. The expedition discovered the Grand Canyon of the Colorado, but since the Spaniards could not even find a trail down from the rim, the discovery did not result in a practical route to the Gulf of California. The failure to find a trail down suggests that perhaps Cárdenas did not have the complete cooperation of his Hopi guides.

In 1583 the Hopi country was revisited by an expedition led by Antonio de Espejo (Pérez de Luxán 1929). The widely held, erroneous belief that Kawaika and not Awatovi was the Hopi town first visited by Tovar in 1540 arises from a misinterpretation of a statement in the journal of Diego Pérez de Luxán, a member of the Espejo expedition. A careful analysis of the documents has established Awatovi as the first point of contact by Tovar (Reed 1942; Montgomery, Smith, and Brew 1949:5-7). Espejo's first contact was Awatovi, which he mentioned by name (Aguato) and where he reported a friendly reception and took possession for His Majesty of Spain.

The last two decades of the sixteenth century and the first three of the seventeenth saw the Spaniards attempting to consolidate their position in the Rio Grande Valley. At times it was touch and go with the colony. The lack of material wealth in the New Mexico Pueblos had been a bitter disappointment to the Spanish merchant-adventurers and military men. In 1608 the abandonment of New Mexico as an "extravagant and unprofitable possession" was actually recommended by the Council of the Indies and seriously considered by the king (Hammond 1927:139). The priests alone had found a crop awaiting them and their eagerness to reap the harvest of souls had much to do with the decision to continue.

### The Franciscan Period

By the end of the third decade of the seventeenth century the Spaniards in the Rio Grande were ready to expand. An influx of 30 new Franciscan friars from Mexico City in 1629 doubled the number available and permitted foundation of establishments to the west (Scholes and Bloom 1944-1945:69-72). The new conversions included Acoma, Zuni, and Hopi. The initial establishment in the Hopi country was at Awatovi. It was not easily achieved. Three Franciscans, Francisco Porras, Andrés Gutiérrez, and Cristóbal de la Concepción (a lay brother), arrived at Awatovi on August 20, 1629. Since that is the feast day of Saint Bernard of Clairvaux, the mission, according to custom, was dedicated to him and henceforth known as San Bernardo de Aguátubi. Subsequently a confusion arose from the fact that San Bernardo and San Bernardino, in abbreviated form, are both written Ber[do]. Bernardo is correct. Saint Bernardine of Siena's feast day is May 20 (Montgomery, Smith, and Brew 1949:9, 124-125).

This was an important day in Hopi history. The events that occurred there then and during subsequent weeks changed radically the ways of the people and eventually led to the downfall of Awatovi. The inhabitants of Awatovi at first resisted conversion but it is said that they submitted in response to a miracle when a cross placed on the eyes of a blind youth by Father Porras restored his sight (Perea 1945; Benavides 1916:28-30). Whether or not something like this actually happened at Awatovi in 1629, the story of it is important and should not be underestimated. For if the citizens of Awatovi 71 years later, in 1700, believed that such a miracle had occurred it would help to explain the unusual strength of their

Fig. 7. Mural paintings from kiva directly under the main altar of San Bernardo de Aguátubi mission (W. Smith 1952:figs. 79a, 81a) (see fig. 8). top, Section of one of a series of similar paintings (Awatovi, Room 788, right wall, design layer 1) extending around 3 walls of the kiva, each composed of a central figure (left) flanked by an ear of corn similar to those used on altars (see Fewkes 1927:pl. 3) and a figure in full dance costume holding a parrot. The central figure, legless but with a black dance kilt and white rain sash, carries what may be a prayer-stick bundle in his left hand. The flanking figure (at right) wears a white dance kilt with red and black designs, a feather headdress, and (probably) a mask. The cloud-terrace symbol emerging from his mouth has been interpreted as a breath cloud or pipe, relating to the ritual symbolism of blowing either breath or smoke (W. Smith 1952:237). bottom, Figure from design layer 4 of the same wall. This figure corresponds in mask, headdress, and complex staff to the Ahul kachina or one of its variants (W. Smith 1952:303–304; see also "Pueblo Fine Arts," fig. 6, this vol.). His mask is half gray and half white, with crosses and a large triangle painted in black, and is topped with eagle-tail and unidentified red feathers. Length of top segment approximately 190 cm, bottom same scale. Slightly reconstructed copies of original murals made by the Peabody Museum Awatovi Expedition, 1935–1939.

Christianity in comparison to that of the remainder of the Hopi. It would be a good reason for their return to the fold, alone of all the Hopi towns after the revolt, against the advice and threats of their neighbors. There must have been strong motivation for their choice to face death and destruction on the side of the Christian God and the Spaniards against their native kachinas and fellow Hopis.

Another factor in the apparent vitality of Awatovi Christianity may lie in the personality of the man who converted them, miracle or no. Father Porras seems to have gained dominance in the minds of Awatovi over the local religious leaders. That dominance was expressed physically and persisted for 70 years. The finest examples of Hopi kiva murals were found at Awatovi, directly under the main altar of church 2 (fig. 7). The kiva was complete, even to the entrance hatchway, and filled to the top with clean sand (fig. 8). Obviously it had been

obtained by the priest from the Hopi owners for the express purpose of "superposition," demonstrating the ascendancy of the new faith over the old. Amid seventeenth-century New Mexico records replete with reports of mistakes, irregularities, and immoralities in the public and private lives of members of the government, the military, and the priesthood, Porras stands out as a man of exceptional ability and probity. The archeological evidence demonstrates that he was a great builder. He also learned to speak Hopi.

Two other missions were established in the first flush of missionary zeal, at Oraibi and Shongopavi, and also two *visitas,* at Walpi and Mishongnovi. The two missions subsequently were demoted to *visitas,* with only occasional visits by a priest. Christian zeal persisted only at Awatovi.

Although the religious effect of the Spanish advent on most Hopis was small, the material effect was great. In addition to domestic animals and new food plants, European goods flowed into the Hopi country, although this stream, like the local watercourses, was intermittent and irregular. Every three years, beginning in 1631, His Majesty's government set aside a considerable sum for the New Mexico missions. This largesse produced a triennial wagon train of iron-tired carts pulled by mules, which carried north the products of workshops in Mexico City, Puebla, Europe, and the Orient.

The outposts of Old World culture in New Mexico were thus at the far end of a remarkable system of procurement. The Manila galleons provided a yearly service for 250 years, 1565 to 1815, bringing Chinese goods to Acapulco, whence they came to Mexico City over the so-called China Road. The Spanish *flota* provided more frequent service to Vera Cruz. So crockery came from the kilns of Puebla in Mexico, Valencia in Spain, and Ching-te-chen in China (Woodward 1949). In addition to silks, tapestries, and tablecloths, the Manila galleons brought nails, sheet iron, tin, and lead. For the Hopi, the most valuable imports were the Spanish woodworking and stoneworking kits: knives, axes, adzes, mattocks, picks, crowbars, saws, chisels, planes, and augers. Religious paraphernalia loomed large in the caravan inventories (Scholes 1930). In September 1627, 18 bells of 200 pounds weight each were brought for New Mexico. Fragments of one of them were found in the excavations at Awatovi, and two still serve the church at Acoma.

Relations between Hopis and clergy during the seventeenth century were varied in character. Under the supervision of the blue-robed priests, Hopis built the churches and friaries, painted decorative murals on the walls (fig. 9), and made pottery utensils for the kitchen and refectory. Soup plates with Hopi designs and a fillet of clay affixed to the base in imitation of Old World wheel-made pottery are found in the ruins (fig. 10). An

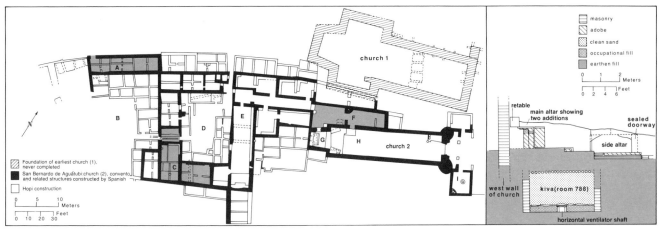

after Montgomery, Smith, and Brew 1949:figs. 4, 10, 34, 39.

Fig. 8. Plan of San Bernardo de Aguátubi and immediately adjacent Hopi structures at Awatovi, based on conjectural reconstruction of the ruins. (For plan of the entire site of Awatovi as excavated by the Peabody Museum Excavations 1935-1939, see Montgomery, Smith, and Brew 1949:fig. 3.) Church and convento complex included: A, storage and shop area; B, service yard; C, kitchen and refectory areas; D, courtyard; E, friar's chapel; F, sacristies; G, nave (containing main altar, which had been twice renovated, and side altars); H, sanctuary; and I, baptistry (font in center). Cross-sectional detail shows position of main altar relative to the filled kiva (room 788), one of many rectangular kivas excavated at Awatovi. The opening under the floor of the kiva is the ventilator shaft.

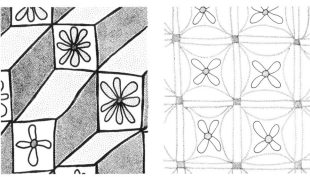

after Montgomery, Smith, and Brew 1949:figs. 55e,g, 60.

Fig. 9. Painted mural designs from the church of San Bernardo de Aguátubi that appeared to either side of the altar. These were probably executed by the Hopis on the basis of designs provided by the friars, apparently in imitation of decorative tiled designs used for altar faces in Spanish and colonial Mexican churches (see Montgomery, Smith, and Brew 1949:291-339). As with kiva murals, different designs were applied to successive layers of plaster, not all of which were decorated. Design at left (in green, ocher, and brown) was applied after the black, brown, and cream design at right. Drawn to scale; width of each section approximately 30 cm.

immense bowl with a hole in the bottom was found in a holy-water font at Awatovi, where the church and friary have been excavated completely (Montgomery, Smith, and Brew 1949:47-339). Friction was commonplace, however, and culminated when the Hopis joined in the Pueblo Revolt of 1680.

## The Pueblo Revolt

Although local rebellions occurred from time to time, except for the rebellion at Zuni, 1632 to 1635, they were short-lived, ending in capitulation or destruction of the recalcitrant Pueblo. In 1680, however, the Pueblo Indians, for the first and only time, acted together. Every Pueblo rose, and the Spaniards were driven from New Mexico with great loss of life to both clergy and laity. Surviving refugees collected in El Paso del Norte (present-day El Paso, Texas) where those who did not go on to Mexico City remained until the reconquest of 1692.

This, their one successful expression of solidarity, was a triumph for the Pueblos. Yet for most of them it lasted less than 20 years. The Spaniards came back stronger than ever. But not to the Hopis. The struggle lost by the Christian God in Tusayán in 1680 stayed lost. The kachinas won and the kachinas have held the field since. From that time on, Spaniards appeared on the Hopi mesas only as unwelcome visitors, except at Awatovi, and Awatovi did not live long to enjoy the reunion.

Little is known of events in the Hopi towns in 1680. The date was sometime between August 10 and 13. All the priests were killed, two at Oraibi, two at Shongopavi, and one at Awatovi. The churches were destroyed and at Awatovi, at least, the Hopis took over the friary and converted it for their own use.

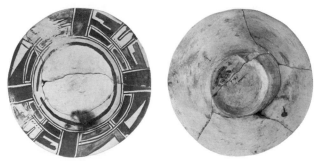

Harvard U., Peabody Mus.: 38-120-10/13668.

Fig. 10. Shallow bowl from Awatovi dating from the 17th century, which combines traditional Sikyatki design and color with European-influenced form. Excavated from the baptistry and friars' chapel of church 2, circular base added to copy European wheel-thrown pottery. Diameter 18.1 cm.

*521*

In 1692 Capt.-Gen. Diego de Vargas effected the reconquest of New Mexico, in the course of which he visited the Hopi towns (Sigüenza y Góngora 1932). His retinue consisted of 63 soldiers and "numerous Indians." The reception was hostile, except at Awatovi, and although the other towns openly submitted to Spanish arms, the submission did not last. It was merely a matter of temporary expediency. Geographically the most remote from Santa Fe, the Hopi country became the refuge of the irreconcilables among the Pueblos of the east who could not bring themselves to bear the Spanish yoke. After the rebellion, the First and Second Mesa towns had moved, for better defense, from the springs of the terraces to the mesa tops, even though they had to carry water. There they were joined by Rio Grande refugees. Some of them established their own towns, of which Hano on First Mesa and now-ruined Payupki on Second Mesa are the best known. Since no Spanish farmers or traders had, as far as is known, ever settled in the Hopi country, the area was of interest only to the priests. Furthermore, when it came to military resistance, the Hopis had allies among the non-Pueblo groups around them who were able fighters. De Vargas in 1692 had found the Hopi leaders supported by Utes, Havasupais, and *Apaches de Navajú* (Navajo).

The attitude of the Hopis is illustrated by the sacking of Awatovi, the only Hopi Pueblo to return to Christianity after the rebellion. Sometime during the winter of 1700–1701, Hopis from the other towns attacked Awatovi. Legend says that the men were killed and the women and children taken captive (Bandelier 1890–1892, 2:371–372). When the Franciscans had returned to Awatovi they had driven the Hopis out of the friary and had established a small church in one side of it. No attempt was made to rebuild the old church, which was the size of the one still in use at Acoma.

Throughout the first half of the eighteenth century, sporadic attempts were made (some by priests without military support) to bring the Hopis back into the fold. None succeeded. In 1701 the governor at Santa Fe sent a military expedition to punish the Hopis for their destruction of the Christian Pueblo of Awatovi. It failed because of the superior military force of the Hopis. This set the pattern for the eighteenth century. Two military expeditions failed in 1707. The most ambitious attempt occurred in 1716 when the governor and the Franciscan custos of New Mexico led a force of soldiers considerably larger than usual to Walpi. The wisdom of the move of the towns to the mesa tops was demonstrated. Walpi proved impregnable and, although there were some deaths and many cornfields were laid waste, the Spaniards again failed. In 1724 two priests vainly attempted to gain a foothold, followed very shortly by a lone priest.

Promises for the future were all that was obtained by these visits.

In 1741 a new and somewhat startling development occurred on paper; it never seemingly passed beyond that stage. The king of Spain, disappointed by the failure of the Franciscans, removed the Hopis from their theoretical charge and handed them over to the Jesuits, who showed no enthusiasm whatever for this opportunity. Although Jesuits tried at least three times to reach Tusayán to have a look at the persistent pagans who had been assigned to them, they never got there. Meanwhile the Franciscans attempted to regain jurisdiction over the Hopis by submitting false reports of thousands of Hopi converts; however, the Hopis remained obstinately and successfully anti-Christian.

In 1775 Father Silvestre Velez de Escalante visited the Hopis in his attempt to reach the Colorado River. His recommendation of a military expedition as the only solution to the Hopi problem was not accepted. Another attempt, by Father Francisco Garcés, failed dismally in 1776. The Hopis would not let him in their houses and spurned his gifts. A final attempt to reduce the Hopis was made in 1780 by Gov. Juan Bautista de Anza, who later founded San Francisco, California. The real aim of this expedition was to secure the neutrality of the Hopis in a campaign planned by de Anza against their then allies, the Apaches. Like all others, this attempt failed.

So the Hopis remained isolated on the mesas. Their valiant stand against the return of the Spaniards bears fruit today. They live in enjoyment of their own indigenous culture when so many American Indian groups have lost all or most of theirs.

## Sources

This section† refers to all the chapters on the Hopi. It is limited to monographs that provide major syntheses or new information based on field research in Hopi communities and to sources of photographs.

Laird's (1977) *Hopi Bibliography* is both comprehensive and annotated and includes some 2,935 references that cover almost every aspect of Hopi life.

Laird (1977:148) notes that Donaldson (in U.S. Census Office. 11th Census 1893) is "the first, and perhaps the only, work ever to attempt a comprehensive coverage of the Hopi," and it is far from complete. Brew (in Montgomery, Smith, and Brew 1949) provides a history of Awatovi, and the Hopi villages generally, from 1540 to 1700, based on both documentary and archeological research. The early attempts to study Hopi history in terms of clan legends were inconclusive, but Nequatewa (1936) has provided a Hopi interpretation of clan legends that is useful.

---

† This sources section was written by Fred Eggan and Alfonso Ortiz; the last paragraph is by Laura J. Greenberg.

General ethnographic coverage varies from mesa to mesa, and from village to village. For First Mesa Stephen's *Hopi Journal* (1936), which covers events from 1891 to 1894, is an indispensable source, and Fewkes utilized much of Stephen's data in his many publications at the turn of the century. For Third Mesa, the Rev. H.R. Voth, a Mennonite missionary who resided at Oraibi from 1893 to 1902, provided, in collaboration with G.A. Dorsey and the Field Museum, Chicago, an outstanding series of accounts of Hopi ceremonies and observations on selected aspects of Hopi life, along with extensive collections of artifacts and reconstructions of altars (see Dorsey and Voth 1901, 1902; Voth 1900, 1901, 1903, 1903a, 1905, 1905a, 1967 for examples). The Second Mesa villages are less adequately covered. Parsons (1939) synthesizes the Hopi materials on ceremonialism with those of the other Pueblos.

More ethnologically oriented studies began with Freire-Marreco's (1914) account of kinship at Tewa Village on First Mesa, and with Lowie's two summers, 1915 and 1916, on First and Second Mesa, which provided the first adequate accounts (1929, 1929a) of the Hopi clan and kinship systems. Curtis (1907-1930, 12) independently provided new and important information on First Mesa to supplement his photographic records. Forde (1931) made an excellent study of Hopi agriculture and land ownership, which clarified the understanding of clan lands.

During the summer of 1932 the Laboratory of Anthropology at Santa Fe sponsored a field training session on the Hopi reservation where Titiev, Kennard, and Eggan began a long-range study of the Hopi. Titiev (1944, 1972) concentrated on the breakup of Old Oraibi in 1906. Kennard became fluent in Hopi, and his account of the kachina cult (Kennard and Earle 1938), his study of linguistic acculturation (1963), and his concern with key concepts in Hopi culture (1972) are important additions. Eggan's monograph (1950) attempted a comparative study of Western Pueblo social structure, based on the Hopi model.

During the period 1935 to 1939 the Peabody Museum's expedition to the no longer occupied historic Hopi town of Awatovi was in operation under the direction of J.O. Brew; the resulting monograph by W. Smith (1952) on kiva mural decorations and his (1971) report on painted ceramics provide an important background to Hopi cultural development.

More specialized studies occupied the war and postwar periods. The autobiography of Don Talayesva (1942) has been published. D. Eggan (1949, 1952, 1955) collected and analyzed Hopi dreams as cultural products. Dennis (1940) studied the Hopi child, Thompson and Joseph (1944) gave an account of the Hopi Way, and Thompson (1950) discussed culture crisis. Brandt (1954) provides an analysis of Hopi ethics based in part on field research. Dozier, himself a Tewa Indian from Santa Clara Pueblo in New Mexico, has written an outstanding monograph (1954) on the Tewa of First Mesa.

In the 1930s Whorf (1946) began the studies of Hopi linguistics that culminated in his grammar of the Mishongnovi dialect and a series of articles on the relation of language to thought (1956a), which have evoked controversy ever since. Kennard (1963) and Dozier (1951, 1955) have contributed to an understanding of linguistic acculturation, and Voegelin and Voegelin (1957, 1960) have continued the study of the Hopi language.

Waters (1963), in collaboration with Oswald White Bear Fredericks, wrote a very personal interpretation of the Hopi. Nagata's (1970) study of modern Moenkopi is an important contribution to the understanding of the processes of modernization among the Hopi villages. Bradfield's (1973) detailed analysis of Hopi ceremonial and world view, in relation to Great Basin Shoshoni backgrounds and possible Maya influences, is controversial.

The literature on Hopi arts and crafts is voluminous. Colton's (1950) analysis of kachina dolls, Whiting's (1939) account of ethnobotany, M.N. Wright's (1972) history of Hopi silversmithing, Harvey's (1970) account of Hopi life in native paintings, and Kabotie's (1977) account of his life as a Hopi Indian artist, illustrated with his own paintings, provide an introduction to these subjects.

Many photographers made important records of the Hopi, especially from about 1890 to about 1910. Well known are Edward S. Curtis (1907-1930, 12); Adam C. Vroman (negatives especially at the Los Angeles County Museum and the Southwest Museum, Los Angeles); G. Wharton James (negatives at the California Historical Society and Southwest Museum, Los Angeles); and Ben Wittick (at Museum of New Mexico, Sante Fe). Less known but well-documented collections are by H.R. Voth (at Mennonite Museum and Archives, North Newton, Kansas); Sumner W. Matteson and Samuel H. Barrett (both at Milwaukee Public Museum); J.H. Bratley (Denver Museum of Natural History); and Emory Kopta (Museum of the American Indian, Heye Foundation, New York). Important works by others such as Jo Mora and Kate Corey were discovered in the 1970s. General collections of historic Hopi photographs are in major anthropological repositories, such as the National Anthropological Archives (Smithsonian Institution), and the Field Museum (Chicago), and in many museums and historical societies in the Southwest.

# Hopi History, 1850–1940

FREDERICK J. DOCKSTADER

## Isolation

By the middle of the nineteenth century, the Hopi were still among the lesser known and more isolated Indian peoples living within the continental United States. Although there is an almost annual mention of them in various documents, which indicates an awareness of their existence, most of these comments refer to earlier records and are not based upon actual visitation. They usually pertain to a single individual or small group—the ubiquitous fur trapper, explorer, or wandering trader in search of food, water, or directions. As far as is known, no major expedition is recorded as having ventured into the Hopi villages after Juan Bautista de Anza; a few stragglers from the gold rush did pass through (Dockstader 1954:147-158).

As a result, the Hopi were able to overcome the effects of the early Spanish interruption of their lives, and it is probable that few indications of this intrusion were evident in their everyday activities. The events leading up to the Pueblo Revolt had become part of legend, and all the interwoven patterns that made up The Hopi Way were again in force. But it should not be thought that the Spanish invasion did not leave its mark. The exposure to Christianity, Spanish military force, and the opportunity to observe from afar what Spanish domination meant to their Pueblo brethren in the Rio Grande area left an indelible impression; however, Hopi culture did not undergo the amalgam of European and Indian social patterns that is so characteristic of the Rio Grande villages. Of even greater importance was the tendency of the Hopi to assign the credit for this ability to withstand external forces to Hopi cultural qualities, rather than other, perhaps more contributory factors: thus, the attitude became, in essence, the Whites versus the kachinas, and the kachinas had won the day. This resulted in a complacency and self-confidence that overshadowed all Hopi-White relations until the end of the nineteenth century.

This was not an entirely tranquil situation, for the Hopi were increasingly preoccupied with attacks from Mexican, Apache, and Navajo raiders in pursuit of plunder, food, or captives to be sold into slavery in Mexico. In fact, the outbreak of the Mexican War had as its major effect a limitation upon Mexican participation in slave raids and the subsequent freeing of the Navajo to raid at will.

To the Hopi this was certainly of far greater importance than any alteration of outside government. Mexico had never implemented sovereignty over the region following its successful revolution against the Spanish Crown, and it is doubtful that the Hopi were ever truly aware of the political change of fortune that had gone on around them.

## Bureau of Indian Affairs Administration

With the end of the Mexican War in 1848, a new world opened up for the Southwest. An official Indian agent was appointed April 7, 1849, in the person of John S. Calhoun. His duties were to establish headquarters at Santa Fe and to oversee the destinies of the Indian inhabitants of the region. An honorable and sincere individual, Calhoun was devoted to the improvement of Indian conditions. Before he died in mid-1852 he put into operation a variety of excellent plans, particularly with reference to control of the increasing Navajo menace (U.S. Office of Indian Affairs 1915).

In addition to Hopi isolation, which protected them, the lack of rich mineral wealth was also to their initial advantage. Were this the only concern, they might have continued without interference or interruption; but the increasing Navajo attacks combined with curiosity about the new political situation caused a group of seven Hopi leaders to journey to Santa Fe to seek a conference with Calhoun on October 6, 1850. While they went primarily to petition for military protection against the Navajo, they were equally uneasy about the intentions of the new government that controlled their homelands. The Hopi leader at this time was Nakwaiyamtewa, the chief at Oraibi, then the major Hopi village (Titiev 1944). There were earlier Hopi emissaries to Santa Fe directed toward Spanish authority, but this is the first known Hopi-American political conference.

During the next decade, Americans are known to have entered Hopi country in increasing numbers. In 1851, Fort Defiance was established as an outpost to protect the region against the marauding Navajo; from it ventured various military personnel, either on official business or simply as early-day tourists. One such was Dr. P.G.S. TenBroeck, who is known to have made several visits in 1851-1852 (Schoolcraft 1851-1857, 4). He was followed by perhaps a half-dozen expeditions seeking a way to the West Coast. Some of these entered the villages, and some did not; no official documents record such visits until that of Lt. J.C. Ives in 1857–1858. The main result of these various contacts was a disastrous smallpox epidemic that devastated the Hopi in 1853–1854, killing hundreds of people. This was followed by a drought, which reduced the already weakened population at Oraibi from 800 to 200 (U.S. Census Office. 11th Census 1894).

In 1858 a new and strong force entered the area, with the advent of Jacob Hamlin, a famed Mormon missionary who was to make many more trips into the Hopi country, remaining on excellent terms with the people throughout his long career. From his work and that of other missionaries, the Mormon faith gained a strong position in the Southwest (Nagata 1970).

With the outbreak of the Civil War, the U.S. Army was withdrawn for service elsewhere, with the immediate result of an increase in Navajo attacks. A particularly serious assault on Fort Defiance occurred in 1860. The next year, John Ward came into the villages to report on the desperate situation; his visit was followed for an entirely different reason by a small party of Rio Grande settlers who attacked the Hopi in the mistaken belief that they were responsible for recent depredations. In 1863 Brig. Gen. James J. Carleton was sent through the region to repel Confederate soldiers, mostly from Texas, who were thought to be in the country; Carleton then returned to New Mexico to continue his efforts against the Navajo. In this, his command was assisted by Kit Carson, and the Navajo were finally rounded up and taken on the Long Walk to Bosque Redondo where they were incarcerated until 1868. This resulted in a period of relative peace for the Hopi, except for the inevitable raids by individual Navajos or Apaches who had escaped the Carson dragnet (K. Bartlett 1936).

In 1864 a far more serious drought struck the mesa country; in that same year John H. Moss was appointed as the first Hopi Indian agent. The drought forced a group of Indians to go to Santa Fe to plead for food to avoid starvation; for famine often strikes in the Hopi country two years following a drought, and from 1866 to 1868 many people died. A commentary upon relations with the Whites may be seen in the first attempt to treat with the newly established territorial government. A party of Hopis went to Prescott in 1866 to ask the governor for help during the famine. Misunderstanding their entirely peaceful purpose, the group was thrown into jail. They were shortly released, but the episode further alienated the Hopi (Dockstader 1954). Attendant upon the famine, a smallpox epidemic, introduced by some soldiers who had come into the villages, took a serious toll in lives. To escape the pestilence, many Hopi fled to Zuni, where they stayed for some years. During their stay, many major influences entered Hopi culture. Although this was but another of the frequent inter-

changes among people from different Pueblos who were accustomed to visiting back and forth for varying periods of time, it does seem to have made changes that persist in the twentieth century. Most particularly, this is seen in changes of pottery designs (fig. 1), religious influences, and language; until this time, apparently few Hopi had need to use Spanish, but following the Zuni sojourn, the number increased considerably. And finally, Sichomovi was abandoned, to be reestablished later by Zuni emigrants (Montgomery, Smith, and Brew 1949).

In 1868 Vincent Colyer, the newly appointed Indian agent, dispatched Maj. A.D. Palmer as a special Hopi agent. In fact, the various changes of political appointees had become so confusing as to make impossible any degree of continuum insofar as the Hopis were concerned.

But the first of several far more serious dislocations came in 1870, with the establishment of a Moravian mission at Oraibi. This was the first non-Hopi religious activity effectively established in the villages since the destruction of Awatovi in 1700. That same year, an independent Hopi Indian Agency was established at Oraibi, which lasted until 1883 when it was incorporated into the Navajo Agency. Next, the Atlantic and Pacific Railroad was started through northern Arizona, and workmen occasionally went into the Hopi country as tourists. The first government buildings for the new agency center were started at Keams Canyon in 1874, and in 1875 the Mormon Church located a mission at Moenkopi, the western colony of Oraibi. At about the same time, Baptists founded a mission at Mishongnovi.

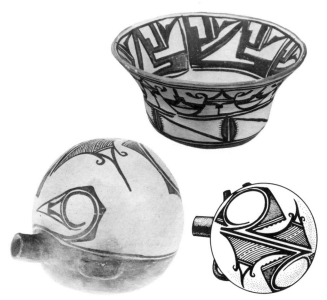

Smithsonian, Dept. of Anthr.: 22602; Mus. of Northern Ariz., Flagstaff: 255/1051.
Fig. 1. Hopi pottery showing Zuni influences. top, Food bowl with Zuni-derived decoration and flared rim; collected early 1870s. bottom, Canteen decorated with black and red Zuni design motifs on crackled grayish-white slip, collected about 1890. Top rim diameter 26 cm, other same scale.

Thus, in five short years, three competing Christian sects had made serious inroads into an area that had not known outside religious contacts since the Pueblo Revolt in 1680 (U.S. Census Office. 11th Census 1894).

The major effect of the Mormon mission was the degree of protection that it offered from the Navajos of the western region. Surprisingly enough, there was very little interaction between the two groups, and almost no successful conversions to Mormonism took place. In effect, the two peoples lived side by side with little reaction. The one primary result of this coexistence was the slow takeover of Hopi land by the Mormons, until the Hopis were reduced to a position of relative peonage on their own lands.

In 1878 the Mormons established Tuba City as their major outpost in northern Arizona and began to expand toward the villages. The hatred felt toward them by non-Mormons, in addition to Indian discontent, caused the U.S. to dispatch W. Crothers as Indian agent in an effort to control the increasing pressures on the Hopis. The completion in 1881 of the Atlantic and Pacific Railroad resulted in more and more people coming into the country, and the towns of Flagstaff, Winslow, and Holbrook sprang up. Located less than 70 miles from the Hopi villages, they provided entry for a wide variety of outsiders: traders, tourists, and teachers, few of whom came to learn, in that period of White supremacy. These towns facilitated access to materials from the East, thus putting in motion the slow transition to a greater degree of non-Indian concepts and objects (Nagata 1970).

## Factionalism

After the death of Nakwaiyamtewa, Kuyingwu had served as acting village chief since the logical candidates, Sakhongyoma and Lololoma, were judged too young to hold office. He was bitterly hostile to Americans, and when his regency ended about 1880, the dual position was terminated, and Lololoma became the formal village chief, carrying on Kuyingwu's antagonistic attitude. The Navajo problem continued to cause trouble, and in an effort to find some means of controlling the raiders, Thomas Varker Keam, an English trader who had been licensed to trade with the Hopis in 1875, took a group of village leaders to Washington to meet with President Chester A. Arthur. Lololoma was apparently deeply impressed by what he saw in the capital. Crediting these wonders to the White educational system, he changed his attitude completely and began to use his influence to persuade his people to send their children to school; thus began the disintegration of Oraibi (Titiev 1944).

With increasing hostility manifested toward Mormon occupancy of the Southwest, federal authorities felt it was necessary to head off their further expansion; one avenue was by way of the establishment of controlled lands. Accordingly, on December 16, 1882, President Arthur signed an executive order establishing a formal reservation bounded by rectangular limits. A section of approximately 55 by 70 miles was set aside for the use of "Hopis and other Indians" (V.H. Jones 1950).

By this time an increasing number of scholars and visitors began to filter into the villages; most of them were deeply interested in and largely sympathetic to Hopi culture. In one way or another they further affected the psychological reactions of the people and added to the widening schism. In late 1880 or early 1881, Alexander M. Stephen arrived in Hopi country. A remarkable Scotsman who lived with the Hopis until his death in mid-1894, Stephen (1936) left what is undoubtedly the best single account of Hopi life of the period. In 1883 the ethnologist Frank H. Cushing came on a trading trip from Zuni; he provided a revealing article concerning his confrontation with hostile village chiefs (Cushing 1922). In 1886–1888 military visitors included Gen. Nelson A. Miles and Lt. John G. Bourke. Both were primarily concerned with the Apache threat.

Internal strife was also becoming more intense; the change of attitude toward Americans demonstrated by Lololoma was by no means universally accepted by the Oraibi people, a majority of whom were extremely conservative. The conservative group soon found a capable and aggressive spokesman in the person of Loma-hongyoma (fig. 2), an important ceremonial leader. In time the two factions became popularly known as Friendlies (to the U.S. government) and Hostiles.

The combination of pressures from inside and outside the village made an explosion inevitable. At this same time, one other element was added to the forces of disruption—the passage of the Dawes Severalty Act in 1887. Although the Indians of the Southwest were not seriously affected by this legislation as were those in other areas of the United States, there was a brief attempt by the Bureau of Indian Affairs to set up land allotments in the Southwest. In brief, the Dawes Act never resulted in dismemberment of Pueblo lands, but it levied some psychological trauma; indeed, some students feel that the firm opposition of Hopi leaders to the program had a major bearing on its abandonment in the Southwest in 1911. A further indication of the constriction of outside contact was the establishment in 1887 of the federal "Moqui School" at Keams Canyon (Thompson and Joseph 1944).

Thus, in the last decade of the nineteenth century, Hopi life entered its most critical phase since contact with Francisco Vásquez de Coronado. In 1890 Lololoma (fig. 4) became the "real" village chief of Oraibi, tantamount at this time to an overall tribal chief of the Hopi, due to the superior position of Oraibi. Missionaries began to arrive in increasing numbers, along with traders, tourists, and settlers. Although this was still perhaps only a few individuals at a time, it meant in effect that the Hopi people were seeing as many White people in a month as

Fig. 2. Lomahongyoma (standing in dark blanket at center) with other Hostiles imprisoned at Alcatraz, Jan. 3–Aug. 7, 1895, following their active opposition to the allotment of clan-held land to individual Hopis (as provided by the Dawes Severalty Act of 1887). Earlier action against the surveying of Hopi lands for this purpose had resulted in imprisonment of many Oraibi men at Fort Wingate (Fewkes 1922:273–282). With Lomahongyoma are, left to right: (front row) Komaletstewa, Yoda, Naquatewa, Kochyouma, Soukhongva, Sekaheptewa, Karshongnewa; (second row) Kochventewa, Beephongva(?), Poolegoiva, Lomanankwosa, Kochadah, Wongnehma; (back row) unidentified, Polingyouma, Hahvema, Masatewa, Quoyahoinema; identifications (H. C. James 1974:115) were provided by Helen Sekaquaptewa. Photograph probably by Isaiah West Taber.

they had formerly experienced in the course of a year, or slightly earlier, in a decade.

In 1899 silversmithing was introduced into the Hopi crafts inventory by Navajo teachers working directly or through Zuni contacts (Adair 1944). The work, accomplished by only a few part-time smiths, was relatively simple, consisting of rings, bracelets, and buttons copying Navajo designs. Another major influence was the arrival of J. Walter Fewkes (1898) (fig. 5), an anthropologist who undertook a concentrated 10-year study of Hopi life. In June 1895 C.E. Vandever was appointed as the new Hopi agent.

With the opening of the new school at Keams Canyon in July 1887 (fig. 6), many of the conservative Hopis refused to allow their children to attend. Several efforts to force compliance with the governmental edict finally resulted in a confrontation between the two groups, and eventually a group of Hopi parents, including Lololoma and Lomahongyoma, were imprisoned for defying the authorities. This overreaction, combining with the coin-

cidental arrival of surveyors working on the land-allotment program, resulted in a cementing of the alienation of the conservative faction.

The Baptist converts were established in 1907 at Polacca, with C.P. Cox as preacher; he was to keep passions stirred up for many years following his appointment. H.R. Voth (fig. 7), who had already established a Mennonite mission at Oraibi in 1893, was an unusual individual who seems to have "turned Hopi"; his journals and writings give an intimate picture of Hopi religious practices of the time (1901, 1903, 1903a, 1912, 1912a). Indeed, the writings of Stephen, Fewkes, and Voth provide the basis for most knowledge of early Hopi social and ceremonial life.

In 1894 the government day school at Polacca was built as well as a second school at Oraibi. This same year saw the development of what may have been the first Indian-operated store in the Southwest: the establishment of a trading post at Polacca by Tom Pavatea, a Hopi from First Mesa. And finally, Toreva Day School

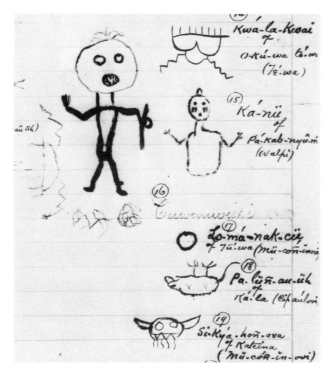

Natl. Arch.: RG 75, 1894–14830 L, p. 4.

Fig. 3. Detail of fourth page of a petition drafted in March 1894 requesting clarification of Hopi land claims, showing Hopi pictographic signatures witnessed by Alexander M. Stephen, Thomas V. Keam, and H.R. Voth. Stephen wrote the annotations here and the explanations in a separate accompanying memorandum (cf. the names in Stephen 1936, 2:1088–1137). The signers' clan "totems" shown here are: 16, Masawu; 14, rain clouds and lightning (for Cloud clan); 15, stone war fetish (for Reed clan); 17, horizon circle (for Earth clan); 18, rat (a rebus for Sun's Forehead clan); 19, Broad-Face mask (for Kachina clan); 14, 18, 19 retouched.

Smithsonian, NAA.

Fig. 4. Lololoma, chief of Oraibi. Photograph by John K. Hillers, probably in 1890 when Lololoma was in Washington, D.C., with a Hopi delegation that met with the commissioner of Indian affairs (Diehl 1961).

was built in 1897, thus closing out a decade of complete breakdown of Hopi isolation and an introduction of day-to-day government relations with the people, which has continued in the twentieth century (U.S. Census Office. 11th Census 1894).

Aggravating this situation was the absolute split that had developed between the two factions within the Oraibi village. Not only did this disrupt the social and political areas, but also it seriously weakened the framework of Hopi religious life, as Lomahongyoma and Lololoma intensified their rivalry for leadership. Another factor was the ambitious Youkioma (fig. 8), a relative of Lomahongyoma who was eager to take over the leadership of the conservative faction. There was also a large number of non-Indians interested in intervening to satisfy their own personal or economic goals; most of these were missionary personnel or settlers. Impartial, sympathetic, or unbiased participants were almost entirely lacking in the struggle (Titiev 1944).

In 1901 H.R. Voth built the Mennonite church at Oraibi (destroyed by lightning in 1942), and in 1903 the Mormons were forced to leave the village as the result of

Mus. of Northern Ariz., Flagstaff: 735/E25.

Fig. 5. Hopi painted pottery tile, believed to date to 1897, possibly depicting the anthropologist J. Walter Fewkes, said to have worn a long coat, carried a lunch bag, and smoked a pipe (Barton Wright, personal communication 1976), or perhaps representing a missionary. Length 14.8 cm; collected before 1934.

528

Fig. 6. Keams Canyon about 1895. This was the site of the trading post built by Thomas Varker Keam near First Mesa, and of the first Hopi (then called Moqui) Agency. It was housed in buildings rented from Keam and subsequently purchased by the Indian Bureau in 1889. A school (lower right) opened in 1887 as the result of a petition by Lololoma and other Friendlies. Other buildings are the trading post and residential structures. Photograph by Ben Wittick.

a very tense conflict. During this period increasing numbers of settlers arrived in northern Arizona, adding further to Hopi discontent.

The factional split came to a dramatic climax in 1906 when the conservative and liberal forces clashed at Oraibi. From 1900 to 1905 tension between the Hostile and Friendly factions had seriously disrupted village life; even religious ceremonies were not free from interference. To gather strength and support, Lomahongyoma invited a number of sympathetic Hopi people from Shongopavi to settle at Oraibi. Outraged at the distribution of their lands to Second Mesa villagers, the Friendlies sought to evict the newcomers. On September 8, 1906, in a memorable clash, they engaged the Hostile forces in a violent push-of-war and forced them back. As agreed, the 298 Hostile members packed their belongings and left Oraibi forever. They went to a site about seven miles northwest on Third Mesa, where they established a new village, Hotevilla (fig. 9). The Friendlies, numbering about 324, stayed behind with Tawaquaptewa (fig. 10) as village chief (Titiev 1944).

The next year, during the arguments over Bureau of Indian Affairs land-allotment efforts, some dissidents tried to return to Oraibi, but their request was refused and they eventually settled nearby, where they built the present-day village of Bacabi.

By 1910 the tribal split was complete. It seems to be the continuation of an old practice that may have been the cause of innumerable divisions in village structure in prehistoric times, for the Pueblo people have had a long history of village mobility, some of which defies logical explanation (Titiev 1944). Oraibi friendliness to Whites was soon put to a test when the government announced that Tawaquaptewa was to be temporarily relieved of his position and taken to Riverside School in California to learn English and to absorb something of White customs. His protests that in view of the tension Oraibi was hardly in a position to be left without a traditional leader were ignored. This enforced absence affected him deeply, for upon his return in 1910 he was a vindictive, bitter man, and this attitude in time caused the decline of the village to a mere shell.

## The Twentieth Century

In 1910 Shongopavi Day School was built, reflecting more forced schooling. Hotevilla parents refused to allow

Smithsonian, NAA.
Fig. 8. Youkioma, Hostile leader and founder of the village of Hotevilla. Photograph by DeLancey Gill, probably at the Bureau of American Ethnology, Washington, D.C., 1910.

top, Milwaukee Public Mus., Wis.; bottom, Mennonite Lib. and Arch., North Newton, Kans.

Fig. 7. Rev. H.R. Voth. top, Inside a kiva during a summer snake ceremony, probably at Oraibi in 1896, 1898 or 1900, or at Mishongnovi in 1901 (Voth 1903; Dorsey and Voth 1902); bottom, apparently proselytizing among the Hopis (he is pointing to a picture of Jesus Christ), probably at Oraibi, date unknown. Photograph by Sumner W. Matteson (top), unknown photographer (bottom).

their children to attend school, and in 1911 military force was again applied to bring the children into schools. This only intensified the anti-White feelings of the Hostiles, and Hotevilla remains in the 1970s the most militant Hopi village.

Very slowly, positions solidified on the three Mesas, and day schools were built in other areas. The Bacabi Day School was erected in 1912; its title and function were changed in 1916 to the Hotevilla-Bacabi School. In 1913 the government opened a hospital at Keams Canyon, which serves both the Hopi and surrounding Indian peoples (Thompson 1950).

During the First World War, approximately one-tenth of the Hopi tribe served in the army; the majority adhered to their longstanding noncombatant tradition. Perhaps the most newsworthy event of the decade was the C.C. Pyle "Bunion Derby" fiasco. This cross-country footrace, from Boston to Los Angeles, was won by Louis Tewanima, whose elimination on a technicality became a *cause célèbre* in the newspapers. In 1924 the Hopi were included among the American Indians officially declared by the Congress to be citizens of the United States.

By 1930 Hopi economic status had declined. Tribal income was primarily gained by farming with a modest amount of off-reservation work and arts and crafts activities. In 1926 the Lee's Ferry Bridge over the Colorado River was built, bringing increased tourist travel into northeastern Arizona. While this more directly affected the Navajo reservation, it also influenced the Hopi, who saw more and more outsiders coming into the villages; following the completion of the Cameron-to-Gallup road this contact and pressure has been intensified.

With wage work an ever more important basis for the economy, Winslow became a key city in the Hopi world, replacing Flagstaff, since it was on a direct line to First Mesa (Nagata 1970). The Depression affected Hopi economic life drastically. Intoxication became a problem for the first time; previously, the Hopi had been widely known as a tribe remarkably free from this vice.

Perhaps the greatest change followed passage in 1934

Fig. 9. First Hostile camp at Hotevilla (shelters at right and on hill, center) following Hostiles' departure from Oraibi. Photograph by Jo Mora, probably Oct. 1906.

of the Wheeler-Howard bill, commonly known as the Indian Reorganization Act. Under the leadership of Interior Secretary Harold L. Ickes and Commissioner of Indian Affairs John Collier, this act offered a well-meant and dramatic change of fortune for Indian people; indeed, it was a complete about-face in federal attitude. Oliver La Farge, a long-time friend of Indian causes,

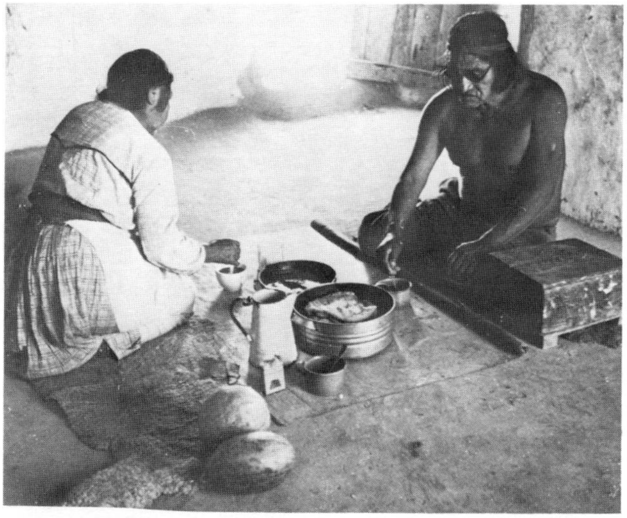

drafted a constitution for the Hopi in 1936 after consulting widely with Hopi people he knew. The tribal council was established in 1935 after an election in which a minority of Hopis voted to accept the terms of the Reorganization Act. The overwhelming majority of eligible Hopi adults had registered their disapproval by just staying away from the polls. The perpetuation of political factions was reflected in the council then, as it was in the 1970s.

The federal stock reduction plan introduced to the Hopi was just as strongly opposed as it was among the Navajo. Eventually Hopis accepted the stock problem and worked to solve it. Oraibi High School, with about 200 pupils, was established in 1939 and has been a strong educational force ever since.

By 1940, then, the Hopi Indians had seen tremendous changes in their own social organization, problems of outside pressures increase radically, and their whole world view undergo new and irreversible alterations. Their major city, Oraibi, had declined from 600 in 1900 to a town of 112; completely new villages had developed, and the traditional centers of population suffered crippling strains (Titiev 1944). Many Hopi people left the reservation for work in the neighboring cities during World War II, and many registered as conscientious objectors, rendering alternative service. By no means of the least significance is the fact that missionary activities were reduced to a minimum, and the influence of traders became less pronounced.

Fig. 10. Tawaquaptewa, village chief, probably at a mid-day meal in his Oraibi home with his wife, Nasingönsi (see Titiev 1972:figs. 8–9). Photograph by unknown photographer, probably in the 1930s.

Population pressures were increasing, and the subtle but steady movement of Navajo settlers brought reservation landholding problems to a critical point. Navajos had been settling closer and closer to the Hopi villages; their population superiority and political dominance gained them a de facto recognition, and the setting aside of part of the Hopi lands under a soil conservation program resulted in the establishment of a subdivision known locally as District Six, which was in actual fact a restriction of Hopi land, diminishing their use to 501,501 acres. This remained in the 1970s a key point of dispute between the two tribes.

The Hopi have seen their isolation completely gone, their independence as a tribal unit disappear, and their internal vitality radically threatened. Almost every facet of their life has been affected: with wage work predominant, ceremonies began to be scheduled more and more on the basis of the European calendar, to accommodate those who work by the week. Architectural changes subtly affected home life, and water-supply programs altered attitudes toward rain ceremonies. The economy changed from a subsistence base with some cash supplement to a completely cash base with small subsistence support. Returning veterans had demonstrated the vital need for a sound education in order to cope with Anglo-American culture, as well as the critical need for political sophistication.

Traditional Hopi anonymity had undergone change; the emergence of recognized individuals by name, particularly in the field of arts and crafts, as well as in certain political areas, gave rise to jealousies. The recognition, at the same time, of some of the aspects of their unique culture provided a degree of comfort and balance to this very considerable internal stress.

Yet even with all of this culture shock, by the end of the period 1850–1940, the Hopi continued to follow a way of life that, in most respects, was perhaps nearer to an aboriginal way of existence than that of any other Indian tribe in the United States.

# Hopi History, 1940–1974

RICHARD O. CLEMMER

The Hopi of the atomic age reflect the kaleidoscope of social, economic, and ideological poses evident in most nations of the modern industrial world. At the same time, fundamental behavior patterns and perceptual modes persist from aboriginal times. Two issues that emerged as central focuses of Hopi concern in the 1950s and 1960s were land and resource use and cultural sovereignty.

Land has always been the mainstay of Hopi culture. The Hopi ceremonial cycle, still practiced at all three mesas in the 1970s, expresses a philosophical imperative mandating proper preparation, use, and appreciation of land and its generative powers. Hopi elders of the 1960s and 1970s still spoke of the land reverently and emotionally, one elder even referring to it as "the Hopis' social security" (Clemmer 1974). These elders refer to Hopi land as a "shrine" that extends far beyond the Hopi villages to the Grand Canyon, the San Francisco Peaks, the northern reaches of Black Mesa, Zuni Salt Lake, and south of Route 66 (Clemmer 1968–1970)

Of course the United States government has never acknowledged such an extensive parcel as exclusively Hopi. The 1882 executive order reservation included only two and one-half million acres and completely excluded the Hopi settlement of Moenkopi (see "Hopi Social Organization," fig. 1, this vol.). By 1900 Navajos had moved onto a good portion of the Hopi reservation, and Hopis began to fear that if this trend continued, they would be surrounded by Navajos whose use of land for stock raising would confine the Hopis to their villages. In 1939 Hopi representatives met with Commissioner of Indian Affairs John Collier to enlist his support in confirming the boundaries of the Hopi shrine and enforcing the exclusivity of at least the 1882 reservation. The meeting produced no tangible results.

Hopis' fears that the United States would not protect Hopis' special relationship to their land were heightened when the Hopi and Navajo reservations were divided into grazing districts. As the main administrative agency concerned with Indian lands, the Bureau of Indian Affairs assumed administration of the districts. In 1943 the BIA's Hopi Indian Agency took charge of District Six as its area, even though District Six included only 631,306 acres (Hopi Indian Agency 1968:6) immediately surrounding the 11 Hopi reservation villages.

Although Hopis were assured that District Six would not become the new Hopi reservation, in fact Hopis' fears were confirmed. The Hopi Agency implemented stock reduction to improve grazing potential only in District Six, leaving the rest of reservation stock reduction to Navajo agencies. For practical purposes, then, the Interior Department's interpretation of the stock reduction procedures shrank the Hopi land base to an almost token fraction of the enshrined area venerated in Hopi ceremonies.

The postwar years brought increased government attempts to establish its presence in Hopi land and also brought, for the first time, conscious action by Hopis to deal with the problems of non-Hopi jurisdiction over their lands. Two of the most important legislative actions accomplishing the government's intent were passage of the Indian Claims Commission Act of 1946 and the Navajo-Hopi Act of 1950. Hopis, for their part, reestablished the Hopi tribal council and evolved a new political group referring to themselves as the Hopi Traditionals.

## Revival of the Council

The Indian Claims Commission was authorized to rule on claims for monetary compensation brought against the United States by any tribal entity recognized as representing a tribe or identifiable Indian group. By far the most common proceedings were those over lands taken by the United States without rendering just compensation or without due process of law. According to Indian Claims Commission statutes, once the award is made and the money is in the hands of the Indians, such payment "shall finally dispose of all rights, claims or demands" that the claimants could make (J.D. Forbes 1965:45).

The BIA officially had nothing to do with the Claims Commission. However, the BIA took responsibility for disseminating information about the claims, calling meetings, and supervising referenda (see J.D. Forbes 1967:248–253, 257–259; Costo 1974). Teachers in the Hopi Day School at Kyakotsmovi (New Oraibi) were encouraged to talk about the claims in class, and the agency superintendent encouraged Hopis to submit a claim.

Hopis from Second Mesa who had spearheaded the attempt to establish the Hopi claim to their shrine for Commissioner Collier were joined by people from First Mesa and Moenkopi in a trip to Washington in 1950. Their intention was to see what they could do about pressing their land claim. In Washington they were told "that the only salvation for the Hopi people was . . . to revive the Hopi Tribal Council," which had been disbanded in 1940 after functioning sporadically and ineffectively for four years (Emmons 1955:310–311). These "progressives" enlisted the aid of the agency superintendent and persuaded 7 of the 13 villages to select representatives to the council. The council was finally reconstituted in 1951, just in time to retain a lawyer and submit a claim (Emmons 1955:312; Clemmer 1973:26) before the deadline expired.

Revival of the council came at a time when a lot of attention was being focused on the Hopi and Navajo reservations. The Navajo-Hopi Act had authorized expenditure of $88,570,000 for general improvement of both reservations. On the Hopi reservation, such improvements were items like wells, stock troughs, fences, flood-control dikes, and roads. Coupled with revival of

the government-supported council, the act intensified the government's presence among the Hopi by providing jobs and services and by encouraging Hopis to think of the United States and its agencies as part of the normal state of affairs.

## Two Strategies

While those who pushed for the council's revival generally supported the government's presence, the legacy of the ideological split of 1906 was reflected in a renewed resistance to government policies. This resistance was publicly expressed to the Indian world when two Hopis spoke against the Navajo-Hopi Act at the annual meeting of the National Congress of American Indians in 1949. The spokesmen presented a viewpoint diametrically opposed to that of council supporters and reflected a growing concern among traditional elders that, without

John S. Boyden, Salt Lake City, Utah.

Fig. 1. Delegation of Hopis meeting in the courtroom of Salt Lake City District Judge for the purpose of signing their first attorney's contract, July 12, 1951. They are: (seated left to right), Homer Homewytewa, Kyakotsmovi; Homer Cooyama, Kyakotsmovi; Roger Honahni, Upper Moenkopi; Lewis Numkena, Upper Moenkopi; John S. Boyden, Salt Lake City attorney retained by the Hopis; Judge A.H. Ellett, Salt Lake City District Judge; Ned Nayatewa, Sichomovi; Andrew Seechoma, Walpi; Hale Secakuku, Shipaulovi; David Talawiftema, Shipaulovi; Julius Toopkema, Bacabi; Howard Talayumptewa, Bacabi; (standing left to right), Samuel Shing, Moenkopi; Dewey Healing, First Mesa (Tewa); Dean Tevaya, Sichomovi; James S. Beck, Bureau of Indian Affairs employee; Logan Koopee, Sichomovi. Photographer unknown.

non-Hopi allies to counter government influence, Hopi cultural sovereignty could easily be compromised.

The ideological basis of the spokesmen's message was expressed in a letter sent to President Harry Truman, also in 1949. This document should have dispelled any thoughts that Hopi religious elders suffered from torpidity born of mystical detachment. It rejected the notion of Hopis "asking the government for land that is ours" through participation in claims proceedings, denied oil companies drilling access to Hopi lands, denounced the Navajo-Hopi Act appropriations as an effort "to reduce the Hopi people under this plan," and refused participation in any military action resulting from the North Atlantic Treaty Organization alliance. It stated, in part: "This land is a sacred home of the Hopi people.... It was given to the Hopi people the task to guard this land . . . by obedience to our traditional and religious instructions and by being faithful to our Great Spirit Massau'u. . . . We have never abandoned our sovereignty to any foreign power or nation. . ." (Talahaftewa et al. 1949).

The document was signed by 24 ceremonial leaders from four villages. Although the letter expressed a militancy unusual for that period, it reflected the firm belief of these elders that Hopi mythic prophecy was unfolding in a manner that necessitated action on their part. Traditionally, a Hopi community adjusts psychologically to stress from the outside through mythic ideology, which regards present and future as the revelation of predictable forces whose seeds were sown in past events (see Whorf 1956:58, 59-60; Loeffler 1971).

The predictive force of Hopi mythology is indicated by a version of the Hopi origin and migration myth told to missionary H.R. Voth (1905:21-26). The storyteller incorporates the White man into the myth as pahá·na, the Hopis' elder brother. Upon emerging from the underworld, the elder brother headed eastward, but if the Hopi ever got into trouble, the elder brother would return and punish those who were causing trouble. The elder brother started out, "and they became the White Men as they traveled eastward. . . . But the Hopi are still looking towards their elder brother. . . . Our old men and ancestors have said that some White Men would be coming to them, but they would not be the White Men like our elder brother, and they would be worrying us."

By 1947 the second generation of elders who had to deal with Whites decided to announce that elder brother was needed. Around that year a clan elder from Second Mesa stated in a kiva meeting that in the early days of his training as a religious leader he was instructed that when a gourd of ashes fell from the sky, he was to tell teachings, prophecies, and traditions that had previously been secret. Other clan elders mentioned similar instructions. A series of meetings brought elders from all three mesas; and clan functions and duties, religious philosophy, and prophecies were discussed. Results of these meetings were an increase in initiates to religious sodalities; communi-

cation of esoteric religious ceremonies to young people; assured perpetuation of ceremonies that were about to disappear; and the start of the counter-campaign to the acculturative pressures of United States jurisdiction, resulting in emergence of the Hopi Traditionals as a political entity.

Obviously by 1950 two definite political strategies with separate leaderships had emerged among the Hopi, each communicating a different ideology to the agencies of non-Indian jurisdiction. The two strategies may manifest what Alice Schlegel (personal communication 1972) refers to as the "linearity and dialectic involved in Hopi cosmology in an almost Hegelian progression of time and space . . . encapsulated in the ceremonial cycle."

This dialectic process is seen in the continuing pursuit of diametrically opposed strategies by the tribal council and the Hopi Traditionals. The Traditionals asserted that the Hopis were an independent nation, not even extending diplomatic recognition to the United States through treaty negotiation, since the Hopi never signed a treaty with the United States. The council supporters, reflecting the influence of 60 years of Christian missionizing efforts, asserted that as "the younger generation of the Hopis who are not baptized into Hopi ceremonial customs," they had "chosen the civilized method of democratic government in dealing with others for the welfare of our people" (Emmons 1955:288).

## Land Issues and Economic Development

For both the Hopi Traditionals and the council supporters, land emerged as the central focus of attention in the 1960s. Just as the Traditionals asserted their caretakership of Mother Earth, the tribal council asserted economic interest in Hopi land resources as a basis for political strength and influence. After filing a claim with the Claims Commission, the council next started negotiations with the Navajos over the areas of the Hopi reservation outside District Six, which by 1953 had become occupied almost exclusively by Navajos. After several years of fruitless negotiations between the Hopi and Navajo tribal councils, Congress passed a bill authorizing the Hopis to sue the Navajos to settle the land question in court. Filed in 1961, the suit was resolved by a three-judge panel in 1962. The panel ruled that Hopis had exclusive right and interest in District Six, but only "joint, undivided and equal rights and interests . . . to all of the executive order reservation . . . lying outside . . . district six" with the Navajos. Hopis were not happy with the decision, since it required them to pursue an aggressive strategy to enforce their rights and officially diminished what was operationally a shrunken land base.

Despite limited access to once exclusive Hopi territory, the tribal council has successfully promoted economic exploitation of land and its resources. A legacy of the Navajo-Hopi Act was a report published by the Bureau of Indian Affairs in 1956 assessing the economic feasibility of mineral exploitation (Kiersch 1955-1956, 1). Between 1961 and 1964 the tribal council secured leases for prospecting, exploring, and drilling for oil, gas, and minerals. These leases brought $3,139,104.43 in royalties (Anonymous 1961; Hopi Indian Agency 1968; Anonymous 1964). Regular income greatly bolstered the council's image and made it more like a real government. From this income, the council authorized payment of $1,000,000 for legal fees and services to their attorney, reserving about $500,000 for operating expenses, a meeting hall and headquarters, and regular compensation for council members.

The remaining $1,600,000 was invested in constructing an undergarment factory for the B.V.D. Company (fig. 2) on lands donated as a "Hopi industrial park" by private individuals and the city of Winslow in that off-reservation town. After two years of operation, the factory threatened to close down in 1971. Worker dissatisfaction, Hopi complaints of B.V.D.'s failure to pay rent, and Indians' lack of enthusiasm for relocating to Winslow indicated that the B.V.D. factory was anything but an unqualified success. Nevertheless, the Hopi and Navajo tribal councils, the Bureau of Indian Affairs, B.V.D., and the city of Winslow launched a cooperative effort to pump new life into this important Hopi investment (Anonymous 1971). This attempt was not successful, and the factory closed in 1975.

Around the same time as the council began its B.V.D. venture, it also began to provide more services and employment for Hopis under the BIA's "buy Indian" policy and under various programs of the federal War on Poverty. Through a grant-loan from the Economic De-

velopment Administration and $144,700 of its own money, the council constructed a motel-café-museum complex on Second Mesa. Known as the Hopi Cultural Center, the building opened in 1970, featuring excellent displays of contemporary Hopi weaving, carving, and visual art.

The largest economic development scheme in which the tribal council has gotten involved is the 1966 leasing of a portion of the joint use area in conjunction with the Navajo Tribe to Peabody Coal Company. Peabody began strip-mining an area of Black Mesa in 1970, agreeing to pay the Hopi Tribe an annual royalty of approximately $500,000. In addition to coal, Peabody also negotiated to pump 38 billion gallons of water from underneath Black Mesa for processing the coal for power plants (McGavock and Levings 1973; Martone 1974).

Although the mining operations guaranteed a steady income to the tribal council, many observers (Clemmer 1970, 1973; Josephy 1971; Aarons 1971; Budnik 1972; Brom 1974) feared that runoff from the mining area could adversely affect Hopi crops, that Peabody's plans for reseeding and recontouring the mined area would not reverse the environmental damage to the fragile ecosystem, that no amount of money could undo the possible harmful effects of pollution from the power plants (see U.S. Department of Health, Education and Welfare 1970), and that pumping operations could seriously deplete accessible water supplies (McGavock and Levings 1973; Martone 1974).

The Hopi Traditionals, after several years of waning support, mustered impressive opposition to the strip-mining (fig. 3). In 1970 village chiefs and ceremonial leaders representing 10 of the 13 villages organized to file a lawsuit against the secretary of the interior and Peabody Coal Company. Filing of the suit in May 1971 followed nearly a year of village meetings at which Hopis, environmental experts and advocates, lawyers, and anthropologists aired their opinions. There was much discussion of Hopi prophecy, the significance of Black Mesa as a portion of the Hopi shrine, and the advisability of subjecting Hopi sovereignty to arbitration under United States law. There were even a couple of dramatic exchanges between Hopi Traditionals and Peabody representatives.

The 1971 suit (Lomayaktewa et al. v. Morton) alleged that the Hopi tribal council did not constitute a proper quorum when it signed the lease (see Clemmer 1973) and charged the secretary of the interior with exceeding his authority when he approved it. The basis of the suit was that the strip-mining violated "the most sacred elements of traditional Hopi religion, culture and way of life." In a statement prepared for the complaint, six Hopi elders explained that Black Mesa was "part of the heart of our Mother Earth" granted to the Hopi to hold "in trust in a spiritual way for the Great Spirit, Massau'u." "Title," they asserted, "is vested in the whole makeup of Hopi life.

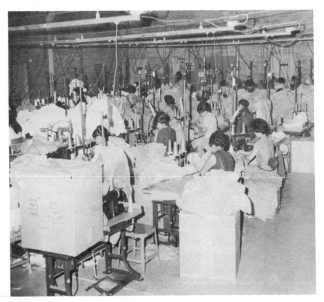

*Winslow Mail*, Ariz.
Fig. 2. B.V.D. factory, Winslow, Ariz. Photograph by unidentified photographer, probably 1969-1971.

Fig. 3. Hopi man viewing the Peabody Coal Company's strip mine at Black Mesa. Photograph by Terrence Moore, 1970.

Fig. 4. One of several meetings called by the Hopi-Navajo Unity Committee to discuss the division of the joint use area. Thomas Banyacya (standing) and Mina Lanza (seated at right) were prominent Hopis on the committee, which was formed to oppose division and relocation. Photograph by Dan Budnick, Shongopavi, May 1972.

. . . If the land is abused, the sacredness of Hopi life will disappear."

Although this view conflicted with the council's strategy of economic development, it is clear that Traditionals and council supporters were alike in valuing land and its resources. Whether land was used for economic purposes or as a basis for religious activity and ritual enactment of the mythic process, land was regarded as the most crucial factor for the perpetuation of the Hopi as a viable Indian nation. In one sense, the tribal council's negotiation of leases with Peabody Coal was an effort at asserting their claim to the "joint use" area that was formerly exclusively Hopi. Certainly the 6,000 Hopis were conscious of their diminished position in relation to the economic and political power of the surrounding Navajo Nation. In 1970 the Navajo tribal council infuriated the Hopis by offering to purchase the Hopis' half-interest in the joint use area (fig. 4). The tribal council denounced and rejected the offer, and the Hopi Traditionals issued their own statement to the same effect, stating that no Hopi land was for sale (C.H. Johnson 1970).

Many Hopis saw land and land resources as crucial for Hopis' ability as an Indian nation to withstand the economic onslaught that development of the Southwest as a major metropolitan area could bring (see Westinghouse Electric Corporation, Systems Operations 1969;

Fig. 5. Sign placed outside Old Oraibi by Mina Lanza, in 1974, closing the village to tourists. (See Hopi 1977). Mina Lanza functioned as "village chief" *(kí·kmòŋʷi)* from 1960 until her death in 1978, although her brother, Myron Poliquaptewa, was also recognized as village chief by some villagers. The sign was put up at the request of villagers because of their experiences with disrespectful tourists. Photograph by Cradoc Bagshaw, 1975.

*537*

Martone 1974). Although by the 1970s there were several hundred Hopis attending college, few could expect reservation employment from federal or tribal agencies dependent on fluctuating government funding. Climatic factors limit agriculture to a subsistence basis, and stock production in the 1970s was severely limited by inadequate land. Efforts to work out a legislative plan for relocating Navajos, enlarging the exclusive Hopi area, and including Moenkopi in a new and diminished Hopi reservation had not solved the Hopi land problem as of 1975.

Although in many respects the tribal council had intensified non-Indian influence over the Hopi after its revival in 1951, the dialectical process of cooperation and resistance manifested by the council and the Traditionals represented multiple strategies aimed at one goal: perpetuation of Hopi cultural sovereignty and the processes that underlie it. It is evident that for Hopis, land—whether it is maintained as the Great Spirit ordained it or is incorporated into non-Indian use patterns—is the crucial variable for maintaining these processes.

# Hopi Social Organization

JOHN C. CONNELLY

The concept of tribe when applied to Hopi is misleading, for the Hopi "do not form a tribe in the ordinary sense of the word" (Colton 1934). The prominent features encompassing the whole of the Hopi population are a distinctive Pueblo life-style and language, although slight but identifiable dialectical differences exist among communities. The Tewa-speaking community of First Mesa has a different language, but its people share in accommodating ways the general Hopi Pueblo culture, while retaining significant elements of their Rio Grande Pueblo culture. Efforts to gain "tribal" unity among the Hopi relate to Hopi social organization only as a contemporary issue, following the enactment of the Indian Reorganization Act of 1934. The problems that attended the efforts to achieve Hopi political unity show that such unity was not encompassed within the traditional social structure and throw some light on why such a perception of unity was antithetical to Hopi culture.

The use of the terms town, Pueblo, or village for the Hopi has also tended to distract from a clear view of the operative social organization. As Euro-American concepts they have tended to impose upon the residence groups an alien expectation of political order. The fact that the Hopi have given place-names to these residence sites and the groups occupying them has given support to the misconception. The term village has become embedded in the literature and in common usage in identifying the different residence groups, but it is used in this chapter without its Euro-American connotations to refer only to the residence sites and the specific Hopi relationships associated with them.

Hopi social structure contains a number of significant interlocking social groupings, named and unnamed. The (village) residence sites, the clans, and the societies are named groups. The households, lineages, and phratries are unnamed groups or named only by reference. Larger areas of residence sites were given American names—First (East) Mesa, Second (Middle) Mesa, and Third (West) Mesa (fig. 1). Connelly (1956) noted cluster relationships among the Hopi-named residence sites in the American-named mesa areas. Hopi individuals frequently refer to a mesa area by naming the most conspicuous village to indicate the whole cluster. It is in the data covering these named and unnamed subgroupings, both studies of their persistence and studies of the

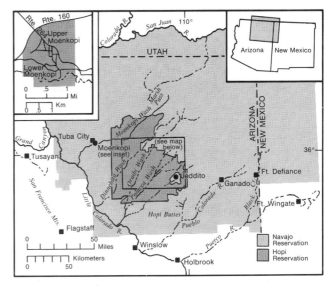

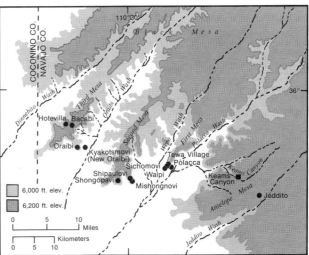

Fig. 1. top, Hopi and part of Navajo Reservations. Hopi Reservation outlined along "Mediator's Line" according to an Order of Partition issued by the U.S. District Court for Ariz., Feb. 10, 1977. bottom, Hopi village area.

changes in them, that the social structure is most clearly seen.

## The Community Clusters

Throughout the dispersed residence sites of the Hopi population there runs a common pattern of socioreligious ceremonialism and an affinity of clan identification. In this broad extension of clan relationships, clans operate on the level of social courtesy and reciprocity, whereas within the residence sites themselves, clan kin demonstrate stronger obligatory relationships. The distinction between nominal relationships and relationships carrying mutual obligation is of help in viewing both the clan system and the other obligatory relationships that form the structure of Hopi social organization.

Significant units within which the obligatory affinity operates may be viewed in terms of orbital relationships or clusters of social units surrounding a core unit. On the minimal level of social organization, the households (within which the nuclear families are contained) are the essential core groups in Hopi social structure. At the other extreme, the clusters of named residence sites constitute the greatest extent of obligatory relationships.

In the precarious natural environment of Hopi, the ceremonies are the instruments of supernatural management, from which arise directives for social control. In the First Mesa area (figs. 2–3) the major ceremonies are in the custody of the mother village, Walpi, and Sichomovi is in a colonial relationship, dependent upon Walpi for reli-

gious initiation. In return, Sichomovi serves as a reservoir of available population. The ceremonials must be maintained with sufficient personnel to insure their performance but protected against excess population competing to usurp ceremonial rights and status. Surplus population may be maneuvered into safe social distance if controlled by dependency relationships.

The other satellite community of First Mesa, Tewa Village, was established in historic times. The oral traditions of Hopi clans give many instances of procrastination and ambivalence attending acceptance of refugee or nomadic groups into the Hopi area and of the contractual arrangements upon which acceptance was based. First Mesa is in an exposed position, and the Tewa immigrants were assigned to protect the Hopi from intrusion (including intrusion of other Tewa) upon Hopi management of land, water, residence, and ceremonial jurisdiction. Social distance was maintained by physical separation on the narrow mesa top, reinforced by separation of role, the Tewa occupying the "prestigeless positions of warriors" (Dozier 1954:290–297). However, the bilingual Hopi-Tewa found a means for enhancing their role as guard-

Southwest Foundation for Audio-Visual Resources, Santa Fe, N.M.

Fig. 2. First Mesa, looking northeast. Walpi is in the foreground, Sichomovi and Tewa Village are beyond the narrowing of the mesa in the middle of the photograph. Photograph by Peter Dechert, June 1977.

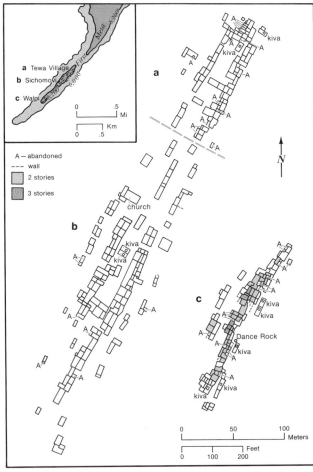

after Stubbs 1950:figs. 22–23.

Fig. 3. First Mesa villages in 1950: a, Tewa Village; b, Sichomovi; c, Walpi.

CONNELLY

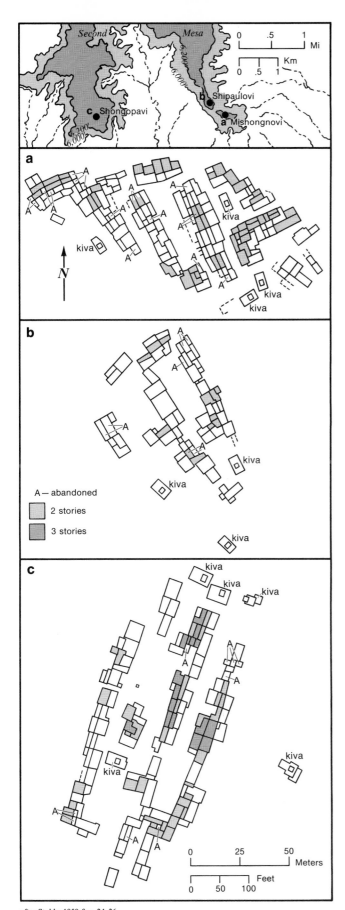

after Stubbs 1950:figs. 24-26.

Fig. 4. Second Mesa villages in 1950: a, Mishongnovi; b,
Shipaulovi; c, Shongopavi.

Southwest Foundation for Audio-Visual Resources, Santa Fe, N.M.

Fig. 5. Part of Second Mesa, looking northeast. Mishongnovi is in
the foreground, part of Shipaulovi is in the distance to the left
(arrow). Photograph by Peter Dechert, June 1977.

Southwest Foundation for Audio-Visual Resources, Santa Fe, N.M.

Fig. 6. Shipaulovi, looking east. Photograph by Peter Dechert, June
1977.

Southwest Foundation for Audio-Visual Resources, Santa Fe, N.M.

Fig. 7. Shongopavi, looking northeast. Photograph by Peter Dechert,
June 1977.

ians by emphasizing Hopi dependence upon them as interpreters (hence buffers) between the Hopi and other peoples. Both Hopi and Tewa people regard Tewa speakers as more competent in English, and often in Spanish, Apache, or Navajo as well as Tewa and Hopi.

In the Second Mesa area (figs. 4-7) Shongopavi is the mother village. Shipaulovi carries a colonial role and Mishongnovi a guard role. The cluster relationship here, older than that of First Mesa, is described in tradition (Nequatewa 1936). According to legend, Crow clan people, led by one Mishon, petitioned for admission to Shongopavi and after long negotiations were assigned a location east of the Shongopavi site and charged with protecting a shrine and maintaining vigilance for the prophesied arrival of *pahá·na* ('white man'). In time they were joined by other clans, but the guard function remains as the assigned role for Mishongnovi.

According to tradition, Shipaulovi was founded by part of the Shongopavi population during the move to the mesa top following the Pueblo Revolt of 1680 (Hargrave 1930). The removal of the population from its original site at a large spring in the sandhills below the mesa to the waterless mesa top undoubtedly created pressure on the population, as the springs higher up in the mesa walls were less abundant. Nequatewa (1936:46) describes the founding of Shipaulovi as a place of refuge in case of the return of the Spanish, charged with keeping account of happenings and preserving the truth in the event of the destruction of Shongopavi. Shipaulovi's colonial status is reaffirmed in the Wuwuchim (*wiwicim*) ceremony, when Shipaulovi men go to Shongopavi for initiation.

The binding relationships of the Second Mesa and First Mesa communities form two separate clusters, which represent Hopi social management in its widest extension.

In the Third Mesa area (figs. 8-11) Oraibi is the mother community. Both Oraibi and Shongopavi traditions hold that Oraibi arose from a division at Shongopavi and that the legitimacy of each would be demonstrated by its growth and prosperity. Whether or not this tradition had an effect upon the growth of Oraibi, the concentration of population at Oraibi at the turn of the century was estimated as almost equal to the six First and Second Mesa communities combined. Throughout the historical period it had been noted for its size and apparent affluence, but Titiev (1944:69) observed that fission existed early in the historical period, based on scarcity of land and water resources, and mounted in intensity for a number of years prior to its climax in 1906. He describes the protest when one faction of the divided community invited allies from Second Mesa to move to Oraibi, and the "warrior" Kokop clan (*kó·kovwiŋʷa*), which had been permitted to settle within rather than as an appendage to the village, had proved a divisive element. Most significant for Hopi social organization and behavior is the fact that the population surplus had allowed competitive religious performances and society groupings to arise within the community. The arrested process of division thus built up to an explosive fragmentation, resulting in a rapid settlement in the six residence sites of Third Mesa. Both European and non-European intrusions appear to have delayed the segmentation process; the need of the population to disperse and reconstitute was held back by fear of a Spanish return and the continuing threat of raiding groups such as Navajo and Ute. The first relief for Oraibi's overpopulation came when the distant farming site at Moenkopi began to develop from a seasonal to a permanent residence site after the raids were controlled.

During the rapid dispersal of Oraibi's population and the occupation of the Third Mesa sites, acculturation was creating new functions and roles for communities as well as individuals. Though new bases for intervillage affiliation emerged during that time, there are indications of the persistence of the clustering pattern. Old Oraibi, Lower Moenkopi, and Hotevilla form one tenuous cluster, as do Kyakotsmovi (New Oraibi), Upper Moenkopi, and Bacabi. Nagata's (1970) study of Moenkopi reveals a significant residue of older cultural patterns. The relation of Lower Moenkopi to Oraibi as a dependent colony is acknowledged in both communities. The relationships of the other Third Mesa communities are more ambiguous and become apparent only when the group behaviors of the villages are analyzed in relation to one another.

## Phratries and Clans

The phratry is the largest exogamous unit; marriage is forbidden with members of all clans in the phratry, and kinship is extended to all members of the phratry. Fewkes (1907) used the name of a prime clan as a means of identification, but the phratry is unnamed in Hopi, and the rationalizations given by informants are of little help in finding any meaningful pattern in the clan groupings that form the phratries. In addition, the variation in clan-phratry grouping among different residence clusters poses a descriptive problem.

In function the phratry system is more than simply an exogamy system. Connelly (1956) made a distinction between descriptive kinship and what he terms operational kinship, a distinction apparent in the contradictions between the observed behavior of individuals or groups and the implications of the structures as described in anthropological literature. Operational analysis, as against descriptive, does not pose an issue of alternatives but adds the dimension of behavioral dynamics to the static identification of status and role.

Hopi ceremony emphasizes unity and cooperation. Operationally in the social structure, unity is evidenced in core groups around which gravitate orbital groups of varying social distance, with varying attachment through role, dependency, or obligation. This produces a competitive sociopsychological environment in which group

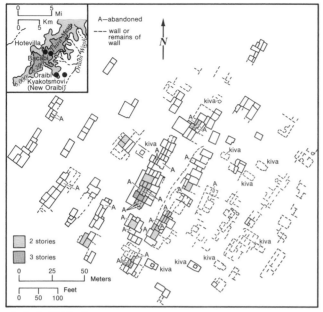

after Stubbs 1950:fig. 27.

Fig. 8. Third Mesa villages (key) and Oraibi in 1950.

Southwest Foundation for Audio-Visual Resources, Santa Fe, N.M.

Fig. 10. Terraced fields on the north slope of Third Mesa (looking south), below Hotevilla. Photograph by Peter Dechert, June 1977.

Southwest Foundation for Audio-Visual Resources, Santa Fe, N.M.

Fig. 9. Oraibi, looking northwest. Photograph by Peter Dechert, June 1977.

Southwest Foundation for Audio-Visual Resources, Santa Fe, N.M.

Fig. 11. Bacabi, looking northwest. Photograph by Peter Dechert, June 1977.

validity and priority fluctuate with changes in physical environment or social change. This cooperative-competitive interplay is present throughout Hopi social structure.

Within the phratry the position, expected behavior, and responsibilities of clans are defined in relation to the prime clan. Clan lore describes the admission of each clan on the basis of its negotiations and commitments for certain ceremonial and secular services to the residence community. The clusters of associated clans thus surround the prime clan in an orbital arrangement of

dependency and support, and a clan's social distance from the center is determined by the significance of its contribution. A satellite clan may shift from one trajectory to another as changing conditions require or as they provide opportunity. A satellite may even move, through the process of role-custody, into the prime position. In Shongopavi the Spider clan became extinct reportedly in the late 1800s. A lineage of the very populous Rope clan eventually took custodial possession of the Spider clan house site and in the 1950s was observed giving Spider

Fig. 12. Women building and whitewashing houses at Oraibi (left) and unidentified Hopi village (right). Roof has brush and grass over two layers of beams, and then earth and adobe on top. Housebuilding is largely women's work, and whitewashing entirely so. Photographs probably by G. Wharton James or Charles C. Pierce, before 1901.

names in infant-naming ceremonies. This maneuver was a persistent process of increasing identification with Spider. A rapid move would have been subject to challenge from associate clans within the phratry, and also from within its own clan, which was at that time so numerous that its lineages had to vie for function and status. Such role transference serves not only to keep the supportive clan roles filled but also to provide roles for the excess lineages of overpopulated clans. Having a large number of lineages poses the threat of competing claims upon a clan's ceremonial functions.

Having overall responsibility for the commitments of the clans in its cluster, the prime clan is in a position to make reassignments of any ceremonial office or duty not being properly carried out. Such an assignment enhances the status of the appointed individual and kinsmen as well. The result is to wean this particular lineage away from the competing lineages in its clan toward closer ties with the prime clan.

The flexible quality of the phratry allows for the managing of population size in a physical environment where either too small or too large a population creates problems. This may explain in part why political organization appears antithetical to Hopi social patterns. Political alliances tend to produce ever larger groupings, with the goal of power to establish and retain territoriality. However, in an environment where the prime enemy is unpredictable climate and weather, large populations have been vulnerable as illustrated by the demise of the Great Pueblos. Hopi history and archeology demonstrate the importance for survival of division and balance in population.

A result of population imbalance is evidenced in the division at Oraibi (Titiev 1944:89). Of the nine phratries in the community at the time, that of Bear and Spider was next to smallest in size, and Bear had only 10 members to Spider's 23. This made the Bear clan vulnerable to challenge by its larger associated clan, the more so because of the total population imbalance in the community, as the basic challenge was to Bear's capability for carrying out its primary function of land management for the total population. Bear had no other associate clan reserves within its phratry to balance against the Spider clan challenge.

As a coordinating unit, the Hopi phratry contains competitive clan elements ready to move in toto or by lineage segments into orbits vacated by extinct or malfunctioning clans. In such maneuvers associated clans within a phratry have priority, but as there are no guarantees for survival of either clan or phratry, the functions of an entire phratry that becomes extinct may be taken over by other clans. Eggan (1950) gives an account of the demise of the Bear clan at Walpi and the last individual survivor of the affiliated Spider clan. The Snake and Horn clans from other phratries moved in, first to give assistance, then eventually to carry on certain Bear clan responsibilities in "custodial" roles.

Through such transference, contributary commitments

Fig. 13. Family meal. Note the standard method of dipping food up with fingers (properly, only thumb, index, and middle fingers and only as far as the first joint). Photograph probably by Adam C. Vroman, 1901.

are assured of continuity and continue to govern the behavior of individuals and groups. Instances of clan extinctions and mergers, clan revivals through adoptions, and clan reidentification all illustrate the remarkable flexibility that the phratry gives to Hopi social organization.

### Households and Lineages

The household, the smallest distinct unit of Hopi society, varies in size of membership and may divide into a number of adjacent or quite separate households. Titiev (1944:51), recognizing the limitations of a genealogical procedure, turned to an examination of households in analyzing population relations in Oraibi. He lists 31 clan houses (presumably the prime households or house sites) and 145 households accommodating a population of 863 people. The Shongopavi population when Connelly began his study (1944–1945) was approximately half that of Oraibi prior to its split. Connelly retained the genealogical approach together with the study of households, which revealed two significant patterns. The first, the process of sloughing off descent-line groups not needed to support a prime descent line, has the effect of proliferating households apart from the core cluster. This separa-

Fig. 14. Two methods of carrying babies: left, placing baby in cradleboard (with Hopi-made blanket); right, carried in (commercial) blanket on mother's back. Woman is using gourd dipper. Photographs probably 1895–1900, photographer not identified.

*545*

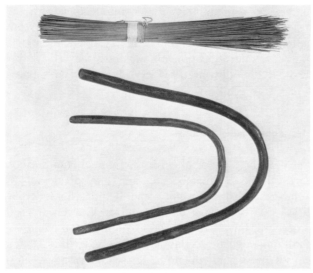

Smithsonian, Dept. of Anthr.: 409584, 128909, 22539.

Fig. 15. Hopi hair-dressing implements. top, Hair brush, a tied bundle of grass stems, collected 1941. bottom, Wooden hair bows over which a young girl's hair is wound to form a whorl, collected 1885 and early 1870s. The length of the hair to be wound determines the width of the bow used. Similar bows (usually smaller) were also used for dressing men's hair. Length of brush 26.5 cm, rest same scale.

Southwest Mus., Los Angeles.

Fig. 16. Women's hair styles. left, Married woman; right, postpubescent girl. Photographs by Adam C. Vroman, 1901, Shongopavi; for additional photographs showing this sequence see Webb and Weinstein (1973:76-79).

tion was often explained on the basis of a "quarrel." A second is the existence of biologically unrelated lineage groups often identified as immigrant. This differentiation placed a certain social distance between the "native" lineage and the other, each developing its own clusters of descent-line households. The kinship system is maintained throughout, but the intensity of obligatory relationship is diminished by degree of social distance.

A household may consist of several biological families: adult married sisters, their husbands and offspring, the mother and her husband, unmarried brothers, and frequently a senior woman. An ideal situation can be described as a prime descent line with one or more reserve descent lines allied in a close working relationship. They may live in the same house structure, in appended house extensions, or in houses placed close together. Proliferation of descent lines may lead to forming of separate households, but these often continue in amiable relations with the prime group (generally the one possessing the recognized clan house, the ʔȉ·yi 'plant (prayer-stick)'—symbol of clan authority—and responsibility for insuring that the clan commitments are met). In a crisis situation, such as drought, crop loss, declining domestic water supply, or overpopulation, the peripheral household groups may be pressed to emigrate.

Shifts of position can take place among households within the lineage clusters, as among clans within the phratry clusters. Occupancy of the clan house and its possessions does not guarantee its residents continuance in this important position; these are custodial holdings for the clan and its continuity. In order to hold its

position, the prime household must insure that respect is maintained for the clan as a whole by the effectiveness with which it conducts its ceremonies and performs its obligatory services. It must have within its own membership the personnel for carrying out these duties, or else have them in ready reserve in satellite lineage households, with which it maintains close working and trusting ties. It must encourage supportive marital ties with other phratries to negate or minimize potential aggression. The central management of the prime household consists of the senior woman and her senior brother. Seniority is less a matter of chronological age than of a recognized

546

capability and dependability in attendance to clan affairs. Succession, likewise, is determined not by chronological age but by serious disposition, interest, and involvement in clan concerns demonstrated by members of the maternal group offspring as they develop—or as Hopi express it, reveal—their qualification. General instruction in clan lore, duties, entitlements, and ceremonies given to all offspring becomes more specific for the potential successor, finally leading to a more consultative role and more responsible participation in the required activities.

Hopi ceremonialism stresses pacification of the natural elements to prevent threatening disturbances in nature. Hopi ideology places equal stress upon pacifying, nonaggressive human behavior to counteract the threat posed by competition within the residence sites. Infant and child-rearing practices and expected behavior within the household manifest this nonaggressive ideology. The flexibility of the social system and its strain for balance operate to control competitive threat and prevent disintegration.

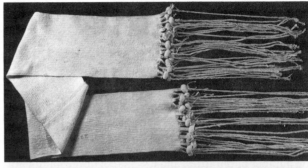

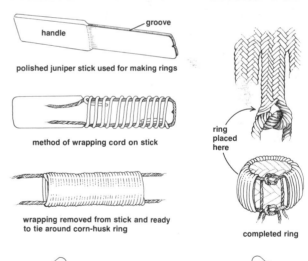

top-center, Smithsonian, Dept. of Anthr.: 22953; bottom, after Kent 1940:figs. 12-16, 8.

Fig. 18. top, Hopi braided cotton wedding sash worn by brides and occasionally by men as part of kachina costumes; length 220 cm, collected early 1870s; center, detail of braiding; bottom, Construction of decorative ring for fringe and method of braiding sash on horizontal loom. The warps are continuous, being strung onto the loom as a complete circle, and the braiding twists are held in place by the insertion of rods (for technique of manufacture see Kent 1940:46-52).

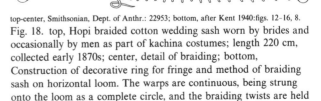

Mus. of Northern Ariz., Flagstaff (top); drawing after Nequatewa 1933:fig. 4.

Fig. 17. Second Mesa wedding ritual. top, New bride leaving the home of her mother-in-law, where she lived and worked while the groom, his closest male relatives and other men in the village wove her wedding robes and belt and prepared the rest of her wedding outfit in the kiva to which he belongs. The wedding outfit consists of the cotton wedding robe that she wears, white ceremonial moccasins (which, like the robe, have been whitened with a fine clay), and the reed suitcase that she carries, which contains another (larger) wedding robe and a plaited cotton belt with long white fringe (visible here). She wears a string of cotton, remaining from the weaving of her robes, in each ear. To the bride's left is her father-in-law, Edmund Nequatewa, who will lead her back to her mother's home, where her husband will meet her (see Nequatewa 1933; Titiev 1944:30-43). Photographer unidentified, probably Oct. or Nov. 1932. insert, Detail showing bottom corner of a wedding robe, which includes a prayer feather, tassel wrapped in black yarn, and plaited red yarn—all of which have symbolic significance.

Titiev's (1944) population study at Oraibi shows a result of a lack of flexibility in balancing population. Between 1900 and 1906 there was a population loss of 28 percent: 18 percent through death, 8 percent through migration, and 2 percent unaccounted for. This reduction still left a population of over 600, still an excessive demand upon land and domestic water supply. Tensions were intensified with the split in the prime phratry, the one charged most specifically with responsibility for passive behavior. Political competition then resulted, for both factions had to gain support from among nonkin groups in their claims for legitimacy. The effect of this division was to release pressure within the other overpopulated clan-phratry groups and provide the prospect for eventual stabilization by a major separation into dispersed residence sites.

By comparison, the Shongopavi community had approximately half the population of Oraibi, less than half the number of phratries, and less than half the number of clans. The situation was more manageable there because of the avoidance of population compression through the development of an interdependent cluster of dispersed residence sites.

## Societies

The ceremonial societies perform a religious function that in Hopi theory includes all life and all people. On the practical level within the society the cross-clan membership of the societies aids in preventing the concentration of power in any one group within a residence site.

Theoretically ceremonies belong to particular clans, though as Eggan's (1950:89–106) analysis shows, there are variations from one community to another as to the clan or clans recognized as being in charge of a given ceremony. Furthermore, the theoretically exclusive possession of a ceremony by a clan is considerably attenuated in practice. The long periods of negotiation for admission into the residence sites suggest that an apprenticeship was involved in such adoptions. It was necessary for the petitioning group to demonstrate the value of its power or service by performance, and the power claimed by the petitioners had to be delineated and shaped into a contributory component of the existing ceremonial order for the group to be admitted. Thus admission was gained after the revelation of many of the petitioners' procedural and instrumental possessions and their submission to accommodative restrictions. The cross-clan membership of the societies, while providing broad support for the individual clans' ceremonial responsibilities and performances, also provides a supervisory control over them. The resources of the broad society membership enable clan-based ceremonies to develop into impressive rituals, but the clearly defined domains of the separate societies disallow overlapping of function and prevent competition for specific ceremonies.

Fig. 19. Hopi burials below Second Mesa, marked by pottery bowls and basketry plaques. Photograph by Sumner W. Matteson, about 1900.

The importance placed upon balance in the memberships of societies is seen in initiation rites. The four men's societies, Wuwuchim, Singer, Horn, and Agave, are involved in both Wuwuchim initiation and the initiation of the kachina cult. If any of the societies does not receive sufficient initiates pledged by their kinsmen, it may refuse to participate, and the initiation must be postponed to a future year (Connelly 1947–1954).

The clustering of clans within a society makes it possible to maintain a ceremony once gained without its being dependent on clan survival, since the transfer of function from one clan to another can prevent the loss of the ceremony to the community.

## Kinship

For the Hopi the kinship system is "the most important element in their social structure. If kinship is considered as based on genealogical relations which are socially recognized and which determine social relations of all kinds between persons so related, the Hopi have emphasized the *social recognition* at the expense of the *genealogi-*

*cal relations* and have used kinship relations and behavior in ceremonial as well as daily life" (Eggan 1950:19).

The Hopi kinship system is a classificatory type with mother and mother's sisters being classed together, and father being classed together with father's brothers. Further refinements of classification are made on the basis of peer generation, supergeneration, and subgeneration. An individual's identity is in the maternal group, reinforced by the close associations with matrilineal kin in the matrilocal residency group. He recognizes maternal kin as those he is involved with on the plane of subsistence. Paternal kin are identified as supportive kin. The rule of exogamy applies to all relatives of the mother's clan, immediate and remote. Although marriage is theoretically disallowed with paternal clan kin also, breaches of this rule are tolerated with the more remote kin of the father.

The degree of intensity in interpersonal affinity among kin is greatest in the close relations of households and allied households and somewhat less with kin in clans of the phratry to which one's own clan is related. In other residence areas kin association tends to operate on the basis of reciprocal social courtesy and hospitality. An individual visiting another village need only locate the houses of his clansmen and hospitality is unquestioned.

The kinship classification of individuals in identifying their relationships extends as well to ceremonial sponsors and associates and to those who have had involvement in the curing of an individual.

Eggan (1950:19-61) has provided the specifics of the kinship terminology, definition, and application. It is sufficient here to observe that the kinship system permeates the whole of Hopi society and allows for easy access from one community to another on a social basis with minimal demand, though in close-range interpersonal relations the obligations are demanding. Most important is the recognition that the kinship system, while widely differential in degree, is, like the rest of the culture, a shared understanding of human relations within a management arrangement.

## Conclusion

Hopi social organization is characterized by a pattern of maneuverable management groups. A theoretical order of social prestige is rooted in the origin myths, which established highest status for the earliest arrivals, with descending positions of importance for later-arriving groups. Living in a semidesert with an unpredictable and narrow growing season and crops subject to destruction from violent spring sandstorms, prolonged drought, or torrential summer rains, the tightly knit small units of social structure are highly significant. The appearance of Hopi society as "an unstable equilibrium" (D.F. Aberle 1951:123) bears modification when it is viewed in the environmental context. Recognizing that survival and enrichment have been maintained and developed over a very long period of time in an environment of unstable equilibrium, the social organization of the Hopi appears instead as a flexible instrument of stability.

The continual process of establishing small household units, held together in strong obligatory kin groups within the manageable bounds of cooperative work groups, has provided a stabilizing effect, making possible production for survival in a natural setting adverse to large concentrations of human population. An increasing population

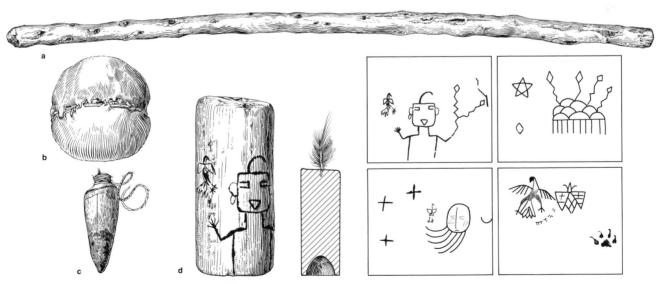

Smithsonian, Dept. of Anthr.: a, 22554; b, 84289; c, 84298; d, 25550.

Fig. 20. Hopi games. a–b, Wooden stick and buckskin ball for shinny, collected 1882 and early 1870s; c, wooden spinning top, collected 1882; d, 1 of set of 4 wooden cups under which objects are hidden in guessing game (Hough 1918:290), collected early 1870s. Diameter of b 11.5 cm, rest same scale. The cross section of the cylinder with its cup-shaped cavity shows the location of a feather decoration now missing on all four specimens. Diagrams to the right indicate what remains of the designs burnt into each of the cylinders.

has resulted in a segmentation process whereby new household groups have emerged as manageable work units, a process of separation and reformation without loss of kinship affinity. The extensions of kinship classification have insured position and identity within a wide range of human associations, but with greater intensity on the subsistence level. The kinship system embracing individuals in household groups of genealogical descent lines extended to include groups having different genealogical descent but accepted as having common ancestry in clan origins. It also extended to encompass other clans in the exogamous phratries. Here on each level were core groups encircled with clusters of kin as support and as reserves to provide social continuity for the ceremonial, service, and economic needs to maintain the residence sites.

In times of crisis a dispersal of population could and did result, without abandonment, as seen in the colonial residence groups of Sichomovi, Shipaulovi, and Moenkopi. The kinship ties of migrant groups were not severed, and linkages to the clan mother house and to kinsmen in the mother community were retained. This had the practical effect of moderating the alienating effects of the separation. At the Oraibi site the delay in the dispersal of population intensified the crisis of division in that area, and the rapidity of the dispersal when it finally occurred did not allow time for defined functional relationships to develop among the new communities, though kinship ties persist among all of them and with the other Hopi communities. The guard functions carried by Mishongnovi at Second Mesa and Tewa Village at First Mesa are not so clearly delineated at Third Mesa, although within Oraibi the aggressive overt behavior of people charged with the warrior-guard function was present, exemplified in the Kokop clan. The idea of guard function goes far back in Hopi thought. In clan legends and within the religious society organization, certain clans and societies hold these responsibilities.

The political organization of the Hopi population became an issue primarily after the Indian Reorganization Act of 1934. The problems of establishing and maintaining a Hopi tribal government devolved mainly upon the Bureau of Indian Affairs. Eggan (1950:116) in his discussion of social integration notes the lack of "a political superstructure" and comments that "the clan and phratry groups tend to assert their position at the expense of the village." Titiev (1944:68) wrote that no town was "free from strife, and never has a leader arisen to mould the autonomous villages into a coordinated unit worthy of being a tribe. Whatever other talents they may possess, the Hopi do not have the gift of statecraft." The issues of tribal and village political organization are contemporary problems still to be resolved by the Hopi in their adaptation to their changing circumstances.

Nagata's (1970) comprehensive study of change and transformation in the Moenkopi communities provides a wealth of detail on changing Hopi life not only at Moenkopi but also elsewhere. The tendency of household groups to move from the refuge on the mesa tops to the older, more convenient pre-Spanish residence sites in the sandy foothills appears in the Polacca area at First Mesa, in Kyakotsmovi at Third Mesa, and to some degree near Shipaulovi and Mishongnovi at Second Mesa. There are other movements of households to residence outside the villages; but such moves, whether to outlying farming sites or to employment locations in towns or cities, do not sever the links of kinship. The emigrant household continues to be identified in Hopi view with its clan and its affiliate clan households in the village residence site, although Nagata (1970:312–314) notes occasional shifts from matrilineal to bilateral kinship ties.

Hopi society developed a cultural and linguistic integration that allowed a sociocultural identity to arise and gave to small wandering subsistence groups a shared identity, a shared value system, and a comparative enriched subsistence. These values more than compensate for the stress produced by the unpredictable environment and ever-present potential for a division and dispersal process that are part of Hopi life. There are certain aspects of the varied socioceremonial activities that provide release from the pressures of nonaggression, obligation, and responsibility required by the tightly interlocked social units.

As Eggan (1950:116) observed:

Hopi integration may be viewed from the standpoint of the major organizations: kinship, clan and phratry, society and kiva. Each of these organizations has various devices for increasing or maintaining its own social solidarity. Each system of organization also overlaps the others in terms of membership, so that an integration of the whole is achieved; the bonds holding individuals to household, clan, society, and kiva groupings interweave in complex fashion.

Hopi social organization in its management of small units of human association provides linkages in kinship that in their practical effect serve to communicate cultural information, to reassure identity, to promote a measure of sharing, and to assure continuity. Concurrently it provides a means for survival that gives preeminence to the survival of the whole rather than any segment, in a sometimes benign but often destructive natural environment.

### Synonymy*

The English name for the Hopi (ˈhōpē) is their name for themselves: *hópi* (pl. *hóhpi* or *hopíti?*) (Whorf 1936:1221),

* This synonymy has been prepared by Albert Schroeder and Ives Goddard. The forms in the Third Mesa dialect of Hopi have been provided by LaVerne Masayesva Jeanne (personal communication 1978). The Shongopavi dialect village names in Kalectaca (1978:176) are identical with the Third Mesa forms except for lacking any indication of the falling accent.

Third Mesa *hópi* (pl. *hopí·t*) (Voegelin and Voegelin 1957:49). The Third Mesa word also means 'good in every respect', while for the Mishongnovi dialect Whorf gives *hóʰpi* 'is good, peaceable' and *hópi* 'is wise, knowing'. Fewkes (1892:4, 67, 117, 1892a:9, 1892b:33) was responsible for the name Hopi being adopted by anthropologists as a replacement for Moqui, when Moqui was found to be offensive. An earlier spelling was Hopees (Dellenbaugh 1877:170). Forms corresponding to *hópi* or Third Mesa *hopísinom* 'Hopi people' (Voegelin and Voegelin 1957:48) were earlier used to refer to all the Pueblo Indians, as distinct from the Navajos, Utes, and others whom the Hopi regarded as more warlike (Harrington 1945:178; Stephen 1936, 2:1221). From *hópi* Jemez has the borrowing *hípé* 'Hopi' (pl. *hípeš*) (Joe Sando, personal communication 1978).

According to information obtained by Harrington (1945:178) from "the chief of Walpi and several old-time Indians," the original self-designation of the Hopi was *mó·kʷi* (phonemicized). Names for the Hopi borrowed from this into other Indian languages are: Southern Paiute *mo·qʷi-* (Sapir 1931:574), Zuni *mu·kʷi* (pl. *ʔa·mu·kʷi*) (Newman 1958:32; Dennis Tedlock, personal communication 1977), and, with phonetic modification, Isleta *búxiek* 'at Hopi' and *buxíde* or *bùxieʔíde* 'a Hopi' (C.T. Harrington 1920:47; William Leap, personal communication 1977) and Keresan names such as Acoma *mú·cʰi* 'Hopi country' and *mù·cʰiṁè·çʰa* 'Hopi tribesmen' (Miller 1965:164). Keresan was the source of the Spanish names used by the Antonio de Espejo party in 1582–1583—Mohose, Mojose, Mohoce, Moje (Pérez de Luxán 1929: 83, 86, 91, 93–94, 96; Bolton 1916:185)—and similar forms continued in use after the arrival of Juan de Oñate in 1598, additional spellings being Mohoze and Moze. From this period comes the first use of the Spanish borrowing of the Zuni (or Hopi?) form of the name, appearing as Mohoqui, Mooque, and Moqui (Hammond and Rey 1953, 1:327, 346, 395–396, 408, 421, 428, 477). After Oñate Moqui, sometimes Mooqui (e.g., Zárate-Salmerón 1966:65), is the standard Spanish, and later English, form until the end of the nineteenth century. The original pronunciation must have been [mókwi], but the ambiguous spelling eventually came to be taken as [móki], in accordance with later Spanish orthographic conventions (Harrington 1945), and was sometimes spelled in English Moki (ˈmōkē). This pronunciation resembled Hopi *mó·ki* 'dies, is dead' and was so offensive to the Hopi that Fewkes undertook to urge that it be replaced by Hopi. In 1923 the local BIA agency officially renamed the Hopi Agency, and the term Moqui was dropped from government usage (Frederick J. Dockstader, personal communication 1978).

The first name thought to have been applied by Europeans to the Hopis was Totonteac, obtained by Fray Marcos de Niza in 1539 while among Sobaipuri Pimas (?)

of southeastern Arizona and used again while among the Yavapais of central Arizona as well as in discussions with a Zuni refugee among them. Data on this name are meager. The Zuni informant placed Totonteac southeast of the Zunis. Diaz, in early 1540, possibly while among Yavapais, reported that this place was seven short days from Cíbola (Zuni), had 12 pueblos, and grew cotton. Francisco Vásquez de Coronado, later in 1540, was told at Zuni that Totonteac had 5 or 6 pueblos, others having been destroyed by war. This is the only use of this name in any of the Coronado documents and occurs prior to any visit to the Hopi villages (Hammond and Rey 1940:70-72, 79, 160, 173). After reaching the Zuni villages, documents of Coronado's expedition refer to the Hopis as Tucano (for Tuçano?), Tusayán, Tuçayán, or Tuzán (ibid.:214, 253, 259, 286, 299). This name was revived by anthropologists in the late nineteenth century as Tusayan (Powell 1891:110).

The name Asay or Osay was applied to the Hopis by the Francisco Sánchez Chamuscado–Agustín Rodríguez party, which did not visit the Hopis but journeyed west only as far as the Zuni pueblos in 1581–1582 (Hammond and Rey 1966:131, 137). This may have been a rendering of the name of the village of Oraibi, though Schroeder (1958:2-3) points out the similarity to the name Axa, which appears on the earliest maps (prior to 1569) as a place-name considerably west of Tiguex (the Tiwas on the Rio Grande), and the Acha of Castañeda, who wrote in 1567, and suggests a derivation from the name of the Tansy Mustard clan (*ʔá·sa*).

Other names for the Hopi are Rio Grande Tewa *xosóʔon*, not now analyzable but said by Harrington (1916:561) to mean 'big legging'; Arizona Tewa *ko·son* (Paul V. Kroskrity, personal communication 1977) or *kʰosoʔon* (Freire-Marreco 1914:272, phonemicized), with the same meaning; Navajo *ʔAyahkiní*, literally 'underneath ones', especially applied to Walpi, and *ʔOozéí*, a generalized use of the name for Oraibi (Robert W. Young, personal communication 1977). Further variants are in Fewkes (1907:567-568).

*First Mesa*

Walpi (ˈwälpē, ˈwôlpē) is *wáLpi* in the Mishongnovi dialect (Whorf 1936:1317) and *walpi* at Third Mesa; the meaning is 'place of the gap' or (Whorf) 'place of the ravine', from *wá·la* 'notch, ravine, narrow gorge'. The people are *wáLpitiʔ*. The Navajo name is *ʔAyahkiní* 'underneath ones', which is also the name for the Hopi in general (Robert W. Young, personal communication 1977). Zuni has Watlpiye (tl=ł) (Kroeber 1916:275). Early Spanish sources have Oalpe or Gaspe, 1582–1583 (Pérez de Luxán 1929:99, 104) and Gualpi, 1765 (Tamarón y Romeral 1937:355) and 1782 (Fewkes 1898:579). Further variants are in Fewkes (1910:902).

Sichomovi (sĭˈchō₁mōvē, sĭˈchōmə₁vē) is (Third Mesa)

sicom°ovi 'flower hill place', and the people are (Mishongnovi) sicómovt (Whorf 1936:1293) and in Navajo 'Ata'kiní. Zuni has šiwin°a 'where there are Zunis' (Kroeber 1916: 275; Dennis Tedlock, personal communication 1977). Though not named separately in the Spanish sources Sichomovi must have existed by 1745, when six villages are mentioned for the Hopi (Hackett 1923-1937, 3:414). Spelling variants include Sichumovi (Titiev 1944:3), Sichimovi (H.C. James 1956:22), and those listed by Hodge (1907-1910, 2:564-565).

Polacca (pō'läku, pə'läku) is named after Tom Polacca (see "Hopi-Tewa," fig. 1, this vol.), a Tewa who built the first store below the mesa in the late nineteenth century.

## Second Mesa

Mishongnovi (mĭ'shäŋnə₁vē) was recorded by Whorf (1936:1255) as mosáŋnɨvi, but other sources indicate ɨ in the first syllable: (Third Mesa) misaŋnɨvi, (First Mesa) müshóŋĭnovi (Stephen 1936, 2:1160, normalized). Spelling variants include Mashongnavi (Mindeleff 1891:136), Mushongnovi (Hough 1915:23), and those listed by Hodge (1907g:871). Stephen (1936, 1:745, 2:1160) wrote that the village was named after a certain large boulder or four stone pillars nearby, but the exact meaning of the name is a matter of dispute; Kalectaca (1978:176) gives 'place of the black man'. Compare the Navajo name Tsétsohk'id 'big boulder hill'. The early Spanish sources have Majanani, 1582-1583 (Pérez de Luxán 1929:101), Masanani, about 1760 (Miera y Pacheco 1760), Mozán, 1765 (Tamarón y Romeral 1937:355), Mossanganabi, 1776 (Auerbach 1943:108), and Mosasnabi, 1782 (Fewkes 1898:579). Whorf also gives mosáŋnɨvt 'people of Mishongnovi'. The Zuni name is mushshailekwe (Kroeber 1916:275).

Shipaulovi (shĭ'päwlə₁vē) is (Third Mesa) sipawlavi, usually translated 'place of the mosquitoes'. Whorf (1936:1290) has sipáwlivt 'people of Shipaulovi' beside sipáwlivi 'a little round midge' and Stephen (1936, 1:745-747) explains that the name is applied to a stone in a shrine, but Curtis (1907-1930, 12:223) indicates disapproval of this interpretation on the part of "Hopi traditionists." The spelling Shipolovi, adopted in 1915 by the U.S. Board on Geographic Names, has generally not been used (except on government maps) because it reflects an incorrect pronunciation. Mindeleff (1891:137) has Shupaulovi. Early Spanish sources have Sesepaulabi, 1776 (Coues 1900, 2:394) and Xipaolabi, 1776 (Auerbach 1943:108). The Zuni name is Shippailemma (Kroeber 1916:275).

Shongopavi (shəŋ'ōpəvē, shĭ'mōpəvē) is (Third Mesa) soŋô·pavi 'sand-grass spring place', named after the reed (Third Mesa) soŋóho (Voegelin and Voegelin 1957:22), identified as Calamovilfa gigantea (Whiting 1939:65). Other recordings are sɨŋópavi and sɨŋóhɨ (Edward Kennard, personal communication 1978) and (First Mesa)

Shüŋópovĭ and shüŋóhü (Stephen 1936, 2:1292, normalized). The spelling Shongopovi was officially adopted by the U.S. Board on Geographic Names in 1915, but Shongopavi is used on the road sign at the village (John C. Connelly, personal communication 1978). Other spellings are Shungopavi (O'Kane 1953:262), Shung-opovi (Nequatewa 1936), Shungopovi (Thompson 1950:4), and, with m for n, Shumopavi (Hough 1915:24), Shumopovi (Dorsey 1903:107), Chimopovy (Titiev 1944:3), Chimopovi, and Shimopovy. Early Spanish spellings include Comupaui (presumably for Çomupavi), 1582-1583 (Hammond and Rey 1953, 1:101), Xumupami, 1598 (Hammond and Rey 1953, 1:360), and Xongopavi, 1680 (Hackett 1942:111). The Spanish mission established about 1629 was San Bartolomé de Jongopavi (Xongopabi, etc.) (Hodge 1910m:554). The people of Shongopavi are soŋópavɨt (Whorf 1936:1292). The Navajo name is Kin Naazt'i' 'strung-around building' (Robert W. Young, personal communication 1977), and Zuni has Shummahpawa (Kroeber 1916:275).

## Third Mesa

Oraibi (ô'rībē, ₁ō'rībē) is (Third Mesa) orayvi 'oray-rock place'. Spanish spellings include Olalla, 1582-1583 (Pérez de Luxán 1929:102), Oraybi, 1598 (Hammond and Rey 1953, 1:360), and Oraibi, 1742 (Hackett 1923-1937, 3:389). Other variants are listed by Hodge (1910l:143). The Navajo name is 'Oozéí, also used for Hopi in general (Robert W. Young, personal communication 1977). Zuni has °ullewa·kʷe 'Oraibi person or people' (Kroeber 1916:275; Dennis Tedlock, personal communication 1977). The name Old Oraibi has often been used to differentiate this village from Kyakotsmovi.

Kyakotsmovi (kyə'kätsmə₁vē) is (Third Mesa) kiqöcmovi 'ruin-hill place'. Beside the official spelling, used here, others are Kiakochomovi (Dockstader 1954:12), Kiakotsmovi, and Kiakatsmovi. The spellings reflect the pronunciation of i before q as, approximately, [ia] (Whorf 1946:161). This village has also been called New Oraibi and Lower Oraibi, to differentiate it from Oraibi (Old Oraibi).

Hotevilla ('hōtə₁vĭlu, 'hōt₁vĭlu) is (Third Mesa) hotvela, said by different speakers to mean 'skins the back' or 'juniper slope'. Other spellings are Hotavilla, Hotavila, and Hotevila. The Navajo name is Tł'ohchintó 'onion spring' (Robert W. Young, personal communication 1977).

Bacabi ('bäkəbē, 'bäkəvē) is (Third Mesa) pa·qavi, the name of the reed Phragmites communis, locally called 'bamboo' (Whiting 1939:47). It is also spelled Bakabi (Dockstader 1954:12), Bacobi, and Bakavi (Titiev 1944:3). Navajo has Tł'ohchin Biyáázh 'offspring of Hotevilla' (Robert W. Young, personal communication 1977).

Moenkopi ('mō(ə)n₁kōpē, 'mōən₁käpē, in origin spelling pronunciations) is (Third Mesa) *mínqapi* 'flowing-stream place' (from *mi·na* 'stream'). Other spellings are Moencopi, Moenkapi (Hodge 1907h), and in early Spanish sources Munque concabe and Muqui concabe, 1776 (Coues 1900, 2:393), referring to a farm site where the village was later founded in the 1870s. The Navajo name is *'Oozéí Biyáázh* 'offspring of Oraibi' (Robert W. Young, personal communication 1977).

# Hopi Economy and Subsistence

EDWARD A. KENNARD

The economy of the Hopi can be best understood historically. The prehistoric foundation was an agriculture based upon the cultivation of corn, beans, squash, gourds, and cotton. During the sixteenth and seventeenth centuries Hopis acquired from the Spaniards domesticated animals—horses, mules, burros, sheep, and cattle. From the same source they derived peaches and apricots. Chili peppers from Mexico were also introduced during this time. The period of American contact, which dates from 1848, has been marked by gradual but accelerating additions of a wide variety of consumption goods, new skills, and a cash economy first supplementing and later displacing the traditional subsistence economy.

## Agriculture

### Land Tenure

Each village is autonomous and has its own land. The cultivated fields of one are separated from another by sight lines and geographic features, projected southward from the mesas. Along the water courses below the mesas, the fields of each village are divided into large sections assigned to the various matrilineal clans of the village. Formerly, each clan allotment was marked by boundary stones, set up at the corners of the fields, with symbols of the clans painted on them (Forde 1931:368). The clan land system of the First and Second Mesa villages and the boundaries between villages are shown in Forde (1931: maps 2, 3, 4).

Within each clan allotment, fields are assigned to women of the clan, and they are planted and cultivated by the men of the household—husbands, brothers, or sons (fig. 1). With the pattern of matrilineal inheritance and matrilocal residence, fields tend to become associated with specific households. Each clan has land in more than one location so that if one fails, either through lack of rain or from sudden flooding that destroys the crop, the other may still be productive.

middle, Calif. Histl. Soc., Los Angeles: Title Insurance Coll.; bottom, Smithsonian, NAA.
Fig. 1. Hopi farming. top, Corn plants in dune field below Hotevilla, photograph by Cradoc Bagshaw, July or Aug. 1975; middle, men roasting unhusked corn in a field near Oraibi, photograph possibly by G. Wharton James or C.C. Pierce, probably about 1900; bottom, terraced gardens at Hotevilla, photograph by O.C. Havens, 1924.

Fig. 2. Hopi uses of gourds. a, Container decorated with black painted human and animal figures, collected 1883; b, painted ceremonial container, collected 1892; c, painted gourd snout for mask worn by some kachina impersonators, collected 1885. Length of c 27 cm, rest same scale.

Formerly, some fields were allocated to the chiefs of ceremonial societies, and they were planted for them by the men of the village, but this custom has disappeared (Parsons 1925a:87; Forde 1931:map 4).

In addition to the clan lands, any man may establish a field in the area beyond them. He has the right to use it as long as he cultivates it and may assign it to another; however, should he abandon it, that land reverts to the common domain. About 1900, the best fields for the floodwater irrigation employed were along the water courses close to the villages. However, as the Polacca, Wepo, and Oraibi washes grew deeper and wider, much of this land was destroyed. Consequently, new fields were developed 20 and 30 miles south, where the water spreads more readily over the flatter land of the valleys. The possession of horses and wagons, and later pickup trucks, facilitated the development of more distant fields.

Hopi agriculture has always been precarious, subject to long-term wet and dry cycles. In the period 1866–1870 there was a nearly total crop failure, and some villages were abandoned, while the people sought refuge with the Pueblos to the east. In a study of land use in the Oraibi valley, it was discovered that the dissection of the wash had over a period of 50 years destroyed approximately one-third of the fields that had been in cultivation (Bradfield 1971). This may have been responsible for the gradual growth of Moenkopi, a satellite of Oraibi, 40 miles to the northwest, where there was a system of irrigation.

There is no private property in grazing land. Horses

Fig. 3. Peaches and squash drying on the rooftops in the east courtyard of Oraibi. Photograph by John K. Hillers, about 1879.

555

and burros are hobbled and permitted to graze where they will. Cattle are permitted to drift in areas where there is a relatively permanent supply of water. Sheep are herded every day and corralled at night. Most sheep owners have shelters or regular Hopi houses in the area where they customarily graze their sheep. Sometimes they have their major cornfields in the same area in places like Coyote Spring and Burro Spring.

Irrigated gardens watered from nearby springs are utilized for the cultivation of chili peppers, onions, and other vegetables; and titles to these small plots are jealously guarded. A Patki clan plot below Wepo spring was planted every year by men from Shongopavi, whose

grandmother had come from the Tewa village at First Mesa (Forde 1931:391).

Although the pattern of land ownership is clear in Hopi theory and reflects the myths of the settlement of each village, adjustments have to be made. Matrilineages vary in size and increase or decrease in a few generations. Should there be a shortage of land in his wife's clan lands, a man may be assigned a field of his own clan's land, or in his father's if there is a surplus (Forde 1931:380). Fields for beans, melons, squash, and gourds are sometimes planted adjacent to a cornfield, but bean fields are also located on the tops of the mesas, as are orchards at both Second Mesa and Hotevilla.

left, Milwaukee Public Mus.; right, Los Angeles Co. Mus. of Nat. Hist.

Fig. 4. Hunting of rabbits done individually or in small groups and as a more organized communal pursuit is connected with ceremonial activities and can itself entail many ritual procedures (Beaglehole 1936:11-17, 23-25). left, Man from Oraibi with a rabbit stick, a throwing stick made in distinctively flat curved shape with a defined handle (and often with painted decoration) that is used to flush out rabbits; photograph by Sumner W. Matteson, perhaps about 1900. right, Rabbit hunters at camp, probably at Kawaika, Ariz., 1901, carrying bows and arrows (also used to hunt rabbits) and apparently mugging for the camera; photograph by Adam C. Vroman or Walter Hough (NAA, BAE original prints).

left, Milwaukee Public Mus.

Fig. 5. Stock raising. left, Woman and children herding sheep and goats, photographed about 1900 by Sumner W. Matteson. In more recent times this, like cattle herding, has been an exclusively men's activity. right, Willie Coin branding a calf; photographed south of Oraibi by Cradoc Bagshaw, July-Sept. 1975.

KENNARD

## Crops

Hopis plant several varieties of corn, classified by color, but most of the fields are devoted to blue and white. Whiting (1939:67-70) lists 24 varieties of Hopi corn. They also cultivate a short-eared variety of sweet corn.

The first planting occurs in April, usually on dune fields close to the mesas, so that it will be mature by the time of the Niman ceremony in mid-July. The main planting, which is announced by the Crier, usually begins in the middle of May and frequently extends through the month of June. Some men plant their fields by themselves, but others have a work party for planting. The men all assemble at the host's field and complete it in a day. In the evening when they return to the village, the host's wife feeds them all an evening meal in payment.

Sweet corn is baked in field pits (fig. 1) and then stored for future use. Most of the corn crop is harvested in October—picked, husked, and hauled to the village in wagons and trucks. It is sorted by color and stored in the rear room of the house, stacked like cordwood.

Hopis grow 23 varieties of beans, some quite old but many recently introduced (Whiting 1939:80-83). Several species of squash, pumpkins, and melons are regularly cultivated. The squash is dried and preserved, but melons are eaten when they are ripe in August and September. They plant gourds in the same fields as squash. They are used as spoons, dippers, cups, rattles, pottery scrapers, medicine containers, and as decorations on kachina masks such as snouts and horns (fig. 2).

Fruit trees do not yield a crop every year. Frequently, late frosts when the trees are in blossom destroy the potential for fruit; however, in good years they yield bountifully and most of the fruit is preserved by drying. The peaches and apricots are pitted, split in halves, and spread out on the roof to dry (fig. 3). Orchards or even individual trees are owned by men. It is the tree and not the land on which it grows that is conceived to be property, and it is inherited by men, usually sons of the previous owner.

The estimated agricultural figures for 1893 show the proportionate production at various communities. At First Mesa, 1,200 acres were planted in corn; at Second Mesa, 800; at Oraibi, 1,600. Of the total corn crop of about 2,500,000 pounds, 1,150,000 pounds were consumed, 100,000 were sold to traders, 150,000 were otherwise traded, 500,000 were bartered to Navajos for sheep, and 600,000 were stored as surplus. In addition, 2,000 acres were sowed with vegetables (beans, melons, squash, pumpkin, chili, onions, gourds), sunflowers, and cotton. Peach and apricot orchards accounted for another 1,000 acres (Stephen 1936, 2:954-955).

## Wild Plants

The Hopis make extensive use of the wild plants in their habitat. The roots of yucca (soapweed) are used in hair washing, which is an essential part of every ceremony—naming, initiations, girl's puberty grinding, marriage. The leaves are split and sewed around a core in making coiled basketry and in making sifting baskets and trays. The Hopi brush, which is an essential tool in every house, is made from the culms of purple hair grass (Whiting 1939:65). A handful is tied with a piece of string near the butt end. The lower end serves as a hair brush, while the upper is used to sweep the meal from the grinding stones, as well as to sweep the floor of houses with adobe floors.

Of 150 plant species identified in their habitat, the Hopi utilized 134: for agriculture and forage, 11 species; art materials, 16; house building, 4; domestic life, 10; dress and ornament, 6; food, 40; medicine, 29; and religious purposes, for example, prayer sticks and kiva fuel, 18 (Hough 1897:43-44).

## Hunting

Hunting has not been important as an economic activity since the sixteenth century when the Hopis acquired domesticated animals. The area is not rich in large game, although deer and antelope were reported to have grazed in the area between the Hopi Buttes and the Little Colorado River. They were formerly hunted by men in pairs, and it was regarded more as a sport than a subsistence quest (Beaglehole 1936).

Rabbit hunting is a regular fall and winter sport (fig. 4). Announcement of the hunt is made in the evening before the hunt. The place of assembly, the direction in which they are going to hunt, the place-names along the route of the hunt, and the route of return are all included in the announcement. In the morning the men assemble with their throwing sticks. They form a surround a mile to a mile and one-half in area, and those at the rear close up the circle. When a rabbit is raised the hunters throw their sticks with a side arm motion at it. When a man hits and stuns one, he runs to it and kills it.

## Livestock

The major forms of men's property are sheep and cattle (fig. 5). Horses, burros, and wagons become important as the distance one has to travel to his fields or to cut and haul firewood increases. The size of the flocks and herds has always been limited by the amount of browse and the availability of water.

From the earliest days of the agency at Keams Canyon the government made systematic efforts to aid Hopi stockmen. Drilling deep wells with windmills, storage tanks, and watering troughs has been one of the most effective ways aiding the growth of the Hopi herds. Efforts were also made to improve the quality by assisting in the purchase of pure bred rams and bulls, but the benefits were limited since the Hopi did nothing to control the breeding. It was not until 1944, when a fenced

557

Fig. 6. Men weaving at Oraibi, about 1898. Both men use vertical looms that are suspended from the ceiling beams. left, Man weaving a brocaded ceremonial sash (fig. 7) of the type traded to the other Pueblos; the red, green, and blue weft elements are wrapped completely around the warp elements to produce the design—the white areas being unwrapped warp threads. right, Man weaving a blanket inside a Hopi house; a kachina doll and braids of corn are suspended against the wall to the right of the loom. Photographs by G. Wharton James, about 1898.

Fig. 7. Man's ceremonial cotton sash with brocaded designs on top surface at each end formed by nonstructural wool wefts (for technique see Douglas 1938:35-38). Brocade table runners, a modification of the traditional sash, are made for tourist sale (see Kent 1976:fig. 27a). Length 224 cm, collected early 1870s.

Fig. 8. Man's wearing blanket of brown and white handspun wool in diagonal twill weave. Length 137 cm, collected about 1930.

pasture for rams and bulls was built by the agency, that the program to improve the quality of the stock became effective.

Sheep owners usually have one or two partners—a pair of brothers, father and son, uncle and nephew. If there are only two, half a man's days must be devoted to sheep herding. A man will spend two or three days at a time herding and then be relieved by his partner. Men who have corrals close to the mesa pen their sheep at night and go out to herd each day. During lambing season all hands are with the flock, and each earmarks the lambs from his own ewes. Table 1 gives five examples of how Oraibi men allocated their work activity in autumn 1933.

In June the flocks are brought close to the village, and

| Type of Work | Luther | King | Cecil | Alex | Don | Total |
|---|---|---|---|---|---|---|
| Herding | 0[a] | 49 | 22 | 17 | 22 | 110 |
| Cornfields | 10 | 10 | 9 | 14.5 | 23 | 66.5 |
| Bean fields | 3 | 1 | 3.5 | 0 | 0 | 7.5 |
| Melon fields | 9.5 | 6 | 3 | 3 | 1.5 | 23 |
| House building | 9.5 | 8 | 20 | 0 | 0 | 37.5 |
| Wood hauling | 1 | 7 | 5 | 1 | 4 | 18 |
| Horses | 0 | 1 | 3.5 | 9.5 | 2.5 | 16.5 |
| Other work | 14.5 | 7 | 6 | 3 | 5.5 | 36 |
| No work | 3.5 | 9 | 10 | 35 | 10.5 | 68 |
| Days noted | 51 | 98 | 82 | 83 | 69 | 383 |

SOURCE: Titiev 1944:196.

[a] Luther owned no sheep.

Mus. of Northern Ariz., Flagstaff: a, E6363; b, E7804; c, E5964; d, E5370.

Fig. 9. Contemporary Hopi and Hopi-Tewa pottery from First Mesa. a, Jar with black and red on orange bear-paw design used by the Nampeyo family; made at Polacca by Dextra Quotskuyva, great granddaughter of Nampeyo, collected 1973. b, White wedding jar with black and red decorations made by Nancy Lewis of Sichomovi, collected 1977. c, Black on red bowl by Ella Mae Talashie of Walpi, collected 1973. d, Orange jar with black painted Sikyatki-type designs, made by Lorna Lomakema of Tewa Village, collected 1974. Diameter of a 22.4 cm, rest same scale.

HOPI ECONOMY AND SUBSISTENCE

work parties assemble to shear the sheep. The wool clip is sold to the traders, and until the end of World War II it was often the only source of money for many men. Most Hopis do not sell their lambs; they are butchered and eaten on all the occasions during the year that require feasts, such dance days, weddings, and initiations. They practically never butcher just to have meat in their diet. What little is not cooked for the immediate occasion is dried in the sun and preserved for future use.

Cattle are always marketed.

In 1937, the total livestock on the Hopi reservation consisted of 11,203 sheep, 317 goats, 7,695 head of cattle, and 5,085 burros and horses (Hack 1942:17). In 1944 the government instituted a stock-reduction program to bring the total number of animals within the carrying capacity of the range. Since it had been preceded by the program of controlled breeding and improved quality, the actual income of the Hopis was not reduced. All stock owners were issued grazing permits, and reductions were made in proportion to the number of head owned at the time.

With the spread of wage work and other forms of cash income on the reservation since 1946, Hopis have been shifting their forms of livestock from sheep to cattle, which do not require constant care. At the same time, the widespread ownership of cars and trucks has reduced the need for horses and burros, freeing that many more range units for cattle.

## Trade

The Hopis have traded with the Najavo for sheep and wool, with the Havasupai for buckskins, and with Zuni and the Eastern Pueblos for turquoise and other goods. Hopi weavers of ceremonial garments have kept the other Pueblos supplied for many years (fig. 6).

A trading post at Keams Canyon was operating in 1881, and Hubbell's post at Oraibi was established in 1919. All other posts and stores on the reservation have been owned and managed by Hopis. Tom Pavatea's post at Polacca was one of the largest and most successful. When he died in 1941, his estate was valued at more than $40,000.

In 1937 of a total of 17 licensed trading posts 15 were owned by Hopis. Many have been started, operated for a number of years, and then abandoned. Clothing, flour, sugar, coffee, and canned goods were sold; and craft products, corn, and wool were taken in payment as well as money when it was available.

With the spread of wage work, both on and off the reservation, and with the completion of a network of paved roads, a cash economy has been gradually displacing the traditional subsistence economy. As a result trading posts have become supermarkets. Bottled gas,

Smithsonian, Dept. of Anthr.: 166452, 213546.

Fig. 10. Basketry plaques. left, Second Mesa coiled basketry plaque; coiled foundation bundles of shredded yucca or grasses are closely sewed with strips of split yucca leaves (O. Mason 1976:257; Underhill 1944:29); collected 1892. right, Third Mesa wicker basketry plaque; two bound groups of peeled and smoothed sumac or willow stems are crossed and lashed to form radiating ribs around which stems of rabbitbrush are woven (Hough 1918:265-266; Underhill 1944:20-25) to form Kwahu (eagle) kachina design; the basket edge is wrapped with yucca leaf strips; collected 1901. Diameter of right 35 cm, other same scale.

top, Calif. Histl. Soc., Los Angeles: Title Insurance Coll.; bottom, U. of Ariz., Ariz. State Mus., Tucson.

Fig. 11. Making coiled plaques, trays and baskets. top, Group of women outside house, probably in a Second Mesa village about 1895-1900. bottom, Annabella Nequatewa (a Shongopavi basketmaker) with her grandchild and her husband, Edmund Nequatewa, who makes kachina dolls (these are on the table between them, with brushes and paints with which he has just been painting them). Photographs by unknown photographer (top) and by Helga Teiwes, Oct. 1973 (bottom).

top, Calif. Histl. Soc., Los Angeles: Title Insurance Coll.; bottom, U. of Ariz., Ariz. State Mus., Tucson.

Fig. 12. Making basketry. top, An Oraibi woman, her hair bound in the style worn by married women, making a wicker basketry plaque. Her husband is knitting, or possibly crocheting, one of a pair of cotton or wool leggings, an item typically manufactured by men. Photograph by G. Wharton James, about 1898. bottom, Marietta Tewa, a resident of the Third Mesa town of Kyakotsmovi, making a twilled yucca ring basket (2 finished baskets on table). Photograph by Helga Teiwes, Oct. 1973.

electricity, and refrigeration permit the sale of fresh meat, frozen vegetables, fruit, and a multiplicity of other foodstuffs.

## Crafts

A supplementary source of income in every household is the production of crafts. Since the beginning of the twentieth century, women's products have tended to become specialized; at First Mesa they make pottery (fig. 9), at Second Mesa coiled basketry (figs. 10–11), and at Third Mesa wicker basketry (figs. 10, 12).

Hopi men do the weaving, and the bulk of their work is in ceremonial garments of cotton and wool. Sashes (fig. 7), kilts, wedding robes, belts, and garters are the most commonly produced forms of the weaver's art. They also make the woolen black dress, which is part of a woman's traditional costume, and knit black or blue leggings, which are worn in dances. Some men also weave a striped woolen blanket (fig. 8).

Since about 1930, the Museum of Northern Arizona in Flagstaff has encouraged the production of the best work, holding an annual exhibition in July. Prizes including cash awards are given for the best pieces, and they are sold to the public at whatever price the craftsman puts upon his work.

The carving and painting of kachina dolls has become increasingly popular since the growth of a cash economy. Originally made for distribution by the kachinas to girls at dances, they are now made in large numbers for sale in the market. They tend to become larger and more elaborately carved and feathered to appeal to the tastes of the buyers.

Until 1946, there were a few Hopi silversmiths, but their work was not distinguishable from that of the Navajo or Zuni. In that year a group of 17 Hopi veterans was taught the art, and a set of traditional Hopi design elements was adapted to the possibilities of the medium. In 1965 there were seven men who worked full time at silver and another 12 who worked during the winter months. They now constitute a guild with its own hallmark (fig. 15).

On top of Second Mesa, at the junction of the roads from Shongopavi and Mishongnovi the Hopi Craft Guild has its own building, where native products are displayed and sold. Any craftsman, potter, basketmaker, weaver, or silversmith can have his work displayed and sold there. The other half of the building is devoted to work benches and supplies for the silversmiths.

## Household Economy

The basic economic unit of production and consumption has always been the household. It is here that the basic division of labor between men's work and women's work, between male property and female property, is focused.

Every Hopi house has a set of three grinding stones, set in a wooden frame (fig. 16). The metates differ in the degree of coarseness. When corn is ground it is first shelled and cracked, and then ground successively on each of the metates until it is as fine as powder. Since almost all Hopi foodstuffs are made of it, plaques piled high with meal are one of the commonest forms of payment in exchanges between households.

The other essential item of equipment is the piki stone (fig. 17), sometimes located in a back room, but more often in a small house built for that purpose. Piki (*píki*) is a wafer-thin bread of finely ground blue cornmeal. A fire is built under the stone, the surface is rubbed with the oil from cotton seeds or watermelon seeds, and a thin batter is spread upon the hot stone by hand. The piki is peeled off the stone, turned over for a minute, and then folded into squares or rolled up like a diploma (fig. 17). It is prepared before all ceremonies, and it is an item of daily consumption. Many houses also have a stone and adobe beehive-shaped oven outside, which is used for baking bread.

In addition to piki, and many other dishes prepared from a cornmeal base, a standard feast dish is hominy and mutton stew (*nöqkwivi*). The women prepare the hominy and the men butcher sheep, which are then boiled together. Child naming on the twentieth day, a girl's grinding following first menses, marriages, boy's initiation, as well as all the ceremonies of the annual cycle require the preparation of these foods.

At marriage a girl spends four days grinding and making piki at her mother-in-law's house. Meanwhile the men who are relatives of the groom are carding and spinning cotton and setting up a loom in a kiva to make the bride's wedding clothes (see "Hopi Social Organization," figs. 17–18, this vol). Until the weaving is finished, the bride stays grinding and cooking. When the clothes are finished, she is dressed in them and returns to her own house accompanied by her mother-in-law, bearing a bowl of hominy stew. After they feast, her mother-in-law's bowl is filled with other Hopi foods as a gift. Later the girl and her mother and female relatives will grind and prepare other kinds of food, which is carried to the house of every man who participated in the weaving. When a boy has his Wuwuchim (*wíwìcim*) initiation, his mother gives ground meal, piki, and other food to his ceremonial father's sister. A woman who sponsors a kachina dance is obligated to prepare food to feed all the dancers as well as the guests who will visit her house.

A man contributes his work, his fruit, his livestock or his income to whatever house he is living in: his wife's when he is married, his mother's before marriage, or his mother's or sister's if he should be divorced.

561

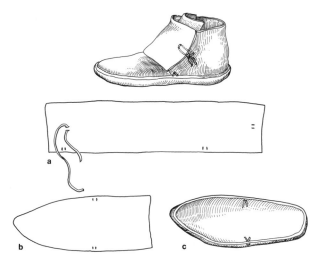

after Hough 1918:fig. 15.

Fig. 13. Construction of ordinary men's and women's moccasins consisting of three sections sewed together: a, ankle wrap and b, vamp with tongue, both of tanned deerskin; c, sole of cow (formerly elk) rawhide (see Kewanwytewa and Bartlett 1946).

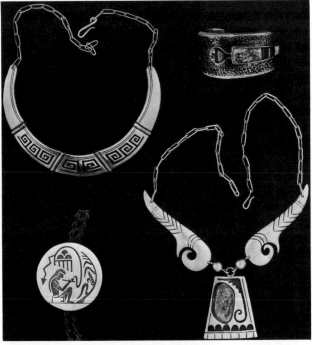

Mus. of Northern Ariz., Flagstaff: E3387, E5949, E6213, E5110.

Fig. 14. Hopi silver jewelry characterized by the silver overlay technique (Bedinger 1973:203–204), minimal use of turquoise, and traditional Hopi pottery and textile designs (M. Wright 1972:38; M.R.F. Colton 1939:2). top left, Overlay choker made by Billy Rae Howee of Shongopavi, collected 1964; top right, cast bracelet in distinctive contemporary style of Charles Loloma of Hotevilla, with gold bezel around Turquoise Girl anthropomorphic figure in turquoise, Italian oxblood coral, lapis lazuli, and ironwood (see M. Wright 1972:69; Fair 1975), collected 1973. bottom left, Bolo tie with overlay design described by silversmiths, Lawrence and Gracilda Saufkie of Shongopavi, as a kiva chief blowing smoke into the clouds to make rain for the corn crops, collected 1973; bottom right, necklace with overlay, turquoise setting, and stamped designs by Morris Robinson of Bacabi, collected 1955. Diameter of bottom left 5.0 cm, rest same scale.

after M. Wright 1972: top, pp. 92, 87, 85, 90; bottom, pp. 87, 81, 83.

Fig. 15. Hopi Silvercraft Guild and silversmith's stamps. top row, left to right, One of the several similar stamps of the Hopi Silvercraft Guild depicting the sun, and personal marks of Hopi silversmiths representing Crow Mother, bear paw, corn plant, feather, and bottom row, lightning, parrot, rain cloud, and tadpole.

Milwaukee Public Mus.

Fig. 16. Unmarried woman grinding cornmeal at Sichomovi; each Hopi house has a set of two to four grinding stones, of graduated fineness, tilted in bins, on which corn is successively ground by rubbing with a long stone mano (3 stand in corner, and one in bin in foreground); photograph by Sumner W. Matteson, about 1900.

Traditionally, the family was of the extended matrilineal type. In more recent years when it became easier to build a house or have it built, young couples moved into houses of their own. As a result, a census of the three Second Mesa villages in 1961 revealed that about one-half the families were nuclear in pattern, the other half reflecting the extended matrilineal form (Kennard 1965:30).

While the effects of contact with the larger society upon the Hopi economy and culture are similar in all villages, the extent is variable. Moenkopi, the westernmost village of all those whose people came from Old Oraibi, has been for many years the most highly acculturated. Only 13 miles from U.S. Highway 89 leading south to Flagstaff, and only two miles from the Western Navajo Agency at Tuba City, it has been a ready reservoir of manpower and skills. With the breakdown of the traditional order at Old Oraibi there has been little to tie them to the traditional way of life. As the population grew from 200 in 1903 to 592 in 1962, even the available irrigated land would have been inadequate to support them (Nagata 1970:224).

KENNARD

Fig. 17. left, Woman identified as Mashongke toasting cornmeal—probably to remove moisture after preliminary grinding—in a jar on the interior cooking fire, stirring it with the basket in her hand, brush of bound grass at left; photograph by G. Wharton James at Oraibi, 1898. center, Piki stone greased with burro fat is over the fire; a thin layer of batter spread on it cooks instantly and is peeled off, then laid on top of the next sheet being baked, then folded and sometimes rolled (Beaglehole 1937:63-64). right, Carrying folded piki bread, perhaps to a ceremony, probably at Oraibi. center and right, by unknown photographer 1917 or before.

HOPI ECONOMY AND SUBSISTENCE

# Hopi Ceremonial Organization

ARLETTE FRIGOUT*

In a sense, all Hopi life is based on the ceremonies, which assure vital equilibrium, both social and individual, and conciliate the supernatural powers in order to obtain rain, good harvests, good health, and peace. Some 300 kachinas (*qacína* sg., *qacínam* pl.),† the mythical heroes, and numerous gods are venerated: the sun (*tá·wa*); *mɨyʔìŋʷa* (god of germination); *másàwɨ* or (Third Mesa) *mâ·sawɨ* (god of death); *tɨwávoŋʸtɨmsi* 'sand-altar young woman' (the earth); *kóʰkaŋwɨʰti* 'Spider Woman'; *talátɨmsi* 'daylight young woman' (Dawn Woman); *sótöqönaŋʷɨ* (the star god); *póqaŋhòyat* (the Twin War Gods); and others. Different names and different forms can correspond to similar beings (Fewkes 1903; Earle and Kennard 1938; Colton 1959). In spite of the presence among the Hopi of various missionaries, religious syncretism such as occurs among the Rio Grande Pueblos does not exist.

## The Villages and Their Calendar

Hopi ceremonial organization is based on the year as a temporal unit and the village or mesa as a spatial unit. The ceremonial importance of each village varies according to its cultural conservatism and its antiquity. First Mesa includes Walpi, Sichomovi, and Tewa Village on top of the mesa, and down below Polacca, which has no dance plaza and no ceremonial life. Second Mesa consists of three villages above, Shongopavi, Mishongnovi, and Shipaulovi. Third Mesa includes Old Oraibi above where ceremonial life has much declined and Kyakotsmovi (New Oraibi) at the base, which organizes secondary ceremonies. Equally a part of Third Mesa, although geographically removed, are Hotevilla and Bacabi, the latter comparable to New Oraibi. Moenkopi, divided into two villages, is on a detached section of the Hopi Reservation surrounded by Navajo territory.

* The original manuscript of this chapter, written in 1972, was translated from French by William C. Sturtevant. After the author's death Louis A. Hieb edited and revised the chapter, and Ives Goddard revised sections on the Hopi calendar.

† Hopi religious and ceremonial vocabulary is poorly known to linguists and anthropologists. The phonemicized terms cited in this paper have been provided by the editors, chiefly from Whorf (1936), who recorded the Mishongnovi dialect; a few forms not directly attested have been made on the analogy of words Whorf recorded. Some Third Mesa forms from anonymous sources have been added when they are particularly different.

In principle, each traditional village organizes its own ceremonies following a general model that permits variation. But the villages of Walpi (until recently), Shongopavi, Mishongnovi, and Hotevilla serve as leaders; when a ceremony cannot be held in one of the less important villages, their occupants can go to "serve" in the principal village of their mesa. The ceremonies are organized only at the village level, never at the tribal one, even though the Hopis believe that it is necessary to pray for all the Hopis and even for all of humanity (Titiev 1944:106). In the early 1970s the cycle of ceremonies outlined here still obtained as a general model, although only Shongopavi performed the full cycle. It was still possible for any Hopi to participate in the whole series of ceremonies although not necessarily in one village or on one mesa in a given year.

Extensive discussions of Hopi ceremonial organization appear in Eggan (1950), Titiev (1944), and Bradfield (1973, 2:46-305).

## The Ceremonial Cycle

The ceremonial cycle is an annual cycle consisting of two major periods, that of the masked and that of the unmasked ceremonies. The masked dancers, called kachinas, arrive in either January or February (depending on the calendar and the village) and depart in July. Their first great ceremony is Powamu (*powámi*), when children are initiated into the kachina and Powamu societies, and their last is the Niman (*nimán-* 'returning-home') ceremony. Thus, their presence marks a season extending from sometime in the month or so following the winter solstice to sometime in the month after the summer solstice (cf. Titiev 1944:109, 175), and their departure coincides with the end of planting the fields. Following this comes the Snake-Antelope ceremony (*cɨʔcɨvti*) or the Flute ceremony (*lé·lenti*), in alternating years in each village. In even-numbered years Shipaulovi, Oraibi-Hotevilla, and Shongopavi have Snake-Antelope, and Walpi and Mishongnovi have Flute; in odd-numbered years the reverse is true. The Butterfly Dance takes place in late summer and the Buffalo Dance (figs. 1-2) following Soyal, though these so-called social dances do not have precise dates. In autumn come the ceremonies of the three women's societies: the Maraw (*máraw*) ceremony of the *mámraWt*, the Lakon (*lakón-*) of the *lálakòNt*, and the

School of Amer. Research, Santa Fe.

Fig. 1. *Hopi Men Getting Ready for A Buffalo Dance*. The man at left is preparing a sun symbol from eagle feathers (worn by the buffalo maidens, fig. 2), while the man at right prepares the headdress worn by the male buffalo dancers. Completed versions of both items hang on the kiva wall behind them, along with rain sashes and ceremonial kilts; lightning sticks (carried by male buffalo dancers) are propped against the wall. Painting by Fred Kabotie, about 1920.

Mus. of Northern Ariz., Flagstaff.

Fig. 2. *Buffalo Dance*. This is one of several so-called social dances (a variant of which is also done among the Eastern Pueblos—see "San Ildefonso Pueblo," figs. 10-12, this vol.). Participants include (left to right): the chorus (some of whom hold standards), 2 buffalo maidens (wearing sun symbols on their backs), and 2 buffalo dancers. (For an almost contemporaneous photograph showing this same scene, see Hightower 1977:120-121). Watercolor painting by Fred Kabotie, about 1920.

Owaqol (ʔowáqölỏ, ʔowáqöl-) of the ʔowáqöLt; the sequence of occurrence differs somewhat among the villages. Then comes Wuwuchim (wíwicìm), the ceremonies of the four men's societies: the kʷáˑkʷaNt (Agave), ʔáˑʔaLt (Horn), wíwicìMt (Wuwuchim), and táˑtawkam (Singers); the Wuwuchim ceremony (fig. 3) takes its name from the Wuwuchim Society, but the name has no other known meaning. Wuwuchim includes in principle an initiation ceremony every fourth year (for Oraibi, which is somewhat different, see Titiev 1944:131), which corre-

Mennonite Lib. and Arch., North Newton, Kansas.

Fig. 3. Wuwuchim ceremonial. Wuwuchim society members dancing in plaza in Oraibi before the village divided. They are led by two Alosaka, priests of the Horn Society, who represent Mountain Sheep. The members dance in a sideways step, with fingers intertwined, and are accompanied by a drummer (center). The songs sometimes taunt the women of the Maraw Society who douse the dancers with water. The hair ornaments are cutouts representing flowers. Photograph by H.R. Voth, before 1906.

sponds to the initiation into manhood; the initiation into the women's ceremonies is not of equivalent importance. Finally comes the most important ceremony of all, Soyal, which marks the winter solstice (fig. 4); the Hopi designation is *soyála* (Third Mesa *soˑyal*), or *soyal-* in compounds.

The dates of the ceremonies are determined by the position of the sun and, to a lesser extent, by the lunar calendar. For most ceremonies the sequence of ritual preparations is begun when the sun is observed to rise or set over a particular landmark on the horizon, the geographic features used being different from village to village. In contrast, the date of *powámi* is determined by that of the new moon of the lunar month *powámiyàw*, at least on First and Third Mesas, and the date of the Snake-Antelope and Flute ceremonies by both the moon of the summer month *páˑmiyàw* and the (solar-determined) date of Niman, which these ceremonies must follow (Stephen 1936, 1:136, 155, 577-767; Titiev 1944:244; McCluskey 1977:188-190).

The lunar calendar has 12 months in most years, but every two or three years (7 or 8 out of every 19) an additional month is intercalated between the eleventh month and the last month. This intercalary month is necessary to keep the lunar year (in which 12 months total only approximately 354.37 days) roughly in step with the solar year of approximately 365.24 days. The eighth through (ordinary) twelfth months of summer have the same names as the first through fifth months of winter, but there are also alternate names for some of the

565

John R. Wilson, Tulsa, Okla.: Mora #173.

Fig. 4. "Opening" the kivas for the kachina season at Walpi. Auhalani (center kachina) and his two corn-maiden sisters, Sikyamana or Yellow Corn Girl (carrying a tray of upright ears of yellow corn) and Sakwapmana or Blue Corn Girl (carrying blue corn) generally appear on the 6th day of the Soyal ceremony and go on a circuit throughout the village, singing what is in effect an announcement of the coming kachina season (Wright 1973:14-16). They have just emerged from the Chief kiva (out of view at right) with Supela, the Soyal Chief, who holds a basket of cornmeal with which he will sprinkle the kachinas. At Oraibi, the Soyal kachina (impersonated by Soyal Chief), rather than Auhalani, inaugurates the kachina season. Photograph by Jo Mora, 1902-1904.

summer months, which, like that of the intercalary month, tend to be given differently in sources from different villages. The outline of the basic lunar calendar in table 1 gives the most firmly attested month names and translations.

The first month, *kélmɨyàw*, is the Initiates' Moon, the time of the Wuwuchim ceremony. An initiate or neophyte in a society is called *ké·le* (pl. *ké·keLɨ*) 'sparrow hawk' (Stephen 1936, 2:1229); *-mɨyaw* is the compounding form of *mɨ·yàwɨ* 'month, moon'. The Dangerous Moon, *ká·mɨyàw,* is the month of the Soyal ceremony, which requires the observance of numerous prohibitions and taboos to prevent misfortune. The name of *pá·mɨyàw* has been taken as the Water (*pá·hɨ*) or Prayer-stick (*pá·ho*) Moon, or as the Play or Foolish Moon. In this month the prohibitions are lifted, and it is the time for pastime dances (Butterfly, Buffalo) and amusements (fig. 6). It is also referred to as *qacínam ʔóki* 'the kachinas return, are back' and *qacínam nóŋa* 'the kachinas come up', a reference to their ascent at this time through the sipapu from their home in the underworld (Parsons in Stephen 1936, 2:1037). *powámɨyàw* is the month of the purification by the kachinas of the first ceremonial plantings inside the kiva and the purification that terminates the Powamu ceremony. *ʔösömɨyàw* is the Whistling Moon (compare *ʔösö* 'gives a low whistle'), when the soft wind whistles, or the Cactus Moon (*ʔösö* 'Opuntia cac-

Mus. of the Amer. Ind., Heye Foundation, New York.

Fig. 5. *Young Men at the Shrine.* Young men placing willow prayer sticks at shrine identified as Somaikoli, a Second Mesa hunt shrine, which is one of many shrines visited at the time of the Soyal ceremonies. Also shown are antler and skull offerings, broken pottery (the bowl with which a newborn baby's hair is washed may be placed at the shrine), and a large pottery canteen containing offerings (Harvey 1970:29). Watercolor painting by Narron Lomayaktewa, one of 270 paintings documenting Hopi life commissioned from 5 Second Mesa Hopis under the aegis of the Mus. of the Amer. Ind., 1964-1965.

Federal Emergency Management Administration, Washington.

Fig. 6. Third Mesa butterfly dancers, posing before the dance in 1978. The men wear traditional white dance kilts with black, red, and green embroidery down one side, and black shirts with colored ribbons. The women wear black mantas, woven belts in red, black, and green, carved and painted tablita headdresses with butterfly and other designs, and fringes of false black hair across their foreheads. Both men and women have vertical red stripes painted on each cheek, similar to the "warriors' markings" described by Titiev (1972:339). Photograph by W. G. Williams, Aug. 1978, at Bacabi.

**Table 1. Hopi Lunar Calendar**

| Month Names | Range of Gregorian Calendar Dates of the New Moon |
|---|---|
| 1. *kélmɨyàw,* Initiates' Moon | mid Oct.–mid Nov. |
| 2. *ká·mɨyàw,* Dangerous Moon | Nov.–Dec. |
| 3. *pá·mɨyàw,* Water Moon | Dec.–Jan. |
| 4. *powámɨyàw,* Purification Moon | Jan.–Feb. |
| 5. *ʔösőmɨyàw,* Whistling or Cactus Moon | Feb.–Mar. |
| 6. *kʷiyámɨyàw,* Windbreak Moon | Mar.–Apr. |
| 7. *hakítonmɨyàw,* Waiting Moon | Apr.–May |
| 8. *kélmɨyàw; ʔɨyí(s)mɨyàw,* Planting Moon | May–June |
| 9. *ká·mɨyàw* ⎫ | ⎰ June–July |
| 10. *pá·mɨyàw* ⎬ also called "nameless moons" | ⎱ July–Aug. |
| 11. *powámɨyàw* ⎭ | Aug.–Sept. |
| (12. *nösánmɨyàw,* Feasting Moon; *höhőqmɨyàw,* Harvest Moon) | (Sept.) |
| 12. or 13. *ʔösőmɨyàw; tohósmɨ·yaw,* Autumn Moon | Sept.–Oct. |

NOTE: The parenthesized 12th month is the intercalary month. The transcriptions of the names have been arrived at by comparing the available sources and may contain errors of detail. The range of dates of the new moon of each Hopi month is from mid-month to mid-month on the Gregorian calendar for the last month and the early months of the Hopi year, falling back gradually to a range of early August to early September for the 11th month; the new moon of the intercalary month comes in early or mid-Sept. For a hypothesis of the specific dates see McCluskey (1977:177), who is followed here with the addition of the intercalary month, which he does not account for. Other sources: Stephen 1936, 2:852, 953, 1037–1040; Whorf 1936; Titiev 1938a, 1944:174; Frigout 1962–1965; Fewkes 1892:151–159, 1897:256–257; Beaglehole 1937:23–25; Curtis 1907–1930, 12:250–251.

tus'). The Windbreak Moon, *kʷiyámɨyàw,* is when rabbit brush (*siváʰpi; Chrysothamnus nauseosus*) is gathered and set out in lines for protection where the seeds are to be planted. The Waiting Moon, *hakítonmɨyàw,* when the favorable moment for planting is awaited, is also called the sweet-corn-planting month (Parsons in Stephen 1936, 2:1037), because it includes the time of the first ceremonial planting of sweet corn. The *kélmɨyàw* of summer is also called (Third Mesa) *ʔɨyimɨya* or (First Mesa?) *ʔɨyísmɨyàw,* Planting Moon (Third Mesa *ʔɨyis* 'early summer, planting time'). The intercalary month is most often said to be called *nösánmɨyàw,* Feasting Moon (compare *nő·sa* 'eats (it)'; Whorf 1936:1260, 1265) or *höhőqmɨyàw,* Harvest Moon (compare Third Mesa *hőhőqö* 'he is harvesting'; Voegelin and Voegelin 1957:21); the first part of the second name is also spelled hüük-, höök-, and hüúkɨ- (Fewkes 1897:257; Curtis 1907–1930, 12:251; Parsons in Stephen 1936, 2:1038). The alternate name of the last month is based on (Third Mesa) *tɨhoʔos* 'autumn' (Voegelin and Voegelin 1957:15) and is also interpreted as Basket-Carrying Moon. Since none of the investigators figured out how the intercalation of the extra month worked, there is particularly extensive disagreement among them over the names of the final months of the Hopi year.

The Niman, Snake-Antelope, and Flute ceremonies, and those of the *mámraWt* and *lálakòNt* societies, have not only an announcement during the month when each is performed but also a preliminary announcement during the winter month that is homonymous with it. The reason why, inversely, Wuwuchim, Soyal, and Powamu are not announced in the summer is not exactly known. A ceremony is announced six months before by means of

a sort of minor celebration of the same ceremony (Fewkes 1898a:67, 1902a:494; Titiev 1944:175).

Some Hopis begin the year with Wuwuchim, which includes a new fire ceremony, others with Soyal and the winter solstice, and still others with Powamu, the first great ceremony of the kachina and the start of the agricultural season (Frigout 1962–1965).

**The Ceremonies**

There is a general plan common to all the ceremonies, although notable differences appear according to the ceremony, the village, and the year.

All the great ceremonies last eight full ceremonial days, grouped into two sets of four, plus a preliminary day for entering into session, hence nine days altogether according to the following scheme (after Stephen 1936, 1:162, 104, 2:930–931; Parsons in Stephen 1936, 2:1041; Titiev 1944:105; Voth 1901:84):

| Day | Meaning |
|---|---|
| 1. *yúŋʸa* | 'they enter, assemble in kiva' |
| 2. *sɨs-tá·la* | 'the first day', or *sós kahími* 'all (do) nothing' |
| 3. *lő́s-tá·la* | 'the second day' |
| 4. *páyis-tá·la* | 'the third day' |
| 5. *ná·lös-tá·la* | 'the fourth day' |
| 6. *sɨs-tá·la* or *sós kahími* | |
| 7. *komóktotòka* | 'wood-carrying sleep (i.e., day)' |
| (Third Mesa *piktotoka* | 'piki(-making) sleep') |
| 8. *totóka* | 'sleep' |
| 9. *tí·kìveʔ* | 'at the dance' |

Short ceremonies last four days, plus the preliminary day. It is also possible to double the duration of the ceremony when it is considered to be particularly important, such as for Wuwuchim in years of initiation (Titiev 1944:104). It consists then generally of two times eight plus one, making 17 days. Sometimes it takes even 20 days. The first days include mostly secret rituals that are principally performed in the kiva, while the second part includes mostly public rites conducted mainly in the plaza, constituting the festive aspect. There are other locations that also play a role, such as the clan house (which replaces the kiva for the Flute ceremony) and various sanctuaries.

The kivas or ceremonial chambers (Hopi *kíva*, sg.) are constructed separately from the dwellings. They are either subterranean or semisubterranean and are rectangular among the Hopi. Ceremonial access is by means of a ladder passing through the trap door constructed in the roof and resting on the floor of the kiva, near the fireplace. The floor is divided into two parts, an elevated platform for the public when they are admitted, and a lower level where the participants perform, which is generally provided with wall benches (see "Hopi World View," fig. 3, this vol.). In the lower level is the sipapu (*sípàpì*, Third Mesa *sípa·pì*), a hole dug in the ground symbolizing the place of emergence, which is supposed to communicate with the underworld. It is covered with a wooden plug in normal times and uncovered when in use (Mindeleff 1891:117, 121, 123; Titiev 1944:103–104). There are several kivas per village. The plaza where the public performances occur is traditionally considered to be the principal place of the village. It generally shelters a sanctuary called *pahóki*, literally 'prayer-stick house'. Shongopavi is the only village where there are two plazas, one with and one without a *pahóki* (Frigout 1962–1965).

At the start of a ceremony, there is first a meeting either in the clan house or in the kiva, where the participants smoke, prepare offerings, and arrange the announcement. This announcement is effectuated on top of a house roof by the Crier chief, the spokesman for the village chief. These religious announcements differ from everyday announcements and are addressed more to the Clouds than to the inhabitants of the village. The beginning of the ceremony as such is marked by the erection of a standard (a decorated pole called a *ná'ci*) at one side or on the ladder of the kiva that houses the ceremony (fig. 7).

Fig. 7. Guard at the entrance to the Antelope kiva at the First Mesa village of Walpi, during the Snake-Antelope ceremony. A standard *(ná'ci)*, composed of a bow to which red horsehair has been attached, hangs on the ladder. The bow standards for the Snake and Antelope societies are similar; on Third Mesa (where the ceremony differs somewhat), the Snake Society bow standard includes animal skins and eagle feathers. In the matting in front of the kiva is a snake whip (whip standard; Voth 1903:285, pl. 155), used in addition to the bow standard, to indicate ceremonial activity within the kiva. Photograph by C. C. Pierce or G. Wharton James (copyright by C. C. Pierce), about 1898.

Fig. 8. Hopi runners, on unknown occasion, approaching Oraibi from Kyakotsmovi (New Oraibi). Races may be run on a variety of ceremonial occasions and may also be run by kiva groups and by racing kachinas who challenge the villagers to race. The kiva races usually involve kicking a specially prepared seed-filled ball around the course. Photograph by L. L. Hargrave, 1929.

Fig. 9. *Clowns Between the Dances*. Ritual clowns shown here include Koyimse clowns or Mudheads (the three figures standing at center with drum) and Chuku (Third Mesa *ciki*) clowns (standing and being offered food by the women at center), who are thought to be the true Hopi clowns. Also shown are kachinas who often appear with the clowns: the Angwusi or Crow kachina (figure seated at left), a warrior kachina who threatens the clowns; Mongkachina 'Great Horned Owl kachina' (standing between Mudheads at center), who with the other warrior kachinas punishes the clowns for their misbehavior; and Kokopelmana, the female counterpart of Kokopeli (the Humpbacked Flute Player) who mimics copulation with selected challengers. (See Wright 1973 for kachina identifications.) Painting by Hopi artist Otis Polelonema, 1966.

Fig. 10. Koyala clowns (with striped decorations) engaged in a mock tug-of-war under the direction of a Chuku or Hopi clown at a kachina dance. The Koyala were introduced by the Tewa from the Rio Grande region and the Koyimse (see fig. 9) are of Zuni origin (see Titiev 1972a). Photograph by Jo Mora at Sichomovi, 1905.

From this moment on no one, unless he is a member of the participating fraternity, can enter the kiva. As for the participants, throughout the ceremony they must observe sexual continence and abstain from salt and meat (Titiev 1944:60, 104).

Inside the kiva the most important ceremonies consist of smoking, singing, praying, and erecting altars. The songs may accompany dances, which may include imitative sequences. Some of these songs and dances, rhythmically accompanied by gourd rattles and by tortoise shells

Smithsonian, Dept. of Anthr.: 212,659, 22,934, 9567.

Fig. 11. Salako and Salako maiden kachina dolls in flat and rounded styles prevalent in the 19th century; in the 20th century there has been a trend toward more realistic, 3-dimensional representations (see "Pueblo Fine Arts," fig. 5, this vol.; Dockstader 1954:95–106; Erikson 1977). left, Salako maiden, carved in the flat style that was probably characteristic of the earliest kachina dolls, collected before 1902. center, Salako carved in a transitional flat-rounded style, probably collected in 1876. right, Salako maiden carved in a rounded style, collected in 1869 and thought to be the earliest collected kachina doll in a museum collection. The Salako and Salako maiden (Colton 1959:47) are only 2 among hundreds of recorded kachina representations (see Fewkes 1903; Colton 1959; Wright 1977). Height of kachina at left 23 cm, others (both virtually destroyed in a 1965 fire) same scale.

attached to the dancers' lower legs, serve as practice for the public performance. The act of smoking is very important because clouds of smoke are considered to favor the appearance of rain clouds (cf. Stephen 1936, 1:106). The altars erected in the kiva consist of vertical slabs, with symbolic or realistic paintings of maize, clouds, lightning, sacred animals, and cult heroes. On the ground in front are displayed objects, in particular: the *típòni,* fetishes of the chiefs (Stephen 1936, 2:1305), effigies of sky and earth gods and of cult patrons (Titiev 1944:105), and the medicine bowl holding spring water. This last is placed in the middle of a figure drawn on sand, with six lines of sacred cornmeal corresponding to the six directions, on each of which is an ear of maize of a color corresponding to the traditional association: yellow for the northwest, turquoise blue for the southwest, red for the southeast, white for the northeast, black for above, and speckled for below (see also "Hopi World View," this vol.). This traditional order of the four or six directions, beginning with the northeast and proceeding counterclockwise in the manner that Fewkes calls the ceremonial circuit, is also followed in numerous ritual acts, such as the sprinkling of water and cornmeal (Fewkes 1892b, 1901:215). Generally on the next to last day the altars are dismantled and the sand paintings erased (Titiev 1944:106).

Usually on the last day or two the most important public performances take place: dances or simply the depositing of offerings at the *pahóki* or at other sacred places, the distribution of provisions, or races that begin at a sanctuary or a sacred spring and tend to lead the clouds or other benefits of the gods into the village (fig. 8). The principal dances on the plaza move according to the counterclockwise ceremonial circuit (Fewkes 1892b:39; Frigout 1962–1965). The public gathers all around the plaza, on benches in front of the houses, and on the roofs.

After these public performances the participants sleep in the kiva and continue their abstinences for four days. Before taking up ordinary life again and mingling with others they must purify themselves by a rite called *ná·vocìwa* 'he exorcizes himself', which consists in sprinkling ashes with the left hand on the participant or the ceremonial object (Parsons 1939, 1:457–460; Titiev 1944:106). Contact with ceremonial secrets is considered to be dangerous; without this purification it may bring on the participants the same sickness that the secret society in question is supposed to control, each society having its specific sickness (Titiev 1944:106).

*Kachinas*

Night dances begin on First and Third Mesas with the Soyal, on Second Mesa after the Powamu. Each kiva in the village organizes its dance, repeats it, and in the evening goes to perform it in all the other kivas. The

Fig. 12. Powamu kachinas in the plaza at Walpi. These kachinas are ogres who go from house to house during Powamu to scare children into obedience to their parents. They are (left to right): Hahaiwuhti (a mother of the kachinas) who leads the procession, a Black Natashka, Soyokmana (Natashka kachina girl), Soyokwuhti (grandmother of Natashka), a White Natashka, 3 Black Natashkas, a White Natashka, and 3 Heheya kachinas (who pretend to copulate with spectators). Photograph by James Mooney, Feb. 1893.

Fig. 13. Humisi ('corn flower') kachinas dancing during a Niman ceremony. The "father" of the kachinas (at right) is a member of the Powamu society who leads the kachinas in and out of the plaza, "feeds" them (by sprinkling them with cornmeal) and represents the village to the kachinas. The melons and cornstalks at right are for distribution by the kachinas to the audience. Not shown are the Humismanas who appear with the Humisi. Photograph by Adam C. Vroman at Shongopavi, 1901.

HOPI CEREMONIAL ORGANIZATION

Fig. 14. Public performance of the Snake-Antelope ceremony at Oraibi, 1898 and 1902. left, Building the bowers to be used in the plaza dances later that afternoon when the Antelope priest dances with vines in his mouth; the bower is constructed of cottonwood boughs and long reeds gathered that morning. Photograph by Adam C. Vroman, 1898. right, Antelope dancers (wearing white kilts with brocaded sashes, and horizontal lines painted just above their mouths) stand in a line in front of the bower beating time with their rattles as the Snake dancers dance in the plaza with live snakes in their mouths on the afternoon of the 9th day; the wooden plank at their feet covers a symbolic sipapu or earth navel. Photograph by C. C. Pierce or G. Wharton James (copyright by C. C. Pierce), 1902. The Snake and Antelope ceremonials were extensively photographed (see Webb and Weinstein 1973:85-102) and written about (see Fewkes 1894b; Voth 1903) during this period.

public, invited by the kiva chief, is then admitted into the kiva (Titiev 1944:112-114). One of the most famous variants of the night dances is the dance of *pá·lölòqaŋʷɨ,* the Horned Water Serpent, in which puppets represent the mythical serpents (Fewkes and Stephen 1893; Stephen 1936, 1:287-324; Titiev 1944:121-123).

The day dances succeed the night dances about April. The masked dancers conducted by their "father," who traces their route in maize flour, arrive in the plaza with the sunrise and dance in place in a line, one behind the others, in several successive locations, generally three. In the intervals between the dances during the day the kachinas distribute gifts, particularly foods, and there are some comical interludes performed by different kinds of clowns (figs. 9-10) (Stephen 1936, 1:350-463; Earle and Kennard 1938:29-33; Titiev 1944:126-128). The very popular Koyimse are kachinas but they also participate in comical acts. For a more thorough discussion of clowning see Titiev (1972a) and Hieb (1972).

There are also some solitary appearances of kachinas, such as that of the Sòyal kachina who comes (on Second Mesa the day after the Soyal, on Third Mesa 16 days before) to open the kivas symbolically for the kachinas coming from all directions (Titiev 1944:110).

At Powamu beans and maize are ritually planted inside the kivas, to assure good harvests and to demonstrate the "good heart" of the participants (Titiev 1944:114-115). Small boys and girls, after having been whipped (or not,

according to whether they are entering the Kachina society or the Powamu society, and according to the village) are shown, by attending a performance of unmasked dancers, that the kachinas are none other than their relatives and other villagers (Talayesva 1942:83-84). The afternoon of the ninth day the kachinas go about in the village (fig. 12), but there is no organized dance (Voth 1901:114-117; Titiev 1944:115, 117-118). The Niman ceremony usually consists of a personification of the male and female Humisi kachinas (fig. 13), the female figures imitating corn grinding (Titiev 1944:128; Stephen 1936, 1:533, 575). Some eagles, previously captured and kept on the house roofs, at the end of the ceremony are ritually suffocated so that they will carry the people's messages to the spirits (Voth 1912a:108; Stephen 1936, 1:568-569). At Powamu as at Niman the kachinas bring many presents, especially to children: kachina dolls for girls; toy bows and arrows, ball games, and rattles for boys (Titiev 1944:232, 115, 117-118).

The kachina masks are considered to be incarnations of the ancestors, more or less individualized, who spend half the year with the Hopis and the other half in the subterranean world (Titiev 1944:109, 129).

### Snake-Antelope and Flute

The Snake and Antelope societies perform a single ceremony, but only the Snake men go to hunt snakes on four days, successively to the northwest, southwest,

Los Angeles Co. Mus.

Fig. 15. Ninth day of the Mishongnovi Flute ceremony, 1902. The Flute ceremony and the Snake-Antelope ceremony are held in alternate years in any given village and follow the same basic pattern of 8 days of nonpublic ritual followed by 1 day of public ritual. Here the Flute men sit at Toreva Springs, the sacred springs below the mesa where the "entrances" to the underworld and the homes of the Horned Water Serpents and the clouds are located; a priest (standing in the springs) is hunting for 3 water jars, which he will symbolically obtain from the underworld, which will then be carried in procession to the plaza. Photograph by Adam C. Vroman.

southeast, and northeast of the village (Voth 1903: 286-290; Stephen 1936, 1:587, 726, 732, 736). The evenings of the fifth and sixth days the two groups gather in the Antelope kiva where a man and a woman are costumed to represent the heroes of the Snake myth (Voth 1903:310). The mornings of the eighth and ninth days there is a race, the winner bringing a gourd full of water to the village (Voth 1903:323-327, 337). The afternoons of the same days the Snakes and the Antelopes dance in the plaza, near the kí·si (a bower of cottonwood erected there for the ceremony). The ninth day the Snakes dance while holding in their mouths living snakes taken out of the kí·si (fig. 14). Afterward the snakes are set free far from the village in sacred places situated at the four Hopi cardinal directions, and the dancers take an emetic (Voth 1903:334-336, 345-348; Stephen 1936, 1:707-709, 712, 754-756, 763-764).

There are two Flute societies: the Blue Flute and the Gray Flute (except at Walpi where there is only one). A particular mythico-historical episode took place at Wal-

pi, when the members of the Flute society returning to the village found their way blocked by the chiefs of the Bear clan and the Snake clan, then by a personage representing ʔálwisàqa, and they did not finally gain access to the village until the promise of bringing rain in the middle of their ceremony (Stephen 1936, 2:769, 805-811). On the evening of the ninth day there is a race like the one for the Snake and Antelope ceremony. In the afternoon the Blue Flutes followed by the Gray Flutes go toward the kí·si while drawing cloud symbols on the ground with maize flour (Stephen 1936, 2:816-817; Titiev 1944:147-148).

Titiev (1944:153-154) classes the Snake-Antelope and Flute ceremonies (fig. 15) among the solar ceremonies, with the Soyal.

## Women's Rites

At the Maraw ceremony the caricature dances can take place on the plaza the next to the last days (Stephen 1936, 2:899). At the Lakon ceremony there is a women's race the eighth day, at least at Walpi, and a men's race the ninth day (Stephen 1936, 2:851-852; Fewkes and Owens 1892:123-125). At the Owaqol ceremony there is a men's race the ninth day (Voth 1903a: 40-41).

On the ninth day two protagonists direct themselves toward the dance circle on the plaza, which is moving at Maraw and at Owaqol, but fixed at Lakon: at Maraw they aim some arrows toward a bundle of vines thrown on the ground (followed at Oraibi by two others with lances and hoops); at Lakon they throw ears of corn (yellow for the northwest, blue for the southwest, red for the southeast, white for the northeast) into the cloud symbols traced in cornmeal; at Owaqol they aim a corn husk at a hoop. Many presents are then thrown by these protagonists toward the spectators at Lakon (fig. 16) and at Owaqol (Voth 1912:66, 1903a:42-43; Fewkes and Owens 1892:126-128; Stephen 1936, 2:855, 909).

The Maraw rites are considered to relate to war and fertility (among other things) while those of Lakon and Owaqol relate particularly to fertility.

## Initiation

When adolescent boys are initiated into the Wuwuchim, Singers, Horns, or Agaves, the four societies gather on the first day in a common kiva for the lighting of a new fire, at which time an Agave member personifies másàwi (Fewkes and Stephen 1892:195; Titiev 1944:131), the god of death and the owner of the earth, who in the myths welcomed men on their emergence from the subterranean world and gave them fire (Titiev 1944:138; Colton 1959:78). The initiation is considered to be like a birth into adult life and is probably at the same time the introduction to the society of spirits to which the individual will belong when he dies (Fewkes and Stephen 1892:197-199; Titiev 1944:136). The fourth day all the roads leading into the village are blocked off, except for one at the northwest by which, at least at Oraibi, tradition

Fig. 16. Basket Dance (in which many specially prepared baskets are thrown to the spectators) performed in the plaza at Oraibi on the 9th day of a Lakon ceremony (see Fewkes 1899b:84–85 for other photographs in this series). The public dances of the Lakon and Owaqol societies are somewhat similar (see Fewkes and Owens 1892; Voth 1903a for extensive descriptions), each generally having two special priestesses or maidens who dress in characteristic headdress and costume. On this occasion there were 4 rather than 2 Lakon Maidens, one of whom can be seen at the opening of the circle throwing a basket. Photographer unknown, possibly G. Wharton James, E.E. Palmer, or G.L. Rose (all credited elsewhere with photographs of this event), Oct. 26, 1898.

says that the dead will return during the night to the abandoned half of the village to eat the food prepared by the women. Some Agaves are sent to the burial grounds, where it is believed that they disinter cadavers in order to borrow their clothes to wear before the initiates (Titiev 1944:135–136).

The Wuwuchim and the Singers dance in public several days in a row, surrounded by the Horns. The ninth day the Agaves trace a path of maize flour on the plaza, departing from the west; then they efface it in order to reestablish the customary dissociation between the dead and the living (Fewkes and Stephen 1892:217; Titiev 1944:132, 136).

The Wuwuchim and the Singers are particularly associated with fertility, the Agaves with war, and the Horns with hunting. The Wuwuchim and Maraw societies are considered to be socio-ceremonially connected (Titiev 1944:168; Eggan 1950:93, 100).

### Winter Solstice

Initiation at Wuwuchim is necessary in order to participate in Soyal. Most of the Soyal rites take place in the kiva. One of the most significant occurs on the evening of the ninth day and consists in a dancer depicting the hesitant course of the sun returning toward the summer solstice. At Oraibi a Star Priest turns a solar symbol; at Walpi a group of Singers forces the carrier of a shield in the form of a sun to return into the correct road (Dorsey and Voth 1901:54–55; Stephen 1936, 1:22–24). The first evening the participants in the Soyal give back to their relatives and friends the prayer-sticks (páˑho, sg.) that they have prepared for their use. These prayer-sticks are then deposited in the proper sanctuaries, generally one by the men, the other by the women in each village (Dorsey and Voth 1901:57; Titiev 1944:144).

The so-called social dances that follow, such as the

# Table 2. Major Hopi Ceremonies and Their Society, Clan, and Kiva Affiliations

| Ceremony and Society | Oraibi before 1900 | | Shongopavi | | Mishongnovi | | Walpi | |
|---|---|---|---|---|---|---|---|---|
| | Controlling Clan | Home Kiva | Controlling Clan | Home Kiva | Controlling Clan | Home Kiva | Controlling Clan | Home Kiva |
| **Initiation (Wuwuchim)** | | | | | | | | |
| Wuwuchim | Sparrow Hawk[a] | Hawiovi | Corn and Bluebird | Bluebird | Coyote and Squash | Badger | [Squash] Mustard | Wikwalovi |
| Singer | Parrot | Singer | Bear and Kachina | Parrot | Parrot[a] | Parrot | Tobacco[a] | Chief |
| Horn | Bow | Middle | Fog[a] and Patki | Horn | Patki | Horn | Bear and Reed | Horn |
| Agave | Masawu | Agave | Kachina, Sun, and Snow | Snow Mountain | Lizard | Kochovi | Patki | Goat |
| Soyal | Bear | Blue Flute | Bear | Parrot | Bear(?), Lizard | Horn | Patki | Chief |
| **Powamu** | | | | | | | | |
| Powamu | Badger | Hochichivi | Kachina and Bear | Parrot | Kachina | Kochovi | Kachina-Parrot | Chief |
| Kachina | Kachina | Hawiovi | Kachina | Parrot | Kachina | Kochovi | Kachina-Parrot | Chief |
| Niman | Kachina | (rotates) | Kachina | (rotates) | Kachina | (rotates) | Kachina-Parrot | (rotates) |
| Blue Flute | Spider | Blue Flute | Patki | (clanhouse) | Parrot | (clanhouse) | Millet | (clanhouse) |
| Gray Flute | Patki | Hawiovi | Bear | (clanhouse) | Squash | (clanhouse) | [Squash] | — |
| Snake | Snake | Snake | Sun and Sun's Forehead | Nuvaovi | Lizard | Badger | Snake-Cactus | Wikwalovi |
| Antelope | Spider | Middle | Carrying Strap | Parrot | Bear | Horn | Snake-Dove | Chief |
| Maraw | Lizard | Maraw | Bluebird | Parrot | Parrot | Badger | [Squash] Snake | Horn |
| Owaqol | Sand | Hawiovi | Bear | Parrot | Badger | Badger | Reed-Eagle | Young Corn Mound |
| Lakon | Parrot | Hawiovi | Snow | Parrot | Lizard | Kochovi | Patki | Goat |

SOURCE: Eggan 1950:103, which gives variations from this summary.

[a] Clan of chief in general charge.

[ ] Extinct clan.

Buffalo, are mixed dances with a chorus of men, performed both for obtaining blessings (moisture, game animals) and for pleasure. Formerly they apparently had some relationship with war (Fewkes 1902a:507, 1910a:588–589; Stephen 1936, 1:125, 126, 128, 130; Titiev 1938a:107).

## War

When the Hopi still made war the Warrior Society (Third Mesa mo·mcit) held an annual ceremony, either in the autumn (reported for Oraibi) or just after Soyal (reported for Walpi), at which a war medicine was prepared and a public dance was performed. In the autumn, after the harvest, was the traditional time for going to war, and when the warriors (qalé[h]taqa, sg.) returned and were welcomed back to the village by the women there was a scalp dance (Mishongnovi ʔósnìna tìva; Third Mesa qalê·ti), also referred to as the Market Dance (Third Mesa ho·winaʔay), though the latter has also been described as a harvest dance of thanksgiving (Mishongnovi hoyna; First Mesa Howina and variants). The celebration of a war dance in the fall continued for some years after the end of traditional warfare (Titiev 1944:156-163; Stephen 1936, 1:83-96, 2:911).

### Societies, Clans, and Kivas

Each ceremony reflected a triple membership in a society, a clan, and a kiva (table 2) but with no precise correspondence between the society and the clan and not with identical systems in each village (Mindeleff 1891: 133-134; Stephen 1936, 2:1169-1179; Eggan 1950: 89-106).

Each ceremony is controlled in principle by a clan, or sometimes by several. The clan and especially a lineage within the clan is in charge of the ceremonial paraphernalia and furnishes the chief official who must of course be initiated in the society and is thus at the intersection of the society and the clan. The charge is transmitted within the lineage, or if this becomes extinct, within the clan; if the clan becomes extinct, it stays in the phratry. In some cases a ceremony can be put on by any person who claims it (Stephen 1936, 2:958-959; Eggan 1950:90).

Mythically the ceremony was "given" by the gods or the heroes to the clan after the emergence, an explanation that is not consistent with the variety of socio-ceremonial associations from village to village (Eggan 1950:90-104). In fact, each ceremony is put on by one or several secret societies, the membership of which does not depend on clan affiliation. Each postulant has a ceremonial father who belongs to another clan and who initiates him to all the societies to which he himself belongs.

In any case, each ceremony is conducted by a village within a given kiva (except in the case of the Flute), which was constructed by one or several clans that are its proprietors. It is difficult to agree with Parsons that the clan association is primary, because the kiva membership is ceremonial (Eggan 1950:96). Each man is basically associated with the kiva of the men's society into which he was initiated; he belongs secondarily to other kivas for other ceremonies. At an earlier age each child or adolescent goes to the kiva where he was initiated into the kachinas. The number of kivas varies with the village: five at Walpi, two at Sichomovi, two at Tewa Village; five at Shongopavi, four at Mishongnovi, three at Shipaulovi; six at Hotevilla, three at Old Oraibi, three at Kyakotsmovi, two at Bacabi, and five at Moenkopi.

Within a ceremony certain rites belong to certain clans; for instance, a man of the Tobacco clan prepares the pipe and a man of the Sand clan brings the sand for the altar (Eggan 1950:102).

# Hopi World View

LOUIS A. HIEB

A people's world view is "their picture of the way things, in sheer actuality are, their concept of nature, of self, of society. It contains their most comprehensive ideas of order" (Geertz 1958:421–422). World view is, thus, to be understood as a people's way of selecting, classifying, and structuring reality and is concerned with the logical properties of belief. However, as Leach (1968:3) has noted, "the components of a religious system are meaningful not only because of their internal coherence but because of their practical integration with the secular life of the congregation." Religion is felt to be not only logically true but also empirically true, that is, its validity is equally derivable from its relationship to everyday realities. A description of world view should, at least in some minimal fashion, attempt to indicate connections with other symbol systems, like art, architecture, and social organization.

## The Bipartite Universe

Titiev (1944:107–108, 171–178) has provided an extensive discussion of the bipartite structure of the Hopi universe. One of the fundamental elements of Hopi world view is:

> the concept of a dual division of time and space between the upper world of the living and the lower world of the dead. This is expressed in the description of the sun's journey on its daily rounds. The Hopi believe that the sun has two entrances, variously referred to as houses, homes or kivas, situated at each extremity of its course. In the morning the sun is supposed to emerge from its eastern house, and in the evening it is said to descend into its western home. During the night the sun must travel underground from west to east in order to be ready to arise at its accustomed place the next day. Hence day and night are reversed in the upper and lower worlds . . . (Titiev 1944:173).

Life and death, day and night, summer and winter are seen not simply as opposed but as involved in a system of alternation and continuity—indeed, a fundamental consubstantiality. Death is "birth" into a new world, and many Hopi burial practices (cf. Stephen 1936, 2:824–825) parallel those of birth except that four black lines of charcoal separate the dead from his home in the village while four white lines of cornmeal mark the walls of a newborn baby's home.

This world and the world of spirits are transformations of each other. At death a cotton mask—a "white cloud mask" (Stephen 1936, 2:825)—is placed on the face of a dead person. The spirits of the dead return to this world as kachinas. All kachinas are believed to take on cloud form—to be cloud people—and their spiritual essence, or navala, is a liquid that is manifested as rainfall. When the kachinas (as ritual figures) depart, they are petitioned, "When you return to your homes bring this message to them that, without delay, they may have mercy for us with their liquid essence [rain] so that all things may grow and life may be bountiful." Everything, in Hopi belief, is dependent on rainfall, which, when combined with Mother Earth, is the essence of all things. Hence navala is also the essence of the individual self, conceived of as a liquid, and a Hopi will say, "I have the liquid essence of my fathers," to express the English notion of being of the same flesh and blood. Through the combination of the rain with the earth and its transformation into corn, the blessings of the kachinas (their navala) become the essence of our bodies (our navala). There is, thus, an essential consubstantiality in the bipartite structure of the Hopi universe that relates cotton masks and clouds, the living and the dead, rain and life.

## The System of Correspondences

In ritual, songs, prayers, masks, and altars, concepts of space, time, color, and number (as both sequence and quantity) are interrelated paradigmatically. Expressed together, they form the basis of an elaborate system of correspondences that orders much of what is significant in the Hopi world by relating a vast number of domains within a bipartite universe. This forms a system of symbolic classification, which is one aspect of the Hopi world view.

Fundamental to this system is the spatial orientation of the traditional Hopi, which is related to the four most distant points reached by the sun in its apparent movement during the year along the eastern and western horizons. These define the four cardinal directions, *kwiníwi* 'northwest' (at the horizon point of the summer-solstice sunset), *té·veŋà* 'southwest' (winter-solstice sunset), *tá·tȫqa* 'southeast' (winter-solstice sunrise), and *hó·pòqa* 'northeast' (summer-solstice sunrise), in addition to which *ʔó·mi* 'above' and *ʔatkámi* 'below' are also treated as primary directions. Certain colors are associated with each direction (fig. 1), and nearly every ritual act expresses this fundamental conception of order in being repeated four or six times in time, or space, or both (Stephen 1898:261-262, 1936, 2:1190-1191). Stephen (1898:261-262) explained that the northwest was yellow "because the anthropomorphic deity who sits there is yellow, wearing a yellow cloud as a mask which covers his head and rests upon his shoulders; a multitude of yellow butterflies constantly flutters before the cloud, and yellow corn grows continually in that yellow land," and that below, associated with all colors, is where there "sits the deity regarded as the maker of all life germs. He sits upon a flowery mound on which grows all vegetation; he is speckled with all the colors, as also is his cloud mask, and before it flutter all the butterflies, and all the sacred birds." These associations have remained strong, even though the Hopi in the twentieth century have come to conform their directions to the cardinal points of the European compass, familiar from local road maps, by making *kwiniwi* north (Hieb 1969-1971; Stephen 1936, 2:1221, 1241, 1301, 1304).

This basic space-time-color-number paradigm provides the logical basis for an elaborate system of correspondences that find expression throughout Hopi ritual. Clouds, butterflies, corn, lightning, rains, winds, birds, animals, trees, shrubs, flowers, beans, and so on are ordered in terms of this schema in song and prayer and in Hopi religious thought. Various ritual paraphernalia are constructed in accordance with this paradigm. However, unlike the Tewa of the Rio Grande (Ortiz 1969) or the Zuni of western New Mexico (Cushing 1896), this schema does not in 1970 serve as a system of classification with practical consequences for social organization and the division of labor during the year's subsistence activities. Nor do the writings of Stephen (1898, 1936), Fewkes (1927), or Voth (1901, 1905, 1912) indicate a correspondence between this system of meaning and any system of action outside the ritual context at the turn of the twentieth century.

*Space*

The Hopi cultural construction of space is a quadripartite one to which are added "up" and "down." This spatial orientation is centrifugal, as illustrated in the Hopi "six directions altar" (fig. 2) (cf. Fewkes 1927). After sand is spread upon the floor of the kiva to form the "earth," a bowl (usually with cloud symbols on its four sides) of water is placed in the center. From this middle place paths of cornmeal radiate outward to the six directions and various objects (including ears of corn, feathers, animal fetishes) are added according to their positions in the system of correspondences. This spatial paradigm is articulated throughout Hopi ceremonialism. Rarely is a ritual act performed once but is, rather, given fourfold or sixfold expression according to the syntagmatic stereotype that derives from the basic paradigm: for example, yellow clouds come from the north, blue clouds from the west.

Unlike the Zuni, the Hopi do not articulate the notion of the "middle" in this schema; however, there are many middles. As prayers radiate centrifugally, the rain-bearing clouds are beckoned centripetally. The Hopi entered

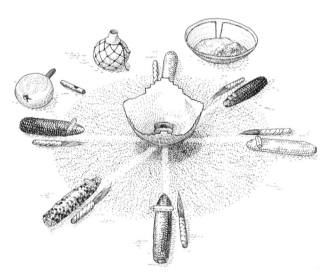

after Fewkes 1927:pl. 1 and Stephen 1936, 1:fig. 296.
Fig. 2. Six directions altar. An appropriately colored ear of corn rests on each end of the directional cornmeal axes. To the right of each is a pollen sprinkler (*makʷáNpi*), made of feathers bound together with either cotton or leather thongs. Pieces of quartz crystal and other minerals have been placed on each ear of corn and in the medicine bowl at the altar's earth center. The peripheral items, which seem to be more variable, are: a net-covered water gourd, a bone whistle, and a gourd rattle. This altar is one section of a more elaborate Niman ceremony altar that was recorded at Walpi in the 1890s by Fewkes (1927:pl. 3) and by Stephen, who in addition described the precise order in which the directions altar was laid out on 2 different days of the ceremony (Stephen 1936, 1:fig. 286, 2:figs. 512-513, 526).

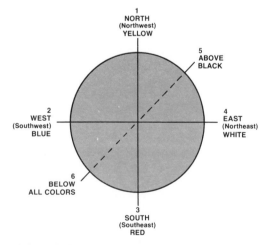

Fig. 1. Schematic diagram showing association of specific colors with each of the traditional 6 directions. When laid out symbolically on the plane surface of a kiva floor (see fig. 2), the up and down directions are represented on a diagonal axis.

this world at its middle, through Sipapu (Hopi *sípàpɨ*), which is said to be at the bottom of the Grand Canyon to the west of the Hopi villages. It is there that the dead travel to find their way to the world, the "house," below. Sipapu is represented, symbolically, by a covered hole in the floor of the kiva. The architectural form of the kiva (fig. 3), the dance positions assumed by the kachinas (*qacínam;* sg. *qacína*), various shrines in and around the village—all reduplicate this middle. To it prayer offerings are made and from it come blessings.

## Time

The dual organization of time provides a structural principle fundamental to Hopi religious belief and ritual action. The organization of the Hopi ritual calendar is based on this notion (see "Hopi Ceremonial Organization," this vol.). Time as quantity or as sequence is given fourfold expression throughout ritual. The major ceremonies of the priestly period begin 16 days after an "event" in the solar or lunar calendar and are followed by four days of prayer and fasting. Observances during the kachina period also involve fourfold expressions, and processions follow the counterclockwise sequence noted in figure 1.

## Color

The ritual construction of the continuum of color is sixfold: red, yellow, blue/green, black, white, and gray. In the system of correspondences the "color" for "down" is "all colors" but this is sometimes given ritual represen-tation by gray. A distinct series of colors is thus established, which makes color an important symbolic classifier: first, because the six colors are easily represented by living things found in nature; and second, because it is easily applied (conceptually or by application of paints or dyes) to a variety of significant elements, for example, clouds, flowers, or corn as they are depicted in altars or on masks. Color may be viewed as an abstract and arbitrary classifier especially in its paradigmatic application. But this sixfold division of color has important natural motivation. According to one early observer, "at least ninety percent of the vegetable food eaten by the Hopi Indians is made of corn" (Owens 1892:163). Hopi corn is yellow, blue, red, white, black, and sweet ("kachina corn"). To the Hopi, corn is their "mother" for "they live on and draw life from the corn as the child draws life from its mother" (Voth 1901:149). A second basic source of food is beans. According to Stephen (1936, 1:354) the "old time beans" of the Hopi seem to be "yellow, blue, red, white, black, speckled." It is here that the system of correspondences is most closely related to Hopi life. Hopi dependence on corn has decreased since the nineteenth century, but corn remains a meaningful symbol of life— its substance and that which sustains it.

## Number

As either quantity or sequence, number is an abstract classifier that derives its significance from the other dimensions of the basic paradigm. Again, the numbers four and six provide a structural principle for dividing

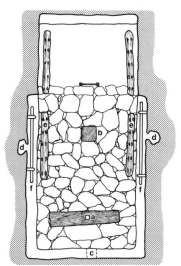

Fig. 3. Plan and interior view of a subterranean Hopi kiva: a, sipapu or symbolic earth navel represented as a hole (which can be covered by a wooden plug) leading from an underground cavity, which is covered over with a cottonwood plank; b, firepit, directly under hatchway that serves as entrance, exit, and chimney; c, kachina house or shrine, a niche in the front ledge (adjacent to northwest wall) in which kachina masks are placed; d, niches in side walls, once used exclusively for pipes, tobacco, and small ritual paraphernalia; e, wooden planks with indentations, used to anchor vertical looms; f, bars from which loom is suspended. The masonry ledge behind the sipapu is used to display ritual paraphernalia. Similar ledges lining the side walls are used as benches by participants in kiva ceremonies, while spectators are relegated to the narrower section of the kiva, which is slightly elevated. The kiva structurally replicates Hopi cosmological organization, with its three distinct levels in which the sipapu leads from the first to the second level, and a ladder leads from the third level through the hatchway to the fourth or outside world (Mindeleff 1891:135; Stephen 1936, 1:151). Plan and reconstruction based on Mindeleff (1891:118-136) and Stephen (1936, 1:719-720).

and classifying reality, and nearly every ritual act is ordered by this notion.

## Reciprocity with the Spirits

For the Hopi, all forms of prayer offering are understood to be prestations requiring reciprocity between the two realms. Prayer offerings in any form are operations of exchange. They are relational but, more important, they make obligatory and compensative requirements of the spirits of the other world. In making prayer offerings to the kachinas, for example, the Hopi "feeds" them. The kachinas are to reciprocate by feeding the Hopis with rains so their crops will grow. The ritual cycle consists, then, in a series of elaborate prayer-prestations between the two worlds. In Hopi belief the peoples of the other world mirror the ritual activities of this world, and there are minor opposite-period observances of all rituals in which reciprocal prayer-prestations are made. As Voth (1912:55) noted: "It is the supposition that the spirits of the departed come and get the food and the prayer-feathers, or rather the *[hík*si]* (breath, essence, soul) of those objects. [There is] the custom of not only informing the ancestors and friends in the other world that a ceremony is in progress here, but also of providing the means to have them share its benefits." Because the dead "eat only the odor or the soul of the food . . . they are not heavy. And that is the reason why the clouds into which the dead are transformed are not heavy and can float in the air" (Voth 1905:116). While one end of ritual in this world is to contribute to the well-being of the spirit world, the spirit world is obligated to contribute to the well-being of this world by providing rain, which is essential to the crops and, hence, to the health of the Hopis (and all living things of this world). Rain is the most common request in Hopi prayer; however, the "gift," "blessing," or "benefit" (Third Mesa *ná(:)maŋ*i;* cf. Voth 1901:146) may take other forms as well. The living and the dead, patterns of subsistence, various rhythms of nature—are all systematically interrelated through an elaborate system of reciprocities. It is this notion that is the most pervasive element in the Hopi world view.

# Hopi Semantics

C.F. VOEGELIN, F.M. VOEGELIN, AND LAVERNE MASAYESVA JEANNE

The major contribution to understanding Hopi semantics, so far, was certainly made by Benjamin Lee Whorf,
who alluded to many semantic problems but, with a few
exceptions, did not have time or opportunity in his brief
career to obtain enough information to fully explicate the
problems; characteristically, he treated these problems in
outline rather than in detail. Perhaps the most successful
semantic treatment of all the Whorf papers is that
concerned with Hopi architecture. Architectural terms,
which have as their referents 'hollow spaces' or empty
spaces (that is, interior three-dimensional spaces such as
would be referred to in English as a room or passageway
or storeroom) are relatively few in number and, like
deictics of location, such as 'here', 'there', 'above' and
'below', and some pronouns, are combinable with loca-
tional suffixes. Such terms are not nouns; unlike nouns,
they are not inflected for nominative or oblique cases or
for possession: Hopi cannot say 'our room' or 'our
passageway'. And terms for hollow spaces are restricted
to a few lexical items in contrast to terms for component
parts of buildings, such as 'door', and for adjuncts of
buildings, such as 'ladders', for which Whorf cites about
a score of lexical items. These terms with referents that
are structural elements or parts of a building are really
nouns; they can be inflected for possession and for the
same cases as other nouns. When Hopi is expanded in
consequence of new social relationships, it sometimes
becomes necessary to speak of a room in town that
belongs to a Hopi renter who will not say in Hopi 'my
room' but he might say in Hopi 'my door' or 'my floor'
"which would acquire the extended meaning of an
individual person's own room, like French *foyer* 'hearth'
meaning one's home" (Whorf 1953:142).

The semantic aspects of Hopi that Whorf analyzed are
related to what he liked to call "linguistic relativity":
Hopi in its way—and Shawnee in another way (Whorf
1940)—is so language-particular in its semantics as to be
sharply differentiated from English as a representative of
what he referred to as Standard Average European. This
higher question or claim of linguistic relativity is challenged by a bolder question (does there exist for all
natural languages a shared semantic core that is lan-
guage-universal rather than language-particular?) that is
in conflict with Whorf's thesis inherited from Edward
Sapir. The main thrust of this chapter will be to balance
what appears to be language-particular in Hopi seman-

tics against what might be claimed to be either language-
universal or at least shared by some Old World languages
rather than being a peculiarity of New World languages
or of Hopi in particular.

## Tense

Whorf (1941:143-145) argues that tense or awareness of
time—that is, "real time"—can be reduced to 'changing
certain relations in an irreversible manner', in short,
'getting later' or 'latering' or 'durating', with a contrast
between what is most recently attended to and what was
attended to earlier.

According to Whorf, scores of languages distinguish
two tenses (later to earlier), while Standard Average
European languages with their "objectification tendency" construct a system of points on a line: past,
present, future. In contrast, there is no "basis for an
objectified time in Hopi verbs."

In 1941 and again in 1946 and 1950 Whorf denied
tense for Hopi, whether or not "objectified," and reinter-
preted as "validity-forms" forms that resemble tenses
semantically. But Whorf's (1936a:127, 1956a:103) first
impression of Hopi was that this language distinguishes
three tenses: a "past" also called a "factual or present-
past" (a "non-future" since the so-called past in Hopi
extends up to and includes the present); a "future"; and
a "usitative" also called "generalized tense" (which may
be classified as an aspect rather than a tense). When the
last two were taken to be "validity-forms" rather than
tenses, the "future" was called "expective" and the
"generalized tense" was called "gnomic"—in Whorf's
spelling "nomic" (for verbal activity that is true generally
or universally).

For verbs in simple, nonconjoined sentences, those to
which the future suffix is attached should be regarded as
future in tense, and those to which the future suffix is not
attached as nonfuture, that is, present or past in tense,
which Whorf (1938:113) calls "reportive"; both tenses in
different sentences can be read with different modal
interpretations—not only expective in the case of future
verbs in some sentences but also desiderative, as in the
interpretation of a sentence with the denominal verb
'want coffee' or 'will have coffee': *ḳaphe* for 'coffee' before
oblique case suffix *-t,* which precedes the future suffix *-ni,*

as in the sentence for 'Do you want coffee?' or 'Will you have coffee?' *(ya ʔɨm ḳaphetni).* *

But the scope of tense in conjoined sentences (and in complex sentences with embedding) often extends beyond the clauses of verbs marked for future or nonfuture, as appears in examples of sentences cited below. And a variety of time adverbs often make it clear whether a verb marked for nonfuture refers to time in the past or in the present, though often enough a nonfuture verb occurs in simple sentences without a time adverb, so that the time referred to by the nonfuture verb is left vague—past or present—though probably not regarded by Hopi speakers as immaterial. Instead, the context or Hopi culture space in which such a sentence is spoken is usually sufficient to refer it to present or past time even when this nonfuture time is unspecified.

Whorf presents an argument against accepting the English kind of tense distinction as a language universal that is shared by Hopi; he exaggerates the possibility of Hopi speakers regarding tense or time to be immaterial in some sentences; and he even seems to claim that time adverbs are not 'words' relevant to time: "the Hopi language is seen to contain no words, grammatical forms, constructions or expressions that refer directly to what we call 'time'. . . . Hence, the Hopi language contains no reference to 'time', either explicit or implicit" (Whorf 1950:67).

Just as Hopi makes a minimum division between future tense and nonfuture tenses, so some linguists, in contrast to the traditional past-present-future division, suggest that English makes a minimum division between past and nonpast tenses. Both languages contain some minimum expression of tense; and this may well be a language universal, even if it turns out that no universal can be found for matching a particular tense in one language with a particular tense in another. This mild caveat on the universality of tense is quite different from Whorf's (1950:72) argument against language universals by counter-example: "the Hopi language gets along perfectly without tenses for its verbs."

Hopi verbs make a minimum division of time in terms of stative or active conditions expected or wanted or predicted or otherwise contemplated, but not yet occurring (future tense or tense-modality) versus conditions occurring now or in the past (nonfuture tense). This is roughly the minimum division that verbs make in respect to two tenses that saliently combine with modality the notion of the time an event or condition occurs. But Hopi sentences are not restricted to this minimum division of time; for example, time adverbs make possible a further distinction of the nonfuture tense into present time and past time.

So far as modality is concerned, Hopi *ʔas* is by no means the only modal adverb in the language, as the examples cited by Whorf (1946:177) suggest. Some of these, like *ʔas*, have a semantic scope not restricted to the clause in which they occur in conjoined sentences (Voegelin and Voegelin 1969). Such sentences also show the interplay of tense between constituent clauses within a given conjoined sentence. Tense or time is clearly involved in two of the four proximate suffixes discussed by Whorf (1946:176), who names the individual proximate suffixes but offers no cover-term for the set of four. The cover-term "proximate" for these four is used here because the functional subject of one clause is the same as (coreferential with) that of another clause in the same sentence; this is in contrast to a set that includes only one suffix on a verb having a functional subject that is obviative or in other words nonidentical with the functional subject of an adjacent clause in the same sentence; when there is switch-reference for the functional subjects of adjacent clauses the verb of one of the clauses is obviative.† Thus, the subject of the first clause in the translation of the Hopi sentence following is 'I' with obviative verb; that of the second clause is 'it', with proximate verb; that of the third clause is coreferential with the 'it' of the second clause: (1) 'I bumped your dish hard' *(nɨ ʔɨ̀·caqaptay hinʔɨr toŋoknaq)*, (2) 'and because it gave out a ring' *(ʔeyomtiqaʔe)*, (3) 'it frightened me' *(nɨy ca·wina)*. The tense is nonfuture for each clause in this sentence.

Compare the following pair of sentences, which have two proximate suffixes that involve tense as well as coreferential agreement between adjacent clauses: *-t*, which Whorf labels "sequential"; and *-kaŋ*, *-ka·kaŋ*, which Whorf labels "concursive" (for singular and plural functional subjects, respectively). The sequential *-t* is attached to each of the verbs in the first four clauses of the next sentence: (1) 'Well, a person doesn't skin prairie dogs' *(pay, hak tɨkat qa siskʷat);* (2) 'he just first takes out entrails from the stomach of one that has its pelt on' *(pay pɨ·kaʔytaqat ponoŋaq mô·ti sicamt);* (3) 'then he washes [the carcass] out' *(pɨʔ ʔaŋq tɨ·vahomt);* (4) 'and he sews [the carcass] back together' *(ʔahoy ʔakʷ kopkinat)*. These four clauses are all in the proximate conjunct mode; the fifth and final clause is in the independent mode, ending in a verb to which neither a proximate nor an obviative conjunct mode suffix is attached. (5) 'then a person always cooks it [the carcass] buried in the hot sand' *(pɨʔ hak pɨt nakʔamŋʷɨ)*. The same noun *(hak)* serves as the functional subject of each clause in this sentence; it is specified in the first and last clauses but is interpreted to

---

† The type of syntactic marking here called obviative has more generally been called switch-reference. The terms obviative and proximate have been borrowed from the grammatical terminology of the Algonquian languages for their convenience but should not be taken to imply any close similarity to the Algonquian categories, which differ from those of Hopi in several important ways.

* All the Hopi forms and sentences in this chapter are in the Third Mesa dialect; see the orthographic footnote in "Hopi Prehistory and History to 1850," this vol.

be the same 'person' even when left unspecified in clauses (2), (3), and (4). Note that the minimum division of time would place the five verbs in the five clauses as nonfuture; but the referential time changes sequentially for each clause. The event or denial of event in clause (1) occurs before the event of taking out the entrails in clause (2), which precedes the event of washing in (3), which in turn precedes the event of sewing in (4), while the last event in the sequence is sand-bury cooking in (5). Note that the sentence final verb of clause (5), *nakʔamŋʷɨ*, ends in the suffix *-ŋʷɨ*, which contributes no time nuance to the nonfuture tense but does add an indication of the gnomic aspect, here translated 'always'.

Now compare the kind of time nuances that the proximate conjunct mode suffix *-t* 'sequential' contributes to the nonfuture tense of the verbs in clauses of the preceding sentence, with the time nuance that the proximate conjunct mode suffix *-kaŋ* 'concursive' contributes to the future tense of the verb in clause (1) of the following sentence. This sentence can be spoken as two pairs of clauses, the first pair ending with the verb of clause (2) in the independent mode and with tense shown by future suffix *-ni;* and the second pair having clause (3), which ends with conditional proximate mode suffix *-eʔ*, preceding clause (4), ending in the same mode and tense as clause (2); the pairs of clauses are separated by a semicolon in the following translation. (1) 'She, it is said, while making piki tomorrow' *(pam yaw qaꞏvo piktani niꞏkaŋ),* (2) 'she will, just then, not be rolling them, it is said' *(yaw pay pam qa mîꞏpantani);* (3) 'just later, under the condition that [she] will finish them, it is said' *(pay yaw ʔason yɨkʔeʔ),* (4) '[she] will then quickly be folding [the piki] over and over' *(pɨʔ nömömnani),* that is, she will then be quickly repeatedly folding flat piki cakes that she did not roll or fold earlier, as mentioned in clause (2).

The same pronoun, *pam* for 'she', serves as the subject of each of the four clauses. The specification of the functional subject, here *pam,* in the initial clause (1), is usual; the repetition of *pam* in clause (2) is optional, and the subject is interpreted to be coreferential with that of (1) and (2) in clauses (3) and (4), but left unspecified in (3) and (4).

The verb of clause (3) has the conditional proximate mode suffix, *-eʔ*, attached to a verb *(yɨkʔeʔ)* in nonfuture tense. Note that an interesting constraint is found for clauses with this conditional proximate mode suffix: they appear only when preceding an independent mode clause inflected for future tense, or else inflected for gnomic aspect, marked by suffix *-ŋʷɨ* instead of future suffix *-ni,* which appears in clause (4).

But this is a one-way constraint. An independent clause with its verb inflected for gnomic aspect or future tense is only optionally preceded by a clause with its verb inflected for conditional proximate mode; see above where clause (1) with concursive *-kaŋ* precedes (2) with future; compare clause (5) of the Hopi sentence before

this, where the independent mode gnomic aspect clause is preceded by sequential proximate mode suffix *-t* ending clauses (1), (2), (3), (4).

Note that the tense of conditional proximate mode clauses in *-eʔ* matches semantically the future tense of the following independent verb, as above; in other words, (3), which is without tense suffix matches semantically the tense of the independent mode clause (4), which is explicitly marked with the future suffix, *-ni*. This much was stated by Whorf (1946:176) who then overstated the case by saying that a parallel semantic matching occurs between 'dependent clause' verb inflected for the conditional proximate mode with a following independent mode clause with verb inflected for gnomic aspect. This kind of semantic matching, as just shown, exists only between a conditional mode clause unmarked for tense, but interpreted as anticipating the tense in the following independent mode clause, where that tense is marked as future tense. The semantic parallel of this does not exist between a conditional mode clause unmarked for tense and a following clause with independent verb marked for gnomic—possibly because gnomic is not a tense as Whorf (1956a:103) claimed in 1937, but an aspect. The clearest counter-examples to Whorf's claim are sentences with conditional clauses like 'if the beans get burned' *(ʔöŋava taqteʔ),* which cannot be interpreted in gnomic aspect, for it is not generally or universally true that beans get burned, even though the following clause is inflected for gnomic: 'they really don't taste good' *(pas qa kʷaŋŋʷɨ).* The second clause can be interpreted as being gnomic in aspect, because it is generally or universally true that beans do not taste good after they are burned in cooking.

## Aspect

Perhaps the most sustained, though not the most successful, of Whorf's selected writings is his treatment of two contrasting aspects—punctual and segmentative—which contrast only in respect to verb stems that permit final syllable reduplication.

The following two separable questions about aspect can be asked in respect to verbs that permit final syllable reduplication. First there is the question of the aspect of the unreduplicated form, of which Whorf (1936a:127) says the "verb is a bare root of the form CVCV, and is in the third person singular intransitive voice, punctual aspect, and present-past tense [nonfuture tense]." Whorf generalizes from his examples, without suffixes added to the "bare root" when it is left unreduplicated. What is the aspect ascribed to the same verbal lexeme when the final syllable is reduplicated? Whorf restricts all his examples of the reduplicated forms to those occurring before suffix *-ta,* which is itself an aspect marking suffix, as he realizes. "The segmentative aspect is formed by final reduplication of this root plus the durative suffix *-ta.* . . ."

The next question is in two parts: how to balance the

aspectual meaning of an aspect suffix, -ta or some other aspect suffix, against the aspect contributed by the final syllable reduplication of the "bare root." And the second part of this question is how the aspectual meaning of the word as a whole is affected by the referential phenomenon of the "bare root." Whorf (1936a:128 ff.) treats the second part of this question but not the first, for which he is content to cite the unreduplicated stem without any suffix, though suffixes may be attached to it. It is true that the reduplicated form cannot occur without suffixes (but -ta is not the only suffix permitted).

In short, Whorf's treatment is restricted to the contrast between two aspects that he labels punctual and segmentative and his exemplification is by contrasting words rather than by contrasting sentences, words that he classifies according to their referential phenomena.

Nonetheless, he argues that this restricted treatment permits him to make the strongest of the many arguments he presents in favor of "linguistic relativity." His restricted or simplified problem is to show that final reduplication changes the meaning of the simplex (the "bare root" without reduplication): the phenomenon denoted by the "bare root" is "manifested about a point"; once the root undergoes final syllable reduplication, the phenomenon "becomes manifested as a series of repeated interconnected segments" (Whorf 1936a:127).

(a). This is true even when the "phenomenon" has "a rigid or semirigid substance for its field of manifestation" (Whorf 1936a:128).

(b). When the "bare root" denotes "a non-rigid or mobile substance . . . for example a liquid or a swarm of mobile particles . . . the punctual [= "bare root"] will denote one pulse of the deformation . . . while the segmentative [=with final syllable reduplication] will refer to the entire train or field of vibrations, both as extending in space and as continuing in time . . . wála it (e.g. a liquid) makes one wave, gives a slosh walálata it is tossing in waves, it is kicking up a sea" (Whorf 1936a:128).

(c). When the "bare root" denotes a phenomenon resulting from torque, the punctual [= "bare root"] will denote a "single oscillation or a single turning," while the segmentative [= with final syllable reduplication] will denote continued rotation (Whorf 1936a:129).

(d). Though a gaseous or etheric medium lacks evidence of extension in space in the "bare root" (ʔɨwi 'it flames up'), the segmentative [= with final syllable reduplication] "denotes only pulsation in time" (ʔɨwiwita 'it is flaming') (Whorf 1936a:130).

(e). Where English occasionally employs two different stems "Hopi simply uses the punctual and segmentative of the same stem," as to denote, respectively, a shock or jar (tiri 'he gives a sudden start') and pulsative phenomenon or a succession of shocks (tiririta 'he is quivering, trembling') (Whorf 1936a:130).

(f). There is an overall semantic constraint on disyllabic stems that permit final syllable reduplication. "It is not applied to 'mental', 'emotional' or other 'inner' or 'psychological' experiences. It concerns only the world of external observation" (Whorf 1936a:130).

Whorf claims that an overall interpretation of the punctual-segmentative contrast is possible, despite the diverse range of phenomena to which the contrast is applicable, as outlined above: to (a) a rigid substance, (b) mobile substance, (c) rigid or mobile substance that permits rotation, (d) gaseous medium, (e) external parts of living beings, but not (f) to internal sensations of living beings. His overall interpretation is that "the Hopi language maps out a certain terrain of what might be termed primitive physics . . . all sorts of vibratile phenomena in nature are classified by being referred to various elementary types of deformation process . . . analysis . . . is freely extensible . . . such extension could be made with great appropriateness to a multiplicity of phenomena belonging entirely to the modern scientific and technical world . . ." (Whorf 1936a:131).

The tenor of this interpretation leads Whorf to his grand conclusion about linguistic relativity, a conclusion that goes beyond his usual claim that Hopi semantics for the most part can be classified as language-particular to the claim that in some semantic resources Hopi is superior to English and other Standard Average European languages: "The Hopi actually have a language better equipped to deal with . . . vibratile phenomena than is our latest scientific terminology. This is simply because their language establishes a general contrast . . . the contrast of particle and field of vibrations . . ." (Whorf 1936a:131).

Note the contrast that Hopi speakers make when their sentences include disyllabic stems that permit final syllable reduplication. Most revealing of all the verbal lexemes that appear in the following sentences are those that include disyllabic stems, which permit not only final syllable reduplication but also initial syllable reduplication; but it must be admitted that such permissive disyllabic stems are relatively rare in number, rarer indeed than those that permit final syllable reduplication but do not also permit initial syllable reduplication, which, in fact, are far outnumbered by verbal stems that permit initial syllable but not final syllable reduplication. (The latter are, in turn, even further outnumbered by nominal stems that permit initial reduplication.)

(1) 'This tape-recorder's wheel is rubbing against its lid' (ʔit tape-recordert ŋölaʔat ʔiʔicpiyat ʔaŋqe rikʷakʷata). The selection of the verb for 'rubbing' when, as here, the friction is fast and continuous is not merely the intransitive stem rikʷa; it includes this stem with final syllable reduplication, rikʷakʷa-, followed by an aspect suffix, -ta. The predictable aspect of the word as a whole, which may be called fast progressive, is derived from both the final reduplication and the aspect suffix under the usual

assumption that the meanings of a word or sentence are built up from the meanings of their constituent processes and parts, unless the combination leads to unpredictable semantic results such as are characteristically encountered in compound words made up of two or more words, and also in some kinds of nominalization and verbalization and in idiomatic sentences.

(2) 'A dog is rubbing himself against the wagon' (pôˑko qareˑtat ʔaŋqaʔy naˑrɨkʷanta). The stem selection for 'rubbing' is the same as in (1), but in (2) there is no reduplication before the suffixes -n-ta; the prefix naˑ- is attached to verbs when the reflexive is expressed. The meaning of the verb in (2) is 'singular subject is rubbing self' with progressive aspect, which is noncommittal as to whether the dog is rubbing himself slowly and rhythmically or in segmentative jerks; the dog is giving more than a 'punctual' rub at any rate, for the final suffix -ta signifies one kind of progressive aspect. What the verb specifies is no more than that the 'rubbing' is or was going on progressively, and since fast rubbing could be expressed, the lack of final reduplication in (2) makes a weak implication that the rubbing was relatively slow.

(3) 'Evidently she is/was/has been smoothing her piki stone' (pam kɨr tɨmay rɨˑrɨkʷa). The stem selection for 'smoothing' in this sentence is the same as that for 'rubbing' in (1) and (2), but the processes signifying progressive aspect are different: reduplication involves the first or initial CV of the CVCV stem in (3), in contrast to reduplication involving the second or final CV of the same CVCV stem as for (1). Final reduplication as in (1) signifies a fast progressive; initial reduplication signifies progressive aspect but is noncommittal as to the speed involved, so far as language-linked semantics is concerned. Part of the interpretation for (3) is derived from culture-linked semantics—namely that the subject was smoothing her piki stone at the appropriate rate for smoothing such stones; and that whether she is, was, or had been doing so depends on the 'evidence' (indicated by kɨr) that the Hopi speaker who reported this had utilized—she saw her doing so, came upon her freshly smoothed stone, or something else—whatever the 'evidence' might be. The gender interpretation (the subject is 'she' rather than 'he') is also derived from culture-linked semantics: in the division of labor among the Hopi, women take care of the piki stones on which they cook piki, but only a male specialist—not just any adult male—knows how to make piki stones. If sentence (3) were altered so as to be translatable as 'Evidently he is making a piki stone', the same pronoun for subject, pam, would be interpreted as 'he' rather than 'she'.

(4) 'Sand drifted down from the kiva top' (pisa kivacʔoŋaq siwɨ). The stem selection for 'drifted down' is siwɨ, lacking both reduplication and suffixes (Whorf's "bare root"); this indicates, as Whorf said, punctual aspect, but not in the sense that a single grain of sand drifted down; tense of the verbal reference is not relevant, but the duration of it is—namely, almost but not quite zero duration, or in other words the duration is nonprogressive; and nonprogressive might be a more suggestive label for this aspect than punctual. There is a parallel between this particular aspect and nonfuture tense; neither is ever explicitly marked by any affix or process.

(5) 'The woman had been sprinkling salt on the meat' (pam wɨˑti ʔöˑŋat siwɨwɨykina sikʷit ʔaŋ). The stem selection in (5) for 'had been sprinkling' is the same as that for 'drifted down' in (4), but here the final syllable of the stem is reduplicated and followed by two suffixes; the first is -yki, a sort of completive or perfective combined with imperfective reading here, but the imperfective or fast progressive is really made explicit by the reduplication process preceding -yki, which in turn is followed by -na to indicate a transitive (or causative) voice, if 'sprinkle' is here taken to mean 'to cause to be drifting down quickly'. Hence it cannot be said that the reduplication process in question is compatible only with intransitive voice; but it can be said (as Whorf implied) that CVCV stems are capable of final syllable reduplication only when the underlying stem is intransitive; from such a stem the derived verb may be made transitive, as here in (5).

(6) 'Sand is trickling down from up there' (pisa ʔayaŋq ʔoˑŋaq siwɨwɨta). Whorf has adequately accounted for sentences like (6), in which the stem, here siwɨ as in (4), has its final syllable reduplicated, and has this process followed by -ta, a suffix for durative aspect (another label for progressive). Yet the detailed nature of the aspectual duration (for all? or for different semantic classes of stems with different referential phenomena?) is open to question. Is it 'segmentative' as Whorf thought? Or is it noncommittal as to segmental division of sand trickling down? Should this particular sentence be interpreted as sand trickling down quite fast rather than in segments—in short, fast progressive?

Sentences (4), (5), and (6) exemplify the type of verb stem that permits reduplication of the final syllable without permitting reduplication of the initial syllable of the stem. Sentences (7) and (8) show the converse of this, the type of verb that permits reduplication of the initial syllable of the stem, but not the final syllable. There are two subtypes of stems of this only-initial reduplication type: in one subtype the reduplication indicates aspect (a progressive aspect—slow or at least non-fast progressive); in the other subtype, the initial reduplication indicates number.

(7) 'Because it [the firewood] didn't flame up' (qa ʔɨwiqqaʔe ʔoˑvi) 'it began to smoke' (kʷicva). Here the CVCV verbal stem is kʷici; the stem final vowel is deleted before the inceptive suffix -va.

(8) 'It keeps smoking from your piki house' (ʔɨˑtɨmcokkiy ʔawŋq kʷiˑkʷici). The stem in (7), kʷici, appears here with reduplication of the initial syllable. Note that verbal stems with reduplication of initial syllable (as here) may appear without following suffix,

585

while stems with reduplication of the final syllable may not.

## Number in Nouns and Verbs

Number—at least the distinction between singular and plural—is marked on both nouns and verbs in Hopi in a variety of ways.

Initial reduplication is used to mark the plural of many nouns, as *so·hɨ* 'star', *so·sohɨ* 'stars', and for some intransitive verbs to mark the fact that they have plural subjects, as for example, *nimani* 'he will go home', *ninmani* 'they will go home'. In these examples the first vowels of the stems are shortened or deleted after the initial syllables are reduplicated.

Suffixes may also mark plural on nouns and verbs—with suffix *-m* for some nouns, as *höya* 'yellowjacket', *höyam* 'yellowjackets', and for other nouns suffix *-t,* as *höwi* 'dove', *höwit* 'doves'. Plural subject of verbs of one type is indicated by suffix *-ya,* as *pô·toyla* 'he counted it', *pô·toylaya* 'they counted it'. Verbs of another type indicate plural by suppletion. For these replacing the singular stem by a different stem is sufficient to mark the plural, as *pitɨ* 'he arrived', *ʔöki* 'they arrived', but the rare type of noun that uses suppletion to mark the plural uses it in combination with a suffix, as *wɨ·ti* 'woman', *momoyam* 'women'. So also, a combination of initial reduplication and the suffix *-ya* is used for the plural of some verbs, as *hɨ·wi* 'he's trapping', *hɨ·hɨwiya* 'they're trapping'.

Whorf (1946:176) speaks of the "*agentive* -qa" that "forms relative clauses and is inflected as a noun" and cites a sentence without head noun, but Masayesva Jeanne (1974; revised in Hale, Masayesva Jeanne, and Platero 1977 and Masayesva Jeanne 1978) cites all sentential examples with head nouns. It is interesting for the consideration of number that all plurals of nominalizations in *-qa* are formed by attaching the suffix *-m* to *-qa,* while nominal stems form their plurals in a variety of ways, as mentioned above.

For nouns Whorf distinguishes those plural forms with suffixes *-t* or *-m* as being "paucal", in the sense of few, as opposed to "multiple", marked by initial reduplication, with the restriction that the multiples of some animate nouns are "paucals with the addition of reduplication, i.e., they have paucal suffixes in all the forms. . . . Some animates use the paucals for all plurals [i.e., they are not reduplicated]" (1946:170). Many Hopi speakers have lost the paucal-multiple distinction for the inanimate nouns for which it may have been formerly made and use one form or the other as their only plural form.

Another number distinction for nouns made only by speakers of some Hopi dialects (Whorf) is the distinction of a dual category (exactly two), marked by a suffix, as opposed to the unmarked singular (one) and the plural (three or more) marked in any one of the ways discussed above.

But all Hopi speakers, whether or not they distinguish dual forms for nouns, do distinguish dual from singular and plural subjects of sentences, not necessarily by utilizing a dual form but by the way in which they combine singular and plural nouns or pronouns and verbs. If the subject of the sentence is singular it always takes the verb form for singular subject and is interpreted as a singular: *pam pitɨ* 'he (or she) arrived'. But if the subject is nonsingular it is used with a plural verb to indicate a plural subject (*pɨma ʔöki* 'they (three or more) arrived'), and with a singular verb to indicate a dual subject (*pɨma pitɨ* 'they (two) arrived').

While suppletion and initial reduplication are both used to mark the fact that the subject is plural for some intransitive verbs like 'arrive', some transitive verbs have suppletive or reduplicated forms that mark the fact that the object is plural, rather than the subject (pluralization of the subject is marked for these verbs by suffix): *tavi* 'he moved it', *taviya* 'they moved it', *ʔoya* 'he moved them', *ʔoyya* 'they moved them'; *lakna* 'he dried it', *la·lakna* 'he dried them'.

The fact that a verb has a plural subject may be marked by suffixes other than the plural suffix *-ya*: certain verb suffixes have one form when the subject of the verb is singular and another when it is plural. When one of these suffixes occurs, its plural form, rather than *-ya,* is used with plural subjects. Thus, the plural of the singular suffix *-ma* is *-wisa* (*mɨmamatima* 'it's rolling along', *mɨmamatiwisa* 'they're rolling along'), and the plural of the singular suffix *-ta* is *-tota* (*qöninita* 'it's whirling around', *qöninitota* 'they're whirling around').

Whorf (1946:175) postulates the semantic interpretation of the suffix cluster *-m-ti* to be an "inner plural" that "pluralizes the single figure of the root within a small local region," but attempts to replicate fully this interpretation have not succeeded. The suffix sequence *-m-ti* does appear after the unreduplicated stem of some, but not all, stems that permit final reduplication, but then usually yields an interpretation of punctual-completive aspect, as in 'The jackrabbit jumped out from the bush' (*cokit ʔaŋqaq sowi coʔomti*). This aspect sometimes has the force of 'became, got', as in 'My bean plants blossomed', or more literally, 'My bean plant's flower evidently became flapped open' (*ʔimoriʔiyiy siʔat kɨr pɨyamti*).

Note that in the last example the words for 'bean plant' and 'flower' are both singular nouns. Indeed, for most plants, plant parts, and fruits, the singular form of the noun is used with plural meaning. When, as in this sentence, the singular noun is subject, the verb agrees with it in also being singular.

# Hopi-Tewa

MICHAEL B. STANISLAWSKI

The Hopi-Tewa (¹hōpē ¹tāwu) are one of the smallest of the Native American societies in the American Southwest, estimated in 1975 to number about 625, approximately 475 of whom were living in their traditional home area on the Hopi Indian Reservation, on or near the easternmost of the Hopi Mesas in northeastern Arizona ("Hopi Social Organization," fig. 1, this vol.). The society includes those people who trace descent through their mother's female lines to immigrant Tano families from the Rio Grande who settled at First Mesa, Arizona, in 1700 and who thus have traditional land rights and houses there (Dozier 1951:57, 1954).

The Hopi-Tewa are often grouped with the Hopi of First Mesa, with whom they have lived for the past 275 years, and with whom they share most cultural patterns. However, even in the late twentieth century the cultures are not identical, and they were even more divergent prior to the beginning of European influences at the end of the nineteenth century (Dozier 1954:259-260, 290-297, 367-371; Eggan 1950:172-175).

## Language

The Hopi-Tewa do not speak the Uto-Aztecan language of the Hopi but a variety of Tewa, a Tanoan language.* The Hopi-Tewa dialect is the modern continuation of Tano, or Southern Tewa, and until A.D. 1700 it was spoken in the Rio Grande Valley, where the closely related Northern Tewa is spoken in several dialects in Santa Clara, San Juan, and the other Rio Grande Tewa

* As analyzed by Yegerlehner (1959) Hopi-Tewa (Arizona Tewa) has the following phonemes (with his "component combinations" interpreted as units): (voiceless stops and affricate) $p, t, c, k^y, k, k^w;$ (aspirated stops) $p^h, t^h, k^{yh}, k^h, k^{wh};$ (voiced stops and continuants) $b$ ([v] or [β]; [b] after $n$), $d, g;$ (glottalized stops and affricate) $\dot{p}, \dot{t}, \dot{c}, \dot{k}^y, \dot{k}, \dot{k}^w;$ (nasals, liquid, sibilant, and glides) $m, n; l; s$ ([s] or [š]); $w, y, \dot{w}, \dot{y}; h, h^y, h^w, ?;$ (vowels) $i, e, a, o, u,$ and their nasalized $(q)$, long $(a\cdot)$, and long nasalized $(q\cdot)$ correspondents; (pitch) high $(\acute{v})$ and low $(v)$. The inventory of sounds given by Dozier (1954:261-262) differs from this in being more similar to that of Rio Grande Tewa as described by Hoijer and Dozier (1949). Arizona Tewa words in italics in the *Handbook* have been written by Paul V. Kroskrity (personal communication 1977) in the orthography used in his doctoral dissertation (Kroskrity 1977), on the basis of information supplied by Albert Yava and Dewey Healing. This orthography differs from Yegerlehner's in recognizing an additional front vowel $(\varepsilon)$, in the marking of aspiration, and in a few other details. Since it has not been possible to reconcile the differences among the available transcriptions the forms cited doubtless contain inaccuracies.

Pueblos. Because of their modern locations these dialects are usually distinguished as Arizona Tewa and Rio Grande Tewa, respectively. The Hopi-Tewa and Rio Grande Tewa can understand each other's speech, but only with some difficulty and after a short period of adjustment. Hopi-Tewa and Hopi, on the other hand, are mutually unintelligible, and their speakers can communicate only if one has learned the other's language or through a shared third language such as English (Dozier 1951:56-57, 1955; Reed 1943a:75).

Almost all adult Hopi-Tewa are trilingual in Hopi, English, and Tewa. They have no language problems when they intermarry with Hopi, but the reverse is not true (Dozier 1951:58-63, 1954:279-292). Many Hopi-Tewa speak Spanish, which is needed in trading with Rio Grande Pueblo peoples, and many also speak Navajo, which was one of the first languages used by Anglo traders, such as Tom Keam, and by scientists, such as Alexander M. Stephen (1936,1:xxvii-xxviii). Thus, many Hopi-Tewa speak five languages: Tewa, Hopi, English, Navajo, and Spanish (Dozier 1954:281).

It is thus clear why the Tewa were the first "speakers" for First Mesa. They were serving as go-betweens in English, Spanish, Navajo, and other languages as early as 1850 and were the official interpreters by the 1870s-1890s (fig. 1), the period of first major Anglo contacts. In the 1970s Hopi-Tewa interpreters were still requested by Hopi chiefs and tribal council members (Crane 1925:136-137; Dozier 1954:291-297, 1966a:27-28).

## Territory and Environment

The society has always had a limited geographical distribution. The two major settlements are mesa-top Tewa Village (Hano) with a 1975 population of 218 (about 200 Hopi-Tewa) and Polacca, the government village founded in 1888 at the east base of First Mesa (shared with the Hopi), which had a 1975 population of 782 (perhaps 650 resident) indicating perhaps 220 Hopi-Tewa ("Hopi Social Organization," figs. 1-3, this vol.). The villages are located in Navajo County, northeastern Arizona, about 80 airline miles northeast of Flagstaff and 55 airline miles north of Winslow. Hopi-Tewa are also settled in Keams Canyon Hopi governmental center, 12 miles to the northeast, whose 1975 population of 252 included 30-40 Hopi-Tewa. In addition, about 20 percent

587

Fig. 1. Tom Polacca (Polaccaca), brother of Nampeyo, member of the Tewa Corn clan, and owner of a small store around which the town of Polacca grew up. Polacca was a speaker of Tewa and Hopi and an interpreter at First Mesa in the 1880s and 1890s. Photograph by an unknown photographer, probably taken about 1890 when Polacca accompanied a Hopi delegation to Washington, D.C.

(100–125) of the population is probably living off the reservation at any one time in Winslow, Holbrook, and Flagstaff, at the Parker Indian Reservation in southwestern Arizona, or out of state. The Hopi-Tewa form about one-third of the population of First Mesa, and about one-tenth of the total Hopi tribal roll, which numbers about 6,600 (Dozier 1954:288–290; Kunitz 1973, 1974:9; Anonymous 1975).

The principal settlement is known as Hano (to outsiders) and as Tewa Village to the Hopi-Tewa (Dozier 1951:56, 1954:259–263). It was founded in A.D. 1700 on the flat, bare, windswept, sandstone top of First Mesa, the southern and easternmost fingerlike extension of Black Mesa, a diamond-shaped area about 60 miles to a side. The mesa is sculpted by the water of two of the southwest-flowing Tusayan washes, Wepo and Polacca, which rise at 8,000 feet at the north mesa edge. The tip of First Mesa has an area of about 10 acres, measuring about 3,500 feet long by 200–350 feet wide (Hoover 1930:427; Forde 1931:358). Where the villages of Tewa, Sichomovi, and Walpi are located, the altitude is 6,190–6,210 feet.

Most of the houses of the new town of Polacca are built on the talus slopes and sand dunes at the eastern base of the mesa at an altitude of about 5,700–5,900 feet. Some new government-built houses are at 5,600–5,700 feet, south of the highway. The vertical face of the mesa near Polacca is about 300 feet high; the talus slope and dunes cover another 200 feet of drop, and finally there is a 150-foot gradual slope to Polacca Wash edge at about 5,650 feet, with water level at about 5,640 feet east of Polacca village.

The smaller settlements and ranches at Bluebird Canyon and at Awatovi on Antelope Mesa (established about 1900) stand at 6,300 feet, and some ranches on the flats below are at 5,600–5,700 feet. The Hopi-Tewa at Keams Canyon numbered about 450 in 1978, with 252 on the Hopi tribal roll. They lived in a government settlement founded about 1887 near a school and trading post at an elevation of 6,200–6,300 feet. There are also a few Hopi-Tewa in Public Health Service housing near the new hospital and at local trailer camps.

Mean annual temperature at Tewa Village (6,200 feet) or Polacca (5,700–5,900 feet) is about 50–52°F., with 9.5–11.0 inches of rain. The growing season is 133–135 days, with the last frost averaging May 18–19. Because the rainfall and growing season vary widely from year to year (5–20 inches of rain), dry farming is always precarious. Heavy winds occur in May and June, and in July and August (the hottest months and the early harvest period) the heaviest rains occur, dropping one-half the year's moisture in torrential cloudbursts, which may wash away the topsoil and crops. Evaporation, runoff, and erosion are thus very high, although humidity readings between the rains may be as low as 5 percent (Forde 1931; Beaglehole 1937; Hack 1942; Bradfield 1971; Ellis 1974b).

Settlement in the Southwest is dependent upon the rare water sources. While arid, the Hopi mesa region is particularly blessed in some ways. Washes provide much annual runoff and there are many permanent springs. The collection area for the wash water supply has been stated at 672 square miles for Polacca Wash and 176 square miles for Wepo Wash (Forde 1931:361; Bradfield 1971:2). The washes flow into the flat plains to the south of the mesa at about 5,600 feet altitude (fig. 2), providing floodwater for irrigation and depositing a large load of sand, which is then blown back, north and east, onto the valley edge and the mesa rim, forming dunes (Hack 1942:5–7). The dunes hold the rainwater, which allows dune farming, and also affects the spring water supply. For it is primarily in the dunes that water is held to percolate to the contact area between the permeable sandstone and the impermeable shale layers, at the 5,900–6,000 foot level, forming the 19 permanent First Mesa springs. However, because of the talus slopes and permanent dunes, the water may actually outcrop at the 5,700–5,800 foot level on the valley floor (Forde 1931:360, maps 2–3; Bradfield 1971:11–12; Hack 1942). The catchment basin of the average spring includes a few hundred acres near the northeast tilting mesa edge, and spring flow is rarely more than 5 to 30 gallons a minute (Hack 1942, 1:12–13, 36). The strongest springs, such as

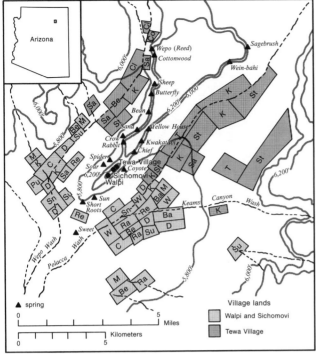

after Forde 1931: maps 2-3.

Fig. 2. First Mesa clan lands. Ba: Badger, Be: Bear, C: Coyote, Cl: Cloud, Co: Corn, D: Deer, K: Kachina, M: Mustard, Pu: Pumpkin, Ra: Rabbit, Re: Reed, Sa: Sand, Sn: Snake, St: Stick, Su: Sun, T: Tobacco, W: Water. The clan names given by Forde have been brought into conformity with usage elsewhere in this chapter.

## Settlements

The day-to-day resident population of Tewa Village is about 165, but 218 individuals claim allegiance. During ceremonial days the population may rise to 400 or more. Hopi-Tewa clan population is about 625 as compared to the 1893 population of 156 (table 1). The majority of the new growth since 1890 has obviously been in new settlements. From 1920 on, the Hopi-Tewa have leased nonclan lands from the tribe for ranches and second homes (Dozier 1954:288, 1966a:22, 1970:122), and it is there at the ranch or "second" home in Keams Canyon or Polacca that they generally live, to take advantage of modern facilities such as piped water and electricity, stores, and schools. Tewa Village is still the "home" settlement for the Hopi-Tewa individual because it is in his mesa home that each person recognizes his primary family relationships and social obligations. This house, generally that of his mother, is the lifelong center of his social life. It may also be the place in which his lineage or clan group's important religious symbols are stored and maintained (Dozier 1954:284-288, 310-312, 1966a:20-22; Eggan 1950:146-147; Titiev 1944:44-58).

Tewa Village in the 1880s was a pyramidal, multistory, hollow-plaza settlement, somewhat atypical of other Hopi mesa villages (Fewkes 1898:642; Mindeleff 1891:61). Early pictures indicate that the north, west, and east house rows all had two- to four-story sections, and there was a 356-foot gap between Tewa and Sichomovi villages, the empty land being on the Tewa side (fig. 3). Today, all Tewa Village houses are one story, and the village has spread out and is contiguous with Sichomovi. Fewkes (1906:90-94, pl. 11) believed that there were three original nuclei of the present Pueblo beginning about 1750-1800: in the middle of the north wing of the main (north) plaza (Corn, Tobacco-Bear clan rooms); east wing (Cloud-Sand-Sun clan rooms); and an early abandoned (pre-1800) room group north of the main plaza (Kachina clan rooms). The west wing began to develop about 1850 when Cloud clan houses were first built there. The continued development of the Pueblo, like that of nearby Hopi towns, has resulted in several hollow plazas and long north-south room lines. Fewkes (1906), Dozier (1954), and Mindeleff (1891:100-225) provide the best maps, descriptions, and architectural details.

In 1975 Tewa Village was still a Hopi-style Pueblo with flat-roofed (earth-covered) adobe material stone houses, but with some new cinder block additions as well. Asphalt and plastic sheeting, board ceilings, and linoleum floors have become common in reconstructed houses. Domed, adobe-plastered, stone-built bread ovens are found by nearly every house. Finally, the modern wage economy has led to familiarity with modern appliances such as radios, televisions, stoves, and refrigerators (Nagata 1970:207-208); but no Tewa Village house yet

Wepo, are found on the northwest side. The water, which is slightly saline and hard, is high in calcium and has a pH of 8.1 (Bradfield 1971:60). Water is also sometimes trapped in rock tanks, both naturally and artificially formed, in the pitted mesa surface. Some of these tanks, near house blocks, are "owned" by individual Hopi-Tewa and are passed along matriclan lines (Hack 1942, 1:10-14; Beaglehole 1937:13).

Much of the water for Hopi-Tewa agriculture and drinking still comes from these traditional springs, and many springs also figure in annual religious observances. Forde's (1931:360, 404-405, maps 2-3) maps of clan lands near First Mesa show a total of 19 named springs that are owned by Hopi or Hopi-Tewa clans (fig. 2). All are classified for domestic use, irrigation, livestock watering, or vegetable and peach tree gardens (Forde 1931:365-366). Coyote Spring, in particular, is important to the Hopi-Tewa, for it probably was the site of the first Tewa settlement at Hopi in 1700 (Fewkes 1899:257, 1900:610, 615; Mindeleff 1891:30), and later it was the site of the beginning of the new town of Polacca (Stephen 1936, 1:510; Fewkes 1898:580). In the 1970s the Hopi-Tewa prefer Sour Spring on the north scarp, or the large Wepo Spring (Reed Spring) located four miles to the north in Wepo Wash. Spider Spring is also used for drinking, and Cottonwood, Wein-bahi, and Yellow House (Sikyatki) springs are used to irrigate gardens.

**Table 1. Clan and Village Population, 1700–1975**

| Date | Clans | Tewa Village | Polacca | Source |
|------|-------|--------------|---------|--------|
| 1700 | 300? | 300[a] | | Hargrave 1951:35 |
| 1775 | | 550[a] | | Fewkes 1899:259 |
| 1853 | | 600[a] | | Page 1940:15 (Leroux) |
| 1865 | | 250[a] | | Page 1940:15 (Ward) |
| 1870 | | 75[a] | | Powell 1895:345 |
| 1883 | | 175[a] | | C. Mindeleff 1900:651 |
| 1884 | | 150[a] | | Bowman 1884:93 |
| 1888 | | | 5[a] | Stephen 1936, 1:590 |
| 1890 | | 161[b] | 10[a] | U.S. Census Office. 11th Census 1893:45; Fewkes 1922:270 |
| 1893 | 156[d] | 163[a] | | Fewkes 1894a:165–166 |
| 1898 | 151[d] | 159[a] | | Fewkes 1899:255, 1900:623 |
| 1900 | | 160[a] | 20[a] | Fewkes 1907:561 |
| 1929 | | 308[a,e] | | Hoover 1930:426 |
| 1932 | | 309[a,e] | 787[a,e] | Colton and Baxter 1932:40 |
| 1951 | 405[c] | 164[a] | | Dozier 1954:288 |
| 1964 | 450[c] | | | Dozier 1970:122 |
| 1966 | 500[c] | 230[a,b] | 530[a] | Dozier 1966a:22; Cox 1967 |
| 1968 | 500[c] | 150[d] | 590[a] | Dozier 1970:122; U.S. Bureau of Indian Affairs 1968 |
| 1972 | | 212[a,b] | 789[a,b] | Kunitz 1972 |
| 1974 | 615 | 225[a,b] | 850[a,b] | Estimated from Kunitz 1972 |
| 1975 | 625[c] | 218[a,b] | 782[a] | Estimated from Kunitz 1972; Anonymous 1975:1 |

NOTE: Figures are sometimes estimated, sometimes by actual count.
[a] All village residents, including non-Hopi-Tewa.
[b] Those who give allegiance to the village as place of birth rather than actual residents.
[c] Total tribal population regardless of habitation.
[d] Only those who were actually counted in the village or on the reservation.
[e] People may be counted in several villages at the same time, i.e., the village of allegiance and the village of residence.

Fig. 3. Main plaza at Tewa Village in 1875, viewed from a north house row rooftop, looking south toward the Hopi First Mesa villages of Sichomovi and Walpi. (For a view from the opposite end of the plaza, see Mindeleff 1891:pl. 17.) At right are Nampeyo and members of her family seated on the roof of their Corn clan house, located at the northeastern corner of the main plaza. (For a map of Tewa Village in 1883 showing settlement pattern by clan, see C. Mindeleff 1900:pl. 25.) Photograph by William H. Jackson.

had a telephone in 1974 although a few houses in Polacca and Keams Canyon did. Many houses in Tewa and Polacca have store-bought lamps, chairs, dining tables, dish cabinets, and beds; religious portraits and photographs of relatives cover the walls, side by side with traditional basketry plaques, kachinas, ceremonial rattles, and bows and arrows (Stanislawski 1968–1974:74).

Polacca village, in contrast, is an open, dispersed, single-family-house, grid-pattern, Anglo settlement, with some traditional stone houses, and some multiroom, peaked-roofed Anglo houses, including government-built modern prefabricated ones and trailers near the highway. Several government buildings, including a post office and a modern grade school, are also located there. House and land ownership continue to follow traditional matrilineal inheritance rules (Dozier 1954; Cox 1967).

Hopi-Tewa religious architecture continues in traditional style. There have been at least three partly subterranean kivas (or men's houses and ceremonial chambers) in use since the 1880s, all in Tewa Village ("Hopi Social Organization," fig. 3, this vol.). Chief kiva (also known as Central Plaza kiva) is found at the northeast edge of the main plaza, where Kachina clan houses were built in the 1800–1850 period (Fewkes 1900:607). Outside kiva is located northeast of the plaza rooms near the entrance road, and the remains of at least one earlier kiva are found there, too (Mindeleff 1891:61; Stephen 1936, 1:483–484). Kiva construction and architectural details are described by Mindeleff (1891:135–137) and Fewkes (1899:265). In general, they are rectangular, semisubterranean, roof-entered rooms with a raised stone platform at one end; they are oriented northwest-southeast (north 44° west). Built by ceremonial societies, clan groups, or individuals, these are used by many different groups of people in different societies and clans as ceremonies are performed, or for the men's leisure activities such as weaving and stone chipping (Stephen 1936; Parsons 1940; Fewkes 1899:265).

## Demography and Health

In 1893 Fewkes (1894a:165–167) found that there were 54 adults and only six families and six living children claiming to be of unmixed Tewa ancestry. Rules against intermarriage with Tewa were strictly enforced by the Hopi during the eighteenth and early nineteenth centuries (Dozier 1954:289–291, 1966a:23–26), but the First Mesa community as a whole is now known to be the least homogeneous, least inbred, and most "mixed" of all of the Hopi areas (Woolf and Dukepoo 1969:34).

By the 1950–1970 period, two-thirds of Hopi-Tewa over 16 were married; 15 to 17 percent were widowed,

590

and 10 to 19 percent were divorced. There has been a very even (±3%) male-female sex ratio at all times (Dozier 1954; U.S. Census Office. 11th Census 1893; U.S. Bureau of Indian Affairs 1968). Age studies show a generally young population, with 15 percent under 6, 48 percent under 20, and only about 17 percent over 55 (U.S. Bureau of Indian Affairs 1968). In the 1890s there were fewer people aged 6 to 19, and in Tewa Village, many less children under 6 (U.S. Census Office. 11th Census 1893). Hopi-Tewa longevity is slightly greater than that of the Hopi, and the population is a slightly older one. The population expanded at an average of 2.1% a year in the 1940-1970 period (Kunitz 1973:3-4, 1974; Thompson and Joseph 1944:30-31). Average family size is about five persons (Kunitz 1974).

Hrdlička (1908, 1935) studied Hopi and Hopi-Tewa anatomy and physiology in the early 1900s; Thompson (1950) summarizes medical, nutritional, psychological, and anatomical data; Kunitz (1973, 1974), Levy and Kunitz (1971), and Kunitz and Euler (1972) discuss health, mental health, fertility, and birth and death ratios. Woolf and Dukepoo (1969) provide general demographic discussions and a detailed analysis of one unusual genetic disease of the area, albinism, which is 100 times more common among Hopis than among Anglos. (Because of the relatively low rate of inbreeding at First Mesa, no Hopi-Tewa albino is known, although local people are carriers.)

## Culture

### Subsistence

The most complete descriptions of the floral environment and the more than 200 plants used by mesa area peoples are found in Bradfield (1971), Hack (1942), Forde (1931), and Whiting (1939). Beaglehole (1936), Page (1940), and L.D. Mason (1965) discuss domestic animals and the fauna; Willey (1969), Beaglehole (1937), and Ellis (1974b) give general ecological surveys. Bradfield, Forde, and Hack discuss traditional farming methods, and Forde mainly used Hopi-Tewa informants.

• ANNUAL CYCLE Traditional dates of subsistence activities and ceremonials are entrusted to officials called Sunwatchers who observe the position of the sun at dawn

**Table 2. Traditional Annual Cycle**

| Month | Agriculture | Hunting and Herding | Wages and Crafts |
|---|---|---|---|
| January | | Hunting, sheep breeding | Pottery making, jewelry, moccasins, tools, games |
| February | Breaking ground, clearing fields 3-4 | Sheep breeding | Crafts |
| March | Preparing seed, terracing/breaks, some green corn 4 | Lambing | Crafts taper off, housebuilding |
| April | Green spring corn 1-2, onions/chili (irrigation) 2-3, early beans and melons 3-4, squash 3-4 | Lambing | |
| May | Musk and watermelons 1, main squash and melons 1-3, beans and sunflowers 3-4, major corn 3-4 | Sheep shearing 3-4 | |
| June | Major corn 1-2, late plants (irrigation) in flood fields and sand dunes. Last plants June 22 | Rabbit hunts, eagle collecting, turtle hunts | Pottery and kachina making, housebuilding |
| July | Weeding and hoeing, harvest first apricots, harvest green corn 3-4 | Eagles killed | Pottery, weaving |
| August | Early peaches picked and dried, weed plants collected | Sheep dipped; cattle branded; deer, antelope, mountain sheep hunting | Pottery |
| September | Melons, beans, squash harvested 1-2; main peaches 4; main corn harvests 3-4 | | Salt trips to Zuni, trading |
| October | Peaches harvested 1-3, peach seeds planted, fruit trees pruned, main corn harvests 1-2 (town chief harvest) | Cattle sold | Salt trips to Zuni, trading |
| November | Final late harvests 1-2 | Sheep herding | Weaving, moccasins, tools, pottery |
| December | | Sheep breeding | Games |

SOURCES: Titiev 1938; Forde 1931; Beaglehole 1937; Ellis 1974b; Parsons 1926; L.D. Mason 1965.
NOTE: Weeks are numbered 1-4.

591

Southwest Mus., Los Angeles.
Fig. 4. Lesho or Lesou, cutting mutton. Meat, cut into thin slices against the grain, was preserved by hanging to dry in the sun; eventually it was boiled, after first soaking to soften it (Underhill 1946:74). Among the Hopi, this meat cutting task was generally performed by the women (Beaglehole 1937:18). Pottery on the ledge is by Lesho's wife, Nampeyo. Photograph by Adam C. Vroman, 1901.

Smithsonian, NAA.
Fig. 5. Nampeyo, one of the most famous Pueblo potters, is credited with the resurgence of a declining Hopi pottery tradition through the Sikyatki revival (Collins 1974; Ashton 1976). This style was inspired by pottery excavated at Sikyatki (Fewkes 1898:631ff.; Frisbie 1973), a site at which Nampeyo's husband, Lesho, was a fieldworker. The coil method of constructing pottery, which entails the progressive addition of coiled pieces of clay, is common to all of the Pueblos (see Douglas 1930). Nampeyo is shown here in her Corn clan house in Tewa Village, seated in front of the traditional graduated grinding bins. Photograph by Adam C. Vroman, 1901.

as it appears above or between selected geographical features on opposite mesas. Dates and months of such appearances are fixed from solstice to solstice (Ellis 1973; Parsons 1925a:74-75). Leslie Agayo, of the Hopi-Tewa Corn clan, drew a Sun chart in 1913 for Tewa Village. There appears to be a 13-month cycle—a dual division of the year in which there are two six-month periods with repeated names, and one unnamed segment (Ellis 1973). Since the 1920s dates have been similar for the Hopi and Hopi-Tewa calendars, varying but a few days from year to year (Parsons 1925a:120), and since 1930, the Tewa have often used a Hopi Sunwatcher (Dozier 1954:345; Forde 1931:385). The traditional annual work cycle as practiced in the 1930s is summarized in table 2. Excellent descriptions of a typical winter and summer work day are given by Beaglehole (1937:17-26).

• DIVISION OF LABOR   During the annual cycle, there is a traditionally strict division of labor by age and sex for both Hopi and Hopi-Tewa peoples, although this is slowly changing due to modern wage work requirements, transportation, and machinery. In general, the Hopi-Tewa male: farms; gathers plants; herds cattle, sheep, horses, and burros; hunts deer, turtles, eagles; builds the houses; spins cotton and wool and weaves all native cloth; makes leather objects, principally leggings, moccasins, and riding gear; makes most jewelry and most kachina carvings; does some pottery decoration; makes most tools, ceremonial objects, and masks; cuts and

stacks wood supplies; collects clay for pottery, paint minerals, and salt; carries water in trucks; trades for shells, turtles, and parrots. In addition, males are generally the shamans or medical specialists, and they do wage work on road crews and fire fighting crews, for instance. They play the active roles in public religious ceremonies, dances, and sings; in politics, language, and political interpretation; as policemen and judges, and in tribal council activities.

Women: also gather plants; gather raw materials for basketry and pottery; make pots (figs. 5-8) and carve some kachinas; prepare foods for eating and storage; cook; care for children; plaster and clean houses and kivas annually; construct and repair bread ovens. They also carry water by hand from springs or pumps. Women also do wage work in the hospital at Keams Canyon and as nurses and secretaries, school cooks, teachers, and maintenance personnel. They conduct trading parties in winter; they organize weddings and funerals. Pregnant women avoid dyeing of clothes, tanning of leather, or preparation of basketry materials, but there are few, if any, menstruation taboos (Beaglehole 1937:18-19; Ellis 1974b:137).

• WILD PLANTS AND ANIMALS   Hopi mesa people still collect about 100 wild plant species in their local area (Whiting 1939:48-50; Beaglehole 1937:50), and an addi-

592

Fig. 6. Four generations of Hopi-Tewa Corn clan women. From right to left, Nampeyo (at age 43), her mother, Kochaka, and Nampeyo's daughter, Annie Nampeyo Healing holding her daughter, Rachel Nampeyo (who became a renowned potter in her own right). Photographer unknown, 1901.

Fig. 8. Joy Navasie, famous modern Hopi-Tewa potter of the Kachina clan. She continues the fine whiteware pottery styles her mother, Paqua Naha, helped originate, and uses her mother's frog identification mark on the bottom of her pots. She appears here in social dance costume in her husband's cornfield on Antelope Mesa, east of First Mesa. Photograph by Ray Manley, 1973.

Fig. 7. Hopi First Mesa pottery jars made by Nampeyo in her famous Sikyatki revival style. Diameter of top about 36 cm, bottom about same scale; both collected 1912.

tional 100 plant species are collected or traded for from distances as great as 200 miles. Whiting states that 65 plants are used for medicine, 37 for ceremonial purposes, 47 for construction or decoration (agriculture, hunting, crafts, housing), 54 for food staples, seasonings, and beverages. Wild-plant collecting is thus still an important activity, but while communal work parties used to collect such plants (Beaglehole 1937:51-52), in 1974 individual Tewa families were more often seen (before the harvest is in) collecting weed plants by the roadside (Stanislawski 1968-1974).

Rabbits, mice, rats, prairie dogs, and other rodents, as well as coyote, turtles, small birds, lizards, and snakes have been hunted since the 1890s. In the 1850s and before, badger, porcupine, deer, antelope, mountain sheep, mountain lions, grizzly bear, and gray wolf were also hunted (Beaglehole 1936:3). Animals were important both for food and for raw materials (fig. 9), and in 1974 rabbit was still a critical resource in times of poor harvests and for ceremonial purposes. Turtles are also collected and their shells used in dance ceremonies as leg rattles. Hopi-Tewa do not have eagle-collecting rights, although they do use Hopi eagles in ceremonial ways. Fish were not caught or eaten (Ellis 1974b:147-153).

• AGRICULTURE Horticultural work is still the traditional center of Hopi-Tewa activity; their lives revolve around problems and ceremonies concerned with farming. Among cultivated plants used by First Mesa peoples Whiting (1939:12) lists as possibly native plants: corn, squash, kidney and tepary beans, sunflower, gourd, and

Smithsonian, NAA.
Fig. 9. Hopi-Tewa women preparing a rabbit-fur blanket (see "Nambe Pueblo," fig. 6, this vol.) on a Tewa Village rooftop. They are probably cutting the skins into long strips. These are twisted together to form a rope, which is arranged on a simple upright loom as a continuous warp, then formed into a blanket by twining across with weft cords (Tanner 1968:43, 58). These blankets are one of the few garments traditionally woven by women as well as men. Photograph by J.H. Bratley, about 1902–1903.

cotton. Spanish introductions, from about 1630, include onions, chili, watermelons, peaches, and wheat. Anglo introductions (1870 on) have been: safflower, sorghum, turban squash, peanut, beet, turnip, cabbage, carrot, tomato, peas, apples, apricots, pears, and cherries. By the 1950s flour corn varieties were preferred to hard flint types because of their ability to store well, and few Anglo hybrid types are used. But all major traditional corn varieties are still grown, because seed is inherited. Vegetables, which take much water, are now more often purchased at the store.

In 1890 First Mesa people planted 3.3 to 3.6 acres per person, about 80 percent in corn. Fifty percent of the corn was used, 25 percent stored, and 25 percent traded (Bradfield 1971:21). Dozier's (1954) 1950 figures seem to indicate an average plot of 1.5 acres per person; thus the average modern farm would be about eight acres for a family of five. By 1950 the population of resident Hopi-Tewa was 400, living on 50 farmers' work, that is, an actual average of little more than one acre a person. Obviously, wage work, herding, and crafts are required to support a modern family, and subsistence farming, while culturally vital, is no longer economically possible for the Hopi-Tewa.

Excellent descriptions of traditional Hopi-Tewa hand tools and planting and harvesting techniques appear in Forde (1931), Hack (1942), and Ellis (1974b). Traditional

planting and harvesting dates and schedules are seen in table 2.

• LAND OWNERSHIP    Hopi-Tewa lands are traditionally upstream or north of lines drawn through the gap north of Tewa Village (fig. 2). Plats have been allocated in order of the traditional arrival of each Tewa clan, but the amount of land does not correspond to clan size; for example, the Corn clan, one of the largest, has the least land. Boundary stones with engraved clan symbols are used to delineate plat borders (Dozier 1954:355; Forde 1931:367–368, map 3). Women are considered the actual owners of land and houses, the rights descending within the matrilineage; however, lands are received in trust, for use only. Thus each matrilineage of each clan has long-term control of lands averaging about 40 to 60 acres (Bradfield 1971:21), and some additional waste lands are held in common by the clans for general use during emergencies (Forde 1931:370–371).

In the 1950s–1970s a new trend emerged. Men moved off clan lands to tribal council-leased, nonclan lands in Hopi territory at Awatovi, north on Antelope Mesa, and near Keams Canyon (Cox 1967:146–147; Stanislawski 1968–1974). Such leased lands may be passed on to a man's own daughters or sons, rather than the nieces in his sister's line; that is, bilateral inheritance may be involved. Tewa men have also received sisters' clan lands when other clan members were few, and some men have given lands to their sons or daughters, who are in different clans (Forde 1931:378–379); however, such lands usually revert to the original clan in the next generation. Finally, if a clan is near extinction, the last members may adopt a woman of another clan to care for houses and fields, as Kosha (ḳosa), the last Hopi-Tewa Sun clan man, adopted a Kachina/Cottonwood girl in the 1890s (Parsons 1925a:91). Land may also be lent, as the land-wealthy Hopi Snake clan did in the 1920s, helping out Hopi-Tewa related by marriage (Forde 1931:382).

• DOMESTIC ANIMALS    Hopi-Tewa had large numbers of black sheep and goats by 1840; large herds of horses, cattle, and sheep are noted by the 1870s to 1890s. Burros became important after 1870; the pig, chicken, and turkey were reintroduced in 1891–1892, according to Fewkes (1900, 1922). Cattle were not generally economically important, with the exception of two Hopi families (Page 1940:29–47).

By 1880 herding was the first major cash industry for First Mesa (Page 1940:29–47, 1940a:29–36; Bradfield 1971:29, 42; U.S. Census Office. 11th Census 1893), and many Hopi-Tewa households were still supported by herding in the 1970s. This is because the Hopi-Tewa were among the first to hire Navajo shepherds and thus go into the herding business (Page 1940:38–39). The men do the work and own their flocks individually, thus giving men a new independence. Hopi-Tewa women may only own shares in flocks (Dozier 1954:356). Range lands are generally nonclan lands held by the villages in common.

Page (1940) provides excellent maps of the locations of corrals and grazing areas on the Hopi Reservation, including Hopi-Tewa areas in Polacca Wash. Ranges may be 10 to 15 miles from the villages, and Hopi-Tewa men often stay for extended periods at the sheep camps and ranches.

In the postwar period, there has been a shift from sheep to cattle raising. Although cattle are more expensive to buy, feed, and care for, they take less continuous care and bring a much higher sales price, vital items in an emerging wage economy. In 1950, 43 Tewa men were livestock owners, about one-half owning sheep (1,602 head) and one-half owning cattle (658 head). About one-quarter were sold each year (Dozier 1954:357). By 1963, nearly half the reservation cattle were at First Mesa (L.D. Mason 1965), and the First Mesa Hopi-Tewa and Hopi were the major cattle ranchers of the reservation.

Some Hopi-Tewa also have a few chickens and one or two pigs; horses or burros are commonly seen in corrals along the mesa edges. Dogs are common in the village, but cats are rare (L.D. Mason 1965).

It is clear that the herding of animals has changed the Hopi-Tewa culture in many ways: wool clothing replaced cotton by 1900; male ownership of herds changed family life; settlement patterns changed as second homes or ranches, 10 to 15 miles from the villages, were built. First Mesa Tewa have done better than most economically; the early First Mesa sheep herding economy has turned into a cattle raising business economy, with Tewas in the lead (L.D. Mason 1965:58-77; Kennard 1965; Nagata 1970:153-175).

• CRAFTS Dozier (1954:359) noted 25 craftsmen in 1950. A minimum of 24 men at First Mesa wove belts, women's wedding robes and ceremonial kilts, sashes, stockings, and other objects in 1970 (Hopi Tribe 1970). Only two or three men in the 1970s still made moccasins, drums, and other leather objects. Special piki cooking stones are collected at Awatovi. Grinding stones, pottery polishing stones, yucca paint brushes, and paint mortars are collected from archeological ruins nearby or are made from local materials. Chipped-stone manufacturing has not been seen in recent years. Almost all local men made kachina dolls, rattles, and bows and arrows to use as gifts at kachina dances (Stanislawski 1968-1974).

Many Tewa women (a minimum of 60 to 65) produced pottery in the 1970s (Stanislawski, Hitchcock, and Stanislawski 1976). A few earned as much as $5,000 to $10,000 a year by ceramic sales. Much of the pottery was sold directly to tourists from Hopi-Tewa homes, but some particularly well-known Tewa potters produced much of their pottery for sale and exhibit at fairs or for specific traders. Specific pottery forms such as mutton stew bowls, ladles, piki mixing bowls, ceremonial jars, and pipes were still widely used by the Hopi and Hopi-Tewa in ceremonies.

• PRODUCTION AND CONSUMPTION The family had been the primary production unit for all Hopi and Tewa reservation people until World War II (Beaglehole 1937:72-81; Kennard 1965; Nagata 1970:181-186, 200-222). Wage work was scarce, even with the start of Works Progress Administration projects during the 1930s; and traditional horticulture, herding, and craft activities were thus the primary economic occupations. Only one Tewa wage earner was noted in 1890 (U.S. Census Office. 11th Census 1893:45), and only six men over 18 on the entire reservation earned wages in 1890.

Quantities of food (particularly bread and fruit), baskets, kachina dolls, and pottery are still produced in Tewa Village for ceremonies, such as initiations, weddings, and kachina dances, and are then recirculated by ceremonial gift giving, producing a leveling effect. The total may approach 15 percent of the foodstuffs, particularly corn (Ford 1972; Nagata 1970:148-149). Thus the traditional annual ceremonial cycle of the Hopi-Tewa and Hopi has a major economic impact on the communities. In the 1970s there were more dances, and they were held more frequently, than in the past; they are longer and more costly and tend to be held on weekends so that off-reservation people may attend (Kennard 1965:29; Dozier 1954:363). Clan and phratry sharing is still vital; Dozier (1954) discusses in detail the traditional cooperative sharing among the Tewa and all peoples of First Mesa.

• MODERN ECONOMY In 1950, 22 percent of the adults were wage earners; 57 percent were still mainly self-employed in farming and crafts (Dozier 1954:356-369). By 1970 population had outstripped the production, and less than 40 percent of the basic requirement of food per person was produced. The majority of income in 1975 must come, therefore, from wage earnings, cash herding, social security payments, and other government funds. Because of reservation status, there is no rent for lands or houses, no property tax, no medical or educational costs for most families (Nagata 1970:116-117, 123-126). The Hopi tribal government also provides facilities such as social service centers, the Cultural Center, schools; U.S. governmental activities and services have created nearby reservation community or agency towns such as Polacca and Keams Canyon, which provide jobs and nontraditional opportunities. The new wage work, well discussed by Dozier (1954, 1966a) and Nagata (1970:176-194, 1971), has caused serious economic and social changes. Hopi-Tewa can choose to stay on underdeveloped reservation areas and remain poor with a semblance of traditional life; or they may migrate to the cities, as encouraged by the government, and have the problems of "city exiles" (Nagata 1971:116). About 20 to 25 percent of the Hopi-Tewa lived off-reservation, but they generally returned to their home villages to take part in local activities (Nagata 1971:144-147; Dozier 1954:353). In addition, the husband's increasing control of his own money and leased lands (neither tied to his wife's holdings) have freed him from some social responsibilities, thus changing relationships in Tewa Village.

Ellis (1974b) noted that the pre-World War II income of the reservation family was about $300, with a per capita mean of about $80. Dozier's (1954:357) figures indicate Hopi-Tewa income of about $350 per capita, and a 1968 census of the Hopi Reservation shows that 45 percent of all reservation Hopis over 16 earned less than $1,000 per year, 65 percent earned less than $3,000, 32 percent earned $5,000 to $10,000, and only 1 percent earned more than $10,000 per year (U.S. Bureau of Indian Affairs 1968:62). The average family income in 1970 was about $2,000, or $400 per person (Dutton 1975:41).

## Clothing and Adornment

In the 1970s Hopi-Tewa wore store-bought Anglo clothes, except during ceremonies and traditional dances. Blue jeans, cotton work shirts, wool jackets, and store-bought shoes were common for men, although long hair (often braided) was still worn. Older men might occasionally wear calico pants and traditional cotton shirts. Older women wore Mother Hubbard dresses with walking shoes. Some men and women still wore their hair in the traditional Dutch bob. Comparisons with the dress and material culture of the 1890s and 1920s may be seen in Fewkes (1922:270-272), Ten Kate (1885:255), and Harshberger (1926).

## Social Organization

The Hopi-Tewa social system is almost identical to the matrilineal, matrilocal, extended-family, exogamous clan system of the Hopi (Dozier 1954, 1955, 1970; Eggan 1950, 1966; Titiev 1944, 1972). The female-oriented household is the important group. It is usually an extended family, composed of several siblings, the mother, her sisters, their children, and also the attached spouses (including father) of different clans. Next in importance are the father's household and clan; linked clans in the mother's line (her phratry group); the father's phratry group; the clans and households of one's sponsors in the kachina initiation rite, kiva group rites, or curing ceremonies. Rules of exogamy are followed. Marriage is forbidden with the mother's or father's linked clans; and also unlike the Hopi case, Hopi-Tewa marriage is traditionally forbidden between cross-cousins (Freire-Marreco 1914:286). There is a joking relationship with father's sisters' husbands. The household group is unnamed, but the matriclan units are named in similar fashion to those of the Hopi (Bradfield 1973). The clans are generally composed of multiple lineages—for example, in 1974 there were two Corn clan lineages and three in the Kachina clan—and are generally connected through a grandmother or great-grandmother, although the relationship may be so vague as to be possibly fictional (Forde 1931:372; Eggan 1950:166). Residence is

matrilocal. The married daughters come to live next to or with the mother, or on her clan lands in her village. Only 11 instances of violation of this rule were found in 1950, and accounts of the 1890s reveal no such violations (Dozier 1954:289-290). This system has helped to preserve Hopi-Tewa independence from the Hopi (Eggan 1966:124).

A few Hopi-Tewa clans are also linked into weak phratries similar to those at Hopi. For example, Bear, Fir/Stick, and a Spider lineage seem to be linked; a Parrot lineage is linked with Kachina/Cottonwood (Dozier 1954:335; Stanislawski 1968-1974). In addition, the two Hopi-Tewa kiva groups are formed of linked clans that "go together" for ceremonies. Bear, Corn, Tobacco, and Fir/Stick (replacing the extinct Sun clan) are linked in the Central Plaza kiva and in the Outer kiva, Earth/Sand, Kachina/Cottonwood, and Cloud (in 1975 almost extinct) "go together." The presence of two kivas suggests the Rio Grande pattern of dual moieties, but Parsons (1926:211) gives objections to this concept. Members of linked clans share ceremonial privileges, extend kin terms to each other, and accept marriage restrictions; and the Hopi-Tewa can also extend their relationships to clans of the Rio Grande Tewa, Navajo, and Hopi in the same way.

Each clan has a senior female head who "feeds" and protects the clan religious symbols and who lives in the clan house. She also controls assigned clan lands. The clan house is the center of religious and economic activity for the clan members, and the eldest woman owns the house, stored food, and its furnishings (Dozier 1954:333). A man has primary authority in his mother's house, not his wife's house. The relative size of these clans has waxed and waned at Tewa Village over the centuries, and since 1870-1880 at least two clans have become extinct. In the 1890s there were eight clans ranging in size from 9 to 28, and six others were claimed to have once existed (Hodge 1896:349-350; Fewkes 1899:253-254). In 1974 there were only six clans (and one remaining Cloud man), but these same units were up to 300 percent larger than in the 1890s. As clan sizes change, so do people's relationships to allocated lands, ceremonies, and housing.

• KINSHIP Hopi-Tewa kinship terminology is classified as a Crow type and, though different in phonemes, is very similar in meaning to that of the Hopi (Dozier 1954:305-311, 1955; Eggan 1950; Freire-Marreco 1914). Only a few words have been borrowed from Hopi. The terms are descriptive, use many reciprocals, and are cognate with Rio Grande Tewa kinship terms; thus, as in the Rio Grande Tewa area, age is a major factor in Hopi-Tewa terminology, and older brothers and sisters are separated from their younger siblings. But while the words used are the same as the Rio Grande Tewa terms, the principles and behaviors associated are mainly those of the Hopi. In short, behavior has changed, but the terminology has stayed the same (Eggan 1950:153; Dozier 1954:310, 1955). Kinship terms are extended to other members of one's linked clans, to Rio Grande Tewa, and to other Indian groups. They are also extended to ceremonial clan relatives such as those godparents taken at kachina initiation ceremonies, who are considered substitute fathers and mothers. The ideal and real kinship behaviors (Dozier 1954:313–325, 1955) are similar to Hopi practices (Eggan 1950; Titiev 1944); but the Hopi-Tewa, in contrast, still do always distinguish between real father and father's brother, and real mother and mother's sister, and seniority rules also apply. Hopi-Tewa behavior is thus partly controlled by relative age, as in the Rio Grande area.

• SOCIAL CONTROL  The Hopi-Tewa connect migration legends with the two kiva groups. The Central Plaza kiva is given priority, and one of its Bear clansmen was village leader in 1950, followed by an associated Corn clansman in the 1960s; however, the early leaders of the late 1800s were Sand, Bear, Tobacco, and Corn clansmen, thus including members of both kiva groups (Dozier 1954: 338; Fewkes 1900:615–616; Parsons 1926:210–211).

The men generally play the official and public political and religious roles, but in their mothers' rather than their wives' clans. Fathers more often discipline their sister's children than their own. The strongest relationships in the family are mother-daughter, aunt-niece in clan, and sibling-sibling, for in these are the continuation of the clan group. Thus, the matrilineal household, including mother's brothers, still provides the authority and training, although affection comes from the father and father's clan. The Hopi-Tewa system also encourages mock fighting and insults with the father's relatives, thus providing a tension release. No witchcraft trials or public accusations seem to occur, although after an unexplained illness a relative with a "bad heart" may be suspect.

The modern wage economy, schooling, and the automobile have deflected younger Hopi-Tewa from traditional patterns. Both men and women are now more protected from gossip and ridicule from the clowns and ogres at dances; ostracism is not so effective in the 1970s. However, officials still warn people of the consequences of bad habits during major ceremonies; and the war chief, traditionally of the Kachina/Cottonwood clan, may still attempt to maintain order (Parsons 1922a:293). The town is generally under very loose ceremonial control; in the past, the winter solstice chief was town head for part of the year, starting in November, and the summer solstice chief was leader for the other part, starting in March (Parsons 1922a:292, 1926:225–226). The Hopi-Tewa are, in part, also governed by the Hopi tribal council, established in 1936 with Hopi-Tewa aid. Polacca, in particular, has supported the council (Nagata 1970:97), and the Tewa group is well represented on the council. The fact that all of First Mesa now acts as one political unit (rare in the Hopi area) may be a result of such Hopi-Tewa influence (Cox 1967, 1968; Dozier 1954:342, 360).

*Religion*

The First Mesa villages cooperate ceremonially, as they do politically. For example, they share most Kachina, Initiation, Snake-Antelope, Flute, and Niman ceremonies (table 3). Kachina dancers often visit all First Mesa kivas during one dance, including Tewa Central Plaza kiva (Fewkes 1903:36). The Hopi-Tewa cooperate with the Hopi religious societies, if asked, and prepare foods, provide transportation, or take part in official religious duties. However, there are differences in ceremonial activity, and before 1900 these differences were even more pronounced (Fewkes 1899:260). Hopi-Tewa may still exclude Hopi from some ceremonies, such as the Tewa Winter Solstice ceremony (*tán-tay*); the Hopi, in turn, may exclude Hopi-Tewa from parts of their Winter Solstice ceremony, the Soyal (Fewkes 1899:273; Parsons 1926:218). They did not borrow each others' ceremonies in the past for fear that the ceremony would· be "polluted" (Dozier 1951:61); this practice has only gradually changed in the twentieth century (Dozier 1954:344; Fewkes 1899:260; Parsons 1926; Eggan 1950:161).

The Central Plaza kiva group is clearly the most powerful and important leadership unit in the village, but the Outer kiva group has its own duties, responsibilities, and powers. For example, the Sunwatcher traditionally was from the Sun clan, and after its extinction, the Cloud clan took over its responsibilities. In 1975 the Cloud clan also controlled the important *sumako·le* curing ceremony. The war chief, traditionally of the Cottonwood/ Kachina clan, punished wrongs, prayed for village health, and maintained warrior groups. Finally, Outer kiva members performed the vital initiation ceremony at the winter solstice, during which 14 to 18 year old boys are taken into kiva groups.

**Table 3. Traditional Ceremonial Round**

| | |
|---|---|
| January | Kachina dances; War ceremony |
| February | Hopi Powamu; Ground Freezing ceremony |
| March | Horned Serpent Dance; seasonal transfer ceremony; hockey games and races |
| April–June | Kachina dances; Summer Solstice ceremony |
| July | Sun Stick making |
| August | *sumako·le* curing ceremony |
| September–October | Harvesting for Tewa Village town chief |
| November–December | Winter Solstice ceremony (*tán-tay*) |

SOURCES: Fewkes 1900:623; Parsons 1926:209–210; Fewkes 1903.

Fig. 10. Tewa clowns performing during a kachina dance (possibly a Niman kachina dance) in the central plaza at Tewa Village, viewed from the south. The men sitting on the roof may be Navajo spectators. Photograph by Robert H. Lowie, 1916.

The Tewa lack Hopi rites such as Niman and most kachina dances, the Snake-Antelope and Flute ceremonies, and nearly all the women's rituals. The War ceremony, Ground Freezing ceremony, Sun Stick making, *sumako·le* curing ceremony, Tewa Horned Serpent ceremony, and Winter Solstice kiva group initiation ceremonies were uniquely and traditionally Tewa (table 3). The Tewa also have one habit irritating to the Hopi: they like to continue kachina dances after the Hopi Niman ceremony, when in Hopi belief the kachinas return home for half the year (Stanislawski 1968–1974). In general, the Hopi ceremonies are basically water and fertility ceremonies, while the Hopi-Tewa ceremonies are curing and village-aid ceremonies. Kachina dances are sponsored by the ill person or his family to help in the curing (Parsons 1925a:75, 104, 107); such a dance to cure a Hopi-Tewa woman of cancer was held during the summer of 1970 (Stanislawski 1968–1974). Members of sacred societies, such as the *sumako·le* society, recruit members from those they cure (Stephen 1936, 1:xl; Parsons 1926:214–215; Dozier 1954:348). Whipper kachinas and shamans may also be used in curing. Hopi-Tewa shamans are widely respected and have a large clientele among Hopi and Navajo, perhaps due to their Rio Grande origins. Exact observance of ritual in dances, prayers, and

ceremonials, and strict obedience to the village chief and senior clansmen, are required to prevent such diseases and accidents from occurring in the first place.

Finally, while the Tewa, like the Hopi, make prayer sticks for all ceremonies, their sticks have always been slightly different in shape (Stephen 1936, 1:392), and the Tewa clowns, similar to Hopi mudheads in function, are quite different in appearance, being dressed in broad black and white horizontal stripes, with painted double horns. They are recruited in the same way as the Hopi clowns, that is, after curing for illness or by trespass (Parsons 1926:215, 223–224). A few Hopi kachinas are thought to be derived from Tewa, such as the Nuvakchina (snow kachina), Chaveyo, Hano mana (Tewa maiden), and Chakwaina warrior maiden (Wright 1973). Good discussions of traditional Tewa Village altars appear in Fewkes (1899, 1903) and Parsons (1926).

It is in the shared Hopi-style kachina ceremonies that the two groups are most similar (Dozier 1951:61, 1954:350–351; Parsons 1926:214–215, 228). Many dances are exchanged with Hopi from other villages and mesas (Parsons 1925a:24, 49, 83–85) as well as games and races such as the hidden ball game, stickball (connected with the war god), and kickball (connected with fertility). Both groups also have extramural ceremonial shrines, central plaza shrines, and four or more shrines marking the boundaries of the villages (Edward P. Dozier, personal communication 1968; Fewkes 1906:357-370), and they each plant prayer sticks in appropriate springs near the mesa (Parsons 1925a:13, 119; Ellis 1974b:172-187).

Acceptance of modern Anglo religions is still slight. The first missionaries arrived in Keams Canyon in 1870, and a Baptist mission was founded at Polacca in 1893. Since that time, the Hopi-Tewa have been in constant contact with Anglo churchmen, and many homes in 1975 had some Christian pictures on the walls; however, few Hopi-Tewa are really serious about Anglo religion, and Dozier (1954:298-300) cites some fascinating anecdotes showing the courteous but casual treatment of missionaries. Missionaries do give food, clothing, transportation, and other material benefits; as long as they do not seriously attempt to stop Tewa ceremonies, they are tolerated. Polacca and Keams Canyon have five churches: a Baptist and a Roman Catholic mission in Keams, and two Baptist missions and an Assembly of God church in Polacca. Mormon missionaries also commonly work at First Mesa (Hopi Tribe 1970:13).

## Life Cycle

There is a traditional series of life events that most Hopi-Tewa still consider to be important. These ceremonies make one a Tewa rather than an Anglo or Navajo.

• BIRTH    Birth takes place in a darkened room with only women, generally aunts or sisters, present. A male shaman is called in case of serious trouble. The woman's husband's mother cuts the cord with an arrowshaft for a male, a corn-stirring stick for a female. She puts ashes on the navel and then washes the baby. The husband's clan women care for the mother and child until the naming ceremony, washing the infant every four days and keeping an ear of fresh white corn by it. On the twentieth day, a naming ceremony occurs, the husband's clan women naming the child with a series of names related to their clan. The parents hold the child up to the sun and choose the "best" name of those given. This is typical also of Hopi practice (Dozier 1954:325; Eggan 1950). The infant then joins his mother's household until he is ready for the local nursery or day school at Polacca.

• PUBERTY    At about age 8 to 10, the male child is given a nonclan ceremonial mother or father and goes through a kachina initiation and whipping rite four days before the Hopi Powamu ceremonies. A new name is given and male children can play kachina roles (such as the Avachhoya) after this time. At about age 14, boys get a new ceremonial father from their proper clan kiva group and are initiated at the Tewa Winter Solstice ceremony. From that point on, they may take part in ceremonial societies and religious and political events. The stories in this ceremony, closed to Hopi, detail the differences between Hopi and Hopi-Tewa and emphasize the Tewa migration legends.

A similar girls' initiation ceremony occurs at the time of first menstruation. It involves seclusion and corn grinding for four days and dressing of the hair into the maiden's traditional "butterfly" whorls.

• MARRIAGE    Weddings usually occur when boys and girls reach 20 to 25 years of age. Courtship is left to the individuals; many children are born shortly before, or after, wedding ceremonies. Weddings are generally planned for January and August in order to avoid the kachina season, during which the weekends are already filled with parties and ceremonies. Relatively elaborate ceremonies are carried on in traditional homes. Clothes are woven by the husband's relatives for the girl's wedding, and in turn the girl grinds corn to be given to the husband's family. Ceremonial mud fights may be held to symbolize the loss of the boy from his family. The girl is then dressed in her new clothing and moved into her new home (generally near her mother). Her hair is dressed in the distinctive Hopi-Tewa married woman's style.

• DEATH    Early death is traditionally thought to result from witchcraft, unkind thoughts, and the failure to maintain proper ceremonial and sacred rules. Natural death is another transition, another rebirth. As in all ceremonies, the washing of the hair is critical, this time with a corn ear. Feathers are tied over the head, and a cotton mask is formed over the face, with a string feather also tied on. The face is painted partly black. These activities make the body "light," like a cloud, and give breath for the other world. The face and body may then be washed, like that of a baby, with cornmeal. A prayer stick is made and the individual is given a new name, because he is now considered a baby in the other world. He will probably be buried in the burial ground near the entrance road east of the mesa, near Coyote Spring. Water and piki bread are placed on, or near, his chest; he is placed in a sitting position with pottery bowls of water nearby. Other pottery bowls, sometimes broken ("killed"), a basket with prayer sticks, and a planting stick are placed on the grave mound. Women traditionally wail throughout the entire ceremony. Shroud clothes and a corn cob are kept at the house for four days, after which the dead person is considered to have finally departed (Parsons 1925a:75-77; Stephen 1936, 2: 824-828). These traditional descriptions do not hold for all recent "Christian" burials, which of course follow normal Anglo procedures.

## Prehistory

The prehistory of the Rio Grande Valley, the original home of the Hopi-Tewa, is still a matter of controversy (Dozier 1954:263-275, 1966a:3-19; Ellis 1967b; Ford,

Schroeder, and Peckham 1972). The Tewa-speaking people probably came from the upper San Juan River area about A.D. 1000-1200 and moved into the Pajarito Plateau or Nambe district, then into the Galisteo Basin (Ellis 1967b:38-42; Ford, Schroeder, and Peckham 1972:31-32). The Galisteo Basin Tewa may then have separated from the Northern Tewa speakers (about 1200-1300), leading to the linguistic and cultural differences that distinguished the two groups by the 1680-1700 period.

## History

Dozier (1954, 1966a), Ellis (1974b), and Montgomery, Smith, and Brew (1949) survey the early history of the Tewa speakers and their contacts with the Spanish invaders and discuss Spanish contacts in the Hopi mesa area. The Tewa groups on the Rio Grande and the Hopi were involved in the Pueblo Revolt of 1680, and according to their traditional oral history the Hopi-Tewa moved as a single village unit to First Mesa at the request of Walpi village chiefs, following the revolts (Fewkes 1899:253, 1900:614-616). They are said to have been asked to guard the mesa trail to Walpi from Utes and Paiutes. The Hopi Asa clans, thought to be related to the Tewa (traditionally the founders of Sichomovi), may also have come at the same time, or shortly before. The Asa clans were said to have come from the Santa Fe or Abiquiu region and to have traveled first to Zuni Pueblo, then to Hopi First Mesa (Ellis 1974b:81-84; Stephen 1936, 2:1085-1086). However, the Hopi-Tewa were in origin definitely Tanos from the Southern Tewa area in the Galisteo Basin, probably from the towns of San Cristóbal and San Lázaro. They moved north of Santa Fe to the town of Tsawarii (Harrington 1916:253) near Santa Cruz, following the Pueblo Revolt of 1680. After continuing pressure from the Spaniards, they left in 1696, traveling through Jemez, Fort Wingate, Fort Defiance, Ganado, and Keams Canyon on their way to First Mesa (Reed 1943a, 1952; Dozier 1951:56-58; Fewkes 1899:257). They may have first built a village near Coyote Spring at the south foot of the present entrance road to Tewa Village, but after defeating the Utes in a battle north of the gap, they were granted permanent farmlands by the Hopi, and their present mesa-top village site (Fewkes 1899:256-259, 1900:614-616; Mindeleff 1891:36).

Narváez (Reed 1943a:74) noted that the "Janos" or "Teguas" were at First Mesa in 1701. Wilson (1972:127-129) cites new evidence to show that in June and July of that year, Spanish soldiers attacked at First Mesa to avenge the previous attacks at Awatovi. Fewkes (1893:368, 1898:633) and Mindeleff (1891:31) state that the Tewa were not at First Mesa until 1700 and were probably not there at the time of the destruction of

Awatovi, which took place in November 1700. The month is known because the attackers came early in the morning during part of Wuwuchim, the tribal initiation ceremony held by the Hopi in November. There is archeological evidence of destruction and burning of Awatovi Pueblo (Fewkes 1893, 1898:601-608) and evidence of a massacred and possibly cannibalized group of 30 victims some 10 miles south of Polacca (Turner and Morris 1970). Thus it appears that Awatovi was destroyed in November 1700 by men from First and Second Mesa Hopi Pueblos as well as some clansmen from Oraibi, before the time of the Tewa arrival. The Hopi-Tewa may have been contacted by a mission of Hopi who visited Santa Fe in October 1700 and thus may have come to First Mesa a few months later (Montgomery, Smith, and Brew 1949:21-24, 222; Mindeleff 1891; Fewkes 1893, 1894a).

The Hopi would presumably have been delighted to have a new guard village at the head of the trail, particularly after their attack on Awatovi, which they no doubt expected would be avenged. In fact, following the Awatovi attack and the migration of the Hopi-Tewa in 1700-1701, the Spaniards did attempt to counterattack in 1701 at First Mesa, and again in 1706 at Payupki at Second Mesa against another Tewa group, and finally in 1716, again at Walpi and Tewa Village. At this time, the Hopi offered to give the Tewas back to the Spaniards, but the Tewa Village military position was too good, and the Spaniards retreated after burning some nearby Polacca Wash farm fields (Dozier 1954:277-283; Montgomery, Smith, and Brew 1949:24-26). Priests attempted to visit the villages several other times in the 1700s, but no military expeditions came again to the mesas, and the Spaniards were no longer to be an influence in the region.

The Navajos and Utes again began to attack the mesas in the late 1700s and early 1800s, and Mexican government officials who took over the territory from Spain in 1823 had neither time nor opportunity to consider the Hopi problems. Anglo trappers reached the mesas in the 1830s, and a few other United States citizens visited in the 1840s. The U.S. control of the territory began in 1848, following the Mexican-American War, and military expeditions and civilian visitors began to visit First Mesa in increasing numbers from 1850 on, particularly after the Civil War. A Hopi agent was appointed in 1869; missionaries and traders settled in Keams Canyon in 1870; a small missionary school was built there in 1875; the Keam trading post was founded in 1878. Anthropologists began to settle and study the First Mesa Hopi and Hopi-Tewa from 1880 on. The reservation was established in 1882, the same year the railroad reached Winslow, and this last was perhaps the most important event of all, for even though 75 miles south of the mesas, the railroad opened the area to tourists, a boom that has continued throughout the twentieth century.

Most Hopi-Tewa under 80 years of age have had some formal education. They were the first group to support the new government reservation school, founded in 1887; 18 Hopi-Tewa were enrolled by 1890, 12 speaking English by then (U.S. Census Office. 11th Census 1893:45; Dozier 1951:64; Fewkes 1922:273; Thompson and Joseph 1944:28-29).

Thompson (1950:92-93, 96-97) showed that First Mesa children, as a group, were more aggressive, more spontaneous, and had less anxiety than other Hopi groups. Their language ability and their "outsider" status have also encouraged them to deal more frequently with Anglos (Dozier 1954:326). As they are going to school, they continue to work either with their fathers in the fields or their mothers and aunts at home. They learn a great deal of traditional and ceremonial life from their grandparents. Most children learn such tasks by doing, or by demonstration, rarely by instruction, in contrast to Anglo education (Bunzel 1929; Dozier 1954:311-325; Stanislawski 1968-1974; Stanislawski, Hitchcock, and Stanislawski 1976).

In 1968 most adults over 25 (68%) had attended at least nine years of school, and more than one-half (54%) had attended high school, with nearly 32 percent graduating (U.S. Bureau of Indian Affairs 1968:56). Median years of education in 1968 were 10.5 (Kunitz 1974:12).

## Synonymy†

The designations Hopi-Tewa and Arizona Tewa are references to the location of this group since 1700. Their original name was what was written in Spanish as Tano, applied to their ancestors while they were still in the Galisteo Basin east of the Rio Grande. In the early 1950s this name was still used by elderly Hopi-Tewas in the self-designation $t^há\cdot nu\ té\cdot wa$ (Dozier 1951:57, 1954:263), and Curtis (1907-1930, 16:260, 262-263) recorded the Rio Grande Tewa form as táno (probably for $t^háno$), with the locative tánoge for 'Tewa Village'. What is probably the same name, recorded as $t^hanuge$, is also applied to the Galisteo Basin and a prominent abandoned Pueblo there (Harrington 1916:104, 481); the exact form in Rio Grande Tewa is uncertain, but translations include 'lower settlement' (assuming $\theta a(\cdot)$- 'dwell') and 'near the sun, on the sunny side' (with $\theta an$ 'sun'). Arizona Tewa $t^há\cdot nu$ was borrowed into Hopi as $há\cdot no$, $há\cdot nòwɨ$ (Whorf 1936:1215) 'Hopi-Tewa Indian' (Third Mesa $ha\cdot no$, pl. $ha\cdot nomɨ$; Voegelin and Voegelin 1957:49); from this comes the English name Hano for Tewa Village and its inhabitants (Reed 1943a:74-75, 1952:17; Curtis 1907-1930, 12:6, 18; Fewkes 1894a; Dozier 1951:56-57). Spanish spellings are

† This synonymy was prepared by Ives Goddard, incorporating material from Michael B. Stanislawski and Albert H. Schroeder (personal communication 1978).

Tagnos, 1680 (Hackett 1942, 1:3, 11, 22); Janos, 1760 (Tamarón y Romeral 1937:355, 1954:74); Thanos, 1779 (Miera y Pacheco map, Auerbach 1943:24); and Tanos, 1782 (Fewkes 1898:579).

When the Hopi constitution was drawn up in 1936 the Hopi-Tewa asked that the name of their Pueblo be changed officially from Hano to Tewa (Dozier 1951:56), and Tewa is now their preferred self-designation. (For the name Tewa and its variants, see the synonymy in "Pueblos: Introduction," this vol.)

The Zuni at one time called the Hopi-Tewa $te\cdot wa$ or $te\cdot wa\cdot k^we$ (Kroeber 1916:275, phonemicized), and their village $te\cdot wan\,^{?}a$, but they now group them with the Hopi and use these names especially for the Rio Grande Tewa (Dennis Tedlock, personal communication 1977). The Navajo call them *Naashashí* or *'Anaashashí* 'bear enemies', a name also applied to the Santa Clara Tewa (Robert W. Young, personal communication 1977).

The Rio Grande Tewa use *téwa* 'Tewa' or *xosó$^?$on* 'Hopi' or combinations of these: *téwa xosó$^?$on* or *xosó$^?$on téwa* (Harrington 1916:569, phonemicized). Jemez has *tǽwa-hípé* 'Tewa Hopi' (Joe Sando, personal communication 1978). Other forms are given by Hodge (1907b: 531-532) and Harrington (1916:569-570).

## Sources

The only major account of the Hopi-Tewa was published by the anthropologist Edward P. Dozier (1954), himself a Tewa from Santa Clara. He also published several preliminary reports (1951, 1955) and a good popular monograph on Tewa Village (1966a). His emphasis was on the social and religious organization of the society and its mechanisms for preserving separate identity in a longstanding culture-contact situation.

A number of early anthropologists wrote brief accounts of the group. Mindeleff (1891) did the best and most detailed study of architecture and settlement of the Hopi mesas. Stephen (1936), who lived at Keams Canyon and on First Mesa in the 1880s until his death at Walpi in 1894, left journals that have some revealing details on Tewa Village and its relations with its Hopi neighbors. A diary by a Hopi-Tewa man, Crow Wing, was edited by Parsons (1925a). Fewkes provided very detailed census counts, clan discussions, religious descriptions, and details of mythology and tradition in Tewa Village in the 1890s, as well as the best early archeological reports of the Hopi area (1894a, 1898, 1899, 1900, 1906). Freire-Marreco did fieldwork at Tewa Village in 1913 and published a detailed and accurate kinship discussion (1914). Parsons, who visited in the 1920s, wrote several fine works on social organization and religion and gave the best picture of the differences in Hopi and Hopi-Tewa ceremonial schedules (1925a, 1926). Bunzel (1929) used Tewa potters as major informants on Pueblo pottery making. Forde's (1931) agricultural study mainly used

601

Hopi-Tewa informants. He also included maps of land ownership rights, which are also discussed by Cox (1967). Reed (1943a, 1952) discussed the basic historical evidence, and the first attempt to summarize the social organization was by Eggan (1950).

Robert Black (1975) has worked with Hopi-Tewa informants on folklore and ethnomusicology and has prepared a biography of Irving Pabanale, a Hopi-Tewa judge. Stanislawski (1969, 1969a, 1969b, 1973, 1974, 1975; Stanislawski and Stanislawski 1975) has done ethno-archeology studies in Tewa Village and Polacca, concentrating on pottery and its relationship to culture in Pueblo society. Yegerlehner (1959, 1959a) has described aspects of the Hopi-Tewa dialect.

Good collections of Hopi-Tewa pottery may be found at the Museum of Northern Arizona, Flagstaff, and at the Smithsonian Institution, among others. The Museum of Northern Arizona also has detailed records and photographs of craft exhibits since 1930, including many Hopi-Tewa craft items. The work of Nampeyo and other Hopi-Tewa potters is exhibited worldwide (Collins 1974; Maxwell Museum of Anthropology 1974).

# Pueblo Fine Arts

J.J. BRODY

The term fine arts, and almost certainly the concept, was introduced to the Pueblos during the course of the twentieth century. Long before then, Pueblo people had produced great quantities of utilitarian artifacts that have since been classified as art, and many of the twentieth-century art objects made in the Pueblos or by Pueblo people simulate these older artifacts and are formally and technically derived from them. Thus, an understanding of Pueblo art history must consider two separate phenomena: the histories of the various Pueblo plastic and visual arts as well as the eclectic expansion of art definitions by the non-Pueblo world that transform artifacts into art.

Throughout the twentieth century, White influence on Pueblo art has been pervasive. Artists have been trained in White-dominated schools, marketing has been controlled by White institutions, and non-Indians have been the principal consumers. Variety of patronage—including art collectors and museums, souvenir-buying tourists, antiquarian curio hunters, and commercial speculators, as well as Pueblo and other Indian peoples—only dramatizes the fundamental difference between ancient and modern Pueblo art.

Most contemporary Pueblo art is a commodity produced by entrepreneurs for sale in an open market. When so made, it is an aspect of an international art movement (Primitive Art) that can be equated with Cubism, Abstract Expressionism, or any other international art activity (Goldwater 1967; Fraser 1971). Ancient Pueblo art became a part of the Primitive Art movement because of the intellectual revolution that made it philosophically valid after about 1912 to reclassify any artifact as art with the act of reclassification (discovery) considered to be art-creative (Lebel 1959:78).

## Before 1880

Before 1880, when the Santa Fe railroad first provided cheap transportation to the American Southwest, the impact of Europe on Pueblo arts was minimal despite more than 300 years of political domination. Political considerations and distance from manufacturing centers in Europe, Mexico, and the eastern United States had inhibited imports, and Spanish and later colonists depended on their own handicrafts or on trade with Pueblo and other Indian people for most manufactured products. Because the Pueblos were usually sellers rather than buyers of artifacts, and because they had a near monopoly, their aesthetic traditions were more affective on than affected by those of their European neighbors and conquerors.

Changes in Pueblo decorative traditions from about 1540 to 1880 were incidental to the demographic, religious, and political effects of contact and conquest. The scores of Pueblo towns of the sixteenth century and earlier were reduced to about 30 by 1900, with negative effects on the quality and quantity of their arts. At the time of contact these included several vigorous traditions in painted pottery; woven textiles decorated by a variety of techniques; basketry; shell, stone, and bone jewelry; mural paintings; stone and wood sculpture; and mask-making. Each had its own history, and most art was made by part-time craftspeople trained within their home communities for use by the people of those places.

Pottery was produced in great quantities and is the best known of these ancient arts. The technology was probably introduced before A.D. 500 when its decoration already had a specific Pueblo (or Anasazi) character. Paint was usually applied to one surface of a hemispherical bowl or globular jar, with line as the essential design element. Picture spaces were architectonically defined into a series of geometrically balanced units that were subdivided and filled with geometric repeat patterns of line or solid color. Except for black and white, colors functioned as passive background fields or as linear elements. Brushwork was tightly controlled and nontextural (fig. 1).

Exceptions, some of great visual impact, can be found for all these attributes. Sikyatki Polychrome made by Hopi potters during the fifteenth and sixteenth centuries used unbalanced design areas, dynamic color fields, and stippling, engraving, and other textures. The Sikyatki painters and the late Mogollon Mimbres phase artists before them had important figurative painting traditions (fig. 2), but whatever the innovation, Pueblo pottery artists ultimately returned to the dominant mode or incorporated their inventions into it.

Most ancient Pueblo pottery was probably made as needed by the women of a town. Except for ritual vessels, their wares were for household use, and paintings on them are an aesthetic aspect of a utilitarian craft that must also have served to proclaim community and personal identity. The design concepts were prefigured in

Field Mus., Chicago: a, 263589; Smithsonian, Dept. of Anthr., Archeol.: b, 336178; c, 336433; d, 334552.

Fig. 1. Prehistoric Pueblo pottery with painted black geometric line designs. a, Mogollon jar, Tularosa phase, Higgins Flat Pueblo, Catron Co., N.M.; b-c, Anasazi bowl and pitcher, Pueblo Bonito, Chaco Canyon, San Juan Co., N.M.; d, Anasazi jar, Pueblo del Arroyo, Chaco Canyon, San Juan Co., N.M. Height of d 35 cm, rest same scale.

the older and less durable media of basketry and textiles. Spanish accounts suggest that contact period textiles were more decorative than can be demonstrated by known specimens, but painted representations of textiles found on kiva murals of the fourteenth to sixteenth centuries support these sources (fig. 3; "Hopi Prehistory and History to 1850," fig. 4, this vol.).

The murals also show that mask-making and body painting were important arts and are themselves evidence of a representational painting tradition ("Hopi Prehistory and History to 1850," fig. 5, this vol.). Wall painting techniques predated the twelfth century, but their pictorial concepts were probably imported from Mexico about A.D. 1350 (Brody 1969-1972, 2:101-110). The earliest known are among the most dynamic. Even though the tradition may have begun in the Rio Grande valley, it seems to have flourished longest in the Hopi towns. Deities, supernaturals, or masked humans impersonating these were the common subjects. Flatly painted figures were isolated as emblems on a wall or grouped in

narrative compositions, sometimes with all walls of a room considered as a continuous picture surface ("Hopi Prehistory and History to 1850," figs. 6-7, this vol.). Because of its representational subject matter, visual complexity, and illusionistic intent, mural art is different in kind from the nonfigurative and geometrically rational Pueblo decorative arts. Sculpture and other ritual arts also differed conceptually from the decoration of utilitarian artifacts.

Religious persecutions in the Rio Grande valley during the seventeenth century forced the Eastern Pueblos to shield their rituals and related arts from outsiders. It became common thereafter for pottery painters to isolate emblems suggestive of ritual symbolism on their utilitarian vessels (fig. 4) (Frank and Harlow 1974). Emblematic pottery painting predated European contact, but its widespread use during the colonial period suggests a fusion of decorative and ritual art concepts when the effects of depopulation, political conquest, warfare, and religious persecution were most traumatic. More recently, the habits of secrecy spread to the Western Pueblos in defense against anthropologists, tourists, curio dealers, and religious proselytizers even as ritual art became almost the only Pueblo art made for Pueblo use. Because of these attitudes discussion of ritual art as art is limited by ignorance and a sense of impropriety.

## 1880-1975

The railroad came to the Southwest at about the time that military defeat of the Plains tribes made popular romantic and sentimental attitudes about all Indian people plausible. Before then, anti-industrial reactions in the industrial world gave intrinsic value to handmade artifacts, while the revolution in perception and definition of art by that world reached a climax only decades later. These events combined to shape the survival, revival, and invention of twentieth-century Pueblo art.

Inexpensive china dishes and metal cooking wares brought in by railroad contributed to a radical decline in manufacture of Pueblo household pottery before 1900 in the communities nearest to Albuquerque and Santa Fe. However, some specialized cooking vessels such as the bean pots of Taos, Picuris, and Tesuque continued to be made. At some Pueblos, potters began to make small and eccentric wares to be sold directly or through curio shops to tourists. At others, the craft died as textile arts did, but production of decorated utilitarian wares continued in the more isolated communities until well into the twentieth century (Bunzel 1929). However, the most isolated of all, Hopi, was the first to produce art pottery.

After 1875 the Keams Canyon Trading Post provided a place for the Hopi to exchange handcrafted goods for industrial ones (McNitt 1962:161). By about 1890 Thomas Keam was distributing art pottery made by Nampeyo (a Hopi-Tewa) and modeled after Sikyatki

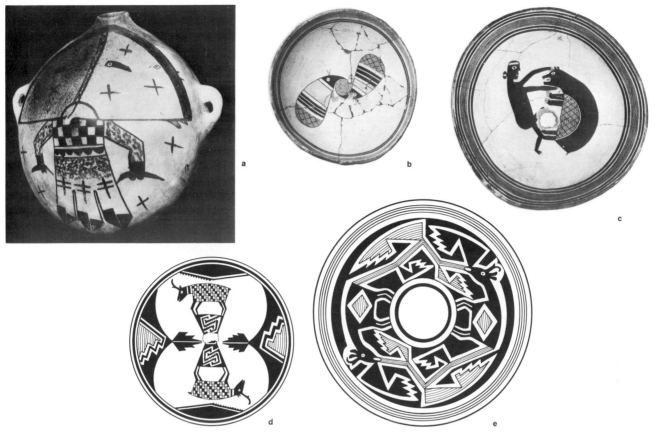

Field Mus., Chicago: a, 21174; Harvard U., Peabody Mus.: b, 10/96024; c, 26-7-10/95879; d-e, after Cosgrove and Cosgrove 1932:pl. 224 d,f.

Fig. 2. Sikyatki and Mimbres pottery. a, Sikyatki polychrome canteen with human figure (possibly Ahul kachina), feather motifs, and crosses; collected before 1894. b-e, Mimbres bowls with pictorial paintings on white slipped interior surface; b, black and beige polychrome insects; c, man with bear; d-e, black and white antelope designs composed of geometric units (Brody 1977). Diameter of b 27 cm, rest same scale.

Harvard U., Peabody Mus.

Fig. 3. Decorated textiles represented in prehistoric mural paintings. left, Figure wearing shirt and kilt with white on black design perhaps representing tie-dye or openwork pattern, and yellow and red tassels; right, kilt, with pattern in red, blue, black, and white probably representing painted fabric. Length of left segment 54 cm, right same scale. Copies of murals by the Peabody Museum Awatovi Expedition, 1935-1939 (W. Smith 1952:figs. 51c, 67d, 67b).

Polychrome and other late prehistoric wares ("Hopi-Tewa," fig. 7, this vol.). These archeological vessels already had value as antiquities. Nampeyo's combination of superior craftsmanship with an appropriate antique model was the prototype for art pottery revivals at other Pueblos and set the pattern for twentieth-century Hopi art pottery (Nequatewa 1943; Frisbie 1973).

Among the upper Rio Grande Pueblos the transition from utilitarian craft to art was more complex and difficult. Contact between craftspeople and patrons was more direct than at Hopi, and there was greater competition among marketing agents including museums. Production of tourist wares (see "Tesuque Pueblo," fig. 7, this vol.) dominated until well after 1920, but by then, Maria and Julian Martinez of San Ildefonso were making art pottery for a specialized audience ("San Ildefonso Pueblo," figs. 7-9, this vol.). Their art, like Nampeyo's, was marketed through institutions that paralleled and in some instances were identical to those of the international fine arts community (Bunzel 1929:5). The high prices paid for their blackwares and their personal fame influenced other potters in their town and at nearby Santa Clara to make similar wares for the art market (Whitman 1947:109). Continued success encouraged art pottery elsewhere, and impressive revivals occurred at Cochiti, 605

Fig. 4. Historic Pueblo polychrome pottery decorated with abstracted triangular feather and stepped cloud motifs. left to right, Two Zuni jars, collected 1904 and 1880, and Hopi jar, collected 1883 (see also Frank and Harlow 1974:figs. 5, 8, 141, 147). Diameter of left 33 cm, others same scale.

Santo Domingo, Zia, and Acoma (examples of characteristic pottery for the Rio Grande Pueblos appear with many of the individual Pueblo chapters, this vol.). Visual differences among wares made at different towns became a sales factor, and by about 1950 emphasis on recognition shifted to individuals who, thereafter, were expected to produce characteristic, signed works. From the time of Nampeyo until about 1965 most Pueblo art pottery was modeled after historic or prehistoric wares, with patrons and artists both finding validation and aesthetic satisfaction in reviving ancient patterns.

Pueblo pottery of this period is generally smaller, more refined, more precise, than that of any past tradition, and emblematic motifs suggesting ritual significance are common. Basic aesthetic concepts and manufacturing methods were identical to or compatible with those of ancient times (Bunzel 1929:49–68; Maxwell Museum of Anthropology 1974). In about 1965 idiosyncratic variation became dominant in the work of some northern Rio Grande artists school-trained or otherwise influenced by individualistic art concepts of White society. Their art is characterized by intense personal rivalries, technical novelties, concentration on surface finish, and, too often, structural formlessness. Visually and metaphorically it summarizes the futility of applying concepts of individualistic creativity to tribal art traditions.

Pottery is the most important of the twentieth-century Pueblo arts to retain the aesthetic character of the past. Blanket weaving, except for an occasional rug-weight blanket woven at Hopi, was an all-but-dead art before the middle of the twentieth century. Belt weaving continues at a number of places, mostly to supply ceremonial needs, and there have been sporadic attempts to revive embroidery, particularly among the Eastern Pueblos.

In sculpture, only Hopi kachina dolls (*tíhü*, pl. *títhü*) are available for study. From the nineteenth century until the 1930s, the kachina carving tradition was directed toward identification of the attributes and personalities of par-

ticular supernaturals. Only significant features such as masks and paraphernalia were detailed, and forms were compact, frontal, and hieratic. Trends toward naturalism were evident before 1900 but became dominant only after significant numbers of Hopis were schooled in White institutions. Since about 1930 proportions have become more natural, physical activity more specific, and irrelevant details such as finger and toe nails treated as visually equal to significant ones. Rather than representing supernaturals, these dolls replicate humans wearing the masks and costumes of the kachinas (fig. 5). Fundamentally powerful formal qualities were replaced by slick surfaces,

Fig. 5. Hopi kachina dolls. left, Simply carved Tukwinong (Cumulus Cloud) kachina in the early static style, height about 38 cm, collected 1890s. right, Contemporary Tumoala (Devils claw) kachina with dynamic stance and added costume details made by Henry Shelton of Hotevilla, height 41.5 cm, collected 1978.

Smithsonian, NAA: Fewkes 1899-1900, 1.
Fig. 6. Two watercolor, pencil, and crayon drawings of Hopi kachinas commissioned and subsequently published by J. Walter Fewkes (1903:pl. VIII, pl. V). The published report cites 2 of the 3 artists by name but does not specify who did which drawings. left, Ahul, the kachina who leads the kachinas in their annual return to the village of Walpi at Powamu (see "Hopi Ceremonial Organization," this vol.). right, Wuwuyomo, a kachina of the Badger clan at the village of Sichomovi, who appears to be a Sichomovi version of Ahul. Fewkes (1903:14) provided materials but "left the execution of the work wholly to the Indians, no suggestion being made save the name of the god whose representation was desired"; drawings commissioned Nov. 1899-March 1900.

and an evocative art form was reduced to a clever craft (Colton 1959; Dockstader 1954).

School training and the influence of curio dealers at Indian art competitions in Flagstaff, Gallup, Albuquerque, and Santa Fe were among the most significant influences on Pueblo sculpture. These same forces played a significant role in the twentieth-century development of Pueblo easel painting. Other than the pictures of kachinas commissioned by J. Walter Fewkes at Hopi about 1900 (fig. 6), no Pueblo easel paintings were made before about 1912 (Fewkes 1903; Dunn 1968). About then, some students at the San Ildefonso Day School made pictures that found a ready market among Santa Fe intelligentsia. By 1918 Pueblo easel painting had all the attributes of a school, including masters, patrons, critics, and exhibit and marketing institutions. Crescencio Martinez ("San Ildefonso Pueblo," fig. 12, this vol.) was the master until his death in 1918 when Alfonso Roybal (Tse Ye Mu) became the dominant artist.

Pueblo genre scenes and nonsecret dances were the common subjects. In the early years, most pictures were of more-or-less realistic figures placed in a blank environment whose parameters were defined by posture and relative position (fig. 7; "Cochiti Pueblo," fig. 17, this vol.). From about 1918 to 1922 other Pueblo young people including Velino (Shije) Herrera (Ma Pe Wi) from Zia and the Hopis Otis Polelonema and Fred Kabotie attending the Santa Fe Indian School also began painting in a similar manner (fig. 8; "History of the Pueblos Since 1821," fig. 7, this vol.). Their illusionistic intentions are quite clear, for they came to use environmental backgrounds, volumetric drawing, and atmospheric color. About 1922 there was reversion to more archeological traditions, perhaps inspired by market forces. Colors were applied flatly, background details were eliminated, and decorative stylizations suggestive of ritual pictures became commonplace. Only a few artists, mostly Hopis inspired by Kabotie, continued to develop the illustrative techniques of the early years, but by about 1930 most of the original group had stopped painting. A few years later, pan-Indian easel painting was invented at the Santa Fe Indian School ("Santa Clara Pueblo," fig. 7, "Jemez Pueblo," fig. 3, this vol.). It combined the Pueblo conventions of the 1920s with a flat, decorative style that had briefly been in vogue among some Oklahoma Kiowas

School of Amer. Research, Santa Fe.
Fig. 8. *Preparing for the Buffalo Dance*. Gouache painting by Otis Polelonema, 1919. For a painting of the same subject by Fred Kabotie at about the same time, see "Hopi Ceremonial Organization," fig. 1, this vol.

Denver Art Mus.
Fig. 7. *Harvest Dance*. Tempera painting by Alfonso Roybal (Awa Tsireh) of San Ildefonso, 1930.

607

about 1928 (Brody 1971:120-126). The Indian School style spread and persists, characterized by sentimental and cliché-ridden subjects, flat and decorative paint application, and the use of one-point perspective (fig. 9).

In 1962 the Institute of American Indian Arts was established on the recommendation of the Indian Arts and Crafts Board by the Bureau of Indian Affairs at the Santa Fe Indian School. In part this was the result of a general feeling that Indian easel painting was aesthetically, emotionally, and financially unsatisfactory (Dockstader 1959). One goal was to prepare young Indians for training as professional artists, thus assimilating them into the mainstream of contemporary art (New 1968:8). Paradoxically, it may be the means by which trained Pueblo painters can develop new community art traditions. In the 1970s a group of young Hopi artists trained at the Institute or influenced by its attitudes organized within their Pueblo to communally produce secular paintings based on ancient prototypes but modified by international art forms. That they are attempting to reconcile nonesoteric tribal art concepts with those that define art objects as their own subjects is no guarantee of failure.

Throughout the twentieth century, self-conscious Pueblo art has largely been conditioned and controlled by marketing forces and patronage. It is mostly a commodity, like any other modern international art, and its success or failure depends on the conviction held by both artist and patron of the validity of a particular way of doing things. Until about 1965 most Pueblo art potters accepted ancient aesthetic attitudes and were firmly convinced of the social and aesthetic value of their work (Maxwell Museum of Anthropology 1974). This conviction was matched by solid patronage, and their art flourished. Easel painters always had patrons, but the artists characteristically became bored with their art as they reached maturity. Social irrelevance of the art was a guarantee of its aesthetic impotence.

Kachina carving in 1975 was sustained by an enormous market demand, but its aesthetic character aborts its social potential to the Pueblos and must alter radically when outside demand slackens. Similarly, Pueblo jewelry, made in enormous quantities for outsiders, has an artistic validity that appears to be irrelevant to its artists. The Pueblos maintain themselves, but their secular utilitarian art products have largely been replaced by industrially made goods, and art has continued mostly as an income-producing activity. Vitality and continuation of the unique Pueblo character of any of the arts seemingly can persist only, as with pottery, when form and content are somehow meaningful to both artist and audience.

## Sources

The literature of Pueblo fine arts is extensive, but no one work satisfactorily covers the field. The most useful publications tend to be those that deal with distinctive art forms. Among these are Bunzel's (1929) study of Zuni pottery, a pioneer work in ethno-aesthetics, and more descriptive works on archeological Hopi pottery by Fewkes (1973), on Mimbres pottery by Brody (1977), on that of modern Santo Domingo by Chapman (1936) and San Ildefonso by Chapman and Harlow (1970). Dockstader's (1954) thoughtful history of kachina doll carving, Colton's (1959) taxonomy of dolls, and Fewkes's (1903) important monograph are basic to study of Hopi carving. Jewelry, particularly silver, is covered in Adair's (1944) definitive book updated by Bedinger (1973). Modern Pueblo painting is perhaps the only art subject whose literature is not oriented toward anthropology; Dunn (1968) and Brody (1971) are the most important. Other nonanthropological texts on any of the arts tend to be surveys that offer few new insights and little new and trustworthy data. Finally, picture books are generally lacking, with that by Frank and Harlow (1974) by far the best of a poor field.

Mus. of Northern Ariz., Flagstaff.

Fig. 9. *The Beginning of the Corn Dance,* casein on colored board, by Rafael Medina of Zia, 1966.

# The Mythological Triangle: Poseyemu, Montezuma, and Jesus in the Pueblos

RICHARD J. PARMENTIER

The story of the culture hero is widespread in the mythologies of the world. He may be a god, a demigod, or a powerful mortal deified by tradition, but his distinguishing characteristic is that he brings mankind the arts of civilization, by stealing fire from the gods, for example, or by instructing people. The Pueblo culture hero, found in almost all the individual Pueblos, is the figure called Poseyemu (*póséyému*) by the Rio Grande Tewa, a name that is also used in this chapter as a general designation, in order to avoid repeatedly listing the equivalent names used in all the languages. At Zuni he is called Poshayanki (*pošaya·nkʔi*); at Taos, Piankettacholla (as spelled by M.L. Miller 1898:44-45; properly *pʔiankʔɔocɋle*); and in the Keresan villages, Boshayanyi (Santa Ana *púšáyâ·ni*, for example). A most interesting aspect of this pan-Pueblo culture hero is that he is consistently identified with the Mexican figure Montezuma and, in some cases, with the Christian deity Jesus Christ. Numerous variants of the Poseyemu legend include exploits of Montezuma and elements from the Christian gospel narrative.

## Tewa Culture Hero Myths

The Poseyemu legend is highly developed among the Rio Grande Tewa. The reason for this may be that the Tewa received the full force of the Roman Catholic missionary and the Spanish military effort; the center of the Spanish government in the Southwest was at Santa Fe, which is within the Tewa world. The Tewa legends are rich in Catholic and Spanish elements and yet have not lost their distinctive native color. As Lévi-Strauss (1969:2) rightly points out, no one variant of a myth or a myth cycle can be considered the ideal type or the best example. Yet one variant may be examined in depth to reveal general themes and relations of the whole cycle. The variant selected does not form the center of a structure but is only one of many possible entries into the mythological spiral. It is best to study a variant that contains few Catholic and Spanish elements in order to form a contrast with those variants that have obvious syncretic features. Such a variant is found in Curtis (1907-1930, 17:170).

> At Posii [*posiʔ* 'Ojo Caliente', the traditional Tewa homeland] lived an old woman and her granddaughter. They were very poor. The people despised them, and children would throw stones at their house and scatter refuse about it. When the cacique announced that it was time to move to the piñon camp, the girl said that she too would go. Her grandmother tried to desuade her: "You are poor, you have only rags. Nobody likes you. Who will bring you wood and water?" Nevertheless the girl followed the others at a distance up toward Rattlesnake Mountain. At noon as she rested alone she heard a voice. She looked up and saw a handsome young man. He asked, "Where are you going?" "I am going to gather piñon nuts." "Do not go," he said. "Will you take some piñons from me?" "Yes," she said. "How many rooms have you?" "Two," she answered. "Take these nuts," he said. "Swallow one, and throw one of the others into each room of your house. Close the door and do not open it until morning." She agreed, took the three piñon nuts, and swallowed one. She returned to the village and tossed a nut into each room and closed the door. Night came, and they slept outside. Early in the morning the girl was astir and went quickly into the house. She found both rooms full of piñons. Four days later, she bore a child. In four days he crept, in six days he walked, on the eighth day he killed a woodrat with a little bow made by the old woman. At twelve days of age he killed rabbits, at fourteen he went hunting antelope. A man spoke to him from behind a bush. "Come here, my son. What are you hunting?" "I come to hunt antelope, but my arrows are small. My bow is weak." "I have brought you a quiver full of good arrows," said the man, "a quiver of cougar-skin. With these you will kill anything. My son, you have no name. You will take this name, Posehweve. I, Sun, am your father." The boy went home, and on the way he killed an antelope. He told his grandmother what had occurred, and she said, "We will call you Poseyemo, because the woman who bore you is stronger than the Sun."

This story introduces several important Tewa themes: a poor girl, a social outcast, is magically impregnated by the Sun; she gives birth to a remarkable boy who grows to maturity quickly and performs difficult tasks easily. In this story the boy's special skill is hunting, while in other variants his skill is prophecy or ritual knowledge. This variant fits easily into the scheme of Kongäs and Maranda (1962): the initial situation is transformed by divine agency into a mediating situation that is then transformed, again by divine agency, into a final resolution.

Several oppositions are clear: poverty/plenty, unnamed/named, no father/father, small game/large game, childlessness/parenthood, small arrows/large arrows. The mediator is also obvious: the Sun, a male principle, is the motivating force for all the reversals; the symbol of this force is the piñon, a traditional Pueblo symbol of fertility. Laski (1959) points out that piñons are

| Minus | Plus |
|---|---|
| Girl lives in poverty | |
| Girl is childless | |
| Girl is husbandless | |
| Girl is socially outcast | |
| | Girl is given piñon by Sun |
| | Girl's house is full of nuts |
| | Girl gives birth to a child |
| | Girl is rendered a woman |
| Poseyemu has no father | |
| Poseyemu has no name | |
| Poseyemu kills only small game | |
| Poseyemu has small arrows | |
| | Poseyemu is given name by the Sun |
| | Poseyemu knows his father |
| | Poseyemu kills big game |
| | Poseyemu is given large arrows |
| | Poseyemu is rendered a man |
| | Girl is stronger than the Sun |

one of several symbols of fertility and prosperity. In the Southwest piñons are fertile in five- or seven-year cycles at a given place (according to either scientific fact or traditional legend) (Parsons 1929:276). This cyclic fertility is echoed in other myths that state that the culture hero visits the Pueblo every seven years. In other myths, the hero returns each year from the lake; whatever the period of the cycle, it is clear that cyclic fertility is associated with both the piñon and the Pueblo culture hero.

The variant from Curtis (1907–1930, 17) also follows the scheme of Kongäs and Maranda (1962) in that the final resolution is not a return to the original state of affairs because Grandmother announces that her granddaughter is stronger than the Sun. The mediator performs a successful permutation of the initial state of affairs rather than merely nullifying that original state. Throughout the myth, the Sun is the motivating force; he is the source of the girl's pregnancy and the giver of the boy's name and hunting equipment; however, the final resolution is an affirmation of the female principle over the male principle, an affirmation strong enough to balance the male and the female forces. The entire narrative is generated by this tension between male and female forces. The poor girl expresses the female principle when she gives birth to a child, but since that child is a male child, the male principle is affirmed. When the boy is given large arrows, which can be interpreted as the means of masculine expression in Pueblo society, the male principle is again affirmed. The final resolution, on

the other hand, expresses the power of the female principle. Without the girl's capacity to bear children, the Sun would have been unable to cause Poseyemu's birth. The importance of the male and female principles and the necessity for their balance will become clearer in other variants.

The identification of the poor girl with White Corn Woman in the variant recorded by Ortiz (1963–1968:47) is the key to the male-female opposition. This identification also enables the myth to be related to Tewa social structure. The Tewa of New Mexico are characterized by a dual organization. Two moieties, the Summer moiety and the Winter moiety, govern the village for unequal portions of the year. The Summer moiety, which rules during the summer months, is concerned with rain and growing crops. Blue cornmeal, representing the blue summer sky, is its symbol. The Winter moiety, which rules during the winter months, prays for snow and for the fertility of seeds. Its symbol is white cornmeal, which represents snow-covered fields. The duality found in the moiety system is also reflected in Tewa thought (Laski 1959:65). The harmony of male and female principles is ultimately a fertility theme. The Tewa fertility ceremonies symbolize the fusion of the father god with the mother earth. Often, this is represented by a breakthrough of the supernatural, the male principle, into the natural, the female principle (Laski 1959).

White Corn Woman presents a contradiction, which generates the structure of the Tewa Poseyemu myths. She embodies a contradiction because she is the mother of the Winter moiety (the male moiety) and, thus, is the symbol of the male principle. On the other hand, she represents the female principle in her maidenhood. Ortiz (1969:169) points out that at least one-third of all Tewa myths deal with White Corn Woman and that she is the closest the Tewa come to a bisexual creator-god. This tension is handled in myth by "initially, designating her as 'maiden,' humanizing her and then proceeding to have her fertilized magically by the Sun or some other transcendental figure" (Ortiz 1969:165). This same ambiguity is present in the Woman's Society, whose leader is called Red Bow Male Youth and whose symbolic mother is White Corn Woman. The head of the society is called "male youth" even though she is a female. The other half of the Woman's Society is represented by Blue Corn Woman, who is the symbol of the Summer moiety (Ortiz 1969:89). The function of the Woman's Society, among other things, is to care for scalps, and a possibly significant connection between scalps and rain is evident in the traditional belief that when it is going to rain the scalps cry.

A relationship among Poseyemu, rain, and scalps has also been suggested on the basis of etymological analyses of the culture hero's name. That his name is significant is shown by the attention paid to it in the myth. In some myths the young boy is mocked because he has no name; in others he is called No-Name. When the Sun bestows a name on the boy his life situation is immediately transformed. Townsfolk remark that his new name is wonderful, unusual, or even unique. The name Poseyemu (póséyému) has been compared to p̌o·se· yemu 'rain shower; falling mist' (p̌o·se· 'light rain, mist, dew, moisture'; yemu 'to fall'; Alfonso Ortiz, personal communications 1971, 1977). Among the suggested translations and interpretations are 'dew falling' (Curtis 1907-1930, 17), 'he who strews the morning dew' (Chavez 1967), and 'moisture from heaven' (Bandelier 1892), and for the alternative name Posehweve (p̌o·se·xʷeve, with xʷeve 'move, scatter'; Harrington 1916:163; Alfonso Ortiz, personal communication 1977) of some myths 'he who comes along strewing moisture in the morning' (Bandelier 1892), 'dew from the sky' (Chavez 1967), and 'he who scatters mist in the morning' (Applegate 1929). The allusions of the name may be understood by reference to the natural phenomena involved. In the Southwest vaporous mist can be seen rising from a still body of water on a hot day. A little imagination creates out of this mist a human form, the culture hero Poseyemu (Alfonso Ortiz, personal communication 1971). Bandelier (1890-1892, 1:47) suggests that similar natural phenomena could inspire the Pueblos into worship. According to Harrington (1916:54) mist is recognized by the Tewa as a cloud and, though rare in Tewa country, it stays for two or three days at a time and "is often seen rising from the river at nightfall in winter." For the significance of clouds, note the resemblance between Tewa oxúwá 'cloud' and o·xuwa 'kachina'. Harrington (1916:54-56) observed that these words were not identical but added that the kachinas "are supposed ever to be present among the clouds, and the close association between them and the clouds probably accounts for the resemblance of the words," which are "doubtless connected etymologically." The impersonation of the kachinas is, of course, an important part of Tewa ritual (Ortiz 1969:92). Finally, an etymological connection between the culture hero's names and scalps is seen in the ritual name for scalps p̌o·se·ʔê· 'little mists', a reflection of the associations with rain that scalps have (Alfonso Ortiz, personal communication 1977; cf. Parsons 1929:138).

The natural-theological conception of Poseyemu as mist rising from water correlates with the Tewa myths in three general ways. First, Poseyemu in the myths is considered to be a universalistic figure. Curtis (1907-1930, 17) regards Poseyemu as the founder of the Summer Society, whose purpose is to pray for rain and the growth of crops for the good of the entire world regardless of tribe or race. This is a remarkable notion for the centripetal Tewas and seems to contradict generalizations made about the nature of the Pueblo world view.

Such universalistic conceptions are also uncharacteristic of archaic religions in general. This universalism is present in the idea of mist, for Poseyemu is always many places at once; he can never be confined to one lake or spring. He is present wherever the natural conditions make his appearance possible. Second, Poseyemu is considered in the myths to be a mediator between heaven and earth, or male and female. This is also shown in his association with mist and dew, for these are the perfect symbols of the fertility given from the sky (male) to enrich the earth (female). Poseyemu is the prophet of rain, which is the principal concern of Pueblo agriculturalists.

The third correlation of this type is found in the Tewa emergence myth (Spinden 1933:355; Haeberlin 1916:21, 29; Harrington 1916:567-569), which is generally the same in most of the other Pueblos as well. The Tewa place of emergence, or Sipapu, is located by some at a particular deep, brackish lake just north of Alamosa, Colorado (see "San Juan Pueblo," this vol.) and at other specific places by the other Pueblo groups. Its Tewa name is si·pófe (locative form si·pófenæ), similar to that in other languages: Santa Ana Keresan šipá·pʰi, Zuni šipa·puliʔma, and Hopi (Second Mesa) sípàpi (Whorf 1936:1295) and (Third Mesa) sípa:pi (Voegelin and Voegelin 1957:44), the source of the English name Sipapu. In the Tewa myth a great Douglas spruce grew out of the lake and served as a ladder for mankind and the animals to climb up out of the underworld, where they originated. According to Spinden (1933:335) some Tewa say that Poseyemu was the first one up, and when he found the earth to be good "he danced and the people down below heard him dancing. That is the reason the people now dance at the . . . shrine at the center of each plaza," called the earth-navel center. The place of emergenge is the center of the universe, both the horizontal and vertical reference point for the Pueblo world view (Ortiz 1969; White 1964). It is the point of contact between the natural world and the supernatural underworld, where the house of the Sun and the Earth Goddess is, where the kachinas live, and where the dead return. The kachinas are primarily those people who did not come out with Poseyemu, but some kachinas are the dead and some are newborn babies who are not yet four days old or not yet christened.

Some other Tewa accounts treat Poseyemu differently. He is sometimes identified with Made Person, or at Nambe with World Man, who lives forever at the lake of emergence (Ortiz 1969:81; Parsons 1929:266-267), though World Man is more commonly identified with the Sun, the father of Poseyemu. On the other hand, Curtis (1907-1930, 17) suggests that Poseyemu might have been an outstanding leader who was a real, historical personage. However, although it may seem inconsistent from the point of view of scientific concepts of space and time, there is no contradiction in the Pueblo mind in having a culture hero present at the emergence, present eternally at the lake of emergence, and present historically at the Spanish conquest.

Another association of Poseyemu is that in Tewa myths between him and Coyote *(pósé-xʷâ·)*. Across the Pueblos, Coyote is usually an old man who acts as a go-between for the kachinas and the townsfolk; often he is a trickster, and often he is a prophet (Parsons 1929). A myth from San Juan says that if the Coyote barks in the summer, rain is coming; if he barks in the winter, snow is coming. In these roles Coyote is remarkably similar to Poseyemu. At Taos there is a myth that Poseyemu was brought up by Coyote. In a Tewa song (Spinden 1933:99) Coyote is invoked in a hunting chant.

All these various associations of Poseyemu with scalps, mist, dew, rain, and Coyote depend on the Pueblo notion of well-being. All Poseyemu's roles can be reduced to a fundamental level; he provides for the general well-being of the Pueblos, whether it be as a symbol of fertility (through rain, piñons, and dew), a successful mediator between heaven and earth (through Sipapu), a hunter and agriculturalist, a leader in warfare (through scalps), or the instrument for social integration (through White Corn Woman). The well-being of the Pueblos during the Spanish contact period depended largely upon the preservation of native religious rituals. Accordingly, Poseyemu plays the role of ritual leader and teacher in many Tewa variants.

Poseyemu's role as ritual leader takes three forms in Tewa mythology. In some variants, Poseyemu institutes dances and rituals during his stay in the village; in others he orders kachina dances to be held underground for protection against the Spaniards; and in others he opposes the alien religious system in direct competition.

The following Tewa myth (Ortiz 1963-1968) tells the story of Poseyemu's confrontation with the Pueblo council after he miraculously kills more buffalo than the experienced hunters. At the meeting Poseyemu declares himself and then institutes the Matachine Dance.

> Today, I have become Po-say-yay-moo [Poseyemu]. Hence from this day forward I am your way of life. I am now your protector, and your savior. You are now my people. Today on I am your Mother and your Father. Even the village officials, the elders and the town crier are now under my guidance. Today you have all become my children and as children I shall lead you. Hand in hand, step by step we shall seek eternal life. . . . You are now on the eve of your redemption. Tomorrow you shall dance the Turtle dance. Through the Turtle dance you shall seek eternal life. There is another dance you must do. It is the Matachina dance. The Matachina dance is done on Christmas day and the Turtle dance is performed the following day (Ortiz 1963-1968:50-51).

The distinction between the Turtle Dance (fig. 1) and the Matachine Dance (fig. 2) is important. The Matachine dance is a Spanish-derived dance, which among the Tewa is governed entirely by Spanish officials. The Turtle

Mus. of N.M., Santa Fe.
Fig. 1. Turtle Dance, as performed at Taos (Parsons 1936:90-91, pl. 13B). For a San Juan Turtle Dance of about the same era, see Parsons (1929:179-185, pls. 21-22). Photograph by an unknown photographer, probably 1915-1920.

Dance, on the other hand, is governed by members of the Warriors' Society *(íowaʔê·)* and is, therefore, distinctively native (Ortiz 1969:158). This variant is not an exhortation to return to native rituals but is rather a warning that both the native and the Spanish dances must be performed in order to secure eternal happiness. Poseyemu is here the mediator between the Spanish and the native customs.

Another variant tells of the coming of Poseyemu to the village of Pojoaque: "The Indians of the village had not learned much then for life was new, and it takes many hundreds of years for people to learn how to live. They ate only herbs, roots, and the sorts of small animals they could catch with their hands or kill with a rock. In those days they had made for themselves no weapons nor knew that they could do so" (A. James 1927:104). The story tells of Poseyemu's skill at hunting and how he taught the people during his four-day stay to hunt big animals with bow and arrow. He taught them that the buffalo would satisfy their needs and he showed them how to kill it. Before he departed, he instituted the Buffalo Dance. The association of Poseyemu with the Buffalo Dance (see "San Ildefonso Pueblo," figs. 10-11, this vol.) is highly significant in respect to the Tewa ritual cycle. This dance, unlike other hunting dances, is held in the spring and is not under the control of the hunt chief. Instead, participants in the buffalo hunt go to the Woman's Society to ask for prayers (Ortiz 1969:172). Ortiz explains this anomaly by the fact that the Buffalo Dance deals with an activity that is outside the Tewa world. The hunts usually take place in the plains to the northeast. Returning hunters must be reintegrated into Pueblo society. Poseyemu, on the weight of logic alone, is the perfect figure to have instituted the Buffalo Dance, for he represents not only the mediation between male and female, heaven and earth, divine and human, but also the mediation between Pueblo and non-Pueblo worlds. He represents the universal, extra-Pueblo world coming into contact with the Pueblo world.

The second religious activity that Poseyemu performs in Tewa mythology is ordering the kachina dances to be held in underground kivas. This was the principal tactic that the Pueblos used to prevent the Franciscans from detecting their native religious practices. While such underground dancing probably took place before Spanish contact, the Spanish presence certainly increased the practice. In one myth Montezuma (Poseyemu) warns the Pueblo: "If you want to dance below [i.e., in the kiva], that same way you are going to follow all your life. You have to keep on in this way until I come back" (Parsons 1926a:113). In another variant, Poseyemu arrives at the Pueblo of Yunque (San Gabriel, an early historic village of the San Juan people) in a strange-looking vehicle and

Fig. 2. Matachine Dance at San Juan, probably Christmas Day, about 1935. This dance, while remaining distinctively Spanish in all the Pueblos, varies somewhat from Pueblo to Pueblo in instrumentation, costuming, and choreography. Characters include two Spanish *abuelos* or grandfathers (one of whom appears, masked and carrying a whip, at left), the *toro* or little bull (center foreground), the *monarca* or lead matachine dancer (seated at right, holding one of the 3-pronged sticks carried by all of the matachina), and the *malinche* or little girl (at right). Composed of several sets or episodes, the Matachine Dance includes a European-style quadrillelike dance, which is performed at San Juan to the accompaniment of guitar and violin. See Parsons (1929:217-222, pls. 35-39) for a detailed description of Matachine performances at San Juan and at Cochiti. Photograph by T. Harmon Parkhurst.

THE MYTHOLOGICAL TRIANGLE: POSEYEMU, MONTEZUMA, AND JESUS IN THE PUEBLOS is thought to be a Spaniard. The gods were dancing in the plaza at the time.

> Thus, when they saw Poseyemu's carriage glistening in the sunlight, and the cloud of dust he was leaving behind, the guards rushed into the plaza and shouted to the people, "Lock them inside! Aliens are coming! Keep them inside!"
>
> When Poseyemu arrived and saw what they had done, he asked, "Why have you hidden them from me?" They answered that they thought he was an alien, and he became angry. He said to them, "Very well, from now on you shall continue to carry these ways on only in the inside" (Ortiz 1963-1968).

Again, Poseyemu is placed at the intersection of two religious traditions. In these two myths he functions as an "early warning system" for the preservation of native religious ceremonies.

In the third set of variants, Poseyemu embodies in actual competition the native Pueblo tradition. The test of magic is the theme of the first two myths. In the first, Poseyemu and Jesus meet in a valley. "Upon finding that they were both supernatural beings, they engaged in a lively discussion as to which one of them should lead the Indians. Poseyemu said, 'The Indians are my people. Therefore, I shall be their leader.' But Jesus replied, 'All people are my people. It is I that should lead them'" (Ortiz 1963-1968). This variant shows that in three contests of magic (eating squash, growing corn, and uprooting a large tree) Poseyemu is victorious. But the myth ends with Poseyemu's refusal to lead the Indian people. The second contest myth (Parsons 1929: 306-307), although it does not end with a similar refusal, ends with Poseyemu's prediction that wherever runs a little water, there the conquering White people will live. Poseyemu's opponent loses the contest, which indicates that the Indian method of life is still superior to the White way, and yet the alien god wins the Indian people. Once more Poseyemu's role is obvious; he stands at the contact point between the Christian system and the native system.

### Pueblo Variants

The culture hero myths can be discussed Pueblo by Pueblo within their ethnographic contexts, or they can be separated into thematic bundles. Each approach captures connections that the other misses. However, the choice of approach is made easier by the fact that the thematic bundles tend to correlate with the different linguistic and geographic divisions of the Pueblos, and that certain themes are more prominent at certain Pueblos than at others. This variation appears to be in part aboriginal and in part the result of different types and degrees of contact with the Spaniards. Parsons (1939, 1:179) summarizes the scope of this thematic variation by pointing out that Poseyemu (Zuni Poshayanki, Keresan Boshayanyi, Isleta Puspiyama) is at Zia "the somewhat Christlike culture

hero, brother and deputy of" Iyatiko, at Zuni the father of the curing societies and "giver of raiment and riches," at Laguna "a despised little boy, a miracle worker or nothing more than a juggler and deceiver who has finally to be killed," and among Acoma Roman Catholics is identified with the serpent in the Garden of Eden. Despite this high degree of variation, though, many of the deeds and personal characteristics of these figures are similar, like their names, and they are all linked with the Mexican figure Montezuma. This combined variation and similarity makes the study of the Pueblo culture hero exceedingly complex. No analysis of Pueblo mythology can be linear, for the myths form never-ending circles or spirals. The problem of circularity appears in two forms. First, mythic thought is circular since it seeks to create an identity between the present, the past, and the future. Second, Pueblo mythology is circular in a special way: there is a high degree of internal reference. For example, in the Tewa myths the complex relationship between scalps, rain, mist, Coyote, Sipapu, and Poseyemu cannot be understood unless all the pieces of the puzzle are present.

One theme found in the culture hero myths at Zuni (which is also prominent in the Tewa variants) is the idea that Poseyemu (Poshayanki at Zuni) delivered men from the underworld. He led the original people from the "City of Mist" (Cushing 1883:16) and taught them the essential skills for cultural life. Poshayanki then disappeared from the earth, either to live with the Sun or to live in the sea beneath the earth. Cushing gives the fullest variant of this Zuni myth.

> Then came among men and the beings, it is said, the wisest of men and the foremost, the all-sacred master, Poshaiyankya [Poshayanki], he who appeared in the waters below, even as did the Sun-father in the waters above, and who arose from the nethermost sea, and pitying men still, won upward, gaining by virtue of his (innate) wisdom-knowledge issuance from that first world-womb through ways so dark and narrow that those who, seeing somewhat, crowded after, could not follow, so eager were they and so mightily did they strive with one another! Alone, then, he fared upward from one womb (cave) to another out into the great breadth of daylight. There, the earth lay, like a vast island in the midst of the great waters, wet and unstable. And alone he fared forth, seeking the Sun-father and supplicating him to deliver mankind and the creatures there below (Cushing 1896:381).

Poshayanki is the mediator between the Sun-father and men, for he is the one who bets with the Sun to permit men to emerge from the underworld. Stephen (1936, 1:281) maintains that the term Poshayanki was applied to the northeast by the Zuni when referring to the emergence myth and that the word is said to be in the language of the below, but according to Dennis Tedlock (personal communication 1974) it is strictly an untranslatable personal name. Cushing elaborates on the role of mediator when he adds that the Pueblos use fetishes to express their prayers to Poshayanki and that he expresses his power through fetishes to men.

The role of Poshayanki as mediator is considered crucial by Lévi-Strauss, who refers to him as the "successful mediator between heaven and earth." Mediation is also the key to understanding the relationship between the culture hero, mist, scalps, and Coyote.

> Coyote (a carrion-eater) is intermediary between herbivorous and carnivorous just as mist between Sky and Earth; as scalp between war and agriculture (scalp is a war crop); as corn smut between wild and cultivated plants; as garments between "nature" and "culture"; as refuse between village and outside; and as ashes (or soot) between roof (sky vault) and hearth (in the ground). This chain of mediators, if one may call them so, not only throws light on entire parts of North American mythology—why the Dew-God may be at the same time the Game-Master and the giver of raiments and be personified as an "Ash-Boy"; or why scalps are mist-producing; or why the Game-Mother is associated with corn smut; etc.—but it also probably corresponds to a universal way of organizing daily experience (Lévi-Strauss 1963:225).

The Zuni culture hero myths have a double focus. Some of the variants concentrate on the hero's role as the leader of the emergence journey and others develop more fully the teaching role of the hero. These roles are separated into two distinct mythological personages, Poshayanki, "the wisest of wise men and the foremost," and Payatamu (payatamu), God of Dew and Dawn (M.L. Miller 1898:46). Cushing has recorded the Payatamu myth at Zuni. Payatamu comes from the east playing the flute (a male fertility symbol), teaches the people proper rituals for growing corn, and then departs into the mist. The role of Payatamu (Bunzel 1932a:530) in Zuni ceremonialism is similar to the role attributed to Poseyemu by Curtis (1907–1930, 17). Since the Zuni name payatamu is a borrowed form of Keresan pʰáyᵃatᵛámɨ (as in Acoma ʔuṣâ·cʰɨ pʰáyᵃatᵛámɨ 'Sun Youth'), it is likely that the mythological character had his origin among the Keresans. Zuni Payatamu "is associated with all things gay and youthful. He is another romantic adventurer in folklore. His prayer stick, significantly, is double and is painted blue and yellow, the colors associated with sex. The flutes of Payatamu are played at the phallic ritual of [ʔololowiwiška]. They are important in the Corn Dance" (Bunzel 1932a:530).

The separation of the emergence leader from the ritual teacher is also found in the mythology of the Keresan Pueblos. The quasi-messiah figure is called Boshayanyi. Boshayanyi (White 1962:277) is a Christ-like culture hero who is born of a virgin at Pecos. He performs miracles, teaches hunting, and vies for the rule of the Pueblo. The people rise up and drive him from the village.

> The day after [Boshayanyi's] death he returned to his wife's home, and when he was seen alive those who tried to destroy him were not only angry but much alarmed; and again he

was captured, and they bound gold and silver to his feet, that after casting him into the lake his body would not rise; but a white fluffy feather of the eagle fell to him, and as he touched the feather the feather rose, and [Boshayanyi] with it, and he lived again, and he still lives, and some time he will come to us (Stevenson 1894:66).

The other figure, the youth, becomes the Sun Youth in Keresan mythology. The Sun's son is a popular figure in all Pueblo mythology, and he figures in as many myths as does the culture hero. He is Zuni payatamu, Hopi Taiowa, Keresan (Acoma) pʰáyᵃatᵛámɨ, Jemez Patyabo, and Rio Grande Tewa θamu yowa eʔnú (Parsons 1939, 1:table 2). Apparent borrowings of the Keresan name appear as the name of the Paiyatamu or Paiakyamu (payákàmɨ, Whorf 1936:1273) clown societies among the Arizona Tewa and the Hopi (Eggan 1950:101–102; Titiev 1944:243; Stephen 1936, 2:1272), who trace their origin to twin sons of the Sun (Stephen 1936, 1:332). According to Parsons, the Sun Youth forms a distinct mythological personage from both the emergence leader and the ritual teacher. This distinction is found in a myth from Acoma. This myth begins with remarkable similarity to the Poseyemu myth from Curtis (1907–1930, 17), but in the Acoma variant, the poor girl is impregnated by Sun Youth, not World Man or the Sun. The identity of Poseyemu and the Keresan Sun Youth is interrupted in this Acoma variant. The myth continues in the manner of the Tewa myth with the exception that the girl bears two children, not one. They are the Twin War Gods, Masewi and Oyoyewi.

The introduction of the Twin War Gods in this Acoma variant opens up a new perspective on the Pueblo culture hero myths. There is not only a confusion between the quasi-messiah Boshayanyi and the Sun Youth, but also a confusion between these two and the Twin War Gods. The essential structure of the Pueblo War Twin myths includes: "The Sun impregnates by magical means a woman, who is obviously an Earth-goddess. She gives birth to twins, who mature rapidly, but always remain diminutive. They go to visit their father, the Sun; after subjecting them to a series of ordeals, he gives them the weapons of war; with these the boys rid the earth of monsters" (Haeberlin 1916:31). Clearly, the Twin War Gods share many characteristics with the culture hero. They both have magical conceptions, they both have remarkable childhoods, and they both are associated with hunting. At Zuni, the Twin War Gods are the patrons of the cult of the Bow Priest, whose function is to keep war fetishes and scalps. Their duty extends further, since they are also in charge of policing the town and defending the Indian people from attack. More interestingly, they are the executive arm of the religious hierarchy and serve as a wall against witchcraft and impurity. In this protective role, the Zuni Bow Priests closely resemble the Tewa Warriors' Society members called the íowaʔê·. Parsons (1929:265) notes that at Jemez the morning star is identified with the war god. When the morning star rises,

615

Masewi rises. The connection between the Twins and the morning star is also found in regard to the culture hero. "In Pueblo myth there are traces of a like identification, through the war god or gods, the two little boys, Ahayuta [ʔahayuʾta] of Zuni, the Towae [ʈowaʾêʾ] of the Tewa. These two, or the one they vaguely merge into are identified with the Morning Star. That Jesus was identified with these little boys when he was first heard about from the Franciscan Friars I long since surmised. Now the Tewan tale of Poseyemu as recorded at San Juan supplies evidence of that identification, at least a few links of evidence" (Parsons 1926a:4-5). The Tewa culture hero Poseyemu, as well as the Twin War Gods, is associated with the morning star, and yet, there are two elements that distinguish the Twin War Gods from the culture hero. The culture hero is prophetic; he tells of coming trouble and predicts a conquering race's arrival. Second, the culture hero leaves the Pueblo to live in the lake or to found Mexico City. In contrast, the Twin War Gods are integrated into Pueblo society. "The boys took off their costumes and hung them up, for they had been told not to wear them until they needed them. They made up ordinary costumes for themselves, and they continued to live as common people in the village" (Stirling 1942:98).

Three of the most interesting culture hero tales are the Taos myth of pʔiankʔɔocǫ́le, the Isleta myth of humúhu, and the Laguna myth of the emergence.

M.L. Miller (1898:44-45) has the fullest account of the myth of pʔiankʔɔocǫ́le. The myth tells how Piankettacholla (as he spells the name) could at any time create a green hill by merely pointing his finger (his name appears to mean 'blue-green mountain maker'). He was born of a virgin about 150 miles north of Taos. His mother conceived him by putting fine pebbles in her belt. Although the people tried to put him to death because he had no father, Piankettacholla escaped and grew into an intelligent and beautiful man. He taught the Pueblo people how to dance, how to make clothes, and how to plant corn, beans, and calabashes. In addition to these skills, Piankettacholla had the magical power to fly; he could fly from Taos to Santa Fe as high as the stars. Piankettacholla is remembered most of all because he recreated the human race out of foam after the flood. It is not a contradiction in the Pueblo mind to see the same mythological character as the emergence leader, the culture hero, and the creator after the flood, for in myth the past and future are frozen in an eternal present. The story concludes: "Before the Pueblo people saw white men, negroes, and other people, this wise man had seen them and told the Pueblo people about them. Of the Americans he had said that some time a people would come who made a noise with their shoes, like men talking on snow. The Indian who told me this added, 'This is true, because we see.' He told them that they would get fewer and fewer, and by and by would all be white men, and then fewer fewer, and by and by would all be white men, and then there would be no more Pueblo people" (M.L. Miller 1898:45). This prophecy is quite different from the prophecy of the Tewa variants. In the Tewa myths, hard times are predicted, but the Pueblos are instructed to resist the new ways. There is no possibility of "cosmic renewal" or cultural rebirth in the Taos variant. The world is changing and there is no way to bring back the precontact times. There is one similarity, however, between the Tewa and the Taos myths. In both, the precontact period is mythologically equated with the beginning of time, ab initio. To resist the influences of the Spanish culture is to recreate the sacred world of the ancestors.

The myth of humúhu is almost exactly the same as the Tewa myth in Curtis (1907-1930, 17). The circumstances surrounding the birth of the hero and his childhood are nearly identical. His skills and ritual knowledge compare with Poseyemu's talents. humúhu inaugurates an era of peace and prosperity. "Grass began to grow up in the mountains. All the animals began to live again, the cattle and sheep that had been dying. And all the springs began to run. Then he began to talk to them all, and they began to work on the ceremony they had used before. From then on all the people lived well together" (Parsons 1932:378). Three elements found in many of the Pueblo culture hero myths are absent from this Isleta variant. The hero does not leave the Pueblo, there is no prophecy, and there is no promised second coming.

The Laguna version of the Boshayanyi myth (Parsons 1920:115) shares many elements with the Taos and the Isleta variants. What is unusual in the Laguna myth is that the culture hero carries a negative value. He arrives at the Pueblo from the north after the elder War Twin Masewi has established prosperity and harmony. The people were already dancing and the rain was already plentiful. Boshayanyi performed tricks of magic and convinced the people that they should believe in him. His acts were so clever that the medicine men (čáyâ·ni) perform them in his memory to this day. As soon as the people were persuaded to believe, Boshayanyi left, traveling first to the northeast, then to the east, and then to the southeast, and finally to Mexico. His circuit is clockwise, while the journey of Masewi, described earlier in the myth, is counterclockwise. "From then on the cheani [čáyâ·ni] had no good fortune. When they had rain dances, the rain did not come. The wind blew. The sun parched their crops . . . They were struck by famine. They would take their own children and jerk off their shoulders and eat the meat" (Parsons 1920:115). Only when Boshayanyi is found and killed does the fortune of the Pueblo turn toward prosperity. This variant is a simple transformation of the Isleta variant.

|  | Isleta | Laguna |
|---|---|---|
| hero accepted | rain | no rain |
| hero rejected | no rain | rain |

PARMENTIER

This discussion of the relationship between the culture hero, the Sun Youth, and the Twin War Gods has used variants that are variously syncretic. While it may be self-evident that the segments of the myths that describe the culture hero's journey to Mexico are not native, it is impossible to unravel the native and the syncretic elements in other types of myths—the sacred-fire legends and the competition stories, for example.

## Montezuma in the Southwest

There are four central questions about the Montezuma legend of the Pueblo Southwest. First, who was Montezuma historically? Second, how did the legend of Montezuma arrive in the Southwest? Third, when did the legend become popular among the Pueblos? And fourth, why does Montezuma become associated with the Pueblo culture hero?

The name Montezuma (in Nahuatl Motecuzoma, Moteuczoma, and variants) refers to two personages in Mexican history. The first, Montezuma I, surnamed Ilhuicamina, was the Aztec king who came to the throne after the death of Itzcoatl in 1440 and led campaigns to the north, east, and south. As king, Montezuma I increased the wealth and prosperity of his people by building an aqueduct from Chapultepec to the city and by building a dike to protect the city from flooding. The second figure, Montezuma II, was the Mexican leader who perished in the custody of Hernando Cortés in 1520. His exploits are recorded in the letters from Cortés to the king of Spain. Cortés was full of awe at the sophisticated ritual and sacrificial system of Aztec religion and admired the powerful military force that Montezuma commanded (Cortés 1908).

The question of how the story of Montezuma arrived in the Southwest has at least three possible solutions. First, the legends about Montezuma I, having become popular among the Indians of central Mexico before the time of Cortés, may have diffused along well-established trade routes into the Pueblos. Second, the legends may have been present aboriginally in the Southwest before the Aztec migration into the valley of Mexico. Third, the legends may have arrived with the Indians who accompanied Francisco Vásquez de Coronado and Juan de Oñate on their expeditions.

Considering the substantial evidence that complex trade routes existed between the Mexican states and the Pueblos, one could logically assume that these same routes might have also functioned as routes for mythological diffusion. If this were so, Montezuma legends would be present in northern Mexico and in the Southwest before the expeditions of Coronado, yet no such evidence has been found in the early journals of the Franciscans, Jesuits, or military leaders (Bandelier 1892:320). Another Spanish writer, Pérez de Ribas, mentions no Montezuma legends in Sonora and Sinaloa in 1645, although he describes in elaborate detail the dances in honor of Montezuma II that were held in Mexico City (Pérez de Ribas 1968:244–246). The lack of positive evidence—not a single mention of southwestern Montezuma legends—makes this first possibility a very dubious one. Of course, the lack of evidence is not, in itself, positive evidence for disproof.

The second possibility takes the migration legends of the Indians seriously and hypothesizes that the Aztecs are derived from the Pueblo Southwest. There is more than mythological evidence that the Aztecs came to the valley of Mexico only after many years of nomadic wandering. Their arrival at Mexico City is estimated at 1340 (Wolf 1959:131); however, the Aztec migration traditions do not locate a point of origin in the Pueblos but refer to a place in northwestern Mexico. The argument for the Pueblo origins of Aztec civilization is encouraged by the ritual and mythological parallels described by Parsons (1933a), who mentions the close similarity between the Aztec Tlalocs, rain gods, and the Pueblo kachinas (especially the Hopi cloud youths). The Aztec gods Uitzilopochtli and Painal resemble the Pueblo Twin War Gods; both are born in the legends and both are impersonated in rituals. Parsons lists an extensive set of ritual parallels, which includes ceremonial fasting, communal hunting, asperging, anti-sunwise ceremonial dancing, and the use of feathers in rituals. At no time does she conclude that these parallels are the result of diffusion. There are two problems, in summary, with this second line of argument. First, even if Montezuma were the leader of the actual migration that, according to legend, began in the Southwest and ended in Mexico City, this fact cannot be correlated with the existence of an actual figure named Montezuma I in 1440. Second, if this position is altered to say that Montezuma is merely a name attached to whoever led the migration and that this name was attributed only after the Aztecs founded Mexico City, then the initial question remains unanswered. If Montezuma and the migration legends are Mexican creations, then the argument for the aboriginal association of the Pueblos and the Aztecs is beside the point. Montezuma's presence in the Southwest remains to be explained. The absurdity of the second possibility is not seen by Ritch (1882:11), who confuses "a written report which is to be found in some of the Pueblos . . . that Pecos pueblo was the birthplace of Montezuma" with the documentation of some legend.

The third possibility is that Montezuma's name and legend are modern creations, transported into the Southwest by Spanish colonists or by their Mexican Indian servants (Chavez in Simpson 1964:19). Montezuma became the name to which all deeds of lesser heroes were ascribed (Bancroft 1874–1876, 3:77). Bandelier (1892) agrees with Chavez and Bancroft but takes the position one step further. He contends that the Montezuma legend brought into the Pueblos was a combination of the    *617* legends surrounding Montezuma I and the historical facts concerning Montezuma II. This fusion can be seen in the reports of missionaries, military leaders, and travelers.

Bandelier (1892:320) claims that the first reference to Montezuma in the Southwest is the mention of "the houses of Montezuma" by Francisco de Gorraez Beaumont and Antonio de Oca Grandes Sarmiento. The identification of Casas Grandes as "the houses of Montezuma" is found in many of the Sonoran Montezuma legends (Ives 1950). The next reference in Spanish documents is a letter written by Antonio de Otermín to the king of Spain on August 20, 1680. Otermín's information comes from the testimony of several Pueblo Indians captured during the Revolt of 1680. They confessed that they were operating under a mandate from an Indian who lived in the north, "from which region Montezuma came" (Hackett 1942, 1:15). Poseyemu and Montezuma were distinct figures in the minds of these Indians. Montezuma was the lieutenant of Poseyemu.

Mention of Montezuma is infrequent during the eighteenth century. In 1746, Father Sedelmair (Ives 1939) links Montezuma with Casa Grande, on the Gila River. He goes so far as to say that Montezuma himself lived in the palaces at Casa Grande and that he ruled his empire from that point. Linking Montezuma with ancient ruins was still done in the nineteenth century, for Bandelier (1892:322) reports that the Indians of El Paso and other areas called such ruins "Montezumas."

If Montezuma is conspicuous by his absence during the eighteenth century, he is even more remarkable for his widespread popularity during the first half of the nineteenth century. Many American travel reports include his legend and many military journals mention his name. The legends fall into four general categories. Some of the legends follow closely the Aztec migration stories in which Montezuma is the leader of a movement from the Pueblos to Mexico City. Other legends, following the Pueblo culture hero myths, deal with Montezuma's promised return from the east. The third category includes legends referring to the sacred fire that Montezuma commanded to be kept burning in his honor. The final group of legends relate the competition between the Roman Catholic god, Dios, and the native god, Montezuma.

The Montezuma migration legends found among the Indians of the Casas Grandes region always tell of the southward migration of Montezuma and his people, during which there were many stops at water holes (Ives 1950:324). In one of the most complete versions of the migration legend (Russell 1908; condensed in Mason 1921), Montezuma is identified with Elder Brother, who is the chief of his people. Montezuma abuses his people by causing famine, drought, and disease. All attempts to kill him fail because Montezuma has the power to rise from the dead. The variant ends with Montezuma's

establishing a new race of people (the invading medicine men) and then dividing the new people into different languages and villages. Another Papago variant (Davidson 1865:131) states more clearly that Montezuma's pride and arrogance displeased the Great Spirit, who threatened the people with calamity if Montezuma remained obdurate. Montezuma continued to disregard the Great Spirit, then led his people southward, subduing many nations, and founded many great cities. Finally, the Great Spirit overtook him by sending the Spaniards from across the ocean. The cooperation between the Great Spirit and the Spanish conquerors is certainly linked with the Jesuit influence on the Papagos. Emory (1857:117) says that the Pimas also consider themselves descendants of Montezuma and the Aztecs. A Pima legend describes Montezuma's departure on horseback to find a new country.

These migration legends are definitely in the Aztec tradition and do not identify Montezuma with the Pueblos; however, there are traditions in the Southwest in which Montezuma is born at the Pueblos (usually Pecos or Ojo Caliente). These legends convey a very different attitude toward Montezuma's mission; in all the variants in which Montezuma is born at a Pueblo he works for the prosperity of the Indian people in harmony with the Great Spirit. Also, Montezuma of the Pueblos is invoked against the Spanish conquerers. The opposition between the Aztec-type Montezuma legends and the Pueblo-type can be shown in a chart.

|  | Aztec-type | Pueblo-type |
|---|---|---|
| Montezuma acts in harmony with the Great Spirit | no | yes |
| Montezuma secures the prosperity of his people | no | yes |
| Montezuma's presence brings prosperity | no | yes |
| Montezuma overcomes the Catholic and Spanish forces | no | yes |
| Montezuma returns to his people as savior | no | yes |

Several of the Pueblo-type legends are found among the Tewa. In one elaborate variant that combines many of the elements of the Poseyemu story, Montezuma teaches the Pueblos to hunt and to grow crops. Then he leaves for Mexico, with a few Indians following him (A.M. Espinosa 1936:101). A second Tewa variant describes in greater detail the founding of Mexico City. Montezuma, in this second legend, is born at Ojo Caliente, north of San Juan Pueblo. After performing great works, guided in all he does by the Great Spirit, Montezuma marries

Malinche, the daughter of the cacique of the Pueblo of Zuni.

> To assist him the Great Spirit sent his sacred eagle to guide Montezuma in his work. The eagle flew ahead of Montezuma and his people, and wherever the eagle alighted a pueblo was built. In this way nearly all the later pueblos in New Mexico were built, and they were populated by the many people who followed Montezuma. Always Montezuma travelled to the southward, and one day travelled a long distance the eagle seized a serpent in his beak and lighted on a cactus plant. This was the sign long awaited by Montezuma, and at this place he stopped and built his capital, where Mexico City now stands, and as his insignia he adopted the sacred eagle sitting on a cactus plant, holding a serpent in its beak (Applegate 1929:175).

Many of the Montezuma migration legends suggest that Montezuma will return to his people. The journals of Abraham Robinson Johnston refer to the second coming of Montezuma and his sacred fire at Pecos (Johnston, Edwards, and Ferguson 1936:102–103). Simpson (1964:19–23) mentions the same tradition at Jemez, where the churches were called the churches of Montezuma, and where the people believed that they would be delivered by a people from the east. A published illustration (Simpson 1850:pl. 9) provides an important piece of evidence (fig. 3), which hints at the complex relationship between Montezuma, who will return from the east, and the Pueblo culture hero, who is often the son of the Sun (which rises in the east) and who is thought to have the power to bring rain.

The sacred-fire legends of Montezuma are found especially at Taos and Pecos. Although Bandelier (1883) has

Academy of Nat. Sciences, Philadelphia.
Fig. 3. Detail of Jemez kiva painting shown to members of the Simpson Expedition by the governor of the Pueblo in 1849. The two small figures blowing trumpets or flutes were reported to be "adjutants of Montezuma, who are sounding a call to him for rain" (Simpson 1964:20). This watercolor by Richard H. Kern, a member of the expedition, was the basis for the lithograph published by Simpson (1850:pl. 9).

demonstrated that in fact the ritual of keeping a sacred fire was present in Pueblo religion before the Spanish contact period (and, therefore, before the Montezuma legend), this fact does not make the practice insignificant for the "children of Montezuma." The sacred fire is a universal symbol of purification and redemption in primitive and archaic religion; the fire is extinguished and then relit at a New Year celebration. In the Pueblos, such rituals may well represent the hope for both purification and the release from oppression. The sacred fire legend at Pecos has been recorded:

> It was related that one day, Montezuma being at Pecos, took hold of a great tree and planted it upside down, remarking at the same time, "that when that tree should disappear, a foreign race would reign over his people, and that rain would cease to fall." He then recommended to the priests to watch over the sacred fire until the fall of the tree, which event would occur when a multitude of white men, coming from the east, should destroy the power of their oppressors; and that he himself would return afterwards to restore his kingdom. Then should the earth be fertilised by abundant rain, and the nation be enriched by the treasures buried in the midst of the mountains (Domenech 1860, 1:165).

In this variant a distinction is made between the Americans and the Spaniards. The Spaniards are the oppressors and the Americans are the deliverers. Another variant highlights this distinction.

> At this last, Montezuma planted a tree upside down, and said that, on his leaving the pueblo, a strange nation should oppress them for many years, years in which there should be no rain, but that they were to persist in watching the sacred fire until the tree fell, when he would return, with a white race which should destroy their enemies; and then rain should fall again and the earth be fertile. It is said that this tree fell from its abnormal position, as the American army entered Santa Fe (Bancroft 1874–1876, 3:170).

In the Domenech variant, Montezuma will return *after* the Americans have destroyed the Spanish oppressors, but in the variant from Bancroft, his return is identical with the coming of the American army. In spite of this slight difference, both legends equate the coming of the Americans with a repudiation of Spanish oppression and with the return of fertility (rain) and a balanced native religious system (the upside-down tree falls).

The last group of Montezuma legends from the Pueblos is composed of those legends which relate a contest between Montezuma, the protector of the native religion, and Dios, the Spanish god. These legends closely resemble the tales of magical combat between the Pueblo culture hero and the Catholic god. If, according to the compartmentalization model (Spicer 1962:508), two religious systems coexist in the Pueblos, then one of the few points of contact between the two traditions is the existence of these legends of competition between the gods. Since it is impossible, at this point, to separate

Montezuma and Poseyemu (Zuni Poshayanki), the legends that set Montezuma against Dios and the myths that set Poseyemu against Dios will be considered together. The Isleta variant given by Parsons (1932:412) is the contest between the Catholic god, *díws,* and the Indian god, *wè?íde,* who is identified with Montezuma. Montezuma uses strictly native means (shooting with a bow and beating on a drum) to defeat *díws,* who uses European methods (shooting with a gun and ringing bells). The Santo Domingo variant is a contest between God and Boshayanyi, who defeats his opponent in five contests: "Then they were going to see who could get some water from Shipap [Sipapu] first. God wrote a letter. [Boshayanyi] made a *wabani* (feather bunch). He got water while someone was reading God's letter. The next was to see who could make the best music. God had a horn and blew on it. [Boshayanyi] used a drum and sang. After a while God got tired and gave up. God went home on a cloud. [Boshayanyi] left on the back of a duck" (White 1935:179). In these legends of competition the culture hero myths confront the Montezuma legends, which are the result of Spanish importation. Montezuma's role as defender of the native religion has behind it at least 300 years of Pueblo-Spanish contact. What was once an Aztec ruler's name has become the symbol for traditional Pueblo religion.

## The Mythological Fusion

Three hypotheses attempt to account for the mythological fusion of Poseyemu, Montezuma, and even Jesus Christ. In order of decreasing concreteness and increasing generality, the three hypotheses are: the hypothesis of political purpose, which argues that the association of Montezuma and Poseyemu is the result of conscious political plotting by the Mexican government; the hypothesis of structural and symbolic similarity, which argues that certain properties in the myths themselves account for the fusion of the three figures; and the hypothesis of religious evolution, which argues that the selection of Poseyemu as Montezuma's counterpart can be explained in terms of the different evolutionary levels of Spanish Catholicism and Pueblo religion. The three hypotheses are neither mutually contradictory nor mutually exclusive.

In the mid-nineteenth century, economic and political strife between Mexicans and Anglos undermined the political stability of New Mexico and placed new importance on the Indian's position at the center of the power game. Mexico sought to unite the entire Mexican territory, including the American Southwest as a geographical-political entity in anticipation of possible territorial claims that would, as they remain, come after the war (David Warren, personal communication 1971).

One possible way, Bandelier suggests, for Mexico to secure the support of the Pueblo Indians was to encourage the fusion of native and Mexican mythological traditions involving the culture hero and Montezuma. He argues that this purpose was served by these legends that connect New Mexico with Mexico through Malinche—historically an Indian woman from Coatzacualco who served Cortés as interpreter and concubine, and was baptized Marina and known as Malintzin in Nahuatl. In the legend, Malinche, the daughter of Montezuma, was born in the Pueblos and later married Cortés, with New Mexico given as part of her dowry to her Spanish husband. The ideological thrust of this tradition was that the Pueblos were aligned "historically" through the legend to Mexico.

How this mythological fusion was to take place is of considerable interest. According to Bandelier (1892) and Ward (1865), a document called the "History of Montezuma" was written in Mexico City in 1864 and copies were circulated among the Pueblos. This document contained the Pueblo culture hero myths (Tewa variants) and the Mexican Montezuma legend. Apparently, this document is the foundation for present-day Montezuma legends in the Southwest. Although he never saw a copy of the document, Bandelier (1892:323-324) speculates that portions of the "History of Montezuma" are merely translations of the letters of Cortés. He suggests that this document was created as a "campaign document," to strengthen the claims of Mexico to the New Mexico region in the view of the Pueblo Indians at a time when an American invasion of New Mexico was expected.

It is possible to evaluate the effect that this "History of Montezuma" had on the Pueblos by examining the journals of Twitchell (1923) and Simpson (1964), who both discuss the Montezuma legend and its relationship to the Indians. They agree that the legend of Montezuma became associated in the native mind with the aboriginal culture hero myth, but they also point out that, as far as political purposes are concerned, the fusion was a complete failure from Mexico's point of view. Not only did the legends not support the claim to New Mexico, but also they encouraged the Indians to see the Americans as deliverers. Montezuma leaves the Pueblos, prophesies a conquering race (Spaniards), and promises to return when a delivering race (Americans) comes from the east.

> The principal chiefs of several tribes of Pueblo Indians presented themselves at the palace and gave in their submission and expressed great satisfaction over the arrival of the American forces. Their interview was long and very interesting, and, as stated by Lieutenant Emory, they narrated what is a tradition for them, that the white man would come from the far east and release them from the bonds and shackles which the Spaniards had imposed, not in the name of, but in a worse form than slavery (Twitchell 1923:34).

Bandelier's hypothesis—that the Montezuma legend in its most recent form is the result of conscious political plotting by the Mexican government—explains many facts from the myths and from historical accounts of New Mexico in his time. His hypothesis explains why more Tewa variants of the Montezuma legend are found, why few legends are found at Hopi, and why there is such a close similarity among the culture hero myths throughout the Pueblos (they are all linked with Montezuma). Unfortunately, there is one major problem that the argument from political purpose cannot handle. Why did Montezuma and Poseyemu, in the 20 years following the circulation of the "History of Montezuma," become so strongly fused that the Pueblo Indians spoke of the "religion of Montezuma" as early as 1864 (Ward 1865:192) and kept sacred fires of Montezuma as early as 1847? In other words, the association of Montezuma and Poseyemu, stimulated first by the Revolt of 1680, developed in the native mind for almost 200 years; therefore, Bandelier is probably confused when he accepts as truth the statement by an Indian from San Juan that "the name of Montezuma has been given to Pose-ueve [Posehweve] but very lately" (Bandelier 1890-1892, 2:310). The "History of Montezuma" cannot explain the origins of this mythological syncretism before 1846, nor can it explain Poseyemu's association in later years with Jesus Christ.

A second hypothesis to explain the fusion of Montezuma, Poseyemu, and Jesus is based on the argument from structural and symbolic similarity. The idea of mediation, which is crucial to the understanding of the function and meaning of the Pueblo culture hero, is the key to the structural similarity among the three figures. Poseyemu mediates heaven and earth, male and female, and the Pueblo and non-Pueblo worlds. His inherent ambiguity is that he can, on the one hand, represent the divine as the son of the Sun and as a sacred emergence leader, and on the other hand, symbolize the essentially human as the foremost agricultural teacher and ritual leader. In these abstract terms, the structural similarity of Poseyemu, Jesus, and Montezuma is apparent. All three are ambiguously human and divine, all three have the power to visit the supernatural world, and all three change the state of their societies in profound ways. The identification of these three figures suggests that mythological syncretism occurs frequently along the lines of structural similarity.

The hypothesis of structural similarity can be applied to the connection between Poseyemu and Jesus. The Pueblo variants present an ambiguous picture of this relationship, for in some myths, especially those dealing with magical competition, Poseyemu and Jesus are carefully separated, while in others a subtle fusion of gospel narrative and native tradition takes place. In other words, some myths compartmentalize Poseyemu and Jesus and others syncretize them. An examination of several variants may explain this apparent paradox.

Even on the surface, the similarities between Jesus and Poseyemu are striking. Both are born of a virgin who was conceived through a magical impregnation, both show early signs of maturity and wisdom, both speak profoundly before religious elders, both depart suddenly from their people, and both promise to return with an era of prosperity and peace. Of course, it is impossible to tell which of these similarities were the results rather than the causes of mythological syncretism. The same logic that brought the Pueblo quasi-messiah into identification with Jesus also assisted the identification of Jesus with Quetzalcoatl. The Franciscans in Mexico likened the Aztec god to the Christian god, and in some cases made a direct identification (David Warren, personal communication 1971).

In one Pueblo myth concerning hunting, Montezuma kills deer by running them over a cliff, an act reminiscent of Matthew 8:32, where Jesus chases a herd of possessed swine over a cliff into the sea. "Montezuma is like Christ. He and Christ are the same thing" (A.M. Espinosa 1936:98). There is a similar case of syncretism in a Cochiti variant in which Montezuma is identified with Boshayanyi. Most of the myth is a Christ myth. Among the Papagos was found "a myth about Montezuma, who returns to life after his people kill him, and who frees them from a cannibalistic giantess and a man-eating bird—a singular mixture of Christ and war god myths" (Dumarest 1919:228).

These two brief examples of Pueblo-Catholic syncretism are countered by other instances in which Christ and Poseyemu are distinguished. A good example of this is provided by Parsons (1926a:108): "When I spoke of Montezuma to my Tesuque informant, Poseyemu was at once mentioned by him. He said, 'Poseyemu came and helped the Indians and Americans. To the Americans he gave money, to the Indians the deer and mountain animals. When Jesus came down he took Poseyemu away.'" The Pueblo and Spanish Catholic figures are not only distinguished; they are thought to be mutually incompatible.

The line between compartmentalization and syncretism is not so sharp as Dozier (1961) makes it. Christ may be *like* Poseyemu and he may *be* Poseyemu in the same myth. The recognition of the native mind that Poseyemu is the Pueblo Christ is followed immediately by the recognition that Jesus is the Christian Poseyemu. Compartmentalization, then, is the first step toward syncretism. To separate the kachinas and the saints or to separate Poseyemu and Jesus is to recognize that in some sense the Catholic tradition is equal to the native tradition.

The hypothesis of political purpose helped to explain the connection of Montezuma and the culture hero after 1846. The hypothesis of structural similarity extended this explanation in time and space by accounting for the possibility of fusion of Poseyemu, Montezuma, and Jesus before 1846. Yet neither hypothesis can explain why Poseyemu is rarely identified with Jesus without the intervention of Montezuma. In other words, the mythological triangle of Poseyemu, Montezuma, and Jesus does not obey the law of transitivity. While Poseyemu and Montezuma are easily associated, and while Montezuma is often linked with Jesus, Poseyemu is rarely identified with Jesus without the reference to Montezuma as an intermediary category. The third hypothesis, based on the evolutionary scheme of Bellah (1964), attempts to overcome the shortcomings of the first two arguments by generalizing about the nature of contact between religions of different evolutionary levels.

The hypothesis used here to explain the selection of Poseyemu as the Indian mythological figure who most fully corresponds to Jesus is based on the assumption that in a situation of direct contact between historic and archaic systems (or between any other two systems), total compartmentalization is impossible. There must be some mechanism of communication between the two systems. It is an error to view compartmentalization as a total absence of communication, for compartmentalization implies the recognition of similarity. The hypothesis, then, is that when religions of different evolutionary levels come in contact, a point of communication will be established by selecting an element (or elements) from the less advanced system that shares characteristics with an element (or elements) in the more advanced system. In the case of Pueblo-Spanish contact, the native element is Poseyemu. The feature that he shares with his historic counterpart, Jesus, is universalism. Poseyemu's universalism has many manifestations. He is universal in that he is omnipresent; like the mist he represents, he is many places at once. Also, he is invoked as the founder of the Tewa religious societies, which pray for the good of the entire world regardless of race or tribe. He is universal in the sense that he founded many of the Pueblos and is found prominently in their various mythologies. The ideological power of his universalism was seen in the Revolt of 1680, when Poseyemu became a symbol for pan-Pueblo religious nationalism. In these ways, Poseyemu resembles the universalism of his Christian counterpart, Jesus. Jesus's role as the savior of mankind applies to all cultures and races; as God-Man, he represents the paradoxical solution to the religious quest for salvation. But universalism is not normally a feature of archaic religions. To see Poseyemu as a universalistic figure is to see him as a potentially historic god. On the other hand, Jesus shares many features of an archaic or mythological god; he is a culture hero, a fertility god, a miracle worker, a prophet, and a mediator between heaven and earth. If Poseyemu and Jesus share this universalism, it would seem logical that they would become easily assimilated according to the principle of structural similarity; however, this is not the case. Many Pueblo variants show that whenever Poseyemu and Jesus come in contact, either positively (through identification) or negatively (through combat), Montezuma intervenes. The name of Montezuma acts as a buffer or shield between the native religion (Poseyemu) and the alien system (Jesus). Of course, it is more important that Montezuma intervene in myths that express a syncretic tendency (Parsons 1926a:108; Dumarest 1919:228). When the Indian culture hero and the Christian god come in contact through combat, the necessity of Montezuma's intervention is not so great, although it does still occur.

In summary, Montezuma serves not only as a mediating symbol to communicate between the two religious traditions but also as a temporal marker for the intrusion of the notion of history in the Pueblos (Emory 1848).

The change in world view, stimulated by the Spanish conquest and motivated by the intensity of the Roman Catholic missionary effort, was a threat to the Pueblo conception of the universe. Through the Montezuma legends, the Indians understood this threat. "The Montezuma tales found just about everywhere among them hint that they grappled, after the coming of the Spaniards, with the prospect of being thrust forever into the ebb and flow of history, but this apparently was not to be" (Ortiz 1972a). Montezuma, finally, is the signpost for the Pueblos' encounter with historical consciousness.

# Contributors

This list gives the academic affiliations of authors at the time this volume went to press. Parenthetical tribal names identify Indian authors. The dates following the entries indicate when each manuscript was (1) first received; (2) accepted after all revisions had been made; and (3) sent to the author (or, if deceased, a substitute) for final approval of editorial work.

ARNON, NANCY S., Santa Fe, New Mexico. Santa Clara Pueblo: 8/16/74; 5/7/75; 12/11/77.

BASSO, KEITH H., Department of Anthropology, University of Arizona, Tucson. History of Ethnological Research: 5/7/75; 12/6/76; 11/9/78.

BODINE, JOHN J., Department of Anthropology, American University, Washington, D.C. Taos Pueblo: 5/18/72; 5/29/74; 10/17/77.

BRANDT, ELIZABETH A., Department of Anthropology, Arizona State University, Tempe. Sandia Pueblo: 5/30/72; 1/18/74; 11/9/77.

BREW, J.O., Peabody Professor, Emeritus, Peabody Museum, Harvard University, Cambridge, Massachusetts. Hopi Prehistory and History to 1850: 9/26/72; 7/7/75; 5/22/78.

BRODY, J.J., Maxwell Museum of Anthropology, University of New Mexico, Albuquerque. Pueblo Fine Arts: 7/21/75; 7/25/75; 6/21/78.

BROWN, DONALD N., Department of Sociology, Oklahoma State University, Stillwater. Picuris Pueblo: 3/31/77; 11/23/77; 3/10/78.

CHAVEZ, FRAY ANGELICO, Santa Fe, New Mexico. Genízaros: 3/22/72; 7/27/78; 9/11/78.

CLEMMER, RICHARD O., Department of Anthropology, California State University, Northridge. Hopi History, 1940-1970: 2/3/75; 7/7/75; 7/3/78.

CONNELLY, JOHN C., School of Education (emeritus), San Francisco State University, San Francisco. Hopi Social Organization: 8/9/74; 8/8/75; 7/10/78.

CORDELL, LINDA S., Department of Anthropology, University of New Mexico, Albuquerque. Prehistory: Eastern Anasazi: 7/3/78; 8/29/78; 10/22/78.

DI PESO, CHARLES C., The Amerind Foundation, Inc., Dragoon, Arizona. Prehistory: O'otam: 9/11/72; 5/29/74; 9/1/78. Prehistory: Southern Periphery: 9/11/72; 5/29/74; 9/15/78.

DOCKSTADER, FREDERICK J., New York City, New York. Hopi History, 1850-1940: 6/20/74; 12/8/77; 6/27/78.

EDELMAN, SANDRA A., San Diego, California. San Ildefonso Pueblo: 10/30/73; 7/9/75; 11/28/77. Tesuque Pueblo: 4/17/74; 5/21/74; 10/18/77.

EGGAN, FRED, Department of Anthropology (emeritus), University of Chicago, Chicago. Pueblos: Introduction: 6/23/76; 1/26/77; 11/18/78. Zuni History, 1850-1970: 8/26/77; 9/22/77; 7/20/78.

ELLIS, FLORENCE HAWLEY, Department of Anthropology (emeritus), University of New Mexico, Albuquerque. Laguna Pueblo: 3/1/73; 11/10/77; 1/13/78. Isleta Pueblo: 9/11/74; 10/25/77; 2/6/78.

FRIGOUT, ARLETTE (deceased), Paris, France. Hopi Ceremonial Organization: 5/11/72; 7/2/75; 9/5/78.

GARCIA-MASON, VELMA (Acoma), Rockville, Maryland. Acoma Pueblo: 1/25/75; 10/25/77; 4/5/78.

GUMERMAN, GEORGE J., Department of Anthropology, Southern Illinois University, Carbondale. Prehistory: Hohokam: 12/10/73; 5/17/74; 7/12/78.

GUNNERSON, JAMES H., University of Nebraska State Museum, Lincoln. Southern Athapaskan Archeology: 2/22/73; 8/28/78; 10/10/78.

HALE, KENNETH, Department of Linguistics and Philosophy, Massachusetts Institute of Technology, Cambridge. Historical Linguistics and Archeology: 8/16/73; 1/18/74; 10/31/78.

HARRIS, DAVID, Electrical Engineering and Computer Science, Massachusetts Institute of Technology, Cambridge. Historical Linguistics and Archeology: 8/16/73; 1/18/74; 10/31/78.

HAURY, EMIL W., Department of Anthropology, University of Arizona, Tucson. Prehistory: Hohokam: 12/10/75; 5/17/74; 7/12/78.

HIEB, LOUIS A., Special Collections, University Library, University of Arizona, Tucson. Hopi World View: 6/9/72; 1/18/74; 10/31/78.

HILL, W.W. (deceased), Department of Anthropology, University of New Mexico, Albuquerque. Santa Clara Pueblo: 8/16/74; 5/7/75; 12/11/77.

HOEBEL, E. ADAMSON, Department of Anthropology (emeritus), University of Minnesota, Minneapolis. Zia Pueblo: 7/2/73; 5/21/74; 1/5/78.

HOUSER, NICHOLAS P., Cuerpo de Paz, United States Embassy, Quito, Ecuador. Tigua Pueblo: 10/30/72; 8/1/75; 10/18/77.

IRWIN-WILLIAMS, CYNTHIA, Department of Anthropology, Eastern New Mexico University, Portales. Post-Pleistocene Archeology, 7000-2000 B.C.: 12/1/72; 8/5/78; 9/1/78.

KENNARD, EDWARD A., Department of Anthropology (emeritus), University of Pittsburgh, Pittsburgh. Hopi Economy and Subsistence: 12/7/72; 1/18/74; 7/7/78.

LADD, EDMUND J. (Zuni), United States Department of the Interior, Honaunau, Kona, Hawaii. Zuni Social and Political Organization: 12/5/77; 3/28/78; 7/14/78. Zuni Economy: 12/7/72; 1/18/74; 8/4/78.

LAMBERT, MARJORIE F., Santa Fe, New Mexico. Pojoaque Pueblo: 4/26/72; 5/5/72; 10/18/78.

LANGE, CHARLES H., Department of Anthropology, Northern Illinois University, DeKalb. Santo Domingo Pueblo: 1/21/74; 6/24/77; 12/22/77. Cochiti Pueblo: 3/7/73; 2/15/74; 2/24/78. Relations of the Southwest with the Plains and Great Basin: 5/14/74; 6/1/78; 10/25/78.

MASAYESVA JEANNE, LAVERNE (Hopi), Department of Linguistics, University of Arizona, Tucson. Hopi Semantics: 9/18/72; 4/20/78; 5/23/78.

MARTIN, PAUL S. (deceased), Department of Anthropology, University of Arizona, Tucson; and Field Museum of Natural History, Chicago. Prehistory: Mogollon: 4/17/72; 7/1/75; 8/2/78.

ORTIZ, ALFONSO (San Juan), Department of Anthropology, University of New Mexico, Albuquerque. San Juan Pueblo: 12/1/77; 1/23/78; 3/7/78. Tesuque Pueblo: 4/17/74; 5/21/74; 10/18/77. Introduction: 11/20/78; 11/20/78; 11/20/78.

PANDEY, T.N., Anthropology Board of Studies, University of California, Santa Cruz. Zuni History, 1850-1970: 7/23/76; 1/26/77; 11/7/78.

PARMENTIER, RICHARD J., Chicago, Illinois. The Mythological Triangle: Poseyemu, Montezuma, and Jesus in the Pueblos: 5/15/72; 8/2/72; 6/4/78.

PLOG, FRED, Department of Anthropology, Arizona State University, Tempe. Prehistory: Western Anasazi: 11/28/77; 11/78; 11/9/78.

SANDO, JOE S. (Jemez), Albuquerque, New Mexico. Jemez Pueblo: 3/20/73; 6/24/74; 12/2/78. The Pueblo Revolt: 4/9/74; 6/24/77; 10/7/78.

SCHROEDER, ALBERT H., National Park Service (retired), Santa Fe, New Mexico. Pueblos Abandoned in Historic Times: 1/20/78; 8/10/78; 10/7/78. Prehistory: Hakataya: 5/26/72; 3/28/73; 9/5/78. History of Archeological Research: 7/7/72; 10/5/72; 9/1/78. Pecos Pueblo: 10/24/72; 10/9/73; 3/30/78.

SIMMONS, MARC, Cerrillos, New Mexico. History of Pueblo-Spanish Relations to 1821: 7/17/72; 8/28/78; 9/12/78. History of the Pueblos Since 1821: 7/17/72; 5/24/78; 9/29/78.

SPEIRS, RANDALL H., Summer Institute of Linguistics, Española, New Mexico. Nambe Pueblo: 12/7/72; 8/12/74; 1/3/78.

STANISLAWSKI, MICHAEL B., Santa Fe, New Mexico. Hopi-Tewa: 9/23/74; 8/25/75; 6/26/78.

STRONG, PAULINE TURNER, Chicago, Illinois. Santa Ana Pueblo: 8/23/77; 9/1/77; 3/27/78. San Felipe Pueblo: 9/22/77; 9/22/77; 3/27/78.

TEDLOCK, DENNIS, Department of Anthropology, Boston University, Boston. Zuni Religion and World View: 6/4/73; 1/31/74; 8/7/78.

VOEGELIN, C.F., Department of Anthropology (emeritus), Indiana University, Bloomington. Hopi Semantics: 9/18/72; 4/20/78; 5/23/78.

VOEGELIN, F.M., Department of Anthropology, Indiana University, Bloomington. Hopi Semantics: 9/18/72; 4/20/78; 5/23/78.

WALKER, WILLARD, Department of Anthropology, Wesleyan University, Middletown, Connecticut. Zuni Semantics: 7/31/72; 7/73; 7/10/78.

WOODBURY, RICHARD B., Department of Anthropology, University of Massachusetts, Amherst. Zuni Prehistory and History to 1850: 8/23/72; 10/5/73; 7/21/78. Agricultural Beginnings, 2000 B.C.-A.D. 500: 7/12/74; 8/7/78; 9/11/78. Prehistory: Introduction: 3/31/73; 7/25/78; 9/5/78.

ZUBROW, EZRA B.W., Department of Anthropology, State University of New York, Buffalo. Agricultural Beginnings, 2000 B.C.-A.D. 500: 7/12/74; 8/7/78; 9/11/78.

# Bibliography

*This list includes all references cited in the volume, arranged in alphabetical order according to the names of the authors as they appear in the citations in the text. Multiple works by the same author are arranged chronologically; second and subsequent titles by the same author in the same year are differentiated by letters added to the dates. Where more than one author with the same surname is cited, one has been arbitrarily selected for text citation by surname alone throughout the volume, while the others are always cited with added initials; the combination of surname with date in text citations should avoid confusion. Where a publication date is different from the series date (as in some annual reports and the like), the former is used. Dates, authors, and titles that do not appear on the original works are enclosed by square brackets. For manuscripts, dates refer to time of composition. For publications reprinted or first published many years after original composition, a bracketed date after the title refers to the time of composition or the date of original publication.*

ARCIA = Commissioner of Indian Affairs
1849-    Annual Reports to the Secretary of the Interior. Washington: U.S. Government Printing Office. (Reprinted: AMS Press, New York, 1976-1977.)

Aarons, Leroy F.
1971    Southwest Colossus: Power and Pollution. *Washington Post*, June 6:A1,A3. Washington.

Abel, Annie H.
1916    The Journal of John Greiner. *Old Santa Fe* 3(11):189-243.

Abel, Leland J.
1955    Pottery Types of the Southwest: Wares 5A, 10A, 10B, 12A, San Juan Red Ware, Mesa Verde Gray and White Ware, San Juan White Ware. Harold S. Colton, ed. *Museum of Northern Arizona Ceramic Series* 3B. Flagstaff.

Aberle, David F.
1951    The Psychosocial Analysis of a Hopi Life-history. *Comparative Psychology Monograph* 21(1). Berkeley.

1954    Comments on Southwestern Studies of Culture and Personality, by Clyde Kluckhohn. *American Anthropologist* 56(4):697-700.

1966    The Peyote Religion Among the Navaho. Chicago: Aldine.

1970    Comments. Pp. 214-223 in Reconstructing Prehistoric Pueblo Societies. William A. Longacre, ed. Albuquerque: University of New Mexico Press.

Aberle, Sophie D.
1948    The Pueblo Indians of New Mexico: Their Land, Economy, and Civil Organization. *Memoirs of the American Anthropological Association* 70. Menasha, Wis.

Aberle, Sophie D., J.H. Watkins, and E.H. Pitney
1940    The Vital History of San Juan Pueblo. *Human Biology* 12(2):141-187.

Abert, James W.
1966    Western America in 1846-1847: The Original Travel Diary of Lieutenant J.W. Abert, Who Mapped New Mexico for the United States Army. John Galvin, ed. San Francisco: John Howell.

———  see also  U.S. Army. Corps of Topographical Engineers

Adair, John J.
1944    The Navajo and Pueblo Silversmiths. Norman: University of Oklahoma Press.

1948    A Study of Culture Resistance: The Veterans of World War II at Zuñi Pueblo. (Unpublished Ph.D. Dissertation in Anthropology, University of New Mexico, Albuquerque.)

Adair, John J., and Evon Z. Vogt
1949    Navaho and Zuni Veterans: A Study of Contrasting Modes of Culture Change. *American Anthropologist* 51(4):547-561.

Adams, Charles
1978    Room Size and Its Relation to Room Function. (Paper Presented at the 43d Annual Meeting of the Society for American Archaeology, Tucson.)

Adams, Eleanor B.
1953-1954    Bishop Tamarón's Visitation of New Mexico, 1760. *New Mexico Historical Review* 28(2):81-114, (3):192-221, (4):291-315; 29(1):41-47.

Adams, Richard N.
1949    Half House: A Pithouse in Chaco Canyon, New Mexico. *Papers of the Michigan Academy of Science, Arts, and Letters* 35:273-295. Ann Arbor.

Adams, William Y., and Nettie K. Adams
1959    An Inventory of Prehistoric Sites on the Lower San Juan River, Utah. *Museum of Northern Arizona Bulletin 31, Glen Canyon Series* 1. Flagstaff.

Adams, William Y., Alexander J. Lindsay, Jr., and Christy G. Turner, II
1961    Survey and Excavations in Lower Glen Canyon, 1952-1958. *Museum of Northern Arizona Bulletin* 36. Flagstaff.

Agenbroad, Larry D.
1967    The Distribution of Fluted Points in Arizona. *The Kiva* 32(4):113-120.

Agogino, George A., and Jim Hester
1956    A Reevaluation of the San José Non-ceramic Culture. *El Palacio* 63(1):6-21.

Agogino, George A., and Frank C. Hibben
1958    Central New Mexico Paleo-Indian Cultures. *American Antiquity* 23(4):422-425.

Aikens, C. Melvin
1963    Kaiparowits Survey, 1961. Pp. 70-100 in Appendix II of 1961 Excavations, Kaiparowits Plateau, Utah, by Don D. Fowler and C. Melvin Aikens. *University of Utah Anthropological Paper 66, Glen Canyon Series* 20. Salt Lake City.

1966    Virgin-Kayenta Cultural Relationships. *University of Utah Anthropological Paper* 79. Salt Lake City.

1966a    Fremont-Promontory-Plains Relationships in Northern Utah. *University of Utah Anthropological Paper* 82. Salt Lake City.

1967    Plains Relationships of the Fremont Culture: A Hypothesis. *American Antiquity* 32(2):198-209.

1970    Hogup Cave. *University of Utah Anthropological Paper* 93. Salt Lake City.

1972    Fremont Culture: Restatement of Some Problems. *American Antiquity* 37(1):61-66.

Aitken, Barbara
1930    Temperament in Native American Religion. *Journal of the Royal Anthropological Institute of Great Britain and Ireland* 60:363-387.

Allen, J.W.
1973    The Tsogue Site: Highway Salvage Excavations Near Tesuque Pueblo, New Mexico. *Museum of New Mexico Laboratory of Anthropology Note* 73. Santa Fe.

Ambler, John R.
1966    Caldwell Village and Fremont Prehistory. (Unpublished Ph.D. Dissertation in Anthropology, University of Colorado, Boulder.)

Ambler, John R., Alexander J. Lindsay, Jr., and Mary Ann Stein
1964    Survey and Excavations on Cummings Mesa, Arizona and Utah, 1960-1961. *Museum of Northern Arizona Bulletin 39, Glen Canyon Series 5.* Flagstaff.

Ames, Oliver et al.
1889    Memorial of Oliver Ames, John G. Whittier, Mary Hemenway, and Others, Praying Legislation for the Protection from Destruction of the Ancient Ruin of the Temple Casa Grande, Situated in Pinal County, Near Florence, Ariz. *U.S. Congress. Senate. 50th Cong., 2d sess. Misc. Doc. No. 60.* Washington: U.S. Government Printing Office.

Amsden, Charles A.
1935    The Pinto Basin Artifacts. Pp. 33-51 in The Pinto Basin Site. E.W.C. Campbell and W.H. Campbell, eds. *Southwest Museum Paper* 9. Los Angeles, Calif.

1936    An Analysis of Hohokam Pottery Design. *Gila Pueblo, Medallion Paper* 23. Globe, Ariz.

1937    The Lake Mohave Artifacts. Pp. 51-97 in The Archeology of Pleistocene Lake Mohave: A Symposium. *Southwest Museum Paper* 11. Los Angeles, Calif.

Anonymous
1886    Cowed by a Woman: A Craven Red Devil Weakens in the Face of a Resolute White Heroine - Exciting Adventure in an Indian Village in Arizona. *Illustrated Police News* 39(1010):9,15.

1899    Protest of the Pueblos: Red Men Visit the Secretary of the Interior. *The Evening Times,* November 15:1. Washington.

1943    Bibliography of Elsie Clews Parsons. *Journal of American Folklore* 56(219):48-56.

1960    Legend, Tradition Surround Gift from Abe Lincoln to Pueblos. *Los Alamos Scientific Laboratory Community News,* February 11:7. Los Alamos, N.M.

1961    Hopis Give Out First Mineral Prospecting Permit. *Phoenix Gazette,* September 15:51. Phoenix, Ariz.

1964    Hopi Council Approves 780,000 for Attorneys. *Arizona Republic,* December 5:21. Phoenix.

1967    [Acoma Land Claims Records.] (Records on File at the Tribal Office, Acomita, N.M.)

1969    Zuni Comprehensive Development Plan for a Better Zuni by '75. Presented by the Pueblo of Zuni with the Cooperation of Local, State, and Federal Agencies. (On File at Zuni Tribal Office, Zuni, N.M.)

1971    BVD to Improve Employee Conditions. *Gallup Independent,* May 26:6. Gallup, N.M.

1975    Population on the Hopi Reservation. *Winslow Mail Hopi Action News,* August 17:1. Winslow, Ariz.

Antevs, Ernst
1948    The Great Basin, with Emphasis on Glacial and Postglacial Times: III, Climatic Changes and Pre-white Man. *University of Utah Bulletin* 38(20):168-191. Salt Lake City.

1952    Arroyo-cutting and Filling. *Journal of Geology* 60(4):375-385.

1955    Geologic-climatic Dating in the West. *American Antiquity* 20(4):317-335.

Applegate, Frank G.
1929    Indian Stories from the Pueblos. Philadelphia: J.B. Lippincott.

1930    Sandia the Tragic. *Southwest Review* 15(3):310-316.

Arizona State Museum
1968    [Acoma Pueblo Oral History. Archives on Doris Duke Project.] (Tape Recordings in Arizona State Museum, Tucson.)

Armelagos, George J.
1967    Future Work in Paleopathology. Pp. 1-8 in Miscellaneous Papers in Paleopathology, I. William W. Wade, ed. *Museum of Northern Arizona Technical Series* 7. Flagstaff.

Arnold, J.R., and W.F. Libby
1949    Age Determinations by Radiocarbon Content: Checks with Samples of Known Age. *Science* 110(2869):678-680.

Arny, William F.M.
1870    [Tabular Statement of Indian Pueblos (Villages) Within the Territory of New Mexico.] (Microcopy in Record Group 75, Records of the Bureau of Indian Affairs Field Papers, Michigan Superintendency, 1854-1871, The National Archives, Washington, 1957.)

1967    Indian Agent in New Mexico: The Journal of Special Agent W.F.M. Arny [1870]. Lawrence R. Murphy, ed. Santa Fe: Stagecoach Press.

Asch, C.M.
1960    Post-Pueblo Occupation at the Willow Creek Ruin, Point of Pines. *The Kiva* 26(2):31-42.

Ascher, Robert, and Francis J. Clune, Jr.
1960    Waterfall Cave, Southern Chihuahua, Mexico. *American Antiquity* 26(2):270-274.

Ashton, Robert, Jr.
1976    Nampeyo and Lesou. *American Indian Art* 1(3):24-33.

Astrov, Margot
1950    The Concept of Motion as the Psychological Leitmotif of Navaho Life and Literature. *Journal of American Folklore* 63(247):45-56.

Athens, J. Stephen
1977    Theory Building and the Study of Evolutionary Process in Complex Societies. Pp. 353-384 in For Theory Building in Archaeology: Essays on Faunal Remains, Aquatic Resources, Spatial Analysis, and Systemic Modeling. Lewis R. Binford, ed. New York: Academic Press.

Auerbach, Herbert S.
1943    Father Escalante's Journal with Related Documents and Maps. *Utah Historical Quarterly* 11. Salt Lake City.

Aveleyra Arroyo de Anda, Luis
1951    Reconocimiento arqueológico en la zona de la presa internacional Falcon, Tamaulipas y Texas. *Revista Mexicana de Estudios Antropológicos* 12:31-59.

Aveleyra Arroyo de Anda, Luis, Manuel Maldonado- Koerdell, and Pablo Martínez del Río
1956-   Cueva de la Candelaria. Vol. 1. *Memorias del Instituto Nacional de Antropología e Historia* 5. Mexico City.

Bailey, Jessie B.
1940    Diego de Vargas and the Reconquest of New Mexico. (Taken from 3000 Handwritten Pages in the National Archives, Mexico City.) Albuquerque: University of New Mexico Press.

Bailey, Lynn (Robison)
1966    Indian Slave Trade in the Southwest: A Study of Slave-taking and the Traffic in Indian Captives. Los Angeles: Westernlore Press.

Baker, Gayla S.
1971    The Riverside Site, Grant County, New Mexico. *Southwestern New Mexico Research Report* 5. Case Western Reserve University, Department of Anthropology. Cleveland.

Bancroft, Hubert H.
1874-1876  The Native Races of the Pacific States of North America. 5 vols. New York: D. Appleton.

1889    History of Arizona and New Mexico, 1530-1888. (The Works of Hubert H. Bancroft 17) San Francisco: The History Company. (Reprinted: Horn and Wallace, Albuquerque, 1962.)

Bandelier, Adolph F.A.
1883 A Report on the Ruins of the Pueblo of Pecos. (A Visit to the Aboriginal Ruins in the Valley of the Rio Pecos) *Papers of the Archaeological Institute of America, American Series* 1(2). 2d ed. Boston.

_____ 1887 Histoire de la colonisation et des missions de Sonora, Chihuahua, Nouveau-Mexique, et Arizona jusqu'à l'année 1700. 7 Pts. (Manuscript Lat. 14111 in Vatican Library, Rome.)

_____ 1890 The Delight Makers. New York: Dodd, Mead and Company. (Reprinted: Harcourt Brace Jovanovich, New York, 1916, 1918, 1946, and 1971.)

_____ 1890a Hemenway Southwestern Archaeological Expedition: Contributions to the History of the Southwestern Portion of the United States. *Papers of the Archaeological Institute of America, American Series* 5. Cambridge, Mass.

_____ 1890-1892 Final Report of Investigations Among the Indians of the Southwestern United States, Carried on Mainly in the Years from 1880 to 1885. 2 vols. *Papers of the Archaeological Institute of America, American Series* 3 and 4. Cambridge, Mass.

_____ 1892 The 'Montezuma' of the Pueblo Indians. *American Anthropologist* 5(4):319-326.

_____ 1892a An Outline of the Documentary History of the Zuñi Tribe. *Journal of American Ethnology and Archaeology* 3(1):1-115.

_____ 1966-1976 The Southwestern Journals of Adolph F. Bandelier. Charles H. Lange and Carroll L. Riley, with Elizabeth M. Lange, eds. 4 vols. Albuquerque: University of New Mexico Press; Santa Fe: The School of American Research Museum of New Mexico Press.

_____ 1969 A History of the Southwest: A Study of the Civilization and Conversion of the Indians in Southwestern United States and Northwestern Mexico from the Earliest Times to 1700. Vol. 1: A Catalogue of the Bandelier Collection in the Vatican Library. Rome and St. Louis: Jesuit Historical Institue.

Bandelier, Adolph F.A., and Edgar L. Hewett
1937 Indians of the Rio Grande Valley. Albuquerque: University of New Mexico Press.

Bannister, Bryant
1964 Tree-ring Dating of the Archeological Sites in the Chaco Canyon Region, New Mexico. *Southwestern Monuments Association Technical Series* 6(2). Coolidge, Ariz.

Barnett, Franklin
1969 Tonque Pueblo: A Report of Partial Excavation of an Ancient Pueblo IV Indian Ruin in New Mexico. Albuquerque: Archaeological Society.

Barth, Fredrik, ed.
1969 Ethnic Groups and Boundaries: The Social Organization of Culture Difference. Bergen-Oslo: Universitets Forlaget; London: G. Allen and Unwin.

Bartlett, John R.
1852 [Senecu Piro Vocabulary.] (Manuscript No. 1627 in National Anthropological Archives, Smithsonian Institution, Washington.)

_____ 1854 Personal Narrative of Explorations and Incidents in Texas, New Mexico, California, Sonora, and Chihuahua, Connected with the United States and Mexican Boundary Commission During the Years 1850, '51, and '53. 2 vols. New York: D. Appleton.

_____ 1909 The Language of the Piro. *American Anthropologist* n.s. 11(3):426-433.

Bartlett, John R., and James Mooney
1897 [Kiowa and Tiwa (Isleta del Sur) Linguistic Notes and Vocabularies.] (Manuscript No. 454 in National Anthropological Archives, Smithsonian Institution, Washington.)

Bartlett, Katharine
1933 Pueblo Milling Stones of the Flagstaff Region and Their Relation to Others in the Southwest: A Study in Progressive Efficiency. *Museum of Northern Arizona Bulletin* 3. Flagstaff.

_____ 1936 Hopi History No. 2: The Navajo Wars 1823-1870. *Museum of Northern Arizona, Museum Note* 8(7):33-37. Flagstaff.

_____ 1943 A Primitive Stone Industry of the Little Colorado Valley, Arizona. *American Antiquity* 8(3):266-268.

Bartlett, Richard A.
1962 Great Surveys of the West. Norman : University of Oklahoma Press.

Basso, Keith H.
1969 Western Apache Witchcraft. *Anthropological Papers of the University of Arizona* 15. Tucson.

_____, ed.
1971 Western Apache Raiding and Warfare: From the Notes of Grenville Goodwin. Tucson: University of Arizona Press.

_____ 1973 Southwestern Ethnology: A Critical Review. *Annual Review of Anthropology* 2:221-252. Palo Alto, Calif.

Batcho, David G.
1978 Report of Investigations at Chavez Pass Ruin, Coconino National Forest, Arizona. (Manuscript on File, Office of Cultural Resource Management, Department of Anthropology, Arizona State University, Tempe.)

Baxter, Sylvester
1882 An Aboriginal Pilgrimage. *Century Magazine* 24:526-536.

Bayard, Don T.
1969 Science, Theory, and Reality in the New Archaeology. *American Antiquity* 34(4):376-384.

Baylor, George W.
1900-1906 [Collection of Historical Stories of the Southwest Published in the *El Paso Herald*, 1900-1906.] (Manuscripts in Special Collections, University of Texas, El Paso.)

Beadle, George W.
1972 The Mystery of Maize. *Field Museum of Natural History Bulletin* 43(10):2-11. Chicago.

Beaglehole, Ernest
1936 Hopi Hunting and Hunting Ritual. *Yale University Publications in Anthropology* 4. New Haven, Conn.

_____ 1937 Notes on Hopi Economic Life. *Yale University Publications in Anthropology* 15. New Haven, Conn.

Beals, Ralph L.
1932 The Comparative Ethnology of Northern Mexico Before 1750. *Ibero-Americana* 2:93-225. Berkeley, Calif.

_____ 1943 Northern Mexico and the Southwest. Pp. 191-199 in El norte de México... Mesa redonda sobre problemas antropológicos de México y Centro América. Mexico, D.F.: Sociedad Méxicana de Antropología.

_____ 1943a Relations Between Meso America and the Southwest. Pp. 245- 252 in El norte de México . . . Mesa redonda sobre problemas antropológicos de México y Centro América. Mexico, D.F.: Sociedad Méxicana de Antropología.

Beals, Ralph L., George W. Brainerd, and Watson Smith
1945 Archaeological Studies in Northeast Arizona. *University of California Publications in American Archaeology and Ethnology* 44(1). Berkeley.

Beattie, George W.
1933 Reopening the Anza Road. *California Pacific Historical Review* 2:52-71.

Beckett, Patrick H.
1973    Cochise Culture Sites in South Central and North Central New Mexico. (Unpublished M.A. Thesis in Anthropology, Eastern New Mexico University, Portales.)

Bedinger, Margery
1973    Indian Silver: Navajo and Pueblo Jewelers. Albuquerque: University of New Mexico Press.

Beeson, William J.
1966    Archaeological Survey Near St. Johns, Arizona: A Methodological Study. (Unpublished Ph.D. Dissertation in Anthropology, University of Arizona, Tucson.)

Bell, Barbara
1975    Zuni: The Art and the People. Photos by Ed Bell. 2 vols. Grants, N.M.: Squaw Bell Traders.

Bell, Betty
1971    Archaeology of Nayarit, Jalisco, and Colima. Pp. 694-753 in *Archaeology of Northern Mesoamerica.* Pt. 2. Gordon F. Ekholm and Ignacio Bernal, eds. Handbook of Middle American Indians. Robert Wauchope, gen. ed. Vol. 11. Austin: University of Texas Press.

Bell, William A.
1965    New Tracks in North America [1869]. Albuquerque: Horn and Wallace.

Bellah, Robert N.
1964    Religious Evolution. *American Sociological Review* 29(3):358-374.

Benavides, Alonso de
1630    Memorial qve Fray Ivan de Santander de la Orden de San Francisco, Commissario General de Indias, presenta a la Magestad Catolica del Rey don Felipe Qvarto nuestro Señor. Madrid: La Imprenta Real.

_____
1916    The Memorial of Fray Alonso de Benavides, 1630. Mrs. Edward E. Ayer, trans. Frederick W. Hodge and Charles F. Lummis, ann. Chicago: Privately Printed. (Reprinted: Horn and Wallace, University of New Mexico Press, Albuquerque, 1965.)

_____
1945    Fray Alonso de Benavides' Revised Memorial of 1634. Frederick W. Hodge, George P. Hammond, and Agapito Rey, eds. Albuquerque: University of New Mexico Press.

Benedict, Ruth (Fulton)
1930    Eight Stories from Acoma. *Journal of American Folk-Lore* 43(167):59-87.

_____
1930a   Psychological Types in the Cultures of the Southwest. Pp. 572-581 in *Proceedings of the 23d International Congress of Americanists.* New York, 1928.

_____
1931    Tales of the Cochiti Indians. *Bureau of American Ethnology Bulletin* 98. Washington.

_____
1932    Configurations of Culture in North America. *American Anthropologist* 34(1):1-27.

_____
1934    Patterns of Culture. Boston and New York: Houghton Mifflin.

_____
1935    Zuni Mythology. *Columbia University Contributions to Anthropology* 21. New York.

Bennett, John W.
1946    The Interpretation of Pueblo Culture: A Question of Values. *Southwestern Journal of Anthropology* 2(4):361-374.

Bennett, Wendell C.
1948    The Peruvian Co-tradition. Pp. 1-7 in A Reappraisal of Peruvian Archaeology. Wendell C. Bennett, ed. *Memoirs of the Society for American Archaeology* 4. Menasha, Wis.

Bennett, Wendell C., and R.M. Zingg
1935    The Tarahumara: An Indian Tribe of Northern Mexico. Chicago: University of Chicago Press.

Bernal, Ignacio
1963    Mexico Before Cortez: Art, History, Legend. Willis Barnstone, trans. Garden City, N.Y.: Dolphin Books, Doubleday.

Biella, J.V., and Richard Chapman
1977    Archeological Investigations in Cochiti Reservoir, New Mexico. Vol. 1: A Survey of Regional Variability. Albuquerque: University of New Mexico, Office of Contract Archeology.

Binford, Lewis R.
1968    Post-Pleistocene Adaptations. Pp. 313-341 in New Perspectives in Archeology. Sally R. Binford and Lewis R. Binford, eds. Chicago: Aldine.

Binford, Lewis R., and W.J. Chasko, Jr.
1976    Nunamiut Demographic History: A Provocative Case. Pp. 63-143 in Demographic Anthropology: Quantitative Approaches. Ezra B.W. Zubrow, ed. Albuquerque: University of New Mexico Press.

Binford, Sally R., and Lewis R. Binford, eds.
1968    New Perspectives in Archeology. Chicago: Aldine.

Bittman, Bente, and Thelma D. Sullivan
1978    The Pochteca. Pp. 211-218 in Mesoamerican Communication Routes and Cultural Contacts. Thomas A. Lee, Jr., and Carlos Navarrete, eds. *Papers of the New World Archaeological Foundation* 40. Provo, Utah.

Black, Robert A.
[1975]  Biography of Irving Pabanale. (Manuscript in Black's Possession.)

Blevins, Byron B., and Carol Joiner
1977    The Archeological Survey of Tijeras Canyon: The 1975 Excavation of Tijeras Pueblo, Cibola National Forest, New Mexico. (Archeological Report 18) Albuquerque: U.S.D.A. Forest Service, Southwestern Regional Office.

Bloom, Lansing B.
1913-1914  New Mexico Under Mexican Administration, 1821-1846. *Old Santa Fe Genealogy and Biography* 1(1):3-49.

_____
1928    A Glimpse of New Mexico in 1620. *New Mexico Historical Review* 3(4):357-380.

_____, ed.
1931    A Campaign Against the Moqui Pueblos Under Governor Phelix Martinez, 1716. *New Mexico Historical Review* 6(2):158-226.

_____, ed.
1933-1938  Bourke on the Southwest, I-XIII. *New Mexico Historical Review* 8(1):1-30; 9(1):33-77; 10(2):159-183; 11(3):273-289, (4):375-435; 10(1):1-35, (4)271-322; 11(1):77-122, (2):188-207, (3):217-282; 12(1):41-77, (4):337-379; 13(2):192-238.

_____
1946    The West Jemez Culture Area. *New Mexico Historical Review* 21(2):120-126.

Bloom, Lansing B., and Lynn B. Mitchell
1938    The Chapter Elections in 1672. *New Mexico Historical Review* 13(1):85-119.

Bloomfield, Leonard
1925    On the Sound-system of Central Algonquian. *Language* 1(4):130-156.

_____
1946    Algonquian. Pp. 85-129 in Linguistic Structures of Native America. *Viking Fund Publications in Anthropology* 6. New York.

Blumenschein, Helen
1956    Excavations in the Taos Area, 1953-1955. *El Palacio* 63(2):53-56.

1958　　Further Excavations and Surveys in the Taos Area. *El Palacio* 65(3):107-111.

1963　　Report on Site 268. *El Palacio* 70(4):48-49.

Boas, Franz
1925-1928　Keresan Texts. 2 Pts. *Publications of the American Ethnological Society* 8. New York.

1939　　Edward Sapir. *International Journal of American Linguistics* 10(1):58-63.

Bodine, John J.
1964　　Symbiosis at Taos: The Impact of Tourism on the Pueblo. (Paper Read at the Annual Meeting of the Central States Anthropological Society, Milwaukee, 1964.)

1967　　Attitudes and Institutions of Taos, New Mexico: Variables for Value System Expression. (Unpublished Ph.D. Dissertation in Anthropology, Tulane University, New Orleans.)

1968　　A Tri-ethnic Trap: The Spanish Americans of Taos. Pp. 145-153 in *Proceedings of the Annual Spring Meeting of the American Ethnological Society*. Detroit, 1968. Seattle: University of Washington Press.

1968a　　Taos Names: A Clue to Linguistic Acculturation. *Anthropological Linguistics* 10(5):23-27.

1971　　The Population Structure of Taos Pueblo. *California Anthropologist* 1(1):1-9.

1972　　Acculturation Processes and Population Dynamics. Pp. 257-285 in New Perspectives on the Pueblos. Alfonso Ortiz, ed. Albuquerque: University of New Mexico Press.

Bohrer, Vorsila L.
1970　　Ethnobotanical Aspects of Snaketown, a Hohokam Village in Southern Arizona. *American Antiquity* 35(4):413-430.

1972　　Paleoecology of the Hay Hollow Site, Arizona. *Fieldiana: Anthropology* 63(1). Chicago.

Bolton, Herbert E., ed.
1916　　Spanish Exploration in the Southwest, 1542-1706. (Original Narratives of Early American History) New York: Charles Scribner's Sons.

1917　　French Intrusions into New Mexico, 1749-1752. Pp. 389-407 in The Pacific Ocean in History. H. Morse Stephens and Herbert E. Bolton, eds. New York: Macmillan.

1936　　Rim of Christendom: A Biography of Eusebio Francisco Kino, Pacific Coast Pioneer. New York: Macmillan.

1949　　Coronado on the Turquoise Trail: Knight of the Pueblos and Plains. Albuquerque: University of New Mexico Press; New York, London, Toronto: Whittlesey House, McGraw-Hill.

1950　　Pageant in the Wilderness: The Story of the Escalante Expedition to the Interior Basin, 1776; Including the Diary of Father Escalante. *Utah Historical Quarterly* 18(1-4). Salt Lake City.

————, ed.
1952　　Spanish Exploration in the Southwest, 1542-1706 [1908]. New York: Barnes and Noble.

1964　　Coronado, Knight of Pueblos and Plains. Albuquerque: University of New Mexico Press.

Bourke, John G.
1884　　The Snake-dance of the Moquis of Arizona... with an Account of the Tablet Dance of the Pueblo of Santo Domingo, New Mexico, etc. New York: Charles Scribner's Sons. (Reprinted: Rio Grande Press, Glorieta, N.M., 1962.)

1892　　The Medicine-men of the Apache. Pp. 443-603 in *9th Annual Report of the Bureau of American Ethnology for the Years 1887-1888*. Washington.

Bowden, Jocelyn J.
1952　　The Ascarate Grant. (Unpublished M.A. Thesis in History, Texas Western College, El Paso.)

Bowman, John H.
1884　　[Tewa Village Population Figures.] P. 93 in Healing *v.* Jones; Defendants Exhibits 1. (Manuscripts in Field Records at the U.S. Bureau of Indian Affairs for 1950. Washington.)

Bradfield, Richard M.
1971　　The Changing Pattern of Hopi Agriculture. *Royal Anthropological Institute of Great Britain and Ireland, Occasional Paper* 30. London.

1973　　A Natural History of Associations: A Study in the Meaning of Community. 2 vols. New York: International Universities Press.

Bradfield, Wesley
1931　　Cameron Creek Village: A Site in the Mimbres Area in Grant County, New Mexico. *Monographs of the School of American Research* 1. Santa Fe.

Bradley, Zorro A.
1971　　Site Bc236, Chaco Canyon National Monument, New Mexico. Washington: National Park Service, Division of Archaeology.

Brand, Donald D.
1935　　The Distribution of Pottery Types in Northwest Mexico. *American Anthropologist* 37(2):287-305.

1938　　Aboriginal Trade Routes for Sea Shells in the Southwest. *Yearbook of the Association of Pacific Coast Geographers* 4:3-10. Cheney, Wash.

Brand, Donald D., Florence M. Hawley, and Frank C. Hibben
1937　　Tseh So, a Small House Ruin, Chaco Canyon, New Mexico (Preliminary Report). *Anthropological Series 2(2), University of New Mexico Bulletin* 308. Albuquerque.

Brandes, Raymond S.
1965　　Frank Hamilton Cushing: Pioneer Americanist. (Unpublished Ph.D. Dissertation in Modern History, University of Arizona, Tucson.)

Brandt, Elizabeth A.
1969　　[Ethnographic and Linguistic Notes from Approximately 5 Months' Fieldwork at Sandía Pueblo, New Mexico.] (Manuscripts in Brandt's Possession.)

1970　　On the Origins of Linguistic Stratification: The Sandia Case. *Anthropological Linguistics* 12(2):46-50.

1970a　　Sandía Pueblo, New Mexico: A Linguistic and Ethnolinguistic Investigation. (Unpublished Ph.D. Dissertation in Anthropology, Southern Methodist University, Dallas.)

1971　　A Proposed Practical Alphabet for the Sandía Language. (Manuscript in Brandt's Possession and Sandía Pueblo, Office of the Governor.)

Brandt, Richard B.
1954　　Hopi Ethics: A Theoretical Analysis. Chicago: University of Chicago Press.

Brant, Charles S.
1950　　Preliminary Data on Tesuque Pueblo, New Mexico. *Papers of the Michigan Academy of Science, Arts and Letters* 34:253-259. Ann Arbor.

Brayer, Herbert O.
1938　　Pueblo Indian Land Grants of the "Rio Abajo," New Mexico. *University of New Mexico Bulletin 334, Historical Series* 1(1). Albuquerque.

Breternitz, David A.
1957     A Brief Archeological Survey of the Lower Gila River. *The Kiva* 22(2-3):1-12.

1959     Excavations at Nantack Village, Point of Pines, Arizona. *Anthropological Papers of the University of Arizona* 1. Tucson.

1959a    Excavations at Two Cinder Park Phase Sites. *Plateau* 31(3):66-72.

1960     Excavation at Three Sites in the Verde Valley, Arizona. *Museum of Northern Arizona Bulletin* 34. Flagstaff.

1966     An Appraisal of Tree-ring Dated Pottery in the Southwest. *Anthropological Papers of the University of Arizona* 10. Tucson.

Brew, John O.
1941     Preliminary Report of the Peabody Museum Awatovi Expedition of 1939. *Plateau* 13(3):37-48.

1943     On the Pueblo IV and on the Katchina-Tlaloc Relations. Pp. 241-245 in El norte de México... Mesa redonda sobre problemas antropológicos de México y Centro América. México, D.F.: Sociedad Méxicana de Antropología.

1946     Archaeology of Alkali Ridge, Southeastern Utah, with a Review of the Prehistory of the Mesa Verde Division of the San Juan and Some Observations on Archaeological Systematics. *Papers of the Peabody Museum of American Archaeology and Ethnology, Harvard University* 21. Cambridge, Mass.

1961     Emergency Archaeology: Salvage in Advance of Technological Progress. *Proceedings of the American Philosophical Society* 105(1):1-10. Philadelphia.

Brew, John O., and Ross G. Montgomery
1951     [Review of] The Mission of San Gregorio de Abó: A Report on the Excavation of a 17th Century New Mexico Mission, by Joseph H. Toulouse, Jr. *El Palacio* 58(10):326-328.

Bright, William
1956     Glottochronologic Counts of Hokaltecan Material. *Language* 32(1):42-48.

Brinton, Daniel G.
1891     The American Race: A Linguistic Classification and Ethnographic Description of the Native Tribes of North and South America. New York: N.D.C. Hodges.

Briuer, Frederick L.
1975     Cultural and Noncultural Deposition Processes in Chevelon Canyon. (Unpublished Ph.D. Dissertation in Anthropology, University of California, Los Angeles.)

Brody, J.J.
1969-1972 The Kiva Murals of Pottery Mound. Pp. 101-110 in Vol. 2 of *Proceedings of the 38th International Congress of Americanists*. 4 vols. Stuttgart-Munich, 1968.

1971     Indian Painters and White Patrons. Albuquerque: University of New Mexico Press.

1977     Mimbres Painted Pottery. Santa Fe: School of American Research; Albuquerque: University of New Mexico Press.

Brom, Thomas
1974     The Southwest: America's New Appalachia. *Ramparts*, 13(4):17-20.

Brown, Donald N.
1973     Structural Change at Picuris Pueblo, New Mexico. (Unpublished Ph.D. Dissertation in Anthropology, University of Arizona, Tucson.)

1974     Social Structure as Reflected in Architectural Units at Picuris Pueblo. Pp. 317-338 in The Human Mirror: Material and Spacial Images of Man. Miles Richardson, ed. Baton Rouge: Louisiana State University Press.

Brown, James A.
1954     Wooden Artifacts. Pp. 181-211 in Caves of the Reserve Area, by Paul S. Martin, John B. Rinaldo, and Elaine Bluhm. *Fieldiana: Anthropology* 42. Chicago.

Browne, Jim
1940     Projectile Points. *American Antiquity* 5(3):209-213.

Brugge, David M.
1963     Navajo Pottery and Ethnohistory. *Navajoland Publications Series* 2. Window Rock, Ariz.

1965     Some Plains Indians in the Church Records of New Mexico. *Plains Anthropologist* 10(29):181-189.

1968     Navajos in the Catholic Church Records of New Mexico, 1694-1875. *Parks and Recreation Department, Research Section, Research Report* 1. Window Rock, Ariz.

Bryan, Bruce
1931     Excavation of the Galaz Ruin, Mimbres Valley, N.M. *Art and Archaeology* 32(1-2):35-42.

Bryan, Kirk
1925     Date of Channel Trenching (Arroyo Cutting) in the Arid Southwest. *Science* 62(1607):338-344.

1926     Recent Deposits of Chaco Canyon, New Mexico, in Relation to the Life of the Pre-historic Peoples of Pueblo Bonito. *Journal of the Washington Academy of Sciences* 16(3):75-76. Washington.

1929     Flood-water Farming. *Geographical Review* 19(3):444-456.

1941     Correlation of the Deposits of Sandia Cave, New Mexico, with the Glacial Chronology. Pp. 45-64 in Evidences of Early Occupation of Sandia Cave, New Mexico, and Other Sites in the Sandia-Manzano Region, by Frank C. Hibben. *Smithsonian Miscellaneous Collections* 99(23). Washington.

1950     Flint Quarries: The Sources of Tools and, at the Same Time, the Factories of the American Indian, with a Consideration of the Theory of the "Blank" and Some of the Techniques of Flint Utilization. *Papers of the Peabody Museum of American Archaeology and Ethnology, Harvard University* 17(3):3-35. Cambridge, Mass.

1950a    The Geology and Fossil Vertebrates of Ventana Cave: Geological Interpretation of the Deposits. Pp. 75-126 in The Stratigraphy and Archaeology of Ventana Cave, Arizona, by Emil W. Haury. Tucson: University of Arizona Press; Albuquerque: University of New Mexico Press.

1954     The Geology of Chaco Canyon, New Mexico, in Relation to the Life and Remains of the Prehistoric Peoples of Pueblo Bonito. *Smithsonian Miscellaneous Collections* 122(7):1-65. Washington.

Bryan, Kirk, and Joseph H. Toulouse, Jr.
1943     The San Jose Non-ceramic Culture and Its Relation to a Puebloan Culture in New Mexico. *American Antiquity* 8(3):269-280.

Bryson, Reid A., David A. Baerreis, and W.M. Wendland
1970     The Character of Late-Glacial and Post-Glacial Climatic Change. Pp. 53-73 in Pleistocene and Recent Environments of the Central Plains. W. Dort and J.K. Jones, eds. Lawrence: University of Kansas Press.

Budnik, Dan
1972     Black Mesa: Progress Report on an Ecological Rape. *Art in America* 60(4):98-105.

Bullard, William R., Jr.
1962     The Cerro Colorado Site and Pithouse Architecture in the Southwestern United States Prior to A.D. 900. *Papers of*

the Peabody Museum of American Archaeology and Ethnology, Harvard University* 44(2). Cambridge, Mass.

Bunker, Robert M.
1956 Other Men's Skies. Drawings by Cliff Ingram. Bloomington: Indiana University Press.

Bunzel, Ruth L.
1929 The Pueblo Potter: A Study of Creative Imagination in Primitive Art. *Columbia University Contributions to Anthropology* 8. New York.

————
1932 Zuñi Katcinas. Pp. 837-1086 in *47th Annual Report of the Bureau of American Ethnology for the Years 1929-1930*. Washington.

————
1932a Introduction to Zuñi Ceremonialism. Pp. 467-544 in *47th Annual Report of the Bureau of American Ethnology for the Years 1929-1930*. Washington.

————
1932b Zuñi Origin Myths. Pp. 545-609 in *47th Annual Report of the Bureau of American Ethnology for the Years 1929-1930*. Washington.

————
1932c Zuñi Ritual Poetry. Pp. 611-835 in *47th Annual Report of the Bureau of American Ethnology for the Years 1929-1930*. Washington.

————
1933 Zuni Texts. *Publications of the American Ethnological Society* 15. New York.

————
1938 The Economic Organization of Primitive Peoples. Pp. 327-408 in General Anthropology. Franz Boas, ed. Boston, New York, Chicago, Atlanta, Dallas, San Francisco, and London: D.C. Heath.

————
1952 Chichicastenango, a Guatemalan Village. *Publications of the American Ethnological Society* 22. Locust Valley, N.Y.

————
1972 The Pueblo Potter: A Story of Creative Imagination in Primitive Art [1929]. New York: Dover.

Burns, Peter E.
1972 The Heron Ruin, Grant County, New Mexico. *Southwestern New Mexico Research Report* 7. Case Western Reserve University, Department of Anthropology. Cleveland.

Burrus, Ernest J.
1966 The Bandelier Collection in the Vatican Library. *Manuscripta* 10(2):67-84.

Burton, Henrietta K.
1936 The Re-establishment of the Indians in Their Pueblo Life Through the Revival of Their Traditional Crafts: A Study in Home Extension Education. New York: Columbia University, Teachers College.

Buschmann, Johann C.E.
1859 Die Spuren der aztekischen Sprache im nördlichen Mexiko und höheren amerikanischen Norden. Pp. 512-516 in *Abhandlungen der Königlichen Akademie der Wissenschaften* Suppl. 2. Berlin.

Calhoun, James S.
1849-1850 Correspondence to Col. W. Medill, Commissioner of Indian Affairs, Washington, D.C., from James S. Calhoun, Indian Agent, Santa Fe, New Mexico. Pp. 204-207, 212-219 in *31st Cong., 1st sess. Senate Exec. Docs. Vol. 9. (Serial No. 557.)* Washington: U.S. Government Printing Office.

Calleros, Cleofás
1953 El Paso's Missions and Indians. El Paso, Tex.: McMath Company.

Calleros, Cleofás, with Marjorie F. Graham
1952 The Mother Mission. El Paso, Tex.: American Printing Company.

————
1953 Tigua Indians, Oldest Permanent Settlers in Texas. El Paso, Tex.: American Printing Company.

Calvin, Ross *see* U.S. Army. Corps of Topographical Engineers

Campbell, Elizabeth W. (Crozer)
1949 Two Ancient Archeological Sites in the Great Basin. *Science* 109(2831):340.

Campbell, Elizabeth W. (Crozer), and William H. Campbell
1935 The Pinto Basin Site: An Ancient Aboriginal Camping Ground in the California Desert. *Southwest Museum Paper* 9. Los Angeles, Calif.

————
1937 The Lake Mohave Site. Pp. 9-44 in The Archeology of Pleistocene Lake Mohave: A Symposium. *Southwest Museum Paper* 11. Los Angeles, Calif.

Campbell, Elsie
1950 Spanish Records of the Civil Government of Ysleta, 1835. 2 Pts. (Unpublished M.A. Thesis in History, Texas Western College, El Paso.)

Campbell, Lyle, and Marianne Mithun
[1978] The Languages of Native America: An Historical and Comparative Assessment. Austin: University of Texas Press. In Press.

Carey, Henry A.
1931 An Analysis of Northwestern Chihuahua Culture. *American Anthropologist* 33(3):325-374.

Carlson, Roy L.
1963 Basketmaker III Sites Near Durango, Colorado. *University of Colorado Studies, Series in Anthropology* 8. Boulder.

————
1970 White Mountain Redware: A Pottery Tradition of East-central Arizona and Western New Mexico. *Anthropological Papers of the University of Arizona* 19. Tucson.

Carneiro, Robert L.
1967 On the Relationship Between Size of Population and Complexity of Social Organization. *Southwestern Journal of Anthropology* 23(3):234-243.

Carroll, Horace B., and Juan V. Haggard, trans.
1942 Three New Mexico Chronicles: The Exposición of Don Pedro Bautista Pino, 1812; The Ojeada of Lic. Antonio Barréiro, 1832; and the Additions by Don José Agustín de Escudero, 1849. Albuquerque: The Quivira Society.

Castaño de Sosa, Gaspar
1965 A Colony on the Move: Gaspar Castaño de Sosa's Journal, 1590-1591. Albert H. Schroeder and Dan S. Matson, eds. and trans. Santa Fe: The School of American Research.

Castetter, Edward F., and Willis H. Bell
1942 Pima and Papago Indian Agriculture. (Interamericana Studies 1) Albuquerque: University of New Mexico Press.

Castetter, Edward F., and Ruth M. Underhill
1935 The Ethnobiology of the Papago Indians. *Biological Series 4(3), University of New Mexico Bulletin* 275. Albuquerque.

Champe, John L.
1949 White Cat Village. *American Antiquity* 14(4):285-292.

Chapman, Kenneth M.
1936 The Pottery of Santo Domingo Pueblo: A Detailed Study of its Decoration. *Memoirs of the Laboratory of Anthropology* 1. Santa Fe. (Reprinted in 1977.)

Chapman, Kenneth M., and Francis H. Harlow
1970 The Pottery of San Ildefonso Pueblo. Albuquerque: Published for the School of American Research by the University of New Mexico Press.

Chard, Chester S.
1940 Distribution and Significance of Ball Courts in the Southwest. *Papers of the Excavators' Club* 1(2). Cambridge, Mass.

Chavez, Fray Angelico
1954    Origins of New Mexico Families in the Spanish Colonial Period. Santa Fe: Historical Society of New Mexico.

_____
1955    José Gonzales, Genízaro Governor. *New Mexico Historical Review* 30(3):190-194.

_____, comp.
1957    Archives, 1678-1900 (of the Archdiocese of Sante Fe). Washington: Academy of American Franciscan History.

_____
1957a   Addenda to New Mexico Families. *El Palacio* 64(5-6):178-190.

_____
1967    Pohé-yemo's Representative and the Pueblo Revolt of 1680. *New Mexico Historical Review* 42(2):85-126.

Clemmer, Richard O.
[1968-1970] [Fieldnotes, from Approximately 12 Months' Fieldwork Among the Hopi, Arizona.] (Manuscripts in Clemmer's Possession.)

1970    Economic Development vs. Aboriginal Land Use: An Attempt to Predict Culture Change on an Indian Reservation in Arizona. (Manuscript in Columbia University, International Affairs Library, New York City.)

1973    Culture Change and the Hopi Nation: The Impact of Federal Jurisdiction. (Manuscript in Columbia University, International Affairs Library, New York City.)

1974    Stripping Black Mesa: The Consequences of Crisis Ideology and Energy Politics. (Manuscript in Columbia University, International Affairs Library, New York City.)

Coan, Charles F.
1925    A History of New Mexico. 3 vols. Chicago and New York:

Cole, Fay-Cooper
1955    Tesuque Rain Gods. *The Living Museum* 16(9):550-551.

Colee, Philips
1969    Ethnohistoric Research on the Southern Tiwa. (Paper Presented at the Third Summer Colloquium, Eastern New Mexico University, Armijo Lake, 1969.)

Collins, John E.
1974    Nampeyo, Hopi Potter: Her Artistry and Her Legacy. Fullerton, Calif.: Muckenthaler Cultural Center.

Collins, John J.
1968    A Descriptive Introduction to the Taos Peyote Ceremony. *Ethnology* 7(4):427-449.

Colton, Harold S.
1934    A Brief Survey of Hopi Common Law. *Museum of Northern Arizona, Museum Note* 7:21-24. Flagstaff.

1936    The Rise and Fall of the Prehistoric Population of Northern Arizona. *Science* 84(2181):337-343.

1938    Names of the Four Culture Roots in the Southwest. *Science* 87(2268):551-552.

1939    Prehistoric Culture Units and Their Relationships in Northern Arizona. *Museum of Northern Arizona Bulletin* 17. Flagstaff.

1939a   The Reducing Atmosphere and Oxidizing Atmosphere in Prehistoric Southwestern Ceramics. *American Antiquity* 4(3):224-231.

1941    Winona and Ridge Ruin, Pt. 2: Notes on the Technology and Taxonomy of the Pottery. *Museum of Northern Arizona Bulletin* 19. Flagstaff.

1945    The Patayan Problem in the Colorado River Valley. *Southwestern Journal of Anthropology* 1(1):114-121.

1946    The Sinagua: A Summary of the Archaeology of the Region of Flagstaff, Arizona. *Museum of Northern Arizona Bulletin* 22. Flagstaff.

1950    Kachina Dolls. *Arizona Highways* 26(7):8-13.

1953    Potsherds: An Introduction to the Study of Prehistoric Southwestern Ceramics and Their Use in Historic Reconstruction. Flagstaff: Northern Arizona Society of Science and Art.

_____, ed.
1955    Pottery Types of the Southwest: Wares 8A, 8B, 9A, 9B, Tusayan Gray and White Ware, Little Colorado Gray and White Ware. *Museum of Northern Arizona Ceramic Series* 3A. Flagstaff.

1956    Pottery Types of the Southwest: Wares 5A, 5B, 6A, 6B, 7A, 7B, 7C, San Juan Red Ware, Tsegi Orange Ware, Homolovi Orange Ware, Winslow Orange Ware, Awatovi Yellow Ware, Jeddito Yellow Ware, Sichomovi Red Ware. *Museum of Northern Arizona Ceramic Series* 3C. Flagstaff.

1958    Pottery Types of the Southwest: Wares 14, 15, 16, 17, 18: Revised Descriptions, Alameda Brown Ware, Tizon Brown Ware, Lower Colorado Buff Ware, Prescott Gray Ware, San Francisco Mt. Gray Ware. *Museum of Northern Arizona Ceramic Series* 3D. Flagstaff.

1959    Hopi Kachina Dolls; with a Key to Their Identification. Rev. ed. Albuquerque: University of New Mexico Press.

1960    Black Sand: Prehistory in Northern Arizona. Albuquerque: University of New Mexico Press.

Colton, Harold S., and Frank C. Baxter
1932    Days in the Painted Desert and the San Francisco Mountains: A Guide. 2d ed. *Northern Arizona Society of Science and Art Bulletin* 2. Flagstaff.

Colton, Harold S., and Lyndon L. Hargrave
1937    Handbook of Northern Arizona Pottery Wares. *Museum of Northern Arizona Bulletin* 11. Flagstaff.

Colton, Mary-Russell (Ferrell)
1939    Hopi Silversmithing: Its Background and Future. *Plateau* 12(1):1-7.

Connelly, John C.
1944-1945   [Fieldnotes from First 18 Months' Teaching at Shungopovi Day School.] (Manuscripts in Connelly's Possession.)

1947-1954   [Census Data and Ethnographic Fieldnotes from Seven Years' Work at Shungopovi Day School, Arizona.] (Manuscripts in Connelly's Possession.)

1956    Descriptive and Operational Kinship. (Paper Presented to the American Anthropological Association, Santa Monica, Calif.)

Cook de Leonard, Carmen
1971    Ceramics of the Classic Period in Central Mexico. Pp. 179-205 in *Archaeology of Northern Mesoamerica*. Pt. 1. Gordon F. Ekholm and Ignacio Bernal, eds. Handbook of Middle American Indians. Robert Wauchope, gen. ed. Vol. 10. Austin: University of Texas Press.

Cordell, Linda S.
1972    Settlement Pattern Changes at Wetherill Mesa, Colorado: A Test Case for Computer Simulation in Archaeology. (Unpublished Ph.D. Dissertation in Anthropology, University of California, Santa Barbara.)

1975    Predicting Site Abandonment at Wetherill Mesa. *The Kiva* 40(3):189-202.

1977    Late Anasazi Farming and Hunting Strategies: One Example of a Problem in Congruence. *American Antiquity* 42(3):449-461.

1977a   Report of the 1976 Season at Tijeras Pueblo, Cibola National Forest, New Mexico. (Archeological Report 18) Albuquerque: U.S.D.A. Forest Service, Southwestern Regional Office.

632

Cortés, Hernando
1908        Letters of Cortes; the Five Letters of Relation from Fer-
            nando Cortes to the Emperor Charles V. Francis A. Mac-
            Nutt, ed. New York: G.P. Putnam's Sons.

Cosgrove, C.B.
1947        Caves of the Upper Gila and Hueco Areas, in New Mex-
            ico and Texas. *Papers of the Peabody Museum of American
            Archaeology and Ethnology, Harvard University* 24(2).
            Cambridge, Mass.

Cosgrove, H.S., and C.B. Cosgrove
1932        The Swarts Ruin: A Typical Mimbres Site in Southwest-
            ern New Mexico. (Report of the Mimbres Valley Expedi-
            tion Seasons of 1924-1927) *Papers of the Peabody Museum
            of American Archaeology and Ethnology, Harvard Univer-
            sity* 15(1). Cambridge, Mass.

Costo, Rupert
1974        The Struggle of the California Indians in Their Claims
            Case Against the U.S. Government, BIA, Their Attor-
            neys. *Wassaja* 2(10):15-16.

Coues, Elliott, ed.
1900        On the Trail of a Spanish Pioneer: The Diary and Itiner-
            ary of Francisco Garcés (Missionary Priest) in His Travels
            Through Sonora, Arizona, and California, 1775-1776. 2
            vols. New York: Francis P. Harper.

Cox, Bruce A.
1967        Hopi Trouble Cases: Cultivation Rights and Homesteads.
            *Plateau* 39(4):145-156.

1968        Law and Conflict Management Among the Hopi. (Un-
            published Ph.D. Dissertation in Anthropology, University
            of California, Berkeley.)

Crampton, C. Gregory
1977        The Zunis of Cibola. Salt Lake City: University of Utah
            Press.

Crane, Leo
1925        Indians of the Enchanted Desert. Boston: Little, Brown.

1928        Desert Drums: The Pueblo Indians of New Mexico,
            1540-1928. Boston: Little, Brown.

Crocchiola, Stanley F. L.
1962        The Picuris, New Mexico, Story. Pantex, Tex.: Privately
            Printed.

1966        The Nambe, New Mexico Story. Pep, Tex.: Privately
            Printed.

Cummings, Byron
1928        Cochise of Yesterday. *Arizona, Old and New* 1(4):9-10, 26-
            28. Phoenix.

Curtis, Edward S.
1907-1930   The North American Indian: Being a Series of Volumes
            Picturing and Describing the Indians of the United States,
            and Alaska. Frederick W. Hodge, ed. 20 vols. Norwood,
            Mass.: Plimpton Press. (Reprinted: Johnson Reprint,
            New York, 1970.)

Cushing, Frank H.
1883        Zuñi Fetiches. Pp. 3-45 in *2d Annual Report of the Bureau
            of American Ethnology for the Years 1880-1881.* Washing-
            ton.

1890        Preliminary Notes on the Origin, Working Hypothesis and
            Primary Researches of the Hemenway Southwestern
            Archaeological Expedition. Pp. 151-194 in *Proceedings of
            the 7th International Congress of Americanists.* Berlin,
            1888.

1896        Outlines of Zuñi Creation Myths. Pp. 321-447 in *13th
            Annual Report of the Bureau of American Ethnology for the
            Years 1891-1892.* Washington.

————, comp. and trans.
1901        Zuñi Folk Tales. New York: G.P. Putnam's Sons. (Re-
            printed: Alfred A. Knopf, New York, 1931.)

1920        Zuñi Breadstuff. *Museum of the American Indian, Heye
            Foundation. Indian Notes and Monographs* 8. New York.
            (Reprinted in 1974.)

1922        Oraibi in 1883. Pp. 253-268 in Contributions to Hopi
            History. *American Anthropologist* 24(3).

1941        My Adventures in Zuñi [1882]. Santa Fe, N.M.: The Peri-
            patetic Press. (Reprinted: American West Publishing
            Company, Palo Alto, Calif., 1970.)

Cutler, Hugh C.
1952        A Preliminary Survey of Plant Remains of Tularosa Cave.
            Pp. 461-479 in Mogollon Cultural Continuity and
            Change: The Stratigraphic Analysis of Tularosa and Cor-
            dova Caves, by Paul S. Martin et al. *Fieldiana: Anthro-
            pology* 40. Chicago.

Cutler, Hugh C., and Thomas W. Whitaker
1961        History and Distribution of the Cultivated Cucurbits in
            the Americas. *American Antiquity* 26(4):469-485.

Cutts, James M.
1965        The Conquest of California and New Mexico by the
            Forces of the United States, in the Years 1846 and 1847.
            Albuquerque: Horn and Wallace.

Daifuku, Hiroshi
1952        A New Conceptual Scheme for Prehistoric Cultures in the
            Southwestern United States. *American Anthropologist*
            54(2):191-200.

1961        Jeddito 264: A Report on the Excavation of a Basket
            Maker III - Pueblo I Site in Northeastern Arizona with a
            Review of Some Current Theories in Southwestern Ar-
            chaeology. (Reports of the Awatovi Expedition 7) *Papers
            of the Peabody Museum of American Archaeology and Eth-
            nology, Harvard University* 33(1). Cambridge, Mass.

Dale, Edward E.
1949        The Indians of the Southwest: A Century of Develop-
            ment Under the United States. Norman: University of
            Oklahoma Press.

Daniel, James M., ed.
1956        Diary of Pedro Jose de la Fuente, Captain of the Presidio
            of El Paso del Norte, January-July, 1765. *Southwestern
            Historical Quarterly* 60(2):260-281.

Danson, Edward B.
1957        An Archaeological Survey of West Central New Mexico
            and East Central Arizona. *Papers of the Peabody Museum
            of American Archaeology and Ethnology, Harvard Univer-
            sity* 44(1). Cambridge, Mass.

1957a       Pottery Type Descriptions. Pp. 219-232 in Excavations,
            1940, at University Indian Ruin, Tucson, Arizona, by Ju-
            lian D. Hayden. *Southwestern Monuments Association
            Technical Series* 5. Gila Pueblo, Globe, Ariz.

Danson, Edward B., and Robert M. Wallace
1956        A Petrographic Study of Gila Polychrome. *American An-
            tiquity* 22(2):180-183.

Davidson, M.O.
1865        Arizona Superintendency. Pp. 129-136 in *Report of the
            Commissioner of Indian Affairs for the Year 1865.* Wash-
            ington.

Davis, Emma Lou
1963        The Desert Culture of the Western Great Basin: A Life-
            way of Seasonal Transhumance. *American Antiquity*
            29(2):202-212.

1965        Small Pressures and Cultural Drift as Explanations for
            Abandonment of the San Juan Area, New Mexico and
            Arizona. *American Antiquity* 30(3):353-355.

1968        Early Man in the Mojave Desert. *Eastern New Mexico
            Contributions in Anthropology* 1(4). Portales.

Davis, Emma Lou, and David E. Fortsch
1970        Extinct Fauna and Early Man in the Mohave Desert,
            California: A Progress Report. (Manuscript in Davis'
            Possession.)

633

Davis, Emma Lou, and Richard Shutler, Jr.
1969    Recent Discoveries of Fluted Points in California and Ne-
        vada. *Miscellaneous Papers on Nevada Archaeology 7, Ne-
        vada State Museum Anthropological Paper* 14.  Carson
        City.

Davis, Emma Lou, and James H. Winkler
1959    A Late Mesa Verde Site in the Rio Puerco Valley. *El Pa-
        lacio* 66(3):92-100.

Davis, Emma Lou, Clark W. Brott, and David L. Weide
1969    The Western Lithic Co-tradition. *San Diego Museum Pa-
        per 6.*  San Diego, Calif.

Davis, Irvine
1959    Linguistic Clues to Northern Rio Grande Prehistory. *El
        Palacio* 66(3):73-84.

_____
1964    The Language of Santa Ana Pueblo. *Anthropological Pa-
        pers 69, Bureau of American Ethnology Bulletin* 191:53-
        190.  Washington.

Davis, James T.
1962    The Rustler Rockshelter Site (SBr-288):  A Culturally
        Stratified Site in the Mohave Desert, California. *University
        of California Archaeological Survey Report* 57(2):25-56.
        Berkeley.

Dean, Jeffrey S.
1969    Chronological Analysis of Tsegi Phase Sites in Northeast-
        ern Arizona. *Papers of the Laboratory of Tree-ring Re-
        search* 3.  Tucson.

_____
1970    Aspects of Tsegi Phase Social Organization:  A Trial Re-
        construction.  Pp. 140-174 in Reconstructing Prehistoric
        Pueblo Societies.  William A. Longacre, ed.  Albuquer-
        que: University of New Mexico Press.

Dean, Jeffrey S., and William J. Robinson
1977    Dendroclimatic Variability in the American Southwest
        A.D. 680 to 1970, Appendix 2.  Final Report to the Na-
        tional Park Service Project:  Southwest Paleoclimate.
        Tucson: University of Arizona, Laboratory of Tree-ring
        Research.

Dean, Jeffrey S., Alexander J. Lindsay, Jr., and William J. Robinson
1978    Prehistoric Settlement in Long House Valley, Northeast-
        ern Arizona.  Pp. 25-44 in Investigations of the Southwest-
        ern Anthropological Research Group.  Robert C. Euler
        and George J. Gumerman, eds.  Flagstaff:  Museum of
        Northern Arizona.

DeBloois, Evan I., and Dee F. Green
1978    SARG Research on the Elk Ridge Project Manti-Lasal
        National Forest, Utah.  Pp. 13-24 in Investigations of the
        Southwestern Anthropological Research Group.  Robert
        C. Euler and George J. Gumerman, eds.  Flagstaff:  Mu-
        seum of Northern Arizona.

De Borhegyi, Stephan
1956    The Excavation of Site 9 Near Apache Creek, Catron
        County, New Mexico. *Highway Salvage Archaeology*
        2(6):1-9.

Decker, Dean A.
1976    A Typology for the Chevelon Flaked Lithic Implements.
        Pp. 92- 106 in Chevelon Archaeological Research Project.
        Fred Plog, James Hill, and Dwight Read, eds. *University
        of California, Department of Anthropology, Archaeological
        Survey Monograph* 2.  Los Angeles.

Decorme, Gerardo P.
[1950]  Las misiones del Valle de El Paso, Texas, 1536-1950.
        (Manuscript in Private Collection of C.L. Sonnichsen, El
        Paso, Tex.)

DeHarport, David L.
1959    An Archaeological Survey of Canyon de Chelly, North-
        eastern Arizona: A Puebloan Community Through Time.
        (Unpublished **Ph.D.** Dissertation in Anthropology, Har-
        vard University, Cambridge, Mass.)

De Huff, Elizabeth (Willis)
1943    Say the Bells of Old Missions:  Legends of Old New Mex-
        ico Churches.  St. Louis and London:  B. Herder Book
        Company.

De Laguna, Frederica
1942    The Bryn Mawr Dig at Cinder Park, Arizona. *Plateau*
        14(4):53-56.

Dellenbough, Frederick S.
1877    The Shinumos:  A Prehistoric People of the Rocky Moun-
        tain Region. *Bulletin of the Society of Natural Sciences*
        3:168-180.  Buffalo.

Deloria, Vine, Jr., ed.
1971    Of Utmost Good Faith.  San Francisco:  Straight Arrow
        Books.

Dennis, Wayne
1940    The Hopi Child.  (University of Virginia Institute for Re-
        search in the Social Sciences, Institute Monograph 26)
        New York and London:  D. Appleton-Century.

Dennis, Wayne, and Marsena G. Dennis
1940    Cradles and Cradling Practices of the Pueblo Indians.
        *American Anthropologist* 42(1):107-115.

Densmore, Frances
1938    Music of Santo Domingo Pueblo, New Mexico. *Southwest
        Museum Paper* 12.  Los Angeles, Cal;f.

Devereux, George
1937    Institutionalized Homosexuality of the Mohave Indians.
        *Human Biology* 9(4):498-527.

_____
1948    The Function of Alcohol in Mohave Society. *Quarterly
        Journal of Studies on Alcohol* 9(2):207-251.

Devereux, George, and Edwin M. Loeb
1943    Some Notes on Apache Criminality. *Journal of Criminal
        Psychopathology* 4(3):424-430.

Diamond, Tom
1966    The Tigua Indians of El Paso.  Denver:  National Con-
        gress of American Indians Fund.

Dick, Herbert W.
1951    Evidences of Early Man in Bat Cave and on the Plains of
        San Augustin, New Mexico.  Pp. 158-163 in Pt. 3 of In-
        dian Tribes of Aboriginal America:  Selected Papers of
        the 29th International Congress of Americanists.  3 vols.
        New York, 1949.

_____
1954    The Bat Cave Pod Corn Complex:  A Note on Its Distri-
        bution and Archaeological Significance. *El Palacio*
        61(5):138-144.

_____
1965    Picuris Pueblo Excavations.  (Document No. PB177047,
        National Technical Information Service, Springfield, Va.)

_____
1965a   Bat Cave. *Monographs of the School of American Research*
        27.  Santa Fe.

_____
1976    Archeological Excavations in the Llaves Area, Santa Fe
        National Forest, New Mexico, 1972-1974. Pt. 1: Architec-
        ture.  (Archeological Report 13)  Albuquerque: U.S.D.A.
        Forest Service, Southwestern Region.

Dickson, Bruce D.
1975    Settlement Pattern Stability and Change in the Middle
        Northern Rio Grande Region, New Mexico:  A Test of
        Some Hypotheses. *American Antiquity* 40(2):159-171.

Diehl, H.C.
1961    [Letter to F.H.H. Roberts, Jr., Dated September 5, 1961,
        with Enclosures.]  (Manuscript in "BAE Correspon-
        dence," National Anthropological Archives, Smithsonian
        Institution, Washington.)

Di Peso, Charles C.
1951    The Babocomari Village Site on the Babocomari River,
        Southeastern Arizona. *Amerind Foundation Publication* 5.
        Dragoon, Ariz.

1953    The Sobaipuri Indians of the Upper San Pedro River Valley, Southeastern Arizona. *Amerind Foundation Publication* 6. Dragoon, Ariz.

1956    The Upper Pima of San Cayetana del Tumacacari: An Archeohistorical Reconstruction of the Ootam of Pimeria Alta. *Amerind Foundation Publication* 7. Dragoon, Ariz.

1958    The Reeve Ruin of Southeastern Arizona: A Study of a Prehistoric Western Pueblo Migration into the Middle San Pedro Valley. *Amerind Foundation Publication* 8. Dragoon, Ariz.

1963    Cultural Development in Northern Mexico. Pp. 1-15 in Aboriginal Cultural Development in Latin America: An Interpretative Review. Betty J. Meggers and Clifford Evans, eds. *Smithsonian Miscellaneous Collections* 146(1). Washington.

1966    Archaeology and Ethnohistory of the Northern Sierra. Pp. 3-25 in *Archaeological Frontiers and External Connections*. Gordon F. Ekholm and Gordon R. Willey, eds. Handbook of Middle American Indians. Robert Wauchope, gen. ed. Vol. 4. Austin: University of Texas Press.

1968    Casas Grandes: A Fallen Trading Center of the Gran Chichimeca. *Masterkey* 42(1):20-37.

1968a   Casas Grandes and the Gran Chichimeca. *El Palacio* 75(4):45-61.

1974    Casas Grandes: A Fallen Trading Center of the Gran Chichimeca. 3 vols. *Amerind Foundation Series* 9. Dragoon, Ariz.

Dittert, Alfred E., Jr.
1957    Salvage Excavations in the Blackwater No. 1 Locality Near Portales, New Mexico. *Highway Salvage Archaeology* 3(10):1-9.

1959    Culture Change in the Cebolleta Mesa Region, Central Western New Mexico. (Unpublished Ph.D. Dissertation in Anthropology, University of Arizona, Tucson.)

1976    Comments. Pp. 126-127 in The 1976 Salado Conference. David E. Doyel and Emil W. Haury, eds. *The Kiva* 42(1).

Dittert, Alfred E., Jr., and R.J. Ruppé, Jr.
1951    The Archaeology of Cebollita Mesa: A Preliminary Report. *El Palacio* 58(4):116-129.

Dittert, Alfred E., Jr., Frank W. Eddy, and Beth L. Dickey
1963    Evidences of Early Ceramic Phases in the Navajo Reservoir District. *El Palacio* 70(1-2):5-12.

Dittert, Alfred E., Jr., James J. Hester, and Frank W. Eddy
1961    An Archaeological Survey of the Navajo Reservoir District, Northwestern New Mexico. *Monographs of the School of American Research* 23. Santa Fe.

Dixon, Keith A.
1963    The Interamerican Diffusion of a Cooking Technique: The Culinary Shoe-pot. *American Anthropologist* 65(3):593-619.

Dixon, Roland B., and Alfred L. Kroeber
1913    New Linguistic Families in California. *American Anthropologist* 15(4):647-655.

Dobyns, Henry F., and Robert C. Euler
1970    Wauba Yuma's People: The Comparative Socio-political Structure of the Pai Indians of Arizona. *Prescott Arizona College Studies in Anthropology* 3. Prescott.

Dockstader, Frederick J.
1954    The Kachina and the White Man: A Study of the Influences of White Culture on the Hopi Kachina Cult. *Cranbrook Institute of Science Bulletin* 35. Bloomfield Hills, Mich.

1959    Directions in Indian Art: Report of a Conference Held at the University of Arizona. Tucson: University of Arizona Press.

Domenech, Emmanuel H.D.
1860    Seven Years' Residence in the Great Deserts of North America. 2 vols. London: Longman, Green, Longman, and Roberts.

Domínguez, Francisco A.
1956    The Missions of New Mexico, 1776; A Description by Fray Francisco Atonasio Domínguez, with Other Contemporary Documents. Eleanor B. Adams and Fray Angelico Chavez, trans. Albuquerque: University of New Mexico Press.

Donaldson, Bruce
1975    An Archeological Sample of the White Mountain Planning Unit, Apache-Sitgreaves National Forest Arizona. *U.S.D.A. Forest Service Southwest Regional Archeological Report* 6. Albuquerque.

Dorsey, George A.
1903    Indians of the Southwest. Chicago: Atcheson, Topeka, and Santa Fe Railway System, Passenger Department.

Dorsey, George A., and Henry R. Voth
1901    The Oraibi Soyal Ceremony. *Field Museum of Natural History Publication 55, Anthropological Series* 3(1):5-59. Chicago.

1902    The Mishongnovi Ceremonies of the Snake and Antelope Fraternities. *Field Museum of Natural History Publication 66, Anthropological Series* 3(3). Chicago.

Douglas, Frederic H.
1930    Pueblo Indian Pottery Making. *Denver Art Museum Leaflet* 6. Denver. (Reprinted in 1935, 1967, and 1973.)

1938    Notes on Hopi Brocading. *Museum of Northern Arizona Bulletin* 11(4):35-38. Flagstaff.

1939    Acoma Pueblo Weaving and Embroidery. *Denver Art Museum Leaflet* 89. Denver.

1939a   Weaving in the Tewa Pueblos: Tesuque, Nambe, San Ildefonso, Santa Clara, San Juan. *Denver Art Museum Leaflet* 90. Denver.

Douglass, Andrew E.
1929    The Secret of the Southwest Solved by Talkative Tree Rings. *National Geographic Magazine* 56(6):736-770.

Doyel, David E.
1974    Excavations in the Escalante Ruin Group, Southern Arizona. *University of Arizona, Arizona State Museum Archaeological Series* 124. Tucson.

Dozier, Edward P.
1951    Resistance to Acculturation and Assimilation in an Indian Pueblo. *American Anthropologist* 53(1):56-66.

1953    Tewa, II: Verb Structure. *International Journal of American Linguistics* 19(2):118-127.

1954    The Hopi-Tewa of Arizona. *University of California Publications in American Archaeology and Ethnology* 44(3):259-376. Berkeley.

1955    Kinship and Linguistic Change Among the Arizona Tewa. *International Journal of American Linguistics* 21(3):242-257.

1956    Two Examples of Linguistic Acculturation: The Yaqui of Sonora and Arizona and the Tewa of New Mexico. *Language* 32(1):146-157.

1958    Spanish-Catholic Influences on Rio Grande Pueblo Religion. *American Anthropologist* 60(3):441-448.

1961    Rio Grande Pueblos. Pp. 94-186 in Perspectives in American Indian Culture Change. Edward H. Spicer, ed. Chicago: University of Chicago Press.

1965    Southwestern Social Units and Archaeology. *American Antiquity* 31(1):38-47.

1966    Factionalism at Santa Clara Pueblo. *Ethnology* 5(2):172-185.

1966a   Hano: A Tewa Indian Community in Arizona. New York: Holt, Rinehart and Winston.

1970    The Pueblo Indians of North America. New York: Holt, Rinehart and Winston.

1970a   Making Inferences from the Present to the Past. Pp. 202-213 in Reconstructing Prehistoric Pueblo Societies. William A. Longacre, ed. Albuquerque: University of New Mexico Press.

Driver, Harold E., and William C. Massey
1957    Comparative Studies of North American Indians. *Transactions of the American Philosophical Society* n.s. 47(2). Philadelphia.

Driver, Harold E., John M. Cooper, Paul Kirchhoff, Dorothy R. Libby, William C. Massey, and Leslie Spier
1953    Indian Tribes of North America. *Indiana University Publications in Anthropology and Linguistics, Memoir* 9. Bloomington.

[1960]  Indian Tribes of North America. (Map, Revision of Driver et al. 1953. Bloomington: Indiana University, Department of Anthropology.)

Duffus, Robert L.
1930    The Santa Fe Trail. London and New York: Longmans, Green.

Dumarest, Noël
1919    Notes on Cochiti, New Mexico. Elsie C. Parsons, ed. *Memoirs of the American Anthropological Association* 6(3). Lancaster, Pa.

Dunn, Dorothy
1968    American Indian Painting of the Southwest and Plains Areas. Albuquerque: University of New Mexico Press.

Dutton, Bertha P.
1963    Sun Father's Way: The Kiva Murals of Kuaua, a Pueblo Ruin, Coronado State Monument, New Mexico. Albuquerque: University of New Mexico Press.

1970    Let's Explore Indian Villages, Past and Present: Tour Guide for Santa Fe Area. Rev. ed. Santa Fe: Museum of New Mexico Press.

1975    Indians of the American Southwest. Englewood Cliffs, N.J.: Prentice Hall.

Dyson-Hudson, Rada, and Eric A. Smith
1978    Human Territoriality: An Ecological Reassessment. *American Anthropologist* 80(1):21-41.

Earle, Edwin, and Edward A. Kennard
1938    Hopi Kachinas. New York: J.J. Augustin.

Eddy, Frank W.
1958    A Sequence of Cultural and Alluvial Deposits in the Ciénega Creek Basin, Southeastern Arizona. (Unpublished M.A. Thesis in Archaeology, University of Arizona, Tucson.)

1961    Excavations at Los Pinos Phase Sites in the Navajo Reservoir District. *Museum of New Mexico Papers in Anthropology* 4. Santa Fe.

1966    Prehistory in the Navajo Reservoir District, Northwestern New Mexico. 2 Pts. *Museum of New Mexico Papers in Anthropology* 15. Santa Fe.

1977    Archaeological Investigations at Chimney Rock Mesa: 1970-1972. *Memoirs of the Colorado Archaeological Society* 1. Boulder.

Eggan, Dorothy
1943    The General Problem of Hopi Adjustment. *American Anthropologist* 45(3):357-373.

1949    The Significance of Dreams for Anthropological Research. *American Anthropologist* 51(2):177-198.

1952    The Manifest Content of Dreams: A Challenge to Social Science. *American Anthropologist* 54(4):469-485.

1955    The Personal Use of Myth in Dreams. *Journal of American Folklore* 68(270):445-453.

Eggan, Fred R.
1950    Social Organization of the Western Pueblos. Chicago: University of Chicago Press. (Reprinted in 1970.)

1966    The Pueblo Indians in Modern Perspective: Unity in Diversity. Pp. 112-141 in The American Indian: Perspectives for the Study of Social Change. Chicago: Aldine.

1972    Summary. Pp. 287-305 in New Perspectives on the Pueblos. Alfonso Ortiz, ed. Albuquerque: University of New Mexico Press.

Eickemeyer, Carl, and Lilian W. Eickemeyer
1895    Among the Pueblo Indians. New York: The Merriam Company.

Ekholm, Gordon F.
1939    Results of an Archeological Survey of Sonora and Northern Sinaloa. Pp. 7-10 in *Revista Mexicana de Estudios Antropológicos* 3. Mexico City.

1940    The Archaeology of Northern and Western Mexico. Pp. 320- 330 in The Maya and Their Neighbors. Clarence L. Hay et al., eds. New York, London: D. Appleton-Century.

1942    Excavations at Guasave, Sinaloa, Mexico. *Anthropological Papers of the American Museum of Natural History* 38(2):23-139. New York.

1958    Regional Sequences in Mesoamerica and Their Relationships. Pp. 15-27 in Middle American Anthropology. Gordon R. Willey, ed. (Social Science Monographs 5) Washington: Pan American Union, Department of Cultural Affairs, Social Science Section.

Ellis, Florence (Hawley)
1945-1953   [Ethnographic Fieldnotes Including Kinship, Social and Religious Organization, Ceremonies, Crafts, Witchcraft, Death, in Isleta Pueblo, New Mexico.] (Manuscripts in Ellis' Possession.)

1951    Patterns of Aggression and the War Cult in Southwestern Pueblos. *Southwestern Journal of Anthropology* 7(2):177-201.

1952    Jemez Kiva Magic and its Relation to Features of Prehistoric Kivas. *Southwestern Journal of Anthropology* 8(2):147-163.

1953    Authoritative Control and the Society System in Jemez Pueblo. *Southwestern Journal of Anthropology* 9(4):385-394.

1959    [Archaeologic and Ethnologic Data Pertaining to Acoma and Laguna Land Claims, 1958-1959.] (Manuscript in New Mexico Archaeological Center, University of New Mexico, Albuquerque.)

1959a   An Outline of Laguna Pueblo History and Social Organization. *Southwestern Journal of Anthropology* 15(4):325-347.

636

1964 A Reconstruction of the Basic Jemez Pattern of Social Organization, with Comparisons to Other Tanoan Social Structures. *University of New Mexico Publications in Anthropology* 11. Albuquerque.

1964a Archaeological History of Nambe Pueblo, 14th Century to the Present. *American Antiquity* 30(1):34-42.

1966 On Distinguishing Laguna from Acoma Polychrome. *El Palacio* 73(3):37-39.

1967 Use and Significance of the Tcamahia. *El Palacio* 74(1):35-43.

1967a Water Rights Studies of Nambe, Pojoaque, Tesuque and San Ildefonso Pueblos. (Manuscript in U.S. Bureau of Indian Affairs, Washington; Copy in Library, Laboratory of Anthropology, Santa Fe.)

1967b Where Did the Pueblo People Come From? *El Palacio* 74(3):35-43.

1968 An Interpretation of Prehistoric Death Customs in Terms of Modern Southwestern Parallels. Pp. 57-68 in *Papers of the Archaeological Society of New Mexico* 1. Santa Fe.

1970 Pueblo Witchcraft and Medicine. Pp. 37-72 in Systems of North American Witchcraft and Sorcery. Deward E. Walker, Jr., ed. *Anthropological Monographs of the University of Idaho* 1. Moscow.

1970a Irrigation and Water Works in the Rio Grande. (Manuscript in Ellis' Possession.)

1973 A Thousand Years of the Pueblo Sun-Moon-Star Calendar. (Paper Presented at the American Association for the Advancement of Science Meeting, June 20, 1973, Mexico City.)

1974 Archaeologic and Ethnologic Data: Acoma - Laguna Land Claims. Pp. 9-99 in American Indian Ethnohistory, Indians of the Southwest: Pueblo Indians, II. New York: Garland.

1974a Anthropology of Laguna Pueblo Land Claims. Pp. 9-120 in American Indian Ethnohistory, Indians of the Southwest: Pueblo Indians, III. New York: Garland.

1974b The Hopi: Their History and Use of Lands. Defendant's Exhibit No. E500, Docket No. 229. Indian Claims Commission. Pp. 25-277 in American Indian Ethnohistory, Indians of the Southwest: Hopi Indians. New York and London: Garland.

————— see also Hawley, Florence M.

Ellis, Florence H., and J.J. Brody
1964 Ceramic Stratigraphy and Tribal History at Taos Pueblo. *American Antiquity* 29(3):316-327.

El-Najjar, Mahmoud Y.
1974 People of Canyon de Chelly: A Study of Their Biology and Culture. (Unpublished Ph.D. Dissertation in Anthropology, Arizona State University, Tempe.)

El Paso County Deed Records
1825 State of Chihuahua to Inhabitants of Ysleta Grant, December 1, 1825; Book B:24, Books D:1,4. (Manuscript in El Paso County Court House, El Paso, Tex.)

Elton, Charles S.
1958 The Ecology of Invasion by Animals and Plants. London: Methuen.

El-Zur, Arieh
1965 Soil, Water and Man in the Desert Habitat of the Hohokam Culture: An Experimental Study in Environmental Archaeology. (Unpublished Ph.D. Dissertation in Anthropology, University of Arizona, Tucson.)

Emmons, Glen L.
1955 Hopi Hearings Conducted by a Team Appointed by Mr. Glen L. Emmons, Commissioner of Indian Affairs and Composed of Mr. Thomas M. Reid, Assistant Commissioner, and Program Officers Joe Jennings and Graham Holmes. Washington: U.S. Government Printing Office.

Emory, William H.
1848 Notes of a Military Reconnoissance, from Fort Leavenworth, in Missouri, to San Diego, in California, Including Part of the Arkansas, Del Norte, and Gila Rivers. Made in 1846-1847. *U.S. Congress. Senate. 31st Cong., 1st sess., Senate Executive Doc. No. 7. (Serial No. 505)* Washington: U.S. Government Printing Office..

1857 Report on the United States and Mexican Boundary Survey. Vol. 1. *U.S. Congress. Senate. 34th Cong., 1st sess., Senate Executive Doc. No. 108. (Serial No. 832-834)* Washington: U.S. Government Printing Office.

Epstein, Jeremiah F.
[1969] The San Isidro Site: An Early Man Campsite in Nuevo Leon, Mexico. *University of Texas Anthropological Series* 7. Austin.

Erickson, Jon T.
1977 Kachinas: An Evolving Hopi Art Form? Phoenix, Ariz.: The Heard Museum.

Escalante, Silvestre Vélez de *see* Vélez de Escalante, Silvestre

Espejo, Antonio
1916 Account of the Journey to the Provinces and Settlements of New Mexico. Pp. 161-195 in Spanish Exploration in the Southwest, 1542-1706. Herbert E. Bolton, ed. New York: Charles Scribner's Sons.

Espinosa, Aurelio M.
1936 Pueblo Indian Folk Tales. *Journal of American Folk-Lore* 49(191-192):69-133.

Espinosa, J. Manuel
1936 Governor Vargas in Colorado. *New Mexico Historical Review* 11(2):179-187.

1940 First Expedition of Vargas into New Mexico, 1692. Albuquerque: University of New Mexico Press.

1942 Crusaders of the Rio Grande: The Story of Don Diego de Vargas and the Reconquest and Refounding of New Mexico. Chicago: Institute of Jesuit History.

Euler, Robert C.
1954 Notes on Land Tenure at Isleta Pueblo. *El Palacio* 61(11):368-373.

1957 A Cohonina Burial. *Plateau* 29(3):59-62.

1963 Archaeological Problems in Western and Northwestern Arizona, 1962. *Plateau* 35(3):78-85.

1963a Edgar Lee Hewett, 1865-1946. *Arizona and the West* 5(4):286-290.

1966 Willow Figurines from Arizona. *Natural History* 75(3):62-67.

Euler, Robert C., and Susan M. Chandler
1978 Aspects of Prehistoric Settlement Patterns in Grand Canyon. Pp. 73-86 in Investigations of the Southwestern Anthropological Research Group. Robert C. Euler and George J. Gumerman, eds. Flagstaff: Museum of Northern Arizona.

Euler, Robert C., and Henry F. Dobyns
1962 Excavations West of Prescott, Arizona. *Plateau* 34(3):69-84.

1971 The Hopi People. Phoenix: Indian Tribal Series.

Euler, Robert C., and George J. Gumerman, eds.
1978 Investigations of the Southwestern Anthropological Research Group: The Proceedings of the 1976 Conference. Flagstaff: Museum of Northern Arizona.

Euler, Robert C., and Alan P. Olson
1965 Split-twig Figurines from Northern Arizona: New Radiocarbon Dates. *Science* 148(3668):368-369.

*637*

Evans, Glen L.
1951    Prehistoric Wells in Eastern New Mexico. *American Antiquity* 17(1):1-9.

Ezell, Paul H.
1954    An Archeological Survey of Northwestern Papagueria. *The Kiva* 19(2-4):1-26.

———    
1956    NA 4274. Pp. 137-139 in Pipeline Archaeology. Fred Wendorf, Nancy Fox, and Orian Lewis, eds. Santa Fe and Flagstaff: Laboratory of Anthropology and Museum of Northern Arizona.

———    
1963    Is There a Hohokam-Pima Culture Continuum? *American Antiquity* 29(1):61-66.

Fair, Susan
1975    Charles Loloma. *American Indian Art* 1(1):54-57.

Falconer, Thomas
1844    Notes of a Journey Through Texas and New Mexico in the Years 1841 and 1842. *Journal of the Royal Geographical Society of London* 13(2):199-222.

Farabee, William C.
1920    Indian Cradles. *University of Pennsylvania Museum Journal* 11(4):183-211.

Farber, Joseph C., and Michael Dorris
1975    Native Americans 500 Years After. New York: Thomas Y. Crowell.

Fay, George E.
1956    Peralta Complex: A Sonoran Variant of the Cochise Culture. *Science* 124(3230):1029.

———    
1958    The Peralta Complex: A Sonoran Variant of the Cochise Culture. Pp. 491-493 in *Proceedings of the 32d International Congress of Americanists*. Copenhagen, 1956.

Fenenga, Franklin, and Fred Wendorf
1956    Excavations at the Ignacio, Colorado, Field Camp: Site LA 2605. Pp. 207-214 in Pipeline Archaeology: Reports of Salvage Operations in the Southwest on El Paso Natural Gas Company Projects, 1950-1953. Fred Wendorf, Nancy Fox, and Orian L. Lewis, eds. Santa Fe and Flagstaff: Laboratory of Anthropology and Museum of Northern Arizona.

Fenton, William N.
1957    Factionalism at Taos Pueblo, New Mexico. *Anthropological Papers 56, Bureau of American Ethnology Bulletin* 164:297-344. Washington.

Ferdon, Edwin N., Jr.
1955    A Trial Survey of Mexican-Southwestern Architectural Parallels. *Monographs of the School of American Research* 21. Santa Fe.

———    
1967    The Hohokam "Ball-Court": An Alternate View of its Function. *The Kiva* 33(1):1-14.

Ferguson, Marjorie
1931    The Acculturation of Sandía Pueblo. (Unpublished M.A. Thesis in Anthropology, University of New Mexico, Albuquerque.)

Fewkes, J. Walter
1890    On the Use of the Phonograph Among the Zuni Indians. *American Naturalist* 24(283):687-691.

———    
1891    Reconnoissance of Ruins in or near the Zuni Reservation. *Journal of American Ethnology and Archaeology* 1(3):93-132.

———    
1892    A Few Summer Ceremonials at the Tusayan Pueblos. *Journal of American Ethnology and Archaeology* 2:1-160.

———    
1892a   A Few Tusayan Pictographs. *American Anthropologist* 5(1):9-26.

———    
1892b   The Ceremonial Circuit Among the Village Indians of Northeastern Arizona. *Journal of American Folk-Lore* 5(16):33-42.

———    
1893    A-WA-TO-BI: An Archeological Verification of a Tusayan Legend. *American Anthropologist* 6(4):363-375.

———    
1894    The Kinship of the Tusayan Indians. *American Anthropologist* 7(4):394-417.

———    
1894a   The Kinship of a Tanoan-speaking Community in Tusayan. *American Anthropologist* 7(2):162-167.

———    
1894b   The Snake Ceremonials at Walpi. *Journal of American Ethnology and Archaeology* 4.

———    
1895    A Comparison of Sia and Tusayan Snake Ceremonials. *American Anthropologist* 8(2):118-141.

———    
1896    Pacific Coast Shells from Prehistoric Tusayan Pueblos. *American Anthropologist* 9(11):359-367.

———    
1896a   Two Ruins Recently Discovered in the Red Rock Country, Arizona. *American Anthropologist* 9(8):263-283.

———    
1896b   The Prehistoric Culture of Tusayan. *American Anthropologist* 9(5):151-174.

———    
1896c   Preliminary Account of an Expedition to the Cliff Villages of the Red Rock Country, and the Tusayan Ruins of Sikyatki and Awatobi, Arizona, in 1895. Pp. 557-588 in *Annual Report of the Smithsonian Institution for 1895*. Washington.

———    
1897    Tusayan Katcinas. Pp. 245-313 in *15th Annual Report of the Bureau of American Ethnology for the Years 1893-1894*. Washington.

———    
1898    Archaeological Expedition into Arizona in 1895. Pp. 519-742 in *17th Annual Report of the Bureau of American Ethnology for the Years 1895-1896. Pt. 2*. Washington.

———    
1898a   The Winter Solstice Ceremony at Walpi. *American Anthropologist* 11(3):65-87, (4):101-115.

———    
1898b   Preliminary Account of an Expedition to the Pueblo Ruins Near Winslow, Arizona, in 1896. Pp.517-539 in *Annual Report of the Smithsonian Institution for 1896*. Washington.

———    
1899    The Winter Solstice Altars at Hano Pueblo. *American Anthropologist* 1(2):251-276.

———    
1899a   Hopi Basket Dances. *Journal of American Folk-Lore* 12(45):81-96.

———, coll.
[1899-1900] ["Codex Hopiensis": Hopi Kachinas. Drawings. 3 vols.] [Manuscript No. 4371 in National Anthropological Archives, Smithsonian Institution, Washington.)

———    
1900    Tusayan Migration Traditions. Pp. 573-634 in *19th Annual Report of the Bureau of American Ethnology for the Years 1897-1898. Pt. 2*. Washington.

———    
1901    The Owakülti Altar at Sichomovi Pueblo. *American Anthropologist* n.s. 3(2):211-226.

———    
1902    The Pueblo Settlements Near El Paso, Texas. *American Anthropologist* n.s. 4(1):57-75.

———    
1902a   Minor Hopi Festivals. *American Anthropologist* n.s. 4(3):482-511.

———    
1903    Hopi Katcinas Drawn by Native Artists. Pp. 13-126 in *21st Annual Report of the Bureau of American Ethnology for the Years 1899-1900*. Washington.

———    
1904    Two Summers' Work in Pueblo Ruins. Pp. 3-195 in *22d Annual Report of the Bureau of American Ethnology for the Years 1900-1901. Pt. 1*. Washington.

———    
1906    The Sun's Influence on the Form of Hopi Pueblos. *American Anthropologist* n.s. 8(1):88-100.

———    
1906a   Hopi Shrines Near the East Mesa, Arizona. *American Anthropologist* n.s. 8(2):346-375.

———    
1907    Hopi. Pp. 560-568 in Vol. 1 of Handbook of American Indians North of Mexico. Frederick W. Hodge, ed. 2 vols. *Bureau of American Ethnology Bulletin* 30. Washington.

1907a     Excavations at Casa Grande, Arizona, in 1906-07. *Smithsonian Miscellaneous Collections* 50(3). Washington.

1909     Antiquities of the Mesa Verde National Park: Spruce Tree House. *Bureau of American Ethnology Bulletin* 41. Washington.

1910     Walpi. Pp. 901-902 in Vol. 2 of Handbook of American Indians North of Mexico. Frederick W. Hodge, ed. 2 vols. *Bureau of American Ethnology Bulletin* 30. Washington.

1910a     The Butterfly in Hopi Myth and Ritual. *American Anthropologist* 12(4):576-594.

1911     Antiquities of the Mesa Verde National Park, Cliff Palace. *Bureau of American Ethnology Bulletin* 51. Washington.

1911a     Preliminary Report on a Visit to the Navajo National Monument, Arizona. *Bureau of American Ethnology Bulletin* 50. Washington.

1912     Casa Grande, Arizona. Pp. 25-179 in *28th Annual Report of the Bureau of American Ethnology for the Years 1906-1907.* Washington.

1912a     Antiquities of the Upper Verde River and Walnut Creek Valleys, Arizona. Pp. 181-220 in *28th Annual Report of the Bureau of American Ethnology for the Years 1906-1907.* Washington.

1916     Excavation and Repair of Sun Temple, Mesa Verde National Park. Washington: U.S. Government Printing Office.

1917     Far View House -- A Pure Type of Pueblo Ruin. *Art and Archaeology* 6:133-141.

1919     Designs on Prehistoric Hopi Pottery. Pp. 207-284 in *33d Annual Report of the Bureau of American Ethnology for the Years 1911-1912.* Washington.

1922     Oraibi in 1890. Pp. 268-283 in Contributions to Hopi History. *American Anthropologist* 24(3).

1927     The Katcina Altars in Hopi Worship. Pp. 469-486 in *Annual Report of the Smithsonian Institution for 1926.* Washington.

1927a     Archaeological Fieldwork in Arizona. *Smithsonian Miscellaneous Collections* 78(7):207-232. Washington.

1973     Designs on Prehistoric Hopi Pottery [1919]. New York: Dover.

Fewkes, J. Walter, and J.G. Owens
1892     The Lǎ-lā-kōn-ta: A Tusayan Dance. *American Anthropologist* 5(2):105-129.

Fewkes, J. Walter, and Alexander M. Stephen
1892     The Nā-ác-nai-ya: A Tusayan Initiation Ceremony. *Journal of American Folk-Lore* 5(18):189-217.

1893     The Pá-lü-lü-koñ-ti: A Tusayan Ceremony. *Journal of American Folk-Lore* 6(23):269-282.

Figgins, Jesse D.
1927     The Antiquity of Man in America. *Natural History* 27(3):229-239.

Fisher, Reginald G.
1931     Second Report of the Archaeological Survey of the Pueblo Plateau: Santa Fe Sub-Quadrangle A. *School of American Research and University of New Mexico Survey Series* 1. Albuquerque.

Fiske, Turbé L., and Keith Lummis
1975     Charles F. Lummis: The Man and His West. Norman: University of Oklahoma Press.

Fitting, James E.
1971     The Hermanas Ruin, Luna County, New Mexico. *Southwestern New Mexico Research Report* 3. Case Western Reserve University, Department of Anthropology. Cleveland.

1971a     The Burris Ranch Site, Dona Ana County, New Mexico. *Southwestern New Mexico Research Report* 1. Case Western Reserve University, Department of Anthropology. Cleveland.

1971b     Excavations at MC 110, Grant County, New Mexico. *Southwestern New Mexico Research Report* 2. Case Western Reserve University, Department of Anthropology. Cleveland.

1972     [Preliminary Notes on Cliff Valley Settlement Patterns.] (Manuscript in Fitting's Possession.)

Fitting, James E., James L. Ross, and B. Thomas Gray
1971     Preliminary Report on the 1971 Intersession Excavations at the Saige-McFarland Site (MC146). *Southwestern New Mexico Research Report* 4. Case Western Reserve University, Department of Anthropology. Cleveland.

Flannery, Kent V.
1968     Archeological Systems Theory and Early Mesoamerica. Pp. 67-87 in Anthropological Archeology in the Americas. Betty J. Meggers, ed. Washington: Anthropological Society of Washington.

1968a     The Olmec and the Valley of Oaxaca: A Model for Interregional Interaction in Formative Times. Pp. 79-110 in Dumbarton Oaks Conference on the Olmec, October 28th-29th, 1967. Elizabeth P. Benson, ed. Washington: Dumbarton Oaks Research Library and Collection.

1972     The Cultural Evolution of Civilizations. *Annual Review of Ecology and Systematics* 3:399-426. Palo Alto, Calif.

1973     The Origins of Agriculture. *Annual Review of Anthropology* 2:271-310. Palo Alto, Calif.

Flinn, Lynn, Christy G. Turner, II, and Alan Brew
1976     Additional Evidence for Cannibalism in the Southwest: The Case of LA 4528. *American Antiquity* 41(3):308-318.

Folmer, Henri
1941     Contraband Trade Between Louisiana and New Mexico in the Eighteenth Century. *New Mexico Historical Review* 16(3):249-274.

Folsom, Franklin
1973     Red Power on the Rio Grande: The American Revolution of 1680. Chicago: Follett.

Fontana, Bernard L., William J. Robinson, Charles W. Cormack, and Ernest E. Leavitt, Jr.
1962     Papago Indian Pottery. (American Ethnological Society Monograph 37) Seattle: University of Washington Press.

Forbes, Anne
1950     A Survey of Current Indian Pueblo Paintings. *El Palacio* 57(8):235-251.

Forbes, Jack D.
1960     Apache, Navaho, and Spaniard. Norman: University of Oklahoma Press.

1965     The "Public Domain" of Nevada and its Relationship to Indian Property Rights. *Nevada State Bar Journal* 30(3):16-47.

————, ed.
1967     Nevada Indians Speak. Reno: University of Nevada Press.

Ford, Richard I.
1968     An Ecological Analysis Involving the Population of San Juan Pueblo, New Mexico. (Unpublished Ph.D. Dissertation in Anthropology, University of Michigan, Lansing.)

1968a     Jemez Cave and Its Place in an Early Horticultural Settlement Pattern. (Paper Presented at the 33d Annual Meeting of the Society for American Archaeology, Santa Fe, N.M.)

1972     Barter, Gift, or Violence: An Analysis of Tewa Intertribal Exchange. Pp. 21-45 in Social Exchange and Interaction. Edwin N. Wilmsen, ed. *University of Michigan Museum of Anthropology, Anthropological Papers* 46:21-45. Ann Arbor.

1972a     An Ecological Perspective on the Eastern Pueblos. Pp. 1-18 in New Perspectives on the Pueblos. Alfonso Ortiz, ed. Albuquerque: University of New Mexico Press.

1977     The Technology of Irrigation in a New Mexico Pueblo. Pp. 139-154 in Material Culture. Heather Lechtman and Robert Merrill, eds. (Proceedings of the American Ethnological Society, 1975) Seattle: University of Washington Press.

Ford, Richard I., Albert H. Schroeder, and Stewart L. Peckham
1972     Three Perspectives on Puebloan Prehistory. Pp. 19-39 in New Perspectives on the Pueblos. Alfonso Ortiz, ed. Albuquerque: University of New Mexico Press.

Forde, C. Daryll
1931     Hopi Agriculture and Land Ownership. *Journal of the Royal Anthropological Institute of Great Britain and Ireland* 61:357-405.

1931a     Ethnography of the Yuma Indians. *University of California Publications in American Archaeology and Ethnology* 28(4):83-278. Berkeley.

Forrest, Earle R.
1929     Missions and Pueblos of the Old Southwest: Their Myths, Legends, Fiestas, and Ceremonies, with Some Accounts of the Indian Tribes and Their Dances; and of the Penitentes. Cleveland: Arthur H. Clark.

Fosberg, Stephen, and John Husler
1977     Pedology in the Service of Archeology: Soil Testing at LA 13086. (Manuscript on File at the Office of Contract Archeology, University of New Mexico, Albuquerque.)

Foster, George M.
1960     Culture and Conquest: America's Spanish Heritage. *Viking Fund Publications in Anthropology* 27. New York.

Fowler, Don D., and Catherine S. Fowler, eds.
1971     Anthropology of the Numa: John Wesley Powell's Manuscripts on the Numic Peoples of Western North America, 1868-1880. *Smithsonian Contributions to Anthropology* 14. Washington.

Fowler, Don D., James H. Gunnerson, Jesse D. Jennings, Robert H. Lister, Dee Ann Suhm, and Ted Weller
1959     The Glen Canyon Archeological Survey, Pts. I, II, and III. *University of Utah, Department of Anthropology, Anthropological Papers 39, Glen Canyon Series 6.* Salt Lake City.

Fox, Robin
1967     The Keresan Bridge: A Problem in Pueblo Ethnology. (*London School of Economics, Monographs on Social Anthropology* 35) London: Athlone Press.

1972     Some Unsolved Problems of Pueblo Social Organization. Pp. 71-85 in New Perspectives on the Pueblos. Alfonso Ortiz, ed. Albuquerque: University of New Mexico Press.

Franciscan Fathers
1910     An Ethnologic Dictionary of the Navaho Language. St. Michaels, Ariz.: The Franciscan Fathers.

Frank, Lawrence P., and Francis H. Harlow
1974     Historic Pottery of the Pueblo Indians, 1600-1800. Photographs by Bernard Lopez. Boston: New York Graphic Society.

Fraser, Douglas
1971     The Discovery of Primitive Art. Pp. 20-36 in Anthropology and Art: Readings in Cross-cultural Aesthetics. Charlotte M. Otten, ed. Garden City, N.Y.: Natural History Press.

Freire-Marreco, Barbara
1914     Tewa Kinship Terms from the Pueblo of Hano, Arizona. *American Anthropologist* 16(2):269-287.

French, David H.
1948     Factionalism in Isleta Pueblo. *Monographs of the American Ethnological Society* 14. Seattle. (Reprinted: University of Oklahoma Press, Norman, 1966.)

Fried, Morton H.
1960     On the Evolution of Social Stratification and the State. Pp. 713-731 in Culture in History: Essays in Honor of Paul Radin. Stanley Diamond, ed. New York: Published for Brandeis University by Columbia University Press.

1967     The Evolution of Political Society: An Essay in Political Anthropology. New York: Random House.

Frigout, Arlette
1962-1965 [Ethnographic Fieldnotes from Approximately 13 Months' Fieldwork Among the Hopi in Arizona.] (Manuscript in Frigout's Possession.)

Frisbie, Charlotte (Johnson)
1967     Kinaaldá: A Study of the Navaho Girl's Puberty Ceremony. Middletown, Conn.: Wesleyan University Press.

Frisbie, Theodore R.
1967     The Excavation and Interpretation of the Artificial Leg Basketmaker III - Pueblo I Sites Near Corrales, New Mexico. (Unpublished M.A. Thesis in Anthropology, University of New Mexico, Albuquerque.)

1973     The Influence of J. Walter Fewkes on Nampeyo: Fact or Fancy? Pp. 231-244 in Changing Ways of Southwestern Indians: A Historic Perspective. Albert H. Schroeder, ed. Glorieta, N.M.: Rio Grande Press.

Fritts, Harold C.
1965     Tree-ring Evidence for Climatic Changes in Western North America. *Monthly Weather Review* 93(7):421-443.

Fritts, Harold C., David G. Smith, and Marvin A. Stokes
1965     The Biological Model for Paleoclimatic Interpretation of Mesa Verde Tree-ring Series. Pp. 101-121 in Contributions of the Wetherill Mesa Archeological Project. *Memoirs of the Society for American Archaeology* 19. Salt Lake City, Utah.

Fritz, John M.
1974     The Hay Hollow Site Subsistence System: East Central Arizona. (Unpublished Ph.D. Dissertation in Anthropology, University of Chicago, Chicago.)

Fulton, William S.
1934     Archaeological Notes on Texas Canyon, Arizona. *Contributions from the Museum of the American Indian, Heye Foundation* 12(1):11-23, (2):9-23. New York.

Fulton, William S., and Carr Tuthill
1940     An Archaeological Site Near Gleeson, Arizona. *Amerind Foundation Publication* 1. Dragoon, Ariz.

Galinat, Walton C.
1970     The Cupule and Its Role in the Origin and Evolution of Maize. *University of Massachusetts Agricultural Experiment Station Bulletin* 585. Amherst.

1971     The Origin of Maize. *Annual Review of Genetics* 5:447-478. Palo Alto, Calif.

Galinat, Walton C., and James H. Gunnerson
1963     Spread of Eight-rowed Maize from the Prehistoric Southwest. *Harvard University Botanical Museum Leaflet* 20(5):117-160. Cambridge, Mass.

Galinat, Walton C., Theodore R. Reinhart, and Theodore R. Frisbie
1970     Early Eight-rowed Maize from the Middle Rio Grande Valley, New Mexico. *Harvard University Botanical Museum Leaflet* 22(9):313-331. Cambridge, Mass.

Gall, Patricia L., and Arthur A. Saxe
1977     The Ecological Evolution of Culture: The State as Predator in Succession Theory. Pp. 255-268 in Exchange Sys-

tems in Prehistory. Timothy K. Earle and Jonathon E. Ericson, eds. New York: Academic Press.

Gallegos Lamero, Hernán
1927    The Rodriguez Expedition to New Mexico. George P. Hammond and Agapito Rey, eds. and trans. *New Mexico Historical Review* 2(3):239-268, (4):334-362.

———    1927a   The Gallegos Relation of the Rodriguez Expedition to New Mexico. George P. Hammond and Agapito Rey, eds. *Historical Society of New Mexico Publications in History* 4. Santa Fe.

Gálvez, Bernardo de
1951    Instructions for Governing the Interior Provinces of New Spain, 1786. Donald E. Worcester, ed. and trans. Berkeley, Calif.: The Quivira Society. (Reprinted: Arno Press, New York, 1967.)

Gatschet, Albert S.
1876    Zwölf Sprachen aus dem Südwesten Nordamerikas. (Pueblos- und Apache-Mundarten; Tonto, Tonkawa, Digger, Utah.) Weimar, Germany: Böhlau.

———    1879    Classification into Seven Linguistic Stocks of Western Indian Dialects Contained in Forty Vocabularies. Pp. 403-485 in *Report upon United States Geographical Surveys West of the One Hundredth Meridian, Archaeology* 7. Washington.

———    1882    Indian Languages of the Pacific States and Territories and of the Pueblos of New Mexico. *Magazine of American History* 4(8):254-263.

———    1899    [Language of the Sandia Pueblo or Nafin ab, in the Central Parts of New Mexico. Tewa Linguistic Family. Obtained in (Washington, D.C.) November 1899 from Mariano Carpintero, Governor of Sandia, for the Bureau of American Ethnology.] (Manuscript No. 614 in National Anthropological Archives, Smithsonian Institution, Washington.)

———    1899a   The Téwa [*sic*] Dialect of Sandía, New Mexico. Obtained in Washington from Governor of Sandía, Mariano Carpintero. November, 1899. (Manuscript No. 1553 in National Anthropological Archives, Smithsonian Institution Washington.)

Geertz, Clifford
1958    Ethos, World-view and the Analysis of Sacred Symbols. *Antioch Review* 17:421-437.

Gerald, Rex E.
[1958]  Davis Ranch Site (ARIZ:BB:11:7), a Prehistoric Pueblo in Southeastern Arizona. (Manuscript Notebook on File at The Amerind Foundation Library, Dragoon, Ariz.)

———    1958a   Two Wickiups on the San Carlos Indian Reservation, Arizona. *The Kiva* 23(3):5-11.

———    1968    Spanish Presidios of the Late 18th Century in Northern New Spain. *Museum of New Mexico Research Record* 7. Santa Fe.

Gifford, Edward W.
1932    The Southeastern Yavapai. *University of California Publications in American Archaeology and Ethnology* 29(3):177-252. Berkeley.

———    1933    The Cocopa. *University of California Publications in American Archaeology and Ethnology* 31(5):257-334. Berkeley.

———    1936    Northeastern and Western Yavapai. *University of California Publications in American Archaeology and Ethnology* 34(4):247-354. Berkeley.

———    1946    Archaeology in the Punta Peñasco Region, Sonora. *American Antiquity* 11(4):215-222.

Gifford, James C.
1957    Archaeological Explorations in Caves of the Point of Pines Region. (Unpublished M.A. Thesis in Anthropology, University of Arizona, Tucson.)

Gillett, James B.
1925    Six Years with the Texas Rangers, 1875 to 1881. M.M. Quaife, ed. New Haven, Conn.: Yale University Press. (Reprinted in 1963.)

Gladwin, Harold S.
1928    Excavations at Casa Grande, Arizona, February 12-May 1, 1927. *Southwest Museum Paper* 2:7-30. Los Angeles.

———    1942    Excavations at Snaketown, III: Revisions. *Gila Pueblo, Medallion Paper* 30. Globe, Ariz.

———    1945    The Chaco Branch Excavations at White Mound and in the Red Mesa Valley. *Gila Pueblo, Medallion Paper* 33. Globe, Ariz.

———    1948    Excavations at Snaketown, IV: Reviews and Conclusions. *Gila Pueblo, Medallion Paper* 38. Globe, Ariz.

———    1957    A History of the Ancient Southwest. Portland, Me.: Bond Wheelwright Company.

Gladwin, Harold S., Emil W. Haury, Edwin B. Sayles, and Nora Gladwin
1937    Excavations at Snaketown, I: Material Culture. *Gila Pueblo, Medallion Paper* 25. Globe, Ariz. (Reprinted: Arizona State Museum, Tucson, 1965.)

Gladwin, Winifred J., and Harold S. Gladwin
1929    The Red-on-Buff Culture of the Gila Basin. *Gila Pueblo, Medallion Paper* 3. Globe, Ariz.

———    1933    Some Southwestern Pottery Types. Series III. *Gila Pueblo, Medallion Paper* 13. Globe, Ariz.

———    1934    A Method for the Designation of Cultures and Their Variations. *Gila Pueblo, Medallion Paper* 15. Globe, Ariz.

———    1935    The Eastern Range of the Red-on-Buff Culture. *Gila Pueblo, Medallion Paper* 16. Globe, Ariz.

Glassow, Michael A.
1972    Changes in the Adaptations of Southwestern Basketmakers: A Systems Perspective. Pp. 289-302 in Contemporary Archaeology: A Guide to Theory and Contributions. Mark P. Leone, ed. Carbondale: Southern Illinois University.

———    1972a   The Evolution of Early Agricultural Facilities Systems in the Northern Southwest. (Unpublished Ph.D. Dissertation in Anthropology, University of California, Los Angeles.)

Goddard, Ives
[1978]  The Languages of South Texas and the Lower Rio Grande. In The Languages of Native America: An Historical and Comparative Assessment. Lyle Campbell and Marianne Mithun, eds. Austin: University of Texas Press. In Press.

Goldfrank, Esther S.
1927    The Social and Ceremonial Organization of Cochiti. *Memoirs of the American Anthropological Association* 33. Menasha, Wis.

———    1945    Socialization, Personality, and the Structure of Pueblo Society (with Particular Reference to Hopi and Zuni). *American Anthropologist* 47(4):516-539.

———    1945a   Irrigation Agriculture and Navaho Community Leadership: Case Material on Environment and Culture. *American Anthropologist* 47(2):262-277.

1948    The Impact of Situation and Personality on Four Hopi Emergence Myths. *Southwestern Journal of Anthropology* 4(3):241-262.

————, ed.
1962    Isleta Paintings. *Bureau of American Ethnology Bulletin* 181. Washington.

1967    The Artist of "Isleta Paintings" in Pueblo Society. *Smithsonian Contributions to Anthropology* 5. Washington.

Goldwater, Robert J.
1967    Primitivism in Modern Art. Rev. ed. New York: Vintage Books.

Goodwin, Grenville
1939    Myths and Tales of the White Mountain Apache. *Memoirs of the American Folklore Society* 33. New York.

1942    The Social Organization of the Western Apache. Chicago: University of Chicago Press.

Goodyear, Albert C., III
1975    HECLA II and III: An Interpretative Study of Archeological Remains from the Lakeshore Project, Papago Reservation, Southcentral Arizona. *Arizona State University Anthropological Research Paper* 9. Tempe.

Goss, James A.
1965    Ute Linguistics and Anasazi Abandonment of the Four Corners Area. Pp. 73-81 in Contributions of the Wetherill Mesa Archeological Project. H. Douglas Osborne, comp. *Memoirs of the Society for American Archaeology* 19. Salt Lake City.

Grange, Roger, Jr.
1952    Wooden Artifacts. Pp. 331-450 in Mogollon Cultural Continuity and Change: The Stratigraphic Analysis of Tularosa and Cordova Caves, by Paul S. Martin et al. *Fieldiana: Anthropology* 40. Chicago.

Grant, Campbell
1968    Rock Drawings of the Coso Range, Inyo County, California. *Maturango Museum Publication* 4. China Lake, Calif.

1978    Canyon de Chelly: Its People and Rock Art. Tucson: University of Arizona Press.

Gratz, Kathleen
1976    Tesuque Rain God. *El Palacio* 82(3):3-8.

Graves, Theodore D.
1970    The Personal Adjustment of Navajo Indian Migrants to Denver, Colorado. *American Anthropologist* 72(1):35-54.

1971    Drinking and Drunkenness Among Urban Indians. Pp. 274-311 in The American Indian in Urban Society. Jack O. Waddell and O. Michael Watson, eds. Boston: Little, Brown.

Green, F.E.
1962    Additional Notes on Prehistoric Wells at the Clovis Site. *American Antiquity* 28(2):230-234.

Green, Ernestene Le Verne
1963    Valdez Phase Occupation Near Taos, New Mexico. (Unpublished M.A. Thesis in Anthropology, University of Arizona, Tucson.)

1976    Valdez Phase Occupation Near Taos, New Mexico. *Fort Burgwin Research Center Publication* 10. Taos, N.M.

Green, Margie
1975    Patterns of Variation in Chipped Stone Raw Materials for the Chevelon Drainage. (Unpublished M.A. Thesis in Anthropology, State University of New York, Binghamton.)

1978    Variation in Chipped Stone Raw Material Use on Black Mesa. (Paper Presented at the 43d Annual Meeting, Society for American Archaeology, Tucson.)

Green, Roger C.
1956    Excavations Near Mayhill, New Mexico. *Highway Salvage Archaeology* 2(7):10-16.

Gregg, Josiah
1844    Commerce of the Prairies; or, The Journal of a Santa Fé Trader, During Eight Expeditions Across the Great Western Prairies, and a Residence of Nearly Nine Years in Northern Mexico. 2 vols. New York: H.G. Langley.

1954    Commerce of the Prairies. Norman: University of Oklahoma Press.

Griffin, James B., and Alex D. Krieger
1947    Notes on Some Ceramic Techniques and Intrusions in Central Mexico. *American Antiquity* 12(3):156-168.

Griffin, William B.
1969    Culture Change and Shifting Populations in Central Northern Mexico. *Anthropological Papers of the University of Arizona* 13. Tucson.

Grosscup, Gordon L.
1960    The Culture History of Lovelock Cave, Nevada. *University of California Archaeological Survey Report* 52. Berkeley.

Guernsey, Samuel J.
1931    Explorations in Northeastern Arizona: Report on the Archaeological Fieldwork of 1920-1923. *Papers of the Peabody Museum of American Archaeology and Ethnology, Harvard University* 12(1). Cambridge, Mass.

Guernsey, Samuel J., and Alfred V. Kidder
1921    Basket-maker Caves of Northeastern Arizona: Report on the Explorations, 1916-17. *Papers of the Peabody Museum of American Archaeology and Ethnology, Harvard University* 8(2). Cambridge, Mass.

Gumerman, George J.
1969    The Archaeology of the Hopi Buttes District, Arizona. (Unpublished Ph.D. Dissertation in Anthropology, University of Arizona, Tucson.)

1970    Black Mesa: Survey and Excavation in Northeastern Arizona, 1968. *Prescott College Studies in Anthropology* 2. Prescott, Ariz.

————, ed.
1971    The Distribution of Prehistoric Population Aggregates. *Prescott College Anthropological Report* 1. Prescott, Ariz.

1975    Alternative Cultural Models for Demographic Change: Southwestern Examples. Pp. 104-115 in Population Studies in Archaeology and Biological Anthropology: A Symposium. Alan C. Swedlund, ed. *Memoirs of the Society for American Archaeology* 30. Salt Lake City, Utah.

Gumerman, George J., and Robert C. Euler, eds.
1976    Papers on the Archaeology of Black Mesa, Arizona. Carbondale and Edwardsville: Southern Illinois University Press.

Gumerman, George J., and R. Roy Johnson
1971    Prehistoric Human Population Distribution in a Biological Transition Zone. Pp. 83-102 in The Distribution of Prehistoric Population Aggregates. George J. Gumerman, ed. Prescott, Ariz.: Prescott College Press.

Gumerman, George J., and S. Alan Skinner
1968    A Synthesis of the Prehistory of the Central Little Colorado Valley, Arizona. *American Antiquity* 33(2):185-199.

Gumerman, George J., Deborah Westfall, and Carol S. Weed
1972    Black Mesa: Archaeological Investigations on Black Mesa, the 1969-1970 Seasons. *Prescott College Studies in Anthropology* 4. Prescott, Ariz.

Gunn, John M.
1917 Schat - chen, History, Traditions and Narratives of the Queres Indians of Laguna and Acoma. Albuquerque, N.M.: Albright and Anderson.

Gunnerson, Dolores A.
1956 The Southern Athabascans: Their Arrival in the Southwest. El Palacio 63(11-12):346-365.

1972 Man and Bison on the Plains in the Protohistoric Period. Plains Anthropologist 17(55):1-10.

1974 The Jicarilla Apaches: A Study in Survival. DeKalb: Northern Illinois University Press.

Gunnerson, James H.
1956 Plains-Promontory Relationships. American Antiquity 22(1):69-72.

1959 Archaeological Survey in Northeastern New Mexico. El Palacio 66(5):145-154.

1960 An Introduction to Plains Apache Archeology: The Dismal River Aspect. Anthropological Papers 58, Bureau of American Ethnology Bulletin 173:131-260. Washington.

1962 Plateau Shoshonean Prehistory: A Suggested Reconstruction. American Antiquity 28(1):41-45.

1964 [Fieldnotes on the Jicarilla Apache.] (Manuscript at the University of Nebraska State Museum, Lincoln.)

1968 Plains Apache Archaeology: A Review. Plains Anthropologist 13(41):167-189.

1969 Apache Archaeology in Northeastern New Mexico. American Antiquity 34(1):23-39.

Gunnerson, James H., and Dolores A. Gunnerson
1970 Evidence of Apaches at Pecos. El Palacio 76(3):1-6.

1971 Apachean Culture: A Study in Unity and Diversity. Pp. 7-27 in Apachean Culture History and Ethnology. Keith H. Basso and Morris E. Opler, eds. Anthropological Papers of the University of Arizona 21. Tucson.

Guthe, Carl E.
1925 Pueblo Pottery Making: A Study at the Village of San Ildefonso. (Papers of the Phillips Academy Southwestern Expedition 2) New Haven, Conn.: Published for Phillips Academy by Yale University Press.

Gwyther, George
1871 Pueblo Indians. Overland Monthly (March):262-264.

Haas, Mary R.
1959 Tonkawa and Algonkian. Anthropological Linguistics 1(2):1-6.

1967 On the Relations of Tonkawa. Pp. 310-320 in Studies in Southwestern Ethnolinguistics. Dell H. Hymes with William E. Bittle, eds. The Hague, Paris: Mouton.

Hack, John T.
1942 The Changing Physical Environment of the Hopi Indians of Arizona. (Reports of the Awatovi Expedition 1) Papers of the Peabody Museum of American Archaeology and Ethnology, Harvard University 35(1). Cambridge, Mass.

1942a Prehistoric Coal Mining in the Jeddito Valley, Arizona. (Reports of the Awatovi Expedition 2) Papers of the Peabody Museum of American Archaeology and Ethnology, Harvard University 35(2). Cambridge, Mass.

Hackenberg, Robert A., ed.
1972 Modernization Research on the Papago Indians. Human Organization 31(2).

Hackett, Charles W., ed.
1923-1937 Historical Documents Relating to New Mexico, Nueva Vizcaya and Approaches Thereto, to 1773. Adolph F.A. Bandelier and Fanny R. Bandelier, colls. 3 vols. Carnegie Institution of Washington Publication 330. Washington.

_____, ed.
1942 Revolt of the Pueblo Indians of New Mexico and Otermín's Attempted Reconquest, 1680-1682. Charmion C. Shelby, trans. 2 vols. Albuquerque: University of New Mexico Press.

Hadlock, Harry L.
1962 Surface Surveys of Lithic Sites on the Gallegos Wash. El Palacio 69(3):174-184.

Haeberlin, H.K.
1916 The Idea of Fertilization in the Culture of the Pueblo Indians. Memoirs of the American Anthropological Association 3:1-55. Lancaster, Pa.

Haile, Berard
1950-1951 A Stem Vocabulary of the Navaho Language. 2 vols. St. Michaels, Ariz.: St. Michaels Press.

Hale, Kenneth L.
1958 Internal Diversity in Uto-Aztecan, I. International Journal of American Linguistics 24(2):101-107.

1962 Jemez and Kiowa Correspondences in Reference to Kiowa-Tanoan. International Journal of American Linguistics 28(1):1-5.

1964 The Sub-grouping of Uto-Aztecan Languages: Lexical Evidence for Sonoran. Pp. 511-517 in Vol. 2 of Proceedings of the 35th International Congress of Americanists. 3 vols. Mexico, 1964.

1967 Toward a Reconstruction of Kiowa-Tanoan Phonology. International Journal of American Linguistics 33(2):112-120.

1970 Jemez Vocabulary. (Manuscript in Hale's Possession.)

Hale, Kenneth L., LaVerne Masayesva Jeanne, and Paul Platero
1977 Three Cases of Overgeneration. Pp. 379-416 in Formal Syntax. Peter W. Culicover, Thomas Wasow and Adrian Akmajian, eds. New York, San Francisco, and London: Academic Press.

Hall, Edward T., Jr.
1942 Archaeological Survey of Walhalla Glades. Museum of Northern Arizona Bulletin 20. Flagstaff.

1944 Early Stockaded Settlements in the Governador, New Mexico: A Marginal Anasazi Development from Basket Maker III to Pueblo I Times. Columbia Studies in Archeology and Ethnology 2(1). New York.

Hall-Quest, Olga (Wilbourne)
1969 Conquistadors and Pueblos: The Story of the American Southwest, 1540-1848. New York: E.P. Dutton.

Hammack, Laurens C.
1969 A Preliminary Report of the Excavations at Las Colinas. The Kiva 35(1):11-28.

Hammack, Laurens C., Stanley D. Bussey, and Ronald Ice
1966 The Cliff Highway Salvage Project: A Preliminary Report Describing the Archaeological Investigations at Three Sites Located Within the Right-of-way of S-1165(18). Santa Fe: Museum of New Mexico.

Hammond, George P.
1927 Don Juan de Oñate, and the Founding of New Mexico. New Mexico Historical Review 2(2):134-174.

Hammond, George P., and Agapito Rey 1927 see Gallegos Lamero, Hernán 1927

_____, eds. and trans.
1928 Obregón's History of Sixteenth Century Explorations in Western America, Entitled: Chronicle, Commentary, or Relation of the Ancient and Modern Discoveries in New Spain New Mexico, and Mexico, 1584. Los Angeles: Wetzel.

————, eds. and trans.
1940    Narratives of the Coronado Expedition, 1540-1542. Albuquerque: University of New Mexico Press.

————, eds.
1953    Don Juan de Oñate, Colonizer of New Mexico, 1598-1628. Santa Fe: University of New Mexico Press.

————
1966    The Rediscovery of New Mexico, 1580-1594: The Explorations of Chamuscado, Espejo, Castaño de Sosa, Morlete, and Leyva de Bonilla and Humaña. Albuquerque: University of New Mexico Press.

Hankins, Russell L.
1962    Fray Francisco de Ayeta in the Service of New Mexico, 1673-1683. (Unpublished M.A. Thesis in History, University of New Mexico, Albuquerque.)

Hargrave, Lyndon L.
1930    Shungopovi. Museum of Northern Arizona, Museum Note 2(10). Flagstaff.

————
1932    Guide to Forty Pottery Types from the Hopi Country and the San Francisco Mountains, Arizona. Museum of Northern Arizona Bulletin 1. Flagstaff.

————
1933    Pueblo II Houses of the San Francisco Mountains, Arizona. Museum of Northern Arizona Bulletin 4. Flagstaff.

————
1938    Results of a Study of the Cohonina Branch of the Patayan Culture in 1938. Museum of Northern Arizona, Museum Note 11(6):43-49. Flagstaff.

————
1939    Bird Bones from Abandoned Indian Dwellings in Arizona and Utah. The Condor 41(5):206-210.

————
1951    First Mesa. Museum of Northern Arizona Reprint Series 2:30-35. (Reprinted from Museum of Northern Arizona, Museum Note 3(8):1-6. Flagstaff, 1931.)

Harlan, Jack R.
1967    A Wild Wheat Harvest in Turkey. Archaeology 20(3):197-201.

Harlow, Francis H.
1970    Historic Pueblo Indian Pottery: Painted Jars and Bowls of the Period 1600-1900. Santa Fe: Museum of New Mexico Press.

Harner, Michael J.
1957    Potsherds and the Tentative Dating of the San Gorgonio-Big Maria Trail. University of California Archaeological Survey Report 37:35-39. Berkeley.

————
1958    Lowland Patayan Phases in the Lower Colorado River Valley and Colorado Desert. University of California Archaeological Survey Report 42:93-97. Berkeley.

Harrill, Bruce G.
1973    The DoBell Site: Archaeological Salvage Near the Petrified Forest. The Kiva 39(1):35-67.

Harrington, Carobeth (Tucker)
1920    [Isleta Language: Texts and Analytical Vocabulary.] (Manuscript No. 2299 in National Anthropological Archives, Smithsonian Institution, Washington.)

Harrington, John P.
1909    [Piro Vocabulary with Added Words in the Sima Dialect of Sandia and Tiwa Language of Isleta del Sur.] (7 Manuscript Pages, Typed, MS. No. 2292 [Missing since 1964] in National Anthropological Archives, Smithsonian Institution, Washington.)

1909a   Notes on the Piro Language. American Anthropologist 11(4):563-594.

1910    A Brief Description of the Tewa Language. American Anthropologist 12(4):497-504.

1910a   An Introductory Paper of the Tiwa Language Dialect of Taos, New Mexico. American Anthropologist 12(1):11-48.

1910b   On Phonetic and Lexic Resemblances Between Kiowan and Tanoan. American Anthropologist 12(1):119-123.

1912    Tewa Relationship Terms. American Anthropologist 14(3):472-498.

1913    [Linguistic Fieldnotes Based on Work with a Speaker of Oraibi Hopi.] (Manuscript in National Anthropological Archives, Smithsonian Institution, Washington.)

1916    The Ethnogeography of the Tewa Indians. Pp. 29-636 in 29th Annual Report of the Bureau of American Ethnology for the Years 1907-1908. Washington.

[1918]  [Taos Vocabulary.] (Manuscript No. 2290 in National Anthropological Archives, Smithsonian Institution, Washington.)

1928    Vocabulary of the Kiowa Language. Bureau of American Ethnology Bulletin 84. Washington.

1940    Southern Peripheral Athapaskawan Origins, Divisions, and Migrations. Smithsonian Miscellaneous Collections 100:503-532. Washington.

1945    Note on the Names Moqui and Hopi. American Anthropologist 47(1):177-178.

1947    Three Tewa Texts. International Journal of American Linguistics 13(2):112-116.

Harrington, John P., and Helen H. Roberts
1928    Picuris Children's Stories with Texts and Songs. Pp. 289-447 in 43d Annual Report of the Bureau of American Ethnology for the Years 1925-1926. Washington.

Harrington, Mark R.
1933    Gypsum Cave, Nevada. Southwest Museum Paper 8. Los Angeles, Calif.

————
1957    A Pinto Site at Little Lake, California. Southwest Museum Paper 17. Los Angeles, Calif.

Harrington, Mark R., and Ruth D. Simpson
1961    Tule Springs, Nevada with Other Evidences of Pleistocene Man in North America. Southwest Museum Paper 18. Los Angeles, Calif.

Harris, Arthur H.
1963    Vertebrate Remains and Past Environmental Reconstruction in the Navajo Reservoir District. (Navajo Project Studies 10) Museum of New Mexico Papers in Anthropology 11. Santa Fe.

Harris, Arthur H., James Schoenwetter, and A.H. Warren
1967    An Archaeological Survey of the Chuska Valley and the Chaco Plateau, New Mexico. Museum of New Mexico Research Record 4. Santa Fe.

Harshberger, John W.
1926    Changes in the Habits of the Hopi Indians, Arizona. Bulletin of the Geographical Society of Philadelphia 24:39-45.

Harvey, Byron, III
1963    Masks at a Maskless Pueblo: The Laguna Colony Kachina Organization at Isleta. Ethnology 2(4):478-489.

————
1970    Ritual in Pueblo Art: Hopi Life in Hopi Painting. Contributions from the Museum of the American Indian, Heye Foundation 24. New York.

Haury, Emil W.
1931    Kivas of the Tusayan Ruin, Grand Canyon, Arizona. Gila Pueblo, Medallion Paper 9. Globe, Ariz.

1932      Roosevelt 9:6: A Hohokam Site of the Colonial Period. *Gila Pueblo, Medallion Paper* 11. Globe, Ariz.

1936      Some Southwestern Pottery Types. *Gila Pueblo, Medallion Paper* 19. Globe, Ariz.

1936a      The Mogollon Culture of Southwestern New Mexico. *Gila Pueblo, Medallion Paper* 20. Globe, Ariz.

1937      Pottery Types at Snaketown. Pp. 169-229 in Excavations at Snaketown, I: Material Culture, by Harold S. Gladwin et al. *Gila Pueblo, Medallion Paper* 25. Globe, Ariz.

1937a      A Pre-Spanish Rubber Ball from Arizona. *American Antiquity* 2(4):282-288.

1937b      The Snaketown Canal. Pp. 50-58 in Excavations at Snaketown, I: Material Culture, by Harold S. Gladwin et al. *Gila Pueblo, Medallion Paper* 25. Globe, Ariz.

1943      A Possible Cochise-Mogollon-Hohokam Sequence. Pp. 260-263 in Recent Advances in American Archaeology: Papers Read Before the American Philosophical Society Annual Meeting April 23, 24, 25, 1942. *Proceedings of the American Philosophical Society* 86(2). Philadelphia.

1945      The Excavation of Los Muertos and Neighboring Ruins in the Salt River Valley, Southern Arizona. *Papers of the Peabody Museum of American Archaeology and Ethnology, Harvard University* 24(1). Cambridge, Mass.

1945a      The Problem of Contacts Between the Southwestern United States and Mexico. *Southwestern Journal of Anthropology* 1(1):55-74.

1950      The Stratigraphy and Archaeology of Ventana Cave, Arizona. Tucson: University of Arizona Press; Albuquerque: University of New Mexico Press.

1953      Artifacts with Mammoth Remains, Naco, Arizona, I: Discovery of the Naco Mammoth and the Associated Projectile Points. *American Antiquity* 19(1):1-14.

————, ed.
1954      Southwest Issue. *American Anthropologist* 56(4).

1957      An Alluvial Site on the San Carlos Indian Reservation, Arizona. *American Antiquity* 23(1):2-27.

1960      Association of Fossil Fauna and Artifacts of the Sulphur Spring Stage, Cochise Culture. *American Antiquity* 25(4):609-610.

1962      The Greater American Southwest. Pp. 106-131 in Courses Toward Urban Life: Archeological Considerations of Some Cultural Alternates. Robert J. Braidwood and Gordon R. Willey, eds. *Viking Fund Publications in Anthropology* 32. New York.

1965      Snaketown: 1964-1965. *The Kiva* 31(1):1-13.

1967      The Hohokam: The First Masters of the American Desert. *National Geographic Magazine* 131(5):670-695.

1976      The Hohokam, Desert Farmers and Craftsmen: Excavations at Snaketown, 1964-1965. Tucson: University of Arizona Press.

Haury, Emil W., and Lyndon L. Hargrave
1931      Recently Dated Pueblo Ruins in Arizona. *Smithsonian Miscellaneous Collections* 82(11). Washington.

Haury, Emil W., and Edwin B. Sayles
1947      An Early Pit House Village of the Mogollon Culture, Forestdale Valley, Arizona. *University of Arizona Social Science Bulletin* 16. Tucson.

Haury, Emil W., Edwin B. Sayles, and William W. Wasley
1959      The Lehner Mammoth Site, Southeastern Arizona. *American Antiquity* 25(1):2-30.

Havighurst, Robert J., and Rea R. Hilkevitch
1944      The Intelligence of Indian Children as Measured by a Performance Scale. *Journal of Abnormal and Social Psychology* 39(4):419-433.

Hawley, Florence M.
1934      The Significance of the Dated Prehistory of Chetro Ketl, Chaco Cañon, New Mexico. *Monograph Series 1(1), University of New Mexico Bulletin* 246. Albuquerque.

1937      Pueblo Social Organization as a Lead to Pueblo History. *American Anthropologist* 39(3):504-522.

1937a      The Place of Tseh So in the Chaco Culture Pattern. Pp. 115-119 in Tseh So, a Small House Ruin, Chaco Canyon, New Mexico. Preliminary Report. Donald D. Brand, Florence M. Hawley, Frank C. Hibben et al., eds. *Anthropological Series 2(2), University of New Mexico Bulletin* 308. Albuquerque.

1950      Big Kivas, Little Kivas, and Moiety Houses in Historical Reconstruction. *Southwestern Journal of Anthropology* 6(3):286-302.

———— see also Ellis, Florence (Hawley)

Hayden, Ferdinand V.
1877      Geological and Geographical Atlas of Colorado and Portions of Adjacent Territory. Washington: U.S. Department of the Interior.

Hayden, Julian D.
1957      Excavations, 1940 at University Indian Ruin Tucson, Arizona. *Southwestern Monuments Association Technical Series* 5. Gila Pueblo, Globe, Ariz.

1970      Of Hohokam Origins and Other Matters. *American Antiquity* 35(1):87-93.

1972      Hohokam Petroglyphs of the Sierra Pinacate, Sonora and the Hohokam Shell Expeditions. *The Kiva* 37(2):74-83.

Hayes, Alden C.
1964      The Archeological Survey of Wetherill Mesa, Mesa Verde National Park, Colorado. *U.S. National Park Service Archeological Research Series* 7A. Washington.

1975      A Survey of Chaco Canyon Archeology. (Manuscript 13, Chaco Center, National Park Service, University of New Mexico, Albuquerque.)

Hayes, Alden C., and James A. Lancaster
1975      Badger House Community, Mesa Verde National Park, Colorado. (Publications in Archeology 7E, Wetherill Mesa Studies) Washington: U.S. Department of the Interior, National Park Service.

Hayes, Alden C., and Thomas C. Windes
1975      An Anasazi Shrine in Chaco Canyon. Pp. 143-156 in Collected Papers in Honor of Florence Hawley Ellis. Theodore R. Frisbie, ed. *Papers of the Archaeological Society of New Mexico* 2. Santa Fe.

Haynes, C. Vance, Jr.
1968      Geochronology and Late Quaternary Alluvium. Pp. 591-631 in Means of Correlation of Quaternary Successions. Roger B. Morrison and Herbert E. Wright, eds. Salt Lake City: University of Utah Press.

Heath, Jeffrey
1977      Uto-Aztecan Morphophonemics. *International Journal of American Linguistics* 43(1):27-36.

Heiser, Charles B., Jr.
1951      The Sunflower Among the North American Indians. *Proceedings of the American Philosophical Society* 95(4):432-448. Philadelphia.

Hemmings, E. Thomas, and C. Vance Haynes
1969      The Escapule Mammoth and Associated Projectile Points, San Pedro Valley, Arizona. *Journal of the Arizona Academy of Science* 5(3):184-188. Tucson.

645

Henderson, Junius, and John P. Harrington
1914    The Ethnozoology of the Tewa Indians. *Bureau of American Ethnology Bulletin* 56. Washington.

Henige, David P.
1970    Colonial Governors from the Fifteenth Century to the Present. Madison, Milwaukee and London: University of Wisconsin Press.

Henry, Jeannette, Vine Deloria, Jr., M. Scott Momaday, Bea Medicine, and Alfonso Ortiz, eds.
1970    Indian Voices: The First Convocation of American Indian Scholars. San Francisco: The Indian Historian Press.

Herold, Laurance, and Ralph A. Luebben
1968    Papers on Taos Archeology. *Fort Burgwin Research Center Publication* 7. Taos, N.M.

Hester, James J.
1962    Early Navajo Migrations and Acculturation in the Southwest. (Navajo Project Studies 5) *Museum of New Mexico Papers in Anthropology* 6. Santa Fe.

Hewett, Edgar L.
1904    Studies on the Extinct Pueblo of Pecos. *American Anthropologist* 6(4):426-439.

1906    Antiquities of the Jemez Plateau, New Mexico. *Bureau of American Ethnology Bulletin* 32. Washington.

1918    Crescencio Martinez - Artist. *El Palacio* 5(5):67-69.

1930    Ancient Life in the American Southwest. Indianapolis: Bobbs-Merill.

1936    The Chaco Canyon and Its Monuments. Albuquerque: University of New Mexico Press.

1938    Pajarito Plateau and Its Ancient People. Albuquerque: University of New Mexico Press.

Hewett, Edgar L., and Bertha P. Dutton, eds.
1945    The Pueblo Indian World: Studies on the Natural History of the Rio Grande Valley in Relation to Pueblo Indian Culture. Albuquerque: University of New Mexico and School of American Research.

Hibben, Frank C.
1937    Excavation of the Riana Ruin and Chama Valley Survey. *University of New Mexico Anthropological Series* 2(1). Albuquerque.

1938    The Gallina Phase. *American Antiquity* 4(2):131-136.

1940    The Gallina Culture of North Central New Mexico. (Unpublished Ph.D. Dissertation in Anthropology, Harvard University, Cambridge, Mass.)

1941    Evidences of Early Occupation in Sandia Cave, New Mexico, and Other Sites in the Sandia-Manzano Region. *Smithsonian Miscellaneous Collections* 99(23):1-64. Washington.

1948    The Gallina Architectural Forms. *American Antiquity* 14(1):32-36.

1949    The Pottery of the Gallina Complex. *American Antiquity* 14(3):194-202.

Hickerson, Harold
1965    The Virginia Deer and Intertribal Buffer Zones in the Upper Mississippi Valley. P. 43-66 in Man, Culture, and Animals: The Role of Animals in Human Ecological Adjustments. Anthony Leeds and Andrew P. Vayda, eds. Washington: American Association for the Advancement of Science.

Hieb, Louis A.
[1969-1971] [Ethnographic Notes, from Approximately 17 Months' Fieldwork Among the Hopi.] (Manuscripts in Hieb's Possession.)

1972    The Hopi Ritual Clown: Life As It Should Not Be. (Unpublished Ph.D. Dissertation in Anthropology, Princeton University, Princeton, N.J.)

Hightower, Jamake
1977    Ritual of the Wind: Northamerican Indian Ceremonies, Music and Dances. New York: Viking Press.

Hill, W.W.
1936    Navaho Warfare. *Yale University Publications in Anthropology* 5. New Haven, Conn.

1938    The Agricultural and Hunting Methods of the Navaho Indians. *Yale University Publications in Anthropology* 18. New Haven, Conn.

1940-1941 [Santa Clara.] (Unpublished Manuscript in the Possession of Mrs. W.W. Hill.)

Hill, James N.
1966    A Prehistoric Community in Eastern Arizona. *Southwestern Journal of Anthropology* 22(1):9-30.

1970    Broken K Pueblo: Prehistoric Social Organization in the American Southwest. *Anthropological Papers of the University of Arizona* 18. Tucson.

1978    Preliminary Report of 1977 Survey on the Pajarito Plateau, Santa Fe National Forest. (Manuscript on File at U.S.D.A. Forest Service, Southwestern Regional Office, Albuquerque, N.M.)

Hill, James N., and Joel Gunn, eds.
1977    The Individual in Prehistory: Studies in Variability in Style in Prehistoric Technologies. New York: Academic Press.

Hodge, Frederick W.
1893    Prehistoric Irrigation in Arizona. *American Anthropologist* 6(3):323-330.

1896    Pueblo Indian Clans. *American Anthropologist* 9(10):345-352.

1907    Cochiti. Pp. 317-318 in Vol. 1 of Handbook of American Indians North of Mexico. Frederick W. Hodge, ed. 2 vols. *Bureau of American Ethnology Bulletin* 30. Washington.

1907a   Jemez. Pp. 629-631 in Vol. 1 of Handbook of American Indians North of Mexico. Frederick W. Hodge, ed. 2 vols. *Bureau of American Ethnology Bulletin* 30. Washington.

1907b   Hano. Pp. 531-532 in Vol. 1 of Handbook of American Indians North of Mexico. Frederick W. Hodge, ed. 2 vols. *Bureau of American Ethnology Bulletin* 30. Washington.

1907c   Hawikuh. Pp. 539-540 in Vol. 1 of Handbook of American Indians North of Mexico. Frederick W. Hodge, ed. 2 vols. *Bureau of American Ethnology Bulletin* 30. Washington.

1907d   Kechipauan. P. 670 in Vol. 1 of Handbook of American Indians North of Mexico. Frederick W. Hodge, ed. 2 vols. *Bureau of American Ethnology Bulletin* 30. Washington.

1907e   Kiakima. P. 681 in Vol. 1 of Handbook of American Indians North of Mexico. Frederick W. Hodge, ed. 2 vols. *Bureau of American Ethnology Bulletin* 30. Washington.

1907f   Matsaki. P. 821 in Vol. 2 of Handbook of American Indians North of Mexico. Frederick W. Hodge, ed. 2 vols. *Bureau of American Ethnology Bulletin* 30. Washington.

1907g    Mishongnovi. P. 871 in Vol. 1 of Handbook of American Indians North of Mexico. Frederick W. Hodge, ed. 2 vols. *Bureau of American Ethnology Bulletin* 30. Washington.

1907h    Moenkopi. P. 919 in Vol. 1 of Handbook of American Indians North of Mexico. Frederick W. Hodge, ed. 2 vols. *Bureau of American Ethnology Bulletin* 30. Washington.

1907i    Keresan Family. P. 675 in Vol. 1 of Handbook of American Indians North of Mexico. Frederick W. Hodge, ed. 2 vols. *Bureau of American Ethnology Bulletin* 30. Washington.

————, ed.
1907-1910    Handbook of American Indians North of Mexico. 2 vols. *Bureau of American Ethnology Bulletin* 30. Washington.

1910    Santo Domingo. P. 462 in Vol. 2 of Handbook of American Indians North of Mexico. Frederick W. Hodge, ed. 2 vols. *Bureau of American Ethnology Bulletin* 30. Washington.

1910a    Taos. Pp. 688-691 in Vol. 2 of Handbook of American Indians North of Mexico. Frederick W. Hodge, ed. 2 vols. *Bureau of American Ethnology Bulletin* 30. Washington.

1910b    Santa Clara. Pp. 456-457 in Vol. 2 of Handbook of American Indians North of Mexico. Frederick W. Hodge, ed. 2 vols. *Bureau of American Ethnology Bulletin* 30. Washington.

1910c    Nambe. Pp. 15 and 325 in Vol. 2 of Handbook of American Indians North of Mexico. Frederick W. Hodge, ed. 2 vols. *Bureau of American Ethnology Bulletin* 30. Washington.

1910d    Sandía. Pp. 429-430 in Vol. 2 of Handbook of American Indians North of Mexico. Frederick W. Hodge, ed. 2 vols. *Bureau of American Ethnology Bulletin* 30. Washington.

1910e    Payupki. P. 218 in Vol. 2 of Handbook of American Indians North of Mexico. Frederick W. Hodge, ed. 2 vols. *Bureau of American Ethnology Bulletin* 30. Washington.

1910f    Pojoaque. P. 274 in Vol. 2 of Handbook of American Indians North of Mexico. Frederick W. Hodge, ed. 2 vols. *Bureau of American Ethnology Bulletin* 30. Washington.

1910g    Sia. Pp. 562-563 in Vol. 2 of Handbook of American Indians North of Mexico. Frederick W. Hodge, ed. 2 vols. *Bureau of American Ethnology Bulletin* 30. Washington.

1910h    Picuris. Pp. 245-246 in Vol. 2 of Handbook of American Indians North of Mexico. Frederick W. Hodge, ed. 2 vols. *Bureau of American Ethnology Bulletin* 30. Washington.

1910i    Tewa. Pp. 737-738 in Vol. 2 of Handbook of American Indians North of Mexico. Frederick W. Hodge, ed. 2 vols. *Bureau of American Ethnology Bulletin* 30. Washington.

1910j    Zuni. Pp. 1015-1020 in Vol. 2 of Handbook of American Indians North of Mexico. Frederick W. Hodge, ed. 2 vols. *Bureau of American Ethnology Bulletin* 30. Washington.

1910k    Tano. Pp. 686-687 in Vol. 2 of Handbook of American Indians North of Mexico. Frederick W. Hodge, ed. 2 vols. *Bureau of American Ethnology Bulletin* 30. Washington.

1910l    Oraibi. Pp. 142-143 in Vol. 2 of Handbook of American Indians North of Mexico. Frederick W. Hodge, ed. 2 vols. *Bureau of American Ethnology Bulletin* 30. Washington.

1910m    Shongopovi. Pp. 553-554 in Vol. 2 of Handbook of American Indians North of Mexico. Frederick W. Hodge, ed. 2 vols. *Bureau of American Ethnology Bulletin* 30. Washington.

1910n    Tigua. Pp. 747-749 in Vol. 2 of Handbook of American Indians North of Mexico. Frederick W. Hodge, ed. 2 vols. *Bureau of American Ethnology Bulletin* 30. Washington.

1929    French Intrusion Toward New Mexico in 1695. *New Mexico Historical Review* 4(1):72-76.

1935    Pueblo Names in the Oñate Documents. *New Mexico Historical Review* 10(1):36-47.

1937    History of Hawikuh, New Mexico: One of the So-called Cities of Cíbola. (Publications of the Frederick Webb Hodge Anniversary Publication Fund 1) Los Angeles: Southwest Museum.

Hodge, William H.
1969    The Albuquerque Navajos. *Anthropological Papers of the University of Arizona* 11. Tucson.

Hoebel, E. Adamson
1943-1950    [Unpublished Fieldnotes on Zia Law.] (Manuscript in Hoebel's Possession.)

1954    Major Contributions of Southwestern Studies to Anthropological Theory. *American Anthropologist* 56(4):720-727.

1968    The Character of Keresan Pueblo Law. *Proceedings of the American Philosophical Society* 112(3):127-130. Philadelphia.

1969    Keresan Pueblo Law. Pp. 92-116 in Law in Culture and Society. Laura Nader, ed. Chicago: Aldine.

Hoijer, Harry
1938    The Southern Athapaskan Languages. *American Anthropologist* 40(1):75-87.

1945-1949    The Apachean Verb: Parts I-V. *International Journal of American Linguistics* 11(4):193-203; 12(1):1-13, (2):51-59; 14(4):247-259; 15(1):12-22.

1956    The Chronology of the Athapaskan Languages. *International Journal of American Linguistics* 22(4):219-232.

1963    The Athapaskan Languages. Pp. 1-29 in Studies in the Athapaskan Languages. Harry Hoijer et al. eds. *University of California Publications in Linguistics* 29. Berkeley.

1971    The Position of the Apachean Languages in the Athapaskan Stock. Pp. 3-6 in Apachean Culture History and Ethnology. Keith H. Basso and Morris E. Opler, eds. *Anthropological Papers of the University of Arizona* 21. Tucson.

1974    A Navajo Lexicon. *University of California Publications in Linguistics* 78. Berkeley.

Hoijer, Harry, and Edward P. Dozier
1949    The Phonemes of Tewa, Santa Clara Dialect. *International Journal of American Linguistics* 15(3):139-144.

Holbrook, Sally J., and James C. Mackey
1976    Prehistoric Environmental Change in Northern New Mexico: Evidence from a Gallina Phase Archaeological Site. *The Kiva* 41(3-4):309-317.

Holden, Jane
1952    The Bonnell Site. *Texas Archaeological and Paleontological Society Bulletin* 23:78-132. Lubbock.

Holmes, William H.
1878    Report on the Ancient Ruins of Southwestern Colorado, Examined During the Summers of 1875 and 1876. Pp.

383-408 in *10th Annual Report of the U.S. Geological and Geographical Survey of the Territories for 1876.* Washington.

1911    Report to the Chief. Pp. 7-14 in *27th Annual Report of the Bureau of American Ethnology for the Years 1905-1906.* Washington.

Holschlag, Stephanie L.
1975    Pot Creek Pueblo and the Question of Prehistoric Northern Tiwa Household Configuration. (Unpublished Ph.D. Dissertation in Anthropology, Washington State University, Pullman.)

Hooton, Earnest A.
1930    The Indians of Pecos Pueblo: A Study of Their Skeletal Remains. (Papers of the Southwestern Expedition 4) New Haven, Conn.: Published for the Phillips Academy by Yale University Press.

Hoover, J.W.
1930    Tusayan: The Hopi Indian Country of Arizona. *Geographical Review* 20(3):425-444.

Hopi Indian Agency
[1968]    [Pamphlet Issued for Tourists.] (Mimeographed Copy in Richard S. Clemmer's Possession.)

Hopi Tribe
1970    The Hopi-Tewa and His Reservation. Oraibi, Ariz.: Hopi Indian Agency.

Hopi: People of Peace. (Motion Picture)
[1977]    Associated Television of Great Britain. Michael Pearce, director. 16 mm. Color. Time: 60 min.

Hopkins, Nicholas A.
1965    Great Basin Prehistory and Uto-Aztecan. *American Antiquity* 31(1):48-60.

Hough, Walter
1897    The Hopi in Relation to Their Plant Environment. *American Anthropologist* 10(2):33-44.

1903    Archeological Field Work in Northeastern Arizona: The Museum-Gates Expedition of 1901. Pp. 279-358 in *Report of the United States National Museum for 1901.* Washington.

1906    Pueblo Environment. *Proceedings of the 55th Meeting of the American Association for the Advancement of Science* 40:447-454. Washington.

1907    Antiquities of the Upper Gila and Salt River Valleys in Arizona and New Mexico. *Bureau of American Ethnology Bulletin* 35. Washington.

1915    The Hopi Indians. Cedar Rapids, Ia.: Torch Press.

1918    The Hopi Indian Collection in the United States National Museum. *Proceedings of the United States National Museum* 54(2231):235-296. Washington.

1920    Exploration of a Pit House Village at Luna, New Mexico. *Proceedings of the United States National Museum* 55(2280):409-431. Washington.

Houghton, Frank E.
1959    Climate of New Mexico. *Climatography of the United States* 60-29. U.S. Department of Commerce, National Oceanic and Atmospheric Administration, Environmental Data Service. Silver Spring, Md.

Houser, Nicholas P.
1966    A Description and Analysis of the Tiwa Community of Ysleta, Texas. (Manuscript in Arizona State Museum Library, University of Arizona, Tucson.)

1966a    Census of the Members of the Ysleta del Sur Indian Community. (Manuscript Submitted to Frederick Smith, Office of Economic Opportunity, Project Bravo, El Paso, Tex.)

1970    The Tigua Settlement of Ysleta del Sur. *The Kiva* 36(2):23-39.

Howard, Calvin D.
1974    The Atlatl: Function and Performance. *American Antiquity* 39(1):102-104.

Howlett, William J.
1908    Life of the Right Reverend Joseph P. Machebeuf, D.D.: Pioneer Priest of Ohio, Pioneer Priest of New Mexico, Pioneer Priest of Colorado, Vicar Apostolic of Colorado and Utah, and First Bishop of Denver. Pueblo, Colo.: Franklin Press.

Hrdlička, Aleš
1908    Physiological and Medical Observations Among the Indians of the Southwestern United States and Northern Mexico. *Bureau of American Ethnology Bulletin* 34. Washington.

1918    Recent Discoveries Attributed to Early Man in America. *Bureau of American Ethnology Bulletin* 66. Washington.

1931    Catalogue of Human Crania in the United States National Museum Collections. *Proceedings of the United States National Museum* 78(4):1-95. Washington.

1935    The Pueblos, with Comparative Data on the Bulk of the Tribes of the Southwest and Northern Mexico. *American Journal of Physical Anthropology* 20(3):235-460.

Hughes, Anne E.
1914    The Beginnings of Spanish Settlement in the El Paso District. *University of California Publications in History* 1(3):295-392. Berkeley. (Reprinted: Press of the El Paso Public Schools, El Paso, Tex., 1935.)

Hume, Bill
1970    Nambe Holding Line Against Cultural Assimilation. *Albuquerque Journal*, August 30:E-1. Albuquerque.

Hunt, Alice P.
1960    Archaeology of the Death Valley Salt Pan, California. *University of Utah Anthropological Paper* 47. Salt Lake City.

Hunt, Alice P., and Dallas Tanner
1960    Early Man Sites Near Moab, Utah. *American Antiquity* 26(1):110-117.

Hunter-Anderson, Rosalind L.
1976    The Negeezi-Carrizo Survey, Results and Conclusions: A Report on an Archeological Survey Carried Out in Summer 1976 by the Wheelwright Museum of Santa Fe. (Manuscript on File at the Wheelwright Museum, Santa Fe, N.M.)

Huscher, Betty H., and Harold A. Huscher
1943    The Hogan Builders of Colorado. *Southwestern Lore* 9(2).

Hymes, Dell H.
1957    A Note on Athapaskan Glottochronology. *International Journal of American Linguistics* 23(4):291-297.

Irwin, Henry T.J.
1967    The Itama: Late Pleistocene Inhabitants of the Plains of the United States and Canada and the American Southwest. (Unpublished Ph.D. Dissertation in Anthropology, Harvard University, Cambridge, Mass.)

Irwin-Williams, Cynthia
1967    Picosa: The Elementary Southwestern Culture. *American Antiquity* 32(4):441-457.

1967a    Associations of Early Man with Horse, Camel, and Mastodon at Hueyatlaco, Valsequillo (Puebla, Mexico). Pp. 337-350 in Pleistocene Extinctions: The Search for a Cause. Paul S. Martin and Herbert E. Wright, Jr., eds. New Haven, Conn.: Yale University Press.

1967b    Prehistoric Cultural and Linguistic Patterns in the South-west Since 5,000 B.C. (Paper Read at the Annual Meeting of the Society for American Archaeology, Portales, N.M., 1967.)

1968    Configurations of Preceramic Development in the South-western United States. *Eastern New Mexico University Contributions in Anthropology* 1(1):1-9. Portales.

1968a    Archaic Culture History in the Southwestern United States. *Eastern New Mexico University Contributions in Anthropology* 1(4):48-54. Portales.

1968b    The Oshara Tradition: Origins of the Anasazi Culture. (Paper Presented at the 1968 Meeting of the Society of American Archaeology, Santa Fe, N.M.)

1968c    The Reconstruction of Archaic Culture in the Southwest-ern United States. *Eastern New Mexico University Contri-butions in Anthropology* 1(3):19-23. Portales.

1970    Report to the National Endowment for the Humanities on Investigations at the Fresnal Shelter, South Central New Mexico. (Manuscript at Eastern New Mexico University, Portales, N.M.)

1971    Report to the Wenner-Gren Foundation on Investigations on Very Early Agriculture in the Southwest. (Manuscript at Eastern New Mexico University, Portales, N.M.)

1971a    Report to the National Endowment for the Humanities on Investigations at the Fresnal Shelter, South Central New Mexico. (Manuscript at Eastern New Mexico University, Portales, N.M.)

————, ed.
1972    The Structure of Chacoan Society in the Northern South-west: Investigations at the Salmon Site - 1972. *Eastern New Mexico University Contributions in Anthropology* 4(3). Portales.

1973    The Oshara Tradition: Origins of Anasazi Culture. *East-ern New Mexico University Contributions in Anthropology* 5(1). Portales.

1977    A Network Model for the Analysis of Prehistoric Trade. Pp. 141-151 in Exchange Systems in Prehistory. Timothy K. Earle and Jonathon E. Ericson, eds. New York: Aca-demic Press.

Irwin-Williams, Cynthia, and P. Beckett
[1973]    Excavations at the Moquino Site: A Cochise Culture Lo-cality in Northern New Mexico. (Manuscript in Irwin-Williams' Possession.)

Irwin-Williams, Cynthia, and C. Vance Haynes, Jr.
1970    Climatic Change and Early Population Dynamics in the Southwestern United States. *Quaternary Research* 1(1):59-71.

Irwin-Williams, Cynthia, and Henry T.J. Irwin
1966    Excavations at Magic Mountain: A Diachronic Study of Plains-Southwest Relations. *Proceedings of the Denver Mu-seum of Natural History* 12. Denver, Colo.

Ives, Joseph C. *see* U.S. Army. Corps of Topographical Engineers

Ives, Ronald L., ed. and trans.
1939    Sedelmayr's Relacion of 1746. *Bureau of American Ethnol-ogy Bulletin* 123(9):97-117. Washington.

1950    The Sonoran "Primer Montezuma" Legends. *Western Folklore* 9(4):321-325.

Jackson, William H.
1875    Descriptive Catalogue of the Photographs of the U.S.G.S. of the Territories for the Years 1869 to 1875 Inclusive. 2d ed. (U.S. Geological Survey of the Territories Miscella-neous Publication 5) Washington: U.S. Government Printing Office.

1876    Ancient Ruins in Southwestern Colorado. Pp. 367-381 in *8th Annual Report of the U.S. Geological and Geographical Survey of the Territories for 1874.* Washington.

1877    Descriptive Catalogue of Photographs of North American Indians. (U.S. Geological Survey of the Territories Mis-cellaneous Publication 9) Washington: U.S. Government Printing Office.

James, Ahlee
1927    Tewa Firelight Tales. New York: Longmans, Green.

James, Harry C.
1956    The Hopi Indians: Their History and Their Culture. Il-lustrations by Harry C. James. Caldwell, Ida.: Caxton Printers.

1974    Pages from Hopi History. Tucson: University of Arizona Press.

James, Thomas
1962    Three Years Among the Indians and Mexicans [1846]. Philadelphia and New York: J.B. Lippincott.

Jeançon, Jean A.
1911    Explorations in Chama Basin, New Mexico. *Records of the Past* 10:92-108.

1923    Excavations in the Chama Valley, New Mexico. *Bureau of American Ethnology Bulletin* 81. Washington.

1929    Archeological Investigations in the Taos Valley, New Mexico During 1920. *Smithsonian Miscellaneous Collec-tions* 81(12):1-21. Washington.

[1931]    [Santa Clara: A New Mexican Tewa Pueblo.] Unpub-lished Manuscript in the Possession of Mrs. W.W. Hill.)

Jeançon, Jean A., and F.H. Douglas, comps.
1931    Indian Musical and Noise-making Instruments. *Denver Art Museum Leaflet* 29. Denver, Colo.

Jelinek, Arthur J.
1967    A Prehistoric Sequence in the Middle Pecos Valley, New Mexico. *University of Michigan Museum of Anthropology, Anthropological Paper* 31. Ann Arbor.

Jenkins, Myra E.
1961    The Baltasar Baca "Grant:" History of an Encroach-ment. *El Palacio* 68(1):47-64.

1966    Taos Pueblo and Its Neighbors, 1540-1847. *New Mexico Historical Review* 41(2):85-114.

1972    Spanish Land Grants in the Tewa Area. *New Mexico His-torical Review* 47(2):113-134.

Jennings, Calvin H.
1971    Early Prehistory of the Coconino Plateau, Northwestern Arizona. (Unpublished Ph.D. Dissertation in Anthro-pology, University of Colorado, Boulder.)

Jennings, Jesse D., ed.
1956    The American Southwest: A Problem in Cultural Isola-tion. Pp. 59-127 in Seminars in Archaeology, 1955. Rob-ert Wauchope, ed. *Memoirs of the Society for American Archaeology* 11. Salt Lake City.

1957    Danger Cave. *University of Utah Anthropological Paper* 27. Salt Lake City.

1957a    Danger Cave. *Memoirs of the Society for American Archae-ology* 14. Salt Lake City, Utah.

1964    The Desert West. Pp. 149-174 in Prehistoric Man in the New World. Jesse D. Jennings and Edward Norbeck, eds. Chicago: University of Chicago Press.

1966    Glen Canyon: A Summary. *University of Utah Anthropo-logical Paper* 81. Salt Lake City.

Jennings, Jesse D., and Georg Neumann
1940    A Variation of Southwestern Pueblo Culture. *New Mexico Archaeological Survey, Laboratory of Anthropology Techni-cal Series Bulletin* 10. Santa Fe.

*649*

Jennings, Jesse D., and Edward Norbeck
1955      Great Basin Prehistory:  A Review. *American Antiquity* 21(1):1-11.

Jett, Stephen C.
1964      Pueblo Indian Migrations:  An Evaluation of the Possible Physical and Cultural Determinants. *American Antiquity* 29(3):281-300.

Jocano, F. Landa
1963      Tesuque Kinship System and Social Organization. (Manuscript in National Museum, Manila, Philippines.)

Joël, Judith
1964      Classification of the Yuman Languages.  Pp. 99-105 in Studies in Californian Linguistics.  William Bright, ed. *University of California Publications in Linguistics* 34. Berkeley.

Johnson, Alfred E.
1960      The Place of the Trincheras Culture of Northern Sonora in Southwestern Archaeology. (Unpublished M.A. Thesis in Anthropology, University of Arizona, Tucson.)

———
1963      The Trincheras Culture of Northern Sonora. *American Antiquity* 29(2):174-186.

———
1964      Archaeological Excavations in Hohokam Sites of Southern Arizona. *American Antiquity* 30(2):145-161.

———
1965      The Development of the Western Pueblo Culture. (Unpublished Ph.D. Dissertation in Anthropology, University of Arizona, Tucson.)

———
1966      Archaeology of Sonora, Mexico.  Pp. 26-37 in *Archaeological Frontiers and External Connections.*  Gordon F. Ekholm and Gordon R. Willey, eds.  Handbook of Middle American Indians.  Robert Wauchope, gen. ed. Vol. 4. Austin:  University of Texas Press.

Johnson, Alfred E., and Raymond H. Thompson
1963      The Ringo Site, Southeastern Arizona. *American Antiquity* 28(4):465-481.

Johnson, Alfred E., and William W. Wasley
1966      Archaeological Excavations Near Bylas, Arizona. *The Kiva* 31(4):205-253.

Johnson, Ann (Stofer)
1958      Similarities in Hohokam and Chalchihuites Artifacts. *American Antiquity* 24(2):126-130.

Johnson, Caleb H.
1970      [Letter to the Editor.] *Navajo Times,* February 26.

Johnston, Abraham R., Marcellus B. Edwards, and Philip G. Ferguson
1936      Marching with the Army of the West, 1846-1848.  Ralph P. Bieber, ed. (Southwest Historical Series 4) Glendale, Calif.:  Arthur H. Clark.

Johnston, Francis J., and Patricia H. Johnston
1957      An Indian Trail Complex of the Central Colorado Desert: A Preliminary Survey. *University of California Archaeological Survey Report* 37:24-34.  Berkeley.

Jones, Oakah L., Jr.
1962      Pueblo Indian Auxiliaries in New Mexico, 1763-1821. *New Mexico Historical Review* 37(2):81-109.

———
1966      Pueblo Warriors and Spanish Conquest.  Norman:  University of Oklahoma Press.

Jones, Volney H.
1935      Ceremonial Cigarettes. *Southwestern Monuments Monthly Report Supplement* (October):287-291.  Coolidge, Ariz.

———
1950      The Establishment of the Hopi Reservation, and Some Later Developments Concerning Hopi Lands. *Plateau* 23(2):17-25.

Jones, Volney H., and Elizabeth Ann Morris
1960      A Seventh-century Record of Tobacco Utilization in Arizona. *El Palacio* 67(4):115-117.

Jorde, Lynn B.
1977      Precipitation Cycles and Cultural Buffering in the Prehistoric Southwest.  Pp. 385-396 in For Theory Building in Archaeology: Essays on Faunal Remains, Aquatic Resources, Spatial Analysis, and Systemic Modeling.  Lewis Binford, ed. New York:  Academic Press.

Josephy, Alvin M., Jr., ed.
1961      The American Heritage Book of Indians.  Narrative by William Brandon.  New York:  American Heritage Publishing Company.

———
1971      Murder of the Southwest.  Pp. 3-9 in Myths and Technofantasies.  Santa Fe:  Black Mesa Defense.

Judd, Neil M.
1922      Archeological Investigations at Pueblo Bonito, New Mexico. *Smithsonian Miscellaneous Collections* 72(15):106-117. Washington.

———
1924      Two Chaco Canyon Pit Houses.  Pp. 399-413 in *Annual Report of the Smithsonian Institution for the Year 1922.* Washington.

———
1926      Archeological Observations North of the Rio Colorado. *Bureau of American Ethnology Bulletin* 82. Washington.

———
1930      The Excavation and Repair of Betatakin. *Proceedings of the United States National Museum* 77(5). Washington.

———
1940      Progress in the Southwest.  Pp. 417-444 in Essays in Historical Anthropology of North America. *Smithsonian Miscellaneous Collections* 100. Washington.

———
1954      The Material Culture of Pueblo Bonito. *Smithsonian Miscellaneous Collections* 124. Washington.

———
1959      Pueblo del Arroyo, Chaco Canyon, New Mexico. *Smithsonian Miscellaneous Collections* 38(1). Washington.

———
1964      The Architecture of Pueblo Bonito. *Smithsonian Miscellaneous Collections* 147(1). Washington.

Judge, W. James
1974      The Excavation of Tijeras Pueblo, 1971-1973: Preliminary Report Cibola National Forest, New Mexico. (Archaeological Report 3) Albuquerque:  U.S.D.A. Forest Service, Southwestern Regional Office.

———
1976      The Development of a Complex Cultural Ecosystem in the Chaco Basin, New Mexico. (Manuscript on File at the Chaco Center, National Park Service, University of New Mexico, Albuquerque.)

Kabotie, Fred
1977      Fred Kabotie, Hopi Indian Artist:  An Autobiography Told with Bill Belknap.  Flagstaff:  Museum of Northern Arizona.

Kalectaca, Milo
1978      Lessons in Hopi.  Ronald W. Langacker, ed.  Tucson: University of Arizona Press.

Kaplan, Bert
1954      A Study of Rorschach Responses in Four Cultures. *Papers of the Peabody Museum of American Archaeology and Ethnology, Harvard University* 42(2).  Cambridge, Mass.

Kaplan, Lawrence
1967      Archaeological Phaseolus from Tehuacan.  Pp. 201-211 in *Environment and Subsistence.*  Douglas S. Byers, ed. The Prehistory of the Tehuacan Valley.  Vol. 1.  Austin and London:  The University of Texas Press.

Kappler, Charles J., comp.
1904-1941   Indian Affairs:  Laws and Treaties.  5 vols.  Washington: U.S. Government Printing Office.  (Reprinted:  AMS Press, New York, 1971.)

Kate, Herman F.C. ten, Jr.
1885   Reizen en Onderzoekingen in Noord-Amerika.  (Travels and Researches in North America)  Leiden, The Netherlands:  E.J. Brill.

1892   Somatological Observations on Indians of the Southwest. *Journal of American Ethnology and Archeology* 3:117-144.

Kayser, D.W., and G.H. Ewing
1971   Salvage Archaeology in the Galisteo Dam and Reservoir Area, New Mexico.  (Manuscript in Laboratory of Anthropology, Museum of New Mexico, Santa Fe.)

Kearney, Thomas H., Robert H. Peebles, John T. Howell, and Elizabeth McClintock
1960   Arizona Flora.  2d ed.  Berkeley and Los Angeles:  University of California Press.

Keleher, William A.
1952   Turmoil in New Mexico, 1846-1868.  Santa Fe, N.M.: Rydal Press.

1964   Maxwell Land Grant:  A New Mexico Item [1942].  New York:  Argosy-Antiquarian.

Keller, Donald R., and Suzanne M. Wilson
1976   New Light on the Tolchaco Problem. *The Kiva* 41(3-4):225-239.

Kelley, J. Charles
1952   Factors Involved in the Abandonment of Certain Peripheral Southwestern Settlements. *American Anthropologist* 54(3):356-387.

1955   Juan Sabeata and Diffusion in Aboriginal Texas. *American Anthropologist* 57(5):981-995.

1956   Settlement Patterns in North-central Mexico.  Pp. 128-139 in Prehistoric Settlement Patterns in the New World. Gordon R. Willey, ed. *Viking Fund Publications in Anthropology* 23.  New York.

1960   North Mexico and the Correlation of Meso-American and Southwestern Cultural Sequences.  Pp. 566-573 in Selected Papers of the 5th International Congress of Anthropological and Ethnological Sciences.  Philadelphia.

1966   Mesoamerica and the Southwestern United States.  Pp. 95-110 in *Archaeological Frontiers and External Connections.*  Gordon F. Ekholm and Gordon R. Willey, eds. Handbook of Middle American Indians.  Robert Wauchope, gen. ed. Vol. 4.  Austin:  University of Texas Press.

1971   Archaeology of the Northern Frontier:  Zacatecas and Durango.  Pp. 768-801 in *Archaeology of Northern Mesoamerica.*  Pt. 2.  Gordon F. Ekholm and Ignacio Bernal, eds. Handbook of Middle American Indians.  Robert Wauchope, gen. ed. Vol. 11.  Austin:  University of Texas Press.

Kelley, J. Charles, and Ellen Abbott
1966   The Cultural Sequence on the North Central Frontier of Mesoamerica.  Pp. 325-344 in Arqueología de Mesoamerica.  A. Guy Stresser-Péan, ed. *Proceedings of the 36th International Congress of Americanists* Vol. 1.  Seville, Spain, 1964.

Kelley, J. Charles, and Ellen A. Kelley
1971   An Introduction to the Ceramics of the Chalchihuites Culture of Zacatecas and Durango, Mexico.  Pt. 1:  The Decorated Wares.  (Mesoamerican Studies 5)  Carbondale:  Southern Illinois University and Museum..

1975   An Alternative Hypothesis for the Explanation of Anasazi Culture History.  Pp. 178-223 in Collected Papers in Honor of Florence Hawley Ellis.  Theodore Frisbie, ed. *Papers of the Archaeological Society of New Mexico* 2.  Albuquerque.

Kelley, J. Charles, and Howard D. Winters
1960   A Revision of the Archaeological Sequence in Sinaloa, Mexico. *American Antiquity* 25(4):547-561.

Kelly, Henry W.
1940   Franciscan Missions of New Mexico, 1740-1760. *New Mexico Historical Review* 15(4):345-368.

1941   Franciscan Missions of New Mexico, 1740-1760. *New Mexico Historical Review* 16(2):148-183.

Kelly, Isabel (Truesdell)
1938   Excavations at Chametla, Sinaloa. *Ibero-Americana* 14:1-107.  Berkeley, Calif..

1945   Excavations at Culiacán, Sinaloa. *Ibero-Americana* 25:1-186.  Berkeley, Calif.

1961   The Hodges Site:  Pottery.  Revised by James E. Officer. (Manuscript in the Arizona State Museum Library, University of Arizona, Tucson.)

Kelly, Lawrence C.
1968   The Navajo Indians and Federal Indian Policy, 1900-1935.  Tucson:  University of Arizona Press.

Kennard, Edward A.
1963   Linguistic Acculturation in Hopi. *International Journal of American Linguistics* 29(1):36-41.

1965   Post-war Economic Changes Among the Hopi.  Pp. 25-32 in Essays in Economic Anthropology.  (Proceedings of the 1965 Annual Spring Meeting of the American Ethnological Society.  Lexington, Ky.)  Seattle:  University of Washington Press.

1972   Metaphor and Magic:  Key Concepts in Hopi Culture and Their Linguistic Forms.  Pp. 468-473 in Studies in Linguistics in Honor of George L. Trager.  M. Estellie Smith, ed.  (Janua Linguarum Series Maior 52)  The Hague: Mouton.

Kennard, Edward A., and Edwin Earle
1938   Hopi Kachinas.  New York:  J.J. Augustin.

Kenner, Charles L.
1969   A History of New Mexican-Plains Indian Relations.  Norman:  University of Oklahoma Press.

Kent, Kate (Peck)
1940   The Braiding of a Hopi Wedding Sash. *Plateau* 12(3):46-52.

1957   The Cultivation and Weaving of Cotton in the Prehistoric Southwestern United States. *Transactions of the American Philosophical Society* 47(3).  Philadelphia.

1976   Pueblo and Navajo Weaving Traditions and the Western World.  Pp. 85-101 in Ethnic and Tourist Arts:  Cultural Expressions from the Fourth World.  Nelson H.H. Graburn, ed. Berkeley, Los Angeles, and London:  University of California Press.

Keur, Dorothy L.
1941   Big Bead Mesa:  An Archaeological Study of Navaho Acculturation, 1745-1812. *Memoirs of the Society for American Archaeology* 1.  Menasha, Wis.

Kewanwytewa, Jim, and Katharine Bartlett
1946   Hopi Moccasin Making. *Plateau* 19(2):21-28.

Kidder, Alfred V.
1915   Pottery of the Pajarito Plateau and of Some Adjacent Regions in New Mexico. *Memoirs of the American Anthropological Association* 2(6):407-462.  Menasha, Wis.

1917 Prehistoric Cultures of the San Juan Drainage. Pp. 108-113 in *Proceedings of the 19th International Congress of Americanists.* Washington, 1917.

1924 An Introduction to the Study of Southwestern Archaeology, with a Preliminary Account of the Excavations at Pecos. (Papers of the Southwestern Expedition 1) New Haven, Conn.: Published for the Phillips Academy by Yale University Press. (Reprinted in 1962.)

1926 Early Pecos Ruins on the Forked Lightning Ranch. *Archaeological Institute of America. Papers of the School of American Research* n.s. 16. Santa Fe.

1927 Southwestern Archeological Conference. *Science* 66(1716):489-491.

1931-1936 The Pottery of Pecos. 2 vols. (Papers of the Southwestern Expedition 7) New Haven, Conn.: Published for Phillips Academy by Yale University Press.

1932 The Artifacts of Pecos. (Papers of the Southwestern Expedition 6) New Haven, Conn.: Published for Phillips Academy by Yale University Press.

1936 Speculations on New World Prehistory. Pp. 143-152 in Essays in Anthropology Presented to Alfred L. Kroeber. Robert H. Lowie, ed. Berkeley: University of California Press.

1958 Pecos, New Mexico: Archaeological Notes. *Papers of the Robert S. Peabody Foundation for Archaeology* 5. Andover, Mass.

1962 An Introduction to the Study of Southwestern Archaeology with a Preliminary Account of the Excavations at Pecos [1924]. New Haven, Conn. and London: Yale University Press.

Kidder, Alfred V., and Samuel J. Guernsey
1919 Archaeological Explorations in Northeastern Arizona. *Bureau of American Ethnology Bulletin* 65. Washington.

Kidder, Alfred V., H.S. Cosgrove, and C.B. Cosgrove
1949 The Pendleton Ruin, Hidalgo County New Mexico. *Contributions to American Anthropology and History 10, Carnegie Institution of Washington Publication* 585:107-152. Washington.

Kidder, Alfred V., Jesse D. Jennings, and Edwin M. Shook
1946 Excavation at Kaminaljuyú, Guatemala. *Carnegie Institution of Washington Publication* 561. Washington.

Kiersch, George
1955-1956 Mineral Resources, Navajo-Hopi Indian Reservations, Arizona-Utah; Geology, Evaluation and Uses. 3 vols. Tucson: University of Arizona Press.

Kino, Eusebio F.
1919 Kino's Historical Memoir of Pimeria Alta: A Contemporary Account of the Beginnings of California, Sonora, and Arizona, by Father Eusebio Francisco Kino, S.J., a Pioneer Missionary Explorer, Cartographer, and Ranchman, 1683-1716. Herbert E. Bolton, ed. Cleveland: Arthur H. Clark.

Kirchhoff, Paul
1954 Gatherers and Farmers in the Greater Southwest: A Problem in Classification. *American Anthropologist* 56(4):529-550.

Kirkpatrick, David T.
1976 Archaeological Investigations in the Cimarron District, Northeastern New Mexico: 1929-1975. *Awanyu* 4(3):6-15.

Kirkpatrick, David T., and Richard I. Ford
1977 Basketmaker Food Plants from the Cimarron District, Northeastern New Mexico. *The Kiva* 42(3-4):257-269.

Klíma, Bohuslav
1954 Paleolithic Huts at Dolní Věstonice, Czechoslovakia. *Antiquity* 28(109):4-14.

Kluckhohn, Clyde
1941 Patterning as Exemplified in Navaho Culture. Pp. 109-130 in Language, Culture, and Personality: Essays in Memory of Edward Sapir. Leslie Spier, A. Irving Hallowell and Stanley S. Newman, eds. Menasha, Wis.: Sapir Memorial Publication Fund. (Reprinted: University of Utah Press, Salt Lake City, 1960.)

1942 Myths and Rituals: A General Theory. *Harvard Theological Review* 35(1):45-79.

1944 Navaho Witchcraft. *Papers of the Peabody Museum of American Archaeology and Ethnology, Harvard University* 22(2). Cambridge, Mass.

1951 Values and Value Orientations in the Theory of Action: An Exploration in Definition and Classification. Pp. 88-433 in Toward a General Theory of Action. Talcott Parsons and Edward Shils, eds. Cambridge, Mass.: Harvard University Press.

1954 Southwestern Studies of Culture and Personality. *American Anthropologist* 56(4):685-697.

Kluckhohn, Clyde, and Dorothea C. Leighton
1946 The Navaho. Cambridge, Mass.: Harvard University Press.

Kluckhohn, Clyde, and Paul Reiter, eds.
1939 Preliminary Report on the 1937 Excavations, Bc 50-51, Chaco Canyon, New Mexico with Some Distributional Analyses. *Anthropological Series 3(2), University of New Mexico Bulletin* 345. Santa Fe.

Kluckhohn, Clyde, and Janine C. Rosenzweig
1949 Two Navaho Children Over a Five-year Period. *American Journal of Orthopsychiatry* 19(2):266-278.

Kluckhohn, Clyde, and Leland C. Wyman
1940 An Introduction to Navaho Chant Practice: With an Account of the Behavior Observed in Four Chants. *Memoirs of the American Anthropological Association* 53. Menasha, Wis.

Kluckhohn, Florence R., and Fred L. Strodtbeck
1961 Variations in Value Orientations. Evanston, Ill. and Elmsford, N.Y.: Row, Peterson.

Kongäs, Elli-Kaija, and Pierre Maranda
1962 Structural Models in Folklore. *Midwest Folklore* 12:133-193.

Krauss, Michael E.
1964 Proto-Athapaskan-Eyak and the Problem of Na-Dene, I: The Phonology. *International Journal of American Linguistics* 30(2):118-131.

1965 Proto-Athapaskan-Eyak and the Problem of Na-Dene, II: Morphology. *International Journal of American Linguistics* 31(1):18-28.

1973 Na-Dene. Pp. 903-978 in *Linguistics in North America.* Current Trends in Linguistics. Thomas A. Sebeok, ed. Vol. 10. The Hague, Paris: Mouton.

[1978] Na-Dene and Eskimo. In The Languages of Native America: An Historical and Comparative Assessment. Lyle Campbell and Marianne Mithun, eds. Austin: University of Texas Press. In Press.

Krieger, Alex D.
1946 Culture Complexes and Chronology in Northern Texas, with Extension of Puebloan Datings to the Mississippi Valley. *University of Texas Publication* 4640. Austin.

1947 The Eastward Extension of Puebloan Datings Toward Cultures of the Mississippi Valley. *American Antiquity* 12(3):141-148.

1962      The Earliest Cultures in the Western United States. *American Antiquity* 28(2):138-143.

Kroeber, Alfred L.
1907      Shoshonean Dialects of California. *University of California Publications in American Archaeology and Ethnology* 4(3):65-165. Berkeley.

1915      Serian, Tequistlatecan, and Hokan. *University of California Publications in American Archaeology and Ethnology* 11(4):279-290. Berkeley.

1916      Thoughts on Zuñi Religion. Pp. 269-277 in Holmes Anniversary Volume: Anthropological Essays Presented to William Henry Holmes in Honor of His Seventieth Birthday. Washington: J.W. Bryan Press.

1916a      Zuñi Potsherds. *Anthropological Papers of the American Museum of Natural History* 18(1):1-37. New York.

1916b      The Speech of a Zuñi Child. *American Anthropologist* 18(4):529-534.

1919      Zuñi Kin and Clan. *Anthropological Papers of the American Museum of Natural History* 18(2):39-204. New York.

1925      Handbook of the Indians of California. *Bureau of American Ethnology Bulletin* 78. Washington.

1928      Native Culture in the Southwest. *University of California Publications in American Archaeology and Ethnology* 23(9):375-398. Berkeley.

1934      Uto-Aztecan Languages of Mexico. *Ibero-Americana* 8:1-27. Berkeley, Calif.

————, ed.
1935      Walapai Ethnography. *Memoirs of the American Anthropological Association* 42. Menasha, Wis.

1939      Cultural and Natural Areas of Native North America. *University of California Publications in American Archaeology and Ethnology* 38. Berkeley.

1943      Elsie Clews Parsons. *American Anthropologist* 45(2):252-255.

1943a      Classification of the Yuman Languages. *University of California Publications in Linguistics* 1(3):21-40. Berkeley.

Kroeber, Alfred L., and Michael J. Harner
1955      Mohave Pottery. *University of California Anthropological Records* 16(1). Berkeley.

Kroskrity, Paul V.
1977      Aspects of Arizona Tewa Language Structure and Language Use. (Unpublished Ph.D. Dissertation in Anthropology, Indiana University, Bloomington.)

Kubler, George A.
1940      Religious Architecture of New Mexico in the Colonial Period and Since the American Occupation. Colorado Springs: The Taylor Museum.

Kuhman, Gary L.
1968      A Preliminary Report on the Clinging Cactus Site, Colfax County, New Mexico. (Manuscript in Anthropology Laboratories, Northern Illinois University, DeKalb.)

Kunitz, Stephen J.
1970      Disease and Death Among the Anasazi: Some Notes on Southwestern Paleoepidemiology. *El Palacio* 76(3):17-22.

1972      [Hopi Population.] (Manuscript in Library of the Museum of Northern Arizona, Flagstaff.)

1973      Demographic Change Among the Hopi and Navajo Indians. *Lake Powell Research Project Bulletin* 2. Los Angeles, Calif.

1974      Factors Influencing Recent Navajo and Hopi Population Changes. *Human Organization* 33(1):7-16.

Kunitz, Stephen J., and Robert C. Euler
1972      Aspects of Southwestern Paleoepidemiology. *Prescott College Anthropological Report* 2. Prescott, Ariz.

Kurath, Gertrude (Prokosch), with Antonio Garcia
1969      Music and Dance of the Tewa Pueblos. *Museum of New Mexico Research Record* 8. Santa Fe.

Kurtz, Ronald J.
1969      Headmen and War Chanters: Role Theory and the Early Canyoncito Navaho. *Ethnohistory* 16(1):83-111.

Ladd, Edmund J.
1963      Zuni Ethno-ornithology. (Unpublished M.A. Thesis in Anthropology, University of New Mexico, Albuquerque.)

Ladd, John
1957      The Structure of a Moral Code: A Philosophical Analysis of Ethical Discourse Applied to the Ethics of the Navaho Indians. Cambridge, Mass.: Harvard University Press.

Lafora, Nicolás de
1958      The Frontiers of New Spain; Nicolás de Lafora's Description, 1766-1768. Lawrence Kinnaird, ed. and trans. (Quivira Society Publications 13) Berkeley, Calif.: The Quivira Society.

Laird, W. David
1977      Hopi Bibliography. Tucson: University of Arizona Press.

Lamar, Howard R.
1970      The Far Southwest, 1846-1912: A Territorial History. New York: W.W. Norton.

Lamb, Sydney M.
1958      Linguistic Prehistory in the Great Basin. *International Journal of American Linguistics* 24(2):95-100.

1964      The Classification of the Uto-Aztecan Languages: A Historical Survey. Pp. 106-125 in Studies in Californian Linguistics. William Bright, ed. *University of California Publications in Linguistics* 34. Berkeley.

Lambert, Marjorie F.
1942-1970      [Fieldnotes on Pojoaque, 1942, 1959, 1970.] (Manuscript in Lambert's Possession.)

1954      Paa-ko, Archaeological Chronicle of an Indian Village in North Central New Mexico. *Monographs of the School of American Research* 19. Santa Fe.

Lamphere, Louise
1969      Symbolic Elements in Navajo Ritual. *Southwestern Journal of Anthropology* 25(3):279-305.

1970      Ceremonial Co-operation and Networks: A Reanalysis of the Navajo Outfit. *Man* n.s. 5(1):39-59.

1971      The Navajo Cultural System: An Analysis of Concepts of Cooperation and Autonomy and Their Relation to Gossip and Witchcraft. Pp. 91-114 in Apachean Culture History and Ethnology. Keith H. Basso and Morris E. Opler, eds. *Anthropological Papers of the University of Arizona* 21. Tucson.

Lancaster, James A., Jean M. Pinkley, Philip F. Van Cleave, and Don Watson
1954      Archaeological Excavations in Mesa Verde National Park, Colorado, 1950. *U.S. National Park Service Archaeological Research Series* 2. Washington.

Landar, Herbert
1968      The Karankawa Invasion of Texas. *International Journal of American Linguistics* 34(4):242-258.

Lang, Richard W.
1977      An Archaeological Survey of Certain State Lands Within the Drainages of Arroyo de la Vega de los Tanos and Tonque, Sandoval County, New Mexico. Santa Fe: The

School of American Research Contract Archaeology Program.

1977a    Archeological Survey of the Upper San Cristobal Arroyo Drainage, Galisteo Basin, Santa Fe County, New Mexico. Santa Fe: The School of American Research Contract Archaeology Program.

Lange, Charles H.
1951    Kings' Day Ceremonies at a Rio Grande Pueblo, January 6, 1940. *El Palacio* 58(1):398-406.

1952    Problems in Acculturation at Cochiti Pueblo, New Mexico. *Texas Journal of Science* 4(4):477-481.

1952a    San Juan's Day at Cochiti Pueblo, New Mexico, 1894 and 1947. *El Palacio* 59(6):175-182.

1953    Culture Change as Revealed in Cochiti Pueblo Hunting Customs. *Texas Journal of Science* 5(2):178-184.

1953a    The Role of Economics in Cochiti Pueblo Culture Change. *American Anthropologist* 55(5):674-694.

1953b    A Reappraisal of Evidence of Plains Influences Among the Rio Grande Pueblos. *Southwestern Journal of Anthropology* 9(2):212-230.

1957    *Tablita*, or Corn, Dances of the Rio Grande Pueblo Indians. *Texas Journal of Science* 9(1):59-74.

1957a    Plains-southwestern Inter-cultural Relations During the Historic Period. *Ethnohistory* 4(2):150-173.

1958    The Keresan Component of Southwestern Pueblo Culture. *Southwestern Journal of Anthropology* 14(1):34-50.

1958a    Recent Developments in Culture Change at Cochiti Pueblo, New Mexico. *Texas Journal of Science* 10(4):399-404.

1959    Cochití: A New Mexico Pueblo, Past and Present. Austin: University of Texas Press. (Reprinted: Southern Illinois University Press, Carbondale, 1968.)

1960    Forces of Change and Tradition at Cochití Pueblo, New Mexico. *Texas Quarterly* 3(3):63-72.

1967    Historical Reconstruction: Problems in Cochiti Culture History. Pp. 69-100 in American Historical Anthropology: Essays in Honor of Leslie Spier. Carroll L. Riley and Walter W. Taylor, eds. Carbondale: Southern Illinois University Press.

1968    The Cochiti Dam Archaeological Salvage Project, Pt. 1: Report on the 1963 Season. Charles H. Lange, ed. *Museum of New Mexico Research Record* 6. Santa Fe.

Lanning, Edward P.
1963    Archaeology of the Rose Spring Site, INY-372. *University of California Publications in American Archaeology and Ethnology* 49(3):237-336. Berkeley.

Laski, Vera
1959    Seeking Life. *Memoirs of the American Folklore Society* 50. Philadelphia.

Lasswell, Harold D.
1935    Collective Autism as a Consequence of Culture Contact: Notes on Religious Training and the Peyote Cult at Taos. *Zeitschrift für Sozialforschung* 4(2):232-246. Frankfurt, Germany.

Layhe, Robert
1977    A Multivariate Approach for Estimating Prehistoric Population Change, Black Mesa, Northeastern Arizona. (Unpublished Master Thesis in Anthropology, Southern Illinois University, Carbondale.)

Layhe, Robert, Steven Sessions, Charles Miksicek, and Stephen Plog
1976    The Black Mesa Archaeological Project: A Preliminary Report for the 1975 Season. *Southern Illinois University Museum, Archaeological Service Report* 48. Carbondale.

Leach, Edmund R.
1968    Introduction. Pp. 1-6 in Dialectic in Practical Religion. Edmund R. Leach, ed. (Cambridge Papers in Social Anthropology 5) London: Cambridge University Press.

Leap, William L.
1970    The Language of Isleta, New Mexico. (Unpublished Ph.D. Dissertation in Anthropology, Southern Methodist University, Dallas.)

1970a    Tiwa Noun Class Semology: A Historical View. *Anthropological Linguistics* 12(2):38-45.

1971    Who Were the Piro? *Anthropological Linguistics* 13(7):321-330.

Lebel, Robert
1959    Marcel Duchamp. George H. Hamilton, trans. London: Trianon Press; New York: Grove Press.

LeBlanc, Steven A.
1978    Settlement Patterns in the El Morro Valley, New Mexico. Pp. 45-52 in Investigations of the Southwestern Anthropological Research Group. Robert C. Euler and George J. Gumerman, eds. Flagstaff: Museum of Northern Arizona.

Lee, Douglas H.K.
1963    Human Factors in Desert Development. Pp. 339-367 in Aridity and Man: The Challenge of the Arid Lands in the United States. Carle Hodge, ed. *American Association for the Advancement of Science Publication* 74. Washington.

Lee, Richard B.
1968    What Hunters Do for a Living, or How to Make Out on Scarce Resources. Pp. 30-48 in Man the Hunter. Richard B. Lee and Irven DeVore, eds. Chicago: Aldine.

1969    !Kung Bushman Subsistence: An Input-output Analysis. Pp. 47- 79 in Environment and Cultural Behavior: Ecological Studies in Cultural Anthropology. Andrew P. Vayda, ed. Garden City, N.Y.: Published for the American Museum of Natural History by The Natural History Press.

Lee, Richard B., and Irven DeVore, eds.
1968    Symposium on Man the Hunter, University of Chicago, 1966. Chicago: Aldine.

Le Free, Betty
1975    Santa Clara Pottery Today. Albuquerque: University of New Mexico Press.

Lehmer, Donald J.
1948    The Jornada Branch of the Mogollon. *Social Science Bulletin 17, University of Arizona Bulletin* 19(2). Tucson.

Leiby, Austin N.
1973    The Marmon Batallion and the Apache Campaign of 1885. Pp. 211-230 in The Changing Ways of Southwestern Indians: A Historic Perspective. Albert H. Schroeder, ed. (Westerners Brand Book 3) Glorieta, N.M.: Rio Grande Press.

Leighton, Alexander H., and Dorothea C. Leighton
1949    Gregorio, the Hand-trembler: A Psychobiological Personality Study of a Navaho Indian. *Papers of the Peabody Museum of American Archaeology and Ethnology, Harvard University* 40(1). Cambridge, Mass.

Leighton, Dorothea C., and John Adair
1966    People of the Middle Place: A Study of the Zuñi Indians. New Haven, Conn.: Human Relations Area Files Press.

Lekson, Stephen, James L. Ross, and James E. Fitting
1971    The Stailey Cave Collection. *Southwestern New Mexico Research Report* 6. Case Western Reserve University, Department of Anthropology. Cleveland.

Lenneberg, Eric H., and John M. Roberts
1956    The Language of Experience: A Study in Methodology. *Indiana University Publications in Anthropology and Linguistics, Memoir* 13. Bloomington.

Lévi-Strauss, Claude
1949    Les Structures élémentaires de la parenté. Paris: Presses Universitaires de France.

1963    Structural Anthropology. New York: Basic Books.

1965    The Future of Kinship Studies: The Huxley Memorial Lecture 1965. Pp. 13-22 in *Proceedings of the Royal Anthropological Institute of Great Britain and Ireland for 1965.* London.

1969    The Raw and the Cooked. John and Dorothea Weightman, eds. New York: Harper and Row.

Levy, Jerrold E., and Stephen J. Kunitz
1971    Indian Reservations, Anomie, and Social Pathologies. *Southwestern Journal of Anthropology* 27(2):97-128.

1974    Indian Drinking: Navajo Practices and Anglo-American Theories. New York: John Wiley.

Li, An-che
1937    Zuni: Some Observations and Queries. *American Anthropologist* 39(1):62-76.

Lightfoot, Kent G.
1978    Food Redistribution in the Prehistoric Southwest. (Paper Presented at the 43d Annual Meeting of the Society for American Archaeology, Tucson.)

Lindsay, Alexander J., Jr.
1969    The Tsegi Phase of the Kayenta Cultural Tradition in Northeastern Arizona. (Unpublished Ph.D. Dissertation in Anthropology, University of Arizona, Tucson.)

Lindsay, Alexander J., Jr., J. Richard Ambler, Mary Ann Stein, and Philip M. Hobler
1969    Survey and Excavations North and East of Navajo Mountain, Utah, 1959-1962. *Museum of Northern Arizona Bulletin 45, Glen Canyon Series* 8. Flagstaff.

Linné, Sigvald
1942    Mexican Highland Cultures: Archaeological Researches at Teotihuacan, Calpulalpan and Chalchicomula in 1934/35. *Ethnological Museum of Sweden Publication* 7. Stockholm.

Linton, Ralph
1944    Nomad Raids and Fortified Pueblos. *American Antiquity* 10(1):28-32.

Lipe, William D.
1967    Anasazi Culture and Its Relationship to the Environment in the Red Rock Plateau Region, Southeastern Utah. (Unpublished Ph.D. Dissertation in Anthropology, Yale University, New Haven, Conn.)

1970    Anasazi Communities in the Red Rock Plateau, Southeastern Utah. Pp. 84-139 in Reconstructing Prehistoric Pueblo Societies. William A. Longacre, ed. Albuquerque: University of New Mexico Press.

Lipe, William D., and R.G. Matson
1975    Archaeology and Alluvium in the Grand Gulch-Cedar Mesa Area, Southeastern Utah. Pp. 67-71 in Canyonlands Country. James E. Fassett, ed. (Four Corners Geological Society Guidebook, 8th Field Conference, Canyonlands, September 22-25, 1975) Durango, Colo.: Four Corners Geological Society.

Lister, Robert H.
1953    The Stemmed, Indented Base Point: A Possible Horizon Marker. *American Antiquity* 18(3):264-265.

1958    Archaeological Excavations in the Northern Sierra Madre Occidental, Chihuahua and Sonora, Mexico. *University of Colorado Studies, Series in Anthropology* 7. Boulder.

1966    Contributions to Mesa Verde Archaeology, III: Site 866, and the Cultural Sequence at Four Villages in the Far View Group, Mesa Verde National Park, Colorado. *University of Colorado Studies, Series in Anthropology* 12. Boulder.

Lister, Robert H., J. Richard Ambler, Florence C. Lister, Lyndon L. Hargrave, and Christy G. Turner, II
1959-1961 The Coombs Site, Parts I, II, and III. *University of Utah Anthropological Papers 41, Glen Canyon Series* 8. Salt Lake City.

Lobeck, Armin K.
1948    Physiographic Diagram of North America. New York: Columbia University, Geographical Press.

Loeffler, Jack
1971    The Shaman's Wisdom. P. 1 in Myths and Technofantasies. Santa Fe: Black Mesa Defense.

Loew, Oscar
1879    Report on the Ruins in New Mexico. Pp. 337-345 in Vol. 7 of Report on U.S. Geographical Surveys West of the 100th Meridian... 7 vols. in 8. Washington: U.S. Government Printing Office.

Longacre, William A.
1966    Changing Patterns of Social Integration: A Prehistoric Example from the American Southwest. *American Anthropologist* 68(1):94-102.

1968    Some Aspects of Prehistoric Society in East-central Arizona. Pp. 89-102 in New Perspectives in Archeology. Sally R. Binford and Lewis R. Binford, eds. Chicago: Aldine.

_____, ed.
1970    Reconstructing Prehistoric Pueblo Societies. Albuquerque: University of New Mexico Press.

1970a   Archaeology as Anthropology: A Case Study. *Anthropological Papers of the University of Arizona* 17. Tucson.

1973    Current Directions in Southwestern Archaeology. *Annual Review of Anthropology* 2:201-219. Palo Alto, Calif.

1976    Paul Sidney Martin, 1899-1974. *American Anthropologist* 78(1):90-92.

Longacre, William A., and Michael W. Graves
1976    Probability Sampling Applied to an Early Multi-component Surface Site in East-central Arizona. *The Kiva* 41(3-4):277-287.

Longacre, William A., and J. Jefferson Reid
1974    The University of Arizona Archaeological Field School at Grasshopper: Eleven Years of Multidisciplinary Research and Teaching. Pp. 3-38 in Behavioral Archaeology at the Grasshopper Ruin. J. Jefferson Reid, ed. *The Kiva* 40:(1-2).

Loomis, Noel M., and Abraham P. Nasatir
1967    Pedro Vial and the Roads to Santa Fe. Norman: University of Oklahoma Press.

Loose, Ann A.
1974    Archeological Excavations Near Arroyo Hondo, Carson National Forest. (Archeological Report 4) Albuquerque: U.S.D.A. Forest Service. Southwestern Region.

López de Llergo, Rita
1959    Principales rasgos geográficos de la república mexicana. Pp. 1-48 in Vol. 1 of Esplendor del México antiguo. 2 vols. Mexico, D.F.: Centro de Investigaciones Antropológicas de México.

Lothrop, Samuel K.
1936    Zacualpa: A Study of Ancient Quiché Artifacts. *Carnegie Institution of Washington Publication* 472. Washington.

Lowie, Robert H.
1929    Notes on Hopi Clans. *Anthropological Papers of the American Museum of Natural History* 30(6):303-360. New York.

655

1929a     Hopi Kinship. *Anthropological Papers of the American Museum of Natural History* 30(7). New York.

Luebben, Ralph A.
1953     Leaf Water Site. Pp. 9-33 in Salvage Archaeology in the Chama Valley, New Mexico. Fred Wendorf, comp. *Monographs of the School of American Research* 17. Santa Fe.

Lumholtz, Karl S.
1902     Unknown Mexico: A Record of Five Years' Exploration Among the Tribes of the Western Sierra Madre; in the Tierra Caliente of Tepic and Jalisco; and Among the Tarascos and Michoacan. 2 vols. New York: C. Scribner and Sons.

Lummis, Charles F.
1894     The Man Who Married the Moon, and Other Pueblo Indian Folk-stories. New York: Century.

1916     A Tramp Across the Continent... [1892.] New York: Scribner.

1925     The Land of Poco Tiempo [1893]. New York: Charles Scribner's Sons.

1925a     Mesa, Cañon and Pueblo: Our Wonderland of the Southwest - its Marvels of Nature - its Pageant of the Earth Building - its Strange Peoples - its Centuried Romance. New York and London: The Century Company.

1968     Bullying the Moqui. Robert Easton and Mackenzie Brown, eds. Flagstaff, Ariz.: Prescott College Press.

Lutes, Eugene
1959     A Marginal Prehistoric Culture of Northeastern New Mexico. *El Palacio* 66(2):59-68.

Lyon, Marcus W., Jr.
1906     Mammal Remains from Two Prehistoric Village Sites in New Mexico and Arizona. *Proceedings of the United States National Museum* 31:647-649. Washington.

Lyons, Thomas R., and Robert K. Hitchcock
1977     Remote Sensing Interpretation of Anasazi Land Route System. Pp. 111-134 in Aerial Remote Sensing Techniques in Archeology. Thomas R. Lyons and Robert K. Hitchcock, eds. (Reports of the Chaco Center 2) Albuquerque: U.S. National Park Service and the University of New Mexico.

McAllister, J. Gilbert
1955     Kiowa-Apache Social Organization. Pp. 99-169 in Social Anthropology of North American Tribes. Fred Eggan, ed. Chicago: University of Chicago Press.

McCluskey, Stephen C.
1977     The Astronomy of the Hopi Indians. *Journal for the History of Astronomy* 8:174-195.

McConville, J. Lawrence
1966     A History of Population in the El Paso-Ciudad Juarez Area. (Unpublished M.A. Thesis in History, University of New Mexico, Albuquerque.)

McCown, B.E.
1945     An Archaeological Survey of San Vicente Lake Bed, San Diego County, California. *American Antiquity* 10(3):255-264.

McGavock, E.H., and Gary W. Levings
1973     Ground Water in the Navajo Sandstone in the Black Mesa Area, Arizona. H.L. James, ed. In Guidebook of Monument Valley and Vicinity: Arizona and Utah. Santa Fe: New Mexico Geological Society.

McGee, WJ
1898     The Seri Indians. Pp. 1-344 in *17th Annual Report of the Bureau of American Ethnology for the Years 1895-1896*. Pt. 1. Washington.

McGehee, Ralph M.
1963     Weather: Complex Causes of Aridity. Pp. 117-143 in Aridity and Man: The Challenge of the Arid Lands in the United States. Carle Hodge and Peter C. Duisberg, eds. *American Association for the Advancement of Science Publication* 74. Washington.

McGilberry, Charles W.
1934     Picuris Pueblo Votes One Hundred Percent Approval of the Wheeler-Howard Bill. *Indians at Work* 2(8):8. Washington.

1935     Indians Build a Community House at Picuris Pueblo. *Indians at Work* 2(13):44. Washington.

1935a     Picuris Community Store. *Indians at Work* 3(5):27-28. Washington.

McGregor, John C.
1937     Winona Village: A 12th Century Settlement with a Ball Court Near Flagstaff. *Museum of Northern Arizona Bulletin* 12. Flagstaff.

1941     Winona and Ridge Ruin, I: Architecture and Material Culture. *Museum of Northern Arizona Bulletin* 18. Flagstaff.

1941a     Southwestern Archaeology. New York: John Wiley and Sons; London: Chapman and Hall.

1951     The Cohonina Culture of Northwestern Arizona. (Museum of Northern Arizona Contribution 178) Urbana: University of Illinois Press.

1955     A Sinagua Kiva. *Plateau* 27(3):11-17.

1965     Southwestern Archaeology. 2d ed. Urbana: University of Illinois Press.

McKern, W.C.
1939     The Midwestern Taxonomic Method as an Aid to Archaeological Culture Study. *American Antiquity* 4(4):301-313.

Mackey, James C., and Sally J. Holbrook
1978     Environmental Reconstruction and the Abandonment of the Largo-Gallina Area, New Mexico. *Journal of Field Archaeology* 5(1):29-49.

McLendon, Sally
1964     Northern Hokan (B) and (C): A Comparison of Eastern Pomo and Yana. Pp. 126-144 in Studies in Californian Linguistics. William Bright, ed. *University of California Publications in Linguistics* 34. Berkeley.

MacNeish, Richard S.
1958     Preliminary Archaeological Investigations in the Sierra de Tamaulipas. *Transactions of the American Philosophical Society* 48(6). Philadelphia.

1964     The Food-gathering and Incipient Agriculture Stage of Prehistoric Middle America. Pp. 413-426 in *Natural Environments and Early Cultures*. Robert C. West, ed. Handbook of Middle American Indians. Robert Wauchope, gen. ed. Vol. 1. Austin: University of Texas Press.

1967     A Summary of the Subsistence. Pp. 290-309 in *Environment and Subsistence*. Douglas S. Byers, ed. The Prehistory of the Tehuacan Valley. Vol. 1. Austin and London: University of Texas Press.

1971     Archaeological Synthesis of the Sierra. Pp. 573-581 in *Archaeology of Northern Mesoamerica*. Pt. 2. Gordon F. Ekholm and Ignacio Bernal, eds. Handbook of Middle American Indians. Robert Wauchope, gen. ed. Vol. 11. Austin: University of Texas Press.

1978     The Science of Archaeology?   North Scituate, Mass.:
         Duxbury Press.

MacNeish, Richard S., Antoinette Nelken-Terner, and Irmgard W.
Johnson
1967     *Non-ceramic Artifacts.*   Douglas S. Byers, ed. The Prehis-
         tory of the Tehuacan Valley. Vol. 2. Austin and London:
         University of Texas Press.

McNitt, Frank
1957     Richard Wetherill: Anasazi. Albuquerque: University of
         New Mexico Press.

1962     The Indian Traders.   Norman:   University of Oklahoma
         Press.

McNutt, Charles H.
1969     Early Puebloan Occupations at Tesuque By-pass and in
         the Upper Rio Grande Valley. *University of Michigan Mu-
         seum of Anthropology, Anthropological Paper* 40. Ann Ar-
         bor.

McNutt, Charles H., and Robert C. Euler
1966     The Red Butte Lithic Sites Near Grand Canyon, Arizona.
         *American Antiquity* 31(3):410-419.

Malde, Harold E.
1964     Environment and Man in Arid America. *Science*
         145(3628):123-129.

Malde, Harold E., and Asher P. Schick
1964     Thorne Cave, Northeastern Utah:   Geology. *American
         Antiquity* 30(1):60-73.

Mangelsdorf, Paul C.
1974     Corn:  Its Origin, Evolution, and Development. Cam-
         bridge, Mass.: Harvard University Press.

Mangelsdorf, Paul C., and Robert H. Lister
1956     Archaeological Evidence on the Evolution of Maize in
         Northwestern Mexico. *Harvard University Botanical Mu-
         seum Leaflet* 17(6):151-178. Cambridge, Mass.

Mangelsdorf, Paul C., and C. Earle Smith, Jr.
1949     New Archaeological Evidence on Evolution in Maize.
         *Harvard University Botanical Museum Leaflet* 13(8):213-
         245. Cambridge, Mass.

Mangelsdorf, Paul C., Richard S. MacNeish, and Walton C. Galinat
1956     Archaeological Evidence on the Diffusion and Evolution
         of Maize in Northeastern Mexico. *Harvard University Bo-
         tanical Museum Leaflet* 17(5):125-150. Cambridge, Mass.

1964     Domestication of Corn. *Science* 143(3606):538-545.

1967     Prehistoric Wild and Cultivated Maize. Pp. 178-200 in
         *Environment and Subsistence.*   Douglas S. Byers, ed. The
         Prehistory of the Tehuacan Valley. Vol. 1. Austin and
         London: University of Texas Press.

Mark, Joan
1976     Frank Hamilton Cushing and an American Science of An-
         thropology. *Perspectives in American History* 10:449-486.

Marquardt, William H.
1974     A Temporal Perspective on Late Prehistoric Societies in
         the Eastern Cibola Area: Factor Analytic Approaches to
         Short-term Chronological Investigation.   (Unpublished
         Ph.D. Dissertation in Anthropology, Washington Univer-
         sity, St. Louis, Mo.)

Marriott, Alice
1948     María: The Potter of San Ildefonso. Norman: University
         of Oklahoma Press.

Martin, Paul S.
1929     The 1928 Archaeological Expedition of the State Histori-
         cal Society of Colorado. *Colorado Magazine* 6(1):1-35.

1940     The SU Site: Excavations at a Mogollon Village, Western
         New Mexico. *Field Museum of Natural History Publication
         476, Anthropological Series* 32(1). Chicago.

1943     The SU Site: Excavations at a Mogollon Village, Western
         New Mexico, Second Season, 1941. *Field Museum of
         Natural History Publication 526, Anthropological Series*
         32(2). Chicago.

1963     The Last 10,000 Years: A Fossil Pollen Record of the
         American Southwest.   Tucson:   University of Arizona
         Press.

1963a    Early Man in Arizona: The Pollen Evidence. *American
         Antiquity* 29(1):67-73.

1967     Hay Hollow Site. *Field Museum of Natural History Bulle-
         tin* 38(5):6-10. Chicago.

1970     Explanation as an Afterthought and as a Goal. Pp. 194-
         201 in Reconstructing Prehistoric Pueblo Societies. Wil-
         liam A. Longacre, ed. Albuquerque: University of New
         Mexico Press.

Martin, Paul S., and Fred T. Plog
1973     The Archaeology of Arizona: A Study of the Southwest
         Region. Garden City, N.Y.:  Doubleday Natural History
         Press.

Martin, Paul S., and John B. Rinaldo
1939     Modified Basket Maker Sites, Ackmen-Lowry Area,
         Southwestern Colorado, 1938. *Fieldiana: Anthropology*
         23(3). Chicago.

1947     The SU Site: Excavations at a Mogollon Village, Western
         New Mexico, Third Season, 1946. *Field Museum of Natu-
         ral History Publication 601, Anthropological Series* 32(3).
         Chicago.

1950     Turkey Foot Ridge Site: A Mogollon Village, Pine Lawn
         Valley, Western New Mexico. *Fieldiana:  Anthropology*
         38(2). Chicago.

1950a    Sites of the Reserve Phase:  Pine Lawn Valley, Western
         New Mexico. *Fieldiana:  Anthropology* 38(3). Chicago.

1951     The Southwestern Co-tradition. *Southwestern Journal of
         Anthropology* 7(3):215-229.

1960     Excavations in the Upper Little Colorado Drainage, East-
         ern Arizona. *Fieldiana: Anthropology* 51(1). Chicago.

1960a    Table Rock Pueblo, Arizona. *Fieldiana:  Anthropology*
         51(2). Chicago.

Martin, Paul S., and James Schoenwetter
1960     Arizona's Oldest Cornfield. *Science* 132(3418):33-34.

Martin, Paul S., Carl Lloyd, and Alexander Spoehr
1938     Archaeological Work in the Ackmen-Lowry Area, South-
         western Colorado, 1937. *Field Museum of Natural History
         Publication 419, Anthropological Series* 23(2):219-304.
         Chicago.

Martin, Paul S., William A. Longacre, and James N. Hill
1967     Chapters in the Prehistory of Eastern Arizona, III. *Fieldi-
         ana: Anthropology* 57. Chicago.

Martin Paul S., George I. Quimby, and Donald Collier
1947     Indians Before Columbus:  Twenty Thousand Years of
         North American History Revealed by Archaeology. Chi-
         cago: University of Chicago Press.

Martin, Paul S., John B. Rinaldo, and Ernst Antevs
1949     Cochise and Mogollon Sites, Pine Lawn Valley, Western
         New Mexico. *Fieldiana: Anthropology* 38(1). Chicago.

Martin, Paul S., John B. Rinaldo, and Eloise R. Barter
1957     Late Mogollon Communities:  Four Sites of the Tularosa
         Phase, Western New Mexico. *Fieldiana:  Anthropology*
         49(1). Chicago.

Martin, Paul S., John B. Rinaldo, and William A. Longacre
1961     Mineral Creek Site and Hooper Ranch Pueblo, Eastern
         Arizona. *Fieldiana: Anthropology* 52. Chicago.

Martin, Paul S., Lawrence Roys, and Gerhardt von Bonin
1936     Lowry Ruin in Southwestern Colorado. *Field Museum of
         Natural History Publication 356, Anthropological Series*
         23(1). Chicago.

Martin, Paul S., John B. Rinaldo, Elaine A. Bluhm, Hugh C. Cutler, and Roger Grange, Jr.
1952      Mogollon Cultural Continuity and Change: The Stratigraphic Analysis of Tularosa and Cordova Caves. *Fieldiana: Anthropology* 40. Chicago.

Martin, Paul S., John B. Rinaldo, William A. Longacre, Constance Cronin, Leslie G. Freeman, Jr., and James Schoenwetter
1962-     Chapters in the Prehistory of Eastern Arizona, I. *Fieldiana: Anthropology* 53. Chicago.

Martin, Paul S., John B. Rinaldo, William A. Longacre, Leslie G. Freeman, Jr., James A. Brown, Richard H. Hevly, and M.E. Cooley
1964      Chapters in the Prehistory of Eastern Arizona, II. *Fieldiana: Anthropology* 55. Chicago.

Martone, Rosalie
1974      The United States and the Betrayal of Indian Water Rights. *Indian Historian* 7(3):3-11.

Masayesva Jeanne, LaVerne
1974      The Relative Clause in Hopi. (Manuscript in Author's Possession; Revised in Hale, Masayesva Jeanne, and Platero 1977, and Masayesva Jeanne 1978.)

1978      Topics in Hopi Syntax. (Unpublished Ph.D. Dissertation in Linguistics, Massachusetts Institute of Technology, Cambridge.)

Mason, J. Alden
1921      The Papago Migration Legend. *Journal of American Folk-Lore* 34(133):254-268.

1927      Mirror of Ancient America. *Pennsylvania University Museum Journal* (June):201-209. Philadelphia.

1936      The Classification of the Sonoran Languages. Pp. 183-198 in Essays in Anthropology Presented to A.L. Kroeber in Celebration of His Sixtieth Birthday, June 11, 1936. Robert H. Lowie, ed. Berkeley: University of California Press.

1940      The Native Languages of Middle America. Pp. 52-87 in The Maya and Their Neighbors. Clarence L. Hay et al., eds. New York, London: D. Appleton-Century.

Mason, Lynn D.
1965      Hopi Domestic Animals: Past and Present. (Manuscript in Library of the Museum of Northern Arizona, Flagstaff.)

Mason, Otis T.
1907      Environment. Pp. 427-430 in Vol. 1 of Handbook of American Indians North of Mexico. Frederick W. Hodge, ed. 2 vols. *Bureau of American Ethnology Bulletin* 30. Washington.

1976      Aboriginal American Indian Basketry: Studies in a Textile Art Without Machinery [1904]. Santa Barbara, Calif.: P. Smith.

Massey, William C.
1959      The Pinto-Gypsum Complex in Baja, California. (Paper Presented at the Society for American Archaeology Meeting, Salt Lake City.)

1966      Archaeology and Ethnohistory of Lower California. Pp. 38-58 in *Archaeological Frontiers and External Connections*. Gordon F. Ekholm and Gordon R. Willey, eds. Handbook of Middle American Indians. Robert Wauchope, gen. ed. Vol. 4. Austin: University of Texas Press.

Mathews, Tom, and Earl H. Neller
1978      Archaic and Basketmaker II Investigations in Chaco Canyon National Monument. (Manuscript on File at the Chaco Center, National Park Service, University of New Mexico, Albuquerque.)

Matson, R.G., and William D. Lipe
1978      Settlement Patterns on Cedar Mesa: Boom and Bust on the Northern Periphery. Pp. 1-12 in Investigations of the Southwestern Anthropological Research Group. Robert C. Euler and George J. Gumerman, eds. Flagstaff: Museum of Northern Arizona.

Matthews, Washington
1887      The Mountain Chant: A Navajo Ceremony. Pp. 379-467 in *5th Annual Report of the Bureau of American Ethnology for the Years 1883-1884*. Washington.

1890      The Gentile System of the Navajo Indians. *Journal of American Folk-Lore* 3(9):89-110.

1902      The Night Chant: A Navaho Ceremony. *Memoirs of the American Museum of Natural History* 6. New York.

Matthews, Washington, J.L. Wortman, and J.S. Billings
1893      Human Bones of the Hemenway Collection in the United States Army Medical Museum. *Memoirs of the National Academy of Sciences* 7(6):141-286. Washington.

Maxwell Museum of Anthropology
1974      Seven Families in Pueblo Pottery. Albuquerque: University of New Mexico, Maxwell Museum of Anthropology.

Mecham, J. Lloyd
1926      The Second Spanish Expedition to New Mexico: An Account of the Chamuscado-Rodriguez Entrada of 1581-1582. *New Mexico Historical Review* 1(3):265-291.

Mehringer, Peter J., Jr.
1965      Late Pleistocene Vegetation in the Mohave Desert of Southern Nevada. *Journal of the Arizona Academy of Science* 3(3):172-188.

1967      Pollen Analysis and the Alluvial Chronology. *The Kiva* 32(3):96-101.

Mehringer, Peter J., Jr., and C. Vance Haynes, Jr.
1965      The Pollen Evidence for the Environment of Early Man and Extinct Mammals at the Lehner Mammoth Site, Southeastern Arizona. *American Antiquity* 31(1):17-23.

Mehringer, Peter J., Jr., Paul S. Martin, and C. Vance Haynes, Jr.
1967      Murray Springs: A Mid Post-glacial Pollen Record from Southern Arizona. *American Journal of Science* 265(9):786-797.

Meighan, Clement W.
1958-1959 Archaeological Resources of Borrego Desert State Park. *Annual Reports of the University of California Archaeological Survey* 1:27-40. Los Angeles.

1960      Prehistoric Copper Objectives from Western Mexico. *Science* 131 (3412):1534.

1971      Archaeology of Sinaloa. Pp. 754-767 in *Archaeology of Northern Mesoamerica*. Pt. 2. Gordon F. Ekholm and Ignacio Bernal, eds. Handbook of Middle American Indians. Robert Wauchope, gen. ed. Vol. 11. Austin: University of Texas Press.

Meline, James F.
1966      Two Thousand Miles on Horseback, Santa Fé and Back: A Summer Tour Through Kansas, Nebraska, Colorado, and New Mexico in the Year 1866 [1868]. Albuquerque: Horn and Wallace.

Mendinueta, Pedro Fermín de
1965      Indian and Mission Affairs in New Mexico, 1773. Marc Simmons, ed. Santa Fe, N.M.: Stagecoach Press.

Mera, Harry P.
1933      A Proposed Revision of the Rio Grande Glaze-paint Sequence. *New Mexico Archaeological Survey, Laboratory of Anthropology Technical Series Bulletin* 5. Santa Fe.

1934      Observations on the Archaeology of the Petrified Forest National Monument. *New Mexico Archaeological Survey, Laboratory of Anthropology Technical Series Bulletin* 7. Santa Fe.

1935      Ceramic Clues to the Prehistory of North Central New Mexico. *New Mexico Archaeological Survey, Laboratory of Anthropology Technical Series Bulletin* 8. Santa Fe.

1938 Some Aspects of the Largo Cultural Phase, Northern New Mexico. *American Antiquity* 3(3):236-243.

1940 Population Changes in the Rio Grande Glaze-paint Area. *New Mexico Archaeological Survey, Laboratory of Anthropology Technical Series Bulletin* 9. Santa Fe.

1943 Pueblo Indian Embroidery. *Memoirs of the Laboratory of Anthropology* 4. Santa Fe.

1943a An Outline of Ceramic Developments in Southern and Southeastern New Mexico. *New Mexico Archaeological Survey, Laboratory of Anthropology Technical Series Bulletin* 11. Santa Fe.

Meyerhoff, Barbara G.
1970 The Deer-Maize-Peyote Symbol Complex Among the Huichol Indians of Mexico. *Anthropological Quarterly* 43(2):64-78.

Mickey, Barbara (Harris)
1956 Acoma Kinship Terms. *Southwestern Journal of Anthropology* 12(3):249-256.

Miller, John P.
1958 Problems of the Pleistocene in Cordilleran North America as Related to Reconstruction of Environmental Changes That Affected Early Man. Pp. 19-49 in Climate and Man in the Southwest. Terah L. Smiley, ed. *University of Arizona Bulletin* 28(4). Tucson.

Miller, Merton L.
1898 Preliminary Study of the Pueblo of Taos, New Mexico. Chicago: University of Chicago Press.

Miller, Wick R.
1959 Some Notes on Acoma Kinship Terminology. *Southwestern Journal of Anthropology* 15(2):179-184.

1959a A Note on Kiowa Linguistic Affiliations. *American Anthropologist* 61(1):102-105.

1961 [Review of] The Sparkman Grammar of Luiseño, by Alfred L. Kroeber and George W. Grace. *Language* 37(1):186-189.

1964 The Shoshonean Languages of Uto-Aztecan. Pp. 145-148 in Studies in Californian Linguistics. William Bright, ed. *University of California Publications in Linguistics* 34. Berkeley.

1965 Acoma Grammar and Texts. *University of California Publications in Linguistics* 40. Berkeley.

1966 Anthropological Linguistics in the Great Basin. Pp. 75-112 in The Current Status of Anthropological Research in the Great Basin: 1964. Warren L. d'Azevedo et al., eds. *Desert Research Institute, Technical Report Series S-H, Social Sciences and Humanities Publication* 1. Reno, Nev.

1967 Uto-Aztecan Cognate Sets. *University of California Publications in Linguistics* 48. Berkeley.

Miller, Wick R., and Irvine Davis
1963 Proto-Keresan Phonology. *International Journal of American Linguistics* 29(4):310-330.

Mills, Jack P., and Vera M. Mills
1969 The Kuykendall Site: A Prehistoric Salado Village in Southeastern Arizona. *El Paso Archaeological Society Special Report for 1967, No.* 6. El Paso, Tex.

Mindeleff, Cosmos
1895 Cliff Ruins of Canyon de Chelly, Arizona. *American Anthropologist* 8(2):153-174.

1896 Casa Grande Ruin. Pp. 289-319 in *13th Annual Report of the Bureau of American Ethnology for the Years 1891-1892*. Washington.

1896a Aboriginal Remains in Verde Valley, Arizona. Pp. 185-261 in *13th Annual Report of the Bureau of American Ethnology for the Years 1891-1892*. Washington.

1897 The Repair of Casa Grande Ruin, Arizona, in 1891. (Extract from the *15th Annual Report of the Bureau of American Ethnology*) Washington: U.S. Government Printing Office.

1897a The Cliff Ruins of Canyon de Chelly, Arizona. Pp. 79-198 in *16th Annual Report of the Bureau of American Ethnology for the Years 1894-1895*. Washington.

1900 Localization of Tusayan Clans. Pp. 635-653 in *19th Annual Report of the Bureau of American Ethnology for the Years 1897-1898*. Pt. 2. Washington.

Mindeleff, Victor
1891 A Study of Pueblo Architecture in Tusayan and Cibola. Pp. 3-228 in *8th Annual Report of the Bureau of American Ethnology for the Years 1886-1887*. Washington.

Minge, Ward A.
1976 Acoma: Pueblo in the Sky. Albuquerque: University of New Mexico Press.

Minnis, Paul E., and Stephen E. Plog
1976 A Study of the Site Specific Distribution of *Agave Parryi* in East Central Arizona. *The Kiva* 41(3-4):299-308.

Mohr, Albert L., and L.L. Sample
1959 San Jose Sites in Southeastern Utah. *El Palacio* 66(4):109-119.

Montgomery, Ross G., Watson Smith, and John O. Brew
1949 Franciscan Awátovi: The Excavation and Conjectural Reconstruction of a 17th Century Spanish Mission Establishment at a Hopi Indian Town in Northeastern Arizona. *Papers of the Peabody Museum of American Archaeology and Ethnology, Harvard University* 36. Cambridge, Mass.

Mooney, James
1897 [Notebook: "Trip 194-5" (Sinecu etc.); Texas Materials Concerning Isleta Pueblo.] (Manuscript No. 1953 in National Anthropological Archives, Smithsonian Institution, Washington.)

1898 Calendar History of the Kiowa Indians. Pp. 129-445 in *17th Annual Report of the Bureau of American Ethnology for the Years 1895-1896*. Pt. 1. Washington.

Moorehead, Warren K.
1906 Explorations in New Mexico. *Phillips Academy, Department of Archaeology Bulletin* 3:33-53. Andover, Mass.

Morgan, Lewis H.
1880 On the Ruins of a Stone Pueblo on the Animas River in New Mexico; With a Ground Plan. *Reports of the Peabody Museum of American Archaeology and Ethnology, Harvard University* 2:536-556. Cambridge, Mass.

Moriarty, James R.
1966 Culture Phase Divisions Suggested by Typological Change Coordinated with Stratigraphically Controlled Radiocarbon Dating at San Diego. *Anthropological Journal of Canada* 4(4):20-30.

Morley, Sylvanus G.
1908 The Excavation of the Cannonball Ruins in Southwestern Colorado. *American Anthropologist* 10(4):596-610.

Morley, Sylvanus G., and Alfred V. Kidder
1917 The Archaeology of McElmo Canyon, Colorado. *El Palacio* 4(4):41-70.

Morris, Donald H.
1969 Red Mountain: An Early Pioneer Period Hohokam Site in the Salt River Valley of Central Arizona. *American Antiquity* 34(1):40-53.

1970    Walnut Creek Village: A Ninth-century Hohokam-Anasazi Settlement in the Mountains of Central Arizona. *American Antiquity* 35(1):49-61.

Morris, Earl H.
1921    Chronology of the San Juan Area. *Proceedings of the National Academy of Sciences* 7:18-22. Washington.

1921a    The House of the Great Kiva at the Aztec Ruin. *Anthropological Papers of the American Museum of Natural History* 26(2). New York.

1925    Exploring in the Canyon of Death: Remains of a People Who Dwelt in Our Southwest at Least 4,000 Years Ago Are Revealed. *National Geographic Magazine* 48(3):263-300.

1938    Mummy Cave. *Natural History* 42(2):127-138. New York.

1939    Archaeological Studies in the La Plata District: Southwestern Colorado and Northwestern New Mexico. *Carnegie Institution of Washington Publication* 519. Washington.

Morris, Earl H., and Robert F. Burgh
1954    Basket Maker II Sites Near Durango, Colorado. *Carnegie Institution of Washington Publication* 604. Washington.

Morris, Elizabeth Ann
1959    Basketmaker Caves in the Prayer Rock District, Northeastern Arizona. (Unpublished Ph.D. Dissertation in Anthropology, University of Arizona, Tucson.)

Morss, Noel
1931    The Ancient Culture of the Fremont River in Utah: Report on the Explorations Under the Claflen-Emerson Fund, 1928-29. *Papers of the Peabody Museum of American Archaeology and Ethnology, Harvard University* 12(3). Cambridge, Mass.

1954    Clay Figurines of the American Southwest: With a Description of the New Pillings Find in Northeastern Utah and a Comparison with Certain Other North American Figurines. *Papers of the Peabody Museum of American Archaeology and Ethnology, Harvard University* 49(1). Cambridge, Mass.

Mueller, James W.
1974    The Use of Sampling in Archaeological Survey. *Memoirs of the Society for American Archaeology* 28. Salt Lake City, Utah.

Mundie, Christine, and Dwight W. Read
1976    Groundstone at Chevelon. Pp. 41-57 in Chevelon Archaeological Research Project. Fred Plog, James Hill, and Dwight Read, eds. *University of California, Department of Anthropology, Archaeological Survey Monograph* 2. Los Angeles.

Murdock, George P.
1949    Social Structure. New York: Macmillan.

Murdock, George P., and Timothy J. O'Leary
1975    Ethnographic Bibliography of North America. 5 vols. New Haven, Conn.: Human Relations Area Files Press.

Nagata, Shuichi
1970    Modern Transformations of Moenkopi Pueblo. *Illinois University Studies in Anthropology* 6. Urbana.

1971    The Reservation Community and the Urban Community: Hopi Indians of Moenkopi. Pp. 114-159 in The American Indian in Urban Society. Jack O. Waddell and O. Michael Watson, eds. Boston: Little, Brown.

Naroll, Raoul
1970    What Have We Learned from Cross-cultural Surveys? *American Anthropologist* 72(6):1227-1288.

Nelson, Nels C.
1914    Pueblo Ruins of the Galisteo Basin, New Mexico. *Anthropological Papers of the American Museum of Natural History* 15(1). New York.

1916    Chronology of the Tano Ruins, New Mexico. *American Anthropologist* 18(2):159-180.

Nequatewa, Edmund
1933    Hopi Courtship and Marriage: Second Mesa. *Museum of Northern Arizona, Museum Note* 5(9):41-54. Flagstaff.

1936    Truth of a Hopi and Other Clan Stories of Shung-opovi. Mary-Russell F. Colton, ed. *Museum of Northern Arizona Bulletin* 8. Flagstaff. (Reprinted: Northland Press, Flagstaff, Ariz., 1967.)

1943    Nampeyo, Famous Hopi Potter. *Plateau* 15(3):40-42.

1967    Truth of a Hopi: Stories Relating to the Origin Myth and Clan Histories of the Hopi. Mary-Russell F. Colton, ed. Flagstaff, Ariz.: Northland Press.

Nesbitt, Paul H.
1938    Starkweather Ruin: A Mogollon-Pueblo Site in the Upper Gila Area of New Mexico, and Affiliative Aspects of the Mogollon Culture. *Logan Museum Publications in Anthropology, Bulletin* 6. Beloit, Wis.

New, Lloyd
1968    Institute of American Indian Arts; Cultural Difference as the Basis for Creative Education. (U.S. Indian Arts and Crafts Board. Native American Arts 1) Washington: U.S. Government Printing Office.

Newhall, Beaumont, and Diana E. Edkins
1974    William H. Jackson. Fort Worth, Tex.: Amon Carter Museum.

Newman, Stanley
1955    Vocabulary Levels: Zuñi Sacred and Slang Usage. *Southwestern Journal of Anthropology* 11(4):345-354.

1958    Zuni Dictionary. *Indiana University Research Center in Anthropology, Folklore, and Linguistics, Publication* 6. Bloomington.

1964    A Comparison of Zuni and California Penutian. *International Journal of American Linguistics* 30(1):1-13.

1965    Zuni Grammar. *University of New Mexico Publications in Anthropology* 14. Albuquerque.

New Mexico State Planning Office
1972    Reconnaissance Survey for Sandía Pueblo. (Manuscript on File, New Mexico State Planning Office, Santa Fe.)

Nordenskiöld, Gustof E.A.
[1893]    The Cliff Dwellers of the Mesa Verde, Southwestern Colorado: Their Pottery and Implements. D. Lloyd Morgan, trans. Stockholm and Chicago: P.A. Norstedt and Söner.

Northern Pueblos Agency
1971    [Population as of January 1, 1971.] (Unpublished Manuscript in Northern Pueblos Agency, Santa Fe.)

1973    [Population Records.] (Unpublished Manuscript in Northern Pueblos Agency, Santa Fe.)

Nusbaum, Jesse L.
1911    The Excavation and Repair of Balcony House, Mesa Verde National Park. *American Journal of Archaeology* 2d ser., Vol. 15:75.

O'Bryan, Deric
1951-1952    The Abandonment of the Northern Pueblos in the Thirteenth Century. Pp. 153-157 in Indian Tribes of Aboriginal America. *Proceedings of the 29th International Congress of Americanists* New York, 1949.

Ocaranza, Fernando
1934    Establecimientos franciscanos en el misterioso reino de Nuevo México. Mexico, D.F.: Privately Printed.

O'Kane, Walter C.
1953      The Hopis: Portrait of a Desert People. Norman: University of Oklahoma Press.

Olguin, John P., and Mary T. Olguin
1976      Isleta - The Pueblo That Roared. *Indian Historian* 9(4):2-13.

Olson, Alan P.
1963      Some Archaeological Problems of Central and Northeastern Arizona. *Plateau* 35(3):93-99.

Opler, Morris E.
1936      The Kinship Systems of the Southern Athapaskan-speaking Tribes. *American Anthropologist* 38(4):620-633.

1936a     A Summary of Jicarilla Apache Culture. *American Anthropologist* 38(2):202-223.

1936b     Some Points of Comparison and Contrast Between the Treatment of Functional Disorders by Apache Shamans and Modern Psychiatric Practice. *American Journal of Psychiatry* 92(6):1371-1387.

1938      Myths and Tales of the Jicarilla Apache Indians. *Memoirs of the American Folklore Society* 31. New York.

1941      An Apache Life-way. Chicago: University of Chicago Press.

1942      Myths and Tales of the Chiricahua Apache Indians. *Memoirs of the American Folklore Society* 37. New York.

1946      Childhood and Youth in Jicarilla Apache Society. *Publications of the Frederick Webb Hodge Anniversary Publication Fund* 5. Los Angeles.

Oppelt, Norman T.
1976      Southwestern Pottery: An Annotated Bibliography and List of Types and Wares. *Occasional Publications in Anthropology of the University of Northern Colorado, Museum of Anthropology Archaeology Series* 7. Greeley.

Orcutt, Janet D.
1974      The Measurement of Prehistoric Population Size. (Unpublished M.A. Thesis in Anthropology, University of California, Los Angeles.)

Orozco y Berra, Manuel
1864      Geografía de las lenguas de México y carta etnográfica de México. Mexico City, D.F.: J.M. Andrade y F. Escalante.

Ortiz, Alfonso
1963-1968  Tewa Traditions. (Unpublished Collection of Stories of Traditional History and Literature in Ortiz's Possession.)

1963-1977  [Unpublished Fieldnotes on San Juan Pueblo.] (Manuscripts in Ortiz's Possession.)

1969      The Tewa World: Space, Time, Being, and Becoming in a Pueblo Society. Chicago: University of Chicago Press.

————, ed.
1972      New Perspectives on the Pueblos. Albuquerque: University of New Mexico Press.

1972a     Ritual Drama and the Pueblo World View. Pp. 135-161 in New Perspectives on the Pueblos. Alfonso Ortiz, ed. Albuquerque: University of New Mexico Press.

1977      Some Concerns Central to the Writing of "Indian" History. *Indian Historian* 10(1):17-22.

Osborn, Douglas, ed.
1965      Contributions of the Wetherill Mesa Archeological Project. *Memoirs of the Society for American Archaeology* 19. Salt Lake City, Utah.

Owens, John G.
1892      Natal Ceremonies of the Hopi Indians. *Journal of American Ethnology and Archaeology* 2(2):161-175.

Pacheco, Joaquín F., and Francisco de Cárdenas y Espejo
1864-1884  Colección de documentos inéditos, relativos al descubrimiento, conquista y organización de las antiguas posesiones españolas de América y Oceania. 42 vols. Madrid.

Page, Gordon B.
1940      Hopi Agricultural Notes. (Manuscript in Soil Conservation Service, U.S. Dept. of Agriculture, Washington.)

1940a     Hopi Land Patterns. *Plateau* 13(2):29-36.

Pailes, Richard A.
1964      An Analysis of the Fitch Site and its Relationship to the Hohokam Classic Period. (Unpublished M.A. Thesis in Archaeology, Arizona State University, Tempe.)

Pandey, Triloki Nath
1967      Factionalism in a Southwestern Pueblo. (Unpublished Ph.D. Dissertation in Anthropology, University of Chicago, Chicago.)

1968      Tribal Council Elections in a Southwestern Pueblo. *Ethnology* 7(1):71-85.

1972      Anthropologists at Zuni. *Proceedings of the American Philosophical Society* 116(4):321-337.

1977      Images of Power in a Southwestern Pueblo. Pp. 195-215 in Anthropology of Power: Ethnographic Studies from Asia, Oceania, and the New World. Raymond D. Fogelson and Richard N. Adams, eds. New York: Academic Press.

Parsons, Elsie (Clews)
1916      The Zuñi A'Doshlě and Suukě. *American Anthropologist* 18(3):338-347.

1917      Notes on Zuni. *Memoirs of the American Anthropological Association* 4(3-4):151-327. Lancaster, Pa.

1919      Increase by Magic: A Zuñi Pattern. *American Anthropologist* 21(3):279-286.

1920      Notes on Ceremonialism at Laguna. *Anthropological Papers of the American Museum of Natural History* 19(4):83-131. New York.

1922      Winter and Summer Dance Series in Zuñi in 1918. *University of California Publications in American Archaeology and Ethnology* 17(3):171-216. Berkeley.

1922a     Contributions to Hopi History: III. Oraibi in 1920. *American Anthropologist* 24(3):283-298.

1923      Notes on San Felipe and Santo Domingo. *American Anthropologist* 25(4):485-494.

1923a     Laguna Genealogies. *Anthropological Papers of the American Museum of Natural History* 19(5):133-292. New York.

1924      The Scalp Ceremonial of Zuni. *Memoirs of the American Anthropological Association* 31. Menasha, Wis.

1924a     Tewa Kin, Clan, and Moiety. *American Anthropologist* 26(3):333-339.

1925      The Pueblo of Jemez. (Papers of the Phillips Academy Southwestern Expedition 3) New Haven, Conn.: Published for the Phillips Academy by Yale University Press.

1925a     A Pueblo Indian Journal, 1920-1921: Introduction and Notes. *Memoirs of the American Anthropological Association* 32. Menasha, Wis.

1926      The Ceremonial Calendar of the Tewa of Arizona. *American Anthropologist* 28(1):209-229.

1926a     Tewa Tales. *Memoirs of the American Folk-Lore Society* 19. New York.

1928      The Laguna Migration to Isleta. *American Anthropologist* 30(4):602-613.

1929      The Social Organization of the Tewa of New Mexico. *Memoirs of the American Anthropological Association* 36. Menasha, Wis.

1929a    Ritual Parallels in Pueblo and Plains Cultures, with a Special Reference to the Pawnee. *American Anthropologist* 31(4):642-654.

1930     Spanish Elements in the Kachina Cult of the Pueblos. Pp. 582-603 in *Proceedings of the 23d International Congress of Americanists*. New York, 1928.

1932     Isleta, New Mexico. Pp. 193-466 in *47th Annual Report of the Bureau of American Ethnology for the Years 1929-1930*. Washington.

1933     Hopi and Zuñi Ceremonialism. *Memoirs of the American Anthropological Association* 39. Menasha, Wis.

1933a    Some Aztec and Pueblo Parallels. *American Anthropologist* 35(4):611-631.

1936     Taos Pueblo. *General Series in Anthropology* 2. Menasha, Wis. (Reprinted: Johnson Reprint, New York, 1971.)

1939     Pueblo Indian Religion. 2 vols. Chicago: University of Chicago Press.

1939a    Picurís, New Mexico. *American Anthropologist* 41(2):206-222.

1940     Relations Between Ethnology and Archaeology in the Southwest. *American Antiquity* 5(3):214-220.

1962     Introduction. Pp. 1-12 in Isleta Paintings. Esther S. Goldfrank, ed. *Bureau of American Ethnology Bulletin* 181. Washington.

Parsons, Elsie (Clews), and Ralph L. Beals
1934     The Sacred Clowns of the Pueblo and Mayo-Yaqui Indians. *American Anthropologist* 36(4):491-514.

Parsons, Francis B.
1975     Early 17th Century Missions of the Southwest, with Historical Introduction. Tucson, Ariz.: D.S. King.

Pattie, James O.
1883     The Personal Narrative of James O. Pattie of Kentucky During an Expedition from St. Louis, Through the Vast Regions Between That Place and the Pacific Ocean... Timothy Flint, ed. Cincinnati: E.H. Flint. (Reprinted: R.R. Donnelly and Sons, Chicago, 1930.)

Pattison, Natalie B.
1968     Nogales Cliff House: A Largo-Gallina Site. (Unpublished M.A. Thesis in Anthropology, University of New Mexico, Albuquerque.)

Paytiamo, James
1932     Flaming Arrow's People, by an Acoma Indian. New York: Duffield and Green.

Pearce, Thomas M., with Ina S. Cassidy and Helen S. Pearce
1965     New Mexico Place Names: A Geographical Dictionary. Albuquerque: University of New Mexico Press.

Peckham, Stewart
1954     A Pueblo III Site at Farmington, New Mexico. *Highway Salvage Archaeology* 1(3):29-40.

1954a    A Pueblo I Site Near San Felipe Pueblo, New Mexico. *Highway Salvage Archaeology* 1(4):41-51.

1957     Three Pithouse Sites Near Albuquerque, New Mexico. *Highway Salvage Archaeology* 3(12):39-70.

1963     Three Sites Near Ranchos de Taos, New Mexico. *Highway Salvage Archaeology* 4:1-28. Santa Fe.

1974     The Palisade Ruin LA 3505: Archaeological Salvage Excavations Near the Abiquiu Dam, Rio Arriba County, New Mexico. (Manuscript on File, Museum of New Mexico, Laboratory of Anthropology, Santa Fe.)

Pendergast, David M.
1962     Metal Artifacts from Amapa, Nayarit, Mexico. *American Antiquity* 27(3):370-379.

Pennington, Campbell W.
1963     The Tarahumar of Mexico: Their Environment and Material Culture. Salt Lake City: University of Utah Press.

Pepper, George H.
1902     The Ancient Basket Makers of Southeastern Utah. *Journal of the American Museum of Natural History* 2(4). Supplement. New York.

1920     Pueblo Bonito. *Anthropological Papers of the American Museum of Natural History* 27. New York.

Perea, Estevan de
1945     Second Report of the Great Conversion [1653]. Pp. 216-221 in Fray Alfonso de Benavides' Revised Memorial of 1634, Appendix 25. Frederick W. Hodge, George P. Hammond, and Agapito Rey, eds. Albuquerque: University of New Mexico Press.

Pérez de Luxán, Diego
1929     Expedition into New Mexico Made by Antonio de Espejo, 1582-1583, as Revealed in the Journal of Diego Pérez de Luxán, a Member of the Party. George P. Hammond and Agapito Rey, eds. Los Angeles: The Quivira Society.

Pérez de Ribas, Andrés
1968     My Life Among the Savage Nations of New Spain [1644]. Tomas A. Robertson, trans. Los Angeles: Ward Ritchie.

Phillips, Philip, James A. Ford, and James B. Griffin
1951     Archaeological Survey in the Lower Mississippi Alluvial Valley, 1940-1947. *Papers of the Peabody Museum of American Archaeology and Ethnology, Harvard University* 25. Cambridge, Mass.

Philp, Kenneth
1970     Albert B. Fall and the Protest from the Pueblos, 1921-1923. *Arizona and the West* 12(3):237-254.

Pimentel, Francisco
1874-1875 Cuadro descriptivo y comparativo de las lenguas indígenas de México, o tratado de filología méxicana. 3 vols. Mexico City: Isidoro Epstein.

Piña Chan, Román
1971     Preclassic or Formative Pottery and Minor Arts of the Valley of Mexico. Pp. 157-178 in *Archaeology of Northern Mesoamerica*. Pt. 1. Gordon F. Ekholm and Ignacio Bernal, eds. Handbook of Middle American Indians. Robert Wauchope, gen. ed. Vol. 10. Austin: University of Texas Press.

Pinart, Alphonse L.
1962     Journey to Arizona in 1876. George H. Whitney, trans. Los Angeles: Zamorano Club.

Plog, Fred T.
1969     An Approach to the Study of Prehistoric Change. (Unpublished Ph.D. Dissertation in Anthropology, University of Chicago, Chicago.)

1974     The Study of Prehistoric Change. New York: Academic Press.

1975     Demographic Studies in Southwestern Prehistory. Pp. 94-103 in Population Studies in Archaeology and Biological Anthropology: A Symposium. Alan C. Swedlund, ed. *Memoirs of the Society for American Archaeology* 30. Salt Lake City, Utah.

_____, ed.
1978     An Analytical Approach to Cultural Resource Management: The Little Colorado Planning Unit. *U.S.D.A. Forest Service Cultural Resources Report 19, Arizona State University Anthropological Research Paper* 13. Tempe.

Plog, Fred T., and Cheryl K. Garrett
1972     Explaining Variability in Prehistoric Southwestern Water Control Systems. Pp. 280-288 in Contemporary Archaeology: A Guide to Theory and Contributions. Mark P. Leone, ed. Carbondale: Southern Illinois University Press.

Plog, Fred T., Richard Effland, and Dee F. Green
1978    Inferences Using the SARG Data Bank. Pp. 139-148 in Investigations of the Southwestern Anthropological Research Group: Proceedings of the 1976 Conference. Robert C. Euler and George J. Gumerman, eds. Flagstaff: Museum of Northern Arizona.

Plog, Fred T., James N. Hill, and Dwight W. Read
1976    Chevelon Archaeological Research Project. *University of California, Department of Anthropology, Archaeological Survey Monograph* 2. Los Angeles.

Plog, Fred T., Jeffrey S. Dean, Richard Effland, and Sylvia W. Gaines
1978    SARG: Future Research Directions. Pp. 177-186 in Investigations of the Southwestern Anthropological Research Group: Proceedings of the 1976 Conference. Robert C. Euler and George J. Gumerman, eds. Flagstaff: Museum of Northern Arizona.

Plog, Stephen
1969    Prehistoric Population Movements: Measurement and Explanation. (Unpublished Manuscript on File at Field Museum of Natural History, Chicago.)

————, ed.
1977    Excavation on Black Mesa, 1976: A Preliminary Report. *Southern Illinois University Museum, Archaeological Service Report* 50. Carbondale.

1977a   A Multivariate Approach to the Explanation of Ceramic Design Variation. (Unpublished Ph.D. Dissertation in Anthropology, University of Michigan, Ann Arbor.)

Plog, Stephen, Fred T. Plog, and Walter Wait
1978    Decision Making in Modern Survey Research. Pp. 383-421 in Vol. 1 of Advances in Archeological Method and Theory. Michael Schiffer, ed. New York: Academic Press.

Powell, John Wesley
1878    The Nationality of the Pueblos. *The Rocky Mountain Presbyterian,* November, 1878. Denver.

1880    Pueblo Indians. *American Naturalist* 14(8):603-605.

1891    Indian Linguistic Families of America North of Mexico. Pp. 1-142 in *7th Annual Report of the Bureau of American Ethnology for the Years 1885-1886.* Washington.

1895    Canyons of the Colorado. Meadville, Pa.: Flood and Vincint. (Reprinted: Argosy-Antiquarian, New York, 1964.)

1900    Administrative Report: Field Research and Exploration. Pp. xiii-xviii in *19th Annual Report of the Bureau of American Ethnology for the Years 1897-1898.* Pt. 1. Washington.

Prince, L. Bradford
1915    Spanish Mission Churches of New Mexico. Cedar Rapids, Ia.: Torch Press.

Prudden, T. Mitchell
1903    The Prehistoric Ruins of the San Juan Watershed in Utah, Arizona, Colorado, and New Mexico. *American Anthropologist* n.s. 5(2):224-288.

1914    The Circular Kivas of Small Ruins in the San Juan Watershed. *American Anthropologist* 16(1):33-58.

1918    A Further Study of Prehistoric Small House Ruins. *Memoirs of the American Anthropological Association* 5:1-50. Lancaster, Pa.

Pueblo of Picuris
1962    [Overall Economic Development Plan.] Mimeo.

Putnam, Frederick W.
1879    Notes on the Implements of Stone, Pottery, and Objects Obtained in New Mexico and Arizona. Pp. 374-390 in Vol. 7 of Reports on U.S. Geographical Surveys West of the 100th Meridian, by George M. Wheeler. Washington: U.S. Government Printing Office.

1879a   Reports Upon Archaeological and Ethnological Collections from the Vicinity of Santa Barbara, California, and from Ruined Pueblos of Arizona and New Mexico, and Certain Interior Tribes. 2 Pts. Reports Upon the U.S. Geographical Surveys West of the 100th Meridian, by George M. Wheeler. Vol. 7: Archaeology. Washington: U.S. Government Printing Office.

Quam, Alvina, trans.
1972    The Zunis: Self-portrayals by the Zuni People. Albuquerque: University of New Mexico Press.

Rapoport, Robert N.
1954    Changing Navaho Religious Values: A Study of Christian Missions to the Rimrock Navahos. *Papers of the Peabody Museum of American Archaeology and Ethnology, Harvard University* 41(2). Cambridge, Mass.

Reed, Erik K.
1942    Kawaika-a in the Historic Period. *American Antiquity* 8(1):119-120.

1943    The Problem of Protohistoric Picuris. *El Palacio* 50(3):65-68.

1943a   The Origins of Hano Pueblo. *El Palacio* 50(4)73-76.

1943b   The Southern Tewa Pueblos in the Historic Period. *El Palacio* 50(11):254-264, (12):276-288.

1944    Aspects of Acculturation in the Southwest. *Acta Americana* 2(1-2):62-69.

1946    The Distinctive Features and Distribution of the San Juan Anasazi Culture. *Southwestern Journal of Anthropology* 2(3):295-305.

1948    The Western Pueblo Archaeological Complex. *El Palacio* 55(1):9-15.

1949    The Significance of Skull Deformation in the Southwest. *El Palacio* 56(4):106-119.

1949a   Sources of Upper Rio Grande Pueblo Culture and Population. *El Palacio* 56(6):163-184.

1950    Eastern-central Arizona Archaeology in Relation to the Western Pueblos. *Southwestern Journal of Anthropology* 6(2):120-138.

1952    The Tewa Indians of the Hopi Country. *Plateau* 25(1):11-18.

1955    Trends in Southwestern Archeology. Pp. 46-58 in New Interpretations of Aboriginal American Culture History. Washington: 75th Anniversary Volume of the Anthropological Society of Washington.

1957    From Some Highway Salvage Excavations in New Mexico. *Highway Salvage Archaeology* 3(14):85-97.

1964    The Greater Southwest. Pp. 175-191 in Prehistoric Man in the Southwest. Jesse D. Jennings and Edward Norbeck, eds. Chicago: University of Chicago Press.

Reichard, Gladys
1950    Navaho Religion: A Study of Symbolism. 2 vols. New York: Pantheon Books.

Reinhart, Theodore R.
1967    The Alameda Phase: An Early Basketmaker III Culture in the Middle Rio Grande Valley, New Mexico. *Southwestern Lore* 33(1):24-32.

1967a   The Rio Rancho Phase: A Preliminary Report on Early Basketmaker Culture in the Middle Rio Grande Valley, New Mexico. *American Antiquity* 32(4):458-470.

*663*

1968        Late Archaic Cultures of the Middle Rio Grande Valley, New Mexico. A Study of the Process of Culture Change. (Unpublished Ph.D. Dissertation in Anthropology, University of New Mexico, Albuquerque.)

Reiter, Paul
1938        The Jemez Pueblo of Unshagi, New Mexico, with Notes on the Earlier Excavations at "Amoxiumqua" and Giusewa. 2 Pts. *Monographs of the School of American Research* 5-6. Santa Fe.

Renaud, Abel E.B.
1942        Reconnaissance Work in the Upper Rio Grande Valley, Colorado and Northern New Mexico. *University of Denver Department of Anthropology, Archaeological Series* 3. Denver, Colo.

Reno, Philip
1965        Rebellion in New Mexico, 1837. *New Mexico Historical Review* 40(3):197-213.

Riley, Carroll L., and Howard D. Winters
1963        The Prehistoric Tepehuan of Northern Mexico. *Southwestern Journal of Anthropology* 19(2):177-185.

Rinaldo, John B.
1964        Notes on the Origin of Historic Zuni Culture. *The Kiva* 29(4):86-98.

Ritch, W.G.
1882        Introductory. New Mexico: A Sketch of its History and Review of its Resources. Appended to The Legislative Blue-book of the Territory of New Mexico... W.G. Ritch, comp. Santa Fe: Charles W. Greene.

Robbins, Wilfred W., John P. Harrington, and Barbara Freire-Marreco
1916        The Ethnobotany of the Tewa Indians. *Bureau of American Ethnology Bulletin* 55. Washington.

Roberts, Frank H.H., Jr.
1929        Shabik'eshchee Village: A Late Basket Maker Site in Chaco Canyon, New Mexico. *Bureau of American Ethnology Bulletin* 92. Washington.

1930        Early Pueblo Ruins in the Piedra District, Southwestern Colorado. *Bureau of American Ethnology Bulletin* 96. Washington.

1931        The Ruins at Kiatuthlanna, Eastern Arizona. *Bureau of American Ethnology Bulletin* 100. Washington.

1932        The Village of the Great Kivas on the Zuñi Reservation, New Mexico. *Bureau of American Ethnology Bulletin* 111. Washington.

1935        A Survey of Southwestern Archaeology. *American Anthropologist* 37(1):1-35.

1937        Archaeology in the Southwest. *American Antiquity* 3(1):3-33.

1939        Archeological Remains in the Whitewater District, Eastern Arizona. Pt. 1: House Types. *Bureau of American Ethnology Bulletin* 121. Washington.

1940        Archeological Remains in the Whitewater District, Eastern Arizona. Pt. 2: Artifacts and Burials. *Bureau of American Ethnology Bulletin* 126. Washington.

Roberts, Helen H.
1932        The Reason for the Departure of the Pecos Indians for Jemez Pueblo. *American Anthropologist* 34(2):359-360.

Roberts, John M.
1956        Zuni Daily Life. *University of Nebraska Laboratory of Anthropology, Note Book 3, Monograph* 1. Lincoln. (Reprinted: Human Relations Area Files Press, New Haven, Conn., 1965.)

1961        The Zuni. Pp. 285-316 in Variations in Value Orientations, by Florence R. Kluckhohn and Fred L. Strodtbeck. Evanston, Ill., and Elmsford, N.Y.: Row, Peterson.

Robinson, William J., John W. Hannah, and Bruce G. Harrill
1972        Tree-ring Dates from New Mexico I, O, V: Central Rio Grande Area. Tucson: University of Arizona, Laboratory of Tree-ring Research.

Rock, James T., and Donald P. Morris, eds.
1975        Environment and Behavior at Antelope House. *The Kiva* 41(1).

Roediger, Virginia (More)
1941        Ceremonial Costumes of the Pueblo Indians: Their Evolution, Fabrication, and Significance in the Prayer Drama. Berkeley and Los Angeles: University of California Press.

Rogers, Malcolm J.
1938        Archaeological and Geological Investigations of the Cultural Levels in an Old Channel of San Dieguito Valley. *Yearbook of the Carnegie Institute of Washington* 37:344-345. Washington.

1939        Early Lithic Industries of the Lower Basin of the Colorado River and Adjacent Desert Areas. *San Diego Museum Paper* 3. San Diego.

1941        Aboriginal Cultural Relations Between Southern California and the Southwest. *San Diego Museum Bulletin* 5(3):1-6.

1945        An Outline of Yuman Prehistory. *Southwestern Journal of Anthropology* 1(2):167-198.

1958        San Dieguito Implements from the Terraces of the Rincon- Pantano and Rillito Drainage System. *The Kiva* 24(1):1-23.

Rogers, Malcolm J., H.M. Wormington, E.L. Davis, and Clark W. Brott
1966        Ancient Hunters of the Far West. Richard F. Pourade, ed. San Diego, Calif.: Union-Tribune Publishing Company.

Rohn, Arthur H.
1963        Prehistoric Soil and Water Conservation on Chapin Mesa, Southwestern Colorado. *American Antiquity* 28(4):441-455.

1971        Mug House, Mesa Verde National Park, Colorado. *U.S. National Park Service Archaeological Research Series* 7-D. Washington.

1977        Cultural Change and Continuity on Chapin Mesa. Lawrence: Regents Press of Kansas.

1978        Chronologies in New World Archaeology. Pp. 201-222 in American Southwest. R.E. Taylor and C.W. Meighan, eds. New York: Academic Press.

Romney, A. Kimball
1957        The Genetic Model and Uto-Aztecan Time Perspective. *Davidson Journal of Anthropology* 3(2):35-41.

Roney, J., and Cynthia Irwin-Williams
1971        Report to the National Forest Service on Excavations in the Lincoln National Forest, 1970-1971. (Manuscript at Eastern New Mexico University, Portales.)

Ruppé, Reynold J., Jr.
1953        The Acoma Culture Province: An Archaeological Concept. (Unpublished Ph.D. Dissertation in Anthropology, Harvard University, Cambridge, Mass.)

1966        The Archaeological Survey: A Defense. *American Antiquity* 31(3):313-333.

Ruppé, Reynold J., Jr., and Alfred E. Dittert, Jr.
1953        Acoma Archaeology: A Preliminary Report of the Final Season in the Cebolleta Mesa Region, New Mexico. *El Palacio* 60(7):259-273.

Russell, Frank
1908    The Pima Indians. Pp. 3-389 in *26th Annual Report of the Bureau of American Ethnology for the Years 1904-1905.* Washington.

Ryan, Dennis
1977    Prehistoric Indian Health in Northeastern Arizona: A Study of the Paleopathology and Paleoepidemiology of the Kayenta Anasazi Indians. (Unpublished Ph.D. Dissertation in Anthropology, Arizona State University, Tempe.)

Sahagún, Bernardino de
1959    General History of the Things of New Spain; Florentine Codex, Book 9: The Merchants [1590]. Charles E. Dibble and Arthur J.O. Anderson, trans. *Monographs of the School of American Research and the Museum of New Mexico* 14(10). Santa Fe.

Sahlins, Marshall D.
1968    Tribesmen. Englewood Cliffs, N.J.: Prentice-Hall.

1972    Stone Age Economics. Chicago: Aldine-Atherton.

Sahlins, Marshall D., and Elman R. Service, eds.
1960    Evolution and Culture. Ann Arbor: University of Michigan Press.

Sample, L.L.
1950    Trade and Trails in Aboriginal California. *University of California Archaeological Survey Report* 8. Berkeley.

Sando, Joe S.
1974    The Pueblo Indian Book of History and Biographies. San Francisco: Indian Historian Press.

1976    The Pueblo Indians. San Francisco: Indian Historian Press.

Santa Ana Governor's Office
[1978]   [Population Data File.] Mimeo.

Sapir, Edward
1913-1914 Southern Paiute and Nahuatl: A Study in Uto-Aztecan. *Journal de la Société des Américanistes de Paris* n.s. 10:379-425, 11:443-488.

1916    Time Perspective in Aboriginal American Culture: A Study in Method. *Anthropological Series 13, Memoirs of the Canadian Geological Survey* 90. Ottawa.

1917    The Position of Yana in the Hokan Stock. *University of California Publications in American Archaeology and Ethnology* 13(1):1-34. Berkeley.

1917a   The Hokan and Coahuiltecan Languages. *International Journal of American Linguistics* 1(4):280-290.

1921    A Birds'-eye View of American Languages North of Mexico. *Science* 54(1400):408.

1925    The Hokan Affinity of Subtiaba in Nicaragua. *American Anthropologist* 27(4):491-527.

1929    Central and North American Indian Languages. Pp. 138-141 in Vol. 5 of Encyclopedia Britannica. (14th ed.) London and New York: Encyclopedia Britannica Company. (Reprinted: Pp. 169-178 in Selected Writings of Edward Sapir in Language, Culture, and Personality. David G. Mandelbaum, ed., University of California Press, Berkeley and Los Angeles, 1949.)

1931    Southern Paiute Dictionary. *Proceedings of the American Academy of Arts and Sciences* 65(3):537-730. Boston.

1931a   The Concept of Phonetic Law as Tested in Primitive Languages by Leonard Bloomfield. Pp. 297-306 in Methods in Social Science: A Case Book. Stuart A. Rice, ed. Chicago: University of Chicago Press.

1936    Internal Linguistic Evidence Suggestive of the Northern Origin of the Navaho. *American Anthropologist* 38(2):224-235.

1942    Navaho Texts. Harry Hoijer, ed. Iowa City: Linguistic Society of America.

Sapir, Edward, and Harry Hoijer
1967    The Phonology and Morphology of the Navajo Language. *University of California Publications in Linguistics* 50. Berkeley.

Sauer, Carl
1934    The Distribution of Aboriginal Tribes and Languages in Northwestern Mexico. *Ibero-Americana* 10. Berkeley, Calif.

Sauer, Carl, and Donald Brand
1930    Pueblo Sites in Southeastern Arizona. *University of California Publications in Geography* 3(7):415-458. Berkeley.

1931    Prehistoric Settlements of Sonora with Special Reference to Cerros de Trincheras. *University of California Publications in Geography* 5(3):67-148. Berkeley.

1932    Aztatlán: Prehistoric Mexican Frontier on the Pacific Coast. *Ibero-Americana* 1. Berkeley, Calif.

Sayles, Edwin B.
1935    An Archaeological Survey of Texas. *Gila Pueblo, Medallion Paper* 17. Globe, Ariz.

1936    An Archaeological Survey of Chihuahua, Mexico. *Gila Pueblo, Medallion Paper* 22. Globe, Ariz.

1936a   Some Southwestern Pottery Types: Series V. *Gila Pueblo, Medallion Paper* 21. Globe, Ariz.

1945    The San Simon Branch: Excavations at Cave Creek and in the San Simon Valley, I: Material Culture. *Gila Pueblo, Medallion Paper* 34. Globe, Ariz.

Sayles, Edwin B., and Ernst Antevs
1935    An Archaeological Survey of Texas. *Gila Pueblo, Medallion Paper* 17. Globe, Ariz.

1941    The Cochise Culture. *Gila Pueblo, Medallion Paper* 29. Globe, Ariz.

1955    Report Given at the 1955 Great Basin Archaeological Conference. *American Antiquity* 20(3):311.

Scantling, Frederick H.
1940    Excavations at Jackrabbit Ruin, Papago Indian Reservation, Arizona. (Unpublished M.A. Thesis in Anthropology, University of Arizona, Tucson.)

Schaafsma, Curtis F.
1976    Archaeological Survey of Maximum Pool and Navajo Excavations at Abiquiu Reservoir, Rio Arriba County, New Mexico: Santa Fe: School of American Research Contract Program.

Schaafsma, Polly
1963    Rock Art in the Navajo Reservoir District. *Museum of New Mexico Papers in Anthropology* 7. Santa Fe.

1975    Rock Art in the Cochiti Reservoir District. *Museum of New Mexico Papers in Anthropology* 16. Santa Fe.

Schaafsma, Polly, and Curtis F. Schaafsma
1974    Evidence for the Origins of the Pueblo Katchina Cult as Suggested by Southwestern Rock Art. *American Antiquity* 39(4):535-545.

Schiffer, Michael B.
1972    Cultural Laws and the Reconstruction of Past Lifeways. *The Kiva* 37(3):148-157.

Schlesier, Karl H.
1972    Rethinking the Dismal River Aspect and the Plains Athapaskans, A.D. 1692-1768. *Plains Anthropologist* 17(56):101-133.

Schneider, David M., and John M. Roberts
1956    Zuñi Kin Terms. *University of Nebraska, Laboratory of Anthropology Notebook* 3. Lincoln. (Reprinted: Human Relations Area Files Press, New Haven, Conn., 1965.)

Schoenwetter, James
1962    The Pollen Analysis of Eighteen Archaeological Sites in Arizona and New Mexico. Pp. 168-209 in Chapters in the Prehistory of Eastern Arizona, I. *Fieldiana: Anthropology* 53(8). Chicago.

———
1966    A Re-evaluation of the Navajo Reservoir Pollen Chronology. *El Palacio* 73(1):19-26.

Schoenwetter, James, and Alfred E. Dittert, Jr.
1968    An Ecological Interpretation of Anasazi Settlement Patterns. Pp. 41-66 in Anthropological Archeology in the Americas. Betty J. Meggers, ed. Washington: Anthropological Society of Washington.

Schoenwetter, James, and Frank W. Eddy
1964    Alluvial and Palynological Reconstruction of Environments, Navajo Reservoir District. *Museum of New Mexico Papers in Anthropology* 13. Santa Fe.

Scholes, France V.
1930    The Supply Service of the New Mexico Missions in the Seventeenth Century. *New Mexico Historical Review* 5(1):93-115, (2)186-210.

———
1936-1937    Church and State in New Mexico, 1610-1650. *New Mexico Historical Review* 11(1):9-76, (2):145-178, (3):283-294, (4):297-349; 12(1):78-106.

———
1937-1938    Troublous Times in New Mexico, 1659-1670. *New Mexico Historical Review* 12(2):134-174, (4):380-452; 13(1):63-84.

———
1938    Notes on the Jemez Missions in the 17th Century. *El Palacio* 44(1-2):61-102.

Scholes, France V., and Lansing B. Bloom
1944-1945    Friar Personnel and Mission Chronology, 1598-1629. *New Mexico Historical Review* 19(4):319-326; 20(1):58-82.

Scholes, France V., and H.P. Mera
1940    Some Aspects of the Jumano Problem. *Contributions to American Anthropology and History 34, Carnegie Institution of Washington Publication* 523. Washington.

Schoolcraft, Henry R.
1851-1857    Historical and Statistical Information Respecting the History, Condition and Prospects of the Indian Tribes of the United States. 6 vols. Philadelphia: Lippincott, Grambo.

Schorsch, Russell L.
1962    A Basket Maker III Pit House Near Albuquerque. *El Palacio* 69(2):114-118.

Schroeder, Albert H.
1940    A Stratigraphic Survey of Pre-Spanish Trashmounds of the Salt River Valley, Arizona. (Unpublished M.A. Thesis in Anthropology, University of Arizona, Tucson.)

———
1947    Did the Sinagua of the Verde Valley Settle in the Salt River Valley? *Southwestern Journal of Anthropology* 3(3):230-246.

———
1952    The Bearing of Ceramics on Developments in the Hohokam Classic Period. *Southwestern Journal of Anthropology* 8(3):320-335.

———
1952a    A Brief Survey of the Lower Colorado River from Davis Dam to the International Border. Boulder City, Nev.: Bureau of Reclamation, Reproduction Unit.

———
1953    The Problem of Hohokam, Sinagua, and Salado Relations in Southern Arizona. *Plateau* 26(2):75-83.

1954    Four Prehistoric Sites Near Mayer, Arizona Which Suggest a New Focus. *Plateau* 26(3):103-107.

1955    Archeology of Zion Park. *University of Utah Anthropological Paper* 22. Salt Lake City.

1957    The Hakataya Cultural Tradition. *American Antiquity* 23(2):176-178.

1958    Castañeda's "Acha"-Picurís, Hopi, or Apache? *El Palacio* 65(1):1-7.

[1959]    A Study of the Apache Indians. Pt. 2. (Manuscript at the U.S. National Park Service, Region Three Headquarters, Santa Fe.)

1960    The Hohokam, Sinagua and Hakataya. *Society for American Archaeology, Archives of Archaeology* 5. Madison, Wis.

1961    The Pre-eruptive and Post-eruptive Sinagua Patterns. *Plateau* 34(2):60-66.

1961a    The Archaeological Excavations at Willow Beach, Arizona, 1950. *University of Utah Anthropological Paper* 50. Salt Lake City.

1961b    An Archeological Survey of the Painted Rock Reservoir, Western Arizona. *The Kiva* 27(1):1-28.

1963    Diffusion North Out of South-central Arizona. *El Palacio* 70(1-2):13-24.

1963a    Navajo and Apache Relationships West of the Rio Grande. *El Palacio* 70(3):5-23.

1963b    Hakataya, Patayan and Hohokam. *U.S. National Park Service, Regional Research Abstract* 309. Santa Fe, N.M.

1964    The Language of the Saline Pueblos, Piro or Tiwa? *New Mexico Historical Review* 39(3):235-249.

1965    Unregulated Diffusion from Mexico into the Southwest Prior to A.D. 700. *American Antiquity* 30(3):297-309.

1966    Pattern Diffusion from Mexico into the Southwest After A.D. 600. *American Antiquity* 31(5):683-704.

1968    Shifting for Survival in the Spanish Southwest. *New Mexico Historical Review* 43(4):291-310.

[1970]    [Unpublished Notes on San Felipe Pueblo.] (Notes in Schroeder's Possession.)

[1970a]    [Unpublished Notes on Santa Ana Pueblo.] (Notes in Schroeder's Possession.)

1972    Rio Grande Ethnohistory. Pp. 41-70 in New Perspectives on the Pueblos. Alfonso Ortiz, ed. Albuquerque: University of New Mexico Press.

1975    The Hohokam, Sinagua and the Hakataya. *Imperial Valley College Museum Society Publications, Occasional Paper* 3. El Centro, Calif.

Schroeder, Gail D.
1964    San Juan Pottery: Methods and Incentives. *El Palacio* 71(1):45-51.

Schwartz, Douglas W.
1956    The Havasupai, 600 A.D. - 1955 A.D.: A Short Culture History. *Plateau* 28(4):77-85.

1966    A Historical Analysis and Synthesis of Grand Canyon Archaeology. *American Antiquity* 31(4):469-484.

1970      Grand Canyon Archeological Research. (Unpublished Manuscript in the Possession of Schwartz.)

1970a      Exploration: The Grand Canyon. Pp. 12-21 in Explorations, 1970. Santa Fe, N.M.: School of American Research, Archaeological Institute of America.

Schwartz, Douglas W., and R.W. Lang
1973      Archaeological Investigations at the Arroyo Hondo Site: Third Field Report - 1972. Santa Fe: School of American Research.

Schwartz, Douglas W., and Milton Wetherill
1957      A Cohonina Cremation. *Plateau* 29(3):63-65.

Schwatka, Frederick
1893      In the Land of Cave and Cliff Dwellers. New York: Cassell Publishing Company.

Scully, Vincent
1975      Pueblo: Mountain, Village, Dance. New York: Viking Press.

Seaman, Timothy J.
1976      Archeological Investigations on the San Juan-to-Ojo 345KV Transmission Line for Public Service Company of New Mexico; Excavation of LA11843: An Early Stockaded Settlement of the Gallina Phase. (Manuscript on File at the Laboratory of Anthropology, Museum of New Mexico, Santa Fe, and U.S.D.A. Forest Service, Southwestern Regional Office, Albuquerque.)

Sedgwick, Mary K. (Rice)
1926      Acoma, the Sky City: A Study in Pueblo-Indian History and Civilization. Cambridge, Mass.: Harvard University Press.

Seltzer, Carl C.
1936      New Light on the Racial History of the Southwest Area. Abstract 30. *American Journal of Physical Anthropology* o.s. 21(2):supp. 2:17.

1944      Racial Prehistory in the Southwest and the Hawikuh Zunis. *Papers of the Peabody Museum of American Archaeology and Ethnology, Harvard University* 23(1). Cambridge, Mass.

Service, Elman R.
1971      Primitive Social Organization: An Evolutionary Perspective. 2d ed. New York: Random House.

Shepard, Anna O.
1942      Rio Grande Glaze Paint Ware: A Study Illustrating the Place of Ceramic Technological Analysis in Archaeological Research. *Contributions to American Anthropology and History 39, Carnegie Institute of Washington Publication 528.* Washington.

Shutler, Richard, Jr.
1950      The Dry Creek Site: A Pre-pottery Lithic Horizon in the Verde Valley, Arizona. *Plateau* 23(1):6-10.

1951      Two Pueblo Ruins in the Verde Valley, Arizona. *Plateau* 24(1):1-9.

1965      Tule Springs Expedition. *Current Anthropology* 6(1):110-111.

Siegel, Bernard J.
1949      Some Observations on the Pueblo Pattern at Taos. *American Anthropologist* 51(4):562-577.

1952      Suggested Factors of Culture Change at Taos Pueblo. Pp. 133- 140 in Vol. 2 of Proceedings and Selected Papers of the 29th International Congress of Americanists. Sol Tax, ed. Chicago: University of Chicago Press.

1959      Some Structure Implications for Change in Pueblo and Spanish New Mexico. Pp. 37-44 in Intermediate Societies, Social Mobility and Communication. Verne F. Ray, ed. (*Proceedings of the 1959 Annual Spring Meeting of the American Ethnological Society*) Seattle: University of Washington Press.

1965      Social Disorganization in Picuris Pueblo. *International Journal of Comparative Sociology* 6(2):199-206.

Siegel, Bernard J., and Alan R. Beals
1960      Pervasive Factionalism. *American Anthropologist* 62(3):394-417.

Sigüenza y Góngora, Carlos de
1932      The Mercurio Volante of Don Carlos de Siguenza y Góngora: An Account of the First Expedition of Don Diego de Vargas into New Mexico in 1692. Irving A. Leonard, trans. and ed. Los Angeles: The Quivira Society.

Siméon, Rémi
1963      Dictionnaire de la langue nahuatl ou mexicaine [1885]. Graz, Austria: Akademische Druck und Verlagsanstalt.

Simmons, Leo W., ed.
1942      Sun Chief: The Autobiography of a Hopi Indian. New Haven, Conn.: Yale University Press; London: Humphrey Milford, Oxford University Press.

Simmons, Marc
1968      Spanish Government in New Mexico. Albuquerque: University of New Mexico Press.

1968a      Two Southwesterners: Charles F. Lummis and Amado Chavez. Cerillos, N.M.: San Marcos Press.

1973      Blacksmithing at Zuni Pueblo. *Masterkey* 47(4):155-157.

1974      Witchcraft in the Southwest: Spanish and Indian Supernaturalism on the Rio Grande. Flagstaff, Ariz.: Northland Press.

Simons, Suzanne (Lee)
1969      The Cultural and Social Survival of a Pueblo Indian Community. Pp. 85-112 in Minorities and Politics. Henry J. Tobias and Charles E. Woodhouse, eds. Albuquerque: University of New Mexico Press.

1969a      Sandía Pueblo: Persistence and Change in a New Mexican Indian Community. (Unpublished Ph.D. Dissertation in Anthropology, University of New Mexico, Albuquerque.)

Simpson, James H.
1850      Journal of a Military Reconnaissance from Santa Fe, New Mexico, to the Navajo Country ... in 1849, by James Simpson, A.M., First Lieutenant Corps of Topographical Engineers. Pp. 56-139 in *31st Cong., 1st sess. Senate Executive Doc. No. 64. (Serial No. 562)* Washington: U.S. Government Printing Office.

1964      Navaho Expedition: Journal of a Military Reconnaissance from Santa Fe, New Mexico, to the Navaho Country Made in 1849. Frank McNitt, ed. Norman: University of Oklahoma Press.

Sitgreaves, Lorenzo
1853      Report of an Expedition Down the Zuni and Colorado Rivers. Washington: U.S. Government Printing Office.

Skinner, S. Alan
1965      The Sedillo Site: A Pit House Village in Albuquerque. *El Palacio* 72(1):5-24.

1968      Two Historic Period Sites in the El Rito Valley, New Mexico. *Plains Anthropologist* 13(39):63-70.

Slatter, Edwin D.
1973      Climate in Pueblo Abandonment of the Chevelon Drainage, Arizona. (Paper Presented at the Annual Meeting of the American Anthropological Association, New Orleans, 1973.)

Smiley, Terah L., ed.
1955      Geochronology, with Special Reference to the Southwestern United States. *University of Arizona Physical Science Bulletin* 2. Tucson.

Smith, Anne M.
1966    New Mexico Indians: Economic, Educational and Social Problems. *Museum of New Mexico Research Record* 1. Santa Fe.

Smith, M. Estellie
1967    Aspects of Social Control Among the Taos Indians. (Unpublished Ph.D. Dissertation in Anthropology, State University of New York, Buffalo.)

1969    Governing at Taos Pueblo. *Eastern New Mexico University Contributions in Anthropology* 2(1). Portales.

Smith, Watson
1952    Kiva Mural Decorations at Awatovi and Kawaika-a, with a Survey of Other Wall Paintings in the Pueblo Southwest. *Papers of the Peabody Museum of American Archaeology and Ethnology, Harvard University* 37. Cambridge, Mass.

1952a   Excavations in Big Hawk Valley, Wupatki National Monument, Arizona. *Museum of Northern Arizona Bulletin* 24. Flagstaff.

1971    Painted Ceramics of the Western Mound at Awatovi. (Reports of the Awatovi Expedition 8) *Papers of the Peabody Museum of American Archaeology and Ethnology, Harvard University* 38. Cambridge, Mass.

Smith, Watson, and John M. Roberts
1954    Zuni Law: A Field of Values. *Papers of the Peabody Museum of American Archaeology and Ethnology, Harvard University* 43(1). Cambridge, Mass.

Smith, Watson, Richard B. Woodbury, and Nathalie F.S. Woodbury
1966    The Excavation of Hawikuh by Frederick Webb Hodge: Report of the Hendricks-Hodge Expedition, 1917-1923. *Contributions from the Museum of the American Indian, Heye Foundation* 20. New York.

Snow, David H.
1973    Prehistoric Southwestern Turquoise Industry. *El Palacio* 79(1):33-51.

1974    The Excavation of Saltbush Pueblo, Bandelier National Monument, New Mexico, 1971. *Museum of New Mexico Laboratory of Anthropology Note* 97. Santa Fe.

Southern Pueblos Agency
1971    [Population of Sandia Pueblo, January 1, 1971.] (Unpublished Manuscript, Census Division, Southern Pueblos Agency, Albuquerque, N.M.)

Speirs, Randall H.
1966    Some Aspects of the Structure of Rio Grande Tewa. (Unpublished Ph.D. Dissertation in Linguistics, State University of New York, Buffalo.)

1968    Tewa Workbook. Santa Ana, Calif.: Summer Institute of Linguistics.

1968a   Tewa Reading Book. Santa Ana, Calif.: Summer Institute of Linguistics.

1969    Pehtsiye'ây [Anecdotes; Goldilocks, etc.]. Santa Ana, Calif.: Summer Institute of Linguistics.

1969a   Téwa Hí [Short Dictionary]. Santa Ana, Calif.: Summer Institute of Linguistics.

1969b   Mark Ita'nannin [Gospel of Mark]. Santa Ana, Calif.: Wycliffe Bible Translators.

1970    Téwa Kháwǎ [Tewa Names]. Santa Ana, Calif.: Summer Institute of Linguistics.

1971    Téwa Pehtsiyeh [Tewa Tales]. Santa Ana, Calif.: Summer Institute of Linguistics.

1971a   Âykha'wamí [Let's Sing; Hymnal]. Santa Ana, Calif.: Wycliffe Bible Translators.

1971b   Jesus-ví Wówátsi Thaa [Life of Jesus]. Santa Ana, Calif.: Wycliffe Bible Translators.

Spence, Michael W.
1971    Some Lithic Assemblages of Western Zacatecas and Durango. (Mesoamerican Studies 8) Carbondale: Southern Illinois University and Museum.

Spicer, Edward H.
1940    Pascua: A Yaqui Village in Arizona. Chicago: University of Chicago Press.

1943    Linguistic Aspects of Yaqui Acculturation. *American Anthropologist* 45(3):410-426.

1954    Spanish-Indian Acculturation in the Southwest. *American Anthropologist* 56(4):663-678.

1954a   Potam: A Yaqui Village in Sonora. *Memoirs of the American Anthropological Association* 77. Menasha, Wis.

——, ed.
1961    Perspectives in American Indian Culture Change. Chicago: University of Chicago Press.

1962    Cycles of Conquest: The Impact of Spain, Mexico, and the United States on the Indians of the Southwest, 1533-1960. Tucson: University of Arizona Press.

1969    A Short History of the Indians of the United States. New York: Van Nostrand Reinhold.

Spicer, Edward H., and Louis R. Caywood
1936    Two Pueblo Ruins in West Central Arizona. *University of Arizona Social Science Bulletin* 10. Tucson.

Spier, Leslie
1917    An Outline for a Chronology of Zuñi Ruins. *Anthropological Papers of the American Museum of Natural History* 18(3):207-331. New York.

1917a   Zuñi Chronology. *Proceedings of the National Academy of Sciences* 3(4):280-283. Washington.

1919    Ruins in the White Mountains, Arizona. *Anthropological Papers of the American Museum of Natural History* 18(5):363-387. New York.

1919a   Notes on Some Little Colorado Ruins. *Anthropological Papers of the American Museum of Natural History* 18(4):333-362. New York.

1928    Havasupai Ethnography. *Anthropological Papers of the American Museum of Natural History* 29(3). New York.

1929    Problems Arising from the Cultural Position of the Havasupai. *American Anthropologist* 31(2):213-222.

1933    Yuman Tribes of the Gila River. Chicago: University of Chicago Press.

1943    Elsie Clews Parsons. *American Anthropologist* 45(2):244-251.

1953    Some Observations on Mohave Clans. *Southwestern Journal of Anthropology* 9(3):324-342.

Spinden, Herbert J.
1912    Notes on the Material Culture of the Rio Grande Pueblos. *American Anthropologist* 14(1):154-155.

1915    Indian Dances of the Southwest. *American Museum Journal* 15(3):103-116.

——, trans.
1933    Songs of the Tewa. New York: The Exposition of Indian Tribal Arts.

Stanislawski, Michael B.
1963    Wupatki Pueblo: A Study in Cultural Fusion and Change in Sinagua and Hopi Prehistory. (Unpublished Ph.D. Dissertation in Anthropology, University of Arizona, Tucson.)

1968-1974  [Fieldnotes on First Mesa Arizona.] (Manuscript in Stanislawski's Possession.)

1969    What Good Is a Broken Pot? An Experiment in Hopi-Tewa Ethno-archaeology. *Southwestern Lore* 35(1):11-18.

1969a   The Ethno-archaeology of Hopi Pottery Making. *Plateau* 42(1):27-33.

1969b   Hopi-Tewa Pottery Making: Styles of Learning. (Paper Presented at the 34th Annual Meeting of the Society for American Archaeology, Milwaukee, Wis.)

1973 [Review of] Archaeology as Anthropology: A Case Study, by William A. Longacre. *American Antiquity* 38(1):117-122.

1974 History of Hopi-Tewa Pottery Making: Etics and Emics. (Paper Presented at the Society for Historic Archeology. Berkeley, 1974.)

1975 What You See Is What You Get: Ethnoarchaeology and Scientific Model Building. (Paper Presented at the Society of American Archaeology Meeting, Dallas, 1975.)

Stanislawski, Michael B., and Barbara B. Stanislawski
1975 Hopi and Hopi-Tewa Ceramic Tradition Networks. Pp. 61-76 in Spatial Organization of Culture. Ian Hodder, ed. London: Duckworth Press.

Stanislawski, Michael B., Ann Hitchcock, and Barbara B. Stanislawski
1976 Identification Marks on Hopi and Hopi-Tewa Pottery. *Plateau* 48(3-4):47-66.

Stanley, F. *see* Crocchiola, Stanley F.L.

Starr, Frederick
1897-1899 A Study of a Census of the Pueblo of Cochiti, New Mexico. *Proceedings of the Davenport Academy of Natural Sciences* 7:33-44. Davenport, Ia.

Steen, Charles R.
1966 Excavations at Tse-ta'a, Canyon de Chelly National Monument, Arizona. *U.S. National Park Service Archaeological Research Series* 9. Washington.

1977 Pajarito Plateau Archaeological Survey and Excavation. Los Alamos, N.M.: Los Alamos Scientific Laboratories.

Stegner, Wallace
1954 Beyond the 100th Meridian: John Wesley Powell and the Opening of the West. Boston: Houghton Mifflin.

Stephen, Alexander M.
1898 Pigments in Ceremonials of the Hopi. (Papers Read at the International Folk-Lore Congress of the World's Columbian Exposition, Chicago, 1893) *Archives of the International Folk-Lore Association* 1:260-265.

1936 Hopi Journal of Alexander M. Stephen. Elsie C. Parsons, ed. 2 vols. *Columbia University Contributions to Anthropology* 23. New York.

Stevenson, James
1883 Illustrated Catalogue of the Collections Obtained from the Indians of New Mexico and Arizona. (Extract from the *2d Annual Report of the Bureau of American Ethnology*) Washington: U.S. Government Printing Office.

Stevenson, Matilda (Coxe)
1887 The Religious Life of the Zuñi Child. Pp. 533-555 in *5th Annual Report of the Bureau of American Ethnology for the Years 1883-1884*. Washington.

1894 The Sia. Pp. 3-157 in *11th Annual Report of the Bureau of American Ethnology for the Years 1889-1890*. Washington.

1904 The Zuñi Indians: Their Mythology, Esoteric Fraternities, and Ceremonies. Pp. 3-634 in *23d Annual Report of the Bureau of American Ethnology for the Years 1901-1902*. Washington.

1911 Dress and Adornment of the Pueblo Indians. (Manuscript No. 2093 in National Anthropological Archives, Smithsonian Institution, Washington.)

1915 Ethnobotany of the Zuñi Indians. Pp. 31-102 in *30th Annual Report of the Bureau of American Ethnology for the Years 1908-1909*. Washington.

Steward, Julian H.
1931 Archaeological Discoveries at Kanosh in Utah. *El Palacio* 30(8):121-130.

1933 Archaeological Problems of the Northern Periphery of the Southwest. *Museum of Northern Arizona Bulletin* 5. Flagstaff.

1936 Pueblo Material Culture in Western Utah. *Anthropological Series 1(3), University of New Mexico Bulletin* 287. Albuquerque.

1937 Ecological Aspects of Southwestern Society. *Anthropos* 32:87-104.

1938 Basin-Plateau Aboriginal Sociopolitical Groups. *Bureau of American Ethnology Bulletin* 120. Washington.

1955 Theory of Culture Change: The Methodology of Multilinear Evolution. Urbana: University of Illinois Press.

Steward, Julian H., and Frank M. Setzler
1938 Function and Configuration in Archaeology. *American Antiquity* 4(1):4-10.

Stiger, Mark A.
1977 Anasazi Diet: The Coprolite Evidence. (Unpublished M.A. Thesis in Anthropology, University of Colorado, Boulder.)

Stirling, Matthew W.
1942 Origin Myth of Acoma and Other Records. *Bureau of American Ethnology Bulletin* 135. Washington.

Stresser-Péan, Guy
1971 Ancient Sources on the Huasteca. Pp. 582-601 in *Archaeology of Northern Mesoamerica*. Pt. 2. Gordon F. Ekholm and Ignacio Bernal, eds. Handbook of Middle American Indians. Robert Wauchope, gen. ed. Vol. 11. Austin: University of Texas Press.

Strong, William D.
1927 An Analysis of Southwestern Society. *American Anthropologist* 29(1):1-61.

1929 Aboriginal Society in Southern California. *University of California Publications in American Archaeology and Ethnology* 26:36-273. Berkeley.

Stubbs, Stanley A.
1950 Bird's-eye View of the Pueblos. Norman: University of Oklahoma Press.

Stubbs, Stanley A., and W.S. Stallings, Jr.
1953 The Excavation of Pindi Pueblo, New Mexico. *Monographs of the School of American Research* 18. Santa Fe.

Stubbs, Stanley A., Bruce T. Ellis, and Alfred E. Dittert, Jr.
1957 "Lost" Pecos Church. *El Palacio* 64(3-4):67-92.

Sullivan, Alan P., and Michael B. Schiffer
1978 A Critical Examination of SARG. Pp. 168-178 in Investigations of the Southwestern Anthropological Research Group: Proceedings of the 1976 Conference. Robert C. Euler and George J. Gumerman, eds. Flagstaff: Museum of Northern Arizona.

Surveyor General's Report
1856 Pojoaque. Santa Fe: New Mexico Record Center and Archives Commission.

Swadesh, Morris
1954 Perspectives and Problems of Amerindian Comparative Linguistics. *Word* 10(2-3):306-332.

1954-1955 Algunas fechas glotocronológicas importantes para la prehistoria Nahua. *Revista Mexicana de Estudios Antropológicos* 14(1):173-192.

1955 Towards Greater Accuracy in Lexico-statistic Dating. *International Journal of American Linguistics* 21(2):121-137.

1956 Problems of Long-range Comparison in Penutian. *Language* 32(1):17-41.

1959 Indian Linguistic Groups of Mexico. Published in Commemoration of the 58th Annual Meeting of the American Anthropological Association, Held in Mexico City in December 1959. Mexico: Escuela Nacional de Antropología e Historia, Instituto Nacional de Antropología e Historia.

1963 Nuevo ensayo de glotocronología Yutonahua. *Anales del Instituto Nacional de Antropología e Historia* 15(44):263-302. Mexico, D.F.

1967     Linguistic Classification in the Southwest. Pp. 281-309 in Studies in Southwestern Ethnolinguistics. Dell H. Hymes with William E. Bittle, eds. The Hague and Paris: Mouton.

Swannack, Jervis D., Jr.
1969     Wetherill Excavations: Big Juniper House, Mesa Verde National Park, Colorado. *U.S. National Park Service Archaeological Research Series* 7-C. Washington.

Swanton, John R.
1915     Linguistic Position of the Tribes of Southern Texas and Northeastern Mexico. *American Anthropologist* 17(1):17-40.

1940     Linguistic Material from the Tribes of Southern Texas and Northeastern Mexico. *Bureau of American Ethnology Bulletin* 127. Washington.

Swanton, John R., and Frank H.H. Roberts, Jr.
1931     Jesse Walter Fewkes. Pp. 609-616 in *Annual Report of the Smithsonian Institution for 1930*. Washington.

Swedlund, Alan C., and Steven E. Sessions
1976     A Developmental Model of Prehistoric Population Growth on Black Mesa, Northeastern Arizona. Pp. 136-148 in Papers on the Archaeology of Black Mesa, Arizona. George J. Gumerman and Robert C. Euler, eds. Carbondale and Edwardsville: Southern Illinois University Press.

Talahaftewa, Don C. et al.
1949     [Letter from Hopi Ceremonial Leaders to President Harry S. Truman, Dated March 28, 1949.] (Manuscript, Copy in Richard S. Clemmer's Possession.)

Talayesva, Don C.
1942     Sun Chief: The Autobiography of a Hopi Indian. Leo W. Simmons, ed. New Haven, Conn.: Yale University Press; London: Oxford University Press.

Tamarón y Romeral, Pedro
1937     Demostración del vastísimo obispado de la Nueva Vizcaya, 1765: Durango, Sinaloa, Sonora, Arizona, Nuevo México, Chihuahua y porciones de Texas, Coahuila y Zacatecas... México: Antigua Librería Robredo, de José Porrúa e Hijos.

1954     Bishop Tamarón's Visitation of New Mexico, 1760. Eleanor B. Adams, ed. (New Mexico Historical Society Publications in History 15) Albuquerque: University of New Mexico Press.

Tanner, Clara (Lee)
1968     Southwest Indian Craft Arts. Tucson: University of Arizona Press.

1973     Southwest Indian Painting: A Changing Art. 2d ed. Tucson: University of Arizona Press.

1976     Prehistoric Southwestern Craft Arts. Tucson: University of Arizona Press.

1978     The Squash Blossom. *American Indian Art* 3(3):36-43.

Tax, Sol, and Sam Stanley
1960     The North American Indians: 1950 Distribution of Descendants of the Aboriginal Population of Alaska, Canada and the United States. (Map) Chicago: University of Chicago, Department of Anthropology.

Taylor, Walter W.
1948     A Study of Archeology. *Memoirs of the American Anthropological Association* 69. Menasha, Wis.

1954     Southwestern Archeology: Its History and Theory. *American Anthropologist* 56(4):561-570.

1956     Some Implications of the Carbon-14 Dates from a Cave in Coahuila, Mexico. *Bulletin of the Texas Archeological Society* 27:215-234. Austin.

1958     A Brief Survey Through the Grand Canyon of the Colorado River. *Museum of Northern Arizona Bulletin* 30:18-30. Flagstaff.

1961     Archaeology and Language in Western North America. *American Antiquity* 27(1):71-81.

1964     Tethered Nomadism and Water Territoriality: An Hypothesis. Pp. 197-203 in Vol. 2 of *Proceedings of the 35th International Congress of Americanists*. 2 vols. Mexico, 1964.

1966     Archaic Cultures Adjacent to the Northeastern Frontiers of Mesoamerica. Pp. 59-94 in *Archaeological Frontiers and External Connections*. Gordon F. Ekholm and Gordon R. Willey, eds. Handbook of Middle American Indians. Robert Wauchope, gen. ed. Vol. 4. Austin: University of Texas Press.

Tedlock, Barbara
1971     Prayer Stick Sacrifice at Zuni. (Manuscript in Department of Anthropology, Wesleyan University, Middletown, Conn.)

1973     Kachina Dance Songs in Zuni Society: The Role of Aesthetics in Social Integration. (Unpublished M.A. Thesis in Anthropology, Wesleyan University, Middletown, Conn.)

Tedlock, Dennis
1965-1966 [Texts and Translations from Fieldwork Among the Zuni.] (Manuscripts in Tedlock's Possession.)

1968     The Ethnography of Tale-telling at Zuni. (Unpublished Ph.D. Dissertation in Anthropology, Tulane University, New Orleans.)

————, trans.
1972     Finding the Center: Narrative Poetry of the Zuni Indians, from Performances in Zuni, by Andrew Peynetsa and Walter Sanchez. New York: Dial Press.

Tedlock, Dennis, and Barbara Tedlock
[1971-1972] [Tapes from Fieldwork Among the Zuni.] (Tapes in the Tedlocks' Possession.)

Ten Kate, Herman F.C., Jr. *see* Kate, Herman F.C. ten, Jr.

Texas. Laws, Statutes, etc.
1898     The Laws of Texas 1822-1897... H.P.N. Gammel, comp. Austin: The Gammel Book Company.

1962     Vernon's Annotated Revised Civil Statutes of the State of Texas. Landlord and Tenant to Lands, Public: Vol. 15a, Articles 5222-5421. Kansas City: Vernon Law Book Company.

Thomas, Alfred B., ed. and trans.
1932     Forgotten Frontiers: A Study of the Spanish Indian Policy of Don Juan Bautista de Anza, Governor of New Mexico, 1777-1787; from the Original Documents in the Archives of Spain, Mexico, and New Mexico. Norman: University of Oklahoma Press.

————, ed. and trans.
1935     After Coronado: Spanish Exploration Northeast of New Mexico, 1696-1727; Documents from the Archives of Spain, Mexico and New Mexico. Norman: University of Oklahoma Press.

1940     The Plains Indians and New Mexico, 1751-1778: A Collection of Documents Illustrative of the History of the Eastern Frontier of New Mexico. Albuquerque: University of New Mexico Press.

Thomas, David H.
1973     An Empirical Test for Steward's Model of Great Basin Settlement Patterns. *American Antiquity* 38(2):155-176.

Thompson, Laura
1945     Logico-aesthetic Integration in Hopi Culture. *American Anthropologist* 47(4):540-553.

1950     Culture in Crisis: A Study of the Hopi Indians. New York: Harper and Brothers.

Thompson, Laura, and Alice Joseph
1944     The Hopi Way. Chicago: University of Chicago Press.

Tichy, Marjorie F.
1944     Exploratory Work at Yuque Yunque. *El Palacio* 51(11): 222-224.

Titiev, Mischa
1938     Dates of Planting at the Hopi Indian Pueblo of Oraibi. *Museum of Northern Arizona, Museum Note* 11(5). Flagstaff.

1938a     The Problem of Cross-cousin Marriage Among the Hopi. *American Anthropologist* 40(1):105-111.

1944     Old Oraibi: A Study of the Hopi Indians of Third Mesa. *Papers of the Peabody Museum of American Archaeology and Ethnology, Harvard University* 22(1). Cambridge, Mass.

1972     The Hopi Indians of Old Oraibi: Change and Continuity. Ann Arbor: University of Michigan Press.

1972a     Some Aspects of Clowning Among the Hopi Indians. Pp. 326-336 in Themes in Culture: Essays in Honor of Morris E. Opler. Mario D. Zamora, J. Michael Mahar and Henry Orenstein, eds. Quezon City, Philippines: Kayumanggi.

Toulouse, Betty
1977     Pueblo Pottery of the New Mexico Indians: Ever Constant, Ever Changing. Santa Fe: Museum of New Mexico Press.

Toulouse, Joseph H., Jr.
1949     The Mission of San Gregorio de Abó: A Report on the Excavation and Repair of a 17th-Century New Mexico Mission. *Monographs of the School of American Research* 13. Santa Fe.

Toulouse, Joseph H., Jr., and Robert L. Stephenson
1960     Excavations at Pueblo Pardo. *Museum of New Mexico Papers in Anthropology* 2. Santa Fe.

Tower, Donald B.
1945     The Use of Marine Mollusca and Their Value in Reconstructing Prehistoric Trade Routes in the American Southwest. *Papers of the Excavators' Club* 2(3). Cambridge, Mass.

Trager, Felicia (Harben)
1968     Picurís Pueblo, New Mexico: An Ethnolinguistic "Salvage" Study. (Unpublished Ph.D. Dissertation in Anthropology, State University of New York, Buffalo.)

1971     Some Aspects of 'Time' at Picuris Pueblo (with an Addendum on the Nootka). *Anthropological Linguistics* 13(7):331-338.

1971a     The Phonology of Picuris. *International Journal of American Linguistics* 37(1):29-33.

Trager, George L.
[1935-1971] [Notes and Tape Recordings of Taos Material - Linguistic and Ethnographic, Collected in Field Sessions in 1935-1937, 1947, 1948, 1954, 1955, 1959, and Every Summer 1961-1971; Picuris Material Recorded in 1937 and, with Felicia Harben Trager, 1965-1971.] (Manuscripts and Recordings in Trager's Possession.)

1938     The Phonemes of the Sandía Language. (Unpublished Manuscript in Trager's Possession.)

1942     The Historical Phonology of the Tiwa Languages. *Studies in Linguistics* 1(5):1-10.

1943     The Kinship and Status Terms of the Tiwa Languages. *American Anthropologist* 45(4):557-571.

1944     Spanish and English Loanwords in Taos. *International Journal of American Linguistics* 10(4):14-18.

1946     An Outline of Taos Grammar. Pp. 184-221 in Linguistic Structures of Native America by Harry Hoijer et al. *Viking Fund Publications in Anthropology* 6. New York.

1948     A Status Symbol and Personality at Taos Pueblo. *Southwestern Journal of Anthropology* 4(3):299-304.

1948a     Taos, I: A Language Revisited. *International Journal of American Linguistics* 14(3):155-160.

1960     The Name of Taos, New Mexico. *Anthropological Linguistics* 2(3):5-6.

1967     The Tanoan Settlement of the Rio Grande Area: A Possible Chronology. Pp. 335-350 in Studies in Southwestern Ethnolinguistics: Meaning and History in the Languages of the American Southwest. Dell H. Hymes with William E. Bittle, eds. The Hague and Paris: Mouton.

1969     Taos and Picuris -- How Long Separated? *International Journal of American Linguistics* 35(2):180-182.

1971     An Annotated Bibliography. *Studies in Linguistics, Occasional Paper* 12. Dallas.

Trager, George L., and Edith C. Trager
1959     Kiowa and Tanoan. *American Anthropologist* 61(6):1078-1083.

Traylor, Diane
1977     Bandelier: Excavations in the Flood Pool of Cochiti Lake, New Mexico. (Manuscript on File at the Southwest Cultural Resource Center, Santa Fe, N.M.)

Treganza, Adan E.
1942     An Archaeological Reconnaissance of Northeastern Baja California and Southeastern California. *American Antiquity* 8(2):152-163.

Trischka, Carl
1933     Hohokam: A Chapter in the History of Red-on-Buff Culture of Arizona. *Scientific Monthly* 37(November):417-433.

Troike, Rudolph C.
1967     A Structural Comparison of Tonkawa and Coahuilteco. Pp. 321-332 in Studies in Southwestern Ethnolinguistics. Dell H. Hymes with William E. Bittle, eds. The Hague and Paris: Mouton.

Trotter, George A.
1955     From Feather, Blanket and Tepee: The Indians' Fight for Equality. New York: Vantage Press.

True, D.L.
1970     Investigation of a Late Prehistoric Complex in Cuyamaca Rancho State Park, San Diego County, California. *University of California Archaeological Survey Monograph* 1. Los Angeles.

Truell, Marcia
1976     Site 628 Summary. (Manuscript on File at Chaco Center, National Park Service, University of New Mexico, Albuquerque.)

Tuan, Yi-Fu
1973     The Climate of New Mexico. Santa Fe: New Mexico State Planning Office.

Tuohy, Donald R.
1960     Two More Wickiups on the San Carlos Indian Reservation, Arizona. *The Kiva* 26(2):27-30.

Turner, Christy G., II
1958     A Human Skeleton from the Cohonina Culture Area. *Plateau* 31(1):16-19.

1962     A Summary of the Archaeological Explorations of Dr. Byron Cummings in the Anasazi Culture Area. *Museum of Northern Arizona Technical Series* 5. Flagstaff.

1971     Revised Dating for Early Rock Art of the Glen Canyon Region. *American Antiquity* 36(4):469-471.

Turner, Christy G., II, and Nancy T. Morris
1970     A Massacre at Hopi. *American Antiquity* 35(3):320-331.

Turner, Paul R.
1967     Seri and Chontal (Tequistlateco). *International Journal of American Linguistics* 33(3):235-239.

671

Turney, Omar A.
1924    The Land of the Stone Hoe. Phoenix: Republican Print Shop.

Tuthill, Carr
1947    The Tres Alamos Site on the San Pedro River, Southeastern Arizona. *Amerind Foundation Publication* 4. Dragoon, Ariz.

————
1950    Notes on the Dragoon Complex. Pp. 51-61 in For the Dean: Essays in Anthropology in Honor of Byron Cummings on His Eighty-ninth Birthday, September 20, 1950. Erik K. Reed and Dale S. King, eds. Tucson: Hohokam Museums Association; Santa Fe: Southwestern Monuments Association.

Twitchell, Ralph E.
1911-1917    The Leading Facts of New Mexican History. 5 vols. Cedar Rapids, Ia.: The Torch Press.

————, comp.
1914    The Spanish Archives of New Mexico. 2 vols. Cedar Rapids, Ia.: The Torch Press.

————, ed. and trans.
1916    The Pueblo Revolt of 1696: Extracts from the Journal of General Don Diego de Vargas. *Old Santa Fe* 3(12):333-373.

————
1923    The Story of the Conquest of Santa Fe, New Mexico, and the Building of Old Fort Marcy. *Publications of the Historical Society of New Mexico* 24. Santa Fe.

U.S. Army. Corps of Topographical Engineers
1855    Report of Exploration of a Route for the Pacific Railroad Near the Thirty-second Parallel of Latitude, from the Red River to the Rio Grande, by Brevet Captain John Pope. *33d Cong., 1st sess. House Doc. No. 129. (Serial No. 739)* Washington: U.S. Government Printing Office.

————
1951    Lieutenant Emory Reports: A Reprint of Lieutenant W.H. Emory's Notes of a Military Reconnoissance. Ross Calvin, ed. Albuquerque: University of New Mexico Press.

————
1962    Abert's New Mexico Report, 1846-1847 [1848]. Albuquerque: Horn and Wallace.

————
1969    Report Upon the Colorado River of the West, by Lt. Joseph C. Ives [1861]. New York: Da Capo Press.

U.S. Bureau of Indian Affairs
1854-1871    [Population Records.] Santa Fe, N.M.

————
1963    U.S. Indian Population (1962) and Land (1963). Washington: U.S. Department of the Interior.

————
1968    Demographic Characteristics: Hopi Indian Reservation, Arizona. Phoenix.

————
1971    Fact Book. Santa Fe: Northern Pueblos Agency.

————
1971a    Pueblo Population (January 1971). Santa Fe: Northern Pueblos Agency.

————
1974    [Population Records.] Santa Fe, N.M.

U.S. Bureau of the Census
1915    Indian Population of the United States and Alaska 1910. Washington: U.S. Government Printing Office.

U.S. Census Office. 11th Census
1893    Moqui Pueblo Indians of Arizona and Pueblo Indians of New Mexico. Extra Census Bulletin, 11th Census, 1890. Washington: U.S. Government Printing Office.

————
1894    Condition of 16 New Mexico Indian Pueblos, 1890. Pt. 3. Pp. 424-446 in Report of Indians Taxed and Indians Not Taxed in the United States (Except Alaska). Extra Census Bulletin, 11th Census, 1890. Washington: U.S. Government Printing Office.

U.S. Congress. House. Committee on Interior and Insular Affairs
1953    Report with Respect to the House Resolution Authorizing the Committee on Interior and Insular Affairs to Conduct an Investigation of the Bureau of Indian Affairs. *82d Cong., 2d sess., House Report No. 2503. (Serial No. 11582)* Washington: U.S. Government Printing Office.

————
1954    Report with Respect to the House Resolution Authorizing the Committee on Interior and Insular Affairs to Conduct an Investigation of the Bureau of Indian Affairs. *83d Cong., 2d sess., House Report No. 2680. (Serial No. 11747)* Washington: U.S. Government Printing Office.

U.S. Congress. House. Indian Affairs Committee
1932    Hearings (No. 597) on HR9071, February 17, 1932: Authorization of Appropriations to Pay in Part Liability of United States to Certain Pueblos. *72d Cong., 1st sess.* Washington: U.S. Government Printing Office.

U.S. Congress. Senate
1889    Memorial of Oliver Ames et al.; Praying Legislation for the Protection from Destruction of the Ancient Ruin of the Temple of Casa Grande Situated in Pinal County, Near Florence, Ariz. *50th Cong., 2d sess. Senate Misc. Doc. No. 60. (Serial No. 2615)* Washington: U.S. Government Printing Office.

U.S. Congress. Senate. Committee on Indian Affairs
1932    Survey of Conditions of the Indians in the United States. Pt. 26. Hearings Before a Subcommittee of the Committee on Indian Affairs, U.S. Senate. *72d Cong., 1st sess.* Washington: U.S. Government Printing Office.

U.S. Congress. Senate. Congressional Record
1882    Indian Antiquities; Dialogue Between Mr. Hoar and Mr. Plumb. *47th Cong., 1st sess.,* May 10, 1882. Washington.

U.S. Department of Commerce
1974    Federal and State Indian Reservations and Indian Trust Areas. Washington: U.S. Government Printing Office.

U.S. Department of Commerce. Economic Development Agency
1971    Federal and State Indian Reservations: An EDA Handbook. Washington: U.S. Government Printing Office.

U.S. Department of Health, Education and Welfare
1970    Estimates of Air Pollution from Four Corners Power Plant, New Mexico. Washington: U.S. Public Health Service, Bureau of Abatement and Control.

U.S. Department of the Interior
1872    Instructions to the Surveyor General of New Mexico (August 21, 1854). Pp. 65-69 in Report of the Commissioner of General Land Office to the Secretary of the Interior for the Year 1871. Washington: U.S. Government Printing Office.

————
1886    Indian Affairs. Pp. 3-21 in Report of the Secretary of the Interior for the Fiscal Year Ending June 30, 1886. Washington: U.S. Government Printing Office.

U.S. National Archives
1880    Military Records: Register of Enlistments of Soldiers Belonging to the First Regiment of United States Infantry. (Manuscript, War Records Branch, Record Group 94 in National Archives, Washington.)

U.S. Office of Indian Affairs
1915    The Official Correspondence of James S. Calhoun While Indian Agent at Santa Fé and Superintendent of Indian Affairs in New Mexico, Collected Mainly from the Files of the Indian Office and Edited Under its Direction by Annie Heloise Abel. Washington: U.S. Government Printing Office.

U.S. Office of Indian Affairs. Indian Land Research Unit
1935    Tewa Basin Study. Eshref Shevky et al., eds. 4 vols. Albuquerque, N.M.: Soil Conservation Service. Mimeo.

U.S. Public Health Service
1966    Topographic Maps: Hopi Villages; First Mesa Water Supply. Washington: U.S. Government Printing Office.

Underhill, Ruth M.
1939      Social Organization of the Papago Indians. *Columbia University Contributions to Anthropology* 30. New York.

1944      Pueblo Crafts. Washington: U.S. Bureau of Indian Affairs, Branch of Education.

1946      Work a Day Life of the Pueblos. Willard W. Beatty, ed. (U.S. Office of Indian Affairs, Indian Life and Customs 4) Phoenix: Phoenix Indian School.

1946a      Papago Indian Religion. *Columbia University Contributions to Anthropology* 33. New York.

1948      Ceremonial Patterns in the Greater Southwest. *Monographs of the American Ethnological Society* 13. New York.

1954      Intercultural Relations in the Greater Southwest. *American Anthropologist* 56(4):645-656.

United Pueblos Agency
1900-1970      Census Records for Sandía Pueblo. (Unpublished Manuscript, Census Division, United Pueblos Agency, Albuquerque, N.M.)

Vaillant, George
1932      Some Resemblances in the Ceramics of Central and North America. *Gila Pueblo, Medallion Paper* 12. Globe, Ariz.

Van Valkenburgh, Sallie
1962      The Casa Grande of Arizona as a Landmark on the Desert, a Government Reservation, and a National Monument. *The Kiva* 27(3):1-31.

Vargas Zapata y Luxán Ponce de León, Diego de
1914      The Re-conquest of New Mexico, 1692. Extracts from the Journal of General Don Diego de Vargas Zapata Lujan Ponce de Leon. *Old Santa Fe* 1(4):420-435.

1940      First Expedition of Vargas into New Mexico, 1692. José M. Espinosa, ed. and trans. Albuquerque: University of New Mexico Press.

Vélez de Escalante, Silvestre
1856      Sesto cuaderno, y primero del año de 1695. Pp. 168-180 in Documentos para la historia antigua de Mexico, 3d ser., Vol. 1. México: J.R. Navarro.

Vetancurt, Agustín de
1960      Teatro mexicano. (Colección Chimalistac de libros y documentos acerca de la Nueva España, 8-11) Madrid: J. Porrúa Turanzas.

Vickery, Lucretia D.
1969      Excavations at TA-26, a Small Pueblo Site Near Taos, New Mexico. (Unpublished M.A. Thesis in Anthropology, Wichita State University, Witchita, Kans.)

Villagrá, Gaspar Pérez de
1900      Historia de la Nueva Mexico. 2 vols. Mexico: Museo Nacional.

1933      History of New Mexico. Gilberto Espinosa, trans. F.W. Hodge, ed. Los Angeles: Quivira Society.

Visher, Stephen S.
1954      Climatic Atlas of the United States. Cambridge, Mass.: Harvard University Press.

Vivian, R. Gordon
1934      The Excavation of Bandelier's Puaray. *El Palacio* 37(19-20):153-161.

1959      The Hubbard Site and Other Tri-wall Structures in New Mexico and Colorado. *U.S. National Park Service Archeological Research Series* 5. Washington.

1964      Excavations in a 17th Century Jumano Pueblo, Gran Quivira. *U.S. National Park Service Archeological Research Series* 8. Washington.

1964a      Gran Quivira: Excavations in a 17th-Century Jumano Pueblo. *U.S. National Park Service Archaeological Research Series* 8. Washington.

1965      The Three-C Site, an Early Pueblo II Ruin in Chaco Canyon, New Mexico. *University of New Mexico Publications in Anthropology* 13. Albuquerque.

Vivian, R. Gordon, and Tom W. Mathews
1964      Kin Kletso, a Pueblo III Community in Chaco Canyon, New Mexico. *Southwestern Monuments Association Technical Series* 6(1). Coolidge, Ariz.

Vivian, R. Gordon, and Paul Reiter
1960      The Great Kivas of Chaco Canyon and Their Relationships. *Monographs of the School of American Research* 22. Santa Fe.

Vivian, R. Gwinn
1965      An Archaeological Survey of the Lower Gila River, Arizona. *The Kiva* 30(4):95-146.

1970      An Inquiry into Prehistoric Social Organization in Chaco Canyon, New Mexico. Pp. 59-83 in Reconstructing Prehistoric Pueblo Societies. William A. Longacre, ed. Albuquerque: University of New Mexico Press.

1974      Conservation and Diversion: Water-control Systems in the Anasazi Southwest. Pp. 95-112 in Irrigation's Impact on Society. Theodore Downing and McGuire Gibson, eds. *Anthropological Papers of the University of Arizona* 25. Tucson.

Vivian, R. Gwinn, and Nancy Clendenen
1965      The Denison Site: Four Pit Houses Near Isleta, New Mexico. *El Palacio* 72(2):5-24.

Voegelin, Charles F., and Florence M. Voegelin
1957      Hopi Domains: A Lexical Approach to the Problem of Selection. *Indiana University Publications in Anthropology and Linguistics, Memoir* 14. Bloomington.

1960      Selection in Hopi Ethics, Linguistics, and Translation. *Anthropological Linguistics* 2(2):48-78.

1965      Languages of the World: Native American Fascicle Two. *Anthropological Linguistics* 7(7):1-150.

1969      Hopi /ʔas/. *International Journal of American Linguistics* 35(2):192-202.

Voegelin, Charles F., Florence M. Voegelin, and Kenneth Hale
1962      Typological and Comparative Grammar of Uto-Aztecan: I (Phonology). *Indiana University Publications in Anthropology and Linguistics, Memoir* 17. Bloomington.

Vogt, Evon Z.
1951      Navaho Veterans: A Study of Changing Values. *Papers of the Peabody Museum of American Archaeology and Ethnology, Harvard University* 41(1). Cambridge, Mass.

Vogt, Evon Z., and Ethel M. Albert, eds.
1966      People of Rimrock: A Study of Value in Five Cultures. Cambridge, Mass.: Harvard University Press.

Voth, Henry R.
1900      Oraibi Marriage Customs. *American Anthropologist* n.s. 2(2):238-246.

1901      The Oraibi Powamu Ceremony. *Field Museum of Natural History Publication 61, Anthropological Series* 3(2):67-158. Chicago.

1903      The Oraibi Summer Snake Ceremony. *Field Museum of Natural History Publication 83, Anthropological Series* 3(4):262-358. Chicago.

1903a      The Oraibi Oáquöl Ceremony. *Field Museum of Natural History Publication 84, Anthropological Series* 6(1):1-46. Chicago.

673

1905    Traditions of the Hopi. *Field Museum of Natural History Publication 96, Anthropological Series 8*. Chicago.

1905a   Oraibi Natal Customs and Ceremonies. *Field Museum of Natural History Publication 97, Anthropological Series 6(2)*. Chicago.

1912    The Oraibi Marau Ceremony. *Field Museum of Natural History Publication 156, Anthropological Series 11(1):1-88*. Chicago.

1912a   Brief Miscellaneous Hopi Papers. *Field Museum of Natural History Publication 157, Anthropological Series 11(2):91-149*. Chicago.

1967    The Henry R. Voth Hopi Indian Collection at Grand Canyon, Arizona. A Catalogue Prepared for the Fred Harvey Company in 1912 by Henry R. Voth. Phoenix: no publisher.

Vytlacil, Natalie, and J.J. Brody
1958    Two Pit Houses Near Zia Pueblo. *El Palacio* 65(5):174-184.

Waddell, Eric
1975    How the Enga Cope with Frost: Responses to Climatic Perturbations in the Central Highlands of New Guinea. *Human Ecology* 3(4):249-273.

Wagner, Henry R.
1934    Father Marcos de Niza. *New Mexico Historical Review* 9(2):184-227.

1967    The Life and Writings of Bartolomé de las Casas. Albuquerque: University of New Mexico Press.

Wait, Walter K., ed.
1976    Star Lake Archeological Report: A Report of the Prehistoric, Historic and Current Cultural Resources of the Star Lake Area, McKinley County, Northwestern, New Mexico. (Manuscript at Southern Illinois University, Carbondale)

Walker, Douglas
1970    Diegueno Plural Formation. *Linguistic Notes from La Jolla* 4:1-16.

Walker, Willard
1964    Reference, Taxonomy, and Inflection in Zuni. (Unpublished Ph.D. Dissertation in Linguistics, Cornell University, Ithaca, N.Y.)

1965    Taxonomic Structure and the Pursuit of Meaning. *Southwestern Journal of Anthropology* 21(3):265-275.

1966    The Responses of Bilingual and Monolingual Zunis to a Zuni Language Questionnaire. (Paper Delivered at the 65th Annual Meeting of the American Anthropological Association at Pittsburgh, Pa., November 19, 1966.)

1966a   Inflectional Class and Taxonomic Structure in Zuni. *International Journal of American Linguistics* 32(3):217-227.

1972    Toward the Sound Pattern of Zuni. *International Journal of American Linguistics* 38(4):240-259.

1974    Palowahtiwa and the Economic Redevelopment of Zuni Pueblo. *Ethnohistory* 21(1):65-75.

Walker, Willard, and John M. Roberts
1965    A Zuni Material Inventory Code. (Manuscripts in Walker's and Roberts' Possession.)

Wallace, Ernest, and E. Adamson Hoebel
1952    The Comanches: Lords of the South Plains. Norman: University of Oklahoma Press.

Wallace, William J.
1962    Prehistoric Cultural Developments in the Southern California Deserts. *American Antiquity* 28(2):172-180.

Wallace, William J., and Edith S. Taylor
1958    An Archeological Reconnaissance in Bow Willow Canyon, Anza-Borrego Desert State Park. *The Masterkey* 32(5):155-166.

1960    The Indian Hill Rockshelter: Preliminary Excavations. *The Masterkey* 34(2):66-82.

Walter, Paul A.F.
1931    The Cities That Died of Fear. Santa Fe: El Palacio Press. (Reprinted from *El Palacio* 3(4):13-74, 1916.)

Walz, Vina E.
1951    History of the El Paso Area, 1680-1692. (Unpublished Ph.D. Dissertation in History, University of New Mexico, Albuquerque.)

Ward, Al, ed.
1978    Limited Activity and Occupation Sites: A Collection of Conference Papers. Albuquerque: Center for Anthropological Studies.

Ward, John
1865    New Mexico Superintendency. Pp. 187-195 in *Report of the Commissioner of Indian Affairs for the Year 1864*. Washington.

Warren, A. Helene
1969    Tonque. *El Palacio* 76(2):36-42.

1969a   The Nambe Project; Archaeological Salvage at Nambe Pueblo, Santa Fe County, New Mexico: Notes on Ceramics and Lithics of the Nambe Pueblo. *Museum of New Mexico, Laboratory of Anthropology Note* 100. Santa Fe.

1970    Centers of Manufacture and Trade of Rio Grande Glazes. (Manuscript on File, Laboratory of Anthropology, Museum of New Mexico, Santa Fe.)

1976    Technological Studies of the Pottery of Chaco Canyon. (Manuscript on File at Chaco Center, National Park Service, University of New Mexico, Albuquerque.)

1977    New Dimensions in the Study of Prehistoric Pottery. Appendix I. Pp. 363-374 in Archeological Investigations in Cochiti Reservoir, New Mexico. Vol. 2: Excavation and Analysis 1975 Season. Richard C. Chapman and Jan V. Biella, eds. Albuquerque: University of New Mexico, Office of Contract Archeology.

1977a   Prehistoric and Historic Ceramic Analysis. Pp. 97-101 in Archeological Investigations in Cochiti Reservoir, New Mexico. Vol. 2: Excavation and Analysis 1975 Season. Richard C. Chapman and Jan V. Biella, eds. Albuquerque: University of New Mexico, Office of Contract Archeology.

Warren, Claude N.
1967    The San Dieguito Complex: A Review and Hypothesis. *American Antiquity* 32(2):168-185.

Warren, Claude N., and Delbert L. True
1960-1961  The San Dieguito Complex and Its Place in California Prehistory. *Annual Reports of the University of California Archaeological Survey* 3:246-338. Los Angeles.

Warren, Nancy
1976    Priscilla Vigil Makes a Classic Tesuque Rain God: A Photo Essay. *El Palacio* 82(3):9-13.

Washburn, Dorothy K.
1975    The American Southwest. Pp. 103-132 in North America. Shirley Gorenstein et al., eds. New York: St. Martin's Press.

Wasley, William W., comp.
1959    Southwest. Pp. 147-149 in Notes and News. *American Antiquity* 25(1).

1959a   Cultural Implications of Style Trends in Southwestern Prehistoric Pottery: Basketmaker III to Pueblo II in West Central New Mexico. (Unpublished Ph.D. Dissertation in Anthropology, University of Arizona, Tucson.)

674

**BIBLIOGRAPHY**

1960      A Hohokam Platform Mound at the Gatlin Site, Gila Bend, Arizona. *American Antiquity* 26(2):244-262.

1966      Classic Period Hohokam. (Paper Presented to the 31st Annual Meeting of the Society for American Archaeology, Reno, Nev.)

1967      [Archaeological Survey in Sonora, Mexico.] (Fieldnotes in Arizona State Museum, Flagstaff.)

Wasley, William W., and Blake Benham
1968      Salvage Excavation in the Buttes Dam Site, Southern Arizona. *The Kiva* 33(4):244-279.

Wasley, William W., and Alfred E. Johnson
1965      Salvage Archaeology in Painted Rocks Reservoir, Western Arizona. *Anthropological Papers of the University of Arizona* 9. Tucson.

Waters, Frank
1950      Masked Gods: Navaho and Pueblo Ceremonialism. Albuquerque: University of New Mexico Press. (Reprinted: Ballantine Books, New York, 1970.)

1963      Book of the Hopi. Drawings and Source Material Recorded by Oswald White Bear Fredericks. New York: Viking Press. (Reprinted: Ballantine Books, New York, 1972.)

Watson, Don
1959      Indians of the Mesa Verde. Mesa Verde National Park, Colo.: Mesa Verde Museum Association.

Wauchope, Robert, ed.
1956      Seminars in Archaeology: 1955. *Memoirs of the Society for American Archaeology* 11. Salt Lake City.

1965      Alfred Vincent Kidder, 1885-1963. *American Antiquity* 31(2):149-171.

Weaver, Donald E., Jr.
1972      Excavations at Pueblo del Monte and the Classic Period Hohokam Problem. *Student Anthropologist* 4(2):66-76. Prescott, Ariz.

1978      Prehistoric Population Dynamics and Environmental Exploitation in the Manuelito Canyon District, Northwestern New Mexico. (Unpublished Ph.D. Dissertation in Anthropology, Arizona State University, Tempe.)

Weaver, Kenneth F.
1967      Magnetic Clues Help Date the Past. *National Geographic Magazine* 131(5):696-701.

Webb, William, and Robert A. Weinstein
1973      Dwellers at the Source: Southwestern Indian Photographs; from the A.C. Vroman Collection at the Natural History Museum of Los Angeles County. New York: Grossman.

Wedel, Waldo R.
1959      An Introduction to Kansas Archeology. *Bureau of American Ethnology Bulletin* 174:1-668. Washington.

Weed, Carol S.
1972      Classic Period Hohokam Lithic Assemblages. (Paper Presented to the 37th Annual Meeting of the Society for American Archaeology, Miami Beach, Fla.)

Weed, Carol S., and Albert E. Ward
1970      The Henderson Site: Colonial Hohokam in Northcentral Arizona: A Preliminary Report. *The Kiva* 36(2):1-12.

Weigand, Phil C., Garman Harbottle, and Edward V. Sayre
1977      Turquoise Sources and Source Analysis: Mesoamerican and the Southwestern U.S.A. Pp. 15-34 in Exchange Systems in Prehistory. Timothy K. Earle and Jonathon E. Ericson, eds. New York: Academic Press.

Wendorf, Fred
1950      The Flattop Site in the Petrified Forest National Monument. *Plateau* 22(3):43-51.

1950a      A Report on the Excavation of a Small Ruin Near Point of Pines, East-central Arizona. *University of Arizona Bulletin 21(3), Social Science Bulletin* 19. Tucson.

1953      Archaeological Studies in the Petrified Forest National Monument. *Museum of Northern Arizona Bulletin* 27. Flagstaff.

———, ass.
1953a      Salvage Archaeology in the Chama Valley. *Monographs of the School of American Research* 17. Santa Fe.

1954      A Reconstruction of Northern Rio Grande Prehistory. *American Anthropologist* 56(2):200-227.

1954      A Reconstruction of Northern Rio Grande Prehistory. *American Anthropologist* 56(2):200-227.

———, ed.
1954-1956      Highway Salvage Archaeology. Whole Vols. 1 and 2. New Mexico State Highway Department and the Museum of New Mexico. Santa Fe.

1956      Some Distributions of Settlement Patterns in the Pueblo Southwest. Pp. 18-25 in Prehistoric Settlement Patterns in the New World. Gordon R. Willey, ed. *Viking Fund Publications in Anthropology* 23. New York.

———, comp.
1961      Paleoecology of the Llano Estacado. *Fort Burgwin Research Center Publication* 1. Santa Fe, N.M.

Wendorf, Fred, and Erik K. Reed
1955      An Alternative Reconstruction of Northern Rio Grande Prehistory. *El Palacio* 62(5-6):131-173.

Wendorf, Fred, and Tully H. Thomas
1951      Early Man Sites Near Concho, Arizona. *American Antiquity* 17(2):107-114.

Wendorf, Fred, Edward N. Ferdon, Jr., and John Bradbury
1963      A Tularosa Phase Pueblo Near Luna, New Mexico. *Highway Salvage Archaeology* 4(16):29-40.

Wendorf, Fred, Nancy Fox, and Orian L. Lewis, eds.
1956      Pipeline Archaeology: Reports of Salvage Operations in the Southwest on El Paso Natural Gas Company Projects, 1950- 1953. Santa Fe and Flagstaff: Laboratory of Anthropology and the Museum of Northern Arizona.

Werner, Oswald, and Kenneth Y. Begishe
1970      A Lexemic Typology of Navajo Anatomical Terms, I: The Foot. *International Journal of American Linguistics* 36(4):247-265.

West, Robert G.
1924      Validity of Certain Land Grants in Texas. *Texas Law Review* 2(4):435-444.

Westinghouse Electric Corporation, Systems Operations
1969      Four Corners Regional Development Study Program; a Study of Development Guidelines Including the Analysis of Economic Potential and the Concept of a New Town for the Four Corners Region. Final Report, SO-503. Baltimore. Mimeo.

Wetherington, Ronald K.
1968      Excavations at Pot Creek Pueblo. *Fort Burgwin Research Center Publication* 6. Taos, N.M.

Whalen, Norman M.
1971      Cochise Culture Sites in the Central San Pedro Drainage, Arizona. (Unpublished Ph.D. Dissertation in Anthropology, University of Arizona, Tucson.)

Wheat, Carl I.
1957-1963      Mapping the Transmississippi West, 1540-1861. 6 vols. San Francisco: The Institute of Historical Cartography.

Wheat, Joe Ben
1954      Crooked Ridge Village (Arizona W:10:15). *University of Arizona Bulletin 25(3), Social Science Bulletin* 24. Tucson.

1955      Mogollon Culture Prior to A.D. 1000. *Memoirs of the American Anthropological Association* 82; *Memoirs of the Society for American Archaeology* 10.

Whipple, Amiel W.
1854-1855      Itinerary, Explorations, and Surveys for a Railroad Route from the Mississippi River to the Pacific Ocean. War

Route Near the Thirty-fifth Parallel Under the Command of Lieut. A.W. Whipple, Topographical Engineers, in 1853 and 1854. Pacific Survey Reports, Vol. 3. *33d Cong., 2d sess. Exec. Doc. No. 78. (Serial No. 760)* Washington: Beverley Tucker.

White, Katherine H.
1961     The Pueblo de Socorro Grant. (Unpublished M.A. Thesis in History, Texas Western College, El Paso.)

White, Leslie A.
1930     A Comparative Study of Keresan Medicine Societies. Pp. 604- 619 in *Proceedings of the 23d International Congress of Americanists.* New York, 1928.

1932     The Pueblo of San Felipe. *Memoirs of the American Anthropological Association* 38. Menasha, Wis.

1932a    The Acoma Indians. Pp. 17-192 in *47th Annual Report of the Bureau of American Ethnology for the Years 1929-1930.* Washington. (Reprinted: Rio Grande Press, Glorieta, N.M., 1973.)

1935     The Pueblo of Santo Domingo, New Mexico. *Memoirs of the American Anthropological Association* 43. Menasha, Wis.

1942     The Pueblo of Santa Ana, New Mexico. *Memoirs of the American Anthropological Association* 60. Menasha, Wis.

1945     Ethnographic Notes on Sandia Pueblo, New Mexico. *Papers of the Michigan Academy of Science, Arts and Letters* 31:215-222. Ann Arbor.

1960     The World of the Keresan Pueblo Indians. Pp. 53-64 in Culture in History: Essays in Honor of Paul Radin. Stanley Diamond, ed. New York: Columbia University Press.

1962     The Pueblo of Sia, New Mexico. *Bureau of American Ethnology Bulletin* 184. Washington.

1964     The World of the Keresan Pueblo Indians. Pp. 83-94 in Primitive Views of the World. Stanley Diamond, ed. New York: Columbia University Press.

Whiteaker, R.J.
1976     Excavation of Portions of LA 11841: A Gallina Phase Pithouse Site, Rio Arriba County, New Mexico. *Museum of New Mexico, Laboratory of Anthropology Note, Series* 111d. Santa Fe.

Whiting, Alfred F.
1939     Ethnobotany of the Hopi. *Museum of Northern Arizona Bulletin* 15. Flagstaff.

1958     Havasupai Characteristics in the Cohonina. *Plateau* 30(3):55-60.

Whitman, William
1940     The San Ildefonso of New Mexico. Pp. 390-460 in Acculturation in Seven American Indian Tribes. Ralph Linton, ed. New York: D. Appleton-Century.

1947     The Pueblo Indians of San Ildefonso: A Changing Culture. *Columbia University Contributions to Anthropology* 34. New York.

Whorf, Benjamin Lee
1935     The Comparative Linguistics of Uto-Aztecan. *American Anthropologist* 37(4):600-608.

1935a    [Review of] Uto-Aztecan Languages of Mexico, by A.L. Kroeber. *American Anthropologist* 37(2):343-345.

1936     [Notes on Hopi Grammar and Pronunciation; Mishongnovi Forms.] Pp. 1198-1326 in Vol. 2 of Hopi Journal of Alexander M. Stephen. Elsie C. Parsons, ed. 2 vols. New York: Columbia University Press.

1936a    The Punctual and Segmentative Aspects of Verbs in Hopi. *Language* 12(2):127-131. (Reprinted: Pp. 51-56 in Language, Thought, and Reality: Selected Writings of Benjamin L. Whorf. John B. Carroll, ed. Cambridge, Mass.: M.I.T. Press; New York: John Wiley, 1956.)

1936b    Appendix to The Classification of the Sonoran Languages, by J. Alden Mason. Pp. 197-198 in Essays in Anthropology Presented to A.L. Kroeber in Celebration of His Sixtieth Birthday, June 11, 1936. Robert H. Lowie, ed. Berkeley: University of California Press.

1938     Some Verbal Categories of Hopi. *Language* 14(4):275-286. (Reprinted: Pp. 112-124 in Language, Thought, and Reality: Selected Writings of Benjamin L. Whorf. John B. Carroll, ed. Cambridge, Mass.: M.I.T. Press; New York: John Wiley, 1956.)

1940     Gestalt Technique of Stem Composition in Shawnee. *Indiana Historical Society, Prehistory Research Series* 1(9):393-406. (Reprinted: Pp. 160-172 in Language, Thought, and Reality: Selected Writings of Benjamin L. Whorf. John B. Carroll, ed. Cambridge, Mass.: M.I.T. Press; New York: John Wiley, 1956.)

1941     The Relation of Habitual Thought and Behavior to Language. Pp. 75-93 in Language, Culture, and Personality: Essays in Memory of Edward Sapir. Leslie Spier, A. Irving Hallowell, and Stanley S. Newman, eds. Menasha, Wis.: Sapir Memorial Publication Fund. (Reprinted: University of Utah Press, Salt Lake City, 1960.)

1946     The Hopi Language, Toreva Dialect. Pp. 158-183 in Linguistic Structures of Native America, by Harry Hoijer et al. *Viking Fund Publications in Anthropology* 6. New York.

1950     An American Indian Model of the Universe. *International Journal of American Linguistics* 16(2):67-72. (Reprinted: Pp. 57-64 in Language, Thought, and Reality: Selected Writings of Benjamin L. Whorf. John B. Carroll, ed. Cambridge, Mass.: M.I.T. Press; New York: John Wiley, 1956.)

1953     Linguistic Factors in the Terminology of Hopi Architecture. *International Journal of American Linguistics* 19(2):141-145. (Reprinted: Pp. 199-206 in Language, Thought, and Reality: Selected Writings of Benjamin L. Whorf. John B. Carroll, ed. Cambridge, Mass.: M.I.T. Press; New York: John Wiley, 1956.)

1956     An American Indian Model of the Universe. Pp. 57-64 in Language, Thought and Reality: Selected Writings of Benjamin Lee Whorf. John B. Carroll, ed. Cambridge: MIT Press; New York: John Wiley.

1956a    Language, Thought, and Reality: Selected Writings of Benjamin Lee Whorf. John B. Carroll, ed. Cambridge: Technology Press of Massachusetts Institute of Technology.

1956b    Discussion of Hopi Linguistics. Pp. 102-111 in Language, Thought, and Reality: Selected Writings of Benjamin L. Whorf. John B. Carroll, ed. Cambridge, Mass.: M.I.T. Press; New York: John Wiley.

Whorf, Benjamin L., and George L. Trager
1937     The Relationship of Uto-Aztecan and Tanoan. *American Anthropologist* 39(4):609-624.

Wilcox, David R.
1975     A Strategy for Perceiving Social Groups in Puebloan Sites. Pp. 120-159 in Chapters in the Prehistory of Eastern Arizona, IV. Paul S. Martin et al., eds. *Fieldiana: Anthropology* 65. Chicago.

Wilder, Carleton S.
1944     Archaeological Survey of the Great Thumb Area, Grand Canyon National Park. *Plateau* 17(2):17-26.

Wilks, Flo
1976        Pablita. *New Mexico Magazine* 54(8):28.

Willey, Elizabeth (Scowcroft)
1969        The Lands and History of the Hopi Indians. (Manuscript in Library of the Museum of Northern Arizona, Flagstaff.)

Willey, Gordon R.
1966        An Introduction to American Archaeology. Vol. 1: North and Middle America. Englewood Cliffs, N.J.: Prentice-Hall.

1967        *Alfred Vincent Kidder. Biographical Memoirs of the National Academy of Sciences* 39:292-322. New York.

Willey, Gordon R., Charles C. Di Peso, William A. Ritchie, Irving Rouse, and John H. Rowe
1956        An Archaeological Classification of Culture Contact Situations. Pp. 1-30 in Seminars in Archaeology: 1955. Robert Wauchope et al., eds. *Memoirs of the Society for American Archaeology* 11. Salt Lake City.

Williams, Pete A., and Robert I. Orlins
1963        The Corn Creek Dunes Site: A Dated Surface Site in Southern Nevada. *Nevada State Museum Anthropological Paper* 10. Carson City.

Wilson, John P.
1969        The Sinagua and Their Neighbors. (Unpublished Ph.D. Dissertation in Anthropology, Harvard University, Cambridge, Mass.)

1972        Awatovi--More Light on a Legend. *Plateau* 44(3):125-130.

1973        Quarai: Living Mission to Monument. *El Palacio* 78(4):15-28.

Wimberly, M.
1972        Training Bulletin for the Tularosa Valley Project. (Manuscript at Human Systems Research Corporation, Albuquerque, N.M.)

Winfrey, Dorman H. et al., eds.
1960        Texas Indian Papers, 1846-1859. 5 vols. Austin: Texas State Library.

Winship, George P.
1896        The Coronado Expedition, 1540-1542. Pp. 329-613 in *14th Annual Report of the Bureau of American Ethnology for the Years 1892-1893*. Pt. 1. Washington.

Winter, Joseph C.
1973        The Distribution and Development of Fremont Maize Agriculture: Some Preliminary Interpretations. *American Antiquity* 38(4):439-452.

1976        The Processes of Farming Diffusion in the Southwest and Great Basin. *American Antiquity* 41(4):421-429.

Winter, Werner
1957        Yuman Languages, I: First Impressions. *International Journal of American Linguistics* 23(1):18-23.

1967        The Identity of the Paipai (Akwa'ala). Pp. 372-378 in Studies in Southwestern Ethnolinguistics. Dell H. Hymes with William E. Bittle, eds. The Hague and Paris: Mouton.

Wissler, Clark
1922        The American Indian: An Introduction to the Anthropology of the New World. 2d ed. New York: Oxford University Press.

1938        The American Indian: An Introduction to the Anthropology of the New World. 3d ed. New York: Oxford University Press.

Withers, Arnold M.
1944        Excavations at Valshni Village: A Site on the Papago Indian Reservation. *American Antiquity* 10(1):33-47.

Witherspoon, Gary J.
1971        Navajo Categories of Objects at Rest. *American Anthropologist* 73(1):110-127.

Wittfogel, Karl A.
1957        Oriental Despotism: A Comparative Study of Total Power. New Haven: Yale University Press.

Wobst, H. Martin
1974        Boundary Conditions for Paleolithic Social Systems: A Simulation Approach. *American Antiquity* 39(2):147-178.

1977        Stylistic Behavior and Information Exchange. Pp. 317-342 in Papers for the Director: Research Essays in Honor of James B. Griffin. Charles E. Cleland, ed. *University of Michigan Museum of Anthropology, Anthropology Paper* 61. Ann Arbor.

Wolf, Eric R.
1959        Sons of the Shaking Earth. Chicago: University of Chicago Press.

Woodbury, Richard B.
1954        Prehistoric Stone Implements of Northeastern Arizona. (Reports of the Awatovi Expedition 6) *Papers of the Peabody Museum of American Archaeology and Ethnology, Harvard University* 34. Cambridge, Mass.

1956        The Antecedents of Zuni Culture. *Transactions of the New York Academy of Sciences* 2d. ser., Vol. 18(6):557-563. New York.

1961        Prehistoric Agriculture at Point of Pines, Arizona. *Memoirs of the Society for American Archaeology* 17. Salt Lake City.

1961a       A Reappraisal of Hohokam Irrigation. *American Anthropologist* 63(3):550-560.

1962        Systems of Irrigation and Water Control in Arid North America. Pp. 301-305 in *Proceedings of the 34th International Congress of Americanists*. Vienna, 1960.

1973        Alfred V. Kidder. New York: Columbia University Press.

Woodbury, Richard B., and James A. Neely
1972        Water Control Systems of the Tehuacan Valley. Pp. 81-153 in *Chronology and Irrigation*. Frederick Johnson, ed. The Prehistory of the Tehuacan Valley. Vol. 4. Austin and London: University of Texas Press.

Woodward, Arthur
1931        The Grewe Site, Gila Valley, Arizona. *Los Angeles Museum of History, Science and Art Occasional Paper* 1. Los Angeles.

1936        A Shell Bracelet Manufactory. *American Antiquity* 2(2):117-125.

1949        Imported China and Crockery at Awatovi. Pp. 94-95 in Franciscan Awatovi. *Papers of the Peabody Museum of American Archaeology and Ethnology, Harvard University* 36. Cambridge, Mass.

Woolf, Charles M., and Frank C. Dukepoo
1969        Hopi Indians, Inbreeding and Albinism. *Science* 164(3875):30-37.

Wormington, H. Marie
1947        Prehistoric Indians of the Southwest. *Denver Museum of Natural History, Popular Series* 7. Denver.

1957        Ancient Man in North America. *Denver Museum of Natural History, Popular Series* 4. Denver.

1969        Prehistoric Indians of the Southwest. *Denver Museum of Natural History, Popular Series* 7. 2d ed. Denver.

Wright, Barton
1954        Excavation of Catclaw Cave, Lower Colorado River. (Unpublished M.A. Thesis in Anthropology, University of Arizona, Tucson.)

1973     Kachinas: A Hopi Artist's Documentary. Flagstaff, Ariz.: Northland Press.

1976     Pueblo Shields from the Fred Harvey Fine Arts Collection. Flagstaff, Ariz.: Northland Press.

1977     Hopi Kachinas: The Complete Guide to Collecting Kachina Dolls. Flagstaff, Ariz.: Northland Press.

Wright, Margaret (Nickelson)
1972     The History and Hallmarks of Hopi Silversmithing: Hopi Silver. Flagstaff, Ariz.: Northland Press.

Wyman, Leland C.
1970     Blessingway; with Three Versions of the Myth Recorded and Translated from the Navajo by Bernard Haile. Tucson: University of Arizona Press.

Yegerlehner, John
1959     Arizona Tewa, I: Phonemes. *International Journal of American Linguistics* 25(1):1-7.

1959a     Arizona Tewa, II: Person Markers. *International Journal of American Linguistics* 25(2):75-80.

Young, Otis E.
1952     The First Military Escort on the Santa Fe Trail, 1829: From the Journal and Reports of Major Bennet Riley and Lieutenant Philip St. George Cooke. Glendale, Calif.: Arthur H. Clark.

Young, Robert W., and William Morgan
1943     The Navaho Language: The Elements of Navaho Grammar with a Dictionary in Two Parts Containing Basic Vocabularies of Navaho and English. Washington: U.S. Indian Service, Education Branch.

Zaharlick, Amy
1977     Picuris Syntax. (Unpublished Ph.D. Dissertation in Linguistics, American University, Washington.)

Zahniser, John L.
1966     Late Prehistoric Villages Southeast of Tucson, Arizona and the Archaeology of the Tanque Verde Phase. *The Kiva* 31(3):103-204.

Zárate Salmerón, Gerónimo de
1966     Relaciones: An Account of Things Seen and Learned by Father Jerónimo de Zárate Salmerón from the Year 1538 to the Year 1626. Alicia R. Milich, trans. Albuquerque: Horn and Wallace.

Zavala, Silvio
1943     New Viewpoints on the Spanish Colonization of America. Philadelphia: University of Pennsylvania Press; London: H. Milford, Oxford University Press.

Zingg, Robert M.
1940     Report on Archaeology of Southern Chihuahua. *Contributions of the University of Denver, Center of Latin American Studies* 1. Denver, Colo.

Zubrow, Ezra B.W.
1971     Carrying Capacity and Dynamic Equilibrium in the Prehistoric Southwest. *American Antiquity* 36(2):127-138.

1971a     A Southwestern Test of an Anthropological Model of Population Dynamics. (Unpublished Ph.D. Dissertation in Anthropology, University of Arizona, Tucson.)

1975     Prehistoric Carrying Capacity: A Model. Menlo Park, Calif.: Cummings Publishing Company.

# Index

*Italic numbers indicate material in a figure caption; roman numbers, material in the text.*

*All variant names of groups are indexed, with the occurrences under* synonymy *discussing the equivalences. Variants of group names that differ from those cited only in their capitalization, hyphenation, or accentuation have generally been omitted; variants that differ only in the presence or absence of one (noninitial) letter or compound element have been collapsed into a single entry with that letter or element in parentheses.*

*The entry* Indian words *indexes, by language, all words appearing in the standard orthographies and some others.*

mythology: 612, 616, 619. orthography: 255. political organization: 219, 261, *263, 264-265.* population: 185, 221, 458. prehistory: 143, 146, 147, 150, 151, 164, 167, 257-259. puberty: 261. religion: 233, 262-264. settlement pattern: 260. settlements: *256, 257, 278.* social organization: 218, 260-261. structures: 260, *261.* subsistence: 255-256, 259, *262.* synonymy: 235, 250, 267. technology: 259-260, 604. territory: *189,* 207, 216, 218. trade: 189, 202. warfare: 195, 208-209.
  *See also* Indian words
Taowa; synonymy: 235
Tapia, Antonio José: 327
Taracahitan language grouping: 170
Tarahumara: 20, 161. language: 170
Tarascan: 157, 193
*ła·θi̧·ge;* synonymy: 335
tâtsürma; synonymy: 335
Tavira: 241
Tawaquaptewa: 529, *531*
Tawas; synonymy: 235
Taxio: 246
Taxumulco Pueblo: 240
Tayberin; synonymy: 250, 267
Tayberon; synonymy: 250, 267
Taycios Pueblo: 243
Tayip Pueblo: 241
*tˀay-kabéde;* synonymy: 351
Taylor, Walter W.: 12
Tay-wa(ug)h; synonymy: 235
*tóanq̌bák;* synonymy: 417
*tóbanq̌;* synonymy: 235
Tecahan Pueblo: 241
technology: 23, 33, 34, 35, *35,* 36, 37, *37,* 40, *40,* 44, 51, 52, 53, 55-59, *58,* 60, 66, *66,* 67-68, 75, 77, 78-82, 87-88, 92, 101, *141,* 157, 305, 403, *404,* 427, 433, 443, 493, *555.* antler: 136. bonework: *42,* 72, *95,* 128, 165, 168, 201, *358, 427,* 434. cordage: *96.* leatherwork: 259, 305, *358,* 397, 403, *404, 425,* 434, 456, *562,* 591, 595. metalwork: 86, *97,* 140, 156, 167, 224, 303, 305, 492, 527. postcontact adaptations: *521.* shell-work: 72, *72,* 77, 79-81, *81,* 84, 85-86, 88, 93, 94, *97,* 98, 100, 101, 105, *114,* 128, 135, 139, *142,* 153, 155, 156, 157, 158-159, *159, 395,* 397, 403, *427.* silverwork: 222, 232, *374,* 375, 479, 492, 495-497, *495-497,* 527, 561, *562.* Spanish introduction: 432, 472. stonework: 71-73, *71, 72,* 79, 83-84, 85, 88, 94, *95, 96,* 100, 101, 113, 115, *115,* 117-118, 127-218, 155, *156,* 157, 159, *159,* 163, 164-165, *165, 166,* 167, 168, 201, *368, 370, 427,* 434. textiles: 51, *65,* 94, *96,* 98, *98,* 113, *114, 118,* 157, *157, 159,* 178, 190, 211, 222, 236, 242, 252, 261, 305, 321, 338, *371,* 397, 403, 416, 427, *428,* 443, *453,* 456, 459, 460, 496, *558,* 559, 561, 590, 591, *594,* 595, 603, 604, *605.* turquoise: 135, 140, *142,* 149, 150, 153, 156, 157, 158, 160, 165, 202, 224, 232, 247, 251, 252, 253, *395, 409, 495-497. See also* art; basketry; beads; pottery; projectile points; tools
*tečúgé;* synonymy: 335
Teewi Pueblo: 145, 239, 250

Teeytzaan Pueblo: 241
Tegua; synonymy: 235
Tegualpa: 249
Tehua(s); synonymy: 235
Tehua; synonymy: 235
Tejon: 250
Tekapo; synonymy: 481. *See also* Zuni
*tekappowa;* synonymy: 481
Tekyapoawa; synonymy: 481
*témá;* synonymy: 234, 377
Tempal: 457
temper; definition: 137, 145. *See also* pottery
Tenabó Pueblo: *239,* 240, 351
Ten Broeck, P.G.S.: 524-525
Téoas; synonymy: 235
*tôotho;* synonymy: 267
Teotihuacán: 158, 160
Tepehuan: 91, 161. Northern: 170. Southern: 170. territory: 91
*tapíanę̌;* synonymy: 235
Tepocoty Pueblo: 248.
Tepotra: 248
Tercao Pueblo: 241
territory; Acoma: 146, 150, *225,* 441, 450-451, 454, 459. Apache: 162-163. Athapaskan: 162. Cochiti: 145, 216, *225,* 366. Hopi: 182, *183.* Hopi-Tewa: 587-589. Isleta: 218, 232, 351. Jemez: 410, 418. Laguna: 146, 150, 207, 216, *225,* 442, 438, 459. Nambe: 317. Pecos: 145, 430, 432. Picuris: 216, 268. Pojoaque: 216, 324-325. Sandia: 343. San Felipe: *225,* 390. San Ildefonso: 308. San Juan: 216, 278-279. Santa Ana: *225,* 398, 408, 307. Santa Clara: 296. Santo Domingo: *225,* 379, 381. Taos: 207, 216, 218. Tesuque: 330. Tigua: 340-341. Zia: *225, 409.* Zuni: 210, 234, 467, 492
Tesuke; synonymy: 335
Tesuki; synonymy: 335
Tesuque Pueblo: 221, 250, 265, 318, 330-335, *330, 331.* ceremonies: 317, 332, *334.* clothing: *320.* curing: 331. disease: 333. economic development: 335. education: 332-333. employment: 334. external relations: 202. history: *189,* 250, 332-335. kinship: 331. language: 296, 330. marriage: 331. mythology: 621. orthography: 330. political organization: 298, 331-332. population: 185, 221, 333. religion: 331-332. settlements: *330, 331.* social organization: 330-332. structures: *330.* subsistence: 332, 332, 333-335, 333. synonymy: 318, 322, 335. technology: *334,* 604. territory: *189,* 330. transportation: *332.* warfare: 195, 196, 332, 333
Tesuqui; synonymy: 335
*tóˀu kwihun ag;* synonymy: 388
Tevas; synonymy: 235
Tevaya, Dean: *534*
Tewa, Marietta: *560*
*te·wa,* synonymy: 235, 364, 601
*téwagˠíˀ;* synonymy: 364
*téwákʷa;* synonymy: 364
*te·wa·kʷe;* synonymy: 601
Tewa language grouping: 227, 259, 308, 317, 330
Téwan; synonymy: 234

*te·wanˀa,* synonymy: 601
Tewanima, Louis: 530
Tewas: 15, 163, 221, 231, 326, 345. ceremonies: 204, 612-613. history: 179, 186, 195, 196, 224, 248, 250-251, 333, 421. language: 296, 319, 321-322, 539, 587, 596-597. mythology: 609-617, 621. population: 185, 221. prehistory: 392, 418, 430, 599-600. religion: 609. social organization: 227, 233, 308, 331, 332. synonymy: 235, 294, 307, 322, 335. trade: 430. warfare: 211. *See also* Nambe Pueblo; Pojoaque Pueblo; San Ildefonso Pueblo; San Juan Pueblo; Tesuque Pueblo
*téwa-łæˀš̌;* synonymy: 235
Tewa Village: *189, 192. See also* Hopi-Tewa
*téwa xosóˀon;* synonymy: 601
*tewě̆ˀlĭnĕ;* synonymy: 235
*tewíˀai;* synonymy: 388
*téwige;* synonymy: 388
Texa Pueblo: 241
textiles. *See* technology
*te·xʷevege ówîngé;* synonymy: 388
Teyas: 162, 248, 436
Teyaxa Pueblo: 241
Teypama Pueblo: 241
Teypana Pueblo: 241
Tezcatlipoca: 94
Tezuque; synonymy: 318, 335
Tezuqui; synonymy: 335
Thanos; synonymy: 601
*tʰanu(ge);* synonymy: 601
*tʰá·nu té·wa;* synonymy: 601
*θa·wíˀ ówîngé;* synonymy: 267
Theguas; synonymy: 235
*thɔ̆-wélene;* synonymy: 267
*thɔ̆wílana;* synonymy: 267
Thezuque; synonymy: 335
Third Mesa: 20, 529, 539, 542, *543,* 550, *560,* 561, 564, *568,* 570
thoxtlawĭamắ; synonymy: 397
*thúhwir taǎ̀ˀi;* synonymy: 267
*thủhwíride* (pl. *thûhwírnin*); synonymy: 267
*thúr-tuà:* 362
Tiara Pueblo: 243
Ticomán: 160
Ticori; synonymy: 276
*tí·čʰíná:* 450
*tí·čiyâ·rha:* 450
*tį́dae* (pl. *tį́dæcóš̌*); synonymy: 406
*tį́dægˠíˀ;* synonymy: 406
Tierra del Padre: 155
ti-gua(n); synonymy: 235
Tigua Pueblo (Ysleta del Sur): 231, 336-342. ceremonies: 336, *338, 339.* external relations: 336-337. history: 220, 241, 338-341, 354. language: 336. political organization: 337, 341. population: 185, 237, 241. religion: 337. settlement pattern: 336. social organization: 337-338. territory: *189,* 336, *336,* 340, 341. technology: 338. synonymy: 341-342, 364
Tiguas; synonymy: 235, 242
ti-gues(h); synonymy: 235
Tiguex: 236, 242, 344, 408; synonymy: 235, 236
Tigüez; synonymy: 235

Tzias: 245
Tziati Pueblo: 243, 250
Tzibola; synonymy: 480
Tziguis, Tziquis, 235, 240
Tzijaatica: 249
Tzios: 243
Tziquis. *See* Tziguis
tziquite; synonymy: 437
Tziymatsi: 243
Tziymatzi Pueblo: 243
Tzooma; synonymy: 250
Tzula Pueblo: 240
Tzuñi: 252. synonymy: 480
Tzyiti; synonymy: 251

**U**
Ubates: 247, 248-250
Ulibarrí, Juan de: 164, 187
*ʔullewa·kʷe;* synonymy: 552
Underhill, Ruth: 19
United States government: 453, 479.
  assistance programs: 266, 272, 274-275,
  282, 292, 293, 306, 348, 364, 595.
  Department of Commerce: 407.
  Department of Health, Education, and
  Welfare: 406, 407, 448, 454. Department
  of Housing and Urban Development: *322,*
  *348, 348,* 397, 406, 411, 448. Department
  of the Interior: 210. Department of
  Labor: 407. Economic Development
  Administration: 306, 536. Forest Service:
  275. Grazing Service: 407. Headstart: 371,
  406, 428, 429, 492. Office of Economic
  Opportunity: 335, 341. Public Health
  Service: 217, 374, 406, 407, 450.
  reservation policy: 209. Soil Conservation
  Service: 407. VISTA: *292.* War
  Department: 210. Works Progress
  Administration: 305, 595. *See also* Bureau
  of Indian Affairs; legislation, United
  States; treaties
Unshagi Pueblo: 143, *239,* 251, 419
Upper Little Colorado province: 122
Uraba; synonymy: 251, 267
Usleta; synonymy: 364
Ute: 201, 203, 204, 207, 209, 551. external
  relations: 151, 162, 164, 190, 255, 398,
  458, 522. prehistory: 514. trade: 146, 305.
  warfare: 189, 199, 200, 211, 271, 410, 442,
  542, 600. *See also* Indian words
Uto-Aztecan language grouping: 154,
  170-171, 173, 174-175, 176, 177, 226, 233,
  587

**V**
Vacus; synonymy: 466
Vahki phase: 54, 57, 77, 78, 79, 92, 93
Valladolid Pueblo: 245, 246, 247. synonymy:
  250, 267
Valle, Martin: 461
Vanderwagen, Andrew: 475-476
Vandever, C.E.: 527
Vargas, Diego de: 4, 151, 186, 187, 198, 224,
  247, 253, 296, 314, 325, 339, 345, 353, 393,
  405, 408, 419, 420-421, 458, 471, 522
Vargas, Eusebio de: 420
Vásquez de Coronado, Francisco. *See*
  Coronado, Francisco Vásquez de

Velarde, Pablita: *222, 300*
Vélez de Escalante, Silvestre: *192, 522*
Vergara, Sánchez: 206
Viareato Pueblo: 243
Victoria, Francisco de: 194
Vicuris; synonymy: 276
Viejo period: 155, 158
Vigil, Antonio José: *321*
Village of the Great Kivas: 468, 469, *471*
Villagrá, Gaspar de: 457
Villarasa Pueblo: 242, 243
Virgin River culture: 103, 127
Vivian, R. Gordon: 11
Vivian, R. Gwinn: 13
Voth, H.R.: 527, 528, *528, 530,* 535
Vsacus; synonymy: 466
Vumaheyn Pueblo: 241

**W**
*wǽhǽča·nįkʷá* pueblo: 419
Walapai: 1, 107
*wàlati·wa;* synonymy: 429
Walatowa: 418. synonymy: 429
*wáLpi(tiʔ);* synonymy: 551
Walpi; synonymy: 551. *See also* Hopi
*wán;* synonymy: 429
*wángé ówîngé;* synonymy: 429
war chiefs and war captains. *See* political
  organization
Ward, John: 525
warfare: 195, 210. equipment: *404, 425.* for
  revenge: 189, 246, 522, 600. guard
  function: 540, 542, 550, 600. intergroup:
  189, 190, 202, 208, 237, 242, 249, 436.
  prisoners: 184, 189, 202, 203, 474. raiding
  for subsistence: 184, 190, 202, 203, 226,
  248, 305, 344, 377, 436, 472, 474, 525.
  ritual: 253. scalping: 184, 208, 265, 360,
  396, 401, 414, 444, 445, 488, 501, 610, 611,
  612, 614, 615. tactics: 188, 202, 252.
  technique: 189, 246, 252, 253, 435.
  warriors' societies: 229, 308, 310, 331, 360,
  361, 386, 396, 401, 412, 414-415, 444, 445,
  488-489, 505-506, 573-574, 575-576, 597.
  weapons: 237. *See also* Pueblo Revolt
Washington, John M.: 474
*wá·śú·ce;* synonymy: 349
water control: 190, 233, 241, 242, 246, 250,
  252, 254, 279, 300, 302, 303, 317, 332, 355,
  364, 367, 368, *382,* 410, 426, 434, 441, 452,
  455, 456, 589. city water systems: 154,
  158, 159. prehistoric: 2, 6, 23, 43, 44, 45,
  48, 49, 51-52, 66, 75, 77, 78, 82, 83, *83,*
  86, 87, 89, 93, 101, 102, 108, 112, 115, 119,
  126, 129, 138, 139-140, *141,* 143, 144, 145,
  146, 149-150, 154, 158, 159, 164, 224, 325.
  reservoirs: 154. wells: 51-52, 77, 158, 241,
  *426*
water rights: 207, 210, 215, 278, 326, 335,
  422, 589, *589*
Watlpiye; synonymy: 551
Wayhusiwa: *489, 490*
wehkʔa·kʷe; synonymy: 388
wehkʔa(na); synonymy: 234, 388
*wehkʔana cʔana;* synonymy: 397
*we·łuwalʔa;* synonymy: 349, 388
Wendorf, Fred: 12

Wenima: 384
wepłapatsa; synonymy: 397
Western Lithic cotradition: 34
Wetherill Mesa: 126
Wetherill, Richard: *8*
Wet Leggett site: *69, 72*
Wheat, J.B.: 62
Wheeler, George M.: 474
Whewa: 19
White, Leslie: 17, *20*
White House: 379, 383-384, 404, 413
White Mound: 119, 123, 468
Whitewater Drought: 33
Whorf, Benjamin Lee: 581
Wichita: *180*
*wílanạ;* synonymy: 276
*wílatho;* synonymy: 276
Wilder, Marshall P.: 6
witchcraft: 186, 237, 281, 318, 353, 354, 358,
  359, 360, 384, 411, 413, 415, 447, 476, 477,
  488, 506, 507, 597, 599, 615
Wongnehma: *527*
world view. *See* cosmology
Wyaco, Virgil: *490*

**X**
Xaimela Pueblo: 247, 248
Xala: 252
Xameca Pueblo: 247, 248
*xaʔp̌o·;* synonymy: 307
Xavier, Francisco: 196
Xay: 249
Xenopue Pueblo: 240
Xiaqeumo Pueblo: 250
Ximena Pueblo: 247, 248
Ximenes, Francisco: 325
Xiomato: 250
Xipaolabi; synonymy: 552
Xoalpe; synonymy: 254
Xólotl: 159
Xomupa; synonymy: 254
Xongopavi; synonymy: 552
*xosóʔon (téwa);* synonymy: 551, 601
Xotre Pueblo: 248
Xumanas; synonymy: 240
Xumupami: 254. synonymy: 552
Xunusta: 246
*xų́·očú teʔi ówîngé;* synonymy: 294

**Y**
Yacco Pueblo: 245. synonymy: 466
Yanamo Pueblo: 241
Yaqui; language: 170, 322
Yates Pueblo: 245
Yatez Pueblo: 245
Yavapai; Northeastern: 107. Southeastern:
  107, 551
Ye, Felipe de: 195
Yellow House interval: 31-32
Yhohota Pueblo: 248
*yíla* (pl. *yíłaeš*); synonymy: 267
*yíłata;* synonymy: 267
Yjar Guayo; synonymy: 251
Yncohocpi: 249
Yoda: *527*
Yohla: 240
Yonalu Pueblo: 248
Youkioma: 528, *530*